$\hat{P}_0$	Intrinsic value of stock today; $\hat{P}_t$ is the expected (intrinsic) value of the stock in Period t
PP	Sales price per unit of product sold
P/E	Price/earnings ratio
PMT	Periodic level payment of an annuity
PV	Present value
PVP	Present value of a perpetuity
PVA_n	Present value of an ordinary annuity for n payments
$PVA(DUE)_n$	Present value of an annuity due for n payments
Q	Quantity produced or sold
r	(1) A percentage discount rate, or cost of capital
	(2) Required rate of return
$\ddot{r}$	Historic, or realized, rate of return
$\bar{r}$	Average historical return
$\hat{r}$	"r hat," an expected rate of return
r*	Real risk-free rate of interest
r_d	Cost of debt
r_{dT}	After-tax cost of debt $= r_d(1 - T)$
r_e	Cost of new common stock (external equity)
r_{EAR}	Effective annual rate of return
r_j	Cost of capital for an individual firm or security
r_M	Rate of return for "the market," or an "average" stock
r_{PER}	Rate per compounding period
r_{ps}	Cost of preferred stock
r_{RF}	Nominal rate of return on a risk-free security
r_s	(1) Cost of retained earnings (internal equity)
	(2) Required return on a stock
r_{SIMPLE}	Nominal (simple) rate of return (interest) $=$ APR
ROA	Return on assets
ROE	Return on equity
RP	Risk premium
RP_M	Market risk premium
S	Sales in dollars
SML	Security Market Line
$\sum$	Summation sign (capital sigma)
σ	Standard deviation (lowercase sigma)
σ^2	Variance
t	Time period
T	Marginal income tax rate
TIE	Times interest earned
v	Variable cost as a percent of selling price
V	Variable cost per unit ($)
V_d	Bond value
VC	Total variable costs ($)
w_i	Weight of Investment i in a portfolio, or the proportion (weight) of a particular type of capital used by a firm
WACC	Weighted average cost of capital
YTC	Yield to call
YTM	Yield to maturity

FOURTH EDITION

Principles of FINANCE

FOURTH EDITION

Principles of FINANCE

Scott Besley
University of South Florida

Eugene F. Brigham
University of Florida

SOUTH-WESTERN
CENGAGE Learning™

Australia · Brazil · Japan · Korea · Mexico · Singapore · Spain · United Kingdom · United States

Principles of Finance, Fourth Edition
Scott Besley, Eugene F. Brigham

Vice President of Editorial, Business:
Jack W. Calhoun

Vice President/Editor-in-Chief:
Alex von Rosenberg

Executive Editor: Mike Reynolds

Developmental Editor: Maggie Kubale

Executive Marketing Manager: Brian Joyner

Marketing Manager: Nathan Anderson

Senior Marketing Communications
Manager: Jim Overly

Senior Content Project Manager:
Tamborah Moore

Media Editor: Scott Fidler

Managing Media Editor: Matt McKinney

Frontlist Buyer, Manufacturing: Kevin Kluck

Production Service: International
Typesetting and Composition

Compositor: International
Typesetting and Composition

Sr. Art Director: Michelle Kunkler

Cover and Internal Designer:
Lou Ann Thesing

Cover Image: © Campbell Laird/Veer, Inc.

For product information and technology assistance, contact us at
Cengage Learning Customer & Sales Support, 1-800-354-9706

For permission to use material from this text or product, submit all requests online at **www.cengage.com/permissions**
Further permissions questions can be emailed to
permissionrequest@cengage.com

ExamView® is a registered trademark of eInstruction Corp. Windows is a registered trademark of the Microsoft Corporation used herein under license. Macintosh and Power Macintosh are registered trademarks of Apple Computer, Inc. used herein under license.

Library of Congress Control Number: 2008931991

ISBN-13: 978-0-324-65588-9

ISBN-10: 0-324-65588-6

South-Western Cengage Learning
5191 Natorp Boulevard
Mason, OH 45040
USA

Cengage Learning products are represented in Canada by Nelson Education, Ltd.

For your course and learning solutions, visit **www.cengage.com**

Purchase any of our products at your local college store or at our preferred online store **www.ichapters.com**

Printed in the United States of America
1 2 3 4 5 6 7 12 11 10 09 08

Brief Contents

Contents

PART 3   FUNDAMENTALS OF VALUATION   313

PART 4   CORPORATE DECISION MAKING   471

Preface

Principles of Finance is intended for use in an introductory finance course. The book represents a survey of key concepts by covering the three general areas of study in finance: (1) financial markets and institutions, (2) investments, and (3) managerial finance. The book begins with a discussion of the principles of financial systems—markets, institutions, and assets. This section is followed by a presentation of general business concepts, including discussions of business organizations and goals and an examination of financial health. The next set of chapters covers valuation concepts, which include the time value of money, valuing financial and real assets, and fundamentals of risk and return. Then, corporate decision making, or managerial finance, is presented. The discussions here center on how financial managers can help maximize their firms' values by making sound decisions in such areas as capital budgeting, choice of capital structure, and working capital management. Finally, in the last two chapters, investment fundamentals are explained. This organization has three important advantages:

1. Explaining early in the book how financial markets operate and how security prices are determined helps students understand how managerial finance can affect the value of the firm as well as how the same concepts can be used to make personal financial decisions. This background helps when coverage of such key concepts as risk analysis, time value of money, and valuation techniques are discussed in the remainder of the book.

2. Structuring the book around markets and valuation enhances continuity because this organization helps students see how the various topics relate to one another.

3. Most students—even those who do not plan to major in finance—are generally interested in investment concepts, such as stock and bond valuation and selection, how financial markets work, how risk and rates of return affect financial decision making, and the like. Because people's ability to learn a subject is a function of their interest and motivation, and because *Principles* begins by showing the relationships among security markets, valuing financial assets, and managerial finance, this organization works well from a pedagogic standpoint.

Although this book is intended to be a survey of general finance, we could not include discussions of every area associated with the field of finance. Thus, we included those topics considered most relevant to presenting a basic understanding of the diversity of finance as an area of study. Because most students who read this book will probably not become finance majors, this book will be their only exposure to finance, including investment concepts that intrigue all of us. For this reason, we have structured the book so that (1) its content is sufficient to provide students with a good basic understanding of finance and (2) it can be used as a reference, or guide, for answering fundamental questions about finance.

RELATIONSHIP OF THIS BOOK WITH OTHER CENGAGE BOOKS

Clearly, it is impossible to provide everything one needs to know about finance in one text, especially an introductory text. This recognition has led us to limit the scope of this book and also to write other texts to deal with the materials that cannot be included in *Principles*. Besley and Brigham have authored a text that emphasizes more detailed material about managerial finance (*Essentials of Managerial Finance*, fourteenth edition). Also, Eugene F. Brigham and Philip R. Daves have coauthored an intermediate undergraduate text (*Intermediate Financial Management*, ninth edition) and Eugene F. Brigham and Michael C. Ehrhardt have coauthored a comprehensive book aimed primarily at MBAs (*Financial Management: Theory and Practice*, twelfth edition).

The relationship between *Principles* and the more advanced books deserves special comment. First, we recognize that the advanced books are often used by students who have also used *Principles* in an introductory finance course. Thus, we wanted to avoid excessive overlap but wanted to be sure to expose students to alternative points of view on controversial subjects. We should note, though, that our students in advanced courses invariably tell us that they find it helpful to have the more difficult materials repeated—they need the review. Students also say they like the fact that the style and notation used in our upper-level books are consistent with those in the introductory text, as this makes learning easier. Regarding alternative points of view, we have made every effort to take a moderate, middle-of-the-road approach, and where serious controversy exists, we have tried to present the alternative points of view. Reviewers were asked to consider this point, and their comments have helped us eliminate potential biases.

INTENDED MARKET AND USE

As noted earlier, *Principles* is intended for use as an introductory text. The key chapters can be covered in a one-term course, and if supplemented with cases and some outside readings, the book can also be used in a two-term course. If it is used in a one-term course, the instructor might cover only selected chapters, leaving the others for students either to examine on their own or to use as reference in conjunction with work in later courses. Also, we have made every effort to write the chapters in a flexible, modular format, which helps instructors cover the material in a different sequence, should they choose to do so.

IMPORTANT FEATURES OF THE BOOK

We must present the material contained in the book in a structured manner to ensure continuity and cogency in the coverage of the topics. To enhance the pedagogy, we have included some important features, which are discussed here.

Learning Objectives and End-of-Chapter Summary

Each chapter now begins with a section called Chapter *Principles*—The Questions, which consists of a set of questions that students should be able to answer when they finish reading the chapter. These questions represent the learning objectives for the chapter. At the end of the chapter, the beginning-of-the-chapter questions are answered in a section called Chapter *Principles*—The Answers, which replaces the typical end-of-chapter summary. This feature helps students to connect the material covered in the chapter with questions that instructors often ask during class or on exams.

Spreadsheets

This edition contains expanded coverage of spreadsheets. The use of spreadsheets to solve financial problems is prominent in the chapter that covers time value of money concepts (Chapter 9) and the chapter that describes capital budgeting techniques (Chapter 13). The interest tables have been taken out of the book because financial calculators and spreadsheets make them obsolete. Because students must use spreadsheets in the business world, they should be exposed to the benefits of this important business tool early in their business curriculum.

Personal Finance

In the years that we have taught the basic course in finance that all business majors are required to complete, we have noticed that many students seem uninterested in the topic. In fact, most admit that they would not take the course if it was not required. As a result, we have tried various methods to get the uninterested students more interested in finance. It seems that one way to get the attention of students is to relate managerial finance topics to personal financial decisions that everyone is exposed to at some point during their lives. Therefore, we added a new feature in each chapter, which is titled Chapter *Principles*—Personal Finance. This section contains discussion that relates the topics covered in the chapter to personal financial decisions. Our hope is that students make the connection between financial concepts presented in the course and the application to decisions that they will face with their personal finances. Perhaps this pedagogy will help to get students more interested in learning some of the important financial concepts.

Ethical Dilemmas

We feel that it is crucial for students who will someday be decision makers in the business world to be exposed to ethical situations to improve their critical-thinking skills. For this reason, we have included ethical dilemma vignettes in every edition of *Principles*. In this edition, we have expanded the ethical dilemmas so that an Ethical Dilemma box is contained in each chapter. Each ethical dilemma vignette is related to the material covered in the chapter and is based on real-world circumstances. These ethical dilemmas (1) expose the students to the relationship between ethics and business, (2) promote the development of critical-thinking and decision-making skills, and (3) provide a vehicle for lively class discussion.

Cash Flow Time Lines and Solutions Approach to TVM Analysis

In our discussions of time value of money topics (Chapter 9), we begin each major section with a verbal discussion of a time value issue, and then we present a time line to show graphically the cash flows that are involved, after which we give the equation that must be solved to obtain the required answer. Finally, we present two methods that can be used to solve the equation: (1) a numerical solution and (2) a financial calculator solution (We also present spreadsheet solutions for some problems.). The cash flow time line helps students visualize the problem at hand and see how to set it up for solution, the equation helps them understand the mathematics, and the two-pronged solution approach helps them see that time value problems can be solved in alternative ways. Each student will focus on the particular solution technique he or she will actually use, which generally calls for using a financial calculator. One advantage of our approach is that it helps students understand that a financial calculator is not a "black box"; rather, it is an efficient tool that can be used to solve time value problems.

Multinational Finance Coverage

Coverage of multinational finance is still included in the chapters where the specific topics are covered rather than in a separate chapter devoted to multinational managerial finance. This placement allows students to better understand how the application of the material presented in the chapter differs in domestic and international settings.

A Managerial Perspective

Each chapter leads off with "A Managerial Perspective," which can be used for student reading, for class lecture, or for both. Although these business anecdotes are not new to this edition of *Principles,* we want to draw attention to them because the content of each is either new to this edition or has been updated since the previous edition.

ANCILLARY MATERIALS

A number of items are available free of charge to adopting *instructors:*

1. *Instructor's Manual.* The comprehensive manual contains answers to all text questions and problems, detailed solutions to integrative problems, sample exam questions, and suggested course outlines.

2. *Lecture Presentation Software.* To facilitate classroom presentations, computer graphics slide shows written in Microsoft PowerPoint are available.

3. *Test Bank and ExamView.* The Test Bank contains more than 1,000 class-tested questions and problems, many of which are new. True/false questions, multiple-choice conceptual questions, multiple-choice problems (which can be easily modified to short-answer problems by removing the answer choices), and financial calculator problems are included for every chapter. For this version of the test bank, we have developed learning objectives and outcomes assessment criteria that satisfy AACSB requirements. Questions that can be used for assessment of outcomes are identified in the test bank. So that they are considered AACSB qualified, these questions were selected by a committee.

    ExamView contains all of the questions in the printed test bank and allows instructors to create, edit, store, and print exams, as well as use them online.

4. *Problem Spreadsheet.* Spreadsheets that contain models for the computer-related end-of-chapter problems are also available.

5. *Web site.* A book-designated Web site with numerous resources for instructors and students can be accessed through http://www.cengage.com/finance/besley.

A number of additional items are available for purchase by *students:*

1. *Cases. Finance Online Case Library,* third edition, by Lin Klein and Eugene F. Brigham, is well suited for use with *Principles.* The cases provide

real-world applications of the methodologies and concepts developed in this book. In addition, all of the cases are available in a customized format, so your students pay only for the cases you decide to use.

2. *Spreadsheet Analysis Book. Financial Analysis with Microsoft Excel*, fourth edition, by Timothy Mayes and Todd Shank, fully integrates the teaching of spreadsheet analysis with the basic finance concepts. This book makes a good companion to *Principles* in courses in which computer work is highly emphasized.

ACKNOWLEDGMENTS

This book reflects the efforts of a number of people over the years. For the fourth edition, we are indebted to the professors listed here who provided their input for improving *Principles:*

John Fay
Santa Clara University

Kristie J. Loescher
The University of Texas at Austin

Joseph H. Meredith
Elon University

Aldo Palles
Palm Beach Atlantic University

Sorin A. Tuluca
Fairleigh Dickinson University

Sinan Yildirim
St. Edward's University

Shaorong Zhang
Marshall University

Next, we would like to thank the following people for their valuable comments and suggestions in previous editions of this book: Nasser Arshadi, Robert E. Chatfield, K. C. Chen, John H. Crockett Jr., Mary M. Cutler, Dean Drenk, David R. Fewings, Shawn M. Forbes, Beverly Hadaway, Wiliam C. Handorf, Jerry M. Hood, Raman Kumar, Robert M. Pavlik, Stephen Peters, Marianne Plunkert, Gary Sanger, Oliver Schnusenberg, Paul J. Swanson, Harold B. Tamule, Sorin Tuluca, David E. Upton, Bonnie Van Ness, and Howard R. Whitney.

ERRORS IN THE TEXT

At this point, most authors make a statement like this: "We appreciate all the help we received from the people listed above, but any remaining errors are, of course, our own responsibility." And in many books, there are plenty of remaining errors. Having experienced difficulty with errors ourselves, both as students and as instructors, we resolved to avoid this problem in *Principles*. As a result of our error-detection procedures, we are convinced that this text is relatively free of mistakes.

Partly due to our confidence that there are few errors in this book, but primarily because we want to correct any errors that might have slipped by so that we can correct them in future printings of the book, we have decided to offer a reward of $10 per error to the *first* person who reports it to us. For purposes of this reward, errors are defined as spelling errors, computational errors not due to rounding, factual errors, and other errors that inhibit comprehension. Typesetting errors, such as spacing, and differences in opinion concerning grammatical or punctuation conventions do not qualify for the reward. Also, given the ever-changing nature of the World Wide Web, changes in Web addresses do not qualify as errors—the Web addresses included in the book are those that existed at the time we wrote it. Finally, any qualifying error that has follow-through effect is counted as two errors only. Please report any errors to Scott Besley either via email at sbesley@coba.usf.edu or by regular mail at the address that follows.

CONCLUSION

Finance is, in a real sense, the cornerstone of the enterprise system—good financial management is vitally important to the economic health of business firms, and hence to the nation and the world. Because of its importance, finance should be widely and thoroughly understood, but this is easier said than done. The field is relatively complex, and it is undergoing constant change in response to shifts in economic conditions. All of this makes finance stimulating and exciting, but also challenging and sometimes perplexing. We sincerely hope that *Principles of Finance,* fourth edition, will meet its own challenge by contributing to a better understanding of our financial system.

Scott Besley
University of South Florida
College of Business Administration, BSN3403
Tampa, FL 33620-5500

Eugene F. Brigham
University of Florida
College of Business
Gainesville, Florida 32611-7160

PART 1

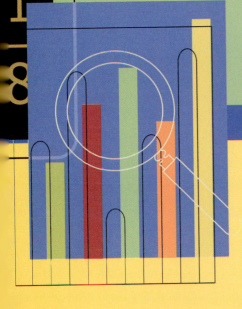

General Finance Concepts

An Overview of Finance

A MANAGERIAL PERSPECTIVE

Do you like money? Then you should like finance because finance deals with money. More importantly, you will discover as you read this text that *finance people* like putting the money they have to work so as to make more money. Sound like a good idea? It is, if you know what you are doing.

How well do you think you understand finance? If you are like most people, the answer is "not very well." According to numerous surveys and quizzes that have been administered to determine the financial literacy of Americans, it can be concluded that too many people are financially illiterate. According to Bankrate.com, the average grade that Americans score for financial literacy is a D. Only 10 percent of the participants earned a score of A on the financial literacy test; 35 percent of the participants earned a failing grade.[1] The results are worse for high schools students. In its 2008 survey of high school seniors, Jump$tart found that the average score on its financial literacy test was 48, which is failing. Although they performed better, college students still received a grade of D with an average score of 62.[2] It has been reported that between 10 and 20 percent of Americans have no financial knowledge at all, and only 55 percent could be rated as possessing a level of financial literacy that is considered average or above average.

The areas in which people seem to have the greatest deficiencies or misconceptions about their finances are retirement needs and personal debt. During the 1990s, the average annual savings rate in the United States declined from approximately 9 percent to nothing (0 percent), which means that, as the new millennium began, Americans were not putting aside any of their income to prepare for either retirement or emergencies. In 2005 and 2006, the personal savings rates were −3.2 percent and −1.6 percent, respectively, which means that Americans spent more money than they earned during this period. Curently, the savings rate is just above 1 percent.[3] To make matters worse, as savings dropped, personal debt increased sharply. For example, in 1990 the average credit card balance was approximately $3,000, and in 2000 the average balance was nearly $8,000. Today (2008), it is estimated that the average American family has between $8,500 and $9,000 in credit card debt. As a student, you should be concerned about your credit because, on average, undergraduate students carry outstanding credit card balances equal to about $3,500, and

---

[1]The sources for the information about financial literacy can be found at Bankrate.com.

[2]The results of the Jump$tart survey are available at http://www.jumpstart.org/.

[3]Sources: The American Savings Education Council (http://www.choosetosave.org/asec/) and the Bureau of Economic Analysis (http://www.bea.gov/).

graduate students carry balances equal to almost $5,600. Approximately 10 percent of graduating students have credit card balances in excess of $7,000. In addition, when they graduate, undergaduate students on average have education loans that amount to between $17,000 and $20,000, and students who pursue graduate degrees owe from $27,000 to $114,000 in student loans.[4]

Finance is a fundamental part of life, so it is important to have some understanding of how it affects you as a person. When you buy a car or a house or plan for retirement, you must deal with the general concepts of finance. As you read this text, try to relate the topics that are presented to future decisions that you will face, including investing in stocks, planning for retirement, and financing such big-ticket items as cars and houses. Even if you pursue a career in a non-finance profession, you will find yourself using finance concepts in both your job and your personal life.

Finance is centuries old. Despite its ancient roots, it remains an evolving discipline, with no limits in sight. As you read this chapter, as well as the rest of the book, keep in mind that this field is dynamic and ever-changing. If you are looking for a career in which you are not likely to become bored, finance just might be the answer.

[4]Sources include Draut, T., "Economic State of Young America," Dēmos: A Network for Ideas & Action (New York, NY), Spring 2008. A pdf version of the report is available at http://www.demos.org/pub1568.cfm. Dickler, J., "Getting Squeezed by Credit Card Companies: Card Issuers Use All Sorts of Tactics to Wrestle Every Penny Out of Customers. Here's What You Need to Know," CNNMoney.com, May 27, 2008. "Taking Charge: America's Relationship with Credit Cards," CreditCards.com, June 6, 2007.

CHAPTER PRINCIPLES
–The Questions

After reading this chapter, you should be able to answer the following questions:

- What is finance, and why should everyone understand basic financial concepts?
- How has the finance discipline changed during the past 100 years?
- What is value, and what does it mean to maximize value?
- What is sustainability?
- What is lean manufacturing? What is lean finance?

"Why should I study finance?" You probably are asking yourself this question right now. To answer this question, you need to answer another question: What is finance?

WHAT IS FINANCE?

finance
The discipline that deals with decisions concerning how money is raised and used by businesses, governments, and individuals.

In simple terms finance is concerned with decisions about money, or more appropriately, cash flows. **Finance** decisions deal with how money is raised and used by businesses, governments, and individuals. To make rational financial decisions, you must understand three general, yet reasonable, concepts (with everything else being equal): (1) more value is preferred to less, (2) the sooner cash is received, the more valuable it is, and (3) less risky assets are more valuable than (preferred to) riskier assets.

In this book we will show that a firm that practices sound financial management can provide better products to its customers at lower prices, pay higher salaries to its employees, and still provide greater returns to investors who put up the funds needed to form and operate the business. Because the economy—both national and worldwide—consists of customers, employees, and investors, sound financial management contributes to the well-being of both individuals and the general population.

When making financial decisions, everyone should keep in mind the primary goal of finance, which is to *maximize value*. In simple terms, financial value is created when funds are used to generate returns that exceed the costs that are associated with using those funds. Although the concept is simple, achieving this goal can be difficult. We will discuss the general goal of value maximization later in this chapter and in greater detail throughout the book.

As you read this book, you will discover that the same concepts that firms apply when making sound business decisions can be used to make informed decisions relating to personal finances. For example, consider the decision you might have to make if you won a state lottery worth $105 million. Which *would* you choose, a lump-sum payment of $54 million today or a payment of $3.5 million each year for the next 30 years? Which *should* you choose? In Chapter 9, we will describe time value of money techniques that can be used to answer this question and other questions that relate to personal finances. In fact, throughout the book we will show how the general finance concepts that are presented in the chapters apply to decisions about personal financial management.

Self-Test Questions

In general terms, what does it mean to maximize value?

What are some common personal finance decisions that individuals face?

GENERAL AREAS OF FINANCE

The study of finance consists of four interrelated areas: (1) financial markets and institutions; (2) investments; (3) financial services; and (4) managerial (business) finance. Because these four areas are interrelated, an individual who works in any one area should have a good understanding of the other areas as well.

Financial Markets and Institutions

Financial institutions, which include banks, insurance companies, savings and loans, and credit unions, are an integral part of the general financial services marketplace. The success of these organizations requires an understanding of factors that cause interest rates to rise and fall, regulations to which financial institutions are subject, and the various types of financial instruments, such as mortgages, auto loans, and certificates of deposit, that financial institutions offer.

Investments

This area of finance focuses on the decisions made by businesses and individuals as they choose securities for their investment portfolios. The major functions in the investments area are (1) determining the values, risks, and returns associated with such financial assets as stocks and bonds and (2) determining the optimal mix of securities that should be held in a portfolio of investments.

Financial Services

Financial services refers to functions provided by organizations that operate in the finance industry. In general, financial services organizations deal with the management of money. Persons who work in these organizations, which include banks, insurance companies, brokerage firms, and other similar companies, provide services that help individuals (and companies) determine how to invest money to achieve such goals as home purchase, retirement, financial stability and sustainability, budgeting, and related activities. The financial services industry is one of the largest in the world.

Managerial (Business) Finance

Managerial finance deals with decisions that all firms make concerning their cash flows. As a consequence, managerial finance is important in all types of businesses, whether they are public or private, deal with financial services, or manufacture products. The types of duties encountered in managerial finance range from making decisions about plant expansions to choosing what types of securities to issue to finance such expansions. Financial managers also have the responsibility for deciding the credit terms under which customers can buy, how much inventory the firm should carry, how much cash to keep on hand, whether to acquire other firms (merger analysis), and how much of the firm's earnings to reinvest in the business and how much to pay out as dividends.

If you pursue a career in finance, you will need some knowledge of each of the areas of finance, regardless of which area you might enter. For example, a banker lending to a business must have a good understanding of managerial finance to judge how well the borrowing company is operated. The same holds true for a securities analyst. Even stockbrokers must understand general financial principles if they are to give intelligent advice to their customers. At the same time, corporate financial managers need to know what their bankers are thinking about and how investors are likely to judge their corporations' performances and thus determine their stock prices.

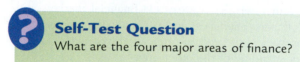

Self-Test Question
What are the four major areas of finance?

THE IMPORTANCE OF FINANCE IN NONFINANCE AREAS

Believe it or not, everyone is exposed to finance concepts almost every day. For example, when you borrow to buy a car or house, finance concepts are used to determine the monthly payments that you are required to make. When you retire, finance concepts are used to determine the amount of the monthly payments you receive from your retirement plan. If you want to start your own business, an understanding of finance concepts is essential for survival. Thus, even if you do not intend to pursue a career in a finance-related profession, it is important that you have some basic understanding of finance concepts. Similarly, if you pursue a career in finance, it is important that you have an understanding of other areas in the business, including marketing, accounting, production, and so forth, to make more informed financial decisions.

Let's consider how finance relates to some of the nonfinance areas in a business.

Management

When we think of management, we often think of personnel decisions and employee relations, strategic planning, and the general operations of the firm. Strategic planning, which is one of the most important activities of management, cannot be accomplished without considering how such plans impact the overall financial well-being of the firm. Personnel decisions such as setting salaries, hiring new staff, and paying bonuses must be coordinated with financial decisions to ensure that any needed funds are available.

For these reasons, managers must have at least a general understanding of financial management concepts to make informed decisions in their areas.

Marketing

If you have taken a basic marketing course, one of the first things you probably learned was that the *four Ps of marketing*—product, price, place, and promotion—determine the success of products that are manufactured and sold by companies. Clearly, the price that should be charged for a product and the amount of advertising a firm can afford for the product must be determined in conjunction with financial managers, because the firm will lose money if the price of the product is too low or too much is spent on advertising. Coordination of the finance function and the marketing function is critical to the success of a company, especially for a small, newly formed firm, because it is necessary to ensure that sufficient cash is generated to survive. For these reasons, people in marketing must understand how marketing decisions affect and are affected by such issues as funds availability, inventory levels, and excess plant capacity.

Accounting

In many firms (especially small ones), it is difficult to distinguish between the finance function and the accounting function. Often, accountants make finance decisions, and vice versa, because the two disciplines are closely related. In fact, you might recognize some of the material in this book from accounting courses that you have already taken. As you will discover, financial managers rely heavily on accounting information because making decisions about the future requires information about the past. As a consequence, accountants must understand how financial managers use accounting information in planning and decision making so that it can be provided in an accurate and timely fashion. Similarly, accountants must understand how accounting data are viewed (used) by investors, creditors, and other outsiders who are interested in the firm's operations.

Information Systems

Businesses thrive by effectively collecting and using information, which must be reliable and available when needed for making decisions. The process by which the delivery of such information is planned, developed, and implemented is costly, but so are the problems caused by a lack of good information. Without appropriate information, decisions relating to finance, management, marketing, and accounting could prove disastrous. Different types of information require different information systems, so information system specialists work with financial managers to determine what information is needed, how it should be stored, how it should be delivered, and how information management will affect the profitability of the firm.

Economics

Finance and economics are so similar that some universities and colleges offer courses related to these areas in the same department or functional area. Many tools used to make financial decisions evolved from theories or models developed by economists. Perhaps the most noticeable difference between finance and economics is that financial managers evaluate information and make decisions about cash flows associated with a particular firm or a small group of firms, whereas economists analyze information and forecast changes in activities associated with entire industries and the economy as a whole. It is important that financial managers understand economics and that economists understand finance—economic activity and policy impact financial decisions, and vice versa.

Finance will be a part of your life no matter what career you choose. There will be a number of times during your life, both in business and in a personal capacity, that you will make finance-related decisions. It is therefore important that you have some understanding of general finance concepts. *There are financial implications in virtually all business decisions, and nonfinancial executives must know enough finance to incorporate these implications into their own specialized analyses.* For this reason, every student of business, regardless of his or her major, should be concerned with finance.

Self-Test Question

Why do people in areas outside financial management need to know something about managerial finance?

THE EVOLUTION OF MODERN FINANCE[5]

In this book, we examine general financial concepts in all of the four interrelated areas that we discussed earlier, but we separate our discusssion into the general areas that many people believe cover the basic topics of finance study: (1) financial markets, (2) investments, and (3) business (managerial) finance. This section provides a brief overview of the evolution of modern finance in these general areas. Later in the book, you will discover that many of the discussions emphasize managerial finance. We have chosen this treatment for two reasons: (1) managerial finance encompasses financial markets and investments and (2) in general, the techniques used in managerial finance can also be applied to financing and investment decisions faced by individuals, and thus to services and products offered by financial services organizations.

Financial Markets

Because the financial markets in the United States are well developed, we have been able to achieve a higher standard of living than otherwise would be possible. Without such financial institutions as banks, credit unions, and savings and loan associations, it would be difficult for us to finance such purchases as houses and automobiles. During the twentieth century, however, both financial markets and financial institutions experienced substantial changes.

In the early 1900s, the "banking" community consisted of thousands of independent banking organizations—mostly small, hometown banks. The larger banks offered a variety of services, including those that we traditionally associate with banks, as well as other financial functions, such as investment services and insurance. By 1920, many of the large commercial banks included investment departments and affiliate organizations that helped companies issue stocks and bonds. A decade later, banks or their affiliates originated nearly 50 percent of all new issues of stocks and bonds. During this period, banks truly were full-service financial organizations.

A series of financial catastrophes during the first third of the twentieth century—including a devastating financial crisis in 1907, the failure of nearly 6,000 banks during the 1920s, and the Great Depression of 1929–1933—resulted in legislation

---

[5]For an excellent discussion of the evolution of finance in the twentieth century, see J. Fred Weston, "A (Relatively) Brief History of Finance Ideas." *Financial Practice and Education,* Spring/Summer 1994, 7–26.

that severely restricted where and how banks could operate and established the foundation of our current banking structure. During this period, branch banking as we know it today did not exist; such expansion was either prohibited by law or condemned by the banking industry. In addition, banking reforms enacted in the 1930s significantly limited the financial activities that banks could undertake. The general sentiment held that unscrupulous banking organizations contributed to earlier financial panics and the Great Depression; consequently, reform was needed to force banks to concentrate on the principal activities associated with the banking industry—taking deposits and making loans. It was felt that such focus could be achieved only through cogent regulation and supervision.

The restrictions imposed on banking operations placed banks at a competitive disadvantage in the financial markets, both domestically and abroad. In the 1970s and 1980s, the financial markets experienced rapid increases in interest rates as well as significant technological advances in communications and information systems. These events resulted in the emergence of nonbank organizations, which soon threatened the presence of banks and other financial institutions. To deal with these issues, a great deal of deregulation has occurred in the banking industry since the 1970s. For example, during the past couple of decades, legislation and legislative proposals have helped tear down barriers to national branch banking and permitted banking organizations to venture into such financial areas as investments and insurance that were prohibited since the 1930s. The deregulation has been supported as a means to improve competition, with proponents arguing that severely restrictive regulation threatens the existence of financial institutions.

In the past, as banking regulations became more restrictive, so did regulation of the financial markets as a whole. It will be interesting to see the sentiment of future legislation, especially given recent problems that have arisen in real estate financing (i.e., subprime mortgages). Generally, when the economy (and thus the financial markets) performs well, there is a tendency to deregulate; the opposite is true during, or immediately after, calamitous economic events.

Investments

The United States has seen a variety of stock markets since the beginning of the twentieth century. In addition, both participation in investments and the types of instruments offered have changed considerably. In the early 1900s, the investments arena was dominated by a small group of wealthy investors and opulent corporations. Few small, individual investors ventured into corporate stocks and bonds because managers rarely disclosed financial information to the public—disclosure of such information was not mandated at the time. Because information was controlled by insiders and those who could afford to pay for it, the small investor was at a considerable disadvantage and was often exploited by the more informed investor. Consequently, most individuals invested in instruments that were considered relatively safe, such as savings accounts at banks and government securities.

Industrialization and the government financing of World War I resulted in increased financial prosperity and provided substantial wealth for people who had invested in the financial markets. Not surprisingly, the performance of the markets soon attracted greater interest from small unsophisticated investors. By the 1920s, the number of investment firms had grown substantially, and corporate stocks and bonds were no longer viewed as investments for the elite only. Unfortunately, as the popularity of the securities markets increased, so did the fraudulent and manipulative practices of investment organizations, including those affiliated with commercial banks. It is interesting to note that mutual funds were introduced to the U.S.

financial markets during this period. Nearly all of these funds focused on common stocks, and the highly speculative nature of many of these funds helped fuel the "fire" associated with the 1929 stock market crash.

From 1929 to 1932, the stock market declined by more than 80 percent—the value of stocks declined from nearly $90 billion to less than $16 billion. Many felt that the market crash was precipitated by unethical trading practices and abuses of investment organizations and individuals. Consequently, during the 1930s, significant pressure was applied to regulate the behavior of the participants in the financial markets. Much of the legislation that established the foundation of today's regulatory tenor was enacted at the time. The principal impetus of the regulation was to ban fraudulent behavior and abusive practices of investors and investment organizations and to require greater disclosure of financial information by issuers of securities. The requirements to disclose more financial information created new opportunities in the investments arena: the accounting profession exploded, investment organizations introduced security analysis, and investments became a popular field of study at many universities.

Post–World War II prosperity and a growing interest in investments by the average individual helped popularize mutual funds in the 1950s and 1960s. The 1970s, on the other hand, was a period of rising interest rates and high inflation, which created a great deal of uncertainty in the economy and caused the securities markets to be extremely volatile. In response, investors withdrew their funds from mutual funds, which basically offered investments only in stocks at the time. As a result, mutual fund companies began introducing new products, such as money market funds (short-term investments) and municipal (government) bond funds, in an attempt to recapture some of the lost demand. Since the 1970s, mutual fund organizations have continued to expand the types of funds offered, mostly to satisfy investors' demands. Currently, you can find mutual funds for just about any type of investment you can imagine. The popularity of any one type of fund shifts with changes in the financial markets. Inevitably, when the stock market is performing well, stock funds are in greater demand; when the economy is stagnant or declining, money market, or short-term, funds are more popular.

Since World War II, both institutional investors (which include pension funds, mutual funds, insurance companies, and the like) and individual investors have increased their presence in the securities markets. For instance, prior to 1950, institutional investors held less than 20 percent of corporate stock; by 2008, however, their share had increased to more than 50 percent. After the 1929 market crash, less than 5 percent of the U.S. population owned stock; today, more than 30 percent of the population invests *directly* in common stock, and more than 70 percent of the population invests *indirectly* either through mutual funds or through company retirement plans. With an increased interest in stocks as personal investments and the ready availability of advanced information technologies, the proportion of individual stockholders surely will increase in the future.

As the attitudes of both investors and regulators have changed, so have the types of investments and the methods used to evaluate investment opportunities. At the beginning of the twentieth century, in most cases the only investments available to individuals were corporate stocks and bonds. Because useful, timely financial information was rarely disclosed publicly, the common investor could generally evaluate securities only by observing the behavior of, and reacting to, those with access to financial information. Over time, as information disclosure became standardized and the common investor obtained greater investment knowledge, greater varieties of investment instruments and investing techniques were introduced, including interest-rate swaps, Treasury strips, program trading, junk bonds, and indexing (described later in the book).

In addition, investment analysis evolved into a more sophisticated process. The analytical tools we use today have their roots in theory developed in the 1930s. During that period, investment experts suggested that there exists a relationship among earnings, dividends, and stock prices such that value should be determined by computing the present value of the future cash flows associated with the stock. Although the techniques we use today are much more sophisticated, as you will discover in later chapters, we still use this same general approach to analyze investments.

Corporate (Managerial) Finance

When managerial finance emerged as a separate field of study in the early 1900s, the emphasis was on the legal aspects of mergers, the formation of new firms, and the various types of securities that firms could issue to raise funds. During this time, industrialization was sweeping the country; *big* was considered to be equivalent to *powerful*, so many takeovers and mergers were used to create large corporations. To illustrate the sentiment of the times, consider the fact that almost 4,300 companies were merged into 300 corporations during the period from 1890 to 1905. The most famous merger involved the combination of eight large steel companies to form U.S. Steel Corporation. The deal was worth $1.4 billion, which was equivalent to 7 percent of the country's gross national product at the time. In today's economy, a comparable merger would be valued at nearly $1 trillion.

Another wave of mergers occurred during the 1920s, fueled primarily by consolidations within the utilities industry. During the Depression era of the 1930s, however, an unprecedented number of business failures caused the emphasis in managerial finance to shift to bankruptcy and reorganization, corporate liquidity, and regulation of security markets. During this period, new rules were enacted that required firms to maintain and publicly disclose certain financial information.

Even with the frenzy of mergers in the early 1900s and throughout the 1920s, and the large number of bankruptcies that followed the Great Depression in the 1930s, finance was mostly a descriptive discipline that emphasized organizational relationships of firms and legal matters. For the most part, finance theory consisted of anecdotes and "rules of thumb." If you read books about financial decision-making practices that were published during this period, you will find few, if any, analytical procedures applied to such complex decisions as appropriate levels of liquidity; instead, many decisions were based on subjective, or "seat-of-the-pants," logic. Analytical models based on time value of money principles sometimes were used to help make decisions about long-term, high-priced capital investments. Even then, however, subjective techniques, such as payback methods, were considered the best methods to make such decisions.[6]

During the 1940s and early 1950s, managerial finance continued to be taught as a descriptive, institutional subject, viewed more from the standpoint of an outsider than from the perspective of management. Financial managers emphasized liquidity—that is, cash budgeting, and management of short-term assets and liabilities were stressed. At the same time, the scope of financial management began to widen somewhat, primarily because the responsibilities associated with proper liquidity management included knowledge of accounts receivable activities, manufacturing operations, and short-term financing alternatives.

In the late 1950s and the 1960s, increased competition in established industries reduced the profit opportunities available to corporations. As a result, financial

---

[6]We describe the techniques that are used to make such decisions, called capital budgeting decisions, in greater detail in Chapter 13.

managers shifted their focus toward techniques used to evaluate investment opportunities. Emphasis was given to finding investments that would improve the firm's ability to generate profits in the future. At roughly the same time, the computer was introduced as a tool for general business use. The focus of managerial finance began to shift more toward the insider's point of view and the importance of financial decision making to the firm. A movement toward theoretical analysis began during the 1960s, and the emphasis of managerial finance shifted to managerial decisions regarding the choice of assets and liabilities necessary to maximize the value of the firm. This era is considered the birth of modern finance, from which many of the decision-making techniques we use today evolved.

The 1970s were marked by increased international competition, fast-paced innovation and technological changes, and, perhaps most important, persistent inflation and economic uncertainty fueled by deficits in government spending and in international trade. Changes in the business arena saw the beginning of a financial revolution of sorts in the late 1970s. Firms discovered innovative ways to manage financial risk and finance their activities. Stockholders became more concerned than before with how firms were managed and how managers' actions affected the firms' value.

The focus on valuation continued through the 1980s, but the analysis was expanded to include several new areas: (1) inflation and its effects on business decisions; (2) deregulation of financial institutions and the resulting trend toward large, broadly diversified financial services companies; (3) the dramatic increase in both the use of computers for analysis and the electronic transfer of information; (4) the increased importance of global markets and business operations; and (5) innovations in the financial products offered to investors. For example, the 1980s saw an increase in the popularity of the leveraged buyout (LBO), which is a transaction in which huge amounts of debt are used to purchase a publicly traded company to form a new privately owned, highly leveraged company.

In today's fast-paced, technologically driven world, the area of managerial finance continues to evolve. Mergers and acquisitions remain an important part of the financial world. The most important trends in the 1990s that have continued into the twenty-first century, however, include (1) the continued globalization of business, (2) ongoing adoption of electronic technology, and (3) the regulatory attitude of the government.

The Globalization of Business

Four factors have made the trend toward globalization mandatory for many businesses:

1. Modern transportation and communications have lowered shipping costs and made international trade more feasible than previously.

2. The political clout of consumers who desire low-cost, high-quality products has helped lower trade barriers designed to protect inefficient, high-cost domestic manufacturers.

3. As technology has advanced, the cost of developing new products has increased; as development costs rise, so too must unit sales if the firm is to remain competitive.

4. In a world populated with multinational firms able to shift production to wherever costs are lowest, a firm whose manufacturing operations are restricted to one country cannot compete unless costs in its home country happen to be low—a condition that does not necessarily exist for many U.S. corporations.

As a result of these four factors, survival requires that most manufacturers produce and sell globally. Service companies, including banks, advertising agencies, and accounting firms, also are being forced to "go global" to better serve their multinational clients that have worldwide operations. There will, of course, always be some purely domestic companies, but you should keep in mind that the most dynamic growth and the best opportunities are often found with companies that operate worldwide.

Not long ago, events in eastern Asia highlighted the interrelationship of the world's marketplaces. Economic catastrophes in Japan and southeast Asia in 1997 and 1998 caused U.S. investors to become skittish, increasing the uncertainty in U.S. financial markets. Many investors sat on the sidelines, waiting to see how the economic problems in Asia would affect large U.S. companies that had multinational operations. A similar event is occuring at the time we write this book in 2008. At a time when the U.S. economy is highly uncertain—it is either stagnant or recessionary—the financial markets around the world are very uncertain. Economic uncertainty in the United States has led to speculation in the world's commodities markets, which has driven the prices of oil to record highs (currently a barrel of oil is selling for greater than $130).

Information Technology

Large companies operate networks of personal computers that are linked to one another, to the firm's own central computers, and to their customers' and suppliers' computers. Some companies, such as General Motors, require their suppliers to be linked electronically so that orders and payments can be made via the computer. As the twenty-first century proceeds, we will see continued advances in the use of electronic and information technology in managerial finance. This technology promises to revolutionize the way financial decisions are made, just as it has in the past. For example, one result of this "electronic revolution" has been the increased use of quantitative analysis via computer models for financial decision making. It is clear that the next generation of financial managers will need stronger computer and quantitative skills than were required of their predecessors.

Regulatory Attitude of the Government

During the past three decades, the government has taken fairly friendly positions with respect to legislative enactments and regulatory enforcements affecting businesses. Much of the legislation has focused on deregulation of such highly regulated industries as financial services, transportation, communications, and utilities. In addition, for the most part, the government has not discouraged mergers and acquisitions. Since 1985, record numbers of mergers at historically high values have taken place. During this period, economic conditions generally were favorable, as evidenced by record levels posted by the stock markets during the 1980s and 1990s, and later in the mid-2000s. However, when economic conditions sour, causing decreases in the securities markets and burdens on consumers, you can bet legislators will favor re-regulation if they believe deregulation contributed to the economic woes of the country. Historically, after the country has experienced economic crises, or when other factors (unethical practices) have caused investors to suffer significant losses, cries for new, tougher regulations have been abundant, and, for the most part, Congress has obliged.

At the time we write this book (2008), economic conditions are uncertain and consumer confidence is low. The economic woes can be attributed to two major factors: (1) a real estate boom that existed for longer than a decade has reversed, which has resulted in substantial declines in real estate values and substantial increases in mortgage defaults and foreclosures during the past year and (2) the cost of oil has risen substantially during the past year, which translates into significantly higher fuel prices and prices of consumer goods and services that are affected by fuel prices. It shouldn't be a surprise that there is an outcry for Congress to enact legislation that will temper the effects of the downturn in the real estate market and lower the price that Americans pay for fuel, and Congress seems to be listening.

 Self-Test Questions

How have financial markets and institutions evolved during the past century?

How have investments evolved during the past century?

How has business (managerial) finance evolved during the past century?

How might a person become better prepared for a career in managerial finance?

THE IMPORTANCE OF MANAGERIAL FINANCE

The historical trends discussed in the previous section have greatly increased the importance of finance, especially managerial finance. Because much of this book is concerned with the decision-making framework faced by corporate financial managers, this section describes the role of managerial finance in business decisions.

The areas of finance we discussed in the previous section are highly related to one another. In fact, in many instances, it is very difficult to distinguish among the functions performed in each area. Consider, for example, the series of events that occurs when a firm needs to raise funds to finance future growth. Generally, if the firm's stock is publicly traded, the amount of funds that is needed is substantial—much greater than can be borrowed at an individual bank or financial institution. For this reason, the firm generally raises the funds by selling (issuing) stocks, bonds, or a combination of these two instruments to individual investors, institutional investors (pension funds, mutual funds, and so forth), or both. When determining the amount of funds needed, the firm uses techniques developed for making managerial finance decisions, including capital budgeting and other valuation techniques. Likewise, when determining whether to invest their funds in the stocks or bonds of a company that wants to fund its future growth opportunities, investors assess the attractiveness of the investment using some of the same valuation techniques.

In essence, a firm decides as to whether to raise funds by using available information to assess the value of the projects for which the funds will be used, and this process is based on the concepts of managerial finance. At the same time, investors make decisions about the attractiveness of the firm by evaluating available information to assess the value—that is, the opportunities—of the firm's decisions to finance growth, and this process is based on investment concepts. The financial markets have an effect on both decisions. Firms "go to" the financial markets to get (raise) funds they need, whereas investors "go to" the financial markets to provide funds to firms hoping that they will earn high returns on their investments. To make informed business decisions, both firms and investors follow essentially the same financial decision-making processes; both parties evaluate the value of their decisions. The major difference is that they are on "different sides of the fence"; that is, the firm seeks funds to invest in growth, whereas the investor is willing to provide such funds if the "price is right." Both parties need some knowledge of the financial markets, because they both "visit" the financial marketplaces to implement their decisions.

At this point, you should have an idea as to the relationships that exist among the general areas of finance. We will explain in greater detail these relationships and some of the techniques that are used to make informed decisions in each of these areas in the remainder of the book. First, however, because it is the foundation of all finance decisions, we are going to give you an idea of what *value* represents.

Self-Test Question
Explain why financial planning is important to today's chief executives.

FINANCIAL DECISIONS AND VALUE (WEALTH) MAXIMIZATION

Investors purchase corporate stocks because they expect to earn good returns on their investments. In fact, everything else equal, we know that investors want to increase their wealth positions as much as possible. Because investors (stockholders) are not involved with firms' day-to-day operations, they expect those who are responsible for daily decisions—that is, executives and managers—to run the businesses with the stockholders' best interests in mind. We will discuss the relationship between stockholders and firms' decision makers later in the text. At this point, however, it is important to note that financial decisions are decisions about value, regardless of whether the decisions concern the operations of a firm or are related to personal finances. When you invest your hard-earned money in stocks, you want those stocks to increase in value as much as possible; likewise, when you invest your money in such assets as houses, you want those assets to maintain or increase in value if possible.

How do we measure value, and what types of actions can be taken to maximize value? Although we will discuss valuation in much greater detail later in the book, we introduce the concept of value here to give you an indication of what value represents and what changes the value of an asset. First, the *value* of any investment, such as a stock, is based on the *cash flows the asset is expected to generate during its life*—both the amount and the timing of the cash flows. Would you invest in an asset that you expect will *not* generate (pay you) any cash flows in the future? Your answer should be "ABSOLUTELY NOT," because it would be irrational for you to give up some of your hard-earned money today and receive nothing in return in the future. Second, investors generally are *risk averse,* which means that they are willing to pay more for investments with more certain future cash flows than investments with less certain, or riskier, cash flows, everything else being equal. For these reasons, all else equal, we know that the value of any asset changes when there are changes in the asset's expected future cash flows (both the amounts and the timings), when there are changes in the certainty of the expected cash flows, or when a combination of these actions occurs.

Figure 1-1 diagrams the general relationships that are involved in the valuation process. As you can see, and as we will discuss in much greater detail throughout the book, valuation is ultimately a function of the cash flows of the firm (or any asset) is expected to generate in the future and the rate of return at which investors are willing to provide funds to the firm for the purposes of financing operations and growth. Many factors affect the determination of the expected cash flows and the rates people demand when investing their funds. Some of these factors are conditions in the economy and financial markets, the competitive environment, and the general operations of the firm, including operating efficiency, labor conditions, and so forth. As we progress through the book, we will discuss these and other factors that affect the value of a firm (and other assets). When we refer to **value,** we mean the

value
The worth of the future cash flows, stated in current dollars, that an asset is expected to generate during its life.

FIGURE 1-1   Value of a Firm

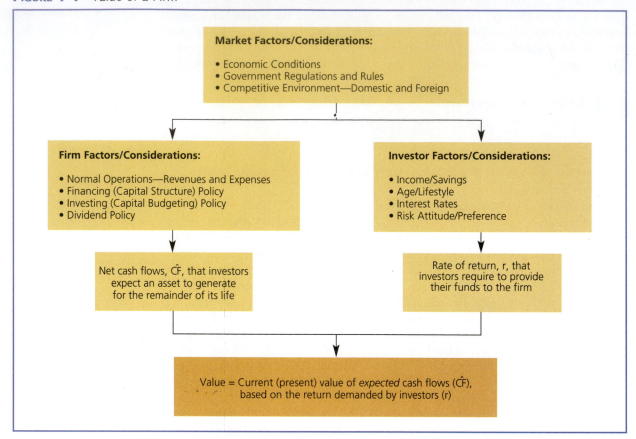

worth of the future cash flows, stated in current dollars,—that is, the present, or current, value of the cash flows the asset is expected to generate during its life.

Self-Test Questions

Identify some decisions made by financial managers that affect the value of the firm.

Identify some factors beyond a firm's control that influence its stock price.

RECENT (FUTURE) DEVELOPMENTS IN BUSINESS AND FINANCE

In recent years, many businesses have focused on two areas when making strategic decisions: (1) sustainability and (2) lean manufacturing. Although some might argue that the concepts espoused in these areas are not "new," the interest in these subjects has exploded in the twenty-first century. As a result, in this section we discuss the role of finance in a strategic decision-making framework that integrates the principle concepts of sustainability and lean manufacturing.

Sustainability

What is sustainability? In its simplest form, sustainability represents the continuing process by which we live and interact with everyone and everything that currently exists and that will exist in the future. Sound sustainable practices recognize that the economy, environment, and civilization are linked in such a way that factors that influence one area directly affect the other areas as well. **Sustainability** is a long-run concept that focuses on improving the quality of life of all stakeholders—that is, humans, animals, businesses, governments, and so forth—for all generations, both current and future. The basic idea is to maintain or improve the quality of life that currently exists without compromising the quality of life that will be available for future generations (stakeholders).

sustainability
The concept that we should improve the quality of life of all stakeholders for all generations, both current and future.

Finance is an important ingredient in the "system" in which we live, both professionally and personally, and, as such, plays an important role in sustainability. Broadly speaking, the "stakeholders" that are affected by firms' decisions can be thought of as the environment in which we live and do business, which includes firms that make the decisions, competitors, customers, governments, the ecology, and any other person, animal, or "thing" that might be affected by firms' decisions. It should be apparent that a firm cannot survive—that is, remain sustainable—unless it fairly treats all stakeholders, whether human, business, government, or environment. A firm that destroys either the trust of its employees, customers, and shareholders or the environment in which it operates destroys itself. Thus, as you will see as we progress through the book, the firm cannot achieve the goal of value maximization without being sustainable.

Lean Manufacturing

Lean manufacturing refers to a "system" that integrates the entire production process so that the least amount of resources is used. The primary goal of lean manufacturing is to eliminate excesses in an effort to more efficiently satisfy customer needs—that is, produce high-quality products at low costs. The mantra of managers who espouse lean manufacturing might be: "Our goal is to create value for our customers, and we accomplish this by developing and generating products and services in the most efficient manner possible."

lean manufacturing
A "system" that integrates the entire production process so that the least amount of resources is used.

The primary goal in finance is to maximize value (wealth); to do so, the "process" must be lean. For example, as an investor, you will find that you want to invest your money to earn the highest rates of return at the lowest costs. Business executives attempt to maximize the prices of their companies' stocks, which, by definition, is accomplished when the *net* cash flows that are generated for stockholders are maximized—that is, the highest cash flows are generated at the lowest costs. Thus, as you will see as we progress through the book, the firm cannot achieve the goal of value maximization without being "lean."

As more firms become "lean thinkers," other business areas and functions are following. For example, recently, firms have begun to explore the possibility of simplifying financial reporting. Traditional financial reporting methods are fairly complex, somewhat redundant, and, in some cases, produce useless (wasteful) data. There is a relatively new initiative to make financial reporting lean—that is, to simplify financial statements such that the appropriate information is reported accurately and in a timely and easily understood manner. At this time, "lean accounting" is still in the evolution stage, so it might be quite some time before most firms adopt the process.

Self-Test Questions

What does the term *sustainability* mean?

In business, what does it mean to be lean?

Ethical Dilemma

Who Has the Money—The Democrat or The Republican?

Sunflower Manufacturing recently applied for a $10 million loan at The Democrat Federal Bank (known simply as The Democrat). The purpose of the loan is to support its working capital needs during the next nine months. Sunflower has been a loyal customer of the bank for many years and has been extended whatever amount of credit it requested in the past.

Sheli Crocker, who is a new, young loan officer at The Democrat, reviewed Sunflower's loan application and decided to turn down the loan for the requested amount. In her report to Henry, her boss and the senior loan officer, Sheli indicated that she thought that Sunflower would have trouble repaying a $10 million loan because its financial position has deteriorated in recent months. Sheli noted that the company's ability to pay its current obligations—that is, its liquidity position—is poor and that analysts are pessimistic about Sunflower's ability to improve its liquidity during the next two years. As a result, Sheli recommended that Sunflower's request for $10 million should be denied. She did indicate, however, that she thought it would be appropriate for the bank to lend a smaller amount, up to a maximum of $2 million.

Earlier today, Henry called Sheli into his office to discuss her report because he wanted her to reconsider her recommendation. Henry told Sheli that he thought the bank should extend the $10 million loan to Sunflower because the company has been a model customer in the past, and the bank should not abandon a loyal customer just because it might have some short-term financial difficulties. Sheli explained that Sunflower's financial numbers indicate that the firm can handle only a $2 million loan. In addition, she said that the cash budget that was provided with the loan application was "suspicious" because the numbers don't seem to match Sunflower's other financial statements and recent activity in the company's bank accounts.

Henry instructed Sheli to return to her office and reevaluate Sunflower's loan application. He suggested that Sheli should consider the loyalty the company has shown to the bank over the years. In fact, Henry told Sheli that he believed customer loyalty should be the primary consideration when determining to whom the bank should lend money. Further, Henry indicated that he thought Sunflower would go to another bank—perhaps to its archrival, The Republican National Bank (affectionately known as The Republican)—for the loan unless The Democrat approved a loan for the entire $10 million that was requested. And, if a competing bank grants Sunflower the loan, The Democrat probably will lose all of the company's business, including its checking account, payroll management, and receivables management.

After reconsidering the financial numbers, Sheli did not change her mind. In fact, she was even more convinced that the loan should not be made because both Sunflower's financial position and its ability to generate the necessary cash flows in recent months suggest that the bank would be making a big mistake if the loan were granted. But, because it is the end of the accounting period and Sheli knew that her department had not generated its quota of loans, she was trying to determine what actions she can take to make the loan application more attractive. In the back of her mind, she can't forget her earlier discussion with Henry in which he reminded her of the importance of meeting loan quotas; he suggested that jobs could be lost if quotas aren't attained.

Another factor that Sheli has to consider is that The Democrat was in a somewhat precarious financial position itself. The Democrat had been losing business to competing banks, especially to The Republican, during the past few years. The loss of business had caused a significant decline in The Democrat's growth. What should Sheli do? What would you do if you were in Sheli's position?

To summarize the key concepts in this chapter, let's answer the questions that were posed at the beginning of the chapter:

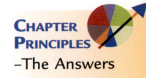

- **What is finance, and why should everyone understand basic financial concepts?** Finance deals with decisions about money—that is, how money is raised and used by companies and individuals. Everyone deals with financial decisions, both in business and in their personal lives. For this reason, and because *there are financial implications in nearly every business-related decision,* it is important that everyone has at least a general knowledge of financial concepts so that they can make informed decisions about money.

- **How has the finance discipline changed during the past 100 years?** During the twentieth century, finance evolved from a more descriptive discipline in which many decisions were driven by rules of thumb to a more technical discipline where the decision-making processes include inputs derived from quantitative models, some of which are complex. The emphasis on the application of quantitative techniques has increased as technology has advanced.

- **What is value, and what does it mean to maximize value?** An asset's value is based on the cash flows that it is expected to generate during its useful life. The value of any asset is determined by translating the future cash flows that the asset is expected to generate into its current equivalents, or present values. Value is created when an individual or a firm can generate investment returns that are higher than the costs associated with the money that is invested; value is lost (destroyed) when the opposite occurs. Thus, to maximize value, you should attempt to invest low-cost funds to generate the highest returns possible. This concept will become clear as we progress through the book.

- **What is sustainability?** Sustainability recognizes the effects that the practices and behaviors we pursue in the current period have on future generations. "Good sustainability" focuses on improving the quality of life of all stakeholders—that is, all interested parties—for all generations, both current and future. A business that does not consider the well-being of either its employees, customers, and shareholders or the environment in which it operates will not survive.

- **What is lean manufacturing? What is lean finance?** Lean manufacturing is the concept that products should be produced using the least amount of resources such that wasted resources are eliminated. The primary goal of lean manufacturing is complete efficiency in the production process. To maximize value, which is a firm's primary goal, it must be lean. As you will discover later in the book, one of the ways a firm attempts to maximize its value is by decreasing the cost of the funds that it uses to finance investments in assets. At the same time, everything else equal, the firm wants to invest at the highest returns possible. Thus, we can say that the goal of the firm is to become "financially lean."

The basic knowledge you learn in this book will help you understand how to make more informed decisions about your personal finances. As we progress through the book, we will show how you can use the concepts that are discussed in the chapters to better ensure that you make "appropriate" personal financial decisions.

Following are the general concepts presented in this chapter as they relate to personal financial decisions.

- **Valuation** Throughout the book, we will show that the concept of value is fairly easy to grasp—that is, value is based on the future cash flows an asset is expected to produce (both the amount and the timing) and the risk associated with those cash flows. You should be able to apply this concept to estimate the values of investments and make informed decisions about these investments based on their current selling prices.

- **Investment Goals** When you invest your money in a company's stock, you would like the value of the stock to increase, hopefully significantly. In essence, you want to earn the highest return on the stock as possible, which means that you want the combination of the dividends paid by the company and the price of the stock to be as high as possible. As a result, you want managers to make decisions that maximize the value of the firm.

- **Sustainability** We humans have a responsibility to preserve the environment for future generations—that is, it is our responsibility to leave the environment in a condition that is at least as "good" as when we began "using" it. When making personal financial decisions, we must consider the extent to which such decisions will impact both our fellow humans and the environment.

QUESTIONS

1-1 How has the study of finance changed since the beginning of the twentieth century?

1-2 Why is it important for business students to study finance, even if the topic is not their major?

1-3 How can knowledge of financial decision making by corporate financial managers help you make personal financial decisions?

1-4 Under what circumstances do you think the government will impose greater regulations on financial markets and businesses? When does the government tend to favor deregulation and take a more laissez-faire attitude toward business?

1-5 In general, how is value measured? What general factors determine value? How does each factor affect value?

1-6 What does it mean to maximize value?

1-7 What does the term *sustainability* mean?

1-8 Can a firm stay in business if it does not consider the impact of its decisions on all stakeholders, including the environment?

1-9 What is lean manufacturing?

1-10 How does the goal of value maximization relate to lean manufacturing?

SELF-TEST PROBLEM

Solution appears in Appendix B.

Key Terms   **ST-1** Define each of the following terms:
   a. Finance
   b. Value
   c. Sustainability
   d. Lean manufacturing

PROBLEM

Integrative Problem

1-1 Samantha Sampson retired a few years ago at the age of 55. Because she is **Finance Basics**
bored with retirement and still relatively young, Sam has considered starting
a business of her own. However, she doesn't know anything about business.
As a result, Sam has hired the consulting firm for which you work to give her
a brief tutorial on business and finance. To begin her lesson, Ms. Sampson
has asked you to answer the following questions:

  a. What is finance, and why is it important to understand finance to run a
successful business?

  b. What are the major areas of the finance discipline?

  c. How has finance changed since the beginning of the twentieth century?

  d. What are some of the financial trends that are currently of interest to
businesses?

  e. What is value, and how is it determined?

  f. What does it mean to maximize value?

  g. What is sustainability, and how is this concept related to finance?

  h. What is lean manufacturing? How is the goal of value maximization
related to lean manufacturing?

Financial Assets (Instruments)

CHAPTER 2

A Managerial Perspective

Recently, a West Virginia man won a $315 million lottery. He chose to take a lump-sum amount equal to $170 million, which left him with approximately $100 million after taxes. Suppose that you were the person who won the lottery. Should you invest the money? If so, which investments would (should) you choose? Would you invest in stocks or bonds? If you decide to invest in stocks, would you invest in preferred stock or common stock? Maybe you like common stock because it has the potential for substantial gains and the stock market seems "hot"; it has received a great deal of publicity lately. But which kind of common stock should you purchase—growth stock or income stock? If bonds are your choice, which types of bonds would you prefer—long-term or short-term, secured or unsecured? What about mutual funds? Are they appropriate for you? Or would you simply put the money in the bank by purchasing a certificate of deposit?

Now suppose that you are the financial manager of a corporation, charged with making decisions about how to finance current operations as well as capital projects needed for future expansion. Should you recommend that the firm issue commercial paper, bonds, common stock, or some other type of financial instrument? If the company issues a bond, should the bond contract have a conversion feature, a call provision, or both? Why might a company choose to raise funds using a common stock issue rather than a bond issue, or vice versa?

Procedures and techniques to answer these questions are described in later chapters. Before we can make such decisions, however, we need to have some understanding of the types of financial assets available both to investors, who use them as savings instruments, and to corporations and governments, which use them as instruments to raise funds. As these questions make clear, many types of financial instruments with numerous characteristics exist. At times, the choices facing investors and borrowers might seem boundless. But, as you will see, not all financial assets serve the same purpose: different circumstances call for different instruments.

As you read this chapter, try to answer the questions posed here. As you read the description of each financial asset, put yourself in the place of an investor and consider the circumstances under which you would invest in that instrument. Then "switch hats"; put yourself in the place of a borrower and think about when it would be appropriate to use the same instrument to raise funds. You should find this exercise quite interesting. By the time you finish this chapter, you should be able to give cursory answers to the questions posed here.

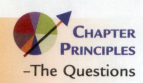

CHAPTER PRINCIPLES –The Questions

After reading this chapter, you should be able to answer the following questions:

- Why are there so many different types of financial instruments?
- What is debt? What types of debt exist and what are some of the characteristics?
- What are bond ratings and why are they important?
- What is equity? What are some of the features/characteristics of equity?
- What are derivatives? What are some of the more familiar types of derivatives?

Chapter 3 introduces the concept of financial markets, which is where financial instruments such as stocks and bonds are traded, and explains how these markets operate. Before delving into the topic of financial markets, however, we describe some of the instruments that are traded in these markets. Some of the *financial assets* that are described in this chapter probably are familiar to you—for example, corporate stocks, government bonds, money market funds, and certificates of deposit; others might be new to you—for example, convertible bonds, futures, and swaps. Many more financial assets exist than we can describe here, so we will describe some of the more popular instruments.

Before describing individual financial assets, we must differentiate between *real assets* and *financial assets,* the two general categories into which we classify assets in the business world. Although any asset generally is regarded as something that provides value to its owner, a significant difference exists between how value is provided by a real asset and how it is provided by a financial asset. A **real asset** sometimes is called a physical asset because it typically is a tangible (that is, physically observable) item, such as a computer, a building, or an inventory item. On the other hand, a **financial asset** is intangible because it represents an expectation, or promise, that future cash flows will be paid to the owner of such an asset.

Different groups of investors prefer different types of financial instruments, and investors' tastes change over time. Thus, corporations and governments offer a variety of securities, and they package their security offerings at each point in time to appeal to the greatest possible number of potential investors. For the most part, however, a financial asset can be classified as debt, equity, or a derivative. Table 2-1 lists some of the more familiar financial instruments that are traded in the various financial markets. In the table, these instruments are arranged in order from those with the shortest maturities to those with the longest maturities.

To give some perspective of the role played by financial instruments in business, this chapter begins with a discussion of some accounting issues that relate to securities used (issued) by firms. The remainder of the chapter describes each security included in Table 2-1, and then provides a brief overview of derivatives. Individuals can invest in each financial instrument described in this chapter either directly or through such intermediaries as pension funds or mutual funds.

real asset
A physically observable, or touchable, item.

financial asset
An asset that represents a promise to distribute cash flows at some future time.

FINANCIAL INSTRUMENTS AND THE FIRM'S BALANCE SHEET

Recall from your accounting courses that a company invests in such *real* assets as inventories and fixed assets to generate positive returns called income. At the same time, a corporation issues *financial* instruments called debt and equity to raise funds to acquire these assets. In other words, the company issues *financial instruments* so that the *assets* necessary to produce and sell inventories can be purchased. In addition, firms use derivatives to hedge, or insure, against a variety of risks. An understanding of the legal and accounting terminology and explanations of financial instruments issued by firms is vital to both investors and financial managers if they are to avoid misinterpretations and the possibility of costly mistakes.

TABLE 2-1   Major Financial Instruments

Instrument	Market Participants	Riskiness	Maturity	Rates on 5/29/08[a]
Treasury bills	Sold to institutional investors by the Treasury to finance government operations	Extremely low risk; no default risk	91 days to 1 year	1.9%
Repurchase agreements	Used by banks to adjust reserves—sell investments with a repurchase promise	Low risk	Very short/overnight	2.3
Federal funds	Interbank loans used to adjust reserves	Low risk	Very short/overnight	2.2
Banker's acceptances	Firms promise to pay (IOU); guaranteed by a bank	Low risk if bank is strong	Up to 180 days	2.5
Commercial paper	Issued by large, financially secure firms	Low default risk	Up to 270 days	2.7
Eurodollars	Dollar denominated deposits in foreign banks	Risk depends on strength of foreign bank	Up to 1 year	2.9
Negotiable CDs	Issued by large, financial sound banks	Riskier than T-bills	Up to a few years	2.8
Money market funds	Invest in T-bills, CDs, and other short-term investments	Low risk	No specific maturity (instant liquidity)	3.5
Treasury notes/bonds	Issued by the U.S. government to finance expenditures	No default risk, but prices change when market rates change	1 to 30 years	4.7
Municipal bonds	Issued by state and local governments	Riskier than Treasury bonds	Up to 30 years	4.8
Term loans	Issued by corporations; negotiated with financial institutions	Depends on borrower; riskier than government bonds	2 to 30 years	5.1
Residential mortgages	Property loans from financial intermediaries	Risk depends on borrower; much riskier than government bonds	Up to 30 years	5.5
Corporate bonds	Debt issued by corporations	Depends on the company; riskier than government bonds; not as risky as stock	Up to 40 years	6.2
Preferred stock	Equity issued by corporations	Riskier than corporate bonds; not as risky as common stock	None	5.4
Common stock	Equity issued by corporations	Risky	None	−10.0[b]

[a]Interest rates are for the longest maturity securities of the type and for the strongest (safest) securities of a given type. Thus, the 5.7 percent interest rate shown for corporate bonds reflects that rate on 30-year, AAA bonds. Lower-rated bonds have higher interest rates.

[b]The rate on common stocks is based on the average return that investors would have earned if they purchased stock on January 2, 2008, and held it until May 29, 2008. The rate was determined by averaging various market indexes, and then annualizing the result.

Sources: Federal Reserve Board (http://www.federalreserve.gov/), *The Wall Street Journal,* and various sites that provide such data on the Internet.

TABLE 2-2   Sydex Corporation Balance Sheet, December 31 ($ millions)

	2010	2009
Assets		
Cash and receivables	$280	$290
Inventory	180	150
Current assets	$460	$440
Net plant and equipment	280	240
Total assets	$740	$680
Liabilities and Equity		
Current liabilities	$230	$220
Long-term debt (bonds)	180	150
Total liabilities	$410	$370
Common stock (75 million shares authorized, 40 million shares outstanding, $1 par)	40	40
Additional paid-in capital	120	120
Retained earnings	170	150
Total common stockholders' equity	$330	$310
Total liabilities and equity	$740	$680

Consider Table 2-2, which shows a simplified balance sheet for Sydex Corporation. At the end of 2010, the book value of Sydex's assets was $740 million. These assets were financed by (1) debt in the form of current liabilities (short term) and bonds (long term), which totaled $410 million, and (2) equity, which totaled $330 million. During the year, Sydex's *investment* in total assets increased by $60 million, rising from $680 million at the beginning of 2010 (end of 2009) to $740 million at the end of the year. The company raised the *funds* needed to purchase the additional assets by using another $10 million in short-term debt (current liabilities increased from $220 million to $230 million), by issuing bonds worth $30 million (long-term debt increased from $150 million to $180 million), and by retaining $20 million of the income earned during the year (retained earnings increased from $150 million to $170 million). The total amount of funds raised during 2010 was $60 million = ($10 million increase in short-term debt) + ($30 million increase in long-term debt) + ($20 million increase in retained earnings).

In 2010, Sydex had total liabilities equal to $410 million, which represented funds borrowed from such creditors as banks, materials suppliers, and investors in the firm's bonds. Thus, the company owes its creditors $410 million. Only $230 million is "current," which means that it must be paid during the year 2011; the rest is due in future years.

As shown in the **common equity** section of the balance sheet, Sydex's owners—its stockholders—have authorized management to issue a total of 75 million shares, and management actually has issued, or sold, 40 million shares thus far. Each share has a **par value** of $1, which is the minimum amount for which each new share of common stock can be issued.[1]

common equity
The sum of the firm's common stock, paid-in capital, and retained earnings, which equals the common stockholders' total investment in the firm stated at book value.

par value
The nominal or face value of a stock or bond.

---

[1]A stock's par value is an arbitrary figure that originally indicated the minimum amount of money stockholders had to put up. Today, firms generally do not have to establish a par value for their stock. Consequently, Sydex Corporation could have elected to use no-par stock, in which case the common stock and additional paid-in capital accounts would have been consolidated into a single account called *common stock,* which would show a 2010 balance of $160 million ($40 million "common stock" plus $120 million "additional paid-in capital").

Sydex's income statement (not included for brevity) shows that the company generated $50 million in net income in 2010. A portion of the earnings was paid out as dividends to stockholders, and the remainder was added to retained earnings. Total dividend payments were $30 million, so $20 million was added to accumulated **retained earnings** to produce the $170 million balance shown at year-end 2010. Thus, Sydex has retained, or plowed back into the company, a total of $170 million since it began business. This money belongs to the common stockholders because it represents funds that could have been paid as dividends in previous years. Instead, the stockholders "allowed" management to reinvest the $170 million in the business to grow the firm.

Now consider the $120 million in **additional paid-in capital.** This account shows the difference between the stock's par value and the amount that stockholders paid when they bought newly issued shares of common stock. For example, in 1990, when Sydex was formed, 15 million shares were issued at par value; the first balance sheet therefore showed $0 for paid-in capital and $15 million in the common stock account. In 1993, to raise funds for expansion projects, Sydex issued 25 million more shares at a market price of $5.80 per share—the total value of the issue was $145 million. At that time, the common stock account was increased by $25 million ($1 par value for the 25 million shares issued), and the remainder of the $145 million stock issued, $120 million, was reported in additional paid-in capital. Sydex has not issued any more stock since 1993, so the only change in the common equity section since that time has occurred in retained earnings.

As Table 2-2 shows, Sydex used both debt and equity to raise funds to support its 2010 operations. The debt and equity instruments issued by the company, which were purchased by individuals, other corporations, and financial institutions, represent some of the financial assets that are traded in the financial markets. The remainder of this chapter describes the characteristics of debt and equity as well as other types of financial instruments.

retained earnings
The balance sheet account that indicates the total amount of earnings the firm has not paid out as dividends throughout its history; these earnings have been reinvested in the firm.

additional paid-in capital
The difference between the value of newly issued stock and its par value.

Self-Test Questions

How can you recognize financial instruments on the balance sheets of firms?

What differences distinguish the stockholders' equity account of a firm that has par value stock from the stockholders' equity account of a firm that has no-par stock?

How does the amount of earnings retained by a firm affect its common equity accounts?

DEBT

Simply stated, **debt** is a loan to a firm, a government, or an individual. Many types of debt instruments exist: home mortgages, commercial paper, term loans, bonds, secured and unsecured notes, and marketable and nonmarketable debt, among others.

debt
A loan to an individual, company, or government.

Debt Features

Often, we identify debt by describing three of its features: the principal repayment value, the interest payments, and the time to maturity. For instance, a $1,000, 10-year, 8 percent bond consists of debt with a $1,000 principal due in 10 years that pays interest equal to 8 percent of the principal amount, or $80, per year. In this section, we explain the meaning of these terms and describe some of the general features associated with debt.

Priority to Assets and Earnings

Debtholders have priority over stockholders with regard to distribution of earnings and liquidation of assets. That is, they must be paid before stockholders can be paid. Interest on debt is paid before stock dividends are distributed, and any outstanding debt must be repaid before stockholders can receive any proceeds from liquidation of the company.

Principal Value, Face Value, Maturity Value, and Par Value

The principal value of debt represents the amount owed to the lender, which must be repaid at some point during the life of the debt. For much of the debt issued by corporations, the principal amount is repaid at maturity. Consequently, we also refer to the principal value as the *maturity value*. In addition, the principal value generally is written on the "face"—that is, the outside cover—of the debt instrument, so it is sometimes called the *face value*. When the market value of debt is the same as its face value, it is said to be selling at *par;* thus the principal amount is also referred to as the *par value*. For most debt, the terms *par value, face value, maturity value,* and *principal value* are used interchangeably to indicate the amount that must be repaid by the borrower.

Interest Payments

In many cases, owners of debt instruments receive periodic payments of interest, which are computed as a percentage of the principal amount. Some debts do not pay interest; to generate a positive return for investors, such financial assets must sell for less than their par, or maturity, values. Securities that sell for less than their par value are said to be selling at a discount. Securities that sell at a discount when issued are called **discounted securities.** If an investor holds a discounted security until its maturity date, the dollar return that he or she earns is the difference between the security's purchase price and its maturity, or face, value. Most discounted debt securities have maturities of 1 year or less.

discounted securities
Securities selling for less than par value when issued.

Maturity Date

The maturity date represents the date on which the principal amount of a debt is due. As long as interest has been paid when due, once the principal amount is repaid, the debt obligation has been satisfied. Some debt instruments, called installment loans, require the principal amount to be repaid in several payments during the life of the loan. In such cases, the maturity date is the date the last installment payment of principal is due. The time to maturity varies—some debt has maturity as short as a few hours, while other debt has no specific maturity.

Control of the Firm (Voting Rights)

Debtholders do not have voting rights, so they cannot attain corporate control. Nevertheless, debtholders can affect the management and the operations of a firm by placing restrictions on the use of the borrowed funds as part of the loan agreement.

Short-Term Debt

Short-term debt generally refers to debt with a maturity of 1 year or less. Some of the more common short-term debt instruments include the following.

Treasury Bills

Treasury bills (T-bills) are *discounted* securities issued by the U.S. government to finance operations. When the U.S. Treasury issues T-bills, the prices are determined by an auction process: interested investors and investing organizations submit competitive bids for the T-bills offered.[2] T-bills are issued electronically with face values ranging from $1,000 to $5 million, and with maturities of 4, 13, or 26 weeks at the time of issue.

Treasury bills (T-bills)
Discounted debt instruments issued by the U.S. government.

Repurchase Agreement (Repo)

A **repurchase agreement** is an arrangement where one firm sells some of its financial assets to another firm with a promise to *repurchase* the securities at a higher price at a later date. The price at which the securities will be repurchased is agreed to at the time the *repo* is arranged. One firm agrees to sell the securities because it needs funds, whereas the other firm agrees to purchase the securities because it has excess funds to invest. Thus, with this arrangement, the repo *seller* effectively borrows funds from the repo *buyer*. Often the parties involved in repurchase agreements are banks, and the securities that are sold and repurchased are government securities, such as T-bills. Although some repos last for days or even weeks, the maturity for most repurchase agreements is overnight.

repurchase agreement
An arrangement where one firm sells some of its financial assets to another firm with a promise to *repurchase* the securities at a later date.

Federal Funds

Often referred to simply as "fed funds," **federal funds** represent overnight loans from one bank to another. Banks generally use the fed funds market to adjust their reserves: banks that need additional funds to meet the reserve requirements of the Federal Reserve borrow from banks with excess reserves, and vice versa. The interest rate associated with such debt is known as the *federal funds rate*. Federal funds have very short maturities, often overnight.

federal funds
Overnight loans from one bank to another.

Banker's Acceptance

A **banker's acceptance** might be best described as a post-dated check. More accurately, a banker's acceptance is a time draft—an instrument, issued by a bank, that obligates the bank to pay a specified amount to the owner of the banker's acceptance at some future date. Generally used in international trade, a banker's acceptance arrangement is established between a bank and a firm to ensure the firm's international trading partner that payment for goods and services essentially is guaranteed at some future date, which is sufficient time to verify the completion of the transaction. Banker's acceptances generally are sold by the original owner before maturity to raise immediate cash. They are sold at a discount, however, because they do not pay interest. Banker's acceptances generally have maturities of 180 days or less.

banker's acceptance
An instrument issued by a bank that obligates the bank to pay a specified amount at some future date.

---

[2]The Treasury also sells T-bills on a noncompetitive basis to investors or investment organizations offering to buy a certain dollar amount. In such cases, the purchase price is based on the average of the competitive bids received by the Treasury.

Commercial Paper

commercial paper
A discounted instrument that is a type of promissory note, or legal IOU, issued by large, financially sound firms.

Commercial paper is a type of promissory note, or legal IOU, issued by large, financially sound firms. Like T-bills, commercial paper does not pay interest, so it must be sold at a discount. The maturity on commercial paper varies from 1 to 9 months, with an average of about 5 months.[3] Generally, commercial paper is issued in denominations of $100,000 or more, so few individuals can afford to *directly* invest in the commercial paper market. Instead, commercial paper is sold primarily to other businesses, insurance companies, pension funds, money market mutual funds, and banks.

Certificate of Deposit (CD)

certificate of deposit
An interest-earning time deposit at a bank or other financial intermediary.

negotiable CD
Certificate of deposit that can be traded to other investors prior to maturity; redemption is made by the investor who owns the CD at maturity.

A **certificate of deposit** represents a time deposit at a bank or other financial intermediary. Traditional CDs generally earn periodic interest and must be kept at the institution for a specified time period. To liquidate a traditional CD prior to maturity, the owner must return it to the issuing institution, which applies an interest penalty to the amount paid out.

Negotiable CDs, however, can be traded to other investors prior to maturity because they can be redeemed by whomever owns them at maturity. Often called jumbo CDs, these financial assets typically come in denominations of $1 million to $5 million. They have maturities that range from a few months to a few years.

Eurodollar Deposit

Eurodollar deposit
A deposit in a foreign bank that is denominated in U.S. dollars.

A **Eurodollar deposit** is a deposit in a bank outside the United States that is not converted into the currency of the foreign country; instead, it is denominated in U.S. dollars. Such deposits are not exposed to exchange rate risk, which is the risk associated with converting dollars into foreign currencies. Eurodollar deposits earn rates offered by foreign banks and are not subject to the same regulations imposed on deposits in U.S. banks. Consequently, the rate that can be earned on Eurodollars is sometimes considerably greater than the rate that can be earned in the United States.

Money Market Mutual Funds

money market mutual funds
Pools of funds, managed by investment companies, that are primarily invested in short-term financial assets.

Money market mutual funds represent funds that are pooled and managed by investment companies for the purpose of investing in short-term financial assets, including those described here. These funds offer individual investors the ability to *indirectly* invest in such short-term securities as T-bills, commercial paper, Eurodollars, and so on, which they otherwise would not be able to purchase because such investments either are sold in denominations that are too large or are not sold to individuals.[4]

Long-Term Debt

Long-term debt refers to debt instruments with maturities greater than 1 year. Owners of such debt generally receive periodic payments of interest. This section discusses some common types of long-term debt.

---

[3]The maximum maturity without SEC registration is 270 days. Also, commercial paper can be sold only to "sophisticated" investors; otherwise, SEC registration would be required even for maturities of less than 270 days.

[4]Mutual funds are discussed in greater detail in Chapter 4.

Term Loans

A **term loan** is a contract under which a borrower agrees to make a series of interest and principal payments on specific dates to the lender. Term loans usually are negotiated directly between the borrowing firm and a financial institution, such as a bank, an insurance company, or a pension fund. For this reason, they are often referred to as private debt. Although term loans' maturities vary from 2 to 30 years, most maturities are in the 3-year to 15-year range.[5]

Term loans have three major advantages over public debt offerings, such as corporate bonds: *speed, flexibility,* and *low issuance costs.* Because they are negotiated directly between the lender and the borrower, formal documentation is minimized. The key provisions of a term loan can be worked out much more quickly than can those for a public issue, and it is not necessary for the loan to go through the Securities and Exchange Commission (SEC) registration process. Another advantage of term loans relates to their future flexibility. If a bond issue is held by many different bondholders, it is virtually impossible to obtain permission to alter the terms of the agreement, even though new economic conditions might make such changes desirable. With a term loan, however, the borrower generally can sit down with the lender and work out mutually agreeable modifications to the contract.

The interest rate on a term loan can be either fixed for the life of the loan or variable. If a fixed rate is used, generally it will be set close to the rate on bonds of equivalent maturity and risk. If the rate is variable, usually it will be set at a certain number of percentage points above an index representing either the prime rate, the commercial paper rate, the T-bill rate, or some other designated rate. When the index rate rises or falls, the rate charged on the outstanding balance of the term loan is adjusted periodically. Generally, when interest rates become more volatile, banks and other lenders are more reluctant to make long-term, fixed-rate loans, so variable-rate term loans become more common.

term loan
A loan, generally obtained from a bank or insurance company, on which the borrower agrees to make a series of payments consisting of interest and principal.

Bonds

A **bond** is a long-term contract under which a borrower agrees to make payments of interest and principal on specific dates to the bondholder. The interest payments are determined by the *coupon rate* and the principal, or face, value of the bond. The **coupon rate** represents the total interest paid each year, stated as a percentage of the bond's face value. Typically, interest is paid semiannually, although bonds that pay interest annually, quarterly, or monthly also exist. For example, a 10 percent coupon bond with a face value equal to $1,000 would commonly pay $50 interest every 6 months, or a total of $100 each year.

Next, we describe some of the more common bonds issued by both governments and corporations.

1. **Government bonds** are issued by the U.S. government, state governments, and local or municipal governments. U.S. government bonds are issued by the U.S. Treasury and are called either *Treasury notes* or *Treasury bonds.* Both types of debt pay interest semiannually. The primary difference between Treasury notes and Treasury bonds is the maturity when the debt is

bond
A long-term debt instrument.

coupon rate
Interest paid on a bond or other debt instrument stated as a percentage of its face, or maturity, value.

government bond
Debt issued by the federal government or by a state or local government.

---

[5]Most term loans are amortized, which means that they are paid off in equal installments over the life of the loan. Amortization protects the lender against the possibility that the borrower will not make adequate provisions for the loan's retirement during the life of the loan. (Chapter 9 reviews the concept of amortization.) Also, if the interest and principal payments required under a term loan agreement are not met on schedule, the borrowing firm is said to have *defaulted,* and it can then be forced into bankruptcy.

issued: the original maturity on notes is from more than 1 year to 10 years, whereas the original maturity on bonds exceeds 10 years.

Municipal bonds, or *munis,* are similar to Treasury bonds, except that they are issued by state and local governments. The two principal types of munis are revenue bonds and general obligation bonds. **Revenue bonds** are used to raise funds for projects that generate *revenues* that contribute to payment of interest and the repayment of the debt. **General obligation bonds** are backed by the government's ability to tax its citizens; special taxes or tax increases are used to generate the funds needed to service such bonds. Generally, the income that an investor earns from munis is exempt from federal taxes.

municipal bond
A bond issued by a state or local government.

revenue bond
A municipal bond that generates revenue, which in turn can be used to make interest payments and repay the principal.

general obligation bond
A municipal bond backed by the local government's ability to impose taxes.

corporate bonds
Long-term debt instruments issued by corporations.

2. As the name implies, **corporate bonds** are issued by businesses called corporations.[6] Although corporate bonds traditionally have been issued with maturities of between 20 and 30 years, bonds with shorter maturities, such as 7 to 10 years, are also common. Corporate bonds resemble term loans, but a bond issue generally is advertised, offered to the public, and sold to many different investors. Indeed, thousands of individuals and institutional investors might purchase bonds when a firm sells a bond issue, whereas generally only one lender is involved with a term loan.[7] With bonds, the interest rate typically remains fixed, although the popularity of floating-rate bonds has grown during the past couple of decades. In addition, several types of corporate bonds exist, the more important of which are discussed in the remainder of this section.

mortgage bond
A bond backed by fixed assets. First mortgage bonds are senior in priority to claims of second mortgage bonds.

3. With a **mortgage bond,** the corporation pledges certain assets as security, or collateral, for the bond. To illustrate, in 2009, Muttle Furniture needed $30 million to build a major regional distribution center. The company issued bonds in the amount of $24 million, secured by a mortgage on the property. (The remaining $6 million was financed with stock, or equity capital.) If Muttle defaults on the bonds, the bondholders can foreclose on the property and sell it to satisfy their claims. At the same time, if Muttle so chooses, it can issue *second mortgage bonds* secured by the same $30 million facility. In the event of liquidation, the holders of these second mortgage bonds would have a claim against the property, but only after the first mortgage bondholders had been paid off in full. Second mortgages are sometimes called *junior mortgages* because they are junior in priority to the claims of *senior mortgages,* or *first mortgage bonds.*

debenture
A long-term bond that is not secured by a mortgage on specific property.

4. A **debenture** is an unsecured bond. As such, it provides no lien, or claim, against specific property as security for the obligation. Therefore, debenture holders are general creditors whose claims are protected by property not otherwise pledged as collateral. In practice, the use of debentures depends on the nature of the firm's assets as well as its general credit strength. An extremely strong company, such as IBM, will tend to use debentures; it simply does not need to put up property as security for its debt. Debentures also are issued by companies in industries in which it would not be practical to provide security through mortgage on fixed assets. For example, large

---

[6]The forms of business organizations—proprietorships, partnerships, and corporations—are described in Chapter 6. At this point, we need note only that corporate bonds are issued by businesses formed as corporations; proprietorships and partnerships cannot use corporate bonds to raise funds.

[7]For very large term loans, 20 or more financial institutions might form a syndicate to grant the credit. Also, note that a bond issue can be sold to one lender (or to just a few); in this case, the issue is said to be "privately placed." Companies that place bonds privately do so for the same reasons that they use term loans—speed, flexibility, and low issuance costs.

mail-order houses and commercial banks characteristically hold most of their assets in the form of inventories or loans, neither of which is satisfactory security for a long-term mortgage bond.

5. A **subordinated debenture** is an unsecured bond that ranks below, or is "inferior to," other debt with respect to claims on cash distributions made by the firm. In the event of bankruptcy, for instance, *subordinated debt* has claims on assets only after senior debt has been paid off. Subordinated debentures might be subordinated either to designated notes payable (usually bank loans) or to all other debt.

subordinated debenture
A bond that has a claim on assets only after the senior debt has been paid off in the event of liquidation.

6. Several other types of corporate bonds are used sufficiently often to merit mention. First, **income bonds** pay interest only when the firm has sufficient income to cover the interest payments. As a consequence, missing interest payments on these securities cannot bankrupt a company. From an investor's standpoint, these bonds are riskier than "regular" bonds.

   Putable bonds are bonds that can be turned in and exchanged for cash at the bondholder's option. Generally, the option to turn in the bond can be exercised only if the firm takes some specified action, such as being acquired by a weaker company or increasing its outstanding debt by a large amount.

   Indexed, or **purchasing power, bonds** are popular in countries plagued by high rates of inflation. With such a bond, the interest payment is based on an inflation index such as the consumer price index. The interest paid rises automatically when the inflation rate rises, thereby protecting bondholders against inflation.

   Floating-rate bonds are similar to *indexed bonds* except the coupon rates on these bonds "float" with market interest rates rather than with the inflation rate. Thus, when interest rates rise, the coupon rates will increase, and vice versa. In many cases, limits are imposed on how high and low (referred to as "caps" and "collars," respectively) the rates on such debt can change, both during each period and over the life of the bond.

income bond
A bond that pays interest to the holder only if the interest is earned by the firm.

putable bond
A bond that can be redeemed at the bondholder's option.

indexed (purchasing power) bond
A bond that has interest payments based on an inflation index to protect the holder from inflation.

floating-rate bond
A bond whose interest rate fluctuates with shifts in the general level of interest rates.

7. During the 1980s, *original issue discount bonds (OIDs)*, commonly referred to as **zero coupon bonds,** were created. These securities were offered at substantial discounts below their par values because they paid little or no coupon interest. OIDs have since lost their attraction for many individual investors, primarily because the interest income that must be reported each year for tax purposes includes any cash interest actually received, which is $0 for zero coupons, plus the annual *prorated* capital appreciation that would be received if the bond was held to maturity. Thus, capital appreciation is taxed before it is actually received. For this reason, most OID bonds currently are held by institutional investors, such as pension funds and mutual funds, rather than by individual investors.[8]

zero coupon bond
A bond that pays no annual interest but is sold at a discount below par, thus providing compensation to investors in the form of capital appreciation.

junk bond
A high-risk, high-yield bond used to finance mergers, leveraged buyouts, and troubled companies.

Another innovation from the 1980s is the **junk bond,** a high-risk, high-yield bond often issued to finance a management buyout (MBO), a merger, or a troubled

---

[8]Shortly after corporations began to issue zeros, investment firms figured out a way to create zeros from U.S. Treasury bonds, which are issued only in coupon form. In 1982, Salomon Brothers bought $1 billion of 12 percent, 30-year Treasuries. Each bond had 60 coupons worth $60 each, which represented the interest payments due every 6 months. Salomon then in effect clipped the coupons and placed them in 60 piles; the last pile also contained the "stripped" bond itself, which represented a promise to pay $1,000 in 2012. These 60 piles of U.S. Treasury promises were then placed with the trust department of a bank and used as collateral for "zero coupon U.S. Treasury Trust Certificates," which are, in essence, zero coupon Treasury bonds. A pension fund that expected to need money in 2010 could have bought 28-year certificates backed by the interest that the Treasury will pay in 2010. Treasury zeros are, of course, safer than corporate zeros, so they are popular with pension fund managers.

company. In junk bond deals, firms generally have significant amounts of debt, so bondholders must bear as much risk as stockholders normally would. The yields on these bonds reflect this fact. For example, at the beginning of 2005, R. J. Tower Automotive, which produces structural components for automobiles, found itself in a troubled financial situation. More than 75 percent of Tower's total financing consisted of debt, which the company was having difficulty servicing—that is, covering the required payments. Its bond issue with a coupon rate equal to 12 percent was selling for 56.5 percent of face value, which meant that investors could buy an R. J. Tower bond with a $1,000 face value for $565 and earn more than 24 percent if they held the bond until its 2013 maturity. At the time, the yield on average-risk corporate bonds was slightly less than 5 percent. The emergence of junk bonds as an important type of debt is an example of how corporations adjust to and facilitate new developments in the financial markets.[9]

 Self-Test Questions

Differentiate between the characteristics of short-term debt and the characteristics of long-term debt.

What are the three major advantages that term loans have over public offerings?

Differentiate between term loans and bonds.

Differentiate between mortgage bonds and debentures.

Define *income bonds, putable bonds,* and *indexed bonds.*

What problem was solved by the introduction of long-term, floating-rate debt, and how is the rate on such bonds actually set?

Why would you expect junk bonds to have higher yields than traditional bonds with similar coupon rates?

BOND CONTRACT FEATURES[10]

A firm's managers are concerned with both the effective cost of debt and any restrictions in debt contracts that might limit the firm's future actions. Investors are concerned with these same factors, but they are on "the opposite side of the fence" from the firm—that is, investors expect to receive a positive return, which, in effect, is paid by the corporations that issue bonds. As a result, a firm's cost of debt represents the rate of return that bondholders (investors) earn, and generally the restrictions that are included in the bond contract are intended to help protect investors' funds from unethical or fraudulent actions that the firm might pursue.

---

[9]The development of junk bond financing has, as much as any other factor, helped to reshape the U.S. financial scene. The existence of these securities led directly to the loss of independence of Gulf Oil and hundreds of other companies, and it prompted major shake-ups in such companies as CBS, Union Carbide, and USX (formerly U.S. Steel). The phenomenal growth of the junk bond market was impressive, but controversial. Significant risk, combined with unscrupulous dealings, produced substantial losses for investors. In 1990, for example, "junk bond king" Michael Milken was sent to jail for his role in misleading investors in this market. Additionally, the realization that high leverage can spell trouble—as when Campeau, with $3 billion in junk financing, filed for bankruptcy in early 1990—has slowed the growth in the junk bond market from its glory days. Recent trends, however, indicate that a slight resurgence has begun.

[10]In this section we discuss bond features from the perspective of corporations. Most of these features also apply to government debt.

This section discusses features that generally are included in bond contracts, which can affect the firm's cost of debt and its future financial flexibility.

Bond Indenture

Bondholders have a legitimate fear that once they lend money to a company and become "locked in" for a period as long as 30 years, the firm will take some action that is designed to benefit stockholders but harm bondholders. For example, in the 1980s when RJR Nabisco was highly rated, it sold 30-year bonds with a low coupon rate, and investors bought those bonds despite the low yield because of their low risk. After the bonds had been sold, the company announced plans to issue much more debt, increasing the expected rate of return to stockholders—as well as the riskiness of the company's bonds. The market value of RJR's bonds fell by 20 percent the week the announcement was made. A number of other companies have made the same move, and their bondholders also suffered heavy losses as the market yields on the bonds rose and drove the prices of the bonds down.

Bondholders attempt to reduce the potential for financial problems by use of legal restrictions designed to ensure, insofar as possible, that the company does nothing to cause the quality of its bonds to deteriorate after they have been issued. An **indenture** is a legal document that spells out any legal restrictions associated with the bond as well as the rights of the bondholders (lenders) and the corporation (bond issuer). A **trustee,** usually a bank, is assigned to represent the bondholders and to guarantee that the terms of the indenture are carried out. The indenture might be several hundred pages long, and it includes **restrictive covenants** that cover such points as the conditions under which the issuer can pay off the bonds prior to maturity, the level at which various financial measures (such as the ability to pay interest) must be maintained if the company is to sell additional bonds, and restrictions against the payment of dividends when earnings do not meet certain specifications. The Securities and Exchange Commission approves indentures for publicly traded bonds and verifies that all indenture provisions have been met before allowing a company to sell new securities to the public.

The trustee is responsible for making sure that any covenants are not violated and for taking appropriate action if they are. What constitutes "appropriate action" varies with the circumstances. Perhaps insisting on immediate compliance would result in bankruptcy, which in turn might lead to large losses on the bonds. In such a case, the trustee might decide that the bondholders would be better served by giving the company a chance to work out its problems rather than by forcing it into bankruptcy.

indenture
A formal agreement (contract) between the issuer of a bond and the bondholders.

trustee
An official who ensures that the bondholders' interests are protected and that the terms of the indenture are carried out.

restrictive covenant
A provision in a debt contract that constrains the actions of the borrower.

Call Provision

Most corporate bonds contain a **call provision,** which gives the issuing corporation the right to call the bonds for redemption prior to maturity. A call provision generally states that the company must pay the bondholders an amount greater than the par value for the bonds when they are called. This additional sum, which is termed a *call premium,* typically equals 1 year's interest if the bonds are called during the first year in which a call is permitted; the premium declines at a constant rate each year thereafter. Bonds usually are not callable until several years (generally 5 to 10) after they are issued; bonds with such *deferred calls* are said to have *call protection.* Call provisions allow firms to refinance debt, much as individuals might refinance mortgages on their houses—when interest rates decline, firms can *recall* (refund) some existing debt and replace it with new, lower-cost debt.

call provision
A provision in a bond contract that gives the issuer the right to redeem the bonds under specified terms prior to the normal maturity date.

Sinking Fund

sinking fund
A required annual payment designed to amortize a bond or preferred stock issue.

A **sinking fund** is a provision that facilitates the orderly retirement of a bond issue. Typically, the sinking fund provision requires the firm to retire a portion of the bond issue each year. On rare occasions, the firm might be required to deposit money with a trustee, which invests the funds and then uses the accumulated sum to retire the bonds when they mature. Failure to meet the sinking fund requirement will throw the bond issue into default, which might force the company into bankruptcy. Obviously, a sinking fund can constitute a dangerous cash drain on the firm.

In most cases, the firm has the right to handle the sinking fund in two ways: by randomly calling for redemption (at par value) a certain percentage of the bonds each year or by purchasing the required amount of bonds in the open market. The firm will choose the lower cost method. If interest rates have risen, causing bond prices to fall, the firm will buy bonds in the open market at a discount; if interest rates have fallen, it will call the bonds and pay the face value. Note that a call for sinking fund purposes is quite different from a refunding call as discussed earlier. A sinking fund call does not require the company to pay a call premium, but only a small percentage of the issue is normally callable in any 1 year.

Convertible Feature

conversion feature
Permits bondholders to exchange their investments for a fixed number of shares of common stock.

A **conversion feature** permits the bondholder (investor) to exchange, or *convert*, the bond into shares of common stock at a fixed price. Investors have greater flexibility with *convertible bonds* than with straight bonds, because they can choose whether to hold the company's bond or convert it into its stock. Convertible securities are discussed in more detail later in this chapter.

Self-Test Questions

How do trustees and indentures reduce potential problems for bondholders?

What are the two ways in which a sinking fund can be handled? Which method will the firm choose if interest rates rise? If interest rates fall?

What is the difference between a call for sinking fund purposes and a refunding call?

Are securities that provide for a sinking fund regarded as riskier than those without this type of provision? Explain.

Why is a call provision so advantageous to a bond issuer? When will the issuer initiate a refunding call? Why?

BOND RATINGS

investment-grade bond
A bond rated A or BBB; many banks and other institutional investors are permitted by law to hold only bonds rated investment grade or better.

Since the early 1900s, bonds have been assigned quality ratings that reflect their probability of going into default. The two major rating agencies are Moody's Investors Service (Moody's) and Standard & Poor's Corporation (S&P). Table 2-3 shows these agencies' rating designations.[11]

The triple-A and double-A bonds are extremely safe. Single-A and triple-B bonds are strong enough to be called **investment-grade bonds;** they are the

[11]In the discussion to follow, a reference to the S&P code is intended to imply the Moody's code as well. Thus *triple-B bonds* mean both BBB and Baa bonds; *double-B bonds* mean both BB and Ba bonds; and so on.

TABLE 2-3 Moody's and Standard & Poor's (S&P) Bond Ratings

| | High Quality | | Investment Grade | | Junk Bonds | | | |
					Substandard		Speculative	
Moody's	Aaa	Aa	A	Baa	Ba	B	Caa	C
S&P	AAA	AA	A	BBB	BB	B	CCC	D

Note: Both Moody's and S&P use "modifiers" for bonds rated below triple-A. S&P uses a plus and minus system; that is, A+ designates the strongest A-rated bonds and A– indicates the weakest. Moody's uses a 1, 2, or 3 designation, with 1 denoting the strongest and 3 the weakest; thus, within the double-A category, Aa1 is the best, Aa2 is average, and Aa3 is the weakest.

lowest-rated bonds that many banks and other institutional investors are permitted by law to hold. Double-B and lower-rated bonds are speculative, or *junk bonds;* they have a significant probability of going into default, and many financial institutions are prohibited from buying them.

Bond Rating Criteria

Bond ratings are based on both qualitative and quantitative factors. Factors considered by the bond rating agencies include the financial strength of the company as measured by various ratios, collateral provisions, the seniority of the debt, restrictive covenants, provisions such as a sinking fund or a deferred call, litigation possibilities, regulation, and so on. Representatives of the rating agencies have consistently stated that no precise formula is used to set a firm's rating; all the factors listed, plus others, are taken into account, but not in a mathematically precise manner. Statistical studies have borne out this contention. Indeed, researchers who have tried to predict bond ratings on the basis of quantitative data have found only limited success, indicating that the agencies use subjective judgment when establishing a firm's rating.[12]

Importance of Bond Ratings

Bond ratings are important to both issuers and investors for several reasons. First, because a bond's rating serves as an indicator of its default risk, the rating has a direct, measurable influence on the bond's interest rate and the firm's cost of using such debt. Second, most bonds are purchased by institutional investors rather than by individuals, and many institutions are restricted to investment-grade or high-quality securities. Therefore, if its bonds fall below a BBB rating, a firm will have a difficult time selling new bonds because many potential purchasers will not be allowed to buy them.

As a result of their higher risk and more restricted market, lower grade bonds offer higher returns than high-grade bonds. Figure 2-1 illustrates this point. In each of the years shown on the graph, U.S. government bonds have the lowest yields, corporate AAA bonds have the next lowest, and corporate BBB bonds have the highest yields. The figure also shows that the gaps between yields on the three types of bonds vary over time, indicating that the cost differentials, or risk premiums, fluctuate from year to year.

Changes in Ratings

Changes in a firm's bond rating affect both its ability to borrow long-term capital and the cost of such funds. Rating agencies review outstanding bonds on a periodic basis,

[12]See Ahmed Belkaoui, *Industrial Bonds and the Rating Process* (London: Quorum Books, 1983).

FIGURE 2-1   Yields on Selected Long-Term Bonds, 1990–2008

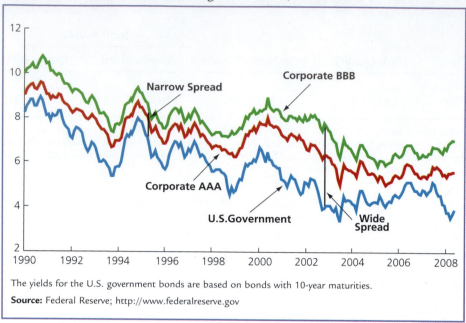

The yields for the U.S. government bonds are based on bonds with 10-year maturities.

Source: Federal Reserve; http://www.federalreserve.gov

occasionally upgrading or downgrading a bond as a result of its issuer's changed circumstances. For example, in September 2007, the debt rating for Forsyth County Water and Sewerage Authority of Georgia was raised from AA to AA+ to reflect its stable financial position. In the same month, JHT Holdings, which is a trucking company, was put on CreditWatch because its financial position had deteriorated.

Self-Test Questions

Name the two major rating agencies and some factors that affect bond ratings.

Why are bond ratings important both to firms and to investors?

STOCK (EQUITY)

Each corporation issues at least one type of stock, or equity, called *common stock*. Some corporations issue more than one type of common stock, and some issue *preferred stock* in addition to common stock. As the names imply, most equity takes the form of common stock, and preferred shareholders have preference over common shareholders when a firm distributes funds to stockholders; dividends, as well as liquidation proceeds resulting from bankruptcy, are paid to preferred stockholders before common stockholders receive any payouts. On the other hand, preferred stockholders generally receive the same dividend every year, regardless of the company's earnings or growth during the year, whereas the dividends paid to common stockholders can vary each year and often depend on current and previous earnings levels and the firm's plans for growth.

The amount of stock sold by a corporation is reflected in the "owner's equity" section of its balance sheet. Returning to Table 2-2, you can see that the owner's equity, or net worth, for Sydex Corporation amounted to $330 million in

2010. The firm's balance sheet also shows that Sydex has issued only common stock.

In this section, we describe the basic characteristics of both preferred and common stock.

Preferred Stock

Preferred stock often is referred to as a *hybrid* security because it is similar to bonds in some respects and similar to common stock in other respects. The hybrid nature of preferred stock becomes apparent when we try to classify it in relation to bonds and common stock. Like bonds, preferred stock has a par, or face, value. Preferred dividends are similar to interest payments in that they are fixed in amount and must be paid before common stock dividends can be distributed. If the preferred dividend is not earned, however, the directors can omit it (or "pass") without throwing the company into bankruptcy. Thus, although preferred stock has a fixed payment like bonds, a failure to make this payment will not lead to bankruptcy.

Accountants classify preferred stock as equity and report it in the equity portion of the balance sheet under "preferred stock" or "preferred equity." Financial analysts, on the other hand, sometimes treat preferred stock as debt and at other times treat it as equity, depending on the type of analysis involved. If the analysis is undertaken by a common stockholder, the key consideration is the fact that the preferred dividend is a fixed charge that reduces the amount that can be distributed to common shareholders; from the common stockholder's point of view, then, preferred stock is similar to debt. Suppose, however, that a bondholder is studying the firm's chance of failure in the event of a decline in sales and income. If the firm's income declines, the debtholders have a prior claim to the available income ahead of preferred stockholders. If the firm eventually fails, these debtholders have a prior claim to assets when the firm is liquidated. Thus, to a bondholder, preferred stock is similar to common equity.

From management's perspective, preferred stock falls between debt and common equity. Because failure to pay dividends on preferred stock will not force the firm into bankruptcy, this type of stock is safer to use than debt. At the same time, if the firm is highly successful, the common stockholders do not share that success with the preferred stockholders because preferred dividends are fixed. Remember, however, that the preferred stockholders do have a higher priority claim than the common stockholders. We see, then, that preferred stock shares some characteristics with debt and some characteristics with common stock, and it is used in situations where neither debt nor common stock is entirely appropriate. For instance, a corporation might find preferred stock to be an ideal instrument when it needs to raise funds and already has a considerable amount of debt. In this situation, its creditors might be reluctant to lend more funds, and, at the same time, its common stockholders might not want their ownership shares diluted.

Preferred stock has a number of features, the most important of which are described next.

Priority to Assets and Earnings

Preferred stockholders have priority over common stockholders with regard to earnings and assets. Thus, dividends must be paid on preferred stock before they can be paid on the common stock, and, in the event of bankruptcy, the claims of the preferred shareholders must be satisfied before the common stockholders receive anything. To reinforce these features, most preferred stocks have coverage requirements similar to those placed on bonds. These restrictions limit the amount of preferred stock that a company can use, and they require a minimum level of retained earnings before the firm can pay any common dividends.

Par Value

Most preferred stock has a par value or its equivalent under some other name—for example, liquidation value. The par value is important for two reasons: (1) it establishes the amount due to the preferred stockholders in the event of liquidation and (2) the preferred dividend generally is stated as a percentage of the par value. For example, in 2008, New York State Electric & Gas (NYSEG), a utility company that is a subsidiary of Energy East, had an issue of preferred stock with a liquidation value of $100 and a stated dividend of 4.5 percent. Investors who held this issue of preferred stock received an annual dividend equal to $4.50 per share.

Cumulative Dividends

cumulative dividends
A protective feature on preferred stock that requires preferred dividends previously not paid to be disbursed before any common stock dividends can be paid.

Most preferred stock provides for **cumulative dividends;** that is, any preferred dividends not paid in previous periods must be paid before common dividends can be distributed. The cumulative feature acts as a protective device. If the preferred stock dividends were not cumulative, a firm could avoid paying preferred and common stock dividends for, say, 10 years, plowing back all of its earnings into the company, and then pay a huge common stock dividend but only the stipulated annual dividend to the preferred stockholders. Obviously, such an action would effectively void the preferred position that the preferred stockholders are supposed to enjoy. The cumulative feature helps prevent such abuses.[13]

Control of the Firm (Voting Rights)

Although most preferred stock is not voting stock, preferred stockholders generally are given the right to vote for directors if the company has not paid the preferred dividend for a specified period, such as 2 years. For example, holders of NYSEG preferred stock can elect a majority of the members of the board of directors if the company misses four consecutive quarterly dividend payments. This feature motivates management to make every effort to pay preferred dividends.

Convertibility

Most preferred stock that has been issued in recent years is convertible into common stock. For example, each share of the Series A preferred stock issued by Chiquita Brands, a food processor, was convertible into 2.63 shares of common stock at the option of the preferred shareholders.

Other Provisions

Some other provisions occasionally found in preferred stocks include the following:

1. *Participating.* A rare type of preferred stock is one that participates with the common stock in sharing the firm's earnings. Participating preferred stocks generally work as follows: (a) the stated preferred dividend is paid—for example, $5 per share; (b) the common stock is then entitled to a dividend in an

---

[13]Most cumulative plans do not provide for compounding—in other words, the unpaid preferred dividends themselves earn no return. Also, many preferred issues have a limited cumulative feature; for example, unpaid preferred dividends might accumulate for only 3 years.

amount up to the preferred dividend; and (c) if the common dividend is raised, say to $5.50, the preferred dividend must likewise be raised to $5.50.

2. *Sinking fund.* In the past (before the mid-1970s), few preferred issues had sinking funds. Today, however, most newly issued preferred stocks have sinking funds that call for the repurchase and retirement of a given percentage of the preferred stock each year.

3. *Call provision.* A call provision gives the issuing corporation the right to call in the preferred stock for redemption. As in the case of bonds, call provisions generally state that the company must pay an amount greater than the par value of the preferred stock, with the additional sum being dubbed a **call premium.** For example, Antigenics Inc., which develops treatments for cancer, has an issue of preferred stock outstanding that is callable in 2013. The call price on the issue is $15.80.

4. *Maturity.* Although preferred stock has no specified maturity date, today most new preferred stock has a sinking fund and thus an effective maturity date with call provisions.

call premium
The amount in excess of par value that a company must pay when it calls a security.

Common Stock

We usually refer to common stockholders as the "owners" of the firm because investors in common stock have certain rights and privileges generally associated with property ownership. The most common characteristics and rights associated with common stock include the following.

Priority to Assets and Earnings

Common stockholders can be paid dividends only after the interest on debt and the preferred dividends are paid. In the event of liquidation resulting from bankruptcy, common stockholders are last to receive any funds. Thus, as investors, the common stockholders are "last in line" to receive any cash distributions from the corporation.

Dividends

The firm has no obligation, contractual or implied, to pay common stock dividends. Some firms pay relatively constant dividends from year to year; other companies do not pay dividends at all. The return that investors receive when they own a company's common stock is based on both the change in the stock's market value (capital gain) and the dividend paid by the company. Some investors prefer current income to future capital gains, so they invest in firms that pay large dividends; thus their returns are based primarily on the dividends earned from owning such stocks. These types of stocks traditionally are called **income stocks.** For example, stocks of utility companies are typically considered income stocks. On the other hand, some investors prefer capital gains to current income, so they invest in firms that pay little or no dividends; thus, their returns are based primarily on the capital gains earned from owning such stocks. Generally, these types of firms retain most, if not all, of their earnings each year to help fund growth opportunities, so their stocks are referred to as **growth stocks.** Microsoft Corporation is a good example of a growth stock. Until 2003, the company did not pay a dividend, but the growth in net income averaged nearly 50 percent from 1995 to 1999. In 2000, a period of decrease for many companies, Microsoft's net income grew by 21 percent over the previous year. Even when it started paying dividends, the estimated growth for Microsoft was greater than 12 percent.

income stocks
Stocks of firms that traditionally pay large, relatively constant dividends each year.

growth stocks
Stocks that generally pay little or no dividends so as to retain earnings to help fund growth opportunities.

Maturity

Like preferred stock, common stock has no specified maturity—that is, it is perpetual. At times, however, companies repurchase shares of their common stock in the financial markets. Stock repurchases might be undertaken when (1) the firm has excess cash but no "good" investment opportunities, (2) the price of the firm's stock is undervalued, or (3) management wants to gain more ownership control of the firm—by repurchasing the stock of other investors, the percentage owned by management increases.

Control of the Firm (Voting Rights)

The common stockholders have the right to elect the firm's directors, who in turn appoint the officers who manage the business. Stockholders also vote on shareholders' proposals, mergers, and changes in the firm's charter. In a small firm, the major stockholder typically assumes the positions of president and chairperson of the board of directors. In a large, publicly owned firm, the managers typically own some stock, but their personal holdings are insufficient to provide voting control. Thus, stockholders can remove the managers of most publicly owned firms if they decide that a management team is not effective.

Numerous state and federal laws stipulate how stockholder control is to be exercised. Corporations must hold an election of directors periodically, usually once each year, with the vote taken at the annual meeting. In many firms, one-third of the directors are elected each year for a 3-year term. Each share of stock normally has one vote, so the owner of 1,000 shares has 1,000 votes. Stockholders of large corporations, such as General Motors, can appear at the annual meeting and vote in person, but typically they transfer their right to vote to a second party by means of an instrument known as a **proxy.** The management of large firms always solicits, and thus usually gets, stockholders' proxies. If earnings are poor and stockholders are dissatisfied, however, an outside group might solicit the proxies in an effort to overthrow management and take control of the business. This kind of battle is known as a **proxy fight.**

The question of corporate control has become a central issue in finance. The frequency of proxy fights has increased, as have attempts by one corporation to take over another by purchasing a large amount of the outstanding stock. This action is called a **takeover.** Well-known examples of takeover battles include Kohlberg Kravis Roberts & Company's (KKR) acquisition of RJR Nabisco, Chevron's acquisition of Gulf Oil, AT&T's takeovers of NCR and Cingular Wireless, and NationsBank's takeovers of Barnett Banks and Bank America Corporation.

Managers who do not have majority control (more than 50 percent of their firms' stock) are very concerned about proxy fights and takeovers, and many attempt to get stockholder approval for changes in their corporate charters that would make takeovers more difficult. For example, companies have persuaded their stockholders to agree to the following provisions: (1) to elect only one-third of the directors each year (rather than electing all directors each year), (2) to require 75 percent of the stockholders (rather than 50 percent) to approve a merger, and (3) to approve a "poison pill" provision that would allow the stockholders of a firm that is taken over by another firm to buy shares in the second firm at a reduced price. The third provision makes the acquisition unattractive and, therefore, wards off hostile takeover attempts. Managements seeking such changes generally cite a fear that the firm will be picked up at a bargain price, but it often appears that managers' concerns about their own positions might be an even more important consideration.

proxy
A document giving one person the authority to act for another, typically the power to vote shares of common stock.

proxy fight
An attempt by a person or group of people to gain control of a firm by getting its stockholders to grant that person or group the authority to vote their shares so as to change the management team.

takeover
An action whereby a person or group succeeds in ousting a firm's management and taking control of the company.

Preemptive Right

Some common stockholders have the right, called a **preemptive right,** to purchase any additional shares sold by the firm. The preemptive right requires a firm to offer existing stockholders shares of a new stock issue in proportion to their ownership holdings before such shares can be offered to other investors. Most common stock issues do not have preemptive rights because most states do not require such rights to be included in corporate charters.

The purpose of the preemptive right is twofold. First, it protects the power of control of current stockholders. If not for this safeguard, the management team of a corporation under criticism from stockholders could prevent stockholders from removing the managers from office by issuing a large number of additional shares and purchasing these shares themselves. Second, and more importantly, a preemptive right protects stockholders against the dilution of value that would occur if new shares were sold at relatively low prices.

> **preemptive right**
> A provision in the corporate charter or bylaws that gives common stockholders the right to purchase on a pro rata basis new issues of common stock (or convertible securities).

Types of Common Stock

Although most firms have only one type of common stock, in some instances **classified stock** is used to meet the special needs of the company. Generally, when special classifications of stock are used, one type is designated Class A, another Class B, and so on. Small, new companies seeking to obtain funds from outside sources frequently use different types of common stock.

For example, when Genetic Concepts went public, its Class A stock was sold to the public and paid a dividend, but this stock did not have voting rights until 5 years after its issue. The company's Class B stock, which was retained by the organizers of the firm, had full voting rights for 5 years, but the legal terms stated that dividends could not be paid on the Class B stock until Genetic Concepts had established its earning power by building up retained earnings to a designated level. The use of classified stock thus enabled the public to take a position in a conservatively financed growth company without sacrificing income, while the founders retained absolute control during the crucial early stages of the firm's development. At the same time, outside investors were protected against excessive withdrawals of funds by the original owners. As is often the case in such situations, the Class B stock was called **founders' shares.**

Note that "Class A," "Class B," and so on have no standard meanings. Most firms have no classified shares, but a firm that does could designate its Class B shares as founders' shares and its Class A shares as those sold to the public. Another firm might reverse these designations. Still other firms could use stock classifications for entirely different purposes.[14]

Some companies are so small that their common stocks are not actively traded; they are owned by only a few people, usually the companies' managers. Such firms are said to be *privately owned,* or **closely held, corporations,** and their stock is called *closely held stock.* In contrast, the stocks of most larger companies are owned by a large

> **classified stock**
> Common stock that is given a special designation, such as Class A, Class B, and so forth, to meet special needs of the company.

> **founders' shares**
> Stock owned by the firm's founders that has sole voting rights but generally pays out only restricted dividends for a specified number of years.

> **closely held corporation**
> A corporation that is owned by a few individuals who are typically associated with the firm's management.

---

[14]When General Motors (GM) acquired Hughes Aircraft for $5 billion in 1985, it paid for the purchase in part with a new Class H common stock (designated as GMH). The GMH stock had limited voting rights and its dividends were tied to Hughes' performance as a GM subsidiary. The company created the new stock for the following reasons: (1) GM wanted to limit voting privileges on the new classified stock because of management's concern about a possible takeover and (2) Hughes' employees wanted to be rewarded more directly based on Hughes' own performance than would have been possible with regular GM stock. GM's deal posed a problem for the New York Stock Exchange, which had a rule against listing any company's common stock if the firm had any nonvoting common stock outstanding. GM made it clear that it was willing to delist if the NYSE did not change its rules. The NYSE concluded that such arrangements as GM had made were logical and were likely to be made by other companies in the future, so it changed its rules to accommodate GM.

number of investors, most of whom are not active in management. Such companies are said to be **publicly owned corporations,** and their stock is called *publicly held stock.*

publicly owned corporation
A corporation that is owned by a relatively large number of individuals who are not actively involved in its management.

 Self-Test Questions

Explain the following statement: "Preferred stock is a hybrid."

Identify and briefly explain some of the key features of preferred stock and common stock.

Identify some actions that companies have taken to make takeovers more difficult.

What are the two primary reasons for the existence of the preemptive right?

What are some reasons that a company might use classified stock?

What is a closely held stock?

DERIVATIVES

derivatives
Financial assets whose values depend on the values of other assets, such as stocks or bonds.

In finance, the term **derivatives** refers to financial assets that have values based on, or *derived* from, the values of other assets, such as stocks or bonds. Without the other assets, derivatives would be worthless. Because the values of derivatives depend on the values of other assets, they can be rather complex investments. A detailed discussion of derivative securities is beyond the scope of this book. To provide some indication of the nature of derivatives, however, we briefly describe options, futures, convertibles, swaps, and hedge funds.

Options

option
A contract that gives the option holder the right to buy (sell) an asset at some predetermined price within a specified period of time.

An **option** is a contract that gives its holder the right to buy (sell) an asset at some predetermined price within a specified period of time. "Pure options" are instruments that are created by outsiders (generally investment firms) rather than by the firm itself; they are bought and sold primarily by investors (or speculators).

The most basic types of options include a *call* and a *put.* A **call option** gives the holder the right to purchase, or *call in,* shares of a stock for purchase at a predetermined price at any time during the option period. In contrast, a **put option** gives the holder the right to sell, or *put out,* shares of a stock at a specified price during the option period. The transaction price established in the option contract—that is, the purchase price for a call and the selling price for a put—is called the **striking, or exercise, price.**

call option
An option to buy shares of stock at a certain price within a specified period.

put option
An option to sell shares of a stock at a specified price during a particular time period.

striking (exercise) price
The price that must be paid (buying or selling) for a share of common stock when an option is exercised.

Because options are created by parties outside the firm, such as investment firms or investors, companies on whose stocks the options are written are not directly involved in the options markets. Therefore, corporations do not raise money in the options markets, and option holders neither receive dividends nor vote for corporate directors (unless they exercise their options to purchase the stock, which few actually do).[15]

---

[15]Corporations sometimes issue options called *warrants.* The holder of a warrant has the right to buy a stated number of shares of stock from the company at a specified price. Generally, warrants are distributed along with debt, and they are used to induce investors to buy a firm's long-term debt at a lower interest rate than otherwise would be required. In many cases, warrants cannot be exercised for several years after their issue, so their lives are longer than those of "pure options." When an investor exercises a warrant, unlike with a "pure option," the issuing company does receive funds, because the investor buys the stock directly from firm.

Convertibles

Convertible securities are bonds or preferred stocks that can be exchanged for, or converted into, common stock at the option of the holder. Conversion does not bring in additional capital for the issuing firm—rather, debt or preferred stock is simply replaced by common stock. Of course, this reduction of debt or preferred stock will strengthen the firm's balance sheet and make it easier to raise additional capital, but this effect represents a separate action. In many cases, a convertible security is issued as a temporary substitute for common stock when the market price of a firm's stock is depressed but is expected to improve in the future. If the company wants to ensure that a convertible security will be converted into common stock once stock prices rise, the original convertible will include a call provision. The firm will then call the bond (or preferred stock) when the market price of the common stock rises to a point where bondholders (preferred stockholders) would prefer to convert the bonds rather than return the bonds to the firm. When the conversion takes place, the firm has issued stock. Once the conversion is made, investors cannot convert back to bonds (preferred stock).

One of the most important provisions of a convertible security is the conversion ratio, which is defined as the number of shares of stock that the convertible holder receives upon conversion. Related to the conversion ratio is the conversion price, which is the effective price paid for the common stock obtained by converting a convertible security. For example, a $1,000 convertible bond with a conversion ratio of 20 can be converted into 20 shares of common stock, so the conversion price is $50 = $1,000/20. If the market value of the stock rises above $50 per share, it would be beneficial for the bondholder to convert the bond into stock (ignoring any costs associated with conversion).

> **convertible security**
> A security, usually a bond or preferred stock, that is exchangeable, at the option of the holder, for the common stock of the issuing firm.

Futures

A **futures contract** represents an arrangement for delivery of an item at some date in the future; the details of the delivery, including the amount to be delivered and the price that will be paid at delivery, are specified when the futures contract is created. Multinational corporations often enter into futures contracts for foreign currencies used in their transactions.

As an example, consider a U.S. firm that has to pay for products purchased from a British manufacturer. The terms of the transactions require the firm to pay £1,000,000 (1 million British pounds) 30 days from today. If the firm exchanges U.S. dollars into British pounds today, it would need $1.8 million because each dollar can be exchanged for approximately 0.556 British pound (each $1.00 buys £0.556, or $1.80 buys £1.00). When the firm makes the payment in 30 days, however, the exchange rate could be different and might cost the firm more than $1.8 million. To avoid the risk of the exchange rate changing in an unfavorable direction, the firm can enter into a futures contract today to purchase £1,000,000 in 30 days at a price specified today—say, $1.82 per £1.00. In 30 days, the firm could take delivery of £1,000,000 and pay $1,820,000 = $1.82 × 1,000,000, no matter what exchange rate exists at that time. The futures contract provides the company with *insurance* against unfavorable changes in exchange rates—the company has hedged its risk.

> **futures contract**
> An arrangement for delivery of an item at some date in the future, where the delivery details are determined when the contract is created.

Swaps

A **swap** is an agreement to exchange, or swap, cash flows or assets at some time in the future. For example, firms might agree to exchange interest payments on outstanding debt. One firm might have fixed-rate debt outstanding but would prefer to have floating-rate debt, whereas the other firm might have floating-rate debt outstanding

> **swap**
> An agreement to exchange, or swap, cash flows or assets at some specified time in the future.

but would prefer to have fixed-rate debt. Perhaps market conditions make it too costly for each firm to refinance or convert their present debt into the desired debt. The firms could, therefore, agree to swap interest payments such that the firm with the fixed-rate debt pays the variable interest on the floating-rate debt, and vice versa. As long as the principal amounts of the two debts are the same, the swap agreement allows the two firms to create the desired interest payments. Such an arrangement is referred to as a "plain vanilla" swap because it is a very simple strategy. More complex arrangements include combination swaps in which multiple items are exchanged; an example would be a combination interest-rate, exchange-rate swap.

Hedge Funds

A hedge fund is a relatively new, innovative, and complex investment that takes many different forms. Although an in-depth discussion is beyond the scope of this book, we include a brief description of hedge funds here because these investments have received a great deal of attention recently and the growth in hedge funds has been extraordinary during the past few years.

hedge fund
A private pool of funds that is constructed for the purpose of generating a specific range of returns, no matter what happens in the general stock market.

In simple terms, a **hedge fund** is a private pool of funds that is constructed for the purpose of generating a specific range of returns, no matter what happens in the general stock market. To do so, hedge fund managers follow complex combinations of investment strategies that include borrowing large amounts of money and taking a variety of investment positions in stocks, bonds, options, swaps, and other derivatives. For example, one of the strategies followed in a hedge fund might be to buy financially distressed firms. As a result, the risks associated with hedge funds can be substantial. Due to their complexities and the amounts that are invested, those who participate in hedge funds are wealthy individuals who are considered to be sophisticated investors—that is, investors who are well informed about the financial risks associated with such investments. Most hedge funds are formed as partnerships that are managed by investment professionals who receive performance fees of 20 percent (or more) of the returns that are generated, which is in addition to normal management fees equal to 1 or 2 percent of the value of the hedge fund's assets.

Because they are "private" and intended for investment-savvy investors, hedge funds are not subject to the same restrictions, regulations, and registration requirements as most other investment instruments, including mutual funds. As a result, little is known about the specific strategies that are followed in the management of hedge funds. Hedge funds should not be compared—or confused with—mutual funds; these two investments differ significantly.

Self-Test Questions

Differentiate between a call option and a put option.

Do the corporations on whose stocks options are written raise money in the options market? Explain.

Does the exchange of convertible securities for common stock bring in additional funds to the firm? Explain.

Why are convertibles with call provisions considered "delayed" equity offerings?

What are future contracts, and how do they reduce risk?

What is a swap agreement?

What is a hedge fund?

FIGURE 2-2   Risk and Returns on Different Classes of Financial Instruments

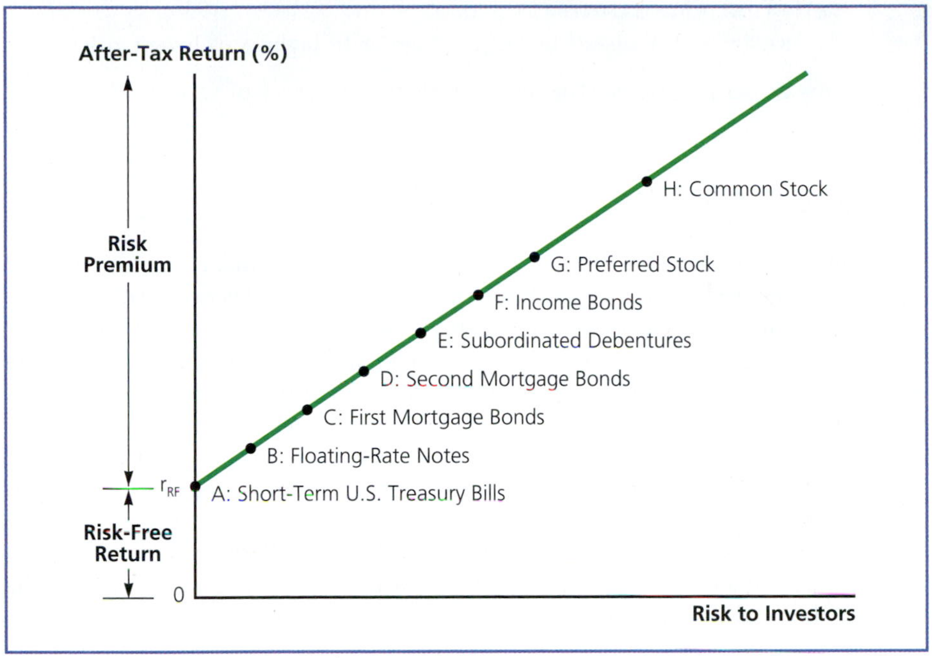

RATIONALE FOR DIFFERENT TYPES OF SECURITIES

Why do so many different types of securities exist? At least a partial answer to this question might be seen in Figure 2-2, which depicts the tradeoff between the risk and expected after-tax return for the various securities issued by Taxton Products.[16] First, U.S. Treasury bills, which represent the risk-free rate, are shown for reference. The lowest-risk, long-term securities offered by Taxton are its floating-rate notes; these securities are free of risk associated with changes in interest rates (interest rate risk), but they are exposed to some risk of default, or nonpayment by the company. The first mortgage bonds are somewhat riskier than the notes (because the bonds are exposed to interest rate risk), and they sell at a somewhat higher after-tax return. The second mortgage bonds are even riskier, so they have an even higher return. Subordinated debentures, income bonds, and preferred stocks are all increasingly risky, and their returns increase accordingly. Taxton's common stock is the riskiest security it issues, so it has the highest return.

Why does Taxton issue so many different classes of securities? Why not offer just one type of bond plus common stock? The answer lies in the fact that different investors have different risk/return tradeoff preferences. Thus, to appeal to the broadest possible market, Taxton must offer securities that attract as many different types of investors as possible. Also, different securities are more popular at different points in time, and firms tend to issue whatever is popular at the time they need money. When used wisely, a policy of selling differentiated securities to take advantage of market conditions can lower a firm's overall cost of funds below what it would be if the firm used only one class of debt or equity.

[16]The yields in Figure 2-2 are shown on an after-tax basis to the recipient. If yields were on a before-tax basis, those on preferred stocks would lie below those on bonds because of the tax treatment of preferred stock (discussed in Chapter 6). In essence, 70 percent of preferred dividends are tax exempt to corporations owning preferred shares, so a preferred stock with a 10 percent pretax yield will have a higher after-tax return to a corporation in the 34 percent tax bracket than will a bond with a 12 percent yield.

WHICH FINANCIAL INSTRUMENT IS BEST?

In this chapter, we have described numerous financial instruments used by firms to raise funds and used by investors as tools for saving funds. At this point, you might be wondering which financial instrument is best. Simply stated, what is best for one individual or firm is not necessarily best for another individual or firm. To complicate matters, what is best for one individual or firm when certain market conditions or circumstances exist might not be best under other market conditions or circumstances. For example, the decisions you make concerning your investments most certainly will change as you approach retirement age. That is, when you first start investing, you probably will take greater chances and, therefore, invest in riskier financial assets than when you are near retirement age. Similarly, your confidence in the financial markets most certainly will change with market conditions and affect the types of financial instruments you purchase. Generally, as your confidence in the markets increases, you are willing to take greater chances, and vice versa.

With this idea in mind, let's consider the circumstances under which firms might prefer to use debt and equity to raise funds as well as situations in which investors might have a preference for one of these investments compared to another.

Issuer's Viewpoint

Traditional bonds (as well as many other forms of debt) require fixed interest payments no matter the level of operating earnings for a firm. Thus, a major advantage associated with debt issues is the firm's ability to limit its financial costs. This ability proves beneficial when the firm prospers because earnings above the interest payments can be distributed to stockholders or reinvested in the firm to fund growth opportunities. Bondholders do not share in the firm's prosperity; only stockholders do. Unfortunately, debt can be a drawback during times of economic and financial adversity, as the interest obligation must be paid even if the firm's operating earnings are low.

Another advantage of using debt financing is that it does not represent ownership, so debtholders do not have voting rights, which means no dilution of ownership occurs when the firm issues additional debt. Many bond indentures and other debt contracts, however, contain clauses that restrict certain actions the firm can make, such as the amount of common stock dividends that can be paid each year. If the firm violates any of the contractual provisions, debtholders might force it to liquidate.

Remember that preferred stock has many of the same characteristics as debt, including a fixed payment and no voting rights. For these reasons, a firm might consider issuing preferred stock if prosperous times are expected so that existing common stockholders do not have to share the prosperity. Unlike debt, preferred stock does not "legally" obligate the firm to make payments to stockholders, and it has no maturity date.

Preferred stock does have a major disadvantage from the issuer's standpoint: it has a higher after-tax cost than debt. The major reason for this higher cost is taxes: preferred dividends are not deductible as a tax expense, whereas interest expense is deductible.[17] This fact makes the cost of preferred stock much greater than that of bonds.

Common stock offers several advantages to the corporation:

1. Like preferred stock, common stock does not legally obligate the firm to make payments to stockholders—only if the company generates earnings and has no pressing internal needs will it pay dividends.

2. Common stock carries no fixed maturity date: it never has to be "repaid" as would a debt issue.

3. The sale of common stock generally increases the creditworthiness of the firm because common stock cushions creditors against losses.

4. If a company's prospects look bright, then common stock often can be sold on better terms than can debt.

Stock appeals to certain groups of investors because it typically carries a higher expected total return (dividends plus capital gains) than does preferred stock or debt. It also provides the investor with a means to hedge against unanticipated inflation because common dividends tend to rise during inflationary periods.[18]

Disadvantages associated with issuing common stock include the following:

1. The sale of common stock gives some voting rights—and perhaps even control—to new stockholders. For this reason, additional equity financing often is avoided by managers who are concerned about maintaining control of the firm.

2. Common stock gives new owners the right to share in the income of the firm. Thus, if profits soar, then new stockholders will share in this bonanza. If debt had been used under the same circumstances, new investors would have received only a fixed return, no matter how profitable the company proved.[19]

3. As discussed in Chapter 3, the costs of underwriting and distributing common stock usually are higher than those for debt or preferred stock.

4. Like preferred stock, under current tax laws, common stock dividends are not deductible as an expense for tax purposes.

Convertible securities can be used to take advantage of some of the benefits associated with both debt and equity. Debt with a conversion feature offers investors greater flexibility by providing them with the opportunity to ultimately be either a debtholder or a stockholder. Thus, such a feature generally allows the firm to sell debt with lower coupon interest rates and with fewer restrictive covenants. Even though convertibles do not bring additional funds into the firm at the time of conversion, they are nevertheless useful features that help the firm achieve "delayed equity financing" when conversion occurs. Convertibles generally are subordinated to mortgage bonds, bank loans, and other senior debt, so financing with these instruments leaves the company's access to "regular" debt unimpaired.

---

[17]You might think that a given firm's preferred stock would carry a higher coupon rate than its bonds because of the preferred stock's greater risk from the holder's viewpoint. In the real world, 70 percent of preferred dividends received by corporate owners are exempt from income taxes, a fact that has made preferred stock very attractive to corporate investors. Today, most preferred stock is owned by corporations. In recent years, high-grade preferred stocks have typically sold on a lower yield basis, before taxes, than have high-grade bonds. On an after-tax basis, however, the yield on preferred stocks generally exceeds the yield on high-grade corporate bonds.

[18]For common stock in general, the rate of increase in dividends has slightly exceeded the rate of inflation since 1970.

[19]This point has given rise to an important theory: If a firm sells a large issue of bonds, the move signals that management expects the company to earn high profits on investments financed by the new capital and that it does not wish to share these profits with new stockholders. On the other hand, if the firm issues stock, it signals that its prospects are not so bright.

In addition, convertibles provide a way of "effectively" selling common stock at prices higher than those prevailing when the issue was made. Many companies actually want to sell common stock and not debt, but they believe that the prices of their stocks are temporarily depressed and "too many" shares would have to be sold to raise a given amount of money. Such firms might use convertibles if they expect the prices of common stocks to rise sufficiently in the future to make conversion attractive; when the conversions take place, the firms have obtained "delayed equity financing" that eliminates the original debt. Conversely, if the stock price does not increase sufficiently, and hence conversion does not occur, the company could be saddled with debt in the face of low earnings, which could prove disastrous.

Convertible securities are useful, but they do have important disadvantages. The use of a convertible feature might, in effect, give the issuer the opportunity to sell common stock at a price higher than it could otherwise. If the price of the common stock increases dramatically, however, the company probably would have been better off if it had used straight debt (despite its higher interest rate) and then later sold common stock to repay the debt. Also, convertibles typically have a low coupon interest rate, an advantage that is lost when conversion occurs.

Investor's Viewpoint

In designing securities, the financial manager must consider the investor's point of view. Both debt and preferred stock provide investors with a steadier, more assured income than does common stock. In addition, debtholders and preferred stockholders have priority over common stockholders in the event of liquidation. The primary advantage of debt from an investor's standpoint is that the firm is legally obligated to make the interest payments. If payments are missed, debtholders have legal recourse that might include forcing the firm into bankruptcy in an attempt to recover what is owed.

Many firms find preferred stock a very attractive investment because 70 percent of the preferred dividends received by corporations is not taxable. For this reason, most preferred stock is owned by corporations. Conversely, preferred stock might seem somewhat unattractive to investors because their returns are limited by the fixed dividend payments, even though preferred stockholders bear some of the ownership risks. For individual investors (as opposed to corporations), *after-tax* bond yields generally are higher than those on preferred stock, even though the preferred stock is the riskier instrument.

From a social viewpoint, common stock is a desirable form of financing because it makes businesses less vulnerable to the consequences of declines in sales and earnings. Common stock financing involves no fixed-charge payments that might force a faltering firm into bankruptcy. From the standpoint of the economy as a whole, if too many firms used too much debt, then business fluctuations would be amplified and minor recessions could turn into major depressions. Not long ago, when the level of leveraged mergers and buyouts was increasing the proportion of debt used by firms, the Federal Reserve and other authorities voiced concern over the possible dangers created by the situation. Congressional leaders, in turn, debated the wisdom of social controls over corporations' use of debt. Like most important issues, this one inspires controversy, and the debate centers around who can better determine an "appropriate" way for firms to raise funds—corporate managers or government officials.[20]

---

[20]When business executives hear someone say, "I'm from Washington and I'm here to help you," they generally cringe—and often with good reason. On the other hand, a stable national economy does require sound businesses, and too much debt can lead to corporate instability.

Investors use derivatives either to manage risk associated with their investment portfolios or to speculate about the direction prices will change in the future. Options and futures essentially are created by investors; firms do not use these instruments to raise funds. Both types of derivatives involve two parties—one on each side of the transaction. In aggregate, such derivatives do not create wealth in the financial markets, because when an investor on one side of the transaction gains from a price movement, the investor on the other side loses an equivalent amount. From an investor's viewpoint, derivatives can be quite complex. You can learn more details about derivatives and other complex investments by taking a course that covers "investments."

Self-Test Questions

What are the advantages and disadvantages of debt and preferred stock from an issuer's viewpoint?

What are the advantages and disadvantages of debt and preferred stock from an investor's viewpoint?

How are convertible securities used to help firms raise funds?

What are some advantages and disadvantages of including convertibles as features in debt indentures?

What are the major advantages and disadvantages of common stock financing?

From a social viewpoint, why is common stock a desirable form of financing?

FINANCIAL INSTRUMENTS IN INTERNATIONAL MARKETS

For the most part, the financial securities of companies and institutions in other countries are similar to those in the United States. Some differences do exist, however, as discussed in this section. Also, some financial securities have been created specifically to permit investors easier access to international investments, such as *American depository receipts.*

American Depository Receipts

Ownership of foreign companies can be traded internationally through *depository receipts,* which represent shares of the underlying stocks of foreign companies. In the United States, most foreign stock is traded through **American depository receipts (ADRs).** ADRs are not foreign stocks; instead they are "certificates" created by organizations such as banks. The certificates represent ownership in stocks of foreign companies that are held in trust by a bank located in the country where the stock is traded. ADRs provide U.S. investors with the ability to invest in foreign companies with less complexity and difficulty than might otherwise be possible.

Each ADR certificate represents a certain number of shares of stock of a foreign company and entitles the owner to receive any dividends paid by the company in U.S. dollars. ADRs are traded in the stock markets in the United States, which often are more liquid than those in foreign markets. All financial information, including values, is denominated in dollars and stated in English, thereby eliminating potential problems with exchange rates and language translations.

American depository receipts (ADRs)
Certificates representing ownership in stocks of foreign companies that are held in trust by a bank located in the country the stock is traded.

In many cases, investors can purchase foreign securities directly. Such investments might be complicated by legal issues, the ability to take funds such as dividends out of the country, and interpretation into domestic terms. Thus, ADRs enable investors to participate in the international financial markets without having to bear risks greater than those associated with the corporations in which the investments are made. The market values of ADRs move in tandem with the market values of the underlying stocks that are held in trust.

Debt Instruments

Like the U.S. debt markets, the international debt markets offer a variety of instruments with many different features. Here, we discuss a few of the more familiar types of debt that are traded internationally.

Any debt sold outside the country of the borrower is called international debt. Two important types of international debt exist: foreign debt and Eurodebt.

foreign debt
A debt instrument sold by a foreign borrower but denominated in the currency of the country in which it is sold.

Foreign debt is debt sold by a foreign borrower but denominated in the currency of the country in which the issue is sold. For instance, Bell Canada might need U.S. dollars to finance the operations of its subsidiaries in the United States. If it decides to raise the needed capital in the domestic U.S. bond market, the bond will be underwritten by a syndicate of U.S. investment firms, denominated in U.S. dollars, and sold to U.S. investors in accordance with SEC and applicable state regulations. Except for the foreign origin of the borrower (Canada), this bond will be indistinguishable from bonds issued by equivalent U.S. corporations. Because Bell Canada is a foreign corporation, however, its bond will be called a *foreign bond*. Foreign bonds generally are labeled according to the country in which they are issued. For example, if foreign bonds are issued in the United States, they are called *Yankee bonds;* if they are issued in Japan, they are called *Samurai bonds;* and if they are issued in the United Kingdom, they are called *Bulldog bonds.*

Eurodebt
Debt sold in a country other than the one in whose currency the debt is denominated.

The term **Eurodebt** is used to designate any debt sold in a country other than the one in whose currency the debt is denominated. Examples include *Eurobonds,* such as a British firm's issue of pound-denominated bonds sold in France or Ford Motor Company's dollar-denominated issue that is sold in Germany. The institutional arrangements by which Eurobonds are marketed are different than those for most other bond issues, with the most important distinction being a far lower level of required disclosure than normally applies to bonds issued in domestic markets, particularly in the United States. Governments tend to be less strict when regulating securities denominated in foreign currencies than they are on home-currency securities, because the purchasers of such bonds generally are more "sophisticated." The lower disclosure requirements result in lower total transaction costs for Eurobonds.

Eurobonds appeal to investors for several reasons. Generally, they are issued in bearer form rather than as registered bonds, so the names and nationalities of investors are not recorded. Individuals who desire anonymity, whether for privacy reasons or for tax avoidance, find Eurobonds to their liking. Similarly, most governments do not withhold taxes on interest payments associated with Eurobonds.

More than half of all Eurobonds are denominated in dollars; bonds in Japanese yen and euros account for most of the rest. Although centered in Europe, Eurobonds truly are international. Their underwriting syndicates include investment firms from all regions of the world, and the bonds are sold to investors not only in

Europe but also in such faraway places as Bahrain and Singapore. Until recently, Eurobonds were issued solely by multinational firms, international financial institutions, and national governments. Today, however, the Eurobond market is also being tapped by purely domestic U.S. firms such as electric utilities, which find that borrowing overseas enables them to lower their debt costs.

Some other types of *Eurodebt* include the following:

1. *Eurocredits.* Eurocredits are bank loans that are denominated in the currency of a country other than that where the lending bank is located. Many of these loans are very large, so the lending bank often forms a loan syndicate to help raise the needed funds and to spread out some of the risk associated with the loan.

   Interest rates on Eurocredits, as well as other short-term Eurodebt forms, typically are tied to a standard rate known by the acronym **LIBOR,** which stands for *London InterBank Offer Rate.* LIBOR is the rate of interest offered by the largest and strongest London banks on deposits of other large banks of the highest credit standing. In May 2008, LIBOR rates were higher than domestic U.S. bank rates on time deposits of the same maturity— 2.5 percent for 3-month CDs versus 2.7 percent for 3-month LIBOR CDs.

2. *Euro-commercial paper (Euro-CP).* Euro-CP is similar to commercial paper issued in the United States. This short-term debt instrument is issued by corporations, and it typically has a maturity of 1, 3, or 6 months. The principal difference between Euro-CP and U.S. commercial paper is that there is not as much concern about the credit quality of Euro-CP issuers.

3. *Euronotes.* Euronotes, which represent medium-term debt, typically have maturities ranging from 1 to 10 years. The general features of Euronotes closely resemble those of longer term debt instruments such as bonds. The principal amount is repaid at maturity, and interest often is paid semiannually. Most foreign companies use Euronotes just as they would a line of credit, continuously issuing notes to finance medium-term needs.

LIBOR
The London InterBank Offer Rate; the interest rate offered by the best London banks on deposits of other large, very creditworthy banks.

Equity Instruments

The equities of foreign companies resemble those of U.S. corporations. The primary difference between stocks of foreign companies and U.S. companies is that U.S. regulations provide greater protection of stockholders' rights than do the regulations of most other countries. In the international markets, equity generally is referred to as "Euro stock" or "Yankee stock."

Euro stock is traded in countries other than the home country of the company, not including the United States. Thus, if the stock of a Japanese company is sold in Germany, it would be considered a Euro stock.

Yankee stock is issued by foreign companies and traded in the United States. If a Japanese company sold its stock in the United States, it would be called Yankee stock in the international markets.

As the financial markets become more global and more sophisticated, the financial instruments offered both domestically and internationally will certainly change. Already, foreign companies and governments have discovered that financial markets in the United States provide excellent sources of funds because of the great variety of financial outlets found in this country. As technology improves and regulations that bar or discourage foreign investment are repealed, the financial markets of other developed countries will become more prominent, and new, innovative financial products will emerge.

Self-Test Questions

Differentiate between foreign debt and Eurodebt.

Why do Eurobonds appeal to investors?

What are Eurocredits, Euro-commercial paper, and Euronotes?

What is a Yankee stock?

What changes do you think will occur in the international markets during the next few decades?

Ethical Dilemma

Should Maria Take a SINful Cruise?

Maria Santos was recently promoted to senior vice president and assistant to the CFO at Paradise Environmental Designs (PED). In her new position, Maria is responsible for raising external funds for PED. When the firm needs to raise capital, her team recommends the type of financial instrument that should be issued, completes the appropriate paperwork, negotiates with PED's investment bankers, and so forth. In a departmental meeting a couple of days ago, the CEO stated that he thought the rate at which PED has been raising capital has been much too high, and he wants any future funds that are raised to have substantially lower costs. Although he blamed her predecessor, the comments were clearly directed at Maria and the members of her department. As a result, Maria felt that she had to come up with some means by which PED can lower the costs of funds in the future.

Because she is fairly new to her position, Maria thought it would be a good idea to meet with others who are more experienced in raising funds for corporations. One of the persons who offered Maria some ideas is Roger, a close friend of hers, who works at Superior Investment Networks (SIN), which is one of the investment banking organizations used by PED. Roger suggested that PED consider issuing convertible bonds rather than straight, or traditional, bonds. He explained that a convertible bond can be issued at a lower interest rate than an identical bond that is not convertible, because the conversion feature is a benefit to investors rather than to

issuers. Roger also explained that convertibles are somewhat complex hybrid securities. Other than the information that Roger gave her, Maria knows nothing about convertibles. But because Roger is a friend and his description of convertibles was intriguing, she decided to investigate whether it would be appropriate for PED to use convertibles.

When she arrived at work this morning, Maria was told that PED plans to raise $400 million as soon as possible to invest in new projects that the CEO wants to purchase within 1 year. Unfortunately, Maria hasn't had a chance to collect more information about convertibles. Even so, she thinks that a convertible might be an appropriate instrument to issue at this time. As a result, Maria called Roger and asked him how she could learn more about convertibles in a short time period. Roger told her that SIN presents a conference each year at which invited participants discuss various aspects of convertibles. The topics that are covered at the conference range from the basics of convertible securities to more complex topics. The conference seems to be exactly what Maria needs in order to become more informed about the advantages and disadvantages of issuing convertibles, so she asked Roger to provide her with specific information about the conference, including the dates, costs, specific session topics, and so forth.

One hour ago, Roger called with details about the SIN conference. The 7-day conference will be

continues

held aboard a cruise ship as it sails to exotic ports in the Mediterranean Sea. The sessions are scheduled during the time the ship is traveling from one port to another, which generally takes 4 or 5 hours. When the ship is in port, the conference coordinator has arranged for the participants to take tours, play golf and tennis, lounge at the beach, and enjoy the local entertainment. The conference sounds great to Maria because she can work and relax at the same time. One thing bothers her, however—all of the costs, including recreation, relaxation, and entertainment activities will be paid for by SIN.

Maria is convinced that she will get the information she needs at the SIN conference. But she is concerned that attending the conference might be considered a conflict of interest, because she knows that SIN representatives will try to convince her to use the company's services to issue convertibles. She also knows that Roger will earn substantial commissions if PED uses SIN to issue convertibles. Further, Maria is concerned that material/information she receives at the conference will be one-sided (biased).

If she is going to attend the conference, Maria needs to register within the next couple of days. As a result, she needs to make a decision soon. What should she do? What would you do if you were Maria?

To summarize the key concepts, let's answer the questions that were posed at the beginning of the chapter:

CHAPTER PRINCIPLES
–The Answers

- **Why are there so many different types of financial instruments?** Because different investors have different risk/return tradeoff preferences, it is necessary to have different financial assets that appeal to a diverse pool of investors. Different securities attract different types of investors. Also, some types of investments are more popular at different points in time, and firms tend to issue whatever is popular at the time they need to raise funds. Firms can raise funds more easily, and thus at lower costs, if they issue the types of securities that investors want.

- **What is debt? What types of debt exist and what are some of the characteristics?** In simple terms, debt represents a loan. A debt agreement, which is called an *indenture,* specifies the principal amount that must be repaid, the amount of interest that is paid on specific dates, and the date the debt matures. There are many types of debt—short-term debt includes Treasury bills, repurchase agreements, federal funds, and commercial paper, to name a few; long-term debt generally includes term loans and bonds (corporate, government, and municipal). Bonds often include such provisions as a call which allows the issuer to "call" the bond in for a refund prior to maturity, a sinking fund, which requires the issuer to repay portions of the bond each year, and a convertible feature, which allows bondholders to convert their bonds into common stock.

- **What are bond ratings and why are they important?** A bond rating, which is based on both quantitative and qualitative factors, gives an indication of the default risk associated with a bond. Bonds with low ratings are perceived as having greater risk than bonds with high ratings; thus, to attract investors, low-rated bonds generally must have higher rates of return than high-rated bonds. Some organizations, such as pension funds and insurance companies (institutional investors), can invest only in high-rated bonds, which means that bond ratings are important to these types of investors.

- **What is equity? What are some of the features/characteristics of equity?** *Equity* generally is defined as the value of assets that are *owned* minus the amount of debt that is *owed*. Thus, if a firm's assets are sold at their *book values* and all debts are paid off, the amount remaining is the equity that can be paid to stockholders. Some firms have two types of stock (equity)—preferred stock and common stock. Preferred stock has preference when the firm distributes cash in the form of dividends or liquidation proceeds. Neither preferred stock nor common stock has a maturity date, thus both have infinite lives. Preferred stockholders generally are paid a constant dividend. Although some common stocks pay constant, or fairly constant, dividends, many common stocks either pay no dividends or pay variable dividends. Common stockholders elect the members of the board of directors, who then appoint the corporate officers who run the day-to-day operations; most preferred stockholders have no voting rights. Common stockholders generally are considered the owners of the firm because they bear most of the risks associated with the firm's operations. It is the common stockholders who benefit most when the firm performs well, but it is the same stockholders who incur the greatest losses when the firm performs poorly.

- **What are derivatives? What are some of the more familiar types of derivatives?** Derivatives are financial assets that have values based on, or *derived* from, the values of other assets, such as stocks or bonds. That is, as the values of the *underlying assets* change, so do the values of the derivatives. Derivatives that are familiar to many investors include options, futures, convertibles, and swaps. A stock option is a contract that sets the prices at which a stock can be purchased (or sold) during a specified time period. A futures contract is a contract that specifies the price at which a commodity or other asset will be delivered at some future date. A convertible security generally is either a bond or preferred stock that can be traded in for (converted into) common stock at some contractually specified price. A swap is a contract where two parties exchange, or swap, payments on such financial assets as bonds or currency futures. For example, perhaps one firm that has variable-rate debt swaps debt payments with another firm that has fixed-rate debt.

CHAPTER PRINCIPLES
–Personal Finance

The concepts presented in this chapter should give you an idea as to what alternative investments are available in the financial markets. There are many types of investment opportunities that range from basic stocks and bonds to complex, exotic combinations of options and convertibles. You should be careful, however, when investing your money. You should not invest in securities that you don't understand; if you do, you might be left wondering why you lost your money.

Following are concepts from this chapter that can be applied to personal finance:

- **How can I use bond ratings to help make investment decisions?** Bond ratings provide an indication of the default risks associated with bond issues. Thus, if you don't mind risking your money to try to earn higher returns, you would invest in lower rated bonds—that is, bonds with greater default risk. If you don't like taking much risk, then you should invest in high-rated bonds.

- **How can I use the concepts discussed in this chapter to help make decisions about borrowing money?** Individuals, like corporations, have credit ratings. The better an individual's credit rating, the lower the interest rate he or she is charged on loans, such as mortgages and automobile loans. To lower the interest you are charged, you need to improve your credit rating.

- **Should I purchase regular preferred stock, convertible preferred stock, regular common stock, Class A common stock, or Class B common stock?** The answer to this question depends on the reason you want to invest in stocks. If you want to receive dividends (income) each year, then you would invest in income-producing stocks, such as preferred stock or the common stock of large, well-established firms that pay relatively constant dividends from year to year. But if you are willing to wait to receive capital gains at some later date, then you should purchase common stocks of companies that pay little or no dividends because such firms invest current earnings to fund future growth. After reading the discussions of the characteristics of different types and classes of stocks given in this chapter, you should be more informed when making decisions about what kind of stock is appropriate to meet your investment needs.

- Options provide some protection against "bad" risk, which means that they can be used to reduce the risks associated with investment positions. Consider, for example, an investor who owns 100 shares of IBM stock. Suppose that the current market value of IBM stock is $92 per share. Perhaps the investor believes that the price of IBM stock is likely to drop during the next few months. Although she does not want to sell the stock today, she does plan to sell the stock within 2 months. To protect against the risk of a significant price decrease, she can purchase a 3-month put option on the IBM stock she owns. The cost to purchase a put position to cover the 100 shares of IBM stock is $380, and the striking price for each put is $95. Consider what happens if the price of IBM's stock declines to $80. The investor will lose $-1,200 = 100(\$80 - \$92)$ on her current position in the stock, but she will realize a net gain equal to $\$1,120 = 100(\$95 - \$80) - \$380$ on the put position. As a result, her net loss on the combined position is $-\$80 = \$1,120 - \$1,200$, which is much less than if she did not have the put position. If the price of IBM stock increases to $100 per share, the investor will let the put options expire because they are worthless. In this case, it effectively costs the investor $380 to insure the 100 shares of IBM stock that she holds from "downside" risk.

QUESTIONS

2-1 In what respect is preferred stock similar to bonds, and in what respect is it similar to common stock?

2-2 Explain the following statement: "Whereas a bond contains a promise to pay interest, common stock provides an expectation but no promise of dividends."

2-3 What is the significance of the par value on a preferred stock? What is the significance of the par value on a common stock?

2-4 What effect do you think each of the following items should have on the interest rate that a firm must pay on a new issue of long-term debt? Indicate whether each factor would tend to raise, lower, or have an indeterminate effect on the interest rate, and then explain why.

   a. The firm uses bonds rather than a term loan.

   b. The firm uses debentures rather than first mortgage bonds.

   c. The firm makes its bonds convertible into common stock.

   d. If the firm makes its debentures subordinate to its bank debt, what will the effect be

      (1) On the cost of the debentures?

      (2) On the cost of the bank debt?

      (3) On the average cost of total debt?

   e. The firm sells income bonds rather than debentures.

f. The firm must raise $100 million, all of which will be used to construct a new plant, and it is debating the sale of first mortgage bonds or debentures. If it decides to issue $50 million of each type, as opposed to $75 million of first mortgage bonds and $25 million of debentures, how will this choice affect

    (1) The cost of debentures?

    (2) The cost of mortgage bonds?

    (3) The overall cost of the $100 million?

g. The firm puts a call provision on its new issue of bonds.

h. The firm includes a sinking fund on its new issue of bonds.

i. The firm's bonds are downgraded from A to BBB.

2-5   Rank the following securities from lowest (1) to highest (8) in terms of their riskiness for an investor. All securities (except the Treasury bond) are for a given firm. If you think two or more securities are equally risky, indicate so.

a. Income bond   _____

b. Subordinated debentures—noncallable   _____

c. First mortgage bond—no sinking fund   _____

d. Common stock   _____

e. U.S. Treasury bond   _____

f. First mortgage bond—with sinking fund   _____

g. Subordinated debentures—callable   _____

h. Term loan   _____

2-6   A sinking fund can be set up in one of two ways:

(1) The corporation makes annual payments to the trustee, who invests the proceeds in securities (frequently government bonds) and uses the accumulated total to retire the bond issue at maturity.

(2) The trustee uses the annual payments to retire a portion of the issue each year, either by calling a given percentage of the issue through a lottery and paying a specified price per bond or by buying bonds on the open market, whichever is cheaper.

Discuss the advantages and disadvantages of each procedure from the viewpoint of both the firm and its bondholders.

2-7   Examine Table 2-2. Suppose Sydex sold 2 million shares of common stock, with the company netting $25 per share. Construct a statement of the equity accounts to reflect this sale.

2-8   It is often said that the primary purpose of the preemptive right is to allow individuals to maintain their proportionate share of the ownership and control of a corporation.

a. How important do you suppose this consideration is for the average stockholder of a firm whose shares are traded on the New York Stock Exchange?

b. Is the preemptive right likely to be of greater importance to stockholders of publicly owned or closely held firms? Explain.

2-9   Should preferred stock be classified as debt or equity? Does it matter if the classification is being made by the firm's (a) management, (b) creditors, or (c) equity investors?

2-10 Evaluate the following statement: "Issuing convertible securities represents a means by which a firm can sell common stock at a price above the existing market price."

2-11 Suppose a company simultaneously issues $50 million of convertible bonds with a coupon rate of 9 percent and $50 million of pure bonds with a coupon rate of 12 percent. Both bonds have the same maturity. Does the fact that the convertible issue has the lower coupon rate suggest that it is less risky than the pure bond? Would you regard the cost of the funds as being lower on the convertible security than on the pure bond? Explain. (*Hint:* Although it might appear at first glance that the convertible's cost is lower, it is not necessarily the case because the interest rate on the convertible understates its cost. Think about this point before answering the questions.)

2-12 In 1936, the Canadian government raised $55 million by issuing bonds at a 3 percent annual rate of interest. Unlike most bonds issued today, which have a specific maturity date, these bonds can remain outstanding forever; they are, in fact, perpetual.

At the time of issue, the Canadian government stated in the bond indenture that cash redemption was possible at face value ($100) on or after September 1966; in other words, the bonds were callable at par after September 1966. Believing that the bonds would actually be called, many investors purchased these bonds in 1965 with the expectation of receiving $100 in 1966 for each perpetual bond they had. In 1965, the bonds sold for $55. A rush of buyers, however, drove the price to slightly less than the $100 par value by 1966, but prices fell dramatically when the Canadian government announced that these perpetual bonds were indeed perpetual and would not be paid off. The bonds' market price declined to $42 in December 1966. Because of their severe losses, hundreds of Canadian bondholders formed the Perpetual Bond Association to lobby for face value redemption of the bonds, claiming that the government had reneged on an implied promise to redeem the bonds. Government officials in Ottawa insisted that claims for face value payment were nonsense—that the bonds were and always had been clearly identified as perpetuals. One Ottawa official stated, "Our job is to protect the taxpayer. Why should we pay $55 million for less than $25 million worth of bonds?"

The following questions relating to the Canadian issue will test your understanding of bonds in general:

a. Do you think it would it make sense for a business firm to issue bonds like the Canadian government bonds described here?

b. Suppose the U.S. government today sold $100 billion each of four types of bonds: 5-year bonds, 50-year bonds, "regular" perpetual bonds, and Canadian-type perpetual bonds. Rank the bonds from the one with the lowest to the one with the highest expected interest rate. Explain your answer.

c. Do you think the Canadian government would have taken the same action with regard to retiring the bonds if the interest rate had fallen rather than risen after they were issued?

d. Do you think the Canadian government was fair or unfair in its actions? Give the pros and cons of its decision, and justify your reason for thinking that one outweighs the other. Would it matter if the bonds had been sold to "sophisticated" as opposed to "naive" purchasers?

SELF-TEST PROBLEMS

Key Terms   **ST-1**   Define each of the following terms:

    a. Term loan; bond

    b. Mortgage bond

    c. Debenture; subordinated debenture

    d. Convertible bond; income bond; putable bond; indexed (purchasing power) bond

    e. Indenture; restrictive covenant

    f. Trustee

    g. Call provision; sinking fund

    h. Zero coupon bond; original issue discount bond (OID)

    i. Floating-rate bond

    j. Junk bond

    k. Investment-grade bond

    l. Common equity; paid-in capital; retained earnings

    m. Proxy; proxy fight; takeover

    n. Preemptive right

    o. Classified stock; founders' shares

    p. Closely held corporation; publicly owned corporation

    q. Cumulative dividends

    r. Option; call option; put option

    s. Convertible security; convertible preferred stock

    t. Swaps

    u. Eurodebt; Yankee stock

Sinking Fund   **ST-2**   The Vancouver Development Company just sold a $100 million, 10-year, 12 percent bond issue. A sinking fund will retire the issue over its life. Sinking fund payments are of equal amounts and will be made *semiannually*, and the proceeds will be used to retire bonds as the payments are made. Bonds can be called at par for sinking fund purposes, or the funds paid into the sinking fund can be used to buy bonds in the open market.

    a. How large must each semiannual sinking fund payment be?

    b. What will happen over time, under the conditions of the problem stated to this point, to the company's debt service requirements (interest and sinking fund payments) per year for this issue?

    c. Now suppose that Vancouver Development sets up its sinking fund so that, at the end of each year, equal annual amounts are paid into a sinking fund trust held by a bank, with the proceeds being used to buy government bonds that pay 9 percent interest. The payments that will be made to the sinking fund each year equal $6,582,009. What are the annual cash requirements for covering bond service costs under this trusteeship arrangement? (*Note:* Interest must be paid on Vancouver's outstanding bonds but not on bonds that have been retired.)

    d. What would have to happen to bond prices to cause the company to buy bonds on the open market rather than call them under the original sinking fund plan?

PROBLEMS

2-1   The Swift Company is planning to finance an expansion. The principal executives of the company agree that an industrial company such as theirs should finance growth by issuing common stock rather than by taking on additional debt. Because they believe that the current price of Swift's common stock does not reflect its true worth, however, they have decided to sell convertible bonds. Each convertible bond has a face value equal to $1,000 and can be converted into 25 shares of common stock.

Convertible Bond

   a. What would be the minimum price of the stock that would make it beneficial for bondholders to convert their bonds? Ignore the effects of taxes or other costs.

   b. What would be the benefits of including a call provision with these bonds?

2-2   Four years ago, Ideal Solutions issued convertible preferred stock with a par value of $50 and a stated dividend of 8 percent. Each share of preferred stock can be converted to four shares of common stock at the option of the investor. When issued, the preferred stock was sold at par value such that Ideal raised $2.5 million to fund expansion of its operations.

Convertible Preferred Stock

   a. What is the annual dividend per share on the preferred stock?

   b. What is the conversion price of the preferred stock? When should an investor consider converting into common stock? (Ignore taxes and other costs that might be associated with conversion.)

   c. If all investors convert their preferred stock to common stock, how many new shares of common stock will Ideal have outstanding?

2-3   Filkins Farm Equipment needs to raise $4.5 million for expansion, and it expects that 5-year zero coupon bonds can be sold at a price of $567.44 for each $1,000 bond.

Zero Coupon Bond

   a. How many $1,000 par value, zero coupon bonds would Filkins have to sell to raise the needed $4.5 million?

   b. What will be the burden of this bond issue on the future cash flows generated by Filkins? What will be the annual debt service costs?

2-4   Suppose you own a call option that permits you to purchase 100 shares of the stock of Silicon Graphics for $15 per share any time in the next 3 months. Silicon Graphics has a current market price of $12 per share.

Gain (Loss) from Stock Options

   a. Should you exercise the option and purchase the stock if its price increases to $18? What would be your gain (loss) if you exercised the option and then immediately sold the stock?

   b. Should you exercise the option and purchase the stock if its price increases to $13? What would be your gain (loss) if you exercised the option and then immediately sold the stock?

   c. Would your answer to part (b) change if the option were a put rather than a call? Remember, a put gives you the right to sell stock at a predetermined price.

2-5   Suppose you own a put option that gives you the right to sell 200 shares of MMM Construction to another investor for $25 per share anytime during the next 6 months. MMM's stock currently sells for $26 per share.

Gain (Loss) Stock Options

   a. Should you exercise the option and sell the stock to the option writer (sells) if the stock price stays at $26 per share?

b. Should you exercise the option if the stock's price increases to $30? What would be your gain (loss) if you bought the stock at $30 and then exercised the option?

c. Should you exercise the option if the stock's price decreases to $20? What would be your gain (loss) if you bought the stock at $20 and then exercised the option?

Balance Sheet Effects of Raising Funds   **2-6**   Two textile companies, Meyer Manufacturing and Haugen Mills, began operations with identical balance sheets. A year later, both required additional manufacturing capacity, which could be attained by purchasing a new machine for $200,000. To raise the needed funds, Meyer issued a 5-year, $200,000 bond with a coupon rate equal to 8 percent. Haugen, on the other hand, decided to sell common stock to raise the $200,000. The stock was sold for $50 per share, and the issue increased the number of outstanding, or existing, shares by 20 percent from the pre-issue level. The balance sheet for each company, before the asset increases, is as follows:

		Debt	$200,000
		Equity	200,000
Total assets	$400,000	Total liabilities and equity	$400,000

a. Show the balance sheet of each firm after the asset is purchased.

b. How many shares of stock did Haugen have outstanding before the equity issue? How many are outstanding after the issue?

c. With the additional manufacturing capacity provided by the machine, the operating earnings (before taxes and interest payments) of each company will increase by $100,000. How much of this amount could be paid to the shareholders of each company? Assume that the tax rate for both companies is 40 percent.

d. How much of the $100,000 operating earnings could be paid as dividends to *each* share of stock for each company (that is, the additional earnings per share)? Assume that both companies had the same number of outstanding shares of stock prior to the purchase of the new machine.

Financing Alternatives   **2-7**   The Cox Computer Company has grown rapidly during the past 5 years. Recently, its commercial bank urged the company to consider increasing its permanent financing. Its bank loan has risen to $150,000 and carries a 10 percent interest rate, and Cox has been 30 to 60 days late in paying its suppliers.

Discussions with an investment banker have resulted in the decision to raise $250,000 at this time. Investment bankers have assured Cox that the following alternatives are feasible (issuing costs will be ignored):

- *Alternative 1.* Sell common stock at $10 per share.
- *Alternative 2.* Sell convertible bonds with a 10 percent coupon, convertible into 80 shares of common stock for each $1,000 bond (that is, the conversion price is $12.50 per share).
- *Alternative 3.* Sell debentures with a 12 percent coupon; each bond will sell at its face value of $1,000 and will have a maturity of 10 years.

Charles Cox, the president, owns 80 percent of Cox's common stock and wishes to maintain control of the company; 50,000 shares are outstanding. The following are summaries of Cox's latest financial statements:

Balance Sheet		Income Statement	
Total assets	$275,000	Sales	$550,000
Short-term debt (bank		All costs except	
loans, etc.)	175,000	interest	(495,000)
Bonds	25,000	EBIT	$ 55,000
Common stock, $1 par	50,000	Interest	(15,000)
Retained earnings	25,000	EBT	$ 40,000
Total liabilities and equity	$275,000	Taxes at 40%	(16,000)
		Net income	$ 24,000
		Shares outstanding	50,000
		Earnings per share	$ 0.48
		Market price of stock	$ 8.64

a. Show the new balance sheet under each alternative. For Alternative 2, show the balance sheet after conversion of the bond into stock. Assume that $150,000 of the funds raised will be used to pay off the bank loan and the rest will be used to increase total assets.

b. Show Charles Cox's control position under each alternative, assuming that he does not purchase additional shares.

c. What is the effect on earnings per share of each alternative if it is assumed that earnings before interest and taxes will be 20 percent of total assets? [*Hint:* Earnings per share = (Net income)/(Shares outstanding).]

d. Which of the three alternatives would you recommend to Charles Cox, and why?

2-8 Atlantic Coast Resources Company had the following balance sheet at the end of 2010:

Book Value Per Share

Atlantic Coast Resources Company: Balance Sheet December 31, 2010

		Accounts payable	$ 64,400
		Notes payable	71,400
		Long-term debt	151,200
		Common stock (30,000 authorized	
		20,000 shares outstanding)	364,000
		Retained earnings	336,000
Total assets	$987,000	Total liabilities and equity	$987,000

Atlantic Coast Resources is concerned about its book value per share, which is computed by dividing the total equity on the balance sheet by the number of outstanding shares of stock.

a. What is the book value per share of Atlantic's common stock?

b. Suppose the firm sold the remaining authorized shares and netted $32.55 per share from the sale. What would be the new book value per share?

2-9 Fibertech Corporation just received an invoice from a Japanese manufacturer. The invoice states that Fibertech must pay the Japanese company 5,500,000 yen (the Japanese currency) in 90 days. If Fibertech pays the bill today, it needs $500,000 because each yen currently costs $0.091 (that is, $1 can purchase 11 yen). Fibertech is considering waiting to pay until the bill is due, because to pay today it would have to borrow the needed funds at a very high interest rate. In 90 days, the firm expects to have collected funds from

Futures Contract

outstanding sales that will be more than sufficient to pay the Japanese manufacturer.

a. Give some reasons why Fibertech might want to pay the bill today rather than wait for 90 days. Give some reasons for not paying the bill until it is due.

b. Suppose Fibertech can obtain a futures contract for delivery of 5,500,000 yen in 90 days, but it will cost $0.095 for each yen at delivery. In U.S. dollars, how much will Fibertech have to pay to settle its bill in 90 days with this contract?

c. Assume that Fibertech chooses not to take the futures contract described in part (b). In U.S. dollars, how much will the company have to pay if the exchange rate in 90 days is $0.10 per yen? If it is $0.085 per yen?

d. What primary benefit would Fibertech derive from entering into the futures contract?

Integrative Problem

Debt/Equity Financing

2-10 Gonzales Food Stores, a family-owned grocery store chain headquartered in El Paso, has hired you to make recommendations concerning financing needs for the following two situations.

Part I: Initial Expansion Gonzales is a closely held corporation considering a major expansion. The proposed expansion would require the firm to raise $10 million in additional capital. Because Gonzales currently has 50 percent debt and because the family members already have all their funds tied up in the business, the owners cannot supply any additional equity, so the company will have to sell stock to the public. The family wants to ensure that it will retain control of the company. This offering would be Gonzales's first stock sale, and the owners are not sure exactly what would be involved. For this reason, they have asked you to research the process and to help them decide how to raise the needed capital. In doing so, you should answer the following questions:

a. What are the advantages to Gonzales of financing with stock rather than with bonds? What are the disadvantages of using stock?

b. Is the stock of Gonzales Food Stores currently publicly held or privately owned? Would this situation change if the company undertook a stock sale?

c. What is classified stock? Would Gonzales find any advantage in designating the stock currently outstanding as founders' shares? What type of common stock should Gonzales sell to the public to allow the family members to retain control of the business?

d. If some members of the Gonzales family wanted to sell some of their own shares to diversify at the same time that the company was selling new shares to raise expansion capital, would this choice be feasible?

Part II: Subsequent Expansions A few years after the initial expansion, Gonzales wants to build a plant and finance an operation that would manufacture and distribute its homemade salsa and related products to supermarkets throughout the United States and Mexico. Mr. Gonzales, CEO and family head, has begun planning this venture, even though construction is not expected to begin until the current expansion is complete and the company is financially stable, which might take several years. Even so, Mr. Gonzales has some ideas that he would like you to examine.

The project's estimated cost is $30 million, which will be used to build a manufacturing facility and to set up the necessary distribution system. Gonzales tentatively plans to raise the $30 million by selling 10-year bonds, and its investment bankers have indicated that the firm can use either regular or zero coupon bonds. Regular coupon bonds would sell at par and would have annual payment coupons of 12 percent; zero coupon bonds would also be priced to yield 12 percent annually. Either bond would be callable after 3 years, on the anniversary date of the issue.

As part of your analysis, you have been asked to answer the following questions:

a. What is the difference between a bond and a term loan? What are the advantages of a term loan over a bond?

b. Suppose Gonzales issues bonds and uses the manufacturing facility (land and buildings) as collateral to secure the issue. What type of bond would this security be? Suppose that instead of using secured bonds, Gonzales decides to sell debentures. How would this choice affect the interest rate that Gonzales would have to pay on the $30 million of debt?

c. What is a bond indenture? What are some typical provisions that the bondholders would require Gonzales to include in its indenture?

d. Gonzales's bonds will be callable after 3 years. If the bonds were not callable, would the required interest rate be higher or lower than 12 percent? What would be the effect on the rate if the bonds were callable immediately? What are the advantages to Gonzales of making the bonds callable?

e. Consider the following:

   (1) Suppose Gonzales's indenture included a sinking fund provision that required the company to retire one-tenth of the bonds each year. Would this provision raise or lower the interest rate required on the bonds?

   (2) How would the sinking fund operate?

   (3) Why might Gonzales's investors require it to use a sinking fund?

   (4) For this particular issue, would it make sense to include a sinking fund?

f. At the time of the bond issue, Gonzales expects to be an A-rated firm. Suppose the firm's bond rating was (1) lowered to BBB or (2) raised to AA. Who would make these changes, and what would they mean? How would these changes affect the interest rate required on Gonzales' new long-term debt and the market value of Gonzales' outstanding debt?

g. What are some factors that a firm such as Gonzales should consider when deciding whether to issue long-term debt, short-term debt, or equity? Why might long-term debt be the company's best choice for this project?

Financial Markets and the Investment Banking Process

A Managerial Perspective

Do you like roller-coaster rides? Consider the ups and downs of the stock market in 2007. The following table gives an indication of the wild ride investors took if they owned stocks similar to those that make up the Dow Jones Industrial Average (DJIA).[1]

The DJIA increased from nearly 12,500 at the beginning of 2007 to a record high of nearly 14,100 at the beginning of October, which translates into a simple annual return equal to 12 percent. As you can see, however, the increase was not steady—there were quite a few periods in which rather significant decreases occurred. Was the stock market a lion or a lamb during 2007? Clearly, many of the movements in the DJIA were extreme, like a lion's roar, but the market could not decide which way to go, much like a lost lamb.

Period	Number of Trading Days	Actual Change in Points	Simple Percent Change[2]	
			Per Period	Annualized
2/27	1	−416.0	−3.3%	−1,202.1%
3/13	1	−242.7	−2.0	−719.0
7/12	1	+283.9	+2.1	+763.1
7/26–7/27	2	−519.6	−3.8	−687.9
8/6–8/8	3	+476.0	+3.6	+439.3
8/9–8/16	6	−812.1	−5.9	−361.7
8/17–8/18	2	+275.6	+2.1	+391.5
9/5–9/7	3	−335.5	−2.5	−303.5
9/18	1	+336.0	+2.5	+914.9
11/7–11/2	4	−673.4	−4.9	−449.8
11/27–11/28	2	+782.0	+4.3	+782.0
12/14−12/17	2	−350.8	−2.6	−473.6

[1]The Dow Jones Industrial Average includes stocks of the 30 largest industrial firms in the United States. Chapter 16 describes the DJIA.

[2]These computations do not consider compounding. For example, if the daily change was 1 percent, the annual rate was computed as $1.0\% \times 365 = 365.0\%$. The effects of compounding and the inclusion of compounding in computations are discussed in Chapter 9. Also, the per period rates were rounded to the nearest 0.1 percent for reporting purposes, but they were not rounded when the computations were performed.

According to the pundits, the primary reasons for the turbulence in the market were the uncertainty of investors about the future of the economy due to the uncertainty about both the war in Iraq and fuel prices, a slump in the housing industry, and the failure of many earnings reports announced by large firms at the time to meet investors' expectations. In addition, economists and investors were uncertain as to how Ben Bernanke, the chairman of the Board of Governors of the Federal Reserve, would guide the monetary policy of the United States.

As the numbers presented here show, the stock market—indeed, any financial market—can send investors (and borrowers) along an exceedingly bumpy path. Consequently, both investors and businesspeople should be informed about why such movements in the financial markets occur. Consider, for example, a business that needs to raise funds for expansion. Should the firm raise the needed funds by issuing either stocks or bonds during periods of significant market fluctuations similar to what was exhibited in the stock market in 2007? This chapter begins the process of answering questions such as this by describing the characteristics of the various financial markets. In addition, it provides an overview of how firms utilize the financial markets to raise funds. As you read this chapter, as well as related chapters later in the book, keep in mind this example of the 2007 market and try to explain why markets experience such drastic changes at times.

CHAPTER PRINCIPLES
–The Questions

After reading this chapter, you should be able to answer the following questions:

- What are financial markets and what role do they play in improving the standard of living in an economy?
- Why is it important for financial markets to be somewhat efficient?
- Why are there so many different types of financial markets? How do we differentiate among various financial markets?
- What is an investment banking house and what role does an investment banking house play when firms want to raise funds in the financial markets?
- How do the financial markets in the United States differ from financial markets in other parts of the world?

Financial markets are extremely important to the economic well-being of the United States.[3] For this reason, it is important that both investors and financial managers understand the environment and markets within which securities are traded and businesses operate. This chapter examines the markets where funds are raised by firms securities are raised, and the prices for stocks and bonds are raised.

WHAT ARE FINANCIAL MARKETS?

Businesses, individuals, and government units often need to raise funds to invest in assets. For example, suppose Florida Power & Light (FP&L) forecasts an increase in the demand for electricity in Florida, and the company decides to build a new power plant. Because FP&L almost certainly will not have the hundreds of millions of dollars necessary to pay for the plant, the company will have to raise these funds in the financial markets. Similarly, if you want to buy a home that costs $150,000, but you have only $20,000 in savings, how can you raise the other $130,000?

---

[3]Throughout much of this chapter and in the next couple of chapters, we primarily refer to corporations as the users, or issuers, of such financial assets as debt and equity. In reality, governments, government agencies, and individuals also issue debt. For example, an individual "issues" a mortgage when he or she finances the purchase of a house. Because corporations issue a variety of debt instruments and can also issue equity, we will identify them as the issuers more often than governments or individuals in the examples.

Whereas some individuals and firms need funds, others have incomes that are greater than their current expenditures. Thus, they have funds available to invest, or save. For example, Alexandra Trottier has an annual income of $50,000, but her expenses (including taxes) are only $40,000. As a result, Alexandra has $10,000 to invest (save) this year.

People and organizations that need money are brought together with those that have surplus funds in the *financial markets*. Note that *markets* is plural—a great many different financial markets exist, each of which includes many institutions and individuals, in a developed economy such as that of the United States. Unlike *physical asset markets*, which deal with products such as wheat, autos, real estate, computers, and machinery, *financial asset markets* deal with stocks, bonds, mortgages, and other *claims on real assets* with respect to the distribution of future cash flows. Individual financial instruments were described in Chapter 2.

In a general sense, the term *financial market* refers to a conceptual "mechanism" rather than a physical location or a specific type of organization or structure. We usually define the **financial markets** as a system that includes individuals and institutions, instruments, and procedures that bring together borrowers and savers, no matter the location. This chapter focuses on the concepts and procedures of financial markets. Chapter 4 describes some of the institutions that participate in borrowing and savings activities that take place in the financial markets.

financial markets
A system consisting of individuals and institutions, instruments, and procedures that bring together borrowers and savers.

Self-Test Questions

What is a financial market?

Why is it important to have a basic understanding of financial markets?

IMPORTANCE OF FINANCIAL MARKETS

The primary role of financial markets is to help bring together *borrowers* and savers *(lenders)* by facilitating the flow of funds from individuals and businesses that have surplus funds to individuals, businesses, and governments that have needs for funds in excess of their incomes.[4] In developed economies, financial markets help efficiently allocate excess funds of savers to individuals and organizations in need of funds for investment or consumption. The more efficient the process of funds flow, the more productive the economy, both in terms of manufacturing and financing.

Flow of Funds

By providing *mechanisms* by which borrowers and lenders get together to transfer funds, the financial markets allow us to consume amounts different than our current incomes. In this way, they provide us with the ability to transfer income through time. When we borrow, for example, we sacrifice future income to increase current income; when we save, or invest, we sacrifice current income in exchange for greater expected income in the future. For example, young adults borrow funds to go to

---

[4]Throughout this chapter, we often refer to the parties involved in financial market transactions as *borrowers* or *lenders*, which implies that only loans are traded in the financial markets. In reality, stocks, options, and many other financial assets also are traded in the financial markets. In our general discussions, we will use the term *borrowers* to refer to parties such as individuals and government units that raise needed funds through various types of loans as well as corporations that use both loans and stock issues to raise needed funds. We will use the term *lenders* to refer to those parties that provide funds, whether the medium is a loan or a stock.

college or to buy such high-priced items as houses or cars, so they tend to save little or nothing. Older adults, when they become established in their careers and reach or are near their peak income years, generally save (invest) greater percentages of their incomes. Finally, when adults retire, they rely on funds accumulated from prior years' savings to provide their retirement income. Consequently, adults go through three general phases that would not be possible without financial markets:

1. Young adults desire to consume more than their incomes, so they must borrow.

2. Older working adults earn more than their consumption needs, so they save.

3. Retired adults use the funds accumulated in earlier years to at least partially replace income lost due to retirement.

Without financial markets, consumption would be restricted to income earned each year plus any amounts put aside (perhaps in a coffee can) in previous years. As a result, our standard of living would be much lower than is now possible.

Funds are transferred from those with surpluses (savers) to those with needs (borrowers) by the three different processes diagrammed in Figure 3-1:

1. A *direct transfer* of money and securities, as shown in the top section, occurs when a business sells its stocks or bonds directly to savers (investors) without going through any type of intermediary or financial institution. The business delivers its securities to savers, who in turn provide the firm the money it needs.

2. As shown in the middle section, a transfer also can go through an *investment banking house,* which serves as a middleman and facilitates the issuance of securities. The company sells its stocks or bonds to the investment bank, which in turn sells these same securities to savers. The business's securities and the savers' money merely "pass through" the investment banking house. For example, the next time IBM raises funds by issuing stock, it probably will utilize the services of an investment banker, such as Goldman Sachs or

FIGURE 3-1   Diagram of the Capital Formation Process

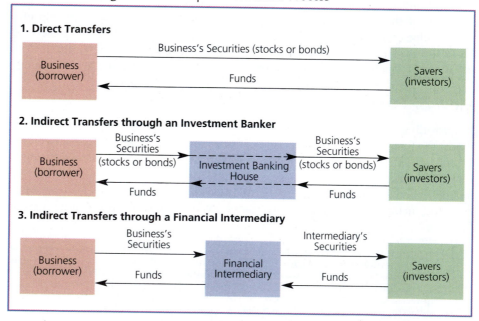

Merrill Lynch, to sell the issue in the financial markets. The investment banking process is described in detail later in this chapter.

3. Transfers can also be made through a *financial intermediary*, such as a bank or a mutual fund. In this case, the intermediary obtains funds from savers and then uses the money to lend out or to purchase other businesses' securities. For example, when you deposit money in a savings account at your local bank, the bank takes those funds along with other depositors' funds and creates such loans as mortgages, business loans, and automobile loans. The existence of intermediaries greatly increases the efficiency of the financial markets. More information concerning the roles and descriptions of financial intermediaries is provided in Chapter 4.

For simplicity, Figure 3-1 assumes that the entity in need of capital is a business, and specifically a corporation. Nevertheless, it is easy to visualize the demander of funds as being a home purchaser or a government unit. Direct transfers of funds from savers to borrowers are possible and do occur on occasion. Generally, however, corporations and government entities use investment bankers to help them raise needed capital in the financial markets, and individual savers use such intermediaries as banks and mutual funds to help them lend their funds or to borrow needed funds.

Market Efficiency

If the financial markets did not provide efficient funds transfers, the economy simply could not function as it now does. Because Florida Power & Light would have difficulty raising needed capital, Miami's citizens would pay more for electricity. Likewise, you would not be able to buy the house you want, and Alexandra Trottier would have no place to invest her savings. Clearly, the level of employment and productivity, and hence our standard of living, would be much lower. Therefore, it is absolutely essential that our financial markets function efficiently—not only quickly, but also at a low cost. When we speak of market efficiency, we generally mean either economic efficiency or informational efficiency.

Economic Efficiency

The financial markets are said to have **economic efficiency** if funds are allocated to their optimal use at the lowest costs. In other words, in economically efficient markets, businesses and individuals invest their funds in assets that yield the highest returns, and the costs of searching for such opportunities are lower than those observed in less efficient markets. Often individuals hire brokers, who charge commissions, to help search for, and then buy or sell, investments in the financial markets. If the commissions and other costs associated with transactions, which are called **transaction costs,** are very high, investments will not be as attractive as when transaction costs are low.

economic efficiency
Funds are allocated to their optimal use at the lowest costs in the financial markets.

transaction costs
Costs associated with buying and selling investments, including commissions, search costs, taxes, and so on.

Informational Efficiency

The prices of investments bought and sold in the financial markets are based on available information. If these prices reflect existing information and adjust quickly when new information becomes available, then the financial markets have achieved **informational efficiency.** When the financial markets have a large number of participants in search of the most profitable investments, informational efficiency generally exists. For instance, in the United States, millions of individual investors

informational efficiency
The prices of investments reflect existing information and adjust quickly when new information enters the markets.

and more than 100,000 highly trained professionals participate in the financial markets. As a consequence, you would expect investment prices to adjust almost instantaneously to new information, because a large number of the market participants will evaluate the new information as soon as possible in an effort to find more profitable investments.

Informational efficiency generally is classified into one of the following three categories:

1. *Weak-form efficiency* states that all information contained in past price movements is fully reflected in current market prices. Therefore, information about recent, or past, trends in investment prices is of no use in selecting "winning" investments; the fact that an investment has risen for the past 3 days, for example, gives us no clues as to what it will do today or tomorrow.

2. *Semistrong-form efficiency* states that current market prices reflect all *publicly available* information. In this case, it does no good to scrutinize such published data as a corporation's financial statements, because market prices will have adjusted to any good news or bad news contained in such reports as soon as they were made public. Insiders (for example, the presidents of companies), even under semistrong-form efficiency, can still make **abnormal returns** on their own companies' investments (stocks). For the purposes of our discussion, abnormal returns are returns that exceed those that are justified by the risks associated with the investments.

3. *Strong-form efficiency* states that current market prices reflect all pertinent information, whether publicly available or privately held. If this form of efficiency holds, even insiders would find it impossible to earn abnormal returns in the financial markets.[5]

The informational efficiency of the financial markets has received a great deal of attention. The results of most of the market efficiency studies suggest that the financial markets are highly efficient in the weak form and reasonably efficient in the semistrong form, but strong-form efficiency does not appear to hold.

Financial markets that are informationally efficient also tend to be economically efficient. This situation arises because investors can expect prices to reflect appropriate information and thus make intelligent choices about which investments will likely provide the best returns.

abnormal returns
Returns that exceed those that are justified by the risks associated with the investments.

Self-Test Questions

What are the three methods by which funds are transferred from savers (lenders) to borrowers?

Why do you think that most transfers of money and securities are indirect rather than direct?

What does it mean to have economically efficient financial markets? What does it mean to have informationally efficient markets?

What are the three forms (degrees) of informational efficiency?

---

[5]Several cases of illegal insider trading have made the news headlines in the past. In a famous case, Ivan Boesky admitted to making $50 million by purchasing the stocks of firms that he knew were preparing to merge. Boesky went to jail and had to pay a large fine, but he helped disprove strong-form efficiency. More recently, Martha Stewart served time in jail because she was convicted of obstructing justice by lying to federal investigators about whether inside information was used to time the sale of stock she owned (ImClone Systems Inc.).

TYPES OF FINANCIAL MARKETS

A number of different financial markets, with a variety of investments and participants, exist today. We generally differentiate among financial markets based on the types of investments, maturities of investments, types of borrowers and lenders, locations of the markets, and types of transactions. There are too many different types of financial markets to discuss here. Instead, we describe only the more common classifications and provide some indication of the function of each type of market.

Money Markets versus Capital Markets

Some borrowers need funds for short periods; others need funds for extended periods. For example, a company that finances its inventories generally uses loans with maturities ranging from 30 to 90 *days*, whereas an individual who purchases a house uses a loan with a maturity from 15 to 30 *years*. Similarly, some investors prefer to invest for short periods, but others invest for longer periods. For example, a college student who has funds that she does not need for another 6 months, perhaps to pay tuition, might invest the extra funds in a 6-month certificate of deposit (CD). On the other hand, a couple who invests for the college education of their 3-year-old child might choose to invest in longer term investments, such as 15-year corporate bonds.

The markets for short-term financial instruments are termed the *money markets,* and the markets for long-term financial instruments are dubbed the *capital markets*. More specifically, the **money markets** include instruments that have maturities equal to 1 year or less when originally issued, and the **capital markets** include instruments with original maturities greater than 1 year. By definition, then, money markets include only debt instruments, because equity instruments (that is, stocks) have no specific maturities, whereas capital markets include both equity instruments and such long-term debt instruments as mortgages, corporate bonds, and government bonds.[6]

The primary function of the money markets is to provide liquidity to businesses, governments, and individuals so that they can meet their short-term needs for cash, because, in most cases, the receipt of cash inflows does not coincide exactly with the payment of cash outflows. The existence of money market instruments with different maturities permits us to better match our cash inflows with cash outflows.

For example, the college student who has funds that are not needed for tuition payments until 6 months from now can invest the funds and earn a positive return rather than allowing the funds to sit in a checking account that earns little or no interest. If she invests in a 6-month CD, the college student will effectively match the timing of her cash inflow (maturity of the CD) with her cash needs (payment of tuition).

On the other hand, consider a corporation that needs to pay for the purchase of inventory, but cash from sales of the inventories will not be received for another 30 days. The company has the opportunity to raise the needed funds through a 30-day loan, so it can match the timing of the cash outflow (payment for inventory) with the timing of the cash inflow (collection for inventory sales).

Individuals, companies, and governments use the money markets similarly—to better align short-term cash flows. Thus, when cash surpluses exist for short periods,

money markets
The segments of the financial markets where the instruments that are traded have original maturities equal to 1 year or less.

capital markets
The segments of the financial markets where the instruments that are traded have original maturities greater than 1 year.

---

[6]The characteristics of various financial instruments, called financial assets, are discussed in Chapter 2.

short-term investments are desirable; when cash deficits exist for short periods, short-term loans (debt instruments) are desirable.

The primary function of the capital markets is to provide us with the opportunity to transfer cash surpluses or deficits to future years—that is, transfer income through time. For example, without the availability of mortgages, most individuals could not afford to buy houses when they are young and just starting their careers because they have little or no savings and their incomes are not sufficient to pay for such houses. Based on our abilities to generate sufficient funds from future years' incomes to repay the debts, mortgages and other long-term loans permit us to borrow funds we do not have today. Thus, we can spend more than our incomes today because we expect to provide greater incomes in the future. Similarly, corporations issue stocks and bonds to get funds to support such current investment needs as expansion, and investors who provide the funds receive promises that cash flows generated by these firms will be distributed at some point in the future. In essence, individuals, corporations, and governments use the capital markets to spend more than the funds generated in the current period in exchange for their ability to spend funds generated in future periods or to invest current income to enable greater consumption in the future.

Debt Markets versus Equity Markets

debt markets
Financial markets where loans are traded.

equity markets
Financial markets where corporate stocks are traded.

Simply stated, the **debt markets** are where loans are traded, and the **equity markets** are where stocks of corporations are traded. A debt instrument is a contract that specifies the amounts, as well as the times, a borrower must repay a lender. In contrast, equity represents "ownership" in a corporation; it entitles the stockholder to share in cash distributions generated from income and from liquidation of the firm.

The debt markets permit individuals, companies, and governments with investment opportunities to consume future income in the current period through loans such as mortgages, corporate bonds, and Treasury bonds. Each of these loans requires repayment, with interest, from income (cash flows) generated during the loan period. Conversely, the equity markets permit corporations to raise funds by selling ownership interests, thereby transferring some risks associated with businesses to individuals and other companies. Purchasers of equity receive the right to distributions of cash flows made by the firm from income generated in the future. Unlike debt, however, equity is not a specific contract guaranteeing that cash distributions will be made or that the investment will be repaid. Because debt typically has a maturity, it can be considered temporary funding; equity is more permanent because it has no specific maturity.

Equity markets, which also are called stock markets, are familiar to most people. In fact, a majority of Americans invest in stocks, either directly or through mutual funds. In addition, more than 10,000 institutions, such as pension funds and insurance companies, invest in the equity markets. Clearly, stock markets are important in the United States. For that reason, we discuss the characteristics of stock markets in more detail in the next section.

Debt markets generally are described according to the characteristics of the debt that is traded. Many different types of debt exist, and thus many different types of debt markets exist. For example, short-term debt instruments, such as those issued by the U.S. Treasury, are traded in the *money markets*. Long-term debt instruments, such as corporate bonds and mortgages, are traded in the *capital markets*. In addition, the debt markets are clearly divided by the type of participant—issuer (borrower) or investor (lender). The portion of the debt markets

TABLE 3-1   Debt Markets in the United States, 2008

Type of Debt	Amount ($ billion)	Percentage of Total
Mortgages	$14,733.30	29.70%
Corporate bonds	10,803.20	21.77
Federal agencies	7,558.20	15.23
Treasury issues	5,299.10	10.68
Consumer loans	2,542.90	5.13
Municipals	2,656.90	5.36
Money market	1,748.60	3.52
Bank loans	2,107.90	4.25
Other loans	2,164.30	4.36
Total Debt	$49,614.40	

Source: *Statistics: Releases and Historical Data,* Federal Reserve Board, http://federalreserve.gov/releases/

where government bonds are traded differs from the corporate bonds market, and the market for consumer debt differs from both of these segments. Thus, the segmentation of the debt markets is based on the maturity of the instrument, the issuer, and the investor.

The largest segment of the debt markets is represented by the bond markets, where government, corporate, and foreign bonds are traded. Table 3-1 shows the values of the various debt markets in the United States in 2008. At that time, the value of the debt markets in the United States amounted to nearly $50 trillion. As you can see, mortgages, corporate bonds, and Treasury issues accounted for greater than 75 percent of the total debt market. Corporate debt is held principally by corporations and such financial institutions as mutual funds and insurance companies.

Primary Markets versus Secondary Markets

The primary markets are where "new" securities are traded, and the secondary markets are where "used" securities are traded.

Primary markets are the markets in which corporations raise new capital. If IBM were to sell a new issue of common stock to raise capital, this activity would be a primary market transaction. The corporation selling the newly created stock receives the proceeds from the sale in a primary market transaction.

Secondary markets are markets in which existing, previously issued securities are traded among investors. Thus, if Jessica Rogers decided to buy 1,000 shares of existing IBM stock, the purchase would occur in the secondary market. The New York Stock Exchange is a secondary market, because it deals in outstanding, or previously issued, stocks and bonds as opposed to newly issued stocks and bonds. Secondary markets also exist for mortgages, other types of loans, and other financial assets. The corporation whose securities are traded in the secondary market is not involved in the transaction and, therefore, does not receive any funds from such a sale (trade).

Derivatives Markets

Options, futures, and swaps are some of the securities traded in the **derivatives markets.** These securities are called derivatives because their values are determined,

primary markets
Markets in which various organizations raise funds by issuing new securities.

secondary markets
Markets where financial assets that have previously been issued by various organizations are traded among investors.

derivatives markets
Financial markets where options, futures, and similar financial instruments are traded.

or "derived," directly from other assets. For example, if an individual owns a call option written on IBM stock, he or she has the ability to purchase shares of IBM at a price specified in the option contract. Because the contract fixes the purchase price of the IBM common stock, the value of the call option changes as the actual *market value* of IBM shares changes.

Although many investors use derivatives to speculate about the movements of prices in the financial markets and the markets for such commodities as wheat and soy beans, these instruments are typically employed to help manage risk. That is, individuals, corporations, and governments use derivatives to *hedge* risk by offsetting exposures to uncertain price changes in the future.

Self-Test Questions

How are the financial markets differentiated?

What are the differences between (1) the money markets and the capital markets, (2) the primary markets and the secondary markets, and (3) the debt markets and the equity markets?

How are the debt markets differentiated?

What types of assets are traded in the derivatives markets?

STOCK MARKETS

In recent years, individuals have expressed greater interest in stocks than ever before. A major reason for this increased interest is the fact that the stock markets generated record-breaking returns during the 1990s. From 1995 to 1999, the annual returns in the stock markets averaged more than 20 percent—an unprecedented level. Much of the record upward movement in the markets was spurred by enthusiastic buying by individual investors who felt they had to join their neighbors in trying to "get rich" by trading stocks. Although the markets slowed and even turned around during the 2000–2008 period, the popularity and intrigue of the stock markets is still evident. This section describes the characteristics of stock markets.

Types of General Stock Market Activities

We can classify general stock market activities into three distinct categories:

1. *Trading in the outstanding, previously issued shares of established, publicly owned companies: the secondary market.* If the owner of 100 shares of IBM sells his or her stock, the trade is said to have occurred in the *secondary market*. The company receives no new money when sales occur in this market.

2. *Additional shares sold by established, publicly owned companies: the primary market.* If IBM decides to sell (or issue) additional shares to raise funds for expansion, this transaction is said to occur in the *primary market*. The company receives the funds that are raised when its securities are sold (issued) in the primary market.

3. *New public offerings by privately held firms: the initial public offering (IPO) market; the primary market.* When Google decided to sell some stock to raise capital needed to grow and expand into new products, it took its stock public.

Whenever stock in a privately held corporation is offered to the public for the first time, the company is said to be **going public.** The market for stock that has recently gone public is called the **initial public offering (IPO) market.**

Nearly all stock transactions occur in the secondary markets. Nevertheless, primary market transactions are important to corporations that need to raise funds for capital projects. In this section, we examine the general characteristics of stock markets, which function principally as secondary markets; the next section considers how stocks and bonds are issued in the primary markets.

Traditionally, we have categorized stock markets in the United States into one of two basic types: (1) *physical stock exchanges,* which include the New York Stock Exchange (NYSE), the American Stock Exchange (AMEX), and several regional exchanges, and (2) the less formal *over-the-counter (OTC) market,* which consists of a network of dealers around the country and includes the well-known NASDAQ market. As a result of heated competition, stock markets have changed significantly in recent years through mergers and by introducing new, more efficient trading systems. As a result, it is now difficult to differentiate between the two categories of stock markets. Even so, we generally still refer to stock markets as having the general characteristics of either a physical stock exchange or the OTC/NASDAQ market.

Physical Stock Exchanges[7]

The **physical security exchanges** are tangible physical entities. The physical exchanges in the United States include national exchanges, such as the NYSE and the AMEX, and regional exchanges, such as the Philadelphia Stock Exchange (PHLX) and the Chicago Stock Exchange (CHX).[8] The prices of stocks listed on the physical stock exchanges are determined by auction processes where investors (through their broker) bid for stocks.

Until the late 1990s, most stock exchanges were not-for-profit organizations that were owned by their members who were said to hold "seats" on the exchange (although everyone stood up). These seats, which were bought and sold, gave the holder the right to trade on the exchange.[9] Organizations such as these that are owned and operated by their members are said to have *mutual ownership* structures.

The current trend of stock exchanges is to convert from not-for-profit mutual ownership organizations to for-profit organizations that are owned by stockholders and are publicly traded. The process of converting an exchange from a mutual ownership organization to a stock ownership organization is called **demutualization.** The first U.S. stock exchange to "demutualize" was the Pacific Exchange (PCX) in 2000. Not long after its conversion, PCX and Archipelago Holdings, Inc. (Arca), which is an Electronic Communications Network (ECN), merged to form ArcaEX. ArcaEx was the first totally electronic stock market in the United States.

going public
The act of selling stock to the general public for the first time by a corporation or its principal stockholders.

initial public offering (IPO) market
The market consisting of stocks of companies that have just gone public.

physical security exchanges
Formal organizations with physical locations that facilitate trading in designated ("listed") securities. The two major U.S. stock exchanges are the New York Stock Exchange (NYSE) and the American Stock Exchange (AMEX).

demutualization
Conversion from mutual ownership to stock ownership.

---

[7]The statistics and other information that are provided in this section are based on information that is reported by the various stock exchanges. Additional statistics and information can be found on the Web sites of the exchanges: http://www.nyse.com, http://amex.com and http://www.chx.com.

[8]The NYSE, which is more than 200 years old, is the largest physical stock exchange in the world in terms of the total value of stocks traded. The PHLX, which was established in 1790, is the oldest physical exchange in the United States; the New York Stock Exchange was started a couple of years later in 1792.

[9]NYSE stocks were not traded continuously until 1871. Prior to that time, stocks were traded sequentially according to their position on a stock roll, or roster, sheet. Members were assigned chairs, or "seats," in which to sit while the roll call of stocks proceeded. The number of "seats" changed as the number of members changed, until the number was fixed at 1,366 in 1868.

In March 2006, the largest merger of stock exchanges took place when the NYSE joined with ArcaEx to form the NYSE Group. When the merger took place, the ownership structure of the NYSE was "demutualized." The previous owners of the NYSE—that is, the "seat" holders—were given stock ownership in the new organization, and *trading licenses* were auctioned off to those companies that wished to have either electronic or physical access to the exchange's facilities and trading services. This marked the end of the NYSE traditional seat membership (ownership) that had existed for more than 210 years.[10] Now, trading licenses are awarded to successful bidders through the SEATS (Stock Exchange Auction Trading System) auction.

At about the same time, the NYSE merged with ArcaEx and became a for-profit organization, the Chicago Stock Exchange "demutualized," and the board of directors of the American Stock Exchange approved "demutualization." Many foreign stock exchanges have also "demutualized" since the late 1990s, including the Australian Stock Exchange, Hong Kong Stock Exchange, Stock Exchange of Singapore, and Toronto Stock Exchange, to name a few. It is estimated that at least 80 percent of the world's developed stock exchanges will be "demutualized" within the next few years. Clearly, the ownership structure of the stock exchanges has changed dramatically in recent years. To trade on an exchange, however, membership similar to a "seat" is still required.

Exchange Members

Exchange members are charged with different trading responsibilities, depending on the type of license (trading permit) they own. For example, trading licenses on the NYSE are classified into one of two categories: floor brokers and specialists. The responsibilities of each NYSE member are given here:

1. *Floor brokers* act as agents for investors who want to buy or sell securities. *House brokers* are floor brokers who are employed by brokerage firms, such as Merrill Lynch and Smith Barney, to execute orders for the firms' clients. *Independent brokers* are freelance brokers who work for themselves or for firms that provide trading services to house brokers rather than for a brokerage firm. Independent brokers "farm out" their services to brokerage firms that need additional help because trading activity is too high for their house brokers to handle.

2. *Specialists* are considered the most important participants in NYSE transactions because their role is to bring buyers and sellers together. Each specialist oversees a particular group of stocks. Specialists are charged with ensuring that the auction process is completed in a fair and efficient manner. To accomplish his or her job, a specialist might have to buy stock when not enough buyers exist or to sell stock when not enough sellers exist; he or she must be ready to *make a market* when either buyers or sellers are needed. To accomplish this task, a specialist must maintain inventories in the stocks he or she is assigned. The specialist posts a *bid price* (the price he or she will pay for the stock) and an *asked price* (the price at which shares will be sold out of inventory) in an effort to keep the inventory in balance. Bid prices are somewhat lower than asked prices, with the difference, or *spread,* representing the specialist's profit

---

[10]The number of seats, or memberships, that were available on each exchange varied—the number of seats on the NYSE was fixed at 1,366, the AMEX had about 850, and the CHX had about 450 members. The cost of exchange membership also has varied considerably. For example, in 2005 a seat on the CHX cost about $19,000, whereas a seat on the NYSE sold for a record $4 million in December 2005.

TABLE 3-2   Initial Listing Requirements for Stock Exchanges and the NASDAQ

	NYSE	AMEX and Regional Exchanges[a]	NASDAQ
Round-lot (100 shares) shareholders	400	400	300
Number of public shares (million)	1.1	0.5	1.0
Market value of public shares ($ million)	$100	$3	$15
Pretax income ($ million)	$2.00	$0.75	$1.00

[a] These numbers are indicative of the listing requirements for larger regional stock exchanges, including the Chicago Stock Exchange, the Pacific Exchange, and the Philadelphia Stock Exchange. The listing requirements for smaller regional exchanges generally are not as restrictive.

margin.[11] If many buy orders start coming in because of favorable developments or if many sell orders come in because of unfavorable events, the specialist will raise or lower prices to keep supply and demand in balance. On the NYSE, supply/demand imbalances require specialists to participate in buying or selling shares only about 10 percent of the time.

Listing Requirements

For a stock to be traded on an exchange, it must be *listed*. Each exchange has established **listing requirements,** which indicate the quantitative and qualitative characteristics that a firm must possess to be listed. Table 3-2 provides examples of the listing requirements for some U.S. exchanges. The primary purpose of these requirements is to ensure that investors have some interest in the company so that the firm's stock will be actively traded on the exchange.

Approximately 2,700 companies in the United States and worldwide have shares listed for trade on the NYSE, about 1,200 firms are listed on the AMEX, more than 150 firms are listed on the Chicago Stock Exchange, and the Philadelphia Stock Exchange and Pacific Exchange each have more than 2,400 listed companies. The NASDAQ (which stands for the National Association of Security Dealers Automated Quotation) has the greatest number of *listed* companies—more than 3,300 firms. The NASDAQ evolved from the OTC market, as described in the next section.

A listed firm pays a relatively small annual fee to the exchange to receive such benefits as the marketability offered by continuous trading activity and the publicity and prestige associated with being an exchange-listed firm. Many people believe that listing has a beneficial effect on the sales of the firm's products, and it probably is advantageous in terms of lowering the return demanded by investors to buy its common stock. Investors respond favorably to a listed firm's increased information and liquidity, and they have confidence that its quoted price is not being manipulated. It is not required that a qualified firm be listed on an exchange—listing is the choice of the firm.

listing requirements
Characteristics a firm must possess to be listed on an exchange.

[11] Special facilities are available to help institutional investors such as mutual funds or pension funds sell large blocks of stock without depressing their prices. In essence, brokerage houses that cater to institutional clients purchase blocks of stocks (defined as 10,000 or more shares) and then resell the stocks to other institutions or individuals. Also, when a firm is preparing to make a major announcement that will likely cause its stock price to fluctuate sharply, it will ask the exchanges to halt trading in its stock until the announcement has been made and digested by investors. For example, when Texaco announced that it planned to acquire Getty Oil, trading in both Texaco and Getty stocks was halted for one day.

The Over-the-Counter (OTC) Market and the NASDAQ

over-the-counter market
A collection of brokers and dealers, connected electronically by telephones and computers, that provides for trading in securities not listed on the physical exchanges.

If a security is not traded on an organized (physical) exchange, it has been customary to say that it is traded in the **over-the-counter market,** which is an intangible trading system that consists of a network of brokers and dealers around the country. An explanation of the term *over-the-counter* helps clarify how the market got its name.

The exchanges operate as auction markets: Buy and sell orders come in more or less simultaneously, and exchange members match these orders. If a stock is traded less frequently, perhaps because it is the stock of a new or a small firm, few buy and sell orders come in, and matching them within a reasonable length of time could be difficult. To avoid this problem, some brokerage firms maintain inventories of such stocks; they buy when individual investors want to sell and sell when investors want to buy. At one time, the inventory of securities was kept in a safe, and the stocks, when bought and sold, literally were passed *over the counter*.

Traditionally, the OTC market has been defined as including all facilities needed to conduct security transactions not conducted on the physical exchanges. These facilities consist of: (1) the *dealers* who hold inventories of OTC securities and who are said to "make a market" in these securities, (2) the *brokers* who act as *agents* in bringing dealers together with investors, and (3) the *electronic networks* that provide a communications link between dealers and brokers. Unlike physical exchanges, the OTC market does not operate as an auction market. The dealers who make a market in a particular stock continuously quote a price at which they are willing to buy the stock (the *bid price*) and a price at which they will sell shares (the *asked price*). Each dealer's prices, which are adjusted as supply and demand conditions change, can be read off computer screens across the country. The spread between the bid and asked price (the *dealer's spread*) represents the dealer's markup, or profit.

Brokers and dealers who participate in the OTC market are members of a self-regulating body known as the *National Association of Security Dealers* (NASD), which licenses brokers and oversees trading practices. The computerized trading network used by NASD is known as the NASD Automated Quotation system, or NASDAQ, and *The Wall Street Journal* and other newspapers provide information on NASDAQ transactions. Today, the NASDAQ is considered a sophisticated market of its own, separate from the OTC market. In fact, unlike the general OTC market, the NASDAQ includes *market makers* who continuously monitor trading activities in various stocks to ensure that such stocks are available to traders who want to buy or sell. The role of the NASDAQ market maker is similar to that of the specialist on the NYSE. Also, companies must meet minimum financial requirements to be *listed,* or included, on the NASDAQ (see Table 3-2); the OTC market has no such requirements.

Electronic Communications Network (ECN)
Electronic systems that transfer information about securities transactions to facilitate the execution of orders by automatically matching buy and sell orders for a large number of investors.

As information technology has evolved, so have the choices to investors as to how to trade securities. Today, most stocks and bonds can be traded electronically using trading systems known as **Electronic Communications Networks (ECN).** ECNs, which are registered with the Securities and Exchange Commission (SEC), are electronic systems that transfer information about securities transactions to facilitate the execution of the orders. ECNs automatically match the buy and sell orders by price for a large number of investors. Investors use ECNs through accounts they have at brokerage firms, such as Charles Schwab, that offer online trading services and subscribe to ECNs. When an order (buy or sell) is placed electronically, the process is seamless in the sense that investors have no indication that an ECN is used to execute their transactions. In essence, ECNs allow investors to submit orders in an "electronic-exchange" market. Generally, the biggest users of ECNs are such institutional investors as mutual funds, pension funds, and so forth. ECNs provide an alternative trading medium, which has increased the competition with the stock exchanges. In fact, as a result of the increased competition and to improve its competitive position, the NYSE merged with the Archipelago Exchange (ArcaEx), an ECN started in 1997, to form the NYSE Group.

According to a study published by the SEC, nearly all the transactions executed by ECNs in 1999 involved NASDAQ stocks (93 percent). The study also reported that few of these transactions (4 percent) occurred "after hours"—that is, after the physical stock exchanges had closed.[12] Today, approximately 50 percent of the total dollar volume of trades in NASDAQ stocks is executed using ECNs, whereas ECNs account for 5 percent of the dollar transactions of securities listed on the physical stock exchanges. As after-hour trading increases in the future, so will the use of ECNs.

In terms of *numbers of issues,* most stocks are traded over-the-counter. Even though the OTC market includes some very large companies, most of the stocks traded over-the-counter involve small companies that do not meet the requirements to be listed on a physical exchange. On the other hand, because the stocks of larger companies generally are listed on the exchanges, approximately two-thirds of the total *dollar volume of stock trading* takes place on the exchanges. In fact, the NYSE generates greater than 50 percent of the daily dollar trading with its listing of nearly 2,700 stocks.

Competition among Stock Markets

Competition among the major stock markets has become increasingly fierce in recent years. In the United States, the major stock markets, especially NYSE and NASDAQ, continuously explore ways to improve their competitive positions. Two factors have changed the competitive arena of the stock markets. First, whereas many years ago stocks could be traded only on the exchanges where they were listed, today many stocks are *dual listed*. A stock with a **dual listing** is eligible (registered) to be traded on more than one stock market (exchange). Dual listing increases liquidity because a stock has more exposure through a greater number of outlets than if it was listed on only one exchange. Various stock markets compete to list stocks that are very actively traded because increased trading activity translates into increased profits.

Second, in 2005, the Securities and Exchange Commission voted to adopt Regulation NMS (National Market Structure), which mandates that the "trade-through rule" be used when securities are traded. The trade-through rule states that a stock trade should be executed at the best price available in all of the stock markets. In other words, a trade order continues to "pass through" markets until the best price is reached; the order cannot be "traded through" to another market once the best trading price is found. The objective of the **trade-through rule** is to provide investors equal access to various stock markets so that they can trade at the best prices. Clearly, this rule requires all of the stock markets—that is, NYSE, NASDAQ, and regional markets—and ECNs to be "connected" electronically. Those markets that have electronic advantages, such as processing speed and cost efficiencies, will be most successful in this extremely competitive environment. Based on the recent changes that have been made by the NYSE and NASDAQ, it seems that Regulation NMS is producing the desired result—that is, increased competition among the stock markets, which ultimately benefits investors in the form of better prices and lower trading costs.

dual listing
When stocks are listed for trading in more than one stock market.

trade-through rule
Provides investors equal access to various stock markets so that they can trade at the best prices.

---

[12]Securities and Exchange Commission, "Special Study: Electronic Communication Networks and After-Hours Trading," June 2000. This study is available at the SEC Web site, which is located at http://www.sec.gov/.

As a result of the increased competition among the stock markets, both the NYSE and NASDAQ have taken actions to improve their competitive positions. For example, we mentioned earlier that in 2006 the NYSE merged with ArcaEx to form the NYSE Group. The "new and improved" NYSE Group effectively consists of two distinct stock (securities) exchanges. The physical stock exchange called the NYSE still exists, and the products and services it offers continue to improve but are similar to what was offered prior to the merger. In addition, the NYSE Group offers a fully electronic exchange through NYSE Arca, which was previously the ArcaEx that evolved from the Archipelago ECN. The NYSE Group was formed to improve the competitive position of the NYSE. For the same reason, later in the same year, the NYSE Group made a bid to merge with Euronext, which operates the stock markets in Paris, Amsterdam, Brussels, and Lisbon. In April 2007, the NYSE Group merged with Euronext to form NYSE Euronext. The union brought together the largest stock market in the world, the NYSE, with key financial markets in Europe to form a truly global marketplace. It is certain that the NYSE will continue such actions in an effort to improve its competitive position in financial markets around the world.

In an effort to become more competitive with other stock markets, especially the NYSE, the NASDAQ, the AMEX, and the Philadelphia Stock Exchange merged in 1998 to form the NASDAQ Amex Market Group. However, the merger did not produce the desired results, so AMEX members bought the exchange back from NASD in 2005. Even so, NASDAQ continues to explore ways to improve its competitive position. Soon after the announcement of the NYSE-ArcaEX merger agreement in 2005, NASDAQ acquired Instinet to improve its ability to compete with the NYSE as an electronic stock exchange. Instinet provided an "electronic exchange" that improved the technology and efficiency of NASDAQ trading. In 2006, NASDAQ tried to acquire the London Stock Exchange (LSE). Even though the takeover attempt was originally rejected, NASDAQ unsuccessfully continued its quest to take over the LSE. In September 2007, NASDAQ liquidated the remaining LSE stock that it held, severing all ties with the LSE. Even so, it is clear that NASDAQ will continue to seek ways to compete better with the NYSE Group. In fact, in 2007, nearly 16 percent of the volume of trades for NYSE-listed companies took place through the NASDAQ market.

Increased competition among global stock markets assuredly will result in similar alliances among various exchanges/markets in the future. Clearly, the playing field on which the exchanges compete will be much different in the future than it has been in the past. Many believe that the playing field is becoming more level for all players.

Self-Test Questions

What are the two basic types of stock markets, and how do they differ?

Are the greatest number of stocks traded over-the-counter or on the physical stock exchanges?

Why do stock exchanges have listing requirements?

What are the types of membership available on the NYSE?

How do stocks traded on the NASDAQ differ from other stocks traded over-the-counter?

THE INVESTMENT BANKING PROCESS

When a business needs to raise funds in the financial markets, it generally enlists the services of an **investment banker** (see panel 2 in Figure 3-1). Merrill Lynch, Morgan Stanley, and Goldman Sachs are all examples of companies that offer investment banking services. Such organizations perform three types of tasks: (1) they help corporations design securities with the features that are most attractive to investors given existing market conditions; (2) they buy these securities from the corporations; and (3) they resell the securities to investors (savers). Although the securities are sold twice, this process is actually one primary market transaction, with the investment banker acting as a middleman (agent) as funds are transferred from savers to businesses.

Investment banking has nothing to do with the traditional banking process as we know it; it deals with the issuance of new securities, not deposits and loans. The major investment banking houses often are divisions of large financial service corporations that engage in a wide range of activities. For example, Merrill Lynch has a brokerage department that operates thousands of offices worldwide as well as an investment banking department that helps companies issue securities, take over other companies, and the like. The firm's brokers sell previously issued stocks as well as stocks that are issued through their investment banking departments. Thus, financial service organizations such as Merrill Lynch sell securities in both the secondary markets and the primary markets.

This section describes how securities are issued in the financial markets and explains the role of investment bankers in this process.

investment banker
An organization that underwrites and distributes new issues of securities; it helps businesses and other entities obtain needed financing.

Raising Capital: Stage I Decisions

The corporation that needs to raise funds makes some preliminary decisions on its own, including the following:[13]

1. *Dollars to be raised.* How much new capital is needed?

2. *Type of securities used.* Should stock, bonds, or a combination of the two be used? Furthermore, if stock is to be issued, should it be offered to existing stockholders or sold to the general public?

3. *Competitive bid versus negotiated deal.* Should the company simply offer a block of its securities for sale to the investment banker that submits the highest bid of all interested investment bankers or should it sit down and negotiate a deal with a single investment banker? These two procedures are called *competitive bids* and *negotiated deals,* respectively. Only a handful of the largest firms on the NYSE, whose securities are already well known to the investment banking community, are in a position to use the competitive bid process. The investment banks would have to do a large amount of investigative work to bid on an issue unless they were already quite familiar with the firm, and the costs involved would be too high to make it worthwhile unless the investment bank was sure of getting the deal. For these reasons, the vast majority of offerings of stocks or bonds are made on a negotiated basis.[14]

4. *Selection of an investment banker.* If the issue is to be negotiated, which investment banker should the firm use? An older firm that has "been to

---

[13]For the most part, the procedures described in this section also apply to government entities. Governments issue only debt, however; they do not issue stock.

[14]On the other hand, by law, most government entities are required to solicit competitive bids for bond issues.

market" before will already have established a relationship with an investment banker, although it is easy enough to change its investment banker if the firm is dissatisfied. A firm that is just going public will have to choose an investment bank, and different investment banking houses are better suited for different companies. The older, larger "establishment houses," such as Morgan Stanley, deal mainly with large companies such as GM, IBM, and ExxonMobil. Other investment bankers specialize in more speculative issues such as initial public offerings. The three largest investment banking companies—Citigroup, Morgan Stanley, and J. P. Morgan Chase—handle approximately 25 percent of the total amount of debt and equity issued.

Raising Capital: Stage II Decisions

Stage II decisions, which are made jointly by the firm and its selected investment banker, include the following:

1. *Reevaluating the initial decisions.* The firm and its investment banker will reevaluate the initial decisions about the size of the issue and the type of securities to use. For example, the firm initially might have decided to raise $100 million by selling common stock, but the investment banker might convince the company's management that it would be better, in view of existing market conditions, to limit the stock issue to $50 million and then raise the other $50 million as debt.

2. *Best efforts or underwritten issues.* The firm and its investment banker must decide whether the investment banker will underwrite the issue or work on a best efforts basis. In an **underwritten arrangement,** the investment banker generally assures the company that the entire issue will be sold, so the investment banker bears significant risks in such an offering. With this type of arrangement, the investment banking firm typically buys the securities from the issuing firm and then sells the securities in the primary markets, hoping to make a profit. In a **best efforts arrangement,** the investment banker does not guarantee that the securities will be sold or that the company will get the cash it needs. With this type of arrangement, the investment banker does not buy the securities from the issuing firm; rather the securities are handled on a contingency basis, and the investment banker receives a commission based on the amount of the issue that is sold. The investment banker essentially promises to exert its best efforts when selling the securities. With a best efforts arrangement, the issuing firm takes the chance the entire issue will not be sold and that all needed funds will not be raised.

3. *Issuance (flotation) costs.* The investment banker's fee must be negotiated, and the firm must estimate the other expenses it will incur in connection with the issue—that is, lawyers' fees, accountants' costs, printing and engraving, and so forth. The investment banker will buy the issue from the company at a discount below the price at which the securities are to be offered to the public. This **underwriter's spread** covers the investment banker's costs and provides for a profit.

Table 3-3 gives an indication of the **flotation costs** associated with public issues of bonds and common stock. As the table shows, costs as a percentage of the proceeds are higher for stocks than for bonds, and they are also higher for small issues than for large issues. The relationship between the size of issue and the flotation costs primarily reflects the existence of fixed costs: certain costs must be incurred regardless of the size of the issue, so the flotation cost percentage is quite high for small issues.

underwritten arrangement
Agreement for the sale of securities in which the investment bank guarantees the sale by purchasing the securities from the issuer, thus agreeing to bear any risks involved in the transaction.

best efforts arrangement
Agreement for the sale of securities in which the investment bank handling the transaction gives no guarantee that the securities will be sold.

underwriter's spread
The difference between the price at which the investment banking firm buys an issue from a company and the price at which the securities are sold in the primary market—it represents the investment banker's gross profit on the issue.

flotation costs
The costs associated with issuing new stocks or bonds.

| TABLE 3-3 | Flotation (Issuance) Costs for Issuing Debt and Equity[a] | | | |

| Issue Size ($ million) | Bonds[b] | | Equity[c] | |
	Straight	Convertible	Seasoned Issues	IPOs
Under 10.0	4.4%	8.8%	13.3%	17.0%
10.0 – 19.9	2.8	8.7	8.7	11.6
20.0 – 39.9	2.4	6.1	6.9	9.7
40.0 – 59.9	1.3	4.3	5.9	8.7
60.0 – 79.9	2.3	3.2	5.2	8.2
80.0 – 99.9	2.2	3.0	4.7	7.9
100.0 – 199.9	2.3	2.8	4.2	7.1
200.0 – 499.9	2.2	2.2	3.5	6.5
500.0 and larger	1.6	2.1	3.2	5.7

[a] The results provided in this table represent the direct costs as a percentage of the size of the issue. Direct costs include underwriting fees, registration fees, legal costs, auditing costs, and other costs directly related to the issue. The numbers presented in this table are intended to provide an indication of the costs associated with issuing debt and equity. Such costs increase somewhat when interest rates are cyclically high; when money is in relatively tight supply, the investment bankers will have a more difficult time placing issues. Thus, actual flotation costs will vary over time.

[b] A straight bond is the traditional type of bond discussed in Chapter 2, in which interest is paid periodically (perhaps every 6 months) and the principal amount is repaid at maturity. A convertible bond resembles a straight bond but can be converted into shares of common stock by the bondholder.

[c] Seasoned equity issues are issues of stock of publicly traded corporations. Initial public offerings (IPOs) are equity issues of privately held companies that are "going public" by offering shares of stock to the general public for the first time.

Source: Lee, Inmoo, Scott Lochhead, and Jay Ritter, 1996, "The Costs of Raising Capital," *Journal of Financial Research* 21 (Spring), 59–74.

4. *Setting the offering price.* If the company is already publicly owned, the **offering price** will be based on the existing market price of the stock or the yield on the firm's bonds. For common stock, the arrangement typically calls for the investment banker to buy the securities at a prescribed number of points below the closing price on the last day of registration, which is the day the issue is released for sale by the Securities and Exchange Commission (SEC). Investment bankers have an easier job if an issue carries a relatively low price, but the issuer of the securities naturally wants as high a price as possible. Therefore, an inherent conflict of interest on price exists between the investment banker and the issuer. If the issuer is financially sophisticated and makes comparisons with similar security issues, however, the investment banker will be forced to price the issue close to the market price.

If the company is going public for the first time (an IPO), it will have no established price (or demand curve). Consequently, the investment banker must estimate the equilibrium price at which the stock will sell after its issuance. If the offering price is set below the true equilibrium price, the stock price will rise sharply after issue, and the company and its original stockholders will have given away too many shares to raise the required capital. If the offering price is set above the true equilibrium price, either the issue will fail or, if the investment bankers succeed in selling the stock, their investment clients will be unhappy when the stock subsequently falls to its equilibrium level. For these reasons, it is important that the equilibrium price be estimated as accurately as possible.

offering price
The price at which common stock is sold to the public.

Selling Procedures

registration statement
A statement of facts filed with the SEC about a company that plans to issue securities.

Prospectus
A document describing a new security issue and the issuing company.

Once the company and its investment bankers have decided how much money to raise, the types of securities to issue, and the basis for pricing the issue, they will prepare and file a registration statement and prospectus with the SEC. The **registration statement** provides financial, legal, and technical information about the company, whereas the **prospectus** summarizes the information in the registration statement and is provided to prospective investors for use in selling the securities. Lawyers and accountants at the SEC examine both the registration statement and the prospectus; if the information is deemed inadequate or misleading, the agency can delay or stop the public offering. The SEC review process generally takes from 20 days to 6 months. The final price of the stock (or the interest rate on a bond issue) is set at the close of business on the day the issue clears the SEC, and the securities are often offered to the public on the following day.

Typically, investment bankers sell the stock within a day or two after the offering begins. On occasion, however, they miscalculate, set the offering price too high, and are unable to move the issue. Alternatively, the market might decline during the offering period, which also would force the investment bankers to reduce the price of the stock. In either instance, on an underwritten offering, the corporation would still receive the agreed-upon price, and the investment bankers would have to absorb any losses.

underwriting syndicate
A group of investment banking firms formed to spread the risk associated with the purchase and distribution of a new issue of securities.

Because they are exposed to large potential losses, investment bankers typically do not handle the purchase and distribution of an issue alone unless it is fairly small. If the amount of money involved is large and the risk of price fluctuations is substantial, an investment banker will form an **underwriting syndicate,** where the issue is distributed to a number of investment firms in an effort to minimize the amount of risk carried by each firm. The investment banking house that sets up the deal is called the *lead,* or *managing, underwriter.*

In addition to the underwriting syndicate, larger offerings might require the services of still more investment bankers as part of a *selling group.* The selling group, which handles the distribution of securities to individual investors, includes all members of the underwriting syndicate plus additional dealers who take relatively small participations (or shares of the total issue) from the syndicate members. Members of the selling group act as selling agents and receive commissions for their efforts: they do not purchase the securities, so they do not bear the same risk the underwriting syndicate does. In other words, the underwriters act as wholesalers and bear the risk associated with the issue, whereas members of the selling group act as retailers. The number of investment banking houses in a selling group depends partly on the size of the issue; for example, the one set up when Communications Satellite Corporation (Comsat) went public included 385 members.

Shelf Registrations

shelf registration
Securities registered with the SEC for sale at a later date; the securities are held "on the shelf" until the sale.

The selling procedures just described, including the 20-day minimum waiting period between registration with the SEC and sale of the issue, apply to many security sales. Often, however, large, well-known public companies that issue securities frequently file a master registration statement with the SEC and then update it with a short-form statement immediately prior to each individual offering. In such a case, a company could decide at 10 a.m. to sell registered securities and have the sale completed before noon. This procedure is known as **shelf registration** because, in effect, the company puts its new securities "on the shelf" and then sells them to investors when it thinks the market is right.

Maintenance of the Secondary Market

In the case of a large, established firm such as General Motors, the investment banking firm's job is finished once it has disposed of the stock and turned the net proceeds over to the company. Conversely, in the case of a company going public for the first time, the investment banker has an obligation to maintain a market for the shares after the issue has been completed. Such stocks typically are traded in the OTC market, and the lead underwriter generally agrees to "make a market" in the stock and keep it reasonably liquid. The company wants a good market to exist for its stock, as do its stockholders. Therefore, if the investment banking house wants to do business with the company in the future, to keep its own brokerage customers happy, and to have future referral business, it will hold an inventory of the shares and help maintain an active secondary market in the stock.

Self-Test Questions

How does an investment bank differ from a commercial bank?

What is the sequence of events that ensues when a firm decides to issue new securities?

What is an underwriting syndicate and why is it important in the investment banking process?

What type of firm would use a shelf registration? Explain.

REGULATION OF SECURITIES MARKETS

Sales of new securities, such as stocks and bonds, as well as operations in the secondary markets, are regulated by the **Securities and Exchange Commission (SEC)** and, to a lesser extent, by each of the 50 states. For the most part, the SEC regulations are intended to ensure that investors receive fair financial disclosure from publicly traded companies and to discourage fraudulent and misleading behavior by firms' investors, owners, and employees to manipulate stock prices.

The primary elements of SEC regulations are as follows:

Securities and Exchange Commission (SEC)
The U.S. government agency that regulates the issuance and trading of securities.

1. The SEC has jurisdiction over nearly all interstate offerings of new securities to the general investing public. As mentioned earlier, firms that wish to issue new stock must file both a registration statement and a prospectus with the SEC. The primary purpose of such filings is to disclose specific information—financial and nonfinancial—concerning the issuing firm and the intended use of the funds to be raised from the issue. When the SEC approves the registration statement and the prospectus, it merely validates that the required information has been furnished. The SEC does not judge the quality or value of the issue; that task is left to potential investors.

2. The SEC regulates all national securities exchanges. Companies whose securities are listed on an exchange must file annual reports similar to the registration statement with both the SEC and the exchange.

3. The SEC exerts control over stock trades by corporate **insiders.** Officers, directors, and major stockholders must file monthly reports of changes in

insiders
Officers, directors, major stockholders, or others who might have inside information on a company's operations.

their holdings of the corporation's stock. Any *short-term* profits from such transactions must be handed over to the corporation.

4. The SEC has the power to prohibit manipulation of securities' prices by such devices as pools (aggregations of funds used to affect prices artificially) or wash sales (sales between members of the same group employed to record artificial trading volume and transaction prices). This prohibition means that deliberate manipulation of securities' prices is illegal.

Self-Test Question

What is the primary purpose for regulating securities trading?

INTERNATIONAL FINANCIAL MARKETS

Financial markets have become much more global during the last few decades. As the economies of countries in southeast Asia and the former Soviet Union have developed and experienced enormous growth in their financial markets, greater numbers of investors have provided funds to these regions. In 1970, U.S. stocks accounted for nearly two-thirds of the value of worldwide stock markets. Today, as Table 3-4 shows, U.S. stock markets represent less than 35 percent of the total value worldwide.[15] The areas of greatest growth lie in the emerging markets of China, Slovenia, India, and Russia. Until the region experienced severe economic difficulties, stock markets in Southeast Asia showed significant growth. At the time we write this book, however, growth in these markets has slowed somewhat. To some extent, the slowdown in this region can be traced to insufficient regulation and monitoring of financial markets, which allowed a few influential individuals or groups to wield significant power and control in determining economic events. Even so, many experts predict that the growth potential in Asian countries will continue to attract investors from around the world for many years to come.

Even with the expansion of stock markets internationally, exchanges in the United States continue to account for the greatest numbers of trades, with respect to both volume and value. Stock trades in the United States are approximately seven times greater than the value of stocks traded in both Japan and the United Kingdom. In fact, U.S. trading activity accounts for approximately 50 percent of worldwide trading activity each year.

The international market for bonds has experienced growth similar to the international stock markets. Table 3-5 shows the values of some of the foreign bond markets at the end 2007. The value of the U.S. bond market is substantial, but the bond markets in such countries as Spain, the Netherlands, and the United Kingdom have experienced substantial growth in the past few years. For example, from 1998 to 2007, the value of bond markets in the United States increased by 128 percent, and the values of bond markets in Spain, the Netherlands, and the United Kingdom increased by 747 percent, 455 percent, and 255 percent, respectively.

On January 1, 1999, the European Monetary Union (EMU) came into force. The EMU, which often is referred to as Euroland, started with 11 member

---

[15]The value given for U.S. stock exchanges is based on the combined values of the New York Stock Exchange, the American Stock Exchange, and NASDAQ.

TABLE 3-4   International Stock Market Values ($ billion)[a]

	Year-End 2007		Year-End 1997		
	Market Value	Percent of Total	Market Value	Percent of Total	10-Year Growth
I. Developed Stock Markets					
United States	$17,446.4	32.4%	$11,308.8	49.3%	54.3%
Japan	4,422.9	8.2	2,216.7	9.7	99.5
France	2,554.8	4.7	674.4	2.9	278.8
United Kingdom	3,665.9	6.8	1,996.2	8.7	83.6
Germany	1,913.8	3.6	825.2	3.6	131.9
Canada	1,811.4	3.4	567.6	2.5	219.1
Switzerland	1,292.0	2.4	575.3	2.5	124.6
Australia	1,272.9	2.4	295.8	1.3	330.3
Italy	1,069.5	2.0	344.7	1.5	210.3
Spain	1,032.5	1.9	290.4	1.3	255.5
Other developed markets	4,726.1	8.8	1,856.2	8.1	154.6
Total developed markets	$41,208.2	76.6%	$20,951.3	91.3%	96.7%
II. Emerging Stock Markets					
China	$ 4,203.2	7.8%	$ 206.4	0.9%	1,936.4%
India	1,411.4	2.6	128.5	0.6	998.4
Russia	1,264.0	2.3	128.2	0.6	886.0
Brazil	1,165.3	2.2	255.5	1.1	356.1
Slovenia	1,030.6	1.9	1.6	0.0	64,312.5
Taiwan	680.2	1.3	287.8	1.3	136.3
South Africa	403.9	0.8	232.1	1.0	74.0
Mexico	399.5	0.7	156.6	0.7	155.1
Malaysia	263.2	0.5	93.6	0.4	181.2
Turkey	240.7	0.4	61.1	0.3	293.9
Other emerging markets	1,528.1	2.8	436.7	1.9	249.9
Total emerging markets	$12,590.1	23.4%	$ 1,988.1	8.7%	533.3%
All stock markets	$53,798.3	100.0%	$22,939.4	100.0%	134.5%

[a]All market values are stated in U.S. dollars. Some of the changes in market values from 1997 to 2007 resulted from changes in the value of the dollar relative to foreign currencies (exchange rate changes). The classification of developed stock markets and emerging stock markets is based on the Standard & Poor's classification. Only the countries listed in the Standard & Poor's 2007 report were used to determine the numbers in this table.

Sources: *Standard & Poor's Global Stock Markets Factbook*, 2007 and *Standard & Poor's Global Stock Market Review: The World By Numbers*, December 2007 (http://www2.standardandpoors.com/spf/pdf/index/011108_WorldbyNumbers-Report.pdf).

countries. The members created a common currency (the euro) and a common debt instrument that is denominated in the euro and traded in a unified financial market called the Euro-market.[16] The emergence of Euroland is intended to reduce or eliminate country boundaries with respect to member countries' economic and trading policies. As the data in Table 3-5 show, in 2007 the size of the Euroland bond market was nearly 30 percent of the size of the world debt market, and 77 percent of the

---

[16]The 11 countries originally included in Euroland were Austria, Belgium, Finland, France, Germany, Ireland, Italy, Luxembourg, the Netherlands, Portugal, and Spain.

TABLE 3-5 Foreign Bond Market Values, December 2007 ($ billion)

	Total Bonds	Percentage of Total	Foreign Bonds	Domestic Bonds	Breakdown of Domestic Bonds Government Bonds	Bonds of Fin. Institutions	Corporate Bonds
I. Developed Countries							
United States	$29,879.2	37.6%	$ 5,565.4	$24,313.8	$ 6,590.6	$14,795.0	$2,928.2
Euroland[a]	23,023.6	28.9	10,272.7	12,750.9	6,436.6	4,597.7	1,716.6
Japan	9,217.6	11.6	361.8	8,855.8	7,145.1	982.5	728.2
United Kingdom	3,844.7	4.8	2,485.7	1,359.0	903.0	432.9	23.1
Canada	1,585.7	2.0	443.6	1,142.1	732.7	276.5	132.9
Australia	1,195.7	1.5	500.5	695.2	118.8	533.6	42.8
Denmark	691.5	0.9	121.3	570.2	83.3	454.4	32.5
Sweden	661.3	0.8	271.9	389.4	145.4	206.6	37.4
Switzerland	640.0	0.8	397.2	242.8	116.1	111.0	15.7
Norway	297.7	0.4	146.1	151.6	53.4	77.9	20.3
Other countries[b]	904.3	1.1	82.5	821.8	612.0	109.6	100.2
Total developed countries	$71,941.3	90.4%	$20,648.7	$51,292.6	$22,937.0	$22,577.7	$5,777.9
II. Developing Countries							
Asia[c]	$ 3,960.5	5.0%	$ 304.6	$ 3,655.9	$ 2,262.7	$892.1	$ 501.1
Latin & South America[d]	1,750.3	2.2	367.0	1,383.3	948.8	390.6	43.9
South Africa	781.0	1.0	660.3	120.7	72.2	31.5	17.0
Europe[e]	760.0	1.0	272.8	487.2	467.2	14.5	5.5
Offshore[f]	369.5	0.5	223.5	146.0	86.6	44.1	15.3
Total developing countries	$ 7,621.3	9.6%	$ 1,828.2	$ 5,793.1	$ 3,837.5	$ 1,372.8	$ 582.8
Total bonds outstanding	$79,562.6	100.0%	$22,476.9	$57,085.7	$26,774.5	$23,950.5	$6,360.7

[a]Includes Austria, Belgium, Finland, France, Germany, Greece, Ireland, Italy, Luxembourg, Netherlands, Portugal, and Spain

[b]Includes Iceland, Cyprus, and New Zealand

[c]Includes China, India, Indonesia, Malaysia, Philippines, South Korea, Taiwan, and Thailand

[d]Includes Argentina, Brazil, Chile, Colombia, Mexico, Peru, Uraguay, and Venezuela

[e]Includes Croatia, Czech Republic, Hungary, Poland, Russia, Slovakia, and Turkey

[f]Includes Hong Kong, Lebanon, and Singapore

Source: Bank for International Settlements, *BIS Quarterly Review*, June 2008. Data are available on the BIS Web site at http://www.bis.org/publ/quarterly.htm.

size of the U.S. bond market. The total increase in the bond markets of countries that were EMU members in 2007 was 241 percent from 1998 through 2007. Clearly, the importance of the Euroland market is poised to increase dramatically during the next few decades. The financial markets truly are global in nature—which means that events that influence the Asian and European markets will also influence the U.S. markets.

Although the globalization of financial markets continues and international markets offer investors greater frontiers of opportunities, investing overseas can be difficult due to restrictions or barriers erected by foreign countries. In many cases, individual investors find it difficult or unattractive to invest directly in foreign stocks.

Many countries prohibit or severely limit the ability of foreigners to invest in their financial markets, or they make it extremely difficult to access reliable information concerning the companies that are traded in the stock markets. For these reasons, most individuals interested in investing internationally do so indirectly, by purchasing financial instruments that represent foreign stocks, bonds, and other investments but that are offered by institutions in the United States. Investors can participate internationally by purchasing American depository receipts (ADRs), mutual funds that hold international stocks, or foreign securities certificates issued in dollar denominations.

Self-Test Questions

Why should investors in the United States be concerned with financial markets in other countries?

How do you think the European Monetary Union will affect the international financial markets?

Ethical Dilemma

Too High Tech ("Smoke and Mirrors" or Real Sales)?

Staci Sutter works as an analyst for Independent Investment BankShares (IIBS), which is a large investment banking organization. She has been evaluating an initial public offering (IPO) that IIBS is handling for a technology company named ProTech Incorporated. Staci is essentially finished with her analysis, and she is ready to estimate the price for which the stock should be offered when it is issued next week. According to her analysis, Staci has concluded that ProTech is financially strong and is expected to remain financially strong long into the future. In fact, the figures provided by ProTech suggest that the firm's growth will exceed 30 percent during the next 5 years. For these reasons, Staci is considering assigning a value of $35 per share to ProTech's stock.

Staci, however, has an uneasy feeling about the validity of the financial figures she has been evaluating. She believes the Protech's CFO has given her what he believes are "quality financial statements." However, yesterday Staci received an e-mail from a friend, who was an executive at ProTech until he was fired a few months ago, that suggests that the company has been artificially inflating its sales by selling products to an affiliate company and then repurchasing the same items a few months later. At the same time, Staci received a memo from her boss, Mr. Baker, who has made it clear that he thinks the ProTech IPO can be extremely profitable to top management "if it is handled correctly." In his memo, Mr. Baker indicates that the issue price of ProTech's stock must be at least $34 per share for the IPO to be considered successful by IIBS. Part of Staci's uneasiness stems from the fact that a coworker confided that she had seen the CEO of ProTech and his wife at an amusement park with Mr. Baker and his wife last month. If ProTech's sales figures are inflated, Staci surely would assign a different value to the company's stock for the IPO, but it will take her at least 2 weeks to completely reevaluate the company using different data. Staci knows that if she stays with her current analysis and she is wrong, the consequences can destroy IIBS because reputation is important in the investment banking business. If you were in Staci's situation, what would you do?

**CHAPTER
PRINCIPLES
–The Answers**

To summarize the key concepts, let's answer the questions that were posed at the beginning of the chapter:

- **What are financial markets and what role do they play in improving the standard of living in an economy?** Financial markets are the "mechanisms" by which borrowers and lenders are brought together. Without financial markets, individuals (companies) with excess funds to invest would either have to personally seek out individuals (companies) who had a need for those funds or simply hold the funds until a future period. If savers had to seek out borrowers, the search costs would be higher and the net returns earned on investments would be lower.

- **Why is it important for financial markets to be somewhat efficient?** When financial markets are *economically efficient,* investors invest in financial assets that yield the highest returns at the lowest cost, and borrowers borrow money at the lowest costs. In both cases, the costs of the transactions (transaction costs) are lower than would exist if efficient financial markets did not exist; thus money is efficiently distributed in the economy. When financial markets are *informationally efficient,* the prices of financial securities reflect available information. Depending on the amount of information that is reflected in securities' prices, the financial markets are considered to have achieved one of three degrees of informational efficiency: weak-form efficiency, semistrong-form efficiency, or strong-form efficiency.

- **Why are there so many different types of financial markets? How do we differentiate among various financial markets?** Different types of financial markets exist because savers (investors) and borrowers have different needs. Some investors (borrowers) want to invest for short periods, whereas others want to invest (borrow) for long periods. Financial markets are categorized according to the type of financial security that is traded, time to maturity, type of participant, location, and type of transaction.

- **What is an investment banking house and what role does an investment banking house play when firms want to raise funds in the financial markets?** An investment banking house is an organization that acts as a middleman, or agent, to help firms and governments raise funds by issuing financial instruments. The investment banker provides advice about the financial markets and helps to sell the securities that are issued. If investment banking houses did not exist, firms and governments would have to issue securities by themselves, which would be much costlier in most cases.

- **How do the financial markets in the United States differ from financial markets in other parts of the world?** The United States has the largest and most active financial markets in the world. There are more participants in the U.S. financial markets than in foreign financial markets. Also, most experts would agree that the U.S. financial markets are generally more efficient than foreign financial markets. A primary difference between U.S. financial markets and foreign financial markets is the participation and structure of financial institutions (intermediaries), which are factors that we discuss further in Chapter 4. There are more independent financial institutions in the United States than in any country in the world. And, although their competitive positions are improving, for the most part, U.S. financial intermediaries are competitively disadvantaged because they face greater restrictions as to the types of business associations they can enter than do their foreign counterparts.

The concepts presented in this chapter should help you understand what factors affect financial markets, the differences among the markets, and in which markets you should invest your money. If you understand the basic concepts contained in this chapter, you should be able to make more informed borrowing decisions.

- **What do financial markets have to do with personal finance?** When you borrow money to purchase a house (or anything else) or you invest some of your income, the transactions take place in the financial marketplace. Because there are differences among financial markets, there are also differences among the interest rates that exist in these markets. When rates are higher in the stock markets than in the bond markets, investors tend to buy stocks rather than bonds, and vice versa. When rates on home equity loans are lower than rates on other consumer loans, individuals tend to borrow money through home equity loans. As a result, if you monitor financial markets on a fairly regular basis, you will make better decisions about borrowing and investing than if you have no knowledge of the activities in these markets; you should be able to plan better as to when to borrow or invest to get the best interest rates. We discuss the determination of factors that affect interest rates in detail in Chapter 5.

- **How can I use knowledge of different financial markets when making investment decisions?** Different financial markets offer different financial instruments, such as stocks, bonds, and derivatives (discussed in Chapter 2). As a result, individuals have many choices as to where to invest their money. If the stock markets are performing poorly, investors who want to invest long term might choose to participate in the debt markets. On the other hand, investors who find it more desirable will invest in money market (short-term) instruments rather than capital market (long-term) instruments. Because the financial markets are so diverse, investors are able to tailor their investment strategies to their financial needs.

QUESTIONS

3-1   What is a financial market? What is the role of a financial market?

3-2   What would happen to the standard of living in the United States if people lost faith in our financial markets? Why?

3-3   How does a cost-efficient capital market help to reduce the prices of goods and services?

3-4   The SEC attempts to protect investors who are purchasing newly issued securities by requiring issuers to provide relevant financial information to prospective investors. The SEC does not provide an opinion about the real value of the securities. Hence, an unwise investor might pay too much for some stocks and consequently lose heavily. Do you think the SEC should, as a part of every new stock or bond offering, render an opinion to investors on the proper value of the securities being offered? Explain.

3-5   How do you think each of the following would affect a company's ability to attract new capital and the flotation (issuing) costs involved in doing so?

   a.   The decision to list a company's stock; the stock now trades in the over-the-counter market

   b.   The decision of a privately held company to go public

   c.   An increasing importance of institutions in the stock and bond markets

    d. The continuing trend toward financial conglomerates as opposed to stand-alone investment banking houses

    e. An increase in the number of shelf registrations

3-6 Before entering into a formal agreement, investment bankers carefully investigate the companies whose securities they underwrite, especially with issues of firms going public for the first time. Because the investment bankers do not themselves plan to hold the securities but intend to sell them to investors as soon as possible, why are they so concerned about making careful investigations?

3-7 Why would management be interested in getting a wide distribution of its shares?

3-8 Both physical stock exchanges and the OTC market are markets for trading stocks. Why do you think companies want to be listed on physical exchanges rather than stay OTC?

3-9 Microsoft and Intel qualify to be listed on the New York Stock Exchange, but both have chosen to be traded on the NASDAQ market. Can you think of reasons why the companies would choose to be traded on the NASDAQ? (*Hint:* Both companies deal with products that relate to electronic/computer media.)

3-10 What types of companies enter the markets for initial public offerings? Why do companies choose to go public? Why not stay private?

SELF-TEST PROBLEMS

Solutions appear in Appendix B.

Key Terms

ST-1 Define each of the following terms:

    a. Informational efficiency; economic efficiency

    b. Money market; capital market

    c. Debt market; equity market

    d. Primary market; secondary market

    e. Over-the-counter (OTC) market; physical stock exchange; Electronic Communications Networks (ECN)

    f. Demutualization; trade-through rule

    g. Floor broker; independent broker; house broker; specialist

    h. Investment banker

    i. Going public; new issue market; initial public offering (IPO)

    j. Prospectus; registration statement

    k. Shelf registration

    l. Best efforts arrangement; underwritten arrangement

    m. Underwriter's spread; flotation costs; offering price

    n. Underwriting syndicate; lead, or managing, underwriter; selling group

    o. Securities and Exchange Commission (SEC); insiders

Flotation Costs and Net Proceeds

ST-2 Global Geotell just hired InvestPro, a local investment banker, to help it issue common stock. The proceeds of the stock offering will be used for research and development of a new satellite tracking system for the

U.S. Navy. The market value of the issue equals $150 million, direct costs incurred by Global Geotell will amount to $225,000, and InvestPro charges a 7 percent fee for its services.

a. What will be the net proceeds to Global Geotell from the $150 million equity issue? That is, how much of the issue will Global Geotell be able to use?

b. If the price per share of the common stock equals $25 at the time of the issue, how many shares of stock must be issued if the total value of the issue is $150 million?

c. How many shares of stock must be issued if Global Geotell actually needs $150 million for its research and development? Assume that the issue price is $25 per share.

PROBLEMS

3-1   Security Brokers Inc. specializes in underwriting new issues by small firms. On a recent offering of Barenbaum Inc., the terms were as follows:

Price to public	$7.50 per share
Number of shares	3 million
Proceeds to Barenbaum	$21,000,000

Profit (Loss) on a New Stock Issue

Security Brokers incurred $450,000 in out-of-pocket expenses in the design and distribution of the issue. What profit or loss would Security Brokers incur if the issue were sold to the public at an average price of _____?

a. $7.50 per share

b. $9.00 per share

c. $6.00 per share

3-2   Eagle Sports Products (ESP) is considering issuing debt to raise funds to finance its growth during the next few years. The amount of the issue will be between $35 million and $40 million. ESP has already arranged for a local investment banker to handle the debt issue. The arrangement calls for ESP to pay flotation costs equal to 7 percent of the total market value of the issue.

Debt Issue

a. Compute the flotation costs that ESP will have to pay if the market value of the debt issue is $39 million.

b. If the debt issue has a market value of $39 million, how much will ESP be able to use for its financing needs? That is, what will be the net proceeds from the issue for ESP? Assume that the only costs associated with the issue are those paid to the investment banker.

c. If the company needs $39 million to finance its future growth, how much debt must ESP issue?

3-3   The Taussig Company, whose stock price is currently $30, needs to raise $15 million by issuing common stock. Underwriters have informed Taussig's management that it must price the new issue to the public at $27.53 per share to ensure that all shares will be sold. The underwriters' compensation will be 7 percent of the issue price, so Taussig will net $25.60 per share. The company will also incur expenses in the amount of $360,000. How many shares must Taussig sell to net $15 million after underwriting and flotation expenses?

Underwriting and Flotation Expenses

Size of Equity Issue   **3-4**   Anderson Anchor Corporation needs to raise $54 million to support its expansion plans. Anderson's investment banker normally charges 10 percent of the market value to handle an equity issue. If the price of Anderson's stock is expected to be $12, how many shares of stock must be issued so that the company receives the needed $54 million?

Underwriting and Flotation Expenses   **3-5**   WonderWorld Widgets (WWW) needs to raise $75 million in debt. To issue the debt, WWW must pay its underwriter a fee equal to 3 percent of the issue. The company estimates that other expenses associated with the issue will total $450,000. If the face value of each bond is $1,000, how many bonds must be issued to net the needed $75 million? Assume that the firm cannot issue a fraction of a bond (that is, 1/2 bond)—only "whole bonds" can be issued.

Equity Issue   **3-6**   Global gum company (GGC) has decided to issue $150 million in common stock to raise funds to finance future growth. GGC's stock currently sells for $25 per share.

　　a. How many shares of stock does GGC plan to issue?

　　b. If flotation costs are 8 percent, how much of the $150 million will GGC be able to use to fund growth?

Equity Issue   **3-7**   Investment Bankers Association (IBA) has an agreement with Northern Airlines to underwrite an equity issue with a market value equal to $11 million.

　　a. If IBA's underwriting fee is 5 percent and its out-of-pocket expenses associated with the issue are $125,000, what is the net amount that IBA will receive under its agreement with Northern?

　　b. Assuming that the information in part (a) does not change and Northern incurs out-of-pocket expenses equal to $240,000 for items such as printing, legal fees, and so on, what will be the net proceeds from the equity issue for Northern?

Flotation Costs   **3-8**   The Sprite Toy Company needs to raise funds for a major expansion of its manufacturing operations. Sprite has determined that it will issue $100 million of financing, but it has not decided whether to issue debt or equity. The company is publicly traded.

　　a. Based on the information given in Table 3-3, compute the flotation costs that Sprite would incur if it raises the needed funds by issuing equity only.

　　b. Based on the information given in Table 3-3, compute the flotation costs that Sprite would incur if it raises the needed funds by issuing straight debt only.

　　c. If Sprite wants to keep its flotation costs low, which form of financing should it use? Discuss some factors other than flotation costs that the company should consider.

IPO and Control   **3-9**   Bluesky.com, which currently is a privately held corporation, is making plans for future growth. The company's financial manager has recommended that Bluesky "go public" by issuing common stock to raise the funds needed to support the growth. The current owners, who are the founders of the company, are concerned that control of the firm will be diluted by this strategy. If Bluesky undertakes an IPO, it is estimated that each share of stock will sell for $5, the investment banking fee will be 15 percent of the total value of the issue, and the costs to the company for items such as lawyer

fees, printing stock certificates, SEC registration, and so on will be approximately 1 percent of the total value of the issue.

   a. If the market value of the stock issue is $42 million, how much will
Bluesky be able to use for growth?

   b. How many shares of stock will Bluesky have to issue to obtain $42
million for growth?

   c. The founders now hold all of the company's stock—10 million shares. If
the company issues the number of shares computed in part (b), what
proportion of the stock will the founders own after the IPO?

   d. If the founders must issue stock to finance the growth of the firm, what
would you recommend they do to protect their controlling interest for at
least a few years after the IPO? (*Hint:* See the discussion of the different
types of common stock in Chapter 2.)

Integrative Problem

3-10 Kampfire, Inc., a very successful manufacturer of camping equipment, is
considering "going public" next month to raise funds to help finance the
company's future growth. The financial manager of Kampfire has approached the investment banking firm at which you work seeking help with
its decision. Your boss asked you to explain the nature of the U.S. financial
markets and the process of issuing equity to the financial manager. To help
with this task, your boss has asked you to answer the following questions in
explaining the U.S. financial system to the financial manager:

Financial Markets

   a. What is a *financial market*? How are financial markets differentiated
from markets for *physical* assets?

   b. Differentiate between *money markets* and *capital markets*.

   c. Differentiate between a *primary market* and a *secondary market*. If
Microsoft decided to issue additional common stock, and an investor
purchased 1,000 shares of this stock from Merrill Lynch, the underwriter, would this transaction be a primary market transaction or a
secondary market transaction? Would it make a difference if the investor
purchased previously outstanding Microsoft stock in the NASDAQ
market?

   d. Describe the three primary ways in which capital is transferred between
savers and borrowers.

   e. Securities can be traded on *physical exchanges* or in the *over-the-
counter market*. Define each of these markets, and describe how stocks
are traded in each one.

   f. Describe the *investment banking process* as it relates to initial public
offerings.

   g. Kampfire estimates that it needs $25 million to support its expected
growth. The underwriting fees charged by the investment banking firm
for which you work are based on the schedule given in Table 3-3. In
addition, it is estimated that Kampfire will incur $245,000 in other ex-
penses related to the IPO. If your analysis indicates that Kampfire's
stock can be sold for $8.20 per share, how many shares must be issued to
net the company the $25 million it needs?

CHAPTER 4

Financial Intermediaries and the Banking System

Are banks becoming less important to Americans? Perhaps. During the last few decades, the visage of banking has changed significantly, primarily as the result of deregulation in the financial services industry. Banks no longer have a monopoly on checking accounts as they did prior to the mid-1970s. Today, checking services, as well as other services traditionally offered by banks, are available at such nonbank organizations as mutual funds and brokerage firms. In 1975, approximately 36 percent of the financial assets held by individuals was located in banks; currently, the amount held in banks is less than 15 percent.

What explains this relative decline in the proportion of individuals' financial assets held in banks? The simple answer is that "nonbanks" are able to offer more of the same products as banks, and they are very good at creating other products with the same qualities as those offered by banks. For example, many people see no real difference between money market mutual funds and savings accounts at banks—both offer a safe medium in which to invest, and funds are easily accessible.

In an effort to regain customers' funds, banks are fighting back by expanding into areas previously considered "taboo." For instance, in 1998, Citicorp, one of the largest banking organizations in the United States, and Travelers Group, which operates large

insurance and investment organizations, agreed to a merger that created the largest financial services organization in the world at the time. The new firm had combined assets in excess of $700 billion. The company created by the Travelers–Citicorp merger, which is now called Citigroup, has been able to offer an array of products and services demanded by a wide range of individuals and other businesses.

Other large bank mergers that also took place in 1998 included the merger of NationsBank Corporation and BankAmerica Corporation, which formed Bank of America, and the merger of Norwest Corporation and Wells Fargo & Company, which formed Wells Fargo Bank. At the end of 2000, the merger of Chase Manhattan Corporation and J.P. Morgan & Company formed J.P. Morgan Chase & Company.

This merger trend illustrates the current attitude of many financial institutions: big is better. Bank of America, J.P. Morgan Chase, and Citigroup have pursued this mantra to create mega financial institutions. In the future, it is expected that banking, as well as the financial services industry in general, will undergo major changes, because the future success of financial institutions depends on their ability to offer a variety of financial products and services. Financial institutions that exist today will have significantly different appearances tomorrow. Both the formation of "mega banks" and the deregulation of the financial services industry will contribute to the expected changes in the characteristics and operations of financial institutions.

Following are the notable bank mergers that have occurred recently. As you can see, big banking organizations are trying to become bigger.

Year	Aquirer/Acquired	Name After Merger	Amount ($ billion)
2004	J.P. Morgan Chase/Bank One	J.P. Morgan Chase & Co.	$58.0
2004	Bank of America/FleetBoston Financial	Bank of America	47.0
2004	Wachovia/SouthTrust	Wachovia	14.3
2005	Bank of America/MBNA Corporation	Bank of America	35.0
2006	Wachovia/Golden West Financial	Wachovia	25.0
2006	Regions Financial Corporation/ AmSouth Bancorporation	Regions Financial Corp	10.0
2007	Bank of America/LaSalle Bank	Bank of America	21.0
2007	Bank of New York/Mellon Financial	Bank of New York Mellon	18.3
2007	Wachovia Bank/World Savings Bank	Wachovia Bank	25.0

As you read this chapter, think about why particular types of financial intermediaries evolved, as well as about how such intermediaries will be transformed in the future. How different will a bank and an insurance company be in the year 2020?

CHAPTER PRINCIPLES
–The Questions

After reading this chapter, you should be able to answer the following questions:

- What is a financial intermediary and what role does a financial intermediary play in the financial markets? Why are there so many different types of intermediaries?
- What functions do financial intermediaries perform? Why were different types of intermediaries created?
- What is a fractional reserve system?
- What are the major characteristics of the U.S. banking system?
- What is the function of the Federal Reserve?
- How do banks in the United States differ from foreign banks?

In Chapter 3, we noted that most people do not provide funds directly to users (that is, borrowers) such as companies, governments, and individuals; rather, they *transfer* funds through firms known as financial intermediaries. This chapter describes in more detail the functions and types of financial intermediaries as well as the banking system and the role of the Federal Reserve as the central bank of the United States. Finally, it describes how the U.S. banking system differs from banking systems in other countries.

financial intermediaries
Specialized financial firms that facilitate the indirect transfer of funds from savers to borrowers by offering savings instruments, such as pension plans and certificates of deposit, and borrowing instruments, such as credit cards and mortgages.

ROLES OF FINANCIAL INTERMEDIARIES

Financial intermediaries include such financial services organizations as commercial banks, savings and loan associations, pension funds, and insurance companies. In simple terms, **financial intermediaries** facilitate the transfer of funds from those who have funds (savers) to those who need funds (borrowers). In reality, however, they do far more than simply transfer money and securities between borrowers and savers—they literally *manufacture* a variety of financial products, including mortgages, automobile loans, NOW accounts, money market mutual funds, and pension

FIGURE 4-1   The Financial Intermediation Process

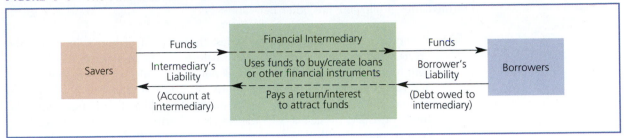

funds. Such products allow savers to provide funds to borrowers *indirectly*, by using whichever savings method (product) is most preferred. At the same time, borrowers can raise funds by using debt instruments created by intermediaries that have characteristics suitable for their needs, including maturity, denomination, and payment structure.

When intermediaries take funds from savers, they issue *securities* with such names as savings accounts, money market funds, and pension plans. These securities represent claims, or liabilities, against the intermediaries. The funds received by intermediaries are, in turn, lent to businesses and individuals via debt instruments created by intermediaries, such as automobile loans, mortgages, and commercial loans. The process by which financial intermediaries transform funds provided by savers into funds used by borrowers is called **financial intermediation.** Figure 4-1 illustrates the financial intermediation process. The arrows at the top of the boxes (pointing to the right) show the flow of funds from savers to borrowers through intermediaries. The arrows at the bottom of the boxes (pointing to the left) indicate the changes in the balance sheets of savers, borrowers, and intermediaries that result from the intermediation process. In essence, savers *exchange* funds for claims, or liabilities, from intermediaries, which include deposits at banks, retirement plans, or money market funds. The intermediaries then *exchange* funds provided by savers for claims, or liabilities, of borrowers that are packaged as debt or other instruments created by the intermediaries, including mortgages, commercial loans, and many other types of loans.

Financial intermediaries have created a variety of products to facilitate the savings and borrowing processes for both individuals and businesses. To illustrate, consider again Alexandra Trottier, who currently has an income equal to $50,000 but spends (consumes) only $40,000 annually. Because a variety of savings instruments are available, Alexandra can choose the instrument that best fits her needs. If she decides to put her funds in a savings instrument offered by Seffner State Bank, the bank will pay her interest on the funds deposited. To pay interest to Alexandra, the bank must create loans for which it receives interest payments from such borrowers as individuals and businesses. The funds that the bank uses to create such loans come from Alexandra's deposits, as well as those of other individuals and businesses. Thus, by depositing money in Seffner State Bank, Alexandra and other depositors *indirectly* lend funds through the bank to individuals and businesses. Without financial intermediaries such as Seffner State Bank, savers would have to provide funds *directly* to borrowers, which would be a difficult task for those who do not possess such expertise; such loans as mortgages and automobile financing would be much more costly, so the financial markets would be much less efficient. Clearly, the presence of intermediaries improves economic well-being. In fact, financial intermediaries were created to fulfill specific needs of both savers and borrowers, and to reduce the inefficiencies that would otherwise exist if users of funds could get loans only by borrowing directly from savers.

financial intermediation
The process by which financial intermediaries transform funds provided by savers into funds used by borrowers.

Improving economic well-being is only one of the benefits associated with intermediaries. Following are other benefits:

1. *Reduced costs.* Without intermediaries, the net cost of borrowing would be greater, and the net return earned by savers would be less, because individuals with funds to lend would have to seek out appropriate borrowers themselves, and vice versa. Intermediaries are more cost-efficient than individuals for two reasons: they create combinations of financial products that better match the funds provided by savers with the needs of borrowers, and they spread the costs associated with these activities over large numbers of transactions. For example, financial intermediaries have greater expertise than individuals when it comes to gathering, verifying, and evaluating information concerning borrowers, because such functions are performed continuously by intermediaries but not by individuals. As a consequence, it is less costly for intermediaries to evaluate the attractiveness of each borrower. Similarly, other costs associated with transforming savings into loans are lower, because intermediaries have expertise and achieve economies of scale that individuals do not. Consider what would happen if you wanted to invest your savings, but you had to personally search for potential borrowers. The costs associated with the time and effort needed to ensure that your funds are invested safely might be so high compared with the potential return that you decide to keep your savings under your mattress or in a coffee can.

2. *Risk/diversification.* The loan portfolios of intermediaries generally are well diversified, because they provide funds to a large number and variety of borrowers by offering many types of loans. Just like investors who purchase varied financial securities, intermediaries spread their risk by "not putting all their financial eggs in one basket."

3. *Funds divisibility/pooling.* Intermediaries can pool funds provided by individuals to offer loans or other financial products with different denominations to borrowers. That is, an intermediary can offer a large loan to a single borrower by combining the funds provided by many small savers. In essence, intermediaries permit the "little guys" to be a part of large loans and the "big guys" to obtain large amounts of funds without having to find individuals with sufficient wealth.

4. *Financial flexibility.* Because intermediaries offer a variety of financial products, both savers and borrowers have greater choices, or financial flexibility, than can be achieved with direct placements. For instance, banks offer savers such products as regular passbook savings accounts, certificates of deposit, and money market accounts, and they offer borrowers such products as commercial loans, mortgages, and lines of credit. Other financial products are offered by other types of intermediaries. In general, the financial products created by intermediaries are quite varied with respect to denominations, maturities, and other characteristics; hence, intermediaries attract many different types of savers and borrowers.

5. *Related services.* A system of specialized intermediaries offers more than just a network of "mechanisms" to transfer funds from savers to borrowers. Many intermediaries provide financial services in areas in which they achieve comparative advantages, such as expertise or economies of scale, relative to individuals. For example, banks provide individuals with a convenient method to make payments through checking accounts, and life insurance companies offer financial protection for individuals' dependents (beneficiaries).

Think about the complications that would arise if we could not pay our bills using checks or we could not borrow funds to purchase cars or houses. In general, financial intermediaries increase the standard of living in the economy. Their financial products help both individuals and businesses invest in opportunities that otherwise might be unreachable. For example, without the mortgages offered by savings and loan associations, individuals would find it much more difficult to purchase houses. Other sources of funds would exist, but great amounts of time, effort, and cost would have to be expended to search for an individual, or group of individuals, willing to lend the correct amount at an appropriate rate. Similarly, financial intermediaries offer loans to businesses that increase growth, thereby improving manufacturing abilities and increasing employment. In summary, intermediaries are good for the economy.

Self-Test Questions

What is the principal role of financial intermediaries?

In what ways do financial intermediaries benefit society?

TYPES OF FINANCIAL INTERMEDIARIES

In the United States, a large set of specialized, highly efficient financial intermediaries has evolved. Competition and government policy have created a rapidly changing arena, however, such that different types of institutions currently create financial products and perform services that previously were reserved for others. This trend, which is destined to continue into the future, has caused the lines among the various types of intermediaries to become blurred. Still, some degree of institutional identity persists, and these distinctions are discussed in this section.

Each type of intermediary originated to satisfy a particular need in the financial markets. For that reason, it has historically been easy to distinguish among the various types of intermediaries based on the characteristics of their assets and liabilities. Even though such organizations are more alike today than at any time in modern history, differences in the specific asset/liability structures persist among the intermediaries. For that reason, as we describe each type of intermediary, we indicate its combination of assets and liabilities. Also, as you will discover, the *types* of loans, deposits, and other products that are available differ among the various intermediaries.

Note that the combinations of assets and liabilities of financial institutions differ from the combinations of assets and liabilities possessed by individuals and non-financial businesses. The assets of financial institutions primarily consist of loans and other instruments that are comparable to the accounts receivable held by businesses. On the other side of the balance sheet, the liabilities of financial institutions largely result from savers providing funds in the form of deposits or shares, which are similar to the accounts payable or notes payable used by businesses to raise funds.

Commercial Banks

Commercial banks, commonly referred to simply as banks, are the traditional "department stores of finance"—that is, they offer a wide range of products and services to a variety of customers. Historically, banks were the institutions that handled checking accounts and provided mechanisms for clearing checks. Also, they traditionally provided the medium through which the supply of money was expanded

commercial bank
"Department stores of finance" that offer a variety of deposits, loans, and other products and services to a variety of customers, especially businesses.

or contracted. Today, however, several other institutions provide checking and check-clearing services and significantly influence the money supply. Conversely, banking companies offer a greater range of services than before, including trust operations, stock brokerage services, and insurance.

Originally, banks were established to serve the needs of commerce, or business—hence the name "commercial banks." Today, commercial banks represent one of the largest groups of depository intermediaries, and their operations affect nearly everyone either directly or indirectly. Most individuals have at least one checking account or savings account at a commercial bank, and many people have borrowed from banks to finance automobile purchases or use bank-issued credit cards. Even individuals who abstain from using such services are nevertheless affected by commercial lending activities, which support business operations. For example, banks provide funds that allow firms to grow, which, in turn, increases wage and employment levels.

Table 4-1 shows the combination of assets and liabilities held by federally insured commercial banks. As the balance sheet shows, almost 60 percent of commercial

TABLE 4-1   FDIC-Insured Commercial Banks: Assets and Liabilities, March 31, 2008

	Amount ($ billion)	Percentage of Total
Assets		
Cash	$ 736.0	6.4%
Securities/Investments		
U.S. Government securities	955.8	8.3
Muncipal securities	140.6	1.2
Other investments	502.6	4.4
Total investments	$ 1,599.1	13.9%
Loans and leases		
Real estate loans	3,681.4	32.0
Comercial (business) loans	1,403.9	12.2
Consumer loans	953.9	8.3
Other loans	576.0	5.0
Total loans	$ 6,615.1	57.5%
Other assets	2,544.6	22.1
Total assets	$11,494.7	100.0%
Liabilities and Equity		
Deposits		
Non-interest-bearing	$ 1,209.2	10.5%
Interest-bearing	6,224.2	54.1
Total deposits	7,433.4	64.7
Borrowed funds	2,547.6	22.2
All other liabilities	355.4	3.1
Total liabilities	$10,336.4	89.9%
Equity capital	1,158.3	10.1
Total liabilities and equity	$11,494.7	100.0%
Number of institutions reporting	7,240	

Note: Totals might not sum to the amounts shown due to rounding.

Source: Federal Deposit Insurance Corporation, *Statistics on Depository Institutions,* http://www.fdic.gov/.

banks' assets takes the form of loans. Almost 77 percent of the loans consists of business loans or real estate financing (mostly commercial land), and less than 15 percent is classified as consumer, or individual, loans. The loans created by banks are funded by liabilities that consist primarily of deposits; according to Table 4-1, deposits from businesses and individuals represent about 65 percent of banks' liabilities.

Credit Unions

A **credit union** is a depository institution that is owned by its depositors, who are members of a common organization or association, such as an occupation, a religious group, or a community. Credit unions operate as nonprofit businesses and are managed by member depositors elected by other members.

The first credit unions can be traced to financial pools, or cooperatives, established in England about 200 years ago. The original purpose of these financial groups was to create savings pools that could be used to provide credit to neighboring farmers who suffered temporary losses of income due to crop failures or other catastrophes. The common bonds possessed by the members generated a "help thy neighbor" attitude within the savings pools. As credit unions developed, they became known as financial institutions that served the "common worker," because many were originally established to serve members of particular occupations, such as the military or railroad workers.

Today, credit unions differ significantly from their earliest forms: they are much larger and hence less personal. Nevertheless, the spirit of credit unions remains unchanged—to serve depositor members. Members' savings are still loaned to other members, but the loans are primarily for automobile purchases, home improvements, and the like. Thanks to the common bond that members possess, loans from credit unions often are the cheapest source of funds for individual borrowers.

Table 4-2 indicates the mix of assets and liabilities held by federally insured credit unions. As you can see, 67 percent of the assets are loans. Most of the loans are made to individuals and take the form of balances outstanding on credit cards (individual loans), home equity loans (real estate), or automobile financing. Indeed, nearly 43 percent of the loans are classified as either individual or automobile. The funds used to make these loans primarily come from members' deposits, which generally take the form of checkable deposits called *share drafts*, regular savings accounts called *share accounts*, or such other types of savings as certificates of deposit and IRA accounts.

credit union
A depository institution owned by depositors who have a common association, such as an occupation or a religion.

Thrift Institutions

Thrifts are financial institutions that cater to savers, especially individuals who have relatively small savings or need long-term loans to purchase houses. Thrifts were originally established because the services offered by commercial banks were designed for businesses rather than individuals, whose needs differed greatly. The two basic types of thrifts are savings and loan associations (S&Ls) and mutual savings banks.

Historically, S&Ls have been viewed as a place to obtain real estate mortgages. In fact, when these institutions were first established, depositors pooled their savings to create loans that were used to help other depositors build houses in a particular geographic area. Each savings association was eventually liquidated when the building goals were achieved and all of the loans were repaid.

Today, S&Ls take the funds of many small savers and then lend this money to home buyers and other types of borrowers. Without institutions such as S&Ls, savers would not be able to invest in mortgages unless they were willing to lend

thrifts
Institutions that cater to savers, especially individuals who have relatively small amounts of money to deposit or need long-term loans to purchase houses.

TABLE 4-2   Federally Insured Credit Unions: Assets and Liabilities, March 31, 2008

	Amount ($ billion)	Percentage of Total
Assets		
Cash	$ 72.0	9.1%
Securities/investments		
U.S. Government securities & municipals	68.4	8.6
Deposits at institutions	45.7	5.8
Other investments	40.6	5.1
Total investments	$154.6	19.5%
Loans and leases		
Consumer loans	53.8	6.8
Automobile loans	173.8	21.9
Real estate loans	279.6	35.3
Other loans	25.7	3.2
Total loans	$532.8	67.3%
Other assets	32.7	4.1
Total assets	$792.2	100.0%
Liabilities and Equity		
Deposits		
Share drafts	$ 75.8	9.6%
Regular shares	177.6	22.4
Money market and savings shares	346.0	43.7
Other shares	65.9	8.3
Nonmember shares	2.4	0.3
Total deposits	$667.7	84.3%
Borrowings	36.8	4.6
Total liabilities	$704.5	88.9%
Equity capital	87.7	11.1
Total liabilities and equity	$792.2	100.0%
Number of credit unions reporting	8,049	

Source: FOIA Data Files, National Credit Union Administration, http://www.ncua.gov/.

directly to borrowers, such as home buyers, which would require funds to be "tied up" for long time periods. Savings accounts provide savers with greater flexibility, because funds do not have to be committed for long periods. In many cases, savings can be easily liquidated (withdrawn) with little or no restriction. Perhaps the most significant economic function of the S&Ls is to "create liquidity" that otherwise would be lacking.

Mutual savings banks, which operate mainly in the northeastern states, are similar to S&Ls, except they are owned and managed by their depositors. Thus, mutual savings banks operate much like credit unions.

Approximately 70 percent of thrifts are savings associations; these associations account for more than 90 percent of all thrift deposits. Table 4-3 shows the mix of assets and liabilities held by federally insured thrift institutions. About 70 percent of the assets are in the form of loans, and 86 percent of these loans are mortgages and other real estate loans. For this reason, thrifts continue to be viewed primarily as mortgage lending institutions. Notice that 60 percent of the liabilities consist of

TABLE 4-3	FDIC-Insured Savings Institutions: Assets and Liabilities, March 31, 2008

	Amount ($ billion)	Percentage of Total
Assets		
Cash	$ 46.6	2.5%
Securities/Investments		
U.S. Government securities	191.8	10.2
Municipals	11.1	0.6
Other investments	151.1	8.1
Total investments	$ 354.0	18.9%
Loans		
Mortgages	939.7	50.1
Other real estate loans	180.5	9.6
Commercial (business) loans	82.0	4.4
Consumer loans	94.5	5.0
Other loans	4.0	0.2
Total loans	$1,300.7	69.4%
Other assets	173.5	9.3
Total assets	$1,874.7	100.0%
Liabilities and Equity		
Deposits		
Non-interest-bearing deposits	$ 57.5	3.1%
Interest-bearing deposits	1,074.9	57.3
Total deposits	$1,132.4	60.4%
Borrowed funds	497.6	26.5
Other liabilities	42.2	2.3
Total liabilities	$1,672.1	89.2
Equity capital	202.7	10.8
Total liabilities and equity	$1,874.7	100.0%
Number of institutions reporting	1,254	

Note: Totals might not sum to the amounts shown due to rounding.

Source: Federal Deposit Insurance Corporation, *Statistics on Depository Institutions,* http://www.fdic.gov/.

deposits, and 95 percent of the deposits are termed "interest-bearing" deposits, which represent some form of savings account or other savings instrument.

Mutual Funds

Mutual funds are *investment companies* that accept money from savers and then use these funds to buy various types of financial assets, including stocks, long-term bonds, short-term debt instruments, and so forth. These organizations pool funds, reducing risks through diversification. They also achieve economies of scale, which lower the costs of analyzing securities, managing portfolios, and buying and selling securities.

Literally, hundreds of different types of mutual funds exist, offering a variety of goals and purposes to meet the objectives of many different savers. For instance, investors who prefer to receive current income can invest in *income funds*. These mutual funds invest primarily in instruments that generate fairly constant annual incomes, including bonds with constant annual interest payments and stocks with constant dividend payments (that is, preferred stock). In contrast, investors who are

mutual funds
Investment companies that accept funds from savers to invest in such financial assets as stocks and bonds.

willing to accept higher risks in hopes of obtaining higher returns can invest in *growth funds*. These mutual funds include investments that generate little or no income each year but exhibit high growth potential that could result in significant increases in the values of the investments (that is, capital gains) in the future.

money market mutual fund
A mutual fund that invests in short-term, low-risk securities and allows investors to write checks against their accounts.

The *money market mutual fund* is a relatively new savings instrument that is available in the financial markets. A **money market mutual fund** includes short-term, low-risk securities and generally allows investors to write checks against their accounts. From their beginning in the mid-1970s, money market funds have experienced unparalleled growth. In 1975, the total value of money market funds was less than $10 *million;* by 2008, this total value exceeded $3 *trillion.* Other mutual funds have shown similar, albeit somewhat slower, growth patterns. With greater than $12 trillion in assets in 2008, mutual fund investment companies represented the largest financial institution in the United States, exceeding the size of banks' assets by more than $500 million. Today, investment companies offer some 8,050 individual mutual funds. According to the Investment Company Institute (ICI), which monitors the performances of mutual funds, 90 percent of these mutual funds are owned by more than 80 million individuals. The primary reason that individuals invest in mutual funds is for retirement. In fact, about 50 percent of individual retirement accounts (IRAs) consist of mutual funds.

The combination of assets and liabilities held by investment companies is readily evident: assets principally include stocks, bonds, and other similar financial instruments, whereas the major liability is represented by investors' (savers') shares, which provide the funds used to purchase the financial assets. The actual composition of the investments held by mutual funds changes as economic and financial market conditions change. Table 4-4 shows the breakdown of the value of mutual funds at the end of April 2008 into stock funds, bond funds (long-term debt), and money market funds (short-term debt). As you can see, stock funds represented about 60 percent of the total value, bonds represented 24 percent, and money market funds represented 10 percent. In contrast, in 1970—before money market funds existed—nearly 95 percent of mutual funds were stock funds and the remaining 5 percent were bond funds. In 1980, when the U.S. economy was in the middle of a recession, the mixture was about 33 percent stock funds, 10 percent bond funds, and 57 percent money market funds. In 1990, the mixture was 23 percent stock funds, about 30 percent bond funds, and nearly 47 percent money market funds. In general, when the economy is doing well and stock markets are moving upward, mutual funds tend to invest greater amounts in stocks; when the economy is stagnant and

---

TABLE 4-4   Mutual Funds Net Assets, April 2008

	Amount ($ billion)	Percentage of Total	Number of Funds	Percentage of Total
Stock (equity)	$ 6,187.6	51.3%	4,810	59.8%
Hybrid securities	699.1	5.8	478	5.9
Taxable bonds	1,374.9	11.4	1,297	16.1
Municipal bonds	380.0	3.2	657	8.2
Money market—taxable	2,947.2	24.4	552	6.9
Money-market—tax-free	479.1	4.0	256	3.2
Total	$12,068.0	100.0%	8,050	100.0%

Note: Totals might not sum to the amounts shown due to rounding.

Source: Investment Company Institute, *Trends in Mutual Fund Investing,* April 2008, http://www.ici.org/stats/mf/.

movements in stock markets are uncertain or exhibit a downward trend, funds tend to make greater investments in short-term, liquid assets (money market instruments).

Whole Life Insurance Companies[1]

Whole life insurance companies differ from other financial institutions in that they provide two services to individuals: insurance and savings. In recent years, many life insurance companies have also offered tax-deferred savings plans designed to provide benefits to participants when they retire.

Broadly speaking, the purpose of life insurance is to provide a beneficiary, such as a spouse or family members, with protection against financial distress or insecurity that might result from the premature death of a "breadwinner," or other wage earner. In a general sense, life insurance can be labeled either term insurance or whole life insurance. *Term life insurance* is a relatively short-term contract that provides financial protection for a temporary period—perhaps for 1 year or for 5 years at a time—and it must be renewed each period to continue such protection. *Whole life insurance* is a long-term contract that provides lifetime protection.

The cost of term insurance, called the *premium,* generally increases with each renewal because the risk of premature death increases as the insured ages. In contrast, the premiums associated with whole life insurance policies are fixed payments computed as an average of the premiums required over the expected life of the insured person. As a consequence, the premiums in the early years exceed what is needed to cover the insured's dependents, and the premiums in the later years are less than what is needed. The excess amounts in the early years are invested to make up for the deficits in later years. These invested amounts provide savings features that create cash values for the whole life insurance policies. In contrast, term life insurance policies do not provide savings features because the premiums are fixed for only a short time period (generally 5 years or less); for this reason, the premiums are based on the existing risks only and change at renewal if risks change. Thus, whole life policies offer both insurance coverage and a savings feature, whereas term life policies do not.[2]

Life insurance companies use statistical tables, called actuarial tables, to estimate the amounts of cash that will be needed each year to satisfy insurance claims. The actuarial tables, which are based on risk factors such as age and lifestyle as well as previous experiences with claims in the life insurance industry, provide companies with fairly accurate forecasts of the amounts and the timings of future claims. Companies that offer whole life insurance can, therefore, project their cash needs with good precision. Because such policies are long-term contracts, the companies invest significant portions of their funds in long-term assets such as corporate bonds, stocks, and government bonds. Table 4-5 indicates the structure of assets and liabilities held by life insurance companies. As you can see, these companies invest primarily in long-term instruments, and the principal source of funds is represented by the reserves associated with the whole life insurance policies and pension plans sold by the companies. The liability labeled "Reserves" represents the obligations that are associated with future commitments derived from life insurance companies' outstanding policies.

whole life insurance companies Firms that receive premiums from individuals; a portion of the funds is invested and a portion is used to cover the dependents of the insured.

---

[1]Insurance is intended to reduce the consequences of risk by transferring some of the economic consequences to others—namely insurance companies—that are better able to absorb such risks. Insurance companies achieve risk reduction by pooling, or diversifying, the risks of individuals, companies, and governments.

[2]Premiums charged by other insurance companies, such as health insurance, property and casualty insurance, and the like, are based only on the risks faced and are changed over time as the risks change. In other words, they reflect the cost of the peril (risk) that is insured at the time at which the premium is paid. There is no savings function because individuals pay only for the insurance services offered by such companies. Such insurance companies do not perform the same intermediary function as life insurance companies do.

TABLE 4-5 Life Insurance Companies: Assets and Liabilities, December 31, 2006		
	Amount ($ billion)	**Percentage of Total**
Assets		
Cash	$ 57.5	1.2%
Investments		
Government securities	579.0	12.0
Corporate bonds	1,882.5	39.0
Corporate stock	1,530.9	31.7
Mortgages	313.7	6.5
Real estate	33.1	0.7
Total investments	$4,339.2	90.0%
Policy loans	112.9	2.3
Other assets	313.2	6.5
Total assets	$4,822.8	100.0%
Liabilities and Equity		
Reserves	$4,226.0	87.6%
Other liabilities	330.9	6.9
Total liabilities	$4,557.0	94.5%
Surplus and net worth	265.9	5.5
Total liabilities and equity	$4,822.8	100.0%
Number of insurance companies	1,072	

Source: *Life Insurers Fact Book*, 2007, American Council on Life Insurance, http://www.acli.com.

Because life insurance companies are able to invest in corporate bonds and stocks, they provide an important source of long-term funds for companies. Table 4-5 shows that investment in corporate bonds and stocks accounts for nearly 71 percent of total assets and 79 percent of total investments. To some degree, life insurance companies compete with commercial banks to provide funds to corporations. For the most part, however, they operate in different financial markets than do banks. Whereas banks focus on helping corporations meet their needs for short-term funds, the accuracy of the actuarial tables used in the life insurance industry allows insurance companies to support long-term funding needs.

Pension Funds

pensions
Employee retirement plans funded by corporations or government agencies.

Pensions are retirement plans funded by corporations or government agencies for their workers that are administered primarily by the trust departments of commercial banks or by life insurance companies. Probably the most famous pension plan is Social Security, which is a government-sponsored plan funded by tax revenues. Most state and municipal governments and large corporations offer pension plans to their employees. Many of these plans have been established to accept both employer and employee contributions, which often are shielded from taxes until the assets are withdrawn from the plan.

The earliest pensions in the United States were created by railroad companies more than a century ago. As the country became more industrialized, pension plans expanded greatly. The growing popularity of pensions was accompanied by new problems associated with managing these plans. Many pensions did not survive the financial turmoil of

TABLE 4-6 Pension and Retirement Programs, December 31, 2007[a]

I. Values of Major Pensions and Retirement Programs

Type of Program	Amount ($ billion)	Percentage of Total
Private Plans		
With life insurance companies	$ 2,454.0	15.6%
Mutual funds	1,537.8	9.8
Individual retirement accounts (IRAs)	4,747.0	30.2
Other private plans	829.2	5.3
Total private plans	$ 9,568.0	60.8%
Public (Government) Plans		
Federal civilian employees	$ 1,171.5	7.5%
State and local governments	2,960.9	18.8
Social Security	2,023.6	12.9
Total public plans	$ 6,156.0	39.2%
Total private and public plans	$15,724.0	100.0%

II. Structure of Assets of Pension Plans

Type of Asset	Amount ($ billion)	Percentage of Total
Private Plans (Excluding Mutual Funds and Insurance Companies)		
Government securities	$ 395.9	7.1%
Bonds	350.1	6.3
Stock (equity)	2,576.6	46.2
Mutual Funds	1,537.8	27.6
Other investments	715.8	12.8
Total private plans	$5,576.2	100.0%
Public Plan (Excluding Social Security)		
Government securities	$ 594.4	14.4%
Bonds	165.9	4.0
Stock (equity)	1,911.7	46.3
Mutual Funds	266.1	6.4
Other investments	1,194.3	28.9
Total public plans	$4,132.4	100.0%

[a]Totals might not sum to the amounts shown due to rounding.

Sources: Federal Reserve Board, *Flow of Funds Accounts of the United States*, http://www.federalreserve.gov, and "A Summary of the 2008 Annual Reports: Status of the Social Security and Medicare Programs," http://www.ssa.gov/OACT/TRSUM/trsummary.html.

the 1920s and 1930s because they were "pay-as-you-go" plans with benefits paid out of the contributions made by the existing employees. "Pay-as-you-go" plans are termed *unfunded pensions*. Social Security, which was established in 1935 to supplement the retirement income provided by private pensions, is the largest unfunded pension.

Since World War II, private pensions have grown significantly compared with government pensions. Today, they account for 61 percent of the total assets held in retirement plans. As panel I in Table 4-6 shows, the assets in Social Security represent about 13 percent of the total value of pensions in the United States.

Like the instruments offered by life insurance companies, pension funds are long-term contracts that provide fairly predictable payments. Not surprisingly, the asset structure of pension plans is similar to that of life insurance companies. As panel II in Table 4-6 shows, pension funds are invested primarily in long-term assets such as stocks, mutual funds, and government securities.

Self-Test Questions

List the major types of financial intermediaries, and briefly describe each one's function.

Why is the primary asset held by savings institutions mortgages?

Why do you think the assets in Social Security represent less than 15 percent of the value of the assets in all pension plans?

SAFETY (RISK) OF FINANCIAL INSTITUTIONS

As discussed in the previous sections, the services provided by financial intermediaries help the economy function more efficiently and increase the general standard of living of the population. Each type of financial institution was originally established to meet certain needs or correct particular inefficiencies that existed in the financial markets. Because intermediaries play such a critical role in the welfare of the economy, the financial services industry has been heavily regulated in an effort to ensure stability and safety in the nation's financial markets. Proponents of regulation argue that the parties involved in the financial intermediation process—savers, borrowers, and intermediaries—do not possess equal levels of expertise or have access to the same information. Legislation is therefore needed to provide a more "even playing field" and maintain public confidence in the financial system. Most of the financial panic experienced by the United States in the past can be traced to actions of intermediaries, which engaged in unscrupulous behavior or took on too much risk, thereby contributing to a public loss of faith in the country's financial system.

The major reason cited for regulating financial institutions is the public's need for protection from financial environments that can result in economic disasters, which are caused by a "domino effect" that can be triggered by the failures of financial intermediaries. When the public loses faith in the financial system, individuals tend to pull funds out of intermediaries. As a result, sources of credit shrink considerably and the economy suffers. Therefore, much of the existing regulation seeks to restrict the activities of financial institutions, presumably to maintain public confidence by helping to assure some degree of safety in the financial system. In addition, the regulations require intermediaries to periodically report certain information. Regulatory attitudes have shaped the structure of the banking system that exists today in the United States.

In the next section, we describe the U.S. banking system and outline how previous regulatory actions shaped the infrastructure of the financial system. In this section, we describe a major aspect of regulation that affects the overall risk associated with various intermediaries: the safety of funds provided by savers.

Individuals and businesses are willing to provide funds to borrowers through intermediaries because they have confidence that their savings will remain safe. If the public lost faith in the safety of intermediaries, few—if any—funds would be available through such institutions. To help maintain confidence, the funds provided to most financial institutions are insured by agencies established through federal or state legislation. The primary purpose of such insurance is to assure the safety of savers' funds even if the financial intermediary fails. In this section, we examine the principal insuring agencies of financial intermediaries.

Banks, Thrifts, and Credit Unions

Probably the most familiar insuring agency is the Federal Deposit Insurance Corporation (FDIC), which insures the deposits at most banks and thrift institutions. Even though the FDIC has changed considerably since it was established in 1933, the primary objective of the federal insurance fund has not changed—to maintain safety and depositor confidence by shifting the risk of losing deposited funds from the saver/depositor to the FDIC. Federal deposit insurance is also available for credit unions through the National Credit Union Share Insurance Funds (NCUSIF). Both the FDIC and the NCUSIF insure deposits for amounts up to $100,000 per individual for most accounts. However, Congress recently passed legislation that increased coverage to $250,000 for such retirement accounts as IRAs and Keoghs (a retirement plan for self-employed individuals). Banks, thrifts, and credit unions that are chartered by the federal government must use a federal insurance fund. Institutions chartered by state governments can use federal insurance if they are qualified; otherwise, they must acquire insurance through the fund provided by the state that charters them.

The Federal Reserve (Fed), which is discussed in the next section, traditionally has been considered the regulatory agency of commercial banking. The Fed also has the power to impose such regulations as reserve requirements on other financial institutions that accept deposits from savers or make conventional loans to borrowers. Although Fed regulations affect thrifts and credit unions, federally chartered thrifts are also regulated/supervised by the Office of Thrift Supervision (OTS), and federally chartered credit unions are regulated/supervised by the National Credit Union Administration (NCUA).

Insurance Companies

Insurance companies are primarily regulated by the states in which they operate. For the most part, regulations in the insurance industry are intended to help assure the financial stability of insurance companies. Insurance companies require prepayment for policies that extend into future periods, so financial stability is important to ensure that policyholders receive the future coverage that they have purchased. The National Association of Insurance Commissioners (NAIC) is a group of state insurance commissioners that meets regularly to discuss concerns in the insurance industry and to coordinate legislative efforts in each state in an effort to provide more uniform regulations nationwide.

Pensions

The major legislation affecting pension plans is the Employee Retirement Income Security Act (ERISA), which became law in 1974. Although this law does not require firms to establish pension plans, it does specify the conditions necessary for a retirement program to receive favorable tax benefits, such as tax-deferred contributions. ERISA and its subsequent improvements have been instrumental in reforming the management of pension plans, thereby enhancing the safety of workers' retirement funds. ERISA includes provisions that mandate the disclosure of certain information by pension funds and provide for insurance of benefits in case an employer defaults or terminates a plan. This act also established the Pension Benefit Guarantee Corporation (PBGC), a federal insurance organization that insured (guaranteed) benefits up to approximately $4,313 per month in 2008, with the maximum amount adjusted for inflation in future periods. Each year, every pension plan must file a statement with the U.S. Department of Labor to report information about the operation and financial position of the fund.

Because some large private pension funds were affected by the recent unethical behavior of executives in large corporations, Congress passed the Pension Protection Act of 2006, which amended ERISA to strengthen pension fund requirements. In general, to better protect individuals' pensions, this piece of legislation set minimum funding requirements and rules as to how pension plans can be managed.

Mutual Funds

The regulation of mutual funds is the responsibility of the Securities and Exchange Commission (SEC), except in a few instances where state regulations apply. Specifically, regulations that apply to mutual funds are specified in the Investment Company Act of 1940 and its subsequent changes. They require that certain information be disclosed to investors, that the funds be diversified, and that managers and employees of funds avoid conflicts of interest associated with the investments held by the funds. In addition, the practices used to sell funds and to compensate for such sales (that is, commissions) should not be considered unethical or appear to take advantage of investors.

Because mutual funds represent investment pools that include such risky assets as stocks, bonds, and options, no federal insurance agency is available to guarantee the safety of savers' funds. Instead, each fund is required to inform investors about the investment goal (for example, income or growth) and the risk associated with pursuing that goal. It is the individual's responsibility to determine the amount of risk he or she is willing to accept. Many different types of mutual funds are available with many different levels of risk, so investors can choose from funds with amounts of risk that range from very low to very high.

 Self-Test Questions

Why is it necessary to regulate financial institutions?

Why have federal insurance agencies been established for financial intermediaries?

Is specific insurance available for mutual funds? Explain.

BANKING SYSTEMS

This section describes the structure of the U.S. banking system and examines the role it plays in our business environment and personal lives. Having a basic knowledge of how the banking system works will allow you to understand how the U.S. monetary policy is managed and the role played by financial intermediaries in this process.

Evolution of Banking Systems

Evidence shows that such banking activities as lending took place in civilizations going back to ancient Babylon. Banking as we know it today probably did not emerge until the Middle Ages, however. During that period, widespread unrest and wars resulted in a great deal of anarchy. Wealthy individuals felt compelled to protect their fortunes by storing their valuables with merchants—usually metal-smiths, such as goldsmiths and silversmiths—who maintained facilities that were considered safe havens for property. When the valuables were *deposited,* the merchants would *issue* a receipt that verified the deposit and ownership of the property. When individuals wanted to purchase goods and services, they would redeem their depository receipts for the needed gold or silver.

Over time, individuals realized that the depository receipts of the better known and more trusted metalsmiths could be used for trade. As a result, metal deposits did not actually have to be withdrawn, which was easier and safer than physically redeeming the depository receipts. Before long, metalsmiths discovered that they always held positive inventories of gold and silver because only a portion of the receipts were redeemed at any point in time. Furthermore, the "safekeepers" re-alized that they could make a profit by lending some of their idle inventories to other merchants and individuals who found themselves temporarily short of funds needed for trade. As this process became more prevalent, metalsmiths began to issue standardized depository receipts that could be used more easily for purchasing goods and services. Often, the depository receipts were also deposited with the issuing metalsmiths, which provided them with additional sources of loans. Thus, metalsmiths found themselves with more depository receipts outstanding than the amount of gold and silver that was held for safekeeping. As they discovered, it was not necessary to hold gold and silver equal to the amount of all deposits as long as all depositors did not demand payment simultaneously. Consequently, the safekeepers needed to maintain metal *reserves* equal to only a fraction of the total deposits.

The use of depository receipts as exchange instruments became more wide-spread as knowledge and confidence in the system improved. Banks, which dealt primarily with deposits and loans, emerged as such transactions became more so-phisticated and specialization became more profitable.[3]

Eventually, the rather simplistic banking operations created by the metalsmiths of the Middle Ages evolved into the more sophisticated banking systems we observe in the world today. An important concept discovered by the metalsmiths was that "money" could be created by lending some of the deposits of others, but only if less than 100 percent of deposits was required to meet depositors' withdrawal demands at any point in time. Thus, the metalsmiths originated the *fractional reserve system,* which forms the basis of our current banking system. Next, we describe how a fractional reserve banking system allows banks to "create" money.

Fractional Reserve System

As noted previously, in a **fractional reserve system,** the amount of reserves maintained to satisfy requests for withdrawal of deposits is less than 100 percent of the total deposits. As the metalsmiths of the Middle Ages discovered, a fractional reserve system actually increases, or creates, money in the economy.

To see how money is created, consider a banking system that includes one bank, which initially has total deposits equal to $100. If the bank is required to maintain reserves equal to 100 percent of deposits, then it would have to keep all $100 in

fractional reserve system
A system in which the amount of reserves maintained by a financial institution to satisfy re-quests for withdrawals is less than 100 percent of total deposits.

---

[3]History seems to indicate that the term *bank* originated from *bancos,* Italian for "benches." Often merchants conducted their transactions from benches at a central meeting location. Merchants who did not honor their deals had their benches broken, preventing them from entering into new transactions; the term *bankrupt* evolved from this practice.

reserves to "back up" deposits; it could not lend any of the funds deposited, so the $100 in deposits would represent exactly $100 in money.

Now suppose that the bank is required to maintain reserves equal to only a fraction of the total deposits—say, 10 percent. Thus, of the original $100 in deposits, $90 would represent **excess reserves,** because the bank is required to maintain reserves of only $10 to "back up" the $100 deposit. The bank could lend the *excess reserves* to an individual or a company. Consider what would happen if an individual borrowed the entire $90 in initial excess reserves and redeposited the funds in the bank. The bank would then have new deposits equal to $90. Because only 10 percent of each deposit must be maintained as reserves, the new deposit would create excess reserves equal to $81 = $90 × (1 − 0.10), which could be loaned to other borrowers. You can imagine what would happen if this process continues until excess reserves are totally eliminated—the $90 excess reserves from the original $100 deposit would become magnified and produce much greater deposits, or funds in the form of money.

The amount of additional money produced by the original deposit depends on the *fraction* that must be held in reserves. If the reserve requirement is 100 percent, then no magnification occurs. If there is no reserve requirement, the magnification is unlimited. In general, the *maximum* change in the money supply created by a *fractional reserve system* is computed as follows:

excess reserves
Reserves at a bank, or another institution affected by reserve requirements, in excess of the amount required; equal to the total reserves minus required reserves.

 **4-1**

$$\text{Maximum change in the money supply} = \frac{\text{Excess reserves}}{\text{Reserve requirement}}$$

Thus, if all excess reserves are loaned to individuals and subsequently redeposited in the bank, the initial $100 deposit would create $900 = ($100 − $10)/(0.10) in *new* money through additional deposits. At the same time, the amount of loans, or credit, created in the banking system would also be $900 because the additional money was created through the loans produced by the bank.

Table 4-7 indicates the changes in deposits and loans associated with this fractional reserve banking system example. Note that when the bank has loaned the maximum amount based on the 10 percent reserve requirement, there are no excess reserves, the total deposits in the banking system equal $1,000, and the total required reserves are $100, the amount of the initial deposit.

TABLE 4-7   Fractional Reserve System

	New Deposits (Loans)	Total Deposits	Total Reserve Requirement	Total Loans
Initial depositor	$100.00	$ 100.00	$ 10.00	$ 0.00
Second depositor	90.00	190.00	19.00	90.00
Third depositor	81.00	271.00	27.10	171.00
Fourth depositor	72.90	343.90	34.39	243.90
	.	.	.	.
	.	.	.	.
	.	.	.	.
Final depositor	$ 0.01	$1,000.00	$100.00	$900.00

This simple example shows how a fractional reserve system can be used to expand money through deposits in a system with a single bank. The same sort of change would occur in a banking system that included many banks or intermediaries as long as the excess reserves are used to create loans that are redeposited in the intermediaries. If deposits are withdrawn from the bank, the expansion process reverses, so the money supply would contract according to Equation 4-1.

The U.S. Banking System (Structure)

The U.S. banking system is a fractional reserve system consisting of various *depository* institutions, such as banks and thrifts, chartered either by the federal government or by the state in which they are located. Institutions whose names contain the words *national* or *federal* have federal charters; similarly, institutions whose names contain the word *state* have state charters. Because the U.S. banking system involves the use of both national and state charters, it is referred to as a **dual banking system.**[4] The roots of the current banking structure can be traced to financial developments that occurred early in the history of the nation.

In the early years of its existence, the U.S. economy was agriculturally oriented, with the populace located in somewhat fragmented farming communities. Similarly, banking structures and financial markets were quite segmented, or territorial, in nature. During this period, large communities created self-sufficient banking systems, which often issued their own bank notes that were used as currency, or money, for transactions with local businesses and residents. Only the currencies of the most reliable banks were accepted in other banking communities. Over time, the federal government tried to form a unified banking system by creating a central, or national, bank. Until the Federal Reserve was established in 1913, however, such attempts were not very successful.

Although banking changed dramatically as the United States became more industrialized, the influence of early banking systems remains readily apparent in contemporary banking. Today's banking system includes 7,300 individual, or unit, banking organizations—far fewer than the 12,500 banks that existed at the beginning of the twentieth century and the 31,000 banks that operated in 1920. Many more banks were needed when transportation and communications were insufficient to support an integrated and efficient banking system.

Fewer individual banks might exist today if federal and state regulations enacted from 1900 to 1930 had not restricted the ability of banks to open multiple offices, or branches, especially across state lines. At the time, such legislation was favored by the banking industry because it was believed that the existence of more banks promoted competition—and, therefore, efficiency—in the banking system. Nevertheless, many bankers feared that unrestricted branching would ultimately concentrate financial power in the hands of a few large banks and that such a banking structure would favor industry and commerce at the expense of agriculture and individuals, resulting in the ruin of the nation's financial system.

Even though legislation passed since 1930 has relaxed some of the branching restrictions, the banking system in the United States remains dominated by a large number of individual banks that generally are allowed to branch within the states in which they are located (**intrastate branching**) but are somewhat limited when it comes to branching across state lines (**interstate branching**). During recent decades, however, interest in unrestricted branch banking has increased greatly.

dual banking system
A banking system in which bank chartering exists both at the national and state levels.

intrastate branching
Establishing branch banks within the same state.

interstate branching
Establishing branch banks in more than one state—that is, across state lines.

---

[4]Banking regulations are enacted both at the federal level and at the state level. When a conflict arises between federal and state laws, generally the more restrictive law applies.

In response, Congress has passed, and will continue to examine, legislation that promotes elimination of the barriers that restrict interstate banking.

Even with the barriers to interstate banking, some banking organizations attained quasi-branch banking via bank holding companies, which were developed in the 1950s. A **bank holding company** is a corporation that owns controlling interest in a single bank or multiple banks. Bank holding companies often were allowed to own multiple banks in the same state, and, in some cases, unusual circumstances led to ownership of banks in other states. Thus, although a particular bank was not able to branch across state lines, a bank holding company could effectively achieve branching by operating separate banks in different states.

Another restriction faced by banks relates to the type of business activities they are permitted to undertake. With the enactment of the Banking Act of 1933, also known as the Glass-Steagall Act, banks were prohibited from engaging in activities that were not directly related to banking services. For instance, they could neither have significant ownership in corporations nor help corporations issue stocks and bonds. This law effectively prohibited banks from combining commerce and banking activities. Recent legislation, which we will discuss in more detail later, has since removed some of these restrictions. Banks can now establish nonbank subsidiaries that engage in finance-related activities. In addition, well-run bank holding companies face fewer barriers to integrating banking operations with nonbank activities.

bank holding company
A corporation that owns controlling interest in one or more banks.

Size of Banks

Table 4-8 shows the 10 largest commercial banks in the United States in March 2008. Mergers and acquisitions of large banks have attracted a great deal of interest in recent years. For example, in 1997, NationsBank, which was the fifth largest banking company at the time, acquired Barnett Banks, the twenty-fifth largest banking company, to form the nation's third largest banking company. In 1998, NationsBank became the largest bank in the United States when it acquired BankAmerica, which was the fourth largest bank at the time, to form Bank of America (BOA). And, in 2004, BOA acquired FleetBoston Financial, which further increased its size. Today, it is estimated that BOA has between 15 percent and 20 percent of all deposits in the United States. Banking experts expect such mergers and acquisitions to continue,

TABLE 4-8   Ten Largest Banks in the United States, March 31, 2008

Rank	Bank Name	Location	Charter[a]	Total Assets ($ billions)	Number of U.S. Branches
1	J.P. Morgan Chase Bank	Columbus, OH	National	$1,407.6	3,153
2	Bank of America	Charlotte, NC	National	1,355.2	5,866
3	Citibank	Las Vegas, NV	National	1,292.5	1,075
4	Wachovia Bank	Charlotte, NC	National	665.8	3,468
5	Wells Fargo Bank	Sioux Falls, SD	National	486.9	4,300
6	U.S. Bank	Cincinnati, OH	National	237.3	2,608
7	HSBC Bank USA	Wilmington, DE	National	188.3	451
8	Sun Trust Bank	Atlanta, GA	State	174.7	1,730
9	FIA Card Service (BOA)	Wilmington, DE	National	159.8	0
10	National City Bank	Cleveland, OH	National	152.5	1,530

[a]National = national charter; State = state charter. All banks are members of the Federal Reserve.

Source: Federal Reserve, http://www.federalreserve.gov.

so the rankings of the banks in Table 4-8 most likely will change during the next few years. The trend is clearly toward fewer, but much larger, banks.

Central Banking—The Federal Reserve System

The **Federal Reserve System,** which was established in 1913, is the central banking system charged with managing the monetary policy of the United States. The *Fed* was established by the Federal Reserve Act to reform the U.S. banking system following the Wall Street Panic of 1907, which resulted in financial ruin for much of the country. Even before the 1907 crisis, the U.S. banking system had been plagued by periods of financial panic and was prone to significant bank failures during economic downturns. Thus, when it was originally created, the primary purpose of the Fed was to supervise banking activities to ensure that bank operations would remain stable and fluctuating economic conditions would not cause widespread ruin in the banking industry. Although it still views banking stability as an important goal, the Fed assumed much greater responsibilities as time passed.

Federal Reserve System
The central banking system charged with managing the monetary policy of the United States.

Structure of the Fed

To ensure that control of the banking system did not become consolidated in the hands of a few, the central bank of the United States was created as a *decentralized* network of regional, or district, banks. The Fed includes 12 independent district banks located in major cities throughout the country. The district banks, which have branches in larger cities within their Federal Reserve districts, provide such services as loans and deposits to banks and other financial institutions, but not to individuals. For this reason, the Fed often is referred to as a *banker's bank*. The Fed is also used by the U.S. government for its banking needs. The Treasury maintains a checking account at the Fed, which is used to collect the taxes we pay and to pay government employees and other expenses.

The Fed banks are supervised by a central governing body called the **Board of Governors.** The members of the Board of Governors are appointed by the U.S. president and approved by the Senate. The Board includes seven members, each of whom is appointed to a 14-year term. Although their terms are staggered to expire every 2 years, many members of the Board do not serve full terms, which sometimes allows the incumbent president to appoint a majority of the board.

Board of Governors
The central governing body of the Federal Reserve System.

In addition to the district banks and the Board of Governors, the other important components of the Federal Reserve are the commercial banks and other financial institutions that are members of the Fed, advisory committees that provide various kinds of recommendations to the Board of Governors and the district banks, and the Federal Open Market Committee, which oversees open market operations, the principal instrument used by the Fed to manage monetary policy.

Responsibilities of the Fed

The Federal Reserve System has the following responsibilities:

1. According to the Federal Reserve Act, the Fed should direct the **monetary policy** of the United States "to promote effectively the goals of maximum employment, stable prices, and moderate long-term interest rates." The primary means by which the Fed attempts to achieve these goals is by changing the nation's money supply through the reserves held at banks and other financial institutions. For instance, if the desire is to increase the nation's money supply, the Fed will take actions to provide excess reserves to

monetary policy
The policy by which the Fed influences economic conditions, especially interest rates, by managing the nation's money supply.

FIGURE 4-2   Diagram of Federal Reserve Open Market Operations

I. **Increase the money supply—Fed buys government securities**

Federal Reserve

Make payment—increase bank reserves

(money flows to the public)

Receive securities from bank/dealer

Bank of Primary Dealer

II. **Decrease the money supply—Fed sells government securities**

Federal Reserve

Receive payment—decrease bank reserves

(money flows from the public)

Deliver securities to bank/dealer

Bank of Primary Dealer

open market operations
Operations in which the Fed buys or sells Treasury securities to expand or contract the U.S. money supply.

primary dealer
A dealer that has established a relationship with the Fed to buy and sell government securities; used by the Fed to modify the money supply.

reserve requirement
Funds that a financial institution must retain "in the vault" to back customers' deposits.

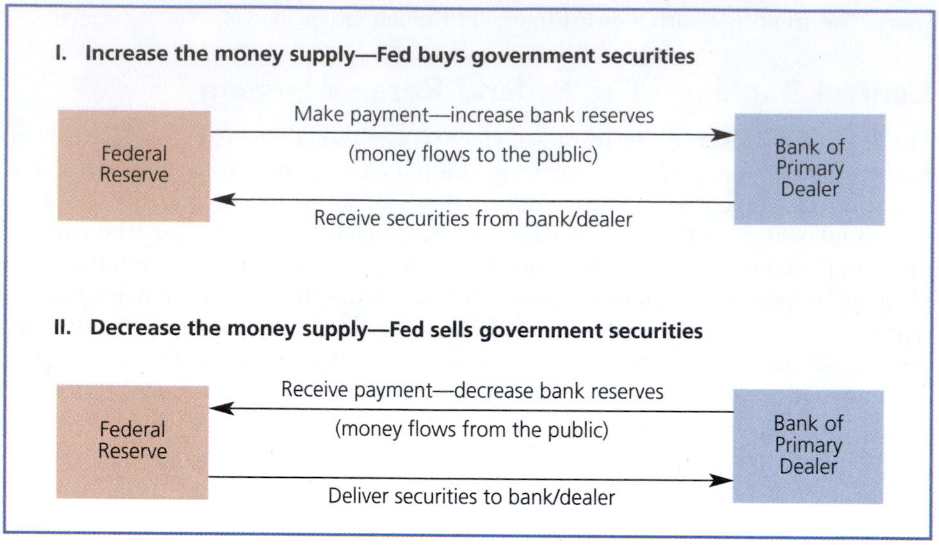

the banking system, which will be channeled into the economy through loans made to individuals and businesses. Because the U.S. banking system is characterized by a fractional reserve system, a $1 addition to reserves will create more than $1 in new loans, or money, in the economy; a contraction will have the opposite effect. The Fed affects reserves in the banking system by using its lending policy, by changing reserve requirements, and by buying and selling U.S. government securities.

The most important tool used by the Fed to manage the supply of money is **open market operations,** which involve buying or selling U.S. Treasury securities to change bank reserves (see Figure 4-2). When the Fed wants to increase the money supply, it purchases government securities from **primary dealers** who have established trading relationships with the Federal Reserve. The Fed pays for the securities by sending funds to the banks where the primary dealers have accounts. This action increases the deposit balances of the dealers, which in turn increases the overall reserves of the banking system. Banks have additional funds to lend, so the money supply increases. The Fed carries out "normal" open market operations on a continuous basis to maintain economic activity within defined limits, and it shifts its open market strategies toward heavier-than-normal buying or selling to make more substantial adjustments.

The amount by which the money supply can change depends on the existing **reserve requirement.** Currently, a reserve requirement applies only to checking (transactions) deposits—this requirement is 10 percent.[5] Thus, for every $1 of government securities purchased through open market operations, the money supply can potentially increase by $9 = $1(1 − 0.10)/0.10 (see Equation 4-1). If the Fed wanted to tighten the money supply, the process would be reversed: government securities would be sold to primary dealers, whose bank accounts would then be decreased.

The Fed can also affect the supply of money by changing the reserve requirement. Consider what would happen if the reserve requirement was

---

[5]Actually, the first $7.0 million of deposits is not subject to reserve requirements, transaction deposits up to $47.6 million are subject to a 3 percent reserve requirement, and all transaction deposits in excess of $47.6 million are subject to a 10 percent reserve requirement.

increased from 10 percent to 20 percent. After the change, 80 percent (rather than the previous 90 percent) of deposits could be loaned to individuals and businesses. How would this change affect the money supply? To find the answer, let's return to the example we used earlier to describe a fractional reserve system, where the reserve requirement was 10 percent. Because the bank needs to hold only a fraction of its deposits as reserves, we discovered that the initial deposit of $100 could be multiplied via the lending process to expand the money supply by an additional $900, such that the total funds in our simple one-bank system were $1,000. If the reserve requirement is set at 20 percent rather than 10 percent, the total funds available would decrease to $500. The $100 now would be able to expand the money supply by $400 = ($100 − $20)/0.2.

As the preceding example illustrates, when the Fed changes the reserve requirement, it has an immediate effect on the ability of banks to lend funds, because it alters the amount of excess reserves in the system. Unlike open market operations, this method is not used by the Fed to manage the money supply on a day-to-day basis. Indeed, reserve requirements change only infrequently.

Another tool used by the Fed to direct monetary policy is the **discount rate,** which is the interest rate that banks and other financial institutions pay when they borrow from a Fed district bank to cover temporary shortages in their required reserves. Changes in the discount rate affect the amounts that banks are willing to borrow, which ultimately affect the money supply. For example, if the Fed lowers the discount rate, banks would tend to depend more on loans from the Fed to meet temporary reserve shortfalls. Consequently, more loans could be made to individuals and businesses than in a situation in which the discount rate was higher.

> **discount rate**
> The rate the Fed charges for loans it makes to banks to meet temporary shortages in required reserves.

In reality, the discount rate is related to the market rates on other types of debt, such as Treasury securities and short-term loans made at commercial banks. Thus, a discount rate change generally is the result, rather than the cause, of movements in other rates. This instrument is neither as effective nor as prominent as open market operations for managing monetary policy.

2. The Federal Reserve is charged with *regulating* and *supervising* depository financial institutions operating in the United States. It monitors such institutions through audits and "bank examinations" to ensure that the U.S. banking system remains sound. In addition, the Fed authorizes bank mergers and any nonbanking activities undertaken by bank holding companies.

3. One important service offered by the Fed is the *check-clearing operations* provided by its payment system, which clears millions of paper checks and electronic payments each day. The Fed's payment system helps ensure that the funds represented by checks or other payment mechanisms are transferred as efficiently as possible among various financial institutions.

The importance of the Fed and its influence on the financial markets cannot be overemphasized. Decisions made by the Fed generally cause significant movements in the financial markets. For example, when the Fed decides to increase interest rates, the markets decline—often substantially.

Deregulation in the U.S. Banking Industry

A great deal of deregulation has occurred in the financial services industry during recent decades. The tenor of the industry has changed significantly since major deregulation began in the late 1970s and the early 1980s. During the 1990s, banking deregulation was fairly fast paced. Although the pace has slowed in recent years, deregulation in the financial services industry is expected to continue in the future. The most influential legislation in banking since 1980 arguably can be traced to the three acts described next.

Depository Institutions Deregulatory and Monetary Control Act (DIDMCA) of 1980

When it was enacted, the DIDMCA was considered perhaps the most significant piece of legislation in the banking industry since the mid-1930s, when most of the original legislation restricting banking activities was passed. The act's general purpose was to improve competition among financial institutions for the benefit of customers and to extend the monetary control of the Federal Reserve. To improve competition, the banking industry began a deregulation process. As part of this process, financial institutions, such as commercial banks, thrifts, and credit unions, were allowed to offer a greater variety of deposit and credit products than before. For example, the act allowed thrifts to provide services previously offered only by banks, and vice versa. Also, ceilings on interest rates were phased out, and the ceiling on insured deposits increased from $40,000 to $100,000. The DIDMCA strengthened the power of the Fed to control monetary policy by requiring all banks and thrifts—even nonmembers—to maintain reserves established by the Fed.

When the DIDMCA was enacted, observers believed that barriers to branch banking, including interstate branching, would soon fall. In fact, in most states branch banking was permitted at least in a limited form. Some states had already entered into or had plans to enter into interstate banking arrangements with other states (called reciprocal banking).

In 1982, Congress passed the Garn–St. Germain Act. This legislation allowed banks and thrifts to offer money market accounts as well as more similar products. A by-product of this act was that some financial institutions were able to branch "across state lines," because their expanded services allowed them to sidestep legal restrictions. That is, in some cases a commercial bank was no longer considered to be simply a bank.

Reigle-Neal Interstate Banking and Branching Efficiency Act of 1994

The Reigle-Neal Interstate Banking Act effectively eliminated barriers that restricted banks and other financial services organizations from expanding geographically. It allowed bank holding companies to acquire banks in any state—that is, to branch into other states—starting in 1997, as long as the state in question did not pass new legislation to prohibit such practices.

Gramm-Leach-Bliley Act of 1999

In effect, this legislation repealed many of the restrictions on banking activities that were established by the Glass-Steagall Act of 1933, which prohibited banks from engaging in activities that were not traditionally considered "normal" banking activities. In particular, the Glass-Steagall Act defined the services that banks could and couldn't offer; banks were prohibited from engaging in activities related to investments, investment banking, insurance, and many other financial services not related to depository and lending functions. The primary reason for this restriction was the belief held by many politicians and regulators that the Great Depression of the late 1920s and early 1930s was either caused by or compounded by banks' activities; before 1933, banks were permitted to offer many services, including investment banking, which some believed presented serious conflicts of interest.

The Gramm-Leach-Bliley Act expanded the powers of banks by abolishing the major restrictions contained in the Glass-Steagall Act. It permits qualified banks to engage in (1) investment banking and related activities, (2) insurance sales and underwriting, and (3) nonfinancial activities that do not substantially increase the risks of the institutions.

Recent Legislation

Much of the legilation that has been passed since 2001 focuses on the protection of bank assets from unethical behavior and terrorist acts. For example, the Sarbanes-Oxley Act of 2002 requires businesses, including financial institutions, to maintain certain standards of corporate governance and financial responsibility. Although this is not specifically banking legislation, the act clearly affects how financial institutions are operated. We will discuss the Sarbanes-Oxley Act in greater detail in Chapter 6.

Along with the Bank Secrecy Act, which was passed in 1970, the USA Patriot Act, which was passed in 2001, requires financial institutions to report suspicious financial activity to the appropriate authorities. In combination, these two acts are intended to stem both money laundering and the funding of terrorist threats to the United States.

U.S. Banking in the Future

Although the banking system of the United States has changed significantly during recent decades, additional changes are certain to emerge in the future. The banking industry has always been heavily regulated, primarily to ensure the safety of the financial institutions and protect depositors. Unfortunately, many of these regulations have tended to impede the free flow of funds around the country and thus have proved detrimental to the efficiency of the financial markets. As mentioned in the previous section, recent legislative changes have removed some of the competitive obstacles created by earlier regulations, and more changes are forthcoming.

During the past several decades, deregulation of depository intermediaries has erased many of the differences between such institutions. For the most part, post-1980 deregulation efforts have encouraged increased competition among various types of financial intermediaries by eliminating some restrictions on the products offered by intermediaries such as commercial banks and savings institutions as well as some limitations on the locations where intermediaries can do business. The move toward deregulation in the financial services industry has led to two major changes: (1) intermediaries have become much more similar in their operations and (2) the number of intermediaries has decreased because legislation has facilitated mergers and acquisitions and branching. The effects of deregulation are evident in the data shown in Table 4-9. The number of commercial banks in the United States has decreased from approximately 31,000 in 1920 to fewer than 7,300 in 2007. Over the same period, the number of bank branches has increased from fewer than 2,000 to approximately 79,000.

The trend in the United States today is toward huge financial services corporations, which own banks, S&Ls, investment banking houses, insurance companies, pension plan operations, and mutual funds, and which have branches across the country and even around the world. Interestingly, at one time, Sears, Roebuck—one

TABLE 4-9   Number of Banks and Branches in the United States, 1900–2007

Year	Banks	Branches	Year	Banks	Branches
			1960	13,126	10,556
2007	7,283	78,867	1950	13,446	4,832
2005	7,526	73,441	1940	13,442	3,489
2000	8,375	62,860	1930	22,500	4,000
1990	12,347	50,406	1920[a]	31,000	1,200
1980	14,434	38,738	1910[a]	25,000	<1,000
1970	13,511	21,839	1900[a]	12,500	<1,000

[a]These figures were estimated from graphs.

Sources: *FDIC Historical Statistics on Banking,* Federal Deposit Insurance Corporation, http://www4.fdic.gov/ hsob/SelectRpt.asp?EntryTyp=10, and *Federal Reserve Chart Book on Financial and Business Statistics, Historical Supplement.*

of the largest retailing organizations in the United States—owned a large insurance company (Allstate Insurance), a leading brokerage and investment banking firm (named Dean Witter at the time), the largest real estate brokerage firm (Coldwell Banker), a mortgage company (Sears Mortgage), a huge credit card business, and a host of other related businesses. By the end of 1994, however, Sears had sold or spun off most of these financial services businesses in an effort to pare down its own operations. Other financial service corporations, most of which started in one area and have now diversified to cover wide financial spectra, include Transamerica, Merrill Lynch, American Express, and Citigroup. In the future, we should see many finance-related companies that have traditionally focused on a single area, such as insurance or real estate, moving into related businesses. In recent times, Congress has shown a willingness to permit financial services organizations greater latitude in the products they offer, and it appears that such sentiment will continue.

In addition to the consolidation of financial institutions and related companies into large mega financial organizations, many experts believe that the financial services organizations will enter business relationships with other industries, including manufacturing and other nonfinancial industries. Such combinations will position U.S. financial services organizations to become better able to compete with international financial services organizations (see the discussion in the next section). At the same time, to ensure customer confidence and the safety of financial services organizations, the U.S. government will surely keep a close eye on the evolution of banking organizations into other industries. And, given recent scandals involving corporate executives (for example, Enron and WorldCom), the executives of financial services organizations will be "under the microscope" when making decisions concerning growth and expansion into nonfinancial areas. The future of banking (financial services) should be very dynamic.

Self-Test Questions

Explain how money is created in a fractional reserve banking system.

Why do so many banks exist in the United States today?

What are the primary roles played by the Federal Reserve System?

What effect do you think regulatory changes and competitive pressures will have on financial institutions in the future?

INTERNATIONAL BANKING

Two notable factors distinguish the banking system in the United States from the banking structures in other countries, both of which can be traced to the regulatory climate that has existed historically in the United States. Generally speaking, U.S. financial institutions have been much more heavily regulated and faced greater limitations with regard to branching activity and nonbanking business relationships than have their foreign counterparts. Such regulations have imposed an organizational structure and competitive environment that have long curbed the ability of individual banking organizations in the United States to grow in size.

First, the U.S. banking system traditionally has been characterized by a large number of independent banks of various sizes rather than a few very large banks, which might exist if branch banking had not been restricted in the past. For that reason, the country has nearly 17,000 individual banks, credit unions, and thrift institutions. In contrast, the banking companies of nearly every other country in the world have been allowed to branch with few, if any, limitations, and as a result, their banking systems include far fewer individual, or unit, institutions than exist in the United States. Japan, for example, has fewer than 160 such institutions, there are about 20 Australian-owned banks (four of which are considered large commercial banks), and Canada has only 70 chartered banks (seven of which operate nationally and internationally). Even India, which has a population nearly four times larger than that of the United States, has fewer than 300 individual banks (about 4 percent of the total number of U.S. banks). In India and other countries, however, each bank generally has many branches. For instance, the State Bank of India alone has more than 13,000 offices (branches).

Second, most foreign banks are allowed to engage in nonbanking business activities whereas U.S. banks' nonbanking activities have been severely restricted until recently. Developed countries such as the United Kingdom, France, Germany, and Switzerland, to name a few, permit banking firms and commercial firms to interact without restriction; banking firms can own commercial firms, and vice versa. Other countries, including Canada, Japan, and Spain, allow the mixing of banking firms and commercial firms with some restrictions. In aggregate, banks in countries that permit banking and commerce to be combined account for approximately 70 percent of the world's banking assets. Regulations that restrict the nonbanking activities of U.S. banks have traditionally put these institutions at a competitive disadvantage internationally. As Congress has demonstrated, however, the legislative trend is to remove existing "competitive restraints," which should allow U.S. institutions to better compete in the global financial arena.

Because foreign banks are less heavily regulated and must comply with fewer restrictions concerning the types of business activities they can pursue than do their U.S. counterparts, they often engage in numerous aspects of multilayer financial deals. For example, a foreign bank might use its investment banking division to help a business raise funds through a new stock issue, even though the bank owns shares of stock and is the primary lender to the company. Being able to operate as a company's lender, owner, investment banker, and insurer permits foreign banking organizations to offer financial products that previously were not available to U.S. banking organizations. In addition, because a single bank can offer such financial products as a package, it is possible to reduce the aggregate costs associated with financial services.

Because they do not have to deal with the restrictive regulations and other limitations on banking activities found in the United States, many foreign banking organizations are large, one-stop financial service institutions. Table 4-10 shows the 10 largest banks in the world at the end of 2006. *At that time,* Bank of America was slightly larger than J.P. Morgan Chase; in 2008, J.P. Morgan Chase was slightly larger (see Table 4-8). As the table shows, Bank of America was ranked as the tenth largest

TABLE 4-10   Ten Largest Banks in the World, 2006

Rank	Bank Name	Country	Total Assets ($ billions)[a]
1	UBS AG	Switzerland	$1,963.2
2	Barclays Bank	United Kingdom	1,951.0
3	The Royal Bank of Scotland	United Kingdom	1,705.7
4	Deutsche Bank AG	Germany	1,485.0
5	BNP Paribas SA	France	1,483.9
6	The Bank of Tokyo-Mitsubishi UFJ	Japan	1,362.6
7	ABN AMRO Holding NV	Netherlands	1,301.5
8	Société Générale	France	1,261.7
9	Crédit Agricole SA	France	1,252.0
10	Bank of America	United States	1,196.1

[a]Represents the assets of the banks at the end of 2006, so the dollar amount of the total assets given for Bank of America does not match the amount in Table 4-8, which shows the 10 largest banks in the United States as of March 31, 2008.

Source: "Top 50 Banks in the World," All Banks, http://www.allbanks.org/top_banks.html.

bank in the world, and the world rankings of J.P. Morgan Chase, Citibank, Wachovia, and Wells Fargo Bank, which were the second through the fifth largest banks in the United States, were 11, 15, 41, and 50, respectively, at the end of 2006. Although these banks are large by U.S. standards, clearly they do not dominate foreign banks.

It should not be surprising that foreign banks dominate international banking activities. Certainly, having to cope with fewer restrictions has helped these banks attain such dominance. In addition, such institutions have been involved in international banking much longer than have U.S. banks. The worldwide presence of foreign banks can be documented as far back as the twelfth century, when banks from Italy dominated international trade—long before the United States became a country. In fact, U.S. banks were not permitted to have operations outside the country until 1913, when the Federal Reserve Act was passed. Until some 40 years ago, however, few U.S. banks operated internationally.

The Federal Reserve Act originally allowed banks with certain qualifications to engage in banking outside the United States. The Edge Act, which was approved in 1919, finally allowed U.S. banks to operate subsidiary organizations in other countries and to offer banking and financial services beyond the traditional "American" banking activities, including investment in stocks of foreign companies. In 1981, the Fed made another move to help U.S. banks compete for international funds by allowing them to create International Banking Facilities (IBFs). IBFs take foreign deposits that are not subject to the same restrictions as domestic deposits, such as reserve requirements and deposit insurance (FDIC). An IBF is not a separate banking organization, but rather a method of accounting for international deposits separately from domestic deposits. In reality, this type of operation consists of a set of financial statements associated with international deposits that is kept separate from the other financial statements of the bank and that is subject to different restrictions.

Whether a bank establishes an Edge Act organization or an IBF, its international banking activities are still subject to limitations imposed by the Fed. And, although U.S. banks generally face fewer restrictions in their overseas operations than they do in their domestic operations, the overseas organizations generally are not allowed to engage in all business activities available to the "native" banks against which they must compete.

The presence of foreign banks in the United States has grown significantly in recent decades. To ensure that foreign banking organizations do not enjoy an unfair competitive edge, Congress has enacted regulations that specifically apply to foreign banks operating in the United States. The International Banking Act (IBA), passed in 1978, essentially obligates foreign banking organizations to follow the same rules that apply to U.S. banks. The Foreign Bank Supervision Enhancement Act (FBSEA), passed in 1991, requires foreign banks to get the Fed's approval before establishing offices in the United States.

Even with the restrictions on U.S. banking operations carried out overseas, the presence of U.S. banks in international banking has grown rapidly in recent years. At the same time, the limitations that overseas banking operations face in the United States have not discouraged the entry of foreign banks, especially in California, where large Japanese banks have claimed significant market shares. As the world continues to become more globally oriented, so will the banking industry—U.S. banks are becoming more important internationally, and foreign banks are increasing their presence in the United States.

Self-Test Questions

How do U.S. financial institutions differ from their counterparts in other countries?

What two factors distinguish the banking system in the United States from banking structures in other countries?

What changes are needed for U.S. financial institutions to become more competitive with financial institutions in other countries? Do you think such changes will occur in the near future?

Ethical Dilemma

Anything for (a) BUC?

The Bank of Universal City (BUC) is a medium-size state banking organization that is located in Louisiana. BUC offers a good variety of products and services, including checking and savings accounts, a bill-paying service, credit cards, business consulting, insurance, and investing services. The CEO of BUC, Chuck Charles, has publicly stated that he intends to grow the bank's assets by 15 percent annually for the next 5 years. Although 15 percent is a fairly robust growth rate, it is not an impossible goal for BUC. In fact, last year, which was the first year the plan was implemented, the bank's assets grew nearly 20 percent. However, much of the growth occurred because there was a significant increase in population when a large manufacturing firm relocated to Universal City 18 months ago.

With only 3 weeks remaining in the current fiscal year, Mr. Charles is concerned that actual growth for the year will fall well short of what is needed to keep the bank on track to achieve its overall growth projections. As a result, Mr. Charles has instructed the vice president in charge of Univest, which is the investment management division of BUC, to find a way to increase the amount of investment funds the bank currently manages.

As the assistant to the vice president of Univest, you are responsible for sales and thus get paid a commission for the funds the division manages. Your boss and the CEO of BUC have given you names (leads) of persons and organizations they think are good prospects for Univest. After contacting the prospects, you discover that the only one who seems interested is Rudolph Radcliff, the head of a radical religious organization based in Universal City. It has been rumored that the

continues

organization, which is called Righteous Freedom Choice (RFC), funds foundations based in countries that are not friendly to the United States. It is suspected that some of the organizations RFC sponsors support terrorist activities around the world. A few days ago, a colleague told you that he thought RFC would be moving its funds to a new investment organization because the firm that currently manages the funds refused to continue as its investment adviser; it was discovered that the funds had been received from organizations that are involved in illicit activities. This information was reported to your colleague during a conversation that he had with two prominent businesspersons at a charity gala the previous weekend. Your colleague noted, however, that the tone of the conversation suggested that the two businesspersons were not on friendly terms with Mr. Radcliff.

When your colleague relayed this information to you, you did not ask questions, such as the names of the businesspersons, because you didn't expect to be involved with RFC. Now, you need to make a decision as to whether to pursue RFC's funds to help Univest and BUC meet their growth objectives. Unfortunately, the colleague who told you the information about RFC is on vacation for the next few weeks and cannot be contacted to answer questions you might have. Univest's sales have been stagnant this year. As a result, if sales don't increase substantially during the next few weeks, the commission you earn will be much lower than normal. And, if your commission does not increase, you and your spouse will have to consider moving from the luxurious house that you purchased 5 years ago. What should you do?

CHAPTER PRINCIPLES –The Answers

To summarize the key concepts, let's answer the questions that were posed at the beginning of the chapter:

- **What is a financial intermediary and what role does a financial intermediary play in the financial markets? Why are there so many different types of intermediaries?** A financial intermediary is an organization that takes "deposits" and uses the money to generate returns by creating loans or other types of investments. There are many different types of financial intermediaries because individuals have different needs, and different intermediaries provide different services for individuals. Because intermediaries facilitate the process by which borrowers and lenders (investors) are brought together, they help to lower costs and provide the best rates to borrowers and lenders; thus, the standard of living in the economy is higher than if the intermediaries did not exist.

- **What functions do financial intermediaries perform? Why were different types of intermediaries created?** The primary function of financial intermediaries is to facilitate the transfer of funds from savers (investors or lenders) to borrowers. Financial institutions, whether they are called banks, credit unions, pension funds, or some other name, help bring together borrowers and lenders. Intermediaries also provide other services, such as check clearing, trust services, safe-deposit boxes, and so forth.

  Many of the types of financial intermediaries that exist today were started more than 200 years ago when the United States was an agrarian (farming) society and long-distance travel was difficult. As a result, financial intermediaries were created to meet specific needs of different groups of people in various locations. For example, commercial banks originally catered to businesses in urban areas, savings and loan associations were established to help farmers build homes and storage facilities, and so forth. Today, however, the customers of most financial intermediaries are diverse such that no particular group is excluded from doing business.

- **What is a fractional reserve system?** According to the fractional reserve system, banks and other financial institutions do not have to retain 100 percent of the funds that customers deposit. Because only a "fraction" of the amount that is deposited needs to be held in reserves, financial intermediaries expand the money supply when amounts in excess of what is required to be held in reserve are used to create loans such as mortgages, automobile loans, and so forth.

- **What are the major characteristics of the U.S. banking system?** The U.S. banking system is based on the fractional reserve system described earlier. Because banks can operate with either a state charter or a federal charter, the U.S. banking system is referred to as a dual banking system. Until fairly recently, the activities of banks have been restricted by legislation such that there are many more independent banks in the United States than in other countries. Although not nearly as severe as in the past, today banks still face some restrictions with respect to both interstate banking and the types of financial services that can be offered. The current trend in the United States is to form mega banks through mergers and acquisitions. Such banking organizations as Bank of America, J.P. Morgan Chase, and Citigroup have grown to "mega bank" status to position themselves to better compete internationally.

- **What is the function of the Federal Reserve?** The Federal Reserve represents the central banking system of the United States. The primary function of the Fed is to direct the monetary policy of the United States. The Fed manages the supply of money by buying and selling U.S. government securities, which is termed *open market operations*. When the Fed wants to decrease interest rates, it will buy securities from investors to put more money in the economy, and vice versa.

  Other responsibilities of the Fed include managing existing reserve requirements of financial institutions. The Fed can change reserve requirements when needed to affect the money supply. The Fed also manages the money supply of the United States by setting the discount rate, which is the rate at which financial institutions can borrow funds from the district banks. In addition to managing the money supply, the Fed is charged with regulating and supervising financial intermediaries that operate in the United States.

- **How do banks in the United States differ from foreign banks?** Most banks in the United States are smaller in size and offer fewer types of services than their foreign counterparts. Past regulations that restricted how and where banks and other financial institutions can operate are responsible for the current structure of the U.S. banking system.

The concepts presented in this chapter should help you better understand financial intermediaries and why different financial institutions exist. If you understand the basic concepts contained in this chapter, you should be able to make more informed decisions about which intermediary to use when you need a loan and which one to use when you want to save some of your money.

CHAPTER PRINCIPLES
–Personal Finance

- **How can knowledge (even a slight amount) of financial intermediaries help me make better decisions about my personal finances?** Different financial intermediaries specialize in different types of financial products. For example, commercial banks primarily service businesses, whereas credit unions primarily service consumers. Generally, you can find better rates and varieties of products/services at financial intermediaries that specialize in the particular products/services you need. For example, savings and loan associations often have better mortgage rates than commercial banks, and credit unions generally offer better rates on automobile loans than either of these institutions. In addition, intermediaries that specialize in particular financial products are better able to service those products because they employ persons who are most familiar with all aspects of those products.

- **How can general knowledge of how the Federal Reserve operates help me make better decisions about my personal finances?** Recently, the Fed lowered interest rates, and in the future, actions taken by the Fed will most certainly change interest rates again. Consumers (and businesses) often try to guess whether the Fed is going to change interest rates, and in which direction, before making decisions about borrowing and investing. Consider, for example, what you would do if you want to buy a house within the next 12 months and you think that the Fed is going to take actions during the year that will lower interest rates. Should you get a mortgage to buy a house now or wait until the Fed lowers rates? Although open market operations directly affect the rates on U.S. Treasury securities, when the Fed acts to change interest rates, there is a "ripple effect" throughout the financial markets. As a result, if the Fed takes actions to lower interest rates on U.S. Treasury securities, rates on other loans, including mortgages, will decrease as well. Thus, you should wait to get a mortgage until the Fed acts to lower rates. On the other hand, if you want to invest money under the circumstances given here, you should invest today and "lock in" a higher rate than you could if you wait for the Fed to lower rates. By timing when you borrow, you can get good rates on loans; by timing when you invest, you can earn higher returns.

QUESTIONS

4-1   What are financial intermediaries, and what economic functions do they perform?

4-2   In what ways do financial intermediaries improve the standard of living in an economy?

4-3   What would happen to the standard of living in the United States if people lost faith in the safety of our financial institutions? Why?

4-4   The federal government has (1) encouraged the development of the savings and loan industry, (2) virtually forced the S&L industry to make long-term, fixed-interest-rate mortgages, and (3) forced S&Ls to obtain most of their capital as deposits that are withdrawable on demand.

    a. Would the S&Ls be better off if rates are expected to increase or to decrease in the future?

    b. Would the S&L industry be better off if the individual institutions sold their mortgages to federal agencies and then collected servicing fees or if the institutions held the mortgages that they originated?

4-5   Name some of the various types of financial intermediaries described in the chapter and indicate the primary reason(s) each was created.

4-6   How has deregulation of the financial services industry affected the makeup of financial intermediaries? How do you think intermediaries' characteristics will change in the future?

4-7   How do banking organizations in the United States differ from banking organizations in other countries? Why are they different?

4-8   How is money created in a banking system that has fractional reserve requirements (that is, a fractional reserve system)?

4-9   Describe the open market operations undertaken by the Federal Reserve. What type of trades would the Fed make if it wanted to increase interest rates?

4-10   How would funds—that is, the money supply—in the United States be affected if the Federal Reserve increases reserve requirements? Give an example.

SELF-TEST PROBLEMS

Solutions appear in Appendix B.

ST-1   Define each of the following terms: **Key Terms**

    a. Financial intermediary; financial intermediation

    b. Commercial bank; thrift institution; credit union

    c. Mutual fund; money market mutual fund

    d. Pension fund

    e. Fractional reserve system; excess reserves

    f. Dual banking system

    g. Branch banking; bank holding company

    h. Federal Reserve System; Board of Governors

    i. Monetary policy; open market operations

ST-2   Assume that the reserve requirement in the United States is 10 percent on   **Money Supply**
all deposits at financial institutions that take deposits. Also, assume that excess reserves do not exist in these institutions—as soon as reserves become excess, they are loaned out.

    a. If the Fed wants to increase the money supply by $110 billion, should it buy or sell Treasury securities? In what amount?

    b. If the Fed wants to decrease the money supply by $50 billion, should it buy or sell Treasury securities? In what amount?

PROBLEMS

4-1   Deposits in all financial institutions equal $2 trillion. The total reserves held   **Reserve Requirements**
by these institutions are $240 billion, $100 billion of which is in excess of reserve requirements.

    a. What is the percentage reserve requirement?

    b. What would the percentage reserve requirement have to be to maintain the existing amount of reserves ($240 billion) but eliminate excess reserves?

    c. What would happen to deposits at all financial institutions if the existing excess reserves were eliminated? Assume that elimination of excess reserves affects deposits only.

4-2   Through its open market operations, the Federal Reserve recently increased   **Effect of Deposit Increase**
deposits at financial institutions by $90 billion. If the reserve requirement for all deposits is 8 percent, what is the maximum effect that the Fed's actions can have on total deposits?

Effect of Reserve Requirements   **4-3**   Compute the maximum change in total deposits that would result if deposits at financial institutions were immediately *increased* by $120 billion, and the reserve requirement applicable to all deposits was _____.

   a. 5 percent

   b. 10 percent

   c. 50 percent

   d. 100 percent

Effect of Reserve Requirements   **4-4**   Compute the maximum change in total deposits that would result if deposits at financial institutions were immediately *decreased* by $120 billion, and the reserve requirement applicable to all deposits was _____.

   a. 5 percent

   b. 10 percent

   c. 50 percent

   d. 100 percent

Change in Reserves   **4-5**   The Federal Reserve has decided that interest rates need to be increased to maintain relatively low inflation in the economy. To accomplish this goal, the Fed has determined that the money supply needs to decrease by $188 billion. It wants to implement this decrease by working through reserves at financial institutions. Assume that the current reserve requirement is 6 percent and applies to all deposits. By how much must reserves be decreased for the Fed to accomplish its goal?

Reserve Requirement   **4-6**   Assume that the reserve requirement is 15 percent for transaction deposits and 4 percent for nontransaction deposits. Compute the reserve requirement for a bank that has $340 billion deposited in transaction accounts and $120 billion deposited in nontransaction accounts.

Excess Reserves   **4-7**   It has been determined that, in aggregate, financial institutions with depository accounts currently hold excess reserves equal to $3 billion—that is, they hold $3 billion more than is necessary to meet the reserve requirements associated with existing deposits. The reserve requirement applicable to *all* deposits is 15 percent. Assume that changes in reserves held by financial institutions affect deposits only (that is, amounts lent out are always redeposited in the financial institutions).

   a. All else being equal, what would be the effect on deposits if financial institutions immediately eliminated all of their excess reserves?

   b. All else being equal, what would be the effect on deposits if financial institutions adjusted their reserves so that excess reserves decreased to $1.2 billion?

   c. Describe the effects that either of the above actions would have on interest rates in the financial markets.

Bank Deposits and Reserve Requirements   **4-8**   According to statistics provided by the Federal Reserve, total reserves of commercial banks currently equal $45.4 billion. Required reserves are $45.1 billion, so excess reserves total approximately $300 million. The reserve requirement is 10 percent on transaction deposits, which include accounts that offer unlimited checking privileges, and there is no reserve requirement on time deposits. Nontransaction deposits currently amount to $600 billion. Assume that changes in reserves held by banks affect transaction deposits only.

   a. According to the information given in the problem, determine the total amount of transaction deposits held in commercial banks.

b. What are total deposits—transaction and nontransaction—at commercial banks?

c. What would happen to deposits if the Fed mandated that commercial banks eliminate their excess reserves?

d. How much would total required reserves be if total deposits remained at the level computed in part (b), but the Fed imposed a 2 percent reserve requirement on nontransaction deposits and maintained the same 10 percent requirement on transaction deposits?

e. Would the existing reserves be sufficient to meet reserve requirements if the Fed imposed a 2 percent requirement for both transaction deposits and existing nontransaction deposits?

4-9   In recent years, the Fed has shown a willingness to decrease existing reserve requirements. Assume that the transaction deposits at banks and other financial institutions total $900 billion and that a reserve requirement of 10 percent applies only to these deposits. Also assume that financial institutions never have excess reserves and all monies that they lend are deposited in transaction accounts (that is, no funds are held as cash or deposited in nontransaction accounts).

Reserve Requirements

a. By what *dollar* amount will transactions deposits increase if the Fed reduces the reserve requirement to 8 percent?

b. By what *percentage* will transaction deposits increase if the Fed changes the reserve requirement to 8 percent?

c. How will transaction deposits change if the Fed increases the reserve requirement to 12 percent?

Integrative Problem

4-10   Assume that you recently graduated with a degree in finance and have just reported to work as an investment adviser at the firm of Balik and Kiefer Inc. Your first assignment is to explain the roles financial intermediaries play in the U.S. banking system to Michelle Delatorre, a professional tennis player who has just come to the United States from Chile. Delatorre is a highly ranked tennis player who expects to invest substantial amounts of money through Balik and Kiefer. She is also extremely bright, and, therefore, she would like to understand in general terms what will happen to her money. Your boss has developed the following questions, which you must answer to help explain the nature of financial intermediaries and the U.S. banking system to Ms. Delatorre.

Financial Intermediaries

a. What is a *financial intermediary?* What is the *financial intermediation process?*

b. What *roles* do financial intermediaries fulfill? How have intermediaries helped improve our standard of living as well as the efficiency of the financial markets?

c. What are the different *types* of financial intermediaries? Give some characteristics that differentiate the various types of intermediaries.

d. Describe the banking system found in the United States. What role does the Federal Reserve play in the U.S. banking system?

e. How does the U.S. banking system differ from banking systems in other countries?

f. How has the U.S. banking system changed in recent years? What are the arguments for and against such changes? What changes are expected in the future?

g. How can Ms. Delatorre utilize the services provided by financial intermediaries?

The Cost of Money (Interest Rates)

CHAPTER 5

A MANAGERIAL PERSPECTIVE

During the period from 2000 through 2004—that is, the beginning of the twenty-first century—for the most part, interest rates trended downward. For example, at the beginning of 2000, the rates on 3-month Treasury bills and 20-year Treasury bonds were 5.4 percent and 6.7 percent, respectively. At the beginning of 2002, the rates on the same investments had dropped to 1.7 percent and 5.8 percent, respectively. And, at the beginning of 2004, the rates had dropped further to 0.9 percent and 5.0 percent, respectively. One reason rates decreased during this period was the recession the U.S. economy experienced during 2001. In the years following the recession, the "investment" confidence of businesses and individuals was fairly low, so there was not much demand for funds to finance such investments as new growth in business or replacement of worn-out assets. Because rates were considered "too low," the Federal Reserve decided to increase rates. From July through December 2004, the Fed increased interest rates six times, such that the rate on 3-month Treasury bills climbed to 2.4 percent. Fearing excessive economic growth and to control inflation, the Fed continued to increase interest rates throughout 2005 and during the first half of 2006, such that the rates on 3-month T-bills and 20-year T-bonds rose to 5 percent and 5.3 percent, respectively. However, the economy began to slow down, and, as a result, the

Fed tried to stimulate the economy by decreasing interest rates at the end of 2007 and the beginning of 2008. At the time we write this book in May 2008, the rate on 3-month T-bills was under 2 percent and the rate on 20-year T-bonds was about 4.6 percent.

Other factors that affected market rates at the beginning of the twenty-first century included the "beating" that technology stocks took in the stock markets, which resulted in a significant loss of value in the technology industry, uncertainty generated by news that a global economic crisis was eminent, and disclosures that the executives of some large U.S. firms approved the use of, or ignored, unethical accounting practices their firms were using to "cook the books." These factors resulted in investors losing confidence in the financial markets, and thus shifting their funds to what they considered safer havens, such as certificates of deposit and savings accounts at banks and savings and loan associations.

When the economy slipped into the 2001 recession and financial markets faltered, companies slowed expansion and borrowed less. To encourage a reversal of this trend and to attempt to prop up a declining economy, the Federal Reserve cut interest rates. The actions both of the Fed and of investors decreased interest rates to their lowest levels in 45 years in 2002 and 2003. Although the low interest rates were not attractive to investors, borrowers found the low rates very attractive. During this period, many borrowers—both

135

individuals and businesses—refinanced their outstanding loans to reduce their interest costs. The increased demand for funds resulted in a moderate increase in interest rates from 2004 to 2006.

As companies become more confident that consumer demand will return to "normal," they will borrow additional amounts to replace deteriorating assets that probably should have been replaced years earlier. Clearly, the behavior of participants in the financial markets— businesses and individuals—is based on expectations about future interest rates. When rates are low, investors have little incentive to purchase stocks and bonds, but borrowers demand more loans, and vice versa.

Whether a business or an individual, when we borrow we would like interest rates to be low. When rates are low, as they were in 2002 and 2003, many firms and individuals refinance to replace higher interest debt with lower interest debt. But, when interest rates are low, those who depend on the income from their investments suffer. It is a fact that interest rates affect all of us. Thus, as you read this chapter, think about (1) all the factors the Fed must consider before attempting to change interest rates and (2) the effects of interest rate changes on inflation, on the financial markets, on you as an individual (student), and on the economy as a whole.

CHAPTER PRINCIPLES

–The Questions

After reading this chapter, you should be able to answer the following questions:

- What is the cost of money, and how is it determined?
- What factors affect interest rates (costs of money)?
- What is a yield curve? Does the yield curve indicate future interest rates?
- How do government actions and business activity affect interest rates?
- How does the level of interest rates (returns) affect the values of stocks and bonds?

In Chapter 3, we stated that the primary role of the financial markets is to help bring together *borrowers* and *lenders* by facilitating the flow of funds from those who have surplus funds (investors) to those who need funds in excess of their current incomes (borrowers).[1] In a free economy such as that of the United States, the excess funds of lenders are allocated to borrowers in the financial markets through a pricing system that is based on the supply of, and the demand for, funds. This system is represented by interest rates, or the cost of money, such that those borrowers who are willing to pay the rates that prevail in the financial markets are able to use funds provided by others. This chapter describes the basic concepts associated with interest rates, including factors that affect rates (returns) and methods for forecasting them.

REALIZED RETURNS (YIELDS)

Before analyzing the factors that affect interest rates, it will be helpful to understand how investors earn returns when providing (supplying) funds to borrowers. Whether the investment instrument is debt or equity, the dollar return earned by an investor can be divided into two categories: (1) income paid by the *issuer* of the financial asset and (2) the change in value of the financial asset in the financial market (capital gains) over some time period.[2] Thus, the dollar return on a financial asset can be stated as follows:

 **5-1**

$$\text{Dollar return} = (\text{Dollar income}) + (\text{Capital gains})$$
$$= (\text{Dollar income}) + (\text{Ending value} - \text{Beginning value})$$

---

[1] Recall from Chapter 3 that savers (investors) and borrowers (issuers of financial assets) can be individuals, firms, and government units.

[2] Various financial assets are described in Chapter 2.

Here "Beginning value" represents the market value of the investment at the beginning of the period and "Ending value" represents its market value at the end of the period.

If the financial asset is debt, the income from the investment consists of the *interest paid* by the borrower. If the financial asset is equity, the income from the investment is the *dividend paid* by a corporation. Also, note that the amount of the capital gains can be negative if the value of the financial asset decreases during the period it is held.

To determine an investment's yield, we state the dollar return as a percentage of the dollar amount that was originally invested. Thus, the yield is computed as follows:

5-2

$$\text{Yield} = \frac{\text{Dollar return}}{\text{Beginning value}} = \frac{\text{Dollar income} + \text{Capital gains}}{\text{Beginning value}}$$

$$= \frac{\text{Dollar income} + (\text{Ending value} - \text{Beginning value})}{\text{Beginning value}}$$

To illustrate the concept of yield, consider the return that you would earn if you purchased a corporate bond on January 1, 2009, for $980.00 and sold it on December 31, 2009, for $990.25. If the bond paid $100.00 interest on December 31, 2009, the total dollar return on your investment would be $110.25; this amount includes $100.00 in interest income and $10.25 = $990.25 − $980.00 in capital gains. Thus the 1-year yield, or percent return, would be:

$$\begin{array}{c}\text{Yield} \\ (\% \text{ return})\end{array} = \frac{\$100.00 + \$10.25}{\$980.00} = \frac{\$110.25}{\$980.00} = 0.1125 = 11.25\%$$

In this example, investors who purchased the bond at the beginning of 2009 and held it until the end of 2009 would have earned a 1-year holding period return equal to 11.25 percent. If we assume that this is the same return that investors expected to earn when they purchased the bond at the beginning of the year, then this yield represents the average rate of return that investors required to provide their funds to the company that issued the bond. In this case, the "cost of money" for such a corporation was essentially 11.25 percent in 2009, because investors demanded the equivalent of a $110.25 return to invest $980.[3] In the remainder of the chapter, we discuss factors that determine the cost of money (returns) and examine what causes the cost of money to change.

Self-Test Questions

What are the two sources of the dollar return associated with an investment?

How is the yield on an investment computed?

---

[3]If we look at the same firm's stock, we would expect the yield, or "cost," to be different because stock has a different risk than debt (bonds). The effects of risk on return will be discussed in detail in Chapter 11.

FACTORS THAT AFFECT THE COST OF MONEY

Four fundamental factors affect the cost of money: (1) production opportunities, (2) time preferences for consumption, (3) risk, and (4) inflation. To see how these factors operate, imagine an isolated island community where the people survive by eating fish. They have a stock of fishing gear that permits them to live reasonably well, but they would like to have more fish. Now suppose Mr. Crusoe has a bright idea for a new type of fishnet that would enable him to increase his daily catch substantially. It would take him 1 year to perfect his design, build his net, and learn how to use it efficiently. Mr. Crusoe probably would starve before he could put his new net into operation. Recognizing this problem, he might suggest to Ms. Robinson, Mr. Friday, and several others that if they would give him one fish each day for 1 year, he would return two fish each day during all of the next year. If someone accepted the offer, then the fish that Ms. Robinson or one of the others gave to Mr. Crusoe would constitute *savings*, these savings would be *invested* in the fishnet, and the extra fish the net produced would constitute a *return on the investment*.

production opportunities
The returns available within an economy from investment in productive (cash-generating) assets.

Obviously, the more productive Mr. Crusoe thought the new fishnet would be—that is, the higher the **production opportunity**—the higher his expected return on the investment would be, and the more he could afford to offer potential investors for their savings. In this example, we assume that Mr. Crusoe thinks he will be able to pay, and thus has offered, a 100 percent rate of return; he has offered to give back two fish for every one he receives. He might have tried to attract savings for less—say, 1.5 fish next year for every one he receives this year.

time preferences for consumption
The preferences of consumers for current consumption as opposed to saving for future consumption.

The attractiveness of Mr. Crusoe's offer for a potential saver would depend in large part on the saver's **time preference for consumption.** For example, Ms. Robinson might be thinking of retirement, and she might be willing to trade fish today for fish in the future on a one-for-one basis. Mr. Friday might be unwilling to "lend" a fish today for anything less than three fish next year because he has a wife and several young children to feed with his current fish. Mr. Friday is said to have a high time preference for consumption, whereas Ms. Robinson has a low time preference for consumption. Note also that if the entire population is living at the subsistence level, time preferences for current consumption would necessarily be high, aggregate savings would be low, interest rates would be high, and capital formation would be difficult.

risk
In a financial market context, the chance that a financial asset will not earn the return promised.

The **risk** inherent in the fishnet project, and thus in Mr. Crusoe's ability to repay the loan, also affects the return required by investors: the higher the perceived risk, the higher the required rate of return. For example, if Mr. Crusoe has a history of not always following through with his ideas, Ms. Robinson, Mr. Friday, and others who are interested in Mr. Crusoe's new fishnet would consider investment to be fairly risky, and thus they might provide Mr. Crusoe with one fish each day this year only if he promises to return four fish each day next year. Also, a more complex society includes many businesses like Mr. Crusoe's, many goods other than fish, and many savers like Ms. Robinson and Mr. Friday. Furthermore, people use money, rather than fish, as a medium of exchange. When the society uses money, its value in the future, which is affected by inflation, comes into play. That is, the higher the expected rate of **inflation,** the greater the required return (interest).

inflation
The tendency of prices to increase over time.

This simple illustration shows that the interest rate paid to savers depends, in a basic way, on (1) the rate of return that producers expect to earn on their invested capital, (2) savers' time preferences for current versus future consumption, (3) the riskiness of the loan, and (4) the expected future rate of inflation. The returns that borrowers expect to earn by investing borrowed funds set an upper limit on how much they can pay for savings. In turn, consumers' time preferences for consumption establish how much consumption they are willing to defer, and hence how much they will save at different levels of interest offered by borrowers. Higher risk and higher inflation also lead to higher interest rates.

Self-Test Questions

What do we call the price paid to borrow money?

What four fundamental factors affect the cost of money?

INTEREST RATE LEVELS

Funds are allocated among borrowers by interest rates: firms with the most profitable investment opportunities are willing and able to pay the most for capital, so they tend to attract it away from less efficient firms or from firms whose products are not in demand. Of course, our economy is not completely free in the sense of being influenced only by market forces. As a result, the federal government supports agencies that help designated individuals or groups obtain credit on favorable terms. Among those eligible for this kind of assistance are small businesses, certain minorities, and firms willing to build facilities in areas characterized by high unemployment. Even with these government interventions, most capital in the U.S. economy is allocated through the price system.

Figure 5-1 shows how supply and demand interact to determine interest rates in two capital markets. Markets A and B represent two of the many capital markets in existence. The going interest rate, which we designate as r for this discussion, initially is 6 percent for the low-risk securities in Market A. That is, borrowers whose credit is strong enough to qualify for this market can obtain funds at a cost of 6 percent, and investors who want to put their money to work without much risk can obtain a 6 percent return. Riskier borrowers must borrow higher-cost funds in Market B. Investors who are willing to take on more risk invest in Market B expecting to earn a 9 percent return, but they also realize that they might actually receive much less (or much more).

FIGURE 5-1   Interest Rates as a Function of Supply and Demand

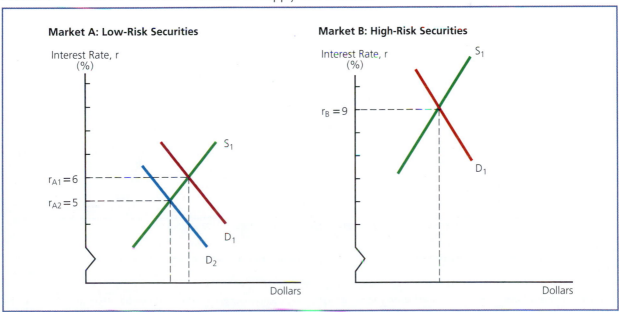

If the demand for funds declines, as it typically does during business recessions, the demand curves will shift to the left, as shown in demand curve D_2 in Market A. The market-clearing, or equilibrium, interest rate in this example then falls to 5 percent. Similarly, you should be able to visualize what would happen if the supply of funds tightens: the supply curve, S_1, would shift to the left, which would raise interest rates and lower the level of borrowing in the economy.

Financial markets are interdependent. For example, if Markets A and B were in equilibrium before the demand shifted to D_2 in Market A, it means that investors were willing to accept the higher risk in Market B in exchange for a 3 percent higher return to compensate for the additional risk that is taken. After the shift to D_2, the risk premium would initially increase to $9\% - 5\% = 4\%$. In all likelihood, this larger premium would induce some of the lenders in Market A to shift to Market B, which in turn would cause the supply curve in Market A to shift to the left (or up) and the supply curve in Market B to shift to the right. The transfer of capital between markets would raise the interest rate in Market A and lower it in Market B, thereby bringing the risk premium closer to the original level, 3 percent. For example, when rates on Treasury securities increase, the rates on corporate bonds and mortgages generally follow suit.

As discussed in Chapter 3, many financial markets are found in the United States and throughout the world. There are markets for short-term debt, long-term debt, home loans, student loans, business loans, government loans, and so forth. Prices are established for each type of fund, and these prices change over time as shifts occur in supply and demand conditions. Figure 5-2 illustrates how long- and short-term interest rates to business borrowers have varied since 1975. Notice that short-term interest rates are especially prone to rise during booms and then fall during recessions. (The shaded areas of the chart indicate recessions.) When the economy is expanding, firms need capital, and this demand for capital pushes rates higher.

FIGURE 5-2 Long- and Short-Term Interest Rates, 1975–2008

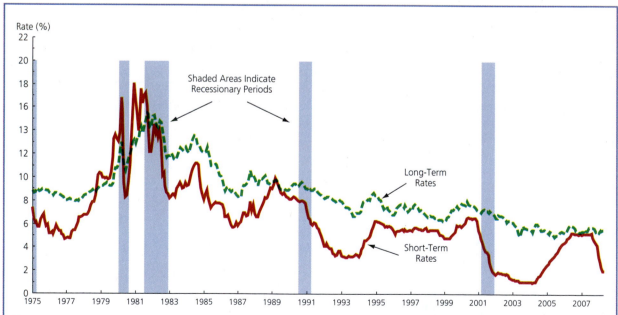

Notes:
Short-term interest rates are measured by 3-month loans to very large, strong corporations, and long-term rates are measured by AAA corporate bonds.
Tick marks on the X axis represent the middle of the year—that is, July 1.

Sources: Interest rates are found at the Federal Reserve Web site at http://www.federalreserve.gov/, and information about recessions can be found at the National Bureau of Economic Research Web site at http://www.nber.org/cycles.html/.

FIGURE 5-3   Relationship between Annual Inflation Rates and Long-Term Interest Rates, 1975–2008

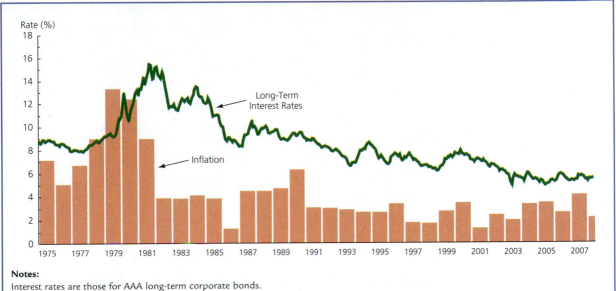

Notes:
Interest rates are those for AAA long-term corporate bonds.
Inflation is measured as the annual rate of change in the Consumer Price Index (CPI).

Sources: Interest rates are found at the Federal Reserve Web site at http://www.federalreserve.gov/; and CPI data are found at the Web site of the U.S. Department of Labor, Bureau of Labor Statistics, at http://www.bls.gov.

Inflationary pressures are strongest during business booms, which also exert upward pressure on rates. Conditions are reversed during recessions, such as those during 1990–1991 and 2001. In these periods, slack business reduces the demand for credit, the rate of inflation falls, and thus interest rates decline.

These tendencies do not hold exactly—just look at the period after 1984. The price of oil fell dramatically in 1985 and 1986, reducing inflationary pressures on other prices and easing fears of serious long-term inflation. In earlier years, these fears had pushed interest rates to record high levels. From 1984 to 1987, the economy was fairly strong, but dwindling fears about inflation more than offset the normal tendency of interest rates to rise during good economic times, and the net result was lower interest rates.[4]

Figure 5-3 highlights the relationship between inflation and long-term interest rates by plotting rates of inflation along with long-term interest rates. Prior to 1965 (not shown), when the average rate of inflation was approximately 1 percent, interest rates on the least risky bonds generally ranged from 4 to 5 percent. As the war in Vietnam accelerated in the late 1960s, the government's demand for funds to finance the war increased, the rate of inflation increased, and interest rates began to rise. The rate of inflation decreased after 1970, leading to a drop in long-term interest rates. The 1973 Arab oil embargo was followed by a quadrupling of oil prices in 1974, which caused a spurt in inflation. In turn, this increase drove interest rates to record highs in 1974 and 1975. Inflationary pressures eased in late 1975 and 1976, but then rose again after 1976. In 1980, inflation rates hit the highest level on record, and fears of continued double-digit inflation pushed interest rates to historic highs. From 1981 through 1986, the inflation rate dropped sharply. Indeed, in 1986 inflation was only 1.1 percent, the lowest level in 25 years. In 1993, interest rates dropped to historical

---

[4]Short-term rates respond to current economic conditions, whereas long-term rates primarily reflect long-run expectations for inflation. As a result, short-term rates are sometimes higher than and sometimes lower than long-term rates. The relationship between long-term and short-term rates is called term structure of interest rates. This topic is discussed later in the chapter.

lows: the Treasury bill yield actually fell below 3 percent. By 2001, rates had dropped further. By the end of the year, inflation was slightly higher than 1 percent, the Treasury bill rate was slightly lower than 2 percent, and interest rates charged to strong corporations for long-term loans was about 6 percent. In May 2008 (at the time this book was written), inflation was approximately 2 percent, the Treasury bill rate was about 1.9 percent, and the rate on AAA corporate bonds was 6.0 percent. Although interest rates have varied since the beginning of the twenty-first century, a particular trend (either upward or downward) had not emerged in 2008.

Self-Test Questions

How are interest rates used to allocate capital among firms?

What happens to market-clearing, or equilibrium, interest rates in a capital market when the demand for funds declines? What happens when inflation increases or decreases?

Why does the price of capital change during economic booms and recessions? How does risk affect interest rates?

How does a change in rates in one financial market affect the rates in other financial markets?

THE DETERMINANTS OF MARKET INTEREST RATES

In general, the quoted (or nominal) interest rate on *any* security, r, is composed of a risk-free rate of interest plus a premium that reflects the riskiness of the security. This relationship can be expressed as follows:

$$\text{Rate of return} = r = \text{Risk-free rate} + \text{Risk premium}$$

This relationship is illustrated in Figure 5-4, which shows that investors require greater returns to invest in securities with greater risks. Although we discuss risk and

FIGURE 5-4   Rate of Return (Interest Rate)

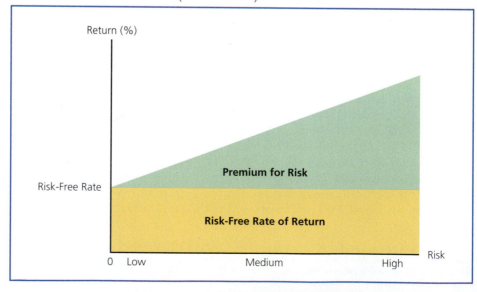

return in detail in Chapter 11, the discussion in this section will give you an indication as to factors that affect interest rates on such debt securities as bonds.

Using this relationship, the interest on *debt* can be expressed as follows:

$$\text{Rate of return} = r = r_{RF} + RP$$
$$= r_{RF} + [DRP + LP + MRP]$$

5-4

The variables in Equation 5-4 are defined as follows:

r = the quoted, or *nominal*, rate of interest on a given security.[5] There are many different securities, hence many different quoted interest rates.

r_{RF} = the quoted risk-free rate of return. Theoretically, this rate is the return associated with an investment that has a guaranteed outcome in the future—that is, it has *no risk*. We generally use the return on U.S. Treasury bills as the risk-free rate because T-bills represent the short-term debt of the U.S. government that is extremely liquid and free of most risks. In other words, the T-bills are considered close to pure risk-free assets.

RP = risk premium, which is the return that exceeds the risk-free rate of return, r_{RF}, and thus represents payment for the risk associated with an investment. $RP = DRP + LP + MRP$.

DRP = default risk premium, which reflects the chance that the borrower—that is, the issuer of the security—will not pay the debt's interest or principal on time.

LP = liquidity, or marketability, premium, which reflects the fact that some investments are more easily converted into cash on a short notice at a "reasonable price" than are other securities.

MRP = maturity risk premium, which accounts for the fact that longer-term bonds experience greater price reactions to particular interest rate changes than do short-term bonds.

We discuss the components whose sum makes up the quoted, or nominal, rate on a given security in the following sections.

The Nominal, or Quoted, Risk-Free Rate of Interest, r_{RF}

The **nominal,** or **quoted, risk-free rate, r_{RF},** is the interest rate on a security that has absolutely no risk at all—that is, one that has a guaranteed outcome in the future, regardless of the market conditions. No such security exists in the real world, hence there is no observable truly risk-free rate. There is, however, one security that is free of *most* risks: a U.S. Treasury bill (T-bill), which is a short-term security issued by the U.S. government.

The nominal risk-free rate, r_{RF}, is composed of two components: the *"real" risk-free rate,* which we designate r^*, and an adjustment for the average inflation that is expected during the life of the investment, which we designate IP, or the *inflation premium*. As a result, $r_{RF} = r^* + IP$ in Equation 5-4.

nominal (quoted) risk-free rate, r_{RF}
The rate of interest on a security that is free of all risk; r_{RF} is proxied by the T-bill rate or the T-bond rate and includes an inflation premium.

---

[5]The term *nominal* as it is used here means the *stated* rate as opposed to the *real* rate, which is adjusted to remove the effects of inflation. If you bought a 10-year Treasury bond in May 2008, the quoted, or nominal, rate was 4.0 percent, but because inflation was expected to average 2 percent over the next 10 years, the real rate was 2.0% = 4.0% − 2.0%.

real risk-free rate of interest, r*
The rate of interest that would exist on default-free U.S. Treasury securities if no inflation were expected.

The **real risk-free rate of interest, r***, is defined as the interest rate that would exist on a security with a *guaranteed* payoff—that is, a risk-free, security—*if inflation is expected to be zero* during the investment period. It can be thought of as the rate of interest that would exist on short-term U.S. Treasury securities in an *inflation-free world*. The real risk-free rate changes over time depending on economic conditions, especially (1) on the rate of return corporations and other borrowers are willing to pay to borrow funds and (2) on people's time preferences for current versus future consumption. It is difficult to measure the real risk-free rate precisely, but most experts think that r* fluctuates in the range of 2 to 4 percent in the United States.

No matter what investments they make, all investors are affected by inflation. For this reason, the minimum rate earned on any security, *no matter its risk,* must include compensation for the loss of purchasing power that is expected during the life of the investment due to inflation. Thus, in addition to the portion that represents the increase in real wealth that investors require to invest their money, r_{RF} must include a component for the average inflation, or purchasing power loss, that investors expect in the future.

If the term *risk-free rate* is used without either the term *real* or the term *nominal,* people generally mean the quoted (nominal) rate, and we will follow that convention in this book. Therefore, when we use the term *risk-free rate,* we mean the nominal risk-free rate, $r_{RF} = r^* + IP$. Also, we generally use the T-bill rate to approximate the short-term risk-free rate and the T-bond rate to approximate the long-term risk-free rate. So, whenever you see the term *risk-free rate,* assume that we are referring either to the quoted T-bill rate or to the quoted T-bond rate.

Inflation Premium (IP)

Inflation has a major effect on interest rates because it erodes the purchasing power of the dollar and lowers the real rate of return on investments. To illustrate, suppose you saved $1,000 and invested it in a certificate of deposit that matures in 1 year and will pay 4.5 percent interest. At the end of the year, you will receive $1,045—your original $1,000 plus $45 of interest. Now suppose the inflation rate during the year is 10 percent, and it affects all items equally. If pizza had cost $1 per slice at the beginning of the year, it would cost $1.10 at the end of the year. Therefore, your $1,000 would have bought $1,000/$1 = 1,000 slices of pizza at the beginning of the year but only $1,045/$1.10 = 950 slices at year's end. *In real terms,* therefore, you would be worse off: you would receive $45 of interest, but that amount would not be sufficient to offset inflation. In this case, you would be better off buying 1,000 slices of frozen pizza (or some other storable asset such as land, timber, apartment buildings, wheat, or gold) than investing in the certificate of deposit.

inflation premium (IP)
A premium for expected inflation that investors add to the real risk-free rate of return.

Investors are well aware of the effect of inflation. When they lend money, therefore, investors build in an **inflation premium (IP)** equal to the *average inflation rate expected over the life of the security.* Thus, if the real risk-free rate of interest, r*, is 3 percent, and if inflation is expected to be 2 percent (and hence IP = 2%) during the next year, then the quoted rate of interest on 1-year T-bills would be 3% + 2% = 5%.[6]

It is important to note that the rate of inflation built into interest rates is the *rate of inflation expected in the future,* not the rate experienced in the past. Thus, although the rates reported by the government indicate that inflation is currently 3 percent,

---

[6]In reality, we should compute the geometric return to account for the effect of inflation on the real rate of return, r*. In other words, in our example $r_{RF} = (1.03)(1.02) - 1.0 = 0.0506 = 5.06\%$. The additional 0.06 percent represents the fact that the purchasing power loss is a compounded effect. We discuss interest compounding in Chapter 9. For this reason, and to simplify our discussion here, we assume that the effect of inflation is additive rather than geometric.

if investors expect inflation to average 5 percent over the next few years, then 5 percent would be built into current interest rates. Note also that the inflation rate reflected in the quoted interest rate of an investment is the *average inflation expected over the life of the investment*. Consequently, the inflation rate that is built into a 1-year bond is the expected inflation rate for the next year, but the inflation rate built into a 30-year bond is the average rate of inflation expected over the next 30 years.

Generally, expectations of future inflation are closely correlated with rates experienced in the recent past. Thus, if the inflation rate reported for the month increased, people would tend to raise their expectations for future inflation. This change in expectations would, in turn, bring about an increase in interest rates.

Default Risk Premium (DRP)

The *risk* that a borrower will *default* on a loan—that is, not pay the interest or the principal—also affects the market interest rate on a security: the greater the default risk, the higher the interest rate that lenders charge (demand). Treasury securities have no default risk because everyone believes that the U.S. government will pay its debt on time. As a result, U.S. Treasury securities (bills, notes, and bonds) generally carry the lowest interest rates on taxable securities in the United States. For corporate bonds, the better the bond's overall credit rating (AAA is the best), the lower its default risk, and, consequently, the lower its interest rate.[7] Following are some representative interest rates on long-term (10-year) corporate bonds that existed in May 2008:

Type of Debt	Amount of Risk	Rate, r	DRP = r − r_{RF}
U.S. Treasury, r_{RF}	No default risk	4.0%	—
AAA corporate bond	Default risk greater than T-bonds	5.6	1.6%
BBB corporate bond	Default risk greater than AAA corporate bonds	6.9	2.9
CCC corporate bond	Default risk much greater than BBB corporate bonds	17.8	13.8

Assuming that these three bonds have identical maturities and debt provisions, the only reason their rates differ is because their default risks differ. As a result, the difference between the quoted interest rate on a T-bond and that on a corporate bond with similar maturity, liquidity, and other features is the **default risk premium (DRP).** Thus, if the bonds listed above were *otherwise similar*, the default risk premium would be DRP = r − r_{RF}. Default risk premiums vary somewhat over time, but in May 2008 the figures were slightly higher than normal compared with levels in recent years.

Liquidity Premium (LP)

Liquidity generally is defined as the ability to convert an asset into cash on short notice and "reasonably" capture the amount initially invested. The more easily an asset can be converted to cash at a price that substantially recovers the initial amount invested, the more liquid it is considered. Clearly, assets have varying degrees of liquidity, depending on the characteristics of the markets in which they

default risk premium (DRP)
The difference between the interest rate on a U.S. Treasury bond and a corporate bond of equal maturity and marketability; compensation for the risk that a corporation will not meet its debt obligations.

[7]Bond ratings, and bond riskiness in general, are discussed in more detail in Chapter 2. For this example, note that bonds rated AAA are judged to have less default risk than are bonds rated AA, AA bonds are less risky than A bonds, and so on.

are traded. For instance, such financial assets as government securities and stocks and bonds trade in extremely active and efficient secondary markets, whereas the markets for real estate are much more restrictive. Also, it generally is easier to convert an asset into cash at a "good" price the closer the asset's life is to its maturity date. Thus, financial assets generally are more liquid than real assets, and short-term financial assets generally are more liquid than long-term financial assets.

liquidity premium (LP)
A premium added to the rate on a security if the security cannot be converted to cash on short notice at a price that is close to its original cost.

Because liquidity is important, investors evaluate liquidity and include **liquidity premiums (LP)** when market rates of securities are established. Although it is difficult to accurately measure liquidity premiums, a differential of at least two and perhaps four or five percentage points exists between the least liquid and the most liquid financial assets of similar default risk and maturity.

Maturity Risk Premium (MRP)

interest rate price risk
The risk of capital losses to which investors are exposed because of changing interest rates.

maturity risk premium (MRP)
A premium that reflects interest rate price risk; bonds with longer maturities have greater interest rate price risk.

The prices of long-term bonds decline sharply whenever interest rates rise. Because interest rates can and do occasionally rise, *all* long-term bonds—even Treasury bonds—have an element of risk called **interest rate price risk.** As a general rule, the bonds of any organization, from the U.S. government to General Motors, have more interest rate price risk the longer the maturity of the bond.[8] Therefore, the required interest rate must include a **maturity risk premium (MRP),** which is higher the longer the time to maturity. Everything else equal, maturity risk premiums raise interest rates on long-term bonds relative to those on short-term bonds. Such a premium, like the other types of premiums, is extremely difficult to measure. Nevertheless, two things seem clear: (1) the MRP appears to vary over time, rising when interest rates are more volatile and uncertain, then falling when interest rates are more stable; and (2) the maturity risk premium on T-bonds with 20 to 30 years to maturity normally is in the range of one or two percentage points.[9]

To illustrate the effect of time to maturity on the prices of bonds, consider two investments that are identical except for their maturity dates. Both investments promise to pay $1,000 at maturity, but Investment A matures in 2 years whereas Investment B matures in 10 years. To simplify this example, let's assume that there is no maturity risk premium so that the return on both investments is currently 10 percent. Under these conditions, the value of Investment A is $826.45 and the value of Investment B is $385.54. What will be the values of these investments if the return on the investments immediately increases to 12 percent? The following table shows the answer to this question as well as the changes in the investments' values stated both in dollars and in percentages.[10]

Investment	Maturity	Value @ 10%	Value @ 12%	$ Change in Value	% Change in Value
A	2 years	$826.45	$797.19	−$29.26	−3.5%
B	10 years	385.54	321.97	−63.57	−16.5

---

[8]For example, if you had bought a 30-year Treasury bond for $1,000 in 1972, when the long-term interest rate was 7 percent, and held it until 1981, when long-term T-bond rates were 14.5 percent, the value of the bond would have declined to $514. That decrease would represent a loss of almost half the money, and it demonstrates that long-term bonds—even U.S. Treasury bonds—are not riskless. If you had purchased short-term T-bills in 1972 and subsequently reinvested the principal each time the bills matured, however, you would still have $1,000. This point will be discussed in detail in Chapter 6.

[9]The MRP has averaged 1.5 percentage points over the last 65 years. See *Stocks, Bonds, Bills, and Inflation: 2007 Yearbook* (Chicago: Ibbotson Associates, 2007).

[10]The values were computed using time value of money techniques (present value), which will be discussed in Chapter 9.

Note that both the dollar change and the percentage change are greater for the investment with the longer term to maturity—that is, Investment B. This simple example, which illustrates the general concept of maturity risk, shows you why investors normally demand higher MRPs for investments with longer terms to maturity.

Although long-term bonds are heavily exposed to interest rate price risk, short-term investments are more vulnerable to **reinvestment rate risk.** When short-term investments mature and the proceeds are reinvested, or "rolled over," a decline in interest rates would necessitate reinvestment at a lower rate, and hence would lead to a decline in interest income. For example, suppose you invested $100,000 in 1-year Treasury bills such that you reinvested your money at the beginning of each year, and you live on the income generated from this investment. In 1981, short-term rates were approximately 15 percent, so your investment would have provided roughly $15,000 in interest income. Because you would have to reinvest the $100,000 each year at the prevailing interest rate, however, your income would have declined to about $9,000 by 1983, to about $1,300 by 2003, and to about $2,000 by 2008. Had you invested your money in long-term—say, 30-year—Treasury bonds in 1981, you would have received a stable annual income of about $13,000.[11] Thus, although "investing short" preserves one's principal, the interest income provided by short-term investments varies from year to year, depending on reinvestment rates.

reinvestment rate risk
The risk that a decline in interest rates will lead to lower income when bonds mature and funds are reinvested.

Self-Test Questions

Write an equation for the nominal interest rate on any debt security.

Distinguish between the *real* risk-free rate of interest, r*, and the *nominal,* or quoted, risk-free rate of interest r_{RF}.

How do investors deal with inflation when they determine interest rates in the financial markets? Explain.

Does the interest rate on a Treasury bond include a default risk premium? Explain.

Briefly explain the following statement: "Although long-term bonds are heavily exposed to interest rate price risk, short-term Treasury bills are more vulnerable to reinvestment rate risk."

Suppose economists have determined that the real risk-free rate of return is 3 percent and that inflation is expected to average 2.5 percent per year long into the future. What should be the rate on a 1-year Treasury bond? Assume that there is no maturity risk premium associated with the bond.   (Answer: 5.5%)

Suppose that economists have determined that the real risk-free rate of return is 3 percent and that inflation is expected to average 2.5 percent per year long into the future. In addition, Treasury bonds with terms to maturity greater than 1 year incur a maturity risk premium equal to 0.1 percent for each year remaining until maturity. What should be the rate on a 5-year Treasury bond?   (Answer: 6.0%)

---

[11]Long-term bonds also have some reinvestment rate risk. To earn the quoted rate on a long-term bond, the interest payments must be reinvested at the quoted rate. If interest rates fall, however, the interest payments must be reinvested at a lower rate. In such a case, the realized return would be less than the quoted rate. Note that the reinvestment rate risk is lower on a long-term bond than on a short-term bond because only the interest payments (rather than the interest plus principal) on the long-term bond are exposed to reinvestment rate risk. Only zero coupon bonds (which are discussed in Chapter 2) are completely free of reinvestment rate risk.

THE TERM STRUCTURE OF INTEREST RATES

term structure of interest rates
The relationship between yields and maturities of securities.

A study of Figure 5-2 reveals that at certain times, such as in 2004 and 2005, short-term interest rates are lower than long-term rates. At other times, such as in 1979-1981, short-term rates are higher than long-term rates. The relationship between long- and short-term rates, which is known as the **term structure of interest rates,** is important to corporate treasurers, who must decide whether to borrow by issuing long- or short-term debt, and to investors, who must decide whether to buy long- or short-term bonds. For these reasons, it is important to understand (1) how long- and short-term rates are related and (2) what causes shifts in their relative positions.

yield curve
A graph showing the relationship between yields and maturities of securities.

The relationship between long- and short-term bonds varies, and is generally dependent on the supply and demand relationship that exists for these bonds at a particular point in time. For example, the tabular section of Figure 5-5 includes interest rates for different maturities on three different dates. The set of data for a given date, when plotted on a graph such as that in Figure 5-5, is called the **yield curve** for that date. The yield curve provides a snapshot of the relationship between short- and long-term rates on a particular date. The yield curve changes both in position and in slope over time. For example, in March 1980, all rates were relatively high, and short-term rates were higher than long-term rates, so the yield curve on that date was *downward sloping*. In July 2003, however, all rates were much lower, and long-term rates were higher than short-term rates, so the

FIGURE 5-5   U.S. Treasury Bonds: Interest Rates on Different Dates

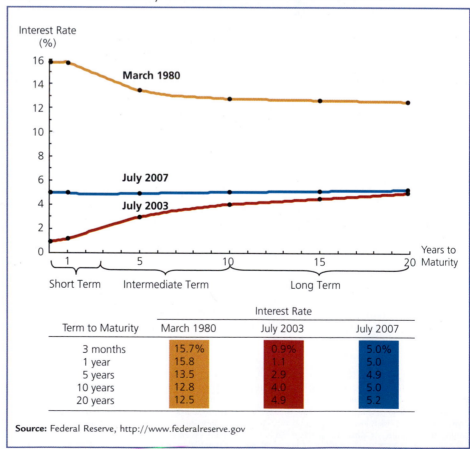

	Interest Rate		
Term to Maturity	March 1980	July 2003	July 2007
3 months	15.7%	0.9%	5.0%
1 year	15.8	1.1	5.0
5 years	13.5	2.9	4.9
10 years	12.8	4.0	5.0
20 years	12.5	4.9	5.2

Source: Federal Reserve, http://www.federalreserve.gov

yield curve at that time was *upward sloping*. And in July 2007, all rates were higher than in 2003, and short- and long-term rates did not differ much, so the yield curve was fairly *flat*, or *horizontal*.

Historically, long-term rates have generally been higher than short-term rates, so the yield curve normally has been upward sloping. For this reason, people often refer to an upward-sloping yield curve as a **"normal" yield curve.** On the other hand, a downward-sloping yield curve is pretty rare, and thus we normally refer to this type of curve as an **inverted,** or **"abnormal," yield curve.** Thus, in Figure 5-5, the yield curve for March 1980 was inverted, but the yield curve for July 2003 was normal. In the next section, we discuss three explanations for the different shapes of the yield curve and explain why an upward-sloping yield curve is considered normal.

"normal" yield curve
An upward-sloping yield curve.

inverted ("abnormal") yield curve
A downward-sloping yield curve.

Self-Test Questions

What is a yield curve, and what information would you need to draw this curve?

How does a "normal" yield curve differ from a flat yield curve and an inverted yield curve?

WHY DO YIELD CURVES DIFFER?

It is clear from Figure 5-5 that the shape of the yield curve at one point in time can be significantly different from the yield curve at another point in time. For example, interest rates were much higher in 1980 than in 2003, and the yield curve was downward sloping in 1980, whereas it was upward sloping in 2003. Remember that interest rates consist of a risk-free return, r_{RF}, which includes the real risk-free return (r^*) and an adjustment for expected inflation (IP), and a risk premium that rewards investors for various risks, including default risk (DRP), liquidity risk (LP), and maturity risk (MRP). Although the real risk-free rate of return, r^*, does change at times, it generally is relatively stable from period to period. As a result, when interest rates shift to substantially different levels, it generally is because investors have changed either their expectations concerning future inflation or their attitudes concerning risk. Because changes in investors' risk attitudes generally evolve over time (years), *inflation expectations represent an important factor in the determination of current interest rates*, and thus the shape of the yield curve.

To illustrate how inflation impacts the shape of the yield curve, let's examine interest rates on U.S. Treasury securities. First, the rate of return on these securities can be written as follows:

$$r_{Treasury} = r_{RF} + MRP = [r^* + IP] + MRP$$

5-5

This equation is the same as Equation 5-4, except the default risk premium (DRP) and the liquidity premium (LP) are not included because we generally consider Treasury securities to be extremely liquid (marketable), default-free investments. As a result, DRP = 0 and LP = 0. The maturity risk premium (MRP) is included in the equation because Treasury securities vary in maturity from as little as a few days to as much as 30 years. All else equal, *investors generally prefer to hold short-term securities* because such securities are less sensitive to changes in interest rates and provide greater investment flexibility than longer-term securities. Investors will, therefore, generally accept lower yields on short-term securities, and this leads to relatively low short-term rates. *Borrowers*, on the other hand, *generally prefer long-term debt* because short-term debt exposes them to the risk of having to refinance the debt under adverse conditions (e.g., higher interest rates). Accordingly, borrowers want to "lock into" long-term funds, which means they are willing to pay a higher rate, other things held constant, for long-term funds than for short-term funds, which also leads to relatively low short-term rates. Taken together, these two sets of preferences imply that under *normal conditions,* a positive maturity risk premium (MRP) exists, and the MRP increases with years to maturity, causing the yield curve to be upward sloping. In economics, the general theory that supports this conclusion is referred to as the **liquidity preference theory,** which simply states that long-term bonds normally yield more than short-term bonds, *all else equal,* primarily because MRP > 0 and MRP increases with time to maturity.

liquidity preference theory
The theory that, all else being equal, lenders prefer to make short-term loans rather than long-term loans, hence they will lend short-term funds at lower rates than they lend long-term funds.

During the past few decades, we have observed three basic shapes to the yield curve associated with Treasury securities. Each of the three shapes is shown in Figure 5-5—that is, a normal, or upward sloping yield curve, an inverted, or downward sloping yield curve, and a flat yield curve. For this reason, although MRP > 0, which supports the *liquidity preference theory,* it appears that this theory does not fully explain the shape of the yield curve. Remember that the nominal risk-free rate of return consists of two components: the real risk-free rate of return, r*, which is considered to be relatively constant from one year to the next, and an adjustment for the inflation expectations of investors, IP. Expectations about future inflation do vary over time. The inflation premium, IP, that is included in interest rates, however, is somewhat predictable because it is the average of the inflation rates that are expected to occur during the life of the investment (a Treasury security in this case). In fact, the yield curve is often used as an aid when forecasting future interest rates because both investors and borrowers base their current decisions on expectations regarding which way interest rates will move in the future. For example, interest rates were at such low levels in 2003 and 2004 (the lowest in 45 years) that most people believed that rates most certainly would have to increase in the future. The attitude was that rates could not possibly drop any lower. During this time, many homeowners refinanced their houses to take advantage of, and thus "lock in," the low rates, whereas most investors purchased short-term securities in hopes that rates would increase in the future, at which time they would be able to "lock in" the higher rates. Clearly, the expectations of the participants in the financial markets—that is, investors and borrowers—greatly impact interest rates. The **expectations theory** states that the yield curve depends on *expectations* concerning future inflation rates. We illustrate how expectations can be used to help *forecast* interest rates in the next section.

expectations theory
The theory that the shape of the yield curve depends on investors' expectations about future inflation rates.

Let's consider the impact of inflation expectations and maturity on the determination of interest rates with two simple examples: (1) inflation is expected to increase in the future and (2) inflation is expected to decrease in the future. Assume the real risk-free rate, r*, is 2 percent and that investors demand a 0.1 percent maturity risk premium for each year remaining until maturity for any debt with a term to maturity greater than 1 year, with a maximum value of 1 percent. For example, if a Treasury bill matures in 1 year, MRP = 0; but, if a Treasury bond matures in 5 years, MRP = 0.5%, and bonds that mature in 10 years or longer have MRP = 1.0%. Also, assume that inflation expectations are as follows for the two situations:

Year	Increasing Inflation	Decreasing Inflation
1	1.0%	5.0%
2	1.8%	4.2%
3	2.0%	4.0%
4	2.4%	3.4%
5	2.8%	3.2%
After Year 5	3.0%	2.4%

Note that these two situations are not related—that is, we are not assuming that the economic conditions in the first year in both cases are the same.

Using this information, we can compute the interest rates for Treasury securities with any term to maturity. To illustrate, consider a bond that matures in 5 years. For the case in which inflation is expected to *increase*, the interest rate, or yield, on this bond should be 4.5 percent: $r^* = 2\%$, $IP = 2\%$, and $MRP = 0.5\%$. Because IP is the average of the rate of inflation that is expected for each year during the life of the bond, $IP = (1.0\% + 1.8\% + 2.0\% + 2.4\% + 2.8\%)/5 = 2.0\%$. Also, $MRP = 0.1\%$ per year for this bond because its term to maturity is greater than 1 year; thus, $MRP = 0.1\% \times 5 \text{ years} = 0.5\%$. As a result, $r = [r^* + IP] + MRP = [2\% + 2\%] + 0.5\% = 4.5\%$.

Figure 5-6 shows the yield curves for both inflationary situations. The yields are given in the tables below the graphs. As the graphs show, when inflation is expected

FIGURE 5-6 Illustrative Yield Curves for Treasury Securities

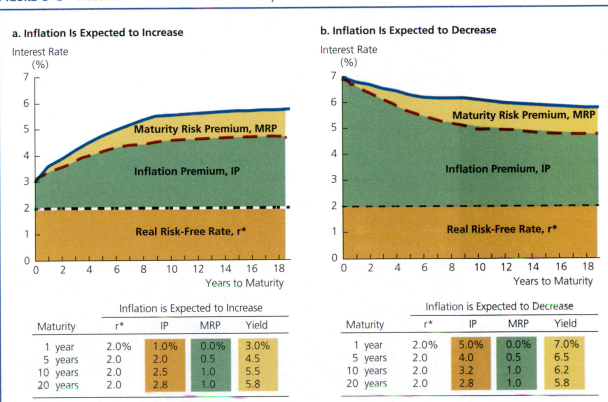

a. Inflation Is Expected to Increase

Inflation is Expected to Increase

Maturity	r^*	IP	MRP	Yield
1 year	2.0%	1.0%	0.0%	3.0%
5 years	2.0	2.0	0.5	4.5
10 years	2.0	2.5	1.0	5.5
20 years	2.0	2.8	1.0	5.8

b. Inflation Is Expected to Decrease

Inflation is Expected to Decrease

Maturity	r^*	IP	MRP	Yield
1 year	2.0%	5.0%	0.0%	7.0%
5 years	2.0	4.0	0.5	6.5
10 years	2.0	3.2	1.0	6.2
20 years	2.0	2.8	1.0	5.8

Note: The inflation premium is the average of the expected inflation rates during the life of the security. Therefore, in the case where inflation is expected to *increase*, IP_{10} is computed as follows:

$$IP_{10} = \frac{1.0\% + 1.8\% + 2.0\% + 2.4\% + 2.8\% + 3.0\% + 3.0\% + 3.0\% + 3.0\% + 3.0\%}{10} = \frac{25\%}{10} = 2.5\%$$

to increase, the yield curve is upward sloping, and vice versa. In either case, economists often use the yield curve to form expectations about the future of the economy. For example, when inflation is high and expected to decline, as panel B of Figure 5-6 indicates, the yield curve generally is downward sloping. In many cases, a downward-sloping yield curve suggests that the economy will weaken in the future: consumers delay purchases because they expect prices to decline in the future, borrowers wait to borrow funds because they believe rates will be lower in the future, and investors provide more funds to the financial markets in an effort to capture higher current rates. All of these actions lead to lower long-term rates in the current period.

There are times when the yield curve exhibits either humps or dips for bonds in a particular range of terms to maturity. Figure 5-7 shows the yield curve for September 2007. The graph "dips" for short-term bonds, and then exhibits a somewhat normal upward slope for bonds with longer maturities. The shape of this yield curve suggests that the supply/demand conditions for bonds with short-term maturities were significantly different than for the longer maturity ranges in September 2007. When supply/demand conditions in one range of maturities is significantly different than in other maturity ranges, interest rates for bonds in that maturity range are either substantially higher or substantially lower than rates in the maturity ranges on either side. In such cases, the resulting yield curve is not smooth or uniform; rather there is a hump in the yield curve if rates are higher, and a dip if rates are lower. The reason these humps and dips occur is because there are instances when investors and borrowers prefer bonds with specific maturity ranges. For example, a person borrowing to buy a long-term asset like a house, or an electric utility borrowing to build a power plant, would want a long-term loan.

FIGURE 5-7   U.S. Treasury Bonds: Yield Curve, September 2007

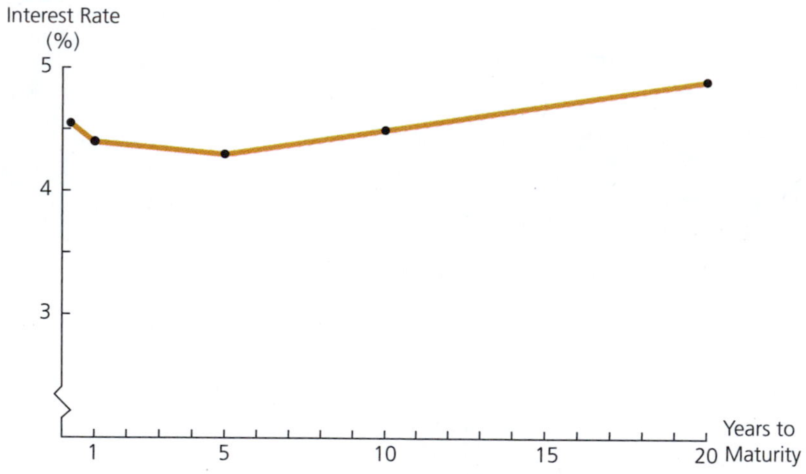

Term to Maturity	Interest Rate
3 months	4.6%
1 year	4.4
5 years	4.3
10 years	4.5
20 years	4.9

Source: Federal Reserve, http://www.federalreserve.gov

However, a retailer borrowing in September to build its inventories for Christmas would prefer a short-term loan. Similar differences exist among savers. For example, a person saving to take a vacation next summer would want to lend (save) in the short-term market, but someone saving for retirement 20 years hence would generally buy long-term securities.

According to the **market segmentation theory** that has been developed by economists, the slope of the yield curve depends on supply/demand conditions in the long- and short-term markets. Thus, the yield curve could at any given time be flat, upward sloping, or downward sloping and have humps or dips. Interest rates would be high in a particular segment compared to other segments when there was a low supply of funds in that segment relative to demand, and vice versa. The hump in the curve shown in Figure 5-7 suggests that the demand for short-term loans was low relative to supply—that is, borrowers sought long-term loans rather than long-term loans, a greater than normal number of investors bought short-term investments so the supply of short-term funds was high, or both conditions existed.

In this section, we use Treasury securities to illustrate concepts relating to the shape of the yield curve. The same concepts apply to corporate bonds. To include corporate bonds in the illustration, however, we would have to determine the default risk premium, DRP, and the liquidity premium, LP, associated with these bonds. In other words, the interest rates on corporate bonds would be determined using Equation 5-6:

market segmentation theory
The theory that every borrower and lender has a preferred maturity and that the slope of the yield curve depends on the supply of and the demand for funds in the long-term market relative to the short-term market.

$$r = r_{RF} + [DRP + LP + MRP] = [r^* + IP] + [DRP + LP + MRP]$$

5-6

For corporate bonds DRP > 0 and LP > 0, which means that interest rates on corporate bonds are greater than interest rates on Treasury securities. The risk-free rate of return for both types of securities is the same, $r_{RF} = r^* + IP$. But because corporate bonds have default risk, liquidity risk, and maturity risk, whereas long-term Treasury securities have only maturity risk, the risk premiums on corporate bonds (MRP + DPR + LP) are greater than the risk premiums on Treasuries (MRP)—that is, $RP_{Corporate} > RP_{Treasury}$. As a result, if we plotted the yield curves for the bonds of a particular corporation, such as Wal-Mart or General Motors (GM), the curves would be higher than for Treasury securities, and it would be higher for riskier corporations. For instance, the yield curve for Wal-Mart's bonds would be below the yield curve for GM's bonds because at the time we write this book GM had financial problems and was considered riskier than Wal-Mart; Wal-Mart's bonds were rated as investment grade because they had low default risk, whereas GM's bonds were rated as "junk bonds" because they had high default risk. Note that although GM's bonds were rated as "junk bonds" at the time we write this book, the rating might be different when you read this book.

Figure 5-8 shows the yield curves for T-bonds, AAA-rated corporate bonds, and BBB-rated corporate bonds in May 2008. The figure illustrates the relationships of the yields for bonds with different risks. Remember that BBB-rated corporate bonds have more risk than AAA-rated corporate bonds, which have more risk than T-bonds. Figure 5-8 verifies that the risk/return relationship shown in Figure 5-4 actually exists in the financial markets—that is, investors demand higher returns to purchase riskier investments such that $r_{BBB} > r_{AAA} > r_{Treasury}$.

FIGURE 5-8   Yield Curves, May 2008: Treasury Bonds, AAA-Rated Corporate Bonds, and BBB-Rated Corporate Bonds

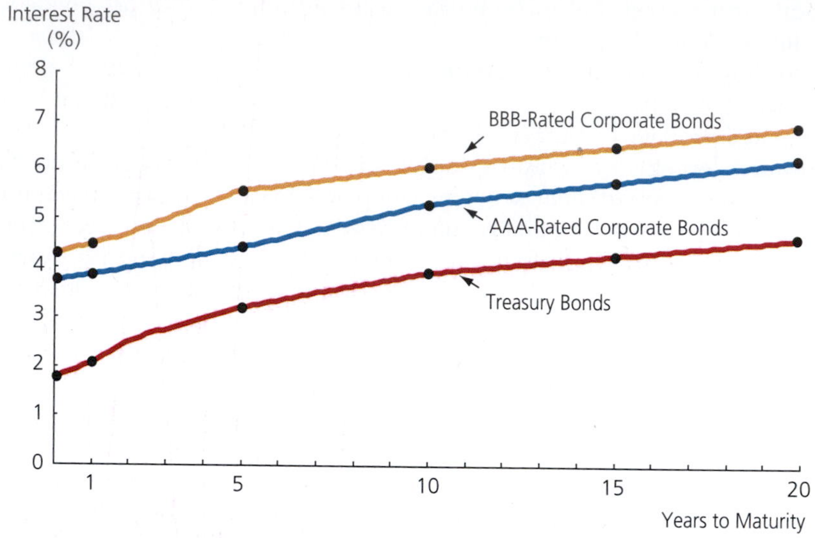

Interest Rate (%)

BBB-Rated Corporate Bonds

AAA-Rated Corporate Bonds

Treasury Bonds

Years to Maturity

Term to Maturity	Treasury Bond	AAA-Rated Corporate Bond	BBB-Rated Corporate Bond
3 months	1.8%	3.7%	4.3%
1 year	2.5	4.0	4.6
5 years	3.2	4.4	5.5
10 years	3.9	5.3	6.1
20 years	4.6	6.2	6.9

Interest Rate, May 2008

Sources: Federal Reserve, http://www.federalreserve.gov; Yahoo! Finance, http://finance.yahoo.com/bonds/composite_bond_rates; and Zions Direct, http://www.zionsbank.com/

Self-Test Questions

How do the various risk premiums affect the yield curve?

Discuss the validity of each of the three theories mentioned in this section that have been proposed to explain the shape of the yield curve.

The interest rate on Cloudy Sun Company's bonds is 8 percent. It has been determined that a portion of this return equal to 3 percent represents compensation for LP and MRP. If $r^* = 2.5\%$ and inflation is expected to be 2 percent every year in the future, what is the DRP associated with Cloudy Sun's bonds? What is r_{RF}?   (Answers: 0.5%, 4.5%)

DOES THE YIELD CURVE INDICATE FUTURE INTEREST RATES?

It was mentioned earlier that the *expectations theory* states that the shape of the yield curve depends on investors' expectations concerning future inflation rates. It was also mentioned that the primary reason interest rates change is because investors change their expectations concerning future inflation rates. If this is true, can we use the yield curve to help forecast future interest rates? In this section, we examine Treasury securities to illustrate how interest rates might be forecasted using information provided by a yield curve. Because there exist many factors that affect interest rates in the real world, models that are used to forecast interest rates are extremely complex and not always very accurate. Therefore, the discussion in this section is very much oversimplified; significantly more analysis than examining a yield curve is needed to forecast interest rates.

Although we know that Treasury securities are exposed to maturity risk, to simplify the discussion here, we assume that MRP = 0 in the determination of interest rates for these securities. If MRP = 0, then all Treasury securities have the same risk, regardless of their terms to maturity, and neither investors nor borrowers should have a preference for securities with particular maturities because all securities are interchangeable. In other words, all else equal, if a person wants to invest for a 5-year period, he or she would not care whether the funds are invested in a Treasury bond that matures in 5 years or a Treasury bill that matures in 1 year and can be "turned over" for the next 5 years. The Treasury securities should be perfect substitutes for each other so that the investor earns the same return if the money is invested in one 5-year Treasury bond or five 1-year Treasury bills that mature one after the other. The reason for this is because the yield on the 5-year T-bond is the average of the yields on the five 1-year T-bills.

To illustrate, suppose that on January 1, 2010, the real risk-free rate of interest is $r^* = 3\%$ and expected inflation rates for the next 3 years are as follows:[12]

Year	Expected Annual (1-Year) Inflation Rate	Expected Average Inflation Rate from January 1, 2010, to December 31 of Indicated Year
2010	2.0%	$IP_1 = \quad (2\%)/1 = 2.0\%$
2011	4.0%	$IP_2 = \quad (2\% + 4\%)/2 = 3.0\%$
2012	6.0%	$IP_3 = (2\% + 4\% + 6\%)/3 = 4.0\%$

Given these expectations, the following interest rate pattern should exist:

Bond Type	Real Risk-Free Rate (r^*)		Inflation Premium: Average Expected Inflation Rate (IP_t)		Nominal Treasury Bond Rate for Each Maturity (r_{RF})
1-year bond	3.0%	+	2.0 %	=	5.0%
2-year bond	3.0%	+	3.0 %	=	6.0%
3-year bond	3.0%	+	4.0 %	=	7.0%

If the yields on these hypothetical bonds were plotted, the yield curve would be upward sloping, similar to the July 2003 yield curve in Figure 5-5.

---

[12]In this example, we compute simple *arithmetic* average. Technically, we should be using *geometric* average, but the differences are not material in this example. These computations will be discussed later in the book.

Had the pattern of expected inflation rates been reversed, with inflation expected to fall from 6 to 2 percent during the 3-year period, the following situation would exist:

Year	Expected Annual (1-Year) Inflation Rate	Expected Average Inflation Rate from January 1, 2010, to December 31 of Indicated Year
2010	6.0%	$IP_1 =$ (6%)/1 = 6.0%
2011	4.0%	$IP_2 =$ (6% + 4%)/2 = 5.0%
2012	2.0%	$IP_3 =$ (6% + 4% + 2%)/3 = 4.0%

Given these expectations, the following interest rate pattern should exist:

Bond Type	Real Risk-Free Rate (r^*)		Inflation Premium: Average Expected Inflation Rate (IP_t)		Nominal Treasury Bond Rate for Each Maturity (r_{RF})
1-year bond	3.0%	+	6.0 %	=	9.0%
2-year bond	3.0%	+	5.0 %	=	8.0%
3-year bond	3.0%	+	4.0 %	=	7.0%

In this case, the pattern of interest rates would produce an inverted yield curve like the March 1980 yield curve in Figure 5-5. As you can see, whenever the annual rate of inflation is expected to decline, according to the expectations theory the yield curve must be downward sloping, or inverted, and vice versa.

We should also be able to forecast the interest rate each year by examining the yields that currently exist on bonds with various maturities. For example, if *The Wall Street Journal* reports that the yield on a 1-year T-bill is 5 percent and the yield on a 2-year T-bond is 6 percent as reported earlier, then because the yield on any bond is the average of the annual interest rates during its life, we know the following relationship exists in this situation:

5-7

$$\text{Yield on a 2-Year Bond} = \frac{\left(\begin{array}{c}\text{Interest rate} \\ \text{in Year 1}\end{array}\right) + \left(\begin{array}{c}\text{Interest rate} \\ \text{in Year 2}\end{array}\right)}{2} = \frac{R_1 + R_2}{2}$$

Here R_1 is the expected interest rate during the first year only (Year 1) and R_2 is the expected interest rate during the second year only (Year 2). Plugging in the known information, we have

$$6\% = \frac{5\% + R_2}{2}$$

Solving for R_2, we have

$$5\% + R_2 = 6\%(2) = 12\%, \text{ so } R_2 = 12\% - 5\% = 7\%$$

This is the yield an investor would expect to earn during 2011 if a 2-year bond is purchased. Therefore, according to this example, investors would expect the interest rate to equal 5 percent in 2010 and 7 percent in 2011. If this is true, then the average yield over the next 2 years would be 6% = (5% + 7%)/2. You can see that the yield curve is upward sloping whenever interest rates are expected to increase in future years because the *average yield* increases as higher interest rates are included in the computation.

This information can also be used to determine the expected inflation rate. In the current example, the interest rate consists of the real risk-free rate, r^*, which is constant, and an adjustment for inflation. Therefore, to determine the expected inflation rate each year, we simply subtract r^* from the nominal interest rate that is expected to occur during the year. Remember that we assumed the real risk-free rate, r^*, is 3 percent per year. As a result, in the current example, investors expect inflation to be 2% = 5% − 3% in 2010 and 4% = 7% − 3% in 2011. These results are the same as the expected inflation rates that were reported earlier.

Self-Test Questions

If interest rates are based solely on the expectations of investors and borrowers, how are long-term interest rates computed?

Suppose that the yield (interest) on a 3-year Treasury bond is 4 percent and the yield (interest) on a 4-year Treasury bond is 4.5 percent. The MRPs for these bonds equal 0 percent. Using the rates on these bonds, estimate the 1-year interest rate in Year 4. If $r^* = 2\%$ each year, what is the expected inflation rate in Year 4? (Answers: 6% = (4.5% × 4 years) − (4% × 3 years), 4% = 6% − 2%)

OTHER FACTORS THAT INFLUENCE INTEREST RATE LEVELS

Factors other than those discussed earlier also influence both the general level of interest rates and the shape of the yield curve. The four most important factors are Federal Reserve policy, the level of the federal budget deficit, the foreign trade balance, and the level of business activity.

Federal Reserve Policy

You probably learned two important points in your economics courses: (1) the money supply has a major effect on both the level of economic activity and the rate of inflation and (2) in the United States, the Federal Reserve controls the money supply. If the Fed wants to control growth in the economy, it slows growth in the money supply. Such an action initially causes interest rates to increase and inflation to stabilize. The opposite effect occurs when the Fed loosens the money supply.

The most important tool used by the Fed to manage the supply of money is **open market operations,** which involve buying or selling U.S. Treasury securities to change bank reserves. When the Fed wants to increase the money supply, it purchases government securities from *primary dealers* who have established trading relationships with the Federal Reserve. The Fed pays for the securities by sending funds to the banks where the primary dealers have accounts. This action increases the deposit balances of the dealers, which in turn increases the overall reserves of the banking system. Banks have additional funds to lend, so the money supply increases. The Fed carries out "normal" open market operations on a continuous basis to maintain economic activity within defined limits, and it shifts its open market strategies toward heavier-than-normal buying or selling to make more substantial adjustments.

open market operations
Operations in which the Federal Reserve buys or sells Treasury securities to expand or contract the U.S. money supply.

During periods when the Fed is actively intervening in the markets, the yield curve will be distorted. Short-term rates will be temporarily "too low" if the Fed is easing credit and "too high" if it is tightening credit. Long-term rates are not affected as much as short-term rates by Fed intervention.

Federal Deficits

If the federal government spends more than it takes in from tax revenues, it runs a deficit. Deficit spending must be covered either by borrowing or by printing money. If the government borrows, the added demand for funds pushes up interest rates. If it prints money, the expectation is that future inflation will increase, which also drives up interest rates. Thus, the larger the federal deficit, other things held constant, the higher the level of interest rates. Whether long- or short-term rates are affected to a greater extent depends on how the deficit is financed. Consequently, we cannot generalize about how deficits will influence the slope of the yield curve.

International Business (Foreign Trade Balance)

Businesses and individuals in the United States buy from and sell to people and firms in other countries. If Americans buy more than we sell (that is, if Americans import more than we export), the United States is said to be running a *foreign trade deficit*. When trade deficits occur, they must be financed, and the main source of financing is debt.[13] Therefore, the larger the trade deficit, the more the United States must borrow. As the country increases its borrowing, interest rates are driven up. Also, foreigners are willing to hold U.S. debt only if the interest rate on this debt is competitive with interest rates in other countries. Therefore, if the Federal Reserve attempts to lower interest rates in the United States, causing U.S. rates to fall below rates abroad, then foreigners will sell U.S. bonds; this activity will depress bond prices and cause U.S. interest rates to increase. As a result, the existence of a deficit trade balance hinders the Fed's ability to combat a recession by lowering interest rates.

The United States has been running annual trade deficits since the mid-1970s, and the cumulative effect of these deficits has been to make the United States the largest debtor nation of all time. As a result, U.S. interest rates are very much influenced by interest rate trends in other countries (higher rates abroad lead to higher U.S. rates). For this reason, U.S. corporate treasurers—and anyone else who is affected by interest rates—must keep up with developments in the world economy.

We mentioned earlier that financial markets in the United States are interdependent in the sense that when rates in one market increase investors tend to take their funds out of other markets to capture the higher rates in the market where the rates first increased. For example, when interest rates increase significantly in the bond markets, investors generally sell their stocks and invest the proceeds in bonds. Of course, borrowers and other users of funds act differently because they want to use the cheaper source of funds, which would be stocks in this case. Clearly such actions affect both markets; the additional funds provided to, and the lower demand for funds in, the bond markets help to decrease interest rates on bonds, whereas the decrease in funds in the stock markets help to

[13]The deficit could also be financed by selling assets, including gold, corporate stocks, entire companies, and real estate. The United States has financed its massive trade deficits by all of these approaches, but the primary method has been by borrowing.

increase rates on stocks. International financial markets are similarly inter-dependent—that is, when rates are higher in one country than in other countries, businesses tend to stay away from the high-interest country when seeking to borrow funds, whereas investors tend to migrate to the high-interest country. As a result, when interest rates are not "properly aligned," investors and borrowers take actions that realign the rates, both in domestic financial markets and in international financial markets.

Business Activity

Business conditions clearly influence interest rates. Inflation increased from the 1960s to 1981, and the general tendency during this period was toward higher interest rates. Since they peaked in 1981, the tendency has been toward lower interest rates. Until 1966, short-term rates were almost always lower than long-term rates. Thus, in those years, the yield curve was almost always "normal" in the sense that it was upward sloping.

We can return to Figure 5-2 to see how economic conditions influence interest rates. Here are the key points revealed by that graph:

1. The shaded areas in Figure 5-2 indicate recessions. During recessions, both the demand for money and the rate of inflation tend to fall, and, at the same time, the Federal Reserve tends to increase the money supply in an effort to stimulate the economy. As a result, interest rates typically decline during recessions. In 2004 and 2005, the U.S. economy showed signs of expanding, so any actions taken by the Fed to change interest rates constituted efforts to discourage too much expansion and to control future growth so that it did not result in high inflation. On the other hand, in the latter part of 2007 and the beginning of 2008, the Fed was concerned that a slowdown would occur in the economy as the result of a housing crisis, high fuel prices, and general uncertainty of consumers. As a result, the Fed lowered interest rates to stimulate business.

2. During recessions, short-term rates decline more sharply than do long-term rates. This situation occurs for two reasons. First, the Fed operates mainly in the short-term sector, so its intervention has the strongest effect here. Second, long-term rates reflect the average expected inflation rate over the next 20 to 30 years. This expectation generally does not change much, even when the current rate of inflation is low because of a recession.

Self-Test Questions

Other than inflationary expectations, liquidity preferences, and normal supply/demand fluctuations, name four additional factors that influence interest rates. Explain their effects.

How does the Fed stimulate the economy? How does it affect interest rates?

INTEREST RATE LEVELS AND STOCK PRICES

Interest rates have two effects on corporate profits. First, because interest is a cost, the higher the rate of interest, the lower a firm's profits, other things held constant. Second, interest rates affect the level of economic activity, and economic activity affects corporate profits. Interest rates obviously affect stock prices because of their effects on profits. Perhaps even more important, they influence stock prices because of competition in the marketplace between stocks and bonds. If interest rates rise sharply, investors can obtain higher returns in the bond market, which induces them to sell stocks and transfer funds from the stock market to the bond market. A massive sale of stocks in response to rising interest rates obviously would depress stock prices. Of course, the reverse occurs if interest rates decline. Indeed, in both December 1991 and October 2002, the Dow Jones Industrial Index rose greater than 10 percent in less than one month, which was caused primarily by sharp drops in long-term interest rates. On the other hand, at least to some extent, the poor performance exhibited by the market in 1994 and 2000, when the prices of common stocks declined, resulted from increases in interest rates.

Nevertheless, as interest rates decline, the stock market generally is the "hot" investment. In the 1990s, rates in the debt markets remained at relatively low to moderate levels, while rates in the stock markets reached historically high levels. In 2004, fearing that the economy would grow too quickly and inflation would escalate significantly, the Federal Reserve began increasing interest rates; in July 2006, the Fed was still increasing interest rates in an attempt to restrict inflationary pressures. When we wrote this book in May 2008, investors were quite concerned about signs of an economic recession. Similar concerns existed in 2005 and 2006 when there was great uncertainty about the future direction of the economy and the expected level of inflation. Generally, the performance of the stock markets during such periods is below average at best.

Self-Test Question

In what two ways do changes in interest rates affect stock prices?

THE COST OF MONEY AS A DETERMINANT OF VALUE

In this chapter, we discussed some of the factors that determine the cost of money. For the most part, these same factors also affect other rates of return, including rates earned on stocks and other investments. In Chapter 1, we mentioned that the value of an asset is a function of the cash flows that it is expected to generate in the future and the *rate of return* at which investors are willing to provide funds to purchase the investment. We know that many factors, including conditions in the economy and financial markets, affect the determination of the expected cash flows and the rate people demand when investing their funds; thus, the process of determining value can be fairly complex. In general, when the cost of money increases, the value of an asset decreases. Let's consider the logic of this statement with a simple example. Suppose that you are offered an investment that will pay you a constant $100 per year forever. If you want to earn a 10 percent return on this investment, you should be willing to pay $1,000 = $100/0.10 to purchase it. But how would the amount you are willing to pay for the investment differ if you decided that a 12.5 percent return was more appropriate than 10 percent? Because the annual payment that you will receive from the investment does not change, to earn 12.5 percent, the amount that you would be willing to pay to receive the $100 each year must be less than $1,000. To earn the higher return, you would be willing to pay only $800 because $100 is 12.5 percent of $800—that is, $100 = 0.125($800).

As you can see, the cost of money—that is, interest rates (returns)—affects the prices of investments. In fact, changes in interest rates can have a significant effect on the prices of stocks and bonds. In general, *when rates in the financial markets increase, the prices (values) of financial assets decrease.* In the next couple of chapters, we discuss the valuation of stocks and bonds to give you a better understanding of this fundamental valuation concept.

Self-Test Question

What is the relationship between the price, or market value, of an investment and the return on the investment?

Ethical Dilemma

Unadvertised Special: Is It a "Shark"?

Skip Stephens recently graduated from college with a degree in business administration. While attending college, Skip built up a large amount of debt, which currently includes student loans, outstanding credit card balances, bank loans, and so forth. Now that he has a good-paying job, Skip wants to clean up his debt position to improve his credit reputation so that he can qualify for a mortgage when he is ready to purchase a house in a few years.

As a result of a conversation with a financial planner, Skip decided that he should consolidate his debt into a single loan. Consolidation will help him to monitor his debt better as he pays it off, and such an action probably will also decrease the interest rate that he is now paying. It took some effort, but Skip was able to find a financial institution that seems willing to offer him the type of loan he needs. The firm, which is named Syndicated Lending, is a new firm that specializes in loans to riskier borrowers, so it appears to be the right fit for Skip. Much of Syndicated's business is conducted electronically via the Internet. Although the company has a Web site that gives some information about loans that Syndicated offers, there is not much information about interest rates, application fees, and other charges associated with getting a loan. When Skip clicked on the "Interest Rate" icon on Syndicated's Web site, a message appeared that said to contact the company directly. After several attempts, Skip was able

to speak to a "real" person at Syndicated. When he asked why more information was not available on the Web site, the employee stated that the company decided not to post interest rates because managers believed it was unfair to publicize low rates to lure customers knowing that most borrowers are unable to qualify for such loans. In other words, managers felt that using the "bait and switch" tactics like those used by competitors was unethical. The employee gave Skip some general information about the loans that Syndicated offers, but she would not tell him interest rates because the company had a policy of not quoting a rate until a thorough credit check was completed. As a result, to get an interest quote, Skip would have to fill out and submit a loan application and he would have to pay a $100 application/credit check fee.

Skip decided that he wanted more information about Syndicated before deciding whether to apply for a loan, so he talked with people in the local area, searched chat boards and consumer opinion Web sites on the Internet, and so forth. Although much of the information he collected was positive, many people complained that Syndicated was a "shady" organization that has a reputation for changing interest rates without notice, and that it is not a customer-friendly firm. Some of the people with whom Skip talked whom went as far as to call Syndicated an unethical "loan shark" that could

continues

get away with unannounced interest rate hikes and other changes in loan agreements because the company knows that its customers cannot borrow from any other financial institution in the local area. Now Skip is wondering whether it is wise to apply for a consolidated loan from Syndicated, even though it appears that he can improve his credit rating and lower his interest payments. What should Skip do? Does it seem like Syndicated follows unethical lending practices? Is it unethical to use "bait and switch" tactics like those that Syndicated accuses other institutions of using?[14] Should interest rates be posted on the company's Web site?

[14]A firm uses a "bait and switch" practice when it advertises a product at a price that it doesn't intend to honor; rather the company plans to sell either the same product or something else at a higher price.

CHAPTER PRINCIPLES
–The Answers

To summarize the key concepts, let's answer the questions that were posed at the beginning of the chapter:

- **What is the cost of money, and how is it determined?** The "cost of money" is simply the interest rate that lenders charge borrowers. Interest rates and such other rates as stock returns are determined by the supply of funds and the demand for those funds. When the demand for borrowed funds increases (decreases) relative to the supply of funds provided by investors, interest rates increase (decrease).

- **What factors affect interest rates (costs of money)?** The major factors that influence interest rates include (1) production opportunities, (2) time preferences for consumption, (3) risk, and (4) inflation. Everything else being equal, interest rates are higher when (1) borrowed funds can be invested in opportunities that provide higher payoffs, because higher interest rates can be paid to attract such funds; (2) fewer people are willing to save, because they either want or need to consume more of their incomes in the current period than normal; (3) risks associated with investing are higher, because investors require higher returns to take on greater risks; and (4) inflation expectations increase, because purchasing power losses are greater with higher inflation rates.

- **What is a yield curve? Does the yield curve indicate future interest rates?** A yield curve is a snapshot of the relationship between short- and long-term interest rates on a particular date. Although a yield curve can be downward sloping or flat, it is normally upward sloping. We know that investors "set" interest rates based on their expectations about the period during which their money is going to be invested, and long-term interest rates represent averages of short-term interest rates. It makes sense then that many believe the yield curve can be used to forecast future interest rates. According to the expectations theory, the direction of the shape of the yield curve indicates the direction interest rates will move in the future—that is, if the yield curve is upward sloping, interest rates are expected to increase in the future, and vice versa.

- **How do government actions and business activity affect interest rates?** When the federal government spends more than it earns (collects in taxes), the additional funds must be borrowed. Government borrowing exerts additional pressure on the demand for borrowed funds and perhaps inflates interest rates compared to what they would be if the government spent only what it collected in taxes. Businesses generally borrow more when interest rates are low, good investment opportunities are plentiful, or both situations exist. Everything else equal, when businesses demand additional loans, whether through the bank or by issuing bonds, interest rates increase. The Federal Reserve carries out the monetary policy of the United States. As a result, when the general level of interest rates is either too high or too low, the Fed will take actions to adjust interest rates to a more "normal" level.

- **How does the level of interest rates (returns) affect the values of stocks and bonds?**
  A fundamental concept mentioned throughout the book is that prices of assets move opposite changes in rates of return—that is, when rates increase, the prices (values) of assets decrease. We show examples of this concept in later chapters.

CHAPTER PRINCIPLES
–Personal Finance

Compared to someone who "has no clue," if you have a basic understanding of interest rates and you plan well, you can possibly (1) lower the cost of borrowing to buy a house, a car, or another high-priced item that generally requires a loan to purchase and (2) increase the average rate of return you earn when investing your money. Consider how you can make better decisions about investing and borrowing if you have a basic idea as to the role interest rates play in the financial markets. For example, if you have an indication, or feeling, as to the direction that interest rates will change in the future, you will be able to make informed decisions about when to invest in long-term (short-term) securities and when to borrow money via long-term (short-term) loans.

Suppose you believe that general interest rates are going to increase during the next 12 to 18 months. What should be your investing strategy and what should be your borrowing strategy? How can some of the concepts presented in this chapter help you make decisions about your personal finances?

- If you are considering purchasing a house in the near future and you thought interest rates were going to increase substantially, it would be better to buy now rather than wait until interest rates increase. If you buy now, your mortgage will have a lower interest rate than if you wait until interest rates are higher. In other words, if you need a loan for a period longer than 12 to 18 months, you should borrow long term to "lock in" today's lower rates.

- On the other hand, if you want to invest money today, you don't want to "lock in" today's lower rates by investing in long-term securities. Instead, you should invest in short-term securities and wait until market rates increase before "locking in" the higher rates.

- From our brief discussion of risk, you should realize that you can possibly earn higher returns if you invest in riskier securities rather than "safer" securities; you can also lose more of your investment when you take greater risks. On the other hand, you can lower the interest rates you pay for loans by taking actions that lower your individual credit risk. Like investors, lending institutions charge higher rates to lend to, or invest in, individuals with greater credit risks. We discuss risk and return in greater detail in Chapter 11.

QUESTIONS

5-1 Explain why the return associated with an investment includes both the income paid by the issuer and the change in value association with the investment.

5-2 Suppose interest rates on residential mortgages of equal risk were 8 percent in California and 10 percent in New York.

    a. Could this differential persist? What forces might tend to equalize rates?

    b. Would differentials in borrowing costs for businesses of equal risk located in California and New York be more or less likely to exist than differentials in residential mortgage rates? Would differentials in the cost of money for California and New York firms be more likely to exist if the firms being compared were very large or very small?

c. What are the implications of the trend for financial institutions to become large mega banking organizations and to engage in nationwide branching?

5-3   Which fluctuate more, short-term or long-term interest rates? Why?

5-4   Suppose a new process was developed that could be used to make oil out of seawater. The equipment required would be quite expensive but would, in time, lead to very low prices for gasoline, electricity, and other types of energy. What effect would this development have on interest rates?

5-5   Suppose a new, highly liberal Congress and presidential administration were elected. The first order of business for these bodies was to take away the independence of the Federal Reserve System and force the Fed to greatly expand the money supply. What effect would this change have on the level and slope of the yield curve in the following circumstances?

    a. Immediately after the announcement

    b. Two or three years in the future

5-6   Suppose interest rates on long-term Treasury bonds rose from 5 to 10 percent as a result of higher interest rates in Europe. What effect would this change have on the price of an average company's common stock?

5-7   How does the Federal Reserve change the money supply in the United States? What action would the Fed take to increase rates? To decrease interest rates?

5-8   How are the values of financial assets affected by changes in interest rates?

5-9   When investors expect interest rates to increase in the future, would they prefer to purchase short-term or long-term investments? Explain.

5-10   Which would be of greater concern to those who hold short-term investments: interest rate price risk or reinvestment rate risk? Explain.

SELF-TEST PROBLEMS

Solutions appear in Appendix B.

Key Terms   **ST-1** Define each of the following terms:

    a. Dollar return on investment; percent return (yield) on investment

    b. Production opportunities; time preferences for consumption; risk

    c. Real risk-free rate of interest, r^*; nominal risk-free rate of interest, r_{RF}

    d. Inflation; inflation premium (IP)

    e. Default risk premium (DRP)

    f. Liquidity; liquidity premium (LP)

    g. Interest rate price risk; maturity risk premium (MRP)

    h. Term structure of interest rates

    i. Yield curve; "normal" yield curve; "inverted" yield curve

    j. Market segmentation theory; liquidity preference theory; expectations theory

    k. Open market operations

ST-2   On January 1, 2010, Garrity Jones purchased 100 shares of Anchor Concrete's common stock for $80 per share. By December 31, 2010, the value of the stock had decreased to $78 per share. During the year, however, Garrity received dividends that totaled $5 per share.

   Realized Return

   a. What is the *dollar* return that Garrity earned during 2010?

   b. Compute the yield (percent return) associated with the investment for 2010.

ST-3   Assume that it is now January 1, 2010. The rate of inflation is expected to be 2 percent throughout 2010. In 2011 and after, increased government deficits and renewed vigor in the economy are expected to push inflation rates higher. Investors expect the inflation rate to be 3 percent in 2011, 5 percent in 2012, and 6 percent in 2013. The real risk-free rate, r*, currently is 3 percent. Assume that no maturity risk premiums are required on bonds with 5 years or less to maturity. The current interest rate on 5-year T-bonds is 8 percent.

   Inflation Rates

   a. What is the average expected inflation rate over the next 4 years?

   b. What should be the prevailing interest rate on 4-year T-bonds?

   c. What is the implied expected inflation rate in 2014, or Year 5, given that bonds that mature in Year 5 yield 8 percent?

PROBLEMS

5-1   Suppose it is now January 1, 2010, and you just sold an investment that you own for $12,500. You purchased the investment 4 years ago for $10,500. During the time you held the investment, it paid income equal to $1,000 each year. What is the 4-year holding period yield that you earned on your investment?

   Investment Yield

5-2   One year ago, Melissa purchased 50 shares of common stock for $20 per share. During the year, the value of her stock decreased to $18 per share. If the stock did not pay a dividend during the year, what yield did Melissa earn on her investment?

   Investment Yield

5-3   Suppose the annual yield on a 2-year Treasury bond is 7.5 percent, the yield on a 1-year bond is 5 percent, r* is 3 percent, and the maturity risk premium is 0.

   Expected Rate of Return

   a. Using the expectations theory, forecast the interest rate on a 1-year bond during the second year. (*Hint:* Under the expectations theory, the yield on a 2-year bond is equal to the average yield on 1-year bonds in Year 1 and Year 2.)

   b. What is the expected inflation rate in Year 1? Year 2?

5-4   Assume that the real risk-free rate is 4 percent and the maturity risk premium is zero. If the nominal rate of interest on 1-year bonds is 11 percent and on comparable-risk 2-year bonds it is 13 percent, what is the 1-year interest rate that is expected for Year 2? What inflation rate is expected during Year 2? Why might the average interest rate during the 2-year period differ from the 1-year interest rate expected for Year 2?

   Expected Rate of Interest

5-5   The rate of inflation for the coming year is expected to be 3 percent, and the rate of inflation in Year 2 and thereafter is expected to remain constant at some level above 3 percent. Assume that the real risk-free rate, r*, is

   Interest Rates

2 percent for all maturities and the expectations theory fully explains the yield curve, so there are no maturity premiums. If 3-year Treasury bonds yield 2 percentage points more than 1-year bonds, what rate of inflation is expected after Year 1?

Expected Inflation Rate   5-6   According to *The Wall Street Journal*, the interest rate on 1-year Treasury bonds is 2.2 percent, the rate on 2-year Treasury bonds is 3.0 percent, and the rate on 3-year Treasury bonds is 3.6 percent. These bonds are considered risk free, so the rates given here are risk-free rates (r_{RF}). The 1-year bond matures 1 year from today, the 2-year bond matures 2 years from today, and so forth. The *real* risk-free rate (r^*) for all 3 years is 2 percent. Using the expectations theory, compute the expected inflation rate for next year—that is, in Year 2.

MRP and DRP   5-7   Suppose economists have determined that the real risk-free rate of return is 3 percent and that inflation is expected to average 2.5 percent per year long into the future. A 1-year Treasury note offers a rate of return equal to 5.6 percent. You are evaluating two corporate bonds: (1) Bond A has a rate of return, r_A, equal to 8 percent; (2) Bond B has a rate of return, r_B, equal to 7.5 percent. Except for their maturities, these bonds are identical—Bond A matures in 10 years, whereas Bond B matures in 5 years. You have determined that both bonds are very liquid, and thus neither bond has a liquidity premium. Assuming that there is an MRP for bonds with maturities equal to 1 year or greater, compute the annual MRP. What is the DRP associated with corporate bonds?

Interest Rate   5-8   Today is January 1, 2010, and according to the results of a recent survey, investors expect the *annual* interest rates for the years 2013–2015 to be:

Year	1-Year Rate
2013	5.0%
2014	4.0
2015	3.0

The rates given here include the risk-free rate, r_{RF}, and appropriate risk premiums. Today, a 3-year bond—that is, a bond that matures on December 31, 2012—has an interest rate equal to 6 percent. What is the yield to maturity for bonds that mature at the end of 2013, 2014, and 2015?

Expected Interest   5-9   Suppose current interest rates on Treasury securities are as follows:

Maturity	Yield
1 year	5.0
2 years	5.5
3 years	6.0
4 years	5.5

Using the expectations theory, compute the expected interest rates (yields) for each security 1 year from now. What will the rates be 2 years from today and 3 years from today?

5-10   Suppose you and most other investors expect the rate of inflation to be 7 percent next year, to fall to 5 percent during the following year, and then to remain at a rate of 3 percent thereafter. Assume that the real risk-free rate, r*, is 2 percent and that maturity risk premiums on Treasury securities rise from 0 percent on very short-term bonds (those that mature in a few days) by 0.2 percentage points for each year to maturity, up to a limit of 1.0 percentage point on 5-year or longer term T-bonds.   **Yield Curve**

   a. Calculate the interest rate on 1-, 2-, 3-, 4-, 5-, 10-, and 20-year Treasury securities and plot the yield curve.

   b. Now suppose IBM, a highly rated company, had bonds with the same maturities as the Treasury bonds. As an approximation, plot a yield curve for IBM on the same graph with the Treasury bond yield curve. (*Hint:* Think about the default risk premium on IBM's long-term bonds versus its short-term bonds.)

   c. Now plot the approximate yield curve of Long Island Lighting Company, a risky nuclear utility.

5-11   Assume that the real risk-free rate of return, r*, is 3 percent, and it will remain at that level far into the future. Also assume that maturity risk premiums on Treasury bonds increase from 0 percent for bonds that mature in 1 year or less to a maximum of 2 percent, and MRP increases by 0.2 percent for each year to maturity that is greater than 1 year—that is, MRP equals 0.2 percent for a 2-year bond, 0.4 percent for a 3-year bond, and so forth. Following are the expected inflation rates for the next 5 years: **Rate of Interest**

Year	Inflation Rate
2010	3.0%
2011	5.0
2012	4.0
2013	8.0
2014	3.0

   a. What is the average expected inflation rate for 1-, 2-, 3-, 4-, and 5-year bonds?

   b. What should be the MRP for 1-, 2-, 3-, 4-, and 5-year bonds?

   c. Compute the interest rate for 1-, 2-, 3-, 4-, and 5-year bonds.

   d. If inflation is expected to equal 2 percent every year after 2014, what should be the interest rate for 10- and 20-year bonds?

   e. Plot the yield curve for the interest rates you computed in parts (c) and (d).

5-12   Today's *Wall Street Journal* reports that the yield on Treasury bills maturing in 30 days is 3.5 percent, the yield on Treasury bonds maturing in 10 years is 6.5 percent, and the yield on a bond issued by Nextel Communications that matures in 6 years is 7.5 percent. Also, today the Federal Reserve announced that inflation is expected to be 2.0 percent during the next 12 months. There is a maturity risk premium (MRP) associated with all bonds with maturities equal to 1 year or more.   **Real Risk-Free Rate, MRP, and DRP**

   a. Assume that the increase in the MRP each year is the same and the total MRP is the same for bonds with maturities equal to 10 years and greater—that is, MRP is at its maximum for bonds with maturities equal to 10 years and greater. What is the MRP per year?

b. What is the default risk premium associated with Nextel's bond.

c. What is the real risk-free rate of return?

Returns   **5-13**   A bond issued by Zephyr Balloons currently has a market price equal to $1,080. The bond pays $120 interest annually.

a. If you buy the bond and its price does not change during the year, what is the total dollar return that you would earn if you sell the bond at the end of the year? Compute the yield for the year.

b. If the price of the bond increases to $1,100 during the year, what is the total dollar return that you would earn if you sell the bond at the end of the year? Compute the yield for the year.

c. If the price of the bond decreases to $1,000 during the year, what is the total dollar return that you would earn if you sell the bond at the end of the year? Compute the yield for the year.

Yield Curves   **5-14**   The following yields on U.S. Treasury securities were published in *The Wall Street Journal* on October 8, 2007:

Term	Rate
6 months	4.2%
1 year	4.2
2 years	4.1
3 years	4.2
4 years	4.2
5 years	4.3
10 years	4.7
20 years	4.9
30 years	4.9

Plot a yield curve based on these data. Discuss how each term structure theory can explain the shape of the yield curve you plot.

Inflation and Interest Rate   **5-15**   It is January 1, 2010. Inflation currently is about 2 percent; throughout 2009, the Fed took action to maintain inflation at this level. Now, the economy is starting to grow too quickly, and reports indicate that inflation is expected to increase during the next 5 years. Assume that the rate of inflation *expected* for 2010 is 4 percent; for 2011, it is *expected* to be 5 percent; for 2012, it is *expected* to be 7 percent; and, for 2013 and every year thereafter, it is *expected* to settle at 4 percent.

a. What was the average expected inflation rate over the 5-year period 2010–2014? (Use the arithmetic average.)

b. What average nominal interest rate would, over the 5-year period, be expected to produce a 2 percent real risk-free rate of return on 5-year Treasury securities?

c. Assuming a real risk-free rate of 2 percent and a maturity risk premium that starts at 0.1 percent and increases by 0.1 percent *each year*, estimate the interest rate in January 2010 on bonds that mature in 1, 2, 5, 10, and 20 years, and then draw a yield curve based on these data.

d. Describe the general economic conditions that could be expected to produce an upward-sloping yield curve.

e. If the consensus among investors in early 2010 had been that the expected rate of inflation for every future year was 5 percent (that is, $\text{Inflation}_{2010} = \text{Inflation}_{2011} = 5\% = \ldots = \text{Inflation}_\infty$), what do you think the yield curve would have looked like? Consider all factors that are likely to affect the curve. Does your answer here make you question the yield curve you drew in part (c)?

Integrative Problem

5-16 In an effort to better understand how her investments are affected by market factors, Michelle Delatorre, the professional tennis player introduced in the Integrative Problem in Chapter 4, has posed some questions about yields and interest rates that she wants answered. Your boss at Balik and Kiefer has asked you to answer the following questions for Ms. Delatorre.

Yields and Interest Rates

a. What is the difference between the *dollar return* and the *percentage return,* or *yield,* on an investment? Show how each return is computed.

b. Ms. Delatorre mentioned that she purchased a stock 1 year ago for $250 per share and that the stock has a current market value equal to $240. She knows she received a dividend payment equal to $25, but she doesn't know what rate of return she earned on her investment. Help Ms. Delatorre by showing her how to compute the rate of return on her investment.

c. What do you call the *price* that a borrower must pay for debt capital? What is the price of equity capital? What are the *four* fundamental factors that affect the cost of money, or the general level of interest rates, in the economy?

d. What is the *real risk-free rate of interest* (r^*) and the *nominal risk-free rate* (r_{RF})? How are these two rates measured?

e. Define the terms *inflation premium (IP), default risk premium (DRP), liquidity premium (LP),* and *maturity risk premium (MRP).* Which of these premiums is included when determining the interest rate on (1) short-term U.S. Treasury securities, (2) long-term U.S. Treasury securities, (3) short-term corporate securities, and (4) long-term corporate securities? Explain how the premiums would vary over time and among the different securities.

f. What is the *term structure* of interest rates? What is a *yield curve?* At any given time, how would the yield curve facing a given company such as IBM or Microsoft compare with the yield curve for U.S. Treasury securities? Draw a graph to illustrate your answer.

g. Several theories have been advanced to explain the shape of the yield curve. The three major ones are the *market segmentation theory,* the *liquidity preference theory,* and the *expectations theory.* Briefly describe each of these theories. Do economists regard one as being "true"?

h. Suppose most investors expect the rate of inflation to be 1 percent next year, 3 percent the following year, and 4 percent thereafter. The real risk-free rate is 3 percent. The maturity risk premium is 0 percent for bonds that mature in 1 year or less, and 0.1 percent for 2-year bonds; the MRP increases by 0.1 percent per year thereafter for 20 years, then becomes stable. What is the interest rate on 1-, 10-, and 20-year Treasury bonds? Draw a yield curve with these data. Is your yield curve consistent with the three term structure theories?

COMPUTER-RELATED PROBLEM

Work the problem in this section only if you are using the computer problem spreadsheet.

Yield Curve   **5-17**   The problem requires you to use File C05 on the computer problem spreadsheet.

    a. Assume today is January 1, 2010, and the expected inflation rates for the next 5 years are as follows:

Year	Inflation Rate
2010	8.0%
2011	6.0
2012	4.0
2013	3.0
2014	5.0

    In 2015 and thereafter, inflation is expected to be 3 percent. The maturity risk premium is 0.1 percent per year to maturity for bonds with maturities greater than 6 months, with a maximum MRP equal to 2 percent. The real risk-free rate of return is currently 2.5 percent, and it is expected to remain at this level long into the future. Compute the interest rates on Treasury securities with maturities equal to 1 year, 2 years, 3 years, 4 years, 5 years, 10 years, 20 years, and 30 years. (The initial spreadsheet solution that you will see is for Problem 5-10.)

    b. Discuss the yield curve that is constructed from the results in part (a).

    c. Rework part (a) assuming 1 year has passed—that is, today is January 1, 2011. All the other information given in part (a) is the same. Rework part (a) again assuming 2, 3, 4, and 5 years have passed.

    d. Assume that all the information given previously is the same and the default risk premium for corporate bonds rated AAA is 1.5 percent whereas it is 4 percent for corporate bonds rated B. Compute the interest rates on AAA- and B-rated corporate bonds with maturities equal to 1 year, 2 years, 3 years, 4 years, 5 years, 10 years, 20 years, and 30 years.

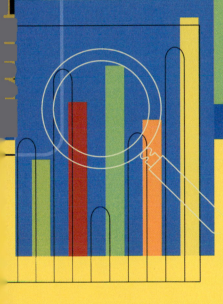

General Business Concepts

PART 2

Business Organizations and the Tax Environment

A MANAGERIAL PERSPECTIVE

When you invest in the common stock of a company, what do you hope (expect) to gain? Rational investors would answer this question with a single word—*wealth*. As you will discover in this chapter, a corporation acts in the best interests of its stockholders when decisions are made that increase the value of the firm, which translates into an increase in the value of the company's stock.

The managers of large corporations generally are encouraged to "act in the best interests" of the firms' stockholders through executive compensation packages that reward "appropriate behavior"—that is, actions that increase firms' values. When managers act in their own best interests and stockholders believe that value is not being maximized, these executives often are ousted from their extremely lucrative positions. Sounds like a good plan, doesn't it?

Although it seems like a good idea to reward managers who run firms with the best interests of the stockholders (owners) in mind, in recent years stockholders have complained that executive compensation plans that are found in many large corporations provide excessive rewards to executives who are interested only in increasing their own wealth positions. Consider, for example, that the CEO of Pfizer was paid $79 million during the period 2001–2005 and the CEOs of Home Depot and Verizon Communications were paid $27 million and $50 million, respectively, during the period from 2004–2005, even though, at the same time, these firms produced negative returns for stockholders.[1] According to Paul Hodgson, senior research associate at The Corporate Library, this is evidence "that the link between long-term value growth and long-term incentive awards is broken at too many companies—if it was ever forged properly in the first place."[2]

In recent years, investors have said: "Enough is enough." Stockholders are now demanding, and more boards of directors are imposing, tougher rules with regard to compensation packages, making it more difficult for executives to earn excessive salaries. In 2006, for example, the shareholders of Pfizer, Merrill Lynch, Morgan Stanley, General Electric, Citigroup, and Raytheon, among others, became much more active in expressing their feelings about "excessive"

[1]Alan Murray, "CEOs of the World, Unite? When Executive Pay Can Be Truly Excessive," *The Wall Street Journal*, April 26, 2006, A2.

[2]"Pay for Failure," The Corporate Library, http://thecorporatelibrary.blogspot.com/. The Corporate Library provides articles and information about corporate governance and executive compensation. Additional reports about CEO compensation can be found by searching http://money.cnn.com/ using the key words "CEO pay."

executive pay plans.[3] In 2007, UBS AG, which is a large Swiss financial institution, enacted a new policy that limited the cash payout to its investment bankers and security traders to $750,000; any additional compensation was paid in stock. Although part of the reason for the change was the fact that the credit markets were in disarray, the decision to limit cash salaries was seen as a move in the right direction.[4]

A compensation plan that has received a great deal of attention recently is the policy of offering "golden parachute" packages that provide executives with excessive payments when they are dismissed from their firms. In the past, a *golden parachute*, which gets its name from the fact that a significant severance pay permits an executive to easily "land on his or her financial feet" after dismissal from the company, often has to be honored no matter the reason for dismissal; one exception would be if a criminal offense was committed by the executive. More companies are now limiting the amount of the severance pay that executives can earn. In addition, large corporations, including ImClone Systems, NCR Corporation, and Walt Disney Company,

are revising their policies so that it is easier to fire executives without having to pay excessive severance pay. More boards of directors are redefining what it means to be fired for "just cause" to include a wider range of actions, or non-actions, for which executives can be dismissed without severance pay. Firms now are including poor firm performance as a justifiable reason for dismissing executives without severance. It seems that stockholders are "speaking their minds," and the boards of directors of many companies are listening.[5]

As you read this chapter, think about some of the issues raised here: As a stockholder in a company, what goal (or set of goals) would you like to see pursued? To what extent should top managers let their own personal goals influence the decisions they make concerning how the firm is run? Would you, as an outside stockholder, feel more comfortable that your interests were being represented better if the firm's top managers also owned large amounts of the firm's stock? What factors should management consider when trying to "boost" the value of the firm's stock?

[3]"Getting Active," The Wall Street Journal Online, May 4, 2006, and Carole Fleck, "The Power of You," *AARP Bulletin,* November 2007, 18–20.

[4]Anita Raghavan and Dana Cimilluca, "A Salary Cap for Bankers" $750,000 Max," *The Wall Street Journal,* November 10, 2007, B1+.

[5]Joann Lublin, "Just Cause: Some Firms Cut Golden Parachute," *The Wall Street Journal,* March 13, 2006, B3, and "Getting Active," The Wall Street Journal Online, May 4, 2006.

In the last few chapters, we described financial markets and the instruments traded in those markets. As we saw then, businesses issue many types of financial instruments to raise funds to support their current operations, replace worn-out assets, and promote future growth. It is reasonable to assume that investors will provide funds to firms only if they believe that those funds will be used "appropriately." But how do investors know when their funds are being used "appropriately," or when a firm is doing well? To answer this question, we need to understand the goals of the firm and the way in which financial managers can contribute to achieving these goals. This chapter provides an overview of business organizations, examining appropriate goals that should be pursued by financial managers and considering how finance fits in a firm's organizational structure. In addition, because taxes affect every financial decision—whether related to individuals or businesses—some key features of the U.S. tax laws are discussed in this chapter.

CHAPTER PRINCIPLES
–The Questions

After reading this chapter, you should be able to answer the following questions:

- What are the different forms of business organization? What are the advantages and disadvantages of each?
- What goal(s) should firms pursue? Do firms always pursue appropriate goals?
- What is the role of ethics in successful businesses?
- Why is it important for a business to have a clear corporate governance policy?
- How do foreign firms differ from U.S. firms?
- Why is it important to consider taxes when making financial decisions?

ALTERNATIVE FORMS OF BUSINESS ORGANIZATION

There are three main forms of business organization: (1) proprietorships, (2) partnerships, and (3) corporations. In terms of numbers, approximately 71 percent of businesses are operated as proprietorships, 9 percent are partnerships, and the remaining 20 percent are corporations. Based on the dollar value of sales, however, almost 85 percent of all business is conducted by corporations, while the remaining 15 percent is generated by both proprietorships (4 percent) and partnerships (11 percent).[6] Because most business is conducted by corporations, we will focus on this form in this book. However, it is important to understand the differences among the three major forms of business as well as the popular "hybrid" forms of business that have evolved from these major forms.

Proprietorship

A **proprietorship** is an unincorporated business owned by one individual. Starting a proprietorship is fairly easy—just begin business operations. In many cases, however, even the smallest business must be licensed by the municipality (city, county, or state) in which it operates.

proprietorship
An unincorporated business owned by one individual.

The proprietorship has three important advantages:

1. It is easily and inexpensively formed.

2. It is subject to few government regulations. Large firms that potentially threaten competition are much more heavily regulated than small "mom-and-pop" businesses.

3. It is taxed like an individual, not a corporation, thus earnings are taxed only once. As we will discuss later, the U.S. Tax Code is composed of only two sections: the individual section and the corporation section. The "corporation section" applies only to businesses that are legal corporations, which means all other forms of business are taxed according to the "individual section."

The proprietorship also has four important limitations:

1. The proprietor has *unlimited personal liability* for business debts. With unlimited personal liability, the proprietor (owner) can potentially lose all of his or her personal assets, even those assets not invested in the business; thus, losses can far exceed the money that he or she has invested in the company.

2. A proprietorship's life is limited to the time the individual who created it owns the business. When a new owner takes over the business, technically the firm becomes a new proprietorship (even if the name of the business does not change).

3. Transferring ownership is somewhat difficult. Disposing of the business is similar to selling a house in that the proprietor must seek out and negotiate with a potential buyer, which generally takes some time.

4. It is difficult for a proprietorship to obtain large sums of capital (long-term funds) because the firm's financial strength generally is based on the financial strength of the sole owner.

For the reasons mentioned here, individual proprietorships are confined primarily to small business operations. In fact, only about 1 percent of all proprietorships have

---

[6]The statistics provided in this section are based on business tax filings reported by the Internal Revenue Service (IRS) in 2007. Additional statistics can be found on the IRS Web site at http://www.irs.ustreas.gov/tax_stats.

assets that are valued at \$1 million or greater; nearly 90 percent have assets valued at \$100,000 or less. Most large businesses, however, start out as proprietorships and then convert to corporations when their growth causes the disadvantages of being a proprietorship—namely, unlimited personal liability—to outweigh the advantages.

Partnership

partnership
An unincorporated business owned by two or more persons.

A **partnership** is the same as a proprietorship, except that it has two or more owners. Partnerships can operate under different degrees of formality, ranging from informal, oral understandings to formal agreements filed with the secretary of the state in which the partnership does business. Most legal experts recommend that partnership agreements be put in writing.

The advantages of a partnership are the same as for a proprietorship:

1. Formation is easy and relatively inexpensive.
2. It is subject to few government regulations.
3. It is taxed like an individual, not a corporation.

The disadvantages are also similar to those associated with proprietorships:

1. *Unlimited personal liability for the owners/partners.* To illustrate the concept of unlimited liability, suppose you invested \$10,000 to become a partner in a business that subsequently went bankrupt, owing creditors \$1 million. Because the owners are liable for the debts of a partnership, as a partner you would be assessed for a share of the company's debt; you could even be held liable for the entire \$1 million if your partners could not pay their shares. Under partnership law each partner is liable for the debts of the business. Therefore, if any partner is unable to meet his or her pro rata claim in the event the partnership goes bankrupt, the remaining partners must make good on the unsatisfied claims, drawing on their personal assets if necessary. Thus, the business-related activities of any of the firm's partners can bring ruin to the other partners, even though those partners are not a direct party to such activities. This is the danger of unlimited liability.
2. *Limited life of the organization.* When the composition of the partnership changes or the business is sold, the original partnership no longer exists.
3. *Difficulty of transferring ownership.*
4. *Difficulty of raising large amounts of capital.* Because there are more owners, everything else equal, partnerships generally find it easier than proprietorships to raise funds.

The first three disadvantages—unlimited liability, impermanence of the organization, and difficulty of transferring ownership—lead to the fourth, the difficulty partnerships have in attracting substantial amounts of funds. This is not a major problem for a slow-growing business. If, however, a business's products really catch on and it needs to raise large amounts of funds to capitalize on its opportunities, the difficulty in attracting funds becomes a real drawback. For this reason, growth companies such as Microsoft and Dell Inc. generally begin life as proprietorships or partnerships, but at some point they find it necessary to convert to corporations.

Corporation

corporation
A legal entity created by a state, separate and distinct from its owners and managers, having unlimited life, easy transferability of ownership, and limited liability.

A **corporation** is a legal entity created by a state. It is separate and distinct from its owners and managers, which permits a corporation to conduct business and enter legal agreements the same as an individual. This separateness gives the corporation four major advantages:

1. A corporation can continue after its original owners and managers no longer have a relationship with the business; thus, it is said to have *unlimited life*.

2. Ownership interests can be divided into shares of stock, which in turn can be *transferred far more easily* than can proprietorship or partnership interests.

3. A corporation offers its owners *limited liability*. The danger of the unlimited liability that affects the owners of a partnership was described earlier. With the limited liability that is associated with ownership of a corporation, an investor is generally liable only for the amount that he or she invests in the company's stock. For example, if you invested $10,000 in the stock of a corporation that then went bankrupt, your potential loss on the investment would be limited to your $10,000 investment.[7]

4. The first three factors—unlimited life, easy transferability of ownership interest, and limited liability—make it much easier for corporations than for proprietorships or partnerships to raise money in the financial markets.

Even though the corporate form of business offers significant advantages over proprietorships and partnerships, it does have two major disadvantages:

1. Setting up a corporation, as well as subsequent filings of required state and federal reports, is more complex and time consuming than for a proprietorship or a partnership. When a corporation is created, (a) a **corporate charter,** which provides general information, including the name of the corporation, types of activities it will pursue, amount of stock, and so forth, must be filed with the secretary of the state in which the firm incorporates and (b) a set of rules, called **bylaws,** that specifies how the corporation will be governed, must be drawn up by the founder(s).

2. Corporate earnings are subject to double taxation—the earnings of the corporation are taxed at the corporate level, and then any earnings paid out as dividends are again taxed as income to stockholders.[8]

corporate charter
A document filed with the secretary of the state in which a business is incorporated that provides information about the company, including its name, address, directors, and amount of capital stock.

bylaws
A set of rules drawn up by the founders of the corporation that indicate how the company is to be governed; includes procedures for electing directors, the rights of the stockholders, and how to change the bylaws when necessary.

Hybrid Business Forms—LLP, LLC, and S Corporation

Alternative business forms that include some of the advantages, as well as avoid some of the disadvantages, of the three major forms of business have evolved over time. These alternative forms of business combine some characteristics of proprietorships and partnerships with some characteristics of corporations. In this section, we provide a brief description of three popular *hybrid business forms* that exist today.

Limited Liability Partnership (LLP)

In the earlier discussion of a partnership, we described the form of business that generally is referred to as a *general partnership,* in which each partner is personally

---

[7]In the case of small corporations, the limited liability feature is often fictitious because bankers and credit managers frequently require personal guarantees from the stockholders of small, weak businesses.

[8]There was a push in Congress in 2003 to eliminate the double taxation of dividends by either treating dividends paid by corporations the same as interest—that is, making them a tax-deductible expense—or allowing dividends to be tax exempt to stockholders. Congress passed neither; instead the tax on dividends received by investors was reduced from the ordinary tax rate to the capital gains rate. Taxes will be discussed briefly later in this chapter.

**limited liability partner-
ship (LLP)**
A partnership wherein
one (or more) partner is
designated the *general
partner(s)* with unlimited
personal financial liability
and the other partners
are *limited partners* whose
liability is limited to
amounts they invested in
the firm.

liable for the debts of the business. It is possible to limit the liability faced by some of the partners by establishing a **limited liability partnership (LLP),** wherein one (or more) partner is designated the *general partner(s)* and the others are *limited partners*. The general partner(s) remains fully personally liable for all business debts, whereas the limited partners are liable only for the amounts they have invested in the business. Only the general partners can participate in the management of the business. If a limited partner becomes involved in the day-to-day management of the firm, then he or she no longer has the protection of limited personal liability. The LLP form of business allows persons to invest in partnerships without exposure to the personal financial liability that general partners face.

Limited Liability Company (LLC)

**limited liability company
(LLC)**
Offers the limited per-
sonal liability associated
with a corporation, but
the company's income is
taxed like a partnership.

A **limited liability company (LLC)** is a legal entity that is separate and distinct from its owners and managers. An LLC offers the limited personal liability associated with a corporation, but the company's income is taxed like a partnership in that it passes through to the owners (it is taxed only once). The structure of the LLC is fairly flexible—owners generally can divide liability, management responsibilities, ownership shares, and control of the business any way they please. Like a corporation, paperwork (articles of organization) must be filed with the state in which the business is set up, and there are certain financial reporting requirements after the formation of an LLC. But, in most cases, the formal paperwork and financial reporting associated with an LLC are less burdensome than for a corporation—for example, some states do not require LLCs to hold formal annual meetings.

The owners of an LLC are referred to as members, and there generally are no restrictions as to how many members there are or who the members are—that is, an LLC can have one owner or several million owners, and owners/members can be individuals, businesses, including other LLCs, foreign companies, or any combination of these. Most states that allow the LLC form of business restrict the type of business that can form as LLCs. For example, generally, financial service companies and related organizations cannot be LLCs.

The two major advantages of an LLC are flexibility of the ownership structure and the ability to elect to be taxed either as a corporation or as a partnership while maintaining limited liability for the owners.

S Corporation

S corporation
A corporation with no
more than 100 stock-
holders that elects to be
taxed the same as pro-
prietorships and partner-
ships so that business
income is taxed only
once.

A domestic corporation that has no more than 100 stockholders and only one type of stock outstanding can elect to file taxes as an **S corporation.** If a corporation elects the S corporation status, then its income is taxed the same as income earned by proprietorships and partnerships—that is, income "passes through" the company to the owners so that it is taxed only once. The major differences between an S corporation and an LLC form of business are that an LLC can have more than 100 stockholders and more than one type of stock. In addition, the owners of S corporations must be individuals who are citizens or legal residents of the United States.

For the following reasons, the value of any business, other than a very small company, probably will be maximized if it is organized as a corporation:

1. Limited liability reduces the risks borne by investors. Other considerations held constant, *the lower the firm's risk, the higher its market value.*

2. *A firm's current value is related to its future growth opportunities,* and corporations can attract funds more easily than can unincorporated businesses to take advantage of growth opportunities.

3. Corporate ownership can be transferred more easily than ownership of either a proprietorship or a partnership. Therefore, all else equal, investors would be willing to pay more for a corporation than a proprietorship or partnership, which means that the corporate form of organization can *enhance the value* of a business.

Most firms are managed with value maximization in mind, and this, in turn, has caused most large businesses to be organized as corporations.

Self-Test Questions

What are the key differences among proprietorships, partnerships, and corporations?

Explain why the value of any business (other than a small firm) will be maximized if it is organized as a corporation.

FINANCE IN THE ORGANIZATIONAL STRUCTURE OF THE FIRM

Organizational structures vary from firm to firm, but Figure 6-1 presents a fairly typical picture of the role of finance within a corporation. The chief financial officer (CFO), who might have the title of vice president of finance, reports to the president. The financial vice president's key subordinates are the treasurer and the controller. In most firms, the treasurer has direct responsibility for managing the firm's cash and marketable securities, planning how funds are raised, selling stocks and bonds to raise funds, and overseeing the corporate pension fund. The treasurer also supervises the credit manager, the inventory manager, and the director of capital budgeting (who analyzes decisions related to investments in

FIGURE 6-1   Role of Finance in a Typical Business Organization

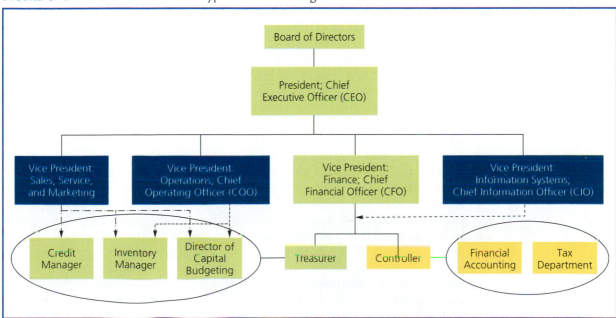

fixed assets). The controller is responsible for the activities of the accounting and tax departments.

Self-Test Question

Identify the two subordinates who report to the firm's chief financial officer, and indicate the primary responsibilities of each.

WHAT GOAL(S) SHOULD BUSINESSES PURSUE?

Depending on the form of business, the primary goal of a firm might differ somewhat, but, in general, every business owner wants the value of his or her investment in the firm to increase. The owner of a proprietorship has direct control over his or her investment in the company because it is the proprietor who runs the business. As a result, a proprietor might choose to work three days per week and play golf or fish the rest of the week as long as the business remains successful and he or she is satisfied living this type of life. On the other hand, the owners (stockholders) of a large corporation have little control over their investments because they generally do not run the business. Because they are not involved in the day-to-day decisions, these stockholders expect that the managers who run the business do so with the best interests of the owners in mind.

Investors purchase the stock of a corporation because they expect to earn an acceptable return on the money they invest. Because we know investors want to increase their wealth positions as much as possible, all else equal, then it follows that managers should behave in a manner that is consistent with enhancing the firm's value. For this reason, throughout this book we operate on the assumption that management's primary goal is **stockholder wealth maximization,** which, as we will see, translates into maximizing the value of the firm as measured by the price of its common stock. Firms do, of course, have other objectives: in particular, managers who make the actual decisions are interested in their own personal satisfaction, in their employees' welfare, and in the good of the community and of society at large. Still, *stock price maximization is the most important goal of most corporations*.

If a firm attempts to maximize its stock price, is this good or is this bad for society? In general, it is good. Aside from such illegal actions as attempting to form monopolies, violating safety codes, and failing to meet pollution control requirements, *the same actions that maximize stock prices also benefit society*. First, note that stock price maximization requires efficient, low-cost plants that produce high-quality goods and services that are sold at the lowest possible prices. Second, stock price maximization requires the development of products that consumers want and need, so the profit motive leads to new technology, new products, and new jobs. Finally, stock price maximization necessitates efficient and courteous service, adequate stocks of merchandise, and well-located business establishments. All of these factors are necessary to maintain a customer base that is required for producing sales and, thus, profits. In addition, to remain sustainable, actions taken by a business must respect all of the stakeholders of the company, which include owners, employees, customers, local residents, the government, and the environment. Therefore, most actions that help a firm increase the price of its stock also are beneficial to society at large. This is why profit-motivated, free-enterprise economies have been so much more successful than socialistic and communistic economic systems.

stockholder wealth maximization
The appropriate goal for management decisions; considers the risk and timing associated with expected cash flows to maximize the price of the firm's common stock.

Because managerial finance plays a crucial role in the operation of successful firms, and because successful firms are necessary for a healthy, productive economy, it is easy to see why finance is important from a social standpoint.[9]

Self-Test Questions

What should be management's primary goal?

How does the goal of stock price maximization benefit society at large?

MANAGERIAL ACTIONS TO MAXIMIZE SHAREHOLDER WEALTH

How do we measure value, and what types of actions can management take to maximize value? Although we will discuss valuation in much greater detail later in the book, we introduce the concept of value here to give you an indication of how management can affect the price of a company's stock. First, the value of any investment, such as a stock, is based on the amount of cash flows the asset is expected to generate during its life. Second, investors prefer to receive a particular cash flow sooner rather than later. And, third, investors generally are risk averse, which means that they are willing to pay more for investments with more certain future cash flows than investments with less certain, or riskier, cash flows, everything else equal. For these reasons, we know that managers can increase the value of a firm by making decisions that increase the firm's expected future cash flows, generate the expected cash flows sooner, increase the certainty of the expected cash flows, or produce any combination of these actions.

The financial manager makes decisions about the expected cash flows of the firm, which include decisions about how much and what types of debt and equity should be used to finance the firm **(capital structure decisions),** what types of assets should be purchased to help generate expected cash flows **(capital budgeting decisions),** and what to do with net cash flows generated by the firm—reinvest in the firm or pay dividends **(dividend policy decisions).** Each of these topics will be addressed in detail later in the book. But, at this point, it should be clear that the decisions financial managers make can significantly affect the firm's value, because they affect the amount, timing, and riskiness of the cash flows the firm produces.

Although managerial actions affect the value of a firm's stock, external factors also influence stock prices. Included among these factors are legal constraints, the general level of economic activity, tax laws, and conditions in the financial markets. Working within the set of external constraints, management makes a set of long-run strategic policy decisions that chart a future course for the firm. These policy decisions, along with the general level of economic activity and government regulations and rules (for instance, tax payments), influence the firm's expected

capital structure decisions
Decisions about how much and what types of debt and equity should be used to finance the firm.

capital budgeting decisions
Decisions as to what types of assets should be purchased to help generate future cash flows.

dividend policy decisions
Decisions concerning how much of current earnings to pay out as dividends rather than retain for reinvestment in the firm.

---

[9]People sometimes argue that firms, in their efforts to raise profits and stock prices, increase product prices and gouge the public. In a reasonably competitive economy, which we have, prices are constrained by competition and consumer resistance. If a firm raises its prices beyond reasonable levels, it will simply lose its market share. Even giant firms like General Motors lose business to the Japanese and Germans, as well as to Ford and Chrysler, if they set prices above levels necessary to cover production costs and earn a "normal" profit. Of course, firms want to earn more, and they constantly try to cut costs or develop new products when attempting to earn above-normal profits. Note, however that if they are indeed successful and do earn above-normal profits, those very profits will attract competition that will eventually drive prices down, so again the main long-term beneficiary is the consumer.

FIGURE 6-2 Value of the Firm

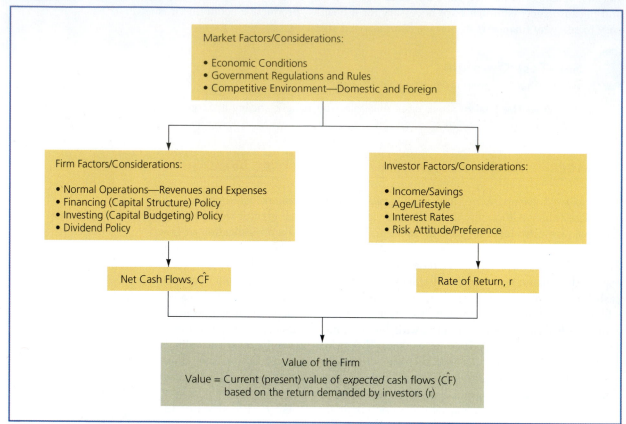

cash flows, the timing of these cash flows and their eventual transfer to stock-holders in the form of dividends, and the degree of risk inherent in the expected cash flows.

Figure 6-2 diagrams the general relationships involved in the valuation process. As you can see, and we will discuss in much greater detail throughout the book, a firm's value is ultimately a function of the cash flows it is expected to generate in the future and the rate of return at which investors are willing to provide funds to the firm for the purposes of financing operations and growth. Many factors, including conditions in the economy and financial markets, the competitive environment, and the general operations of the firm, affect the determination of the expected cash flows and the rate people demand when investing their funds. As we progress through the book, we will discuss these and other factors that affect a firm's value. For now, however, it is important to know that when we refer to **value,** we mean the worth of the expected future cash flows stated in current dollars—that is, the present, or current, value of the future cash flows.

value
The present, or current, value of the cash flows an asset is expected to generate in the future.

 Self-Test Questions

Identify some decisions made by financial managers that affect the firm's value.

Identify some factors beyond a firm's control that influence its stock price.

SHOULD EARNINGS PER SHARE (EPS) BE MAXIMIZED?

Will **profit maximization** also result in stock price maximization? In answering this question, we introduce the concept of **earnings per share (EPS),** which equals net income (NI) divided by the number of outstanding shares of common stock (Shares)—that is, NI/Shares. Many investors use EPS to gauge the value of a stock. A primary reason EPS receives so much attention is the belief that net income, and thus EPS, can be used as a barometer for measuring the firm's potential for generating future cash flows. Although current earnings and cash flows are generally highly correlated, as we mentioned earlier, a firm's value is determined by the cash flows it is expected to generate in the future as well as the risk associated with these expected cash flows. Thus, financial managers who attempt to maximize earnings might not maximize value, because earnings maximization is a shortsighted goal. Most managers who focus solely on earnings generally do not consider the impact maximizing earnings in the current period has on either future earnings (timing) or the firm's future risk position.

First, think about the *timing of the earnings*. Suppose Xerox has a project that will cause earnings per share to rise by $0.20 per year for 5 years, or $1 in total, whereas another project would have no effect on earnings for 4 years but would increase EPS by $1.25 in the fifth year. Which project is better—in other words, is $0.20 per year for 5 years better or worse than $1.25 in Year 5? The answer depends on which project contributes the most to the value of the firm, which in turn depends on the time value of money to investors. Thus, timing is an important reason to concentrate on wealth as measured by the price of the stock rather than on earnings alone.

Second, consider *risk*. Suppose one project is expected to increase EPS by $1, while another is expected to increase earnings by $1.20 per share. The first project is not very risky. If it is undertaken, earnings will almost certainly rise by approximately $1 per share. The other project is quite risky, however. Although our best guess is that earnings will rise by $1.20 per share, we must recognize the possibility that there might be no increase whatsoever, or that the firm might even suffer a loss. Depending on how averse stockholders are to risk, the first project might be preferable to the second.

In many instances, firms have taken actions that increased earnings per share, yet the stock price decreased because investors believed that either the higher earnings would not be sustained in the future or the riskiness of the firm would be increased substantially. Of course, the opposite effect has been observed as well. We see, then, that the firm's stock price, and thus its value, is dependent on (1) the cash flows the firm is expected to provide in the future, (2) when these cash flows are expected to occur, and (3) the risk associated with these cash flows. As we proceed through the book, you will discover that, everything else equal, the firm's value increases if the cash flows the firm is expected to provide increase, they are received sooner, their risk is lowered, or some combination of these actions occurs. Every significant corporate decision should be analyzed in terms of its effect on the firm's value, and hence the price of its stock.

profit maximization
Maximization of the firm's net income each year.

earnings per share (EPS)
Net income divided by the number of shares of common stock outstanding.

Self-Test Questions

Will profit maximization always result in stock price maximization?

Identify three factors that affect the value of the firm, and explain the effects of each.

MANAGERS' ROLES AS AGENTS OF STOCKHOLDERS

Because they generally are not involved in the day-to-day operations, stockholders of large corporations "permit" (empower) the managers to make decisions as to how the firms are run. Of course, even though the stockholders want the managers to make decisions that are consistent with the goal of wealth maximization, managers' interests can potentially conflict with stockholders' interests.

An *agency relationship* exists when one or more individuals, who are called the *principals,* hire another person, the *agent,* to perform a service and delegate decision-making authority to that agent. An **agency problem** arises when the agent makes decisions that are not in the best interests of the principals.

agency problem
A potential conflict of interest between outside shareholders (owners) and managers who make decisions about how to operate the firm.

If a firm is a proprietorship managed by the owner, the owner-manager will presumably operate the business in a fashion that will improve his or her own welfare, with welfare measured in the form of increased personal wealth, more leisure, or perquisites.[10] If, however, the owner-manager incorporates and sells some of the firm's stock to outsiders, a potential conflict of interests immediately arises. For example, the owner-manager might now decide not to work as hard to maximize shareholder wealth because less of the firm's wealth will go to him or her, or the owner-manager might decide to take a higher salary or enjoy more perquisites because part of those costs will fall on the outside stockholders. This potential conflict between two parties—the principals (outside shareholders) and the agents (managers)—is an agency problem.

The potential for agency problems is greatest in large corporations with widely dispersed ownership—for example, IBM and General Motors—because individual stockholders own only very small proportions of the companies and managers have little, if any, of their own wealth tied up in these companies. For this reason, managers might be more concerned about pursuing their own agendas, such as increased job security, higher salary, or more power, than maximizing shareholder wealth.

What can be done to ensure that management treats outside stockholders fairly at the same time the goal of wealth maximization is pursued? Several mechanisms are used to motivate managers to act in the shareholders' best interests. These include:

1. *Managerial compensation (incentives).* A common method used to motivate managers to operate in a manner consistent with stock price maximization is to tie managers' compensation to the company's performance. Such compensation packages should be developed so that managers are rewarded on the basis of the firm's performance over a long period of time, not on the performance in any particular year.

   One compensation plan that many firms use is to give managers **performance shares.** Under this plan, shares of stock are awarded on the basis of the firm's performance—as measured by earnings per share, return on assets, or return on equity, for example—and the executive's tenure with the firm. For example, Dell Inc. uses performance targets based on growth in sales and profit margins relative to industry measures and such nonfinancial factors as customer satisfaction and product leadership. If the company achieves a targeted average growth in earnings per share, managers earn 100 percent of their shares. If the corporate performance is above the target,

performance shares
A type of incentive plan in which managers are awarded shares of stock on the basis of the firm's performance over given intervals with respect to earnings per share or other measures.

---

[10]Perquisites are executive fringe benefits, such as luxurious offices, use of corporate planes and yachts, personal assistants, and general use of business assets for personal purposes.

Dell's managers can earn even more shares. But if growth is below the target, they get less than 100 percent of the shares.

Many large corporations also offer **executive stock options,** which allow managers to purchase stock at some future time at a given price. Because the value of the options is tied directly to the price of the stock, it is assumed that granting options will provide an incentive for managers to take actions that will maximize the stock's price. This type of managerial incentive lost favor in the 1970s, however, because the general stock market declined, and stock prices did not necessarily reflect companies' earnings growth. Incentive plans should be based on those factors over which managers have control, and because they cannot control the general stock market, stock option plans that reward increases in stock prices regardless of economic conditions are not good incentive devices. Today, these plans are based on the performance of the firm's stock price relative to some standard, such as the performance of other stocks in the same industry or the market as a whole during a comparable time period.

> **executive stock option**
> A type of incentive plan that allows managers to purchase stock at some future time at a given price.

There has been a recent movement to replace executive stock options with a fairly new compensation program, **restricted stock grants.** Firms that use this program grant what is termed *restrictive stock* to employees as an incentive for reaching certain financial and nonfinancial goals. The stock given to employees is restricted in the sense that an employee is not vested in the stock—that is, does not have the right to ownership—until some period in the future, say, 5 years. Once vested, the employee can trade the stock for its existing market value. Companies, especially those in technology industries, prefer restricted stock grants because, unless the price of the company's stock drops to $0, the stock that was granted to the employee will have value when he or she is vested. On the other hand, stock options would be worthless at the time they become exercisable if the market value of the stock is less than the exercise price (the price at which the stock can be purchased using the option—that is, exercising it).

> **restricted stock grants**
> Stock is granted to employees based on the firm's performance, but the stock is restricted in the sense that an employee is not vested—that is, does not have the right to ownership of the stock—until some period in the future.

All incentive compensation plans are designed to accomplish two things: (a) provide inducements to executives to act on those factors under their control in a manner that will contribute to stock price maximization and (b) attract and retain top-level executives. Well-designed plans can accomplish both goals.

2. *Shareholder intervention.* More than 25 percent of the individuals in the United States invest *directly* in stocks. Along with such institutional stockholders as pension funds and mutual funds, individual stockholders are "flexing their muscles" to ensure that firms pursue goals that are in the best interests of shareholders rather than managers (where conflicts might arise). Many institutional investors, especially pension funds such as TIAA-CREF and Laborers International Union of North America, routinely monitor top corporations to ensure that managers pursue the goal of wealth maximization. When it is determined that action is needed to "realign" management decisions with the interests of investors, these institutional investors exercise their influence by suggesting possible remedies to management or by sponsoring proposals that must be voted on by stockholders at the annual meeting. Stockholder-sponsored proposals are not binding, but the results of the votes are surely noticed by corporate management.

In situations where large blocks of the stock are owned by a relatively few large institutions, such as pension funds and mutual funds, and they have enough clout to influence a firm's operations, these institutional owners often have enough voting power to overthrow management teams that do not act in the best interests of stockholders. Examples of major corporations whose managements have been ousted in recent years include Coca-Cola, Disney, General Motors, IBM, Lucent Technologies, United Airlines, and Xerox.

hostile takeover
The acquisition of a company over the opposition of its management.

3. *Threat of takeover.* **Hostile takeovers,** instances in which management does not want the firm to be taken over, are most likely to occur when a firm's stock is undervalued relative to its potential, which often is caused by poor management. In a hostile takeover, the managers of the acquired firm generally are fired, and those who do stay on typically lose the power they had prior to the acquisition. Thus, managers have a strong incentive to take actions that maximize stock prices. In the words of one company president, "If you want to keep control, don't let your company's stock sell at a bargain price."

Wealth maximization is a long-term goal, not a short-term goal. For this reason, when executives are rewarded for maximizing the price of the firm's stock, the reward should be based on the long-run performance of the stock. Because the goal of wealth maximization is achieved over time, management must be able to convey to stockholders that their best interests are being pursued. As you proceed through the book, you will discover that many factors affect the value of a stock, which make it difficult to determine precisely when management is acting in the stockholders' best interests. However, a firm's management team will find it difficult to "fool" investors, both in general and for a long period—stockholders can generally recognize when a firm makes a major decision that is value increasing, and vice versa.

Self-Test Questions

What is an agency relationship?

Give some examples of potential problems between stockholders and managers.

List some factors that motivate managers to act in the best interests of stockholders.

STOCKHOLDERS' ROLES AS AGENTS OF CREDITORS

Conflicts between stockholders and creditors (debtholders) can also exist. Creditors lend funds to the firm at rates that are based on (1) the riskiness of the firm's existing assets, (2) expectations concerning the riskiness of future asset additions, (3) the firm's existing capital structure (that is, the amount of debt financing it uses), and (4) expectations concerning future capital structure changes. These factors determine the riskiness of the firm's debt, so creditors (lenders) base the interest rates they charge on expectations regarding these factors.

Suppose that the stockholders, acting through management, cause the firm to take on new ventures that have much greater risk than was anticipated by the creditors. This increased risk will cause the value of the outstanding debt to fall because new investors in the debt will demand a higher rate of return. If the risky ventures prove successful, all of the benefits will go to the stockholders because the creditors receive a fixed return. If things go sour, however, the bondholders will have to share the losses. From the stockholders' point of view, this activity amounts to a game of "heads I win, tails you lose," which obviously is not a good game for the bondholders.

Similarly, if the firm increases its use of debt in an effort to boost the return to stockholders, the value of the old debt will decrease, because the increased debt will result in a greater risk to debtholders. Again we have a "heads I win, tails you lose" situation.

Can and should stockholders, through their managers/agents, try to expropriate wealth from the firm's creditors? In general, the answer to this question is no. First, because such attempts have been made in the past, creditors today protect themselves reasonably well against stockholder actions through restrictions in credit agreements (called covenants). Second, if potential creditors perceive that a firm will try to take advantage of them in unethical ways, they will either refuse to deal with the firm or require a much higher than normal rate of interest to compensate for the risk of such "sneaky" actions. In the end, firms that try to deal unfairly with creditors either lose access to the debt markets or become saddled with higher interest rates, both of which decrease the long-run value of their stock.

In view of these constraints, it follows that the goal of maximizing shareholder wealth requires fair play with creditors: stockholder wealth depends on continued access to capital markets, and access depends on fair play and abiding by both the letter and the spirit of credit agreements. Managers, as agents of both the creditors and the stockholders, must act in a manner that fairly balances the interests of these two classes of security holders. Similarly, because of other constraints and sanctions, management actions that would expropriate wealth from any of the firm's **stakeholders** (employees, customers, suppliers, and the like) will ultimately prove detrimental to shareholders. Maximizing shareholder wealth requires the fair treatment of all stakeholders.

stakeholders
Those who are associated with a business; stakeholders include managers, employees, customers, suppliers, creditors, stockholders, and other parties with an interest in the firm.

Self-Test Question
Give an example of how an agency problem might arise between stockholders and creditors.

BUSINESS ETHICS

The word *ethics* can be defined as "standards of conduct or moral behavior." **Business ethics** can be thought of as a company's attitude and conduct toward its employees, customers, community, and stockholders. High standards of ethical behavior demand that a firm treat each party with which it deals in a fair and honest manner. A firm's commitment to business ethics can be measured by the tendency of the firm and its employees to adhere to laws and regulations relating to such factors as product safety and quality, fair employment practices, fair marketing and selling practices, the use of confidential information for personal gain, community involvement, bribery, and illegal payments to foreign governments to obtain business.

business ethics
A company's attitude and conduct toward its stakeholders—employees, customers, stockholders, and so forth; ethical behavior requires fair and honest treatment of all parties.

Although most firms have policies that espouse ethical business conduct, there are many instances of large corporations that have engaged in unethical behavior. For example, companies such as Arthur Andersen, Enron, and World-Com MCI have fallen or been changed significantly as the result of unethical, and sometimes illegal, practices. In some cases, employees (generally top management) have been sentenced to prison for illegal actions that resulted from their unethical behavior. In recent years, the number of high-profile instances in which unethical behavior has resulted in substantial gains to executives at the expense of stockholders' positions has increased to the point where public outcry resulted in legislation aimed at arresting the apparent tide of unethical behavior in the corporate world. As a result of the large number of recent scandals disclosed by major corporations, Congress passed the Sarbanes-Oxley Act of 2002. A major reason for the legislation was that accounting scandals resulted in public skepticism as to the validity of accounting and financial information reported by large U.S. corporations. Simply put, the public no longer trusted what managers said. Investors felt that executives were pursuing interests that too often resulted in large gains for themselves and large losses for stockholders.

The 11 "titles" in the Sarbanes-Oxley Act of 2002 establish standards for accountability and responsibility of reporting financial information for major corporations. The act provides that a corporation must (1) have a committee that consists of outside directors to oversee the firm's audits, (2) hire an external auditing firm that will render an unbiased (independent) opinion concerning the firm's financial statements, and (3) provide additional information about the procedures used to construct and report financial statements. In addition, the firm's CEO and CFO must certify financial reports submitted to the Securities and Exchange Commission. The act also stiffens the criminal penalties that can be imposed for producing fraudulent financial information and provides regulatory bodies with greater authority to enact prosecution for such actions.

Despite the recent decline in investor trust of financial reporting by corporations, the executives of most major firms in the United States believe their firms should, and do, try to maintain high ethical standards in all of their business dealings. Further, most executives believe that there is a positive correlation between ethics and long-run profitability because ethical behavior (1) avoids fines and legal expenses, (2) builds public trust, (3) attracts business from customers who appreciate and support ethical policies, (4) attracts and keeps employees of the highest caliber, and (5) supports the economic viability of the communities where these firms operate.

Today, most firms have in place strong codes of ethical behavior, and they conduct training programs designed to ensure that all employees understand the correct behavior in different business situations. It is imperative that top management—the company's chairman, president, and vice-presidents—be openly committed to ethical behavior, and that they communicate this commitment through their own personal actions as well as through company policies, directives, and punishment/reward systems. Clearly, investors expect nothing less.

Self-Test Questions

How would you define *business ethics*?

Is "being ethical" good for profits and firm value in the long run? In the short run?

CORPORATE GOVERNANCE

corporate governance
The "set of rules" that a firm follows when conducting business; these rules identify who is accountable for major financial decisions.

The term *corporate governance* has become an important part of business vocabulary in recent years. As a result of the scandals uncovered at Arthur Andersen, Enron, World-Com MCI, and many other companies, stockholders, managers, and Congress have become quite concerned with how firms are operated. **Corporate governance** deals with the "set of rules" that a firm follows when conducting business. Together these rules provide the "road map" that managers follow to pursue the various goals of the firm, including maximizing its stock price. It is important for a firm to clearly specify its corporate governance structure so that individuals and entities that have an interest in the well-being of the business understand how their interests will be pursued. A good corporate governance structure should provide those who have a relationship with a firm—that is, the stakeholders—with an understanding as to how executives run the business and who is accountable for important decisions. As a result of the Sarbanes-Oxley Act of 2002 and increased stockholder pressure, in recent years, most firms have revised their corporate governance policies so that all stakeholders—managers, stockholders, creditors, customers, suppliers, and employees—better understand their rights and responsibilities.[11] And, from our previous discussions, it should be clear that maximizing shareholder wealth requires the fair treatment of all stakeholders.

Studies show that firms that follow good corporate governance generate higher returns to stockholders. Good corporate governance includes a board of directors with members that are independent of the company's management. An independent board generally serves as a "checks and balances" system that monitors important management decisions, including executive compensation. It has also been shown that firms that develop governance structures that make it easier to identify and correct accounting problems and potentially unethical or fraudulent practices perform better than firms that have poor governance policies (internal controls).[12]

Self-Test Question
Why is it important for a firm to have a good corporate governance policy?

FORMS OF BUSINESSES IN OTHER COUNTRIES

Large U.S. corporations can best be described as "open" companies because they are publicly traded organizations that, for the most part, are independent of one another and of the government. As we described earlier, such companies offer limited liability to owners who usually do not participate in the day-to-day operations and who can easily transfer ownership by trading stock in the financial markets. Although most developed countries with free economies have business organizations that are similar to U.S. corporations, some differences exist relating to ownership structure and management of operations. Because a comprehensive discussion is beyond the scope of this book, this section provides fairly simple examples of differences between U.S. companies and non-U.S. companies.

Firms in most developed economies, such as corporations in the United States, offer equities with limited liability to stockholders that can be traded in domestic financial markets. However, such firms are not always called corporations. For instance, a comparable firm in England is called a "public limited company," or PLC, whereas in Germany it is known as an *Aktiengesellschaft*, or AG. In Mexico,

---

[11]Broadly speaking, the term *stakeholders* should include the environment in which we live and do business. It should be apparent that a firm cannot survive—that is, remain sustainable—unless it fairly treats both human stakeholders and environmental stakeholders. A firm that destroys the trust of its employees, customers, and shareholders, or the environment in which it operates, destroys itself.

[12]See, for example, Reshma Kapadia, "Stocks Reward Firms' Good Behavior," *The Wall Street Journal Online*, March 18, 2006, and David Reilly, "Checks on Internal Controls Pay Off," *The Wall Street Journal*, May 8, 2006, C3.

Spain, and Latin America such a company is called a *Sociedad Anónima,* or SA. Some of these firms are publicly traded, whereas others are privately held.

Like corporations in the United States, most large companies in England and Canada are "open," and their stocks are widely dispersed among a large number of different investors. Of note, however, is that two-thirds of the traded stocks of English companies are owned by institutional investors rather than individuals. On the other hand, in much of continental Europe, stock ownership is more concentrated; major investor groups include families, banks, and other corporations. In Germany and France, for instance, the primary group of corporate shareholders is other companies, followed by families. Although banks do not hold a large number of shares of stock, they can greatly influence companies because many shareholders assign banks their **proxy votes** for the directors of the companies. Also, often the family unit has concentrated ownership, and thus is a major influence in many large companies in developed countries such as these. The ownership structures of these firms and many other non-U.S. companies, including very large organizations, often are concentrated in the hands of relatively few investors or investment groups. Such firms are considered "closed" because shares of stock are not publicly traded, relatively few individuals or groups own the stock, and major stockholders often are involved in the firms' daily operations.

The primary reason non-U.S. firms are likely to be more closed, and thus have more concentrated ownership, than U.S. firms results from the "universal" banking relationships that exist outside the United States. Financial institutions in other countries generally are less regulated than in the United States, which means foreign banks, for instance, can provide businesses a greater variety of services, including short-term loans, long-term financing, and even stock ownership. These services are available at many locations, or branches, throughout the country. As a result, non-U.S. firms tend to have close relationships with individual banking organizations that also might take ownership positions in the companies. What this means is that banks in countries like Germany often can meet all of the financing needs of family-owned businesses, even if they are very large. Therefore, such companies need not "go public," and thus relinquish control, to finance additional growth. Consider the fact that in both France and Germany approximately 75 percent of the gross domestic product (GDP) comes from firms not publicly traded—that is, closed businesses. The opposite is true in the United States, where large firms do not have "one-stop" financing outlets; hence, their growth generally must be financed by bringing in outside owners, which results in more widely dispersed ownership.

In some parts of the world, firms belong to **industrial groups,** which are organizations comprised of companies in different industries with common ownership interests and, in some instances, shared management. Firms in the industrial group are "tied" by a major lender, typically a bank, which often also has a significant ownership interest along with other firms in the group. The objective of an industrial group is to include firms that provide materials and services required to manufacture and sell products—that is, to create an organization that ties together all the functions of production and sales from start to finish. Thus, an industrial group encompasses firms involved in manufacturing, financing, marketing, and distribution of products, which includes suppliers of raw materials, production organizations, retail stores, and creditors. A portion of the stocks of firms that are members of an industrial group might be traded publicly, but the "lead" company, which is typically a major creditor, controls the management of the entire group. Industrial groups are most prominent in Asian countries. In Japan, an industrial group is called a *keiretsu,* and it is called a *chaebol* in Korea. Well-known *keiretsu* groups include Mitsubishi, Toshiba, and Toyota, while the best-known *chaebol* probably is Hyundai. The success of industrial groups in Japan and Korea has

---

proxy votes
Voting power that is assigned to another party, such as another stockholder or institution.

industrial groups
Organizations comprised of companies in different industries with common ownership interests, which include firms necessary to manufacture and sell products—a network of manufacturers, suppliers, marketing organizations, distributors, retailers, and creditors.

inspired the formation of similar organizations in developing countries in Latin America and Africa as well as other parts of Asia.

The differences in ownership concentration of non-U.S. firms might cause the behavior of managers, and thus the goals they pursue, to differ. For instance, often it is argued that the greater concentration of ownership of non-U.S. firms permits managers to focus more on long-term objectives, especially wealth maximization, than short-term earnings because firms have easier access to credit in times of financial difficulty. In other words, creditors who also are owners generally have greater interest in supporting long-term survival. On the other hand, it also has been argued that the ownership structures of non-U.S. firms create an environment where it is difficult to change managers, especially if they are significant stockholders. Such entrenchment could be detrimental to firms if management is inefficient (ineffective). Consider, for example, the fact that firms in Japan generally are reluctant to fire employees because losing one's job is a disgrace in the Japanese culture. Whether the ownership structure of non-U.S. firms is an advantage or a disadvantage is debatable. However, we do know that the greater concentration of ownership in non-U.S. firms permits greater monitoring and control by individuals or groups than the more dispersed ownership structures of U.S. firms, which suggests that there are fewer agency problems associated with these businesses.

Self-Test Questions

What is the primary difference between U.S. corporations and non-U.S. firms?

What is an industrial group?

What are some of the names given to firms in other countries?

MULTINATIONAL CORPORATIONS

Large firms, both in the United States and in other countries, generally do not operate in a single country; rather, they conduct business throughout the world. In fact, the largest firms in the world truly are multinational rather than domestic operations. Managers of such multinational companies face a wide range of issues that are not present when a company operates in a single country. This section highlights the key differences between multinational and domestic corporations and the impact these differences have on managerial finance for U.S. businesses.

The term **multinational corporation** is used to describe a firm that operates in two or more countries. Rather than merely buying resources from foreign concerns, multinational firms make direct investments in fully integrated operations, with worldwide entities controlling all phases of the production process, from extraction of raw materials, through the manufacturing process, to distribution to consumers throughout the world. Today, multinational corporate networks control a large and growing share of the world's technological, marketing, and productive resources.

Companies "go international" for the following major reasons:

1. *To seek new markets.* After a company has saturated its home market, growth opportunities often are better in foreign markets. As a result, such home-grown firms as Coca-Cola and McDonald's have aggressively expanded into overseas markets, and foreign firms such as Sony and Toshiba are major competitors in the U.S. consumer electronics market.

multinational corporation
A firm that operates in two or more countries.

2. *To seek raw materials.* Many U.S. oil companies, such as ExxonMobil, have major subsidiaries around the world to ensure they have continued access to the basic resources needed to sustain their primary lines of business.

3. *To seek new technology.* No single nation holds a commanding advantage in all technologies, so companies scour the globe for leading scientific and design ideas. For example, Xerox has introduced more than 80 different office copiers in the United States that were engineered and built by its Japanese joint venture, Fuji Xerox.

4. *To seek production efficiency.* Companies in countries where production costs are high tend to shift production to low-cost countries. For example, General Motors has production and assembly plants in Mexico and Brazil, and even Japanese manufacturers have shifted some of their production to lower cost countries in the Pacific Rim. The ability to shift production from country to country has important implications for labor costs in all countries. For example, when Xerox threatened to move its copier rebuilding work to Mexico, its union in Rochester, New York, agreed to work rules and productivity improvements that kept the operation in the United States.

5. *To avoid political and regulatory hurdles.* Many years ago, Japanese auto companies moved production to the United States to get around U.S. import quotas. Now, Honda, Nissan, and Toyota all assemble automobiles or trucks in the United States. Similarly, one of the factors that prompted U.S. pharmaceutical maker SmithKline and U.K. drug company Beecham to merge in 1989 was the desire to avoid licensing and regulatory delays in their largest markets. Now, GlaxoSmithKline, as the company is known, can identify itself as an inside player in both Europe and the United States.

Since the 1980s, investments in the United States by foreign corporations have increased significantly. This "reverse" investment has created concerns for U.S. government officials, who contend it could erode the doctrine of independence and self-reliance that has traditionally been a hallmark of U.S. policy. Just as U.S. corporations with extensive overseas operations are said to use their economic power to exert substantial economic and political influence over host governments around the world, it is feared that foreign corporations might gain similar influence over U.S. policy. These developments also suggest an increasing degree of mutual influence and interdependence among business enterprises and nations, to which the United States is not immune. Political and social developments that influence the world economy also influence U.S. businesses and financial markets.

Self-Test Questions

What is a multinational corporation?

Why do companies "go international"?

MULTINATIONAL VERSUS DOMESTIC MANAGERIAL FINANCE

In theory, the concepts and procedures discussed in the remaining chapters of this book are valid for both domestic and multinational operations. However, several problems uniquely associated with the international environment increase the complexity of the manager's task in a multinational corporation, and they often force the manager to change the way alternative courses of action are evaluated and compared. Six major factors distinguish managerial finance as practiced by firms operating entirely within a single country from firms that operate in several different countries:

1. *Different currency denominations.* Cash flows in various parts of a multinational corporate system often are denominated in different currencies. It is clear that the price at which one country's currency can be converted into another country's currency at any point in time has a significant effect on the amount of cash the firm has available for investing in other parts of its operations. Hence, an analysis of **exchange rates** and the effects of fluctuating currency values must be included in all financial analyses.

2. *Economic and legal ramifications.* Each country in which the firm operates has its own unique political and economic institutions, and institutional differences among countries can cause significant problems when a firm tries to coordinate and control the worldwide operations of its subsidiaries. For example, differences in tax laws among countries can cause a particular transaction to have strikingly dissimilar after-tax consequences, depending on where it occurred. Also, differences in legal systems of host nations complicate many matters, from the simple recording of a business transaction to the role played by the judiciary in resolving conflicts. Such differences can restrict multinational corporations' flexibility to deploy resources as they wish and can even make procedures illegal in one part of the company that are required in another part. These differences also make it difficult for executives trained in one country to operate effectively in another.

3. *Language differences.* The ability to communicate is critical in all business transactions. Persons born and educated in the United States often are at a disadvantage because they generally are fluent only in English, whereas European and Japanese businesspeople usually are fluent in several languages, including English. As a result, it is often easier for international companies to invade U.S. markets than it is for Americans to penetrate international markets.

4. *Cultural differences.* Even within geographic regions long considered fairly homogeneous, different countries have unique cultural heritages that shape values and influence the role of business in the society. Multinational corporations find that such matters as defining the appropriate goals of the firm, attitudes toward risk taking, dealing with employees, and the ability to curtail unprofitable operations can vary dramatically from one country to the next.

5. *Role of governments.* Most traditional models in finance assume the existence of a competitive marketplace in which the terms of trade are determined by the participants. The government, through its power to establish basic ground rules, is involved in this process, but its participation is minimal. Thus, the market provides both the primary barometer of success and the indicator of the actions that must be taken to remain competitive. This view of the process is reasonably correct for the United States and a few other major industrialized nations, but it does not accurately describe the situation in most of the world. Frequently, the terms under which companies compete, the actions that must be taken or avoided, and the terms of trade on various transactions are determined not in the marketplace but by direct negotiation between the host government and the multinational corporation. This is essentially a political process, and it must be treated as such.

6. *Political risk.* The distinguishing characteristic that differentiates a nation from a multinational corporation is that the nation exercises sovereignty over

exchange rates
The prices at which the currency from one country can be converted into the currency of another country.

the people and property in its territory. Hence, a nation is free to place constraints on the transfer of corporate resources and even to *expropriate*— that is, take for public use—the assets of a firm without compensation. This is political risk, and it tends to be largely a given rather than a variable that can be changed by negotiation. Political risk varies from country to country, and it must be addressed explicitly in any financial analysis. Another aspect of political risk is terrorism against U.S. firms or executives abroad. For example, in the past, U.S. executives have been captured and held for ransom in several South American and Middle Eastern countries.

These six factors complicate managerial finance within multinational firms, and they increase the risks these firms face. Prospects for high profits, however, often make it worthwhile for firms to accept these risks and to learn how to minimize or at least live with them.

Self-Test Question

Identify and briefly explain the major factors that complicate managerial finance within multinational firms.

THE FEDERAL INCOME TAX SYSTEM

The values of financial assets, including stocks, bonds, and mortgages, as well as the values of most real assets, such as manufacturing plants or even entire firms, depend on the stream of net cash flows produced by the assets. By *net cash flows* we mean "investable," or after-tax, cash flows. For this reason, in this section we briefly describe the U.S. tax system. By the time you read this section, tax rates and other factors probably will be different from those described here. Even so, this discussion should give you an idea as to how taxes affect "investable" cash flows, and thus value.

The U.S. Federal Tax Code is separated into two sections:

- Tax laws that are applicable to individuals
- Tax laws that are applicable to corporations[13]

The individual tax code applies to both individuals and families, and the corporate tax code applies to businesses that are organized as corporations. For businesses that are not corporations, the corporate tax code is not applicable; as a result, the taxes of proprietorships and partnerships are based on the individual tax code.

progressive tax
A tax that requires a higher percentage payment on higher incomes. The personal income tax in the United States is progressive.

taxable income
Gross income minus exemptions and allowable deductions as set forth in the Tax Code.

Individual Income Taxes

Individuals pay taxes on wages and salaries, on investment income (dividends, interest, and profits from the sale of securities), and on the profits of *proprietorships* and *partnerships*. The U.S. tax rates are **progressive**—that is, the higher one's income, the larger the percentage paid in taxes. Table 6A-1 in the appendix to this chapter provides the individual federal tax rates for 2008. Here, we discuss some of the general topics applicable to those who are affected by the individual tax code section.

1. **Taxable income** is defined as gross income minus a set of exemptions and deductions that are spelled out in the instructions to the tax forms that

---

[13]Tax information is available at U.S. post offices and on the Internal Revenue Service Web site, http://www.irs.ustreas.gov.

individuals must file. When filing a tax return in 2009 for the tax year 2008, every taxpayer will receive an exemption of $3,500 for each dependent, including the taxpayer. Also, certain expenses, such as mortgage interest paid, state and local income taxes paid, and charitable contributions, can be deducted to reduce taxable income. Individuals can either itemize allowed expenses or take the standard deduction that is available to all taxpayers ($5,450 for single taxpayers and $10,900 for married taxpayers filing joint returns).

2. The **marginal tax** rate is defined as the tax on the last unit of income. It is represented by the tax bracket in which you are placed. For example, if you are single and your taxable income is $50,000, then your marginal tax rate is 25 percent. As Table 6A-1 shows, marginal rates begin at 10 percent, rise to 15 percent, then to 25 percent, and so on.

> **marginal tax rate**
> The tax applicable to the last unit (dollar) of income.

3. The **average tax rate** equals the percentage of taxable income that is paid in taxes. For example, if Jill Smith, a single individual, had taxable income of $50,000, her tax bill would be $8,843.75 = $4,481.25 + ($50,000 − $32,550) (0.25). Her average tax rate would be $8,843.75/$50,000 = 17.7 percent versus a marginal rate of 25 percent. If Jill received a raise of $1,000, bringing her income to $51,000, she would have to pay $250 of her extra income as taxes, so her after-tax raise would net her $750. In addition to regular income taxes, her Social Security and Medicare taxes would increase.

> **average tax rate**
> Taxes paid divided by taxable income.

Taxes on Interest Income

Interest income received by individuals from investments is added to other income and taxed at the rates shown in Table 6A-1. It should be noted that under U.S. tax laws, interest on most state and local government bonds (municipal bonds) is not subject to federal income taxes. Thus, investors get to keep all of the interest received from most municipal bonds but only a fraction of the interest received from bonds issued by corporations or the U.S. government. This means that a lower yielding municipal bond can provide the same after-tax return as a higher yielding corporate bond. For example, a taxpayer in the 25 percent marginal tax bracket who could buy a municipal bond that yields 6 percent would have to receive a before-tax yield of 8 percent on a corporate bond or a U.S. Treasury bond to receive the same after-tax income:

6-1

$$\frac{\text{Equivalent pretax yield}}{\text{on a taxable investment}} = \frac{\text{Yield on a tax-free investment}}{1 - \text{Marginal tax rate}}$$

$$= \frac{6.0\%}{1 - 0.25} = 8.0\%$$

If we know the yield on the taxable bond (investment), we can use the following equation to find the *equivalent yield* on a municipal bond or other tax-free investment:

6-2

$$\frac{\text{Yield on}}{\text{tax-free investment}} = \left(\begin{array}{c}\text{Pretax yield on}\\ \text{taxable income}\end{array}\right) \times (1 - \text{Marginal tax rate})$$

$$= 8.0\% \times (1 - 0.25) = 8.0\%(0.75) = 6.0\%$$

The exemption from federal taxes stems from the separation of federal and state power. Its primary effect is to help state and local governments borrow at lower rates than otherwise would be available to them.

Interest Paid by Individuals

For the most part, the interest paid by individuals on loans is *not* tax deductible. The principal exception is the interest paid on mortgage financing used to purchase a house for a personal residence, which is tax deductible. The effect of tax-deductible interest payments is to lower the actual cost of the mortgage to the taxpayer. For example, if Staci Jones has a 7 percent mortgage on her house and an *average* tax rate equal to 26 percent, the after-tax rate of her mortgage is calculated as follows:

$$\text{After-tax rate} = 7\%(1 - 0.26) = 5.18\%$$

Taxes on Dividend Income

Prior to 2003, dividends received from corporations were taxed just like interest income. However, Congress lowered the tax rates on dividends in 2003 to help mitigate the *double taxation* of corporate income—that is, dividends are paid out of after-tax corporate income and then are taxed again when individuals receive them. Now, taxpayers whose marginal tax rates (tax brackets) are lower than 25 percent pay only 5 percent taxes on qualified dividends received, and taxpayers in higher tax brackets pay 15 percent taxes on qualified dividends that they receive. To qualify for these lower tax rates, the taxpayer must hold the stock of the company that pays the dividend for more than 60 days.

Capital Gains versus Ordinary Income

capital gain (loss)
The profit (loss) from the sale of a capital asset for more (less) than its purchase price.

Assets such as stocks, bonds, and real estate are defined as *capital assets*. If you buy a capital asset and later sell it for more than your purchase price, the profit is called a **capital gain;** if you suffer a loss, it is called a **capital loss.** An asset sold within 1 year of the time it was purchased produces a *short-term gain or loss*, whereas one held for 1 year or longer produces a *long-term gain or loss*.

There has been a great deal of controversy regarding the proper tax rate for capital gains. It has been argued that lower tax rates on capital gains (1) stimulate the flow of venture capital to new, start-up businesses, which generally provide capital gains as opposed to dividend income and (2) cause companies to retain and reinvest a high percentage of their earnings to provide their stockholders with lightly taxed capital gains as opposed to highly taxed dividend income. The proponents of preferential capital gains tax rates lost the argument in 1986, but in 1990, 1998, and 2003 they succeeded in getting the rates capped at levels lower than the top marginal tax rate. In 2007, the long-term gains rate was 15 percent (5 percent if the taxpayer's marginal tax rate was less than 25 percent); the short-term capital gains rate was the same as the taxpayer's marginal tax rate (tax bracket). In 2008, the capital gains rate was reduced to 0 percent for taxpayers with marginal tax rates less than 25 percent.

Business versus Personal Expenses

Individuals pay taxes on the income generated by proprietorships and partnerships they own—the income *passes through* to the owners of these types of businesses. Therefore, we need to differentiate business expenses, which are tax deductible, from personal expenses, which are not tax deductible. Generally speaking, an allowable business expense is a cost that is incurred to generate business revenues. On the other hand, if the expense is incurred for personal benefit (use), it is considered a personal expense.

To illustrate, consider Loretta Kay, who owns a house in which she lived until last month. At that time, she moved and rented the house to a group of college students. Three months ago, the water pipes burst in the kitchen, and Loretta had to call a plumber for repairs. The repairs cost $1,000. Is this a tax-deductible expense? No, because the house was Loretta's personal residence at the time. Last night, Loretta had to call the plumber again to fix pipes that had burst in the house she currently has rented to the students; this time, the repairs cost $1,200. Is this a tax-deductible expense? Yes, because the expense was incurred for business purposes; the house is now rental property, which is considered a business operation.

Example of Individual Income Tax Computation

To illustrate the computation of individual income taxes, suppose Ron Matthews owns a small business that he operates as a sole proprietorship. During 2007, the business generated $180,000 in sales revenues and incurred $80,000 in general operating expenses, including salaries for all employees except himself. The company paid $10,000 in interest to the bank. It also earned interest on invested funds equal to $2,000. Ron's personal income includes a salary of $50,000 that he paid himself from the operating income of the business and $1,500 in interest that he earned on funds invested in a certificate of deposit. Additional funds were received from 100 shares of common stock that Ron sold for $15 per share; he purchased the stock, which did not pay a dividend, in 1999 for $10 per share. Ron also paid interest equal to $2,150 on a loan that he used to finance his personal automobile (the business does not require the use of the car). Ron, who is single, currently lives in a house that he rents from a friend. What is Ron's tax liability?

First, because the business is a proprietorship, all revenues and expenses associated with the business must be recognized by Ron when computing his taxes, even if some of the income is left (reinvested) in the firm; the revenues and expenses of the business are said to "pass through" to the owner. Thus, Ron is personally responsible for all taxable income associated with the firm even if he doesn't take all of it out of the firm to compensate himself. In addition, Ron must report all other personal income, but he can adjust his personal income only by allowable exemptions and deductions. For example, he cannot deduct the $2,150 interest payment associated with the automobile loan, because this expense is considered a personal—not business—expense in this case.

Ron's tax liability is computed as follows:

Business revenues:		
Operating revenues	$180,000	
Interest income	2,000	
Business expenses:		
Operating expenses	(80,000)	
Interest expense	(10,000)	
Business income	92,000	
Personal income:		
Income from proprietorship	$ 92,000	
Interest income from CD	1,500	
Personal exemption	(3,500)	
Standard personal deduction	(5,450)	
Taxable personal income	$ 84,550	
Tax liability:		
Tax on personal income	$ 17,652.25	= $16,056.25 + 0.28($84,550 − $78,850)
Tax on capital gains	75.00	= [($15 − $10)(100)] × 0.15
Total tax liability	$ 17,727.25	

Note that all of the income earned by the proprietorship "passes through" to Ron, even if he doesn't "withdraw" the entire amount from the business. The same principle applies to partnerships, except that the business income is divided among the partners according to the partnership agreement. For example, if one partner is responsible for 60 percent of the firm, then 60 percent of the business income "passes through" to him or her.

Corporate Income Taxes

Although the corporate tax code and the individual tax code differ significantly in many areas, the corporate tax rates are progressive, like the rates for individual taxpayers. In this section, we discuss some of the important topics included in the corporate tax code.

Interest and Dividend Income Received by a Corporation

Interest income received by a corporation is taxed as ordinary income at regular corporate tax rates. However, 70 percent of the dividends received by one corporation from another corporation are excluded from taxable income, while the remaining 30 percent are taxed at the ordinary tax rate.[14] Thus, a corporation that earns $20 million and has a marginal tax rate of 35 percent would pay only $0.30 \times 0.35 = 0.105 = 10.5\%$ of its dividend income as taxes—that is, its effective tax rate on intercorporate dividends would be 10.5 percent. If this firm received $10,000 in dividends from another corporation, its after-tax dividend income would be $8,950:

$$
\begin{aligned}
\text{After-tax income} &= \text{Before-tax income} - \text{Taxes} \\
&= \$10,000 - \$10,000(0.30 \times 0.35) \\
&= \$10,000 - \$1,050 \\
&= \$10,000(1 - 0.105) = \$10,000(0.895) = \$8,950
\end{aligned}
$$

If the corporation that receives dividends distributes its own after-tax income to its stockholders as dividends, the income ultimately is subjected to triple taxation: (1) the original corporation is taxed first, (2) then the second corporation is taxed on the dividends it receives, and (3) the individuals who receive the final dividends are taxed again. This is the reason for the 70 percent exclusion on intercorporate dividends.

Interest and Dividends Paid by a Corporation

A firm can finance its operations with either debt or equity capital. If the firm uses debt, it must pay interest on this debt (to banks and to bondholders), whereas if it uses equity, it might pay dividends to the stockholders. *Interest paid to creditors is a tax deductible expense,* whereas *dividends paid to stockholders are not tax deductible.* Therefore, a firm needs $1 of pretax income to pay $1 of interest; but if it is in the 35 percent tax bracket, it needs $1.54 of pretax income to pay $1 of dividends:

$$
\frac{\text{Pretax income needed}}{\text{to pay \$1 of dividends}} = \frac{\$1}{1 - \text{Tax rate}} = \frac{\$1}{1 - 0.35} = \$1.54
$$

---

[14]The size of the dividend exclusion actually depends on the degree of ownership. Corporations that own less than 20 percent of the stock of the dividend-paying company can exclude 70 percent of the dividends received; firms that own at least 20 percent but less than 80 percent can exclude 80 percent of the dividends; and firms that own more than 80 percent can exclude the entire dividend payment. Because most companies own less than 20 percent of other companies, we will assume a 70 percent dividend exclusion.

Of course, generally it is not possible to finance exclusively with debt capital, and the risk of doing so would offset the benefits of the tax deductibility of interest payments. Even so, the fact that interest is a tax-deductible expense has a profound effect on the way businesses are financed—the U.S. tax system favors debt financing over equity financing. This point is discussed in more detail in Chapter 14.

Corporate Capital Gains

Before 1987, corporate long-term capital gains were taxed at lower rates than ordinary income, as is true for individuals. Under the current U.S. Tax Code, however, corporate capital gains are taxed at the same rate as operating income.

Corporate Loss Carryback and Carryover

Ordinary corporate operating losses can be carried back (**carryback**) to each of the preceding 2 years and carried forward (**carryover**) for the next 20 years to offset taxable income in those years. For example, an operating loss reported in 2008 can be carried back and used to reduce taxable income in 2006 and 2007, and carried forward, if necessary, to offset positive operating income in 2009, 2010, and so on, to the year 2028. The loss must be applied first to the earliest year, then to the next earliest year, and so on, until it has been used up or the 20-year carryover limit has been reached.

To illustrate, consider the partial income statements for Apex Corporation shown in Table 6-1. In 2006 and 2007, Apex produced positive taxable income amounts, and it paid the appropriate taxes in each of those years, which totaled $154 million. In 2008, however, the company experienced a taxable loss equal to $840 million. The carryback feature allows Apex to write off this taxable loss

tax loss carryback (carryover)
Losses that can be carried backward (forward) in time to offset taxable income in a given year.

TABLE 6-1   Apex Corporation: Partial Income Statements for 2006–2008 ($ million)

	2006	**2007**	**2008**
Original Statement			
Taxable income	$260	$180	$(840)
Taxes (35%)	(91)	(63)	
Net income	$169	$117	

			Total Effect of Carryback
Adjusted Statement			
Original taxable income	$260	$180	
Carryback credit	(260)	(180)	$440
Adjusted taxable income	0	0	
Taxes (35%)	0	0	
Adjusted net income	$ 0	$ 0	
Taxes originally paid	$ 91	$ 63	$154

Tax refund = $154
Loss available to carry forward in 2009–2028 = $840 − $440 = $400

against positive taxable income beginning in 2006. Note that the loss is large enough that the *adjusted* taxable incomes for 2006 and 2007 equal $0. Apex would amend the tax forms that it filed in 2006 and 2007, and it would receive a tax refund equal to $154 million. After adjusting the previous 2 years' tax forms, Apex still would have $400 million of unrecovered loss from 2008 to carry forward through the year 2028, if necessary. The purpose of permitting firms to treat losses in this manner is to avoid penalizing corporations whose incomes fluctuate substantially from year to year.

Depreciation

Depreciation plays an important role in income tax calculations. Congress specifies, in the Tax Code, the life over which assets can be depreciated for tax purposes and the methods of depreciation that can be used. Because these factors have a major influence on the amount of depreciation that a firm can take in a given year, and thus on its taxable income, depreciation has an important effect on taxes paid and cash flows from operations. We will discuss the calculation of depreciation and its effects on income and cash flows in Chapter 13, when we discuss the subject of capital budgeting.

Example of Corporate Income Tax Computation

In 2008, Ibis International had a taxable income of $2,500,000 from operations. During that year, the company paid $600,000 interest on its outstanding debt, which included bank loans and bonds, and it paid its common stockholders $220,000 in dividends. Ibis received $180,000 in interest from its investments in the debts of other companies, and it also received $80,000 in dividends from its investments in other companies' common stock. What is the company's tax liability and its after-tax income?

Operating income	$2,500,000
Interest received	180,000
Dividends received (taxable amount)	$24,000 = \$80,000(1.0 - 0.7)$
Interest expense (paid)	(600,000)
Taxable income	2,104,000
Tax liability	$715,360 = \$113,900 + 0.34\ (\$2,104,000 - \$335,000)$
After-tax income	$1,388,640

Taxation of Small Businesses: S Corporations

The Internal Revenue Code provides that small businesses (those with fewer than 100 stockholders) that meet certain restrictions can be set up as corporations and receive the benefits of the corporate form of organization—especially limited liability—yet still be taxed as proprietorships or partnerships. These corporations are called S corporations. For a corporation that elects S corporation status for tax purposes, all of the income of the business is reported as personal income by the owners, and these funds are taxed at the rates that apply to individuals. This approach would be preferred by owners of small corporations in which all or most of the income earned each year is distributed as dividends because, the income would be taxed only once at the individual level.

CORPORATE TAX RATES IN OTHER COUNTRIES

Earlier in the chapter, we described some of the major differences between the organizational structures of U.S. firms and foreign firms. We discovered that much of the difference can be attributed to the regulatory environments that prevail in other countries: for the most part, foreign firms are subject to less regulation than their U.S. counterparts. In addition, businesses in other countries do not face complicated tax laws like those found in the United States. Although a discussion of the structure of taxes in foreign countries is beyond the scope of this chapter, we can give you some indication of the tax rates faced by multinational organizations. Table 6-2 shows the tax rates applied to corporate earnings in several countries as reported by KPMG International in its annual tax rate survey.[15] For comparison, the rates for 1997 and 2007 are given in the table.

The corporate tax rates differ significantly among countries. For example, according to the KPMG International survey, the corporate tax rate of 10 percent in Bulgaria, Cyprus, and Paraguay is lowest in the world, whereas the rates in Japan and the United States are approximately 40 percent and the rate in the United Arab Emirates is 55 percent, which is the highest rate reported in the survey. On average, the tax rates of countries with developed markets are approximately 5 percent higher than the rates of countries with emerging economies/markets. The low corporate tax rates in developing countries generally help to attract some of the operations of foreign firms, which helps to bolster the economic conditions in these countries.

It is intersting to note that worldwide corporate tax rates have declined substantially during the past decade, from an average of 33 percent in 1997 to 27 percent in 2007. Clearly, the corporate income tax rate is a major factor used by countries to attract and retain foreign business, and the competition among countries has forced tax rates downward in recent years. Although most countries have decreased corporate income tax rates, to maintain tax revenues, many of these same countries have added or increased "special" taxes that apply to sales and inventories.

---

[15]*KPMG Corporate and Indirect Tax Rate Survey, 2007,* June 2007. The survey is available at http://kpmg.com/Services/Tax/Business/IntCorp/CTR/.

TABLE 6-2   Corporate Tax Rates for Selected Countries, 1997 and 2007[a]

	Tax Rates			Tax Rates	
	1997	2007		1997	2007
I. Developed Markets			*II. Emerging Markets*		
Australia	34.0	30.0%	Brazil	25.0	34.0%
Canada	44.6	36.1	Chile	15.0	17.0
France	36.7	33.3	China	33.0	33.0
Germany	57.5	38.4	India	35.0	34.0
Italy	53.2	37.3	Indonesia	30.0	30.0
Japan	51.6	40.7	Korea	30.8	27.4
Netherlands	35.0[b]	25.5	Malaysia	30.0	27.0
Switzerland	28.5	21.3	Mexico	34.0	28.0
United Kingdom	31.0	30.0	Philippines	35.0	35.0
United States	40.0	40.0	Thailand	30.0	30.0

[a]The base average corporate tax is adjusted for regional taxes, surcharges, and so forth.

[b]This is the 1998 tax rate; the 1997 rate is not reported.

Source: *KPMG Corporate and Indirect Tax Rate Survey, 2007*, June 2007. The survey is available at http://kpmg.com/Services/Tax/Business/IntCorp/CTR/.

Self-Test Question

Why might one country have a lower corporate tax rate than other countries?

Ethical Dilemma

Chances Are, What They Don't Know Won't Hurt Them!

Futuristic Electronic Technologies (FET) recently released a new advanced electronic micro system to be used by financial institutions, large corporations, and governments to process and store financial data such as taxes and automatic payroll payments. Even though FET developed the technology used in the creation of the product, FET's competitors are expected to possess similar technology soon. To beat the competition to the market, FET introduced its new micro system a little earlier than originally planned. In fact, laboratory testing had not been fully completed before the product reached the market. The tests are complete now, and the final results suggest the micro system might be flawed with respect to how some data are retrieved and processed. The tests are not conclusive, however. Even if additional testing proves that a flaw does exist, FET managers believe it is of minuscule importance because the problem seems to occur for only one out of 100 million retrieval and processing attempts. The financial ramifications associated with the flaw are unknown at this time.

Assume you are one of FET's senior executives whose annual salary is based on the performance of the firm's common stock. You realize that if FET recalls the affected micro system, the stock price will suffer; thus, your salary for the year will be less than you expected. To complicate matters, you just purchased an expensive house based on your salary expectations for the next few years—expectations

continues

that will not be realized unless the new micro system is a success for FET. As one of the senior executives, you will help determine what course of action FET will follow with respect to the micro system. What should you do? Should you encourage FET to recall the micro system until further testing is completed? Or can you suggest another course of action?

To summarize the key concepts, let's answer the questions that were posed at the beginning of the chapter:

CHAPTER PRINCIPLES
–The Answers

- **What are the different forms of business organization? What are the advantages and disadvantages of each?** The three main forms of business organization are the *proprietorship,* the *partnership,* and the *corporation.* Although proprietorships and partnerships are easy to start, the major disadvantage to these forms of business is that the owners have unlimited personal liability for the debts of the businesses. On the other hand, a corporation is more difficult to start than the other forms of business, but owners have limited liability. Most business is conducted by corporations because this organizational form maximizes firms' values.

- **What goal(s) should firms pursue? Do firms always pursue appropriate goals?** The primary goal of management should be to maximize stockholders' wealth, which in turn means maximizing the price of the firm's stock. Further, actions that maximize stock prices also increase social welfare. The price of a firm's stock depends on the firm's projected cash flows and the timing and riskiness of these cash flows.

    There are times when managers might be tempted to act in their own best interests rather than pursue the goal of wealth maximization. The potential for such an *agency problem,* or conflict of interests, can be lessened by providing managers with incentives, or motivations, to act in the best interests of the stockholders.

- **What is the role of ethics in successful businesses?** Most firms have established strict *codes of conduct,* or guidelines, to ensure that managers "behave" ethically when dealing with stakeholders. Executives believe that there is a positive correlation between business ethics and the long-run success of their firms—that is, "ethical firms" prosper, whereas "unethical firms" do not.

- **Why is it important for a business to have a clear corporate governance policy?** A firm's corporate governance policy spells out the "rules" that managers must follow when conducting business. A firm should have a clearly defined corporate governance structure so that those who have an interest in the well-being of the business—that is, the stakeholders—have a good understanding as to how executives run the business and who is accountable for important decisions. Firms that develop governance structures that make it easier to correct potential accounting problems and unethical practices generally are more successful than firms that have poor governance policies (internal controls).

- **How do foreign firms differ from U.S. firms?** Non-U.S. firms generally have more concentrated ownership than U.S. firms. International operations have become increasingly important to individual firms and to the national economy. Companies go "international" to seek new markets, seek raw materials, seek new technology, seek production efficiency, and avoid trade barriers.

    The major factors that distinguish managerial finance as practiced by domestic firms from that of multinational companies include (1) different currency denominations, (2) economic and legal ramifications, (3) languages, (4) cultural differences, (5) role of governments, and (6) political risk.

- **Why is it important to consider taxes when making financial decisions?** Simply stated, taxes must be paid in cash, and we know that a key factor in valuation is the cash flow stream that an asset is expected to generate during its life. As a result, the effects of taxes on cash flows must be considered when making financial decisions. Whereas taxes reduce the cash flows generated from operations that can be reinvested in the firm, taxes also decrease the effective cost of borrowing to finance the firm.

CHAPTER PRINCIPLES
–Personal Finance

The basic knowledge you learn in this book will help you understand how to (1) review companies and industries to determine their prospects for future growth and their ability to maintain the safety of your investment, (2) determine how much risk you are willing to take with your investment position, and (3) evaluate how well your investments are performing so that you can better ensure that your funds are invested "appropriately."

Following are the general concepts presented in this chapter as they relate to personal financial decisions:

- **Valuation** Throughout the book, we will show that the concept of value is fairly easy to grasp—that is, value is based on the future cash flows an asset is expected to produce (both the amount and the timing) and the risk associated with those cash flows. If you can apply this concept, you should be able to estimate the values of investments and make informed decisions about these investments based on their current selling prices.

- **Investment Goals** When you invest your money in a company's stock, you hope that the value of the stock increases significantly—that is, you want the value of the stock to be maximized. Thus, you want managers to make decisions that maximize the value of the firm. When managers make decisions that are in their own best interests rather than in the best interests of stockholders—that is, an agency problem exists—you will have a tendency to sell the stock of that firm and invest in firms where managers "do the right thing."

- **Ethics** When investing, you should behave ethically—that is, your interaction with and conduct toward other investors should be fair and honest. Also, you will tend to invest in firms that are considered ethical because firms that have good corporate governance policies have proven to be better investments than firms that have poor corporate governance policies.

- **Taxes** Don't forget taxes! When investing or borrowing, you should always consider the effects of taxes before making decisions. Except for tax-exempt investments, taxes reduce the return that is earned on investments. For example, suppose that you are in the 25 percent tax bracket and you invest $1,000 in a stock that you sell 6 months later for $1,100. For tax purposes, you must include $100 as taxable income, which means you will pay $25 = $100(0.25) in taxes on your investment income. As a result, your after-tax investment income is $75 and your after-tax return is 7.5 percent, which is lower than the 10 percent return that was earned before taxes. When making investment decisions, you should always compare the after-tax returns of investments. The same logic applies when comparing loan alternatives.

QUESTIONS

6-1   What are the three principal forms of business organization? What are the advantages and disadvantages of each?

6-2   What does it mean to maximize the value of a corporation?

6-3   Should stockholder wealth maximization be thought of as a long-term or a short-term goal? For example, if one action would probably increase the firm's stock price from a current level of $20 to $25 in 6 months and then to $30 in 5 years, but another action would probably keep the stock at $20 for several years, but then increase it to $40 in 5 years, which action would be better? Can you think of some specific corporate actions that might have these general tendencies?

6-4   Would the management of a firm in an oligopolistic industry or in a competitive industry be more likely to engage in "socially conscious" practices? Explain your reasoning.

6-5   What is the difference between stock price maximization and profit maximization? What conditions might promote profit maximization but not lead to stock price maximization?

6-6   If you were the president of a large, publicly owned corporation, would you make decisions to maximize stockholders' welfare or your own personal interests? What are some actions that stockholders could take to ensure that management's interests and those of stockholders coincide? What are some other factors that might influence management's actions?

6-7   The president of United Semiconductor Corporation made this statement in the company's annual report: "United's primary goal is to increase the value of the common stockholders' equity over time." Later in the report, the following announcements were made:

   a.   The company contributed $1.5 million to the symphony orchestra in San Francisco, its headquarters city.

   b.   United is spending $500 million to open a new plant in Mexico. No revenues will be produced by the plant for 4 years, so earnings will be depressed during this period versus what they would have been had the company not opened the new plant.

   c.   The company is increasing its relative use of debt. Assets were formerly financed with 35 percent debt and 65 percent equity, henceforth the financing mix will be 50-50.

   d.   The company uses a great deal of electricity in its manufacturing operations, and it generates most of this power itself. United plans to utilize nuclear fuel rather than coal to produce electricity in the future.

   e.   The company has been paying out half of its earnings as dividends and retaining the other half. Henceforth, it will pay out only 30 percent as dividends.

   Discuss how United's stockholders, customers, and labor force would react to each of these actions, and describe how each action might affect United's stock price.

6-8   Why do U.S. corporations build manufacturing plants abroad when they could build them at home?

6-9   Compared to the ownership structure of U.S. firms, which are "open" companies, what are some advantages of the ownership structure of foreign firms, many of which are "closed" companies? Can you think of any disadvantages?

6-10   In general terms, how is value measured? What are the three factors that determine value? How does each factor affect value?

6-11   What is corporate governance? Does a firm's corporate governance policy relate to whether it conducts business in an ethical manner? Explain.

6-12   Can a firm sustain its operations by maximizing stockholders' wealth at the expense of other stakeholders?

6-13   Compared to purely domestic firms, what are some factors that make financial decision making more complicated for firms that operate in foreign countries?

6-14   Suppose you own 100 shares of General Motors stock, and the company earned $6 per share during the last reporting period. Suppose also that GM could either pay all of its earnings out as dividends (in which case you would receive $600) or retain the earnings in the business, buy more assets, and cause the price of the stock to increase by $6 per share (in which case the value of your stock would rise by $600).

    a.   How would the tax laws influence what you, as a typical stockholder, would want the company to do?

    b.   Would your choice be influenced by how much other income you had? Why might the desires of a 35-year-old doctor differ with respect to corporate dividend policy from the desires of a retiree living on a small income?

    c.   How might the corporation's decision with regard to the dividends it pays influence the price of its stock?

6-15   What does *double taxation of corporate income* mean?

6-16   If you were starting a business, what tax considerations might cause you to prefer to set it up as a proprietorship or a partnership rather than as a corporation? Would you consider the average tax rate or the marginal tax rate to be more relevant when making the decision?

6-17   Explain how the federal income tax structure affects the choice of financing (use of debt versus equity) of U.S. business firms.

SELF-TEST PROBLEMS

Solutions appear in Appendix B.

Key Terms   **ST-1**   Define each of the following terms:

    a.   Proprietorship; partnership; corporation

    b.   Limited liability partnership (LLP); limited liability company (LLC); S corporation

    c.   Corporate charter; bylaws

    d.   Stockholder wealth maximization

    e.   Capital structure decisions; capital budgeting decisions; dividend policy decisions

    f.   Value

    g.   Profit maximization; earnings per share

    h.   Agency problem

    i.   Hostile takeover

    j.   Business ethics; corporate governance

    k.   Stakeholders

    l.   Multinational corporation

m. Industrial group; *chaebol; keiretsu*

n. Exchange rate

o. Progressive tax

p. Marginal and average tax rates

q. Capital gain or loss

r. Tax loss carryback and carryover

ST-2 John Thompson is planning to start a new business, JT Enterprises, and he must decide whether to incorporate or to do business as a sole proprietorship. Under either form of business, John will initially own 100 percent of the firm, and tax considerations are important to him. He plans to finance the firm's expected growth by drawing a salary just sufficient for his family's living expenses, which he estimates will be about $40,000, and by reinvesting all other income in the business. As a married man with one child, John has income tax exemptions of 3 × $3,500 = $10,500 and he estimates that his itemized deductions for each of the 3 years will be $12,000. He expects JT Enterprises to earn an income of $60,000 in 2010, $90,000 in 2011, and $110,000 in 2012. Which form of business organization will allow John to pay the lower taxes (and retain the most income) during the period 2010–2012? Assume that the tax rates given in the appendix to this chapter are applicable for all future years. (John would also have to pay Social Security taxes, but you can ignore them here.)

Form of Business and Taxes

PROBLEMS

Note: *By the time this book is published, Congress most certainly will have changed tax rates, other provisions of current tax law, or both. Work all problems on the assumption that the information in the chapter and the tax rates shown in Table 6A-1 and Table 6A-2 in the appendix at the end of this chapter are still current.*

6-1 The Ramjah Corporation had $200,000 of taxable income from operations in 2010.

a. What is the company's federal income tax bill for the year?

b. Assume that the firm receives an additional $40,000 of interest income from the bonds it owns. What is the tax on this interest income?

c. Assume that Ramjah does not receive the interest income, but does receive an additional $40,000 in dividends on some stock it owns. What is the tax on this dividend income?

Corporate Tax Liability

6-2 The Zocco Corporation has a 2010 taxable income of $365,000 from operations after all operating costs, but before (1) interest charges of $50,000, (2) dividends received of $15,000, (3) dividends paid of $25,000, and (4) income taxes.

a. What is the firm's income tax liability and its after-tax income?

b. What are the company's marginal and average tax rates on taxable income?

Corporate Tax Liability

6-3 A few days ago, Deanna Watson purchased 100 shares of Microsoft common stock for $35 per share. Deanna is single, and her taxable income (after all deductions and exemptions) is $75,000. Compute the capital gains tax liability for the following situations:

a. Deanna holds the stock for 5 months and then sells it for $40 per share.

b. Deanna sells the stock for $45 per share 13 months after she purchased it.

Capital Gains, Tax Liability

    c. Deanna doesn't sell the stock until 4 years from today, when the selling price is $105 per share.

Capital Gains, Tax Liability **6-4** Compute the capital gains tax liability for each of the following cases:

    a. An individual sold a municipal bond for $1,150, 2 years after it was purchased for $950.

    b. An individual sold 100 shares of a stock for $12 per share, 2 years after it was purchased at a price equal to $10 per share.

    c. A corporation bought 100 shares of stock of another company for $55 per share, and then sold it for $57 per share 2 years later.

Loss Carryback/ Carryover **6-5** The Angell Company has earned $150,000 before taxes during each of the last 15 years, and it expects to earn $150,000 per year before taxes in the future. In 2010, however, the firm incurred a loss of $650,000. It will claim a tax credit at the time it files its 2010 income tax return, and it will receive a check from the U.S. Treasury. Show how Angell calculates this credit, and then indicate the firm's tax liability for each of the next 5 years. Assume a 30 percent tax rate on all income to simplify the calculations.

Loss Carryback/ Carryover **6-6** The projected taxable income of the Glasgo Corporation, formed in 2009, is indicated in the following table. (Losses are shown in parentheses.) What is the corporate tax liability for each year? Use the tax rates shown in the appendix to this chapter.

Year	Taxable Income
2009	$ (95,000)
2010	70,000
2011	55,000
2012	80,000
2013	(150,000)

Form of Business **6-7** Kate Brown has operated her small repair shop as a sole proprietorship for several years, but projected changes in her business's income have led her to consider incorporating. Kate is married and has two children. Her family's only income, her annual salary of $55,000, comes from operating the business. (The business actually earns more than $55,000, but Kate reinvests the additional earnings in the business.) She itemizes deductions, and she is able to deduct $19,500. These deductions, combined with her four personal exemptions for 4 × $3,500 = $14,000, give her a personal taxable income of $21,500 = $55,000 − $19,500 − $14,000. Of course, her actual taxable income, if she does not incorporate, would be higher by the amount of reinvested income. Kate estimates that her business earnings before salary and taxes for the period 2010 to 2011 will be as follows:

Year	Earnings Before Salary and Taxes
2010	$ 90,000
2011	120,000
2012	150,000

a. What would Brown's total taxes (corporate plus personal) be in each year under

(1) A corporation? (2010 tax = $7,672.50)

(2) A proprietorship? (2010 tax = $7,672.50)

b. Should Brown incorporate? Discuss.

6-8   Margaret Considine has the following situation for the year 2010: salary of $60,000; dividend income of $10,000; interest on IBM bonds of $5,000; interest on State of Florida municipal bonds of $10,000; proceeds of $22,000 from the sale of IBM stock purchased in 1998 at a cost of $9,000; and proceeds of $22,000 from the November 2010 sale of IBM stock purchased in October 2010 at a cost of $21,000. Margaret gets one exemption ($3,500), and she has allowable itemized deductions of $6,500; these amounts will be deducted from her gross income to determine her taxable income.

Personal Taxes

a. What is Margaret's federal tax liability for 2010?

b. What are her marginal and average tax rates?

c. If she had some money to invest and was offered a choice of either State of Florida bonds with a yield of 9 percent or more IBM bonds with a yield of 11 percent, which should she choose, and why?

d. At what marginal tax rate would Margaret be indifferent in her choice between the Florida munis and the IBM bonds?

6-9   Lexy Ballinger and her 4-year-old son currently live in an apartment owned by Lexy's parents. Her parents charge her very little for rent—$200 per month for a luxurious two-bedroom townhouse. Lexy works at a local hospital as a physician's assistant, where she earns $45,200 per year.

Personal Taxes

a. What is Lexy's tax liability?

b. How would Lexy's tax liability change if she had a $15,000 automobile loan with monthly payments equal to $484 and the interest paid on the loan this year was $1,300?

6-10   Donald Jefferson and his wife, Maryanne, live in a modest house located in a Los Angeles suburb. Donald has a job at Pittsford Cast Iron that pays him $50,000 annually. In addition, he and Maryanne receive $2,500 interest from bonds that they purchased 10 years ago. To supplement his annual income, Donald bought rental property a few years ago. Every month he collects $3,500 in rent from all of the property he owns. Maryanne manages the rental property, and she is paid $15,000 annually for her work. During 2010, Donald had to have the plumbing fixed in the houses that he rents as well as the house in which he and Maryanne live. The plumbing bill was $1,250 for the rented houses and $550 for the Jeffersons' personal residence. In 2010, Donald paid $18,000 for mortgage interest and property taxes—$12,650 was for the rental houses, and the remaining $5,350 was for the house occupied by him and his wife. The couple has three children who have graduated from medical school and now are working as physicians in other states.

Tax Liability

a. What is the Jeffersons' tax liability for 2010?

b. What would the tax liability be if the Jeffersons did not have the rental property? (Assume that Maryanne would not get another job if the Jeffersons did not own the rental property.)

c. Why is the plumbing expense a tax deduction for the rental property but not for the house in which the Jeffersons live?

Integrative Problems

Forms of Business **6-11** Marty Kimble, who "retired" many years ago after winning a huge lottery jackpot, wants to start a new company that will sell authentic sports memorabilia. He plans to name the company Pro Athlete Remembrances, or PAR for short. Marty is still in the planning stages, so he has a few questions about how PAR should be organized when he starts the business and what he should do if the company becomes extremely successful in the future. Marty has little knowledge of finance concepts. To answer his questions and learn more about finance in general, Mr. Kimble has hired Sunshine Business Consultants (SBC). Assume that you are a new employee of SBC and your boss has asked you to answer the following questions for Mr. Kimble:

a. What are the alternative forms of business organization? What are the advantages and disadvantages of each?

b. What form of business organization do you recommend that Mr. Kimble use when starting PAR? Why?

c. Assume that PAR is organized as a proprietorship when it starts business. If PAR becomes extremely successful and grows substantially, would you recommend that Mr. Kimble change the business organization to either a partnership or a corporation? Explain your answer.

d. What goal should Mr. Kimble pursue when operating PAR?

e. Assume that PAR is organized as a proprietorship when it starts business and that Mr. Kimble plans to convert the business to a corporation at some point in the future. What are some potential problems that Mr. Kimble, as one of the owners, might face after converting to a corporation? Discuss some solutions to these potential problems.

f. Mr. Kimble would like PAR to grow so that at some point in the future the company can conduct business in other countries. Why do firms "go global"?

g. Discuss any differences and problems that Mr. Kimble should be aware of when conducting business in foreign markets.

Taxes **6-12** Working with Michelle Delatorre, the tennis pro discussed in the Integrative Problems in Chapters 4 and 5, has required you to put in a great deal of overtime, so you have had little time to spend on your personal finances. It is now April 1, and you have only two weeks left to file your income tax return. You have managed to gather together all of the information that you will need to complete your return.

a. The firm for which you work, Balik and Kiefer, Inc., paid you a salary of $50,000, and you received $3,000 in dividends from common stock that you own. You are single and plan to use the standard deduction rather than itemize expenses.

(1) On the basis of the information given in the problem and the 2005 individual tax rate schedule, what is your tax liability?

(2) What are your marginal and average tax rates?

b. You also compute the taxes for the corporation that your parents own. This company has $100,000 of taxable income from operations plus $5,000 of interest income and $100,000 of dividend income. During the previous year, the company paid dividends equal to $8,000. What is its tax liability?

   c. Assume that after paying your personal income tax, as calculated in part (a), you have funds to invest. You have narrowed your investment choices to California bonds with a yield of 7 percent or IBM bonds with a yield of 10 percent. Which investment should you choose, and why? At what marginal tax rate would you be indifferent between choosing the California bonds and the IBM bonds?

COMPUTER-RELATED PROBLEM

Work the problem in this section only if you are using the problem spreadsheet.

6-13 This problem requires you to rework Problem 6-7 using the information that follows. Use the spreadhsheet model in File C06 to solve this problem.

   Taxes

   a. Suppose Kate decides to pay out (1) 50 percent or (2) 100 percent of the after-salary corporate income each year as dividends. Would such dividend policy changes affect her decision about whether to incorporate?

   b. Suppose business improves, and the firm's actual earnings before salary and taxes in each year are twice the original estimate. Assume that if Kate chooses to incorporate, she will continue to receive a salary of $55,000 and to reinvest additional earnings in the business. (No dividend would be paid.) What would be the effect of this increase in business income on her decision to incorporate?

2008 Tax Rate Schedules   APPENDIX 6A

Table 6A-1 gives the 2008 tax rate for individuals and Table 6A-2 gives the 2008 tax rates for corporations. Even though rates are applicable only for taxes in 2008, they should be used for all of the problems in this chapters that require the computation of tax liabilities.

TABLE 6A-1   Individual Tax Rates for 2008

Single Taxpayer

Taxable Income Bracket			Base Tax Amount	Plus This Percentage	of the Amount Over		Average Tax Rate at the Top of the Bracket
$ 0	–	$ 8,025	$ 0.00	+ 10.0%	$	0	10.0%
8,026	–	32,550	802.50	+ 15.0		8,025	13.8
32,551	–	78,850	4,481.25	+ 25.0		32,550	20.4
78,851	–	164,550	16,056.25	+ 28.0		78,850	24.3
164,551	–	357,700	40,052.25	+ 33.0		164,550	29.0
357,701	–		103,791.75	+ 35.0		357,700	35.0

Married Taxpayer Filing Jointly

Taxable Income Bracket			Base Tax Amount	Plus This Percentage of the Amount Over			Average Tax Rate at the Top of the Bracket
$ 0	–	$ 16,050	$ 0.00	+	10.0%	$ 0	10.0%
16,051	–	65,100	1,605.00	+	15.0	16,050	13.8
65,101	–	131,450	8,962.50	+	25.0	65,100	19.4
131,451	–	200,300	25,550.00	+	28.0	131,450	22.4
200,301	–	357,700	44,828.00	+	33.0	200,300	27.1
357,701	–		96,770.00	+	35.0	357,700	35.0

Notes:

a. The personal exemption for 2008 was $3,500 per person (dependent). The total amount of this exemption can be deducted from income to compute taxable income. For example, for a family of four, the total personal exemption would be $14,000 = $3,500 × 4.

b. If the taxpayer does not want to itemize allowed deductions, such as mortgage interest payments and charitable contributions, the standard deduction can be taken. In 2008, the standard deduction for a single taxpayer was $5,450, and it was $10,900 for a married taxpayer filing a joint return.

c. Both the personal exemption and the standard deduction are phased out for taxpayers with high incomes.

d. The tax rate applied to capital gains on investments held less than 12 months (short term) was the marginal tax rate of the taxpayer. If the asset was held for one year or longer (long term), the amount of the capital gains was taxed at 15 percent (0 percent for taxpayers whose marginal tax rate was either 10 percent or 15 percent).

TABLE 6A-2 Corporate Tax Rates for 2008

Taxable Income Bracket			Base Tax Amount	Plus This Percentage of the Amount Over			Average Tax Rate at the Top of the Bracket
$ 0	–	$ 50,000	$ 0	+	15%	$ 0	15.0%
50,001	–	75,000	7,500	+	25	50,000	18.3
75,001	–	100,000	13,750	+	34	75,000	22.3
100,001	–	335,000	22,250	+	39	100,000	34.0
335,001	–	10,000,000	113,900	+	34	335,000	34.0
10,000,001	–	15,000,000	3,400,000	+	35	10,000,000	34.3
15,000,001	–	18,333,333	5,150,000	+	38	15,000,000	35.0
18,333,334	–		6,416,667	+	35	18,333,333	35.0

Note:

a. Capital gains are taxed at the same rate as ordinary income.

Analysis of Financial Statements

CHAPTER 7

A MANAGERIAL PERSPECTIVE

U.S. firms are required to make "full and fair" disclosure of their operations by publishing various financial statements and other reports required by the Securities and Exchange Commission (SEC), the Financial Accounting Standards Board (FASB), and the American Institute of Certified Public Accountants (AICPA). One such report that firms publish is the annual report, which is often used to convey more than financial results. For example, some corporations view the annual report as an opportunity to showcase top management and sell the future of the company, without regard to the financial information. It is not unusual for work on the report to begin as much as six months before its publication, and many firms hire professional designers and writers to ensure that the final product looks sharp and reads well. Some firms pride themselves on the unique packaging designs used for their annual reports. For example, since 1977, McCormick & Company has used one of the spices or seasonings it produces to scent the paper on which its annual report is printed—the scent for 2007 was Chinese five-spice, which is a mixture of anise, Szechuan peppercorn, cinnamon, cloves, and fennel seed.

In many instances, the puffery contained in annual reports detracts from the reports' nominal purpose of providing objective financial information about the firm. Of course, some companies use the annual report as originally intended—to communicate the financial position of the firm. One such firm is Berkshire Hathaway, whose legendary chairman Warren Buffett says, "I assume I have a very intelligent partner who has been away for a year and needs to be filled in on all that's happened." Consequently, in his letters, he often admits mistakes and emphasizes the negative. Buffett also uses his letters to educate his shareholders and to help them interpret the data presented in the rest of the report. Berkshire Hathaway's annual reports contain little, if any, puffery, freeing readers to focus on the company's financial statements and Buffett's interpretation of them. Some CEOs might contend that such a bare-bones approach is too dull for the average stockholder and that some readers might actually be intimidated by an overload of financial information. However, the manner in which Buffett presents financial information for Berkshire Hathaway seems to work, because the firm's stockholders are considered more sophisticated than the average investor. If you would like to examine some of the statements made by Warren Buffett, visit Berkshire Hathaway's Web site at http://berkshirehathaway.com; even the company Web site lacks glitter.

More and more, firms are recognizing that the "slick" annual report has lost its credibility with serious seekers of financial information and that it has become ever more expensive to produce. In addition, today's technology has allowed firms to post their annual reports on their Web sites. In many cases, the online version of a firm's annual report is devoid of the frills that traditionally exist in the paper version.

As you read this chapter, think about the kinds of information that corporations provide to their stockholders. Do you think the basic financial statements provide adequate data for making investment decisions? What other information might be helpful? Also, consider the pros and cons of Buffett's decision to include frank, and frequently self-critical, letters in his company's annual reports. Would you suggest that other companies follow suit?

CHAPTER PRINCIPLES
–The Questions

After reading this chapter, you should be able to answer the following questions:

- What financial statements do corporations publish, and what information does each statement provide?
- How do investors utilize financial statements?
- What is ratio analysis and why are the results of such an analysis important to both managers and investors?
- What are some potential problems (caveats) associated with financial statement analysis?
- What is the most important ingredient (factor) in financial statement analysis?

In Chapter 6, we stated that managers should strive to maximize the value of the firm's stock. We also noted that a stock's value is determined by the cash flows that the firm is expected to generate in the future. Thus, to estimate value, both managers and investors must be able to estimate future cash flows. In this chapter, we give some indication as to how financial statements that are constructed by firms can be used to accomplish this task.

Financial statement analysis involves analysis of a firm's financial position to identify its current strengths and weaknesses and to suggest actions that the firm might pursue to take advantage of those strengths and correct any weaknesses. In this chapter, we discuss how to evaluate a firm's current financial position using its financial statements. In later chapters, we will examine the types of actions that a firm can take to improve its financial position in the future, thereby increasing the market price of its stock.

RECORDING BUSINESS ACTIVITY—FINANCIAL STATEMENTS

A brief discussion of the history and evolution of accounting and the production of financial statements provides an indication as to why such records are needed and how they are used.[1] Many people believe that the birth of accounting took place more than 4,000 years ago in ancient Mesopotamia as the result of the Code of Hammurabi, which required merchants to provide prices of goods and services in writing so that sales agreements were recorded. Merchants also kept written histories of transactions to ensure that disputed sales could be settled; without written proof of the terms, transactions often were invalidated. As a result, it was important for merchants to keep accurate records of their transactions, which included prices, quantity and quality of the products sold, and so forth.

---

[1]Much of the information provided in this section can be found in the History of Accounting page on the Web site of the Association of Charted Accountants in the United States (ACAUS), which is located at http://www.acaus.org/acc_his.html. For more information about the history of accounting, visit this Web site.

As societies became more sophisticated and governments provided more and more services to the citizens, "accountants" became an important factor in the determination and collection of the taxes that were used to finance government services. Bookkeepers kept the tax records during these times. The penalties for "accounting irregularities" included fines, disfigurement, or even death. As a result, bookkeepers/accountants were motivated to provide reliable, accurate records.

According to all accounts, it wasn't until the fifteenth century that the birth of modern accounting began when Benedetto Cotrugli introduced the double-entry bookkeeping system, which was more formally developed by Luca Pacioli a few decades later. In his writings, Pacioli stated that to be successful, a merchant must have access to funds (cash or credit) to support daily operations and a system that permits the merchant to easily determine his financial position. He also recommended that merchants record all assets and liabilities, both personal and business, before starting business, and he noted that these records should be kept current.

As you can see from this brief history lesson, "financial books" have historically provided important information about the financial well-being of businesses. Today, financial statements provide similar information, which is important to a firm's stakeholders. Information that is included in these statements can be used by managers to improve the firm's performance and by investors (either stockholders or creditors) to evaluate the firm's financial position when making investment decisions.

Financial Reports

Of the various reports that corporations provide to their stockholders, the **annual report** is arguably the most important. This report provides two types of information. First, it includes a verbal section, often presented as a letter from the chairman, that describes the firm's operating results during the past year and discusses new developments that will affect future operations. Second, the annual report presents four basic financial statements: the balance sheet, the income statement, the statement of cash flows, and the statement of retained earnings. Taken together, these statements give an accounting picture of the firm's operations and financial position. Detailed data are provided for the two most recent years, along with historical summaries of key operating statistics for the past 5 or 10 years.[2]

annual report
A report issued by a corporation to its stockholders that contains basic financial statements, as well as the opinions of management about the past year's operations and the firm's future prospects.

The quantitative and verbal information contained in the annual report are equally important. The financial statements indicate what actually happened to the firm's financial position and to its earnings and dividends over the past few years, whereas the verbal statements attempt to explain why things turned out the way they did. To illustrate how annual reports can prove helpful, we will use data taken from a fictitious company called Argile Textiles, a manufacturer and distributor of a wide variety of textiles and clothing items. Formed in 1990 in North Carolina, Argile has grown steadily and has earned a reputation for selling quality products.

In the most recent annual report, management reported that earnings dropped 6.25 percent due to losses associated with a poor cotton crop and from increased costs caused by a 3-month employee strike and a retooling of the factory. Management then went on to paint a more optimistic picture for the future, stating that full operations had been resumed, several unprofitable businesses had been

---

[2]Firms also provide quarterly reports, but they are much less comprehensive than the annual report. In addition, larger firms file even more detailed statements, giving breakdowns for each major division or subsidiary, with the Securities and Exchange Commission (SEC). These reports, called *10-K reports*, are made available to stockholders upon request to a company's corporate secretary. Many companies also post these reports on their Web sites. Finally, many larger firms also publish *statistical supplements*, which give financial statement data and key ratios going back 10 to 20 years.

eliminated, and profits were expected to rise sharply next year. Of course, an increase in profitability might not occur, and analysts should compare management's past statements with subsequent results to determine whether this optimism is justified. In any event, investors use the information contained in an annual report to form expectations about future earnings and dividends. Clearly, then, investors are quite interested in the annual report.

Because this book is intended to provide an introduction to finance, Argile's financial statements are constructed so that they are simple and straightforward. At this time, the company uses only debt and common stock to finance its assets—that is, Argile does not have outstanding preferred stock, convertible financing instruments, or derivatives. Also, the company has only the basic assets that are required to conduct business, including cash and marketable securities, accounts receivable, inventory, and ordinary fixed assets. For this reason, Argile does not have assets that require complex accounting applications.

Self-Test Questions

Identify the two types of information given in the annual report.

Why are investors interested in a firm's annual report?

FINANCIAL STATEMENTS

Before we analyze how Argile's financial position compares to other firms' financial positions, let's take a look at the financial statements the company publishes. Information contained in the financial statements is used by investors to estimate the cash flows that the company is expected to generate in the future.

The Balance Sheet

balance sheet
A statement that shows the firm's financial position—assets and liabilities and equity—at a specific point in time.

The **balance sheet** represents a picture taken *at a specific point in time (date)* that shows a firm's assets and how those assets are financed (debt or equity). Figure 7-1 shows the general setup for a simple balance sheet. Table 7-1 shows Argile's balance sheets on December 31 for the years 2009 and 2010. December 31 is the end of the fiscal year, which is when Argile "takes a snapshot" of its existing assets, liabilities, and equity to construct the balance sheet. In this section, we concentrate on the more recent balance sheet—for December 31, 2010.

Assets, which represent the firm's investments, are classified as either short-term (current) or long-term (see Figure 7-1). Current assets generally include items that will be liquidated and thus converted into cash within 1 year, whereas long-term, or fixed, assets include investments that help generate cash flows over longer periods. As Table 7-1 shows, at the end of 2010 Argile's current assets, which include cash and equivalents, accounts receivable (amounts due from customers), and inventory, totaled $235 million; its long-term assets, which include the building and equipment used to manufacture the textile products, had a net value equal to $190 million; thus, its total assets were $425 million. Table 7-1 shows that 55 percent of Argile's assets was in the form of current, or short-term, assets, whereas the remaining 45 percent was in the form of plant and equipment (long-term assets).

To finance its assets, a firm "issues" debt, equity (stock), or both forms of financing. Debt represents the loans the firm has outstanding, and it generally is divided into two categories—short-term debt and long-term debt (see Figure 7-1).

FIGURE 7-1   Simple Balance Sheet

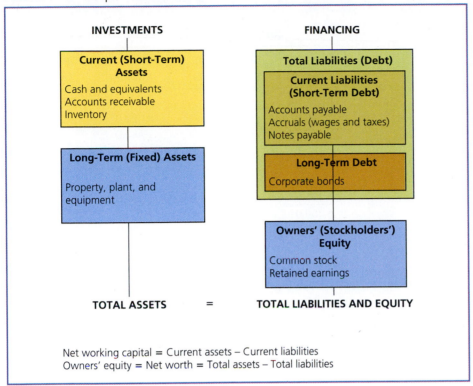

Net working capital = Current assets – Current liabilities
Owners' equity = Net worth = Total assets – Total liabilities

Short-term debt, which is labeled current liabilities, includes accounts payable (amounts owed to suppliers), accruals (amounts owed to employees and state and federal governments), and notes payable (amounts owed to the bank). Current liabilities represent debt that is due within 1 year—that is, these debts are expected to be paid off within 12 months. Table 7-1 shows that Argile's short-term debt totaled $65 million. Long-term debt includes the bonds and similar debt instruments that the firm has issued in previous years that are paid off over a period longer than 1 year. At the end of 2010, Argile had outstanding bonds equal to $152 million. In combination, then, the total amount of debt Argile used to finance its assets was $217 million. Thus, according to Table 7-1, about 51 percent of the firm's assets were financed using debt, most of which was in the form of long-term bonds (70 percent of total liabilities).

Equity represents stockholders' ownership, which, unlike debt, does not have to be "paid off." Total equity is the amount that would be paid to stockholders if the firm's assets could be sold at the values reported on the balance sheet and its debt paid off in the amounts reported on the balance sheet. Thus, the firm's **common stockholders' equity,** or **net worth,** equals total assets minus total liabilities. Table 7-1 shows that Argile's net worth was $208 million at the end of 2010. This implies, but does not mean, that common stockholders would receive $208 million if Argile liquidates its assets and pays off all of its outstanding debt. However, suppose that all of the accounts receivable cannot be collected or some inventory had to be sold for less than the amount shown on the balance sheet. If liabilities remain constant, the value of the stockholders' equity would be less because the firm's creditors (debtholders) would want to be paid the full amount they are owed before stockholders got paid anything. For example, if Argile could collect only $400 million by liquidating all

common stockholders' equity (net worth)
The funds provided by common stockholders—common stock, paid-in capital, and retained earnings.

TABLE 7-1   Argile Textiles: December 31 Comparative Balance Sheets ($ million)

	2010		2009	
	Amount	**Percent of Total Assets**	**Amount**	**Percent of Total Assets**
Assets				
Cash and marketable securities	$ 10.0	2.4%	$ 20.0	5.3%
Accounts receivable	90.0	21.2	80.0	21.3
Inventories	135.0	31.7	101.0	26.9
Total current assets	$ 235.0	55.3%	$ 201.0	53.5%
Gross plant and equipment	345.0		300.0	
Less: Accumulated depreciation	(155.0)		(125.0)	
Net plant and equipment	$ 190.0	44.7	$ 175.0	46.5
Total assets	$ 425.0	100.0%	$ 376.0	100.0%
Liabilities and Equity				
Accounts payable	$ 15.0	3.5%	$ 8.0	2.1%
Accruals	30.0	7.1	27.0	7.2
Notes payable	20.0	4.7	18.0	4.8
Total current liabilities	$ 65.0	15.3%	$ 53.0	14.1%
Long-term bonds	152.0	35.8	128.0	34.0
Total liabilities	$ 217.0	51.1%	$ 181.0	48.1%
Common stock (11 million shares)	66.0	15.5	66.0	17.6
Retained earnings	142.0	33.4	129.0	34.3
Owners' equity	$ 208.0	48.9%	$ 195.0	51.9%
Total liabilities and equity	$ 425.0	100.0%	$ 376.0	100.0%
Book value per share = (Common equity)/Shares	$ 18.91		$ 17.73	
Market value per share (stock price)	$ 20.00		$ 20.00	
Additional Information:				
Net working capital = Current assets − Current liabilties	$ 170.0		$ 148.0	
Net worth = Total assets − Total liabilities	$ 208.0		$ 195.0	

Note: Argile has no preferred stock, so owners' equity includes common equity only.

of its assets today, then the amount that would be left over and that could be distributed to stockholders after paying debts would be $183 million ($400 million liquidation proceeds minus $217 million needed to pay off liabilities), not the $208 million shown in the equity section on the balance sheet. This simple example shows that the risk of asset value fluctuations is borne by the stockholders. Note, however, that if asset values rise, these benefits will accrue exclusively to the stockholders. The change in the firm's net worth is reflected by changes in the retained earnings account; if bad debts are written off in the asset section of the balance sheet, for example, the retained earnings balance is reduced in the equity section.

Notice that the common equity section shown in Table 7-1 is comprised of two accounts—common stock and retained earnings. The common stock account shows the amount that stockholders paid to Argile when the company issued stock to raise funds. Argile has issued stock only once—when it was formed in 1990—so the amount shown in the common stock account has remained constant at $66 million since that time. The amount shown in the **retained earnings** account effectively represents the total amount of income that Argile has saved and reinvested in assets since the firm started business. It is important to note that the amount reported on the balance sheet in the retained earnings account shows the cumulative amount of income the company has kept rather than paid out as dividends over the years. According to Table 7-1, Argile has kept $142 million of all the income generated since 1990. This amount could have been paid to stockholders as dividends over the years, but Argile instead decided to use these funds to finance some of its investment in assets over the years.

retained earnings
The portion of the firm's earnings that has been reinvested in the firm rather than paid out as dividends.

Note that in Table 7-1 the assets are listed in order of their "liquidity," or the length of time it typically takes to convert them to cash. The claims (liabilities and equity) are listed in the order in which they generally must be paid. Accounts payable generally must be paid within 30 to 45 days, accruals are payable within 60 to 90 days, and so on, down to the stockholders' equity accounts, which represent ownership and need never be "paid off." The practice of listing assets and liabilities in this order began in the fifteenth century when Luca Pacioli suggested that items should be listed based on "mobility" such that cash and other assets that can be converted to cash easily should be listed first on the financial books.[3]

Notice that the assets, liabilities, and equity reported on the balance sheets in Table 7-1 are stated both in dollars and as a percent of total assets. When items on a balance sheet are stated as percentages, it is termed a **common size balance sheet.** The resultant percentage statement can be easily compared with statements of larger or smaller firms, or with those of the same firm over time. For example, we noted that 51 percent of Argile's assets were financed with debt in 2010. We can compare this percent with other textile firms to determine whether Argile has too much debt. We discuss such comparisons later in the chapter.

common size balance sheet
Dollar amounts on the balance sheet are stated as a percent of total assets.

Some additional points about the balance sheet are worth noting:

1. *Cash and equivalents versus other assets.* Although the assets are all stated in terms of dollars, only the "cash and equivalents" account represents actual money that can be spent. Receivables are bills that others owe to Argile; inventories show the dollars that the company has invested in raw materials, work-in-process, and finished goods available for sale; and net fixed assets reflect the amount of money that Argile paid for its plant and equipment when it acquired those assets less the amount that has been written off (depreciated) since the assets' acquisitions. The noncash assets should produce cash over time, but they do not represent cash in hand. The amount of cash they would bring in if sold today could be either higher or lower than the values that are reported on the balance sheet (their *book values*). At the end of 2010, Argile had $10 million cash and equivalents that could be used to pay the bills. Of course, in 2011, most customers that owe Argile money at the end of 2010 will pay their bills, Argile will sell some inventory for cash, and Argile will pay most of its bills. As a result, the amount in the cash and equivalents account will vary throughout the year. It is important that Argile has enough cash on hand to pay bills when they are due. But Argile doesn't want to keep too much cash because cash is an idle asset in the sense that it does not earn a positive return for the firm.

---

[3]See the History of Accounting page on the Web site of the Association of Chartered Accountants in the United States (ACAUS), which is located at http://www.acaus.org/acc_his.html.

2. *Accounting alternatives.* Not every firm uses the same method to determine the account balances shown on the balance sheet. For instance, Argile uses the FIFO (first-in, first-out) method to determine the inventory value shown on its balance sheet. It could have used the LIFO (last-in, first-out) method instead. During a period of rising prices, compared to LIFO, FIFO will produce a higher balance sheet inventory value but a lower cost of goods sold, and thus a higher net income.

In some cases, a company might use one accounting method to construct financial statements provided to stockholders and another accounting method for tax purposes, internal reports, and so forth. For example, companies generally use the most accelerated method permissible to calculate depreciation for tax purposes because accelerated methods lower taxable incomes, and thus taxes that must be paid. The same companies might use straight line depreciation for constructing financial statements reported to stockholders because this method results in higher net incomes. There is nothing illegal or unethical about this practice, but when evaluating firms, users of financial statements must be aware that more than one accounting alternative is available for constructing financial statements.

3. *Breakdown of the common equity account.* The equity section of Argile's balance sheet contains two accounts: common stock and retained earnings. The common equity sections of some firms include three accounts: common stock at par, paid-in capital, and retained earnings. We mentioned earlier that the retained earnings account is built up over time as the firm saves, or reinvests, a part of its earnings rather than paying everything out as dividends. The other two accounts arise from the issuance of stock to raise funds (capital). When a firm issues common stock to raise funds to invest in assets, the amount that investors pay for the stock must be reported in the equity section of the balance sheet. For example, Argile issued 11 million shares of stock at $6 to raise $66 million when it started business. Thus, Argile's stockholders provided the company with $66 million of funds to invest in its assets. Because Argile's common stock does not have a par value, the entire amount of the issue is reported in the "common stock" account.

If Argile's common stock had a par value equal to $2 per share, then the funds raised through the stock issue would have to be reported in two accounts: common stock at par and paid-in capital. The amount reported in the "common stock at par" account would equal the total value of the stock issue stated in terms of its par value, and it would be computed as follows:

$$\text{Common stock at par} = \text{Total shares issued} \times \text{Per-share par value}$$
$$= 11 \text{ million} \times \$2 = \$22 \text{ million}$$

The amount that was paid above the par value is reported in the "paid-in capital" account. In this case, because the total value of the issue was $66 million, the remaining $44 million would be reported in the paid-in capital account. This amount can also be computed by multiplying the portion of the selling price per share that exceeds the stock's par value by the number of shares that were issued. If Argile's stock had a par value equal to $2 and each share was issued at $6, then the additional $4 per share is considered paid-in capital. Therefore, the amount reported in the paid-in capital would be $44 million = ($6 − $2) × 11 million shares.

The breakdown of the common equity accounts shows whether the company actually earned the funds reported in its equity accounts or the funds came mainly from selling (issuing) stock. This information is important to both creditors and stockholders. For instance, a potential creditor would be interested in the amount of money that the owners put up, and stockholders would want to know the form of stockholders' funds.

4. *Book values versus market values.* The values, or accounting numbers, that are reported on the balance sheet are called *book values,* and they are generated using generally accepted accounting principles (GAAP). In many cases, these book values are not the same as the prices (values) for which the assets can actually be sold in the marketplace. That is, the **book values** of assets often do not equal their **market values.** For example, when Argile built its original distribution center in 1990, the value of the building was $45 million, which represented the market value at the time. Today, in 2010, the book value of the building is $15 million because $30 million has been depreciated over the years. However, the appraised (market) value of the building is $25 million. Thus, the market value of the building ($25 million) is greater than its book value ($15 million).

book values
Amounts reported in financial statements— accounting numbers.

market values
Value of an item—asset, liability, or equity—in the marketplace outside the firm.

Whereas the book values of assets often are not equal to their market values, the book values of a firm's debt generally are either equal to or very close to the market values of the firm's liabilities. Because most debt represents a contractual obligation to pay a certain amount at a specific time, the amounts reported on the balance sheet normally are the amounts that the firm owes its creditors.

The equity section of the balance sheet must equal the book value of assets minus the book value of liabilities (see Figure 7-1). As we mentioned, it is likely that book values of assets *differ from* their market values, but it is likely that the book values of liabilities are *close to* their market values. As a result, the difference between the book value and market value of equity primarily depends on the differences between the book values and market values of the firm's assets. If the aggregate book value of the firm's assets is much lower than their aggregate market value, then the book value of equity will be much lower than the market value of the firm's common stock, and vice versa.

5. *The time dimension.* The balance sheet can be thought of as a snapshot of the firm's financial position *at a point in time.* The balance sheet changes every day as inventories are increased or decreased, as fixed assets are added or retired, as liabilities are increased or decreased, and so on. Companies whose businesses are seasonal experience especially large changes in their balance sheets during the year. For example, most retailers have large inventories just before Christmas but low inventories and high accounts receivable just after this holiday. As a result, firms' balance sheets will change over the year, depending on the dates on which the statements are constructed.

The Income Statement

The **income statement,** which is also referred to as the profit and loss statement, presents the results of business operations *during a specified period of time* such as a quarter or a year. It summarizes the revenues generated and the expenses incurred by the firm during the accounting period. Table 7-2 gives the 2009 and 2010 income statements for Argile Textiles. Net sales are shown at the top of the statement, followed by various costs, including income taxes, that are subtracted to determine the net income (earnings) available to common stockholders. A report on earnings and dividends per share appears at the bottom of the statement. In managerial finance, earnings per share (EPS) is called "the bottom line" because EPS is often

income statement
A statement summarizing the firm's revenues and expenses over an accounting period, generally a quarter or a year.

TABLE 7-2   Argile Textiles: Income Statement for Years Ending December 31 ($ million, except per-share data)

	2010		2009	
	Amount	**Percent of Net Sales**	**Amount**	**Percent of Net Sales**
Net sales	$ 750.0	100.0%	$ 700.0	100.0%
Cost of goods sold	(600.0)	80.0	(560.0)	80.0
Gross profit	$ 150.0	20.0	140.0	20.0
Fixed operating expenses except depreciation	(55.0)[a]	7.3	(50.0)	7.1
Earnings before interest, taxes, depreciation, and amortization (EBITDA)	$ 95.0	12.7	$ 90.0	12.9
Depreciation	(30.0)	4.0	(24.0)	3.4
Net operating income (NOI)				
= Earnings before interest and taxes (EBIT)	$ 65.0	8.7	$ 66.0	9.4
Interest	(20.0)	2.7	(18.0)	2.6
Earnings before taxes (EBT)	$ 45.0	6.0	48.0	6.9
Taxes (40%)	(18.0)	2.4	(19.2)	2.7
Net income	$ 27.0	3.6	$ 28.8	4.1
Preferred dividends[b]	0.0		0.0	
Earnings available to common shareholders (EAC)	$ 27.0		$ 28.8	
Common dividends	(14.0)		(13.0)	
Addition to retained earnings	$ 13.0		$ 15.8	
Per-share Data (11 Million Shares):				
Earnings per share (EPS) = (EAC)/Shares	$ 2.45		$ 2.62	
Dividends per share (DPS) = (Common dividends)/Shares	$ 1.27		$ 1.18	

[a]Here, and throughout the text, parentheses are used to denote negative numbers.

[b]Argile has no preferred stock. The amount of preferred dividends, which is $0, is shown here to inidcate that preferred dividends are paid before common dividends.

considered to be the most important item on the income statement. Argile earned $2.45 per share in 2010, down from $2.62 in 2009, but it still raised the per-share dividend from $1.18 to $1.27.

Should Identical Firms Report the Same Net Income?

The obvious answer is yes. However, even though two firms might have identical operating structures—that is, facilities, employees, and production methods—they might be financed differently. For example, one firm might be financed with a substantial amount of debt, whereas the other firm might be financed only with stock. Interest payments to debtholders are tax deductible; dividend payments to stockholders are not. The firm that is financed with debt will have greater tax-deductible expenses as a result of the interest expense and thus will report a lower net income than the firm that is financed with equity only. For this reason, when comparing the operations of two firms, analysts often examine the *net operating income (NOI)*, also known as the *earnings before interest and taxes (EBIT)*, because this figure represents the result of normal operations before considering the effects of the firm's financial structure. Argile's EBIT was $65 million in 2010. A firm that has the same operating structure (and follows the same accounting procedures) as Argile should have reported EBIT equal to $65 million as well, even if it does not use the same amount of debt as Argile to finance its assets.

Does Net Income Determine Value?

Investors often focus on the net income that a firm generates when determining how well the firm has performed during a particular time period. But, if investors are concerned with whether management is pursuing the goal of maximizing the firm's stock price, net income might not be the appropriate measure to examine.

Recall from your accounting courses that, for most corporations, the income statement is generated using the accrual method of accounting. That is, revenues are recognized when they are earned, not when the cash is received, and expenses are recognized when they are incurred, not when the cash is paid. As a result, not all of the amounts shown on the income statement represent cash flows. Remember, however, that the value of an investment, such as the firm's stock price, is determined by the cash flows it generates. Therefore, although the firm's net income is important, cash flows are even more important because cash is needed to continue normal business operations such as the payment of financial obligations, the purchase of assets, and the payment of dividends. As a result, in finance we focus on *cash flows* rather than on net income.

One item on Argile's income statement that we know is a noncash item is depreciation. The cash payment for a fixed asset, such as a building, occurs when the asset is originally purchased. But because the asset is used to generate revenues and its life extends for greater than 1 year, depreciation is the method that is used to *match* the expense associated with the decrease in the value of the asset with the revenues that the asset helps to generate. For example, Table 7-2 shows that Argile's net income for 2010 was $27 million and the depreciation expense for the year was $30 million. Because depreciation was not an expense that required a cash payment, Argile's net cash flow must be at least $30 million higher than the $27 million that is reported as net income. If the only noncash item on its income statement is depreciation, then the net cash flow that Argile generated in 2010 was $57 million.

When a firm sells its products for cash and pays cash for all of the expenses reported on its income statement, except depreciation and amortization, its net cash flow can be computed using this simple equation:

7-1

$$\text{Net cash flow} = \text{Net income} + \text{Depreciation and amortization}$$

$$= \$27 \text{ million} + \$30 \text{ million} = \$57 \text{ million}$$

Managers and analysts often use this equation to estimate the net cash flow generated by a firm, even when some customers have not paid for their purchases or the firm has not paid all of the bills for supplies, employees' salaries, and the like. In such cases, Equation 7-1 can be used only to estimate the net cash flow generated by the firm. To get a better estimate of net cash flow, as well as to examine in detail which of the firm's actions provided cash and which actions used cash, a statement of cash flows should be constructed. We discuss the statement of cash flows in the next section.

For our purposes, it is useful to divide cash flows into two categories: (1) operating cash flows and (2) other cash flows. **Operating cash flows** arise from normal operations, and they represent, in essence, the difference between cash collections and cash expenses associated with the manufacture and sale of inventory. Other cash flows arise from borrowing, from the sale of fixed assets, or from the repurchase of common stock. Our focus here is on operating cash flows.

operating cash flows Those cash flows that arise from normal operations; the difference between cash collections and cash expenses associated with the manufacture and sale of inventory.

accounting profits
A firm's net income as reported on its income statement.

We know that operating cash flows can differ from **accounting profits** (or operating income) for two primary reasons: (1) when a firm sells on credit and (2) when some operating expenses are not cash costs. For example, we know that the depreciation and amortization expense is a cost that does not use cash. For this reason, analysts often compute a firm's earnings before interest, taxes, depreciation, and amortization (EBITDA) when evaluating its operations. Because both depreciation, which recognizes the decline in the values of tangible assets, and amortization, which recognizes the decline in the values of intangible assets (patents, trademarks, and so forth) are noncash expenses, EBITDA provides an indication of the cash flows that are generated by normal operations. Argile's EBITDA was $95 million in 2010 (see Table 7-2). This is higher than the reported EBIT of $65 million because the depreciation expense was $30 million; Argile has no amortization expense.

Statement of Cash Flows

statement of cash flows
A statement that reports the effects of a firm's operating, investing, and financing activities on cash flows over an accounting period.

The **statement of cash flows** is designed to show how the firm's operations have affected its cash position by examining the firm's investment decisions (uses of cash) and financing decisions (sources of cash). The information contained in the statement of cash flows can help answer questions such as the following: Is the firm generating the cash needed to purchase additional fixed assets for growth? Does it have excess cash flows that can be used to repay debt or to invest in new products? Because this information is useful for both financial managers and investors, the statement of cash flows is an important part of the annual report.

Constructing a statement of cash flows is relatively easy. First, to some extent, the income statement shows the cash flow effects of a firm's operations. For example, Argile reported its 2010 net income as $27 million, which we know includes a $30 million depreciation expense that is a noncash operating cost. As reported earlier, if the $30 million depreciation expense is added back to the $27 million net income, we *estimate* that the cash flow generated from normal operations is $57 million. For most firms, however, some of the reported revenues have not been collected and some of the reported expenses have not been paid at the time the income statement is constructed. To adjust the estimate of cash flows obtained from the income statement and to account for cash flow effects not reflected in the income statement, we need to examine the implications of changes in the balance sheet accounts during the period in question (fiscal year 2010 for Argile). Looking at the changes in the balance sheet accounts from the beginning to the end of the year, we want to identify which items provided cash (a source) and which items used cash (a use) during the year. To determine whether a change in a balance sheet account was a source or a use of cash, we follow these simple rules:

Sources of Cash	Uses of Cash
Increase in a Liability or Equity Account	***Decrease in a Liability or Equity Account***
Borrowing funds or selling stock provides the firm with cash.	Paying off a loan or buying back stock uses cash.
Decrease in an Asset Account	***Increase in an Asset Account***
Selling inventory or collecting receivables provides cash.	Buying fixed assets or buying more inventory uses cash.

Using these rules, we can identify which changes in Argile's balance sheet accounts provided cash and which changes used cash during 2010. Table 7-3 shows the

TABLE 7-3   Argile Textiles: Cash Sources and Uses, 2010 ($ million)

	Account Balance as of:		Change	
	12/31/10	**12/31/09**	**Sources**	**Uses**
Balance Sheet Changes				
Cash and marketable securities	$ 10.0	$ 20.0	$ 10.0	
Accounts receivable	90.0	80.0		$ (10.0)
Inventory	135.0	101.0		(34.0)
Gross plant and equipment	345.0	300.0		(45.0)
Accounts payable	15.0	8.0	7.0	
Accruals	30.0	27.0	3.0	
Notes payable	20.0	18.0	2.0	
Long-term bonds	152.0	128.0	24.0	
Common stock (11 million shares)	65.0	65.0	—	—
Income Statement Information				
Net income	$ 27.0			
Add: Depreciation	30.0			
Gross cash flow from operations	$ 57.0		57.0	
Dividend payment	14.0			(14.0)
Totals			$103.0	$103.0

results of this identification. In addition, the table includes the cash flow information contained in Argile's 2010 income statement. This information can be used to construct the statement of cash flows that is shown in Table 7-4.[4]

Each balance sheet change in Table 7-4 is classified as resulting from (1) operations, (2) long-term investments, or (3) financing activities. Operating cash flows are those associated with the production and sale of goods and services. The *estimate* of cash flows obtained from the income statement is the primary operating cash flow, but changes in accounts payable, accounts receivable, inventories, and accruals are also classified as operating cash flows, because these accounts are directly affected by the firm's day-to-day operations. Investment cash flows primarily arise from the purchase or sale of plant, property, and equipment. Financing cash inflows result when the firm issues debt or common stock. Financing cash outflows occur when the firm pays dividends, repays debt (loans), or repurchases stock. The cash inflows and outflows from these three activities are summed to determine their effect on the firm's liquidity position, which is measured by the change in the cash and equivalents account from 1 year to the next.

The top part of Table 7-4 shows cash flows generated by and used in operations. For Argile, operations provided net cash flows of $23 million. The operating cash flows are generated principally from the firm's day-to-day operations, and this amount can be determined by adjusting the net income figure to account for noncash items. In 2010, Argile's day-to-day operations provided $57 million of funds ($27 million net income plus $30 million depreciation), but the increase in inventories and

---

[4]The cash flow statement is presented in either of two formats. The method used here is called the *indirect method.* Cash flows from operations are calculated by starting with net income, adding back expenses not paid out of cash and subtracting revenues that do not provide cash. With the *direct method,* operating cash flows are found by summing all revenues that provide cash and then subtracting all expenses that are paid in cash. Both formats produce the same result, and both are accepted by the Financial Accounting Standards Board.

TABLE 7-4   Argile Textiles: Statement of Cash Flows for the Period Ending December 31, 2010 ($ million)

Cash Flows from Operating Activities

Net income	$ 27.0	
Additions (adjustments) to net income		
Depreciation[a]	30.0	
Increase in accounts payable	7.0	
Increase in accruals	3.0	
Subtractions (adjustments) from net income		
Increase in accounts receivable	(10.0)	
Increase in inventory	(34.0)	
Net cash flow from operations		$ 23.0

Cash Flows from Long-Term Investing Activities

Acquisition of fixed assets		$(45.0)

Cash Flows from Financing Activities

Increase in notes payable	$ 2.0	
Increase in long-term bonds	24.0	
Dividend payment	(14.0)	
Net cash flow from financing		$ 12.0
Net change in cash		$(10.0)
Cash at the beginning of the year		20.0
Cash at the end of the year		$ 10.0

[a]Depreciation is a noncash expense that was deducted when calculating net income. It must be added back to show the correct cash flow from operations.

investment in receivables during the year accounted for a combined use of funds equal to $44 million, whereas increases in accounts payable and accruals provided only $10 million in additional operating (short-term) funds. The second section in Table 7-4 shows the company's long-term investing activities. Argile purchased fixed assets totaling $45 million, which was its only investment activity during 2010. Argile's financing activities, shown in the bottom section of Table 7-4, included borrowing from banks (notes payable), selling new bonds, and paying dividends to its common stockholders. The company raised $26 million by borrowing, but it paid $14 million in dividends, so its net inflow of funds from financing activities was $12 million.

When we total all of these sources and uses of cash, we see that Argile had a $10 million cash shortfall during 2010—that is, Argile's cash outflows were $10 million greater than its cash inflows. It met this shortfall by drawing down its cash and equivalents from $20 million to $10 million, as shown in Table 7-1 (the firm's balance sheet).

Argile's statement of cash flows should raise some concerns for the financial manager and outside analysts. The company generated $23 million in cash from operations, it spent $45 million on new fixed assets, and it paid out another $14 million in dividends. These cash outlays were covered by borrowing heavily, selling off marketable securities (cash equivalents), and drawing down its bank account. Obviously, this situation cannot continue indefinitely, so something must be done. We will consider some of the actions that the financial manager might recommend later in this chapter.

TABLE 7-5 Argile Textiles: Statement of Retained Earnings for the Year Ending December 31, 2010 ($ million)	
Balance of retained earnings, December 31, 2009	$129.0
Add: 2010 net income	27.0
Less: 2010 dividends to stockholders	(14.0)
Balance of retained earnings, December 31, 2010	$142.0

Statement of Retained Earnings

Changes in the common equity accounts between balance sheet dates are reported in the **statement of retained earnings.** Argile's statement is shown in Table 7-5. Of the $27 million that it earned, Argile decided to keep $13 million for reinvestment in the business. Thus, the balance sheet item called "Retained earnings" increased from $129 million at the end of 2009 to $142 million at the end of 2010.

It is important to realize that the retained earnings account represents a claim *against assets*, not assets per se. Firms retain earnings primarily to expand the business, which means funds are invested in plant and equipment, in inventories, and so forth, *not* necessarily in a bank account (cash). Changes in retained earnings represent the recognition that income generated by the firm during the accounting period was reinvested in various assets rather than paid out as dividends to stockholders. *As a result, the amount of retained earnings as reported on the balance sheet does not represent cash and is not "available" for the payment of dividends or anything else.*[5]

statement of retained earnings
A statement reporting the change in the firm's retained earnings as a result of the income generated and retained during the year. The balance sheet figure for retained earnings is the sum of the earnings retained for each year that the firm has been in business.

 Self-Test Questions

Describe the four basic financial statements: the balance sheet, the income statement, the statement of cash flows, and the statement of retained earnings.

Explain the following statement: "Retained earnings as reported on the balance sheet do not represent cash and are not 'available' for the payment of dividends or anything else."

Differentiate between operating cash flows and other cash flows.

List two reasons why operating cash flows might differ from net income.

In accounting, the emphasis is on the determination of net income. What is emphasized in finance, and why is that focus important?

Describe the general rules for identifying whether changes in balance sheet accounts represent sources of cash or uses of cash.

---

[5]A positive number in the retained earnings account indicates only that in the past, according to generally accepted accounting principles, the firm has earned income, but its dividends have been less than its reported income. Even though a company reports record earnings and shows an increase in the retained earnings account, it still might be short of cash. The same situation holds for individuals. You might own a new BMW (no loan), lots of clothes, and an expensive stereo and, therefore, have a high net worth. If you had only 25¢ in your pocket plus $5 in your checking account, you would still be short of cash.

How Do Investors Use Financial Statements?

The previous section gives you an indication as to how financial statements are constructed and some of the cautions that should be taken when interpreting the numbers contained on statements published by companies. In this section, we give you an indication as to how investors use financial statements to provide useful information when attempting to determine the value of a company. Although this discussion is not meant to be exhaustive, it should give you an idea about some of the information that investors "glean" from financial statements.

Working (Operating) Capital

The term *working capital* generally refers to a firm's current assets because investment in these assets is necessary to keep the firm's day-to-day operations "working." For example, without inventory, the firm has no products to sell, and a firm that does not permit customers to purchase on credit, which generates accounts receivable, might not be able to sell finished products. These "working assets" often are termed *spontaneous assets* because their values change on a daily basis as the result of the firm's normal operations, not because formal decisions were made to effect such changes. Although some of the financing of working capital assets is provided by outside investors, such as stockholders, much of the funding for these short-term assets is acquired from "loans" provided by suppliers, employees, and the government. Suppliers provide funding by allowing the firm to purchase raw materials on credit; employees provide funding by allowing the firm to pay salaries once (twice) each week (month) rather than requiring payment at the end of each day; and the government provides funding by allowing the taxes the firms collect to be paid periodically rather than at the time of a sale or payment of salaries. These sources of funds are "free" in the sense that the firm does not have to pay interest to use them. In addition, these liabilities are often termed *spontaneously generated funds* or *spontaneous liabilities* because they change spontaneously as the firm's normal operations change, not because the firm makes a conscious effort or enters a contractual agreement to change short-term financing. On the other hand, more formal financing arrangements, such as bank loans, require specific, conscious actions by the firm, and rent, or interest, must be paid for using these funds.

Investors are interested in a firm's operating capital for two reasons: (1) short-term financing arrangements must be paid off in the short term and (2) short-term investments generally earn lower returns than long-term investments. A couple of the measures that are used to evaluate a firm's working capital position include net working capital and net operating working capital. We briefly discuss each of these measures, and show you the result of the computation for Argile Textiles in 2010.

Net working capital | **Net working capital** is defined as:
The amount of current assets that is financed with long-term sources of funds—equals current assets minus current liabilities.

$$\text{Net working capital} = \text{NWC} = \text{Current assets} - \text{Current liabilities}$$
$$= \$235.0 - \$65.0 = \$170.0$$

This computation shows that of the $235 million in current assets, $65 million is financed with short-term financing arrangements; thus, the remaining $170 million is financed with long-term funds, which include bonds and common stock.

Net operating working capital is defined as:

$$\begin{matrix} \text{Net operating} \\ \text{working capital} \end{matrix} = \text{NOWC} = \left(\begin{matrix} \text{Current assets} \\ \text{required for operations} \end{matrix} \right) - \left(\begin{matrix} \text{Non-interest-bearing} \\ \text{current liabilities} \end{matrix} \right)$$

$$= \$235.0 - (\$15.0 + \$30.0) = \$190.0$$

Argile's current assets include cash and equivalents, accounts receivable, and inventory. All of these assets are part of the firm's normal operations. Because the $20 million in notes payable represents interest-bearing, short-term loans from the bank, non-interest-bearing current liabilities include only accounts payable ($15 million) and accruals ($30 million). In 2009, Argile's NOWC was $166 million, so its NOWC increased by $24 million in 2010. Looking at Argile's balance sheets for the 2 years, we see that operating assets increased by $34 million (primarily because inventory increased $34 million) whereas non-interest-bearing liabilities increased by only $10 million (from $35 million in 2009 to $45 million in 2010). We discuss the ramifications of this trend later in this chapter when we use ratio analysis to examine Argile's financial position.

Operating Cash Flows

Earlier we mentioned that when a firm sells it products for cash and pays cash for all of its expenses except depreciation and amortization, we can compute the net cash flow by adding the depreciation and amortization expense to the net income amount shown on the income statement. As a result, Argile's net cash flow in 2010 was $57 million. Another measure that managers and investors examine is the operating cash flow generated by a firm. The *operating cash flow* is defined as:

$$\begin{matrix} \text{Operating} \\ \text{cash flow} \end{matrix} = [\text{NOI}(1 - \text{Tax rate})] + \left(\begin{matrix} \text{Depreciation and} \\ \text{amortization expense} \end{matrix} \right)$$

$$= \left(\begin{matrix} \text{Net operating} \\ \text{profits after taxes} \end{matrix} \right) + \left(\begin{matrix} \text{Depreciation and} \\ \text{amortization expense} \end{matrix} \right)$$

$$= \$65.0(1 - 0.40) + \$30.0 = \$69.0$$

The operating cash flow represents the cash flow that the firm would have available for investing in assets if it had no debt. In other words, Argile would generate $69 million if all of its assets were financed only with common stock and the funds were invested in only operating assets, which include current and fixed assets that are used in the normal operation of the firm. Looking at Argile's balance sheet, we see that the company is financed with 51 percent debt. The income statement shows that Argile paid interest equal to $20 million in 2010. Because interest is a tax-deductible expense that reduces the total amount of taxes that must be paid, it really didn't cost Argile $20 million for its outstanding debt. Rather, the net cash flow associated with the debt was $12 million = $20 million × (1 − 0.40). Thus, Argile paid $12 million in "net interest" for its outstanding debt, which means that its net cash flow would have been $57 million = $69 million − $12 million if all sales were collected in cash and all expenses, except depreciation, were paid in cash during 2010. Clearly, this was not the case, as the statement of cash flows given in Table 7-4 shows.

Free Cash Flow

We mentioned earlier that depreciation is used to recognize the decline in the value over time of an asset that has a life longer than 1 year. Because such assets are required to maintain normal operations, the firm must be able to replace worn-out assets sometime in the future. If the costs of these long-term assets do not change significantly over time, then the firm should be able to put aside cash in the amount of the depreciation expense each year and have sufficient funds to replace the assets when they wear out. Even if they don't put aside cash each year, managers recognize that plans must be made to replace "used up" assets at some point in time if the firm is going to remain in business. If the firm paid out the net cash flows generated each year to investors, it might not be able to replace necessary assets. For this reason, investors are concerned with the *free cash flow* that a firm generates.

Free cash flow
A measure of the cash flow that the firm is free to pay to investors after considering cash investments that are needed to continue operations.

Free cash flow measures the cash flow that the firm is *free* to pay to investors (both bondholders and stockholders) after considering the cash investments that are needed to continue operations, including investments in fixed assets needed to manufacture products, working capital needed to continue operations, and new opportunities that will grow the stock price. We compute the free cash flow by subtracting the amount that is needed to fund investments during the year from operating cash flow:

$$\text{Free Cash Flow (FCF)} = \text{Operating cash flow} - \text{Investments}$$
$$= \text{Operating cash flow} - (\Delta \text{ in fixed assets} + \Delta \text{NOWC})$$
$$= \$69.0 - (\$45.0 + \$24.0) = \$10.0$$

We determined that Argile's operating cash flow was $69 million in 2010 and the change in net operating working capital (ΔNOWC) was $24 million (an increase from $166 million in 2009 to $190 million in 2010). Table 7-1 shows that the company purchased an additional $45 million of fixed assets in 2010. As a result, Argile generated a free cash flow equal to $10 million during the year. According to its income statement, the company paid interest equal to $20 million and a common stock dividend equal to $14 million in 2010. These amounts were much greater than the free cash flow that was generated during the year. Although Argile paid a dividend that was much greater than the free cash flow would suggest was appropriate, investors, especially bondholders, probably would not complain as long as the firm is experiencing robust, profitable growth in operations. We will evaluate Argile's growth as well as its financial position later in this chapter.

economic value added (EVA)
After-tax operating earnings adjusted for the costs associated with the firm's financing—shows how much a firm's economic value increased during a particular period.

Economic Value Added (EVA)[6]

The **economic value added (EVA)** measure is based on the concept that the earnings from actions taken by a company must be sufficient to compensate the suppliers of funds—both the bondholders and the stockholders.

To determine a firm's EVA, we adjust the operating income reported on the income statement to account for the costs associated with both the debt and the

---

[6]The basic EVA approach was developed by Stern Stewart Management Services. Another measure developed by Stern Stewart is market value added (MVA), which is the difference between the market value and book value of a firm's equity.

equity that the firm has outstanding. Recall that the computation of net income includes interest expense, which is a reflection of the cost of debt, but the dividends paid to stockholders, which is an indication of the cost of equity, are recognized after net income is determined. The general concept underlying EVA is to determine how much a firm's economic value is increased by the decisions it makes. Thus, we can write the basic EVA equation as follows:

$$EVA = NOI(1 - \text{Tax rate}) - [(\text{Invested capital})$$
$$\times (\text{After-tax cost of capital as a percent})]$$

Here, invested capital is the amount of funds provided by investors (both bondholders and stockholders), and the cost of capital is the average rate of return associated with these funds.

The EVA measure gives an estimate of the true economic profit that is generated by a firm. If the EVA is positive, the actions of the firm should increase its value. Conversely, if the EVA is negative, the actions of the firm should decrease its value.

If we assume that Argile's total capital, which includes its bonds and common stock, has an average cost equal to 10 percent, then the EVA would be:

$$EVA = \$65.0(1 - 0.40) - [\$425.0 - (\$15.0 + \$30.0)] \times 0.10 = \$39.0 - \$38.0 = \$1.0$$

To compute this value, we deducted the amount of "free" financing that is provided by spontaneous current liabilities from total liabilities and common equity to determine the amount of "costly" financing for which Argile pays either interest or dividends. We discuss the concepts of capital financing and cost of capital in detail later in the book. At this point, we can say that according to the EVA computation, in 2010 Argile generated $39 million net operating profit after taxes and the dollar cost associated with its financing structure was $38 million. As a result, the economic profit generated in 2010 was $1 million, which suggests that the value of the firm should have increased in 2010. Because investors consider other factors when estimating the firm's future cash flows, we will wait to pass judgment about Argile's financial position until after the next section.

Self-Test Questions

What is net working capital and net operating working capital?

How is operating cash flow measured?

What is free cash flow, and why is it an important factor in determining the value of a firm?

What is EVA and how does it differ from accounting income?

Consider a firm that reported net operating income (NOI) equal to $40,000 this year. Examination of the company's balance sheet and income statement shows that the tax rate was 40 percent, the depreciation expense was $5,000, $25,000 was invested in assets during the year, and invested capital equals $200,000. (1) What was the operating cash flow that the firm generated during the year? (2) What was the firm's free cash flow? (3) What was the firm's EVA if its average cost of funds is 8 percent after taxes?   (Answers: $29,000, $4,000, and $8,000)

FINANCIAL STATEMENT (RATIO) ANALYSIS

As we discovered in previous sections, financial statements provide information about a firm's position at a point in time as well as its operations over some past period. Nevertheless, the real value of financial statements lies in the fact that they can be used to help predict the firm's financial position in the future and to determine expected earnings and dividends. From an investor's standpoint, *predicting the future is the purpose of financial statement analysis;* from management's standpoint, *financial statement analysis is useful both as a way to anticipate future conditions and, more important, as a starting point for planning actions that will influence the future course of events.*

The first step in a financial analysis typically includes an evaluation of the firm's ratios. The ratios are designed to show relationships between financial statement accounts *within* firms and *between* firms. Translating accounting numbers into relative values, or ratios, allows us to compare the financial position of one firm with the financial position of another firm, even if their sizes are significantly different.

In this section, we calculate the 2010 financial ratios for Argile Textiles and then evaluate those ratios in relation to the industry averages. Note that all dollar amounts used in the ratio calculations given here are in millions, except where per-share values are used. Also, note that there are literally hundreds of ratios that are used by management, creditors, and stockholders to evaluate firms. In this book, we show only a few of the most often used ratios.

Liquidity Ratios

liquid asset
An asset that can be easily converted into cash without significant loss of the amount originally invested.

A **liquid asset** is one that can be easily converted to cash without significant loss of its original value. Converting assets—especially current assets such as inventory and receivables—to cash is the primary means by which a firm obtains the funds needed to pay its current bills. Therefore, a firm's "liquid position" deals with the question of how well the company is able to meet its current obligations. Short-term, or current, assets are more easily converted to cash (more liquid) than are long-term assets. In general, then, one firm would be considered more liquid than another firm if it has a greater proportion of its total assets in the form of current assets.

liquidity ratios
Ratios that show the relationship of a firm's cash and other current assets to its current liabilities; they provide an indication of the firm's ability to meet its current obligations.

According to its balance sheet, Argile has debts totaling $65 million that must be paid off within the coming year—that is, current liabilities equal $65 million. Will it have trouble satisfying those obligations? A full liquidity analysis requires the use of cash budgets (described in Chapter 15). Nevertheless, by relating the amount of cash and other current assets to the firm's current obligations, ratio analysis provides a quick, easy-to-use measure of liquidity. Two commonly used **liquidity ratios** are discussed in this section: current ratio and quick (acid text) ratio.

Current Ratio

current ratio
A ratio calculated by dividing current assets by current liabilities. It indicates the extent to which current liabilities are covered by assets expected to be converted to cash in the near future.

The **current ratio** is calculated as follows:

$$\text{Current ratio} = \frac{\text{Current assets}}{\text{Current liabilities}}$$

$$= \frac{\$235.0}{\$65.0} = 3.6 \text{ times}$$

$$\text{Industry average} = 4.1 \text{ times}$$

Current assets normally include cash and equivalents, accounts receivable, and inventories. Current liabilities consist of accounts payable, short-term notes payable, long-term debt that matures in the current period (current maturities of long-term debt), accrued taxes, and other accrued expenses (principally wages).

When a company experiences financial difficulty, it pays its bills (accounts payable) more slowly, borrows more from its bank, and so forth. If current liabilities are rising more rapidly than current assets, the current ratio will fall, which could spell trouble. Because the current ratio provides the best single indicator of the extent to which the claims of short-term creditors are covered by assets that are expected to be converted to cash fairly quickly, it is the most commonly used measure of short-term solvency. You should be careful when examining the current ratio, however, just as you should when examining any ratio individually. For example, just because a firm has a low current ratio (even one less than 1.0), this does not mean that the current obligations cannot be met. Consider a firm with a current ratio equal to 0.9, which suggests that if all current assets are liquidated at their book values, only 90 percent of the current liabilities can be covered. If the firm manufactures and sells a substantial amount of inventory for cash and collects much of its current accounts receivables long before suppliers, employees, and short-term creditors need to be paid, then it really does not face a liquidity problem.

Argile's current ratio of 3.6 is below the average for its industry, 4.1, so its liquidity position is somewhat weak. Because current assets are scheduled to be converted to cash in the near future, it is highly probable that they can be liquidated at close to their stated value. With a current ratio of 3.6, Argile could liquidate current assets at only 28 percent of book value and still pay off its current creditors in full.[7]

Although industry average figures are discussed later in this chapter in some detail, at this point you should note that an industry average is not a magic number that all firms should strive to maintain. In fact, some well-managed firms might be above the average, whereas other good firms might be below it. If a firm's ratios are far removed from the average for its industry, however, an analyst should question why this deviation has occurred. A significant deviation from the industry average should signal the analyst (or management) to *check further,* even if the deviation is considered to be in the "good" direction. For example, we know that Argile's current ratio is below average. But, what would you conclude if Argile's current ratio was nearly twice that of the industry—perhaps 8.0? Is this difference good? Maybe not. Because current assets, which are liquid, safe assets, generally generate lower rates of return than do long-term assets, it might be argued that firms with too much liquidity are not investing wisely.

Quick (Acid Test) Ratio

The **quick,** or **acid test, ratio** is calculated as follows:

$$\text{Quick (acid test) ratio} = \frac{\text{Current assets} - \text{Inventory}}{\text{Current liabilities}}$$

$$= \frac{\$235.0 - \$135.0}{\$65.0} = \frac{\$100.0}{\$65.0} = 1.5 \text{ times}$$

$$\text{Industry average} = 2.1 \text{ times}$$

Inventories typically are the least liquid of a firm's current assets, so they are the assets on which losses are most likely to occur in the event of a "quick" liquidation.

quick (acid test) ratio
A ratio calculated by deducting inventories from current assets and dividing the remainder by current liabilities. It is a variation of the current ratio.

---

[7]Argile's current ratio is 3.6154, and 1/3.6154 = 0.2766, which is 28 percent when rounded to two decimal places. Note that 0.2766($235.0) = $65, which is the amount of current liabilities.

Therefore, a measure of the firm's ability to pay off short-term obligations without relying on the sale of inventories is important.

The textile industry's average quick ratio is 2.1, so Argile's ratio value of 1.5 is low in comparison with the ratios of its competitors. This difference suggests that Argile's level of inventories is relatively high. Even so, if the accounts receivable can be collected, the company can pay off its current liabilities even without having to liquidate its inventory.

Our evaluation of its liquidity ratios suggests that Argile's liquidity position currently is fairly poor. To get a better idea of why Argile is in this position, we must examine its asset management ratios.

Asset Management Ratios

asset management ratios
A set of ratios that measures how effectively a firm is managing its assets.

The second group of ratios, the **asset management ratios,** measures how effectively (efficiently) the firm is managing its assets. These ratios are designed to answer the following question: Does the total amount of each type of asset as reported on the balance sheet seem reasonable, too high, or too low in view of current and projected sales levels?

Firms invest in assets to generate revenues both in the current period and in future periods. To purchase their assets, Argile and other companies must borrow or obtain funds from other sources. If firms have too many assets, their interest expenses will be too high, hence their profits will be depressed. On the other hand, because production is affected by the capacity of assets, if assets are too low, profitable sales might be lost because the firm is unable to manufacture enough products.

Inventory Turnover Ratio

inventory turnover ratio
A ratio calculated by dividing cost of goods sold by inventories.

The **inventory turnover ratio** is defined as follows:[8]

$$\text{Inventory turnover ratio} = \frac{\text{Cost of goods sold}}{\text{Inventory}} = \frac{\text{Variable operating costs}}{\text{Inventory}}$$

$$= \frac{\$600.0}{\$135.0} = 4.4 \text{ times}$$

$$\text{Industry average} = 7.4 \text{ times}$$

As a rough approximation, each item of Argile's inventory is sold out and restocked, or "turned over," 4.4 times per year (every 82 days), which is considerably lower than the industry average of 7.4 times (every 49 days).[9] This ratio suggests that Argile is holding excess stocks of inventory; excess stocks are, of course, unproductive and represent an investment with a low or 0 percent rate of return. With such a low turnover, we must wonder whether Argile is holding damaged or obsolete goods (for example, textile types, styles, and patterns from previous years) that are not actually worth their stated value.

---

[8]*Turnover* is a term that originated many years ago with the old Yankee peddler, who would load up his wagon with goods then go off on his route to peddle his wares. The merchandise was his "working capital" because it was what he actually sold, or "turned over," to produce his profits. His "turnover" was the number of trips that he took each year. Annual sales divided by inventory equaled turnover, or trips per year. If the peddler made 10 trips per year, stocked 100 pans, and made a gross profit of $5 per pan, his annual gross profit would be 100 × $5 × 10 = $5,000. If the peddler went faster and made 20 trips per year, his gross profit would double, other things held constant.

[9]Some compilers of financial ratio statistics, such as Dun & Bradstreet, use the ratio of sales to inventories carried at cost to depict inventory turnover. If this form of the inventory turnover ratio is used, the true turnover will be overstated because sales are given at market prices whereas inventories are carried at cost.

You should use care when calculating and using the inventory turnover ratio, because purchases of inventory (and thus the cost of goods sold) occur over the entire year, whereas the inventory figure applies to one point in time (perhaps December 31). For this reason, it is better to use an average inventory measure.[10] If the firm's business is highly seasonal, or if a strong upward or downward sales trend has occurred during the year, it is essential to make such an adjustment. To maintain comparability with industry averages, however, we did not use the average inventory figure in our computations.

Days Sales Outstanding

Days sales outstanding (DSO), also called the *average collection period (ACP)*, is used to evaluate the firm's ability to collect its credit sales in a timely manner. DSO is calculated as follows:[11]

days sales outstanding (DSO)
A ratio calculated by dividing accounts receivable by average sales per day, which indicates the average length of time it takes the firm to collect for credit sales.

$$\text{Days sales outstanding (DSO)} = \frac{\text{Accounts receivable}}{\text{Average daily sales}} = \frac{\text{Accounts receivable}}{\left[\dfrac{\text{Annual sales}}{360}\right]}$$

$$= \frac{\$90.0}{\left[\dfrac{\$750.0}{360}\right]} = \frac{\$90.0}{\$2.08} = 43.2 \text{ days}$$

$$\text{Industry average} = 32.1 \text{ days}$$

The DSO represents the average length of time that the firm must wait after making a credit sale before receiving cash—that is, its average collection period. Argile has about 43 days of sales outstanding, somewhat higher than the 32-day industry average. The DSO also can be evaluated by comparing it with the terms on which the firm sells its goods. For example, Argile's sales terms call for payment within 30 days, so the fact that sales are outstanding an average of 43 days indicates that customers generally are not paying their bills on time. If the trend in DSO over the past few years has been rising, but the credit policy has not been changed, it would be even stronger evidence that the company should take steps to improve the time it takes to collect accounts receivable. This situation seems to be the case for Argile because its 2009 DSO was 41 days.

Fixed Assets Turnover Ratio

The **fixed assets turnover ratio** measures how effectively the firm uses its plant and equipment to help generate sales. It is computed as follows:

fixed assets turnover ratio
A ratio calculated by dividing sales by net fixed assets.

$$\text{Fixed assets turnover ratio} = \frac{\text{Sales}}{\text{Net fixed assets}}$$

$$= \frac{\$750.0}{\$190.0} = 3.9 \text{ times}$$

$$\text{Industry average} = 4.0 \text{ times}$$

---

[10]Preferably, the average inventory value should be calculated by dividing the sum of the monthly figures during the year by 12. If monthly data are not available, you could add the beginning-of-year and end-of-year figures and divide by 2; this calculation will adjust for growth but not for seasonal effects. Using this approach, Argile's average inventory for 2010 would be $118 = ($135 + $101)/2, and its inventory turnover would be 5.1 = $600/$118, which still is well below the industry average.

[11]To compute DSO using this equation, we must assume that all of the firm's sales are on credit. We usually compute DSO in this manner because information on credit sales is rarely available. Because all firms do not have the same percentage of credit sales, the days sales outstanding could be misleading. Also, note that by convention the financial community generally uses 360 rather than 365 as the number of days in the year.

Argile's ratio of 3.9 is almost equal to the industry average, indicating that the firm is using its fixed assets about as efficiently as the other members of its industry. Argile seems to have neither too many nor too few fixed assets in relation to other similar firms.

Take care when using the fixed assets turnover ratio to compare the performance of different firms. Recall from accounting that most balance sheet accounts are stated in terms of historical costs. Inflation might cause the value of many assets that were purchased in the past to be seriously understated. Therefore, if we are comparing an old firm that acquired many of its fixed assets years ago at low prices with a new company that acquired its fixed assets only recently, we probably would find that the old firm has a higher fixed assets turnover ratio. Because financial analysts typically do not have the data necessary to make inflation adjustments to specific assets, they must simply recognize that a problem exists and deal with it using their best judgment. In Argile's case, the issue is not a serious one because all firms in the industry have been expanding at about the same rate; in this instance, the balance sheets of the comparison firms are indeed comparable.

Total Assets Turnover Ratio

total assets turnover ratio
A ratio calculated by dividing sales by total assets; shows how many times assets are "turned over" to generate revenues.

The **total assets turnover ratio** measures the turnover of all of the firm's assets. It is calculated as follows:

$$\text{Total assets turnover ratio} = \frac{\text{Sales}}{\text{Total assets}}$$

$$= \frac{\$750.0}{\$425.0} = 1.8 \text{ times}$$

$$\text{Industry average} = 2.1 \text{ times}$$

Argile's ratio is somewhat lower than the industry average, indicating that the company is not generating a sufficient volume of business given its investment in total assets. To become more efficient, Argile should increase its sales, dispose of some assets, or pursue a combination of these steps.

Our examination of Argile's asset management ratios shows that its fixed assets turnover ratio is very close to the industry average, but its total assets turnover is below average. The fixed assets turnover ratio excludes current assets, whereas the total assets turnover ratio includes them. Therefore, comparison of these ratios confirms our conclusion from the analysis of the liquidity ratios: Argile seems to have a liquidity problem. The fact that the company's inventory turnover ratio and average collection period are worse than the industry averages suggests, at least in part, that the firm might have problems with inventory and receivables management. Slow sales and tardy collections of credit sales suggest that Argile might rely more heavily on external funds, such as loans, than the industry to pay current obligations. Examining the debt management ratios will help us to determine whether this assessment actually is the case.

Debt Management Ratios

The extent to which a firm uses debt financing has three important implications:

1. By raising funds through debt, the firm avoids diluting stockholder ownership.
2. Creditors look to the equity, or owner-supplied funds, to provide a margin of safety. If the stockholders have provided only a small proportion of the total financing, the risks of the enterprise are borne mainly by its creditors.

3. If the firm earns more on investments financed with borrowed funds than it pays in interest, the return on the owners' capital is magnified, or "leveraged."

Financial leverage, or borrowing, affects the expected rate of return realized by stockholders for two reasons. First, the interest on debt is tax deductible whereas dividends are not, so paying interest lowers the firm's tax bill, everything else being equal. Second, the rate a firm earns from its investments in assets usually differs from the rate at which it borrows. If the firm has healthy operations, it typically invests the funds it borrows at a rate of return that is greater than the interest rate on its debt. In combination with the tax advantage that debt offers compared to stock, the higher investment rate of return produces a magnified positive return to the stockholders. Under these conditions, leverage works to the advantage of the firm and its stockholders.

Unfortunately, financial leverage is a double-edged sword. When the firm experiences poor business conditions, typically sales are lower and costs are higher than expected, but the cost of borrowing, which generally is fixed, still must be paid. The *costs* (interest payments) associated with borrowing are contractual and do not vary with sales, and they must be paid to avoid the threat of bankruptcy. Therefore, the required interest payments might impose a significant burden on a firm that has liquidity problems. In fact, if the interest payments are high enough, a firm with a positive operating income could end up with a negative return to stockholders. Under these conditions, leverage works to the detriment of the firm and its stockholders.

Detailed discussions of financial leverage are given in Chapters 8 and 14. For the purposes of ratio analysis in this chapter, we need to understand that firms with relatively high debt ratios have higher expected returns when business is normal or good, but they are exposed to risk of loss when business is poor. Thus, firms with low debt ratios are less risky, but they also forgo the opportunity to "leverage up" their return on equity. The prospects of high returns are desirable, but the average investor is averse to risk. Therefore, decisions about the use of debt require firms to balance the desire for higher expected returns against the increased risk that results from using more debt. Determining the optimal amount of debt for a given firm is a complicated process, and we will defer discussion of this topic until Chapter 14. Here, we will simply look at two procedures that analysts use to examine the firm's debt in a financial statement analysis: (1) they check balance sheet ratios to determine the extent to which borrowed funds have been used to finance assets and (2) they review income statement ratios to determine how well operating profits can cover fixed charges such as interest. These two sets of ratios are complementary, so analysts use both types.

> **financial leverage**
> The use of debt financing.

Debt Ratio

The **debt ratio** measures the percentage of the firm's assets financed by creditors (borrowing). It is computed as follows:

$$\text{Debt ratio} = \text{Debt-to-total-assets ratio} = \frac{\text{Total liabilities}}{\text{Total assets}}$$

$$= \frac{\$217.0}{\$425.0} = 0.511 = 51.1\%$$

$$\text{Industry average} = 42.0\%$$

> **debt ratio**
> A ratio calculated by dividing total debt by total assets; indicates the percentage of total funds provided by creditors.

Total debt includes both current liabilities ($65 million) and long-term debt ($152 million). Creditors prefer low debt ratios, because the lower the ratio the greater the cushion against creditors' losses in the event of liquidation. The owners, on the other hand, can benefit from leverage because it magnifies earnings, thereby increasing the return to stockholders. Too much debt often leads to financial difficulty, which eventually could cause bankruptcy.

Argile's debt ratio is 51 percent, which means that its creditors have supplied slightly more than one-half of the firm's total financing. Because the average debt ratio for the industry is 42 percent, Argile might find it difficult to borrow additional funds without first raising more equity capital through a stock issue. Creditors might be reluctant to lend the firm more money, and management might be subjecting the firm to a greater chance of bankruptcy if it sought to increase the debt ratio much further by borrowing additional funds.[12]

Times Interest Earned Ratio

times interest earned (TIE) ratio
A ratio calculated by dividing earnings before interest and taxes (EBIT) by interest charges; measures the ability of the firm to meet its annual interest payments.

The **times interest earned (TIE) ratio** is defined as follows:

$$\text{Times interest earned ratio (TIE)} = \frac{\text{Earnings before interest and taxes}}{\text{Interest charges}}$$

$$= \frac{\text{EBIT}}{\text{Interest charges}} = \frac{\$65.0}{\$20.0} = 3.3 \text{ times}$$

$$\text{Industry average} = 6.5 \text{ times}$$

The TIE ratio measures the extent to which a firm's earnings before interest and taxes (EBIT), also called *net operating income (NOI)*, can decline before these earnings are unable to cover annual interest costs. Failure to meet this obligation can bring legal action by the firm's creditors, possibly resulting in bankruptcy. Note that EBIT, rather than net income, is used in the numerator. Because interest is paid with pretax dollars, the firm's ability to pay current interest is not affected by taxes.

Argile's interest is covered 3.3 times. Because the industry average is 6.5 times, compared to firms in the same business, Argile is covering its interest charges by a low margin of safety (about one-half of the industry average). Its TIE ratio reinforces our conclusion based on the debt ratio that Argile probably would face difficulties if it attempted to borrow additional funds.

Fixed Charge Coverage Ratio

fixed charge coverage ratio
A ratio calculated by dividing earnings available to cover all fixed financing charges by all fixed financing charges; a variation of the TIE ratio.

The **fixed charge coverage ratio** is similar to the TIE ratio, but it is more inclusive because it recognizes that many firms lease rather than buy assets and also must make sinking fund payments.[13] Leasing is widespread in certain industries, making this ratio preferable to the TIE ratio for many purposes. Argile's annual long-term lease payments total $5 million, and the company must make an annual $4 million required payment to help retire its debt. Because sinking fund payments must be paid with after-tax dollars, whereas interest and lease payments are paid with pretax

---

[12]The ratio of debt to equity also is used in financial analysis. The debt-to-assets (D/A) and debt-to-equity (D/E) ratios are simply transformations of each other because total debt plus total equity must equal total assets:

$$D/E = \frac{D/A}{1 - D/A}, \quad \text{and} \quad D/A = \frac{D/E}{1 - D/E}$$

[13]Generally, a long-term lease is defined as one that extends for more than 1 year. Thus rent incurred under a 6-month lease would not be included in the fixed charge coverage ratio, but rental payments under a 1-year or longer lease would be defined as a fixed charge and would be included. A sinking fund is a required annual payment designed to reduce the balance of a bond or preferred stock issue.

dollars, the sinking fund payments must be divided by $(1 - \text{Tax rate})$ to determine the before-tax income required to pay taxes and still have enough left to make the sinking fund payment. In this case, $\$4/(1 - 0.4) = \$6.67$. Therefore, if the company had pretax income of $6.67 million, it could pay taxes at a 40 percent rate and have $4 million left to make the sinking fund payment.

Because fixed charges include interest, annual long-term lease obligations, and sinking fund payments, the fixed charge coverage ratio is calculated as follows:

$$\text{Fixed charge coverage ratio} = \frac{\text{EBIT} + \text{Lease payments}}{\dfrac{\text{Interest}}{\text{charges}} + \dfrac{\text{Lease}}{\text{payments}} + \left[\dfrac{\text{Sinking fund payments}}{(1 - \text{Tax rate})}\right]}$$

$$= \frac{\$65.0 + \$5.0}{\$20.0 + \$5.0 + \left[\dfrac{\$4.0}{(1 - 0.4)}\right]} = \frac{\$70.0}{\$31.67} = 2.2 \text{ times}$$

$$\text{Industry average} = 5.8 \text{ times}$$

In the numerator of the fixed charge coverage ratio, the lease payments are added to EBIT because we want to determine the firm's ability to cover its fixed financing charges from the income generated before any fixed financing charges are considered (deducted). The EBIT figure represents the firm's operating income net of lease payments, so the lease payments must be added back.

Argile's fixed charges are covered only 2.2 times, compared to the industry average of 5.8 times. Again, this difference indicates that the firm is weaker than average, and it points out the difficulties that Argile probably would encounter if it attempted to increase its debt or other fixed financial obligations.

Our examination of Argile's debt management ratios indicates that the company has a debt ratio that is *higher than* the industry average, and it has coverage ratios that are substantially *lower than* the industry averages. This finding suggests that Argile is in a somewhat dangerous position with respect to leverage (debt). In fact, the firm might have great difficulty borrowing additional funds until its debt position improves. If the company cannot pay its current obligations, it might be forced into bankruptcy. To see how Argile's debt position has affected its profits, we next examine its profitability ratios.

Profitability Ratios

Profitability is the net result of a number of policies and decisions. The ratios examined thus far provide some information about the way the firm is operating, but the **profitability ratios** show the combined effects of liquidity management, asset management, and debt management on operating results.

profitability ratios
A group of ratios showing the effect of liquidity, asset management, and debt management on operating results.

Net Profit Margin

The **net profit margin,** which gives the profit per dollar of sales, is calculated as follows:

$$\text{Net profit margin} = \frac{\text{Net profit}}{\text{Sales}}$$

$$= \frac{\$27.0}{\$750.0} = 0.036 = 3.6\%$$

$$\text{Industry average} = 4.9\%$$

net profit margin
A ratio calculated by dividing net income by sales; measures net income per dollar of sales.

Argile's net profit margin is lower than the industry average of 4.9 percent, indicating that its sales might be too low, its costs might be too high, or both. Recall that, according to its debt ratio, Argile has a greater proportion of debt than the industry average, and the TIE ratio shows that Argile's interest payments on its debt are not covered as well as the rest of the industry. This partly explains why Argile's profit margin is low. To see this fact, we can compute the ratio of EBIT (operating income) to sales, which is called the *operating profit margin*. Argile's operating profit margin of 8.7 percent is exactly the same as the industry average, so the cause of its low net profit margin is the relatively high interest attributable to the firm's higher than average use of debt.

Return on Total Assets

return on total assets (ROA)
A ratio calculated by dividing net income by total assets; provides an idea of the overall return on investment earned by the firm.

The **return on total assets (ROA)** is computed as follows:

$$\text{Return on total assets (ROA)} = \frac{\text{Net income}}{\text{Total assets}}$$
$$= \frac{\$27.0}{\$425.0} = 0.064 = 6.4\%$$
$$\text{Industry average} = 11.5\%$$

Argile's 6.4 percent return is well below the 11.5 percent average for the textile industry. This low return results from the company's higher than average use of debt.

Return on Common Equity

return on common equity (ROE)
A ratio calculated by dividing net income by common equity; measures the rate of return on common stockholders' investments.

The **return on common equity (ROE),** or the *rate of return on stockholders' investment,* is computed as follows:[14]

$$\text{Return on equity (ROE)} = \frac{\text{Net income available to common stockholders}}{\text{Common equity}}$$
$$= \frac{\$27.0}{\$208.0} = 0.130 = 13.0\%$$
$$\text{Industry average} = 17.7\%$$

Argile's 13.0 percent return is lower than the 17.7 percent industry average. This result follows from the company's greater use of debt (leverage), a point that is analyzed further later in this chapter.

Our examination of Argile's profitability ratios shows that the company's operating results have suffered due to its poor liquidity position, its poor asset management, and its above-average debt. In the final group of ratios, we will examine Argile's market value ratios to see how investors feel about the company's current position.

Market Value Ratios

market value ratios
A set of ratios that relate the firm's stock price to its earnings and book value per share.

The **market value ratios** relate the firm's stock price to its earnings and book value per share. They give management an indication of what investors think of the

---

[14]Net income available to common stockholders is computed by subtracting preferred dividends from net income. Because Argile has no preferred stock, the net income available to common stockholders is the same as the net income.

company's future prospects based on its past performance. If the firm's liquidity ratios, asset management ratios, debt management ratios, and profitability ratios are all good, then its market value ratios will be high, and its stock price will probably be as high as can be expected. Of course, the opposite also is true.

Price/Earnings Ratio

The **price/earnings (P/E) ratio** shows how much investors are willing to pay per dollar of reported profits. To compute the P/E ratio, we need to know the firm's earnings per share (EPS):

$$\text{Earnings per share (EPS)} = \frac{\text{Net income available to common stockholders}}{\text{Number of common shares outstanding}}$$

$$= \frac{\$27.0}{11.0} = \$2.45$$

Argile's stock sells for $20. With an EPS of $2.45, its P/E ratio is therefore 8.2:

$$\text{Price/Earnings (PE) ratio} = \frac{\text{Market price per share}}{\text{Earnings per share}}$$

$$= \frac{\$20.00}{\$2.45} = 8.2 \text{ times}$$

$$\text{Industry average} = 15.0 \text{ times}$$

Other things held constant, P/E ratios are higher for firms with high growth prospects and lower for riskier firms. Because Argile's P/E ratio is lower than those of other textile manufacturers, it suggests that the company is regarded as being somewhat riskier than most of its competitors, as having poorer growth prospects, or both. From our analysis of its debt management ratios, we know that Argile has higher than average risk associated with leverage. However, we do not know if its growth prospects are poor.

Market/Book Ratio

The ratio of a stock's market price to its book value gives another indication of how investors regard the company. The stocks of companies with relatively high rates of return on equity generally sell at higher multiples of book value than those with low returns. First, we find Argile's book value per share:

$$\text{Book value per share} = \frac{\text{Common equity}}{\text{Number of common shares outstanding}}$$

$$= \frac{\$208.0}{11.0} = \$18.91$$

Next, we divide the market value per share by the book value per share to get a **market/book (M/B) ratio** of 1.4 for Argile:

$$\text{Market/book (M/B) ratio} = \frac{\text{Market price per share}}{\text{Book value per share}}$$

$$= \frac{\$20.00}{\$18.91} = 1.1 \text{ times}$$

$$\text{Industry average} = 2.5 \text{ times}$$

Investors are willing to pay less for Argile's book value than for that of an average textile manufacturer. This finding should not be surprising, because we discovered earlier that Argile has generated below-average returns with respect to both total assets and common equity. Generally, the stocks of firms that earn high rates of return on their assets sell for prices well in excess of their book values. For extremely successful firms, the market/book ratio can be as much as 10 to 15.

Our examination of Argile's market value ratios indicates that investors are not excited about the future prospects of the company's common stock as an investment. Perhaps they believe that Argile is headed toward bankruptcy unless the firm takes action to correct its liquidity and asset management problems and to improve its leverage position. One approach used to determine the direction in which a firm is headed is to evaluate the trends of the ratios over the past few years and thereby answer the following question: Is the firm's position improving or deteriorating?

Trend Analysis

trend analysis
An evaluation of changes (trends) in a firm's financial position over a period of time, perhaps years.

Our analysis of Argile's ratios indicates that the firm's current financial position is poor as compared to the industry norm. Note, however, that this analysis does not tell us whether the company is in a better or a worse financial position than it was in previous years. To determine the direction in which the firm is headed, we must analyze trends in ratios. By examining the paths taken in the past, **trend analysis** provides information about whether the firm's financial position is more likely to improve or deteriorate in the future.

A simple approach to trend analysis is to construct graphs containing both the firm's ratios and the industry averages for the past 5 years. Using this approach, we can examine both the direction of the movement in, and the relationships between, the firm's ratios and the industry averages.

Figure 7-2 shows that Argile's return on equity has declined since 2006, even though the industry average has steadily increased at a moderate rate. We could

FIGURE 7-2   Argile's Rate of Return on Common Equity (ROE), 2006–2010

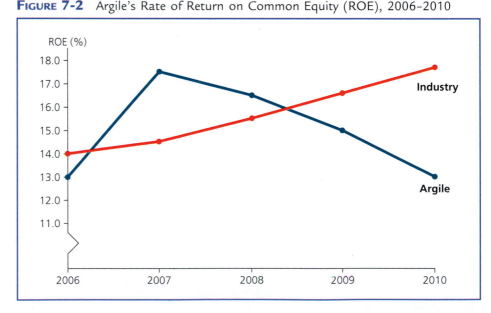

analyze other ratios in a similar fashion. If we were to compare Argile's ratios from 2010 with those from 2009, we would discover that Argile's financial position has deteriorated, not strengthened—not a good trend.

> ### Self-Test Questions
>
> Identify two ratios that are used to analyze a firm's liquidity position and write out their equations.
>
> Identify four ratios that are used to measure how effectively a firm is managing its assets and write out their equations.
>
> Identify three ratios that are used to measure the extent to which a firm uses debt financing and write out their equations.
>
> Identify three ratios that show the combined effects of liquidity, asset management, and debt management on profitability and write out their equations.
>
> Identify two ratios that relate a firm's stock price to its earnings and book value per share and write out their equations.

SUMMARY OF RATIO ANALYSIS: THE DU PONT ANALYSIS

Management and analysts often evaluate ratios using the Du Pont approach, named after the company whose managers developed the evaluation technique. The idea is to attain greater detail by dissecting a single ratio into two or more related ratios. Using the basic approach, we compute the return on assets (ROA) by multiplying the net profit margin by the total assets turnover. The formula, which is called the **Du Pont equation,** is:

Du Pont equation
A formula that gives the rate of return on assets by multiplying the profit margin by the total assets turnover.

$$ROA = \text{Net profit margin} \times \text{Total assets turnover}$$
$$= \frac{\text{Net income}}{\text{Sales}} \times \frac{\text{Sales}}{\text{Total assets}}$$

In 2010 Argile made a profit of 3.6 percent, or 3.6 cents, on each dollar of sales, and assets were "turned over" nearly 1.8 times during the year. The company earned a return of 6.4 percent on its assets. Using the Du Pont equation, we have:

$$ROA = \frac{\$27}{\$750} \times \frac{\$750}{\$425} = 0.036 \times 1.765 = 0.0635 = 6.4\%$$

If the company were financed only with common equity—that is, if it had no debt— the ROA and the ROE would be the same, because total assets would equal the amount of common equity. But, 51 percent of Argile's financing consists of debt, both long term and short term. Thus, as earlier computations show, the ROA and ROE are not equal. Instead, because ROA is defined as *net income available to common stockholders* divided by total assets, the ROA of 6.4 percent all goes to common stockholders. Because the common equity represents less than 100 percent of Argile's capital, the return to the common stockholders, ROE, must be greater than the ROA of 6.4 percent. To translate the ROA into the ROE, we must multiply ROA by the *equity multiplier,* which is the ratio of assets to common equity, or the number of times that the total assets exceed the amount of common equity (it is also the inverse of the percent of total assets that is financed with equity). Using this approach, we can write ROE as follows:

7-3

$$ROE = ROA \times \text{Equity multiplier}$$
$$= \frac{\text{Net income}}{\text{Total assets}} \times \frac{\text{Total assets}}{\text{Common equity}}$$

$$= 6.353\% \times \frac{\$425.0}{\$208.0} = 6.35\% \times 2.043 = 13.0\%$$

We can combine Equations 7-2 and 7-3 to form the *extended* Du Pont equation, which is written as follows:

7-4

$$ROE = \left[\binom{\text{Profit}}{\text{margin}} \times \binom{\text{Total assets}}{\text{turnover}} \right] \times \binom{\text{Equity}}{\text{multiplier}}$$
$$= \left[\frac{\text{Net income}}{\text{Sales}} \times \frac{\text{Sales}}{\text{Total assets}} \right] \times \frac{\text{Total assets}}{\text{Common equity}}$$

$$ROE_{\text{Argile}} = 3.6\% \times 1.765 \times 2.043 = 13.0\%$$
$$ROE_{\text{Industry}} = 4.9\% \times 2.100 \times 1/(1 - 0.42) = 17.7\%$$

Note that the equity multiplier for the industry is computed as the inverse of the equity to total assets ratio ($= 1 -$ debt ratio). Thus, the industry's equity multiplier is $1/[1 - (\text{debt ratio})] = 1/(1 - 0.42) = 1.72$.

The Du Pont computation shows that Argile's ROE is lower than that for the industry because Argile's profit margin and total assets turnover (efficiency) are lower than that for the industry. Argile's management can use the Du Pont system to analyze ways of improving the firm's performance. Focusing on the net profit margin, Argile's marketing personnel can study the effects of raising prices (or lowering them to increase volume), of selling new products or moving into markets with higher margins, and so forth. The company's cost accountants can study various expense items and, working with engineers, purchasing agents, and other operating personnel, seek ways of holding down costs. To improve the assets turnover, Argile's financial analysts, working with both production and marketing personnel, can investigate ways of minimizing the investment in various types of assets. At the same time, its treasury staff can analyze the effects of alternative financing strategies, seeking to hold down interest expense and the risk of debt while still using leverage to increase the rate of return on equity.

As a result of a Du Pont analysis, Sally Anderson, Argile's president, recently announced a series of moves designed to cut the company's operating costs by more than 20 percent per year. Anderson also announced that the company intends to concentrate its capital in markets where profit margins are reasonably high. If competition increases in certain product markets (such as the low-price end of the textiles market), Argile will withdraw from those segments. The company is seeking a high return on equity, and Anderson recognizes that if competition drives profit margins too low in a particular market, it becomes impossible to earn high returns on the capital invested to serve that market. To achieve a high ROE, Argile might have to develop new products and shift capital into new areas. The company's future depends on this type of analysis, and if the firm succeeds in the future, then the Du Pont system will have helped Argile achieve that success.

Self-Test Questions

Explain how the Du Pont equation combines multiple ratios to reveal the basic determinants of ROA and ROE?

Suppose a firm has determined that its ROA is 10 percent and its total assets turnover is 4.0. What is the firm's net profit margin?   (Answer: 2.5%)

Suppose ratio analysis shows a firm has an ROE equal to 15 percent, total assets turnover equal to 3.0, and a net profit margin equal to 4 percent. What is the firm's debt to total assets (debt) ratio?   (Answer: The equity multiplier is 1.25, so the percent of total assets financed with equity is 80 (0.80 = 1/ 1.25); thus, the debt ratio equals 20% = 100% − 80%.)

COMPARATIVE RATIOS (BENCHMARKING)

The preceding analysis of Argile Textiles involved a **comparative ratio analysis**— that is, the ratios calculated for Argile were compared with those of other firms in the same industry. Table 7-6 summarizes the results of our analysis. Comparative ratios, similar to those provided in the table, for a large number of industries and are available from several sources, including Dun & Bradstreet (D&B), Robert Morris Associates, and the U.S. Department of Commerce. Trade associations and individual firms' credit departments also compile industry average financial ratios. Finally, financial statement data for thousands of publicly owned corporations are available from various databases. Because brokerage houses, banks, and other financial institutions have access to these data, security analysts can and do generate comparative ratios tailored to their specific needs. Table 7-7 provides a sample of industry ratios provided by the *Almanac of Business and Industrial Financial Ratios.*

Each of the data-supplying organizations uses a somewhat different set of ratios designed for its own purposes. For example, D&B deals mainly with small firms, many of which are proprietorships, and it sells its services primarily to banks and other lenders. Therefore, D&B is concerned largely with the creditor's viewpoint, and its ratios emphasize current assets and liabilities, not market value ratios. When you select a comparative data source, make sure that your emphasis is similar to that of the agency whose ratios you plan to use. Additionally, there are often definitional differences in the ratios presented by different sources. Therefore, before using any source, you should verify the exact definitions of the ratios to ensure consistency with your work.

comparative ratio analysis
An analysis based on a comparison of a firm's ratios with those of other firms in the same industry.

Self-Test Questions

How is comparative ratio analysis carried out?

How does comparative ratio analysis compare with trend analysis?

TABLE 7-6   Argile Textiles: Summary of 2010 Financial Ratios ($ million, except per-share dollars)

Ratio	Formula for Calculation	Computation	Ratio Value	Industry Average	Comment
Liquidity					
Current	$= \dfrac{\text{Current assets}}{\text{Current liabilities}}$	$\dfrac{\$235.0}{\$65.0}$	$= 3.6\times$	$4.1\times$	Low
Quick, or acid test	$= \dfrac{\text{Current assets} - \text{Inventory}}{\text{Current liabilities}}$	$\dfrac{\$100.0}{\$65.0}$	$= 1.5\times$	$2.1\times$	Low
Asset Management					
Inventory turnover	$= \dfrac{\text{Cost of goods sold}}{\text{Inventory}}$	$\dfrac{\$600.0}{\$135.0}$	$= 4.4\times$	$7.4\times$	Low
Days sales outstanding (DSO)	$= \dfrac{\text{Accounts receivable}}{\left[\dfrac{\text{Annual sales}}{360}\right]}$	$\dfrac{\$90.0}{\$2.08}$	$= 43.2$ days	32.1 days	Poor
Fixed assets turnover	$= \dfrac{\text{Sales}}{\text{Net fixed assets}}$	$\dfrac{\$750.0}{\$190.0}$	$= 3.9\times$	$4.0\times$	OK
Total assets turnover	$= \dfrac{\text{Sales}}{\text{Total assets}}$	$\dfrac{\$750.0}{\$425.0}$	$= 1.8\times$	$2.1\times$	Low
Debt Management					
Debt-to-total-assets	$= \dfrac{\text{Total liabilities}}{\text{Total assets}}$	$\dfrac{\$217.0}{\$425.0}$	$= 51.1\%$	42.0%	Poor
Times interest earned (TIE)	$= \dfrac{\text{EBIT}}{\text{Interest charges}}$	$\dfrac{\$65.0}{\$20.0}$	$= 3.3\times$	$6.5\times$	Low
Fixed charge coverage	$= \dfrac{\text{EBIT} + \text{Lease payments}}{\dfrac{\text{Interest}}{\text{charges}} + \dfrac{\text{Lease}}{\text{payments}} + \left[\dfrac{\text{Sinking fund payments}}{(1-\text{Tax rate})}\right]}$	$\dfrac{\$70.0}{\$31.7}$	$= 2.2\times$	$5.8\times$	Low
Profitability					
Net profit margin	$= \dfrac{\text{Net income}}{\text{Sales}}$	$\dfrac{\$27.0}{\$750.0}$	$= 3.6\%$	4.9%	Poor
Return on total assets (ROA)	$= \dfrac{\text{Net income}}{\text{Total assets}}$	$\dfrac{\$27.0}{\$425.0}$	$= 6.4\%$	11.5%	Poor
Return on equity (ROE)	$= \dfrac{\text{Net income available to common stockholders}}{\text{Common equity}}$	$\dfrac{\$27.0}{\$208.0}$	$= 13.0\%$	17.7%	Poor
Market Value					
Price/Earnings (P/E)	$= \dfrac{\text{Market price per share}}{\text{Earnings per share}}$	$\dfrac{\$20.00}{\$2.45}$	$= 8.2\times$	$15.0\times$	Low
Market/Book (M/B)	$= \dfrac{\text{Market price per share}}{\text{Book value per share}}$	$\dfrac{\$20.00}{\$18.91}$	$= 1.1\times$	$2.5\times$	Low

USES AND LIMITATIONS OF RATIO ANALYSIS

As noted earlier, three main groups use ratio analysis:

- *Managers,* who employ ratios to help analyze, control, and thus improve the firm's operations
- *Credit analysts,* such as bank loan officers or bond rating analysts, who analyze ratios to help ascertain a company's ability to pay its debts

TABLE 7-7 Ratios for Selected Industries

NAICS Code[a] Line of Business (Number of Firms)	Type of Operations	Current Ratio (×)	Quick Ratio (×)	Debt Ratio (%)	TIE Ratio (×)	DSO (days)	Inventory Turnover (×)	Total Assets Turnover (×)	Profit Margin (%)	Return on Assets (%)	Return on Equity (%)
221210 Natural Gas Distribution (895)	Utilities	0.9	0.6	93.9	1.3	225.0	14.0	0.4	0.6	2.7	3.9
325410 Pharmaceuticals (1,131)	Manufacturing	1.1	0.8	67.3	4.9	200.0	4.0	0.4	8.9	6.5	10.1
325600 Soaps, Cleaners, & Toilet Goods (1,517)	Manufacturing	1.0	0.6	59.6	4.1	73.5	9.9	0.7	5.4	8.0	9.8
335310 Electrical Equipment (1,757)	Manufacturing	1.1	0.8	38.9	3.9	116.1	6.9	0.6	4.8	5.3	4.4
423300 Lumber & Construction (13,599)	Wholesale	1.8	1.0	62.9	6.5	38.3	8.6	2.8	2.8	10.7	21.3
424700 Petroleum & Products (8,835)	Wholesale	1.3	0.8	49.6	4.2	22.8	44.7	2.5	1.3	6.1	6.3
444130 Hardware Stores (7,904)	Retail	2.8	0.9	52.0	4.3	20.2	3.5	2.3	1.9	6.4	9.1
445310 Beer, Wine, & Liquor Stores (15,173)	Retail	2.2	0.7	70.4	3.1	5.6	6.0	3.3	1.2	6.4	12.9

[a]NAICS is the North American Industry Classification System, which replaced the Standard Industrial Classification (SIC) in 1997. NAICS is the result of efforts by the United States, Canada, and Mexico to provide comparable statistics about business activity throughout North America.

Source: *Almanac of Business and Industrial Financial Ratios, 2008 Edition,* (Chicago, IL: CCH, 2007).

- *Security analysts* (or *investors*), including stock analysts, who are interested in a company's efficiency and growth prospects, and bond analysts, who are concerned with a company's ability to pay interest on its bonds and the liquidation value of the firm's assets in the event that the company fails

Although ratio analysis can provide useful information concerning a company's operations and financial condition, it does have inherent problems and limitations that necessitate care and judgment. Some potential problems follow:

1. *Many large firms operate a number of divisions in very different industries.* In such cases, it is difficult to develop a meaningful set of industry averages for comparative purposes. Consequently, ratio analysis tends to be more useful for small, narrowly focused firms than for large, multidivisional ones.

2. *Most firms want to be better than average, so merely attaining average performance is not necessarily good.* As a target for high-level performance, it is best to focus on the industry leaders' ratios.

3. *Inflation might distort firms' balance sheets.* For example, if recorded values are historical, they could be substantially different from the "true" values. Furthermore, because inflation affects both depreciation charges and inventory costs, it also affects profits. For these reasons, a ratio analysis for one firm over time, or a comparative analysis of firms of different ages, must be interpreted using judgment.

4. *Seasonal factors can distort a ratio analysis.* For example, the inventory turnover ratio for a textile firm will be radically different if the balance sheet figure used for inventory is the one just before the fall fashion season versus the one just after the close of the season. You can minimize this problem by using monthly averages for inventory (and receivables) when calculating ratios such as turnover.

5. *Firms can employ* **"window dressing" techniques** *to make their financial statements look stronger.* To illustrate, consider a Chicago builder that borrowed on a 2-year basis on December 28, 2009, held the proceeds of the loan as *cash* for a few days, and then paid off the loan ahead of time on January 4, 2010. This activity improved the company's current and quick ratios, and it made the firm's year-end 2009 balance sheet look good. The improvement was strictly window dressing, however; a week later, the balance sheet was back at the old level.

6. *Different accounting practices can distort comparisons.* As noted earlier, inventory valuation and depreciation methods can affect financial statements, and thus the fact that different methods can be used make comparisons among firms difficult.

7. *It is difficult to generalize about whether a particular ratio is "good" or "bad."* For example, a high current ratio might indicate a strong liquidity position, which is good, or excessive cash, which is bad (because excess cash in the bank is a non-earning asset). Similarly, a high fixed assets turnover ratio might denote either a firm that uses its assets efficiently or one that is undercapitalized and cannot afford to buy enough assets.

8. *A firm might have some ratios that look "good" and others that look "bad," making it difficult to tell whether the company is, on balance, strong or weak.* Statistical procedures can be used to analyze the net effects of a set of ratios, and thereby clarify the situation. Many banks and other lending organizations use statistical procedures to analyze firms' financial ratios, and, on the basis of their analyses, classify companies according to their probability of getting into financial trouble.[15]

"window dressing" techniques
Techniques employed by firms to make their financial statements look better than they actually are.

---

[15]The technique used is called discriminant analysis. For a discussion of this technique, see Edward I. Altman, "Financial Ratios, Discriminant Analysis, and the Prediction of Corporate Bankruptcy," *Journal of Finance,* September 1968, 589–609, or Eugene F. Brigham and Phillip R. Daves, *Intermediate Financial Management,* 9th ed. (Cincinnati, OH: South-Western College Publishing, 2007), Chapter 24.

Ratio analysis is useful, but analysts should be aware of these problems and make adjustments as necessary. When conducted in a mechanical, unthinking manner, however, this type of analysis is dangerous. Used intelligently and with good judgment, it can provide useful insights into a firm's operations. *Probably the most important and most difficult input to successful financial statement (ratio) analysis is the judgment used when interpreting the results to reach an overall conclusion about the firm's financial position.*

Self-Test Questions

Name three types of users of ratio analyses. What type of ratio does each group emphasize?

List several potential problems with ratio analysis.

Ethical Dilemma

Hocus-Pocus—Look, An Increase in Sales!

Dynamic Energy Wares (DEW) manufactures and distributes products that are used to save energy and to help reduce and reverse the harmful environmental effects of atmospheric pollutants. DEW relies on a relatively complex distribution system to get the products to its customers. Large companies, which account for nearly 30 percent of the firm's total sales, purchase directly from DEW. Smaller companies and retailers that sell to individuals are required to make their purchases from one of the 50 independent distributors that are contractually obligated to *exclusively* sell DEW's products.

DEW's accountants have just finished the firm's financial statements for the third quarter of the fiscal year, which ended 3 weeks ago. The results are terrible. Profits are down 30 percent from this time last year, when a downturn in sales began. Profits are depressed primarily because DEW continues to lose market share to a competitor that entered the field nearly 2 years ago.

Senior management has decided that it needs to take action to boost sales in the fourth quarter so that year-end profits will be "more acceptable." Starting immediately, DEW will (1) eliminate all direct sales, which means that large companies must purchase products from DEW's distributors just as the smaller companies and retailers do, (2) require distributors to maintain certain minimum inventory levels, which are much higher than previous levels, and (3) form a task force to study and propose ways that the firm can recapture its lost market share.

The financial manager, who is your boss, has asked you to attend a hastily called meeting of DEW's distributors to announce the implementation of these operational changes. At the meeting, the distributors will be informed that they must increase inventory to the required minimum level before the end of DEW's current fiscal year or face losing the distributorship. According to your boss, the reason for this requirement is to ensure that distributors can meet the increased demand they will face when the large companies are no longer permitted to purchase directly from DEW. The sales forecast you have been developing over the past few months, however, indicates that distributors' sales are expected to decline by almost 10 percent during the next year. As a consequence, the added inventories might be extremely burdensome to the distributors. When you approached your boss to discuss this potential problem, she said, "Tell the distributors not to worry! We won't require payment for 6 months, and any additional inventory that remains unsold after 9 months can be returned. But they *must* take delivery of the inventory within the next 2 months."

It appears that the actions implemented by DEW will produce favorable year-end sales results for the current fiscal year. Do you agree with the

continues

decisions made by DEW's senior management? Will you be comfortable announcing the changes to DEW's distributors? How would you respond to a distributor who says the following: "DEW doesn't care about us. The company just wants to look good, no matter who gets hurt. That's unethical." What will you say to your boss? Will you attend the distributors' meeting?

CHAPTER PRINCIPLES
–The Answers

To summarize the key concepts, let's answer the questions that were posed at the beginning of the chapter:

- **What financial statements do corporations publish, and what information does each statement provide?** A company publishes a number of financial statements— including a balance sheet, income statement, statement of cash flows, and statement of retained earnings—to provide management and investors with information about the firm's operations. The balance sheet shows a "snapshot" at one point in time of the firm's assets and how those assets are financed (debt, equity, or both). The income statement reports the effects of the firm's operations during an accounting period; the revenues that were earned and the expenses that were incurred are netted out to compute the bottom line net income figure. The statement of cash flows shows the activities that generated funds and the activities that used funds during the accounting period—it shows how and why the firm's cash position changed during the period. The statement of retained earnings shows what caused changes in the firm's common equity during the accounting period—that is, it shows whether new stock was issued or outstanding stock was repurchased and whether dividends were paid.

- **How do investors utilize financial statements?** The information contained in the financial statements helps investors (both debtholders and stockholders) determine the financial position of a firm, which helps them to estimate the cash flows the firm will generate in the future. Debtholders want to estimate future cash flows to determine whether the debt contracts will be fully honored; stockholders estimate future cash flows to determine the value of the firm's common stock.

- **What is ratio analysis and why are the results of such an analysis important to both managers and investors?** Ratio analysis is used to evaluate a firm's current financial position and the direction this position is expected to take in the future. By determining the firm's financial position, investors form opinions about future conditions of the firm and the safety of their investments. Managers use the information provided by ratio analyses to plan actions that will correct the firm's weaknesses and take advantage of its strengths.

- **What are some potential problems (caveats) associated with financial statement analysis?** Limitations to financial statement analysis include the following: problems are associated with classifying a large conglomerate firm into a particular industry or finding firms that can be used for comparative analysis; inflation might distort some of the numbers reported on financial statements; seasonal firms experience wide swings in their operating accounts; firms can use different generally accepted accounting principles to "manipulate" financial numbers; and it is difficult to make general conclusions when some ratios look good and others look bad.

- **What is the most important ingredient (factor) in financial statement analysis?** To form general impressions about a firm's financial position, judgment must be used when interpreting financial ratios. Because judgment is involved, different analysts might reach different conclusions, and conclusions will not always be correct.

The concepts presented in this chapter should help you understand how to evaluate your own financial position to determine your "operating cash flow," "free cash flow," and whether your debt position is appropriate given your income.

- **Disposable Income (Operating Cash Flow)** An individual's after-tax income is called *disposable income* because this is the amount that is left to pay current bills, spend on groceries, save (invest) to provide funds in the future, and so forth. Disposable income is effectively your "take-home" pay (from all income sources), because it can be "disposed of" in whatever manner you choose. It is important for you to know how much income you have at your disposal so that you can determine how much you can afford to pay for housing, food, and transportation. You must "live within your means"—that is, you cannot buy a house or drive a car that cannot be supported on your income. Disposable income is the key input to constructing a financial budget that can be used to guide spending and investment.

- **Discretionary Income (Free Cash Flow)** Because you *must* pay certain bills for necessities, including housing, utilities, food, and transportation, you cannot spend all of your disposable income as you please. *Discretionary income* is the amount of disposable income that can be spent for things you want rather than for things you need. If you know how much of your disposable income is discretionary, you can better plan for retirement by determining how much of your income can be contributed to a retirement fund each year. If you develop a personal financial budget, you will find that any discretionary income that remains after planned savings (e.g., for retirement) represents funds that can be used to pay for entertainment, to buy non-essential items, and so forth.

- **Debt Position (Ratios)** Lenders consider many factors when they decide whether to grant loans (especially mortgages) to individuals. Some key ratios that are evaluated include the debt-to-income ratio, housing expense ratio, and loan-to-value ratio. The *debt-to-income ratio* is computed by dividing monthly debt payments (mortgage, automobile, credit cards, and other loans) by disposable income. Many mortgage lenders require this ratio to be less than 35 percent. Mortgage lenders also prefer that your total monthly house payment (principal, interest, property taxes, and insurance) be less than 25 to 30 percent of your gross monthly income—that is, your *housing expense ratio* should not exceed about 30 percent. The *loan-to-value (LTV) ratio* is computed by dividing the amount that is owed on the mortgage by the market value of a house or other property. An LTV equal to 70 percent indicates that the borrower has 30 percent equity in the property. Many mortgage lenders want the LTV to be less than 80 percent.

  Just as managers and investors use financial statements and ratio analysis to evaluate the financial position of a firm, you should use personal financial ratios to evaluate your financial position. You should also apply the concepts we discussed in this chapter to your personal finances—that is, you should determine what your current financial position is and forecast what you expect your financial position to be in the future. Living within your financial means and planning for your financial future are key ingredients to sustaining a happy and successful "financial" life.

QUESTIONS

7-1   What four financial statements appear in most annual reports?

7-2   If a "typical" firm reports $20 million of retained earnings on its balance sheet, could its directors declare a $20 million cash dividend without any qualms? Explain why or why not.

7-3   Describe the changes in balance sheet accounts that would constitute sources of funds. What changes would be considered uses of funds?

7-4   Financial ratio analysis is conducted by four types of analysts: managers, equity investors, long-term creditors, and short-term creditors. What is the primary emphasis of each of these groups in evaluating ratios?

7-5   What are some steps that must be taken when using ratio analysis? What is the most important aspect of ratio analysis?

7-6   Profit margins and turnover ratios vary from one industry to another. What differences would you expect to find between a grocery chain, such as Safeway, and a steel company? Think particularly about the turnover ratios and the profit margin, and consider the effect on the Du Pont equation.

7-7   If a firm's ROE is low and management wants to improve it, explain how using more debt might help. Could using too much debt prove detrimental?

7-8   How might (a) seasonal factors and (b) different growth rates distort a comparative ratio analysis? Give some examples. How might these problems be alleviated?

7-9   Explain the difference between net income, or accounting profit, and net cash flow. Why do these numbers generally differ?

7-10   Explain the difference between net cash flow and operating cash flow. What causes these two numbers to differ?

7-11   What is "free cash flow"? Can a company have a negative free cash flow and still be considered successful?

7-12   Following are the balance sheets for Batelan Corporation for the fiscal years 2009 and 2010. In the column to the right of the balance sheet amounts, indicate whether the change in the account balance represents a source or a use of cash for the firm. Place a (+) in the space provided to indicate a source of funds, a (−) to indicate a use of funds, or a (0) if the effect cannot be determined with the information provided.

	2010	2009	Source (+) or Use (−)?
Cash	$ 400	$ 500	_____
Accounts receivable	250	300	_____
Inventory	450	400	_____
Current assets	$1,100	$1,200	
Net property and equipment	1,000	950	_____
Total assets	$2,100	$2,150	
Accounts payable	$ 200	$ 400	_____
Accruals	300	250	_____
Notes payable	400	200	_____
Current liabilities	$ 900	$ 850	
Long-term debt	800	900	_____
Total liabilities	$1,700	$1,750	
Common stock	250	300	_____
Retained earnings	150	100	_____
Total equity	$ 400	$ 400	
Total liabilities and equity	$2,100	$2,150	

From these balance sheets, can you tell whether Batelan generated a positive or negative net income during 2010? Can you tell whether dividends were paid? Explain.

7-13   Indicate the effects of the transactions listed in the following table on total current assets, current ratio, and net income. Use (+) to indicate an increase, (−) to indicate a decrease, and (0) to indicate either no effect or an indeterminate effect. Be prepared to state any necessary assumptions, and assume the initial current ratio is greater than 1.0. (*Note:* A good accounting background is necessary to answer some of these questions; if yours is not strong, just answer the questions you can handle.)

	Total Current Assets	Current Ratio	Effect on Net Income
a. Cash is acquired through issuance of additional common stock.	_____	_____	_____
b. Merchandise is sold for cash.	_____	_____	_____
c. Federal income tax due for the previous year is paid.	_____	_____	_____
d. A fixed asset is sold for less than its book value.	_____	_____	_____
e. A fixed asset is sold for more than its book value.	_____	_____	_____
f. Merchandise is sold on credit.	_____	_____	_____
g. Payment is made to trade creditors for previous purchases.	_____	_____	_____
h. A cash dividend is declared and paid.	_____	_____	_____
i. Cash is obtained through short-term bank loans.	_____	_____	_____
j. Marketable securities are sold below cost.	_____	_____	_____
k. Advances are made to employees.	_____	_____	_____
l. Current operating expenses are paid.	_____	_____	_____
m. Short-term promissory notes are issued to trade creditors in exchange for past due accounts payable.	_____	_____	_____
n. Long-term bonds are issued to pay accounts payable.	_____	_____	_____
o. Accounts receivable are collected.	_____	_____	_____
p. Equipment is purchased with short-term notes.	_____	_____	_____
q. Merchandise is purchased on credit.	_____	_____	_____

SELF-TEST PROBLEMS

Solutions appear in Appendix B.

Key Terms

ST-1   Define each of the following terms:

    a.   Annual report; income statement; balance sheet; common size balance sheet

    b.   Stockholders' equity, or net worth; paid-in capital; retained earnings

c. Statement of retained earnings; statement of cash flows

d. Book value; market value

e. Operating cash flows; accounting profits

f. Net working capital; net operating working capital

g. Free cash flow; economic value added (EVA)

h. Liquidity ratios: current ratio; quick, or acid test, ratio

i. Asset management ratios: inventory turnover ratio; days sales outstanding (DSO); fixed assets turnover ratio; total assets turnover ratio

j. Financial leverage ratios: debt ratio; times-interest-earned (TIE) ratio; fixed charge coverage ratio

k. Profitability ratios ratios: net profit margin; return on total assets (ROA); return on common equity (ROE)

l. Market value ratios: price/earnings (P/E) ratio; market/book (M/B) ratio; book value per share

m. Trend analysis; comparative ratio analysis

n. Du Pont analysis; Du Pont equation

o. "Window dressing"; seasonal effects on ratios

Debt Ratio   **ST-2**   K. Billingsworth & Company had earnings per share of $4 last year, and it paid a $2 dividend. Total retained earnings increased by $12 million during the year, and book value per share at year end was $40. Billingsworth has no preferred stock, and no new common stock was issued during the year. If the company's year-end debt (which equals its total liabilities) was $120 million, what was its year-end debt/assets ratio?

Cash Flows   **ST-3**   Refreshing Pool Corporation reported net operating income equal to $120,000 this year. Examination of the company's balance sheet and income statement shows that the tax rate was 40 percent, the depreciation expense was $25,000, $150,000 was invested in assets during the year, and invested capital equals $500,000. The firm's average after-tax cost of funds is 12 percent. What was the firm's (1) operating cash flow, (2) free cash flow, and (3) economic value added (EVA)?

Ratio Analysis   **ST-4**   The following data apply to A. L. Kaiser & Company ($ million):

Cash and equivalents	$ 100.00
Fixed assets	$ 283.50
Sales	$1,000.00
Net income	$ 50.00
Quick ratio	2.0×
Current ratio	3.0×
DSO	40.0 days
ROE	12.0%

Kaiser has no preferred stock—only common equity, current liabilities, and long-term debt.

a. Find Kaiser's (1) accounts receivable (A/R), (2) current liabilities, (3) current assets, (4) total assets, (5) ROA, (6) common equity, and (7) long-term debt.

b. In part (a), you should have found Kaiser's accounts receivable (A/R) to be $111.1 million. If Kaiser could reduce its DSO from 40 days to

30 days while holding other things constant, how much cash would it generate? If this cash were used to buy back common stock (at book value) and thereby reduce the amount of common equity, how would this action affect the company's (1) ROE, (2) ROA, and (3) total debt/ total assets ratio?

PROBLEMS

7-1 Hindelang Corporation has $1,312,500 in current assets and $525,000 in current liabilities. Its initial inventory level is $375,000, and it will raise funds through additional notes payable and use them to increase inventory. How much can Hindelang's short-term debt (notes payable) increase without pushing its current ratio below 2.0? What will be the firm's quick ratio after Hindelang has raised the maximum amount of short-term funds?

Liquidity Ratio

7-2 W. F. Bailey Company had a quick ratio of 1.4, a current ratio of 3.0, an inventory turnover of five times, total current assets of $810,000, and cash and equivalents of $120,000 in 2010. If the cost of goods sold equaled 86 percent of sales, what were Bailey's annual sales and DSO?

Ratio Calculations

7-3 Wolken Corporation has $500,000 of debt outstanding, and it pays an interest rate of 10 percent annually. Wolken's annual sales are $2 million; its average tax rate is 20 percent; and its net profit margin is 5 percent. If the company does not maintain a TIE ratio of at least 5.0 times, its bank will refuse to renew the loan, and bankruptcy will result. What is Wolken's TIE ratio?

TIE Ratio

7-4 Coastal Packaging's ROE last year was only 3 percent, but its management has developed a new operating plan designed to improve things. The new plan calls for a total debt ratio of 60 percent, which will result in interest charges of $300 per year. Management projects an EBIT of $1,000 on sales of $10,000, and it expects to have a total assets turnover ratio of 2.0×. Under these conditions, the average tax rate will be 30 percent. If the changes are made, what return on equity (ROE) will Coastal earn? What is the ROA?

Return on Equity

7-5 Barbell Corporation's income statement reports that the company's "bottom line" was $180,000 in 2008. The statement also shows that the company had depreciation and amortization expenses equal to $50,000 and taxes equal to $120,000. What was Barbell's net cash flow?

Net Cash Flow

7-6 Last year Z&B Paints reported its net income as $650,000. A review of its income statement shows that Z&B's operating expenses (fixed and variable), excluding depreciation and amortization, were $1,500,000, its depreciation and amortization expense was $300,000, and its company's tax rate was 35 percent. Z&B has no debt—that is, the firm is financed with stock only.

Net Cash Flow

    a. What were Z&B's sales revenues last year?

    b. What was Z&B's net cash flow last year?

    c. What was Z&B's operating cash flow last year?

7-7 Psyre Company reported net operating income (NOI) equal to $150,000 this year. Examination of the company's balance sheet and income statement

Economic Value

shows that the tax rate was 40 percent, the depreciation expense was $40,000, $120,000 was invested in assets during the year, and invested capital currently is $1,100,000. If Psyre's average after-tax cost of funds is 10 percent, what is the firm's EVA?

Ratio Calculation   **7-8**   Assume that you are given the following relationships for Zumwalt Corporation:

Sales/total assets	1.5×
Return on assets (ROA)	3.0%
Return on equity (ROE)	5.0%

Calculate Zumwalt's net profit margin and debt ratio.

Return on Equity   **7-9**   Earth's Best Company has sales of $200,000, a net income of $15,000, and the following balance sheet:

Cash	$ 10,000	Accounts payable	$ 30,000
Receivables	50,000	Other current liabilities	20,000
Inventories	150,000	Long-term debt	50,000
Net fixed assets	90,000	Common equity	200,000
Total assets	$300,000	Total liabilities and equity	$300,000

a. The company's new owner thinks that inventories are excessive and can be lowered to the point where the current ratio is equal to the industry average, 2.5, without affecting either sales or net income. If inventories are sold off and not replaced so as to reduce the current ratio to 2.5, if the funds generated are used to reduce common equity (stock can be repurchased at book value), and if no other changes occur, by how much will the ROE change?

b. Now suppose we wanted to take this problem and modify it for use on an exam—that is, to create a new problem that you have not seen to test your knowledge of this type of problem. How would your answer change if we made the following changes: (1) We doubled all of the dollar amounts? (2) We stated that the target current ratio was 3.0? (3) We said that the company had 10,000 shares of stock outstanding, and we asked how much the change in part (a) would increase EPS? (4) What would your answer to (3) be if we changed the original problem to state that the stock was selling for twice the book value, so common equity would not be reduced on a dollar-for-dollar basis?

c. Explain how we could have set the problem up to have you focus on changing accounts receivable, or fixed assets, or using the funds generated to retire debt (we would give you the interest rate on outstanding debt), or how the original problem could have stated that the company needed *more* inventories and it would finance them with new common equity or with new debt.

Statement of Cash Flows   **7-10**   The consolidated balance sheets for Lloyd Lumber Company at the beginning and end of 2010 follow. The company bought $50 million worth of fixed assets. The charge for depreciation in 2010 was $10 million. Net income was $33 million, and the company paid out $5 million in dividends.

a. Fill in the amount of the source or use in the appropriate column.

Lloyd Lumber Company:
Balance Sheets at Beginning and End of 2010 ($ million)

	Jan. 1	Dec. 31	Change Source	Use
Cash	$ 7	$ 5	_____	_____
Marketable securities	0	11	_____	_____
Net receivables	30	22	_____	_____
Inventories	53	75	_____	_____
Total current assets	$ 90	$ 23		
Gross fixed assets	75	125	_____	_____
Less: Accumulated depreciation	(25)	(235)		
Net fixed assets	$ 50	$ 90		
Total assets	$140	$ 213		
Accounts payable	$ 18	$ 15	_____	_____
Notes payable	3	15	_____	_____
Other current liabilities	15	7	_____	_____
Long-term debt	8	24	_____	_____
Common stock	29	57	_____	_____
Retained earnings	67	95		
Total liabilities and equity	$140	$ 213		

Note: Total sources must equal total uses.

b. Prepare a statement of cash flows.

c. Briefly summarize your findings.

7-11 Montejo Corporation expects 2010 sales to be $12 million. Operating costs other than depreciation are expected to be 75 percent of sales, and depreciation is expected to be $1.5 million in 2010. All sales revenues will be collected in cash, and costs other than depreciation must be paid during the year. Montejo's interest expense is expected to be $1 million, and it is taxed at a 40 percent rate.

Income and Cash Flow Analysis

a. Set up an income statement and a cash flow statement (use two columns on one page) for Montejo. What is the expected cash flow from operations?

b. Suppose Congress changed the tax laws so that Montejo's depreciation expenses doubled in 2010, but no other changes occurred. What would happen to the net income and cash flow from operations expected in 2010?

c. Suppose that Congress, rather than increasing Montejo's 2010 depreciation, reduced it by 50 percent. How would the income and cash flows be affected?

d. If this company belonged to you, would you prefer that Congress increase or decrease the depreciation expense allowed your company? Explain why.

7-12 Data for Argile Textiles' 2009 financial statements are given in Tables 7-1 and 7-2 in the chapter.

Ratio Analysis

a. Compute the 2009 values of the following ratios:

	2009 Values	
Ratio	Argile	Industry
Current ratio	_____	3.9×
Days sales outstanding	_____	33.5 days
Inventory turnover	_____	7.2×
Fixed assets turnover	_____	4.1×
Debt ratio	_____	43.0%
Net profit margin	_____	4.6%
Return on assets	_____	9.9%

b. Briefly comment on Argile's 2009 financial position. Can you see any obvious strengths or weaknesses?

c. Compare Argile's 2009 ratios with its 2010 ratios, which are presented in Table 7-6. Comment on whether you believe Argile's financial position improved or deteriorated during 2010.

d. What other information would be useful for projecting whether Argile's financial position is expected to improve or deteriorate in the future?

Ratio Analysis   7-13 Data for Campsey Computer Company and its industry averages follow.

a. Calculate the indicated ratios for Campsey.

b. Construct the Du Pont equation for both Campsey and the industry.

c. Outline Campsey's strengths and weaknesses as revealed by your analysis.

d. Suppose Campsey had doubled its sales as well as its inventories, accounts receivable, and common equity during 2010. How would that information affect the validity of your ratio analysis? (*Hint:* Think about averages and the effects of rapid growth on ratios if averages are not used. No calculations are needed.)

Campsey Computer Company:
Balance Sheet as of December 31, 2010

Cash	$ 77,500	Accounts payable	$129,000
Receivables	336,000	Notes payable	84,000
Inventories	241,500	Other current liabilities	117,000
Total current assets	$655,000	Total current liabilities	$330,000
Net fixed assets	292,500	Long-term debt	256,500
		Common equity	361,000
Total assets	$947,500	Total liabilities and equity	$947,500

Campsey Computer Company:
Income Statement for Year Ended December 31, 2010

Sales	$ 1,607,500
Cost of goods sold	(1,353,000)
Gross profit	$ 254,500
Fixed operating expenses except depreciation	(143,000)
Earnings before interest, taxes, depreciation, and	
amortization (EBITDA)	$ 111,500
Depreciation	(41,500)

Earnings before interest and taxes (EBIT)		$ 70,000
Interest		(24,500)
Earnings before taxes (EBT)		$ 45,500
Taxes (40%)		(18,200)
Net income		$ 27,300

Ratio	Campsey	Industry Average
Current ratio	_____	2.0×
Days sales outstanding	_____	35.0 days
Inventory turnover	_____	5.6×
Total assets turnover	_____	3.0×
Net profit margin	_____	1.2%
Return on assets (ROA)	_____	3.6%
Return on equity (ROE)	_____	9.0%
Debt ratio	_____	60.0%

7-14   Complete the balance sheet and sales information in the table that follows for Isberg Industries using the following financial data: **Balance Sheet**

Debt ratio: 50%

Quick ratio: 0.80×

Total assets turnover: 1.5×

Days sales outstanding: 36.5 days

Gross profit margin on sales: (Sales − Cost of goods sold)/Sales = 25%

Inventory turnover ratio: 5.0×

Balance Sheet

Cash	_____	Accounts payable	_____
Accounts receivable	_____	Long-term debt	$60,000
Inventories	_____	Common stock	_____
Fixed assets	_____	Retained earnings	$97,500
Total assets	$300,000	Total liabilities and equity	=========
Sales	_____	Cost of goods sold	_____

7-15   The Finnerty Furniture Company, a manufacturer and wholesaler of high-quality home furnishings, has experienced low profitability in recent years. As a result, the board of directors has replaced the president of the firm with a new president, Elizabeth Brannigan, who has asked you to make an analysis of the firm's financial position using the Du Pont chart. The most recent industry average ratios and Finnerty's financial statements are as follows: **Du Pont Analysis**

Industry Average Ratios

Current ratio	2.0×	Fixed assets turnover	6.0×
Debt ratio	30.0%	Total assets turnover	3.0×
Times interest earned	7.0×	Profit margin on sales	3.0%
Inventory turnover	8.5×	Return on total assets	9.0%
Days sales outstanding	24.0 days	Return on common equity	12.9%

Finnerty Furniture Company:
Balance Sheet as of December 31, 2010 ($ million)

Cash	$ 45	Accounts payable	$ 45
Marketable securities	33	Notes payable	45
Net receivables	66	Other current liabilities	21
Inventories	159	Total current liabilities	$111
Total current assets	$303	Long-term debt	24
		Total liabilities	$135
Gross fixed assets	225	Common stock	114
Less: Depreciation	(78)	Retained earnings	201
Net fixed assets	$147	Total stockholders' equity	$315
Total assets	$450	Total liabilities and equity	$450

Finnerty Furniture Company:
Income Statement for Year Ended December 31, 2010 ($ million)

Net sales	$ 795.0
Cost of goods sold	(660.0)
Gross profit	$ 135.0
Selling expenses	(73.5)
Depreciation expense	(12.0)
Earnings before interest and taxes (EBIT)	$ 49.5
Interest expense	(4.5)
Earnings before taxes (EBT)	$ 45.0
Taxes (40%)	(18.0)
Net income	$ 27.0

a. Calculate those ratios that you think would be useful in this analysis.

b. Construct a Du Pont equation for Finnerty and compare the company's ratios to the industry average ratios.

c. Do the balance sheet accounts or the income statement figures seem to be primarily responsible for the low profit?

d. Which specific accounts seem to be most out of line compared with those of other firms in the industry?

e. If Finnerty had a pronounced seasonal sales pattern, or if it grew rapidly during the year, how might that affect the validity of your ratio analysis? How might you correct for such potential problems?

Ratio Analysis   7-16 Cary Corporation's forecasted 2011 financial statements follow, along with industry average ratios.

a. Calculate Cary's 2011 forecasted ratios, compare them with the industry average data, and comment briefly on Cary's projected strengths and weaknesses.

b. What do you think would happen to Cary's ratios if the company initiated cost-cutting measures that allowed it to hold lower levels of inventory and substantially decrease the cost of goods sold? No calculations are necessary. Think about which ratios would be affected by changes in these two accounts.

Cary Corporation: Forecasted Balance Sheet as of December 31, 2011

Cash	$ 72,000	Accounts and notes payable	$ 432,000
Accounts receivable	439,000	Accruals	170,000
Inventories	894,000	Total current liabilities	$ 602,000
Total current assets	$1,405,000	Long-term debt	404,290
Land and building	238,000	Common stock	575,000
Machinery	132,000	Retained earnings	254,710
Other fixed assets	61,000		
Total assets	$1,836,000	Total liabilities and equity	$1,836,000

Cary Corporation: Forecasted Income Statement for 2011

Sales	$ 4,290,000
Cost of goods sold	(3,580,000)
Gross operating profit	$ 710,000
General administrative and selling expenses	(236,320)
Depreciation	(159,000)
Miscellaneous	(134,000)
Earnings before taxes (EBT)	$ 180,680
Taxes (40%)	(72,272)
Net income	$ 108,408
Number of shares outstanding	23,000

Per-Share Data

EPS	$ 4.71
Cash dividends per share	$ 0.95
P/E ratio	5.0×
Market price (average)	$23.57

Industry Financial Ratios (2011)[a]

Quick ratio	1.0×
Current ratio	2.7×
Inventory turnover[b]	5.8×
Days sales outstanding	32 days
Fixed assets turnover[b]	13.0×
Total assets turnover[b]	2.6×
Return on assets	9.1%
Return on equity	18.2%
Debt ratio	50.0%
Profit margin on sales	3.5%
P/E ratio	6.0×

[a]Industry average ratios have been constant for the past 4 years.

[b]Based on year-end balance sheet figures.

Integrative Problem

7-17 Donna Jamison was recently hired as a financial analyst by Computron Industries, a manufacturer of electronic components. Her first task was to conduct a financial analysis of the firm covering the last 2 years. To begin, she gathered the following financial statements and other data:

Financial Statement Analysis

Balance Sheets	2010	2009
Assets		
Cash	$ 52,000	$ 57,600
Accounts receivable	402,000	351,200
Inventories	836,000	715,200
Total current assets	$1,290,000	$1,124,000
Gross fixed assets	527,000	491,000
Less: Accumulated depreciation	166,200	146,200
Net fixed assets	$ 360,800	$ 344,800
Total assets	$1,650,800	$1,468,800
Liabilities and Equity		
Accounts payable	$ 175,200	$ 145,600
Notes payable	225,000	200,000
Accruals	140,000	136,000
Total current liabilities	$ 540,200	$ 481,600
Long-term debt	424,612	323,432
Common stock (100,000 shares)	460,000	460,000
Retained earnings	225,988	203,768
Total equity	$ 685,988	$ 663,768
Total liabilities and equity	$1,650,800	$1,468,800

Income Statements	2010	2009
Sales	$ 3,850,000	$ 3,432,000
Cost of goods sold	(3,250,000)	(2,864,000)
Other expenses	(430,300)	(340,000)
Depreciation	(20,000)	(18,900)
Total operating costs	$ 3,700,300	$ 3,222,900
EBIT	$ 149,700	$ 209,100
Interest expense	(76,000)	(62,500)
EBT	$ 73,700	$ 146,600
Taxes (40%)	(29,480)	(58,640)
Net income	$ 44,220	$ 87,960
EPS	$ 0.442	$ 0.880

Statement of Cash Flows (2010)

Operating Activities		
Net income	$ 44,220	
Other additions (sources of cash)		
Depreciation	20,000	
Increase in accounts payable	29,600	
Increase in accruals	4,000	
Subtractions (uses of cash)		
Increases in accounts receivable	(50,800)	
Increase in inventories	(120,800)	
Net cash flow from operations		$(73,780)
Long-Term Investing Activities		
Investment in fixed assets		$(36,000)

Financing Activities

Increase in notes payable	$ 25,000	
Increase in long-term debt	101,180	
Payment of cash dividends	(22,000)	
Net cash flow from financing		$104,180
Net reduction in cash account		$(5,600)
Cash at beginning of year		57,600
Cash at end of year		$ 52,000

Other Data	2010	2009
December 31 stock price	$ 6.00	$ 8.50
Number of shares	100,000	100,000
Dividends per share	$ 0.22	$ 0.22
Lease payments	$ 40,000	$ 40,000

Industry Average Data for 2010

Ratio	Industry Average
Current	2.7×
Quick	1.0×
Inventory turnover	6.0×
Days sales outstanding (DSO)	32.0 days
Fixed assets turnover	10.7×
Total assets turnover	2.6×
Debt ratio	50.0%
TIE	2.5×
Fixed charge coverage	2.1×
Net profit margin	3.5%
ROA	9.1 %
ROE	18.2%
Price/earnings	14.2×
Market/book	1.4×

Assume that you are Donna Jamison's assistant and that she has asked you to help her prepare a report that evaluates the company's financial condition. Answer the following questions:

a. What can you conclude about the company's financial condition from its statement of cash flows?

b. What is the purpose of financial ratio analysis, and what are the five major categories of ratios?

c. What are Computron's current and quick ratios? What do they tell you about the company's liquidity position?

d. What are Computron's inventory turnover, days sales outstanding, fixed assets turnover, and total assets turnover ratios? How does the firm's utilization of assets stack up against that of the industry?

e. What are the firm's debt, times-interest-earned, and fixed charge coverage ratios? How does Computron compare to the industry with respect to financial leverage? What conclusions can you draw from these ratios?

f. Calculate and discuss the firm's profitability ratios—that is, its net profit margin, return on assets (ROA), and return on equity (ROE).

g. Calculate Computron's market value ratios—that is, its price/earnings ratio and its market/book ratio. What do these ratios tell you about investors' opinions of the company?

h. Use the Du Pont equation to provide a summary and overview of Computron's financial condition. What are the firm's major strengths and weaknesses?

i. Use the following simplified 2010 balance sheet to show, in general terms, how an improvement in one of the ratios—say, the DSO—would affect the stock price. For example, if the company could improve its collection procedures and thereby lower the DSO from 38.1 days to 27.8 days, how would that change "ripple through" the following financial statements ($ thousands) and influence the stock price?

Accounts receivable	$ 402	Debt	$ 965
Other current assets	888		
Net fixed assets	361	Equity	686
Total assets	$1,651	Total liabilities and equity	$1,651

j. Although financial statement analysis can provide useful information about a company's operations and its financial condition, this type of analysis does have some potential problems and limitations, and it must be used with care and judgment. What are some problems and limitations?

COMPUTER-RELATED PROBLEM

Work the problem in this section only if you are using the computer problem spreadsheet.

Ratio Analysis   **7-18**   Use the computerized model in File C07 to solve this problem.

a. Refer to Problem 7-16. Suppose Cary Corporation is considering installing a new computer system that would provide tighter control of inventories, accounts receivable, and accounts payable. If the new system is installed, the following data are projected (rather than the data given in Problem 7-16) for the indicated balance sheet and income statement accounts:

Accounts receivable	$ 395,000
Inventories	$ 700,000
Other fixed assets	$ 150,000
Accounts and notes payable	$ 275,000
Accruals	$ 120,000
Cost of goods sold	$3,450,000
Administrative and selling expenses	$ 248,775
P/E ratio	6.0×

How do these changes affect the projected ratios and the comparison with the industry averages? (Note that any changes to the income statement will change the amount of retained earnings; therefore, the model is set up to calculate 2011 retained earnings as 2010 retained earnings plus net income minus dividends paid. The model also adjusts the cash balance so that the balance sheet balances.)

b. If the new computer system were even more efficient than Cary's management had estimated and thus caused the cost of goods sold to decrease by $125,000 from the projections in part (a), what effect would it have on the company's financial position?

c. If the new computer system were less efficient than Cary's management had estimated and caused the cost of goods sold to increase by $125,000 from the projections in part (a), what effect would it have on the company's financial position?

d. Change, one by one, the other items in part (a) to see how each change affects the ratio analysis. Then think about and write a paragraph describing how computer models such as this one can be used to help make better decisions about the purchase of such items as a new computer system.

CHAPTER 8

Financial Planning and Control

Benjamin Mays, who was a mentor to Martin Luther King Jr., once said: "The tragedy of life [failure] does not lie in not reaching your goal. The tragedy [failure] lies in having no goal to reach." Over time, this quote has been modified somewhat. Now the adage is: "People don't plan to fail, they fail to plan." Applied to business, this maxim would be: "Businesses don't plan to fail, they fail to forecast (plan)."

Indeed, planning is a critical ingredient in achieving success in business. Inadequate financial planning is the principal reason businesses fail. Statistics show that approximately 80 percent of business failures can be linked to poor financial planning. Of all the businesses that will begin operations this year, only about 10 percent will still be in business in 5 years. More than three-quarters of all new businesses fail in their first year. Why? Because the firms either don't have formal business plans or their plans are inadequate.

If you read literature about "how to succeed in business," you will discover a common mantra: "Develop a financial plan that can be used as a 'to-do list'

to guide the future of the firm." A financial plan for a business is comparable to a road map for a traveler; it is designed to help the firm stay on course in its attempt to achieve the goal of wealth maximization. Many companies have learned the hard way—either by going out of business or by suffering through difficult financial times—that a good financial plan is critical to survival.

As you read this chapter, think about businesses with which you might be familiar—perhaps you have read about them in business magazines or newspapers—that have suffered through financial adversity. In nearly every case, you will find that much of the difficulty could have been avoided if the firm had a viable financial plan and a control system in place. The *plan* gives the directions for operating the firm in the future, whereas the *control system* ensures the plan is implemented and modified to account for the dynamic environment the company faces. If you are considering starting your own business someday, *make sure you have a plan so that you have a clue as to which direction the business is headed—give your business a chance at success.*

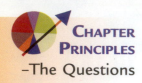

CHAPTER PRINCIPLES
–The Questions

After reading this chapter, you should be able to answer the following questions:

- Why are financial planning and financial control critical to the survival of a firm?
- What are pro forma financial statements? What is the purpose of constructing such statements?
- What is operating breakeven? How is breakeven analysis used in financial decision making?
- What is leverage? What types of leverage are used in financial analysis?
- How can a firm use knowledge of leverage in the financial forecasting and control process?
- Why is it important for a firm to construct a cash budget? What information is provided by a cash budget?

Chapter 7 focused on the use of financial statement analysis to evaluate the existing financial position of a firm. In this chapter, we will see how a financial manager can take advantage of some of the information provided by financial statement analysis to help with financial planning and control of the firm's future operations.

Well-run companies generally base their operating plans on a set of forecasted financial statements. The **financial planning** process begins with a sales forecast for the next few years. The assets required to meet the sales targets are then determined, and a decision is made concerning how to finance the required assets. At that point, income statements and balance sheets can be projected, and earnings and dividends per share, as well as the key ratios, can be forecasted.

Once the "base case" forecasted statements and ratios have been prepared, top managers want to know (1) how realistic the results are, (2) how to attain the results, and (3) how changes in operations would affect the forecasts. At this stage, which is called the **financial control** phase, the firm is concerned with implementing the financial plans (forecasts) and with managing the feedback and adjustment process needed to ensure that the goals of the firm are pursued appropriately.

The first part of this chapter is devoted to financial planning using projected financial statements, or forecasts. The second part focuses on financial control using budgeting and the analysis of leverage to determine how changes in operations affect financial forecasts.

financial planning
The projection of sales, income, and assets based on alternative production and marketing strategies, as well as the determination of the resources needed to achieve these projections.

financial control
The phase in which financial plans are implemented; the feedback and adjustment process required to ensure adherence to plans and modification of plans because of unforeseen changes.

sales forecast
A forecast of a firm's unit and dollar sales for some future period; generally based on recent sales trends plus forecasts of the economic prospects for the country, region, industry, and so forth.

SALES FORECASTS

Forecasting is an essential part of the planning process, and a **sales forecast** is the most important ingredient of financial forecasting. The sales forecast generally starts with a review of sales during the past 5 to 10 years, which can be expressed in a graph such as that shown in Figure 8-1. The first part of the graph shows 5 years of historical sales for Argile Textiles, the textile and clothing manufacturer we analyzed in Chapter 7. The graph could have covered 10 years of sales data, but Argile typically focuses on sales figures for the latest 5 years because the firm's studies have shown that future growth is more closely related to its recent history than to its distant past.

Argile had its ups and downs during the period from 2006 to 2010. In 2008, poor cotton production in the United States and diseased sheep in Australia resulted in low textile production, which caused the firm's sales to fall below the 2007 level. In 2009, a significant increase in both the supply of cotton and the supply of wool pushed Argile's sales up by more than 13 percent. Based on a regression analysis,

FIGURE 8-1   Argile Textiles: 2011 Sales Projection

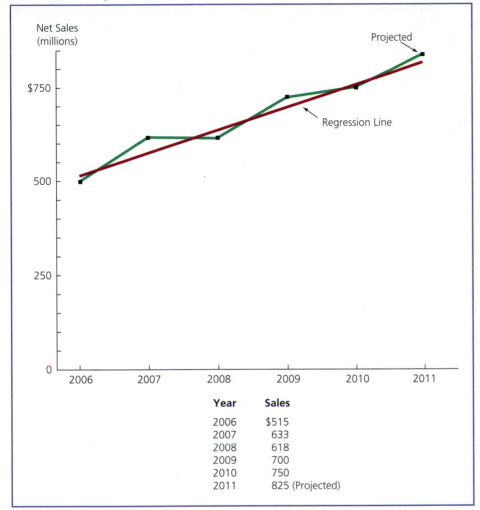

Year	Sales
2006	$515
2007	633
2008	618
2009	700
2010	750
2011	825 (Projected)

the company's forecasters determined that the average annual growth rate in sales over the past 5 years was nearly 10 percent.

To forecast sales growth for 2011, some of the factors that Argile considered included projections of expected economic activity, competitive conditions, and product development and distribution in both its current markets and the markets that it plans to enter in the future. Often, firms develop mathematical models such as regression equations to take into consideration these issues when forecasting future sales. Based on its historical sales trend, plans for new product and market introductions, and its forecast for the economy as a whole, the firm's planning committee projected a 10 percent growth rate for sales during 2011. That is, 2011 sales are expected to reach $825 million, an amount that is 10 percent higher than the company's 2010 sales of $750 million.

If the sales forecast is inaccurate, the consequences can be serious. First, if the market expands significantly *more* than Argile has anticipated, the company probably will not be able to meet demand. Customers will buy competitors' products, and Argile will lose market share, which could prove difficult to regain. Conversely, if the projections are overly optimistic, Argile could end up with too much plant, equipment, and inventory. This excess would translate into low turnover ratios, high costs for depreciation and storage, and, possibly, write-offs of obsolete or unusable inventory. The result would be a low rate of return on equity, which in turn would depress the company's stock price. If Argile had financed an unnecessary expansion with debt, its problems would, of course, be compounded. Recall from our analysis of the firm's 2010 financial statements in Chapter 7 that Argile's current financial position is considered poor. Thus, an accurate sales forecast is critical to the well-being of the firm.[1]

Self-Test Questions

How do past trends affect a sales forecast?

Briefly explain why an accurate sales forecast is critical to a firm's success.

PROJECTED (PRO FORMA) FINANCIAL STATEMENTS

Any forecast of financial requirements involves determining how much money the firm will (1) need during a given period, (2) generate internally during the same period (internally generated funds), and (3) have to raise externally by borrowing, issuing new stock, or both (externally generated funds). One method used to estimate the amount of funds that needs to be raised externally is to construct a *projected,* or *pro forma, balance sheet.*

The projected balance sheet method is straightforward. Simply project the asset requirements for the coming period, then project the liabilities and equity that will be generated under normal operations—that is, without additional external financing—and subtract the projected liabilities and equity from the required assets to estimate the *additional funds needed (AFN)* to support the level of forecasted operations. The steps in the procedure are explained next.

Step 1. Forecast the 2011 Income Statement

projected balance sheet method
A method of forecasting financial requirements based on forecasted financial statements.

The **projected balance sheet method** begins with a forecast of sales. Next, the income statement for the coming year is projected to obtain an initial estimate of the amount of retained earnings that the company will generate during the year. This step requires assumptions about the operating cost ratio, tax rate, interest charges, and dividend payments. In the simplest case, it is assumed that costs will increase at the same rate as sales; in more complicated situations, cost changes are forecasted separately. Whatever the case, the objective of this part of the analysis is to determine how much income the company will earn and then retain for reinvestment in the business during the period that is forecasted.

Table 8-1 shows Argile's actual 2010 income statement and the initial forecast of the 2011 income statement if the firm's operating costs change at the same rate as sales. Thus, to create the 2011 forecasted income statement, we assume that sales and variable operating costs will be 10 percent greater in 2011 than in 2010. In addition, it is assumed that Argile currently *operates at full capacity,* which means it

---

[1]A sales forecast is actually the *expected value of a probability distribution* with many possible levels of sales. Because any sales forecast is subject to a greater or lesser degree of uncertainty, for financial planning we are often just as interested in the degree of uncertainty inherent in the sales forecast (σ_{sales}) as we are in the expected value of sales. The concepts of probability distribution measures as they apply to corporate finance will be discussed in Chapter 11.

TABLE 8-1   Argile Textiles: Actual 2010 and Projected 2011 Income Statements ($ million, except per-share data)

	2010 Actual Results	Forecast Basis[a]	2011 Initial Forecast
Net sales	$ 750.0	× 1.10	$ 825.0
Cost of goods sold	(600.0)	× 1.10	(660.0)
Gross profit	$ 150.0		$ 165.0
Fixed operating costs except depreciation	(55.0)	× 1.10	(60.5)
Depreciation	(30.0)	× 1.10	(33.0)
Earnings before interest and taxes (EBIT)	$ 65.0		71.5
Interest	(20.0)	⟶	(20.0)[b]
Earnings before taxes (EBT)	$ 45.0		$ 51.5
Taxes (40%)	(18.0)		(20.6)
Net income	$ 27.0		$ 30.9
Common dividends	(14.0)		(15.4)[c]
Addition to retained earnings	$ 13.0		$ 15.5
Earnings per share	$ 2.45		$ 2.81
Dividends per share	$ 1.27		$ 1.40
Number of common shares (millions)	11.00		11.00

[a] × 1.10 indicates "times (1 + g)"; it is used for items that grow proportionally with sales.

[b] Indicates a 2010 figure carried over for the preliminary forecast. See discussion for explanation.

[c] Indicates a projected figure. See discussion for explanation.

will need to expand its plant capacity in 2011 to handle the additional operations. Thus, to achieve its forecasted growth in 2011, we assume that Argile will need to increase plant and equipment by 10 percent. This assumption is made so that we can simplify the forecasting process. Later in the chapter, we discuss adjustments that are needed when a firm operates at less than full capacity.

Because Argile is operating at full capacity, in Table 8-1, the 2011 forecasts of sales and *all* operating costs, including depreciation, are 10 percent greater than their 2010 levels. The result is that earnings before interest and taxes (EBIT) is forecasted to be $71.5 million in 2011, which is 10 percent higher than it was in 2010.

To complete the *initial* forecast of 2011 income, we assume that there is no change in the financing of the firm because, at this point, we don't know whether additional funds are needed to support the forecasted increase in sales. But it is apparent that the 2011 interest expense will change if the amount of debt (borrowing) that the firm needs to support the forecasted increase in operations changes. To forecast the 2011 dividends, we simply assume that the dividend per share (DPS) increases at the same rate as the expected growth. If the dividend is increased by 10 percent, then $DPS_{2011} = \$1.27 \times 1.10 = \$1.40$. Because there currently are 11 million shares of common stock outstanding, the total common dividends forecasted for 2011 would be $15.4 million = 11 million shares × $1.40 if the company does not issue new common stock. Like the interest expense amount, however, the amount of total dividends used to create this initial forecast will change if Argile needs to sell new stock to raise funds to support the new operations.

From the initial forecast of 2011 income, we can see that $15.5 million dollars initially is *expected* to be added to retained earnings in 2011. As it turns out, this addition to retained earnings represents the amount Argile is expected to invest in itself (internally generated funds) to support the increase in operations in 2011 if the conditions described here exist. So the next step is to determine what impact this level of internal investment will have on Argile's forecasted 2011 balance sheet.

Step 2. Forecast the 2011 Balance Sheet

If we assume the assets Argile had in place at the end of 2010 were just sufficient to support 2010 operations—that is, the firm operated at full capacity—then, for Argile's sales to increase in 2011, the company's assets also must grow. Because the company was operating at full capacity in 2010, *each* asset account must increase in 2011 for the firm to attain the higher forecasted sales level. In other words, more cash will be needed for transactions, higher sales will lead to higher receivables, additional inventory will have to be stocked, and new plant and equipment must be added to increase production.

Further, if Argile's assets increase, the firm's liabilities and equity also must increase, because the additional assets must be financed in some manner. Some liabilities will increase spontaneously due to normal business relationships. For example, as sales increase, so will Argile's purchases of raw materials, and these larger purchases will spontaneously lead to higher levels of accounts payable. Similarly, a higher level of operations will require more labor, and higher sales will result in higher taxable income. Therefore, both accrued wages and accrued taxes will increase. In general, current liabilities that change naturally with changes in sales provide **spontaneously generated funds,** which increase at the same rate as sales.

spontaneously generated funds
Funds that are obtained from routine business transactions.

Notes payable, long-term bonds, and common stock will not change spontaneously with sales. Rather, the projected levels of these accounts will depend on conscious financing decisions that have to be made once management determines how much external financing is needed to support the projected operations. Therefore, for the *initial* forecast, it is assumed that these account balances remain unchanged from their 2010 levels, because, at this point, management does not know whether or how much additional external financing is needed to support forecasted sales in 2011.

Table 8-2 contains Argile's 2010 actual balance sheet and an initial forecast of its 2011 balance sheet. The mechanics of the balance sheet forecast are similar to those used to develop the forecasted income statement. First, those balance sheet accounts that are expected to increase directly with sales are multiplied by 1.10 to determine the initial 2011 forecasts. For example, 2011 cash is projected to be $10 \times 1.10 = \$11$ million, accounts receivable are projected to be $\$90 \times 1.10 = \$99$ million, and so on. In our example, all assets increase with sales, so once the individual assets have been forecasted, they can be summed to complete the asset portion of the forecasted balance sheet.

Next, we project the spontaneously increasing liabilities (accounts payable and accruals). Then those liability and equity accounts whose values are the result of specific (conscious) management decisions—notes payable, long-term bonds, and common stock—*initially are forecasted* to remain at their 2010 levels. The reason the *nonspontaneous* sources of financing are not changed in the intitial forecast will be because at this stage it is not known whether, or how much, additional funding is needed to finance the required increased investment in assets. If it is determined that the firm needs to raise additional funds by borrowing from the bank, by issuing new bonds, by issuing new common stock, or by using some combination of these actions, the *nonspontaneous* sources of funds will be increased accordingly at that stage of the forecasting process. Thus, the amount of 2011 notes payable initially is set at $20 million, the long-term bond account is set at $152 million, and so forth. The forecasted 2011 level of retained earnings will equal the 2010 level plus the

TABLE 8-2   Argile Textiles: Actual 2010 and Projected 2011 Balance Sheets ($ million)

	2010 Actual Balances	Forecast Basis[a]	2011 Initial Forecast	Change
Cash	$ 10.0	× 1.10	$ 11.0	$ 1.0
Accounts receivable	90.0	× 1.10	99.0	9.0
Inventories	135.0	× 1.10	148.5	13.5
Total current assets	$235.0		$258.5	
Net plant and equipment	190.0	× 1.10	209.0	19.0
Total assets	$425.0		$467.5	$42.5
Accounts payable	$ 15.0	× 1.10	$ 16.5	$ 1.5
Accruals	30.0	× 1.10	33.0	3.0
Notes payable	20.0	⟶	20.0[b]	0.0
Total current liabilities	$ 65.0		$ 69.5	
Long-term bonds	152.0	⟶	152.0[b]	0.0
Total liabilities	$217.0		$221.5	
Common stock	66.0	⟶	66.0[b]	0.0
Retained earnings	142.0	+$15.5[d]	157.5	15.5
Total owners' equity	$208.0		$223.5	
Total liabilities and equity	$425.0		$445.0	$20.0
Additional funds needed (AFN)			$ 22.5[c]	$22.5

[a] × 1.10 indicates "times $(1 + g)$"; it is used for items that grow proportionally with sales.

[b] Indicates a 2010 figure carried over for the initial forecast.

[c] The additional funds needed (AFN) is computed by subtracting the amount of total liabilities and equity from the amount of total assets.

[d] The $15.5 million represents the "addition to retained earnings" from the 2011 projected income statement given in Table 8-1.

forecasted addition to retained earnings, which was computed as $15.5 million in the projected income statement we created in Step 1 (Table 8-1). That is, the amount in retained earnings is initially forecast to be $157.5 million ($142.0 million balance at the end of 2010 plus the $15.5 million addition in 2011).

The forecast of total assets in Table 8-2 is $467.5 million, which indicates that Argile must add $42.5 million of new assets (compared to 2010 assets, which equaled $425 million) to support the higher sales level expected in 2011. According to the *initial* forecast of the 2011 balance sheet, however, the total liabilities and equity sum to only $445.0 million; this amount represents an increase of only $20 million from the 2010 amount of $425 million. So the amount of assets needed to support the forecasted growth is $22.5 million = $467.5 million − $445.0 million greater than the amount of funding (total liabilities and equity) that will be available if the firm does not raise additional funds through nonspontaneous fincancing sources. This indicates that $22.5 million of the forecasted increase in total assets will not be financed by liabilities that spontaneously increase with sales (accounts payable and accruals) or by an increase in retained earnings. Argile can raise the extra $22.5 million, which we designate **additional funds needed (AFN),** by borrowing from the bank as notes payable, by issuing long-term bonds, by selling new common stock, or by taking some combination of these actions.

additional funds needed (AFN)
Funds that a firm must raise externally through borrowing or by selling new stock.

The initial forecast of Argile's financial statements shows that (1) higher sales must be supported by higher asset levels, (2) some of the asset increases can be financed by spontaneous increases in accounts payable and accruals and by retained earnings, and (3) any shortfall must be financed from external sources, either by borrowing or by selling new stock.

Step 3. Raise the Additional Funds Needed (AFN)

Argile's financial manager will base the decision of exactly how to raise the $22.5 million in additional funds needed on several factors, including the firm's ability to handle more debt, conditions in the financial markets, and restrictions imposed by existing debt agreements. The decisions concerning how to best finance the firm are discussed in Chapter 14. At this point, it is important to understand that, regardless of how Argile raises the $22.5 million of AFN, the initial forecasts of both the income statement and the balance sheet will be affected. If Argile takes on new debt, its *total* interest expenses will increase. If the firm sells additional shares of common stock, its *total* dividend payments will increase if the *same dividend per share* is paid to all common stockholders. Each of these changes, which we term *financing feedbacks*, will affect the amount of additional retained earnings that was originally forecasted, which in turn will affect the amount of additional funds needed that was computed in Step 2.

Recall from our ratio analysis in Chapter 7 that Argile has a below-average debt position. Consequently, Argile has decided that any additional funds needed to support future operations will be raised mainly by issuing new common stock. Following this financing policy should help improve Argile's debt position as well as its overall profitability.

Step 4. Adjust Forecasts for Financing Feedbacks

financing feedbacks
The effects on the income statement and balance sheet of actions taken to finance forecasted increases in assets.

As mentioned in Step 3, one complexity that arises in financial forecasting relates to **financing feedbacks.** The external funds raised to pay for new assets create additional financing expenses that must be reflected in the income statement, which lowers the amount that was initially forecasted as the addition to retained earnings. As a result, even more external funds are needed to make up for the lower amount added to retained earnings. In other words, if Argile raised the $22.5 million of AFN by issuing new debt and new common stock, it would find that both the interest expense and the total dividend payments would be higher than the amounts shown in the income statement that was initially forecasted in Step 1 (Table 8-1). Consequently, after adjusting for the higher interest and dividend payments, the forecasted addition to retained earnings would be lower than the initial forecast of $15.5 million. Because the retained earnings will be lower than projected, a financing shortfall will exist even after the original AFN of $22.5 million is considered. In other words, Argile must raise more than $22.5 million to account for the financing feedbacks that affect the amount of internal financing that is expected to be generated from the increase in its operations. To determine the amount of external financing actually needed, the initial forecasts of both the income statement (Step 1) and the balance sheet (Step 2) have to be adjusted to reflect the effects of raising the additional external financing. This process has to be repeated until AFN = 0 in Table 8-2, which means that Step 1 and Step 2 might have to be repeated several times to fully account for the financing feedbacks.

Table 8-3 contains the adjusted 2011 preliminary forecasts for Argile's income statement and balance sheet after all of the financing effects are considered.

TABLE 8-3 Argile Textiles: 2011 Adjusted Forecast of Financial Statements ($ million)

	Initial Forecast	Adjusted Forecast	Financing Adjustment
Income Statement[a]			
Earnings before interest and taxes (EBIT)	$ 71.5	$ 71.5	
Interest	(20.0)	(20.7)	(0.7)
Earnings before taxes (EBT)	$ 51.5	$ 50.8	(0.7)
Taxes (40%)	(20.6)	(20.3)	0.3
Net income	$ 30.9	$ 30.5	(0.4)
Common dividends	(15.4)	(16.6)	1.1
Addition to retained earnings	$ 15.5	$ 14.1	(1.4)[b]
Earnings per share	$ 2.81	$ 2.61	
Dividends per share	$ 1.40	$ 1.40	
Number of common shares (millions)	11.00	11.67	
Balance Sheet[a]			
Total assets	$467.5	$467.5	
Accounts payable	$ 16.5	$ 16.5	
Accruals	33.0	33.0	
Notes payable	$ 20.0	$ 23.6	3.6
Total current liabilities	$ 69.5	$ 73.1	
Long-term bonds	$152.0	$156.8	4.8
Total liabilities	$221.5	$229.9	
Common stock	66.0	81.5	15.5
Retained earnings	$157.5	$156.1	(1.4)[b]
Total owners' equity	$223.5	$237.6	
Total liabilities and equity	$445.0	$467.5	
Additional funds needed (AFN)	$ 22.5	$ 0.0	22.5[c]

Financing Adjustment column bracket for Notes payable (3.6), Long-term bonds (4.8), and Common stock (15.5): AFN = 23.9

[a] Because the operating section of the income statement and the asset section of the balance sheet are not affected by financing feedbacks, these sections are not shown in the table.

[b] The financing adjustment for the addition to retained earnings in the income statement is the same as the financing adjustment for retained earnings in the balance sheet.

[c] The total AFN (or external financing needs) equals $22.5 million plus the $1.4 million decrease in retained earnings from the initial forecast. Thus, the total external funds needed equal $23.9 million—$3.6 million will be from new bank notes, $4.8 million will come from issuing new bonds, and the remaining $15.5 million will be raised by issuing new common stock.

To generate the adjusted forecasts, it is assumed that of the total external funds needed, 65 percent will be raised by selling new common stock at $20 per share, 15 percent will be borrowed from the bank at an interest rate of 7 percent, and 20 percent will be raised by selling long-term bonds with a coupon interest of 10 percent. Under these conditions, Argile actually needs $23.9 million to support the forecasted increase in operations, not the $22.5 million contained in the initial forecast. The additional $1.4 million is required because the added amounts of debt and common stock will increase the firm's interest and dividend payments, which in turn will decrease the contribution to retained earnings by $1.4 million.[2]

---

[2] Appendix 8A at the end of the chapter provides a more detailed description of the iterations required to generate the final forecasts.

TABLE 8-4 Argile Textiles: Key Ratios			
	2010	**Adjusted Preliminary 2011**	**Industry Average**
Current ratio	3.6×	3.5×	4.1×
Inventory turnover	4.4×	5.6	7.4×
Days sales outstanding	43.2 days	43.2 days	32.1 days
Total assets turnover	1.8×	1.8×	2.1×
Debt ratio	51.1%	49.2%	42.0%
Times interest earned	3.3×	3.5×	6.5×
Net profit margin	3.6%	3.7%	4.9%
Return on assets	6.4%	6.5%	11.5%
Return on equity	13.0%	12.8%	17.7%

Analysis of the Forecast

The 2011 forecast developed here represents a *preliminary* forecast, because we have completed only the first stage of the total forecasting process. Next, we must analyze the projected financial statements to determine whether the forecast meets the firm's financial targets. If the statements do not meet the targets, then we must modify elements of the forecast.

Table 8-4 shows Argile's 2010 ratios as they were reported in Chapter 7 (in Table 7-6), plus the projected 2011 ratios based on the preliminary forecast and the industry average ratios. As noted in Chapter 7, the firm's financial condition at the close of 2010 was relatively weak, with many ratios being well below the industry averages. The preliminary final forecast for 2011 (after financing feedbacks are considered), which assumes that Argile's past practices will continue into the future, shows an improved debt position. The overall financial position is still somewhat weak, however, and this condition will persist unless management takes action to improve things.

Argile's management actually plans to take steps to improve its financial condition. The plans are to (1) close down certain operations, (2) modify the credit policy to reduce the collection period for receivables, and (3) better manage inventory so that products are turned over more often. These proposed operational changes will affect both the income statement and the balance sheet, so we must revise the preliminary forecast to reflect the effects of such changes. When this process is complete, management will have its final forecast. To keep things simple, we do not show the final forecast here. Instead, for the remaining discussions, we assume that the preliminary forecast after considering financing feedbacks is not substantially different and use it as the final forecast for Argile's 2011 operations.

As we have shown, forecasting is an iterative process, both in the way that the financial statements are generated and in the way that the financial plan is developed. For planning purposes, the financial staff develops a preliminary forecast based on a continuation of past policies and trends. This effort provides the executives with a starting point, or "straw man" forecast. Next, the staff members modify the model to see how alternative operating plans would affect the firm's earnings and financial condition. This step results in a revised forecast.

Self-Test Questions

What is the AFN, and how do you use the projected balance sheet method to estimate it?

What is a financing feedback, and how do financing feedbacks affect the estimate of AFN?

Why must the forecasting process be iterative?

OTHER CONSIDERATIONS IN FORECASTING

We have presented a simple method for constructing pro forma financial statements under rather restrictive conditions. In this section, we describe some other conditions that should be considered when creating forecasts.

Excess Capacity

The construction of Argile's 2011 forecasts was based on the assumption that the firm operated at full capacity in 2010, so any increase in sales would require additional assets, especially plant and equipment. If Argile did *not* operate at full capacity in 2010, then plant and equipment would not have to be increased unless the additional sales (operations) forecasted in 2011 exceeded the unused capacity of the existing assets. For example, if Argile actually utilized only 75 percent of its fixed assets' capacity to produce 2010 sales of $750 million, then

$$\$750.0 \text{ million} = 0.75 \times (\text{Plant capacity})$$

$$\text{Plant capacity} = \frac{\$750 \text{ million}}{0.75} = \$1,000 \text{ million}$$

In this case, Argile could increase sales to $1 billion, or by one-third of 2010 sales, before full capacity is reached and plant and equipment would have to be increased. In general, we can use the following equation to compute the sales capacity of the firm if we know what percentage of assets is utilized to produce a particular level of sales:

8-1

$$\text{Full capacity sales} = \frac{\text{Sales level}}{(\text{Percent of capacity used to generate sales level})}$$

If Argile does not have to expand its plant and equipment, net fixed assets would remain at the 2010 level of $190 million and the amount of AFN actually would be negative, which means that the amount of internally generated funds would be more than sufficient to support (finance) the forecasted 10 percent increase in sales in 2011. Argile could use this excess to increase the dividend it pays to stockholders by more than 50 percent.

In addition to the excess capacity of fixed assets, the firm could have excess amounts of other assets that might be used to support increases in operations. For instance, in Chapter 7, we concluded that perhaps Argile's inventory level at the end of 2010 was higher than it should have been. If so, then some increase in 2011 forecasted sales might be absorbed by drawing down the higher than normal inventory, and production would not have to be increased until inventory levels reach normal levels—a step that requires no additional financing.

In general, *excess capacity means less external financing is required to support increases in operations than would be needed if the firm previously operated at full capacity.*

Economies of Scale

Economies of scale exist with the use of many types of assets. When such economies occur, a firm's variable cost of goods sold ratio is likely to change as the size of the firm changes (either increases or decreases) substantially. Currently, Argile's variable cost ratio is 80 percent of sales; this ratio might decrease to 78 percent of sales if operations increase significantly. If everything else remains the same, *changes in the variable cost ratio affect the addition to retained earnings, which in turn affects the amount of AFN.*

Lumpy Assets

lumpy assets
Assets that cannot be acquired in small increments; instead, they must be obtained in large, discrete amounts.

In many industries, technological considerations dictate that if a firm is to be competitive, it must add fixed assets in large, discrete units; such assets often are referred to as **lumpy assets.** For example, in the paper industry, strong economies of scale exist in basic paper mill equipment. As a result, when a paper company expands capacity, it must do so in large, lumpy increments. *Lumpy assets primarily affect the turnover of fixed assets and, consequently, the financial requirements associated with expansion of operations.* For instance, if Argile needed an additional $25 million (rather than $19 million) in fixed assets to increase its operations by 10 percent, the AFN would be greater. With *lumpy assets*, a small projected increase in sales could potentially mandate a significant increase in plant and equipment, which would lead to a very large financial requirement.

Self-Test Questions

Discuss three factors that might cause "spontaneous" assets and liabilities to change at a different rate than sales.

Suppose that a firm that currently operates at 75 percent capacity generates $150 million in sales. What is the firm's level of full capacity sales?   (Answer: $200 million)

FINANCIAL CONTROL—BUDGETING AND LEVERAGE

In the previous sections, we focused on financial forecasting, emphasizing how growth in sales requires additional investment in assets, which in turn generally requires the firm to raise new funds externally. In the next few sections, we consider the planning and control systems used by financial managers when implementing the forecasts. First, we look at the relationships that exist between sales volume and profitability under different operating conditions. These relationships provide information that managers use to plan for changes in the firm's level of operations, financing needs, and profitability. Later, we examine the control phase of the planning and control process. A good control system is essential for two reasons: (1) to ensure that plans are executed properly and (2) to facilitate a timely modification of plans if the assumptions upon which the initial plans are based turn out to be inaccurate.

The planning process can be enhanced by examining the effects of changing operations on the firm's profitability, both from the standpoint of profits from operations and from the standpoint of profitability after financing effects are considered.

Self-Test Question

How can a good financial control system enhance the financial planning process?

BREAKEVEN ANALYSIS

The relationship between sales volume and operating profitability is explored in cost-volume-profit planning, or breakeven analysis. **Breakeven analysis** is a method of determining the point at which sales will just cover operating costs—that is, the point at which the firm's operations will break even. It also shows the magnitude of the firm's operating profits or losses if sales exceed or fall below that point.

Breakeven analysis is important in the planning and control process because the cost-volume-profit relationship can be influenced greatly by the firm's investment in fixed assets. A sufficient volume of sales must be anticipated and achieved if the firm hopes to cover its fixed and variable costs, or else the firm will incur losses from operations. In other words, if a firm is to avoid accounting losses, its sales must cover all costs—those that vary directly with production as well as those that remain constant even when production levels change. Costs that vary directly with the level of production are the firm's **variable operating costs,** which generally include the labor and materials needed to produce and sell the product. **Fixed operating costs** generally include costs such as depreciation, rent, and insurance expenses that are incurred regardless of the firm's production level.

The breakeven analysis presented here deals only with the upper portion of the income statement—the portion from sales to net operating income (NOI), also known as earnings before interest and taxes (EBIT). This area is generally referred to as the *operating section* of the income statement. We emphasize the operating section, which contains the revenues and expenses associated with normal production operations of the firm because, at this point, we are concerned with the firm's *operating plan* and how changes in sales affect its general operating results.

Table 8-5 gives the operating section of Argile's forecasted 2011 income statement, which was shown in Table 8-3. In the ensuing discussion, we assume that all of Argile's products sell for $27.50 each and the variable cost of goods sold per unit is $22.00, which is 80 percent of the selling price.

Breakeven Graph

Table 8-5 shows Argile's net operating income if the company manufactures and sells 30 million units of the product during the year. But what if Argile doesn't sell 30 million products? Certainly, the firm's net operating income will be something other than $71.5 million.

Figure 8-2 shows Argile's total operating costs (panel A) and total revenues (panel B) at various levels of sales, beginning with $0. According to the information

breakeven analysis
An analytical technique for studying the relationship among sales revenues, operating costs, and profits.

variable operating costs
Operating costs that vary with production; variable costs are $0 when there is no production and high when production is high.

fixed operating costs
Operating costs that remain the same (constant) regardless of the level of production.

TABLE 8-5 Argile Textiles: 2011 Forecasted Operating Income ($ million)	
Sales (S)	$ 825.0
Variable cost of goods sold (VC)	(660.0)
Gross profit (GP)	165.0
Fixed operating costs (F)	(93.5)
Net operating income (NOI = EBIT)	$ 71.5

Notes:

Selling price per unit = $27.50

Sales in units = $825 million/$27.50 = 30 million units

Variable costs per unit = $660.0/30.0 = $22.00

Fixed operating costs = $93.5 million, which includes $33.0 million depreciation and $60.5 million in other fixed costs, such as rent, insurance, and general office expenses.

given in Table 8-5, Argile has fixed costs, which include depreciation, rent, insurance, and so on, equal to $93.5 million. Because this amount must be paid even if the firm produces and sells nothing, the $93.5 million fixed cost is represented by a horizontal line in panel A of Figure 8-2.

Each unit that Argile sells costs $22 to produce in addition to the fixed operating costs—that is, the variable cost per unit is $22. Thus, for each unit of product that Argile sells, the total operating costs increase by $22. This means that the total operating costs at any level of sales can be computed as follows:

$$\text{Total operating costs} = \text{Total fixed operating costs} + \text{Total variable operating costs}$$
$$\text{TOC} \quad = \quad \text{F} \quad + \quad \text{VC}$$
$$= \quad \text{F} \quad + \quad (\text{V} \times \text{Q})$$

where F = total fixed operating costs, VC = total variable operating costs, V = variable cost per unit, and Q = the number of units sold. If we assume that total

FIGURE 8-2   Argile Textiles: Total Operating Costs and Sales Revenues

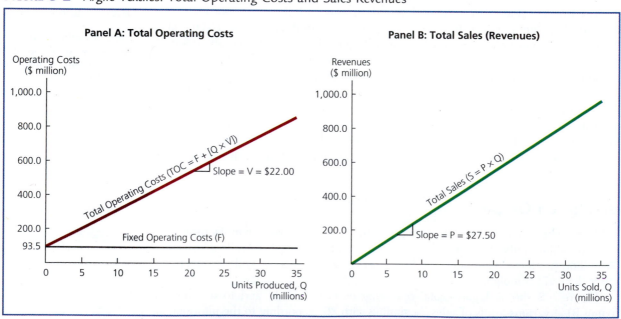

fixed costs (F) and the variable cost *per unit* (V) are constant, the total operating costs (TOC) change only when the number of units produced changes. If the firm produces one additional unit of the product, then TOC increases by $22, which is the variable cost per unit.

From the previous discussion, we know that Argile's operating costs will equal at least $93.5 million, which is the fixed cost associated with operations. We also know that total operating costs will increase by the variable cost that is directly associated with the production of each unit that Argile sells, which equals $22 per unit. As a result, the line in panel A of Figure 8-2 that shows Argile's total operating costs intersects the vertical axis at $93.5 million, which is the fixed operating cost, and it has a slope equal to $22, which is the amount by which total operating costs increase for each additional unit that is produced (the variable cost per unit, V).

Panel B of Figure 8-2 shows Argile's revenues at various levels of sales. If Argile sells nothing, its revenues will be $0. But *for each unit the firms sells,* revenues increase by $27.50, which is the selling price per unit. Therefore, the line shown in panel B of Figure 8-2 intersects the vertical axis at $0, which represents Argile's revenues if no products are sold, and it has a slope equal to $27.50, which is the amount by which revenues increase for each additional unit that is sold (the selling price per unit, P).

Figure 8-3 shows what happens when we combine the graphs in panel A and panel B of Figure 8-2. In Figure 8-3, the operating costs and sales revenues for various levels of sales are shown on the same graph. The point at which the total revenue line intersects the total cost line is the **breakeven point.** It marks the point at which the revenues generated from *sales just cover the total operating costs* of the firm. Notice that prior to the breakeven point, the total cost line is above the total revenue line, which indicates that Argile will suffer operating losses because the total costs cannot be covered by the sales revenues. After the breakeven point, the total revenue line is above the total cost line because

breakeven point
The level of production and sales where operating income is $0. At this point, revenues from sales just equal total operating costs.

FIGURE 8-3   Argile Textiles: Breakeven Chart

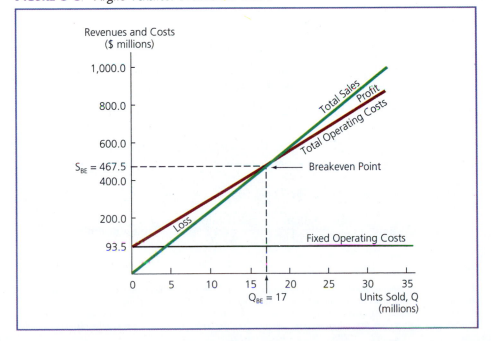

revenues are more than sufficient to cover total operating costs, so Argile will realize operating profits.[3]

Breakeven Computation

Figure 8-3 shows that Argile must sell 17 million units to reach the breakeven point. If the firm sells 17 million products, it will generate $467.5 million = 17 million × $27.50 in sales revenues, which will be just enough to cover the $467.5 million total operating costs—$93.5 million fixed costs and $374.0 million variable costs (17 million units × $22.00 per unit). If we do not have a graph like Figure 8-3, how can we determine the breakeven point? Actually, the procedure is quite simple. Remember, the breakeven point is where the revenues generated from sales just cover the total operating costs, which include both the costs directly attributable to producing each unit and the costs that remain constant no matter the production level. As long as the selling price associated with each unit (the slope of the total revenue line) is greater than the variable operating cost of each unit (the slope of the total operating cost line), each unit sold will generate revenues that help cover the fixed operating costs. For Argile, this contribution (termed the *contribution margin*) is $5.50, which is the difference between the $27.50 selling price and the $22.00 variable cost of each unit. Thus, to compute the breakeven point for Argile, we must determine how many units need to be sold to cover the fixed operating cost of $93.5 million if each unit has a contribution margin equal to $5.50. To do so, simply divide the $93.5 million fixed cost by the $5.50 contribution margin and you will discover that the breakeven point is 17 million units, which equates to $467.5 million in sales revenues.

More formally, we can find the breakeven point by setting the total revenues equal to the total operating costs so that net operating income (NOI) is $0. In equation form, NOI = 0 if

$$\underset{\text{revenues}}{\text{Sales}} = \underset{\text{costs}}{\text{Total operating}} = \underset{\text{costs}}{\text{Total variable}} + \underset{\text{costs}}{\text{Total fixed}}$$

$$(P \times Q) = TOC = (V \times Q) + F$$

where P is the sales price per unit, Q is the number of units produced and sold, V is the variable operating cost per unit, and F is the total fixed operating costs. Solving for the quantity, Q, produces a formula that we can use to find the number of units that need to be sold to achieve operating breakeven.

8-2

$$Q_{\text{OpBE}} = \frac{F}{\text{Contribution margin}} = \frac{F}{P - V}$$

Thus, the breakeven point for Argile is:

$$Q_{\text{OpBE}} = \frac{\$93.5 \text{ million}}{\$27.50 - \$22.00} = \frac{\$93.5 \text{ million}}{\$5.50} = 17 \text{ million units}$$

---

[3]In Figure 8-2, we assume that the operating costs can be divided into two distinct groups—fixed costs and variable costs. In reality, some costs are considered semivariable (or semifixed). These costs remain fixed for a certain range of operations but change if operations either exceed or fall short of this range. For the analysis that follows, we have assumed that the firm has no semivariable costs, so the operating costs can be classified as either fixed or variable.

In the remainder of the chapter, we will omit the word *million* in the computations, including it only in the final answer.

From Equation 8-2, we can see that the breakeven point is lower (higher) if the numerator is lower (higher) or if the denominator is higher (lower). Therefore, all else being equal, one firm will have a *lower breakeven* point than another firm if its *fixed costs are lower,* if the *selling price* of its product *is higher,* if its *variable operating cost per unit is lower,* or if some combination of these conditions exists. For instance, if Argile could increase the sales price per unit from $27.50 to $28.25 without affecting either its fixed operating costs ($93.5 million) or its variable cost per unit ($22), then its breakeven point would fall to approximately 15 million units.

The breakeven point can also be stated in terms of the total sales revenues needed to cover total operating costs. At this point, we just need to multiply the sales price per unit by the breakeven quantity we found using Equation 8-2, which yields $467.5 million for Argile. Alternatively, we can restate the contribution margin as a percentage of the sales price per unit (this percentage is called the gross profit margin), and then apply the following equation:

$$S_{OpBE} = \frac{F}{\text{Gross profit margin}} = \frac{F}{1 - \left(\dfrac{V}{P}\right)}$$

8-3

Solving Equation 8-3 for Argile, the breakeven point based on dollar sales is

$$S_{OpBE} = \frac{\$93.5}{1 - \left(\dfrac{\$22.00}{\$27.50}\right)} = \frac{\$93.5}{1 - 0.80} = \frac{\$93.5}{0.20} = \$467.5 \text{ million}$$

Equation 8-3 shows that 20¢ of every $1 of sales goes to cover the fixed operating costs, so $467.5 million worth of the product must be sold to break even.

Breakeven analysis based on dollar sales rather than on units of output is useful in determining the breakeven volume for a firm that sells many products at varying prices. This analysis requires only that total sales, total fixed costs, and total variable costs at a given level of operations are known.

Using Breakeven Analysis

Breakeven analysis can shed light on four important types of business decisions:

1. When making new product decisions, breakeven analysis can help determine how large the sales of a new product must be for the firm to achieve profitability.

2. Breakeven analysis can be used to study the effects of a general expansion in the level of the firm's operations. An expansion would cause the levels of both fixed and variable costs to rise, but it also would increase expected sales.

3. When considering modernization and automation projects, where the fixed investment in equipment is increased in an effort to lower the firm's variable costs (and particularly the cost of labor), breakeven analysis can help management analyze the consequences of purchasing these projects.

4. Breakeven analysis can help a firm determine the riskiness of its operations. A firm that operates just above its breakeven point is considered riskier than a firm that operates well above its breakeven point. Firms that operate closer

to (well above) their breakeven points have less (greater) cushion to cover fixed operating costs when sales are below normal.

You must take care when using breakeven analysis, however. To apply breakeven analysis as we have discussed it here requires that the sales price *per unit,* the variable cost *per unit,* and the *total* fixed operating costs do not change with the level of the firm's production and sales. Within a narrow range of production and sales, this assumption probably is not a major issue. But what if the firm expects to produce a much greater (or fewer) number of products than normal? What if it plans to expand its plant and equipment significantly? Will the numbers change? Most likely, the answer is yes.

Given these facts, use of a single breakeven chart like the one presented in Figure 8-3 is impractical. Such a chart provides useful information, but it cannot deal with changes in the price of the product, changes in the variable cost rates, or changes in fixed cost levels. This shortcoming suggests that we need a more flexible type of analysis. Today, such analysis is provided by computer simulation. Functions such as those expressed in Equations 8-2 and 8-3 (or more complicated versions of these equations) can be put into a spreadsheet or similarly modeled with other computer software, and variables such as sales price (P), the variable cost per unit (V), and the level of fixed costs (F) can then be changed. The model can instantaneously produce new versions of Figure 8-3, or a whole set of such graphs, to show what the breakeven point would be under different production setups and price-cost situations.

Self-Test Questions

Give the equations used to calculate the breakeven point in units and in dollar sales.

Provide some examples of business decisions for which breakeven analysis might prove useful.

Identify some limitations to the use of a single breakeven chart.

Suppose that Nixon Hardware sells screwdrivers for $12 each. The screwdrivers cost $9.60 to produce, and Nixon's fixed operating costs equal $144,000. What is Nixon's operating breakeven point?   (Answer: Q_{OpBE} = 60,000; S_{OpBE} = $720,000)

LEVERAGE

If a firm has high fixed costs, a small decrease in sales might lead to a large decrease in profits and ROE. Thus, all else being equal, higher fixed costs are associated with a greater risk that the firm will not generate expected profits if sales fall short of the forecasted level. For this reason, the financial manager should understand how the presence of fixed costs can affect the firm's expected profits. Because fixed costs create leverage, we generally evaluate the effect of fixed costs on expected profits by analyzing the *degree of leverage* that exists in a firm.

In physics, leverage implies the use of a lever to raise a heavy object with a small amount of force. In politics, people who have leverage can accomplish a great deal with their smallest word or action. *In business terminology, a high degree of leverage, other things held constant, means that a relatively small change in sales will result in a large change in expected profits.* In this section, we will discuss the two types of leverage that exist in a firm—leverage associated with the existence of fixed operating costs *(operating leverage)* and leverage associated with fixed financing costs *(financial leverage).*

Operating Leverage

If a high percentage of a firm's total operating costs are fixed, the firm is said to have a high degree of **operating leverage.** Operating leverage arises because the firm has fixed *operating costs* that must be covered no matter its level of production and sales. The effect of the leverage, however, depends on the actual operating level of the firm.

For example, Argile has $93.5 million in fixed operating costs, which are covered rather easily because the firm expects to sell 30 million products. Thus, Argile is well above its operating breakeven point of 17 million units. What would happen to operating income if Argile sold more or less than forecasted? To answer this question, we must determine the *degree of operating leverage* that is associated with Argile's 2011 forecasted operations.

Operating leverage can be defined more precisely in terms of how a given change in sales volume affects operating income (NOI). To measure the effect of a change in sales volume on NOI, we calculate the **degree of operating leverage (DOL).** This value is defined as the percentage change in NOI associated with a given percentage change in sales, and it can be computed as follows, where the variables are as previously defined:[4]

> **operating leverage**
> The existence of fixed operating costs such that a change in sales will produce a larger change in operating income (EBIT).

> **degree of operating leverage (DOL)**
> The percentage change in NOI (or EBIT) associated with a given percentage change in sales.

$$\text{DOL} = \frac{\text{Gross profit}}{\text{NOI}} = \frac{(Q \times P) - (Q \times V)}{(Q \times P) - (Q \times V) - F} = \frac{S - VC}{S - VC - F}$$

8-4

In effect, the DOL is an index number that measures the effect of a change in sales on operating income.

Using the information shown in Table 8-5, we find that the DOL for Argile at 30 million units of sales is:

$$\text{DOL}_{Q=30} = \frac{\$165}{\$71.5} = 2.31\times$$

Taken literally, Argile's DOL of 2.31 indicates that if sales change by 1 percent—from the $825 million that is forecasted—operating income (NOI) will change by 2.31 percent. Suppose that Argile actually sells 33 million units of its product, which is 10 percent greater than the 30 million units that we forecasted earlier. At this level of sales, by how much will Argile's NOI differ from the forecasted amount of $71.5 million? Because DOL = 2.31, the actual NOI should be 23.1% = 10% × 2.31 greater than the amount that was forecasted. Table 8-6 compares the operating incomes that would be generated at both 30 million units of sales and 33 million units of sales. As the numbers in the table show, because Argile's fixed operating costs of $93.5 million do not change with the level of sales, a 10 percent increase in forecasted sales will result in a 23.1 percent increase in net operating income. This shows the magnification effect of operating leverage.

[4]Recall that the net operating income (NOI) is equivalent to the earnings before interest and taxes (EBIT).

TABLE 8-6 Argile Textiles: Operating Income at Sales Levels of 30 Million Units and 33 Million Units ($ million)

	2011 Forecasted Operations	Sales with 10% Increase	Unit Change	Percent Change
Sales in units (millions) (Q)	30.0	33.0	3.0	+10.0%
Sales revenues (Q × $27.50)	$ 825.0	$ 907.5	$ 82.5	+10.0%
Variable cost of goods sold (Q × $22)	(660.0)	(726.0)	(66.0)	+10.0%
Gross profit	165.0	181.5	16.5	+10.0%
Fixed operating costs	(93.5)	(93.5)	(0.0)	0.0%
Net operating income (EBIT)	$ 71.5	$ 88.0	$ 16.5	+23.1%

The value of DOL indicates the *change* in operating income that results from a *change* in the level of operations, regardless of whether the change is an increase or a decrease. Thus, if Argile sells 10 percent fewer products than expected, its NOI would be 23.1 percent lower that the original forecast. It should be apparent that the greater the DOL, the greater the effect of a change in operations on EBIT, whether the change is an increase or a decrease. Although we discuss the concept of risk in detail later in the book, at this point we note that *risk* is synonomous with *variability*. Thus, because a higher DOL indicates greater variability in NOI, we generally consider firms with higher DOLs to have riskier operations than firms with lower DOLs.

The DOL value found by using Equation 8-4 is the degree of operating leverage at a specific level of sales. For Argile, that sales level is 30 million units, or $825 million. The DOL value would differ if the level of operations differed. For example, if Argile's operating cost structure was the same, but sales were forecasted to be only 20 million units, the DOL would be much higher than 2.31:

$$\text{DOL}_{Q=20} = \frac{20(\$27.50 - \$22.00)}{20(\$27.50 - \$22.00) - \$93.5} = \frac{\$110}{\$16.5} = 6.67\times$$

The DOL at 20 million units of sales is nearly three times greater than the DOL at 30 million units. Thus, from a base sales of 20 million units, a 10 percent decrease in sales—that is, from 20 million to 18 million units—would result in a $66.7\% = 6.67 \times 10\%$ decrease in operating income—from $16.5 million to $5.5 million $= (\$16.5$ million$) \times (1 - 0.667)$. Clearly, when Argile's operations are closer to its operating breakeven point of 17 million units, the company's degree of operating leverage is higher. Thus, we can conclude that the firm's operations are riskier the closer its operations are to the breakeven point.

In general, given the same operating cost structure, if a firm's level of operations decreases, its DOL increases. Stated differently, *the closer a firm is to its operating breakeven point, the greater is its degree of operating leverage.* This situation occurs because, as Figure 8-3 indicates, the closer a firm is to its operating breakeven point, the more likely it is to incur an operating loss due to a decrease in sales; the buffer in operating income that exists to absorb a decrease in sales and still be able to cover the fixed operating costs is relatively small. Similarly, at the same level of production and sales, a firm's degree of operating leverage will be higher if the contribution margin for its products is lower: With a lower contribution margin, each product that is sold is less able to help cover the fixed operating costs, and the firm operates closer to its breakeven point. Therefore, *the higher the DOL for a particular firm, the closer the firm is to its operating breakeven point*, and the more sensitive its operating income is to a change in sales volume. *Greater sensitivity generally implies greater risk, so firms with higher DOLs generally are considered to have riskier operations than firms with lower DOLs.*

Financial Leverage

Whereas operating leverage considers how changing sales volume affects operating income, **financial leverage** considers how changing operating income (EBIT) affects earnings per share (EPS). *Financial leverage takes over where operating leverage leaves off, further magnifying the effects on earnings per share of changes in the level of sales.* Like operating leverage, financial leverage arises because fixed costs exist. In this case, the fixed costs are associated with how the firm is financed. The **degree of financial leverage (DFL)** is defined as the percentage change in earnings per share (EPS) that results from a given percentage change in operating income (EBIT). DFL at a particular level of EBIT is computed as follows:[5]

financial leverage
The existence of fixed financial costs, such as interest; when a change in EBIT results in a larger change in EPS.

degree of financial leverage (DFL)
The percentage change in EPS that results from a given percentage change in EBIT.

$$DFL = \frac{EBIT}{EBIT - I}$$

8-5

where I is the firm's interest expense, and the other variables are as previously defined.

Using this equation to compute the DFL for Argile at 30 million units of sales, we find:

$$DFL_{Q=30} = \frac{\$71.5}{\$71.5 - \$20.7} = 1.407 \approx 1.41\times$$

The interpretation of the DFL value is the same as that for the DOL value, except that the starting point for evaluating financial leverage is the operating income, or earnings before interest and taxes (EBIT), and the ending point is earnings per share (EPS). Because the DFL for Argile is 1.41, the company can expect a 1.41 percent change in EPS for every 1 percent change in EBIT; a 23.1 percent increase in EBIT will result in a 32.5 percent (23.1% × 1.407) increase in earnings available to common stockholders and, therefore, the same percentage increase in EPS (the number of common shares outstanding does not change). Unfortunately, the opposite is also true—if Argile's 2011 sales are 10 percent below expectations, its EPS will be 32.5 percent lower than the forecast of $2.61, or $1.76. To confirm this result, the financing section of Argile's forecasted income statement and the effect of a 23.1 percent change in expected NOI are shown in

---

[5]If Argile had preferred stock, the DFL would be computed using the following equation:

$$DFL = \frac{EBIT}{EBIT - [\text{Financial BEP}]} = \frac{EBIT}{EBIT - \left[I + \frac{D_{ps}}{(1 - T)}\right]}$$

The term $D_{ps}/(1 - T)$ represents the before-tax dollars that the firm needs to generate to be able to pay preferred dividends out of after-tax dollars. Because most firms do not have preferred stock, to simplify our analysis, we do not use this form of the equation here.

TABLE 8-7	Argile Textiles: Earnings Per Share at Sales Levels of 30 Million Units and 33 Million Units ($ million, except per-share data)[a]			

	2011 Forecasted Operations	**Sales Increase**	**Dollar Change**	**Percent Change**
Sales in units (millions)	30.0	33.0		
Earnings before interest and taxes (EBIT)	$ 71.5	$ 88.0	$16.5	+23.1%
Interest (I)	(20.7)	(20.7)	(0.0)	+ 0.0%
Earnings before taxes (EBT)	$ 50.8	$ 67.3	$16.5	+32.5%
Taxes (40%)	(20.3)	(26.9)	(6.6)	+32.5%
Net income	$ 30.5	$ 40.4	$ 9.9	+32.5%
Earning per share (11.67 million shares)	$ 2.61	$ 3.46	$ 0.85	+32.5%

[a] A spreadsheet was used to generate the results in this table. Only the final results are rounded, so there might be some rounding differences if you rely on some of the values in the table, which are the rounded values, to compute the other values.

Table 8-7. The value of the degree of financial leverage found using Equation 8-5 pertains to one specific EBIT level, which is $71.5 million in the case of Argile. Thus, Argile's DFL will be lower (higher) if the base forecast of its EBIT is higher (lower) than $71.5 million.

In general, *the more difficulty a firm has in covering its fixed financing costs with operating income, the greater its degree of financial leverage.* Therefore, the higher the DFL for a particular firm, the lower the firm's times-interest-earned (TIE) ratio and the more sensitive its earnings per share are to a change in operating income. *Greater sensitivity implies greater risk, so firms with higher DFLs generally are considered to have greater financial risk than firms with lower DFLs.*

Combining Operating and Financial Leverage (DTL)

Our analysis of operating leverage and financial leverage has shown two points:

1. The greater the degree of operating leverage, or fixed operating costs for a particular level of operations, the more sensitive EBIT will be to changes in sales volume; thus, operating risk is higher.

2. The greater the degree of financial leverage, or fixed financial costs for a particular level of operations, the more sensitive EPS will be to changes in EBIT; thus, financial risk is higher.

Combining operating leverage and financial leverage for a particular firm gives an indication of its total risk. If a firm has a considerable amount of both operating and financial leverage, then even small changes in sales will produce wide fluctuations in EPS. Look at the effect that leverage has on Argile's 2011 forecasted operations. If the sales volume increases by 10 percent, Argile's EBIT will increase by 23.1 percent (Table 8-6), and if its EBIT increases by 23.1 percent, EPS will increase by 32.5 percent (Table 8-7). Thus, in combination, a 10 percent increase in sales volume will produce a 32.5 percent increase in EPS (Table 8-6 and Table 8-7). This example illustrates the effects of total leverage, which is the combination of both operating leverage and financial leverage, with respect to Argile's forecasted operations.

The **degree of total leverage (DTL)** is defined as the percentage change in EPS resulting from a percentage change in sales volume. This relationship can be written as follows:

degree of total leverage
The percent change in EPS that results from a one percent change in sales.

8-6

$$
\begin{aligned}
\text{DTL} &= \quad \text{DOL} \quad \times \quad \text{DFL} \\
&= \frac{\text{Gross profit}}{\text{EBIT}} \times \frac{\text{EBIT}}{\text{EBIT} - \text{I}} \\
&= \frac{\text{Gross profit}}{\text{EBIT} - \text{Interest}} = \frac{\text{S} - \text{VC}}{\text{EBIT} - \text{I}} = \frac{\text{Q}(\text{P} - \text{V})}{[\text{Q}(\text{P} - \text{V}) - \text{F}] - \text{I}}
\end{aligned}
$$

Using Equation 8-6, the DTL for Argile would be:

$$
\text{DTL}_{Q=30} = \frac{30(\$27.50 - \$22.0)}{[30(\$27.50 - \$22.0) - \$93.5] - \$20.7} = \frac{\$165.0}{\$71.5 - \$20.7} = 3.25\times
$$

According to Equation 8-6, we could have arrived at the same result for DTL by multiplying the degree of operating leverage by the degree of financial leverage. That is, the DTL for Argile would be $2.31 \times 1.41 = 3.25$ (after rounding). This value indicates that for every 1 percent change in sales volume, Argile's EPS will change by 3.25 percent; a 10 percent increase in sales will result in a 32.5 percent increase in EPS. This result is exactly the effect expected (see Table 8-6 and Table 8-7).

The degree of combined (total) leverage concept is useful primarily because it provides insights into the joint effects of operating and financial leverage on earnings per share. This concept can be used to show management, for example, that a decision to automate a plant and to finance the new equipment with debt would produce a situation where a 10 percent decline in sales would result in a nearly 50 percent decline in earnings. Conversely, with a different operating and financial package, a 10 percent sales decline might cause earnings to decline by only 15 percent. Having the alternatives stated in this manner gives decision makers a better idea of the ramifications of alternative actions with respect to the firm's level of operations and the financing used for those operations.

Self-Test Questions

Give the general equation used to calculate the degree of operating leverage. Compare the equation for DFL to the equation for the times-interest-earned ratio given in Chapter 7.

What does the term *high degree of operating leverage* imply, and what are some implications of having a high degree of operating leverage?

What does the term high degree of *financial leverage* imply, and what are some implications of having a high degree of financial leverage?

What information is provided by the degree of total (combined) leverage?

Suppose that when a firm generates a gross profit equal to $660,000, its operating income is $440,000; the firm pays interest equal to $220,000; and it has no preferred stock. If the firm's marginal tax rate is 30 percent, what is its degree of total operating leverage, degree of financial leverage, and degree of total leverage?   (Answer: DOL = 1.5×, DFL = 2.0, DTL = 3.0)

USING LEVERAGE AND FORECASTING FOR CONTROL

From the discussion in the previous sections, it should be clear how Argile Textiles' income would be affected if the firm's 2011 sales did not match the forecasted level. If sales exceed the expectations, both operating and financial leverage will magnify the "bottom line" effect on EPS (DTL = 3.25). The opposite case also holds. Consequently, if Argile does not meet its forecasted sales level, leverage will produce a magnified loss in income compared to what is expected. In this case, perhaps production facilities are expanded too dramatically, inventories are built up too quickly, and so on. The end result might be that the firm suffers a significant income loss. This loss will result in a lower than expected addition to retained earnings, which means the plans for additional external funds needed to support the firm's operations will be inadequate. Likewise, if the sales forecast is too low and the firm is operating at full capacity, it will not be able to meet the additional demand, and sales opportunities will be lost—perhaps forever.

In the previous sections, we showed only how changes in operations (2011 forecasts) affect the income generated by the firm. We did not continue the process to show how these events alter the balance sheet and the financing needs of the firm. To determine the effect on the financial statements, the financial manager needs to repeat the steps discussed in the first part of this chapter. That is, the financial manager needs to evaluate and act on the feedback received from the forecasting and budgeting processes. In effect, the forecasting (planning) and control of the firm is an ongoing activity—a vital function that influences the long-run survival prospects of any firm.

The forecasting and control functions described in this chapter are important for several reasons. First, if the projected operating results are unsatisfactory, management can "go back to the drawing board," reformulate its plans, and develop more reasonable targets for the coming year. Second, it is possible that the funds required to meet the sales forecast simply cannot be obtained; if so, it is clearly better to know this fact in advance and to scale back the projected level of operations than to suddenly run out of cash and have operations grind to a halt in midstream. Third, even if the firm can raise the required funds, it is desirable to plan for their acquisition well in advance. Finally, any deviation from the projections needs to be evaluated to improve future forecasts and the predictability of the firm's operations, thereby ensuring that the goals of the firm are pursued appropriately.

Self-Test Question

Why is it important for the forecasting and control to be ongoing activities for a firm?

THE CASH BUDGET[6]

One of the most important procedures in budgeting and control is the construction of a cash budget. The cash budget helps management plan investment and borrowing strategies. It also provides feedback and control to improve the efficiency of financial management in the future.

The firm estimates its general needs for cash as a part of its overall budgeting, or forecasting, process. First, it forecasts its operating activities, such as expenses and

---

[6]Coverage of this section can be postponed until Chapter 15 without loss of continuity.

revenues for the period in question. Next, it projects the financing and investment activities necessary to attain that level of operations. Such forecasts entail the construction of pro forma financial statements, which were discussed earlier in this chapter. The information provided from the pro forma balance sheet and income statement is combined with projections of the delay in collecting accounts receivable, of the delay in paying suppliers and employees, tax payment dates, dividend and interest payment dates, and so on. All of this information is summarized in the **cash budget,** which shows the firm's projected cash inflows and cash outflows over some specified period. Generally, firms use a monthly cash budget forecasted over the next year plus a more detailed daily or weekly cash budget for the coming month. The monthly cash budgets are employed for planning purposes, and the daily or weekly budgets are utilized for actual cash control.

> **cash budget**
> A schedule showing cash receipts, cash disbursements, and cash balances for a firm over a specified time period.

The cash budget provides much more detailed information concerning a firm's future cash flows than do the forecasted financial statements. Reviewing Argile Textiles' forecasted financial statements, we find that net income in 2011 is expected to be $30.5 million. Using the 2010 balance sheet and the forecasts given in Table 8-3, we find that the net cash flow (in millions of dollars) generated from operations in 2011 is expected to be $45.5 million:

Net income	$ 30.5
Add: Noncash expenses (depreciation)	33.0
Gross cash flow from operations	$ 63.5
Adjustments to gross cash flow:	
Increase in accounts receivable	(9.0)
Increase in inventories	(13.5)
Increase in accounts payable	1.5
Increase in accruals	3.0
Total adjustments to gross cash flow	$(18.0)
Net cash flow from operations	$ 45.5

Thus, in 2011, Argile expects to generate $45.5 million cash inflow through its normal production and sales operations. Much of this cash will be used to support the firm's financing and investment activities. Even after these activities are considered, Argile's cash account is projected to increase by $1 million in 2011. Does this growth mean that Argile doesn't worry about cash shortages during the year? To answer this question, we must construct Argile's cash budget for 2011.

To simplify the construction of Argile's cash budget, we consider only the latter half of 2011 (July through December). Furthermore, we do not list every cash flow that is expected to occur, but instead focus on the operating cash flows.

Argile's sales peak occurs in September. All sales are made on terms that allow customers to take a 2 percent cash discount on payments made within 10 days of purchase; if this discount is not taken, the full amount is due in 30 days. Like most companies, Argile finds that some of its customers delay payment for more than 90 days. Experience has shown that payment on 20 percent of Argile's *dollar sales* occurs within 10 days of the sales; these transactions are the discount sales. On 70 percent of sales, payment is made during the month immediately following the month of sale. Payment is made on the remaining 10 percent of sales 2 months or more after the initial sales. To simplify the cash budget, we will assume that the last 10 percent of sales is collected 2 months after the sale and that there are no bad debts.

Argile's costs for cotton, wool, and other cloth-related materials average 60 percent of the sales prices of the finished products. These purchases generally are made 1 month before the firm expects to sell the finished products, but Argile's suppliers do

TABLE 8-8   Argile Textiles: 2011 Cash Budget ($ million)

	May	June	July	Aug	Sept	Oct	Nov	Dec
Credit sales	$50.0	$60.0	$ 75.0	$100.0	$125.0	$ 90.0	$ 65.0	$ 50.0
Credit purchases								
= 60% of next month's sales		45.0	60.0	75.0	54.0	39.0	30.0	
Cash Receipts								
Collections from this month's sales								
= 0.2 × 0.98 × (current month's sales)			14.7	19.6	24.5	17.6	12.7	9.8
Collections from previous month's sales								
= 0.7 × (previous month's sales)			42.0	52.5	70.0	87.5	63.0	45.5
Collections from sales 2 months previously								
= 0.1 × (sales 2 months ago)			5.0	6.0	7.5	10.0	12.5	9.0
Total cash receipts			61.7	78.1	102.0	115.1	88.2	64.3
Cash Disbursements								
Payments for credit purchases (1-month lag)			45.0	60.0	75.0	54.0	39.0	30.0
Wages and salaries (20.0% of monthly sales)			15.0	20.0	25.0	18.0	13.0	10.0
Rent			4.5	4.5	4.5	4.5	4.5	4.5
Other expenses			3.5	4.0	5.5	5.0	2.5	2.0
Taxes					8.0			5.0
Payment for plant construction						10.0		
Total cash disbursements			68.0	88.5	118.0	91.5	59.0	51.5
Net cash flow (receipts − disbursements)			$(6.3)	$(10.4)	$(16.0)	$ 23.6	$ 29.2	$ 12.8
Beginning cash balance			4.0	(2.3)	(12.7)	(28.7)	(5.1)	24.2
Ending cash balance			(2.3)	(12.7)	(28.7)	(5.1)	24.2	37.0
Target (minimum) cash balance			(2.0)	(2.0)	(2.0)	(2.0)	(2.0)	(2.0)
Surplus (shortfall) cash			$(4.3)	$(14.7)	$(30.7)	$(7.1)	$ 22.2	$ 35.0

target (minimum) cash balance
The minimum cash balance that a firm desires to maintain while conducting business.

disbursements and receipts method (scheduling)
Net cash flow is determined by estimating the cash disbursements and the cash receipts expected to be generated each period.

not require *payment* for materials until 30 days after the purchase. Accordingly, if July sales reach the forecasted amount of $75 million, then purchases during June will amount to $45 million (0.60 × $75 million), and this bill will actually be paid in July.

Other cash expenses such as wages (20 percent of sales) and rent are built into the cash budget as well. In addition, Argile must make estimated tax payments of $8 million in September and $5 million in December; it must make a $10 million payment for a new plant in October. Assuming that Argile's **target,** or **minimum, cash balance** is $2 million and that the company projects $4 million to be on hand on July 1, 2011, what will the firm's monthly cash surpluses or shortfalls be for the period from July through December?

Table 8-8 presents Argile's 2011 cash budget for July through December. The approach used to construct this cash budget generally is termed the **disbursements and receipts method** (also referred to as **scheduling**) because the cash disbursements and cash receipts are estimated to determine the net cash flow expected to be generated each month. The format used in Table 8-8 is quite simple in that it resembles balancing a checkbook. That is, the cash receipts are lumped into one category and the cash disbursements are placed into another category to determine the net effect that monthly cash flows have on the cash position of the firm. More detailed formats can be used, depending on how the firm prefers to present the cash budget information.

The first line of Table 8-8 gives the sales forecast for the period from May through December. These estimates are necessary to determine collections for July through December. Similarly, the second line of the table gives the credit purchases expected each month based on the sales forecasts, allowing us to determine the monthly payments for credit purchases.

The cash receipts category shows cash collections based on credit sales originating in 3 months—sales in the current month and in the previous 2 months. Take a look at the collections expected in July. Remember that Argile expects 20 percent of the dollar sales to be collected in the month of the sales and, therefore, to be affected by the 2 percent cash discount offered; 70 percent of the dollar sales will be collected 1 month after the sales; and the remaining 10 percent of the dollar sales will be collected 2 months after the sales (it is assumed the company has no bad debts). For example, in July, Argile will collect $14.7 million = 0.20 × [(1 − 0.02) × $75] million from sales that occur in July; $42.0 million = 0.70 × $60.0 million from sales that occurred in June; and $5.0 million = 0.10 × $50 million from sales that occurred in May. Thus, the total collections received in July represent 20 percent of July sales (minus the discount) plus 70 percent of June sales plus 10 percent of May sales—$61.7 million in total.

The cash disbursements category shows payments for raw materials, wages, rent, and so on. Raw materials are purchased on credit 1 month before the finished goods are expected to be sold, but payments for the materials are not made until 1 month later (that is, the month of the expected sales). The cost of the raw materials is expected to equal 60 percent of sales. July sales are forecasted at $75 million, so Argile will purchase $45 million = 0.6($75 million) of materials in June and pay for these purchases in July. Additional monthly cash disbursements include employees' salaries (which equal 20 percent of monthly sales), rent (which remains constant), and other operating expenses (which vary with respect to production levels). Cash disbursements that are not expected to occur monthly include taxes (September and December) and payment for the construction of additional facilities (October).

The line labeled "Net cash flow" indicates whether Argile's operations are expected to generate positive or negative net cash flows each month. This information is merely the beginning of the story, however. We also need to examine the firm's cash position based on the cash balance at the beginning of the month and based on the *target (minimum) cash balance* desired by Argile. The bottom line provides information as to whether Argile can expect a monthly cash surplus that it can invest temporarily in short-term financial assets (that is, money market instruments) or a monthly cash shortfall that the firm must finance with external sources of funds.

At the beginning of July, Argile will have cash equal to $4 million. During that month, the firm is expected to generate a negative $6.3 million net cash flow; in other words, July cash disbursements are expected to exceed cash receipts by $6.3 million. Because Argile has only $4 million in cash to begin July, ignoring any financing requirements, its cash balance at the end of July is expected to be a negative $2.3 million. In effect, if the firm doesn't find additional funding, its checking account will be overdrawn by $2.3 million. To make matters worse, Argile has a target cash balance equal to $2 million. Without any additional financing, then, its cash balance at the end of July is expected to fall $4.3 million short of its target. The company must make arrangements to borrow $4.3 million in July to bring the cash account balance up to the target balance of $2 million. Assuming that this amount is indeed borrowed, loans outstanding will increase by a total of $4.3 million during July to support the firm's operating needs.

The cash surplus or required loan balance (shortfall) is given on the "bottom line" of the cash budget. A positive value indicates a cash surplus, whereas a negative value (in parentheses) indicates a loan requirement. Note that the surplus cash or loan requirement shown is a *cumulative amount*. That is, Argile must borrow $4.3 million in July, and because it has a cash shortfall during August of $10.4 million as reported on the "Net cash flow" line, its total loan requirement for July and August is $14.7 million. This amount includes the $4.3 million needed to support Argile's July operations and the $10.4 million in additional financing needed to support operations in August. Argile's arrangement with the bank permits it to increase its outstanding loans on a daily basis, up to a prearranged maximum (termed a line of credit), just as you could increase the amount you owe on a credit card. The firm will use any surplus funds it generates to pay off its loans. If Argile generates a "bottom line" cash surplus after repaying its short-term loans, it will invest those funds in short-term financial assets.

The same procedure is used in the following months to calculate the firm's cash position. Sales will peak in September, accompanied by increased payments for purchases, wages, and other items. Receipts from sales will also increase, but the firm will still be left with a $16 million net cash outflow during September. The total loan requirement will hit a peak of $30.7 million during this month.

Sales, purchases, and payments for past purchases will fall sharply in October. During that month, however, collections will be the highest of any month because they will reflect the high September sales. As a result, Argile will enjoy a healthy $23.6 million net cash gain during October. It will use this net gain to pay off borrowings, so loans outstanding will decline by $23.6 million, to $7.1 million.

Argile will have an even larger cash surplus in November, which will permit it to pay off all of its short-term loans. In fact, the company is expected to have $22.2 million in surplus cash by month's end, and another cash surplus in December will swell its excess cash to $35 million. With such a large amount of unneeded funds, Argile's treasurer certainly will want to invest in interest-bearing securities or put the funds to use in some other way. Various types of investments into which Argile might put its excess funds were discussed in Chapter 2.

Before concluding our discussion of the cash budget, we should make some additional points:

1. For simplicity, our illustrative budget for Argile omitted many important cash flows that are anticipated for 2011, such as dividends and proceeds from stock and bond sales. Some of these cash streams are projected to occur in the first half of the year, but we could easily add those that are projected for the July through December period to the example. The final cash budget should contain all projected cash inflows and outflows.

2. Our cash budget example does not reflect interest on loans or income from investing surplus cash. We could readily include this refinement.

3. If cash inflows and outflows are not uniform during the month, we might seriously understate the firm's peak financing requirements. The data in Table 8-8 show the situation expected on the last day of each month. On any given day during the month, however, the firm's position might be quite different. For example, if all payments had to be made on the fifth day of each month, but collections came in uniformly throughout the month, the firm would need to borrow much larger amounts than those shown in Table 8-8. In this case, we would have to prepare a cash budget identifying requirements on a daily basis.

4. Because depreciation is a noncash charge, it does not appear on the cash budget other than through its effect on taxable income and hence on taxes paid.

5. Because the cash budget represents a forecast, all values in the table are *expected* values. If actual sales, purchases, and so on differ from the forecasted levels, then the projected cash deficits and surpluses will also differ.

6. Spreadsheets are particularly well suited for constructing and analyzing cash budgets, especially with respect to the sensitivity of cash flows to changes in sales levels, collection periods, and the like. We could change any assumption—for example, the projected monthly sales or the time that customers pay—and the cash budget would automatically and instantly be recalculated. This endeavor would show us exactly how the firm's borrowing requirements would change if various other events occurred.

7. The target cash balance probably will be adjusted over time, rising and falling with seasonal patterns and with long-term changes in the scale of the firm's operations. For example, Argile might want to maintain larger cash balances during August and September than at other times; then as the company grows, so will its required cash balance. Also, the firm might set the target cash balance at $0; this strategy is feasible if the firm purchases a portfolio of marketable securities that could be sold to replenish the cash account or if its bank permits Argile to borrow any funds needed on a daily basis. In that event, the target cash balance would simply be equal to $0. Note, however, that most firms would find it difficult to operate with a zero-balance bank account, just as you would, and the costs of such an operation would typically offset the costs associated with maintaining a positive cash balance. For these reasons, most firms set a positive target cash balance. Factors that influence the target cash balance are discussed later in the book.

Self-Test Questions

What is the purpose of a cash budget?

Suppose a firm's cash flows do not occur uniformly throughout the month. How might this variability affect the accuracy of the forecasted borrowing requirements?

Is depreciation reflected in a cash budget? Explain.

Ethical Dilemma

Competition-Based Planning—Promotion or Payoff?

A few months ago, Kim Darby, financial manager of Republic Communications Corporation (RCC), contacted you about a job opening in the financial planning division of the company. RCC is a well-established firm that has offered long-distance phone service in the United States for more than three decades. Recent deregulation in the telecommunications industry has RCC concerned because competition has increased significantly: today,

many more firms offer long-distance services than did so 5 years ago. In fact, RCC has seen its profits decline along with market share since deregulation began. Kim indicated that RCC wants to reverse this trend by improving the company's planning function so that long-distance rates can be set to better attract and keep customers in the future. According to her, that is the reason she contacted you.

continues

When she first called, Kim told you RCC would like to hire you because you are one of the "up-and-comers" in the telecommunications industry. You have worked at National Telecommunications, Inc. (NTI), one of RCC's fiercest competitors, since you graduated from college 4 years ago, helping to develop its rate-setting program, which many consider the best in the industry.

Taking the position at RCC would be comparable to a promotion with a $30,000 salary increase, and it provides greater chances for advancement than does your current position at NTI. After interviewing with RCC and talking to friends and family, a couple of days ago you informally accepted the job at RCC. You have not yet notified NTI of your decision, however.

Earlier today, Kim called to see if you could start your new position in a few weeks. RCC would like you to begin work as soon as possible because it wants to redesign its rate-setting plan in an effort to regain market share. During the conversation, Kim mentioned that it would be helpful if you could bring NTI's rate-setting program and some

rate-setting information with you to your new job—it will help RCC rewrite its rate-setting program. In an attempt to allay any reservations you might have, Kim told you that NTI sells its software to other companies and any rate-setting information is available to the public through states' public service commissions, so everything you bring is already well known in the industry and should be considered in the public domain. According to Kim, RCC will not copy the rate-setting program. Her attitude is, "What is wrong with taking a look at it as long as we don't copy the program?" If you provide RCC with NTI's rate-setting program, you know it will help the company to plan better, and better planning will lead to increased market share and higher stock prices. An improved rate-setting plan might net RCC as much as $200 million each year, and RCC has a very generous bonus system to reward employees who help the company improve its market position. If you do not provide the software, you might start your new job "off on the wrong foot." What should you do?

Chapter Principles –The Answers

To summarize the key concepts, let's answer the questions that were posed at the beginning of the chapter:

- **Why are financial planning and financial control critical to the survival of a firm?** Financial planning requires the firm to forecast future operations. Such forecasts are needed so that the firm can make arrangements for expected changes in production, future financing needs, and so forth. A financial plan represents a road map for the firm to follow to attain future goals. The process doesn't stop when financial forecasts are completed because the firm needs to monitor operations as the financial plan is implemented to determine whether modifications are needed.

- **What are pro forma financial statements? What is the purpose of constructing such statements?** Pro forma financial statements represent a firm's projections about future operations. The firm projects what it thinks the balance sheet and income statement will look like if future expectations come true. It is important for a firm to construct pro formas so that it can make plans to raise any needed external funds, to expand plant and equipment, and so forth to attain forecasted growth.

- **What is operating breakeven? How is breakeven analysis used in financial decision making?** The operating breakeven point is the level of production and sales that a firm needs to attain so that operating income (EBIT = NOI) equals $0—that is, it is the level of sales where the firm just covers its operating expenses. Breakeven analysis can help determine how large the sales of a new product must be for the firm to achieve profitability. It also is used to determine the effects of expansion and modernization on a firm's operations. In general, breakeven analysis can provide information about the risk associated with a firm's operations. For example, because there is less cushion to cover fixed operating costs when sales are below normal, firms that operate closer to their breakeven points are often considered riskier than firms that operate well above their breakeven points.

- **What is leverage? What types of leverage are used in financial analysis?** Leverage is fixed costs—that is, a firm that has fixed costs, whether they are operating, financial, or both, has leverage.

     Operating leverage represents the fixed operating costs of the firm. The degree of operating leverage (DOL) states these operating costs on a relative basis, and it indicates by what percent the firm's operating income will change if sales change. Everything else equal, because firms with higher DOLs operate closer to their operating breakeven points, they are considered riskier than firms with lower DOLs.

     Financial leverage represents the fixed financial costs of the firm. The degree of financial leverage (DFL) states these financial costs on a relative basis, and it indicates by what percent the firm's EPS will change if EBIT changes. Everything else equal, firms with higher DFLs are considered riskier than firms with lower DFLs.

- **How can a firm use knowledge of leverage in the financial forecasting and control process?** In general, a firm that has a higher degree of leverage is considered riskier than a similar firm that has a lower degree of leverage. A firm uses the concept of leverage to estimate how fixed costs, both operating and financial, affect its "bottom line" net income. Everything else equal, a firm can decrease its risk by decreasing its relative fixed costs, increasing sales, or by attaining both actions. As we will discuss in later chapters, when a firm reduces its risk, its cost of funds (financing) decreases, and thus its value increases.

- **Why is it important for a firm to construct a cash budget? What information is provided by a cash budget?** Constructing a cash budget is one of the most important procedures in budgeting and control because it (1) helps management plan investment and borrowing strategies and (2) provides feedback and control to improve the efficiency of the management of the firm's finances. Because it generally must prearrange (make plans for) loans and other sources of funds, it is important that the firm knows when such external funds are needed. The cash budget provides the information that a firm needs to make such financing arrangements by indicating both when external funds are needed and the amounts that are needed. Similarly, a firm should plan to invest funds that are not needed to support operations in the current period, and the cash budget provides information about when such funds can be invested. To construct a cash budget, management must also construct pro forma financial statements.

The concepts presented in this chapter should help you to understand the importance of financial planning. If you understand the concepts presented in this chapter, you should be able to develop a financial plan that will help you make more informed financial decisions.

CHAPTER PRINCIPLES
–Personal Finance

- **How can I use "sales" forecasts to make better personal financial decisions?** Like firms, it is important for you to develop "sales" forecasts so that you can plan your financial future. In your case, however, a "sales" forecast is a prediction of your future income. Such forecasting is important to your financial survival. For example, if you want to purchase a house, you must determine the "amount of house" you can afford, which is dependent on the income you expect to generate in the future. Even if you construct an unsophisticated financial plan, it is important that you plan your financial future; otherwise, you might find yourself in financial distress. Your financial plan should include more than your expectations about purchasing such high-priced items as a house or an automobile; it should also include plans for retirement, plans for a child's education, plans for the financial security of dependents, and so forth. Financial plans necessarily become more complicated as you grow in your career and as your family ages because your finances become more complicated.

If we slightly change the mantra that is included in the Managerial Perspective at the beginning of the chapter, we can say: "People don't plan to fail financially, they fail to develop financial plans." You should keep these words in mind when dealing with financial matters.

- **How can I use breakeven analysis concepts to better manage my personal finances?** As we discovered in the chapter, firms want to determine their breakeven points so that they know what levels of operations must be attained to earn profits. You, too, should want to determine your breakeven point so that you know when you have funds available to invest in your retirement fund, to buy a car, or to take a dream vacation. Determining your breakeven point should be an integral part of your financial plan.

- **Can leverage help me magnify my investment returns?** In the chapter, we discussed how leverage affects the income generated by a firm. Consider how you can use leverage to your advantage, as well as how leverage can be harmful to your financial position. Remember that when leverage exists, returns are magnified. Consequently, when a person uses leverage, his or her returns are magnified; when returns are positive, there is a "good" magnification, but when returns are negative, there is a "bad" magnification. For example, suppose that you borrow $1,000 at 10 percent and you add the borrowed money to $1,000 of your own money to invest in a stock. If the $2,000 earns a 15 percent return, the *total dollar return* from the investment is $300. Because you have to pay the lender only $100 interest for the money that you borrowed, you get to keep $200 of the amount that is earned. Thus, the percent return on *your* $1,000 is 20% = $200/$1,000. The 20 percent return you earn on your $1,000 is greater than the 15 percent return that the $2,000 investment earned because you do not have to share your additional profits with the lender—that is, you have a fixed financial cost equal to $100. But, if the $2,000 earns only 6 percent, then the *total dollar return* would be $120. You still have to pay the lender $100 interest, thus you earn only $20 on your $1,000 investment. This translates to a 2 percent rate of return (= $20/$1,000). The 2 percent return you earn on your $1,000 is much less than the 6 percent return that the $2,000 investment earns because you have to pay the lender $100 interest regardless of what you do with the money—that is, you have a fixed financial cost equal to $100. As you can see, the fixed financial cost—that is, $100 in interest—magnifies the return you earn, regardless of whether you earn a "good" return or you earn a "bad" return.

- **Why is it important for me to construct a cash budget?** A key ingredient for forecasting your finances is the cash budget. There is a good chance that you already budget your cash, although it might be in a very unsophisticated manner. For example, how do you decide how much cash you should have in your wallet? Often individuals make such decisions by estimating what purchases will be made during the day. Such an estimate represents a rudimentary cash budget. To effectively manage your cash position, however, you should construct a formal cash budget. A cash budget will show you where your money is being spent, when you can expect cash shortfalls that must be financed, and when you might have cash surpluses that can be invested for short periods.

QUESTIONS

8-1 Certain liability and net worth items generally increase spontaneously with increases in sales. Put a check (✔) by those items that typically increase spontaneously:

Accounts payable   _____

Notes payable to banks   _____

Accrued wages   _____

Accrued taxes   _____

Mortgage bonds   _____

Common stock   _____

Retained earnings   _____

8-2 Suppose a firm makes the following policy changes. If the change means that external, nonspontaneous financial requirements (AFN) will increase, indicate this situation with a (+); indicate a decrease with a (−); and indicate an indeterminate or no effect with a (0). Think in terms of the immediate, short-run effect on funds requirements.

  a. The dividend payout ratio is increased.   _____

  b. The firm contracts to buy, rather than make, certain components used in its products.   _____

  c. The firm decides to pay all suppliers on delivery, rather than after a 30-day delay, to take advantage of discounts for rapid payment.   _____

  d. The firm begins to sell on credit (previously all sales had been on a cash basis).   _____

  e. The firm's profit margin is eroded by increased competition; sales remain steady.   _____

  f. Advertising expenditures are stepped up.   _____

  g. A decision is made to substitute long-term mortgage bonds for short-term bank loans.   _____

  h. The firm begins to pay employees on a weekly basis (previously it had paid them at the end of each month).   _____

8-3 What benefits can be derived from breakeven analysis? What are some problems with breakeven analysis?

8-4 What data are required to construct a breakeven graph?

8-5 Explain how profits or losses will be magnified for a firm with high operating leverage as opposed to a firm with lower operating leverage.

8-6 Explain how profits or losses will be magnified for a firm with high financial leverage as opposed to a firm with lower financial leverage.

8-7 Discuss the relationship between a firm's degree of total leverage and its perceived risk.

8-8 What would be the effect of each of the following events on a firm's breakeven point? Indicate the effect in the space provided with a (+) for an increase, a (−) for a decrease, and a (0) for no effect. When answering this question, assume that everything except the change indicated is held constant.

  a. An increase in the sales price   _____

  b. A reduction in variable labor costs   _____

   c. A decrease in fixed operating costs   _____

   d. Issuing new bonds   _____

8-9 Assume that a firm is developing its long-run financial plan. What period should this plan cover—1 month, 6 months, 1 year, 3 years, 5 years, or some other period? Justify your answer.

8-10 What is a cash budget? For what purposes should cash budgets be created?

8-11 Why is a cash budget important even when the firm has plenty of cash in the bank?

SELF-TEST PROBLEMS

Solutions appear in Appendix B.

Key Terms   **ST-1** Define each of the following terms:

   a. Sales forecast

   b. Projected balance sheet method

   c. Spontaneously generated funds

   d. Pro forma financial statement

   e. Additional funds needed (AFN)

   f. Financing feedback

   g. Financial planning; financial control

   h. Breakeven analysis; breakeven point, Q_{OpBE}

   i. Operating leverage; degree of operating leverage (DOL)

   j. Financial leverage; degree of financial leverage (DFL)

   k. Combined (total) leverage; degree of total leverage (DTL)

   l. Cash budget

Operating Leverage and Breakeven Analysis   **ST-2** Olinde Electronics, Inc., produces stereo components that sell for $100. Olinde's fixed costs are $200,000; the firm produces and sells 5,000 components each year; EBIT is currently $50,000; and Olinde's assets (all equity financed) are $500,000. The firm estimates that it can change its production process, adding $400,000 to investment costs and $50,000 to fixed operating costs. This change will reduce variable costs per unit by $10 and increase output by 2,000 units, but the sales price on all units must be lowered to $95 to permit sales of the additional output. Olinde has tax loss carryovers that cause its tax rate to be 0 percent. It uses no debt, and its average cost of funds is 10 percent.

   a. Should Olinde make the change?

   b. Would Olinde's degree of operating leverage increase or decrease if it made the change? What about its operating breakeven point?

   c. Suppose Olinde could not raise additional equity financing and had to borrow the $400,000 to make the investment at an interest rate of 8 percent. Use the Du Pont equation (Chapter 7) to find the expected ROA of the investment. Should Olinde make the change if it must use debt financing?

   d. What would Olinde's degree of financial leverage be if it borrowed the $400,000 at the 8 percent interest rate?

PROBLEMS

8-1   Following is information about the Super Shoe Store (SSS):   Operating Leverage and Breakeven

Selling price per unit	$ 50
Variable cost per unit	$ 30
Fixed operating costs	$120,000

   a. What is SSS's operating income (NOI) when sales are 5,000 units (boxes of shoes)?

   b. How many pairs of shoes does SSS have to sell to break even with its operations?

   c. If the firm normally sells 10,000 pairs of shoes, what is SSS's degree of operating leverage?

8-2   Premier Primer Pumps (PPP) sells sump pumps for $2,500 each. The variable costs associated with the manufacture of each pump is $1,750 and fixed operating costs are $150,000 annually. PPP normally sells 300 pumps each year, has an interest expense equal to $30,000, and its marginal tax rate is 40 percent. Given this information, what is PPP's operating breakeven point?   Operating Breakeven

8-3   Analysts have evaluated the Sivar Silver Company and discovered that if sales are $800,000 the following will exist: Leverage Analysis

Degree of operating leverage (DOL)	4.0×
Degree of financial leverage (DFL)	2.0×
Earnings before interest and taxes (EBIT)	$50,000
Earnings per share (EPS)	$4.00

   According to this information, what will Sivar's EBIT be if sales actually turn out to be $720,000 rather than $800,000? What will the EPS be?

8-4   Gordon's Plants has the following partial income statement for 2010:   Financial Leverage

Earnings before interest and taxes	$ 4,500
Interest	(2,000)
Earnings before taxes	$ 2,500
Taxes (40%)	(1,000)
Net income	$ 1,500
Number of common shares	1,000

   What is the degree of financial leverage for Gordon's? What does this value mean?

8-5   The Niendorf Corporation produces tea kettles, which it sells for $15 each. Fixed costs are $700,000 for output up to 400,000 units. Variable costs amount to $10 per kettle.   Operating Leverage

   a. What is the firm's gain or loss at sales of 125,000 units? Of 175,000 units?

   b. What is the breakeven point? Illustrate your answer with a graph.

   c. What is Niendorf's degree of operating leverage at sales of 125,000 units? Of 150,000 units? Of 175,000 units?

8-6   At year-end 2010, total assets for Shome, Inc., amounted to $1.2 million and accounts payable were $375,000. Sales, which totaled $2.5 million in 2010,   Financing Needs are expected to increase by 25 percent in 2011. Total assets and accounts payable are proportional to sales, and that relationship will be maintained in the future. Shome typically has no current liabilities other than accounts payable. The value of its common stock amounted to $425,000 in 2010, and retained earnings were $295,000. Shome plans to sell new common stock in the amount of $75,000. The firm's profit margin on sales is 6 percent, and 40 percent of earnings will be paid out as dividends.

a. What was Shome's total debt in 2010?

b. How much new, long-term debt financing will be needed in 2011? (*Hint:* AFN − New stock = New long-term debt.) Do not consider any financing feedback effects.

Breakeven Analysis and Leverage
8-7 Straight Arrow Company manufactures golf balls. The following income statement information is relevant for Straight Arrow in 2011:

Selling price per sleeve of balls (P)	$5.00
Variable cost of goods sold as a percentage of price (V)	75%
Fixed operating costs (F)	$50,000
Interest expense (I)	$10,000
Preferred dividends (D_{ps})	$ 0.00
Marginal tax rate (T)	40%
Number of common shares	20,000

a. What level of sales does Straight Arrow need to achieve in 2011 to break even with respect to *operating income?*

b. At its breakeven point, what will be Straight Arrow's EPS?

c. If Straight Arrow expects its sales to reach $300,000 in 2011, what is its degree of operating leverage, its degree of financial leverage, and its degree of total (combined) leverage? Based on the degree of total leverage, compute the EPS you would expect in 2011 if sales actually turn out to be $270,000.

Additional Funds Needed
8-8 The McGill Company's sales are forecasted to increase from $1,000 in 2010 to $2,000 in 2011. Following is the December 31, 2010, balance sheet:

Cash	$ 100	Accounts payable	$ 50
Accounts receivable	200	Notes payable	150
Inventories	200	Accruals	50
Current assets	$ 500	Current liabilities	$ 250
Net fixed assets	500	Long-term debt	400
		Common stock	100
		Retained earnings	250
Total assets	$1,000	Total liabilities and equity	$1,000

McGill's fixed assets were used to only 50 percent of capacity during 2010, but its current assets were maintained at their appropriate levels. All assets except fixed assets increase at the same rate as sales, and fixed assets would also increase at the same rate if the current excess capacity did not exist. McGill's after-tax profit margin is forecasted to be 5 percent, and its dividend payout ratio (percent of earnings paid as dividends) will be 60 percent.

What is McGill's additional funds needed (AFN) for the coming year? Ignore financing feedback effects.

8-9   Craig Computers makes bulk purchases of small computers, stocks them in conveniently located warehouses, and ships them to its chain of retail stores. Following is Craig's balance sheet as of December 31 (all figures are in millions of dollars):

Pro Forma Statements and Ratios

Cash	$ 3.5	Accounts payable	$ 9.0
Receivables	26.0	Notes payable	18.0
Inventories	58.0	Accruals	8.5
Current assets	$ 87.5	Current liabilities	$ 35.5
Net fixed assets	35.0	Long-term bonds	6.0
		Common stock	15.0
		Retained earnings	66.0
Total assets	$122.5	Total liabilities and equity	$122.5

The firm's sales totaled $350 million in 2010, and its net income for the year was $10.5 million. Craig paid dividends of $4.2 million to common stockholders. Sales are projected to increase by $70 million, or 20 percent, during 2011. The firm is operating at full capacity.

a.   Construct Craig's pro forma balance sheet for December 31, 2011. Assume that all external capital requirements are met by bank loans, which are reflected in notes payable. Do not consider any financing feedback effects.

b.   Calculate the following ratios, based on your projected December 31, 2011, balance sheet. Craig's 2010 ratios and industry average ratios are shown here for comparison:

	Craig Computers		Industry Average
	12/31/11	**12/31/10**	**12/31/10**
Current ratio	_____	2.5×	3.0×
Debt/total assets	_____	33.9%	30.0%
Return on equity	_____	13.0%	12.0%

c.   Assume that Craig grows by the same $70 million but that the growth is spread over 5 years—that is, sales grow by $14 million each year. Do not consider any financing feedback effects.

   (1)   Construct a pro forma balance sheet as of December 31, 2015, using notes payable as the balancing item.

   (2)   Calculate the current ratio, debt ratio, and return on equity as of December 31, 2015. (*Hint:* Use total sales, which amount to $1,960 million, to calculate retained earnings, but use 2015 profits to calculate the rate of return on equity. That is, ROE = [2015 profits] ÷ [12/31/15 equity].)

d.   Do the plans outlined in parts (a) and (c) seem feasible to you? That is, do you think Craig could borrow the required capital, and would the company be raising the odds of its bankruptcy to an excessive level in the event of some temporary misfortune?

Additional Funds Needed   **8-10**   Noso Textile's 2010 financial statements follow.

Noso Textile: Balance Sheet as of December 31, 2010 ($ thousand)

Cash	$ 1,080	Accounts payable	$ 4,320
Receivables	6,480	Accruals	2,880
Inventories	9,000	Notes payable	2,100
Current assets	$16,560	Current liabilities	$ 9,300
Net fixed assets	12,600	Long-term bonds	3,500
		Common stock	3,500
		Retained earnings	12,860
Total assets	$29,160	Total liabilities and equity	$29,160

Noso Textile: Income Statement for December 31, 2010 ($ thousand)

Sales	$ 36,000
Operating costs	(32,440)
Earnings before interest and taxes	$ 3,560
Interest	(560)
Earnings before taxes	$ 3,000
Taxes (40%)	(1,200)
Net Income	$ 1,800
Dividends (45%)	$ 810
Addition to retained earnings	$ 990

a. Suppose 2011 sales are projected to increase by 15 percent relative to 2010 sales. Determine Noso's additional funds needed. Assume that the company was operating at full capacity in 2010, that it cannot sell off any of its fixed assets, and that any required financing will be borrowed as notes payable. Also, assume that assets, spontaneous liabilities, and operating costs are expected to increase by the same percentage as sales. Use the projected balance sheet method to develop a pro forma balance sheet and income statement for December 31, 2011. (Do not incorporate any financing feedback effects. Use the pro forma income statement to determine the addition to retained earnings.)

b. Use the financial statements developed in part (a) to incorporate the financing feedback as a result of the addition to notes payable. (That is, do the next financial statement iteration.) For the purpose of this part, assume that the interest rate on the notes payable is 10 percent. What is the AFN for this iteration?

Degree of Leverage   **8-11**   Following is Van Auken Lumber's 2010 income statement.

Van Auken Lumber: Income Statement for December 31, 2010 ($ thousand)

Sales	$ 36,000
Cost of goods sold	(25,200)
Gross profit	$ 10,800
Fixed operating costs	(6,480)
Earnings before interest and taxes	$ 4,320
Interest	(2,880)
Earnings before taxes	$ 1,440
Taxes (40%)	(576)
Net Income	$ 864
Dividends (50%)	$ 432

a. Compute the degree of operating leverage (DOL), degree of financial leverage (DFL), and degree of total leverage (DTL) for Van Auken Lumber.

b. Interpret the meaning of each of the numerical values you computed in part (a).

c. Briefly discuss some ways that Van Auken can reduce its degree of total leverage.

8-12 Following are the 2010 balance sheet and income statement for the Woods Company.

External Financing Requirements (AFN)

Woods Company: Balance Sheet as of December 31, 2010 ($ thousand)

Cash	$ 80	Accounts payable	$ 160
Accounts receivable	240	Accruals	40
Inventories	720	Notes payable	252
Current assets	$1,040	Current liabilities	$ 452
Fixed assets	3,200	Long-term debt	1,244
		Common stock	1,605
		Retained earnings	939
Total assets	$4,240	Total liabilities and equity	$4,240

Woods Company: Income Statement for the Year Ending December 31, 2010 ($ thousand)

Sales	$ 8,000
Operating costs	(7,450)
Earnings before interest and taxes	$ 550
Interest	(150)
Earnings before taxes	$ 400
Taxes (40%)	(160)
Net income	$ 240
Per-Share Data	
Common stock price	$ 16.96
Earnings per share (EPS)	$ 1.60
Dividends per share (DPS)	$ 1.04

a. The firm operated at full capacity in 2010. During 2011, it expects sales to increase by 20 percent and dividends per share to increase to $1.10. Use the projected balance sheet method to determine how much outside financing is required; develop the firm's pro forma balance sheet and income statement, and use AFN as the balancing item.

b. If the firm must maintain a current ratio of 2.3 and a debt ratio of 40 percent, how much financing, after the first pass, will be obtained using notes payable, long-term debt, and common stock?

c. Create the second-pass financial statements by incorporating financing feedbacks and using the ratios calculated in part (b). Assume that the interest rate on debt averages 10 percent.

8-13 The Weaver Watch Company manufactures a line of ladies' watches that is sold through discount houses. Each watch is sold for $25; the fixed costs are $140,000 for 30,000 watches or less; variable costs are $15 per watch.

Breakeven Analysis

a. What is the firm's gain or loss at sales of 8,000 watches? Of 18,000 watches?

b. What is the breakeven point? Illustrate your answer with a graph.

c. What is Weaver's degree of operating leverage (DOL) at sales of 8,000 units? Of 18,000 units?

d. What happens to the operating breakeven point if the selling price rises to $31? What is the significance of the change to the financial manager?

e. What happens to the breakeven point if the selling price rises to $31 but variable costs increase to $23 per unit?

Breakeven Analysis   **8-14**   The following relationships exist for Dellva Industries, a manufacturer of electronic components. Each unit of output is sold for $45; the fixed costs are $175,000, of which $110,000 are annual depreciation charges; variable costs are $20 per unit.

a. What is the firm's gain or loss at sales of 5,000 units? Of 12,000 units?

b. What is the operating breakeven point?

c. Assume that Dellva is operating at a level of 4,000 units. Are creditors likely to seek the liquidation of the company if it is slow in paying its bills?

Cash Budgeting   **8-15**   Patricia Smith recently leased space in the Southside Mall and opened a new business, Smith's Coin Shop. Business has been good, but Smith frequently runs out of cash. This shortcoming has necessitated late payment on certain orders, which in turn is beginning to cause a problem with suppliers. Smith plans to borrow from the bank to have cash ready as needed, but first she needs to forecast how much she must borrow. Accordingly, she has asked you to prepare a cash budget for the critical period around Christmas, when the business's needs will be especially high.

Sales are made on a cash basis only. Smith's purchases of materials must be paid for during the month following the purchases. Smith pays herself a salary of $4,800 per month, and the store's rent is $2,000 per month. In addition, Smith must make a tax payment of $12,000 in December. The current cash on hand (on December 1) is $400, but Smith has agreed to maintain an average bank balance of $6,000—this amount is her target cash balance. (Disregard till cash, which is insignificant because Smith keeps only a small amount on hand to lessen the chances of robbery.)

The firm's estimated sales and purchases for December, January, and February are shown following. Purchases during November amounted to $140,000.

	Sales	Purchases
December	$160,000	$40,000
January	40,000	40,000
February	60,000	40,000

a. Prepare a cash budget for December, January, and February.

b. Suppose that Smith started selling on a credit basis on December 1, giving customers 30 days to pay; all customers accept these terms (paying 30 days after purchases); and all other facts in the problem remain unchanged. What would the company's loan requirements be at the end of February in this case? (*Hint:* The calculations required to answer this question are minimal.)

8-16   Carol Moerdyk, owner of Carol's Fashion Designs, Inc., is planning to re-   **Cash Budgeting**
quest a line of credit from her bank. She has estimated the following sales
forecasts for the firm for parts of 2011 and 2012:

May	2011	$180,000
June		180,000
July		360,000
August		540,000
September		720,000
October		360,000
November		360,000
December		90,000
January	2012	180,000

Collection estimates obtained from the credit and collection department are
as follows: collections within the month of sale, 10 percent; collections during
the month following the sale, 75 percent; collections during the second
month following the sale, 15 percent. Payments for labor and raw materials
are typically made during the month following the one in which these costs
are incurred. Total labor and raw materials costs are estimated for each
month as follows:

May	2011	$ 90,000
June		90,000
July		126,000
August		882,000
September		306,000
October		234,000
November		162,000
December		90,000

General and administrative salaries will amount to approximately $27,000 per
month; lease payments under long-term lease contracts will be $9,000
per month; depreciation charges will be $36,000 per month; miscellaneous
expenses will amount to $2,700 per month; income tax payments of $63,000
will be due in both September and December; and a progress payment of
$180,000 on a new design studio must be paid in October. Cash on hand on
July 1 will amount to $132,000, and the firm will maintain a minimum cash
balance of $90,000 throughout the cash budget period.

a.   Prepare a monthly cash budget for the last 6 months of 2011.

b.   Estimate the required financing (or excess funds)—that is, the amount
of money that Carol will need to borrow (or will have available to
invest)—for each month during that period.

c.   Assume that receipts from sales come in uniformly during the month
(that is, cash receipts come in at the rate of one-thirtieth each day), but
all outflows are paid on the fifth day of the month. Will this pattern have
an effect on the cash budget—that is, will the cash budget you have
prepared be valid under these assumptions? If not, how can you create a
valid estimate of peak financing requirements? No calculations are required, although calculations can be used to illustrate the effects.

d. Carol's production follows a seasonal pattern. Without making any cal-culations, discuss how the company's current ratio and debt ratio would vary during the year assuming that all financial requirements were met by short-term bank loans. Could changes in these ratios affect the firm's ability to obtain bank credit?

Integrative Problem

Forecasting, Breakeven Analysis, and Leverage

8-17 Sue Wilson is the new financial manager of Northwest Chemicals (NWC), an Oregon producer of specialized chemicals that are sold to farmers for use in fruit orchards. She is responsible for constructing financial forecasts and for evaluating the financial feasibility of new products.

Part I. Financial Forecasting Sue must prepare a financial forecast for 2011 for NWC. The firm's 2010 sales amounted to $2 billion, and the marketing department is forecasting a 25 percent increase for 2011. Sue thinks the company was operating at full capacity in 2010, but she is not sure about her assumption. The 2010 financial statements, plus some other data, are given in Table IP8-1.

TABLE IP8-1   Financial Statements and Other Data on NWC ($ million)

A. 2010 Balance Sheet

Cash and securities	$ 20	Accounts payable and accruals	$ 100
Accounts receivable	240	Notes payable	100
Inventories	240	Total current liabilities	$ 200
Total current assets	$ 500	Long-term debt	100
		Common stock	500
Net fixed assets	500	Retained earnings	200
Total assets	$ 1,000	Total liabilities and equity	$1,000

B. 2010 Income Statement

Sales	$ 2,000.00
Variable costs	(1,200.00)
Fixed costs	(700.00)
Earnings before interest and taxes	$ 100.00
Interest	(16.00)
Earnings before taxes	$ 84.00
Taxes (40%)	(33.60)
Net income	$ 50.40
Dividends (30%)	(15.12)
Addition to retained earnings	$ 35.28

C. Key Ratios

	NWC	Industry	Comment
Net profit margin	2.52	4.00	
Return on equity	7.20	15.60	
Days sales outstanding (360 days)	43.20 days	34.00 days	
Inventory turnover	5.00×	8.00×	
Fixed assets turnover	4.00×	5.00×	
Total assets turnover	2.00×	2.50×	
Total debt ratio	30.00%	36.00%	
Times interest earned	6.25×	9.40×	
Current ratio	2.50×	3.00×	
Dividend payout ratio (dividends/NI)	30.00%	30.00%	

Assume that you were recently hired as Sue's assistant, and your first major task is to help her develop the forecast. Sue has asked you to begin by answering the following questions:

a. Assume that NWC was operating at full capacity in 2010 with respect to all assets. Estimate the 2011 financial requirements using the projected financial statement approach, making an initial forecast plus one additional iteration to determine the effects of financing feedbacks. Make the following assumptions: (1) all assets, as well as payables, accruals, and fixed and variable costs, grow at the same rate as sales; (2) the dividend payout ratio is held constant at 30 percent; (3) external funds needed are financed 50 percent by notes payable and 50 percent by long-term debt (no new common stock will be issued); and (4) all debt carries an interest rate of 8 percent.

b. Calculate NWC's forecasted ratios, and compare them with the company's 2010 ratios and with the industry averages. How does NWC compare with the average firm in its industry? Is the company's performance expected to improve during the coming year?

c. Suppose you now learn that NWC's 2010 receivables and inventories were in line with required levels, given the firm's credit and inventory policies, but that excess capacity existed with regard to fixed assets. Specifically, fixed assets were utilized at only 75 percent of the full capacity.

  (1) What level of sales could have existed in 2010 with the available fixed assets? What would the fixed assets/turnover ratio have been if NWC had been operating at full capacity?

  (2) How would the existence of excess capacity in fixed assets affect the additional funds needed during 2011?

d. Without actually working out the numbers, how would you expect the ratios to change in the situation where excess capacity in fixed assets exists? Explain your reasoning.

e. After comparing NWC's days sales outstanding (DSO) and inventory turnover ratios with the industry average figures, does it appear that NWC is operating efficiently with respect to its inventories and accounts receivable? If the company could bring these ratios into line with the industry averages, what effect would this change have on its AFN and its financial ratios?

f. How would changes in the following items affect the AFN: (1) the dividend payout ratio, (2) the profit margin, (3) the plant capacity, and (4) NWC begins buying from its suppliers on terms that permit it to pay after 60 days rather than after 30 days? (Consider each item separately and hold all other things constant.)

Part II. Breakeven Analysis and Leverage One of NWC's employees recently proposed that the company expand its operations and sell its chemicals in retail establishments such as Home Depot and Lowe's Home Improvement. To determine the feasibility of this idea, Sue needs to perform a breakeven analysis. The fixed costs associated with producing and selling the chemicals to retail stores would be $60 million, the selling price per unit is expected to be $10, and the variable cost ratio would be the same as it is now.

a. What is the breakeven point, in terms of both dollars and number of units, for the employee's proposal?

b. Sketch a breakeven graph for the proposal. Should the employee's proposal be adopted if NWC can produce and sell 20 million units of the chemical?

c. If NWC can produce and sell 20 million units of its product to retail stores, what would be its degree of operating leverage for the chemical? What would be NWC's percentage increase in operating profits if sales actually were 10 percent higher than expected?

d. Assume that NWC has excess capacity, so it does not need to raise any additional external funds to implement the proposal—that is, its 2011 interest payments remain the same as the 2010 payments. What would be its degree of financial leverage and its degree of total leverage? If the actual sales turned out to be 10 percent greater than expected, how much greater (in percent) would the earnings per share be?

e. Explain how Sue can use breakeven analysis and leverage analysis in planning the implementation of this proposal.

COMPUTER-RELATED PROBLEM

Work the problem in this section only if you are using the problem spreadsheet.

Forecasting   **8-18**   Use the model in File C08 to solve this problem. Stendardi Industries' 2010 financial statements are shown in the following table.

Stendardi Industries: Balance Sheet as of December 31, 2010 ($ million)

Cash	$ 4.0	Accounts payable	$ 8.0
Receivables	12.0	Notes payable	5.0
Inventories	16.0	Current liabilities	$13.0
Current assets	$32.0	Long-term debt	12.0
Net fixed assets	40.0	Common stock	20.0
		Retained earnings	27.0
Total assets	$72.0	Total liabilities and equity	$72.0

Stendardi Industries: Balance Sheet as of December 31, 2010 ($ million)

Sales	$ 80.0
Operating costs	(71.3)
Earnings before interest and taxes	$ 8.7
Interest	(2.0)
Earnings before taxes	$ 6.7
Taxes (40%)	(2.7)
Net income	$ 4.0
Dividends (40%)	$ 1.60
Addition to retained earnings	$ 2.40

Assume that the firm has no excess capacity in fixed assets, that the average interest rate for debt is 12 percent, and that the projected annual sales growth rate for the next 5 years is 15 percent.

a. Stendardi plans to finance its additional funds needed with 50 percent short-term debt and 50 percent long-term debt. Using the projected balance sheet method, prepare the firm's pro forma financial statements for 2011 through 2015. Determine the following: (1) the additional funds needed, (2) the current ratio, (3) the debt ratio, and (4) the return on equity.

b. Sales growth could be five percentage points higher or lower than the projected 15 percent. Determine the effect of such variances on AFN and the key ratios.

c. Perform an analysis to determine the sensitivity of AFN and the key ratios for 2015 to changes in the dividend payout ratio as specified in the following, assuming that sales grow at a constant 15 percent. What happens to Stendardi's AFN if the dividend payout ratio (1) increases from 40 percent to 70 percent or (2) decreases from 40 percent to 20 percent?

Projected Financial Statements—Including Financing Feedbacks

APPENDIX 8A

In the chapter, we discussed the procedure used to construct pro forma financial statements. In this process, the first step is to estimate the level of operations. Next, we project the effect that such operations will have on the financial statements of the firm. In our discussion, we found that when a firm needs additional external financing, its existing interest and dividend payments will change, thereby altering the values initially projected for the financial statements. To recognize these *financing feedbacks*, we must use an iterative process to construct the projected financial statements.

This appendix describes the iterative process for constructing the pro forma statements for Argile Textiles. Table 8A-1 contains the initial projected statements shown in Tables 8-1 and 8-2, then a subsequent "pass" used to adjust the forecasted statements is given.

In the discussion earlier in the chapter, we constructed the first set of forecasted statements by assuming that only retained earnings and spontaneous financing are available to support the forecasted operations. This "first pass" provides an indication of the additional external funds that are needed—Argile needs $22.51 million. If Argile raises this additional amount by borrowing from the bank and by issuing new bonds and new common stock, however, its interest and dividend payments will increase. We can see this effect by examining the income statement that was constructed in the second pass, which reveals the effects of raising the $22.51 million in additional funds needed. Because Argile would carry additional debt, it would have to pay $0.69 million more in interest. Also, because more shares of the company's common stock are outstanding, the firm would have to pay $0.89 million more in dividends. Consequently, as the second-pass balance sheet shows, if Argile raises only the $22.51 million in AFN initially computed, it would find that it needs still more funds—the AFN would be $1.30 million of additional after-tax interest payments [$0.41 = $0.69(1 − 0.4)] plus additional dividends ($0.89)—because the addition to retained earnings would be lower than originally anticipated. In fact, Argile would need to raise $23.9 million to support the forecasted 2011 operations—$3.6 million from notes, $4.8 million from bonds, and $15.5 million from stock.

TABLE 8A-1   Argile Textiles: 2011 Forecast of Financial Statements ($ million)[a]

	Initial Pass	Feedback	Second Pass	Feedback	Final Pass
Income Statement[b]					
Earnings before interest and taxes (EBIT)	$ 71.50		$ 71.50		$ 71.50
Interest	(20.00)	+0.69	(20.69)	+0.04	(20.73)
Earnings before taxes (EBT)	$ 51.50		$ 50.81		$ 50.77
Taxes (40%)	(20.60)	−0.27	(20.33)	−0.02	(20.31)
Net income	$ 30.90		$ 30.49		$ 30.46
Common dividends	(15.40)	+0.89	(16.29)	+0.06	(16.35)
Addition to retained earnings	$ 15.50	−1.31	$ 14.19	−0.08	$ 14.11
Earnings per share	$ 2.81		$ 2.62		$ 2.61
Dividends per share	$ 1.40		$ 1.40		$ 1.40
Number of common shares (millions)	11.00		11.64		11.68
Balance Sheet[b]					
Total assets	$467.50		$467.50		$467.50
Accounts payable	$ 16.50		$ 16.50		$ 16.50
Accruals	33.00		33.00		33.00
Notes payable	20.00	+3.38	23.38	+0.20	23.58
Total current liabilities	69.50		72.88		73.08
Long-term bonds	152.00	+4.50	156.50	+0.28	156.78
Total liabilities	221.50		229.38		229.86
Common stock	66.00	+14.63	80.63	+0.90	81.53
Retained earnings	157.49	−1.30	156.19	−0.08	156.11
Total owner's equity	223.49		236.82		237.64
Total liabilities and equity	$444.99	+21.21	$466.20	+1.30	$467.50
Additional funds needed (AFN)	$ 22.51		$ 1.30		$ 0.00

[a]A spreadsheet was used to generate the results in this table, which are carried to two decimal places to show some of the more subtle changes that occur. Even so, you will find some rounding differences when summing the feedback amounts.

[b]Because the operating section of the income statement and the asset section of the balance sheet are not affected by financing feedbacks, these sections are not shown in the table.

PART 3

Fundamentals of Valuation

The Time Value of Money

CHAPTER 9

A MANAGERIAL PERSPECTIVE

Even as a student, you should be thinking about retirement. Chances are that unless you create a savings plan for retirement as soon as you start your career, either you will have to work longer than you had planned to attain the retirement lifestyle you desire or you will have to live below the standard of living that you planned for your retirement years. According to the experts, it's never too soon to start saving for retirement. Unfortunately, most Americans are professional procrastinators when it comes to saving and investing for retirement. The savings rate in the United States is the lowest of any developed country. During the 1980s, individuals saved an average of approximately 9 percent of their income, during the 1990s the savings rate dropped to about 5 percent, and since 2000 the savings rate has averaged approximately 1.5 percent. The recent trend has not improved—in 2005, 2006, and 2007 the savings rate was negative, which means that people borrowed more than they saved on average.

Some people believe that they don't need to save much to live comfortably when they retire because they expect to receive Social Security benefits. But don't bet on it! The ratio of workers paying into Social Security to retirees receiving benefits, which was 16.5 in 1950, was down to 3.3 in 2007, and it is expected to be 2.1 by the year 2031. What does all this mean? Current projections are that the government retirement system will go bankrupt within the next 40 years. There are a number of reasons the future of Social Security is in doubt. First, the life expectancy of Americans has increased by more than 15 years, from 67 to more than 80, since the inception of Social Security in 1935, and it is expected to increase further in the future. Second, the number of elderly as a percent of the American population has increased substantially. By the year 2040, it is expected that 25 percent of the U.S. population will be age 65 or older, which is twice today's proportion. Third, more than 77 million "baby boomers" born between 1946 and 1964 are beginning to retire, which is adding a tremendous burden to the system. At some point in the future, there might be more retirees receiving Social Security benefits than workers making contributions to the plan, because birthrates since the mid-1960s have fallen sharply. From 1946 to 1964, the average family had three children; since the mid-1970s the average number of children per family (fertility rate) has been two.

What does the retirement plight of the baby boomers (and their children) have to do with the time value of money? Actually, a great deal. According to a survey conducted by the Employee Benefit Research Institute (EBRI), many Americans are not confident that they will have sufficient funds at retirement to live comfortably. And, although most people indicate that they have saved for retirement, few have any idea as to the amount they need to save to meet their retirement goals. To retire comfortably, 10 to 20 percent of your income should be set aside each year. For example, it is estimated that a 35-year-old who is earning $55,000 would need at least $1 million to retire at the current standard of living in 30 years. To achieve this goal, the individual would have to save about $10,600 each year at 7 percent return, which represents nearly a 20 percent annual savings. The annual savings would have been less than one-half this amount if the individual had begun saving for retirement at age 25.

The techniques and procedures covered in this chapter are exactly the ones used by experts to forecast the boomers' retirement needs, their probable wealth at retirement, and the resulting shortfall. If you study this chapter carefully, perhaps you can avoid the trap into which many people seem to be falling—spending today rather than saving for the future.

Sources: "The 2007 Annual Report of the Board of Trustees of the Federal Old-Age and Survivors Insurance and Disability Insurance Trust Funds" and other reports that are available at the Web site of the Social Security Administration, which is located at http://www.ssa.gov, and "Saving for Retirement in America" and other reports that are available at the Employee Benefit Research Institute Web site, which is located at http://www.ebri.org. Other resources include the Bureau of Economic Analysis, which can be accessed at http://www.bea.gov/, and articles and information found on The Motley Fool, which can be accessed at http://www.fool.com/ ("Our National Savings Rate Is Embarrassing," by Selena Maranjian, January 17, 2007, and "Our Savings Rate Is Abysmal," by Mary Dalrymple, February 2, 2007).

CHAPTER PRINCIPLES
–The Questions

After reading this chapter, you should be able to answer the following questions:

- Why is it important to understand and be able to apply time value of money concepts?
- What is the difference between a present value amount and a future value amount?
- What is an annuity? What are the two types of annuities, and how do their values differ?
- What is the difference between the Annual Percentage Rate (APR) and the Effective Annual Rate (EAR)? Which is more appropriate to use?
- What is an amortized loan? How are amortized loan payments and loan payoffs determined?
- How is the return (interest rate) on an investment (loan) determined?

In Chapter 1, we mentioned that, all else equal, a dollar received sooner is worth more (has more value) than a dollar received at some later date. The logic is simple—*the sooner a dollar is received the more quickly it can be invested to earn a positive return*. So does this mean that an investment that will return $7,023 in 5 years is more valuable than an investment that will return $8,130 in 8 years? Not necessarily, because the 8-year investment promises a higher dollar payoff than the 5-year investment. To determine which investment is more valuable, we need to compare the dollar payoffs for the investments at the same point in time. For example, we can compare these two investments by restating, or revaluing, their future payoffs in terms of current (today's) dollars. The concept used to revalue payoffs such as those associated with these investments is termed the **time value of money.** It is essential that both financial managers and investors have a clear understanding of the time value of money and its effect on the value of an asset. Time value of money concepts are discussed in this chapter, where we show how the timing of cash flows affects the values of assets and rates of return.

The principles of time value analysis that are developed in this chapter have many applications, ranging from setting up schedules for paying off loans to decisions about whether to acquire new equipment. In fact, *of all the techniques used in finance, none is more important than the concept of the time value of money*. Because this concept is used throughout the remainder of the book, it is vital that you understand the time value of money principles presented here before you move on to other topics.

time value of money
The principles and computations used to revalue cash payoffs at different times so they are stated in dollars of the same time period; used to convert dollars from one time period to those of another time period.

CASH FLOW TIME LINES

The first step in time value of money analysis is to construct a **cash flow time line,** which, much like a road map, is used to help visualize the situation that is being analyzed. To illustrate the time line concept, consider the following diagram:

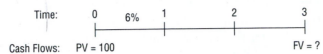

On the time line, Time 0 is today; Time 1 is one period from today, or the end of Period 1; Time 2 is two periods from today, or the end of Period 2; and so on. Often the periods are years; but other time intervals, such as semiannual periods, quarters, months, or even days, are also used. Note that each tick mark corresponds to the end of one period as well as the beginning of the next period—that is, the tick mark at Time 1 represents both the end of Year 1 and the beginning of Year 2.[1]

Cash flows are placed directly below the tick marks, and the interest rate is shown directly above the time line. Unknown cash flows, which we are trying to determine in the analysis, are indicated by question marks. Here $100 is invested at Time 0, and we want to determine how much this investment will be worth in 3 years if it earns 6 percent interest each year.

The cash flow time line is an essential tool that will help you to better understand time value of money concepts—even experts use cash flow time lines to analyze complex problems. We will use cash flow time lines throughout the book, and you should get into the habit of using them when you work problems.

Self-Test Questions

Why is it helpful to draw a cash flow time line when performing a time value of money analysis?

Draw a cash flow time line to illustrate the following situation: You invest $5,000 today in a 4-year savings instrument that pays 7 percent interest each year.

FUTURE VALUE

A dollar in hand today is worth more than a dollar to be received in the future, because, if you had the money now, you could invest it, earn interest, and end up with more than $1 in the future. The process of converting a value stated as a current dollar amount, which is termed the **present value (PV)**, to a **future value (FV)** is called **compounding.** To illustrate, suppose you deposit $100 in a bank account that pays 6 percent interest each year. This is the situation depicted on the cash flow time line in the previous section. How much would you have at the end of 3 years? To begin, we define the following terms:

PV = Present value, or beginning amount, that is invested (or received).
     Here PV = $100.

cash flow time line
An important tool used in time value of money analysis; it is a graphical representation used to show the timing of cash flows.

present value (PV)
The value today—that is, current value—of a future cash flow or series of cash flows.

future value (FV)
The amount to which a cash flow or series of cash flows will grow over a given period of time when compounded at a given interest rate.

compounding
The process of determining the value of a cash flow or series of cash flows sometime in the future when compound interest is applied.

---

[1]For our discussions, the difference between the end of one period and the beginning of the next period is the same as one day ending and the next day beginning—it occurs in less than one second.

r = Interest rate the bank pays on the account each year. The interest earned is based on the balance in the account at the beginning of each year, and we assume that it is paid at the end of the year. Here r = 6%, or, expressed as a decimal, r = 0.06.

INT = Dollars of interest you earn during the year = (Beginning-of-year-amount) × r. Here INT = $100 × 0.06 = $6 in the first year.

FV_n = Future value, or value of the account at the end of n periods (years in this case), after the interest earned has been added to the account.

n = Number of periods interest is earned. Here n = 3.

When computing the future value of an amount invested today, we determine by how much the amount will increase as the result of the interest it earns each year. In our example, the $100 that you invest today will earn 6 percent interest each year for the next 3 years. So, to what amount will your $100 grow in 3 years if it is left in the bank account to accumulate interest? Following is a cash flow time line that is set up to show the amount that will be in the bank account at the end of each year. To compute the end-of-year balance, the amount that is in the bank account at the beginning of the year is multiplied by (1 + r) = 1.06, which accounts for the 6 percent increase that occurs as a result of the annual interest payment.

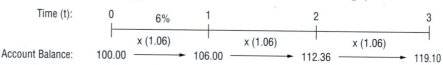

Note the following points:

1. You start by depositing $100 in the bank account—this amount is shown at time t = 0.

2. You earn $100 × 0.06 = $6 of interest during the first year, so the amount at the end of Year 1 is $100 + $6 = $106 = $100(1.06).

3. You start the second year with $106. In the second year, you earn 6 percent interest both on the $100 you invested originally and on the $6 paid to you as interest in the first year—that is, $6.36 total interest is earned in the second year. The $6.36 interest earned in the second year is higher than the first year's interest of $6 because you earn an additional $0.36 =$6 × 0.06 interest by leaving the $6 interest received in Year 1 in the account to earn interest in Year 2. This is an example of *compounding*, which occurs when interest is earned on interest.

4. This process continues. And because the beginning balance is higher in each succeeding year, the amount of interest earned increases each year.

5. The balance in the bank account at the end of Year 3 is $119.10.

As you can see, the total interest earned, $19.10, is greater than $6 per year ($18 for three years), which is 6 percent of the *original* $100 investment. Because the interest earned each year is left in the bank account to earn additional interest the following year, an additional $1.10 = $19.10 − $18.00 is earned compared to what would be earned if the interest payments are withdrawn each year. When interest is left in the account (or reinvested) to earn additional interest, as in our example, the investment is said to earn **compounded interest.**

In this chapter, we will show four different approaches to solve a time value of money problem. We will solve the problem using (1) the cash flow time line to compute the value at the end of each period, which we refer to as the *time line solution*, (2) the appropriate equation, which we refer to as the *equation (numerical)*

compounded interest
Interest earned on interest that is reinvested.

solution, (3) the time value of money functions that are programmed into a financial calculator, which we refer to as the *financial calculator solution*, and (4) the time value of money functions that are programmed into a spreadsheet, which we refer to as the *spreadsheet solution*. Each approach will give the same answer to a particular problem, because each is performing the same computation—we simply use different approaches to perform the computation.

TIME LINE SOLUTION

We showed the time line solution to the current time value of money problem in the previous section. Based on the time line solution, we know that the end-of-the-year balances in the bank account will be $106.00, $112.36, and $119.10 in Year 1, Year 2, and Year 3, respectively.

EQUATION (NUMERICAL) SOLUTION

According to the time line solution, we can compute the balance in the bank account at the end of each year by multiplying the balance at the beginning of each of the three years by $(1 + r) = (1.06)$. As a result, in our example, we would get the same ending balance of $119.10 if we multiplied the initial $100 investment by $(1.06)^3$. That is,

$$FV_3 = \$100(1.06)^3 = \$100(1.191016) = \$119.10$$

When this concept is generalized, the future value of an amount invested today can be computed by applying this equation:

$$FV_n = PV(1 + r)^n$$

9-1

According to Equation 9-1, to compute the future value (FV) of an amount invested today (PV) we need to determine by what multiple the initial investment will increase in the future. As you can see, the multiple by which any amount will increase depends on both the interest rate (r) and the length of time (n) interest is earned—that is, $(1 + r)^n$. The solution for $(1 + r)^n$ can be found with a regular calculator by using the exponential function to raise $(1 + r)$ to the nth power. To solve using the exponential function key on your calculator, which generally is labeled y^x, you would enter 1.06 into your calculator, press the $\boxed{y^x}$ function key, enter 3, and then press the $\boxed{=}$ key. The result displayed on your calculator should be 1.191016, which when multiplied by $100 gives the final answer, $119.1016, or $119.10 when rounded.

FINANCIAL CALCULATOR SOLUTION

Equation 9-1 and most other time value of money (TVM) equations have been programmed directly into *financial calculators*, and such calculators can be used to find future values. These calculators have five keys that correspond to the five most commonly used TVM variables:

| N | I/Y | PV | PMT | FV |

These key designations correspond to the TVM keys that are on a Texas Instruments BAII PLUS financial calculator, which is the calculator that we use throughout this book. Here:

N = The number of periods. This key corresponds to n in Equation 9-1.

I/Y = Interest rate per period. This key corresponds to r in Equation 9-1.

PV = Present (today's) value. This key corresponds to PV in Equation 9-1.

PMT = Annuity payment. This key is used only if the cash flows involve a series of equal, or constant, payments (an annuity). If there are no periodic payments in the particular problem, then PMT = 0. We will use this key later in the chapter.

FV = Future (ending) value. This key corresponds to FV in Equation 9-1.

Throughout the book, we show the values that need to be entered into the financial calculator above the keys and the result of the computation below the keys. For the current example, the inputs and the result are:

Inputs:	3	6	−100	0	?
	N	I/Y	PV	PMT	FV
Output:					= 119.10

Financial calculators require that all cash flows be designated as either inflows or outflows because the computations are based on the fact that we generally pay, which is a **cash outflow,** to receive a benefit, which is a **cash inflow.** As a result, you must enter cash outflows as negative numbers. In our illustration, you deposit the initial amount, which is a cash outflow to you, and you take out, or receive, the ending amount, which is a cash inflow to you. Thus, for this problem, the PV should be entered as −100.[2] If you forget the negative sign and enter 100, then the calculator assumes that you receive $100 in the current period and that you must pay it back with interest in the future, so the FV appears as −119.10, a cash outflow. Sometimes the convention of changing signs can be confusing, but, if you think about what you are doing, you should not have a problem with whether the calculator gives you a positive or a negative answer.[3]

cash outflow
A payment, or disbursement, of cash for expenses, investments, and so forth.

cash inflow
A receipt of cash from an investment, an employer, or other sources.

SPREADSHEET SOLUTION[4]

You probably will use a calculator to solve time value of money problems that are assigned for homework and appear on your exams. However, because most businesses use spreadsheets to solve these problems, you need to have some familiarity with the applications of the TVM functions that are programmed into spreadsheets. You should be able to understand the discussion that follows even if you have not used spreadsheets much.

To access the time value of money functions that are programmed into Excel 2007, you must click the Insert Function option, which is designated f_x and can be found in the Formulas menu on the toolbar at the top of the spreadsheet.[5] Each preprogrammed function is standardized so that numbers must be entered in a specific order to solve the problem correctly. In this chapter, we show the inputs,

---

[2]To reduce clutter, we do not show the dollar signs for the time line solution or the financial calculator solution.

[3]We should note that financial calculators permit you to specify the number of decimal places that are displayed. For most calculators, at least 12 significant digits are used in the actual calculations. But for the purposes of reporting the results of the computations, generally we use two places for answers when working with dollars or percentages and four to six places when working with decimals. *The nature of the problem dictates how many decimal places should be displayed*—to be safe, you might want to set your calculator so that the floating decimal format is used and round the final results yourself.

[4]If you are not familiar with spreadsheets, Appendix A at the end of the book provides a short tutorial.

[5]The Insert Function selection can also be found on the Home menu under the summation sign, Σ.

FIGURE 9-1   Using Excel's FV Function to Compute Future Value

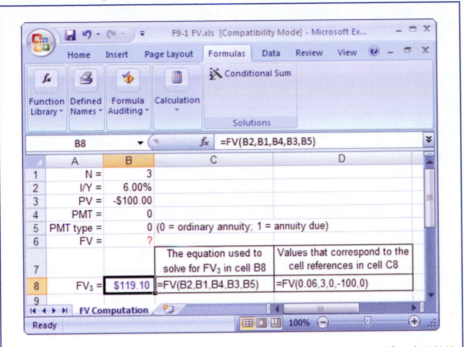

Note: According to the equation shown in cell C8, the input values must be entered in a specific order: I/Y, N, PMT, PV, and PMT type (not used for this problem). It's a good idea to set up a table that contains the data needed to solve the problem, and then refer to the cell where each number is located when you apply the FV equation. If you follow this technique, you can change any number in the table you set up, and the result of the change will immediately show in the cell where the equation is located. For example, if the current problem is changed so that $500 rather than $100 is deposited in a bank account, you would change the value in cell B3 to −$500, and the result of $595.51 would appear in cell B8.

the format of the spreadsheet function, and the results. For a more detailed discussion of how to set up the spreadsheet to solve TVM problems, see Appendix A at the end of the book.

Figure 9-1 shows the setup and the results of using the FV function to compute the future value in 3 years of $100 invested today at 6 percent. Because a financial calculator is programmed much like a spreadsheet to solve time value of money problems, the labels given in Rows 1 through 6 of Column A correspond to the TVM keys on a financial calculator. Note that the $100 invested today is entered into the spreadsheet as a negative value, just like it is when using a financial calculator to solve the problem. When entering values, there is one difference between a financial calculator and a spreadsheet—the interest rate is entered as a percentage (6.0 in our example) in the financial calculator, whereas it is entered as a decimal (0.06 in our example) in the spreadsheet. (In Figure 9-1, even though 0.06 was entered in cell B2 for the interest rate, it appears as 6.00% because the cell was formatted so that the number appears as a percent.)

Graphic View of the Compounding Process: Growth

Figure 9-2 shows how $1 (or any other sum) grows over time at various interest rates. The data used to plot the curves were obtained by solving Equation 9-1 for different values of r and n. We used a spreadsheet to generate the values and draw the curves shown in Figure 9-2. The figure shows that (1) the future value of an amount invested at

FIGURE 9-2   Relationship among Future Value, Growth or Interest Rates, and Time

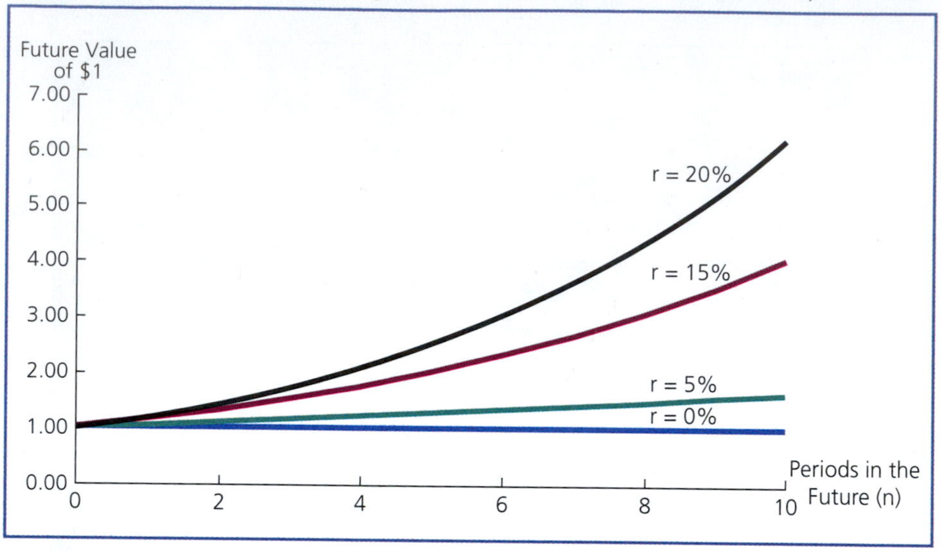

a positive interest rate today will grow to a higher amount the longer it is invested, and (2) the higher the rate of interest, the faster the rate of growth of an amount invested today. In other words, the higher the interest rate, the greater the effect of interest compounding. The *interest rate is*, in fact, *a growth rate:* if a sum is deposited and earns 6 percent interest, then the funds on deposit will grow at a rate of 6 percent per period.

? Self-Test Questions

Explain what the following statement means: "A dollar in hand today is worth more than a dollar to be received next year."

What is compounding? What is "interest on interest"?

Assume that you invest $2,500 today. How much will this amount be worth in 5 years if the interest rate is 4 percent? How would your answer change if the interest rate is 6 percent?   (Answers: $3,041.63; $3,345.56)

PRESENT VALUE

opportunity cost rate
The rate of return on the best available alternative investment of equal risk.

In the example presented in the previous section, we saw that an initial amount of $100 invested at 6 percent per year would grow to $119.10 at the end of 3 years. This means that you should be indifferent between the choice of receiving $100 today or $119.10 at the end of 3 years if you have the opportunity to earn 6 percent interest per year. The $100 that would be invested today is defined as the present value, or PV, of $119.10 due in 3 years when the **opportunity cost rate** is 6 percent. Suppose that someone offered to sell you an investment that promises to pay $119.10 in 3 years for $95 today. Should you buy this investment if your opportunity cost is 6 percent? You should definitely buy it because, as we discovered in the previous section, it would cost you exactly $100 to produce $119.10 in 3 years if you earn a 6 percent return. Therefore, if you could find another investment with the same risk that would produce the same future amount—that is, $119.10—but its cost is less than $100, then you would earn a return higher than 6 percent by purchasing the investment. On the other hand, if the price of the security is greater than $100, you should not buy it because it would cost you only $100 to produce the same future amount at 6 percent per year.

In general, *the present value of a cash flow due n years in the future is the amount that, if it were on hand today, would grow to equal the future amount at a particular rate of return.* Because $100 will grow to $119.10 in 3 years at a 6 percent interest rate, $100 is the present value of $119.10 due 3 years in the future when the opportunity cost rate is 6 percent.

The process of finding present values is called **discounting.** Discounting simply is the reverse of compounding—that is, rather than adding interest to a current amount to determine its future value, we take interest out of a future amount to determine its present value. In essence, when we compute the present value of a future amount, we "strip out" the interest that the amount earns during the investment period. Consequently, if we solve for PV in Equation 9-1, we have an equation that can be used to solve for the present value of a future dollar amount:

discounting
The process of determining the present value of a cash flow or a series of cash flows received (paid) in the future; the reverse of compounding.

$$PV = FV_n \left[\frac{1}{(1+r)^n} \right]$$

9-2

TIME LINE SOLUTION

Applying Equation 9-2 to the current situation gives the following:

Time (t):	0		1		2		3
		6%					
		÷ (1.06)		÷ (1.06)		÷ (1.06)	
Account Balance:	100.00		106.00		112.36		119.10

EQUATION (NUMERICAL) SOLUTION

Applying Equation 9-2 to the current situation using the equation (numerical) approach gives the following:

$$PV = \$119.10 \left[\frac{1}{(1.06)^3} \right] = \$119.10(0.839619) = \$100.00$$

FINANCIAL CALCULATOR SOLUTION

Enter N = 3, I/Y = 6, PMT = 0, and FV = 119.10; then solve for PV = −100.00.

Inputs:	3	6	?	0	119.10
	N	I/Y	PV	PMT	FV
Output:			= −**100.00**		

SPREADSHEET SOLUTION

Figure 9-3 shows the setup and the results of using the spreadsheet's PV function to compute the present value of $119.10 to be received in 3 years if the interest rate is 6 percent. Note that the setup is the same as in Figure 9-1, except we now enter FV = $119.10 and we solve for PV rather than entering PV = −$100.00 and solving for FV.

FIGURE 9-3   Using Excel's PV Function to Compute Present Value

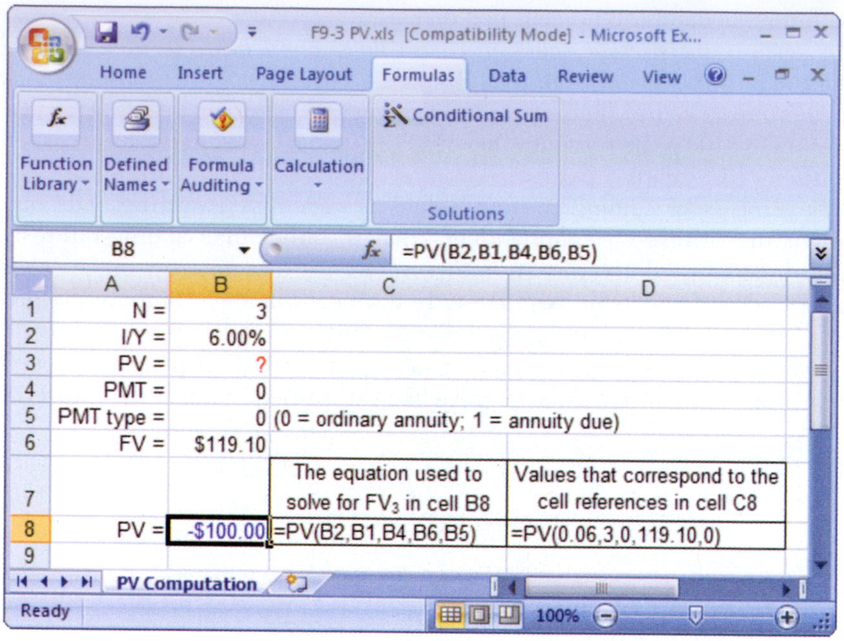

	A	B	C	D
1	N =	3		
2	I/Y =	6.00%		
3	PV =	?		
4	PMT =	0		
5	PMT type =	0	(0 = ordinary annuity; 1 = annuity due)	
6	FV =	$119.10		
7			The equation used to solve for FV₃ in cell B8	Values that correspond to the cell references in cell C8
8	PV =	-$100.00	=PV(B2,B1,B4,B6,B5)	=PV(0.06,3,0,119.10,0)
9				

Cell reference box: B8 f_x =PV(B2,B1,B4,B6,B5)

Note: According to the equation shown in cell C8, the input values must be entered in a specific order: I/Y, N, PMT, FV, and PMT type (not used in this computation).

Graphic View of the Discounting Process

Figure 9-4 shows how the present value of $1 (or any other sum) to be received in the future diminishes as the time to receipt or the interest rate increases. Again, we used a spreadsheet to generate the values and draw the curves shown in Figure 9-4. The figure shows that (1) the present value of a sum to be received at some future date decreases and approaches 0 as the payment date is extended further into the future and (2) the present value of a future amount is lower the higher the interest (discount) rate. At relatively high interest rates, funds due in the future are worth very little today, and even at relatively low discount rates, the present value of an amount due in the very distant future is quite small. For example, at a 20 percent discount rate, $5 million due in 100 years is worth only 6¢ today; conversely, 6¢ would grow to approximately $5 million in 100 years if it is invested at 20 percent.

Self-Test Questions

What is meant by the term *opportunity cost rate*?

What is discounting? How is discounting related to compounding?

Assume that you have the opportunity to purchase an investment that promises to pay you $3,277 in 4 years and your opportunity cost is 7 percent. How much should you be willing to pay for this investment today? How would your answer change if your opportunity cost is 5 percent?   (Answers: $2,500; $2,696)

FIGURE 9-4   Relationship among Present Value, Growth or Interest Rates, and Time

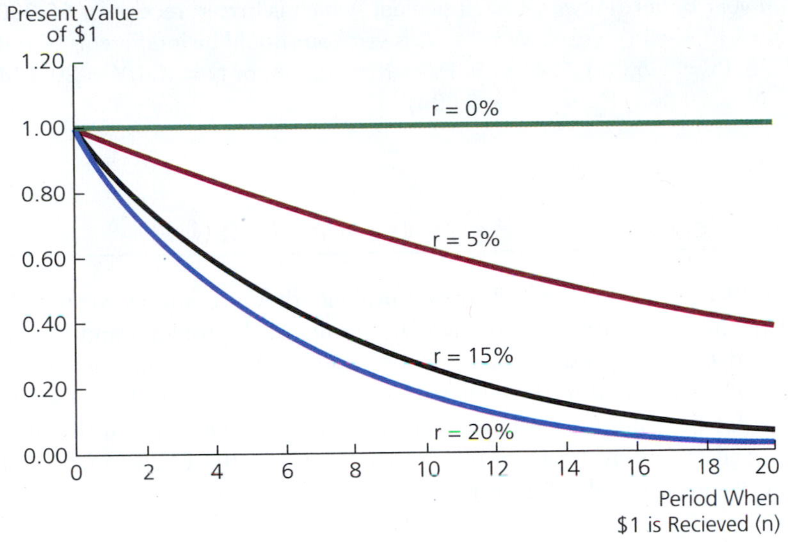

COMPARISON OF FUTURE VALUE WITH PRESENT VALUE

In the previous sections, we showed that $100 invested today at 6 percent will grow to $119.10 in 3 years, and an amount equal to $119.10 to be received in 3 years is worth $100 today if the opportunity cost is 6 percent. Let's assume that you win a raffle that allows you to choose one of two prizes—$100 that will be paid to you today or $119.10 that will be paid to you in 3 years. If your opportunity cost is 6 percent, which prize *should* you choose? Believe it or not, you should flip a coin to make your choice, because both prizes are equally desirable. Whichever prize you receive can be used to create the other prize. For example, if you are given the prize that pays you $100 today, you can invest the money at 6 percent and it will grow to $119.10 in 3 years. Conversely, if you are given the prize that pays you $119.10 in 3 years, you can sell the prize for $100 today. What if you need money today to help pay your rent? Shouldn't you choose the prize that pays you $100 today? The answer is the same as before—it doesn't matter which prize you choose, because you can convert the payoff you receive from one prize into the payoff that you would receive from the other prize. In other words, even if you receive the prize with the future payoff, you should be able to turn it into cash today by selling it.

This simple example shows that when we work time value of money problems, we simply restate (convert) dollars (values) from one time period into their *equivalent* values at some other point in time. Simply stated, when we determine the future value of a current amount, we add the interest that the amount will earn if it is invested today and then is liquidated at some future time. Conversely, when we determine the present value of a future amount, we take out the interest that the amount will earn during the time period to determine how much has to be invested today to create the same future amount—you might say that we "de-interest" the future amount. If you understand this concept, you will have little difficulty grasping the material presented in the rest of the book.

Self-Test Question

If your opportunity cost is 20 percent, which is better: receipt of $5,000 today or $10,368 in 4 years? Why?   (Answer: You should be indifferent; N = 4, I/Y = 20, PV = −5,000, PMT = 0, FV = ? = 10,368, or N = 4, I/Y = 20, PMT = 0, FV = 10,368, PV = ? = −5,000)

SOLVING FOR INTEREST RATES (r) AND TIME (n)

Equation 9-1 and Equation 9-2 are equivalent; they are simply arranged differently. Equation 9-1 is arranged to solve future value (FV) problems and Equation 9-2 is arranged to solve present value (PV) problems. These equations include four variables: PV, FV, r, and n. If we know the values of any three of these variables, we can solve for the value of the fourth. To this point, we have known the number of years, n, and the interest rate, r, plus either the PV or the FV. In many situations, however, we need to solve for either r or n.

Solving for r

Suppose you can buy a security at a price of $78.35 that will pay you $100 after 5 years. What rate of return will you earn if you purchase the security? Here you know PV, FV, and n, but you do not know r, the interest rate you will earn on your investment. We can solve this problem as follows:

TIME LINE SOLUTION

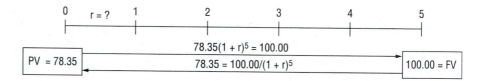

EQUATION (NUMERICAL) SOLUTION

Plugging the known values into Equation 9-1, we have:

$$FV_n = PV(1 + r)^n$$

$$\$100.00 = \$78.35(1 + r)^5$$

In this case, solving for r is not difficult. However, because it is easier to solve for r using either a financial calculator or a spreadsheet, we do not show the numerical solution here.[6]

---

[6]If you are interested, we can solve for r using simple algebra:

$$(1 + r)^5 = \frac{\$100.00}{\$78.35} = 1.27632$$

$$(1 + r) = (1.27632)^{1/5} = (1.27632)^{0.2} = 1.05$$

$$r = 1.05 - 1 = 0.05 = 5.0\%$$

Figure 9-5   Using Excel's RATE Function to Compute r for a Lump-Sum Amount

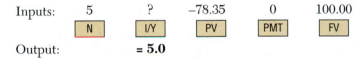

	A	B	C	D
			F9-5 RATE.xls [Compatibility Mode] - Microsoft Excel	
			B8 ▼ f_x =RATE(B1,B4,B3,B6,B5)	
1	N =	5		
2	I/Y =	?		
3	PV =	-$78.35		
4	PMT =	0		
5	PMT type =	0	(0 = ordinary annuity; 1 = annuity due)	
6	FV =	$100.00		
7			The equation used to solve for RATE in cell B8	Values that correspond to the cell references in cell C8
8	RATE =	5.00%	=RATE(B1,B4,B3,B6,B5)	=RATE(5,0,-78.35,100.00,0)
9				

RATE Computation

Note: According to the equation shown in cell C8, the input values must be entered in a specific order: N, PMT, PV, FV, and PMT type (not used in this computation).

FINANCIAL CALCULATOR SOLUTION

Enter the known values into the appropriate locations—that is, N = 5, PV = −78.35, PMT = 0, and FV = 100; then solve for the unknown value:

Inputs:	5	?	−78.35	0	100.00
	N	I/Y	PV	PMT	FV
Output:		= **5.0**			

SPREADSHEET SOLUTION

Figure 9-5 shows how to use the RATE function that is built into Excel to solve for r in our example. According to the answer, if you invest $78.35 today at 5 percent, in 5 years your investment will be worth $100—that is, $FV_5 = \$78.35(1.05)^5 = \$100$.

Solving for n

Suppose you know that a security will provide a return of 10 percent per year, it will cost $68.30, and you will receive $100 at maturity. In how many years does the security mature? In this case, we know PV, FV, and r, but we do not know n, the number of periods.

TIME LINE SOLUTION

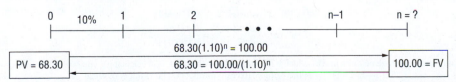

0	10%	1	2	...	n−1	n = ?
PV = 68.30			$68.30(1.10)^n = 100.00$			
			$68.30 = 100.00/(1.10)^n$			100.00 = FV

EQUATION (NUMERICAL) SOLUTION

Plugging the known values into Equation 9-1, we have:

$$FV_n = PV(1 + r)^n$$
$$\$100.00 = \$68.30(1.10)^n$$

One method of finding the value of n is to use a trial-and-error process in which you insert different values of n into the equation until you find a value that "works" in the sense that the right side of the equation equals $100. You would eventually find that the solution is n = 4—that is, it takes 4 years for $68.30 to grow to $100 if interest equal to 10 percent is paid each year.[7] $FV_4 = \$68.30(1.10)^4 = \$100$.

FINANCIAL CALCULATOR SOLUTION

Enter I/Y = 10, PV = −68.30, PMT = 0, and FV = 100; then solve for n = 4.

Inputs:	?	10	−68.30	0	100.00
	N	I/k	PV	PMT	FV

Output: = **4.0**

SPREADSHEET SOLUTION

Figure 9-6 shows how to use the NPER function that is built into Excel to solve for n in our example. Simply enter the required information into the NPER function and you will find that the answer is n = 4.

Self-Test Questions

Suppose that you just called the East Key State Bank and found that the balance in your savings account is $1,269.50. If you deposited $800 6 years ago, what rate of return have you earned on the savings account?   (Answer: 8.0 percent)

Assume that you can invest $1,000 today at 7 percent interest. If you plan to sell the investment when its value reaches $1,500, for how long will your money have to be invested?   (Answer: 6 years)

ANNUITY PAYMENTS

In the previous sections, we showed how to find both the future value of a single amount invested today and the present value of a single amount to be received in the future. But many investments provide a series of cash flows over time—for

---

[7]The value of n also can be found as follows:

$$\$100 = \$68.30(1.10)^n$$
$$(1.10)^n = \frac{\$100}{\$68.30} = 1.46413$$
$$\ln[(1.10)^n] = n[\ln(1.10)] = \ln(1.46413)$$
$$n = \frac{\ln(1.46413)}{\ln(1.10)} = \frac{0.38126}{0.09531} = 4.0$$

You can use your calculator to find ln, which is the natural logarithm. For most calculators, you insert the number—in this case, 1.46413—and then press the LN key (or its equivalent). The result is 0.38126.

FIGURE 9-6   Using Excel's NPER Function to Compute n for a Lump-Sum Amount

	F9-6 NPER.xls [Compatibility Mode] - Microsoft Excel

Home   Insert   Page Layout   **Formulas**   Data   Review   View

Function Library   Defined Names   Formula Auditing   Calculation   Conditional Sum

Solutions

B8 f_x =NPER(B2,B4,B3,B6,B5)

	A	B	C	D
1	N =	?		
2	I/Y =	10.00%		
3	PV =	-$68.30		
4	PMT =	0		
5	PMT type =	0	(0 = ordinary annuity; 1 = annuity due)	
6	FV =	$100.00		
7			The equation used to solve for NPER in cell B8	Values that correspond to the cell references in cell C8
8	NPER =	4.00	=NPER(B2,B4,B3,B6,B5)	=RATE(0.10,0,-68.30,100,0)
9				

NPER Computation

Ready   100%

Note: According to the equation shown in cell C8, the input values must be entered in a specific order: I/Y, PMT, PV, FV, and PMT type (not used in this computation).

example, if you buy a bond, you might receive a $100 interest payment every year for the life of the bond. When cash flows, such as interest payments on a bond, are constant and are received at equal time intervals, such as once every 12 months, the cash flow series is called an **annuity.** The annuity payments are given the symbol PMT, and they can occur either at the beginning or at the end of each period. If the payments occur at the end of each period, as they typically do in business trans- actions, the annuity is called an **ordinary,** or **deferred, annuity.** If payments are made at the beginning of each period, the annuity is an **annuity due.** Because ordinary annuities are more common in finance, when the term *annuity* is used in this book, you should assume that the payments occur at the end of each period unless otherwise noted.

Suppose Alice decides to deposit $100 each year for 3 years in a savings account that pays 5 percent interest per year. If Alice makes her first deposit 1 year from today, the series of deposits would be considered an *ordinary annuity.* The cash flow time line for this annuity is:

Ordinary Annuity Cash Flow Time Line (Alice's Deposits)

Suppose that Alice's twin brother, Alvin, thinks that his sister's savings plan is a good idea, so he decides to copy her by also depositing $100 each year for 3 years in a savings account that pays 5 percent interest per year. But, Alvin decides to make his

annuity
A series of payments of an equal amount at fixed, equal intervals for a specified number of periods.

ordinary (deferred) annuity
An annuity with pay- ments that occur at the end of each period.

annuity due
An annuity with pay- ments that occur at the beginning of each period.

first deposit today rather than 1 year from today. This series of deposits is an *annuity due,* and its cash flow time line is:

Annuity Due Cash Flow Time Line (Alvin's Deposits)

As you can see from these cash flow time lines, the only difference between an ordinary annuity (Alice's deposits) and an equivalent annuity due (Alvin's deposits) is the timing of the cash flows. Both annuities have the same total amount (cash flows) deposited over the 3-year period, but each deposit is made earlier if the cash flow series represents an annuity due. Do you think that the values of these two annuities are the same? Based on what we covered earlier in the chapter, you should have answered "NO!" to this question. We know that $100 deposited today is not the same as $100 deposited in 1 year. In our example, we know that the *first* $100 that Alvin deposits today has a different (higher) "time value" than the *first* $100 that Alice deposits in 1 year. Which annuity is the better annuity? We can answer this question by computing the future values of the two annuities.

In the sections that follow, we show you how to compute both the future value and the present value of an annuity. We also show you how to determine the interest rate you pay on such annuities as automobile loans and how much you have to invest each year (or other period) to achieve such goals as accumulating a specific amount—say, $2,000,000 in a retirement plan.

As you read this section, keep in mind that, to be considered an annuity, the series of cash flows must (1) be constant and (2) occur at equal intervals. If a cash flow series is lacking one or both of these requirements, then it is not an annuity, and the procedures used to determine the values of annuities do not apply.

Self-Test Questions

What is the difference between an ordinary annuity and an annuity due?

Under what circumstances would you prefer a series of cash flows to be an annuity due? When would you prefer a series of cash flows to be an ordinary annuity? (*Hint:* Consider those instances when you receive the annuity payments versus when you pay the annuity payments.)

FUTURE VALUE OF AN ANNUITY

In this section, we will use the example that was introduced in the previous section to show you how to compute the future values of the two annuities—that is, the ordinary annuity (Alice's deposits) and the annuity due (Alvin's deposits).

FUTURE VALUE OF AN ORDINARY ANNUITY

Remember that Alice has decided to deposit $100 each year for 3 years in a savings account that pays 5 percent interest per year, and the first deposit will be made 1 year from today. In this section, we show you how to compute the amount that Alice will have in her savings account at the end of 3 years.

TIME LINE SOLUTION

One way to determine the future value of an ordinary annuity, which we designate FVA_n, is to compute the future value of *each* annuity payment using Equation 9-1 and then sum the results. Using this approach, the computation of the future value of Alice's deposits (annuity) is:

FVA_n
The future value of an *ordinary* annuity over n periods.

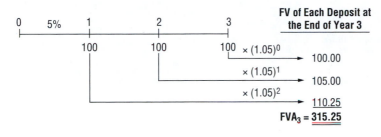

EQUATION (NUMERICAL) SOLUTION

The time line solution shows that we can compute the future value of the annuity simply by determining the future values of the individual payments and then summing the results. Thus, we can write an equation for the future value of an ordinary annuity as a series of solutions to Equation 9-1:

$$\begin{aligned} \text{FVA}_n &= \text{PMT}(1+r)^0 + \text{PMT}(1+r)^1 + \text{PMT}(1+r)^2 + \cdots + \text{PMT}(1+r)^{n-1} \\ &= \text{PMT}[(1+r)^0 + (1+r)^1 + (1+r)^2 + \cdots + (1+r)^{n-1}] \\ &= \text{PMT}\left[\sum_{t=0}^{n-1}(1+r)^t\right] \end{aligned}$$

The first line of Equation 9-3 presents the annuity payments in reverse order of payment where the superscript in each term indicates the number of periods of interest each payment receives. In the current example, Alice deposits the first $100 at the end of Year 1, so interest is earned in Year 2 and Year 3 only (see the cash flow time line). Note that the last $100 deposit is made at the same time the computation is made, so there is no time for this deposit to earn interest. Because the deposit each year (PMT) is the same—that is, $\text{PMT}_1 = \text{PMT}_2 = \ldots = \text{PMT}_n = \text{PMT}$—we can simplify the first line of Equation 9-3 to produce the next two lines. Further simplification of Equation 9-3 produces a general equation that can be used to solve for the future value of an ordinary annuity:[8]

$$\text{FVA}_n = \text{PMT}\left[\sum_{t=0}^{n-1}(1+r)^n\right] = \text{PMT}\left[\frac{(1+r)^n - 1}{r}\right]$$

Using Equation 9-4, the future value of $100 deposited at the end of each year for 3 years in a savings account that earns 5 percent interest per year is:

$$\text{FVA}_3 = \$100\left[\frac{(1.05)^3 - 1}{0.05}\right] = \$100(3.15250) = \$315.25$$

---

[8]The simplification shown in Equation 9-4 is found by applying the algebra of geometric progressions.

FIGURE 9-7 Using Excel's FV Function to Compute the Future Value
of an Ordinary Annuity

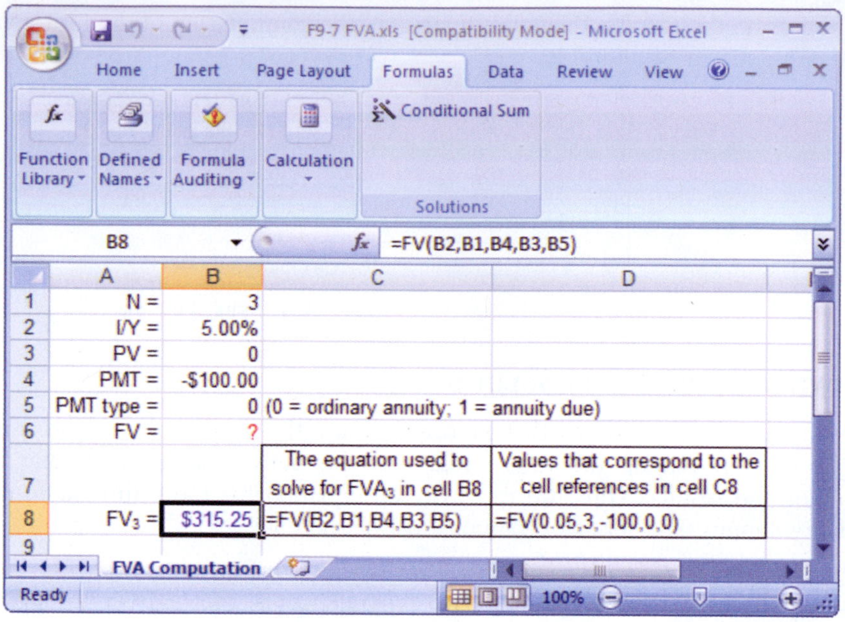

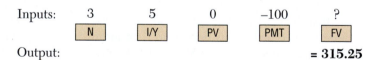

Note: According to the equation shown in cell C8, the input values must be entered in a specific order: I/Y, N, PMT, PV, and PMT type.

FINANCIAL CALCULATOR SOLUTION

To solve for FVA_3 using a financial calculator, we must use the PMT (annuity) key. In our example, because the annuity payment equals $100 per year, PMT = −100. Enter N = 3, I/Y = 5, PV = 0, and PMT = −100; then solve for FV:

Inputs:	3	5	0	−100	?
	N	I/Y	PV	PMT	FV
Output:					**= 315.25**

SPREADSHEET SOLUTION

Figure 9-7 shows how to set up and solve the current situation using an Excel spreadsheet. Notice that we use the same financial function that we used to solve for the future value of a single payment, which is shown in Figure 9-1. To solve for the future value of an annuity, however, we must enter a value for PMT so that the value in cell B4 is −$100. Also, because we are solving for the future value of an ordinary annuity, the value in cell B5 is 0. The value in cell B5 is like an on-off switch that tells the FV function in the spreadsheet whether the annuity payment represents an ordinary annuity, in which case cell B5 = 0, or an annuity due, in which case cell B5 = 1.

Future Value of an Annuity Due

Because Alvin intends to make his deposits at the *beginning* of each year, his series of deposits represents an *annuity due.* To determine the future value of an annuity due, we must adjust our computation to recognize that each annuity payment earns interest for 1 additional year (period).

TIME LINE SOLUTION

The cash flow time line that depicts Alvin's deposits is the same as for Alice's deposits except each payment is made 1 year earlier, which means that each deposit earns interest for 1 additional year.

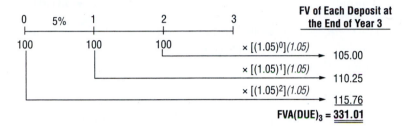

Here we designate the future value of an annuity due as **FVA(DUE)$_n$**. As you can see, the future value of the annuity due ($331.01) is greater than the future value of the equivalent ordinary annuity ($315.25). As the time line shows, the future value of *each deposit* is greater for an annuity due than for an ordinary annuity because each deposit receives (earns) interest for 1 additional year.

FVA(DUE)$_n$
The future value of an annuity *due* over n periods.

EQUATION (NUMERICAL) SOLUTION

The time line solution shows that the computation of the future value of the annuity due is the same as the computation of the future value of an ordinary annuity except that each deposit is multiplied by an additional $(1 + r) = (1.05)$ to account for the fact that interest is earned for 1 additional year. If we make this same adjustment to Equation 9-4, the numerical solution for FVA(DUE)$_n$ is:

9-5

$$\text{FVA(DUE)}_n = \text{PMT}\left[\sum_{t=1}^{n}(1+r)^t\right] = \text{PMT}\left[\left\{\frac{(1+r)^n - 1}{r}\right\} \times (1+r)\right]$$

Using Equation 9-5, we find that the future value of Alvin's annuity is:

$$\text{FVA(DUE)}_3 = \$100\left[\left\{\frac{(1.05)^3 - 1}{0.05}\right\} \times (1.05)\right]$$

$$= \$100[3.15250 \times 1.05] = \$100[3.310125] = \$331.01$$

FINANCIAL CALCULATOR SOLUTION

Financial calculators have a switch, or key, generally marked DUE or BEG, that allows you to switch from end-of-period payments (ordinary annuity) to beginning-of-period payments (annuity due). When the beginning mode is activated, the display normally will show the word BEGIN, or the letters BGN. Thus, to deal with annuities due, switch your calculator to BEGIN and proceed as before. For example, if you are using a Texas Instruments BAII PLUS financial calculator, to "flip" the switch to solve annuity due problems you would press the following keys in sequence: `2ND`, `PMT` (the PMT key has BGN written above it, which is a secondary function), and `2ND`, `ENTER` (the ENTER key has SET written above it, which is a secondary function). After you are finished pressing these keys, you should see BGN in the upper-right corner of the display, which indicates that the calculator will now solve problems for annuity payments that occur at the beginning of the period. For our problem, the solution is:

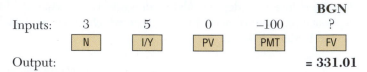

					BGN
Inputs:	3	5	0	−100	?
	N	I/Y	PV	PMT	FV
Output:					= **331.01**

Because most problems specify end-of-period cash flows—that is, ordinary annuities—*you should always switch your calculator back to the END mode after you work an annuity due problem.*

SPREADSHEET SOLUTION

Figure 9-8 shows how to set up and solve the current situation using an Excel spreadsheet. Notice that inputs to the spreadsheet are the same as in Figure 9-7, where we computed the future value of an ordinary annuity, except that cell B5 contains a 1 rather than a 0. Entering a 1 for the PMT type indicates to the spreadsheet that the cash flow series is an annuity due.

Because each of the payments from the annuity due (Alvin's deposits) is received 1 year earlier than the corresponding payment from the ordinary annuity (Alice's deposits), the annuity due payments earn greater total interest than the ordinary annuity. For this reason, everything else equal, $FVA(DUE)_n$ *will always be greater than* FVA_n—that is, $FVA(DUE)_n > FVA_n$.

FIGURE 9-8   Using Excel's FV Function to Compute the Future Value of an Annuity Due

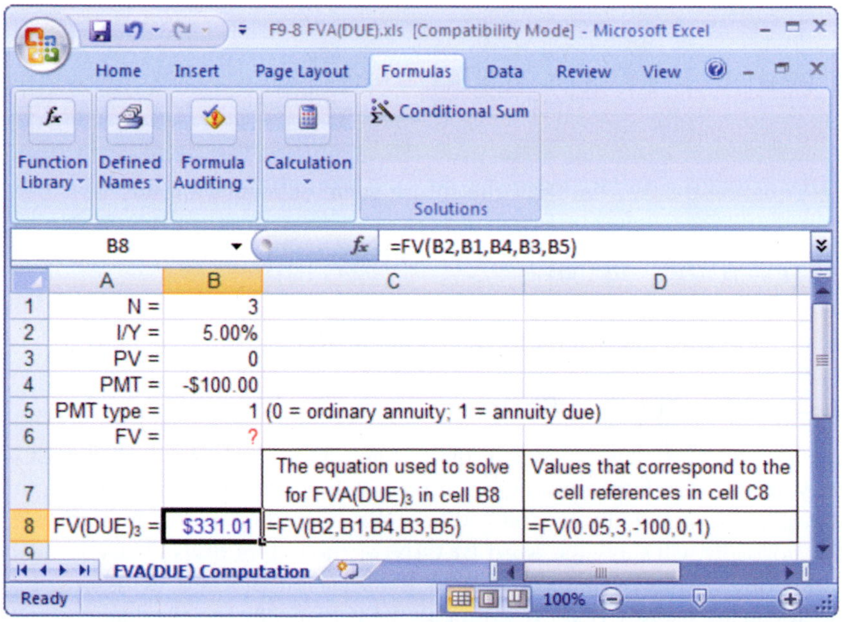

	A	B	C	D
			B8 ▼ fx =FV(B2,B1,B4,B3,B5)	
1	N =	3		
2	I/Y =	5.00%		
3	PV =	0		
4	PMT =	-$100.00		
5	PMT type =	1	(0 = ordinary annuity; 1 = annuity due)	
6	FV =	?		
7			The equation used to solve for FVA(DUE)₃ in cell B8	Values that correspond to the cell references in cell C8
8	FV(DUE)₃ =	$331.01	=FV(B2,B1,B4,B3,B5)	=FV(0.05,3,-100,0,1)

Note: According to the equation shown in cell C8, the input values must be entered in a specific order: I/Y, N, PMT, PV, and PMT type.

PRESENT VALUE OF AN ANNUITY

Suppose that Alice is trying to decide whether to make a single lump-sum deposit today rather than depositing $100 each year for the next 3 years. Alice's twin, Alvin, is also considering this option. How much must the lump-sum payment be so that it is equivalent to the $100 annuity? We can answer this question by computing the present value of the annuity. Remember that we compute the present value of a future amount by taking out interest that the amount earns during the investment period—that is, we discount the future amount by the interest it earns. We apply this concept when computing the present value of an annuity.

Present Value of an Ordinary Annuity

Alice wants to know how much she has to deposit today as a lump-sum amount to end up with the same future value as she would have if she deposited $100 each year, beginning in 1 year, for the next 3 years in a savings account that pays 5 percent interest per year. Because the three $100 deposits represent an ordinary annuity, in this section we show how to compute the present value of an ordinary annuity.

TIME LINE SOLUTION

One way to determine the present value of an ordinary annuity, which we designate **PVA$_n$,** is to compute the present value of *each* annuity payment using Equation 9-2 and then sum the results. Here is the computation of the present value of Alice's deposits (annuity):

PVA$_n$
The present value of an *ordinary* annuity with n payments.

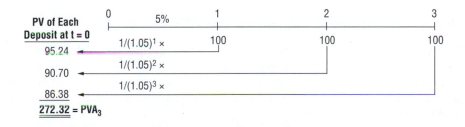

EQUATION (NUMERICAL) SOLUTION

The time line solution shows that we can compute the present value of the annuity simply by computing the PVs of the individual payments and summing the results. The general equation used to find the PV of an ordinary annuity is a series of solutions to Equation 9-2, which can be written as follows:

9-6

$$PVA_n = PMT\left[\frac{1}{(1+r)^1}\right] + PMT\left[\frac{1}{(1+r)^2}\right] + \cdots + PMT\left[\frac{1}{(1+r)^n}\right]$$

$$= PMT\sum_{t=1}^{n}\left[\frac{1}{(1+r)^t}\right] = PMT\left[\frac{1 - \dfrac{1}{(1+r)^n}}{r}\right]$$

Using Equation 9-6, the PV of the 3-year annuity with end-of-year payments of $100 and an opportunity cost of 5 percent is:

$$PVA_3 = \$100\left[\frac{1 - \dfrac{1}{(1.05)^3}}{0.05}\right] = \$100(2.72325) = \$272.32$$

FINANCIAL CALCULATOR SOLUTION

Enter N = 3, I/Y = 5, PMT = −100, and FV = 0; then solve for PV:

Inputs:	3	5	?	−100	0
	N	I/Y	PV	PMT	FV
Output:			= 272.32		

SPREADSHEET SOLUTION

Figure 9-9 shows how to set up and solve the current situation using an Excel spreadsheet. To solve for the present value of an annuity, notice that we use the same financial function that we used to solve for the present value of a single payment, which is shown in Figure 9-3, except we enter a value for PMT so that the value in cell B4 is −$100.

In this section, we found that the present value of a 3-year $100 ordinary annuity that earns 5 percent interest each year is $272.32. As a result, if Alice deposits $272.32 today and earns 5 percent interest for the next 3 years, her bank account will have the same balance in 3 years as it would if she deposits $100 at the end of each of the next 3 years—that is, $315.25 = 272.32(1.05)^3.

Present Value of an Annuity Due

Now let's compute the present value of Alvin's series of deposits, which represent an *annuity due*. To compute the present value of an annuity due, the PVA_n computation must be adjusted to recognize the fact that each annuity payment is at the beginning of the year rather than at the end of the year—that is, each payment must be *discounted for 1 less year*.

FIGURE 9-9   Using Excel's PV Function to Compute the Present Value of an Ordinary Annuity

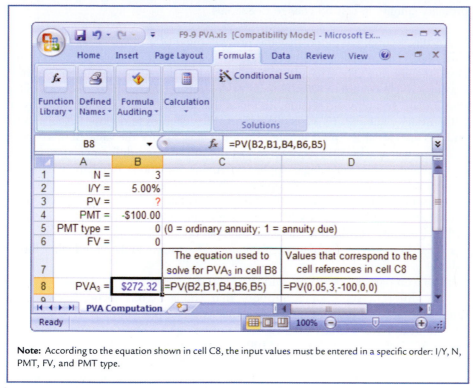

Note: According to the equation shown in cell C8, the input values must be entered in a specific order: I/Y, N, PMT, FV, and PMT type.

TIME LINE SOLUTION

Following is the cash flow time line that depicts Alvin's deposits:

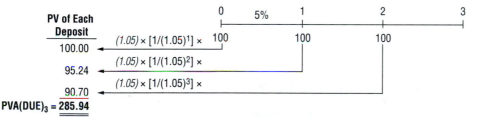

FINANCIAL CALCULATOR SOLUTION

Switch to the beginning-of-period mode (BEGIN) and enter N = 3, I/Y = 5, PMT = −100, and FV = 0; then compute PV = 285.94. Again, because most problems deal with end-of-period cash flows, *don't forget to switch your calculator back to the END mode.*

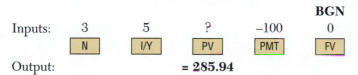

SPREADSHEET SOLUTION

The inputs to the spreadsheet are the same as in Figure 9-9, where we computed the present value of an ordinary annuity, except that cell B5 contains a 1 rather than a 0, which indicates to the spreadsheet that the cash flow series is an annuity due. When you enter 1 cell in B5, you should see the result that was shown for the ordinary annuity in cell B8 change to $285.94.

In this section, we found that the present value of a 3-year $100 annuity that earns 5 percent annual interest is $272.32 if it is an ordinary annuity and $285.94 if it is an annuity due. These results tell us that Alice should be indifferent between making a single deposit of $272.32 today or depositing $100 at the end of each of the next 3 years. In a previous section, we found that the future value of the same 3-year $100 ordinary annuity, FVA_3, is $315.25. If Alice chooses to deposit $272.32 today and this money earns 5 percent interest for the next 3 years, the value of this deposit in 3 years will also be $315.24 = $272.32(1.05)^3$. (There is a difference of $0.01 due to rounding.) This same logic applies to Alvin's situation. Why, though, is the present value of Alvin's series of deposits ($285.94) greater than the present value of Alice's series of deposits ($272.32)? The answer is fairly simple: the future value of Alvin's annuity due in 3 years ($331.01) is greater than the future value of Alice's ordinary annuity ($315.25) at the same time period and the same interest rate. As a result, Alvin has to deposit a greater amount today to accumulate the higher future value.

PVA(DUE)$_n$

The present value of an annuity *due* over n periods.

The comparison of PVA_n and **PVA(DUE)$_n$** can also be viewed from a slightly different standpoint. Suppose that you are considering investing an amount today at 5 percent interest so that you can pay yourself $100 per year for the next 3 years. According to the solutions given here, you would have to invest $272.32 today if the first $100 withdrawal from the investment will be in 1 year (ordinary annuity). On the other hand, you would have to invest $285.94 today if the first $100 is withdrawn today (annuity due). It makes sense that the annuity due has the higher value today, because if the first $100 annuity payment is withdrawn today it will not earn any interest and only $185.94 = $285.94 − $100.00 will be available to earn 5 percent interest in the first year.

Self-Test Questions

How do you compute the present value of an annuity?

All else equal, which annuity has the greater present value: an ordinary annuity or an annuity due? Why?

Suppose that you are considering an investment that pays $5,000 per year for 10 years and your opportunity cost is 7 percent interest. If you don't receive the first $5,000 payment until 1 year from today, what is the most you should be willing to pay for the investment? How much would you be willing to pay if you receive the first $5,000 payment today? (Answers: $35,118; $37,576)

COMPARISON OF **FVA** WITH **PVA**—WHAT **TVM** REALLY MEANS

In the previous two sections, we showed that (1) the future value of a 3-year $100 ordinary annuity is equal to $315.25 if the opportunity rate of return is 5 percent compounded annually and (2) the present, or current, value of the same $100 annuity is $272.32 at the same opportunity rate. Now, let's suppose that you just won a contest that allows you to choose one of the following prizes:

Prize	Payoff
A	$272.32 lump-sum payment today
B	$315.25 lump-sum payment in 3 years
C	$100.00 annuity payment at the end of each of the next 3 years

If there is no risk associated with any of these prizes—that is, the payoffs are guaranteed—which one would (should) you choose (prefer)?

Based on discussions earlier in this chapter, you should recognize that all of the prizes are the same. That is, it doesn't matter which prize you choose, because you can create whichever payoff you prefer from each of the other prizes. To see that this is the case, suppose that three different colored marbles (red, blue, and yellow) are placed in a hat, and you must reach in and select one of the marbles without looking to determine your prize. If you pull out the red marble, you will receive Prize A, if you pull out the blue marble, you will receive Prize B, and if you pull out the yellow marble, you will receive Prize C.

Because your rent is due soon and you are short of funds, you were hoping to pull out the red marble so that you receive $272.32 today. But, you pull out the blue marble instead and, as a result, you are given a piece of paper that is redeemable for $315.25 in 3 years. You should not be upset that you didn't pick the red marble, because, assuming that everyone's opportunity cost is 5 percent, you can sell your prize immediately to someone else for $272.32. Remember that these amounts are equivalent; the present value of $272.32 is simply the future value amount of $315.25 after the interest has been removed. To show that this is true, consider how much money you would have in 3 years if you invest $272.32 today at 5 percent compounded annually:

$$FV = \$272.32(1.05)^3 = \$272.32(1.157625) = \$315.24 \text{ (rounding difference)}$$

The previous exercise shows that you should be indifferent between receiving $272.32 today and receiving $315.25 in 3 years if your opportunity cost is 5 percent (annual compounding). Now suppose that you chose the blue marble when you really wanted the yellow marble that represents the 3-year $100 annuity. How can you create the annuity payments with your prize? If you sell your prize and invest the $272.32 you receive at 5 percent compounded annually, you can create the 3-year $100 ordinary annuity for yourself. The following table shows how you can pay yourself $100 at the end of each of the next 3 years:

Year	Beginning Amount	Interest Earned = (Beginning Amt) × 0.05	Ending Amount before Withdrawal = Beginning Amt + Interest	Withdrawal
1	$272.32	$13.62 = $272.32(0.05)	$285.94 = $272.32 + $13.62	$100
2	185.94	9.30 = 185.94(0.05)	195.24 = 185.94 + 9.30	100
3	95.24	4.76 = 95.24(0.05)	100.00 = 95.24 + 4.76	100

In this section we have shown that, if you invest $272.32 at 5 percent compounded annually, you can either pay yourself $100 at the end of each of the next 3 years or allow the investment to accumulate to $315.25 at the end of 3 years. Previously, we showed that if $100 is invested at the end of each of the next 3 years at 5 percent compounded annually, the investment will grow to $315.25 in 3 years. As a result, it should be clear that each of the three payoffs (prizes) mentioned in this section are equivalent. The only difference among each prize is the time period in which it is stated, and thus the amount of interest that is included in the dollar value that is given.

This simple illustration shows the principal tenet of time value of money: *when the opportunity cost is greater than 0 percent, values from different time periods should never be compared; values should be compared only when they are stated in identical time-period dollars.* For example, to determine whether receiving $500 today is preferable to receiving $1,000 in 9 years if your opportunity cost is 8 percent, you must determine how much $500 invested today will grow to in 9 years and compare it to the $1,000 alternative (that is, find the future value of the $500 lump-sum amount), determine how much you would need to invest today to end up with $1,000 in 9 years (that is, find the present value of the $1,000 lump-sum amount), and compare the amount to the $500 alternative, or restate and compare both amounts at some other common time period—say, 5 years from today. If both alternatives are guaranteed, you will find that the $1,000 lump-sum payment in 9 years is slightly better (more valuable) than the $500 lump-sum payment today. You should perform the computations to prove that this is the case.

Self-Test Questions

Why is it improper to compare values that are stated in different time-period dollars?

What is the present value of $1,000 to be received in 9 years if the opportunity cost is 6 percent?   (Answer: $500.25)

What is the future value in 9 years of $500 invested today if the opportunity cost is 6 percent?   (Answer: $999.50)

COMPUTING ANNUITY PAYMENTS (PMT), INTEREST RATES (r), AND TIME (n)

The equations used to solve for either FVA or PVA contain four variables: either FVA or PVA, depending on whether we are looking for the future value or the present value of an annuity, n, r, and PMT. If we know the values of all the variables except one, we can solve for the value of the unknown variable. In this section, we set up three examples to show you how to solve for (1) annuity payments (PMT), (2) the annual interest rate that is earned (paid) on an annuity (r), and (3) how long it takes (n) to achieve a financial goal with an annuity. Because the solutions to these situations are fairly simple when we use either a financial calculator or a spreadsheet, we use only these approaches to solve the problems.

Computing Annuity Payments, PMT

Suppose that you want to start your own business in 10 years, and you plan to deposit an amount in a savings account every year so that you have sufficient funds to start the business. You have determined that you need $100,000 in 10 years, and you have decided to make the first deposit at the end of this year. If the savings account pays an annual interest equal to 5 percent, how much must you deposit each year to reach your $100,000 goal?

FINANCIAL CALCULATOR SOLUTION

Enter N = 10, I/Y = 5, PV = 0, and FV = 100,000. Solving for PMT, we find that you must deposit $7,950.46 at the end of each year to have $100,000 in 10 years:

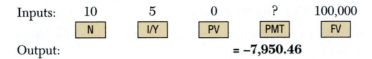

Inputs: 10   5   0   ?   100,000
          N   I/Y   PV   PMT   FV

Output: = –7,950.46

What would the answer be if you decided that the first deposit should be made today rather than 1 year from today? Switch your calculator to the BGN mode, and you should find that the answer is $7,571.86. Because each deposit is made 1 year earlier—that is, we now have an annuity due—each deposit earns more interest, and consequently the annual deposit needed to reach the goal of $100,000 in 10 years is lower than for the ordinary annuity.

SPREADSHEET SOLUTION

Figure 9-10 shows the setup and the inputs used to solve this problem using the PMT function that is available in Excel. The solution shown in Figure 9-10 assumes that the series of deposits represents an ordinary annuity. If the deposits are made at the beginning of the year such that the series is an annuity due, simply enter a 1 in cell B5, and the solution for an annuity due, $7,571.86, will appear in cell B8.

FIGURE 9-10   Using Excel's PMT Function to Compute the Annuity Payment for an Ordinary Annuity

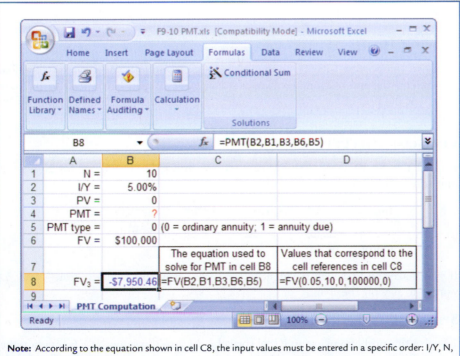

Note: According to the equation shown in cell C8, the input values must be entered in a specific order: I/Y, N, PV, FV, and PMT type.

Solving for r

Suppose you borrow $1,000, and the loan agreement requires you to pay $282 per year for the next 4 years. If the payments are made at the end of each year, what interest rate are you paying on the loan?

FINANCIAL CALCULATOR SOLUTION

Enter N = 4, PV = 1,000, PMT = −282, and FV = 0. Solving for I/Y, we find that r equals 5 percent.

Inputs:	4	?	1,000	−282	0
	N	I/Y	PV	PMT	FV
Output:		= 5.0			

In this problem, the information that was given included the amount of the annuity payment, the *present value* of the annuity, and the number of years the annuity payment is received. If the *future value* of the annuity is given instead of the present value, to find r, we would follow the same procedure outlined here. Also, we follow the same steps to solve this problem if the loan payments are made at the beginning of the year (annuity due) rather than at the end of the year (ordinary annuity). Simply switch your calculator to the BGN mode. You should find that I/Y equals 8.7 percent if the $282 payments represent an annuity due. Think about why the interest rate is much higher for the annuity due than for the ordinary annuity, everything else equal.

SPREADSHEET SOLUTION

To solve this problem using an Excel spreadsheet, use the same RATE function that is described in Figure 9-5. Simply enter the values in the appropriate cells, and the answer, 5.00%, will appear in cell B8.

Solving for n

Suppose you borrow $18,000 to make home improvements. According to the loan agreement, the interest on the loan is 13 percent. If you can afford to pay only $4,070 at the end of each year, how many payments must you make to pay off the loan?

FINANCIAL CALCULATOR SOLUTION

Enter I/Y = 13, PV = 18,000, PMT = −4,070, and FV = 0. Solving for N, we find that n equals 7 years.

Inputs:	?	13.0	18,000	−4,070	0
	N	I/Y	PV	PMT	FV
Output:	= 7.0				

If you make the first loan payment immediately, it would take less time—only 5.8 years—to pay off the loan.

SPREADSHEET SOLUTION

To solve this problem using an Excel spreadsheet, use the same NPER function that is described in Figure 9-6. Simply enter the values in the appropriate cells, and the answer, 7 years, will appear in cell B8.

Self-Test Questions

Suppose that you just won a lottery prize equal to $100,000. You plan to use the winnings to help pay for your college education for the next 5 years (your plans include graduate school). If you can invest your winnings at 6 percent, how much can you withdraw from the investment each year to pay for your education? Assume that the withdrawals represent an annuity due—that is the first withdrawal is today.   (Answer: $22,396)

Suppose you pay $846.80 for an investment that promises to pay you $250 per year for the next 4 years. If the payments are made at the end of each year, what interest rate (rate of return) will you earn on this investment?   (Answer: 7.0%)

Suppose you pay $1,685 for an investment that promises to pay you $400 per year. If the payments are made at the end of each year, how many payments must you receive to earn a 6 percent return?   (Answer: 5 years)

PERPETUITIES

Most annuities call for payments to be made over some finite period of time—for example, $100 per year for 3 years. However, some annuities go on indefinitely, or perpetually. These *perpetual annuities* are called **perpetuities.** The present value of a perpetuity is found by applying the following equation:[9]

perpetuity
A stream of equal payments expected to continue forever.

$$PVP = \frac{\text{Payment}}{\text{Interest rate}} = \frac{PMT}{r}$$

9-7

Perpetuities can be illustrated by British securities that were issued after the Napoleonic Wars. In 1815, the British government sold a huge bond issue and used the proceeds to pay off many smaller bonds that were issued in prior years to pay for the wars. Because the purpose of the bonds was to consolidate past debts, the bonds were called **consols.** The consols paid constant interest, but did not have maturities—that is, the consols were perpetuities. Suppose each consol promised to pay $100 per year in perpetuity. (Actually, interest was stated in pounds.) What would each bond be worth if the opportunity cost rate, or discount rate, was 5 percent? The answer is $2,000:

consol
A perpetual bond issued by the British government to consolidate past debts; in general, any perpetual bond.

$$PVP = \frac{\$100}{0.05} = \$2,000$$

Suppose the interest rate increases to 10 percent. What would happen to the consol's value? The value would drop to $1,000:

$$PVP = \frac{\$100}{0.10} = \$1,000$$

We see that the value of a perpetuity changes dramatically when interest rates change. This example demonstrates an important financial concept: everything else

---

[9]The derivation of Equation 9-7 is given in the Web Extension to Chapter 5 in Eugene F. Brigham and Phillip R. Daves, *Intermediate Financial Management,* 9th ed. (Cincinnati, OH: South-Western Cengage Learning, 2007).

equal, when the *interest rate changes, the value of an investment changes in an opposite direction.* In our example, the value of the consol dropped dramatically when the interest rate increased from 5 to 10 percent. If in subsequent periods the interest rate declines, the value of the consol will increase. This is a fundamental valuation concept that we will discuss in greater detail in Chapter 10.

Self-Test Questions

What happens to the value of a perpetuity when interest rates increase? What happens when rates decrease?

What is the present value of a $3,500 annuity that will be paid forever beginning in 1 year if the interest rate is 7 percent? What is the value of this perpetuity if the interest rate increases to 10 percent? (Answers: $50,000; $35,000)

UNEVEN CASH FLOW STREAMS

The definition of an annuity includes the words *constant amount*—in other words, annuities involve payments that are the same for every period. Although many financial decisions do involve constant payments, some important decisions involve uneven, or nonconstant, cash flows. For example, common stocks typically pay an increasing stream of dividends over time, and fixed asset investments such as new equipment normally do not generate constant cash flows. Consequently, it is necessary to extend our time value of money discussion to include **uneven cash flow streams.**

Throughout the book, we use the term **payment (PMT)** to identify annuity situations where the cash flows are constant, and we use the term **cash flow (CF)** to denote a cash flow series in general, which includes both uneven cash flows and annuities. When all cash flows in a series are nonconstant, $CF_1 \neq CF_2 \neq CF_3 \neq \ldots \neq CF_n$, which represents an *uneven cash flow stream;* when all cash flows in a series are equal, $CF_1 = CF_2 = CF_3 = \ldots = CF_n, = PMT$, which represents an annuity.

Present Value of an Uneven Cash Flow Stream

To find the present value (PV) of an uneven cash flow stream, we must sum the PVs of the individual cash flows included in the stream. The PV is found by applying this general present value equation, which is simply a series of PV solutions to Equation 9-2:

9-8

$$PV = \frac{CF_1}{(1+r)^1} + \frac{CF_2}{(1+r)^2} + \cdots + \frac{CF_n}{(1+r)^n} = \sum_{t=1}^{n} \frac{CF_t}{(1+r)^t}$$

Note that Equation 9-8 is the same as Equation 9-6, which is used to compute PVA, except that CF is substituted for PMT. Unlike Equation 9-6, however, we cannot simplify Equation 9-8 further because the cash flows are not necessarily equal.

To illustrate the application of Equation 9-8, let's assume that you are considering buying an investment that promises to pay $500, $800, and $300 over the next 3 years. The first payment will be received 1 year from today, and your opportunity cost is 8 percent. How much should you pay for this investment?

uneven cash flow stream A series of cash flows in which the amount varies from one period to the next.

payment (PMT) This term designates constant cash flows—that is, the amount of an annuity payment.

cash flow (CF) This term designates cash flows in general, including uneven cash flows.

TIME LINE SOLUTION

One way to find the present value of the cash flow stream in our example is to compute the PV of each individual cash flow and then sum these values—that is, solve for PV using Equation 9-8.

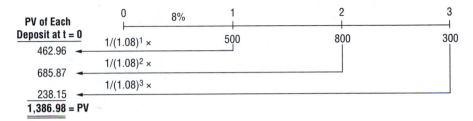

You can find the *present value of any cash flow stream by summing the present values of the individual cash flows* as shown here. When the cash flows are the same—that is, constant—we can simplify the computations by applying the annuity solutions discussed earlier. The annuity equations (solutions) can be used to compute only the present value of cash flows that are all the same, whereas Equation 9-8 can be used to find the present value for any cash flow stream (constant or nonconstant).

FINANCIAL CALCULATOR AND SPREADSHEET SOLUTIONS

Problems involving uneven cash flows can be solved in one step with most financial calculators and spreadsheets. Using a financial calculator, first input the individual cash flows in chronological order into the *cash flow register*. Cash flows usually are designated CF_0, CF_1, CF_2, CF_3, and so on. Next, enter the interest rate. At this point, you have entered all the known values of Equation 9-8, so you only need to press the NPV key to find the present value of the cash flow stream. The calculator has been programmed to find the PV of each cash flow, including CF_0, and then to sum these values to find the PV of the entire stream. To input the cash flows for this problem, enter 0 (because $CF_0 = 0$), 500, 800, and 300 in that order into the cash flow register, enter I = 8, and then press NPV to get the answer, $1,386.98. NPV stands for Net Present Value.

Using a spreadsheet, follow a similar procedure by setting up the spreadsheet so that the cash flows are ordered sequentially. Then using the NPV function, solve for the present value of the nonconstant cash flow series. Because we discuss the application of this function in much greater detail in Chapter 13, we will wait until then to describe in detail the process of solving for NPV using both a financial calculator and a spreadsheet.

Future Value of an Uneven Cash Flow Stream

The future value of an uneven cash flow stream, sometimes called the **terminal value,** is found by compounding each payment to the end of the stream and then summing the future values.[10]

terminal value
The future value of a cash flow stream.

---

[10]Some financial calculators have a net future value (NFV) key that, after the cash flows and interest rate have been entered into the calculator, can be used to compute the future value of an uneven cash flow stream. In any event, it is easy enough to compound the individual cash flows to the terminal year, and then sum them to find the FV of the stream.

TIME LINE SOLUTION

The future value of our illustrative uneven cash flow stream is $1,747.20.

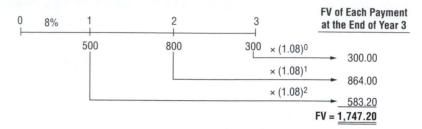

Alternatively, because we already know the present value of the cash flow series, we could have used Equation 9-1 to find the future value of the cash flows. The computation for our situation would be as follows:

$$FV_n = PV(1 + r)^n$$
$$= \$1,386.98(1.08)^3 = \$1,386.98(1.259712) = \$1,747.20$$

We generally are more interested in the present value of an asset's cash flow stream than in the future value, because the present value represents today's value, which we can compare with the price of the asset.

Solving for r with Uneven Cash Flow Streams

To solve for r for an uneven cash flow stream without a financial calculator or a spreadsheet, you must go through tedious trial-and-error calculations. With a financial calculator, however, it is fairly easy to find the value of r. Simply input the CF values into the cash flow register, and then press the IRR key. IRR stands for *internal rate of return,* which is the return on an investment. Spreadsheets have a built-in IRR function that can also be used to solve for r. We will defer further discussion of this calculation for now, but we will take it up later in the book (Chapter 13).

Self-Test Questions

Give two examples of financial decisions that would typically involve uneven flows of cash.

What is meant by the term *terminal value*?

Consider the following uneven cash flow stream: $1,000 at the end of Year 1, $5,000 at the end of Year 2, $800 at the end of Year 3, and $2,000 at the end of Year 4. If your opportunity cost is 10 percent, what is the most you should pay for an investment with these payoffs? If you were to invest each cash flow when you receive it, how much would your investment be worth at the end of 4 years?   (Answers: $7,008.40; $10,261)

annual compounding
The process of determining the future (or present) value of a cash flow or series of cash flows when interest is paid once per year.

SEMIANNUAL AND OTHER COMPOUNDING PERIODS

In all of our examples to this point, we have assumed that interest is compounded once per year, or annually. This is called **annual compounding.** Suppose, however, that you deposited $100 in a bank that pays a 6 percent annual interest rate, but that interest is paid every 6 months. This is called **semiannual compounding.**[11] To illustrate semiannual compounding, first consider again what happens when interest is *compounded annually.*

TIME LINE AND EQUATION SOLUTIONS—6 PERCENT INTEREST COMPOUNDED ANNUALLY

Following is the cash flow time line with the future value computation using Equation 9-1:

Time (t):	0		1	2	3
		6%			
		x (1.06)	x (1.06)	x (1.06)	
Account Balance:	100.00 $\longrightarrow$		106.00 $\longrightarrow$	112.36 $\longrightarrow$	119.10

$$FV_n = PV(1 + r)^n = 100(1.06)^3 = 119.10$$

FINANCIAL CALCULATOR SOLUTION—6 PERCENT INTEREST COMPOUNDED ANNUALLY

Input N = 3, I/Y = 6, PV = −100, and PMT = 0; then compute FV = 119.10.

SPREADSHEET SOLUTION—6 PERCENT INTEREST COMPOUNDED ANNUALLY

The spreadsheet solution is shown in Figure 9-1.

How would the future value change if interest is paid twice each year—that is, semiannually? To find the future value, we must make two adjustments: (1) convert the annual interest rate to a rate per period, which is called the *periodic rate*, and (2) convert the number of years to the total number of interest payments (compounding periods) during the life of the investment. These conversions are as follows:

9-9

$$\text{Periodic rate} = r_{PER} = \frac{\text{Stated annual interest rate}}{\text{Number of interest payments per year}} = \frac{r_{SIMPLE}}{m}$$

9-10

$$\text{Number of interest periods} = n_{PER} = \text{Number of years} \times \text{Interest payments per year}$$
$$= \quad n_{YRS} \quad \times \quad m$$

Here, m is the number of interest compounding periods per year, r_{SIMPLE} is the simple (noncompounded) annual interest rate, r_{PER} is the rate of interest that is paid *each* compounding period, n_{YRS} is the number of years interest is earned, and n_{PER} is the total number of interest payments during the n_{YRS} years. Note that $r_{PER} = r_{SIMPLE}$ and $n_{PER} = n_{YRS}$ only when interest is compounded annually.

In our current example, if interest is paid semiannually, there are $n_{PER} = 2 \times 3 = 6$ interest payments during the life of the investment, and interest is paid at a rate equal to $r_{PER} = r_{SIMPLE}/m = 6\%/2 = 3\%$ every 6 months. Here is the value of the $100 at the end of 3 years at 6 percent with semiannual compounding.

---

[11]Note that financial institutions, such as banks and credit unions, generally pay interest more often than every 6 months; often, interest is paid on a daily basis. But, in our example, we assume interest is paid semiannually so that we can more easily illustrate the effect of multiple interest payments each year.

TIME LINE AND EQUATION SOLUTIONS—6 PERCENT INTEREST COMPOUNDED SEMIANNUALLY

Following is the cash flow time line with the future value computation using Equation 9-1 after converting r_{YRS} to r_{PER} and n_{YRS} to n_{PER}:

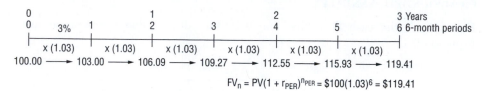

$$FV_n = PV(1 + r_{PER})^{n_{PER}} = \$100(1.03)^6 = \$119.41$$

FINANCIAL CALCULATOR SOLUTION—6 PERCENT INTEREST COMPOUNDED SEMIANNUALLY

Input $N = 3 \times 2 = 6$, $I/Y = 6/2 = 3$, $PV = -100$, and $PMT = 0$; then compute $FV = 119.41$

SPREADSHEET SOLUTION—6 PERCENT INTEREST COMPOUNDED SEMIANNUALLY

Make the same conversions as you do when entering the values into the financial calculator, and then input the converted values into the appropriate cells shown in Figure 9-1. The result that appears in cell B8 will be $119.41.

The FV is larger under semiannual compounding because, compared to annual compounding, the first interest payment is sooner—that is, in 6 months rather than 1 year—and interest is compounded more often—that is, interest is earned on previously paid interest more frequently.

How would the result change if interest is paid quarterly? In this case, $r_{PER} = 6\%/4 = 1.5\%$ and $n_{PER} = 3 \times 4 = 12$ compounding periods. If you make these changes in your calculator—that is, $N = 12$ and $I/Y = 1.5$—you will find that the future value of the $100 deposit is $119.56. This amount is greater than the future value when interest is compounded semiannually. Our results show us that FV (quarterly compounding) = $119.56 > FV (semiannual compounding) = $119.41 > FV (annual compounding) = $119.10. This relationship demonstrates an important financial concept: everything else equal, an amount invested today will be worth more in the future when compounding occurs more often than once per year; and *the more often compounding occurs each year, the higher the future value of an amount invested today.*

The preceding discussion was concerned with finding the future value of a lump-sum amount that is invested today if interest is compounded more than once per year. The same adjustments must be made to compute the present value of a future amount when interest is compounded more than once per year. For example, let's compute the present value of a $500 obligation that must be paid in 4 years when the opportunity cost is 8 percent. If interest is compounded annually, to find the present value using a financial calculator, enter $N = 4$, $I/Y = 8$, $PMT = 0$, and $FV = -500$; the solution is $367.51. If interest is compounded quarterly, enter $N = 4 \times 4 = 16$, $I/Y = 8/4 = 2$, $PMT = 0$, and $FV = -500$; the solution is $364.22. This example shows that *when there is more interest compounding during the year, everything else equal, the present value of a future amount is lower.* More compounding generates greater interest, which means that less would have to be put aside (invested) today to meet a specific future financial goal (obligation).

Self-Test Questions

What changes must you make in your calculations to determine the future value of an amount that is compounded at 8 percent semiannually versus one that is compounded annually at 8 percent?

Why is semiannual compounding better than annual compounding from a saver's standpoint?

Suppose you have $1,000 that you want to invest today. How much would you have in 10 years if you put your money in a savings account that pays 10 percent compounded annually? How much would you have if the bank pays 10 percent compounded quarterly?   (Answers: $2,593.74; $2,685.06)

COMPARISON OF DIFFERENT INTEREST RATES

In the previous section, we showed that the dollar interest earned on an investment is greater when interest is computed (compounded) more than once per year. In simple terms, this means that the *effective* return earned on an investment is higher than the stated, or simple, return (r_{SIMPLE}) when there are multiple interest compounding periods during the year. For example, in the previous section, we found that $100 invested for 3 years at 6 percent will grow to $119.10 when interest is compounded annually, whereas the same $100 will grow to $119.41 when interest is compounded semiannually. Because the $100 investment earns more interest when interest is compounded semiannually, the *effective* annual return is higher with semiannual compounding than with annual compounding. This important financial principle can be summarized as follows: everything else equal, *the greater the number of compounding periods per year, the greater the effective rate of return on an investment.*

Different compounding periods are used for different types of investments. For example, banks generally compute interest on a daily, or even continuous, basis; most bonds pay interest semiannually; and stocks generally pay dividends quarterly.[12] If we are to properly compare the returns that are earned on investments with different compounding periods, we need to put them on a common basis. This requires us to distinguish between the *simple (or quoted) interest rate* and the *effective annual rate (EAR):*

- The **simple,** or **quoted, interest rate** (r_{SIMPLE}) in our example is 6 percent. On all types of contracts, interest is always quoted as an annual rate, and if compounding occurs more frequently than once per year, that fact is stated along with the rate. In our example, the quoted rate is *6 percent, compounded semiannually.* The simple rate is also called the **Annual Percentage Rate,** or **APR.** This is the rate that is reported to you by banks, credit card companies, automobile dealerships, student loan officers, and other lenders when you borrow money. The APR is a noncompounded interest rate because it does not consider the effect that compounding has when interest is paid more than once per year. In other words, you could have two loans (or investments) that have the same stated APR—say, 6 percent—but you could actually be paying different effective rates because the number of loan payments per year differs (annual

simple (quoted) interest rate (r_{SIMPLE})
The rate quoted by borrowers and lenders that is used to determine the rate earned per compounding period (periodic rate, r_{PER}).

Annual Percentage Rate (APR)
Another name for the simple interest rate, r_{SIMPLE}; does not consider the effect of interest compounding.

---

[12]For a discussion of continuous compounding, see the Web Extension to Chapter 8 in Eugene F. Brigham and Michael Ehrhardt, *Financial Management,* 12th ed. (Cincinnati, OH: Cengage Learning South-Western, 2008).

versus semiannual). As a result, to compare loans (or investments) where interest is paid at different times during the year, we must compare the loans' (investments') effective annual interest rates, not their APRs.

effective (equivalent) annual rate (r_{EAR})
The annual rate of interest actually being earned, as opposed to the quoted rate, considering the compounding of interest.

- The **effective (equivalent) annual rate (r_{EAR})** is defined as the rate that would produce the same ending (future) value if annual compounding had been used. To find r_{EAR}, we adjust the APR to include the effect of interest compounding—that is, we convert the APR to its equivalent annual rate of return based on the number of interest payments (compounding periods) each year.

- If interest is computed once each year—that is, compounded annually—$r_{EAR} = r_{SIMPLE} = APR$. But, *if compounding occurs more than once per year, the effective annual rate is greater than the simple, or quoted, interest rate*—that is, $r_{EAR} > r_{SIMPLE}$.

In our example, r_{EAR} is the rate that will grow a $100 investment to $119.41 at the end of 3 years. This is the rate at which you would need to invest $100 today to produce $119.41 at the end of Year 3 if interest is paid one time each year—that is, when annual equivalent compounding exists. Here is the cash flow time line that shows this situation:

0		1	2	3 Years
	$r_{EAR} = ?$			

$$FV_n = PV(1 + r_{EAR})^{n_{YR}} = \$100(1 + r_{EAR})^3 = \$119.41$$

100.00 ⟶ 119.41

We can compute the effective annual rate, r_{EAR}, given the simple rate, r_{SIMPLE}, and the number of compounding periods per year, m, by solving the following equation:

9-11

$$\text{Effective annual rate (EAR)} = r_{EAR} = \left(1 + \frac{r_{SIMPLE}}{m}\right)^m - 1.0$$

$$= (1 + r_{PER})^m - 1.0$$

Here r_{SIMPLE} is the simple, or quoted, interest rate—that is, the APR—and m is the number of compounding periods (interest payments) per year. For example, to find the effective annual rate if the simple rate is 6 percent and interest is paid semiannually, we solve the following:

$$\text{Effective annual rate}_{(EAR)} = r_{EAR} = \left(1 + \frac{0.06}{2}\right)^2 - 1.0$$

$$= (1.03)^2 - 1.0 = 1.0609 - 1.0 = 0.0609 = 6.09\%$$

Using a financial calculator, enter N = 3, PV = −100, PMT = 0, and FV = 119.41; then solve for I/Y = 6.09.

Based on what we discussed here and the discussion in the previous section, semiannual compounding (or any non-annual compounding) can be handled in either of two ways:

ALTERNATIVE 1: *State everything on a periodic basis rather than on an annual basis.* As we showed in the previous section, we can compute the interest rate per period (periodic rate, $r_{PER} = r_{SIMPLE}/m$) and the total number of interest payments ($n_{PER} = n_{YRS} \times m$) during the life of the investment, or loan, when finding its present value or future value. In our example, you would use

$n_{PER} = 3 \times 2 = 6$ periods rather than 3 years, and use $r_{PER} = 6/2 = 3$ interest rate per period rather than 6 percent interest per year.

ALTERNATIVE 2: *Find the effective annual rate (r_{EAR})* by applying Equation 9-11, and then use this rate as an annual rate over the given number of years, n_{YRS}. In our example, use $r_{EAR} = 6.09\%$ and $n_{YRS} = 3$ years.

Here are the time line solutions and equation (numerical) solutions for the two alternatives that can be applied to compute the future value of $100 invested for 3 years at 6 percent interest compounded semiannually:

ALTERNATIVE 1: USE THE RATE PER PERIOD (r_{PER})— STATE EVERYTHING ON A PERIODIC BASIS

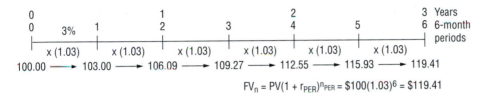

$$FV_n = PV(1 + r_{PER})^{n_{PER}} = \$100(1.03)^6 = \$119.41$$

Using a financial calculator, enter N = 6, I/Y = 3.0, PV = −100, and PMT = 0; then solve for FV = 119.41.

ALTERNATIVE 2: USE THE EFFECTIVE ANNUAL RATE (r_{EAR})— STATE EVERYTHING ON AN ANNUAL BASIS

$$FV_n = PV(1 + r_{EAR})^{n_{YR}} = \$100(1.0609)^3 = \$119.41$$

Using a financial calculator, enter N = 3, I/Y = 6.09, PV = −100, and PMT = 0; then solve for FV = 119.41.

Both procedures give the same result, $119.41. That is, the account balance at the end of each of the 3 years is the same regardless of which alternative is used. Thus, as these time lines show, 6 percent interest compounded semiannually is equivalent to 6.09 percent compounded annually.

Suppose that you've decided to deposit $100 in a bank account that pays 6 percent interest compounded semiannually (the current situation), but you expect to leave the money in the bank account for 18 months rather than 3 years. How much will the balance in the account be in 18 months? Either Alternative 1 or Alternative 2 can be used to solve this problem. Using Alternative 1, the equation (numerical) solution is:

$$FV = \$100(1.03)^3 = \$100(1.092727) = \$109.27$$

In this case, $n_{PER} = 3$ because three interest payments are made during the 18-month period.

Converted into years, $n_{PER} = 3$ is the same as $n_{YRS} = 1.5$—that is, 18 months equates to $1\frac{1}{2}$ years. Therefore, using Alternative 2, the equation (numerical) solution is:

$$FV = \$100(1.0609)^{1.5} = \$100(1.092727) = \$109.27$$

The solution given here illustrates the use of *fractional time periods* to compute the present value of a single payment, or lump-sum amount, using the effective annual rate (r_{EAR}). Using a financial calculator, enter N = 1.5, I/Y = 6.09, PV = −100, and PMT = 0; then compute FV = 109.27.

The points made in this section can be generalized for other situations when compounding occurs more frequently than once per year. When computing either the future value or the present value of a lump-sum amount, either (1) convert the simple annual interest rate (APR = r_{SIMPLE}) to the periodic interest rate (r_{PER}) and the number of years (n_{YRS}) to the total number of compounding periods (n_{PER}) during the life of the investment (loan) or (2) convert the APR to the effective annual rate (r_{EAR}) and use the number of years (n_{YRS}).

Self-Test Questions

What do the terms *annual percentage rate (APR)*, *effective annual rate (r_{EAR})*, and *simple interest rate (r_{SIMPLE})* mean?

How are the simple rate, the periodic rate, and the effective annual rate related? Can you think of a situation where all three of these rates will be the same?

Suppose that you are considering depositing $400 in one of two banks. Bank A offers to pay 12 percent interest compounded monthly, whereas Bank B offers to pay 12.5 percent compounded annually. Which bank offers the better effective rate? (Answer: r_{EAR} at Bank A = 12.7 percent; r_{EAR} at Bank B = 12.5 percent)

AMORTIZED LOANS

amortized loan
A loan that requires equal payments over its life; the payments include both interest and repayment of the debt.

One of the most important applications of compound interest involves loans that are paid off in installments over time. Included in this category are automobile loans, home mortgages, student loans, and some business debt. If a loan is to be repaid in equal periodic amounts (monthly, quarterly, or annually), it is said to be an **amortized loan.**[13]

To illustrate, suppose a firm borrows $15,000, and the loan is to be repaid in three equal payments at the end of each of the next 3 years. The lender will charge 8 percent interest on the loan balance that is outstanding at the beginning of each year. Our first task is to determine the amount the firm must repay each year—that is, the annual payment. To find this amount, recognize that the $15,000 represents the present value of an annuity (PVA) of PMT dollars per year for 3 years, discounted at 8 percent:

Using a financial calculator, the solution is:

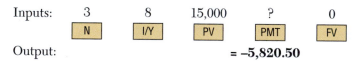

Enter N = 3, I/Y = 8, PV = 15,000 (the firm receives the cash), and FV = 0; then compute PMT = −5,820.50.

Thus, the firm must pay the lender $5,820.50 at the end of each of the next 3 years, in which case the percentage cost to the borrower, which is also the rate of return to

[13]The word *amortized* comes from the Latin *mors,* meaning "death," so an amortized loan is one that is "killed off" over time.

TABLE 9-1   Loan Amortization Schedule, 8 Percent Interest Rate

Year	Beginning of Year Balance (1)	Payment (2)	Interest @ 8%[a] $(3) = (1) \times 0.08$	Repayment of Principal[b] $(4) - (2) - (3)$	Remaining Balance[c] $(5) = (1) - (4)$
1	$15,000.00	$5,820.50	$1,200.00	$4,620.50	10,379.50
2	10,379.50	5,820.50	830.36	4,990.14	5,389.36
3	5,389.36	5,820.50	431.15	5,389.35	0.01

[a] Interest is calculated by multiplying the loan balance in Column 1 by the interest rate (0.08). For example, the interest in Year 2 is $10,379.50 × 0.08 = $830.36.

[b] Repayment of principal is equal to the payment of $5,820.50 in Column 2 minus the interest charge for each year in Column 3. For example, the repayment of principal in Year 2 is $5,820.50 − $830.36 = $4,990.14.

[c] The $0.01 remaining balance at the end of Year 3 results from a rounding difference.

the lender, will be 8 percent. Each payment consists partly of interest and partly of repayment of the amount borrowed (principal). This breakdown is given in the **amortization schedule** shown in Table 9-1. The interest component is largest in the first year, and it declines as the outstanding balance of the loan decreases. For tax purposes, a business borrower reports the interest component shown in Column 3 as a deductible cost each year, whereas the lender reports this same amount as taxable income.

Column 5 in Table 9-1 shows the outstanding balance that is due for our illustrative loan at the end of each year. If you do not have an amortization schedule, such as the one shown in Table 9-1, you can still determine the outstanding balance of the loan by computing the present value of the *remaining* loan payments. For example, after the first loan payment of $5,820.50 is made at the end of Year 1, the loan agreement calls for two more payments equal to $5,820.50 each. If you compute the present value of the two remaining payments at 8 percent interest per year, you will find that $PVA_2 = $10,379.50$, which is the remaining balance at the end of Year 1 that is shown in Column 5 in Table 9-1. The same logic that is presented in Table 9-1 can be used to create amortization schedules for home mortgages, automobile loans, and other amortized loans.

Financial calculators and spreadsheets are programmed to calculate amortization tables—you simply enter the data and apply the appropriate built-in function. If you have a financial calculator, it is worthwhile to read the appropriate section of the manual and learn how to use its amortization feature. Similarly, it is worth your time to learn how to set up an amortization table using a spreadsheet. For the sake of brevity, we show the steps that are required to set up the amortization schedule in Table 9-1 using both a financial calculator and a spreadsheet in the appendix at the end of this chapter.

amortization schedule
A schedule showing precisely how a loan will be repaid. It gives the required payment on each payment date and a breakdown of the payment, showing how much is interest and how much is repayment of principal.

Self-Test Questions

To construct an amortization schedule, how do you determine the amount of the periodic payments?

How do you determine the amount of each payment that goes to interest and to repay the debt?

Suppose that you have an outstanding automobile loan with 2 years remaining until it is paid off. The interest rate on the loan is 6 percent, and you are required to pay $452.07 *per month*. If you want to pay off the loan today, for how much should you write the check?   (Answer: $10,200)

Ethical Dilemma

It's All Chinese to Me!

Teri Zupita is currently considering how to invest the modest amount of money she recently inherited ($48,000). Based on her knowledge of different types of investments, as well as the advice of friends, Teri thinks that she should invest her inheritance in a long-term U.S. Treasury bond that promises to pay her $3,690 interest every 6 months for 10 years. At lunch today, however, Teri asked her best friend Mike how he would invest the money. Mike responded that he thought she could invest in something other than the T-bond and earn a much higher rate of return. In fact, he told Teri that he attended a company social a few nights ago where he overheard a few people talking about a U.S. automobile manufacturer that is partnering with the Chinese government to open a manufacturing operation in Shanghai. The firm, named Universal Autos (UA), would have exclusive rights to manufacture U.S. automobiles in China. One of the men involved in the conversation stated that he thought the arrangement presented a huge opportunity for UA to substantially increase its profits during the next 10 years, which should translate into significant increases in the company's stock price. All of the other persons involved in the discussion agreed.

Intrigued, Teri thought it would be a good idea to investigate UA as a potential investment, so she sought advice from her friends and relatives. One friend advised against UA as an investment because she had heard from another friend that the company planned to use child labor in its Chinese manufacturing plant. Another friend advised against the investment because he had heard rumors that the laborers in such plants are physically abused on a regular basis. And Teri's uncle, who works in the U.S. State Department, said that he had heard that UA paid a huge bribe to the Chinese government before the deal was signed, and it is illegal for U.S. firms to offer or pay such kickbacks. However, Teri's boyfriend, who happens to be Chinese, thinks that she should invest her money in UA. According to information provided by his family and friends in China, the agreement between UA and China represents a historic business deal that the Chinese government intends to support fully, so there is little risk associated with the investment. In fact, according to her boyfriend, Teri's $48,000 could grow to $112,500 in 10 years if she invests it in UA. If you were Teri, what would you do? Should you invest in a company that might knowingly use child labor, use workers who are abused, or pay bribes to foreign governments?

CHAPTER PRINCIPLES
–The Answers

To summarize the key concepts, let's answer the questions that were posed at the beginning of the chapter:

- **Why is it important to understand and be able to apply time value of money concepts?** It is essential that you have at least a basic understanding of time value of money concepts so that you are able to compare various investments. When we apply time value of money concepts, we restate dollars from one time period into equivalent dollars from another time period. Consider the question that was posed at the beginning of the chapter: Which is better, an investment that will return $7,023 in 5 years or an investment that will return $8,130 in 8 years? If your opportunity cost is 5 percent, the two investments are identical, because their present values are the same (PV = $5,502.70). Once the future values of these investments are translated into dollars at the same time period (Period 0 in this case), they can be compared. For these two investments, we could determine what the value of the 5-year investment would be when the 8-year investment matures by restating the dollars at the end of Year 5—that is, $7,023—into equivalent dollars at the end of Year 8. In Year 8, the 5-year investment would be worth FV = $7,023(1.05)^3 = $8,130, which is the same as the amount that the 8-year investment will return at the end of Year 8. A basic time value of money concept or "rule" is that dollars are comparable only when they are stated at the same time period; *dollars from different time periods should never be compared because their values are not the same.* (The only exception to this rule is when the interest rate equals 0 percent, which is highly unlikely.)

- **What is the difference between a present value amount and a future value amount?** When we compute the future value of an amount invested today, we add the interest that is earned during the investment period—that is, the current amount is compounded to a future period. When we compute the present value of a future amount, we take out the interest that is earned during the investment period—that is, we discount, or "de-interest," the future amount to restate it in current dollars.

- **What is an annuity? What are the two types of annuities, and how do their values differ?** An annuity is a series of equal payments that occur at equal time intervals. For example, a rent payment equal to $700 per month is an annuity. Further, the rent payment is called an *annuity due,* because it must be paid at the beginning of the month (period). If the annuity payment is at the end of the period, then it is called an *ordinary annuity.* Determining the present (future) value of an annuity is based on the same concept that is used to determine the present (future) value of a lump-sum, or single payment, amount. Because the annuity payments occur one period earlier and thus have the opportunity to earn one additional interest payment, both the present value and the future value of an annuity due are greater than the present value and future value of an ordinary annuity.

- **What is the difference between the Annual Percentage Rate (APR) and the Effective Annual Rate (EAR)? Which is more appropriate to use?** The APR is a simple interest rate (r_{SIMPLE}) that is quoted on loans, certificates of deposit, and so forth; it does not consider the effects of compounded interest. The EAR, r_{EAR}, is the actual interest rate, or rate of return, that an investment (loan) earns (costs) considering the effects of interest compounding. If interest is compounded more than once per year, $r_{EAR} > r_{SIMPLE}$; if interest is compounded annually, $r_{EAR} = r_{SIMPLE}$.

  APR is used to compute r_{PER} to determine the dollar amount of interest that is paid each interest payment period, whereas r_{EAR} is used to determine the actual return that is earned (paid) on an investment (loan). If you want to know the "true" return (cost) on an investment (loan), you must compute r_{EAR}.

- **What is an amortized loan? How are amortized loan payments and payoffs determined?** An amortized loan is one that is paid off in equal payments over a specified period. Each payment consists partly of interest and partly of repayment of the amount borrowed. In the early years, a large portion of each payment represents the interest charge, whereas in later years a large portion of each payment represents the repayment of the amount borrowed. For an amortized loan, the amount that is owed at any point in time can be determined by computing the present value of the remaining loan (annuity) payments. An amortization schedule shows how much of each payment constitutes interest, how much is used to repay the debt, and the remaining balance of the loan at each point in time.

- **How is the return (interest rate) on an investment (loan) determined?** If we know both the cost of an investment and the amount to which the investment will grow in the future, we can determine its return. For example, suppose that you just purchased an investment for $3,500 that promises to pay you $6,885 in 10 years. The return on this investment is 7 percent (using a financial calculator, enter N = 10, PV = −3,500, PMT = 0, and FV = 6,885; solve for I/Y = 7.0).

CHAPTER PRINCIPLES

–Personal Finance

Following are the general concepts presented in this chapter as they relate to personal financial decisions.

- **How can I use the valuation concepts presented in this chapter to make more informed personal financial decisions?** As was mentioned in Chapter 1, an asset's value is based on the future cash flows it is expected to produce (both the amount and the timing) during its life. In this chapter, we introduced the basic techniques used to determine value, which are based on time value of money concepts. You should now be able to determine the value of a stream of cash flows, regardless of whether the stream represents an annuity or an uneven cash flow series. Consider, for example, an investment that promises to pay investors $500 per year for the next 4 years. If investors demand a 6 percent annual return from this investment, what is its value? (Answer: $1,732.55)

  We apply this basic technique to value other types of investments later in the book.

- **Can time value of money concepts help me evaluate personal loans?** After reading this chapter, you should be able to determine the characteristics associated with loans that you will acquire in the future—that is, you should be able to compute the monthly (or any other period) payments, amount that needs to be borrowed, or interest rate when given enough information about a loan. For example, suppose that your budget indicates that you can only afford to make monthly payments equal to $400 to purchase an automobile, and you want to pay off the loan used for the purchase over 4 years. If the rate on automobile loans is 6.96 percent, "how much car can you buy"— that is, what is the maximum net purchase price you can afford? (Answer: $16,717, which is not much)

  If after three years you decide to pay off the automobile loan early, how much would you need? (Answer: $4,624)

- **How can I use the techniques presented in this chapter to set up a retirement plan?** You should now understand that it is important that you begin planning for retirement today. Suppose that you have determined you will need $1.5 million when you retire in 40 years so that you can live the lifestyle you desire during your retirement years. If your opportunity cost is 8 percent compounded annually, beginning in 1 year how much will you have to contribute each year to a retirement fund to reach your goal? (Answer: $5,790)

  If you wait 20 years to start making contributions, how much will you have to invest each year to reach the same retirement goal? (Answer: $32,778)

  As you can see, depending on when you start contributing to a retirement plan, there is quite a difference in the annual payments required to meet the same retirement goal. This simple example should show the sooner you start investing for retirement, the sooner you start earning interest, and thus the lower the contributions that are needed to reach your particular retirement goal.

QUESTIONS

9-1   What is an *opportunity cost rate*? How is this rate used in time value analysis, and where is it shown on a cash flow time line? Is the opportunity rate a single number that is used in all situations?

9-2   An *annuity* is defined as a series of payments of a fixed amount for a specific number of periods. Thus, $100 a year for 10 years is an annuity, but $100 in Year 1, $200 in Year 2, and $400 in Years 3 through 10 does *not* constitute an annuity. However, the second series *contains* an annuity. Is this a correct statement? Explain.

9-3   If a firm's earnings per share grew from $1 to $2 over a 10-year period, the total *growth* would be 100 percent, but the *annual growth rate* would be *less than* 10 percent. True or false? Explain. Under what conditions would the annual growth rate *actually* be 10 percent per year?

9-4   Would you rather have a savings account that pays 5 percent interest compounded semiannually or one that pays 5 percent interest compounded daily? Explain.

9-5   Give a verbal definition of the term *present value* and illustrate it using a cash flow time line with data from an example that you construct. As a part of your answer, explain why present values are dependent on interest rates.

9-6   To find the present value of an uneven series of cash flows, you must find the PVs of the individual cash flows and then sum them. Annuity procedures can never be of use, even if some of the cash flows constitute an annuity (for example, $100 each for Years 3, 4, 5, and 6), because the entire series is not an annuity. Is this a correct statement? Explain.

9-7   The present value of a perpetuity is equal to the payment on the annuity, PMT, divided by the interest rate, r: $PVP = PMT/r$. What is the *sum,* or *future value,* of a perpetuity of PMT dollars per year? (*Hint:* The answer is infinity, but explain why.)

9-8   When financial institutions, such as banks or credit unions, advertise the rates on their loans, they report the APR. If you wanted to compare the interest rates on loans from different financial institutions, should you compare the APRs? Explain.

9-9   Under what conditions would the simple interest rate, or APR (remember $r_{SIMPLE} = APR$), equal the effective annual rate, r_{EAR}?

9-10   What is an amortized loan? What is an amortization schedule and how is it used?

SELF-TEST PROBLEMS

Solutions appear in Appendix B at the end of the book.

ST-1   Define each of the following terms: **Key Terms**
  a.   PV; r; INT; FV_n; n; PVA_n; FVA_n; PMT
  b.   Opportunity cost rate
  c.   Annuity; lump-sum payment; cash flow; uneven cash flow stream
  d.   Ordinary (deferred) annuity; annuity due
  e.   Perpetuity; consol
  f.   Cash outflow; cash inflow; cash flow time line
  g.   Compounding; discounting
  h.   Annual, semiannual, quarterly, monthly, and daily compounding
  i.   m; simple (quoted) interest rate, r_{SIMPLE}; APR; effective annual rate, r_{EAR}; periodic rate, r_{PER}
  j.   Amortized loan; amortization schedule; principal component versus interest component of a payment
  k.   Terminal value

Rates of Return **ST-2** Suppose that you are evaluating two investments, both of which require you to pay $5,500 today. Investment A will pay you $7,020 in 5 years, whereas Investment B will pay you $8,126 in 8 years.

    a. Based only on the return you would earn from each investment, which is better?

    b. Can you think of any factors other than the expected return that might be important to consider when choosing between the two investment alternatives?

Future Value **ST-3** Assume that it is now January 1, 2010. On January 1, 2011, you will deposit $1,000 into a savings account that pays 8 percent.

    a. If the bank compounds interest annually, how much will you have in your account on January 1, 2014?

    b. What would your January 1, 2014, balance be if the bank used quarterly compounding rather than annual compounding?

    c. Suppose you deposited the $1,000 in four payments of $250 each on January 1 of 2011, 2012, 2013, and 2014. How much would you have in your account on January 1, 2014, based on 8 percent annual compounding?

    d. Suppose you deposited four equal payments in your account on January 1 of 2011, 2012, 2013, and 2014. Assuming an 8 percent interest rate, how large would each of your payments have to be for you to obtain the same ending balance as you calculated in part (a)?

Time Value of Money **ST-4** Assume that it is now January 1, 2010, and you will need $1,000 on January 1, 2014. Your bank compounds interest at an 8 percent annual rate.

    a. How much must you deposit on January 1, 2011, to have a balance of $1,000 on January 1, 2014?

    b. If you want to make equal payments on each January 1 from 2011 through 2014 to accumulate the $1,000, how large must each of the four payments be?

    c. If your father were to offer either to make the payments calculated in part (b) ($221.92) or to give you a lump sum of $750 on January 1, 2011, which would you choose?

    d. If you have only $750 on January 1, 2011, what interest rate, compounded annually, would you have to earn to have the necessary $1,000 on January 1, 2014?

    e. Suppose you can deposit only $186.29 each January 1 from 2011 through 2014, but you still need $1,000 on January 1, 2014. At what interest rate, with annual compounding, must you invest to achieve your goal?

    f. To help you reach your $1,000 goal, your father offers to give you $400 on January 1, 2011. You will get a part-time job and make six additional payments of equal amounts each 6 months thereafter. If all of this money is deposited in a bank that pays 8 percent, compounded semi-annually, how large must each of the six payments be?

    g. What is the effective annual rate being paid by the bank in part (f)?

Effective Annual Rates **ST-5** Bank A pays 8 percent interest, compounded quarterly, on its money market account. The managers of Bank B want the rate on its money market account to equal Bank A's effective annual rate, but interest is to be compounded on a monthly basis. What simple, or quoted, rate must Bank B set?

PROBLEMS

9-1 If you invest $500 today in an account that pays 6 percent interest compounded annually, how much will be in your account after 2 years?

FV—Lump Sum

9-2 What is the present value of an investment that promises to pay you $1,000 in 5 years if you can earn 6 percent interest compounded annually?

PV—Lump Sum

9-3 What is the present value of $1,552.90 due in 10 years at (1) a 12 percent discount rate and (2) a 6 percent rate.

PV—Different Interest Rates

9-4 To the closest year, how long will it take a $200 investment to double if it earns 7 percent interest? How long will it take if the investment earns 18 percent?

Time to Double a Lump Sum

9-5 Which amount is worth more at 14 percent: $1,000 in hand today or $2,000 due in 6 years?

TVM Comparisons

9-6 Martell Corporation's 2009 sales were $12 million. Sales were $6 million 5 years earlier. To the nearest percentage point, at what rate have sales grown?

Growth Rate

9-7 Find the future value of the following *ordinary annuities:*

  a. $400 per year for 10 years at 10 percent.

  b. $200 per year for 5 years at 5 percent.

FV—Ordinary Annuity

9-8 Find the future value of the following *annuities due:*

  a. $400 per year for 10 years at 10 percent.

  b. $200 per year for 5 years at 5 percent.

FV—Annuity Due

9-9 Find the present value of the following *ordinary annuities:*

  a. $400 per year for 10 years at 10 percent.

  b. $200 per year for 5 years at 5 percent.

PV—Ordinary Annuity

9-10 Find the present value of the following *annuities due:*

  a. $400 per year for 10 years at 10 percent.

  b. $200 per year for 5 years at 5 percent.

PV—Annuity Due

9-11 What is the present value of a perpetuity of $100 per year if the appropriate discount rate is 7 percent? If interest rates in general were to double and the appropriate discount rate rose to 14 percent, what would happen to the present value of the perpetuity?

Perpetuity

9-12 Find the *present values* of the following cash flow streams under the following conditions:

PV—Uneven Cash Flow Stream

Year	Cash Stream A	Cash Stream B
1	$100	$300
2	400	400
3	400	400
4	300	100

  a. The appropriate interest rate is 8 percent.

  b. The appropriate interest rate is 0 percent.

9-13 Find the amount to which $500 will grow in 5 years under each of the following conditions:

FV—Lump Sum, Various Compounding Periods

  a. 12 percent compounded annually.

  b. 12 percent compounded semiannually.

       c. 12 percent compounded quarterly.

       d. 12 percent compounded monthly.

PV—Lump Sum, Various Compounding Periods

9-14 Find the present value of $500 due in 5 years under each of the following conditions:

       a. 12 percent simple rate, compounded annually.

       b. 12 percent simple rate, compounded semiannually.

       c. 12 percent simple rate, compounded quarterly.

       d. 12 percent simple rate, compounded monthly.

FV—Ordinary Annuity, Various Compounding Periods

9-15 Find the future values of the following *ordinary* annuities:

       a. FV of $400 each 6 months for 5 years at a simple rate of 12 percent, compounded semiannually.

       b. FV of $200 each 3 months for 5 years at a simple rate of 12 percent, compounded quarterly.

       c. The annuities described in parts (a) and (b) have the same amount of money paid into them during the 5-year period and both earn interest at the same simple rate, yet the annuity in part (b) earns $101.75 more than the one in part (a) over the 5 years. Why does this occur?

PV—Ordinary Annuity, Various Compounding Periods

9-16 Find the present values of the following *ordinary* annuities:

       a. PV of $400 each 6 months for 5 years at a simple rate of 12 percent, compounded semiannually.

       b. PV of $200 each 3 months for 5 years at a simple rate of 12 percent, compounded quarterly.

       c. The annuities described in parts (a) and (b) have the same amount of money paid into them during the 5-year period and both earn interest at the same simple rate, yet the present value of the annuity in part (b) is $31.46 greater than the one in part (a). Why does this occur?

Required Lump-Sum Payment

9-17 To complete your last year in business school and then go through law school, you will need $30,000 per year for 4 years, starting next year (that is, you will need to withdraw the first $30,000 one year from today). Your rich uncle offers to put you through school, and he will deposit in a bank paying 7 percent interest annually a sum of money that is sufficient to provide the four payments of $30,000 each. His deposit will be made today.

       a. How large must the deposit be?

       b. How much will be in the account immediately after you make the first withdrawal? After the last withdrawal?

PMT—Loan Payments

9-18 Sue wants to buy a car that costs $12,000. She has arranged to borrow the total purchase price of the car from her credit union at a simple interest rate equal to 12 percent. The loan requires quarterly payments for a period of 3 years. If the first payment is due in 3 months (one quarter) after purchasing the car, what will be the amount of Sue's quarterly payments on the loan?

Repaying a Loan, n

9-19 While Steve Bouchard was a student at the University of Florida, he borrowed $12,000 in student loans at an annual interest rate of 9 percent. If Steve repays $1,500 per year, how long, to the nearest year, will it take him to repay the loan?

Reaching a Financial Goal

9-20 You need to accumulate $10,000. To do so, you plan to make deposits of $1,750 per year, with the first payment being made 1 year from today, in a bank account that pays 6 percent annual interest. Your last deposit will be more than $1,750 if more is needed to round out to $10,000. How many years will it take you to reach your $10,000 goal, and how large will the last deposit be?

9-21 Jack just discovered that he holds the winning ticket for the $87 million mega lottery in Missouri. Now he needs to decide which alternative to choose: (1) a $44 million lump-sum payment today or (2) a payment of $2.9 million per year for 30 years; the first payment will be made today. If Jack's opportunity cost is 5 percent, which alternative should he choose?

TVM Comparisons—Lottery Winner

9-22 Consider the decision you might have to make if you won a state lottery worth $105 million. Which *would* you choose: a lump-sum payment of $54 million today or a payment of $3.5 million each year for the next 30 years? Which *should* you choose?

TVM Comparisons—Lottery Winner

  a. If your opportunity cost is 6 percent, which alternative should you select?

  b. At what opportunity cost would you be indifferent between the two alternatives?

9-23 Find the interest rates, or rates of return, on each of the following:

Effective Interest Rate, r_{EAR}

  a. You borrow $700 and promise to pay back $749 at the end of 1 year.

  b. You lend $700 and receive a promise to be paid $749 at the end of 1 year.

  c. You borrow $85,000 and promise to pay back $201,229 at the end of 10 years.

  d. You borrow $9,000 and promise to make payments of $2,684.80 per year for 5 years.

9-24 The First City Bank pays 7 percent interest, compounded annually, on time deposits. The Second City Bank pays 6.5 percent interest, compounded quarterly.

r_{EAR} **versus** r_{SIMPLE}

  a. Based on effective interest rates, in which bank would you prefer to deposit your money?

  b. Assume that funds must be left on deposit during the entire compounding period to receive any interest. Could your choice of banks be influenced by the fact that you might want to withdraw your funds during the year as opposed to at the end of the year?

9-25 Krystal Magee invested $150,000 18 months ago. Currently, the investment is worth $168,925. Krystal knows the investment has paid interest *every 3 months (i.e., quarterly)*, but she doesn't know what the yield on her investment is. Help Krystal. Compute both the annual percentage rate (APR), r_{SIMPLE}, and the effective annual rate (EAR) of interest, r_{EAR}.

r_{EAR} **and** r_{SIMPLE}

9-26 Your broker offers to sell you a note for $13,250 that will pay $2,345.05 per year for 10 years. If you buy the note, what rate of interest (to the closest percent) will you be earning?

Effective Rate of Return

9-27 A mortgage company offers to lend you $85,000; the loan calls for payments of $8,273.59 per year for 30 years. What is the effective annual interest rate, r_{EAR}, that the mortgage company is charging you?

EAR, r_{EAR}

9-28 Suppose you found a house that you want to buy, but you still have to determine what mortgage to use. Bank of Middle Texas has offered a 30-year fixed mortgage that requires you to pay 6.9 percent interest compounded monthly. If you take this offer, you will have to pay "3.5 points," which means you will have to make a payment equal to 3.5 percent of the amount

Loan Evaluation—Mortgage

borrowed at the time you sign the mortgage agreement. Bank of South Alaska has offered a 30-year fixed mortgage with no points, but at an interest rate equal to 7.2 percent compounded monthly. For either mortgage, the first payment would not be made until 1 month after the mortgage agreement is signed. The purchase price of the house is $250,000, and you plan to make a down payment equal to $40,000.

a. If you make a down payment equal to $40,000 and borrow the rest of the purchase price of the house from Bank of Middle Texas, how much will you have to pay for the "3.5 points" when you sign the mortgage agreement?

b. Assume that the "points" charged by Bank of Middle Texas can simply be added to the mortgaged amount so that the total amount borrowed from the bank includes the points that must be paid at the time the mortgage is signed plus the net purchase price of the house (purchase price less the down payment). For example, the points that apply to a $100,000 mortgage would be $3,500, so the mortgage amount would be $103,500. Which bank offers the lower monthly payments?

c. What would the "points" on the Middle Texas Bank mortgage have to equal for you to be indifferent between the two mortgages?

Loan Amortization **9-29** Assume that your aunt sold her house on January 1 and that she took a mortgage in the amount of $10,000 as part of the payment. The mortgage has a quoted (or simple) interest rate of 10 percent, but it calls for payments every 6 months, beginning on June 30, and the mortgage is to be amortized over 10 years. Now, 1 year later, your aunt must file a Form 1099 with the IRS and with the person who bought the house, informing them of the interest that was included in the two payments made during the year. (This interest will be income to your aunt and a deduction to the buyer of the house.) To the closest dollar, what is the total amount of interest that was paid during the first year?

Amortization Schedule **9-30** Lorkay Seidens Inc. just borrowed $25,000. The loan is to be repaid in equal installments at the end of each of the next 5 years, and the interest rate is 10 percent.

a. Set up an amortization schedule for the loan.

b. How large must each annual payment be if the loan is for $50,000? Assume that the interest rate remains at 10 percent and that the loan is paid off over 5 years.

c. How large must each payment be if the loan is for $50,000, the interest rate is 10 percent, and the loan is paid off in equal installments at the end of each of the next 10 years? This loan is for the same amount as the loan in part (b), but the payments are spread out over twice as many periods. Why are these payments not half as large as the payments on the loan in part (b)?

Effective Rates of Return **9-31** Assume that AT&T's pension fund managers are considering two alternative securities as investments: (1) Security Z (for zero intermediate year cash flows), which costs $422.41 today, pays nothing during its 10-year life, and then pays $1,000 at the end of 10 years, and (2) Security B, which has a cost today of $500 and pays $74.50 at the end of each of the next 10 years.

a. What is the rate of return on each security?

b. Assume that the interest rate that AT&T's pension fund managers can earn on the fund's money falls to 6 percent immediately after the securities are purchased and is expected to remain at that level for the next 10 years. What would the price of each security be after the change in interest rates?

   c. Now assume that the interest rate rises to 12 percent (rather than falls to 6 percent) immediately after the securities are purchased. What would the price of each security be after the change in interest rates? Explain the results.

9-32 Jason worked various jobs during his teenage years to save money for college. Now it is his twentieth birthday, and he is about to begin his college studies at the University of South Florida (USF). A few months ago, Jason received a scholarship that will cover all of his college tuition for a period not to exceed 5 years. The money he has saved will be used for living expenses while he is in college; in fact, Jason expects to use all of his savings while attending USF. The jobs he worked as a teenager allowed him to save a total of $10,000, which currently is invested at 12 percent in a financial asset that pays interest monthly. Because Jason will be a full-time student, he expects to graduate 4 years from today, on his twenty-fourth birthday.

   a. How much can Jason withdraw every month while he is in college if the first withdrawal occurs today?

   b. How much can Jason withdraw every month while he is in college if he waits until the end of this month to make the first withdrawal?

PMT—Ordinary Annuity versus Annuity Due

9-33 Sue Sharpe, manager of Oaks Mall Jewelry, wants to sell on credit, giving customers 3 months in which to pay. However, Sue will have to borrow from her bank to carry the accounts payable. The bank will charge a simple 15 percent, but with monthly compounding. Sue wants to quote a simple rate to her customers (all of whom are expected to pay on time) that will exactly cover her financing costs. What simple annual rate should she quote to her credit customers?

r_{SIMPLE}, *Simple Interest Rate*

9-34 Brandi just received her credit card bill, which has an outstanding balance equal to $3,310. After reviewing her financial position, Brandi has concluded that she cannot pay the outstanding balance in full; rather, she has to make payments over time to repay the credit card bill. After thinking about it, Brandi decided to cut up her credit card. Now she wants to determine how long it will take to pay off the outstanding balance. The credit card carries an 18 percent simple interest rate, which is compounded monthly. The minimum payment that Brandi must make each month is $25. Assume that the only charge Brandi incurs from month to month is the interest that must be paid on the remaining outstanding balance.

Loan Repayment—Credit Card

   a. If Brandi pays $150 each month, how long will it take her to pay off the credit card bill?

   b. If Brandi pays $222 each month, how long will it take her to pay off the credit card bill?

   c. If Brandi pays $360 each month, how long will it take her to pay off the credit card bill?

9-35 Brandon just graduated from college. Unfortunately, Brandon's education was fairly costly; the student loans that he took out to pay for his education total $95,000. The provisions of the student loans require Brandon to pay interest equal to the prime rate, which is 8 percent, plus a 1 percent margin— that is, the interest rate on the loans is 9 percent. Payments will be made

Loan Repayment— Student Loan

monthly, and the loans must be repaid within 20 years. Brandon wants to determine how he is going to repay his student loans.

a. If Brandon decides to repay the loans over the maximum period—that is, 20 years—how much must he pay each month?

b. If Brandon wants to repay the loans in 10 years, how much must he pay each month?

c. If Brandon pays $985 per month, how long will it take him to repay the loans?

Financing Alternatives— Automobile Loans   **9-36**   Assume that you are on your way to purchase a new car. You have already applied and been accepted for an automobile loan through your local credit union. The loan can be for an amount up to $25,000, depending on the final price of the car you choose. The terms of the loan call for monthly payments for a period of 4 years at a stated interest rate equal to 6 percent. After selecting the car you want, you negotiate with the sales representative and agree on a purchase price of $24,000, which does not include any rebates or incentives. The rebate on the car you chose is $3,000. The dealer offers "0% financing," but you forfeit the $3,000 rebate if you take the "0% financing."

a. What are the monthly payments that you will have to make if you take the "0% financing"? (*Hint:* Because there is no interest, the total amount that has to be repaid is $24,000, which also equals the sum of all the payments.)

b. What are the monthly payments if you finance the car with the credit union loan?

c. Should you use the "0% financing" loan or the credit union loan to finance the car?

d. Assume that it is 2 years later, and you have decided to repay the amount you owe on the automobile loan. How much must you repay if you chose the dealer's "0% financing"? The credit union loan?

Reaching a Financial Goal—Saving for College   **9-37**   A father is planning a savings program to put his daughter through college. His daughter is now 13 years old. She plans to enroll at the university in 5 years, and it should take her 4 years to complete her education. Currently, the cost per year (for everything—food, clothing, tuition, books, transportation, and so forth) is $12,500, but these costs are expected to increase by 5 percent—the inflation rate—each year. The daughter recently received $7,500 from her grandfather's estate; this money, which is invested in a mutual fund paying 8 percent interest compounded annually, will be used to help meet the costs of the daughter's education. The rest of the costs will be met by money that the father will deposit in the savings account. He will make equal deposits to the account in each year beginning today until his daughter starts college—that is, he will make a total of six deposits. These deposits will also earn 8 percent interest.

a. What will be the present value of the cost of 4 years of education *at the time the daughter turns 18*? (*Hint:* Calculate the cost increase, or growth, at 5 percent inflation, or growth for each year of her education, discount three of these costs at 8 percent back to the year in which she turns 18, then sum the four costs, which include the cost of the first year of college.)

b. What will be the value of the $7,500 that the daughter received from her grandfather's estate *when she starts college at age 18*? (*Hint:* Compound for 5 years at 8 percent.)

     c. If the father is planning to make the first of six deposits today, how large must each deposit be for him to be able to put his daughter through college? (*Hint:* Be sure to draw a cash flow time line to depict the timing of the cash flows.)

9-38 As soon as she graduated from college, Kay began planning for her retirement. Her plans were to deposit $500 semiannually into an IRA (a retirement fund) beginning 6 months after graduation and continuing until the day she retired, which she expected to be 30 years later. Today is the day Kay retires. She just made the last $500 deposit into her retirement fund, and now she wants to know how much she has accumulated for her retirement. The fund earned 10 percent compounded semiannually since it was established.

     a. Compute the balance of the retirement fund assuming all the payments were made on time.

     b. Although Kay was able to make all of the $500 deposits she planned, 10 years ago she had to withdraw $10,000 from the fund to pay some medical bills incurred by her mother. Compute the balance in the retirement fund based on this information.

Reaching a Financial Goal—Saving for Retirement

9-39 Sarah is on her way to the local Chevrolet dealership to buy a new car. The list, or "sticker," price of the car is $13,000. Sarah has $3,000 in her checking account that she can use as a down payment toward the purchase of a new car. Sarah has carefully evaluated her finances, and she has determined that she can afford payments that *total* $2,400 per year on a loan to purchase the car. Sarah can borrow the money to purchase the car either through the dealer's "special financing package," which is advertised as 4 percent financing, or from a local bank, which has automobile loans at 12 percent interest. Each loan would be outstanding for a period of 5 years, and the payments would be made quarterly (every 3 months). Sarah knows the dealer's "special financing package" requires that she will have to pay the "sticker" price for the car. But if she uses the bank financing, she thinks she can negotiate with the dealer for a better price. Assume Sarah wants to pay $600 per payment regardless of which loan she chooses, and the remainder of the purchase price will be a down payment that can be satisfied with the money Sarah has in her checking account. Ignoring charges for taxes, tag, and title transfer, how much of a reduction in the "sticker price" must Sarah negotiate to make the bank financing more attractive than the dealer's "special financing package"?

Automobile Loan Computation

9-40 Janet just graduated from a women's college in Mississippi with a degree in business administration, and she is about to start a new job with a large financial services firm based in Tampa, Florida. From reading various business publications while she was in college, Janet has concluded that it probably is a good idea to begin planning for her retirement now. Even though she is only 22 years old and just beginning her career, Janet is concerned that Social Security will not be able to meet her needs when she retires. Fortunately for Janet, the company that hired her has created a good retirement/investment plan that permits her to make contributions every year. Janet is now evaluating the amount she needs to contribute to satisfy her financial requirements at retirement. She has decided that she would like to take a trip as soon as her retirement begins (a reward to herself for many years of excellent work). The estimated cost of the trip, including all expenses such as meals and souvenirs, will be $120,000, and it

PMT—Retirement Plan

will last for 1 year (no other funds will be needed during the first year of retirement). After she returns from her trip, Janet plans to settle down to enjoy her retirement. She estimates she will need $70,000 each year to be able to live comfortably and enjoy her "twilight years." The retirement/ investment plan available to employees where Janet is going to work pays 7 percent interest compounded annually, and it is expected this rate will continue as long as the company offers the opportunity to contribute to the fund. When she retires, Janet will have to move her retirement "nest egg" to another investment so she can withdraw money when she needs it. Her plans are to move the money to a fund that allows withdrawals at the beginning of each year; the fund is expected to pay 5 percent interest compounded annually. Janet expects to retire in 40 years, and, after taking an online "life expectancy" quiz, she has concluded that she will live another 20 years after she returns from her around-the-world "retirement trip." If Janet's expectations are correct, how much must she contribute to the retirement fund to satisfy her retirement plans if she plans to make her first contribution to the fund 1 year from today, and the last contribution will be made on the day she retires?

Integrative Problem

TVM Analysis   **9-41**   Assume that you are nearing graduation and that you have applied for a job with a local bank. As part of the bank's evaluation process, you have been asked to take an exam that covers several financial analysis techniques. The first section of the test addresses time value of money analysis. See how you would do by answering the following questions:

a. Draw cash flow time lines for (1) a $100 lump-sum cash flow at the end of Year 2, (2) an ordinary annuity of $100 per year for 3 years, (3) an uneven cash flow stream of $50, $100, $75, and $50 at the end of Years 0 through 3.

b. (1) What is the future value of an initial $100 after 3 years if it is invested in an account paying 10 percent annual interest?

(2) What is the present value of $100 to be received in 3 years if the appropriate interest rate is 10 percent?

c. We sometimes need to find how long it will take a sum of money (or anything else) to grow to some specified amount. For example, if a company's sales are growing at a rate of 20 percent per year, approximately how long will it take sales to triple?

d. What is the difference between an ordinary annuity and an annuity due? What type of annuity is shown in the following cash flow time line? How would you change it to the other type of annuity?

e. (1) What is the future value of a 3-year ordinary annuity of $100 if the appropriate interest rate is 10 percent?

(2) What is the present value of the annuity?

(3) What would the future and present values be if the annuity were an annuity due?

f. What is the present value of the following uneven cash flow stream? The appropriate interest rate is 10 percent, compounded annually.

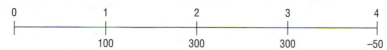

g. What annual interest rate will cause $100 to grow to $125.97 in 3 years?

h. **(1)** Will the future value be larger or smaller if we compound an initial amount more often than annually—for example, every 6 months, or *semiannually*—holding the stated interest rate constant? Why?

(2) Define the stated, or simple (quoted), rate (r_{SIMPLE}), annual percentage rate (APR), the periodic rate (r_{PER}), and the effective annual rate (r_{EAR}).

(3) What is the effective annual rate for a simple rate of 10 percent, compounded semiannually? Compounded quarterly? Compounded daily?

(4) What is the future value of $100 after 3 years under 10 percent semiannual compounding? Quarterly compounding?

i. Will the effective annual rate ever be equal to the simple (quoted) rate? Explain.

j. **(1)** What is the value at the end of Year 3 of the following cash flow stream if the quoted interest rate is 10 percent, compounded semiannually?

(2) What is the PV of the same stream?

(3) Is the stream an annuity?

(4) An important rule is that you should never show a simple rate on a time line or use it in calculations unless what condition holds? (*Hint:* Think of annual compounding, when $r_{SIMPLE} = r_{EAR} = r_{PER}$.) What would be wrong with your answer to parts (1) and (2) if you used the simple rate of 10 percent rather than the periodic rate of $r_{SIMPLE}/2 = 10\%/2 = 5\%$?

k. **(1)** Construct an amortization schedule for a $1,000 loan that has a 10 percent annual interest rate that is repaid in three equal installments.

(2) What is the annual interest expense for the borrower and the annual interest income for the lender during Year 2?

l. Suppose on January 1 you deposit $100 in an account that pays a simple, or quoted, interest rate of 11.33463 percent, with interest added (compounded) daily. How much will you have in your account on October 1, or after 9 months?

m. Now suppose you leave your money in the bank for 21 months. Thus, on January 1 you deposit $100 in an account that pays 11.33463 percent compounded daily. How much will be in your account on October 1 of the following year?

n. Suppose someone offered to sell you a note that calls for a $1,000 payment 15 months from today. The person offers to sell the note for $850. You have $850 in a bank time deposit (savings instrument) that pays a 6.76649 percent simple rate with daily compounding, which is a 7 percent effective annual interest rate; and you plan to leave this money in the bank unless you buy the note. The note is not risky—that is, you are sure it will be paid on schedule. Should you buy the note? Check the decision in three ways: (1) by comparing your future value if you buy the note versus leaving your money in the bank, (2) by comparing the PV of the note with your current bank investment, and (3) by comparing the r_{EAR} on the note with that of the bank investment.

o. Suppose the note discussed in part (n) costs $850, but calls for five quarterly payments of $190 each, with the first payment due in 3 months rather than $1,000 at the end of 15 months. Would it be a good investment?

COMPUTER-RELATED PROBLEM

Work the problem in this section only if you are using the problem spreadsheet.

Amortization Schedule   **9-42**   Use the computerized model in the File C09 to solve this problem.

a. Set up an amortization schedule for a $30,000 loan to be repaid in equal installments at the end of each of the next 20 years at an interest rate of 10 percent. What is the annual payment?

b. Set up an amortization schedule for a $60,000 loan to be repaid in 20 equal annual installments at an interest rate of 10 percent. What is the annual payment?

c. Set up an amortization schedule for a $60,000 loan to be repaid in 20 equal annual installments at an interest rate of 20 percent. What is the annual payment?

APPENDIX 9A   Generating an Amortization Schedule—Financial Calculator Solution and Spreadsheet Solution

The amortization schedule that is shown in Table 9-1 was generated using a regular calculator to compute each value. Although there is nothing wrong with this procedure, it can be tedious and time consuming when there are numerous installment payments. Therefore, in this section, we show you how to generate an amortization schedule using both a financial calculator and a spreadsheet.

In the chapter, we assumed that a firm borrows $15,000, and the loan is to be repaid in equal payments at the end of each of the next 3 years. The interest on the loan is 8 percent. To set up the amortization schedule for this situation, we first determined the amount of the payment that the firm must make each year. Using either a financial calculator or a spreadsheet that, we find that the annual payment must be $5,820.50.

FINANCIAL CALCULATOR SOLUTION

The following steps show you how to generate an amortization schedule using a Texas Instruments BAII PLUS. For more information or if you have a different type of calculator, refer to the manual that came with your calculator.

1. Enter the information for the amortized loan into the TVM registers as described in the chapter:

Inputs: 3   8   15,000   ?   0
         [N]   [I/Y]   [PV]   [PMT]   [FV]
Output: = **−5,820.50**

2. Enter the amortization function by pressing **2ND** **PV**, which has "AMORT" written above it (a secondary function). P1 = 1 is displayed, which indicates that the starting point for the amortization schedule is the first period. Press ▮, and P2 = 1 is displayed, which indicates the ending point for the first set of computations is the first period.

3. **a.** Press ▮, and BAL = 10,379.49729 is displayed. This result indicates that the remaining principal balance at the end of the first year is $10,379.50.

   b. Press ▮, and PRN = −4,620.502711 is displayed, which indicates that the amount of principal repaid in the first period is $4,620.50.

   c. Press ▮, and INT = −1,200 is displayed, which indicates that the amount of interest paid in the first period is $1,200.

4. Press ▮ **CPT**, and P1 = 2 is displayed. Next, press ▮, and P2 = 2 is displayed. This information indicates that the next series of computations relates to the second payment. Follow the procedures given above in Step 3:

   a. Press ▮; the display shows BAL = 5,389.354362.

   b. Press ▮; the display shows PRN = −4,990.142928.

   c. Press ▮; the display shows INT = −830.3597831.

   These values represent the ending loan balance, the amount of principal repaid, and the amount of interest paid, respectively, for the second year.

5. Press ▮ **CPT**, and P1 = 3 is displayed; then press ▮, and P2 = 3 is displayed. This information indicates that the next series of computations relate to the third payment. Follow the procedures given in Step 3:

   a. Press ▮; the display shows BAL = −0.000000.

   b. Press ▮; the display shows PRN = −5,389.354362.

   c. Press ▮; the display shows INT = −431.1483489.

   These values represent the ending loan balance, the amount of principal repaid, and the amount of interest paid, respectively, for the third, and final, year.

If you combine the results from steps 3 through 5 in a table, you would find that it contains the same values given in Table 9-1. If you use a calculator to construct a complete amortization schedule, you must repeat Step 3 for each year the loan exists—that is, Step 3 must be repeated 10 times for a 10-year loan. If you would like to know the balance, principal repayment, or interest paid in a particular year, you need only set P1 and P2 equal to that particular year to display the desired values.

SPREADSHEET SOLUTION

To set up the amortization schedule using Excel, we use two financial functions: IPMT and PPMT. IPMT gives the interest payment for a particular period, given the amount borrowed and the interest rate. PPMT gives the principal repayment for a particular period, given the amount borrowed and the interest rate. The following spreadsheet shows the content of each cell that is required to construct an amortization schedule for our illustrative loan:

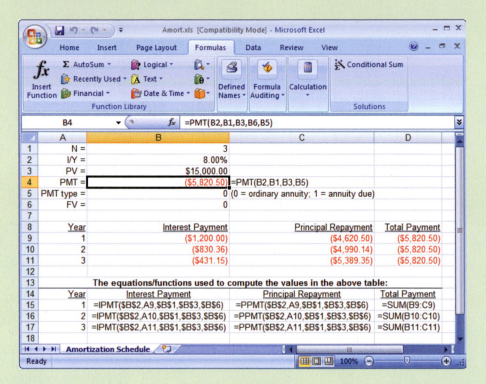

Note that the $ sign is used when referring to cells in the equations to fix the locations of the cells that contain common values that are required for each computation. Fixing the cell locations allows you to use the copy command to copy the relationships from row 9 to rows 10 and 11.

Valuation Concepts

CHAPTER 10

A MANAGERIAL PERSPECTIVE

In June 2003, 10-year Treasury bonds were selling at prices that promised investors an average return equal to 3.2 percent. As a result, a 10-year Treasury bond with a face, or par, value equal to $10,000 that paid $160 interest every 6 months had a market value equal to $10,000 at that time. One year later, in June 2004, the value of the same bond was $8,842, because the market interest rate on similar risk investments had risen to 4.8 percent. Thus, if you had purchased the bond 1 year earlier, at least on paper, you would have incurred a capital loss equal to $1,158. Your "paper loss" would have shrunk somewhat if you still owned the bond in 2005 when its market value was $9,391, because the interest rate on similar risk investments had dropped to 4.1 percent. Unfortunately, if you held on to the bond for the next couple of years hoping that its price would increase, you would have been disappointed, because in June 2007 its value declined to $8,980, when interest rates on such bonds were 5.2 percent. But, by June 2008 the bond's market value had climbed again, this time to its face value of $10,000, because interest rates declined significantly to 3.2 percent during the previous year. Although you would have incurred a "paper gain" equal to $0 during this period, you would have received interest payments that totaled $1,600 ($160 each 6 months).

Why did the market value of the Treasury bond change? The primary reason the value of this investment, as well as other debt instruments, changed was because market interest rates changed several times during the 2003–2008 period. If you purchased a 10-year Treasury bond in June 2003 when interest rates were at historically low levels, and then sold the same bond in June 2007, after interest rates had increased to 5.2 percent, you would have earned an average annual return (noncompounded) equal to approximately 0.7 percent. The return would have consisted of a capital loss equal to $-1,020 = $8,980 - $10,000 and interest payments totaling $1,280 ($320 for 4 years), which would have resulted in a net dollar *gain* equal to $260. On the other hand, if you waited until June 2008 to sell the bond, your annual return would have averaged 3.2 percent (total dollar return = $1,600 = $0 + $1,600; capital gain = $0 = $10,000 - $10,000 and interest = $1,600 = 10 interest payments of $160). And, if you continued to hold the bond beyond June 2008, you would find that its value would change each time interest rates change. This illustration shows that a bond's value changes when market interest rates change; whether the change is an increase or a decrease depends on the direction of the interest rate change.

As you read this chapter, think about why the value of the Treasury bonds first decreased and then increased during the 2003–2008 period, which was characterized first by increasing interest rates and then by decreasing interest rates. What happens to the value of bonds when the returns demanded by investors—that is, interest rates—change? Are bonds and stocks affected the same? Answering these questions will help you to get a basic understanding of how stocks and bonds are valued in the financial markets. Such an understanding will help you make investment decisions, including those that are critical when establishing a retirement plan.

CHAPTER PRINCIPLES
–The Questions

After reading this chapter, you should be able to answer the following questions:

- How are bond prices determined?
- How are bond yields (market rates) determined?
- What is the relationship between bond prices and interest rates? Why is it important for investors to understand this relationship?
- In general, how are stock prices determined?
- How are stock returns (yields) determined?
- What factors affect stock prices?

In Chapter 9, we examined time value of money (TVM) analysis. In this chapter, we show how the TVM concepts are used to determine the values of assets (investments) by examining the cash flows the assets are expected to generate in the future. Knowledge of valuation is important to investors and financial managers, because all important financial decisions should be analyzed in terms of how they affect value, regardless of whether the decisions relate to such real assets as plant and equipment or such financial assets as stocks and bonds. Also, recall from Chapter 6 that the goal of managerial finance is to maximize the value of the firm. Thus, it is critical that we understand the valuation process because it allows us to determine factors that affect the value of the firm.

BASIC VALUATION

After learning about the time value of money, you should realize that the *value* of anything, whether it is a financial asset like a stock or a bond or a real asset like a building or a piece of machinery, *is based on the present value of the cash flows that the asset is expected to produce in the future*. On a cash flow time line, value can be depicted as follows:

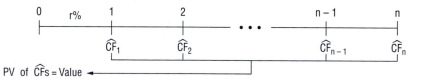

According to this time line, the value of any asset can be expressed in general form as follows:

10-1

$$\text{Asset value} = V = \frac{\widehat{CF}_1}{(1+r)^1} + \frac{\widehat{CF}_2}{(1+r)^2} + \cdots + \frac{\widehat{CF}_{n-1}}{(1+r)^{n-1}} + \frac{\widehat{CF}_n}{(1+r)^n}$$

Here:

$\widehat{CF}_t$ = The cash flow expected to be generated by the asset in Period t. $\widehat{CF}_t$ is pronounced "CF hat t." The "hat" ($\wedge$) indicates that the cash flow, CF, is an expected value that is not known with certainty.

r = The return that investors consider appropriate for holding such an asset. This return is usually termed the *required rate of return*. We discuss risk/return concepts in Chapter 11.

According to Equation 10-1, the value of an asset is affected by the cash flows it is expected to generate, $\widehat{CF}_t$, and the return required by investors, r. Equation 10-1 depicts two important concepts in valuation: (1) the higher the cash flows an asset is expected to generate in the future, the greater its value, and (2) the lower the return investors demand, the greater the asset's value. In the remainder of this chapter, we discuss how to apply Equation 10-1 to determine the values of financial assets (bonds and stocks). In Chapter 13 we apply the same process to value real assets (machines and buildings).

Self-Test Questions

Describe the general methodology used to value any asset.

All else equal, how would an increase in an asset's expected future cash flows affect its value? How would an increase in the required rate of return affect the asset's value?

VALUATION OF BONDS

Recall from our discussion in Chapter 2 that a **bond** is a long-term promissory note issued by a business or governmental unit. The bond's terms are contractually specified such that investors know the principal amount (or par value), the coupon interest rate, the maturity date, and any other features of the security. For example, suppose on January 2, 2009, Genesco Manufacturing borrowed $25 million by selling 25,000 individual bonds for $1,000 each. Genesco received the $25 million, and it promised to pay the holders of each bond interest equal to $100 per year and to repay the $25 million at the end of 10 years.[1] The lenders, who wanted to earn a 10 percent return on their investment, were willing to give Genesco $25 million, so the value of the bond on the date it was issued was $25 million. But how did investors decide that the bond was worth $25 million? Would the value have been different if they had demanded a different rate of return—say, 12 percent?

A bond's market price is determined primarily by the cash flows that it generates—that is, the interest that it pays—which depends on its coupon interest rate. Other things held constant, the higher the coupon rate, the higher the market price of the bond, because the cash flows that are paid to investors in the form of interest are higher. At the time a bond is issued, the coupon rate of interest generally is set at a level that will cause the market price of the bond to equal its par (principal) value. With a lower coupon rate, investors would not be willing to pay $1,000 for the bond. With a higher coupon rate, investors would clamor for the bond

bond
A long-term debt instrument (loan).

---

[1] Actually, Genesco would receive some amount less than $25 million, because of costs associated with issuing the bond, such as legal fees, investment banking fees, and so forth. For our discussion here, we choose to ignore issuing costs to simplify the explanations. Chapter 3 describes the topic of issuing costs and the investment banking process.

and bid its price up over $1,000. Investment bankers can judge quite precisely the coupon rate that will cause a bond to sell at its $1,000 par value. As a result, a newly issued bond generally sells at, or very close to, its par value. On the other hand, because the dollar interest payment is constant, the price of an outstanding bond will vary significantly from its par value when economic conditions change from what existed when the bond was issued. In the following sections, we show how to value bonds and how bonds' values vary when economic conditions vary.

The Basic Bond Valuation Model[2]

In the case of a bond, the cash flows that are paid to investors consist of interest payments during the life of the bond plus a return of the principal amount borrowed (generally the par value) when the bond matures. In a cash flow time line format, here is the situation:

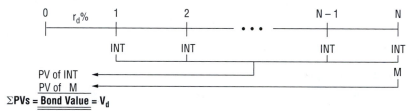

Here:

r_d = The average rate of return investors require to invest in the bond. For the Genesco bond issue, r_d = 10%.[3] In financial calculator terminology, r_d = I/Y = 10.

N = The number of years before the bond matures. For the Genesco bonds, N = 10. Note that N declines each year after the bond has been issued, so a bond that had a maturity of 10 years when it was issued (original maturity = 10) will have N = 9 after 1 year, N = 8 after 2 years, and so on. Note also that at this point we assume that the bond pays interest once per year, or annually, so N is measured in years. Later, we will examine semiannual payment bonds, which pay interest every 6 months.[4] In financial calculator terminology, N = 10.

INT = Dollars of interest paid each year = Coupon rate × Par value. In our example, each bond issued by Genesco requires an interest payment equal to $100. The coupon rate for these bonds must be 10 percent, because $100 = 0.10($1,000). In financial calculator terminology, INT = PMT = 100.

M = The par, or face, value of the bond = $1,000. This amount must be paid off at maturity. In financial calculator terminology, M = FV = 1,000.

---

[2]In finance, the term *model* refers to an equation or a set of equations designed to show how one or more variables affect some other variable. A bond valuation model, then, shows the mathematical relationship between a bond's price and the set of variables that determine the price.

[3]The appropriate interest rate on debt securities was discussed in Chapter 5. The bond's riskiness, liquidity, and years to maturity, as well as supply and demand conditions in the capital markets, all influence the interest rate on bonds.

[4]Some bonds have been issued that either pay no interest during their lives *(zero coupon bonds)* or pay very low coupon rates. Such bonds are sold at a discount below par, so they are called *original issue discount bonds*. The "interest" earned on a zero coupon bond comes at the end when the company pays off at par ($1,000) a bond that was purchased for, say, $321.97. The discount of $1,000 − $321.97 = $678.03 substitutes for interest.

If we redraw the cash flow time line to show the cash flows that investors expect to receive if they purchase Genesco's bond, we have:

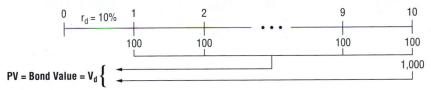

Recognizing the particular cash flows that are associated with a bond, Equation 10-1 can be modified to produce the following general equation that can be used to find the value of any bond:

$$\begin{aligned}
\text{Bond value} = V_d &= \left[\frac{INT}{(1+r_d)^1} + \frac{INT}{(1+r_d)^2} + \cdots + \frac{INT}{(1+r_d)^N}\right] + \frac{M}{(1+r_d)^N} \\[2mm]
&= \left[\sum_{t=1}^{N}\frac{INT}{(1+r_d)^t}\right] + \frac{M}{(1+r_d)^N} \\[2mm]
&= INT\left[\frac{1 - \dfrac{1}{(1+r_d)^N}}{r_d}\right] + M\left[\frac{1}{(1+r_d)^N}\right]
\end{aligned}$$

Notice the interest payments represent an annuity, and repayment of the par value at maturity represents a single, or lump-sum, payment.

Inserting the values relevant to Genesco's bond, we have:

$$\begin{aligned}
V_d &= \left[\frac{\$100}{(1.10)^1} + \frac{\$100}{(1.10)^2} + \cdots + \frac{\$100}{(1.10)^{10}}\right] + \frac{\$1,000}{(1.10)^{10}} \\[2mm]
&= \$100\left[\frac{1 - \dfrac{1}{(1.10)^{10}}}{0.10}\right] + \$1,000\left[\frac{1}{(1.10)^{10}}\right] \\[2mm]
&= \$100(6.14457) + \$1,000(0.38554) \\[1mm]
&= \$614.46 + \$385.54 = \$1,000
\end{aligned}$$

Before continuing our discussion, we show you how to determine the value of a bond using the different approaches that were discussed in Chapter 9—that is, the time line solution, the equation (numerical) solution, the financial caluclator solution, and the spreadsheet solution.

TIME LINE SOLUTION

Figure 10-1 shows how to determine the value of Genesco's bond using the cash flow time line. As you can see, each cash flow is discounted back to the present and then the PVs are summed to find the value of the bond. This method is not very efficient, especially if the bond has many years to maturity.

EQUATION (NUMERICAL) SOLUTION

The value of a bond that pays a constant dividend can be determined by plugging the appropriate future values into Equation 10-2 and completing the math. As we discovered earlier using Equation 10-2, the value of Genesco's bond is $1,000.

FIGURE 10-1   Cash Flow Time Line for Genesco Manufacturing 10% Coupon Bonds; $r_d = 10\%$

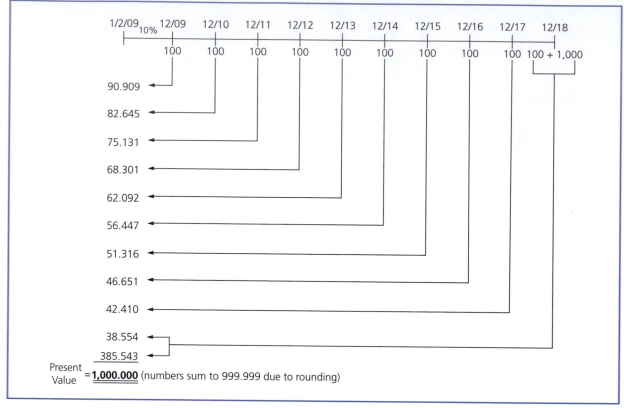

FINANCIAL CALCULATOR SOLUTION

In Chapter 9, we worked problems where we used only four of the five time value of money (TVM) keys on a financial calculator. All five keys are used with bond problems. Here is the setup:

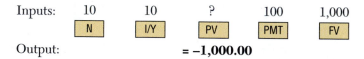

Inputs: 10   10   ?   100   1,000

             N   I/Y   PV   PMT   FV

Output: = −1,000.00

Input N = 10, I/Y = 10, PMT = 100, and FV = 1,000; then solve for PV = −1,000. Because the PV is an outflow to the investor, it is shown with a negative sign.

SPREADSHEET SOLUTION

Figure 10-2 shows the setup and the results of using the spreadsheet's PV function to compute the value of Genesco's bond. Note that the setup is the same as we used in Chapter 9, except that we must input values for four variables—N, I/Y, PMT, and FV—to compute the fifth variable, the value of the bond.[5]

    To simplify the discussion, we solve the situations that we set up in the rest of the chapter using the financial calculator approach. Although we do not show the spreadsheet solutions, you can set up a spreadsheet as shown in Figure 10-2 and

---

[5]For a more detailed discussion about how to use a spreadsheet to solve time value of money problems, see Chapter 9 and Appendix A at the end of the book.

FIGURE 10-2   Using Excel's PV Function to Compute the Value of a Bond

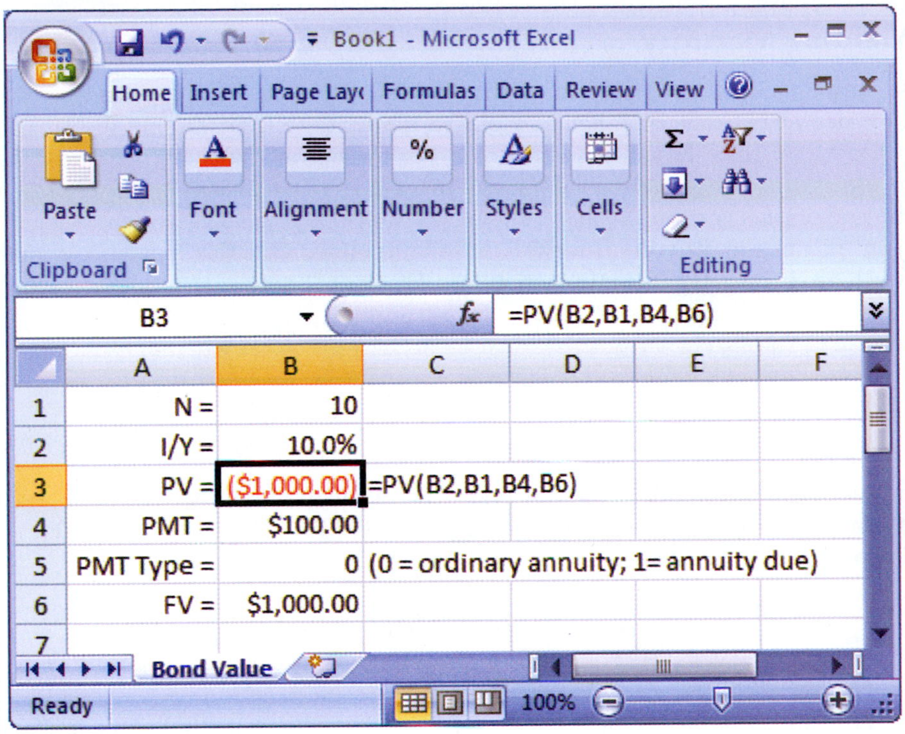

	A	B	C	D	E	F
			fx	=PV(B2,B1,B4,B6)		
1	N =	10				
2	I/Y =	10.0%				
3	PV =	($1,000.00)	=PV(B2,B1,B4,B6)			
4	PMT =	$100.00				
5	PMT Type =		0 (0 = ordinary annuity; 1= annuity due)			
6	FV =	$1,000.00				
7						

Bond Value

Ready   100%

Note: The input values must be entered in a specific order: I/Y, N, PMT, FV, and PMT type (equal to 0 in the computation).

simply change the appropriate values to find the solution to the situation at hand. Likewise, if you prefer to use the equation (numerical) approach, you can set up an equation in the form shown in Equation 10-2 and plug in the appropriate future values to determine the value of the bond being discussed.

? Self-Test Questions

Write a formula that can be used to determine the value of a bond.

Acme Corporation's $1,000 face value bonds have a coupon rate equal to 6 percent. Interest is paid annually. If the bonds mature in 10 years, for what price should they be selling in the financial markets if similar bonds offer an 8 percent rate of return?   (Answer: $865.80)

FINDING BOND YIELDS (MARKET RATES)

Suppose that you were offered a 19-year, 7 percent coupon, $1,000 par value bond at a price of $821. What rate of interest, or yield, would you earn if you bought this bond? In this section, we show you how to compute the yield, or return, you would earn if you purchase a bond with these characteristics. Before we begin, we want to remind you that both the par, or principal, value of the bond and its coupon rate of interest are contractually set, so the cash flows provided by the bond do not change during its life. It is important to remember this fact, because when *market* interest rates change, market values of bonds must change so as to equate their returns to the new market rates that other similar-risk bonds will provide new investors.

Yield to Maturity

yield to maturity (YTM)
The average rate of return earned on a bond if it is held to maturity.

If you buy a bond and hold it until it matures, the average rate of return you will earn per year is called the bond's **yield to maturity (YTM)**. To find the yield to maturity, we solve Equation 10–2 for r_d. For the current situation, we know that investors expect the bond's dollar payoffs to include $70 = \$1,000 \times 0.07$ interest at the end of each year for the next 19 years and a $1,000 principal payment when the bond matures in 19 years. Investors have determined that this bond is currently worth $821. Plugging this information into Equation 10-2, we have:

$$V_d = \frac{\$70}{(1+r_d)^1} + \frac{\$70}{(1+r_d)^2} + \cdots + \frac{\$70+\$1,000}{(1+r_d)^{19}} = \$821$$

$$= \frac{\$70}{(1+YTM)^1} + \frac{\$70}{(1+YTM)^2} + \cdots + \frac{\$70+\$1,000}{(1+YTM)^{19}} = \$821$$

It is easy to solve for $YTM = r_d$ with a financial calculator. Input N = 19, PV = −821 (this is a cash outflow when you buy the bond), PMT = 70, and FV = 1,000; then compute I/Y = 9.0 (the yield to maturity, r_d):[6]

Inputs:	19	?	−821	70	1,000
	N	I/Y	PV	PMT	FV
Output:		= 9.0			

For this bond, the "going rate of return," or yield, currently is 9 percent. Thus, an investor who purchases this bond today and holds it until it matures in 19 years will earn an *average* return of 9 percent each year.[7]

Notice that YTM = 9% > Coupon = 7%. When the bond was issued, which might have been 5 to 10 years ago, the yield for similar bonds was 7 percent. We know that this is the case because a firm sets the coupon rate on a bond immediately before it is issued so that the bond's issuing price equals its face (par) value. As market conditions change, however, the bond's yield to maturity changes to reflect changes in market interest rates, which causes its market price to change. In our example, market interest rates have increased since the time the bond was issued, so the price (value) of the bond has decreased below its face value. In reality, the calculated YTM, and thus the price of a bond, will change frequently before it matures because market conditions change frequently. We will discuss the relationship between YTM changes and price changes in greater detail later in the chapter.

Yield to Call

yield to call (YTC)
The average rate of return earned on a bond if it is held until the first call date.

Bonds that contain call provisions (callable bonds) often are called by the firm prior to maturity. In cases where a bond issue is called, investors do not have the opportunity to earn the yield to maturity (YTM), because the bond issue is retired before the maturity date arrives. Thus, for callable bonds, we generally compute the **yield to call (YTC)**

---

[6]If you do not have a financial calculator, you can compute the *approximate* yield to maturity using the following equation:

$$\text{Approximate yield to maturity} = \frac{\left(\begin{array}{c}\text{Annual}\\\text{interest}\end{array}\right) + \left(\begin{array}{c}\text{Accrued}\\\text{capital gains}\end{array}\right)}{\text{Average value of the bond}} = \frac{INT + \left(\frac{M-V_d}{N}\right)}{\left[\frac{2(V_d)+M}{3}\right]}$$

[7]In reality, an investor would earn a 9 percent return only if interest rates do not change during the life of the bond and he or she reinvests all of the interest received from the bond investment. The same logic applies to the value we find for a bond's yield to call (YTC), which is discussed next.

rather than the yield to maturity. The computation for YTC is the same as that for YTM, except that we substitute the **call price** of the bond for the maturity (par) value and we substitute the number of years until the bond can be called for the years to maturity. To calculate the YTC, then, we modify Equation 10-2, and solve the following equation for r_d:

call price
The price a firm has to pay to recall a bond; generally equal to the principal amount plus some interest.

$$V_d = \frac{INT}{(1+r_d)^1} + \frac{INT}{(1+r_d)^2} + \cdots + \frac{INT + Call\ price}{(1+r_d)^{N_c}}$$

$$= \frac{INT}{(1+YTC)^1} + \frac{INT}{(1+YTC)^2} + \cdots + \frac{INT + Call\ price}{(1+YTC)^{N_c}}$$

Here N_c is the number of years until the company can call the bond; Call price is the price that the company must pay to call the bond on the first call date (it is often set equal to the par value plus 1 year's interest); and r_d now represents the yield to call (YTC).

To solve for the YTC, we proceed just as we did to solve for the YTM of a bond. For example, suppose the bond we are currently examining has a call provision that "kicks in" 9 years from today—that is, the bond is callable 10 years before it matures. If it calls the bond on the first date possible, the firm will have to pay a call price equal to $1,070. The setup for computing the YTC for this bond is:

$$V_d = \frac{\$70}{(1+r_d)^1} + \frac{\$70}{(1+r_d)^2} + \cdots + \frac{\$70 + \$1,070}{(1+r_d)^9} = \$821$$

$$= \frac{\$70}{(1+YTC)^1} + \frac{\$70}{(1+YTC)^2} + \cdots + \frac{\$70 + \$1,070}{(1+YTC)^9} = \$821$$

Using your calculator, you would find the YTC equals 10.7 percent:

Inputs:	9	?	–821	70	1,070
	N	I/Y	PV	PMT	FV

Output: = **10.7**

Input N = 9 (years to first call date), PV = −821 (this is a cash outflow when you buy the bond), PMT = 70, and FV = 1,070 (the call price); then compute I/Y = 10.7 = YTC. Thus, investors who purchase the bond today will earn an average annual return equal to 10.7 percent if the bond is called in 9 years.

Self-Test Questions

What does it mean when we say that a bond's yield to maturity is 10 percent?

What is the difference between a bond's coupon rate of interest and its yield to maturity?

Write a formula that can be used to determine the yield to maturity of a bond. Can the same equation be used to compute the bond's yield to call?

Prizor Corporation has an outstanding bond that has a face value equal to $1,000 and a 10 percent coupon rate of interest. The bond, which matures in 6 years, currently sells for $1,143. If interest is paid annually, what is the bond's yield to maturity (YTM)?   (Answer: 7 percent)

Prizor Corporation has another bond that has a face value equal to $1,000 and an 8 percent coupon rate of interest. The bond, which matures in 15 years, is callable at $1,080 in 8 years. If the bond's current market price is $1,044, what is its yield to call (YTC)?   (Answer: 8 percent)

INTEREST RATES AND BOND VALUES

Even though the interest payment, maturity value, and maturity date of a bond do not change regardless of the conditions in the financial markets, the market values of bonds fluctuate continuously as a result of changing market conditions. To see why the values of bonds change, let's again examine Genesco's bonds to see what happens when market interest rates change.

First, let's assume that you purchased one of Genesco's bonds on the day it was issued. On the issue date, the bond had 10 years remaining until maturity, a 10 percent coupon rate of interest, and the market interest rate at the time of issue was 10 percent. As we showed earlier, under these conditions, you would have paid $1,000 to purchase the bond. Suppose that *immediately after* you purchased the bond, interest rates on similar bonds increased from 10 to 12 percent. How would the value of your bond be affected?

Because the cash flows associated with the bond—that is, interest payments and principal repayment—remain constant, the value of the bond will decrease when interest rates increase. In Equation 10-2, the values in the numerators do not change, but the values in the denominators increase, which results in a lower value for the bond. In present value terms, the decrease in value makes sense. If you want to mimic the Genesco bond—that is, pay yourself $100 each year for 10 years and then pay yourself $1,000 at the end of the tenth year—you must deposit $1,000 in a savings account that pays 10 percent interest annually. But if you found a savings account that pays 12 percent interest annually, you could deposit some amount less than $1,000 and pay yourself the same cash flows because your deposit would earn greater interest. The same logic applies when we consider how an interest rate change affects the value of Genesco's bond or any other bond. As we show next, at 12 percent, the amount you would have to deposit to provide the same cash flows as Genesco's bond is $887.

If market rates *increase* from 10 to 12 percent *immediately after you purchase* Genesco's bond, the value of the bond would decrease to $887:

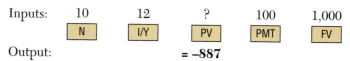

Output: = –887

Input N = 10, I/Y = 12, PMT = 100, and FV = 1,000; then compute PV = –$887.

What would happen to the price of Genesco's bond if interest rates had *decreased* from 10 to 8 percent *immediately after it was issued?*

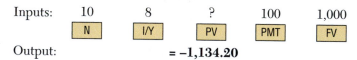

Output: = –1,134.20

Input N = 10, I/Y = 8, PMT = 100, and FV = 1,000; then compute PV = –$1,134.20.

The arithmetic of the bond value increase should be clear, but what sort of logic lies behind it? The fact that r_d has declined to 8 percent means that if you had $1,000 to invest, you could buy *new* bonds such as Genesco's, except that these new bonds would pay $80 of interest each year rather than the $100 interest paid by Genesco. Naturally, you would prefer $100 to $80, so you would be willing to pay more than $1,000 for Genesco's bonds to get its higher coupons. Because all investors would recognize these facts, the Genesco Manufacturing bonds would be bid up in price to $1,134.20. At that point, they would provide the same rate of return to potential investors as the new bonds—that is, 8 percent.

Following is a table that summarizes the relationship between the value of Genesco's bond and its yield to maturity.

Relationship of Market Rate, r_d = YTM, and Coupon Rate, C	Bond Value, V_d (N = 10, PMT = 100, FV = 1,000, and I/Y = r_d)	Relationship of Market Price, V_d, and Maturity Value, M = $1,000
r_d = 10% = C = 10%	$1,000.00	V_d = M; bond sells at par
r_d = 12% > C = 10%	887.00	V_d < M; bond sells at a discount
r_d = 8% < C = 10%	1,134.20	V_d > M; bond sells at a premium

These same relationships exist for all bonds—that is, when the market yield (YTM) and the coupon rate of interest are equal, the bond sells for its *par value;* when the market yield is greater than the coupon rate of interest, the bond sells for less than its par value, or at a *discount;* and when the market yield is less than the coupon rate of interest, the bond sells for greater than its par value, or at a *premium.* A bond that sells for less than its face value is called a **discount bond,** whereas a bond that sells for greater than its face value is called a **premium bond.** This exercise demonstrates an important fundamental concept in finance that was mentioned earlier: when interest rates change, the values of bonds change in an opposite direction— that is, *when rates increase, bond prices decrease, and vice versa.*

discount bond
A bond that sells below its par value. This occurs whenever the going rate of interest rises above the coupon rate.

premium bond
A bond that sells above its par value. This occurs whenever the going rate of interest falls below the coupon rate.

Self-Test Questions

What is the relationship between a bond's yield to maturity and its market value?

Terry's Towel Company has an outstanding bond that has a $1,000 face value and pays $90 interest per year. The existing market rate is 11 percent and the bond matures in 8 years. What was the market interest rate when the bond was issued 12 years ago? What will happen to the price of the bond if the interest rate on similar bonds decreases to 9 percent?   (Answers: 9 percent, which is the coupon rate; market price will increase from $897 to $1,000)

CHANGES IN BOND VALUES OVER TIME

Let's again assume that immediately after Genesco issued its bond market interest rates fell from 10 to 8 percent. In the previous section, we showed that the price of the bond would increase to $1,134.20. Assuming that interest rates remain constant at 8 percent for the next 10 years, what would happen to the value of Genesco's bond as time passes and its maturity date approaches? It would decrease gradually from $1,134.20 at present to $1,000 at maturity, when Genesco would redeem each bond for $1,000. We can illustrate this point by calculating the value of the bond 1 year from now, when it has 9 years remaining to maturity.

Inputs:	9	8	?	100	1,000
	N	I/Y	PV	PMT	FV

Output: = –1,124.94

As you can see, the value of the bond will decrease from $1,134.20 to $1,124.94, or by $9.26. If you were to calculate the bond's value at other future dates using

$r_d = 8\%$, its price would continue to decline as the maturity date is approached—when $N = 8$, $V_d = \$1,114.93$, when $N = 7$, $V_d = \$1,104.13$, and so on. At maturity, the value of the bond must equal its par value of $1,000 (as long as the firm does not go bankrupt).

Suppose that Sherman Sheridan purchased a Genesco bond just after the market rate dropped to 8 percent, so he paid $1,134.20 for the bond. If he sold the bond 1 year later for $1,124.94, Sherman would realize a capital *loss* of $9.26, and a total dollar return of $90.74 = $100.00 − $9.26. The percentage rate of return that Sherman earned on the bond would consist of an **interest yield** (also called a **current** yield) plus a **capital gains yield.** These yields are calculated as follows:

 **10-4**

$$\text{Bond yield} = \text{Current (interest) yield} + \text{Capital gains yield}$$
$$= \frac{\text{INT}}{V_{d,\text{Begin}}} + \frac{V_{d,\text{End}} - V_{d,\text{Begin}}}{V_{d,\text{Begin}}}$$

Here, $V_{d,\text{Begin}}$ represents the value of the bond at the beginning of the year (period) and $V_{d,\text{End}}$ is the value of the bond at the end of the year (period).

In the current situation, the yields for Genesco's bond after 1 year are computed as follows:

$$\text{Current yield} = \$100.00/\$1,134.20 = 0.0882 = 8.82\%$$
$$\text{Capital gains yield} = -\$9.26/\$1,134.20 = -0.0082 = \underline{-0.82\%}$$
$$\text{Total rate of return (yield)} = \$90.74/\$1,134.20 = 0.0800 = \underline{8.00\%} = r_d$$

Had interest rates risen from 10 to 12 percent rather than fallen immediately after issue, the value of the bond would have immediately decreased to $887. If the rate remains at 12 percent, the value of the bond at the end of the year will be $893.44.

Inputs:	9	12	?	100	1,000
	N	I/Y	PV	PMT	FV

Output: $= -893.44$

The total expected future yield on the bond would again consist of a current yield and a capital gains yield, but now the capital gains yield would be positive. The total yield on the bond would be 12 percent, r_d. The capital gain for the year is $893.44 − $887.00 = $6.44. The current yield, capital gains yield, and total yield are calculated as follows:

$$\text{Current yield} = \$100.00/\$887 = 0.1127 = 11.27\%$$
$$\text{Capital gains yield} = \$6.44/\$887 = 0.0073 = \underline{0.73\%}$$
$$\text{Total rate of return (yield)} = \$106.44/\$887 = 0.1200 = \underline{12.00\%} = r_d$$

What would happen to the value of the bond if market interest rates remain constant at 12 percent until maturity? Because the bond's value must equal the principal, or par, amount at maturity (as long as bankruptcy does not occur), its value will gradually increase from the current price of $893.44 to its maturity value of $1,000. For example, the value of the bond would increase to $900.65 at $N = 8$, its value would be $908.72 at $N = 7$, and so forth. Table 10-1 shows the value of Genesco's bond at the end of each year as it approaches the maturity date assuming the market rate, r_d, remains at 12 percent.

Figure 10-3 graphs the value of Genesco's bond over time, assuming that the market interest rate, which was 10 percent when the bond was issued, (1) remains constant at 10 percent to maturity, (2) falls to 8 percent and then remains constant at

TABLE 10-1 Genesco Bonds: Coupon = 10%, r_d = 12%

Years to Maturity	Ending Value ($)	Capital Gains ($)	Interest ($)	Capital Gains Yield (%)	+	Current Yield (%)	=	Total Yield (%)
10	887.00							
9	893.44	6.44	100	0.73		11.27		12.00
8	900.65	7.21	100	0.81		11.19		12.00
7	908.72	8.08	100	0.90		11.10		12.00
6	917.77	9.05	100	1.00		11.00		12.00
5	927.90	10.13	100	1.10		10.90		12.00
4	939.25	11.35	100	1.22		10.78		12.00
3	951.96	12.71	100	1.35		10.65		12.00
2	966.20	14.24	100	1.50		10.50		12.00
1	982.14	15.94	100	1.65		10.35		12.00
0	1,000.00	17.86	100	1.82		10.18		12.00

that level to maturity, or (3) rises to 12 percent and remains constant at that level to maturity. Of course, if the interest rate does not remain constant, then the price of the bond will fluctuate. *Regardless of what interest rates do in the future, however, the bond's price will approach its face value ($1,000) as it nears its maturity date* (barring bankruptcy, in which case the bond's value might drop to $0).

FIGURE 10-3 Time Path of the Value of a 10% Coupon, $1,000 Par Value Bond When the Market Interest Rate is 8%, 10%, or 12%

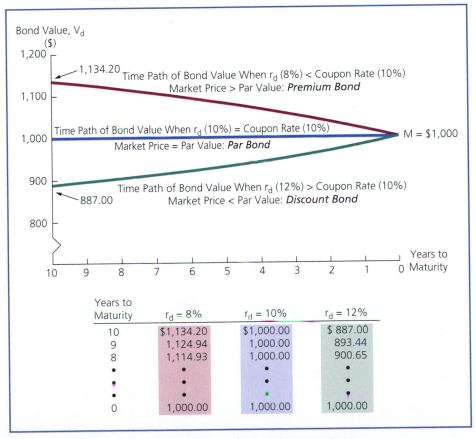

Figure 10-3 illustrates the following key points, which were discussed in this section:

1. Whenever the going rate of interest, r_d, equals the coupon rate, a bond will sell at its par value.

2. Interest rates change over time, but the coupon rate remains fixed after the bond has been issued. Whenever the going rate of interest is greater than the coupon rate, a bond's price will fall below its par value (a discount bond); whenever the going rate of interest is less than the coupon rate, a bond's price will rise above its par value (a premium bond).

3. An increase in interest rates will cause the price of an outstanding bond to fall, whereas a decrease in rates will cause it to rise.

4. The market value of a bond will always approach its par value as its maturity date approaches, provided that the firm does not go bankrupt.

These points are important because they show that bondholders can suffer capital losses or make capital gains, depending on whether market interest rates rise or fall after the bond is purchased. Of course, as we saw in Chapter 5, interest rates do change over time.

Self-Test Questions

Consider a bond that is currently selling at a premium. If market interest rates remain constant, what will happen to the bond's value as the maturity date approaches? What would happen to the bond's value if the bond is currently selling at a discount?

Suppose you purchase a 10-year bond that has a current market price equal to $929.76. The bond has a face value equal to $1,000, and it pays $60 interest each year. Assuming that the going rate of interest remains at its current level, which is 7 percent, what will be the value of the bond at the end of the year? What will be its value 5 years from now?   (Answers: $934.85; $959.00)

BOND VALUES WITH SEMIANNUAL COMPOUNDING

Although some bonds pay interest annually, *most* pay interest semiannually. To evaluate semiannual payment bonds, we must modify the bond valuation equation just as we did in Chapter 9 when discussing interest compounding that occurs more than once per year. As a result, Equation 10-2 becomes:

10-5

$$V_d = \left(\frac{INT}{2}\right)\left[\frac{1 - \dfrac{1}{\left(1 + \dfrac{r_d}{2}\right)^{2 \times N}}}{\left(\dfrac{r_d}{2}\right)}\right] + \frac{M}{\left(1 + \dfrac{r_d}{2}\right)^{2 \times N}}$$

To illustrate, assume that Genesco's bonds pay $50 interest every 6 months rather than $100 at the end of each year. Each interest payment is now only half as large as before, but there are twice as many payments. When the going (simple) rate of interest is 8 percent with semiannual compounding, the value of the bond when there are 9 years remaining until maturity is found as follows:

Inputs:	18	4	?	50	1,000
	N	I/Y	PV	PMT	FV

Output: $= -1,126.59$

Input N = 18 = 9 × 2, I/Y = 4 = 8/2, PMT = 50 = 100/2, and FV = 1,000; then compute PV = $-$1,126.59.

The value with semiannual interest payments ($1,126.59) exceeds the value when interest is paid annually ($1,124.94). This higher value occurs because interest payments are received, and therefore can be reinvested, somewhat more rapidly under semiannual compounding.[8]

Students sometimes want to discount the *maturity (par) value* at 8 percent over 9 years rather than at 4 percent over 18 interest (6-month) periods. This approach is incorrect. Logically, all cash flows in a given contract must be discounted at the same periodic rate—the 4 percent semiannual rate in this instance—because it is the investor's opportunity rate.

Self-Test Questions

What adjustments must be made when using Equation 10-2 to compute the value of a bond that pays interest semiannually?

Suppose that you are considering investing in a 20-year, 11 percent coupon bond that has a $1,000 face value. Interest is paid every 6 months. If the market rate of return is 8 percent, what is the market value of the bond? (Answer: $1,296.89)

INTEREST RATE RISK ON A BOND

When market interest rates change, bondholders are affected in two ways. First, an increase in interest rates leads to a decline in the values of outstanding bonds. For example, at $r_d = 10\%$, the value of Genesco's 10-year bond was $1,000, but at $r_d = 12\%$, $V_d = \$887$ (assuming annual interest payments). Because interest rates can rise, bondholders face the risk of suffering similar losses in the values of their portfolios. This risk is called **interest rate price risk.** Second, many bondholders (including such institutional bondholders as pension funds and life insurance companies) buy bonds to build funds for some future use. These bondholders reinvest the cash flows they receive—that is, each interest payment is reinvested when it is received, and the principal repayment is reinvested when it is received at maturity (or when the bond is called). If interest rates decline—say, from 10 to 8 percent—the bondholders will earn a lower rate of return on *reinvested cash flows*, which will reduce the future values of their portfolios relative to the values they would have accumulated if interest rates had not fallen. This risk is called **interest rate reinvestment risk.**

interest rate price risk
The risk of changes in bond prices to which investors are exposed due to changing interest rates.

interest rate reinvestment risk
The risk that income from a bond portfolio will vary because cash flows must be reinvested at current market rates.

---

[8]We also assume a change in the effective annual interest rate, from 8 percent to $r_{EAR} = (1.04)^2 - 1 = 0.0816 = 8.16\%$. Most bonds pay interest semiannually, and the rates quoted are simple rates compounded semiannually. Therefore, effective annual rates for most bonds are somewhat higher than the quoted rates, which, in effect, represent the APRs for the bonds.

FIGURE 10-4   Value of Long- and Short-Term 10% Annual Coupon Rate Bonds at Different Market Interest Rates (r_d)

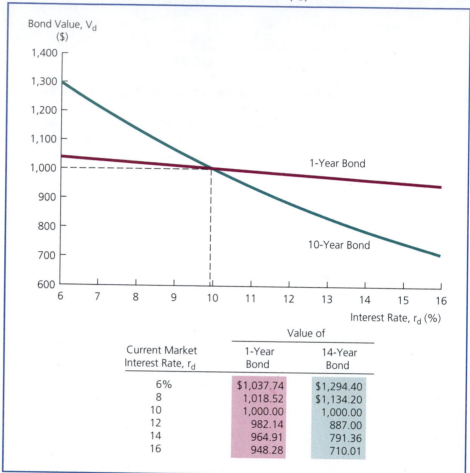

Current Market Interest Rate, r_d	Value of 1-Year Bond	Value of 14-Year Bond
6%	$1,037.74	$1,294.40
8	1,018.52	$1,134.20
10	1,000.00	1,000.00
12	982.14	887.00
14	964.91	791.36
16	948.28	710.01

We can see, then, that, any given change in interest rates has two separate effects on bondholders: it changes the current values of their portfolios (price risk), and it changes the rates of return at which the cash flows from their portfolios can be reinvested (reinvestment risk). These two risks tend to offset each other. For example, an increase in interest rates will lower the current value of a bond portfolio. But, because the future cash flows produced by the portfolio will be reinvested at higher rates of return, the future value of the portfolio will increase.

An investor's exposure to interest rate price risk is higher on bonds with long maturities than on those that mature in the near future. We can demonstrate this fact by considering how the value of a 1-year bond with a 10 percent coupon fluctuates with changes in r_d and then comparing these changes with the effects on a 10-year bond as calculated previously. Figure 10-4 shows the values for a 1-year bond and a 10-year bond at several different market interest rates, r_d. The values for the bonds were computed by assuming that the coupon interest payments for the bonds occur annually. Notice how much more sensitive the price of the long-term bond is to changes in interest rates. At a 10 percent interest rate, both the long- and short-term bonds are valued at $1,000. When rates rise to 12 percent, the value of the long-term bond decreases to $887, or by 11.3 percent, but the value of the short-term bond falls to only $982.14, which is a 1.8 percent decline.[9]

For bonds with similar coupons, this differential sensitivity to changes in interest rates always holds: *the longer the maturity of the bond, the more significantly its price changes in response to a given change in interest rates.* Thus, if two bonds have exactly the same risk of default, the bond with the longer maturity typically is exposed to more price risk from a change in interest rates.

The logical explanation for this difference in interest rate price risk is simple. Suppose that you bought a 10-year bond that yielded 10 percent, or $100 per year. Now suppose that interest rates on comparable-risk bonds increased to 12 percent. You would be stuck with only $100 of interest for the next 10 years. On the other hand, had you bought a 1-year bond, you would have received a low return for only 1 year. At the end of the year, you would get your $1,000 back, and you could then reinvest it and receive 12 percent, or $120 per year, for the next 9 years. As you can see, interest rate price risk reflects the length of time one is committed to a given investment. As we described in Chapter 5, the longer a bond's term to maturity, the higher its maturity risk premium (MRP), which accounts for its higher interest rate risk.

Although a 1-year bond has less interest rate price risk than a 10-year bond, the 1-year bond exposes the buyer to more interest rate reinvestment risk. Suppose that you bought a 1-year bond that yielded 10 percent, and then interest rates on comparable-risk bonds fell to 8 percent such that newly issued bonds now pay $80 interest. After 1 year, when you got your $1,000 back, you would have to invest your funds at only 8 percent. As a result, you would lose $100 − $80 = $20 in annual interest. Had you bought the 10-year bond, you would have continued to receive $100 in annual interest payments even if rates fell. If you reinvested those coupon payments, you would have to accept a lower rate of return, but you would still be much better off than if you had been holding the 1-year bond.

Self-Test Questions

Differentiate between interest rate price risk and interest rate reinvestment risk.

When interest rates increase, which risk would be considered positive, interest rate price risk or interest rate reinvestment risk? Which risk is positive when interest rates decrease?

BOND PRICES IN RECENT YEARS

From Chapter 5, we know that interest rates fluctuate. We have also just seen that the prices of outstanding bonds rise and fall inversely with changes in interest rates. When interest rates fall, many firms "refinance" by issuing new, lower cost debt and using the proceeds to repay higher cost debt. For example, in 2003, interest rates dropped to levels that had not been seen in more than 45 years, and not surprisingly, firms that had issued higher cost debt in earlier years refinanced much of their debt

---

[9]If a 5-year bond were plotted in Figure 10-4, its curve would lie between the curves for the 10-year and 1-year bonds. The curve of a 1-month bond would be almost horizontal, indicating that its price would change very little in response to an interest rate change. A perpetuity would have a very steep slope.

FIGURE 10-5   Value of a $1,000 Bond Issued June 1, 1997, that Matures on May 31, 2012

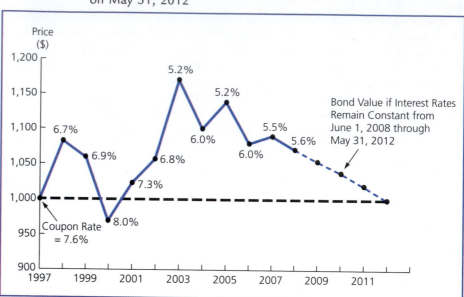

at that time. Because rates have generally increased since 2003, many of the corporate bonds that exist today were originally issued in 2003.[10]

Let's assume a company issued a 15-year bond on June 1, 1997, when the market average interest rate on AAA-rated bonds was 7.6 percent. Assume further that this bond still existed in late May 2008. Figure 10-5 shows what has happened to the price since it was issued in 1997, as well as what will happen to the price if interest rates remain constant from June 1, 2008, until the bond matures on May 31, 2012. Because the interest rate on similar risk bonds was 7.6 percent when the bond was originally issued in 1997, the coupon rate of interest was set at 7.6 percent so that the bond was issued at its par value—that is, $1,000. But, as market interest rates changed, so did the value of the bond. Notice from Figure 10-5 that interest rates decreased in 1998 and 1999, so that the bond was selling for a premium in these years ($1,081 and $1,059, respectively). In 2000 rates increased to greater than the coupon rate of interest, so the bond was selling at a discount ($970). As Figure 10-5 shows, when the market interest rates were (1) less than the bond's coupon rate, which occurred in every year except one—that is, $r_d < 7.6\%$—the plot of the price of the bond was above the $1,000 dashed horizontal line, which means the bond was selling at a premium $(V_d > M)$; (2) greater than the bond's coupon rate—that is, $r_d > 7.6\%$—the plot of the price of the bond was below the $1,000 dashed horizontal line, which means the bond was selling at a discount $(V_d < M)$; and (3) approximately equal to the bond's coupon rate—that is, $r_d = 7.6\%$—the plot of the price of the bond was nearly on the $1,000 dashed horizontal line, which means the bond was selling at par $(V_d = M)$.

When you read this book, interest rates might be much higher or much lower than they were in May 2008. But, as Figure 10-5 shows, the value of the bond that was issued in 1997 will continue to approach its par value of $1,000 until the maturity date, at which time the bond's price should equal $1,000. This is the case

---

[10]In some cases, corporate bonds could not be refinanced at the lower rates due to restrictions that existed in the debt contracts or because firms were not financially sound.

for any corporate bond as long as the issuing firm is financially strong enough to pay both the interest when it is due and the face value of the debt on the maturity date. The prices of other bonds that existed during the period from 1997 through 2008 would have exhibited a similar pattern of changes as the prices of the bond discussed in this example.

 Self-Test Question
How have bond prices fluctuated in recent years?

VALUATION OF EQUITY (STOCK)

A stock's value is found using the same process that is used to determine the values of other assets—that is, compute the present value of the expected future cash flow stream. A stock provides an expected future cash flow stream that consists of two elements: the dividends expected in each year and the price that investors expect to receive when they sell the stock.

In this section, we apply the general valuation process to value stock. We begin by introducing a general stock valuation model. We then apply this model to three scenarios: (1) when there is no growth in dividends, so the amount paid each year remains constant (the same as preferred stock dividends); (2) when dividends increase at a constant rate each year; and (3) when dividends grow at different, or nonconstant rates.

Definitions of Terms Used in the Stock Valuation Models

Before we give the general stock valuation model, let's define some terms and notations that we will use in the remainder of the chapter.

$\hat{D}_t$ = The dividend that the stockholder expects to receive at the end of Year t (pronounced "D hat t"); we designate expected value by placing a "hat" (^) above the variable. D_0 is the most recent dividend, which already has been paid; $\hat{D}_1$ is the next dividend expected to be paid at the end of this year; $\hat{D}_2$ is the dividend expected at the end of 2 years; and so forth. $\hat{D}_1$ represents the first cash flow that a new purchaser of the stock will receive. Note that D_0, the dividend that was just paid, is known with certainty (which explains why there is no "hat" over the D). All future dividends are *expected* values, so the estimate of $\hat{D}_1$ might differ among investors.[11]

$P_0 = V_s$ = The actual **market price (value)** of the stock today.

$\hat{P}_t$ = The expected price of the stock at the end of each Year t. $\hat{P}_0$ is the **intrinsic,** or *theoretical,* **value** of the stock today as seen by the particular investor doing the analysis; $\hat{P}_1$ is the price *expected* at the end of (Year 1); and so on. Note that $\hat{P}_0$ is the intrinsic value of the stock today based on a particular investor's estimate of the stock's expected dividend stream and the riskiness of that stream.

market price, P_0
The price at which a stock currently sells in the market.

intrinsic value, $\hat{P}_0$
The value of an asset that, in the mind of a particular investor, is justified by the facts; $\hat{P}_0$ can be different from the asset's current market price, its book value, or both.

[11]Stocks generally pay dividends quarterly, so theoretically we should evaluate them on a quarterly basis. In stock valuation, however, most analysts work on an annual basis because the data generally are not precise enough to warrant refinement to a quarterly model.

Whereas P_0 is fixed and is identical for all investors because it represents the *actual price* at which the stock currently can be purchased in the stock market, $\hat{P}_0$ can differ among investors depending on what they feel the firm actually is worth. An investor would buy the stock only if his or her estimate of $\hat{P}_0$ is equal to or greater than the current selling price, P_0.

Because many investors participate in the market, many values for $\hat{P}_0$ are possible. We can imagine there exists a group of "average," or "marginal," investors whose actions actually determine the market price. For these average investors, P_0 must equal $\hat{P}_0$; otherwise, a disequilibrium would exist, and buying and selling in the market would change P_0 until $P_0 = \hat{P}_0$.

growth rate, g
The expected rate of change in dividends per share.

g = The expected **growth rate** in dividends as predicted by an average investor. (If we assume that dividends are expected to grow at a constant rate, then g is also equal to the expected rate of growth in the stock's price.) Different investors might use different growth rates to evaluate a firm's stock, but the market price, P_0, reflects the value for g estimated by average investors.

required rate of return, r_s
The minimum rate of return on a common stock that stockholders consider acceptable.

r_s = The minimum acceptable, or **required, rate of return** on the stock, considering both its riskiness and the returns available on other investments. Again, this term generally relates to average investors. The determinants of r_s are discussed in detail in Chapter 11.

dividend yield
The expected dividend divided by the current price of a share of stock, $\hat{D}_1/P_0$.

$\dfrac{\hat{D}_1}{P_0}$ = The expected **dividend yield** on the stock during the coming year. If the stock is expected to pay a dividend of $1 during the next 12 months, and if its current price is $10, then the expected dividend yield is $1/$10 = 0.10 = 10\%$.

capital gains yield
The change in price (capital gain) during a given year divided by the price at the beginning of the year, $(\hat{P}_1 - P_0)/P_0$.

$\dfrac{\hat{P}_1 - P_0}{P_0}$ = The expected **capital gains yield** on the stock during the coming year; it is the expected change in the stock's value stated as a percent. Suppose a stock sells for $10 today and its price is expected to rise to $10.50 at the end of 1 year. The expected capital gain is $\hat{P}_1 - P_0 = \$10.50 - \$10.00 = \$0.50$, and the expected capital gains yield is $0.50/$10 = 0.05 = 5\%$.

expected rate of return, $\hat{r}_s$
The rate of return on a common stock that an individual stockholder expects to receive. It is equal to the expected dividend yield plus the expected capital gains yield, $\hat{r}_s = \hat{D}_1/P_0 + (\hat{P}_1 - P_0)/P_0$.

$\hat{r}_s$ = The **expected rate of return,** which is the return that an investor who buys the stock expects to receive. The value of $\hat{r}_s$ could be above or below the required rate of return, r_s, but an investor should buy the stock only if $\hat{r}_s$ is equal to or greater than r_s— that is, a stock is considered a good investment if $\hat{r}_s \geq r_s$. $\hat{r}_s$ = expected dividend yield plus expected capital gains yield; in other words,

$$\hat{r}_s = \frac{\hat{D}_1}{P_0} + \frac{\hat{P}_1 - P_0}{P_0}$$

In our example, the expected total return is $\hat{r}_s = 10\% + 5\% = 15\%$.

actual (realized) rate of return, $\ddot{r}_s$
The rate of return on a common stock actually received by stockholders; $\ddot{r}_s$ can be greater than or less than the expected return, $\hat{r}_s$, and/or the required return, r_s.

$\ddot{r}_s$ = The **actual,** or **realized,** *after-the-fact* **rate of return.** You might expect to obtain a return equal to 15 percent if you buy a stock today, but if the market goes down, you might end up next year with an actual realized return that is much lower—perhaps even negative. For example, if $\ddot{r}_s = 8\%$, then $\ddot{r}_s = 8\% < \hat{r}_s = 15\%$, and those who invested in this stock would be disappointed because the return they actually earned was lower than the return that they expected.

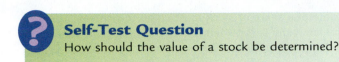

Self-Test Question

How should the value of a stock be determined?

EXPECTED DIVIDENDS AS THE BASIS FOR STOCK VALUES

In our discussion of bonds, we found that the value of a bond is the present value of the interest payments over the life of the bond plus the present value of the bond's maturity (par) value. Stock prices are likewise computed as the present value of a stream of cash flows, and the basic stock valuation equation resembles the bond valuation equation (Equation 10-2).

What cash flows do corporations provide to their stockholders? First, think of yourself as an investor who buys a stock with the intention of holding it (in your family) forever. In this case, even though in some years dividends might not be paid, you and your heirs will receive a stream of dividends that continues forever. Thus, the value of the stock today is calculated as the present value of an infinite stream of dividends, which is depicted on a cash flow time line as follows:

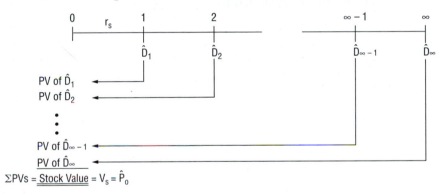

Thus, to compute the value of the stock, we must solve this equation:

$$\text{Stock value} = V_s = \hat{P}_0 = \frac{\hat{D}_1}{(1+r_s)^1} + \frac{\hat{D}_2}{(1+r_s)^2} + \cdots + \frac{\hat{D}_{\infty-1}}{(1+r_s)^{\infty-1}} + \frac{\hat{D}_\infty}{(1+r_s)^\infty}$$

$$= \sum_{t=1}^{\infty} \frac{\hat{D}_t}{(1+r_s)^t}$$

10-6

How do you determine the value of $\hat{P}_0$ when you plan to hold the stock for a specific (finite) period and then sell it? This is the typical scenario followed by investors. Unless the company is likely to be liquidated and therefore disappear, the value of the stock is still determined by Equation 10-6. To see why, recognize that for any *individual investor*, the expected cash flows consist of expected dividends plus the expected price of the stock when it is sold. However, the sale price that the current investor receives depends on the dividends that the *future investor expects* to be paid by the company from that point forward. As a consequence, for all present and future investors, expected cash flows include *all* of the expected future dividends. Put another way, unless a firm is liquidated or sold to another concern, the cash flows that it provides to its stockholders will consist only of a stream of dividends. Therefore, the value of a share of stock must equal the present value of the dividend stream that the company is expected to pay throughout its life.

The general validity of Equation 10-6 can be confirmed by considering the following scenario: suppose you buy a stock and expect to hold it for 1 year. You will receive dividends during the year plus the value of the stock when you sell it at the end of the year. What will determine the value of $\hat{P}_1$? $\hat{P}_1$ equals the present value of the dividends during Year 2 plus the stock price at the end of that year, which in turn is determined as the present value of another set of future dividends and an even more distant stock price. This process can be continued forever, with the ultimate result being Equation 10-6.

Equation 10-6 is a generalized stock valuation model in the sense that over time the value of $\hat{D}_t$ can follow any pattern: $\hat{D}_t$ can be rising, falling, or constant, or it can even be fluctuating randomly. In any event, Equation 10-6 will still hold. Often, however, the projected stream of dividends follows a systematic pattern, in which case we can develop a simplified (easier to apply) version of the stock valuation model expressed in Equation 10-6. In the following sections, we consider the cases of zero growth, constant growth, and nonconstant growth.

Valuing Stock with Zero Growth

zero growth stock
A common stock whose future dividends are not expected to grow at all; that is, $g = 0$, and $D = \hat{D}_1 = \hat{D}_2 = \ldots = \hat{D}_\infty$.

Suppose a firm's dividends are expected to stay the same every year. In this case, we have a **zero growth stock,** for which the dividends expected in future years equal some constant amount—the current dividend. That is, $\hat{D}_1 = \hat{D}_2 = \cdots = \hat{D}_\infty = D_0 = D$. In this case, we can drop the subscripts and the "hats" on D because we are certain about the value of the future dividends, which are all the same, and rewrite Equation 10-6 as follows:

10-7

$$\hat{P}_0 = \frac{D}{(1 + r_s)^1} + \frac{D}{(1 + r_s)^2} + \cdots + \frac{D}{(1 + r_s)^{\infty-1}} + \frac{D}{(1 + r_s)^\infty}$$

$$= \frac{D}{r_s} = \text{Value of a zero growth stock}$$

As we noted in Chapter 9 in connection with the British consol bond, a security that is expected to pay a constant amount every year forever is called a perpetuity. *A zero growth stock is a perpetuity.* Recall that the value of any perpetuity is simply the cash payment divided by the discount rate, which is the term on the lower line in Equation 10-7.

Suppose that we have a stock that is expected to always pay a dividend equal to $1.60, and the required rate of return associated with such an investment is 20 percent. The stock's value would be computed as follows:[12]

$$\hat{P}_0 = \frac{\$1.60}{0.20} = \$8.00$$

---

[12]If you think that having a stock pay dividends forever is unrealistic, then think of it as lasting only for 50 years. Here you would have an annuity of $1.60 per year for 50 years. The PV of a 50-year annuity of $1.60 with an opportunity rate of interest equal to 20 percent would be 1.60(4.9995) = 7.999, which rounds to the same value as we computed for the perpetuity. Thus, the dividends from Year 51 to infinity contribute very little to the current value of the stock.

Expected Rate of Return on a Zero Growth Stock

Generally, we can find the price of a stock and the most recent dividend paid to the stockholders by looking online or in a financial newspaper such as *The Wall Street Journal*. Therefore, if we have a stock with constant dollar dividends, we can solve for the expected rate of return by rearranging Equation 10-7 as follows:[13]

$$\hat{r}_s = \frac{D}{P_0}$$

10-8

Because we are dealing with an *expected rate of return*, we put a "hat" on the r value. Thus, if you buy a stock at a price of $8 and you expect to receive a constant dividend equal to $1.60, your expected rate of return would be:

$$\hat{r}_s = \frac{\$1.60}{\$8.00} = 0.20 = 20\%$$

By now, you probably have recognized that Equation 10-7 can be used to value preferred stock. Recall from our discussion in Chapter 2 that preferred stocks entitle their owners to receive regular, or fixed, dividend payments. If the payments last forever, the issue is a *perpetuity* whose value is defined by Equation 10-7. We can use Equation 10-7 to value any asset, including common stock, with expected future cash flows that exhibit the properties of a perpetuity—that is, constant cash flows forever.

Valuing Stocks with Constant, or Normal, Growth

In general, investors expect the earnings and dividends of most companies to increase each year. Even though expected growth rates vary from company to company, it is not uncommon for investors to expect dividend growth to continue in the foreseeable future at about the same rate as that of the nominal gross national product (real GNP plus inflation). On this basis, we might expect the dividend of an average, or "normal," company to grow at a rate of 3 to 5 percent per year. Thus, if the last dividend paid by a **normal,** or **constant, growth** company was D_0, the firm's dividend in any future Year t can be forecasted as $\hat{D}_t = D_0(1 + g)^t$, where g is the constant expected rate of growth. For example, if a firm just paid a dividend of $1.60—that is, $D_0 = \$1.60$—and investors expect a 5 percent growth rate, then the estimated dividend 1 year hence would be $\hat{D}_1 = \$1.60(1.05) = \$1.68$, $\hat{D}_2$ would be $\$1.60(1.05)^2 = \$1.764$, and so on.

Using this method for estimating future dividends, we can determine the current stock value, $\hat{P}_0$, by using Equation 10-6. That is, we can find the expected future cash flow stream (the dividends), calculate the present value of each dividend

normal (constant) growth
Growth that is expected to continue into the foreseeable future at about the same rate as that of the economy as a whole; g = a constant.

---

[13]The r_s value of Equation 10-7 is a *required* rate of return. When we transform this equation to get Equation 10-8, we are finding an *expected* rate of return. Obviously, the transformation requires that $r_s = \hat{r}_s$. This equality holds if the stock market is in equilibrium, a condition that will be discussed in Chapter 11.

payment, and sum these present values to find the value of the stock. But because g is constant, we can rewrite Equation 10-6 as follows:[14]

10-9

$$\hat{P}_0 = \frac{D_0(1+g)^1}{(1+r_s)^1} + \frac{D_0(1+g)^2}{(1+r_s)^2} + \cdots + \frac{D_0(1+g)^{\infty-1}}{(1+r_s)^{\infty-1}} + \frac{D_0(1+g)^\infty}{(1+r_s)^\infty}$$

$$= \frac{D_0(1+g)}{r_s - g} = \frac{\hat{D}_1}{r_s - g} = \text{Value of a constant growth stock}$$

Inserting values into the final version of Equation 10-9, we find that the value of our illustrative stock is $11.20:

$$\hat{P}_0 = \frac{\$1.60(1.05)}{0.20 - 0.05} = \frac{\$1.68}{0.15} = \$11.20$$

constant growth model
Also called the Gordon model, it is used to find the value of a stock that is expected to experience constant growth.

The **constant growth model** as set forth on the second line of Equation 10-9 is sufficiently general to encompass the zero growth case described earlier.[15] When $g = 0$, Equation 10-9 simplifies to Equation 10-7. Note also that a necessary condition for the derivation of the simplified form of Equation 10-9 is that r_s be greater than g. In situations where r_s is not greater than g, the results will be meaningless. For example, when $r_s < g$, the denominator in the simplified form of Equation 10-9 is negative, which gives a negative value for $\hat{P}_0$; $\hat{P}_0 < 0$ doesn't make sense in the world of finance.

Figure 10-6 illustrates the concept underlying the valuation process for a constant growth stock. Dividends are growing at the rate $g = 5\%$. Because $r_s > g$, however, the present value of each future dividend is declining. For example, the dividend in Year 1 is $\hat{D}_1 = D_0(1 + g)^1 = \$1.60(1.05) = \$1.68$. The present value of this dividend, discounted at 20 percent, is $PV(\hat{D}_1) = \$1.68/(1.20)^1 = \$1.40$. The dividend expected in Year 2 grows to $\$1.68(1.05) = \$1.764$, but the present value of this dividend falls to $1.225. Continuing, $\hat{D}_3 = \$1.8522$ and $PV(\hat{D}_3) = 1.0719$, and so on. As you can see, the expected dividends are growing, but the present value of each successive dividend is declining because the dividend growth rate, 5 percent, is less than the rate used for discounting the dividends to the present, 20 percent.

If we summed the present values of each future dividend, this summation would equal the value of the stock, $\hat{P}_0$. When g is a constant, this summation is equal to $\hat{D}_1/(r_s - g)$, as shown in Equation 10-9. Therefore, if we extended the lower step function curve in Figure 10-6 to infinity and added up the present values of each future dividend, the summation would be identical to the value given by solving Equation 10-9, $11.20.

Growth in dividends occurs primarily as a result of growth in *earnings per share* (*EPS*). Earnings growth, in turn, results from a number of factors, including inflation, the amount of earnings that the company retains and reinvests, and the rate of return that the company earns on its equity (ROE). Regarding inflation, if output (in units) remains stable and if both sales prices and input costs rise at the inflation rate, then EPS will also grow at the inflation rate. Likewise, EPS will grow as a result of the reinvestment, or plowback, of earnings. If the firm's earnings are not all paid out as dividends (that is, if the firm retains some fraction of its earnings), the dollars

---

[14]In essence, the full-blown version of Equation 10-9 is the sum of a geometric progression, and the last term is the solution value of the progression.

[15]The final form of Equation 10-9 is often called the Gordon model, after Myron J. Gordon, who did much to develop and popularize it.

FIGURE 10-6 Present Value of Dividends of a Constant Growth Stock:
$D_0 = \$1.60$, $g = 5\%$, $r_s = 20\%$

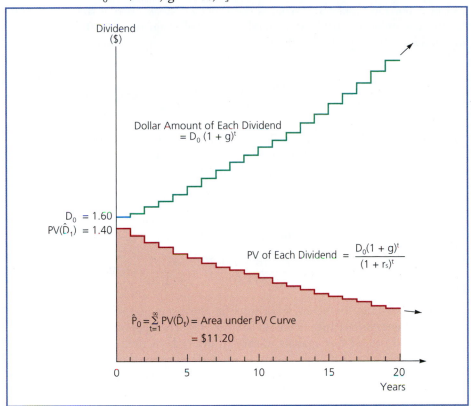

of investment behind each share will increase over time, which should lead to growth in future earnings and dividends.

Expected Rate of Return on a Constant Growth Stock

We can solve Equation 10-9 for r_s, again using the "hat" to denote that we are dealing with an expected rate of return:

$$\hat{r}_s \quad = \quad \frac{\hat{D}_1}{P_0} \quad + \quad g$$

$$\begin{array}{ccc}
\text{Expected rate} & = & \text{Expected} & + & \text{Expected growth rate} \\
\text{of return} & & \text{dividend yield} & & \text{(capital gains yield)}
\end{array}$$

For example, suppose you buy a stock for a price $P_0 = \$11.20$ and you expect the stock to pay a dividend $\hat{D}_1 = \$1.68$ 1 year from now and to grow at a constant rate $g = 5\%$ in the future. In this case, your expected rate of return will be 20 percent:

$$\hat{r}_s = \frac{\$1.68}{\$11.20} + 0.05 = 0.15 + 0.05 = 0.20 = 20.0\%$$

In this form, we see that $\hat{r}_s$ is the *expected total return* and that it consists of an *expected dividend yield*, $\hat{D}_1/P_0 = 15\%$, plus an *expected growth rate or capital gains yield*, $g = 5\%$.

Suppose we had conducted this analysis on January 1, 2009. That is, $P_0 = \$11.20$ is the January 1, 2009, stock price and $\hat{D}_1 = \$1.68$ is the dividend expected at the end of 2009 (December 31). What is the expected stock price at the end of 2009 (or the beginning of 2010)? We would again apply Equation 10-10, but this time we would use the expected 2010 dividend, $\hat{D}_2 = \hat{D}_1 (1 + g) = \hat{D}_{2010} = \hat{D}_{2009} (1+g) = \$1.68(1.05) = \$1.764$, and solve for $\hat{P}_1$ as follows:

$$\hat{P}_1 = \hat{P}_{1/1/10} = \frac{\hat{D}_{12/31/10}}{r_s - g} = \frac{\$1.764}{0.20 - 0.05} = \$11.76$$

Notice that $\hat{P}_1 = \$11.76$ is 5 percent greater than P_0, the $\$11.20$ price on January 1, 2009—that is, $\hat{P}_{1/1/10} = \$11.20(1.05) = \$11.76$. In this case, we would expect to earn a capital gain of $\$0.56 = \$11.76 - \$11.20$ during the year. This amount represents a capital gains yield of 5 percent:

$$\text{Capital gains yield} = \frac{\text{Capital gains}}{\text{Beginning price}} = \frac{\hat{P}_1 - P_0}{P_0}$$

$$= \frac{\$11.76 - \$11.20}{\$11.20} = \frac{\$0.56}{\$11.20} = 0.05 = 5.0\%$$

Here P_0 represents the actual stock price at the beginning of the period and $\hat{P}_1$ represents the expected price of the stock at the end of one period (1 year in this case).

We could extend this analysis further, if desired. In each future year, the expected capital gains yield would equal $g = 5\%$, the expected dividend growth rate. Continuing, we could estimate the dividend yield in 2009 as follows:

$$\text{Dividend yield}_{2009} = \frac{\hat{D}_1}{P_0} = \frac{\hat{D}_{12/31/09}}{P_{1/1/09}} = \frac{\$1.68}{\$11.20} = 0.15 = 15.0\%$$

We could also calculate the dividend yield for 2010, which would again be 15 percent. Thus, for a constant growth stock, the following conditions must hold:

1. The dividend is expected to grow forever at a constant rate, g. The stock price is expected to grow at this same rate, g. As a result, the expected capital gains yield is also constant, and it is equal to g.
2. The expected dividend yield, $\hat{D}_1/P_0$, is a constant.
3. The expected total rate of return, $\hat{r}_s$, is equal to the expected dividend yield plus the expected growth rate: $\hat{r}_s = \hat{D}_1/P_0 + g$.

We should clarify the meaning of the term *expected* here. It means expected in a probabilistic sense, as the statistically expected outcome. Thus, if we say the growth rate is expected to remain constant at 5 percent, we mean that the best prediction for the growth rate in any future year is 5 percent. We do not literally expect the growth rate to be exactly equal to 5 percent in each future year. In this sense, the constant growth assumption is a reasonable one for many large, mature companies.

Valuing Stocks with Nonconstant Growth

Firms typically go through *life cycles*. During the early part of their lives, their growth greatly exceeds that of the economy as a whole. Later, their growth matches

FIGURE 10-7   Illustrative Dividend Growth Rates

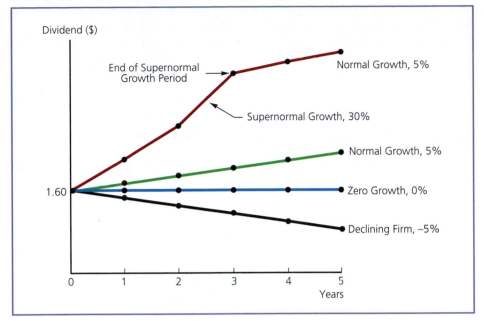

the economy's growth. In the final stage of its life, a firm's growth lags behind that of the economy.[16] Automobile manufacturers in the 1920s, computer software firms such as Microsoft in the 1990s, and the Wi-Fi industry in the 2000s are examples of firms in the early part of this cycle. Today, firms, such as those in the tobacco industry or coal industry, are in the waning stages of their life cycles: that is, their growth is not keeping pace with the general economic growth (in some cases, their growth actually is negative). Firms with growth rates that do not match the economy's growth are called **nonconstant growth** firms. Figure 10-7 illustrates nonconstant growth and compares it with constant growth (both positive and negative) and zero growth.[17]

In Figure 10-7, the dividends of the supernormal growth (growth much greater than the economy's growth) firm are expected to grow at a 30 percent rate for 3 years. The growth rate is then expected to fall to 5 percent, the assumed average for the economy, and remain at that level for the remainder of the firm's life. The value of this firm, like the value of any other firm, is the present value of its expected future dividends as determined by Equation 10-6. In the case in which $\hat{D}_t$ is

nonconstant growth
The part of the life cycle of a firm in which its growth either is much faster or is much slower than that of the economy as a whole.

---

[16]The concept of a life cycle could be broadened to include a *product cycle*, which would include both small, start-up companies and large companies such as IBM, which periodically introduce new products that boost sales and earnings. We should also mention *business cycles*, which alternately depress and boost sales and profits. The growth rate just after a major new product has been introduced, or just after a firm emerges from the depths of a recession, is likely to be much higher than the "expected long-run average growth rate," which is the proper value to use for evaluating the project.

[17]A negative growth rate indicates a declining company. A mining company whose profits are falling because of a declining ore body is an example. Someone buying such a company would expect its earnings, and consequently its dividends and stock price, to decline each year, which would lead to capital losses rather than capital gains. Obviously, a declining company's stock price will be relatively low, and its dividend yield must be high enough to offset the expected capital loss and still produce a competitive total return. Students sometimes argue that they would not be willing to buy a stock whose price was expected to decline. If the annual dividends are large enough to *more than offset* the falling stock price, however, the stock still could provide a good return.

growing at a constant rate, we discovered that Equation 10-6 can be simplified to $\hat{P}_0 = \hat{D}_1/(r_s - g)$. In the supernormal case, however, the expected growth rate is not a constant for all years in the future; it is only constant after the period of supernormal growth ends. To find the value of such a stock, or of any nonconstant growth stock when the *growth rate will eventually stabilize*, we proceed in three steps:

Step 1. Compute the value of the dividends that are affected by nonconstant growth, and then find the present value of these dividends.

Step 2. *Find the price of the stock at the end of the nonconstant growth period, at which point it becomes a constant growth stock.* It is at this point that we can use a modified version of Equation 10-9 to compute $\hat{P}_t$ because all future dividends from that point forward will grow at a constant rate, g_{norm}. In this case the future stock price, $\hat{P}_t$, is computed as follows:

$$\hat{P}_t = \frac{\hat{D}_t(1 + g_{norm})}{r_s - g_{norm}} = \frac{\hat{D}_{t+1}}{r_s - g_{norm}}$$

Here g_{norm} is the rate at which dividends will grow when constant, or normal, growth is attained. $\hat{P}_t$ represents the value in Year t of the dividends that are expected to be paid in Year t + 1 and beyond. In other words, $\hat{P}_t = (PV_t \text{ of } \hat{D}_{t+1}) + (PV_t \text{ of } \hat{D}_{t+2}) + \ldots + (PV_t \text{ of } \hat{D}_\infty)$, where PV_t represents the present value in Year t. In our example, nonconstant growth ends at the end of Year 3, and thus dividends start growing at a constant rate ($g_{norm} = 5\%$) *immediately after* the dividend for Year 3 is paid—that is, during Year 4. The constant growth model can be applied as soon as nonconstant growth ends. Thus, because the first dividend to grow at the constant rate of 5 percent is the Year 4 dividend, $\hat{D}_4$, we can apply the constant growth model at the end of Year 3 to compute $\hat{P}_3$. After we compute $\hat{P}_t$ ($\hat{P}_3$ in our example), we discount this value to the present period—that is, Year 0. PV of $\hat{P}_t = \hat{P}_t/(1 + g)^t$.

Step 3. We add the two present value components computed in Steps 1 and 2 to find the intrinsic value of the stock, $\hat{P}_0$. Thus, $\hat{P}_0 = (PV \text{ of nonconstant growth dividends}) + (PV \text{ of } \hat{P}_t)$.

To determine the value of the stock for our example, we assume the following conditions exist:

r_s = Stockholders' required rate of return; r_s = 20%. This rate is used to discount the cash flows.

n_{super} = The number of years of supernormal growth n_{super} = 3 years.

g_{super} = The rate of growth in both earnings and dividends during the supernormal growth period; g_{super} = 30%. (*Note:* The growth rate during the supernormal growth period could vary from year to year.)

g_{norm} = The rate of normal (constant) growth after the supernormal period; g_{norm} = 5%.

D_0 = The *last* dividend paid by the company; D_0 = $1.60.

To begin the valuation process, let's take a look at the cash flow time line for our situation:

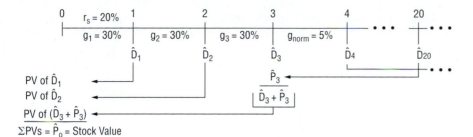

Following the steps outlined in this section, we compute the value of our stock as:

Step 1. Calculate the dividends for each year during the nonconstant growth period:

$$\hat{D}_t = D_0(1 + g_{super})^t$$

$$\hat{D}_1 = D_0(1 + g_{super})^1 = \$1.600(1.30)^1 = \$2.0800$$

$$\hat{D}_2 = D_0(1 + g_{super})^2 = \$1.600(1.30)^2 = \hat{D}_1(1 + g_{super}) = 2.0800(1.30) = \$2.7040$$

$$\hat{D}_3 = D_0(1 + g_{super})^3 = \$1.600(1.30)^3 = \hat{D}_2(1 + g_{super}) = 2.7040(1.30) = \$3.5152$$

Show these values on the cash flow time line as cash flows for Years 1 through 3. Compute the present value of these nonconstant dividends:

Year	Dividend, $\hat{D}_t$	PV at $r_s = 20\%$
1	$2.0800	$1.7333 = \$2.0800/(1.20)^1$
2	2.7040	$1.8778 = 2.7040/(1.20)^2$
3	3.5152	$2.0343 = 3.5152/(1.20)^3$
		PV = $5.6454

Step 2. The price of the stock is the PV of dividends from Year 1 to infinity (∞). In theory, we could continue projecting each future dividend beyond Year 3, when normal growth of 5 percent occurs. In other words, we could use $g_{norm} = 5\%$ to compute $\hat{D}_4$, $\hat{D}_5$, and so on, with $\hat{D}_3 = \$3.5152$ being the base dividend for normal growth:

$$\hat{D}_4 = D_3(1 + g_{norm})^1 = \$3.5152(1.05)^1 = \$3.6910$$

$$\hat{D}_5 = D_3(1 + g_{norm})^2 = \$3.5152(1.05)^2 = \$3.8755$$

$$\cdot$$
$$\cdot$$
$$\cdot$$

$$\hat{D}_{20} = D_3(1 + g_{norm})^{17} = \$3.5152(1.05)^{17} = \$8.0569$$

We can continue this process, and then find the PV of this stream of dividends. After $\hat{D}_3$ has been paid in Year 3, however, the stock becomes a constant growth stock. Thus, we can apply the constant growth formula at that point and find $\hat{P}_3$, which is the PV of the dividends from Year 4 through infinity as evaluated in Year 3. After the firm has paid the Year 3 dividend, all of the future dividends will grow at a constant rate equal to 5 percent, so:

$$\hat{P}_3 = \frac{\hat{D}_4}{r_s - g_{norm}} = \frac{\$3.6910}{0.20 - 0.05} = \$24.6067$$

FIGURE 10-8   Determining the Value of a Nonconstant Growth Stock

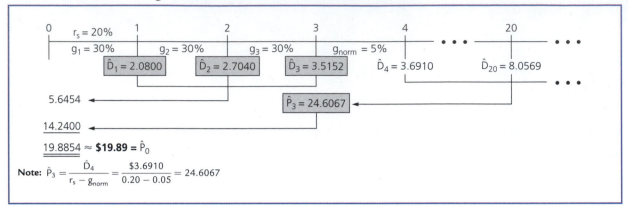

This $24.6067 appears on the cash flow time line as a *second cash flow* in Year 3. The $24.6067 is a Year 3 cash flow in the sense that the owner of the stock *could* sell it for $24.6067 at the end of Year 3 and also in the sense that $24.6067 is the present value equivalent of the dividend cash flows from Year 4 to infinity.

Compute the present value of the price in Year 3:

$$PV(\hat{P}_3) = \$24.6067/(1.20)^3 = \$14.2400$$

Step 3. Figure 10-8 shows the cash flow time line with the actual cash flows we determined in Step 1 and Step 2. Summing the present values that we computed in these two steps, we find that the price of the stock, $\hat{P}_0$, is:

$$\hat{P}_0 = \text{PV of nonconstant dividends} + \text{PV of } \hat{P}_3$$
$$= \$5.6454 + \$14.2400 = \$19.8854 \approx \$19.89$$

This is the result shown to the left below the cash flow time line in Figure 10-8.

To give a different perspective of the valuation process presented in Steps 1 through 3, let's assume that the same situation exists for the stock that we are currently evaluating, except investors expect the company to pay dividends for the next 50 years and then go bankrupt rather than continue to pay dividends forever. Table 10-2 shows the dividend that would be paid each year as well as the present value of all of the dividends that would be paid during the 50-year period. Notice that the present value of the dividends equals $19.8584, which is about $0.03 less than the result we computed earlier (shown in Figure 10-8). Because the only difference between the result shown in Table 10-2 and the result shown in Figure 10-8 is that Table 10-2 excludes the dividends that would be received beyond Year 50, $0.03 represents the present value of the dividends from Year 51 to infinity. This is an extremely small value.

Clearly, it is easy to compute the dividends and their present values for 50 years using a spreadsheet if we know the annual growth rates. It is, however, easier to compute the dividends during the nonconstant growth period, use the modified version of Equation 10-9 to compute the value of the stock at the point when nonconstant growth ends, and then add the present values of these future cash flows to determine $\hat{P}_0$.

TABLE 10-2 Present Value of the Dividends Received from a Stock Investment During a 50-Year Period

Information: Last dividend payment, $D_0 = \$1.60$
Dividend growth rates: $g_{super} = g_1 = g_2 = g_3 = 30\%$; $g_{norm} = g_4 = \ldots = g_\infty = 5\%$
Required rate of return, $r_s = 20\%$

Year	Growth Rate, g_t	Dividend $\hat{D}_t =$ $\hat{D}_{t-1}(1+g_t)$	PV of Dividend $= \hat{D}_t/(1.20)^t$	Year	Growth Rate, g_t	Dividend $\hat{D}_t$ $= \hat{D}_{t-1}(1+g_t)$	PV of Dividend $= \hat{D}_t/(1.20)^t$
1	30%	$ 2.0800	$1.7333	26	5%	$10.7970	$ 0.0943
2	30	2.7040	1.8778	27	5	11.3369	0.0825
3	30	3.5152	2.0343	28	5	11.9037	0.0722
4	5	3.6910	1.7800	29	5	12.4989	0.0632
5	5	3.8755	1.5575	30	5	13.1238	0.0553
6	5	4.0693	1.3628	31	5	13.7800	0.0484
7	5	4.2727	1.1924	32	5	14.4690	0.0423
8	5	4.4864	1.0434	33	5	15.1925	0.0370
9	5	4.7107	0.9130	34	5	15.9521	0.0324
10	5	4.9462	0.7988	35	5	16.7497	0.0284
11	5	5.1936	0.6990	36	5	17.5872	0.0248
12	5	5.4532	0.6116	37	5	18.4666	0.0217
13	5	5.7259	0.5352	38	5	19.3899	0.0190
14	5	6.0122	0.4683	39	5	20.3594	0.0166
15	5	6.3128	0.4097	40	5	21.3774	0.0145
16	5	6.6284	0.3585	41	5	22.4462	0.0127
17	5	6.9599	0.3137	42	5	23.5685	0.0111
18	5	7.3078	0.2745	43	5	24.7470	0.0097
19	5	7.6732	0.2402	44	5	25.9843	0.0085
20	5	8.0569	0.2102	45	5	27.2835	0.0075
21	5	8.4597	0.1839	46	5	28.6477	0.0065
22	5	8.8827	0.1609	47	5	30.0801	0.0057
23	5	9.3269	0.1408	48	5	31.5841	0.0050
24	5	9.7932	0.1232	49	5	33.1633	0.0044
25	5	10.2829	0.1078	50	5	34.8215	0.0038

$\sum$ PV of Dividends $= \underline{\underline{\$19.8584}}$

Self-Test Questions

In general, how should the value of a stock be determined?

Write out a simple equation that can be used to compute the value of a stock that exhibits constant dividend growth. Can this equation be used for stocks that exhibit zero growth in dividends?

What are the two elements of a stock's expected return?

How do you calculate the capital gains yield and the dividend yield of a stock?

How do you determine the value of a stock with nonconstant growth?

Suppose that the last dividend paid by a company was $3.00, dividends are expected to grow at a constant rate equal to 3 percent forever, and stockholders require 13 percent to invest in similar types of investments. What is the value of the company's stock?   (Answer: $30.90)

Suppose that Winding Road Map Company just paid a dividend equal to $5. For the past few years, the company has been growing at a rate equal to 20 percent. This growth is expected to continue for another 2 years, and then for every year thereafter the company's growth is expected to be 5 percent. If investors require a return equal to 15 percent to invest in Winding Road Map, what is the value of its stock?   (Answer: $67.83)

ACTUAL STOCK PRICES AND RETURNS IN RECENT YEARS

So far, our discussion has focused on expected stock prices and expected rates of return. Anyone who has ever invested in the stock market knows that there can be—and generally are—large differences between expected and realized prices and returns.

Figure 10-9 shows how the price of an average share of stock has varied in recent years, as well as how total realized returns have varied. The overall trend has been strongly up, but the market has gone up in some years and down in others. Likewise, the stocks of individual companies have gone up and down. From theory, we know that expected returns as estimated by a marginal investor are always positive. In some years, however, negative returns have been realized. Of course, some individual companies do well even in bad years, so the "name of the game" in security analysis is to pick the

FIGURE 10-9   S&P 500 Index: Value and Total Returns (Capital Gains Plus Dividend Yield), 1985–2008

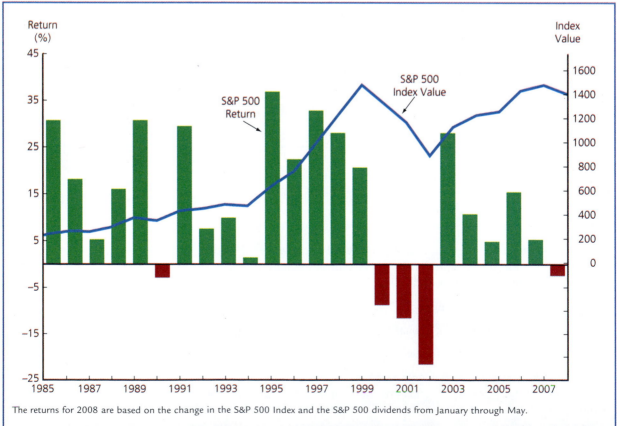

The returns for 2008 are based on the change in the S&P 500 Index and the S&P 500 dividends from January through May.

winners. Financial managers attempt to take actions that will put their companies into the winners' column, but they don't always succeed. In subsequent chapters, we will examine the actions that managers can take to increase the odds that their firms will do relatively well in the marketplace.

Self-Test Question

What causes differences between expected returns and realized returns?

Ethical Dilemma

Which ARM Should You Choose—The Left or the Right?

Alan recently joined Friendly Investment and Financing Options (FIFO) as a loan officer. FIFO is a national company that specializes in mortgage lending. One of Alan's responsibilities is to increase the amount of mortgages FIFO initiates. In a meeting he had with the CEO yesterday, Alan was told about a new mortgage that FIFO intends to market. The new mortgage is called a homeowner's option adjustable rate mortgage, or an OptARM for short, and its most attractive feature is that homeowners can choose to make relatively low monthly payments at the beginning of the mortgage period. However, the payments increase significantly later in the life of the mortgage. In fact, depending on the amount the borrower chooses (hence, the term *option*) to pay at the beginning of the mortgage, the amounts that must be paid later could be substantial; perhaps as much as four to five times the initial payments. In many cases, when a homeowner chooses to pay the minimum amount or an amount that he or she can afford, the mortgage turns "upside down," in which case the amount due on the mortgage is greater than the value of the house.

The primary benefit of OptARMs to borrowers is that such loans allow those who cannot afford the monthly payments associated with conventional mortgages the opportunity to purchase houses. A borrower with income that is lower than is needed to qualify for a conventional mortgage can borrow using OptARMs, choose an affordable (lower than conventional) payment in the early years of the mortgage, and then make the higher payments in later years when his or her income presumably will be higher. Thus, option ARMs permit those who can't afford conventional mortgages to buy houses today that they otherwise couldn't afford until years into the future.

Lenders such as FIFO like selling option ARMs because they can recognize as current revenues the monthly payments that would be required if the loans were conventional mortgages, regardless of the amounts that the borrowers opt to pay. In other words, companies can "book" revenues that will not be collected for a few years.

Unlike most people, including many professionals, Alan understands the complexities of OptARMs. He knows that many borrowers who choose such mortgages will lose their houses 3 to 5 years after buying them because the payments increase so significantly after the low-payment option period expires that these borrowers cannot afford the new, higher monthly payments. And, although they would like to refinance with conventional mortgages, often these homeowners do not have good enough credit to do so. This scenario is quite disturbing to Alan. He would like to explain to his customers in clear terms the possible pitfalls of OptARMs, but the CEO of FIFO has instructed Alan that he should provide only the information that is required by law and to follow company policy, which states that lending officers should provide basic printed material, give simple advice, and answer questions that might provide negative information only when asked.

Alan has a bad feeling about OptARMs. He knows that they are great lending/borrowing tools when used as intended. He is afraid, however, that FIFO is more concerned with booking revenues than with the financial well-being of its customers (borrowers). What should Alan do? How would you handle this situation if you were Alan? Should the OptARMs be called HARMs?

CHAPTER PRINCIPLES –The Answers

To summarize the key concepts, let's answer the questions that were posed at the beginning of the chapter:

- **How are bond prices determined?** The price of a bond is computed as the present value of the cash flows the bond is expected to pay during its life. As a result, a bond's market price is determined by the interest paid during its life, which depends on the bond's coupon rate of interest, and the principal amount that must be repaid at maturity.

- **How are bond yields (market rates) determined?** A bond's yield to maturity (YTM) is the average annual rate of return that an investor will earn if he or she buys the bond at the current market price and holds it until it matures. A bond's yield to call (YTC) is the same as its yield to maturity, except the period that is examined ends on the first date that the bond can be called rather than on the maturity date and its terminal value is the call price rather than the maturity value. To determine the YTM, we compute the rate that equates the market value of the bond to the present value of both the future interest payments and the repayment of the principal amount. For example, if a bond currently sells for $950, the YTM is the rate where the present value of all the future cash flows associated with the bond equals $950.

- **What is the relationship between bond prices and interest rates? Why is it important for investors to understand this relationship?** Bond prices and interest rates are negatively related—that is, when interest rates increase, bond prices decrease, and vice versa. Further, for a particular interest rate change, prices of bonds with longer terms to maturity exhibit greater changes (both in dollar amounts and percentages) than prices of shorter term bonds. Understanding these relationships is important to both investors and borrowers. If investors expect that interest rates will increase in the near term, then they should invest in short-term debt because the market values of bonds will decrease when interest rates increase, at which time longer term bonds can be purchased for much lower prices. In addition, the values of the short-term bonds will decrease less than the values of long-term bonds when the rates increase. Borrowers would follow the opposite strategy—that is, they would borrow using long-term debt to "lock in" existing rates if they expected interest rates to increase in the near term.

- **In general, how are stock prices determined?** We mentioned in Chapter 9 that the value of any asset is equal to the present value of the future cash flows the asset is expected to generate. The same concept is used to determine stock prices. In other words, the price (value) of a stock is equal to the present value of the dividends stockholders expect to receive during the company's life. The model that we often use to determine the value of a stock is called the dividend discount model (DDM)—all the future dividends are discounted to the present period to determine the stock's current value. Even if an investor does not intend to hold a stock for the life of the company, its value is computed as the present value of the dividends the company is expected to pay in the future because the price the investor receives when the stock is sold at some later date is the present value of the dividends that the company is expected to pay from that date forward.

- **How are stock returns (yields) determined?** The total return that a stockholder earns each year is based on the dividend that the company pays and the change in the market value of the stock during the year. These two components of total return are referred to as the dividend yield and the capital gains yield, respectively. The dividend yield is computed by dividing the dividend received during the year by the beginning-of-year stock price—that is, dividend yield = $\hat{D}_1/P_0$. The capital gains yield equals the change in the market value of the stock stated as a percent—that is, capital gains yield $= (\hat{P}_1 - P_0)/P_0$. Some investors prefer stocks that pay high dividends, and thus have high dividend yields, whereas other investors prefer stocks that produce large capital gains, and thus have high capital gains yields.

- **What factors affect stock prices?** The primary reason that stock prices change is because investors change their expectations about the returns the firm will generate in the future. Stockholders earn returns in two forms: (1) dividends and (2) capital gains. If investors expect either of these components to increase (decrease), the market value of the stock increases (decreases). Stockholders also demand a minimum rate of return to invest in a company. If this return, which is termed the required rate of return, increases (decreases), the price of the company's stock decreases (increases). Both the return that investors expect to earn by investing in a stock and the return that they require to invest in a stock are affected by business and economic conditions.

In this chapter, we first showed how to value a bond or an investment with similar characteristics. We also showed how changes in interest rates and risk affect bond values. Based on these discussions, you should be able to answer the questions that follow—your answers will help you make better personal financial decisions.

CHAPTER PRINCIPLES
–Personal Finance

- **How can I use knowledge of, or expectations about, interest rate changes to help make investment decisions?** We know that bond prices decrease (increase) when interest rates increase (decrease). As a result, if interest rates are expected to increase, investors generally wait to invest their money in ("lock into") long-term bonds until the rates peak. When interest rates are increasing, investors still want to "put their money to work," so they generally invest in short-term bonds (debt) until rates are finished increasing.

- **How does knowledge of bond valuation help me to make investment decisions?** If you understand why bond prices change, then you understand why the returns you earn via your bond investments change, and vice versa.

- **How can I use knowledge of bond valuation to make decisions about whether to repay loans early or to refinance my debt?** You should use the same logic that businesses use when determining whether to refinance their debt. In other words, you should compare the cost of your existing debt to the cost that you would have to pay if you took on new loans. If the interest rates on new loans are substantially lower than the interest rates on your existing debt, you probably should refinance your debt—that is, take on new lower interest loans and use the money to pay off the existing higher interest loans. Also, remember that most long-term consumer debt is paid off in installments; thus, each payment includes both interest that is due and repayment of some of the principal amount (outstanding balance). For such loans, you can determine the amount of principal you owe, which is the amount that would have to be paid off to liquidate the loan, by computing the present value of all the remaining payments using the loan's interest rate as r_d. As we showed in Chapter 9, you must "strip" the remaining loan payments of the interest charges—that is, you must "deinterest" the payments.

Our discussion of stock valuation should help you understand what factors affect stock prices and why stock prices change as investors' expectations change. If you understand the basic concepts we discussed, you should be able to determine a "rough" estimate for the value of stocks that you might be interested in purchasing (or you already own), and thus make more informed decisions about your investment positions.

- **How can the concepts presented in the chapter help me to determine whether a stock's market value is appropriate?** There is no scientific process that can be used to value stock. However, we know that the market value of a stock is based on the future cash flows it is expected to provide investors. We also know that, theoretically, the "intrinsic" value of a stock can be determined by computing the present value of these expected future cash flows. Although it isn't always easy to forecast the future cash flows that a stock will generate, you can gather information from various sources—for example, investment sites on the Internet, professional analysts, knowledgeable friends, and so forth—to form your own opinions about a stock's potential cash flows. Using this information, you can use the techniques described in the chapter to get a "ballpark" estimate of the stock's value.

- **How do I know how well my investment in a stock is performing?** As we mentioned in the chapter, the return that is earned on an investment in a stock is a combination of the dividend that is paid by the company and the change in the market value of the stock. Thus, to determine how well your investment is performing, you should compute the total return that the stock provides—that is, the combination of the dividend yield and the capital gains yield. Some stocks generate high dividend yields along with low capital gains yields, whereas other stocks provide low dividend yields but produce high capital gains yields. Depending on your personal tax position, you might prefer to invest in a stock that generates high dividend yields or high capital gains yields, but not both.

- **How do expectations affect stock prices?** As we mentioned, the value of a stock is based on the cash flows it is expected to generate throughout its life. If investors change their expectations about a stock's future cash flows, then the market price of the stock changes. For example, if Pfizer announces that it has developed a drug that cures all types of cancers, investors view this event as good news in the sense that they expect the company's future earnings and thus payouts to stockholders to be greater than before the new drug was developed. As a result, the market price of Pfizer's stock should increase; the present value of the expected future cash flows, which are higher than before the development of the drug, is higher. Pay attention to announcements that are made by companies, and try to determine what impact such announcements will have on the companies' stock prices. Generally, when the announcement is considered "good news," the market price of a stock increases, and vice versa. To make your conclusions, consider whether the announcement suggests that the future cash flows generated by the firm will increase or whether they will decrease.

QUESTIONS

10-1 Describe how the value of any asset is determined.

10-2 The rate of return that you would earn if you bought a bond and held it to its maturity date is called the bond's yield to maturity (YTM). If interest rates in the economy rise after a bond has been issued, what will happen to the bond's price and to its YTM? Does the length of time to maturity affect the extent to which a given change in interest rates will affect the bond's price?

10-3 A bond that pays interest forever and has no maturity date is a perpetual bond. How is the yield to maturity on such a bond determined?

10-4 Suppose that a bond has a yield to call (YTC) equal to 6.5 percent and a yield to maturity (YTM) equal to 6.3 percent. Explain the meanings of these numbers to bond investors.

10-5 Two investors are evaluating IBM's stock for possible purchase. They agree on the expected value of D_1 and on the expected future dividend growth rate. They also agree on the riskiness of the stock. One investor normally holds stocks for 2 years, and the other normally holds stocks for 10 years. On the basis of the type of analysis presented in this chapter, they should both be willing to pay the same price for IBM's stock. Is this statement correct? Explain.

10-6 If you bought a share of common stock, you would typically expect to receive dividends plus capital gains. Would you expect the distribution between the dividend yield and the capital gains yield to be influenced by the firm's decision to pay more dividends rather than to retain and reinvest more of its earnings?

10-7 How will the price of AT&T's stock change if investors decide they want to earn a higher return for purchasing the stock? Assume all else remains constant. Will the price of AT&T's stock change if the CEO announces that the company must pay a 10-year, $10 billion fine for unfair trade practices? Explain your rationale.

10-8 How might an investor's tax situation affect his or her decision to purchase stocks of companies in the early stages of their lives, when they are growing rapidly and paying little or no dividends, versus stocks of older, more mature firms that provide relatively low capital gains?

10-9 How does the par value of common stock relate to its market value?

10-10 Everything else equal, how would each of the following affect the market value of a stock? Indicate by a plus $(+)$, minus $(-)$, or zero (0) if the factor would increase, decrease, or have an indeterminate effect. Be prepared to justify your answer.

    a. Investors require a higher rate of return to buy the stock.

    b. The company increases dividends.

    c. The company's growth rate increases.

    d. Investors become more risk averse.

10-11 How do you think that the process of valuing a real asset, such as a building, differs from the process of valuing a financial asset, such as a stock or a bond?

SELF-TEST PROBLEMS

Solutions appear in Appendix B.

ST-1 Define each of the following terms: **Key Terms**

    a. Bond

    b. Premium bond; discount bond

    c. Current yield (on a bond); yield to maturity (YTM)

    d. Interest rate price risk; interest rate reinvestment risk

    e. Intrinsic value, $\hat{P}_0$; market price (P_0)

    f. Growth rate, g; required rate of return, r_s; expected rate of return, $\hat{r}_s$; actual (realized) rate of return, $\ddot{r}_s$

    g. Capital gains yield; dividend yield

    h. Zero growth stock

    i. Normal (constant) growth; nonconstant growth

Bond Valuation   **ST-2** The Pennington Corporation issued a new series of bonds on January 1, 1985. The bonds were sold at par value, which is $1,000, have a 12 percent coupon, and mature in 30 years, on December 31, 2014. Coupon payments are made semiannually (on June 30 and December 31).

    a. What was the YTM on Pennington's bonds on January 1, 1985?

    b. What was the price of the bond on January 1, 1990 (5 years later), assuming that the level of interest rates has fallen to 10 percent?

    c. Find the current yield and capital gains yield on the bond on January 1, 1990, given the price determined in part (b).

    d. On July 1, 2008, Pennington's bonds sold for $916.42. What was the YTM at that date?

    e. What were the current yield and capital gains yield on July 1, 2008?

Constant Growth   **ST-3** Ewald Company's current stock price is $36, and its last dividend was
Stock Valuation $2.40. In view of Ewald's strong financial position and its consequent low risk, its required rate of return is only 12 percent. If dividends are expected to grow at a constant rate, g, in the future, and if r_s is expected to remain at 12 percent, what is Ewald's expected stock price 5 years from now?

Nonconstant Growth   **ST-4** Snyder Computer Chips, Inc., is experiencing a period of rapid growth.
Stock Valuation Earnings and dividends are expected to grow at a rate of 15 percent during the next 2 years, at 13 percent in the third year, and at a constant rate of 6 percent thereafter. Snyder's *last* dividend was $1.15, and the required rate of return on the stock is 12 percent.

    a. Calculate the value of the stock today.

    b. Calculate $\hat{P}_1$ and $\hat{P}_2$.

    c. Calculate the dividend yield and capital gains yield for Years 1, 2, and 3.

Stock Growth Rates   **ST-5** You are considering buying the stocks of two companies that operate in
and Valuation the same industry. Both firms have similar characteristics except for their dividend payout policies, and both are expected to earn $6 per share this year. Company D (for "dividend") is expected to pay out all of its earnings as dividends, whereas Company G (for "growth") is expected to pay out only one-third of its earnings, or $2 per share. Company D's stock price is $40. Both firms are equally risky. Which of the following is most likely to be true?

    a. Company G will have a faster growth rate than Company D, so G's stock price should be greater than $40.

    b. Although G's growth rate should exceed D's growth rate, D's current dividend exceeds that paid by G, which should cause D's price to exceed G's price.

    c. An investor in Company D will get his or her money back faster because D pays out more of its earnings as dividends. Thus, in a sense, D is like a short-term bond, and G is like a long-term bond. If economic shifts cause r_d and r_s to increase, and if the expected streams of dividends from D and G remain constant, the stocks of both companies will decline, but D's price should decline more.

d. Company D's expected and required rate of return is $\hat{r}_s = r_s = 15\%$. Company G's expected return will be higher because of its higher expected growth rate.

e. On the basis of the available information, the best estimate of G's growth rate is 10 percent.

PROBLEMS

10-1   Buner Corp.'s outstanding bond has the following characteristics: **Bond Valuation**

Years to maturity	6.0
Coupon rate of interest	8.0%
Face value	$1,000

If investors require a rate of return equal to 12 percent on similar risk bonds and *interest is paid semiannually*, what should be the market price of Buner's bond?

10-2   Rick bought a bond when it was issued by Macroflex Corporation 14 years ago. The bond, which has a $1,000 face value and a coupon rate equal to 10 percent, matures in 6 years. Interest is paid every 6 months; the next interest payment is scheduled for 6 months from today. If the yield on similar risk investments is 14 percent, what is the current market value (price) of the bond?   **Bond Valuation**

10-3   Suppose Ford Motor Company sold an issue of bonds with a 10-year maturity, a $1,000 par value, a 10 percent coupon rate, and semiannual interest payments.   **Bond Valuation**

a. Two years after the bonds were issued, the going rate of interest on bonds such as these fell to 6 percent. At what price would the bonds sell?

b. Suppose that the interest rate remained at 6 percent for the next 8 years. What would happen to the price of the Ford Motor Company bonds over time?

10-4   Suppose that 5 years ago Cisco Systems sold a 15-year bond issue that had a $1,000 par value and a 7 percent coupon rate. Interest is paid semiannually.   **Bond Valuation**

a. If the going interest rate has risen to 10 percent, at what price would the bonds be selling today?

b. Suppose that the interest rate remained at 10 percent for the next 10 years. What would happen to the price of Cisco's bonds over time?

10-5   Many years ago, Minnow Bait and Tackle issued preferred stock. The stock pays an annual dividend equal to $6.80. If the required rate of return on similar risk investments is 8 percent, what should be the market value of Minnow's preferred stock?   **Preferred Stock Valuation**

10-6   The Ape Copy Company's preferred stock pays an annual dividend equal to $16.50. If investors demand a return equal to 11 percent to purchase Ape's preferred stock, what is its market value?   **Preferred Stock Valuation**

10-7   Jones Brothers Clothing just issued preferred stock with a face value equal to $80 that pays a 10 percent annual dividend. If the stock currently yields 8 percent, what is its market value?   **Preferred Stock Valuation**

Constant Growth Stock Valuation

10-8 Advanced Corporation's growth has slowed to a constant rate during the past few years. As a result, the company expects its common stock dividend to grow at a constant 4 percent for the remainder of the company's life. A few days ago, Advanced paid common stockholders a $5 dividend. If the required rate of return on the company's stock is 12 percent, what is the value of the stock today?

Constant Growth Stock Valuation

10-9 Ms. Manners Catering (MMC) has paid a constant $1.50 per share dividend to its common stockholders for the past 25 years. Beginning with the next dividend, MMC expects to increase the dividend at a constant rate equal to 2 percent per year into perpetuity. Investors require a 12 percent rate of return to purchase MMC's common stock. What is the market value of ·MMC's common stock?

Constant Growth Stock Valuation

10-10 McCue Mining Company's ore reserves are being depleted, so the firm's sales are falling. Also, its pit is getting deeper each year, so its costs are rising. As a result, the company's earnings and dividends are declining at a constant rate of 5 percent per year. If $D_0 = \$5$ and $r_s = 15\%$, what is the value of McCue Mining's stock?

Constant Growth Dividend

10-11 The common stock of Union Jack Flags is currently selling for $28 per share. The company's stock has been growing at a constant annual rate of 4 percent, and this growth is expected to continue for an infinite period. The required rate on the stock is 11 percent. If you buy the stock today, what is the next dividend you would receive?

Bond Valuation

10-12 The Desreumaux Company has two bond issues outstanding. Both bonds pay $100 annual interest plus $1,000 at maturity. Bond L has a maturity of 15 years and Bond S has a maturity of 1 year.

a. What will be the values of these bonds when the going rate of interest is (1) 5 percent, (2) 7 percent, and (3) 11 percent? Assume that there is only one more interest payment to be made on Bond S.

b. Why does the longer term (15-year) bond fluctuate more when interest rates change than does the shorter term bond (1-year)?

Constant Growth Stock Valuation

10-13 Your broker offers to sell you some shares of Wingler & Company common stock, which paid a dividend of $2 *yesterday*. You expect the dividend to grow at a rate of 5 percent per year into perpetuity. The appropriate rate of return for the stock is 12 percent.

a. If you purchase the Wingler & Company stock with the intent of selling it in 3 years, what cash flows will you receive each year?

b. What is the market value of Wingler's stock?

Nonconstant Growth Stock Valuation

10-14 Assume that the average firm in your company's industry is expected to grow at a constant rate of 6 percent, and its dividend yield is 7 percent. Your company is considered as risky as the average firm in the industry, but it has just successfully completed some R&D work that leads you to expect that its earnings and dividends will grow at a rate of 50 percent $[\hat{D}_1 = D_0(1 + g_{super}) = D_0(1.50)]$ this year and 25 percent the following year. After that period, growth should match the 6 percent industry average rate. The last dividend paid (D_0) was $1. What is the value per share of your firm's stock?

Nonconstant Growth Stock Valuation

10-15 Microtech Corporation is expanding rapidly. Because it needs to retain all of its earnings, it does not currently pay any dividends. Investors expect Microtech to begin paying dividends eventually, with the first dividend of $1 coming 3 years from today. The dividend should grow rapidly—at a rate of 50 percent per year—during Years 4 and 5. After Year 5, the company should grow at a constant rate of 8 percent per year. If the required return on the stock is 15 percent, what is the value of the stock today?

10-16 Bayboro Sails is expected to pay dividends of $2.50, $3.00, and $4.00 in the next 3 years—that is, $\hat{D}_1 = \$2.50$, $\hat{D}_2 = \$3.00$, and $\hat{D}_3 = \$4.00$, respectively. After 3 years, the dividend is expected to grow at a constant rate of 4 percent per year indefinitely. Stockholders require a return of 14 percent to invest in Bayboro's common stock. Compute the value of Bayboro's common stock today.

Nonconstant Growth Stock Valuation

10-17 Intercontinental Baseball Manufacturers (IBM) has an outstanding bond that matures in 10 years. The bond, which pays $25 interest every 6 months ($50 per year), is currently selling for $598.55. What is the bond's yield to maturity?

Yield to Maturity

10-18 Filkins Farm Equipment needs to raise $4.5 million for expansion, and it expects that 5-year, zero coupon bonds can be sold at a price of $567.44 for each $1,000 bond. What is the yield to maturity (YTM) on the bonds?

YTM—Zero Coupons

10-19 A corporation has an outstanding bond with the following characteristics:

Yield to Maturity

Coupon interest rate	6.0%
Interest payments	semiannually
Face value	$1,000.00
Years to maturity	8
Current market value	$ 902.81

What is the yield to maturity (YTM) for this bond?

10-20 It is now January 1, 2010, and you are considering the purchase of an outstanding Puckett Corporation bond that was issued on January 1, 2008. The Puckett bond has a 9.5 percent annual coupon and a 30-year original maturity (it matures on December 31, 2037). Interest rates have declined since the bond was issued, and the bond is now selling at 116.575 percent of the par value, or $1,165.75. What is the yield to maturity in 2010 for the Puckett bond?

Yield to Maturity

10-21 The Severn Company's bonds have 4 years remaining to maturity. Interest is paid annually, the bonds have a $1,000 par value, and the coupon interest rate is 9 percent.

Yield to Maturity

   a. Compute the yield to maturity for the bonds if the current market price is (1) $829 or (2) $1,104.

   b. Would you pay $829 for one of these bonds if you thought that the appropriate rate of interest was 12 percent—that is, if $r_d = 12\%$? Explain your answer.

10-22 Robert bought a new issue of a 10-year bond with a coupon rate equal to 8 percent. If Robert sells the bond at the end of the year when its market price is $925, what return would he earn? What portion of the return is capital gains and what portion is the current yield?

Yields on Bonds

10-23 What will be the rate of return on a perpetual bond with a $1,000 par value, an 8 percent coupon rate, and a current market price of (a) $600, (b) $800, (c) $1,000, and (d) $1,500? Assume that interest is paid annually.

Rate of Return for a Perpetual Bond

10-24 As investment manager of Pasco Electric Company's pension plan (which is exempt from income taxes), you must choose between IBM bonds and AT&T preferred stock. The bonds have a $1,000 par value, mature in

Effective Annual Rate

20 years, pay $40 every 6 months, and sell at a price of $897.40 per bond. The preferred stock is a perpetuity; it pays a dividend of $2 each quarter, and it sells for $95 per share. What is the effective annual rate of return (EAR) on the *higher yielding* security?

Simple Interest Rate

10-25 Tapley Corporation's 14 percent coupon rate, semiannual payment, $1,000 par value bonds mature in 30 years. The bonds sell at a price of $1,353.54, and their yield curve is flat. Assuming that interest rates in the general economy are expected to remain at their current level, what is the best estimate of Tapley's simple interest rate on *new* bonds?

Rates of Return on Stock

10-26 Nancy Cotton bought NuTalk for $15 per share. One year later, Nancy sold the stock for $21 per share, just after she received a $0.90 cash dividend from the company. What total return did Nancy earn? What was the dividend yield and the capital gains yield?

Rates of Return on Stock

10-27 Ralph Rafferty purchased Gold Depot at the beginning of January for $25 per share. Ralph received a $1.25 dividend payment from the company at the end of December. At that time, the stock was selling for $27.50 per share. What is Ralph's return on his investment for the year? What portion of the total return is the dividend yield and what portion is the capital gains yield?

Return on Preferred Stock

10-28 Sanger Music Company's preferred stock, which currently sells for $105 per share, pays an annual dividend equal to $12.60. What is the yield—that is, the rate of return—that Sanger's preferred stockholders earn?

Return on Preferred Stock

10-29 Tando Airlines has preferred stock outstanding that has a par value equal to $100. Preferred dividend payments equal 8 percent of the stock's par value. If Tando's preferred stock currently sells for $160, what is the rate of return that preferred stockholders earn? What portion of this return is the dividend yield and what portion is the capital gains yield? (*Hint:* Think about the growth rate that is associated with preferred stock.)

Returns on Common Stock

10-30 You buy a share of Damanpour Corporation stock for $21.40. You expect it to pay dividends of $1.07, $1.1449, and $1.2250 in Years 1, 2, and 3, respectively. You also expect to sell the stock at a price of $26.22 at the end of 3 years.

  a. Calculate the growth rate in dividends.

  b. Calculate the expected dividend yield.

  c. Assuming that the calculated growth rate is expected to continue, you can add the dividend yield to the expected growth rate to determine the expected total rate of return. What is this stock's expected total rate of return?

Yields on Bonds

10-31 On January 2, 2009, a Sunny Communications $1,000 face value, 6-year bond sold for $889. Investors who bought this particular bond will be paid interest equal to $40 every 6 months. Market interest rates did not change until December 31, 2009, when they decreased significantly. On January 2, 2010, the price of the bond was $1,042.

  a. What was the bond's yield to maturity on January 2, 2009?

  b. What was the bond's yield to maturity on January 2, 2010?

  c. What return did investors who bought the bond on January 2, 2009, earn if they sold the bond 1 year later? What were the capital gains yield and the current yield on the bond in 2009?

10-32 Using the information provided in 10-30, compute the value of the bond on January 2, 2011, assuming interest rates do not change. What return would investors earn in 2010? What would be the capital gains yield and the current yield?

Valuation/Yields

10-33 The bonds of the Lange Corporation are perpetuities with a 10 percent coupon. Bonds of this type currently yield 8 percent, and their par value is $1,000.

Perpetual Bond Valuation

  a. What is the price of the Lange bonds?

  b. Suppose interest rate levels rise to the point where such bonds now yield 12 percent. What would be the price of the Lange bonds?

  c. At what price would the Lange bonds sell if the yield on them was 10 percent?

  d. How would your answers to parts (a), (b), and (c) change if the bonds were not perpetuities but rather had a maturity of 20 years?

10-34 In January 2006, the yield on AAA-rated corporate bonds averaged approximately 5 percent; 1 year later, the yield on these same bonds had climbed to about 6 percent because the Federal Reserve increased interest rates during the year. Assume that IBM issued a 10-year, 5 percent coupon bond on January 1, 2006. On the same date, Microsoft issued a 20-year, 5 percent coupon bond. Both bonds pay interest *annually*. Also assume that the market rate on similar risk bonds was 5 percent at the time that the bonds were issued.

Bond Valuation, Capital Gains, and Current Yield

  a. Compute the market value of each bond at the time of issue.

  b. Compute the market value of each bond 1 year after issue if the market yield for similar risk bonds was 6 percent on January 1, 2007.

  c. Compute the 2006 capital gains yield for each bond.

  d. Compute the current yield for each bond in 2006.

  e. Compute the total return that each bond would have generated for investors in 2006.

  f. If you invested in bonds at the beginning of 2006, would you have been better off if you held long-term or short-term bonds? Explain.

  g. Assume that interest rates stabilize at the January 2006 rate of 6 percent, then they stay at this level indefinitely. What would be the price of each bond on January 1, 2012, after 6 years have passed? Describe what should happen to the prices of these bonds as they approach their maturities.

10-35 Investors require a 15 percent rate of return on Goulet Company's stock ($r_s = 15\%$).

Constant Growth Stock Valuation

  a. What will be Goulet's stock value if the previous dividend was $D_0 = \$2$ and if investors expect dividends to grow at a constant compound annual rate of (1) −5 percent, (2) 0 percent, (3) 5 percent, and (4) 10 percent?

  b. Using data from part (a), calculate the value for Goulet's stock if the required rate of return is 15 percent and the expected growth rate is (1) 15 percent or (2) 20 percent. Are these results reasonable? Explain.

  c. Is it reasonable to expect that a constant growth stock would have $g > r_s$?

10-36 The stock of Gerlunice Company has a rate of return equal to 15.5 percent.

Constant Growth Stock Valuation

  a. If the dividend expected during the coming year, $\hat{D}_1$, is $2.25, and if g remains constant at 5 percent, at what price should Gerlunice's stock sell?

b. Suppose that the Federal Reserve increases the money supply, causing the risk-free rate to drop. The return expected for investing in Gerlunice will fall to 13.5 percent. How should this change affect the price of the stock?

c. In addition to the change in part (b), suppose that investors' risk aversion declines; this fact, combined with the decline in r_{RF}, causes r_s for Gerlunice's stock to fall to 12 percent. At what price would the stock sell?

d. Now suppose Gerlunice undergoes a change in management. The new group institutes policies that increase the expected constant growth rate to 6 percent. Also, the new management stabilizes sales and profits, which causes the return demanded by investors to decline to 11.6 percent. After all these changes, what is the firm's new equilibrium price?

Nonconstant Growth Stock Valuation

10-37 It is now January 1, 2010. Swink Electric, Inc., has just developed a solar panel capable of generating 200 percent more electricity than any solar panel currently on the market. As a result, Swink is expected to experience a 15 percent annual growth rate for the next 5 years. When the 5-year period ends, other firms will have developed comparable technology, and Swink's growth rate will slow to 5 percent per year indefinitely. Stockholders require a return of 12 percent on Swink's stock. The firm's most recent annual dividend (D_0), which was paid yesterday, was $1.75 per share.

a. Calculate Swink's expected dividends for 2010, 2011, 2012, 2013, and 2014.

b. Calculate the value of the stock today. Proceed by finding the present value of the dividends expected at the end of 2010, 2011, 2012, 2013, and 2014, plus the present value of the stock price that should apply at the end of 2014. You can find the year-end 2014 stock price by using the constant growth equation (Equation 10-10). To find the December 31, 2014, price, use the dividend expected in 2015, which is 5 percent greater than the 2014 dividend.

c. Calculate the dividend yield, $\hat{D}_1/P_0$, the capital gains yield expected in 2010, and the expected total return (dividend yield plus capital gains yield) for 2010. (Assume that $\hat{P}_0 = P_0$, and recognize that the capital gains yield is equal to the total return minus the dividend yield.) Calculate these same three yields for 2014.

d. Suppose your boss believes that Swink's annual growth rate will be only 12 percent during the next 5 years and that the firm's normal growth rate will be only 4 percent. Without doing any calculations, explain the general effect that these growth-rate changes would have on the price of Swink's stock.

e. Suppose your boss also regards Swink as being quite risky and believes that the required rate of return for this firm should be 14 percent, not 12 percent. Without doing any calculations, explain how the higher required rate of return would affect the price of the stock, its capital gains yield, and its dividend yield.

Supernormal Growth Stock Valuation

10-38 Tanner Technologies Corporation (TTC) has been growing at a rate of 20 percent per year in recent years. This same growth rate is expected to last for another 2 years.

a. If $D_0 = \$1.60$, $r_s = 10\%$, and $g_{norm} = 6\%$, what is TTC's stock worth today? What are its expected dividend yield and capital gains yield at this time?

b. Assume that TTC's period of supernormal growth lasts another 5 years rather than 2 years. Without doing any calculations, explain how this change would affect its price, dividend yield, and capital gains yield.

c. What will be TTC's dividend yield and capital gains yield once its period of supernormal growth ends? (*Hint:* These values will be the same regardless of whether you examine the case of 2 or 5 years of supernormal growth; the calculations are easy.)

d. Of what interest to investors is the changing relationship between dividend yield and capital gains yield over time?

Integrative Problems

10-39 Robert Campbell and Carol Morris are senior vice presidents of the Mutual of Chicago Insurance Company. They are co-directors of the company's pension fund management division, with Campbell having responsibility for fixed income securities (primarily bonds) and Morris responsible for equity investments. A major new client, the California League of Cities, has requested that Mutual of Chicago present an investment seminar to the mayors of the represented cities. Campbell and Morris, who will make the actual presentation, have asked you to help them by answering the following questions.

Bond Valuation

a. What are the key features of a bond?

b. How do you determine the value of any asset whose value is based on expected future cash flows?

c. How do you determine the value of a bond? What is the value of a 1-year, $1,000 par value bond with a 10 percent annual coupon if its required rate of return is 10 percent? What is the value of a similar 10-year bond?

d. **(1)** What would be the value of the 10-year bond described in part (c) if, just after it had been issued, the expected inflation rate rose by three percentage points, causing investors to require a 13 percent return? Is the security now a discount bond or a premium bond?

   (2) What would happen to the bond's value if inflation fell, and r_d declined to 7 percent? Would it now be a premium bond or a discount bond?

   (3) What would happen to the value of the 10-year bond over time if the required rate of return remained at (i) 13 percent or (ii) remained at 7 percent?

e. **(1)** What is the yield to maturity on a 10-year, 9 percent annual coupon, $1,000 par value bond that sells for $887.00? That sells for $1,134.20? What does the fact that a bond sells at a discount or at a premium tell you about the relationship between r_d and the bond's coupon rate?

   (2) What is the current yield, the capital gains yield, and the total return in each case in the preceding question?

f. Suppose that the bond described in part (e) is callable in 5 years at a call price equal to $1,090. What is the yield to call (YTC) on the bond if its market value is $887? What is the YTC on the same bond if its current market price is $1,134.20?

g. What is *interest rate price risk?* Which bond in part (c) has more interest rate price risk, the 1-year bond or the 10-year bond?

h. What is *interest reinvestment rate risk?* Which bond in part (c) has more interest rate reinvestment rate risk, assuming a 10-year investment horizon?

i. Redo parts (c) and (d), assuming that the bonds have semiannual rather than annual coupons.

j. Suppose you could buy, for $1,000, either a 10 percent, 10-year, annual payment bond or a 10 percent, 10-year, semiannual payment bond. Both bonds are equally risky. Which would you prefer? If $1,000 is the proper price for the semiannual bond, what is the proper price for the annual payment bond?

k. What is the value of a perpetual bond with an annual coupon of $100 if its required rate of return is 10 percent? 13 percent? 7 percent? Assess the following statement: "Because perpetual bonds match an infinite investment horizon, they have little interest rate price risk."

Stock Valuation   **10-40** A major new client has requested that Mutual of Chicago present an investment seminar to illustrate the stock valuation process. As a result, Campbell and Morris have asked you to analyze the Bon Temps Company, an employment agency that supplies word processor operators and computer programmers to businesses with temporarily heavy workloads. You are to answer the following questions:

a. What is the difference between common stock and preferred stock? What are some of the characteristics of each type of stock?

b. What is the difference between a publicly held company and a privately held company? How can the two types of companies be identified?

c. What is classified stock? When "going public, why might a small company designate some stock currently outstanding as "founders' shares"?

d. **(1)** Write a formula that can be used to value any stock, regardless of its dividend pattern.

   (2) What is a constant growth stock? How do you value a constant growth stock?

   (3) What happens if the growth is constant, and $g > r_s$? Will many stocks have $g > r_s$?

e. Bon Temps has an issue of preferred stock outstanding that pays stockholders a dividend equal to $10 each year. If the appropriate required rate of return for this stock is 8 percent, what is its market value?

f. Assume that Bon Temps is a constant growth company whose last dividend (D_0, which was paid yesterday) was $2 and whose dividend is expected to grow indefinitely at a 6 percent rate. The appropriate rate of return for Bon Temps' stock is 16 percent.

   (1) What is the firm's expected dividend stream over the next 3 years?

   (2) What is the firm's current stock price?

   (3) What is the stock's expected value 1 year from now?

   (4) What are the expected dividend yield, the capital gains yield, and the total return during the first year?

g. Assume that Bon Temps' stock is currently selling at $21.20. What is the expected rate of return on the stock?

h. What would the stock price be if its dividends were expected to have zero growth?

i. Assume that Bon Temps is expected to experience supernormal growth of 30 percent for the next 3 years, then to return to its long-run constant growth rate of 6 percent. What is the stock's value under these conditions? What are its expected dividend yield and its capital gains yield in Year 1? In Year 4?

j. Suppose Bon Temps is expected to experience zero growth during the first 3 years and then to resume its steady-state growth of 6 percent in the fourth year. What is the stock's value now? What are its expected dividend yield and its capital gains yield in Year 1? In Year 4?

k. Assume that Bon Temps' earnings and dividends are expected to decline by a constant 6 percent per year—that is, $g = 26\%$. Why might someone be willing to buy such a stock, and at what price should it sell? What would be the dividend yield and capital gains yield in each year?

COMPUTER-RELATED PROBLEM

Work the problem in this section only if you are using the computer problem spreadsheet.

10-41 Use the model in File C10 to solve this problem.

Nonconstant Growth Stock Valuation

  a. Refer to Problem 10-37. Rework part (d) using the computerized model to determine what Swink's expected dividends and stock price would be under the conditions given.

  b. Suppose your boss regards Swink as being quite risky and believes that the required rate of return should be higher than the 12 percent originally specified. Rework the problem under the conditions given in part (d), except change the required rate of return to (1) 13 percent, (2) 15 percent, and (3) 20 percent to determine the effects of the higher required rates of return on Swink's stock price.

Risk and Rates of Return

CHAPTER 11

A Managerial Perspective

The performance of the major stock markets from 1995 through 1998 can best be described as remarkable—a period that investors would love to repeat again and again. During that 4-year stretch, stocks traded on U.S. stock markets earned an average return greater than 20 percent per year. In 1998, companies such as Microsoft and MCI WorldCom more than doubled in value. The value of some Internet companies, such as America Online, Amazon.com, and Yahoo!, increased by more than 500 percent. Consider the return that you would have earned in 1998 if you had purchased Amazon.com at the beginning of the year for $30.13 and then sold it at the end of the year for $321.25: a 1-year return of 966 percent. On the other hand, if you waited until January 2000 to buy Amazon.com and then held it until the end of the year, you would have lost approximately 80 percent of your investment, because the company's stock decreased significantly during the year. In fact, during 2000, the values of most Internet company stocks declined significantly. Indeed, many Internet companies did not survive the "Internet skepticism" that existed during the year. By comparison, if you had purchased the stock of Enron at the beginning of 2000, your investment would have nearly doubled in value by the end of the year. But, if you still held Enron in mid-2003, the value of your investment would have declined to $0.05 per share, because the

company was in bankruptcy at that time. More recently, if you held either Amazon.com or Apple during 2007, your investment would have grown by more than 130 percent, but if you held either E*Trade Financial or Countrywide Financial you would have lost between 80 percent and 85 percent of your investment.

If you had bet all your money on the stock of a single company, you would have essentially "put all your eggs in one basket" and faced considerable risk. For example, you would have won big if you had chosen to invest in Amazon.com for 1 year either in 1998 or 2002. But you would have lost big if you had chosen to invest in Amazon.com in 2000. Investors who diversified by spreading their investments among many stocks, perhaps through mutual funds, would have earned a return somewhere between the extraordinary increases posted by Amazon.com in 1998 and 2002 and the extraordinary decreases posted by Amazon.com and other Internet companies in 2000. Large "baskets" of such diversified investments would have earned returns fairly close to the average of the stock markets.

Investing is risky! Although the stock markets performed well from 1995 through 1998, they have also gone through periods characterized by decreasing prices or negative average returns. For instance, in 1990, 1994, and 2000, the average stock listed on the New York

Stock Exchange decreased in value by 7.5 percent, 3.1 percent, and 5.9 percent, respectively. More recently, at the beginning of 2008, the Dow Jones Industrial Average (DJIA) was 13,265; but 6 months later the DJIA was 10,990, which means that stocks on average decreased in value by 17 percent. Because it was a presidential election year and there was much trepidation about the health of the economy, 2008 promised to take investors on a wild roller coaster ride! What risk!

During the first 6 months of 2008 when we write this book, we cannot predict what will happen in the financial markets. At this time, many so-called market pundits disagree as to which direction the market will move both prior to and following the November presidential elections. We do know, however, that stock prices will change, because the stock market is risky. When you read this book, the market could be trending upward (referred to as a "bull" market), or it could be trending downward (referred to as a "bear" market). Whatever the case, as times change, investment strategies and portfolio mixes need to be changed to meet new conditions. For this reason, you need to understand the basic concepts of risk and return and to recognize how diversification affects investment decisions. As you will discover, investors can create portfolios of securities to reduce risk without reducing the average return on their investments. After reading this chapter, you should have a better understanding of how risk affects investment returns and how to evaluate risk when selecting investments such as those described here.

CHAPTER PRINCIPLES
–The Questions

After reading this chapter, you should be able to answer the following questions:

- What does it mean to take risk when investing?
- How are the risk and return of an investment measured? How are the risk and return of an investment related?
- For what type of risk is an average investor rewarded?
- How can investors reduce risk?
- What actions do investors take when the return they require to purchase an investment is different from the return the investment is expected to produce?

In this chapter we take an in-depth look at how investment risk should be measured and how it affects assets' values and rates of return. Recall that in Chapter 5, when we examined the determinants of interest rates, we defined the real risk-free rate, r^*, to be the rate of interest on a risk-free security in the absence of inflation. The actual interest rate on a particular debt security was shown to be equal to the real risk-free rate plus several premiums that reflect both inflation and the riskiness of the security in question. In this chapter we define the term *risk* more precisely in terms of how it relates to investments, we examine procedures used to measure risk, and we discuss the relationship between risk and return. Both investors and financial managers should understand these concepts and use them when considering investment decisions, whether the decisions concern financial assets or real assets.

We will demonstrate that each investment—each stock, bond, or physical asset—is associated with two types of risk: diversifiable risk and nondiversifiable risk. The sum of these two components is the investment's total risk. Diversifiable risk is not important to rational, informed investors because its effects can be diversified away. The really significant risk is nondiversifiable risk; this risk is bad in the sense that it cannot be eliminated, and if you invest in anything other than riskless assets, such as short-term Treasury bills, you will be exposed to it. In the balance of the chapter, we will describe these risk concepts and consider how risk enters into the investment decision-making process.

DEFINING AND MEASURING RISK

Most dictionaries define *risk* as "peril," "exposure to loss or injury," "the possibility of loss," or some combination of these descriptions.[1] As these definitions suggest, *risk* refers to the chance that some unfavorable event will occur. If you engage in sky-diving, you are taking a chance with your life because skydiving is risky. If you bet on the horses, you risk losing your money. If you invest in speculative stocks (or, really, *any* stock), you are taking a risk in the hope of receiving an appreciable return.

Most people view risk in the manner just described—as a chance of loss. In reality, however, *risk occurs any time we cannot be certain about the outcome of a particular activity or event*—that is, when we are not sure what will happen in the future. Consequently, risk results from the fact that an action such as investing can produce *more than one possible outcome in the future*. When multiple outcomes are possible, some of the possible outcomes are considered "good" and some of the possible outcomes are considered "bad."

To illustrate the riskiness of financial assets, suppose you have a large amount of money to invest for 1 year. You could buy a Treasury security that has an expected return equal to 5 percent. This investment's anticipated rate of return can be determined quite precisely, because the chance of the government defaulting on Treasury securities is negligible; the outcome is essentially guaranteed, which means that the security is a risk-free investment.

Alternatively, you could buy the common stock of a newly formed company that has developed technology that can be used to extract petroleum from the mountains in South America without defacing the landscape and without harming the ecology. The technology has yet to be proved economically feasible, so the returns that the common stockholders will receive in the future remain uncertain. Experts who have analyzed the common stock of the company have determined that the *expected*, or average long-run, return for such an investment is 30 percent. Each year, the investment could yield a positive return as high as 900 percent. Of course, there also is the possibility that the company might not survive, in which case the entire investment will be lost and the return will be −100 percent. The return that investors receive each year cannot be determined precisely because more than one outcome is possible; this stock is a risky investment. Because there is a significant danger of earning considerably less than the expected return, investors probably would consider the stock to be quite risky. There is also a very good chance that the actual return will be greater than expected, which, of course, is an outcome you would gladly accept. But, this possibility could not exist if the stock did not have risk.

Thus, when we think of investment risk, along with the chance of receiving less than expected, we should consider the chance of receiving more than expected. If we consider investment risk from this perspective, then we can define **risk** as the chance of receiving an actual return other than expected. This definition simply means that there is *variability in the returns* or outcomes from the investment. Therefore, investment risk can be measured by the variability of all the investment's returns, both "good" and "bad."

Investment risk, then, is related to the possibility of earning an actual return other than the expected one. *The greater the variability of the possible outcomes, the riskier the investment.* We can define risk more precisely, however, and it is useful to do so.

risk
The chance that an outcome other than the expected one will occur.

---

[1]For example, see *Merriam Webster's Collegiate Dictionary*, 10th Edition, 1996 (Merriam-Webster, Incorporated), page 1011.

Probability Distributions

An event's *probability* is defined as the chance that the event will occur. For example, a weather forecaster might state, "There is a 40 percent chance of rain today and a 60 percent chance that it will not rain." If all possible events, or outcomes, are listed, and if a probability is assigned to each event, the listing is called a **probability distribution.** For our weather forecast, we could set up the following simple probability distribution:

probability distribution
A listing of all possible outcomes, or events, with a probability (chance of occurrence) assigned to each outcome.

Outcome	Probability	
Rain	0.40 =	40%
No rain	0.60 =	60
	1.00	100%

Here the possible outcomes are listed in the left column, and the probabilities of these outcomes, expressed both as decimals and as percentages, are given in the right column. Notice that the probabilities must sum to 1.0, or 100 percent.

Probabilities can also be assigned to the possible outcomes (or returns) from an investment. If you buy a bond, you expect to receive interest on it; those interest payments will provide you with a rate of return on your investment. This investment has two possible outcomes: (1) the issuer makes the interest payments or (2) the issuer fails to make the interest payments. The higher the probability of default on the interest payments, the riskier the bond; the higher the risk, the higher the rate of return you would require to invest in the bond. If you invest in a stock instead of buying a bond, you will again expect to earn a return on your money. Again, the riskier the stock—that is, the greater the variability of the possible payoffs—the higher the stock's expected return must be to persuade you to invest in it.

With this idea in mind, consider the possible rates of return (dividend yield plus capital gain or loss) that you might earn next year on a $10,000 investment in the stock of either Martin Products, Inc., or U.S. Electric. Martin manufactures and distributes equipment for the data transmission industry. Because its sales are cyclical, the firm's profits rise and fall with the business cycle. Furthermore, its market is extremely competitive, and some new company could develop better products that could force Martin into bankruptcy. U.S. Electric, on the other hand, supplies electricity, which is considered an essential service. Because it has city franchises that protect it from competition, this firm's sales and profits are relatively stable and predictable.

Table 11-1 shows the rate-of-return probability distributions for these two companies. As shown in the table, there is a 20 percent chance of a boom, in which

TABLE 11-1   Probability Distributions for Martin Products and U.S. Electric

State of the Economy	Probability of This State Occurring	Rate of Return on Stock if Economic State Occurs	
		Martin Products	U.S. Electric
Boom	0.2	110%	20%
Normal	0.5	22	16
Recession	0.3	−60	10
	1.0		

case both companies will have high earnings, pay high dividends, and enjoy capital gains. There is a 50 percent probability that the two companies will operate in a normal economy and offer moderate returns. There is a 30 percent probability of a recession, which will mean low earnings and dividends as well as potential capital losses. Notice, however, that Martin's rate of return could vary far more dramatically than that of U.S. Electric. There is a fairly high probability that the value of Martin's stock will vary substantially, possibly resulting in a loss of 60 percent or a gain of 110 percent; conversely, there is no chance of a loss for U.S. Electric, and its maximum gain is 20 percent.[2]

Self-Test Questions

What does "investment risk" mean?

Set up illustrative probability distributions for (1) a bond investment and (2) a stock investment.

EXPECTED RATE OF RETURN

Table 11-1 provides the probability distributions showing the possible outcomes for investing in Martin Products and U.S. Electric. We can see that the most likely outcome is for the economy to be normal, in which case Martin will return 22 percent and U.S. Electric will return 16 percent. Other outcomes are also possible, however, so we need to summarize the information contained in the probability distributions into a single measure that considers all these possible outcomes. That measure is called the expected value, or *expected rate of return*, for the investments.

Simply stated, the **expected value (return)** is the *weighted average* of the outcomes, where the weights we use are the probabilities that the possible returns will occur. Table 11-2 shows how we compute the expected rates of return for Martin Products and U.S. Electric. We multiply each possible outcome by the

expected value (return)
The rate of return expected to be realized from an investment; the mean value of the probability distribution of possible results.

TABLE 11-2   Calculation of Expected Rates of Return: Martin Products and U.S. Electric

		Martin Products		**U.S. Electric**	
State of the Economy (1)	Probability of This State Occurring (2)	Return if This State Occurs (3)	Product: (2) × (3) = (4)	Return if This State Occurs (5)	Product: (2) × (5) = (6)
Boom	0.2	110%	22%	20%	4%
Normal	0.5	22	11	16	8
Recession	0.3	−60	−18	10	3
	1.0		$\hat{r}_{Martin} = 15\%$		$\hat{r}_{US} = 15\%$

---

[2]It is, of course, completely unrealistic to think that any stock has no chance of a loss. Only in hypothetical examples could this situation occur.

probability that it will occur, and then sum the results. We designate the expected rate of return, r̂, which is termed *r-hat*.[3] We insert the "hat" over the r to indicate that this return is uncertain because we do not know when each of the possible outcomes will occur in the future. For example, Martin products will return its stockholders 110 percent when the economy is booming, but we do not know in which year(s) the economy will be booming.

The expected rate of return can be calculated using the following equation:

 **11-1**

$$\text{Expected rate of return} = \hat{r} = Pr_1r_1 + Pr_2r_2 + \cdots + Pr_nr_n$$

$$= \sum_{i=1}^{n} Pr_ir_i$$

Here, r_i is the ith possible outcome, Pr_i is the probability that the ith outcome will occur, and n is the number of possible outcomes. Thus, r̂ is a weighted average of the possible outcomes (the r_i values), with each outcome's weight being its probability of occurrence. Using the data for Martin Products, we compute its expected rate of return as follows:

$$\hat{r} = Pr_1(r_1) + Pr_2(r_2) + Pr_3(r_3)$$
$$= 0.2(110\%) + 0.5(22\%) + 0.3(-60\%) = 15.0\%$$

Notice that the expected rate of return does not equal any of the possible payoffs for Martin Products given in Table 11-1. Stated simply, the expected rate of return represents the average payoff that investors will receive from Martin Products if the probability distribution given in Table 11-1 remains the same over a long period of time. If this probability distribution is correct, then 20 percent of the time the future economic condition will be termed a boom, and investors will earn a 110 percent rate of return; 50 percent of the time the economy should be normal, and the investment payoff will be 22 percent; and 30 percent of the time the economy should be in a recession, and the payoff will be a loss equal to 60 percent. On average, then, Martin Products' investors should earn 15 percent over some period of time, say, 10 years.

We can graph the rates of return to obtain a picture of the variability of possible outcomes, as shown in Figure 11-1. The height of each bar in the figure indicates the probability that a given outcome will occur. The probable returns for Martin Products range from +110 percent to −60 percent, with an expected return of 15 percent. The expected return for U.S. Electric is also 15 percent, but its range is much narrower.

Continuous versus Discrete Probability Distributions

So far, we have assumed that only three states of the economy can exist: recession, normal, and boom. Under these conditions, the probability distributions given in Table 11-1 are called **discrete** because the number of outcomes is limited, or finite. In reality, of course, the state of the economy could actually range from a deep depression to a fantastic boom, with an unlimited number of possible states in between. Suppose we had the time and patience to assign a probability to each possible state of the economy (with the sum of the probabilities still equaling 1.0) and to assign a rate of return to each stock for each state of the economy.

discrete probability distribution
The number of possible outcomes is limited, or finite.

---

[3]In Chapter 10 we used r_d to signify the return on a debt instrument and we used r_s to signify the return on a stock. In this section, however, we discuss only returns on stocks; thus, the subscript "s" is unnecessary, and we use the term r̂ rather than $\hat{r}_s$ to represent the expected return on a stock.

FIGURE 11-1   Probability Distribution of Martin Products' and U.S. Electric's Rates of Return

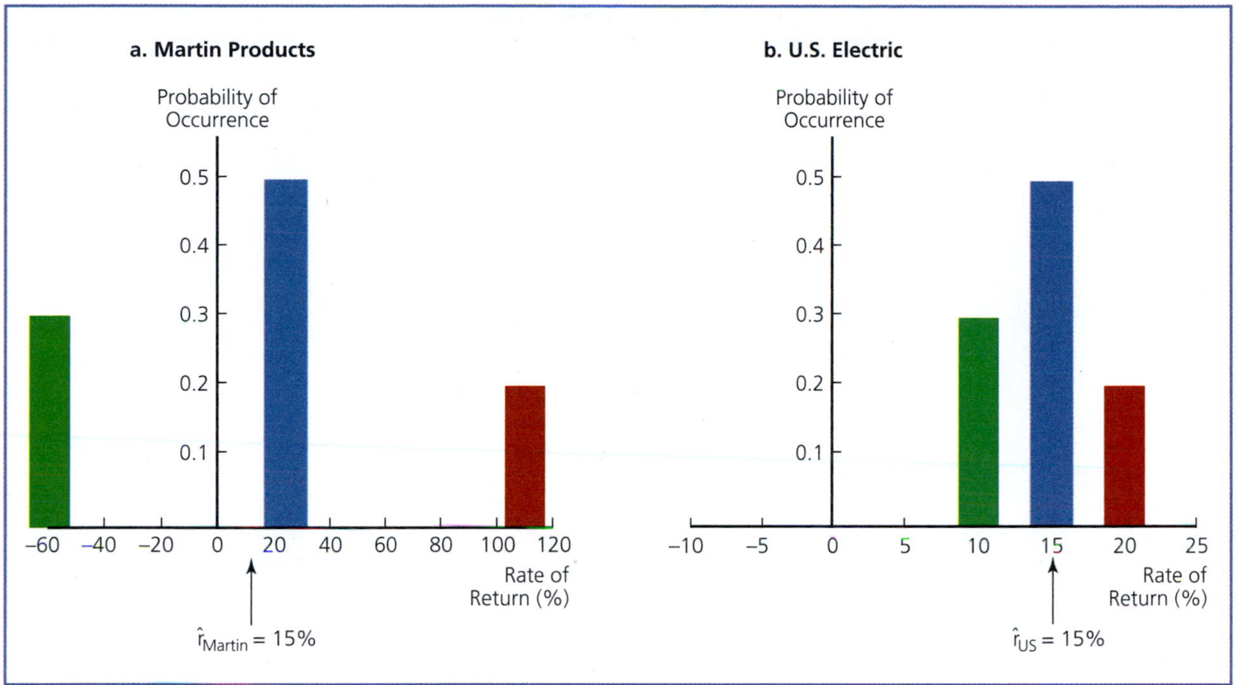

We would then have a table similar to Table 11-1, except that it would include many more entries in each column. We could use this table to calculate the expected rates of return as described previously, and we could approximate the probabilities and outcomes by constructing continuous curves such as those presented in Figure 11-2. In this figure, we have changed the assumptions so that there is essentially a zero probability that Martin Products' return will be less than −60 percent or more than 110 percent, or that U.S. Electric's return will be less than 10 percent or more than 20 percent. Virtually any return within these limits is possible, however. Such probability distributions are called **continuous,** because the number of possible outcomes is unlimited. For example, U.S. Electric's return could be 10.01 percent, 10.001 percent, and so on.

The *tighter the probability distribution, the less variability* there is and the more likely it is that the actual outcome will approach the expected value. Consequently, under these conditions, it becomes less likely that the actual return will differ dramatically from the expected return. Thus, *the tighter the probability distribution, the lower the risk assigned to a stock.* Because U.S. Electric has a relatively tight probability distribution, its *actual* return is likely to be closer to its 15 percent expected return than is that of Martin Products, which means that U.S. Electric would be considered less risky than Martin Products.

continuous probability distribution
The number of possible outcomes is unlimited, or infinite.

Measuring Total (Stand-Alone) Risk: The Standard Deviation

Because we have defined *risk* as the variability of returns, we can measure it by examining the tightness of the probability distribution associated with the possible outcomes. In general, the width of a probability distribution indicates the amount of scatter, or variability, of the possible outcomes. To be most useful, any measure of risk should have a definite value; thus, we need a measure of the tightness of the probability distribution.

FIGURE 11-2 Continuous Probability Distributions of Martin Products' and U.S. Electric's Rates of Return

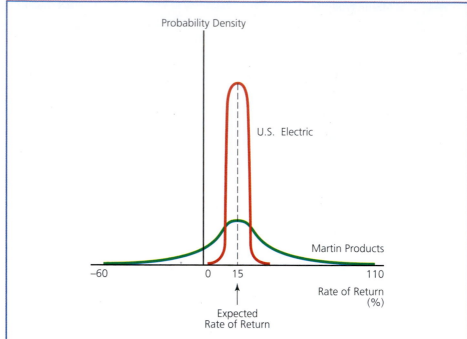

Note: The assumptions regarding the possibilities of various outcomes have been changed from those in Figure 11-1. There, the probability of obtaining exactly 16 percent return for U.S. Electric was 50 percent; here, it is *much smaller,* because there are many possible outcomes instead of just three. With continuous distributions, it is more appropriate to ask what the probability is of obtaining at least some specified rate of return than to ask what the probability is of obtaining exactly that rate. This topic is covered in detail in statistics courses.

standard deviation, σ
A measure of the tightness, or variability, of a set of outcomes.

The measure we use most often is the **standard deviation,** the symbol for which is σ, the Greek letter "sigma." The smaller the standard deviation, the tighter the probability distribution, and, accordingly, the lower the *total* risk associated with the investment. To calculate the standard deviation, we take the following steps, as shown in Table 11-3:

1. Calculate the expected rate of return using Equation 11-1. For Martin, we previously found $\hat{r} = 15\%$.

2. Subtract the expected rate of return, $\hat{r}$, from each possible outcome, r_i, to obtain a set of deviations from $\hat{r}$: Deviation$_i = r_i - \hat{r}$.

   The deviations are shown in Column 3 of Table 11-3.

3. Square each deviation (shown in Column 4), multiply the result by the probability of occurrence for its related outcome (Column 5), and then sum these products to obtain the **variance, σ²,** of the probability distribution, which is shown in Column 6.

variance, σ²
The standard deviation squared.

These three steps are summarized in the following equation:

11-2

$$\text{Variance} = \sigma^2 = (r_1 - \hat{r})^2 Pr_1 + (r_2 - \hat{r})^2 Pr_2 + \cdots + (r_n - \hat{r})^2 Pr_n$$

$$= \sum_{i=1}^{n} (r_i - \hat{r})^2 Pr_i$$

TABLE 11-3   Calculating Martin Products' Standard Deviation

Payoff r_i (1)		Expected Return $\hat{r}$ (2)		Deviation $r_j - \hat{r}$ (1) − (2) = (3)	$(r_j - \hat{r})^2$ = (4)	Probability (5)	$(r_j - \hat{r})^2 Pr_i$ (4) × (5) = (6)
110%	−	15%	=	95	9,025	0.2	9,025 × 0.2 = 1,805.0
22	−	15	=	7	49	0.5	49 × 0.5 = 24.5
−60	−	15	=	−75	5,625	0.3	5,625 × 0.3 = 1,687.5
						Variance = σ^2 =	3,517.0
						Standard deviation = $\sigma = \sqrt{\sigma^2} = \sqrt{3{,}517} = 59.3\%$	

4. Take the square root of the variance to get the standard deviation shown at the bottom of Column 6:

$$\text{Standard deviation} = \sigma = \sqrt{(r_1 - \hat{r})^2 Pr_1 + (r_2 - \hat{r})^2 Pr_2 + \cdots + (r_n - \hat{r})^2 Pr_n}$$

$$= \sqrt{\sum_{i=1}^{n} (r_i - \hat{r})^2 \, Pr_i}$$

As you can see, the standard deviation is a weighted average deviation from the expected value, and it gives an idea of how far above or below the expected value the actual value is likely to be. As shown in Table 11-3, Martin's standard deviation is $\sigma = 59.3\%$. Using these same procedures, we find U.S. Electric's standard deviation to be 3.6 percent. The larger standard deviation for Martin indicates a greater variation of returns for this firm, and hence a greater chance that the actual, or realized, return will differ significantly from the expected return. Consequently, Martin Products would be considered a riskier investment than U.S. Electric according to this measure of risk.

To this point, the example we have used to compute the expected return and standard deviation is based on data that take the form of a known probability distribution. That is, we know or have estimated all of the future outcomes and the chances that these outcomes will occur in a particular situation. In many cases, however, the only information we have available consists of data over some *past period*. For example, suppose we have observed the following returns associated with a common stock:

Year	$\hat{r}$
2007	15%
2008	−5
2009	20
2010	22

We can use this information to *estimate* the risk associated with the stock by estimating standard deviation of returns. The estimated standard deviation can be computed using a series of past, or observed, returns to solve the following formula:

11-4

$$\text{Estimated } \sigma = s = \sqrt{\dfrac{\sum\limits_{t=1}^{n} (\ddot{r}_t - \bar{r})^2}{n - 1}}$$

Here, $\ddot{r}_t$ represents the past realized rate of return in Period t, and $\bar{r}$ ("r bar") is the arithmetic average of the annual returns earned during the last n years. We compute $\bar{r}_t$ as follows:

11-5

$$\bar{r} = \dfrac{\ddot{r}_1 + \ddot{r}_2 + \cdots + \ddot{r}_n}{n} = \dfrac{\sum\limits_{t=1}^{n} \ddot{r}}{n}$$

Continuing with our current example, we would determine the arithmetic average and estimate the value for σ as follows:[4]

$$\bar{r} = \dfrac{15 + (-5) + 20 + 22}{4} = 13.0\%$$

$$\text{Estimated } \sigma = s = \sqrt{\dfrac{(15 - 13)^2 + (-5 - 13)^2 + (20 - 13)^2 + (22 - 13)^2}{4 - 1}}$$

$$= \sqrt{\dfrac{458}{3}} = 12.4\%$$

The historical standard deviation is often used as an estimate of the future standard deviation. Much less often, and generally incorrectly, $\bar{r}_t$ for some past period is used as an estimate of $\hat{r}_t$, the *expected* future return. Because past variability is likely to be repeated, s might be a good estimate of future risk, but it is much less reasonable to expect that the past *level* of return (which could have been as high as +100 percent or as low as −50 percent) is the best expectation of what investors think will happen in the future.

coefficient of variation (CV)
A standardized measure of the risk per unit of return. It is calculated by dividing the standard deviation by the expected return.

Coefficient of Variation (Risk/Return Ratio)

Another useful measure to evaluate risky investments is the **coefficient of variation (CV),** which is the standard deviation divided by the expected return:

11-6

$$\text{Coefficient of variation} = CV = \dfrac{\text{Risk}}{\text{Return}} = \dfrac{\sigma}{\hat{r}}$$

The coefficient of variation shows the risk per unit of return, which provides a more meaningful basis for comparison when the expected returns on two alternatives differ. Because both U.S. Electric and Martin Products have the *same*

---

[4]You should recognize from statistics courses that a sample of four observations is not sufficient to make a good estimate. We use four observations here only to simplify the illustration.

FIGURE 11-3   Comparison of Probability Distributions and Rates of Return for U.S. Electric and Biobotics Corporation

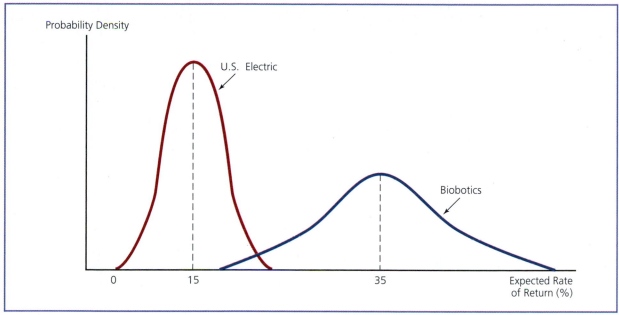

expected return, *it is not necessary to compute the coefficient of variation* to compare the two investments. In this case, most people would prefer to invest in U.S. Electric, because it offers the same expected return with lower risk. The firm with the larger standard deviation, Martin, must have the larger coefficient of variation because the expected returns for the two stocks are equal, but the numerator in Equation 11-6 is greater for Martin. In fact, the coefficient of variation for Martin is 59.3%/15% = 3.95; for U.S. Electric, CV = 3.6%/15% = 0.24. Thus, Martin is more than 16 times riskier than U.S. Electric using this criterion.

The coefficient of variation is more useful when we consider investments that have different expected rates of return *and* different levels of risk. For example, Biobotics Corporation is a biological research and development firm that, according to stock analysts, offers investors an expected rate of return equal to 35 percent with a standard deviation of 7.5 percent. Biobotics offers a higher expected return than U.S. Electric, but it is also riskier. With respect to both risk and return, is Biobotics or U.S. Electric a better investment? If we calculate the coefficient of variation for Biobotics, we find that it equals 7.5%/35% = 0.21, which is slightly less than U.S. Electric's coefficient of variation of 0.24. Thus, Biobotics actually has less risk per unit of return than U.S. Electric, even though its standard deviation is higher. In this case, the additional return offered by Biobotics is more than sufficient to compensate investors for taking on the additional risk.

Figure 11-3 graphs the probability distributions for U.S. Electric and Biobotics. As you can see in the figure, U.S. Electric has the smaller standard deviation, and hence the more peaked probability distribution. As the graph clearly shows, however, the chances of a really high return are much better with Biobotics than with U.S. Electric, because Biobotics' expected return is so high. *Because the coefficient of variation captures the effects of both risk and return, it is a better measure than the standard deviation for evaluating total risk in situations where investments differ with respect to both their amounts of total risk and their expected returns.*

Risk Aversion and Required Returns

Suppose you have worked hard and saved $1 million, which you now plan to invest. You can buy a 10 percent U.S. Treasury note, and at the end of 1 year you will have a sure $1.1 million—that is, your original investment plus $100,000 in interest. Alternatively, you can buy stock in R&D Enterprises. If R&D's research programs are successful, the value of your stock will increase to $2.2 million. Conversely, if the firm's research is a failure, the value of your stock will go to $0, and you will be penniless. You regard R&D's chances of success or failure as being 50-50, so the expected value of the stock investment is 0.5($0) + 0.5($2,200,000) = $1,100,000. Subtracting the $1 million cost of the stock leaves an expected profit of $100,000, or an expected (but risky) 10 percent rate of return:

$$\frac{\text{Expected rate}}{\text{of return}} = \frac{\text{Expected ending value} - \text{Beginning value}}{\text{Beginning value}}$$

$$= \frac{\$1,100,000 - \$1,000,000}{\$1,000,000} = \frac{\$100,000}{\$1,000,000} = 0.10 = 10.0\%$$

In this case, you have a choice between a sure $100,000 profit (representing a 10 percent rate of return) on the Treasury note and a risky expected $100,000 profit (also representing a 10 percent expected rate of return) on the R&D Enterprises stock. Which one would you choose? If you choose the less risky investment, you are risk averse. Most investors are risk averse, and certainly the average investor is risk averse, at least with regard to his or her "serious money." Because this is a well-documented fact, we shall assume **risk aversion** throughout the remainder of the book.

risk aversion
Risk-averse investors require higher rates of return to invest in higher risk securities.

What are the implications of risk aversion for security prices and rates of return? The answer is that, other things held constant, the higher a security's risk, the higher the return investors demand, and thus the less they are willing to pay for the investment. To see how risk aversion affects security prices, we can analyze the situation with U.S. Electric and Martin Products, stocks. Suppose each stock sold for $100 per share and had an expected rate of return of 15 percent. Investors are averse to risk, so they would show a general preference for U.S. Electric because there is less variability in its payoffs (less uncertainty). People with money to invest would bid for U.S. Electric stock rather than Martin stock, and Martin's stockholders would start selling their stock and using the money to buy U.S. Electric stock. Buying pressure would drive up the price of U.S. Electric's stock, and selling pressure would simultaneously cause Martin's price to decline. These price changes, in turn, would alter the expected rates of return on the two securities. Suppose, for example, that the price of U.S. Electric stock was bid up from $100 to $125, whereas the price of Martin's stock declined from $100 to $75. This development would cause U.S. Electric's expected return to fall to 12 percent, whereas Martin's expected return would rise to 20 percent. The difference in returns, 20% − 10% = 8%, is a **risk premium (RP).** In this case, the risk premium represents the compensation that investors require for assuming the *additional* risk of investing in Martin's stock.

risk premium (RP)
The portion of the expected return that can be attributed to the additional risk of an investment. It is the difference between the expected rate of return on a given risky asset and the expected rate of return on a less risky asset.

This example demonstrates a very important principle: in a market dominated by risk-averse investors, *riskier securities must have higher expected returns*, as estimated by the average investor, than less risky securities. If this situation does not hold, investors will buy and sell investments and prices will continue to change until the higher risk investments have higher expected returns than the lower risk investments. Figure 11-4 illustrates this relationship. We will consider the question of how much higher the returns on risky securities must be later in the chapter, after we examine how diversification affects the way risk should be measured.

FIGURE 11-4   Risk/Return Relationship

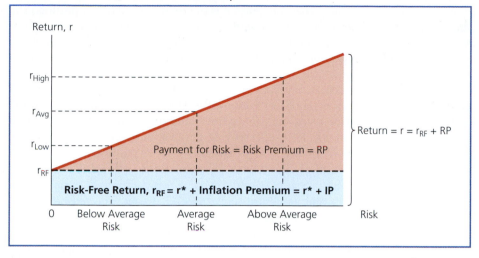

Self-Test Questions

Which of the two stocks graphed in Figure 11-2 is less risky? Why?

How do you calculate the standard deviation associated with an investment? Why is the standard deviation used as a measure of total, or stand-alone, risk?

Which is a better measure of *total* risk: the standard deviation or the coefficient of variation? Explain.

What is meant by the following statement: "Most investors are risk averse"? How does risk aversion affect relative rates of return?

Suppose that you own a stock that provided returns equal to 5 percent, 8 percent, −4 percent, and 15 percent during the past 4 years. What is the average annual return and standard deviation of the stock?   (Answer: $\bar{r} = 6\%$, $s = 7.9\%$)

PORTFOLIO RISK—HOLDING COMBINATIONS OF ASSETS

In the preceding section, we considered the riskiness of investments held in isolation—that is, the *total* risk of an investment if it is held by itself. Now we analyze the riskiness of investments held in portfolios.[5] As we shall see, holding an investment—whether a stock, bond, or other asset—as part of a portfolio generally is less risky than holding the same investment all by itself. In fact, most financial assets are not held in isolation, but rather as parts of portfolios. Banks, pension funds, insurance companies, mutual funds, and other financial institutions are required by law to hold diversified portfolios. Even individual investors—at least those whose security holdings constitute a significant part of their total wealth—generally hold stock portfolios rather than the stock of only one

---

[5]A *portfolio* is a collection of investment securities or assets. If you owned some General Motors stock, some ExxonMobil stock, and some IBM stock, you would be holding a three-stock portfolio. For the reasons set forth in this section, the majority of all stocks are held as parts of portfolios.

firm. From an investor's standpoint, then, the fact that a particular stock goes up or down is not very important. What is important is the return on his or her portfolio and the portfolio's risk. Logically, *the risk and return characteristics of an investment should not be evaluated in isolation; instead, the risk and return of an individual security should be analyzed in terms of how that security affects the risk and return of the portfolio in which it is held.*

To illustrate, consider an investment in Payco American, a collection agency company that operates several offices nationwide. The company is not well known, its stock is not very liquid, its earnings have fluctuated quite a bit in the past, and it doesn't even pay a dividend. This suggests that Payco is risky and that its required rate of return, r, should be relatively high. Even so, Payco's r always has been quite low relative to the rates of return offered by most firms with similar risk. This information indicates that investors regard Payco as being a low-risk company despite its uncertain profits and its nonexistent dividend stream. The reason for this somewhat counterintuitive fact relates to diversification and its effect on risk. Payco's stock price rises during recessions, whereas the prices of other stocks tend to decline when the economy slumps. Therefore, holding Payco in a portfolio of "normal" stocks tends to stabilize returns on the entire portfolio.

expected return on a portfolio, $\hat{r}_p$
The weighted average expected return on stocks held in a portfolio.

Portfolio Returns

The **expected return on a portfolio, $\hat{r}_p$,** is simply the weighted average of the expected returns on the individual stocks in the portfolio, with each weight being the proportion of the total portfolio invested in each stock:

11-7

$$\text{Portfolio return} = \hat{r}_p = w_1\hat{r}_1 + w_2\hat{r}_2 + \cdots + w_N\hat{r}_N$$

$$= \sum_{j=1}^{N} w_j\hat{r}_j$$

Here, the $\hat{r}_j$ values are the expected returns on the individual stocks, the w_j values are the weights, and the portfolio includes N stocks. Note two points: (1) w_j is the proportion of the portfolio's dollar value invested in Stock j, which is equal to the value of the investment in Stock j divided by the total value of the portfolio, and (2) the w_js must sum to 1.0.

Suppose security analysts estimate that the following returns could be expected on four large companies:

Company	Expected Return, $\hat{r}$
AT&T	8%
Citigroup	13
General Electric	19
Microsoft	16

If we formed a $100,000 portfolio, investing $25,000 in each of these four stocks, our expected portfolio return would be 14.0 percent:

$$\hat{r}_p = w_{ATT}\hat{r}_{ATT} + w_{citi}\hat{r}_{citi} + w_{GE}\hat{r}_{GE} + w_{Micro}\hat{r}_{Micro}$$
$$= 0.25(8\%) + 0.25(13\%) + 0.25(19\%) + 0.25(16\%) = 14.0\%$$

Of course, after the fact and 1 year later, the actual **realized rates of return, r̈,** on the individual stocks will almost certainly differ from their expected values, so r̈$_p$ will be somewhat different from r̂$_p = 14\%$. For example, Microsoft's stock might double in price and provide a return of $+100$ percent, whereas General Electric's stock might have a terrible year, see its price fall sharply, and provide a return of -75 percent. Note, however, that those two events would somewhat offset each other, so the portfolio's return might still approach its expected return, even though the individual stocks' actual returns were far from their expected returns.

realized rate of return, r̈
The return that is actually earned. The actual return (r̈) usually differs from the expected return (r̂).

Portfolio Risk

As we just saw, the expected return of a portfolio is simply a weighted average of the expected returns of the individual stocks in the portfolio. Unlike returns, the riskiness of a portfolio (σ_P) generally is *not* a weighted average of the standard deviations of the individual securities in the portfolio. Instead, the portfolio's risk usually is *smaller* than the weighted average of the individual stocks' standard deviations. In fact, it is theoretically possible to combine two stocks that by themselves are quite risky as measured by their standard deviations and form a completely riskless, or risk-free, portfolio—that is, a portfolio with $\sigma_P = 0$.

To illustrate the effect of combining securities, consider the situation depicted in Figure 11-5. The bottom section of the figure gives data on the rates of return for Stock W and Stock M individually, as well as rates of return for a portfolio invested 50 percent in each stock. The three top graphs show the actual historical returns for each investment from 2005 through 2009, and the lower graphs show the probability distributions of returns, assuming that the future is expected to be like the past. The two stocks would be quite risky if they were held in isolation. When they are combined to form Portfolio WM, however, they are not risky at all. (*Note:* These stocks are called W and M because their returns graphs in Figure 11-5 resemble a W and an M.)

The reason Stocks W and M can be combined to form a riskless portfolio is because their returns move in opposite directions. That is, when W's returns are low, M's returns are high, and vice versa. The relationship between any two variables is called *correlation,* and the **correlation coefficient, ρ,** measures the direction and the strength of the relationship between the variables.[6] In statistical terms, we say that the returns on Stock W and Stock M are perfectly *negatively correlated,* with $\rho = -1.0$.[7]

correlation coefficient, ρ
A measure of the degree of relationship between two variables.

The opposite of perfect negative correlation—that is, $\rho = -1.0$—is perfect positive correlation—that is, $\rho = +1.0$. Returns on two perfectly positively correlated stocks would move up and down together, and a portfolio consisting of two such stocks would be exactly as risky as the individual stocks. This point is illustrated in Figure 11-6, where we see that the portfolio's standard deviation equals that of

---

[6]The *correlation coefficient, ρ,* can range from $+1.0$ (denoting that the two variables move in the same direction with exactly the same degree of synchronization every time movement occurs) to -1.0 (denoting that the variables always move with the same degree of synchronization, but in opposite directions). A correlation coefficient of zero suggests that the two variables are not related to each other—that is, changes in one variable occur *independently* of changes in the other.

[7]Following is the computation of the correlation coefficient that measures the relationship between Stock W and Stock M shown in Figure 11-5. The average return and standard deviation for both stocks are the same: $\bar{r} = 15\%$ and $s = 22.6\%$.

$$\text{Covariance} = \frac{(40-15)(-10-15) + (-10-15)(40-15) + (35-15)(-5-15) + (-5-15)(35-15) + (15-15)(15-15)}{5-1} = -512.5$$

$$\text{Correlation} = \rho = \text{Covariance}/(s_W s_M) = -512.5/[(22.6)(22.6)] = -1.0$$

FIGURE 11-5   Rate of Return Distribution for Two Perfectly Negatively Correlated Stocks ($\rho = -1.0$) and for Portfolio WM

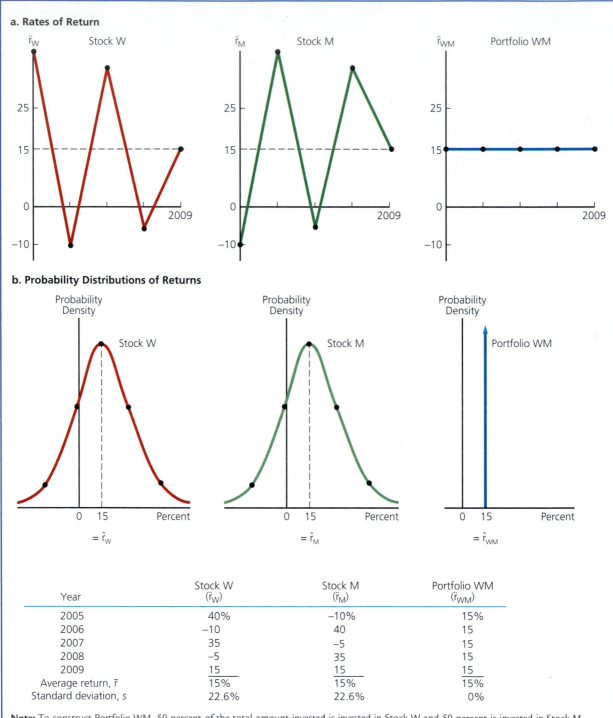

a. Rates of Return

b. Probability Distributions of Returns

Year	Stock W $(\ddot{r}_W)$	Stock M $(\ddot{r}_M)$	Portfolio WM $(\ddot{r}_{WM})$
2005	40%	−10%	15%
2006	−10	40	15
2007	35	−5	15
2008	−5	35	15
2009	15	15	15
Average return, $\bar{r}$	15%	15%	15%
Standard deviation, s	22.6%	22.6%	0%

Note: To construct Portfolio WM, 50 percent of the total amount invested is invested in Stock W and 50 percent is invested in Stock M.

FIGURE 11-6   Rate of Return Distributions for Two Perfectly Positively Correlated Stocks ($\rho = +1.0$) and for Portfolio MM'

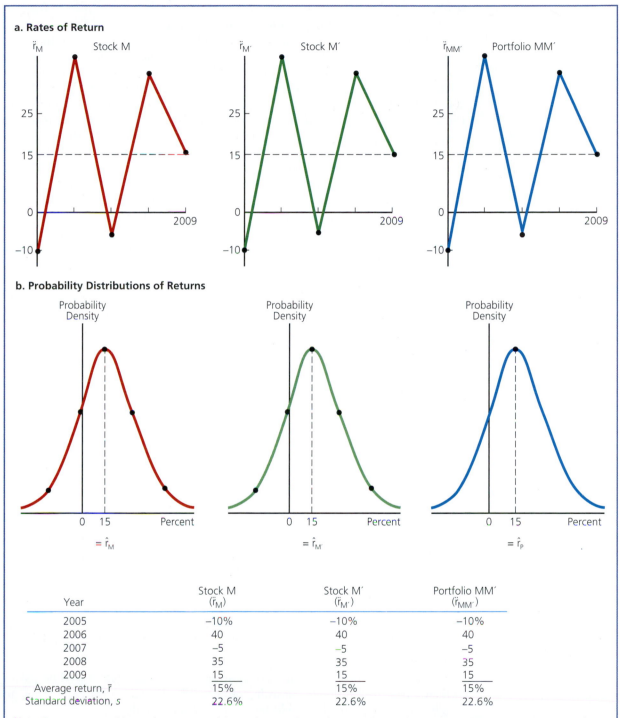

a. Rates of Return

b. Probability Distributions of Returns

Year	Stock M $(\ddot{r}_M)$	Stock M' $(\ddot{r}_{M'})$	Portfolio MM' $(\ddot{r}_{MM'})$
2005	−10%	−10%	−10%
2006	40	40	40
2007	−5	−5	−5
2008	35	35	35
2009	15	15	15
Average return, $\bar{r}$	15%	15%	15%
Standard deviation, s	22.6%	22.6%	22.6%

Note: To construct Portfolio MM', 50 percent of the total amount invested is invested in Stock M and 50 percent is invested in Stock M'.

the individual stocks. As you can see, there is no diversification effect in this case—that is, risk is not reduced if the portfolio contains perfectly positively correlated stocks.

Figures 11-5 and 11-6 demonstrate that when stocks are perfectly negatively correlated ($\rho = -1.0$), all risk can be diversified away; conversely, when stocks are perfectly positively correlated ($\rho = +1.0$), diversification is ineffective. In reality, most stocks are positively correlated, but not perfectly so. On average, the correlation coefficient for the returns on two randomly selected stocks would be about $+0.4$. For most pairs of stocks, ρ would lie in the range of $+0.3$ to $+0.6$. *Under such conditions, combining stocks into portfolios reduces risk but does not eliminate it completely.* Figure 11-7 illustrates this point with two stocks for which the correlation coefficient is $\rho = +0.67$. Both Stock W and Stock Y have the same average return and standard deviation—$\bar{r} = 15\%$ and $s = 22.6\%$. A portfolio that consists of 50 percent of both stocks has an average return equal to 15.0 percent, which is exactly the same as the average return for each of the two stocks. The portfolio's standard deviation, however, is 20.6 percent, which is less than the standard deviation of either stock. Thus, the portfolio's risk is *not* an average of the risks of its individual stocks—diversification has reduced, but not eliminated, risk.

From these two-stock portfolio examples, we have seen that *risk can be completely eliminated in one extreme case ($\rho = -1.0$), whereas diversification does no good in the other extreme case ($\rho = +1.0$). In between these extremes, combining two stocks into a portfolio reduces, but does not eliminate, the riskiness inherent in the individual stocks.*

What would happen if the portfolio included more than two stocks? *As a rule, the riskiness of a portfolio will be reduced as the number of stocks in the portfolio increases.* If we added enough stocks, could we completely eliminate risk? In general, the answer is no, but the extent to which adding stocks to a portfolio reduces its risk depends on the *degree of correlation* among the stocks: *the smaller the positive correlation among stocks included in a portfolio, the lower its total risk.* If we could find a set of stocks whose correlations were negative, we could eliminate all risk. *In the typical case, where the correlations among the individual stocks are positive but less than $+1.0$, some—but not all—risk can be eliminated.*

To test your understanding, consider the following question: Would you expect to find higher correlations between the returns on two companies in the same industry or in different industries? For example, would the correlation of returns on Ford's and General Motors' stocks be higher, or would the correlation coefficient be higher between either Ford or GM and Procter & Gamble (P&G)? How would those correlations affect the risk of portfolios containing them?

Answer: Ford's and GM's returns have a correlation coefficient of approximately 0.9 with each other because both are affected by the factors that affect auto sales. They have a correlation efficient of only 0.4 with the returns of P&G.

Implications: A two-stock portfolio consisting of Ford and GM would be riskier than a two-stock portfolio consisting of either Ford or GM plus P&G. Thus, to minimize risk, portfolios should be diversified *across* industries.

Firm-Specific Risk versus Market Risk

As noted earlier, it is difficult—if not impossible—to find stocks whose expected returns are not positively correlated. Most stocks tend to do well when the national

FIGURE 11-7   Rate of Return Distributions for Two Partially Correlated Stocks ($\rho = +0.67$) and for Portfolio WY

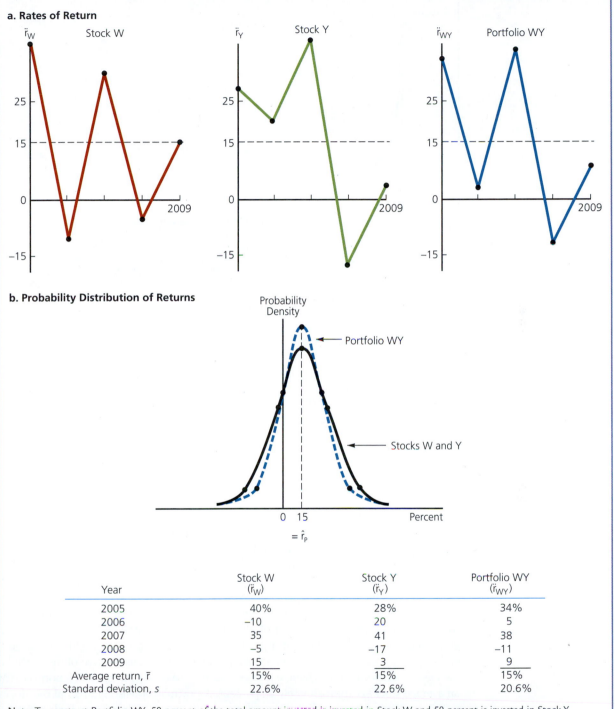

a. Rates of Return

b. Probability Distribution of Returns

Year	Stock W ($\bar{r}_W$)	Stock Y ($\bar{r}_Y$)	Portfolio WY ($\bar{r}_{WY}$)
2005	40%	28%	34%
2006	−10	20	5
2007	35	41	38
2008	−5	−17	−11
2009	15	3	9
Average return, $\bar{r}$	15%	15%	15%
Standard deviation, s	22.6%	22.6%	20.6%

Note: To construct Portfolio WY, 50 percent of the total amount invested is invested in Stock W and 50 percent is invested in Stock Y.

FIGURE 11-8   Effects of Portfolio Size on Portfolio Risk for Average Stocks

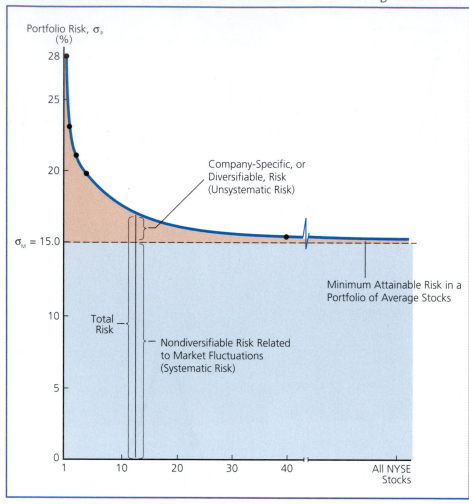

economy is strong and tend to do poorly when it is weak.[8] Thus, even large port-folios end up with substantial amounts of risk, though the risks generally are less than if all of the money was invested in only one stock.

To see more precisely how portfolio size affects portfolio risk, consider Figure 11-8. This figure shows how portfolio risk is affected by forming ever larger portfolios of randomly selected stocks listed on the New York Stock Exchange (NYSE). Standard deviations are plotted for an average one-stock portfolio, for a two-stock portfolio, and so on, up to a portfolio consisting of all common stocks listed on the NYSE. As the graph illustrates, the riskiness of a portfolio consisting of average NYSE stocks gen-erally tends to decline and to approach some minimum limit as the size of the portfolio increases. According to the data, σ_1, the standard deviation of a one-stock portfolio (or an average stock) is approximately 28 percent. A portfolio consisting of all of the stocks in the market, which is called the *market portfolio*, would have a standard deviation, σ_M, of about 15 percent (shown as the horizontal dashed line in Figure 11-8).

---

[8]It is not too difficult to find a few stocks that happened to rise because of a particular set of circumstances in the past while most other stocks were declining. It is much more difficult to find stocks that could logically be *expected* to go up in the future when other stocks are falling. Payco American, the collection agency discussed earlier, is one of those rare exceptions.

Figure 11-8 shows that almost half of the riskiness inherent in an average individual stock can be eliminated if the stock is held as part of a reasonably well diversified portfolio—namely, a portfolio containing 40 or more stocks. Some risk always remains, so it is virtually impossible to diversify away the effects of broad stock market movements that affect almost all stocks.

The part of the risk of a stock that can be eliminated is called *diversifiable,* or *firm-specific,* or *unsystematic, risk*; the part that cannot be eliminated is called *nondiversifiable,* or *market,* or *systematic, risk*. Although the name given to the risk is not especially important, the fact that a large part of the riskiness of any individual stock can be eliminated through portfolio diversification is vitally important.

Firm-specific, or **diversifiable, risk** is caused by such things as lawsuits, loss of key personnel, strikes, successful and unsuccessful marketing programs, the winning and losing of major contracts, and other events that are unique to a particular firm. Because the actual outcomes of these events are essentially random (unpredictable), their effects on a portfolio can be eliminated by diversification—that is, bad events in one firm will be offset by good events in another. **Market, or nondiversifiable, risk,** on the other hand, stems from factors that *systematically* affect all firms, such as war, inflation, recessions, and high interest rates. Because most stocks tend to be affected similarly (negatively) by these *market* conditions, systematic risk cannot be eliminated by portfolio diversification.

We know that investors demand a premium for bearing risk. That is, the riskier a security, the higher the expected return required to persuade investors to buy (or to hold) it. If, however, investors really are primarily concerned with *portfolio risk* rather than the risk of the individual securities in the portfolio, how should we measure the riskiness of an individual stock? The answer is this: *the relevant riskiness of an individual stock is its contribution to the riskiness of a well-diversified portfolio*. In other words, the riskiness of General Electric's stock to a doctor who has a portfolio of 40 stocks or to a trust officer managing a 150-stock portfolio is the contribution that the GE stock makes to the entire portfolio's riskiness. A stock might be quite risky if held by itself, but if much of this total risk can be eliminated through diversification, then its **relevant risk**—that is, its *contribution to the portfolio's risk*—is much smaller than its total, or stand-alone, risk.

A simple example will help clarify this point. Suppose you are offered the chance to flip a coin once. If a head comes up, you win $20,000; if the coin comes up tails, you lose $16,000. This proposition is a good bet: the expected return is $2,000 = 0.5($20,000) + 0.5(−$16,000). It is a highly risky proposition, however, because you have a 50 percent chance of losing $16,000. For this reason, you might refuse to make the bet. Alternatively, suppose you were offered the chance to flip a coin 100 times; you would win $200 for each head but lose $160 for each tail. It is possible that you would flip all heads and win $20,000. It is also possible that you would flip all tails and lose $16,000.[9] The chances are very high, however, that you would actually flip about 50 heads and about 50 tails, winning a net of about $2,000. Although each individual flip is a risky bet, collectively this scenario is a low-risk proposition because most of the risk has been diversified away. This concept underlies the practice of holding portfolios of stocks rather than just one stock. Note that all of the risk associated with stocks cannot be eliminated by diversification: those risks related to broad, systematic changes in the economy that affect the stock market will remain.

firm-specific (diversifiable) risk
That part of a security's risk associated with random outcomes generated by events, or behaviors, specific to the firm. It *can* be eliminated by proper diversification.

market (nondiversifiable) risk
The part of a security's risk associated with economic, or market, factors that systematically affect most firms. It *cannot* be eliminated by diversification.

relevant risk
The portion of a security's risk that cannot be diversified away; the security's market risk. It reflects the security's contribution to the risk of a portfolio.

---

[9]The probability that tails (or heads) will be flipped 100 times in a row is $(0.5)^{100}$, which is approximately 0 when rounded to 20 decimals places.

Are all stocks equally risky in the sense that adding them to a well-diversified portfolio would have the same effect on the portfolio's riskiness? The answer is no. Different stocks will affect the portfolio differently, so different securities have different degrees of relevant (systematic) risk. How can we measure the relevant risk of an individual stock? As we have seen, all risk except that related to broad market movements can, and presumably will, be diversified away. After all, why accept risk that we can easily eliminate? As our discussion suggests, risk that can be diversified should not be a concern, which means that diversifiable (firm-specific) risk is irrelevant when making decisions about which investments to include in a well-diversified portfolio. However, because market (nondiversifiable) risk cannot be eliminated, it is relevant and should be the primary concern when making portfolio decisions. *The risk that remains after diversifying is market risk (that is, risk that is inherent in the market), and it can be measured by evaluating the degree to which a given stock tends to move up and down with the market.*

The Concept of Beta

Recall that the relevant risk associated with an individual stock is based on its systematic risk, which in turn depends on the sensitivity of the firm's operations to economic events such as interest rate changes and inflationary pressures. Because the general movements in the financial markets reflect movements in the economy, we can measure the market risk of a stock by observing its tendency to move with the market or with an average stock that has the same characteristics as the market. The measure of a stock's sensitivity to market fluctuations is called its **beta coefficient,** which is designated with the Greek letter β.

beta coefficient, β
A measure of the extent to which the returns on a given stock move with the stock market.

An *average-risk stock* is defined as one that tends to move up and down in step with the general market as measured by some index—that is, it is a stock that "behaves" just like the market—such as the Dow Jones Industrial Index, the S&P 500 Index, or the New York Stock Exchange Composite Index. Such a stock will, *by definition*, have a beta (β) of 1.0. This value indicates that, in general, if the market moves up by 10 percent, the stock price will also increase by 10 percent; if the market falls by 10 percent, the stock price will decline by 10 percent. A portfolio composed of such β = 1.0 stocks will move up and down with the broad market averages, and it will be just as risky as the averages. If β = 0.5, the stock's relevant (systematic) risk is only half as volatile as the market, and a portfolio of such stocks will be half as risky as a portfolio that includes only β = 1.0 stocks—it will rise and fall only half as much as the market. If β = 2.0, the stock's relevant risk is twice as volatile as an average stock, so a portfolio of such stocks will be twice as risky as an average portfolio. The value of such a portfolio could double—or halve—in a short period of time. If you held such a portfolio, you could quickly become a millionaire—or a pauper.

Figure 11-9 graphs the relative volatility of three stocks. The data below the graph *assume* that in 2007 the "market," defined as a portfolio consisting of all stocks, had a total return (dividend yield plus capital gains yield) of $r_M = 14\%$, and Stocks H, A, and L (for High, Average, and Low risk) also had returns of 14 percent. In 2008, the market rose sharply, and the return on the market portfolio was $r_M = 28\%$. Returns on the three stocks also increased: the return on H soared to 42 percent; the return on A reached 28 percent, the same as the market; and the return on L increased to only 21 percent. In 2009, the market dropped, with the market return falling to $r_M = -14\%$. The three stocks' returns also fell, H plunging to −42 percent, A falling to −14 percent, and L declining to 0 percent. As you can see, all three stocks moved in the same direction as the market, but H was by far the most volatile; A was just as volatile as the market; and L was less volatile than the market.

FIGURE 11-9   Relative Volatility of Stocks H, A, and L

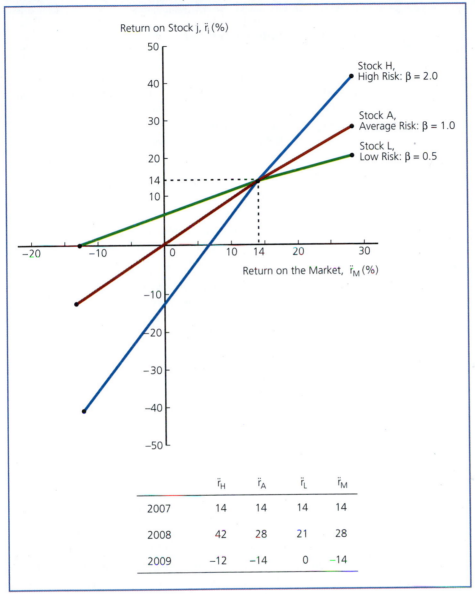

	$\ddot{r}_H$	$\ddot{r}_A$	$\ddot{r}_L$	$\ddot{r}_M$
2007	14	14	14	14
2008	42	28	21	28
2009	−12	−14	0	−14

The beta coefficient measures a stock's volatility relative to an average stock (or the market), which has $\beta = 1.0$. We can calculate a stock's beta by plotting a line like those shown in Figure 11-9. The slopes of these lines show how each stock moves in response to a movement in the general market. Indeed, *the slope coefficient of such a "regression line" is defined as a beta coefficient*. Betas for literally thousands of companies are calculated and published by Merrill Lynch, *Value Line*, and numerous other organizations. Table 11-4 provides the beta coefficients for some well-known companies. Most stocks have betas in the range of 0.50 to 1.50, and the average for all stocks is 1.0 by definition.[10]

---

[10]In theory, betas can be negative. For example, if a stock's returns tend to rise when those of other stocks decline, and vice versa, the regression line in a graph such as Figure 11-9 will have a downward slope, and the beta will be negative. Note, however, that only a few stocks have negative betas. Payco American, the collection agency company, probably has a negative beta.

TABLE 11-4   Beta Coefficients for Selected Companies

Company	Beta	Industry/Product
I. Above Average Market Risk: $\beta > +1.0$		
Nortel Networks Corporation	4.18	Communications equipment/telephone equipment
Yahoo! Inc.	3.40	Computer services/global Internet communications
E*TRADE Group Inc.	2.87	Investment services/online financial services
Sun Microsystems	2.80	Computers and peripherals
eBay	1.76	Retail (specialty nonapparel)/Web-based auction
II. Average Market Risk: $\beta = 1.0$		
Dow Jones & Company	1.02	Publishing and printing (newspapers)
Ryland Group	1.01	Home building
Scotts Corporation	0.99	Pesticide, fertilizer, and agricultural chemicals
Krispy Kreme	0.99	Snack and nonalcoholic beverage bars
Toyota Motor Corporation	0.99	Auto and truck manufacturers
III. Below Average Market Risk: $\beta < 1.0$		
Barnes & Noble	0.75	Specialty retailing/bookstores
Kroger Company	0.50	Food retailing/supermarkets
Walgreen Company	0.28	Retail (drugs)/pharmacies and drugstores
Gillete Company	0.28	Personal and household products
Progress Energy	0.17	Electric utilities/electric power generation

Data from: _Standard & Poor's Research Insight_, 2007.

If we add a higher-than-average beta stock ($\beta > 1.0$) to an average beta ($\beta = 1.0$) portfolio, then the beta, and consequently the riskiness, of the portfolio will increase. Conversely, if we add a lower-than-average-beta stock ($\beta < 1.0$) to an average-risk portfolio, the portfolio's beta and risk will decline. _Thus, because a stock's beta measures its contribution to the riskiness of a portfolio, theoretically beta is the correct measure of the stock's riskiness._

The preceding analysis of risk in a portfolio setting is part of the CAPM. We can summarize our discussion to this point as follows:

1. A stock's risk consists of two components: _market risk_ and _firm-specific risk._

2. _Firm-specific risk_ can be eliminated through diversification. Most investors do diversify, either by holding large portfolios or by purchasing shares in mutual funds. We are left, then, with _market risk,_ which is caused by general movements in the stock market and which reflects the fact that most stocks are systematically affected by major economic events such as war, recessions, and inflation. _Market risk is the only risk that is relevant to a rational, diversified investor,_ because he or she should already have eliminated firm-specific risk.

3. Investors must be compensated for bearing risk. That is, _the greater the riskiness of a stock, the higher its required return._ Such compensation is required only for risk that cannot be eliminated by diversification. If risk premiums existed on stocks with high diversifiable risk, well-diversified investors would start buying these securities and bidding up their prices, and their final (equilibrium) expected returns would reflect only nondiversifiable market risk.

An example might help clarify this point. Suppose half of Stock A's risk is market risk (it occurs because Stock A moves up and down with the market).

The other half of Stock A's risk is diversifiable. You hold only Stock A, so you are exposed to all of its risk. As compensation for bearing so much risk, *you want* a risk premium of 8 percent higher than the 5 percent Treasury bond rate. That is, you demand a return of 13 percent (= 5% + 8%) from this investment. But suppose other investors, including your professor, are well diversified; they also hold Stock A, but they have eliminated its diversifiable risk and thus are exposed to only half as much risk as you are for holding Stock A. Consequently, their risk premium will be only half as large as yours, and they will *require* a return of only 9 percent (= 5% + 4%) to invest in the stock.

If the stock actually yielded more than 9 percent in the market, other investors, including your professor, would buy it. If it yielded the 13 percent you demand, you would be willing to buy the stock, but the well-diversified investors would compete with you for its acquisition. They would bid its price up and its yield down, which would keep you from getting the stock at the return you need to earn to be compensated for taking on its *total risk*. In the end, you would have to accept a 9 percent return or keep your money in the bank. Thus, risk premiums in a market populated with *rational in-vestors*—that is, those who diversify—will reflect only market risk.

4. The market (systematic) risk of a stock is measured by its *beta coefficient*, which is an index of the stock's relative volatility. Some benchmark values for beta follow:
   $\beta = 0.5$: the stock's relevant risk is only half as volatile, or risky, as the average stock.
   $\beta = 1.0$: the stock's relevant risk is of average risk.
   $\beta = 2.0$: the stock's relevant risk is twice as volatile as the average stock.

5. *Because a stock's beta coefficient determines how the stock affects the riskiness of a diversified portfolio, beta (β) is a better measure of a stock's relevant risk than is standard deviation (σ), which measures total, or stand-alone, risk.*

Portfolio Beta Coefficients

A portfolio consisting of low-beta securities will itself have a low beta, because the beta of any set of securities is a weighted average of the individual securities' betas:

$$\text{Portfolio beta} = \beta_p = w_1\beta_1 + w_2\beta_2 + \cdots + w_N\beta_N$$

$$= \sum_{j=1}^{N} w_j\beta_j$$

11-8

Here β_P, the beta of the portfolio, reflects how volatile the portfolio is in relation to the market; w_j is the fraction of the portfolio invested in the jth stock; and β_j is the beta coefficient of the jth stock. For example, if an investor holds a $105,000 portfolio consisting of $35,000 invested in each of three stocks, and each of the stocks has a beta of 0.7, then the portfolio's beta will be $\beta_{P1} = 0.7$:

$$\beta_{P1} = (1/3)(0.7) + (1/3)(0.7) + (1/3)(0.7) = 0.7$$

Such a portfolio will be less risky than the market, which means it should experience relatively narrow price swings and demonstrate relatively small rate-of-return fluctuations. When graphed in a fashion similar to Figure 11-9, the slope of its regression line would be 0.7, which is less than that for a portfolio of average stocks.

Now suppose one of the existing stocks is sold and replaced by a stock with $\beta_j = 2.5$. This action will increase the riskiness of the portfolio from $\beta_{P1} = 0.7$ to $\beta_{P2} = 1.3$:

$$\beta_{P2} = (1/3)(0.7) + (1/3)(0.7) + (1/3)(2.5) = 1.3$$

Had a stock with $\beta_j = 0.4$ been added, the portfolio beta would have declined from 0.7 to 0.6. Adding a low-beta stock, therefore, would reduce the riskiness of the portfolio.

Self-Test Questions

What is meant by perfect positive correlation, by perfect negative correlation, and by zero correlation?

In general, can we reduce the riskiness of a portfolio to zero by increasing the number of stocks in the portfolio? Explain.

What is meant by diversifiable risk and nondiversifiable risk? What is an average-risk stock?

Why is beta the theoretically correct measure of a stock's riskiness?

If you plotted the returns on a particular stock versus those on the Dow Jones Industrial Average index over the past 5 years, what would the slope of the line you obtained indicate about the stock's risk?

Suppose that you have a portfolio that includes two stocks. You invested 60 percent of your total funds in a stock that has a beta equal to 3.0 and the remaining 40 percent of your funds in a stock that has a beta equal to 0.5. What is the portfolio's beta?   (Answer: 2.0)

THE RELATIONSHIP BETWEEN RISK AND RATES OF RETURN— THE CAPITAL ASSET PRICING MODEL (CAPM)

In the preceding section, we saw that beta is the appropriate measure of a stock's relevant risk. Now we must specify the relationship between risk and return. For a given level of beta, what rate of return will investors require on a stock to compensate them for assuming the risk? To determine an investment's required rate of return, we use a *theoretical* model called the **Capital Asset Pricing Model (CAPM).** The CAPM shows how the relevant risk of an investment as measured by its beta co-efficient is used to determine the investment's appropriate required rate of return.

Let's begin by defining the following terms:

Capital Asset Pricing Model (CAPM)
A model used to determine the required return on an asset, which is based on the proposition that any asset's return should be equal to the risk-free return plus a risk premium that reflects the asset's nondiversifiable risk.

$\hat{r}_j$ = *Expected* rate of return on the jth stock, based on the probability distribution for the stock's returns; $\hat{r}_j$ is the rate that investors *expect* to earn if they purchase the stock.

r_j = *Required* rate of return on the jth stock; r_j is the rate that *investors demand* for investing in Stock j. If $\hat{r}_j < r_j$, you would not purchase this stock, or you would sell it if you owned it; if $\hat{r}_j > r_j$, you would want to buy the stock; and, you would be indifferent if $\hat{r}_j = r_j$.

r_{RF} = Risk-free rate of return. In this context, r_{RF} is generally measured by the return on long-term U.S. Treasury securities.

β_j = Beta coefficient of the jth stock. The beta of an average stock is $\beta_A = 1.0$.

r_M = Required rate of return on a portfolio consisting of all stocks, which is the market portfolio. r_M is also the required rate of return on an average ($\beta_A = 1.0$) stock.

$RP_M = (r_M - r_{RF})$ = Market risk premium. This is the additional return above the risk-free rate required to compensate an average investor for assuming an average amount of risk ($\beta_A = 1.0$).

$RP_j = (r_M - r_{RF})\beta_j$ = Risk premium on the jth stock = $(RP_M)\beta_j$. The stock's risk premium is less than, equal to, or greater than the premium on an average stock, depending on whether its relevant risk as measured by beta (β_j) is less than, equal to, or greater than an average stock, respectively. If $\beta_j = \beta_A = 1.0$, then $RP_j = RP_M$; if $\beta_j > 1.0$, then $RP_j > RP_M$; and, if $\beta_j < 1.0$, then $RP_j < RP_M$.

The **market risk premium (RP$_M$)** depends on the degree of aversion (attitude) that investors, on average, show when taking on risk.[11] Let's assume that at the current time, Treasury bonds yield $r_{RF} = 5\%$ and an average share of stock has a required return of $r_M = 11\%$. In this case, the market risk premium is 6 percent:

> **market risk premium (RP$_M$)**
> The additional return over the risk-free rate needed to compensate investors for assuming an average amount of risk.

$$RP_M = r_M - r_{RF} = 11\% - 5\% = 6\%$$

It follows that if one stock has twice the relevant risk as another, its *risk premium* should be twice as high. Conversely, if a stock's relevant risk is only half as much as that of another stock, its *risk premium* should be half as large. Furthermore, we can measure a stock's relevant risk by finding its beta coefficient. Therefore, if we know the market risk premium, RP_M, and the stock's risk as measured by its beta coefficient, β_j, we can find its risk premium as the product $RP_M \times \beta_j$. For example, if $\beta_j = 0.5$ and $RP_M = 6\%$, then RP_j is 3 percent:

$$\text{Risk premium for Stock } j = RP_M \times \beta_j \qquad \textbf{11-9}$$

$$= 6\% \times 0.5$$
$$= 3.0\%$$

---

[11]This concept, as well as other aspects of CAPM, is discussed in more detail in Chapter 3 of Eugene F. Brigham and Phillip R. Daves' *Intermediate Financial Management*, 9th edition (Cincinnati, OH: South-Western College Publishing, 2007). Note that we cannot measure the risk premium of an average stock, $RP_M = r_M - r_{RF}$, with great precision because we cannot possibly obtain precise values for the expected future return on the market, r_M. Empirical studies suggest that where long-term U.S. Treasury bonds are used to measure r_{RF} and where r_M is an estimate of the expected return on the S&P 500, the market risk premium varies somewhat from year to year. It has generally ranged from 4 to 8 percent during the last 20 years.

Chapter 3 of *Intermediate Financial Management* also discusses the assumptions embodied in the CAPM framework. Some of the assumptions of the CAPM theory are unrealistic. As a consequence, the theory does not hold exactly.

As Figure 11-4 shows, the required return for any investment j can be expressed in general terms as:

 **11-10**

$$\text{Required return} = \text{Risk-free return} + \text{Premium for risk}$$
$$r_j \qquad = \qquad r_{RF} \qquad + \qquad RP_j$$

Based on our previous discussion, Equation 11-10 can also be written as:

 **11-11**

$$r_j = r_{RF} + (RP_M)\,\beta_j \qquad = \text{Capital Asset Pricing Model (CAPM)}$$
$$= r_{RF} + (r_M - r_{RF})\,\beta_j$$

$$= 5\% + (11\% - 5\%)(0.5)$$
$$= 5\% + 6\%(0.5) = 8\%$$

Security Market Line (SML)

The line that shows the relationship between risk as measured by beta and the required rate of return for individual securities.

Equation 11-11, which is the CAPM equation for equilibrium pricing, is called the **Security Market Line (SML).**

If some other stock was riskier than Stock j and had $\beta_{j2} = 2.0$, then its required rate of return would be 17 percent:

$$r_{j2} = 5\% + (6\%)\,2.0 = 17\%$$

An average stock, with $\beta = 1.0$, would have a required return of 11 percent, the same as the market return:

$$r_A = 5\% + (6\%)\,1.0 = 11\% = r_M$$

Equation 11-11 (the SML equation) is often expressed in graph form. Figure 11-10, for example, shows the SML when $r_{RF} = 5\%$ and $r_M = 11\%$. Note the following points:

1. *Required rates of return* are shown on the vertical axis, and risk (as measured by beta) is shown on the horizontal axis. This graph is quite different from the one shown in Figure 11-9, where the returns on individual stocks are plotted on the vertical axis and returns on the market index are shown on the horizontal axis. The slopes of the three lines in Figure 11-9 represent the three stocks' betas. In Figure 11-10, these three betas are plotted as points on the horizontal axis.

2. Riskless securities have $\beta_j = 0$; therefore, r_{RF} appears as the vertical axis intercept in Figure 11-10.

3. The slope of the SML reflects the degree of risk aversion in the economy. The greater the average investor's aversion to risk, (a) the steeper the slope of the line, (b) the greater the risk premium for any stock, and (c) the higher the required rate of return on stocks.[12] These points are discussed further in a later section.

4. The values we worked out for stocks with $\beta_j = 0.5$, $\beta_j = 1.0$, and $\beta_j = 2.0$ agree with the values shown on the graph for r_{Low}, r_A, and r_{High}.

---

[12]Students sometimes confuse beta with the slope of the SML. This is a mistake. The slope of any line is equal to the "rise" divided by the "run," or $(Y_1 - Y_0)/(X_1 - X_0)$. Consider Figure 11-10. If we let $Y = r$ and $X = \beta$, and we go from the origin to $\beta = 1.0$, we see that the slope is $(r_M - r_{RF})/(\beta_M - \beta_{RF}) = (11\% - 5\%)/(1 - 0) = 6\%$. Thus, the slope of the SML is equal to $(r_M - r_{RF})$, the market risk premium. In Figure 11-10, $r_j = 5\% + (6\%)\beta_j$, so a doubling of beta (for example, from 1.0 to 2.0) would produce an eight-percentage-point increase in r_j.

FIGURE 11-10   The Security Market Line (SML)

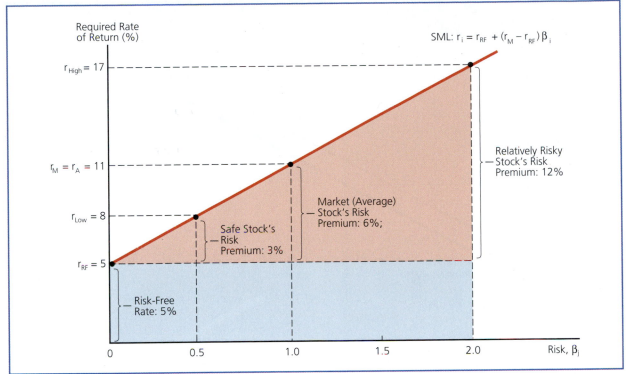

Both the SML and a company's position on it change over time because of changes in interest rates, investors' risk aversion, and individual companies' betas. Such changes are discussed in the following sections.

The Impact of Inflation

As we learned in Chapter 5, interest amounts to "rent" on borrowed money, or the price of money. In essence, then, r_{RF} is the price of money to a riskless borrower. We also learned in Chapter 5 that the risk-free rate as measured by the rate on U.S. Treasury securities is called the *nominal,* or *quoted,* rate, and it consists of two elements: (1) a *real inflation-free rate of return,* r^*, and (2) *an inflation premium, IP,* equal to the anticipated rate of inflation.[13] Thus, $r_{RF} = r^* + IP$.

If the expected rate of inflation rose by 2 percent, r_{RF} would also increase by 2 percent. Figure 11-11 illustrates the effects of such a change. Notice that under the CAPM, the increase in r_{RF} also causes an *equal increase in the rate of return on all risky assets* because the inflation premium is built into the required rate of return of both riskless and risky assets.[14] For example, the risk-free return increases from

---

[13]Long-term Treasury bonds also contain a maturity risk premium (MRP). Here we include the MRP in r^* to simplify the discussion.

[14]Recall that the inflation premium for any asset is equal to the average expected rate of inflation over the life of the asset. In this analysis, we must therefore assume either that all securities plotted on the SML graph have the same life or that the expected rate of future inflation is constant.

   Also note that r_{RF} in a CAPM analysis can be proxied by either a long-term rate (the T-bond rate) or a short-term rate (the T-bill rate). Traditionally, the T-bill rate was used, but a movement toward use of the T-bond rate has occurred in recent years because a closer relationship exists between T-bond yields and stocks than between T-bill yields and stocks. See *Stocks, Bonds, Bills, and Inflation, 2007 Yearbook* (Chicago: Ibbotson & Associates, 2008) for a discussion.

FIGURE 11-11   Shift in the SML Caused by a 2 Percent Increase in Inflation

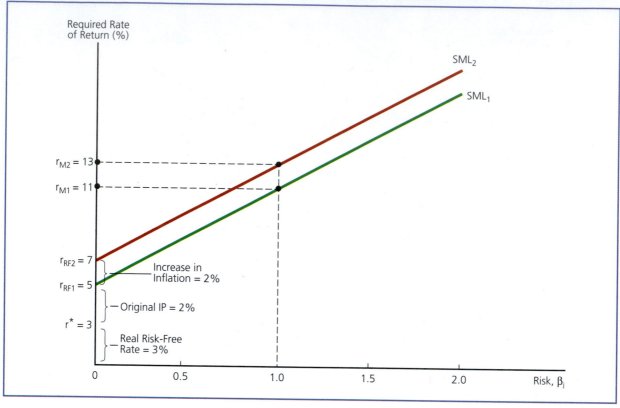

5 to 7 percent, and the rate of return on an average stock, r_M, increases from 11 to 13 percent. Thus, all securities' returns increase by two percentage points.

Changes in Risk Aversion

The slope of the Security Market Line reflects the extent to which investors are averse to risk. The steeper the slope of the line, the greater the average investor's risk aversion. If investors were *indifferent* to risk, and if r_{RF} was 5 percent, then risky assets would also provide an expected return of 5 percent. If there was no risk aversion, there would be no risk premium, so the SML would be horizontal. *As risk aversion increases, so does the risk premium* and, therefore, so does the slope of the SML.

Figure 11-12 illustrates an increase in risk aversion. In this case, the market risk premium increases from 6 to 8 percent, and r_M increases from $r_{M1} = 11\%$ to $r_{M2} = 13\%$. The returns on other risky assets also rise, with the effect of this shift in risk aversion being *more pronounced on riskier securities*. For example, the required return on a stock with $\beta_j = 0.5$ increases by only one percentage point, from 7 to 8 percent. By comparison, the required return on a stock with $\beta_j = 2.0$ increases by four percentage points, from 17 to 21 percent. Because $\Delta RP_j = \Delta RP_M(\beta_j) = (13\% - 11\%)\beta_j = (2\%)\beta_j$, the changes in these risk premiums are computed as follows:

1. If $\beta_j = 0.5$, $\Delta RP_j = (2\%)0.5 = 1\%$

2. If $\beta_j = 2.0$, $\Delta RP_j = (2\%)2.0 = 4\%$

Thus, when the average investor's aversion to risk changes, investments with higher beta coefficients experience greater changes in their required rates of return than investments with lower betas.

FIGURE 11-12   Shift in the SML Caused by Increased Risk Aversion

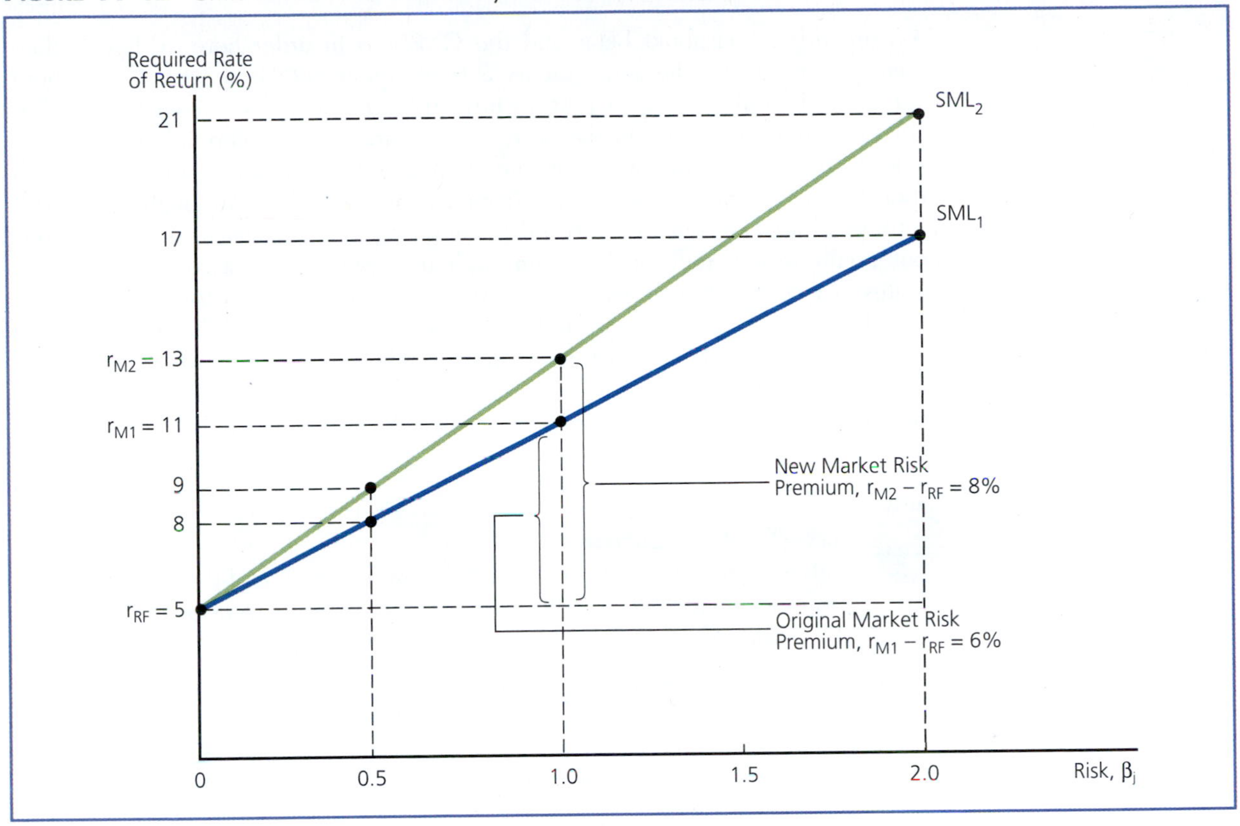

Changes in a Stock's Beta Coefficient

As we will see later in this book, a firm can affect its beta risk by changing the composition of its assets and by modifying its use of debt financing. External factors, such as increased competition within a firm's industry or the expiration of basic patents, can also alter a company's beta. When such changes occur, the required rate of return, r, changes as well, and, as we saw in Chapter 10, this change will affect the price of the firm's stock. For example, consider Genesco Manufacturing with a beta equal to 1.0. Suppose some action occurred that caused this firm's beta to increase from 1.0 to 1.5. If the conditions depicted in Figure 11-10 held, Genesco's required rate of return would increase from

$$r_1 = r_{RF} + (r_M - r_{RF})\beta_j$$
$$= 5\% + (11\% - 5\%)1.0$$
$$= 11\%$$

to

$$r_2 = 5\% + (11\% - 5\%)1.5$$
$$= 14\%$$

Any change that affects the required rate of return on a security, such as a change in its beta coefficient or in expected inflation, will affect the price of the security.

A Word of Caution

A word of caution about betas and the CAPM is in order here. Although these concepts are logical, the entire theory is based on *ex ante*, or *expected*, conditions, yet we have available only *ex post*, or *past*, data. The betas we calculate show how volatile a stock has been in the past, but conditions could certainly change. The stock's *future volatility*, which is the item of real concern to investors, might therefore differ quite dramatically from its past volatility. Although the CAPM represents a significant step forward in security pricing theory, it does have some potentially serious deficiencies when applied in practice. As a consequence, estimates of r_j found through use of the SML might be subject to considerable error. For this reason, many investors and analysts use the CAPM and the concept of β to provide "ballpark" figures for further analysis. The concept that investors should be rewarded only for taking relevant risk makes sense, and the CAPM provides an easy way to get a "rough" estimate of the relevant risk and the appropriate required rate of return of an investment.

Self-Test Questions

Differentiate between the expected rate of return ($\hat{r}$) and the required rate of return (r) on a stock. Which would have to be larger to persuade you to buy the stock?

What are the differences between the relative volatility graph (Figure 11-9), where "betas are made," and the SML graph (Figure 11-10), where "betas are used"? Consider the methods of constructing the graphs and the purposes for which they were developed.

What happens to the SML graph (1) when inflation increases or (2) when inflation decreases?

What happens to the SML graph (1) when risk aversion increases or (2) when risk aversion decreases? What would the SML look like if investors were indifferent to risk—that is, had zero risk aversion?

How can a firm influence its market, or beta, risk?

Stock E has a beta coefficient equal to 1.2. If the risk-free rate of return equals 4 percent and the expected market return equals 10 percent, what is Stock E's required rate of return?   (Answer: $r_E = 11.2\%$)

STOCK MARKET EQUILIBRIUM

Based on our previous discussion, we know that we can use the CAPM to find the *required return* for an investment (say, Stock Q), which we designate as r_Q. Suppose the risk-free return is 5 percent, the market *risk premium* is 6 percent, and Stock Q has a beta of 1.5 ($\beta_Q = 1.5$). In this case, the marginal, or average, investor will require a return of 14 percent on Stock Q:

$$r_A = 5\% + 6\%(1.5) = 14\%$$

This 14 percent return is shown as a point (Q) on the SML in Figure 11-13.

The average investor will want to buy Stock Q if the expected rate of return exceeds 14 percent, will want to sell it if the expected rate of return is less than 14 percent, and

FIGURE 11-13   Expected and Required Returns on Stock Q

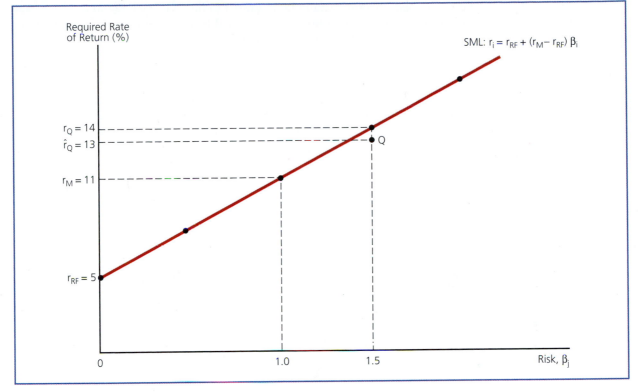

will be indifferent (and therefore will hold but not buy or sell Stock Q) if the expected rate of return is exactly 14 percent. Now suppose the investor's portfolio contains Stock Q, and he or she analyzes the stock's prospects and concludes that its earnings, dividends, and price can be expected to grow at a constant rate of 4 percent per year forever. The last dividend paid was $D_0 = \$3$, so the next expected dividend is:

$$\hat{D}_1 = \$3.00(1.04) = \$3.12$$

Our "average" (marginal) investor observes that the current price of the stock, P_0, is $34.67. Should he or she purchase more of Stock Q, sell the present holdings, or maintain the present position?

Recall from Chapter 10 that we can calculate Stock Q's *expected rate of return* as follows (Equation 10-10):

$$\hat{r}_Q = \frac{\hat{D}_1}{P_0} + g = \frac{\$3.12}{\$34.67} + 0.04 = 0.09 + 0.04 = 0.13 = 13\%$$

This value is plotted on Figure 11-13 as Point Q, which is below the SML. Because the expected rate of return, $\hat{r}_Q = 13\%$, is less than the required return, $r_Q = 14\%$, this marginal investor would want to sell the stock, as would other holders. Because few people would want to buy at the $34.67 price, the present owners would be unable to find buyers unless they cut the price of the stock. The price would therefore decline, and this decline would continue until the stock's price reaches $31.20. At that point, the market for this security would be in **equilibrium** because the expected rate of return, 14 percent, would be equal to the required rate of return:

$$\hat{r}_Q = \frac{\$3.12}{\$31.20} + 0.04 = 0.10 + 0.04 = 0.14 = 14\%$$

equilibrium
The condition under which the expected return on a security is just equal to its required return, $\hat{r} = r$, and the price is stable.

Had the stock initially sold for less than $31.20—say, $28.36—events would have been reversed. Investors would have wanted to buy the stock because its expected rate of return ($\hat{r} = 15\%$) would have exceeded its required rate of return, and buy orders would have driven the stock's price up to $31.20.

To summarize, two conditions must hold in equilibrium:

1. The expected rate of return as seen by the marginal investor must equal the required rate of return: $\hat{r}_j = r_j$.

2. The actual market price of the stock must equal its intrinsic value as estimated by the marginal investor: $P_0 = \hat{P}_0$.

Of course, some individual investors might believe that $\hat{r}_j > r_j$ or $\hat{P}_0 > P_0$, hence, they would invest most of their funds in the stock. Other investors might ascribe to the opposite view and sell all of their shares. Nevertheless, it is the marginal investor who establishes the actual market price. For this investor $\hat{r}_j = r_j$ and $P_0 = \hat{P}_0$. If these conditions do not hold, trading will occur until they do hold.

Self-Test Questions

When a stock is in equilibrium, what two conditions must hold?

If a stock is not in equilibrium, explain how financial markets adjust to bring it into equilibrium.

Suppose that Porter Pottery's stock currently sells for $26.00. The company, which is growing at a constant rate, recently paid a dividend equal to $2.50. Analysts have determined that the market value of the stock is currently in equilibrium and that investors require a rate of return equal to 14 percent to purchase the stock. If the price of the stock increases to $28.89 tomorrow, after Porter's year-end financial statements are made public, what is the stock's expected return? Assume that the company's growth rate remains constant.   (Answer: 13%)

CHANGES IN EQUILIBRIUM STOCK PRICES

Stock market prices undergo violent changes at times. For example, on October 19, 1987, the Dow Jones Industrial Average (DJIA) dropped 508 points, and the average stock lost about 23 percent of its value in just one day. Some stocks lost more than half of their value that day. More recently, during January 2008, the DJIA dropped by approximately 1,100 points; during a 7-day trading period in the middle of the month, the Dow dropped nearly 900 points.

To see how such changes can occur, let's take another look at Stock Q, which would sell at a price of $31.20 per share under the conditions presented earlier. Now consider what would happen to the price of Stock Q if the value of any of the variables used to compute the current price changes. For instance, how would the price be affected if investors demand a higher rate of return—say, 16 percent rather than 14 percent? If we change the value of r to 16 percent in the previous computation, we find that the value of Stock Q would be:

$$\hat{P}_0 = \frac{\hat{D}_1}{r_s - g} = \frac{\$3.00(1.04)}{0.16 - 0.04} = \frac{\$3.12}{0.12} = \$26.00$$

The new price is lower because investors demand a higher return—that is, 16 percent rather than 14 percent—for receiving the same future cash flows.

How would the price change if the expected cash flows differ, but the required rate of return is the same as in the original situation—that is, r = 14%? Consider the effect if the company's growth rate is 3 percent rather than 4 percent:

$$\hat{P}_0 = \frac{\hat{D}_1}{r_s - g} = \frac{\$3.00(1.03)}{0.14 - 0.03} = \frac{\$3.09}{0.11} = \$28.09$$

Again, the new price is lower. In this case, however, the price is lower because investors demand the same return as before, but the cash flows (dividends) that the stock is expected to provide are smaller than expected previously ($\hat{D}_1$ is \$3.09 rather than \$3.12).

From this simple example, you should have concluded that changes in stock prices occur because (1) investors change the rates of return they require to invest in stocks or (2) expectations about the cash flows associated with stocks change. More specifically, the examples show that *stock prices move opposite changes in rates of return, but they move the same as changes in cash flows expected from the stock in the future.* Therefore, if investors demand higher (lower) returns to invest in stocks, prices or values should fall (increase). If investors expect their investments to generate lower (higher) future cash flows, prices also should fall (increase).

Evidence suggests that stocks—especially those of large NYSE companies—adjust rapidly to disequilibrium situations. Consequently, equilibrium ordinarily exists for any given stock, and, in general, required and expected returns are equal. Stock prices certainly change, sometimes violently and rapidly, but these changes simply reflect different conditions and expectations. Of course, sometimes a stock continues to react for several months to a favorable or unfavorable development, but this reaction does not signify a long adjustment period; rather, it illustrates that as more new pieces of information about the situation become available, the market adjusts to them.

Self-Test Questions

When a stock is in equilibrium, what two conditions must hold?

If a stock is not in equilibrium, explain how financial markets adjust to bring it into equilibrium.

PHYSICAL ASSETS VERSUS SECURITIES

In this chapter, much of the discussion has focused on the riskiness of financial assets, especially stocks. It might seem that financial managers should be more concerned with the riskiness of such business (real) assets as plant and equipment. Why not examine the riskiness of real assets? The reason is that *for a financial manager whose goal is stock price maximization, the overriding consideration is the riskiness of the firm's stock, and the relevant risk of any physical asset must be measured in terms of its effect on the stock's risk.* For example, suppose that Goodyear Tire Company is considering making a major investment in a new product, recapped tires. Sales of recaps and, hence, earnings on the new operation are highly uncertain, so the new venture would appear to be quite risky. Now suppose that returns on the recap business are negatively correlated with Goodyear's regular operations. That is, when times are good and people have plenty of money, they buy new tires; when times are bad, they tend to buy more recaps. Therefore, returns would be high on regular operations and low on the recap division during good times, but the opposite situation would occur during recessions. The result might be a pattern like that shown in Figure 11-5 for Stocks W and M. Thus, what appears to be a risky investment when viewed on a stand-alone basis might not be very risky when viewed within the context of the company as a whole.

We can extend this analysis to the corporation's owners, the stockholders. Because the stock of Goodyear is owned by a diversified group of stockholders, the real issue when the company undertakes a major asset investment can be stated as follows: How does this investment affect the risk of the firm's stockholders? Again, the stand-alone risk of an individual project might appear quite high, but it might not be large when viewed in the context of the project's effect on stockholders' risk. We will address this subject again in Chapter 13, where we will examine the effects of capital budgeting projects on companies' beta coefficients and thus on their risk to stockholders.

Self-Test Questions

Explain the following statement: "The stand-alone risk of an individual project may appear quite high, but the project's risk might not be large when viewed in the context of the project's effect on stockholders' risk."

How would the correlation between returns on the project and other assets' returns affect the preceding statement?

DIFFERENT TYPES OF RISK

In Chapter 5, we introduced the concept of risk in our discussion of interest rates, or the cost of money. At that point, we stated that the nominal, or quoted, rate of return, r, can be written as follows:

$$\text{Rate of return (interest)} = r = \text{Risk-free rate} + \text{Risk premium}$$
$$= r_{RF} + RP$$
$$= [r^* + IP] + [DRP + LP + MRP]$$

Remember that here:

  r = the quoted, or *nominal,* rate of interest on a given security. There are many different securities, hence many different quoted interest rates.

 r_{RF} = the nominal risk-free rate of return.

  r^* = real risk-free rate of interest, which is the interest rate that would exist on a security with a *guaranteed* payoff if inflation is expected to be zero during the investment period.

  IP = inflation premium, which equals the average inflation rate expected over the life of the security.

 DRP = default risk premium, which reflects the chance that the borrower will not pay the debt's interest or principal on time.

  LP = liquidity, or marketability, premium, which reflects the fact that some investments are more easily converted into cash on short notice at a "reasonable price" than are other securities.

 MRP = maturity risk premium, which accounts for the fact that longer term bonds experience greater price reactions to interest rate changes than do short-term bonds.

The discussion in Chapter 5 presented an overall view of interest rates and general factors that affect these rates. We did not, however, discuss risk evaluation in detail; rather, we described some of the factors that determine the total risk associated with debt, such as default risk, liquidity risk, and maturity risk. In reality, these risks also affect other types of investments, including equity. Equity does not represent a legal contract that requires the firm to pay defined amounts of dividends at particular times or to "act" in specific ways. There is, however, an expectation that positive returns will be generated through future distributions of cash because dividends will be paid, capital gains will be generated through growth, or both events will occur. Investors also expect the firm to behave "appropriately." If these expectations are not met, investors generally consider the firm in "default" of their expectations. In such cases, as long as no laws have been broken, stockholders generally do not have legal recourse as would be the case for a default on debt. As a result, investors penalize the firm by selling their stock, which causes the value of the firm's stock to decline.

In this chapter, we build on the general concept that was introduced in Chapter 5 by showing how the risk premium associated with any investment should be determined (at least in theory). The basis of our discussion is Equation 5-3, which we develop further in this chapter as follows:

$$r_j = \text{Risk-free rate} + \text{Risk premium}$$
$$= \quad r_{RF} \quad + (r_M - r_{RF})\beta_j = \text{CAPM}$$

According to the CAPM, investors should not expect to be rewarded for all of the risk associated with an investment—that is, its total, or stand-alone risk—because some risk can be eliminated through diversification. The *relevant risk,* and thus the risk for which investors should be compensated, is that portion of the total risk that cannot be "diversified away." Thus, in this chapter we show the following:

$$
\begin{aligned}
\text{Total risk} = \sigma = &\quad \text{Systematic risk} && + \text{Unsystematic risk} \\
= &\quad \text{Market (economic) risk} && + \text{Firm-specific risk} \\
= &\quad \text{Nondiversifiable risk} && + \text{Diversifiable risk} \\
= &\quad \text{Cannot be eliminated} && + \text{Can be eliminated} \\
\text{Relevant risk} = &\quad \text{Nondiversifiable risk} && + \text{\sout{Divesifiable risk}} \text{ (eliminated)} \\
= &\quad \text{Systematic risk}
\end{aligned}
$$

Systematic risk is represented by an investment's beta coefficient, β, in Equation 11-11.

The specific types and sources of risk to which a firm or an investor is exposed are numerous and vary considerably depending on the situation. A detailed discussion of all the different types of risks and the techniques used to evaluate risks is beyond the scope of this book, but you should recognize that risk is an important factor in the determination of the required rate of return (r), which, according to the following equation, is one of the two variables we need to determine to find the value of an asset:

$$\text{Value} = \frac{\widehat{CF}_1}{(1+r)^1} + \frac{\widehat{CF}_2}{(1+r)^2} + \cdots + \frac{\widehat{CF}_n}{(1+r)^n} = \sum_{t=1}^{n} \frac{\widehat{CF}_t}{(1+r)^t}$$

This computation was first introduced in Chapter 1, and it was discussed in detail in Chapter 10. What is important to understand here is that the value of an asset, which could be a stock, a bond, or any other asset, is based on the cash flows that the asset is expected to generate during its life and the rate of return investors require to "put up" their money to purchase the investment. In this chapter, we provide you with an indication as to how the required rate of return, r, should be determined, and we show that investors demand higher rates of return to compensate them for taking greater amounts of "relevant" risks.

Because it is an important concept and has a direct effect on value, we will continue to discuss risk in the remainder of the book. Although there are instances where the discussions focus on the risk to which investors are exposed, most of the discussions focus on risks that affect businesses. Because we discuss different types of risk throughout the book, we thought it might be a good idea to summarize and describe these risks in brief terms. Table 11-5 shows the risks that are discussed in

TABLE 11-5   Different Types (Sources) of Risk

General Type of Risk	Name of Risk	Brief Description
I. Systematic Risks (nondiversifiable risk; market risk; relevant risk)	Interest rate risk	When interest rates change, (1) the values of investments change (in opposite directions) and (2) the rate at which funds can be reinvested also changes (in the same direction).
	Inflation risk	The primary reason interest rates change is because investors change their expectations about future inflation.
	Maturity risk	Long-term investments experience greater price reactions to interest rate changes than do short-term bonds.
	Liquidity risk	This is a reflection of the fact that some investments are more easily converted into cash on a short notice at a "reasonable price" than are other securities.
	Exchange rate risk	Multinational firms deal with different currencies; the rate at which the currency of one country can be *exchanged* into the currency of another country—that is, the exchange rate—changes as market conditions change.
	Political risk	Any action by a government that reduces the value of an investment.
II. Unsystematic Risks (diversifiable risk; firm-specific risk)	Business risk	Risk that would be inherent in the firm's operations if it used no debt—factors such as labor conditions, product safety, quality of management, competitive conditions, and so forth, affect firm-specific risk.
	Financial risk	Risk associated with how the firm is financed—that is, its credit risk.
	Default risk	Part of financial risk—the chance that the firm will not be able to service its existing debt.
III. Combined Risks (some systematic risk and some unsystematic risk)	Total risk	The combination of systematic risk and unsystematic risk; also referred to as stand-alone risk, because this is the risk an investor takes if he or she purchases only one investment, which is tantamount to "putting all your eggs into one basket."
	Corporate risk	The riskiness of the firm without considering the effect of stockholder diversification; based on the combination of assets held by the firm (inventory, accounts receivable, plant and equipment, and so forth). Some diversification exists because the firm's assets represent a portfolio of investments in real assets.

the book and indicates whether each risk is considered a component of systematic (nondiversifiable) or unsystematic (diversifiable) risk. Note that (1) this table oversimplifies risk analysis because some risks are not easily classified as either systematic or unsystematic and (2) some of the risks included in the table will be discussed later in the book. Even so, this table shows the relationships among the different risks discussed in the book.

Self-Test Question

Classify default risk, maturity risk, and liquidity risk as either diversifiable or nondiversifiable risk.

Ethical Dilemma

RIP—Retire in Peace

Retirement Investment Products (RIP) offers a full complement of retirement planning services and a diverse line of retirement investments that have varying degrees of risk. With the investment products available at RIP, investors could form retirement funds with any level of risk preferred, from risk-free to extremely risky. RIP's reputation in the investment community is impeccable, because the service agents who advise clients are required to fully inform their clients of the risk possibilities that exist for any investment position, whether it is recommended by an agent or requested by a client. Since 1950, RIP has built its investment portfolio of retirement funds to $60 billion, which makes it one of the largest providers of retirement funds in the United States.

You work for RIP as an investment analyst. One of your responsibilities is to help form recommendations for the retirement fund managers to evaluate when making investment decisions. Recently, Howard, a close friend from your college days who now works for SunCoast Investments, a large brokerage firm, called to tell you about a new investment that is expected to earn very high returns during the next few years. The investment is called a "Piggyback Asset Investment Device," or PAID for short. Howard told you that he really does not know what this acronym means or how the investment is constructed, but all the reports he has read indicate PAIDs should be a hot investment in the future, so the returns should be

handsome for those who get in now. The one piece of information he did offer was that a PAID is a rather complex investment that consists of a combination of securities whose values are based on numerous debt instruments issued by government agencies, including the Federal National Mortgage Association, the Federal Home Loan Bank, and so on. Howard made it clear that he would like you to consider recommending to RIP that PAIDs be purchased through SunCoast Investments. The commissions from such a deal would bail him and his family out of a financial crisis that resulted because they had bad luck with their investments in the 2001 financial markets. Howard has indicated that somehow he would reward you if RIP invests in PAIDs through SunCoast, because, in his words, "You would literally be saving my life." You told Howard you would think about it and call him back.

Further investigation into PAIDs has yielded little additional information beyond what previously was provided by Howard. The new investment is intriguing because its expected return is extremely high compared with similar investments. Earlier this morning, you called Howard to quiz him a little more about the return expectations and to try to get an idea concerning the riskiness of PAIDs. Howard was unable to adequately explain the risk associated with the investment, although he reminded you that the debt of U.S. government agencies is

continues

involved. As he says, "How much risk is there with government agencies?"

The PAIDs are enticing because RIP can attract more clients if it can increase the return offered on its investments. If you recommend the new investment and the higher returns pan out, you will earn a sizable commission. In addition, you will be helping Howard out of his financial situation because his commissions will be substantial if the PAIDs are purchased through SunCoast Investments. Should you recommend the PAIDs as an investment?

Chapter Principles –The Answers

To summarize the key concepts, let's answer the questions that were posed at the beginning of the chapter:

- **What does it mean to take risk when investing?** In finance, *risk* is defined as the chance of receiving a return other than the one that is expected. Thus, an investment is considered risky if more than one outcome (payoff) is possible. Every *risky* investment has both "bad" risk—that is, the chance that it will return less than expected—and "good" risk—that is, the chance that it will return more than expected. In simple terms, *risk* can be described using one word: *variability*.

- **How are the risk and return of an investment measured? How are the risk and return of an investment related?** An investment's risk is measured by the variability of its possible payoffs (returns). Greater variability in returns indicates greater risk. Investors require higher returns to take on greater risk. Thus, generally speaking, investments with greater risks also have higher returns. The expected return of an investment is measured as a weighted average of all of the possible returns the investment might generate in the future, with the weights being the probability that the particular return will occur.

- **For what type of risk is an average investor rewarded?** Investors should only be rewarded for risk that they must take. Because firm-specific, or unsystematic, risk can be reduced or eliminated through diversification, investors, even those who do not diversify their investment portfolios, should not be rewarded for taking such risk. Consequently, an investment's *relevant* risk is its systematic, or market, risk, which is the risk for which investors should be rewarded. Systematic risk cannot be reduced through diversification. An investment's "irrelevant" risk is its firm-specific, or unsystematic, risk because it is this portion of the total risk that can be eliminated (at least theoretically) through diversification.

- **How can investors reduce risk?** Risk can be reduced through diversification. Investors achieve diversification by forming portfolios that contain numerous financial securities (perhaps stocks and bonds) that are not significantly positively related to each other. For example, an investor can form a well-diversified portfolio by purchasing the stocks of 40 or more companies in different industries, such as transportation, utilities, healthcare, entertainment, food services, and so forth. Total risk, which is equal to market (systematic) risk plus firm-specific (unsystematic) risk, can be reduced through diversification because little or no unsystematic risk should exist in a well-diversified investment portfolio.

- **What actions do investors take when the return they require to purchase an investment is different from the return the investment is expected to produce?** Investors will purchase a security only when its expected return, $\hat{r}$, is greater than its required return, r. When $\hat{r} < r$, investors will not purchase the security and those who own the security tend to sell it, which causes the security's price to decrease and its expected return to increase until $\hat{r} = r$.

The concepts presented in this chapter should help you to better understand the relationship between investment risk and return, which is an important concept in finance. If you understand the basic concepts we discussed, you should be able to construct an investment portfolio that has the level of risk with which you are comfortable.

- **What important principles should I remember from this chapter when investing?** First, remember that risk and return are positively related. As a result, in most cases, when you are offered an investment that promises to pay a high return, you should conclude that the investment has high risk. When considering possible investments, *never* separate "risk" and "return"—that is, do not consider the return of an investment without also considering its risk. Second, remember that you can reduce some investment risk through diversification, which can be achieved by purchasing different investments that are not highly positively related to each other. In many instances, you can reduce risk without reducing the expected rate of return associated with your investment position.

- **How can I diversify if I don't have enough money to purchase 40 different securities?** Mutual funds, which we discuss in Chapter 2, provide investors with the opportunity to diversify their investments because these investments consist of large portfolios often containing greater than 50 to 100 securities that are well diversified. Many types of mutual funds with various investment objectives exist. Shares in most mutual funds can be purchased for as little as $500; thus, you don't have to be rich to diversify. Individuals are well advised to follow an old adage when investing: "Don't put all your eggs in one basket."

- **How can I use the concepts presented in the chapter to construct a portfolio that has a level of risk with which I am comfortable?** Remember that (1) a stock's (investment's) beta coefficient gives a measure of its "relevant" risk and (2) a portfolio's beta equals the weighted average of the betas of all of the investments contained in the portfolio. Thus, if you can determine their beta coefficients, you can choose those investments that provide the risk level you prefer when they are combined to form a portfolio. If you prefer lower risk to higher risk, you should purchase investments with low betas, and vice versa. In addition, you can adjust the riskiness of your portfolio by adding or deleting stocks with particular risks—that is, to reduce a portfolio's risk, you can either add securities with low betas or delete from the portfolio (sell) securities with high betas. Beta coefficients for most large companies' stocks are easy to find—they are posted on numerous Internet sites, contained in various financial publications that are available in public libraries, published by investment organizations, and so forth.

- **How can I determine the required and expected rates of return for an investment?** Many investors examine the past performance of an investment to determine its expected return. Care must be taken with this approach because past returns often do not reflect future returns. Even so, you might be able to get a "rough" idea as to what you expect a stock's long-term growth will be in the future by examining its past growth, especially if the firm is fairly stable. Investors also rely on information provided by professional analysts to form opinions about expected rates of return.

   To determine an investment's required rate of return, investors often evaluate the performances of similar risk investments. In addition, as we discussed in this chapter, some investors use the CAPM to get a "ballpark figure" for an investment's required rate of return. The beta coefficients for most large companies can be obtained from many sources, including the Internet; the risk-free rate of return can be estimated using the rates on existing Treasury securities; and the expected market return can be estimated by evaluating market returns in recent years, the current trend in the market, and predictions made by economists and investment analysts.

When investing your money, keep these words of wisdom in mind: "If you lose sleep over your investments or are more concerned with the performance of your portfolio than with your job, then your investment position probably is too risky." If you find yourself in such a position, use the concepts discussed in this chapter to adjust the riskiness of your portfolio.

QUESTIONS

11-1 "The probability distribution of a less risky expected return is more peaked than that of a riskier return." Is this a correct statement? Explain.

11-2 What shape would the probability distribution have for (a) completely certain returns and (b) completely uncertain returns?

11-3 Give some events that affect the price of a stock that would result from unsystematic risk. What events would result from systematic risk? Explain.

11-4 Explain why systematic risk is the "relevant" risk of an investment and why investors should be rewarded only for this type of risk.

11-5 Explain the following statement: "A stock held as part of a portfolio is generally less risky than the same stock held in isolation."

11-6 Security A has an expected return of 7 percent, a standard deviation of expected returns of 35 percent, a correlation coefficient of −0.3 with the market, and a beta coefficient of −0.5. Security B has an expected return of 12 percent, a standard deviation of returns of 10 percent, a correlation coefficient of 0.7 with the market, and a beta coefficient of 1.0. Which security is riskier? Why?

11-7 Suppose you owned a portfolio consisting of $250,000 of long-term U.S. government bonds.

   a. Would your portfolio be riskless?

   b. Now suppose you hold a portfolio consisting of $250,000 of 30-day Treasury bills. Every 30 days your bills mature and you reinvest the principal ($250,000) in a new batch of bills. Assume that you live on the investment income from your portfolio and that you want to maintain a constant standard of living. Is your portfolio *truly* riskless?

   c. Can you think of any asset that would be completely riskless? Could someone develop such an asset? Explain.

11-8 A life insurance policy is a financial asset. The premiums paid represent the investment's cost.

   a. How would you calculate the expected return on a life insurance policy?

   b. Suppose the owner of a life insurance policy has no other financial assets—the person's only other asset is "human capital," or lifetime earnings capacity. What is the correlation coefficient between returns on the insurance policy and returns on the policyholder's human capital?

   c. Insurance companies have to pay administrative costs and sales representatives' commissions, hence the expected rate of return on insurance premiums is generally low, or even negative. Use the portfolio concept to explain why people buy life insurance despite the negative expected returns.

11-9 If investors' aversion to risk increased, would the risk premium on a high-beta stock increase more or less than that on a low-beta stock? Explain.

11-10 Do you think it is possible to construct a portfolio of stocks that has an expected return that equals the risk-free rate of return?

11-11 Suppose the beta coefficient of a stock doubles from $\beta_1 = 1$ to $\beta_2 = 2$. Logic says that the required rate of return on the stock should also double. Is this logic correct? Explain.

SELF-TEST PROBLEMS

Solutions appear in Appendix B.

ST-1 Define the following terms using graphs or equations to illustrate your answers wherever feasible:

    a. Risk; probability distribution

    b. Expected rate of return, $\hat{r}$; required rate of return, r

    c. Continuous probability distribution; discrete probability distribution

    d. Standard deviation, σ; variance, σ^2; coefficient of variation, CV

    e. Risk aversion; realized rate of return, $\ddot{r}$

    f. Risk premium for Stock j, RP_j; market risk premium, RP_M

    g. Expected return on a portfolio, $\hat{r}_p$

    h. Correlation coefficient, ρ

    i. Market risk; company-specific risk; relevant risk

    j. Beta coefficient, β; average stock's beta, β_M

    k. Capital Asset Pricing Model (CAPM); Security Market Line (SML); SML equation

    l. Slope of SML as a measure of risk aversion

Key Terms

ST-2 Of the $10,000 invested in a two-stock portfolio, 30 percent is invested in Stock A and 70 percent is invested in Stock B. If Stock A has a beta equal to 2.0 and the beta of the portfolio is 0.95, what is the beta of Stock B?

Beta Coefficient

ST-3 If the risk-free rate of return, r_{RF}, is 4 percent and the market return, r_M, is expected to be 12 percent, what is the required rate of return for a stock with a beta, β, equal to 2.5?

Required Rate of Return

ST-4 Stock A and Stock B have the following historical returns:

Realized Rates of Return

Year	Stock A's Returns, $\ddot{r}_A$	Stock B's Returns, $\ddot{r}_B$
2005	−10.00%	−3.00%
2006	18.50	21.29
2007	38.67	44.25
2008	14.33	3.67
2009	33.00	28.30

    a. Calculate the average rate of return for each stock during the period 2005–2009. Assume that someone held a portfolio consisting of 50 percent Stock A and 50 percent Stock B. What would have been the realized rate of return on the portfolio in each year from 2005 through 2009? What would have been the average return on the portfolio during this period?

b. Calculate the standard deviation of returns for each stock and for the portfolio. Use Equation 11-4.

c. Looking at the annual returns data on the two stocks, would you guess that the correlation coefficient between returns on the two stocks is closer to 0.9 or to −0.9? Explain your answer.

Probability Distributions   **ST-5**   Stocks R and S have the following probability distributions of returns:

		Returns	
Probability		**Stock R**	**Stock S**
0.5		−2%	20%
0.1		10	12
0.4		15	2

a. Calculate the expected return for each stock.

b. Calculate the expected return of a portfolio consisting of 50 percent of each stock.

c. Calculate the standard deviation of returns for each stock and for the portfolio. Which stock is considered riskier with respect to total risk?

d. Compute the coefficient of variation for each stock. According to the coefficient of variation, which stock is considered riskier?

e. If you added more stocks at random to the portfolio, which of the following statements most accurately describes what would happen to σ_p?

   (1) σ_p would remain constant.

   (2) σ_p would decline to somewhere in the vicinity of 15 percent.

   (3) σ_p would decline to zero if enough stocks were included.

PROBLEMS

Expected Return   **11-1**   Based on the following probability distribution, what is the security's expected return?

State	Probability	r
1	0.2	−5.0%
2	0.3	10.0
3	0.5	30.0

Expected Return   **11-2**   What is the expected return of the following investment?

Probability	Payoff
0.3	30.0%
0.2	10.0
0.5	−2.0

Portfolio Beta   **11-3**   Susan's investment portfolio currently contains three stocks that have a total value equal to $100,000. The beta of this portfolio is 1.5. Susan is considering investing an additional $50,000 in a stock that has beta equal to 3. After she adds this stock, what will be the portfolio's new beta?

11-4   Suppose that $r_{RF} = 5\%$, $r_M = 12\%$. What is the appropriate required rate of return for a stock that has a beta coefficient equal to 1.5?   **Required Return**

11-5   The current risk-free rate of return, r_{RF}, is 4 percent and the market *risk premium*, RP_M, is 5 percent. If the beta coefficient associated with a firm's stock is 2.0, what should be the stock's required rate of return?   **Required Return**

11-6   Following is information for two stocks: **Coefficient of Variation**

Investment	Expected Return, $\hat{r}$	Standard Deviation, σ
Stock D	10.0%	8.0%
Stock E	36.0	24.0

Which investment has the greatest *relative* risk?

11-7   ZR Corporation's stock has a beta coefficient equal to 1.8 and a required rate of return equal to 16 percent. If the expected return on the market is 10 percent, what is the risk-free rate of return, r_{RF}?   **Risk-Free Return**

11-8   Currently, the risk-free return is 3 percent and the expected market rate of return is 10 percent. What is the expected return of the following three-stock portfolio?   **Portfolio Return**

Amount Invested	Beta
$400,000	1.5
500,000	2.0
100,000	4.0

11-9   The market and Stock S have the following probability distributions: **Expected Returns**

Probability	r_M	r_S
0.3	15%	20%
0.4	9	5
0.3	18	12

a. Calculate the expected rates of return for the market and Stock S.

b. Calculate the standard deviations for the market and Stock S.

c. Calculate the coefficients of variation for the market and Stock S.

11-10 Marvin has investments with the following characteristics in his portfolio: **Portfolio Return**

Investment	Expected Amount Return, $\hat{r}$	Invested
ABC	30%	$10,000
EFG	16	50,000
QRP	20	40,000

What is the expected return of Marvin's portfolio of investments, $\hat{r}_P$?

Expected Returns   **11-11** Stocks X and Y have the following probability distributions of expected future returns:

Probability	r_X	r_Y
0.1	−10%	−35%
0.2	2	0
0.4	12	20
0.2	20	25
0.1	38	45

a. Calculate the expected rate of return for Stock Y, $\hat{r}_Y$ ($\hat{r}_X = 12\%$).

b. Calculate the standard deviation of expected returns for Stock X ($\sigma_Y = 20.35\%$). Also, calculate the coefficient of variation for Stock Y. Is it possible that most investors might regard Stock Y as being less risky than Stock X? Explain.

Required Return   **11-12** Yesterday, Susan determined that the risk-free rate of return, r_{RF}, is 3 percent, the required return on the market portfolio, r_M, is 10 percent, and the required rate of return on Stock K, r_K, is 17 percent. Today, Susan received new information that indicates investors are more risk averse than she thought, such that the market risk premium, RP_M, actually is 1 percent higher than she estimated yesterday. When Susan considers the effect of this change in risk premium, what will she determine the new r_K to be?

Portfolio Beta   **11-13** Terry recently invested equal amounts in five stocks to form an investment portfolio, which has a beta equal to 1.2—that is, $\beta_P = 1.2$. Terry is considering selling the riskiest stock in the portfolio, which has a beta coefficient equal to 2.0, and replacing it with another stock. If Terry replaces the stock that has a β equal to 2.0 with a stock that has a β equal to 1.0, what will be the *new beta* of his investment portfolio? Assume that equal amounts are invested in each stock in the portfolio.

Portfolio Beta   **11-14** Thomas has a five-stock portfolio that has a market value equal to $400,000. The portfolio's beta is 1.5. Thomas is considering selling a particular stock to help pay some university expenses. The stock is valued at $100,000, and if he sells it the portfolio's beta will increase to 1.8. What is the beta of the stock Thomas is considering selling?

Portfolio Beta   **11-15** Suppose that you hold a diversified portfolio consisting of 20 different stocks, with $7,500 invested in each of the stocks. The portfolio beta is equal to 1.12. You have decided to sell one of the stocks in your portfolio with a beta equal to 1.0 for $7,500 and to use the proceeds to buy another stock for your portfolio. Assume that the new stock's beta is equal to 1.75. Calculate your portfolio's new beta.

Beta Computation   **11-16** Suppose $r_{RF} = 8\%$, $r_M = 11\%$, and $r_B = 14\%$.

a. Calculate Stock B's beta, β.

b. If Stock B's beta were 1.5, what would be B's new required rate of return?

SML and CAPM   **11-17** Suppose $r_{RF} = 9\%$, $r_M = 14\%$, and $\beta_X = 1.3$.

a. What is r_X, the required rate of return on Stock X?

b. Now suppose r_{RF} (1) increases to 10 percent or (2) decreases to 8 percent. The slope of the SML remains constant. How would each change affect r_M and r_X?

c. Assume r_{RF} remains at 9 percent, but r_M (1) increases to 16 percent or (2) decreases to 13 percent. The slope of the SML does not remain constant. How would these changes affect r_X?

11-18 Stock R has a beta of 1.5, Stock S has a beta of 0.75, the expected rate of return on an average stock is 15 percent, and the risk-free rate of return is 9 percent. By how much does the required return on the riskier stock exceed the required return on the less risky stock?

Required Rates of Return

11-19 Suppose you are the money manager of a $4 million investment fund. The fund consists of four stocks with the following investments and betas:

Portfolio Required Return

Stock	Investment	Beta
A	$ 400,000	1.50
B	600,000	−0.50
C	1,000,000	1.25
D	2,000,000	0.75

If the market required rate of return is 14 percent and the risk-free rate is 6 percent, what is the fund's required rate of return?

11-20 Following is information about Investment A, Investment B, and Investment C:

Expected Returns

Economic Condition	Probability	Return on Investment: A	B	C
Boom	0.5	25.0%	40.0%	5.0%
Normal	0.4	15.0	20.0	10.0
Recession	0.1	−5.0	−40.0	15.0
$\hat{r}$		18.0%	24.0%	_____
σ		_____	23.3%	3.3%

a. Compute the expected return, $\hat{r}$, for Investment C.

b. Compute the standard deviation, σ, for Investment A.

c. Based on total risk and return, which of the investments should a risk-averse investor prefer?

11-21 Suppose you won the Florida lottery and were offered a choice of $500,000 in cash or a gamble in which you would get $1 million if a head were flipped but $0 if a tail came up.

Expected Returns

a. What is the expected value of the gamble?

b. Would you take the sure $500,000 or the gamble?

c. If you choose the sure $500,000, are you a risk averter or a risk seeker?

d. Suppose you take the sure $500,000. You can invest it in either a U.S. Treasury bond that will return $537,500 at the end of 1 year or a common stock that has a 50-50 chance of being either worthless or worth $1,150,000 at the end of the year.

  (1) What is the expected *dollar* profit on the stock investment? (The expected profit on the T-bond investment is $37,500.)

  (2) What is the expected *rate* of return on the stock investment? (The expected rate of return on the T-bond investment is 7.5 percent.)

  (3) Would you invest in the bond or the stock?

(4) Exactly how large would the expected profit (or the expected rate of return) have to be on the stock investment to make you invest in the stock, given the 7.5 percent return on the bond?

(5) How might your decision be affected if, rather than buying one stock for $500,000, you could construct a portfolio consisting of 100 stocks with $5,000 invested in each? Each of these stocks has the same return characteristics as the one stock—that is, a 50-50 chance of being worth either $0 or $11,500 at year-end. Would the correlation between returns on these stocks matter?

Security Market Line   **11-22** The McAlhany Investment Fund has total capital of $500 million invested in five stocks:

Stock	Investment	Stock's Beta Coefficient
A	$160 million	0.5
B	120 million	2.0
C	80 million	4.0
D	80 million	1.0
E	60 million	3.0

The current risk-free rate is 8 percent. Market returns have the following estimated probability distribution for the next period:

Probability	Market Return
0.1	10%
0.2	12
0.4	13
0.2	16
0.1	17

a. Compute the expected return for the market.

b. Compute the beta coefficient for the investment fund. (Remember, this problem involves a portfolio.)

c. What is the estimated equation for the Security Market Line?

d. Compute the fund's required rate of return for the next period.

e. Suppose John McAlhany, the president, receives a proposal for a new stock. The investment needed to take a position in the stock is $50 million, it will have an expected return of 18 percent, and its estimated beta coefficient is 2.0. Should the firm purchase the new stock? At what expected rate of return should McAlhany be indifferent to purchasing the stock?

Realized Rates of Return   **11-23** Stock A and Stock B have the following historical returns:

Year	Stock A's Returns, $\ddot{r}_A$	Stock B's Returns, $\ddot{r}_B$
2005	−18.00%	−14.50%
2006	33.00	21.80
2007	15.00	30.50
2008	−0.50	−7.60
2009	27.00	26.30

a.   Calculate the average rate of return for each stock during the period 2005–2009.

b.   Assume that someone held a portfolio consisting of 50 percent Stock A and 50 percent Stock B. What would have been the realized rate of return on the portfolio in each year from 2005 through 2009? What would have been the average return on the portfolio during this period?

c.   Calculate the standard deviation of returns for each stock and for the portfolio. Use Equation 11-4.

d.   Calculate the coefficient of variation for each stock and for the portfolio.

e.   If you are a risk-averse investor, would you prefer to hold Stock A, Stock B, or the portfolio? Why?

Integrative Problem

11-24   Assume that you recently graduated with a major in finance, and you just landed a job in the trust department of a large regional bank. Your first assignment is to invest $100,000 from an estate for which the bank is trustee. Because the estate is expected to be distributed to the heirs in approximately 1 year, you have been instructed to plan for a 1-year holding period. Furthermore, your boss has restricted you to the following investment alternatives, shown with their probabilities and associated outcomes. (For now, disregard the items at the bottom of the data; you will fill in the blanks later.)

Risk and Rates of Return

State of the Economy	Probability	T-Bills	**Estimated Returns on Alternative Investments** High Tech	Collections	U.S. Rubber	Market Portfolio	Two–Stock Portfolio
Recession	0.1	8.0%	−22.0%	28.0%	10.0%	−13.0%	_____
Below Average	0.2	8.0	−2.0	14.7	−10.0	1.0	_____
Average	0.4	8.0	20.0	0.0	7.0	15.0	_____
Above Average	0.2	8.0	35.0	−10.0	45.0	29.0	_____
Boom	0.1	8.0	50.0	−20.0	30.0	43.0	_____
$\hat{r}$		_____	_____	_____	_____	_____	_____
σ		_____	_____	_____	_____	_____	_____
CV		_____	_____	_____	_____	_____	_____

The bank's economic forecasting staff has developed probability estimates for the state of the economy, and the trust department has a sophisticated computer program that was used to estimate the rate of return on each alternative under each state of the economy. High Tech, Inc., is an electronics firm, Collections, Inc., collects past due debts, and U.S. Rubber manufactures tires and various other rubber and plastic products. The bank also maintains an "index fund" that includes a market-weighted fraction of all publicly traded stocks; by investing in that fund, you can obtain average stock market results. Given the situation as described, answer the following questions:

a.   (1) Why is the risk-free return independent of the state of the economy? Do T-bills promise a completely risk-free return? (2) Why are High Tech's returns expected to move with the economy whereas Collections' are expected to move counter to the economy?

b. Calculate the expected rate of return on each alternative and fill in the row for $\hat{r}$ in the table.

c. You should recognize that basing a decision solely on expected returns is appropriate only for risk-neutral individuals. Because the beneficiaries of the trust, like virtually everyone, are risk averse, the riskiness of each alternative is an important aspect of the decision. One possible measure of risk is the *standard deviation* of returns. (1) Calculate this value for each alternative and fill in the row for σ in the table. (2) What type of risk does the standard deviation measure? (3) Draw a graph that shows *roughly* the shape of the probability distributions for High Tech, U.S. Rubber, and T-bills.

d. Suppose you suddenly remembered that the coefficient of variation (CV) is generally regarded as being a better measure of total risk than the standard deviation when the alternatives being considered have widely differing expected returns. Calculate the CVs for the different securities and fill in the row for CV in the table. Does the CV measurement produce the same risk rankings as the standard deviation?

e. Suppose you created a two-stock portfolio by investing $50,000 in High Tech and $50,000 in Collections. (1) Calculate the expected return ($\hat{r}_p$), the standard deviation (σ_p), and the coefficient of variation (CV_p) for this portfolio and fill in the appropriate rows in the table. (2) How does the riskiness of this two-stock portfolio compare to the riskiness of the individual stocks if they were held in isolation?

f. Suppose an investor starts with a portfolio consisting of one randomly selected stock. What would happen (1) to the riskiness and (2) to the expected return of the portfolio as more randomly selected stocks are added to the portfolio? What is the implication for investors? Draw two graphs to illustrate your answer.

g. (1) Should portfolio effects influence the way that investors think about the riskiness of individual stocks? (2) If you chose to hold a one-stock portfolio and consequently were exposed to more risk than diversified investors, could you expect to be compensated for all of your risk? That is, could you earn a risk premium on the part of your risk that you could have eliminated by diversifying?

h. The expected rates of return and the beta coefficients of the alternatives as supplied by the bank's computer program are as follows:

Security	Return ($\hat{r}$)	Risk (β)
High Tech	17.4%	1.29
Market	15.0	1.00
U.S. Rubber	13.8	0.68
T-bills	8.0	0.00
Collections	1.7	−0.86

(1) What is a *beta coefficient*, and how are betas used in risk analysis? (2) Do the expected returns appear to be related to each alternative's market risk? (3) Is it possible to choose among the alternatives on the basis of the information developed thus far? (4) Use the data given at the beginning of the problem to construct a graph that shows how the T-bill's,

High Tech's, and Collections' beta coefficients are calculated. Discuss what beta measures and explain how it is used in risk analysis.

i. (1) Write out the SML equation, use it to calculate the required rate of return on each alternative, and then graph the relationship between the expected and required rates of return. (2) How do the expected rates of return compare with the required rates of return? (3) Does the fact that Collections has a negative beta coefficient make any sense? What is the implication of the negative beta? (4) What would be the market risk and the required return of a 50-50 portfolio of High Tech and Collections? Of a 50-50 portfolio of High Tech and U.S. Rubber?

j. (1) Suppose investors raised their inflation expectations by three percentage points over current estimates as reflected in the 8 percent T-bill rate. What effect would higher inflation have on the SML and on the returns required on high- and low-risk securities? (2) Suppose, instead, that investors' risk aversion increased enough to cause the market risk premium to increase by three percentage points (inflation remains constant). What effect would this change have on the SML and on returns of high- and low-risk securities?

COMPUTER-RELATED PROBLEM

Work the problem in this section only if you are using the computer problem spreadsheet.

11-25 Using the model in File C11, rework Problem 11-23, assuming that a third stock, Stock C, is available for inclusion in the portfolio. Stock C has the following historical returns:

Year	Stock C's Return, $\ddot{r}_C$
2005	32.00%
2006	−11.75
2007	10.75
2008	32.25
2009	−6.75

a. Calculate (or read from the computer screen) the average return, standard deviation, and coefficient of variation for Stock C.

b. Assume that the portfolio now consists of 33.33 percent Stock A, 33.33 percent Stock B, and 33.33 percent Stock C. How does this composition affect the portfolio return, standard deviation, and coefficient of variation versus when 50 percent was invested in A and in B?

c. Make some other changes in the portfolio, making sure that the percentages sum to 100 percent. For example, enter 25 percent for Stock A, 25 percent for Stock B, and 50 percent for Stock C. (Note that the program will not allow you to enter a zero for the percentage in Stock C.) Notice that $\hat{r}_p$ remains constant and that σ_p changes. Why do these results occur?

d. In Problem 11-23, the standard deviation of the portfolio decreased only slightly because Stocks A and B were highly positively correlated with each other. In this problem, the addition of Stock C causes the standard deviation of the portfolio to decline dramatically, even though $\sigma_C = \sigma_A = \sigma_B$. What does this change indicate about the correlation between Stock C and Stocks A and B?

e. Would you prefer to hold the portfolio described in Problem 11-23 consisting only of Stocks A and B or a portfolio that also includes Stock C? If others react similarly, how might this fact affect the stocks' prices and rates of return?

PART 4

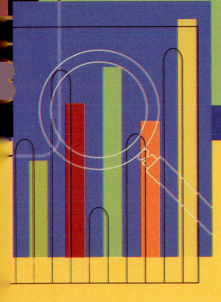

Corporate Decision Making

CHAPTER 12

The Cost of Capital

A MANAGERIAL PERSPECTIVE

Firms raise capital in the financial markets, where interest rates and other yields change continuously. As interest rates change, so do the costs associated with the various types of capital. For instance, in 2000 and 2001, interest rates on corporate debt increased while stock prices dropped. As a consequence, companies had to pay higher costs for using investors' funds. Indeed, many companies curtailed their plans to expand or invest funds in long-term projects because the price of the funds needed for such investments had risen so high. For example, Burlington Northern Santa Fe Corporation (BNSF), a railroad company, estimated that if new funds were raised in 2001, the cost to the firm for the funds would be as much as 12 percent. At the time, however, the expected returns on BNSF's investment opportunities were less than 10 percent. Clearly, the firm would lose money if it paid 12 percent for funds that would provide a return of only 10 percent. Would BNSF's stockholders be upset if the company raised funds and knowingly invested those monies in projects that earned returns less than the cost of the funds? Absolutely! For that reason, Burlington Northern postponed a large portion of its planned investments for 2001 until the cost of funds decreased. When interest rates on corporate debt declined in 2002 and 2003, the estimated cost of funds for BNSF had dropped to less than 7 percent. During the first

6 months of 2003, interest rates had dropped to levels not seen during the previous 50 years. Although they began to increase slowly at the end of 2003 and the beginning of 2004, rates remained at historically low levels. As a result, not only did BNSF resume its investment program, it also refinanced much of its older, more expensive debt (much like homeowners refinanced their homes during the same period). BNSF's executives recognized that, to remain sustainable, the company must earn enough to cover the costs of the funds it uses for investments.

As interest rates slowly increased in 2005, 2006, and most of 2007, fewer firms and individuals refinanced their debt. Even so, some firms used other methods to lower their costs of funds. For example, in 2006, both Ford Motor Company and its competitor General Motors (GM) made plans to sell some of their operations in an effort to improve their fledgling financial positions. The two companies felt that their financing costs would decline if they divested themselves of money-losing operations. Ford and GM were hoping that selling portions of their companies would improve the firms' financial positions, which would decrease the rate of return that investors would demand in the future to provide funds to these companies by investing in their stocks and bonds.

At the end of 2007 and the beginning of 2008, because investors and companies expressed fears that the economy was heading into a recession, the Federal Reserve began to lower interest rates. Even with lower interest rates, businesses reported lower-than-expected earnings for 2007, which suggested that they were not earning enough to cover the costs of the funds that were invested in assets. The economic conditions that existed at the beginning of 2008 were similar to those that we observed in 1999 when Baker Hughes, an oil-services company, initiated a plan that tied executive bonuses to the firm's cost of funds. At the time, the company's stock value was the lowest it had been in 10 years, and although the reported revenues were in the billions of dollars, high operating costs resulted in lackluster profits. As a result, the new executive bonus plan encouraged executives to lower costs substantially to ensure that Baker Hughes generated enough profit to cover the cost of funds. In 2008, firms that find they cannot cover their costs of funds with profits might decide to follow the Baker Hughes plan.

As you read this chapter, keep in mind that firms need funds provided by investors to take advantage of acceptable investment opportunities. The financial marketplace, which consists of investors like you, determines the "price" that firms must pay for these funds. It is essential for us to be able to determine the "price," or the cost, of the capital used by a firm so that we can determine whether the funds are being invested appropriately.

CHAPTER PRINCIPLES –The Questions

After reading this chapter, you should be able to answer the following questions:

- What types of capital do firms use to finance investments?
- What is the cost of capital?
- How is the cost of capital used to make financial decisions?
- Why do funds generated through retained earnings have a cost?
- Who determines a firm's cost of capital?

cost of capital
The firm's average cost of funds, which is the average return required by the firm's investors—what must be paid to attract funds.

required rate of return
The return that must be earned on invested funds to cover the cost of financing such investments; also called the *opportunity cost rate*.

It is vitally important that a firm knows how much it pays for the funds used to purchase assets. The average return required by the firm's investors determines how much must be paid to attract funds. This required rate of return represents the firm's average cost of funds, which is termed its **cost of capital.** The firm's cost of capital represents the minimum rate of return that must be earned from investing in projects to ensure the value of the firm does not decrease. In other words the cost of capital is the firm's **required rate of return.** For example, if investors provide funds at an average cost of 15 percent, the firm's value will decrease if the funds are used to generate returns less than 15 percent, its value will not change if exactly 15 percent is earned, and its value will increase if the funds are used to generate returns greater than 15 percent.

In this chapter, we discuss the concept of cost of capital, how the average cost of capital is determined, and how the cost of capital is used in financial decision making. Most of the models and formulas used in this chapter are the same ones we developed in Chapter 10, where we described how stocks and bonds are valued by investors. A firm's cost of funds is based on the return demanded by investors. If the return offered by the firm is not high enough, investors will not provide sufficient funds. In other words, *the rate of return an investor earns on a corporate security effectively is a cost to the firm that uses those funds,* so the same models are used by both investors and corporate treasurers to determine their required rates of return.

The first topic in this chapter is the logic of the weighted average cost of capital. Next, we consider the costs of the major types of capital, after which we see how the costs of the individual components of the capital structure are brought together to form a weighted average cost of capital.

THE LOGIC OF THE WEIGHTED AVERAGE COST OF CAPITAL (WACC)

The items in the liability and equity section of a firm's balance sheet—various types of debt, preferred stock, and common equity—are its **capital components.** Any increase in total assets must be financed by an increase in one or more of these capital components. The *costs of capital* represent the rates of return that the firm pays to investors to use various forms of capital funds.

It is possible to finance a firm entirely with equity funds by issuing only stock. In that case, the cost, or required rate, that should be used to analyze investments is the company's required return on equity; however, most firms raise a substantial portion of their funds as long-term debt, and some also use preferred stock. For these firms, their required rates of return (costs of capital) must reflect the average costs of the various sources of long-term funds used, not just the firms' costs of equity.

Assume that Daflex Textiles has a 10 percent cost of debt and a 14 percent cost of equity. Further, assume that Daflex has made the decision to finance next year's projects by selling debt only. The argument is sometimes made that the cost of capital for these projects is 10 percent because only debt will be used to finance them; however, this position is incorrect. If Daflex finances a particular set of projects with debt, the firm will be using up some of its potential for obtaining new debt in the future. As expansion occurs in subsequent years, Daflex will at some point find it necessary to raise additional equity to prevent the proportion of debt from becoming too large.

To illustrate, suppose Daflex borrows heavily at 10 percent during 2010, using up its debt capacity in the process, to finance projects yielding 11 percent. In 2011, it has new projects available that yield 13 percent, well above the return on 2010 projects, but it cannot accept them because they would have to be financed with 14 percent equity funds. To avoid this problem, Daflex should be viewed as an ongoing concern, and *the cost of capital used when making investment decisions should be calculated as a weighted average, or combination, of the various types of funds generally used, regardless of the specific financing used to fund a particular project.*

> **capital components**
> The particular types of capital used by the firm—that is, its debt, preferred stock, and common equity.

Self-Test Question

Why should the cost of capital used when making investment decisions be calculated as a weighted average of the various types of funds the firm generally uses, regardless of the specific financing used to fund a particular project?

BASIC DEFINITIONS

Capital is a necessary factor of production, and, like any other factor, it has a cost. The cost of each component is called the *component cost* of that particular type of capital. For example, if Daflex can borrow money at 10 percent, its component cost of debt is 10 percent.[1] Throughout this chapter we concentrate on debt, preferred

---

[1]We will see shortly that there is both a before-tax and after-tax cost of debt. For now it is sufficient to know that 10 percent is the before-tax component cost of debt.

stock, retained earnings, and new issues of common stock, which are the major capital components. We use the following symbols to designate specific component costs of capital:

r_d = Interest rate on the firm's debt = before-tax component cost of debt. That is, r_d is the component cost of debt before taxes are considered. For Daflex, $r_d = 10.0\%$.

r_{dT} = $r_d(1 - T)$ = After-tax component cost of debt, where T is the firm's marginal tax rate. r_{dT} is the debt cost used to calculate the weighted average cost of capital. For Daflex, $T = 40\%$, so $r_{dT} = r_d(1 - T) = 10.0\%(1 - 0.4) = 10.0\%(0.6) = 6.0\%$.

r_{ps} = Component cost of preferred stock. Daflex has no preferred stock at this time, but as new funds are raised, the company plans to issue preferred stock. The cost of preferred stock, r_{ps}, will be 11 percent.

r_s = Component cost of retained earnings (or internal equity). It is identical to the r_s developed in Chapters 10 and 11, which was defined as the required rate of return on common stock that is demanded by investors. As we will see shortly, for Daflex, $r_s = 14\%$.

r_e = Component cost of external equity obtained by issuing new common stock as opposed to retaining earnings. As we shall see, it is necessary to distinguish between common equity needs that can be satisfied by retained earnings and the common equity needs that are satisfied by selling new stock. This is why we distinguish between internal and external equity, r_s and r_e, respectively. Further, r_e is always greater than r_s. For Daflex, $r_e = 15\%$.

WACC = The weighted average cost of capital. In the future, when Daflex needs *new* capital to finance asset expansion, it will raise part of the new funds as debt, part as preferred stock, and part as common equity (with common equity coming either from retained earnings or from the issuance of new common stock).[2] We will calculate WACC for Daflex Textiles shortly.

These definitions and concepts are explained in detail in the remainder of the chapter, where we develop a marginal cost of capital (MCC) schedule that can be used to make investment decisions. Later, in Chapter 14, we will extend the analysis to determine the mix of types of capital, which is termed the **capital structure,** that will minimize the firm's cost of capital and thereby maximize its value.

capital structure
The combination or mix of different types of capital used by a firm.

Self-Test Question
Identify the firm's major capital structure components, and give their respective component cost symbols.

---

[2]Firms try to keep their debt, preferred stock, and common equity in optimal proportions. We will learn how firms establish these proportions in Chapter 14. However, firms do not try to maintain any proportional relationship between the common stock and retained earnings accounts as shown on the balance sheet—for capital structure purposes, common equity is common equity, whether it comes from selling new common stock or from retaining earnings.

COST OF DEBT, r_{dT}

after-tax cost of debt, r_{dT}
The relevant cost of new debt, taking into account the tax deductibility of interest.

The **after-tax cost of debt, r_{dT},** is the interest rate on debt, r_d, less the tax savings that result because interest is deductible. This is the same as r_d multiplied by $(1 - T)$, where T is the firm's marginal tax rate:

$$
\begin{aligned}
\text{After-tax component} &= r_{dT} = \left(\begin{array}{c}\text{Bondholders' required}\\\text{rate of return}\end{array}\right) - \left(\begin{array}{c}\text{Tax}\\\text{savings}\end{array}\right)\\
\text{cost of debt} &= \qquad\quad r_d \qquad\quad - \quad r_d \times T\\
&= r_d(1 - T)
\end{aligned}
$$

In effect, the government pays part of the cost of debt because interest is tax deductible. Therefore, if Daflex can borrow at an interest rate of 10 percent, and if it has a marginal tax rate of 40 percent, then its after-tax cost of debt is 6 percent:

$$r_{dT} = r_d(1 - T) = 10.0\%(1.0 - 0.4) = 10.0\%(0.6) = 6.0\%$$

We use the after-tax cost of debt because the value of the firm's stock, which we want to maximize, depends on *after-tax* cash flows. Because interest is a deductible expense, it produces tax savings that reduce the net cost of borrowing, making the after-tax cost of debt less than the before-tax cost. We are concerned with after-tax cash flows, so after-tax rates of return are appropriate.[3]

Note that the cost of debt is the interest rate on *new* debt, not that on already outstanding debt; in other words, we are interested in the *marginal* cost of debt. Our primary concern with the cost of capital is to use it for investment decisions—for example, a decision about whether to obtain the capital needed to acquire a new machine tool or build a new distribution center. The rate at which the firm has borrowed in the past is a sunk cost, and it is irrelevant for cost of capital purposes.

In Chapter 10, we solved the following equation to find r_d, the rate of return, or yield to maturity (YTM), for a bond:

$$\text{Bond value} = V_d = \frac{INT}{(1 + r_d)^1} + \frac{INT}{(1 + r_d)^2} + \cdots + \frac{INT + M}{(1 + r_d)^N}$$

Here, INT is the dollar coupon interest paid per period, M is the face value repaid at maturity, and N is the number of interest payments remaining until maturity. The r_d, which is the bond's YTM, is the rate of return that investors require to purchase the firm's bonds.

Assume that Daflex issued a new bond a few years ago. The bond has a face value of $1,000, 20 years remain until it matures, and $90 interest is paid annually. Daflex is going to issue new bonds in a couple days that have the same general characteristics as this outstanding bond. If the market price of the outstanding bond is $915, what should the r_d be for the new bond? We would expect that the return investors demand for the new bond should be approximately the same as the return for the outstanding bond because both bonds have the same characteristics. The solution for determining r_d is set up as follows:

$$\$915 = \frac{\$90}{(1 + r_d)^1} + \frac{\$90}{(1 + r_d)^2} + \cdots + \frac{\$1,090}{(1 + r_d)^{20}}$$

Whether you use the trial-and-error method or the time value of money functions on your calculator, you should find r_d is 10 percent, which is the before-tax cost of debt for this bond.[4] As a result, the coupon rate of interest on the *new* bonds must be set at 10 percent if Daflex wants to issue these bonds at their \$1,000 par value. And, in this case, because Daflex's marginal tax rate is 40 percent, the after-tax cost of debt, r_{dT}, is $6.0\% = 10.0\%(1 - 0.40)$.

Self-Test Questions

Why is the after-tax cost of debt rather than the before-tax cost used to calculate the weighted average cost of capital?

Is the relevant cost of debt the interest rate on already outstanding debt or that on new debt? Why?

Payment American currently has bonds outstanding that have the following characteristics: maturity value (M) = \$1,000, coupon rate of interest (C) = 6%, years to maturity (N) = 5, and interest is paid annually. If the bond's market value is \$959, what is its before-tax component cost of debt—that is, its yield to maturity (YTM)—associated with these bonds?   (Answer: $r_d = 7\%$)

cost of preferred stock, r_{ps}
The rate of return investors require on the firm's preferred stock. r_{ps} is calculated as the preferred dividend, D_{ps}, divided by the net issuing price, NP.

COST OF PREFERRED STOCK, r_{ps}

In Chapter 10, we found that the dividend associated with preferred stock, D_{ps}, is constant and that preferred stock has no stated maturity. Thus, D_{ps} represents a perpetuity, and the component **cost of preferred stock, r_{ps},** is the preferred dividend, D_{ps}, divided by the net issuing price, NP, or the price the firm receives after deducting the costs of issuing the stock, which are called *flotation costs*:

    12-3

$$\begin{array}{c}\text{Component cost} \\ \text{of preferred stock}\end{array} = r_{ps} = \frac{D_{ps}}{NP_0} = \frac{D_{ps}}{P_0 - \text{Flotation costs}} = \frac{D_{ps}}{P_0(1 - F)}$$

---

[4]It should also be noted that we have ignored flotation costs (the costs incurred for new issuances) on debt because nearly all debt issued by small and medium-sized firms and by many large firms is privately placed and, hence, has no flotation costs. If, however, bonds are publicly placed and do involve flotation costs, the solution value of r_d in the following formula is used as the before-tax cost of debt:

$$V_d(1 - F) = \sum_{t=1}^{N} \frac{INT}{(1 + r_d)^t} + \frac{M}{(1 + r_d)^N}$$

Here, F is the percentage amount (in decimal form) of the bond flotation, or issuing, cost; N is the number of periods to maturity; INT is the dollars of interest per period; M is the maturity value of the bond; and r_d is the cost of debt adjusted to reflect flotation costs. If we assume that the bond in the example calls for annual payments, that it has a 20-year maturity, and that F = 2%, then the flotation-adjusted, before-tax cost of debt is 10.23 percent versus 10 percent before the flotation adjustment:

$$\$915(1 - 0.02) = \frac{\$90}{(1 + r_d)^1} + \cdots + \frac{\$1090}{(1 + r_d)^{20}}$$

Here, F is the percentage (in decimal form) cost of issuing preferred stock and P_0 is the current market price of the preferred stock.

To illustrate, Daflex plans to issue preferred stock that pays a $12.80 dividend per share and sells for $120 per share in the market. It will cost 3 percent, or $3.60 per share, to issue the new preferred stock, so Daflex will net $116.40 per share. Therefore, Daflex's cost of preferred stock is 11 percent:

$$r_{ps} = \frac{\$12.80}{\$120.00(1 - 0.03)} = \frac{\$12.80}{\$116.40} = 0.11 = 11.0\%$$

No tax adjustments are made when calculating r_{ps} because preferred dividends, unlike interest expense on debt, are not tax deductible, so there are no tax savings associated with the use of preferred stock.

Self-Test Questions

Does the component cost of preferred stock include or exclude flotation costs? Explain.

Is a tax adjustment made to the cost of preferred stock? Why or why not?

Payment American expects to issue preferred stock that pays a $6.84 dividend per share each year for $80. If it costs Payment America 5 percent to issue the new preferred stock, what is the company's component cost of preferred stock?   (Answer: $r_{ps} = 9\%$)

COST OF RETAINED EARNINGS, OR INTERNAL EQUITY, r_s

The costs of debt and preferred stock are based on the returns investors require on these securities. Similarly, the **cost of retained earnings, r_s,** is the rate of return stockholders require on equity capital the firm obtains by retaining earnings that otherwise could be distributed to common stockholders as dividends.[5]

cost of retained earnings, r_s
The rate of return required by stockholders on a firm's existing common stock.

The reason we must assign a cost to retained earnings involves the *opportunity cost principle*. The firm's after-tax earnings literally belong to its common stockholders. Bondholders are compensated by interest payments, and preferred stockholders by preferred dividends, but the earnings that remain after interest and preferred dividends are paid belong to the common stockholders, and these earnings help compensate common stockholders for the use of their capital. Management can either pay out the earnings in the form of dividends or retain earnings and reinvest them in the business. If management decides to retain earnings, there is an opportunity cost involved—stockholders could have received the earnings as dividends and invested this money for themselves in other stocks, in bonds, in real estate, or in anything else. Thus, the firm must earn a return on earnings it retains that is at least as great as the return stockholders themselves can earn on alternative investments of comparable risk; otherwise, investors would demand that the earnings be paid as dividends so they can invest the money themselves.

---

[5]The term *retained earnings* can be interpreted to mean either the balance sheet item "retained earnings," consisting of all the earnings retained in the business throughout its history, or the income statement item "additions to retained earnings." The income statement item is used in this chapter; for our purpose, *retained earnings* refers to that part of current earnings not paid out in dividends and, hence, available for reinvestment in the business this year.

What rate of return can stockholders expect to earn on equivalent-risk investments? First, recall from Chapter 11 that stocks normally are in equilibrium, with the expected rate of return and required rate of return being equal: $\hat{r}_s = r_s$. Therefore, we can assume that Daflex's stockholders expect to earn a return of r_s on their money. *If the firm cannot invest retained earnings and earn at least r_s, it should pay these funds to its stockholders and let them invest directly in other assets that do provide this return.*[6]

Whereas debt and preferred stocks are obligations that have easily determined costs, it is not as easy to measure r_s. We can, however, employ the principles developed in Chapters 10 and 11 to produce reasonably good cost of common equity estimates. To begin, we know that if a stock is in equilibrium (which is the typical situation), then its required rate of return, r_s, is equal to its expected rate of return, $\hat{r}_s$. Further, its required return is equal to a risk-free rate, r_{RF}, plus a risk premium, RP, whereas the expected return on a constant growth stock is equal to the stock's dividend yield, $\hat{D}_1/P_0$, plus its expected growth rate, g. That is:

 **12-4**

$$\text{Required rate of return} = \text{Expected rate of return}$$
$$r_s \qquad = \qquad \hat{r}_s$$
$$r_{RF} + RP \qquad = \qquad \frac{\hat{D}_1}{P_0} + g$$

Because the two must be equal, we can estimate r_s using either the left side or the right side of Equation 12-4. Actually, three methods are commonly used for finding the cost of retained earnings:

1. The CAPM approach (left side of Equation 12-4)

2. The discounted cash flow (DCF) approach (right side of Equation 12-4)

3. The bond-yield-plus-risk-premium approach

These three approaches are discussed next.

CAPM Approach (Required Rate of Return, r_s)

The capital asset pricing model (CAPM) we developed in Chapter 11 is stated as follows:

 **12-5**

$$r_s = r_{RF} + RP$$
$$= r_{RF} + (r_M - r_{RF})\beta_s$$

Equation 12-5 shows that the CAPM estimate of r_s begins with the risk-free rate, r_{RF}, to which is added a risk premium that is based on the stock's relation to the market as measured by its beta coefficient, β_s, and the magnitude of the market risk premium, RP_M, which is the difference between the market return, r_M, and the risk-free rate, r_{RF}.

---

[6]Dividends and capital gains are taxed differently, with long-term gains taxed at a lower rate than dividends for most stockholders. That makes it beneficial for companies to retain earnings rather than to pay them out as dividends, and that, in turn, results in a relatively low cost of capital for retained earnings. This point is discussed in Chapter 14.

To illustrate the CAPM approach, assume that $r_{RF} = 6\%$, $r_M = 11\%$, and $\beta_s = 1.5$ for Daflex's common stock. Using the CAPM approach, Daflex's cost of retained earnings, r_s, is calculated as follows:

$$r_s = 6.0\% + (11.0\% - 6.0\%)(1.5) = 6.0\% + 7.5\% = 13.5\%$$

Although the CAPM approach appears to yield an accurate, precise estimate of r_s, there actually are several problems with it. First, as we saw in Chapter 11, if a firm's stockholders are not well diversified, they might be concerned with total risk rather than with market risk only (measured by β); in this case, the firm's true investment risk will not be measured by its beta, and the CAPM procedure will understate the correct value of r_s. Further, even if the CAPM method is valid, it is difficult to obtain correct estimates of the inputs required to make it operational because (1) there is controversy about whether to use long-term or short-term Treasury yields for r_{RF} and (2) both β_s and r_M should be estimated values, which often are difficult to obtain.

Discounted Cash Flow (DCF) Approach (Expected Rate of Return, $\hat{r}_s$)

In Chapter 10, we learned that both the price and the expected rate of return on a share of common stock depend, ultimately, on the dividends the stock is expected to pay. The value of a share of stock can be written as follows:

$$P_0 = \frac{\hat{D}_1}{(1+r_s)^1} + \frac{\hat{D}_2}{(1+r_s)^2} + \frac{\hat{D}_3}{(1+r_s)^3} + \cdots + \frac{\hat{D}_\infty}{(1+r_s)^\infty}$$

12-6

Here, P_0 is the current market price of the stock; $\hat{D}_t$ is the dividend *expected* to be paid at the end of Year t; and r_s is the required rate of return. If dividends are expected to grow at a constant rate, then, as we saw in Chapter 10, Equation 12-6 reduces to:

$$P_0 = \frac{D_0(1+g)}{r_s - g} = \frac{\hat{D}_1}{r_s - g}$$

12-6a

We can solve Equation 12-6a for r_s to estimate the required rate of return on common equity, which for the marginal investor is also equal to the expected rate of return, $\hat{r}_s$:

$$\hat{r}_s = \frac{\hat{D}_1}{P_0} + g = r_s$$

12-7

Thus, investors expect to receive a dividend yield, $\hat{D}_1/P_0$, plus a capital gain, g, for a total expected return of $\hat{r}_s$. In equilibrium, this expected return is also equal to the required return, r_s. From this point on, we will assume that equilibrium exists, and we will use the terms r_s and $\hat{r}_s$ interchangeably, so we will drop the "hat," ^, above r_s.

It is relatively easy to determine the dividend yield, but it might be difficult to establish the proper growth rate. If past growth rates in earnings and dividends have been relatively stable, and if investors appear to be projecting a continuation of past trends, then g can be based on the firm's historical growth rate. However, if the company's past growth has been abnormally high or low, either because of its own unique situation or because of general economic fluctuations, then historical growth probably should not be used. Security analysts regularly make earnings and dividend growth forecasts, looking at such factors as projected sales, profit margins, and competitive factors. For example, *Value Line*, which is available in most libraries, provides growth rate forecasts for approximately 1,700 companies, and Merrill Lynch, Salomon Smith Barney, and other organizations make similar forecasts. Therefore, someone making a cost of capital estimate can obtain several analysts' forecasts, average them, and use the average as a proxy for the growth expectations, g.[7]

To illustrate the DCF approach, suppose Daflex's common stock sells for $50 per share; the common stock dividend expected to be paid at the end of the year is $4.75 per share; and its expected long-term growth rate is 5 percent. Daflex's expected and required rate of return, and hence its cost of retained earnings, is 14.5 percent:

$$r_s = \frac{\$4.75}{\$50.00} + 0.05 = 0.095 + 0.05 = 0.145 = 14.5\%$$

This 14.5 percent is the minimum rate of return that management must expect to earn to justify retaining earnings and plowing them back into the business rather than paying them out to stockholders as dividends.

Bond-Yield-Plus-Risk-Premium Approach ($r_s = r_d + RP$)

Although it is a subjective procedure, analysts often estimate a firm's cost of common equity by adding a risk premium of three to five percentage points to the *before-tax* interest rate on the firm's own long-term debt. It is logical to think that firms with risky, low-rated, and consequently high-interest-rate debt will also have risky, high-cost equity. Using this logic to estimate the cost of common stock is relatively easy—we simply add a risk premium to a readily observable debt cost. For example, Daflex's cost of equity might be estimated as follows:

$$
\begin{aligned}
r_s &= \text{Bond yield} + \text{Risk premium} \\
&= \quad r_d \quad + \quad RP \\
&= \quad 10.0\% \quad + \quad 4.0\% \quad = 14.0\%
\end{aligned}
$$

Because the 4 percent risk premium is a judgmental estimate, the estimated value of r_s also is judgmental. Empirical work suggests that the risk premium over a firm's own bond yield generally has ranged from three to five percentage points, so this method is not likely to produce a precise cost of equity—about all it can do is get us "into the right ballpark."

We have used three methods to estimate the cost of retained earnings, which should be a single number. To summarize, we found the cost of common equity to be (1) 13.5 percent using the CAPM method; (2) 14.5 percent using the constant growth model, the DCF approach; and (3) 14.0 percent with the bond-yield-plus-risk-premium approach. It is not unusual to get different estimates because each of the approaches is based on different assumptions. The CAPM assumes investors are well diversified, the constant growth model assumes the firm's dividends and

---

[7]Analysts' growth-rate forecasts are usually for 5 years into the future, and the rates provided represent the average growth rate over that 5-year horizon. Studies have shown that analysts' forecasts represent the best source of growth-rate data for DCF cost of capital estimates. See Robert Harris, "Using Analysts' Growth Rate Forecasts to Estimate Shareholder Required Rates of Return," *Financial Management,* Spring 1986, 58–67.

earnings will grow at a constant rate far into the future, and the bond-yield-plus-risk-premium approach assumes the cost of equity is closely related to the firm's cost of debt. Which estimate should be used? Probably all of them. Many analysts use multiple approaches to estimate a single value, then average the results. For Daflex, then, the average of the estimates is 14.0% = (13.5% + 14.5% + 14.0%)/3.

People experienced in estimating equity capital costs recognize that both careful analysis and sound judgment are required. It would be nice to pretend that judgment is unnecessary and to specify an easy, precise way of determining the exact cost of equity capital. Unfortunately, this is not possible—finance is in large part a matter of judgment, and we simply must face that fact.

Self-Test Questions

Why must a cost be assigned to retained earnings?

What are the three approaches for estimating the cost of retained earnings?

Identify some problems with the CAPM approach.

What is the reasoning behind the bond-yield-plus-risk-premium approach?

Which of the components of the constant growth DCF formula is most difficult to estimate? Why?

Payment American has common stock that currently sells for $35. The company's next dividend, $\hat{D}_1$, is expected to be $2.45 and its growth rate is a constant 4 percent. What is Pay America's component cost of retained earnings?   (Answer: $r_s = 11\%$)

COST OF NEWLY ISSUED COMMON STOCK, OR EXTERNAL EQUITY, r_e

The **cost of new common equity, r_e,** or external equity capital, is similar to the cost of retained earnings, r_s, except it is higher because the firm incurs *flotation costs* when it issues new common stock. The **flotation costs,** which are the expenses associated with issuing new securities (equity or debt), reduce the amount of funds the firm receives, and hence the amount that can be used for investments. Only the amount of funds that is left after paying flotation costs—that is, the *net* amount received by the firm—is available for investing. As a result, *the cost of issuing new common stock (external equity), r_e, is greater than the cost of retained earnings, r_s,* because there are no flotation costs associated with retained earnings (internal equity) financing.

In general, the cost of issuing new equity, r_e, can be found by modifying the DCF formula (Equation 12-7) that we used to compute the cost of retained earnings, r_s, to obtain the following equation:

cost of new common equity, r_e
The cost of external equity; based on the cost of retained earnings but increased for flotation costs.

flotation costs
The expenses incurred when selling new issues of securities.

$$\hat{r}_e = \frac{\hat{D}_1}{NP_0} + g = \frac{\hat{D}_1}{P_0(1 - F)} + g$$

12-8

Here, F is the percentage flotation cost (in decimal form) incurred in selling the new stock issue, so $P_0(1 - F)$ is the net price per share received by the company. Note that if $F = 0$, Equation 12-8 simplifies to Equation 12-7, which is the form of the DCF formula that we used to compute the cost of retained earnings.

If Daflex can issue new common stock at a flotation cost of 11 percent, r_e is computed as follows:

$$\hat{r}_e = \frac{\$4.75}{\$50.00(1 - 0.05)} + 0.05$$

$$= \frac{\$4.75}{\$47.50} + 0.05 = 0.15 = 15.0\%$$

Using the DCF approach to estimate the cost of retained earnings, we found that investors require a return of $r_s = 14\%$ on the stock. Because of flotation costs, however, the company must earn more than 14 percent on funds obtained by selling stock if it is to provide a 14 percent return to stockholders. Specifically, if the firm earns 15 percent on funds obtained from new stock, then earnings per share will not fall below previously expected earnings, the firm's expected dividend can be maintained, and, as a result, the price per share will not decline. If the firm earns less than 15 percent, then earnings, dividends, and growth will fall below expectations, causing the price of the stock to decline. If it earns more than 15 percent, the price of the stock will rise.

The reason for the adjustment for flotation costs can be made clear by a simple example. Suppose Coastal Realty Company has $100,000 of assets and no debt, it earns an 18 percent return (or $18,000) on its assets, and it pays all earnings out as dividends, so its growth rate is zero. The company has 1,000 shares of stock outstanding, so EPS = DPS = $18 = $18,000/1,000, and $P_0 = \$100 = \$100,000/$ 1,000. Coastal's cost of equity is thus $r_s = \$18/\$100 + 0 = 18.0\%$. Now suppose Coastal can get a return of 18 percent on new assets. Should it sell new stock to acquire new assets? If it sold 1,000 new shares of stock to the public for $100 per share, but it incurred a 4 percent flotation cost on the issue, it would net $100 − 0.04($100) = $96 per share, or $96,000 in total. It would then invest this $96,000 and earn 18 percent, or $17,280. Its new *total* earnings would be $35,280, which would consist of $18,000 generated from the *old* assets plus $17,280 from the *new* assets. But the $35,280 would have to be distributed equally to the 2,000 shares of stock now outstanding. Therefore, Weaver's EPS and DPS would decline from $18 to $17.64 = $35,280/2,000. Because its EPS and DPS would fall, the price of the stock would also fall from $P_0 = \$100$ to $P_1 = \$17.64/0.18 = \$98.00$. This result occurs because investors put up $100 per share, but the company received and invested only $96 per share. Thus, we see that the firm must earn more than 18 percent when it invests the $96 if it is going to provide investors with an 18 percent return ($18 dividend) on the $100 they put up.

We can use Equation 12-8 to compute the return Coastal must earn on the $96,000 of new assets—that is, the amount raised with the new issue:

$$r_e = \frac{\$18}{\$100(1 - 0.04)} + 0.0 = 0.1875 = 18.75\%$$

If Weaver invests the funds from the new common stock issue at 18.75%, here is what would happen:

New total earnings = Earnings on old assets + Earnings on new assets

= $18,000 + $96,000(0.1875) = $36,000

New EPS and DPS = $36,000/2,000 = $18

New price = $18/0.18 = $100 = Original price

Thus, if the return on the new assets is equal to r_e as calculated by Equation 12-8, then EPS, DPS, and the stock price will all remain constant. If the return on the new assets exceeds r_e, then EPS, DPS, and P_0 will rise. Because of flotation costs, the cost of external equity exceeds the cost of equity raised internally from retained earnings—that is, $r_e > r_s$. If $F = 0$, however, then $r_e = r_s$.

Self-Test Questions

Why is the cost of external equity capital higher than the cost of retained earnings?

How can the DCF model be changed to account for flotation costs?

Payment American has common stock that currently sells for $35. The company's next dividend, $\hat{D}_1$, is expected to be $2.45 and its growth rate is a constant 4 percent. If Pay America issues new common stock, flotation costs will be 12.5 percent. What is Pay America's component cost of new common equity?   (Answer: $r_s = 12\%$)

WEIGHTED AVERAGE COST OF CAPITAL, WACC

Each firm has an optimal capital structure, or mix of debt, preferred stock, and common equity, that causes its stock price to be maximized. Therefore, a rational, value-maximizing firm will establish a **target (optimal) capital structure** and then raise new capital in a manner that will keep the actual capital structure on target over time. In this chapter we assume that the firm has identified its optimal capital structure, it uses this optimum as the target, and it raises funds so that it constantly remains on target. How the target is established will be examined in Chapter 14.[8]

The target proportions of debt, preferred stock, and common equity, along with the component costs of capital, are used to calculate the firm's **weighted average cost of capital (WACC).** The WACC simply represents the average cost of each dollar of financing, no matter its source, that the firm uses to purchase assets. That is, WACC represents the minimum return the firm must earn on its investments (assets) to maintain its current level of wealth; it is the firm's *required rate of return.*

To illustrate, suppose Daflex Textiles has determined that in the future it will raise new capital according to the following proportions: 40 percent debt, 10 percent preferred stock, and 50 percent common equity (retained earnings plus new common stock). In the preceding sections, we found that its before-tax cost of debt, r_d, is 10 percent, so its *after-tax* cost of debt, r_{dT}, is 6 percent; its cost of preferred stock, r_{ps}, is 11 percent; and its cost of common equity is 14 percent if all of its equity financing comes from retained earnings (r_s) and 15 percent if its equity financing comes from selling new common stock (r_e). Now we can calculate Daflex's weighted average cost of capital (WACC) as follows:

target (optimal) capital structure
The combination (percentages) of debt, preferred stock, and common equity that will maximize the price of the firm's stock.

weighted average cost of capital (WACC)
A weighted average of the component costs of debt, preferred stock, and common equity.

$$\text{WACC} = \left[\left(\begin{array}{c}\text{Proportion}\\\text{of}\\\text{debt}\end{array}\right) \times \left(\begin{array}{c}\text{After-tax}\\\text{cost of}\\\text{debt}\end{array}\right)\right] + \left[\left(\begin{array}{c}\text{Proportion}\\\text{of preferred}\\\text{stock}\end{array}\right) \times \left(\begin{array}{c}\text{Cost of}\\\text{preferred}\\\text{stock}\end{array}\right)\right] + \left[\left(\begin{array}{c}\text{Proportion}\\\text{of common}\\\text{equity}\end{array}\right) \times \left(\begin{array}{c}\text{Cost of}\\\text{common}\\\text{equity}\end{array}\right)\right]$$

$$= [\quad w_d \quad \times \quad r_{dT} \quad] + [\quad w_{ps} \quad \times \quad r_{ps} \quad] + [\quad w_s \quad \times \quad (r_s \text{ or } r_e) \quad]$$

12-9

---

[8]Notice that only long-term debt is included in the capital structure. Daflex uses its cost of capital in the investment process, which involves long-term assets, and it finances those assets with long-term capital. Thus, current liabilities do not enter the calculation. We will discuss this point in more detail in Chapter 14.

Here, w_d, w_{ps}, and w_s are the weights used for debt, preferred stock, and common equity, respectively.

If its new financing needs do not require new common stock, then every dollar of new capital that Daflex obtains consists of 40¢ of debt with an after-tax cost of 6 percent, 10¢ of preferred stock with a cost of 11 percent, and 50¢ of common equity (all from additions to retained earnings) with a cost of 14 percent. In this case, the company's WACC is calculated as follows:

$$\text{WACC} = 0.4(6.0\%) + 0.1(11.0\%) + 0.5(14\%) = 10.5\%$$

The average cost of each whole dollar, WACC, is 10.5 percent as long as these conditions continue. If the component costs of capital change when new funds are raised in the future, then WACC changes. We discuss changes in the component costs of capital in the next section.

Determining a firm's WACC is more complicated than simply plugging numbers into Equation 12-9 and performing the math. Most large firms have numerous types of debt (and sometimes different "classes" of common stock) that have different component costs so that there is not one cost of debt (cost of equity). As a result, in practice, the cost of debt, r_d, that is used to compute the firm's WACC is a weighted average of the costs of the various types of debt the firm has issued. Similarly, when a firm raises capital by issuing new common stock, the total amount of equity capital often includes both the amount of earnings retained during the year and the amount raised with the new common stock issue, which means the cost of common equity should be a weighted average of r_s and r_e. To simplify our discussions and the subsequent computations, however, we assume that the firm issues only one type of bond each time it raises new funds using debt, and when new common stock is issued that the average cost to the firm for *all* common equity used to finance new investments is the cost of the new common stock, r_e, even if retained earnings have provided some of the common equity capital.

Self-Test Questions

How is the weighted average cost of capital calculated? Write out the equation.

Payment America's capital structure consists of 40 percent debt, 15 percent preferred stock, and 45 percent common equity. The company's component costs of capital are $r_{dT} = 5\%$, $r_{ps} = 8\%$, and $r_s = 14\%$. What is Payment America's WACC?   (Answer: WACC = r = 9.5%)

THE MARGINAL COST OF CAPITAL, MCC

marginal cost of capital (MCC)
The cost of obtaining another dollar of new capital; the weighted average cost of the last dollar of new capital raised.

The marginal cost of any item is the cost of another unit of that item. For example, the marginal cost of labor is the cost of adding one additional worker. The marginal cost of labor might be $25 per person if 10 workers are added but $35 per person if the firm tries to hire 100 new workers because it will be harder to find that many people willing and able to do the work. The same concept applies to capital. As the firm tries to attract more new dollars, at some point, the cost of each dollar will increase. Thus, the **marginal cost of capital (MCC)** *is defined as the cost of the last dollar of new capital that the firm raises, and the marginal cost rises as more and more capital is raised during a given period.*

In the preceding section, we computed Daflex's WACC to be 10.5 percent. As long as Daflex keeps its capital structure on target, and as long as its debt has an after-tax cost of 6 percent, its preferred stock has a cost of 11 percent, and its common equity has a cost of 14 percent (because new stock does not need to be issued), then its weighted average cost of capital will be 10.5 percent. Each dollar the firm raises will consist of some long-term debt, some preferred stock, and some common equity, and the cost of the whole dollar will be 10.5 percent—that is, its marginal cost of capital (MCC) will be 10.5 percent.

The MCC Schedule

A graph that shows how the WACC changes as more and more new capital is raised by the firm is called the **MCC (marginal cost of capital) schedule.** Figure 12-1 shows Daflex's MCC schedule if the cost of debt, cost of preferred stock, and cost of common equity *never change.* Here the dots represent dollars raised, and because each dollar of new capital will have an average cost equal to 10.5 percent, the marginal cost of capital (MCC) for Daflex is constant at 10.5 percent under the assumptions we have used to this point.

Do you think Daflex actually could raise an unlimited amount of new capital at the 10.5 percent cost? Probably not. As a practical matter, as a company raises larger and larger amounts of funds during a given time period, the costs of those funds begin to rise, and as this occurs, the weighted average cost of each new dollar also rises. Thus, companies cannot raise unlimited amounts of capital at a constant cost. At some point, the cost of each new dollar will increase, no matter what its source (debt, preferred stock, or common equity).

MCC (marginal cost of capital) schedule
A graph that relates the firm's weighted average cost of each dollar of capital to the total amount of new capital raised.

FIGURE 12-1   Marginal Cost of Capital (MCC) Schedule for Daflex Inc.

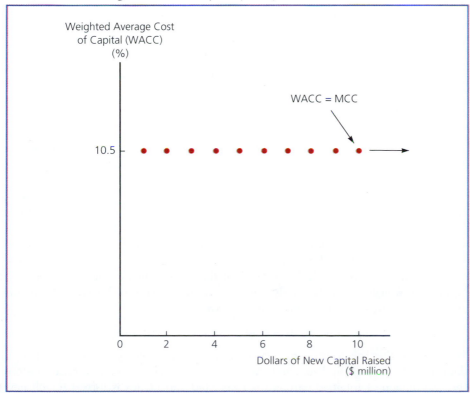

Why does the cost of capital increase as more funds are raised? In Chapter 11, we learned that the return demanded by investors to purchase such financial assets as corporate bonds and stock depends on the riskiness of the instrument. In particular, the higher the risk associated with the investment, the higher the return demanded by investors. Now consider a firm that continues to issue bonds—that is, borrow from investors. Generally speaking, as the firm's percentage of debt (as measured by its debt ratio) increases, so does the chance that the firm will not be able to service the debt, which ultimately could lead to its bankruptcy. Thus, all else equal, as the firm increases its relative amount of debt, its financial risk increases. Investors would likely demand higher rates of return to provide funds to this firm, which means that its WACC would be higher.

How much can Daflex raise before the cost of its funds increases? As a first step to determining the point at which the MCC begins to rise, suppose that the company's current balance sheet shows total long-term capital of $800 million, all of this capital was raised in the past, and these funds have been invested in assets that are now being used in operations. If Daflex wants to raise any new (marginal) capital so that the total amount consists of 40 percent debt, 10 percent preferred stock, and 50 percent common equity, then to raise $10 million in new capital, the company should issue $4 million of new debt, $1 million of new preferred stock, and $5 million of additional common equity. The additional common equity could come from two sources: (1) retained earnings, defined as that part of this year's profits that management decides to retain in the business rather than pay out as dividends (but not earnings retained in the past, because these amounts have already been invested in existing assets) or (2) proceeds from the sale of new common stock.

We know that Daflex's WACC will be 10.5 percent as long as the after-tax cost of debt is 6 percent, the cost of preferred stock is 11 percent, and the funds needed from common equity can be satisfied by retained earnings with a cost of 14 percent ($r_s = 14\%$). But what happens if Daflex expands so rapidly that the retained earnings for the year are not sufficient to meet the common equity needs, forcing the firm to sell new common stock? Earlier, we determined that the cost of issuing new common stock, r_e, will be 15 percent because the flotation costs associated with the new issue will be 5 percent. Because the cost of common equity increases when common stock has to be issued, the WACC also increases at this point.

How much new capital can Daflex raise before it exhausts its retained earnings and is forced to sell new common stock? In other words, where will an increase in the MCC schedule occur?

Suppose that Daflex's net income this year is expected to be $80 million; $30 million of the income will be paid out as dividends, leaving $50 million to be added to retained earnings (the payout ratio is 37.5 percent, so the retention ratio is 62.5 percent). In this case, Daflex can invest in capital projects to the point where the common equity needs equal $50 million before new common stock must be issued. Remember, though, that when Daflex needs new funds, the target capital structure indicates that only 50 percent of the total should come from common equity; the remainder of the funds should come from issues of bonds (40 percent) and preferred stock (10 percent). Thus, we know that:

$$\text{Common equity} = 0.50 \times \text{Total new capital raised}$$

We can use this relationship to determine how much *total new capital*—that is, debt, preferred stock, and retained earnings in combination—can be raised before the $50 million of retained earnings is exhausted and Daflex is forced to sell new common stock. Just set the common equity needs equal to the retained earnings amount, then solve for the *total* new capital amount:

$$\text{Retained earnings} = \$50 \text{ million} = 0.50 \left(\begin{array}{c} \text{Total new} \\ \text{capital raised} \end{array} \right)$$

$$\left(\begin{array}{c} \text{Total new} \\ \text{capital raised} \end{array} \right) = \frac{\$50 \text{ million}}{0.50} = \$100 \text{ million}$$

As long as Daflex needs $100 million or less to finance its new investments, the common equity portion—that is, 50 percent—can be satisfied with retained earnings, or internal, financing. If the firm needs more than $100 million, however, it must sell new common stock to finance the new investments, and the cost of common equity will increase.

If Daflex needs exactly $100 million in total new capital, the breakdown of the amount that would come from each source of capital and the computation for the weighted average cost of capital (WACC) would be as follows:

Capital Source	Weight (1)	Amount in Millions $100 × (1) = (2)	After-Tax Component Cost (3)	WACC (1) × (3) = (4)
Debt	0.40	$ 40.0	6.0%	2.4%
Preferred stock	0.10	10.0	11.0	1.1
Common equity	0.50	50.0	14.0	7.0
	1.00	$100.0		10.5% = WACC$_1$

Therefore, if Daflex needs *exactly* $100 million in new funds this year, retained earnings will be just enough to satisfy the common equity requirement, so the firm will not need to sell new common stock and its weighted average cost of capital (WACC) will be 10.5 percent. But what will happen if Daflex needs more than $100 million in new capital? If Daflex needs $110 million, for example, the $50 million of retained earnings will not be sufficient to cover the $55 million common equity requirements (50 percent of the total funds), so new common stock will have to be sold.

The cost of issuing new common stock, r_e, is greater than the cost of retained earnings, r_s, hence, the WACC will be greater. If Daflex raises $110 million in new capital, the breakdown of the amount that would come from each source of capital and the computation for the weighted average cost of capital (WACC) would be as follows:

Capital Source	Weight (1)	Amount in Millions $110 × (1) = (2)	After-Tax Component Cost (3)	WACC (1) × (3) = (4)
Debt	0.40	$ 44.0	6.0%	2.4%
Preferred stock	0.10	11.0	11.0	1.1
Common equity	0.50	55.0	15.0	7.5
	1.00	$110.0		11.0% = WACC$_2$

FIGURE 12-2   Marginal Cost of Capital Schedule for Daflex Inc. Using Both Retained Earnings and New Common Stock

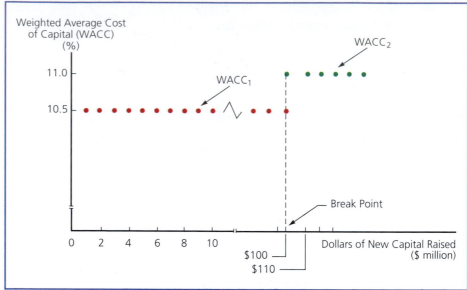

break point (BP)
The dollar value of new capital that can be raised before an increase in the firm's weighted average cost of capital occurs.

The WACC will be greater because Daflex will have to sell new common stock, which has a higher component cost than retained earnings (15 percent versus 14 percent).[9] Consequently, if Daflex's investment needs are greater than $100 million, new common stock will need to be sold, and its WACC will increase. The $100 million in total new capital is defined as the *retained earnings break point,* because above this amount of total capital, a break, or jump, in Daflex's MCC schedule occurs. In general, a **break point (BP)** is defined as the dollar of *new total capital* that can be raised before an increase in the firm's WACC occurs. If the firm raises $1 of additional capital, the WACC will "jump" to a higher level.

Figure 12-2 graphs Daflex's marginal cost of capital schedule with the retained earnings break point. Each dollar has a weighted average cost of 10.5 percent until the company raises more than $100 million. If Daflex raises exactly $100 million, $40 million will be new debt with an after-tax cost of 6 percent, $10 million will be preferred stock with a cost of 11 percent, and $50 million will be retained earnings with a cost of 14 percent. However, if Daflex raises one dollar over $100 million, each new dollar will contain 50¢ of equity *obtained by selling new common stock such that all common equity will cost 15 percent.* As a result, WACC jumps from 10.5 percent to 11.0 percent, as calculated previously and shown in Table 12-1.

Of course, the MCC does not jump by precisely 0.5 percent when we raise $1 over $100 million. Figure 12-2 should be regarded as an approximation rather than as a precise representation of reality. We will return to this point later in the chapter.

---

[9]Remember that to simplify our discussion we have assumed that when new common stock is issued the average cost to the firm for *all* common equity used to finance new investments—that is, retained earnings and new common stock—is the cost of new common stock, r_e.

> **TABLE 12-1**   WACC and Break Points for Daflex's MCC Schedule

I. Break Points

1. $BP_{retained\ earnings} = \$50,000,000/0.50 = \$100,000,000$
2. $BP_{debt} = \$60,000,000/0.40 = \$150,000,000$

II. Weighted Average Cost of Capital (WACC)

1. If the Firm's New Capital Needs Range from $1 to $100,000,000

Capital Source	Breakdown of Funds if $100,000,000 Is Raised	Weight of Capital	×	After-Tax Component Cost	=	WACC
Debt, r_{dT1}	$ 40,000,000	0.40	×	6.0%	=	2.4%
Preferred stock, r_{ps}	10,000,000	0.10	×	11.0	=	1.1
Common equity, r_s	50,000,000	0.50	×	14.0	=	7.0
	$100,000,000	1.00				10.5% = WACC$_1$

2. If the Firm's New Capital Needs Range from $100,000,001 to $150,000,000

Capital Source	Breakdown of Funds if $150,000,000 Is Raised	Weight of Capital	×	After-Tax Component Cost	=	WACC
Debt, r_{dT1}	$ 60,000,000	0.40	×	6.0%	=	2.4%
Preferred stock, r_{ps}	15,000,000	0.10	×	11.0	=	1.1
Common equity, r_e	75,000,000	0.50	×	15.0	=	7.5
	$150,000,000	1.00				11.0% = WACC$_2$

3. If the Firm's New Capital Needs are Greater than $150,000,000

Capital Source	Breakdown of Funds if $160,000,000 Is Raised	Weight of Capital	×	After-Tax Component Cost	=	WACC
Debt, r_{dT2}	$ 64,000,000	0.40	×	7.2%	=	2.9%
Preferred stock, r_{ps}	16,000,000	0.10	×	11.0	=	1.1
Common equity, r_e	80,000,000	0.50	×	15.0	=	7.5
	$160,000,000	1.00				11.5% = WACC$_3$

Note: Each boxed number indicates which component cost differs from the WACC that is computed in the previous range. For example, if the amount of funds that Daflex needs to raise is from $100,000,001 to $150,000,000, new common equity must be issued, and thus equity will have a cost, r_e, equal to 15.0 percent, which is greater than the cost of equity if the firm needs funds equal to $100,000,000 or less ($r_s = 14\%$). Remember that the break point associated with retained earnings is $100,000,000; at this point, the amount of retained earnings is "used up."

Other Breaks in the MCC Schedule

There is a jump, or break, in Daflex's MCC schedule at $100 million of new capital because new common stock needs to be sold. Could there be other breaks in the schedule? Yes, there could. For example, suppose Daflex could obtain only $60 million of debt at a before-tax rate of 10 percent (6 percent after-tax cost), with any additional debt costing 12 percent (7.2 percent after taxes). This would result in a second break point in the MCC schedule, at the point where the $60 million of 10 percent debt is exhausted. At what amount of *total* financing would the 6 percent debt be used up? We know that this total financing will amount to $60 million of debt plus some amount of preferred stock and common equity. If we let BP_{Debt} represent the total financing at this second break point, then we know that 40 percent of BP_{Debt} will be debt, so:

$$0.4(BP_{Debt}) = \$60 \text{ million}$$

Solving for BP_{Debt}, we have:

$$BP_{debt} = \frac{\$60 \text{ million}}{0.4} = \$150 \text{ million}$$

$$= \frac{\text{Maximum amount of 10\% debt}}{\text{Proportion of debt}}$$

As you can see, there will be another break in the MCC schedule after Daflex has raised a total of $150 million, and this second break results from an increase in the cost of debt. The higher after-tax cost of debt (7.2 percent versus 6.0 percent) will result in a higher WACC. For example, if Daflex needs $160 million for investment projects, the WACC would be 11.5 percent:

Capital Source	Weight (1)	Amount in Millions $160 × (1) = (2)	After-Tax Component Cost (3)	WACC (1) × (3) = (4)
Debt	0.40	$ 64.0	7.2%	2.9%
Preferred stock	0.10	16.0	11.0	1.1
Common equity	0.50	80.0	15.0	7.5
	1.00	$160.00		11.5% = WACC₃

In other words, the next dollar beyond $150 million will consist of 40¢ of 12 percent debt (7.2 percent after taxes), 10¢ of 11 percent preferred stock, and 50¢ of new common stock at a cost of 15 percent (retained earnings were used up much earlier), and this marginal dollar will have a cost of $WACC_3 = 11.5\%$.

The effect of this second WACC increase is shown in Figure 12-3. Now there are two break points, one caused by using up all the retained earnings and the other by using up all the 10 percent debt. With the two breaks, there are three different WACCs: $WACC_1 = 10.5\%$ for the first $100 million of new capital; $WACC_2 = 11.0\%$ in the interval between $100 million and $150 million; and $WACC_3 = 11.5\%$ for all new capital beyond $150 million.[10]

There could, of course, be still more break points; they would occur if the cost of debt continued to increase with more debt, if the cost of preferred stock increased

---

[10]When we use the term *weighted average cost of capital,* we are referring to the WACC, which is the cost of $1 raised partly as debt, partly as preferred stock, and partly as common equity. We could also calculate the average cost of all the capital the firm raised during a given year. For example, if Daflex raised $160 million, the first $100 million would have a cost of 10.5 percent, the next $50 million would cost 11 percent, and the last $10 million would cost 11.5 percent. The entire $160 million would have an average cost of:

$$\left(\frac{\$100}{\$160}\right) \times (10.5\%) + \left(\frac{\$50}{\$160}\right) \times (11.0\%) + \left(\frac{\$10}{\$160}\right) \times (11.5\%) = 10.72\%$$

In general, this particular cost of capital should not be used for financial decisions—it usually has no relevance in finance. The only exception to this rule occurs when the firm is considering a very large asset that must be accepted in total or else rejected, and the capital required for it includes capital with different WACCs. For example, if Daflex is considering one $160 million project, that project should be evaluated with a 10.72 percent cost.

FIGURE **12-3**   Marginal Cost of Capital Schedule for Daflex Inc. Using Retained
Earnings, New Common Stock, and Higher-Cost Debt

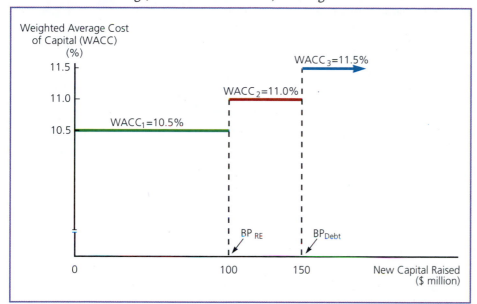

at some level(s), or if the cost of common equity rose as more new common stock is sold.[11] In general, a break point will occur whenever the cost of one of the capital components increases, and the break point can be determined by applying the following equation:

$$\text{Break point} = \frac{\text{Maximum amount of lower cost of capital of a given type}}{\text{Proportion of this type of capital in the capital structure}}$$

12-10

As you can imagine, numerous break points are possible. At the extreme, an MCC schedule might have so many break points that it rises almost continuously beyond some given level of new financing. Such an MCC schedule is shown in Figure 12-4.

The easiest sequence for calculating MCC schedules is as follows:

Step 1. Use Equation 12-10 to determine each point at which a break occurs. A break will occur any time the cost of one of the capital components rises. (It is possible, however, that two capital components could both increase at the same point.) After determining the exact break points, make a list of them.

Step 2. Determine the cost of capital for each component in the intervals between breaks.

---

[11]The first break point is not necessarily the point at which retained earnings are used up; it is possible for low-cost debt to be exhausted *before* retained earnings have been used up. For example, if Daflex had available only $30 million of 10 percent debt, BP_{Debt} would occur at $75 million:

$$BP_{\text{debt}} = \frac{\$30 \text{ million}}{0.40} = \$75 \text{ million}$$

In this case, the break point for debt would occur before the break point for retained earnings, which occurs at $100 million.

FIGURE 12-4   Smooth, or Continuous, Marginal Cost of Capital Schedule

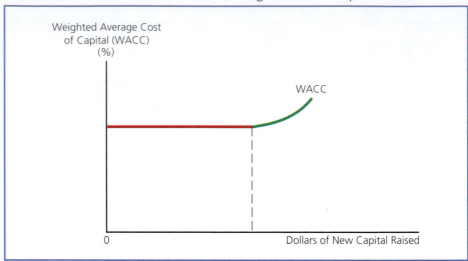

Step 3. Calculate the weighted averages of these component costs to obtain the WACCs in each interval, as we did in Table 12-1. The WACC is constant within each interval, but it rises at each break point.

Notice that if there are n separate breaks, there will be n + 1 different WACCs. For example, in Figure 12-3 we see two breaks and three different WACCs. Also, we should note again that a different MCC schedule will result if a different capital structure—that is, proportions of debt and equity—is used.

Constructing an MCC Schedule—An Illustration

To further illustrate the construction of an MCC schedule, let's assume the following information is known about a firm's capital structures and the current market values of its debt and equity:

Capital Source	Capital Structure	Market Value Per Share	Dividend/Interest Payment Per Share
Debt	35.0%	$1,067.10	$90.00
Preferred stock	5.0	75.00	7.20
Common equity	60.0	35.00	3.00

The face value of the debt is $1,000, and interest is paid annually. The firm is expected to grow at a constant rate of 5 percent far into the future, and retained earnings are forecast to increase by $120 million in the coming year. The flotation costs associated with issuing new debt are negligible, but the costs associated with issuing new preferred stock equal 2 percent of the selling price as long as the amount issued is $15 million or less; amounts of preferred stock exceeding $15 million will have flotation costs of 4 percent. The cost to issue new common stock is 5 percent if $90 million or less is issued; this cost rises to 10 percent for amounts exceeding $90 million. The firm's investment banker estimates that the firm can issue new 10-year debt with the same characteristics as its existing debt up to a maximum of $105 million; any amount in excess of $105 million will have the same characteristics, except that the issue price will match the face value. Preferred stock and common stock can be issued at the current market values given in the preceding table. The firm's marginal tax rate is 40 percent.

Based on the information provided, we construct the MCC schedule as follows:

Step 1. Compute the break points. In this case, at most four break points are possible: (1) if the common equity financing needs exceed the $120 million expected retained earnings because new common stock must be issued and new equity has a higher cost than retained earnings; (2) if the debt financing needs exceed $105 million because additional debt must be sold for the face value ($1,000), which is less than the current market value of the debt ($1,067.10); (3) if preferred stock financing needs exceed $15 million because additional preferred stock will have higher flotation costs; and (4) if the firm needs to issue *new* common equity in excess of $90 million because it will incur higher flotation costs than if lower amounts are issued. If the firm issues new common stock, then its common equity financing needs consist of the $120 million addition to retained earnings that is expected this year plus any new common stock that is issued.

Using Equation 12-10, we can calculate the four break points:

$$BP_{debt} = \frac{\$105 \text{ million}}{0.35} = \$300 \text{ million}$$

$$BP_{preferred\ stock} = \frac{\$15 \text{ million}}{0.05} = \$300 \text{ million}$$

$$BP_{retained\ earnings} = \frac{\$120 \text{ million}}{0.60} = \$200 \text{ million}$$

$$BP_{new\ common\ equity} = \frac{\$120 \text{ million} + \$90 \text{ million}}{0.60} = \$350 \text{ million}$$

In this case, there are three *different* break points. The costs of both debt and preferred stock will increase at the same point, creating one common break point at $300 million of total financing.

Step 2. Next, we compute the cost of capital for each component in the intervals between breaks.

1. *Debt*—$1,000 face; INT = $90, paid annually; N = 10 years; negligible flotation costs:

   a. If the firm's debt financing needs range from $1 to $105 million, the bond can be sold for its market value of $1,067.10. Thus, r_{d1} is:

   $$\$1,067.10 = \frac{\$90}{(1 + r_d)^1} + \frac{\$90}{(1 + r_d)^2} + \cdots + \frac{\$1,090}{(1 + r_d)^{10}}$$

   Using a financial calculator, we find $r_{d1} = 8\%$:

Inputs:	10	?	−1,067.10	90	1,000
	N	I/Y	PV	PMT	FV

   Output: = **8.0**

   b. If debt financing needs are greater than $105 million, the market value of the bond will be $1,000. Thus, r_{d2} is:

   $$\$1,000 = \frac{\$90}{(1 + r_d)^1} + \frac{\$90}{(1 + r_d)^2} + \cdots + \frac{\$1,090}{(1 + r_d)^{10}}$$

Using a financial calculator, we find that $r_{d2} = 9$ percent:

Inputs: 10   ?   −1,000   90   1,000

| N | I/Y | PV | PMT | FV |

Output: = 9.0

2. *Preferred stock*—$P_0 = \$75$; $D_{ps} = \$7.20$:

   a. If preferred stock financing needs range from $1 to $15 million, flotation costs are 2 percent. Using Equation 12-3, we find $r_{ps1} = 9.8$ percent:

$$r_{ps1} = \frac{D_{ps}}{P_0(1 - F)} = \frac{\$7.20}{\$75.00(1 - 0.02)} = \frac{\$7.20}{\$73.50} = 0.098 = 9.8\%$$

   b. If preferred stock financing needs are greater than $15 million, flotation costs increase to 4 percent. In this case, $r_{ps2} = 10.0$ percent:

$$r_{ps2} = \frac{\$7.20}{\$75.00(1 - 0.04)} = \frac{\$7.20}{\$72.00} = 0.10 = 10.0\%$$

3. *Common equity*—$P_0 = \$35$, $D_0 = \$3$; $g = 5\%$:

   a. Expectations are that the addition to retained earnings this year will be $120 million, which represents the amount of internal financing that the firm has available for new investments. Using Equation 12-7, the cost of retained earnings, r_s, is:

$$r_s = \frac{\hat{D}_1}{P_0} + g = \frac{D_0(1 + g)}{P_0} + g = \frac{\$3.00(1.05)}{\$35.00} + 0.05 = \frac{\$3.15}{\$35.00} + 0.05$$
$$= 0.09 + 0.05 = 0.14 = 14.0\%$$

   b. If common equity financing needs are greater than can be satisfied with retained earnings—that is, greater than $120 million—then the firm must sell new common stock to raise the additional amount. The flotation costs for new common stock in amounts from $1 to $90 million are 6 percent. Using Equation 12-8, the cost of new equity, r_{e1}, is:

$$r_{e1} = \frac{\hat{D}_1}{P_0(1 - F)} + g = \frac{\$3.00(1.05)}{\$35.00(1 - 0.05)} + 0.05 = \frac{\$3.15}{\$33.25} + 0.05$$
$$= 0.095 + 0.05 = 0.145 = 14.5\%$$

Thus, the cost of common equity is 14.5 percent if the common equity financing needs exceed the $120 million available from retained earnings but are less than or equal to $210 million, which includes the $120 million in retained earnings plus $90 million in new common stock.

   c. If the amount of new common stock issued exceeds $90 million, the flotation costs are 8 percent. In this case—that is, *total* common equity financing is greater than $210 million—the cost of equity is:

$$r_{e2} = \frac{\hat{D}_1}{P_0(1 - F)} + g = \frac{\$3.00(1.05)}{\$35.00(1 - 0.10)} + 0.05 = \frac{\$3.15}{\$31.50} + 0.05$$
$$= 0.100 + 0.05 = 0.15 = 15.0\%$$

Step 3. Calculate the weighted averages of these component costs to obtain the WACCs in each interval. Remember, there are three break points:

- At $200 million—the break results from a higher cost of common equity because all internal financing (retained earnings) will be used up at this point.

- At $300 million—the break occurs because cheaper debt *and* cheaper preferred stock will be used up at this point.

- At $350 million—the break occurs because greater amounts of new equity will have a higher cost.

With these break points, the WACC will be constant from $1 to $200 million financing. It will increase to a new level that will remain constant from $200 million plus $1 to $300 million because the firm has exhausted its internal financing and must raise common equity funds by issuing new stock that has a higher cost. It will increase to a higher level that will remain constant from $300 million plus $1 to $350 million because both debt and preferred stock financing are more expensive beyond $300 million. Finally, it will increase to an even higher level at $350 million plus $1 because the cost of issuing new common equity is higher.

Table 12-2 shows the computations for the WACCs for each interval of new financing. If you compare the numbers in the column labeled "After-tax component cost" for consecutive intervals, you will see which type of capital caused the WACC to increase from one interval to the next (the boxed values).

Self-Test Questions

What are break points, and why do they occur in MCC schedules? Write out and explain the equation for determining break points.

How is an MCC schedule constructed? If there are n breaks in the MCC schedule, how many different WACCs are there? Why?

Payment America can issue up to $120,000 of new debt for a cost of 6 percent; amounts above $120,000 will cost 8 percent. If Payment America's capital structure contains 40 percent debt, how much can the company raise in total funds before the cost of debt increases to 8 percent? (Answer: $BP_{Debt} = \$300,000$)

COMBINING THE MCC AND INVESTMENT OPPORTUNITY SCHEDULES (IOS)

Now that we have constructed the MCC schedule, we can use it to determine the appropriate rate of return for making investment decisions. That is, we can use the MCC schedule to find the appropriate cost of capital and then compare this cost, or required rate of return, to the returns generated by investment opportunities to determine which ones should be purchased. *Investments should be purchased only if their expected returns exceed the cost of capital,* WACC, that is associated with the level of financing needed to purchase the investments.

To understand how the MCC schedule is used when making investment decisions, assume that Daflex Textiles has three financial executives: a financial vice president (VP), a treasurer, and a director of investment analysis (DIA). The financial VP asks the treasurer to develop the firm's MCC schedule, and the treasurer produces the schedule shown earlier in Figure 12-3. At the same time, the financial VP

TABLE 12-2   MCC Schedule Illustration

1. New Capital Needs: Interval = $1–$200,000,000

Capital Source	Breakdown of Funds at $200,000,000	Weight of Capital	×	After-Tax Component Cost	=	WACC
Debt, $r_{dT1} = r_{d1}(1-T)$	$ 70,000,000	0.35	×	4.8%	=	1.68%
Preferred stock, r_{ps1}	10,000,000	0.05	×	9.8	=	0.49
Common equity, r_s	120,000,000	0.60	×	14.0	=	8.40
	$200,000,000	1.00		$WACC_1$	=	10.57% ≈ 10.6%

2. New Capital Needs: Interval = $200,000,001–$300,000,000

Capital Source	Breakdown of Funds at $300,000,000	Weight of Capital	×	After-Tax Component Cost	=	WACC
Debt, $r_{dT1} = r_{d1}(1-T)$	$105,000,000	0.35	×	4.8%	=	1.68%
Preferred stock, r_{ps1}	15,000,000	0.05	×	9.8	=	0.49
Common equity, r_{e1}	180,000,000	0.60	×	14.5	=	8.70
	$300,000,000	1.00		$WACC_2$	=	10.87% ≈ 10.9%

3. New Capital Needs: Interval = $300,000,001–$350,000,000

Capital Source	Breakdown of Funds at $350,000,000	Weight of Capital	×	After-Tax Component Cost	=	WACC
Debt, $r_{dT2} = r_{d2}(1-T)$	$122,500,000	0.35	×	5.4%	=	1.89%
Preferred stock, r_{ps2}	17,500,000	0.05	×	10.0	=	0.50
Common equity, r_{e1}	210,000,000	0.60	×	14.5	=	8.70
	$350,000,000	1.00		$WACC_3$	=	11.09% ≈ 11.1%

4. New Capital Needs: Interval = Above $350,000,000

Capital Source	Breakdown of Funds at $360,000,000	Weight of Capital	×	After-Tax Component Cost	=	WACC
Debt, $r_{d2} = r_{d2}(1-T)$	$126,000,000	0.35	×	5.4%	=	1.89%
Preferred stock, r_{ps2}	18,000,000	0.05	×	10.0	=	0.50
Common equity, r_{e2}	216,000,000	0.60	×	15.0	=	9.00
	$360,000,000	1.00		$WACC_4$	=	11.39% ≈ 11.4%

investment opportunity schedule (IOS)
A graph of the firm's investment opportunities ranked in order of the projects' expected rates of return.

asks the DIA to draw up a list of all projects that are potentially acceptable. The list shows each project's cost, projected annual net cash inflows, life, and expected rate of return. These data are presented at the bottom of Figure 12-5. For example, Project A has a cost of $26 million, it is expected to produce inflows of $7 million per year for 5 years, and, therefore, it has an expected return of 10.8 percent. Similarly, Project C has a cost of $37 million, it is expected to produce inflows of $9 million per year for 6 years, and thus it has an expected return of 12.0 percent. For simplicity, we assume that any combination of the projects can be purchased—that is, Daflex can purchase any one project, any combination of two projects, any combination of three projects, any combination of four projects, or all five projects. In this example, the risk associated with each project is equal to the average risk of the firm's existing assets.

The DIA then plots the expected returns shown at the bottom of Figure 12-5 as the **investment opportunity schedule (IOS)** shown in the graph. The IOS schedule shows, in rank order, how much money Daflex can invest at different rates of return.

FIGURE 12-5   Combining the MCC and IOS Schedules to Determine
the Optimal Investment

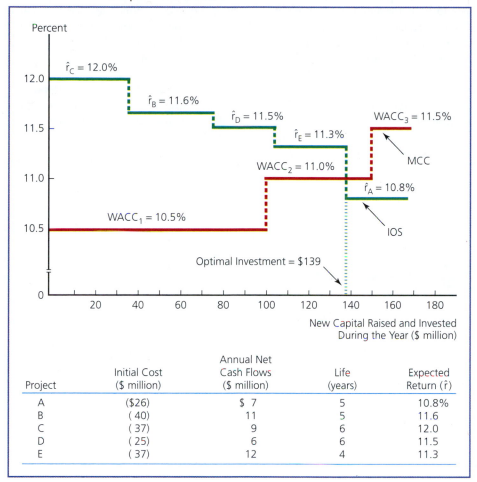

Project	Initial Cost ($ million)	Annual Net Cash Flows ($ million)	Life (years)	Expected Return ($\hat{r}$)
A	($26)	$ 7	5	10.8%
B	(40)	11	5	11.6
C	(37)	9	6	12.0
D	(25)	6	6	11.5
E	(37)	12	4	11.3

Figure 12-5 also shows Daflex's MCC schedule as it was developed by the treasurer and plotted in Figure 12-3. Now consider Project C: its expected return is 12.0 percent, and it can be financed with capital that costs only 10.5 percent; consequently, it should be accepted. If a project's expected rate of return exceeds its cost of capital, then it is deemed a good investment because the firm captures (gets to keep) the return in excess of the cost of capital, which in turn increases the firm's value. Using the same logic, Projects B, D, and E can be analyzed similarly. They are all acceptable because their expected returns exceed the WACC at the level of financing needed to purchase the projects. Project A, on the other hand, should be rejected because, at the necessary level of financing, its expected return is less than the WACC.

People sometimes ask this question: "If we took Project A first, it would be acceptable because its 10.8 percent return would exceed the 10.5 percent cost of money used to finance it. Why couldn't we do this?" The answer is that we are seeking, in effect, to maximize the excess of *returns over costs*, or the area that is above the WACC but below the IOS. We accomplish this by graphing (and accepting) the most profitable projects first.

Another question that sometimes arises is this: What would happen if the MCC cut through one of the projects? For example, suppose the second break point in the MCC schedule had occurred at $120 million rather than at $150 million, causing the MCC schedule to cut through Project E. Should we then accept Project E? If Project E could be accepted in part, we would take on only part of it. Otherwise, the answer would be determined by (1) finding the average cost of the funds needed to finance Project E (some of the money would cost 11.0 percent and some would cost 11.5 percent) and (2) comparing the average cost of this money with the 11.3 percent return on the project. We should accept Project E if its return exceeds the average cost of the $37 million needed to finance it.

The preceding analysis as summarized in Figure 12-5 reveals a very important point: *The cost of capital used in investment decisions is determined at the intersection of the IOS (marginal revenue) and MCC (marginal cost) schedules. If the cost of capital at the intersection is used (WACC$_2$ = 11%), then the firm will make correct investment decisions and its level of financing and investment will be optimal. If it uses any other rate, its investment decision will not be optimal.*

The firm should use the WACC intersection as determined in Figure 12-5 to make investment decisions concerning new projects that are roughly as risky as the firm's existing assets. This WACC should be adjusted up or down when the company is evaluating investments with higher or lower risk than the average project.

Self-Test Questions

Differentiate between the MCC and IOS schedules.

How is the marginal cost of capital that is used to evaluate average risk projects found?

As a general rule, do you think a firm's cost of capital as determined in this chapter should be used to evaluate all of its investment projects? Explain.

PROJECT RISK AND WACC

In the previous section, we saw how the WACC is used to make decisions about investment opportunities that have the same degree of risk as existing assets. Should all projects be evaluated with the same WACC, even if their risks differ significantly from the firm's existing assets? The answer to this question is no. As we saw in Chapter 11, investments that have higher risk must promise higher returns to entice investors to purchase them. The same logic applies to projects in which a firm is considering investing. The difficulty with incorporating risk into the analysis of an investment other than a financial asset, however, relates to the difficulty involved in developing a specific *measure* of project risk. Nevertheless, one might argue that it is possible to evaluate whether one project is riskier than another in a general sense.

In reality, most firms incorporate project risk into their investment decisions by adjusting the required rate of return (WACC) used to evaluate projects with risks that are substantially different from the firm's average risk. Average-risk projects would require an "average" rate of return, which would be the firm's WACC. Above-average-risk projects would require a higher-than-average rate of return, which means that the WACC would be adjusted upward. Conversely, below-average-risk projects would require a lower-than-average rate of return, so the WACC would be adjusted downward. Unfortunately, because we cannot measure risk precisely, we have no accurate way of specifying exactly how much higher or lower the WACC should be. As a result, *risk adjustments are necessarily judgmental and somewhat arbitrary.*

Although the process is not an exact science, many companies use a two-step procedure to develop risk-adjusted WACCs for making investment decisions.

TABLE 12-3   Investment Decisions Using Risk-Adjusted WACCs

Project	Project Risk	Required Return	Estimated Life	Initial Cost	Annual Net Cash Flows	Expected Return	Decision
A	Low	12%	5	$(10,000)	$2,850	13.1%	Accept
B	Average	15	5	(11,000)	3,210	14.1	Reject
C	Average	15	5	(9,000)	2,750	16.0	Accept
D	High	20	5	(12,000)	3,825	17.9	Reject

Project Risk Classification	Required Rate of Return
Low	12%
Average	15
High	20

First, the WACC is determined as described in previous sections, and this rate is considered the required rate of return that should be used to evaluate projects whose risk is similar to the firm's existing assets. Second, all projects are classified into one of three categories: high risk, average risk, and low risk. The firm or division then uses the average required rate of return to evaluate average-risk projects, reduces the average rate by 1 to 3 percent when evaluating low-risk projects, and raises the average rate by several percentage points for high-risk projects.

As an example, assume that a firm has determined its WACC to be 15 percent. The firm should use this rate of return to evaluate projects with average risk. Next, assume the firm has decided that a 20 percent rate should be used for high-risk projects and a 12 percent rate should be used for low-risk projects.

Table 12-3 shows an example application of risk-adjusted rates for the evaluation of four projects. Each of the four projects has a 5-year life, and each is expected to generate a constant cash flow stream during its lifetime. The analysis shows that only projects A and C are acceptable when risk is considered. When the average required rate of return is used to evaluate all of the projects, however, projects C and D would be considered acceptable because their expected rates of return exceed 15 percent. Thus, *if project risk is not considered when evaluating investments, incorrect decisions are possible.*

The approach described here for adjusting the WACC for risk is far from precise. Nevertheless, it recognizes that different projects have different risks, and it incorporates the idea that projects with different risks should be evaluated using different required rates of return.

Self-Test Question

Briefly explain the two-step process that many companies use to develop risk-adjusted WACCs for evaluating investment opportunities.

WACC VERSUS REQUIRED RATE OF RETURN OF INVESTORS

In Chapter 10, we showed how time value of money techniques are used to determine the values of financial assets, such as stocks and bonds. In that chapter, we briefly discussed the concept of the required rate of return of investors. Then, in Chapter 11 we introduced the concept of risk and discussed the effect of risk on required rates of return. It was in these chapters that we discovered investors demand higher rates of return to be compensated for higher levels of risk. We also discovered that, everything else equal, an asset's value is inversely related to the rate of return investors require to invest in it. The following equation, with which you should be familiar by now, shows this relationship:

$$\text{Value} = \frac{\widehat{CF}_1}{(1+r)^1} + \frac{\widehat{CF}_2}{(1+r)^2} + \cdots + \frac{\widehat{CF}_n}{(1+r)^n}$$

This concept, which was first introduced in Chapter 1, shows that the value of any asset—real or financial—is based on (1) the cash flows that the asset is expected to generate during its life, $\widehat{CF}_t$, and (2) the rate of return that investors require to "put up" their money to purchase the investment (asset), r. As a result, we know that investors purchase a firm's stocks and bonds—and thus provide funds to the firm—only when they expect to receive a return that sufficiently compensates them for the risks associated with those stocks and bonds. Consequently, the investors who purchase a firm's stocks and bonds determine the rates of return, or costs, that the firm must pay to raise funds to invest in investment projects.

In Chapter 10, we discussed valuation from the standpoint of investors. For example, we described r_s as the required rate of return of common stockholders—that is, the rate of return investors demand to purchase the firm's common stock and thus provide funds to the firm. In this chapter, we described r_s as the cost of internal common equity, which represents the return that the firm must earn to satisfy investors' demands. Which description is correct? They both are. This point can be illustrated with a simple analogy. Assume that Randy borrows money from his credit union to invest in common stocks. The loan agreement requires Randy to repay the amount borrowed and 10 percent interest at the end of 1 year. The 10 percent interest rate represents both Randy's cost of borrowing—that is, cost of debt—and his required rate of return. If he does not invest the borrowed funds in stocks that earn at least 10 percent return, then Randy will lose wealth because he has to pay the credit union, and thus it costs him 10 percent interest to use the money. The 10 percent interest rate also represents the return the credit union demands to lend money to Randy based on his credit risk—that is, 10 percent is the credit union's required rate, or the return it demands to lend money to (invest in) Randy. Although the situation is much more complex, this same relationship exists for firms that use funds provided by investors. Investors are similar to the credit union in the sense that they provide funds to the firms, whereas firms are similar to Randy in the sense that they use the funds provided by investors and must pay a return that is sufficient to attract such funds. And, much like the credit union determines the interest rate that Randy must pay for his loan, investors determine the rates that firms must pay to use their funds.

We first introduced and discussed rates of return in Chapter 10 and then further expanded this discussion in Chapter 11. These discussions were developed primarily from the perspective of investors. In this chapter, we used the information introduced in earlier chapters to explain the concept of cost of capital, which was discussed from the perspective of the firm. You should have noticed that the general concepts presented in this chapter are similar to the general concepts presented in Chapters 10 and 11—that is, determination of required rates of return and the impact on value. In reality, these chapters present the same relationships from two perspectives—the investor (Chapter 10 and Chapter 11) and the firm (this chapter). The rates of return, or component costs of capital, discussed in this chapter are the same rates that were introduced in Chapters 10 and Chapter 11. For this reason, we thought it might be a good idea to summarize these rates here. Table 12-4 shows the

TABLE 12-4   WACC versus Required Rates of Return

Investor's Required Rate of Return/Firm's Cost of Capital:

$$\text{Investor's required rate of return} = r = r_{RF} + \left[\begin{array}{c}\textbf{Risk}\\\textbf{premium}\end{array}\right] = r_d,\ r_{ps},\ \text{or}\ r_s = \begin{array}{c}\textbf{Firm's component}\\\textbf{cost of capital}\end{array}$$

Financial Asset	Financial Asset's Market Value	Return to Investors	Cost to Firms
Debt, r_d	$P_0 = \dfrac{INT}{(1+YTM)^1} + \cdots + \dfrac{INT+M}{(1+YTM)^N}$	$YTM = r_d$ = return investors require to purchase the firm's debt	$r_d = YTM$ = before-tax cost of debt $r_{dT} = r_d(1-T)$ = after-tax cost of debt
Preferred Stock, r_{ps}	$P_0 = \dfrac{D_{ps}}{r_{ps}}$	$r_{ps} = \dfrac{D_{ps}}{P_0}$ = return investors require to purchase the firm's preferred stock	$r_{ps} = \dfrac{D_{ps}}{P_0(1-F)}$ = cost of preferred stock
Common Equity, r_s*(internal)* or r_e*(external)*	$P_0 = \dfrac{\hat{D}_1}{r_s - g}$; (constant growth firm)	$r_s = \dfrac{\hat{D}_1}{P_0} + g$ = return investors require to purchase the firm's common stock	$r_s = \dfrac{\hat{D}_1}{P_0} + g$ = cost of retained earnings (internal) $r_e = \dfrac{\hat{D}_1}{P_0(1-F)} + g$ = cost of new common equity (external)

Variable Definitions:

r_{RF} = nominal risk-free rate of return

P_0 = market value of the financial asset

INT = dollar interest payment

M = maturity (face) value

N = number of remaining interest payments

g = constant growth rate of the firm

YTM = yield to maturity

T = the firm's marginal tax rate

D_{ps} = preferred stock dividend

$\hat{D}_1$ = next period's common stock dividend

F = cost of issuing new stock (in decimal form)

rates of return discussed in Chapters 10 and 11 and compares them to the component costs of capital discussed in this chapter. Note that the equations shown in the column labeled "Return to Investors" are the same as those shown in the column labeled "Cost to Firms," except for adjustments for taxes and flotation costs.

Self-Test Questions

Who determines a firm's component costs of capital?

Why is r the required rate of return for both investors and the firm?

Ethical Dilemma

How Much Should You Pay to be "Green"?

Tracey works in the investment department of Sustainable Solutions (SS), which is a company that manufactures products and consults on issues that relate to the protection and preservation of the earth's environment. Tracey's primary responsibility is to estimate the company's cost of capital, which is the "hurdle" rate that is used to make final investment decisions.

During the 10 years that Tracey has worked at SS, she has been pleased with the service that the company has provided to other companies and environmentalists. Tracey is compassionate about environmental issues, and she tries to get involved in movements and do everything she can to help clean up and protect the environment.

Last week, Manual, a coworker who works in the investment department as a project analyst, told Tracey about a project that he is currently evaluating. Although he doesn't completely understand the technology, Manual told Tracey that he thought that purchasing the project would allow the firm to significantly increase its presence in the "green" industry and it would also propel SS into the leadership role in the quest to clean up and protect the environment.

Tracey was ecstatic after talking with Manual, but her excitement was short-lived, because another coworker who is part of the team that is evaluating the new project indicated that the analyses that have been completed to date suggest that the project might not be purchased because its expected rate of return appears to be below the firm's required rate of return. It will be a few weeks until the investment analyses are complete.

Because she feels that the environmental benefits the project offers far outweigh its possible financial drawbacks, Tracey is trying to think of ways that she can help "sway" the final investment decision in favor of purchasing the project. As luck would have it, Tracey is close to completing a revised evaluation of the firm's cost of capital. She knows that the results of her evaluation will be used to help decide whether the new project is acceptable. As she pored over her numbers, Tracey realized that if she used a different approach to determine the proportions of debt and equity that are used to compute the firm's weighted average cost of capital (WACC), a higher weight would be given to debt, which has the lowest component cost of capital. It has been the policy of the company to compute the weights for the capital components using the market values of the firm's debt and equity. However, Tracey discovered that debt, which has a substantially lower cost than equity, will have a higher weight if book values are used. If the WAAC is computed using the higher weight given to debt, the required rate of return that is used to evaluate the new project probably will be low enough to ensure that the new project is accepted. Tracey doesn't feel like she is "cheating" by making the change because she doesn't think

continues

that market values should be used to determine the weights for the capital components; she feels that books values are more appropriate. Tracey is convinced that she can justify the deviation from policy if her bosses question why she used book values to determine the weights. Do you think that it is okay for Tracey to change the way she computes SS's WACC? What would you do if you were Tracey?

To summarize the key concepts, let's answer the questions that were posed at the beginning of the chapter:

CHAPTER PRINCIPLES
–The Answers

- **What types of capital do firms use to finance investments?** When we refer to a firm's capital, we generally mean the sources of long-term funds that are used to purchase plant and equipment (long-term investments). Long-term funds generally are classified as either debt or equity. *Debt* refers to the firm's bond issues, whereas *equity* refers to the firm's stock issues. Equity comes in two basic forms—preferred stock and common equity. Common equity includes the common stock that has been issued plus any earnings that have been retained during the life of the firm.

- **What is the cost of capital?** A firm's cost of capital is the average "price" that it pays for the funds it uses to purchase (invest in) assets. The cost for each component of capital differs—the after-tax cost of debt, r_d, is lower than the cost of preferred stock, r_{ps}, which is lower than the cost of common stock, r_s. To make decisions, a firm determines the average cost of all of the funds that it uses. Therefore, the firm computes its weighted average cost of capital, WACC, which is simply the average of each dollar of funding based on the proportion of the total funds of each type of capital that the firm uses. In other words, if WACC = 10%, then the firm pays an average cost of 10 percent for each dollar that it uses for investments.

- **How is the cost of capital used to make financial decisions?** A firm's WACC is its required rate of return. Thus, when evaluating investments, the firm should invest in projects that are expected to provide returns greater than its WACC. The WACC is a cost. If a firm does not earn a return that is greater than or equal to its WACC, then the firm's value decreases.

- **Why do funds generated through retained earnings have a cost?** The earnings that a firm retains over time represent amounts that could have been paid to common stockholders in the form of dividends in previous periods. Thus, a firm is able to retain earnings only if those earnings are reinvested in assets that generate returns greater than the returns that can be earned by the investors to whom those earnings could have been paid as dividends. In other words, a firm is "allowed" to retain earnings as long as it can reinvest the earnings at a higher rate than stockholders can earn elsewhere. If the firm reinvests the earnings at a rate that is lower than stockholders require, then these investors will demand that the firm pay out the earnings as dividends rather than retaining them.

- **Who determines a firm's cost of capital?** A firm's cost of capital is the rate of return that investors require to provide the funds that are used to purchase assets. Investors will not provide funds to a firm unless they expect to receive returns that are high enough to compensate them for the investment risk they take. Thus, if investors demand a 10 percent return, the firm must earn at least a 10 percent return on its assets.

CHAPTER PRINCIPLES
—**Personal Finance**

The concepts presented in this chapter should help you to better understand how to determine the rate of return that you should demand when investing your money. If you apply the concepts presented in this chapter, you should be able to make more informed borrowing and investment decisions.

- **What is my WACC?** You can apply the techniques presented in the chapter to determine the average interest rate that you are paying for all the loans you have outstanding. If you are like most people, you have a mortgage, an automobile loan, and perhaps other debt in smaller amounts. Generally, a mortgage represents 75 to 80 percent of the total amount of the outstanding loans, so the average interest rate you are paying for your loans is fairly close to the rate on your outstanding mortgage. The average interest you pay on your outstanding loans is your required rate of return.

- **How can knowledge of my WACC help me to make better investment decisions?** If you borrow funds to invest—perhaps to purchase stocks—you should choose investments that you expect will earn a return that is greater than the average interest rate that you are paying on the loan(s). If you invest at a rate that is lower than the average interest rate on the loan(s), your wealth will decrease—the difference between the return you earn on the invested money and the average interest rate on the loan(s) "comes out of your pocket." If, however, your investments earn an average return that is greater than the interest you are paying on the loans, the excess "goes in your pocket," and your wealth increases.

- **How do flotation costs affect my cost of borrowing funds?** Using the approaches discussed in the chapter, you should be able to compute the "true" costs of your loans. When you borrow funds from a bank, credit union, or any other source, it is comparable to a firm issuing a stock or bond. You as the borrower are effectively issuing debt to the lending institution; the lender is equivalent to an investor who buys a corporate stock or bond. Much like the flotation costs that corporations incur when issuing stocks and bonds, you incur issuing costs, which might be referred to as points, service fees, and so forth. For instance, many mortgages require the borrower to pay points at the time the loan is initiated. The amount that must be paid to cover the loan's points simply represents a prepayment of some interest. If the loan requires 1 point to be paid, then 1 percent of the amount borrowed is paid at the time the borrower gets the loan. Often the amount that must be paid for the points is paid out of the amount borrowed such that the amount of money from the loan that the borrower has available for use is decreased. This effect is much like the effect that flotation costs have on the cost of issuing new equity—that is, the cost of new equity is higher when flotation costs are higher. In addition, borrowers generally are required to pay other charges when borrowing money, and these other charges increase the cost of the debt. For example, suppose that you want to borrow $100,000 from your bank. The various fees that the bank charges total 2 percent of the loan, or $2,000, and the stated interest rate on the loan is 6 percent. The loan agreement requires you to repay the loan at the end of 1 year with interest; there will be no interest or principal payments made during the year. What is the cost of the loan? Following the procedure shown in the chapter, the cost of the loan can be computed as follows:

$$\text{Cost of the loan} = \frac{\text{Interest}}{\text{Net proceeds}} = \frac{\$100{,}000(0.06) + \$2{,}000}{\$100{,}000 - \$2{,}000} = \frac{\$8{,}000}{\$98{,}000}$$
$$= 0.082 = 8.2\%$$

Here, the $2,000 of fees that are paid are included as a charge for borrowing the money, which effectively is additional interest, or additional rent that is paid on the borrowed money. Because the $2,000 fee is taken out of the amount that is borrowed, you would get only $98,000 of the $100,000 loan to use as you please. Thus, as this example shows, everything else equal, when the dollar interest is higher, the loan proceeds are lower, or should any combination of these two events occur, the cost of the loan is higher.

QUESTIONS

12-1 In what sense does the marginal cost of capital schedule represent a series of average costs?

12-2 The financial manager of a large national firm was overheard making the following statement: "We try to use as much retained earnings as possible for investment purposes because there is no *explicit* cost to these funds, and this allows us to invest in relatively low-yielding projects that would not be feasible if we had to issue new common stock. We actually use retained earnings to invest in projects with yields below the coupon rate on our bonds." Comment on the validity of this statement.

12-3 How would each of the following affect a firm's after-tax cost of debt, r_{dT}; its cost of equity, r_s; and its weighted average cost of capital, WACC? Indicate by a plus (+), a minus (−), or a zero (0) if the factor would increase, decrease, or have an indeterminate effect on the item in question. Assume other things are held constant. Be prepared to justify your answer, but recognize that some of the parts probably have no single correct answer; these questions are designed to stimulate thought and discussion.

	Effect on		
	r_{dT}	r_s	WACC
a. The corporate tax rate is lowered.	____	____	____
b. The Federal Reserve tightens credit.	____	____	____
c. The firm significantly increases the proportion of debt it uses.	____	____	____
d. The dividend payout ratio (percent of earnings paid as dividends) is increased.	____	____	____
e. The firm doubles the amount of capital it raises during the year.	____	____	____
f. The firm expands into riskier new areas.	____	____	____
g. The firm merges with another firm whose earnings are countercyclical both to those of the first firm and to the stock market.	____	____	____
h. The stock market falls drastically, and the value of the firm's stock falls along with the rest.	____	____	____
i. Investors become more risk averse.	____	____	____
j. The firm is an electric utility with a large investment in nuclear plants. Several states propose a ban on nuclear power generation.	____	____	____

12-4 Suppose a firm estimates its MCC and IOS schedules for the coming year and finds that they intersect at the point 10 percent, $10 million. What cost of capital should be used to evaluate average-risk projects, high-risk projects, and low-risk projects?

12-5 Clear Glass Company's investment banker has determined that the following rate schedule would apply if the firm raises funds by issuing new debt (bonds):

Amount of New Debt	Cost, r_d
$ 1 – $ 250,000	8.0%
$ 250,001 – $1,000,000	10.0
$1,000,001 – $5,000,000	14.0
Greater than $5,000,000	20.0

For Clear Glass, how many break points are *associated with debt* when computing the weighted average cost of capital (WACC)? Explain.

12-6 What impact will investors' expectations about inflation have on a firm's cost of debt? Will the firm's cost of equity be affected? Explain.

12-7 Explain why, for a particular firm, the cost of retained earnings, r_s, will always be *less than* the cost of new equity, r_e.

12-8 Suppose a firm invests in projects that are much riskier than its average investments. Do you think the firm's weighted average cost of capital will be affected? Explain.

12-9 In what sense is a firm's WACC also the rate of return that should be earned on its investments?

12-10 Why is there a cost to the firm for retaining earnings to fund investments?

SELF-TEST PROBLEMS

Solutions appear in Appendix B.

Key Terms   **ST-1** Define each of the following terms:
   a. After-tax cost of debt, r_{dT}; capital component cost
   b. Cost of preferred stock, r_{ps}; cost of retained earnings, r_s
   c. Cost of new common equity, r_e
   d. Flotation cost, F
   e. Target capital structure; capital structure components
   f. Weighted average cost of capital, WACC
   g. Marginal cost of capital, MCC
   h. Marginal cost of capital schedule; break point, BP
   i. Investment opportunity schedule, IOS

Optimal Capital Budget   **ST-2** Lancaster Engineering Inc. (LEI) has the following capital structure, which it considers to be optimal:

Debt	25%
Preferred stock	15
Common equity	60
	100%

LEI's expected net income this year is $34,285.72; its established dividend payout ratio is 30 percent; its marginal tax rate is 40 percent; and investors expect earnings and dividends to grow at a constant rate of 9 percent in the future. LEI paid a dividend of $3.60 per share last year, and its stock currently sells at a price of $60 per share.

LEI can obtain new capital in the following ways:

Common stock: New common stock has a flotation cost of 10 percent for up to $12,000 of new stock and 20 percent for all common stock over $12,000.

Preferred stock: New preferred stock with a dividend of $11 can be sold to the public at a price of $100 per share; however, flotation costs of $5 per share will be incurred for up to $7,500 of preferred stock, and flotation costs will rise to $10 per share, or 10 percent, on all preferred stock over $7,500.

Debt: Up to $5,000 of debt can be sold at an interest rate of 12 percent; debt in the range of $5,001 to $10,000 must carry an interest rate of 14 percent; and all debt over $10,000 will have an interest rate of 16 percent.

LEI has the following independent investment opportunities:

Project	Cost at t = 0	Annual Cash Flow	Net Life	Expected Return
A	$10,000	$2,191.20	7 years	12.0%
B	10,000	3,154.42	5	17.4
C	10,000	2,170.18	8	14.2
D	20,000	3,789.48	10	13.7
E	20,000	5,427.84	6	?

a. Find the break points in the MCC schedule.

b. Determine the cost of each capital structure component.

c. Calculate the weighted average cost of capital (WACC) in the interval between each break in the MCC schedule.

d. Calculate the expected return for Project E. (*Hint:* Use the procedure discussed in Chapter 9.)

e. Construct a graph showing the MCC and IOS schedules.

f. Which projects should LEI accept?

PROBLEMS

12-1   Neotech Corporation's 14 percent coupon rate, semiannual payment, $1,000 par value 30-year bonds currently sell at a price of $1,353.54. If its marginal tax rate is 40 percent, what is Neotech's after-tax cost of debt?   **Cost of Debt**

12-2   The McDaniel Company's financing plans for next year include the sale of long-term bonds with a 10 percent coupon. The company believes it can sell the bonds at a price that will provide a yield to maturity of 12 percent. If the marginal tax rate is 34 percent, what is McDaniel's after-tax cost of debt?   **Cost of Debt**

12-3   A corporation has an outstanding bond with the following characteristics: **Cost of Debt**

Coupon interest rate	6.0%
Interest payments	semiannually
Face value	$1,000.00
Years to maturity	8
Current market value	$ 902.81

What is the yield to maturity (YTM = r_d) for this bond?

Cost of Preferred Stock   **12-4** Maness Industries plans to issue some $100 par preferred stock with an 11 percent dividend. The stock is selling on the market for $97.00, and Maness must pay flotation costs of 5 percent of the market price. What is the cost of the preferred stock for Maness?

Cost of Preferred Stock   **12-5** Hybrid Hydro Plants, Inc., which has a marginal tax rate equal to 34 percent, has preferred stock that pays a constant dividend equal to $15 per share. The stock currently sells for $125. If the company incurs a 3 percent flotation cost each time it issues preferred stock, what is the cost of issuing preferred stock?

Cost of Retained Earnings   **12-6** The common stock of Omega Corporation is currently selling for $50 per share. It is expected that Omega will pay a dividend equal to $5 per share this year. In addition, analysts have indicated that the company has been growing at a constant rate of 3 percent, and this growth is expected to continue forever. What is Omega's cost of retained earnings?

Cost of Common Equity   **12-7** Analysts of the ICM Corporation have indicated that the company is expected to grow at a 5 percent rate for as long as it is in business. Currently, ICM's stock is selling for $70 per share. The most recent dividend paid by the company was $5.60 per share. If ICM issues new common stock, it will incur flotation costs equal to 7 percent. ICM's marginal tax rate is 35 percent. What is its cost of retained earnings—that is, its internal equity? What is its cost of new equity?

Cost of New Common Equity   **12-8** The Choi Company's next expected dividend, $\hat{D}_1$, is $3.18; its growth rate is 6 percent; and its stock currently sells for $36. New stock can be sold to net the firm $32.40 per share.

   a. What is Choi's percentage flotation cost, F?

   b. What is Choi's cost of new common stock, r_e?

Cost of Common Equity   **12-9** Following is information about the common equity of Funtastic Furniture Company:

Current selling price	$68.00
Constant growth rate	8.0%
Most recently paid dividend, D_0	$3.50
Flotation costs	10.0%
Marginal tax rate	40.0%

   a. What is Funtastic's cost of retained earnings?

   b. What is Funtastic's cost of new common stock?

Cost of Debt   **12-10** A company's 6 percent coupon rate, semiannual payment, $1,000 par value bond that matures in 30 years sells at a price of $515.16. The company's marginal tax rate is 40 percent. What is the firm's component cost of debt for purposes of calculating the WACC? (*Hint:* Base your answer on the simple rate, not the effective annual rate, r_{EAR}.)

Cost of Equity   **12-11** Chicago Paints Corporation has a target capital structure of 40 percent debt and 60 percent common equity. The company expects to have $600 of after-tax income during the coming year, and it plans to retain 30 percent of its earnings. The current stock price is $P_0 = $30, the last dividend paid was $D_0 = $2.00, and the dividend is expected to grow at a constant rate of 7 percent. New stock can be sold at a flotation cost of F = 25%. What will Chicago Paints' marginal cost of equity capital be if it raises a total of $500 of new capital?

12-12 Magnificent Metal Mining (MMM) expects to generate $60,000 in earnings that will be retained for reinvestment in the firm this year. If MMM's capital structure consists of 25 percent debt and 75 percent common equity, stated in total funds, what is the weighted average cost of capital (WACC) break point that is associated with retained earnings?

Break Point

12-13 Roberson Fashion's capital structure consists of 30 percent debt and 70 percent common equity. Roberson is considering raising new capital to finance its expansion plans. The company's investment banker has compiled the following information about the cost of debt if the firm issues debt:

Break Point

Amount of Debt	After-Tax Cost of Debt
$ 1 – $150,000	6.5%
150,001 – 450,000	7.8
450,001 – 840,000	9.0
above 840,000	11.0

Roberson expects to generate $350,000 in retained earnings next year. For any new equity that is issued, Roberson will incur flotation costs of 6 percent. What are the break points that Roberson faces when computing its marginal cost of capital?

12-14 You are given the following information about a firm:

Marginal Cost of Capital

Type of Capital	After-Tax Cost	Proportion of the Capital Structure
Debt	5.0%	20.0%
Common equity—retained earnings	11.0	80.0
Common equity—new issue	14.0	

The firm expects to retain $160,000 in earnings this year to invest in investment projects. If the firm's capital budget is expected to equal $180,000, what required rate of return, or marginal cost of capital, should be used when evaluating investment projects?

12-15 The CFO of Mega Munchies recently received a report that contains the following information:

Optimal Capital Investment

Project	Cost	Expected Return	Type of Capital	Proportion
E	$200,000	19.0%	Debt	40.0%
F	300,000	17.0	Preferred stock	0.0
G	200,000	14.0	Common equity	60.0

The weighted average cost of capital (WACC) is 12 percent if the firm does *not* have to issue new common equity; if new common equity is needed, the WACC is 15 percent. If Mega Munchies expects to generate $240,000 in retained earnings this year, which project(s) should be purchased? Assume that the projects are independent.

12-16 Sam's Orthodontic Services (SOS) will retain for reinvestment $300,000 of the net income it expects to generate next year. Recently, the CFO determined that the firm's after-tax cost of debt, r_{dT}, is 5 percent, its cost of internal equity (retained earnings), r_s, is 10 percent, and its cost of external

Marginal Cost of Capital

equity (new common stock), r_e, is 13 percent. Next year, SOS expects to finance investment projects so as to maintain its current capital structure, which consists of 60 percent debt. SOS has no preferred stock. What will SOS's marginal cost of capital be if its total investment needs are $700,000 for next year?

Weighted Average Cost of Capital

12-17 The Gupta Company's cost of equity is 16 percent. Its before-tax cost of debt is 13 percent, and its marginal tax rate is 40 percent. The stock sells at book value. Using the following balance sheet, calculate Gupta's after-tax weighted average cost of capital:

Assets		Liabilities and Equity	
Cash	$ 120	Long-term debt	$1,152
Accounts receivable	240	Equity	1,728
Inventories	360		
Net plant and equipment	2,160		
Total assets	$2,880	Total liabilities and equity	$2,880

Optimal Investment

12-18 The Mason Corporation's present capital structure, which is also its target capital structure, calls for 50 percent debt and 50 percent common equity. The firm has only one potential project, an expansion program with a 10.2 percent expected return and a cost of $20 million, which is completely divisible—that is, Mason can invest any amount up to $20 million. The firm expects to retain $3 million of earnings next year. It can raise up to $5 million in new debt at a before-tax cost of 8 percent, and all debt after the first $5 million will have a before-tax cost of 10 percent. The cost of retained earnings is 12 percent, and the firm can sell any amount of new common stock desired at a constant cost of 15 percent. The firm's marginal tax rate is 40 percent. What is the firm's optimal capital budget?

Optimal Investment

12-19 The management of Ferri Phosphate Industries (FPI) is planning next year's capital budget. FPI projects its net income at $7,500, and its payout ratio is 30 percent. The company's earnings and dividends are growing at a constant rate of 5 percent, the last dividend paid, D_0, was $0.90, and the current stock price is $8.59. FPI's new debt will cost 14 percent. If FPI issues new common stock, flotation costs will be 20 percent. FPI is at its optimal capital structure, which is 40 percent debt and 60 percent equity, and the firm's marginal tax rate is 40 percent. FPI has the following independent, indivisible, and equally risky investment opportunities:

Project	Cost	Expected Return
A	$15,000	17%
B	20,000	14
C	15,000	16
D	12,000	15

What is FPI's optimal capital budget?

Optimal Investment

12-20 Refer to Problem 12-19. Management now decides to incorporate project risk differentials into the analysis. The new policy is to add two percentage points to the cost of capital of those projects significantly riskier than average and to subtract two percentage points from the cost of capital of those that are substantially less risky than average. Management judges Project A to be of high risk, projects C and D to be of average risk, and Project B to be of low risk. None of the projects is divisible. What is the optimal capital budget after adjustment for project risk?

12-21 Florida Electric Company (FEC) uses only debt and equity. It can borrow unlimited amounts at an interest rate of 10 percent as long as it finances at its target capital structure, which calls for 45 percent debt and 55 percent common equity. Its last dividend was $2, its expected constant growth rate is 4 percent, its stock sells at a price of $25, and new stock would net the company $20 per share after flotation costs. FEC's marginal tax rate is 40 percent, and it expects to have $100 million of retained earnings this year. Two projects are available: Project A has a cost of $200 million and an expected return of 13 percent, and Project B has a cost of $125 million and an expected return of 10 percent.

> All of the company's potential projects are equally risky.

a. What is FEC's cost of equity from newly issued stock?

b. What is FEC's marginal cost of capital—that is, what WACC cost rate should it use to evaluate investment projects (these two projects plus any others that might arise during the year, provided the cost of capital schedule remains as it is currently)?

12-22 The earnings, dividends, and stock price of Talukdar Technologies Inc. are expected to grow at 7 percent per year in the future. Talukdar's common stock sells for $23 per share, its last dividend was $2.00, and the company will pay a dividend of $2.14 at the end of the current year.

a. Using the discounted cash flow approach, what is its cost of retained earnings?

b. If the firm's beta is 1.6, the risk-free rate is 9 percent, and the average return on the market is 13 percent, what will be the firm's cost of equity using the CAPM approach?

c. If the firm's bonds earn a return of 12 percent, what will r_s be, using the bond-yield-plus-risk-premium approach? (*Hint:* Use the midpoint of the risk premium range discussed in the chapter.)

d. Based on the results of parts (a) through (c), what would you estimate Talukdar's cost of retained earnings to be?

12-23 The Shrieves Company's EPS was $6.50 in 2009 and $4.42 in 2004. The company pays out 40 percent of its earnings as dividends, and the stock sells for $36.

a. Calculate the past growth rate in earnings. (*Hint:* This is a 5-year growth period.)

b. Calculate the *next* expected dividend per share, $\hat{D}_1$. ($D_0 = 0.4(\$6.50) = \$2.60$.) Assume that the past growth rate will continue.

c. What is the cost of retained earnings, r_s, for the Shrieves Company?

12-24 The Simmons Company expects earnings of $30 million next year. Its dividend payout ratio is 40 percent, and its proportion of debt (debt/assets ratio) is 55 percent. Simmons uses no preferred stock.

a. What amount of retained earnings does Simmons expect next year?

b. At what amount of financing will there be a break point in the MCC schedule?

c. If Simmons can borrow $12 million at an interest rate of 11 percent, another $12 million at a rate of 12 percent, and any additional debt at a rate of 13 percent, at what points will rising debt costs cause breaks in the MCC schedule?

Growth and Earnings

12-25 Rowell Products' stock is currently selling for $60 a share. The firm is expected to earn $5.40 per share this year and to pay a year-end dividend of $3.60.

    a. If investors require a 9 percent return, what rate of growth must be expected for Rowell?

    b. If Rowell reinvests retained earnings in projects whose average return is equal to the stock's expected rate of return, what will be next year's earnings per share?

Weighted Average Cost of Capital

12-26 The total assets of the Dexter Company are $270 million, and the firm's present capital structure, which follows, is considered to be optimal. Assume that there is no short-term debt.

Long-term debt	$135,000,000
Common equity	135,000,000
Total liabilities and equity	$270,000,000

New bonds will have a 10 percent coupon rate and will be sold at par. Common stock, currently selling at $60 per share, can be sold to net the company $54 a share. Stockholders' required rate of return is estimated to be 12 percent, consisting of a dividend yield of 4 percent and an expected growth rate of 8 percent. (The next expected dividend is $2.40, so $2.40/$60 = 4%.) Retained earnings are estimated to be $13.5 million. The marginal tax rate is 40 percent. Dexter has determined that acceptable investment opportunities total $70 million.

    a. To maintain the present capital structure, how much of the total investment opportunities must Dexter finance by equity?

    b. How much of the new equity funds needed will be generated internally? Externally?

    c. Calculate the cost of each of the equity components.

    d. At what level of capital expenditure (investment) will there be a break in Dexter's MCC schedule?

    e. Calculate the WACC (1) below and (2) above the break in the MCC schedule.

    f. Plot the MCC schedule. Also, draw in an IOS schedule that is consistent with both the MCC schedule and the projected capital budget. (Any IOS schedule that is consistent will do.)

Weighted Average Cost of Capital

12-27 The following table gives earnings per share figures for the Brueggeman Company during the preceding 10 years. The firm's common stock, 7.8 million shares outstanding, is now (January 1, 2010) selling for $65 per share, and the expected dividend at the end of the current year (2010) is 55 percent of the EPS expected in 2010. Because investors expect past trends to continue, g can be based on the earnings growth rate. (Note that 9 years of *growth* are reflected in the data.)

Year	EPS	Year	EPS
2000	$3.90	2005	$5.73
2001	4.21	2006	6.19
2002	4.55	2007	6.68
2003	4.91	2008	7.22
2004	5.31	2009	7.80

The current before-tax interest rate on debt is 9 percent. The firm's marginal tax rate is 40 percent. Its capital structure, considered to be optimal, is as follows:

Debt	$104,000,000
Common equity	156,000,000
Total liabilities and equity	$260,000,000

a. Calculate Brueggeman's after-tax cost of new debt and of common equity, assuming that new equity comes only from retained earnings. Calculate the cost of equity as $r_s = \hat{D}_1/P_0 + g$.

b. Find Brueggeman's WACC, again assuming that no new common stock is sold and that all debt costs 9 percent before taxes.

c. How much can be spent on capital investments before external equity must be sold? (Assume that retained earnings available for 2010 are 45 percent of 2010 earnings. Obtain 2010 earnings by multiplying the expected 2010 EPS by the shares outstanding.)

d. What is Brueggeman's WACC (cost of funds raised in excess of the amount calculated in part (c)) if new common stock can be sold to the public at $65 a share to net the firm $58.50 a share? The cost of debt is constant.

12-28 Ezzell Enterprises has the following capital structure, which it considers to be optimal under present and forecasted conditions: **Optimal Investment**

Debt (long-term only)	45%
Common equity	55
Total liabilities and equity	100%

For the coming year, management expects after-tax earnings of $2.5 million. Ezzell's past dividend policy of paying out 60 percent of earnings will continue. Present commitments from its banker will allow Ezzell to borrow according to the following schedule:

Loan Amount	Interest Rate
$ 0 to $500,000	9% on this increment of debt
$500,001 to $900,000	11% on this increment of debt
$900,001 and above	13% on this increment of debt

The company's marginal tax rate is 40 percent, the current market price of its stock is $22 per share, its *last* dividend was $2.20 per share, and the expected growth rate is 5 percent. External equity (new common) can be sold at a flotation cost of 10 percent.

Ezzell has the following investment opportunities for the next year:

Project	Cost	Annual Cash Flows	Project Life	Expected Return
1	$675,000	$155,401	8 years	?
2	900,000	268,484	5	15.0%
3	375,000	161,524	3	?
4	562,500	185,194	4	12.0
5	750,000	127,351	10	11.0

Management asks you to help determine which projects (if any) should be undertaken. You proceed with this analysis by answering the following questions (or performing the tasks) as posed in a logical sequence:

a. How many breaks are there in the MCC schedule? At what dollar amounts do the breaks occur, and what causes them?

b. What is the weighted average cost of capital in each of the intervals between the breaks?

c. What are the expected returns for Projects 1 and 3?

d. Graph the IOS and MCC schedules.

e. Which projects should Ezzell's management accept?

f. What assumptions about project risk are implicit in this problem? If you learned that projects 1, 2, and 3 were of above-average risk, yet Ezzell chose the projects that you indicated in part (e), how would this affect the situation?

g. The problem stated that Ezzell pays out 60 percent of its earnings as dividends. How would the analysis change if the payout ratio were changed to zero, to 100 percent, or somewhere in between? (No calculations are necessary.)

Integrative Problem

Cost of Capital   **12-29** Assume that you were recently hired as assistant to Jerry Lehman, financial VP of Coleman Technologies. Your first task is to estimate Coleman's cost of capital. Lehman has provided you with the following data, which he believes is relevant to your task:

1. The firm's marginal tax rate is 40 percent.

2. The current price of Coleman's 12 percent coupon, semiannual payment, noncallable bonds with 15 years remaining to maturity is $1,153.72. Coleman does not use short-term, interest-bearing debt on a permanent basis. New bonds would be privately placed with no flotation cost.

3. The current price of the firm's 10 percent, $100 par value, quarterly dividend, perpetual preferred stock is $113.10. Coleman would incur flotation costs of $2 per share on a new issue.

4. Coleman's common stock is currently selling at $50 per share. Its last dividend (D_0) was $4.19, and dividends are expected to grow at a constant rate of 5 percent in the foreseeable future. Coleman's beta is 1.2, the yield on Treasury bonds is 7 percent, and the market risk premium is estimated to be 6 percent. For the bond-yield-plus-risk-premium approach, the firm uses a four-percentage-point risk premium.

5. Up to $300,000 of new common stock can be sold at a flotation cost of 15 percent. Above $300,000, the flotation cost would rise to 25 percent.

6. Coleman's target capital structure is 30 percent long-term debt, 10 percent preferred stock, and 60 percent common equity.

7. The firm is forecasting retained earnings of $300,000 for the coming year.

To structure the task somewhat, Lehman has asked you to answer the following questions:

a. (1) What sources of capital should be included when you estimate Coleman's weighted average cost of capital (WACC)?

    (2) Should the component costs be figured on a before-tax or an after-tax basis? Explain.

    (3) Should the costs be historical (embedded) costs or new (marginal) costs? Explain.

b. What is the market interest rate on Coleman's debt and its component cost of debt?

c. (1) What is the firm's cost of preferred stock?

    (2) Coleman's preferred stock is riskier to investors than its debt, yet the yield to investors is lower than the yield to maturity on the debt. Does this suggest that you have made a mistake? (*Hint:* Think about taxes.)

d. (1) Why is there a cost associated with retained earnings?

    (2) What is Coleman's estimated cost of retained earnings using the CAPM approach?

e. What is the estimated cost of retained earnings using the discounted cash flow (DCF) approach?

f. What is the bond-yield-plus-risk-premium estimate for Coleman's cost of retained earnings?

g. What is your final estimate for r_s?

h. What is Coleman's cost for up to $300,000 of newly issued common stock, r_{e1}? What happens to the cost of equity if Coleman sells more than $300,000 of new common stock?

i. Explain in words why new common stock has a higher percentage cost than retained earnings.

j. (1) What is Coleman's overall, or weighted average, cost of capital (WACC) when retained earnings are used as the equity component?

    (2) What is the WACC after retained earnings have been exhausted and Coleman uses up to $300,000 of new common stock with a 15 percent flotation cost?

    (3) What is the WACC if more than $300,000 of new common equity is sold?

k. (1) At what amount of new investment would Coleman be forced to issue new common stock? To put it another way, what is the largest capital budget the company could support without issuing new common stock? Assume that the 30/10/60 target capital structure will be maintained.

    (2) At what amount of new investment would Coleman be forced to issue new common stock with a 25 percent flotation cost?

    (3) What is a marginal cost of capital (MCC) schedule? Construct a graph that shows Coleman's MCC schedule.

l. Coleman's director of investment analysis has identified the following potential projects:

Project	Cost	Life	Cash Flow	Expected Return
A	$700,000	5 years	$218,795	17.0%
B	500,000	5	152,705	16.0
B*	500,000	20	79,881	15.0
C	800,000	5	219,185	11.5

Projects B and B* are mutually exclusive, whereas the other projects are independent. All of the projects are equally risky.

(1) Plot the IOS schedule on the same graph that contains your MCC schedule. What is the firm's marginal cost of capital for investment purposes?

(2) What are the dollar size and the included projects in Coleman's optimal capital budget? Explain your answer fully.

(3) Would Coleman's MCC schedule remain constant at 12.8 percent beyond $2 million regardless of the amount of capital required?

(4) If WACC$_3$ had been 18.5 percent rather than 12.8 percent, but the second WACC break point had still occurred at $1,000,000, how would that have affected the analysis?

m. Suppose you learned that Coleman could raise only $200,000 of new debt at a 10 percent interest rate and that new debt beyond $200,000 would have a yield to investors of 12 percent. Trace back through your work and explain how this new fact would change the situation.

COMPUTER-RELATED PROBLEM

Work the problem in this section only if you are using the computer problem spreadsheet.

Optimal Capital Budget

12-30 Use the model in File C12 to work this problem.

a. Refer back to Problem 12-28. Now assume that the debt ratio is increased to 65 percent, causing all interest rates to rise by one percentage point, to 10 percent, 12 percent, and 14 percent, and causing g to increase from 5 to 6 percent. What happens to the MCC schedule and the optimal amount of investment?

b. Assume the facts as in part (a), but suppose Ezzell's marginal tax rate falls (1) to 20 percent or (2) to 0 percent. How would this affect the MCC schedule and the optimal investment?

c. Ezzell's management would now like to know what the optimal investment would be if earnings were as high as $3.25 million or as low as $1 million. Assume a 40 percent marginal tax rate.

d. Would it be reasonable to use the model to analyze the effects of a change in the payout ratio without changing other variables?

Capital Budgeting

I n 1989, when RJR Nabisco (now R. J. Reynolds Tobacco Company) canceled its smokeless cigarette project, called Premier, *The Wall Street Journal* called it "one of the most stunning new product disasters in recent history." Introduced just 2 years earlier, RJR had spent more than $300 million on the Premier brand. The company had even built a new plant, intending to produce smokeless cigarettes in huge quantities. However, the smokeless cigarette had two fatal flaws—it had to be lit with a special lighter and even then it was hard to light, and many, if not most, smokers didn't like the taste. Further, smokers didn't really like the fact that there was no smoke to blow out or ashes to flick, because Premier heated the tobacco rather than burning it. When the Premier brand was introduced, these problems were well known, yet RJR still pumped a substantial amount of money into the project.

What led RJR's top managers to downplay the flaws and to invest more than $300 million in a bad product (investment)? According to industry observers, managers were hesitant to voice their concerns about the Premier brand because they did not want to offend top executives. The executives were so infatuated with their "new toy" that they assumed consumers would embrace the smokeless cigarette despite its obvious flaws. Interestingly, most of the top managers smoked, but none smoked the new Premier cigarette!

Intent on salvaging its investment in the failed Premier brand, in 1996, RJR introduced a second smokeless cigarette called Eclipse. Even though an additional $150 million was invested in the Eclipse brand, it too was a flop. Trying to resurrect its smokeless cigarette, in 2000, RJR once again tested the potential market for Eclipse. This time, however, the smokeless cigarette was touted as a smoking alternative that provided a lower chance of contracting some of the maladies that had been associated with traditional tobacco products. The fact that RJR was marketing Eclipse as a "safer" cigarette showed that the company still held hope for salvaging its investment in its smokeless cigarette projects.

The Eclipse brand was still alive and kicking in 2003 when RJR began expanding its distribution to convenience stores nationwide. At the same time, the company continued to test the merits of Eclipse as a safer alternative to the traditional cigarette. The thought was that as people became more health conscious, perhaps the Eclipse brand would find its niche and finally start to pay off for RJR. Unfortunately, tests by independent researchers suggested that Eclipse cigarettes contained more harmful amounts of cancer-causing ingredients than some light cigarettes. As a result, in 2005, the attorney general of Vermont filed a lawsuit against R. J. Reynolds for misleading advertising. Although the lawsuit is still pending in 2008, it appears that RJR has abandoned the Eclipse brand. In an effort to support some of its aging products, however, RJR continues to explore new tobacco products. Currently, the company is test marketing a "smokeless, spitless" tobacco product called the Camel Snus. The company hopes that this innovative product will be developed into a new category of tobacco products.

Had RJR's top managers followed the procedures set forth in this chapter, perhaps they would not have sunk as much money into the smokeless cigarette projects. Instead, they would have discovered that the Premier project should have been rejected initially because it was not expected to generate the cash flows

necessary to make it a viable investment. If RJR is more diligent with its evaluation of the Camel Snus, perhaps a more rational decision will be made concerning the introduction of this new product. The principles set forth in this chapter offer insights into how capital budgeting decisions such as these are made. As you read this chapter, consider the analyses that RJR should perform before making decisions as to whether it should invest hundreds of millions of dollars in the proposed smokeless, spitless tobacco product.

Sources: Various articles are available on the Dow Jones Interactive® Publications Library located at http://www.wsj.com, and the Web site of Reynolds American, which is the parent company of R. J. Reynolds Tobacco Company (http://www.reynoldsamerican.com/).

CHAPTER PRINCIPLES
–The Questions

After reading this chapter, you should be able to answer the following questions:

- What are the relevant cash flows associated with a capital budgeting project? How are these cash flows identified and used in capital budgeting analysis?
- How do firms make decisions about whether to invest in costly, long-lived real assets, such as buildings and equipment?
- How does a firm make a choice between two (or more) acceptable investments when only one can be purchased?
- How are different capital budgeting techniques related? Which methods do firms actually use?
- How is risk incorporated in capital budgeting analysis?
- How do capital budgeting analyses/decisions differ for multinational firms?

In earlier chapters, we saw how to value assets and determine required rates of return. In this chapter, we apply these concepts to investment decisions involving the fixed assets of a firm, or *capital budgeting*. Here the term *capital* refers to fixed assets used in production, and a *budget* is a plan that details projected cash inflows and cash outflows during some future period. Thus, the capital budget is an outline of planned expenditures on fixed assets, and **capital budgeting** is the process of analyzing projects and deciding which are acceptable investments and which acceptable investments should be purchased.

capital budgeting
The process of planning expenditures on assets whose cash flows are expected to extend beyond 1 year.

Our treatment of capital budgeting focuses on two general areas. First, we consider how the cash flows associated with capital budgeting projects are estimated. Next, we describe the basic techniques used in capital budgeting analysis and examine how investment decisions are made.

THE IMPORTANCE OF CAPITAL BUDGETING

A number of factors combine to make capital budgeting decisions perhaps the most important ones that financial managers must make.

1. First, capital budgeting has *long-term effects*, so the firm loses some decision-making flexibility when it purchases capital projects. For example, when a

firm invests in an asset with a 15-year economic (useful) life, its operations are affected for 15 years; the firm is "locked in" by the capital budgeting decision.[1] Furthermore, because asset expansion is fundamentally related to expected future sales, a decision to buy a fixed asset that is expected to last 15 years involves an implicit 15-year sales forecast. An error in the forecast of asset requirements can have serious consequences. That is, investing too much will result in unnecessarily heavy expenses, whereas investing too little might create inefficient production and inadequate capacity that result in lost sales.

2. *Timing* is also important in capital budgeting. Capital assets must be ready to come "on line" when they are needed; otherwise, opportunities could be lost. A firm that forecasts its needs for capital assets in advance will have an opportunity to purchase and install the assets before they are needed. Unfortunately, many firms do not order capital goods until they approach full capacity or must replace worn-out equipment; then the purchases might come too late, especially if competitors are able to attract the firm's customers while capital projects are being put on line.

3. Finally, capital budgeting is important because the acquisition of fixed assets typically involves *substantial expenditures*. Before a firm can spend a large amount of money, it must have the funds available; large amounts of money are not available automatically. Therefore, a firm contemplating a major capital expenditure program must arrange its financing well in advance to ensure that the necessary funds are available.

Because a firm's growth as well as its ability to remain competitive and to survive depend on a constant flow of ideas for new products, ways to make existing products better, and ways to produce output more efficiently, a well-managed firm will go to great lengths to develop good capital budgeting proposals. And, because some of the capital investment ideas will be good and others will not, the firm must be able to evaluate the worth of such projects. The remainder of this chapter focuses on the evaluation of the acceptability of capital budgeting projects.

Self-Test Question

Why are capital budgeting decisions so important to the success of a firm?

PROJECT CLASSIFICATIONS

Capital budgeting decisions generally are termed either *replacement decisions* or *expansion decisions*. **Replacement decisions** involve determining whether capital projects should be purchased to take the place of (replace) existing assets that might be worn out, damaged, or obsolete. Replacement projects are necessary to maintain or improve profitable operations using *existing* production levels. On the other hand, if a firm is considering whether to *increase* operations by adding capital

replacement decisions
Decisions about whether to purchase capital assets to take the place of existing assets so as to maintain existing operations.

---

[1]In reality, a firm can "exit" a project prior to the end of its life by selling it. Such a decision is called an "abandonment decision," and, in general, the analysis of whether to take such an action is the same as we discuss in the rest of the chapter. Abandonment decisions are discussed in detail in more advanced managerial finance texts.

expansion decisions
Decisions about whether to purchase capital projects and add them to existing assets so as to increase existing operations.

independent projects
Projects whose cash flows are not affected by the acceptance or non-acceptance of other projects.

mutually exclusive projects
A set of projects where the acceptance of one project means that other projects cannot be purchased.

projects to existing assets so as to produce either more of its existing products or entirely new products, **expansion decisions** are made.

Some capital budgeting decisions involve *independent projects*, whereas others involve *mutually exclusive projects*. **Independent projects** are projects whose cash flows are not affected by any other projects, so the acceptance of one project does not affect the acceptance of other projects. As a result, *all independent projects can be purchased if they all are acceptable*. For example, if Cengage Learning, which publishes this book, decided to purchase the ABC television network, it still could publish a new textbook. Conversely, if a capital budgeting decision involves **mutually exclusive projects,** then accepting one project means that other projects must be rejected. *Only one mutually exclusive project can be purchased, even if all of them are acceptable.* For example, imagine that Alldome Sports, Ltd. has a parcel of land on which it wants to build either a children's amusement park or a domed baseball stadium. The land is not large enough for both alternatives, so if Alldome chooses to build the amusement park, it could not build the stadium, and vice versa.

Self-Test Question

Identify and briefly explain how capital project classification categories are used.

STEPS IN THE VALUATION PROCESS

Capital budgeting decisions involve valuation of assets, or projects. Not surprisingly, then, capital budgeting involves the same steps used in general asset valuation, as described in Chapters 10 and 11. These steps can be summarized as follows:

1. Determine the cost, or purchase price, of the asset.
2. Estimate the future cash flows expected to be generated by the asset.
3. Evaluate the riskiness of the projected cash flows to determine the appropriate rate of return to use for computing the present value of the estimated cash flows.
4. Compute the present value of the expected cash flows. In other words, solve the following:

$$PV \text{ of } CF = \frac{\widehat{CF}_1}{(1+r)^1} + \frac{\widehat{CF}_2}{(1+r)^2} + \cdots + \frac{\widehat{CF}_n}{(1+r)^n}$$

5. Compare the present value of the expected future cash flows with the initial investment, or cost, that is required to acquire the asset. Alternatively, the expected rate of return on the project can be calculated and compared with the firm's required rate of return (WACC).

If a firm invests in a project with a present value greater than its cost, the value of the firm will increase. A very direct link therefore exists between capital budgeting and stock values: the more effective the firm's capital budgeting procedures, the higher the price of its stock. In the remainder of the chapter, we discuss the application of the steps outlined here as applied to the capital budgeting process.

Self-Test Questions

List the steps in the capital budgeting process and compare them with the steps in security valuation.

Explain how capital budgeting is related to the wealth-maximization goal that should be pursued by the financial manager of a firm.

ESTIMATING A PROJECT'S CASH FLOWS

Before we can compute a project's value, we must estimate the cash flows—both current and future—associated with it. We therefore begin by discussing cash flow estimation, which is the most important, and perhaps the most difficult, step in the analysis of a capital project. The process of cash flow estimation is problematic because it is difficult to accurately forecast the costs and revenues associated with large, complex projects or projects that are expected to affect operations for long periods of time. Consider, for example, the Alaska Pipeline: the original cost estimates were in the neighborhood of $700 *million*, but the final cost was closer to $7 *billion*. Nevertheless, such estimates are required for evaluation of capital budgeting projects. The individuals responsible for developing reliable estimates of relevant cash flows must use the methods they believe are most appropriate in carrying out this task. This section gives you some sense of the inputs involved in the estimation of the cash flows associated with a capital project.

Relevant Cash Flows

Many variables are involved in cash flow estimation, and many individuals and departments participate in the process. For example, the marketing group typically makes the forecasts of unit sales and prices, the engineering and product development staffs determine the capital outlays associated with a new product, and cost accountants, production experts, and other personnel estimate the operating costs. When all of the information about a project is collected, financial managers use these data to create estimates of its **cash flows**—the investment outlays and the net cash flows expected after the project is purchased.

    Although estimating the *cash flows* can be rather difficult, two cardinal rules can help financial analysts avoid making mistakes:

1. Capital budgeting decisions must be based on *cash flows after taxes,* not accounting income.

2. Only *incremental cash flows* are *relevant* to the analysis.

cash flows
The actual cash, as opposed to accounting profits, that a firm receives or pays during some specified period.

Cash Flow versus Accounting Income

Capital budgeting analysis relies on *after-tax cash flows, not accounting profits;* after all, it is cash that pays the bills and can be invested in capital projects, not profits. Cash flows and accounting profits can be very different. To illustrate, consider Table 13-1, which shows the relationship between accounting profits and cash flows for Argile Textiles. We assume that Argile is planning to start a new division at the end of 2010; that sales and all costs, except depreciation, represent actual cash flows and are projected to remain constant over time; and that the new

TABLE 13-1   Argile Textiles' Accounting Profits versus Net Cash Flow ($ thousand)

	Accounting Profits	Cash Flows
I. 2011 Situation		
Sales	$ 25,000	$ 25,000
Costs except depreciation	(12,500)	(12,500)
Depreciation	(7,500)	
Net operating income or cash flow	$ 5,000	$ 12,500
Taxes based on operating income (30%)	(1,500)	(1,500)
Net income or net cash flow	$ 3,500	$ 11,000
Net cash flow = Net income plus depreciation = $3,500 + $7,500 = $11,000		
II. 2016 Situation		
Sales	$ 25,000	$ 25,000
Costs except depreciation	(12,500)	(12,500)
Depreciation	(2,500)	
Net operating income or cash flow	$ 10,000	$ 12,500
Taxes based on operating income (30%)	(3,000)	(3,000)
Net income or net cash flow	$ 7,000	$ 9,500
Net cash flow = Net income plus depreciation = $7,000 + $2,500 = $9,500		

division will use accelerated depreciation, which will cause its reported depreciation charges to decline over time.[2]

The top section of the table shows the situation in the first year of operations, 2011. Accounting profits are $3.5 million, but the division's net cash flow—money that is available to Argile—totals $11 million. The $3.5 million profit is the *return on the funds* originally invested, and the $7.5 million of depreciation is a *return of part of the funds* originally invested. Thus, the $11 million cash flow consists of both a return *on* and a return *of* part of the invested capital.

The bottom part of the table shows the situation projected for 2016. In that year, reported profits have doubled because of the decline in depreciation, but net cash flow is down sharply because taxes have doubled. The amount of money received by the firm is represented by the cash flow figure, not the net income figure. As we noted in Chapter 10, although accounting profits are important for some purposes, cash flows have greater relevance for the purposes of valuing an asset. Cash flows can be reinvested to create value, whereas profits cannot.[3]

---

[2]Depreciation procedures are discussed in detail in accounting courses, but Appendix 13A at the end of this chapter provides a summary and review of them. The tables in Appendix 13A are used to calculate the depreciation charges for the chapter examples. In some instances, we have simplified the depreciation assumptions so as to make the arithmetic less complex. Because Congress changes depreciation procedures frequently, you should always consult the latest tax regulations before developing actual capital budgeting cash flows.

[3]In Table 13-1, net cash flows are defined as net income plus depreciation. Actually, net cash flow should be adjusted to reflect all noncash charges—not just depreciation. For most projects, however, depreciation is by far the largest noncash charge. Also, note that Table 13-1 ignores interest charges, which would apply if the firm used debt. Most firms do use debt, and hence finance part of their capital budgets with debt. As a result, the question has been raised as to whether capital budgeting cash flow analysis should incorporate interest charges. The consensus is that interest charges should *not* be dealt with explicitly in capital budgeting. Rather, the effects of debt financing are reflected in the cost of capital used to discount the cash flows. If interest were subtracted, and cash flows were then discounted, we would double-count the cost of debt.

Incremental Cash Flows

In evaluating a capital project, we are concerned only with those cash flows that occur as a direct result of accepting the project. To determine whether a specific cash flow is considered relevant, we must determine whether it is affected by the purchase of the project. Cash flows that will change because the project is purchased are **incremental cash flows** that should be included in the capital budgeting evaluation. Cash flows that are not affected by the purchase of the project are not relevant to the particular capital budgeting decision.

Unfortunately, identifying the relevant cash flows for a project is not always as simple as it seems. Notable problems in determining incremental cash flows include the following:

1. *Sunk costs.* A **sunk cost** is an outlay that already has been committed or that already has occurred, which will not change if the project is purchased. Because it is not affected by the decision under consideration, it should *not* be included in the cash flow analysis. To illustrate, in 2009 Argile Textiles hired a consulting firm to examine the feasibility of building a distribution center in New England. The study, which cost $100,000, was expensed for tax purposes in 2009. This expenditure is *not* a cost that should be included in the capital budgeting evaluation, because Argile cannot recover this money, regardless of whether it builds the new distribution center.

2. *Opportunity costs.* Another potential problem relates to **opportunity costs,** defined here as the cash flows that could be generated from assets that the firm already owns if they are not used for the project in question. For example, Argile currently owns a piece of land in New England that is suitable for a distribution center; this land could be sold for $1.5 million. When evaluating the prospective center, the cost of the land is considered an opportunity cost associated with the project, because use of the site for the distribution center would require forgoing a cash inflow equal to $1.5 million. Note that the proper land cost in this example is the $1.5 million market-determined value, no matter what Argile originally paid for the property.

3. *Externalities: effects on other parts of the firm.* Another potential problem relates to the effects of a project on other parts of the firm; economists call these effects **externalities.** For example, Argile has some existing retailers (customers) in New England who would use the new distribution center because its location would be more convenient than the firm's current North Carolina–based distribution center. The sales, and hence profits, generated by these customers would not be new to Argile, but rather would represent a transfer from one distribution center to another. The net cash flows produced by these customers should not be included in the capital budgeting decision. Although they often are difficult to quantify, externalities must be estimated so that they are not mistakenly included as new (incremental) cash flows in the capital budgeting analysis.

4. *Shipping and installation costs.* When a firm acquires fixed assets, it often must pay substantial costs for shipping and installing the equipment. These charges are important because they require cash payments. In addition, for depreciable assets, *the total amount that can be depreciated (known as the depreciable basis) includes the purchase price and any additional expenditures required to make the asset operational, including shipping and installation.* Although depreciation is a noncash expense (cash is not needed to pay the depreciation expense each year), depreciation affects the taxable

incremental cash flow
The change in a firm's net cash flow attributable to an investment project.

sunk cost
A cash outlay that already has been incurred and that cannot be recovered regardless of whether the project is accepted or rejected.

opportunity cost
The return on the best alternative use of an asset; the highest return that will not be earned if funds are invested in a particular project.

externalities
The way in which accepting a project affects the cash flows in other parts (areas) of the firm.

income of a firm. In this way, it affects the amount of taxes paid by the firm, which is a cash flow.

5. *Inflation.* Inflation is a fact of life, and it should be recognized in capital budgeting decisions. If expected inflation is not built into the determination of expected cash flows, then the asset's calculated value and expected rate of return will be incorrect. That is, both of these values will be artificially low. It is easy to avoid inflation bias: simply build inflationary expectations into the cash flows used in the capital budgeting analysis. The firm does not have to adjust its required rate of return (weighted average cost of capital, WACC) to account for inflation expectations, because investors include such expectations when establishing the rate at which they are willing to permit the firm to use their funds. In other words, investors decide the rates at which a firm can raise funds in the capital markets, and these rates include an inflation premium.

Identifying Incremental (Relevant) Cash Flows

Generally, when we identify the incremental cash flows associated with a capital project, we separate them according to when they occur during the life of the project. In most cases, we can classify a project's incremental cash flows into one of three categories:

1. Cash flows that occur *only at the start* of the project's life—time Period 0—which represent the amounts that are initially invested in the project.

2. Cash flows that *continue throughout* the project's life—time Periods 1 through n—which represent changes in the firm's operating cash flows that are associated with investing in the project.

3. Cash flows that occur *only at the end,* or the termination, of the project—time Period n—which represent the amounts that are associated with the disposal, or termination, of the project at the end of its life.

We discuss these three incremental cash flow classifications and identify some of the relevant cash flows next.

Initial Investment Outlay

initial investment outlay
The incremental cash flows associated with a project that will occur only at the start of a project's life, CF_0.

The **initial investment outlay** refers to the incremental cash flows that *occur only at the start of a project's life,* CF_0. It includes such cash flows as the purchase price of the new project and shipping and installation costs. If the capital budgeting decision is a replacement decision, then the initial investment also must take into account the cash flows associated with the disposal of the old, or replaced, asset; this amount includes any cash received or paid to scrap the old asset and any tax effects associated with its disposal.

In many cases, the addition or replacement of a capital asset also affects the firm's short-term assets and liabilities, which are known as the working capital accounts. For example, additional inventories might be required to support a new operation, and increased inventory purchases will increase accounts payable. The difference between the required increase in current assets and the increase in current liabilities is the *change in net working capital*. If this change is positive (as it generally is for expansion projects), then additional financing, over and above the cost of the project, is needed to fund the increase.[4] Thus, *the change in net*

---

[4]In some instances, the change in net working capital associated with a capital project actually produces a decrease in the firm's current funding requirements, which frees up cash flows for investment. Usually, this situation occurs when the project under consideration is much more efficient than the existing assets.

working capital that results from the acceptance of a project is an incremental cash flow that must be considered in the capital budgeting analysis. Because the change in net working capital requirements occurs at the start of the project's life, this incremental cash flow must be included as a part of the initial investment outlay.

Incremental Operating Cash Flow

Incremental operating cash flows are the changes in day-to-day operating cash flows that result from the purchase of a capital project. They occur throughout the life of the project, continuing to affect the firm's cash flows until the firm disposes of the asset.

In most cases, we can compute the incremental operating cash flows for each year directly by using the following equation:

$$\text{Incremental operating CF}_t = \Delta\text{Cash revenues}_t - \Delta\text{Cash expenses}_t - \Delta\text{Taxes}_t$$
$$= \Delta\text{NOI}_t \times (1 - T) + \Delta\text{Depr}_t$$
$$= (\Delta S_t - \Delta OC_t - \Delta\text{Depr}_t) \times (1 - T) + \Delta\text{Depr}_t$$
$$= (\Delta S_t - \Delta OC_t) \times (1 - T) + T(\Delta\text{Depr}_t)$$

incremental operating cash flows
The changes in day-to-day cash flows that result from the purchase of a capital project and continue until the firm disposes of the asset.

13-1

The symbols in Equation 13–1 are defined as follows:

Δ = The Greek letter delta, which indicates the change in something.

$\Delta\text{NOI}_t = \text{NOI}_{t,\,accept} - \text{NOI}_{t,\,reject}$ = The change in net operating income in Period t that results from accepting the capital project; the subscript *accept* indicates the firm's operations that would exist if the project is accepted, and the subscript *reject* indicates the level of operations that would exist if the project is rejected (the existing situation *without* the project).

$\Delta\text{Depr}_t = \text{Depr}_{t,\,accept} - \text{Depr}_{t,\,reject}$ = The change in depreciation expense in Period t that results from accepting the project.

$\Delta S_t = S_{t,\,accept} - S_{t,\,reject}$ = The change in sales revenues in Period t that results from accepting the project.

$\Delta OC_t = OC_{t,\,accept} - OC_{t,\,reject}$ = The change in operating costs, excluding depreciation, in Period t that results from accepting the project.

T = Marginal tax rate.

A few points about the application of Equation 13-1 are warranted here. First, previously we have emphasized that depreciation is a *noncash* expense. We include the change in depreciation expense when computing incremental operating cash flows because, when depreciation changes, both taxable income and hence the amount of income taxes paid change, and the amount of taxes paid is a cash flow. Second, when identifying the relevant cash flows, the effects of financing the new project are omitted. Instead, financing effects, such as interest charges, are reflected in the cost of capital (required return) that is used to evaluate the attractiveness of a project. For this reason, financing effects should not be included in the cash flows. For example, if we included interest in the analysis, and then compared the expected return on the asset to the firm's required rate of return (that is, the firm's weighted average cost of capital, as discussed in Chapter 12), we would double-count the cost of debt.

Terminal Cash Flow

terminal cash flow
The net cash flow that occurs at the end of the life of a project, including the cash flows associated with (1) the final disposal of the project and (2) the return of the firm's operations to their state prior to the project's acceptance.

The **terminal cash flow** occurs at the end of the life of the project. It is associated with (1) the final disposal of the project and (2) the return of the firm's operations to their state prior to the project's acceptance. Consequently, the terminal cash flow includes the salvage value, which could be either positive (selling the asset) or negative (paying for its removal), and the tax effects of the disposition of the project.

Because we assume that the firm returns to the operating level that existed prior to the acceptance of the project, any changes in net working capital that occurred at the beginning of the project's life will be *reversed* at the end of its life. For example, as an expansion project's life approaches termination, we assume that inventories will be sold off and not replaced; the firm will therefore receive an end-of-project cash inflow equal to the net working capital requirement, or cash outflow, that occurred when the project was begun.

Self-Test Questions

Briefly explain the difference between accounting income and net cash flow. Which should you use in capital budgeting? Why?

Explain what the following terms mean and assess their relevance in capital budgeting: *incremental cash flow, sunk cost, opportunity cost, externality, shipping plus installation costs,* and *depreciable basis.*

How should inflation expectations be included in the analysis of capital projects?

Identify the three classifications for the incremental cash flows associated with a project and give examples of each.

Why are the changes in net working capital recognized as incremental cash flows both at the beginning and the end of a project's life?

CASH FLOW ESTIMATION—ILLUSTRATIONS OF EXPANSION PROJECTS AND REPLACEMENT PROJECTS

In the previous section, we discussed important aspects of cash flow analysis. Here we describe two examples intended to illustrate the estimation of cash flows for expansion projects and for replacement projects.

Expansion Projects

Recall that an *expansion project* calls for the firm to invest in new assets in an effort to *increase* sales. Here we illustrate expansion project analysis by examining a project that is being considered by Household Energy Products (HEP), a Dallas-based technology company. HEP wants to decide whether it should proceed with full-scale production of a computerized home appliance control device that will increase a home's energy efficiency by simultaneously controlling all household appliances.

The marketing vice president estimates that annual sales would be 15,000 units if the device's selling price is $2,000 each, so total annual sales are forecasted to be $30 million. The engineering department has determined that the firm would need no additional manufacturing or storage space; it would just need the new machinery required to manufacture the devices. The necessary equipment, which would be purchased and installed in late 2010, would cost $9.5 million, not including the $500,000 that HEP would have to pay for its shipping and installation. Although the equipment's estimated economic, or useful, life is 4 years, it would fall into the MACRS 5-year class for the purposes of depreciation (see Appendix 13A at the end of the chapter). At the end of its useful life, the equipment would have a market value of $2 million and a book value of $1.7 million.

The proposed project would require an initial increase in net working capital of $4 million, primarily because the raw materials required to produce the devices will increase HEP's inventory needs when the manufacturing equipment is installed. The production department has estimated that variable manufacturing costs will total 60 percent of sales, and fixed overhead costs, excluding depreciation, will be $5 million per year. Depreciation expenses will vary from year to year in accordance with the MACRS rates.

HEP's marginal tax rate is 40 percent. For capital budgeting purposes, the company's policy is to assume that operating cash flows occur at the end of each year. Thus, because manufacture of the new product would begin on January 1, 2011, the first *incremental operating cash flows* would occur on December 31, 2011.

Analysis of the Cash Flows

The first step in the analysis is to summarize the initial investment outlays required for the project, as shown in the 2010 column of Table 13-2. For HEP's appliance control device project, the cash outlays consist of the purchase price of the needed equipment, the cost of shipping and installation, and the required investment in net working capital. Notice that these cash flows do not carryover in the years 2011 through 2014: they occur only at the start of the project. Thus, the *initial investment outlay* is $14 million.

Having estimated the initial investment requirements, we next estimate the cash flows that will occur once production begins; these estimates appear in the 2011–2014 columns of Table 13-2. The operating cash flow estimates reflect the information provided by HEP's various departments. We obtained the depreciation amounts by multiplying the depreciable basis (purchase price plus shipping and installation, which equals $10 million) by the MACRS recovery allowance rates as explained in the table footnote. As you can see from the values given in Table 13-2, the *incremental operating cash flow* differs each year only because the depreciation expense—and, therefore, depreciation's effect on taxes—differs each year.

The final cash flow component we must compute is the terminal cash flow. In this example, the $4 million investment in net working capital will be recovered in 2014. We must also estimate the net cash flows from the disposal of the equipment in 2014. Table 13-3 shows the calculation of the net salvage value for the equipment. It is expected that the equipment will be sold for more than its book value, which means that the company must pay taxes on the gain. In essence, the equipment was depreciated too quickly, allowing HEP to reduce its tax liability by too much in the years 2011–2014. The net cash flow from salvage is simply the sum of the salvage value and the tax impact resulting from the sale of the equipment, or $1.88 million in this case. Thus, the *terminal cash flow* is $5.88 million = $4 million + $1.88 million.

Notice that the total net cash flow for 2014 in Table 13-2 is the sum of the incremental cash flow for the year and the terminal cash flow. Thus, in the final year of a project's economic life, the firm incurs two types of cash flows: the final year's incremental operating cash flow and the terminal cash flow associated with the end of the project's life. For the appliance control device project that HEP is considering, the total expected net cash flow in 2014 is $10.56 million.

TABLE 13-2 HEP Expansion Project Net Cash Flows, 2010–2014 ($ thousand)

	2010	2011	2012	2013	2014
I. Initial Investment Outlay					
Cost of new asset	$(9,500)				
Shipping and installation	(500)				
Increase in net working capital	(4,000)				
Initial investment	$(14,000)				
II. Incremental Operating Cash Flow[a]					
Sales revenues		$ 30,000	$ 30,000	$ 30,000	$ 30,000
Variable costs (60% of sales)		(18,000)	(18,000)	(18,000)	(18,000)
Fixed costs		(5,000)	(5,000)	(5,000)	(5,000)
Depreciation on new equipment[b]		(2,000)	(3,200)	(1,900)	(1,200)
Earnings before taxes (EBT)		$ 5,000	$ 3,800	$ 5,100	$ 5,800
Taxes (40%)		(2,000)	(1,520)	(2,040)	(2,320)
Net income		$ 3,000	$ 2,280	$ 3,060	$ 3,480
Add back depreciation		2,000	3,200	1,900	1,200
Incremental operating cash flows		$ 5,000	$ 5,480	$ 4,960	$ 4,680
III. Terminal Cash Flow					
Return of net working capital					$ 4,000
Net salvage value (see Table 13-3)					1,880
Terminal cash flow					$ 5,880
IV. Incremental Cash Flows					
Total net cash flow per period	$(14,000)	$ 5,000	$ 5,480	$ 4,960	$ 10,560

[a]Using Equation 13-1, the incremental operating cash flows can be computed as follows:

Year	Incremental Operating Cash Flow Computation
2011	$ 5,000 = ($30,000 − $18,000 − $5,000)(1 − 0.4) + $2,000(0.4)
2012	$ 5,480 = ($30,000 − $18,000 − $5,000)(1 − 0.4) + $3,200(0.4)
2013	$ 4,960 = ($30,000 − $18,000 − $5,000)(1 − 0.4) + $1,900(0.4)
2014	$10,560 = ($30,000 − $18,000 − $5,000)(1 − 0.4) + $1,200(0.4)

[b]Depreciation for the new equipment was calculated using MACRS (see Appendix 13A at the end of this chapter):

Year	2011	2012	2013	2014
Percent Depreciated	20%	32%	19%	12%

These percentages are multiplied by the depreciable basis of $10,000 to get the depreciation expense each year. For example, the depreciation expense in 2012 is $3,200 = $10,000 × 0.32.

The following cash flow time line summarizes the data for HEP's expansion project. The amounts are in thousands of dollars, just as in Table 13-2. The firm's required rate of return is 15 percent.

Cash Flow Time Line for HEP's Appliance Control Device Project

We discuss the evaluation of these cash flows later in the chapter.

TABLE 13-3	HEP Expansion Project Net Salvage Value, 2014 ($ thousand)

I. Book Value of HEP's Project, 2014

Cost of new asset, 2010	$ 9,500
Shipping and installation	500
Depreciable basis of asset	$10,000
Depreciation, 2011–2014	(8,300) = (0.20 + 0.32 + 0.19 + 0.12) × $10,000
Book value, 2014	$ 1,700

II. Tax Effect of the Sale of HEP's Project, 2014

Selling price of asset, 2014	$ 2,000
Book value of asset, 2014	(1,700)
Gain (loss) on sale of asset	$ 300
Taxes (40%)	$ 120 = $300 × 0.4

III. Net Salvage Value, 2014

Cash flow from sale of project	$ 2,000
Tax effect of sale	(120)
Net salvage value cash flow	$ 1,880

Replacement Analysis

At some point, all companies must make decisions about replacing existing assets. Identifying the incremental cash flows is more complicated with a replacement project than with an expansion project, because the *cash flows from both the new asset and the old asset must be considered*. The net difference between the "new" and "old" cash flows must be taken into account because a replacement decision involves comparing two mutually exclusive projects—that is, retaining the old asset versus buying a new one. If the new project replaces the old project, then the new cash flows replace the old cash flows. We will illustrate replacement analysis with another HEP example.

Ten years ago, HEP purchased a lathe for trimming molded plastics at a cost of $7,500. The machine had an expected life of 15 years at the time of purchase. Management originally estimated—and still believes—that the salvage value will be $0 (5 years from now). The machine is being depreciated on a straight line basis, so its annual depreciation charge is $500, and its present book value is $2,500 = $7,500 − 10($500).

Currently, HEP is considering the purchase of a special-purpose machine to replace the lathe. The new machine, which can be purchased for $12,000 (including shipping and installation), will reduce labor and raw materials usage sufficiently to cut operating costs by $3,500 per year; sales revenues will not change. The new machine will have a useful life of 5 years, after which it will be sold for $2,000. By an IRS ruling, the new machine falls into the 3-year MACRS class. The current market value of the old machine is $1,000. Net working capital requirements will increase by $1,000 if HEP replaces the lathe with the new machine; this increase will occur at the time of replacement.

Table 13-4 shows the worksheet format that HEP uses to analyze proposed replacement projects. To determine the relevant cash flows for a *replacement decision*, we need to consider the fact that *the cash flows associated with the new asset will take the place of the cash flows associated with the old asset*. As a consequence, we must compute the increases or decreases in cash flows that result from the replacement of the old asset with the new asset.

TABLE 13-4   HEP Replacement Project Net Cash Flows, 2010–2015 ($ thousand)

	2010	2011	2012	2013	2014	2015
I. Initial Investment Outlay						
Cost of new asset	$(12,000)					
Change in net working capital	(1,000)					
Net cash flow from sale of old asset[a]	1,600					
Initial investment	$(11,400)					
II. Incremental Operating Cash Flows						
Δ Operating costs		$ 3,500	$ 3,500	$ 3,500	$ 3,500	$ 3,500
Δ Depreciation[b]		(3,460)	(4,900)	(1,300)	(340)	500
Δ Operating income before taxes (EBT)		40	(1,400)	2,200	3,160	4,000
Δ Taxes (40%)		(16)	560	(880)	(1,264)	(1,600)
Δ Net operating income		24	(840)	1,320	1,896	2,400
Add back Δ depreciation		3,460	4,900	1,300	340	(500)
Incremental operating cash flows		$ 3,484	$ 4,060	$ 2,620	$ 2,236	$ 1,900
III. Terminal Cash Flow						
Return of net working capital						$ 1,000
Net salvage value of new asset[c]						1,200
Terminal cash flow						$ 2,200
IV. Incremental Cash Flows						
Total net cash flow per period	$(11,400)	$ 3,484	$ 4,060	$ 2,620	$ 2,236	$ 4,100

[a]The net cash flow from the sale of the old (replaced) asset is computed as follows:

Selling price (market value)	$ 1,000
Subtract book value	(2,500)
Gain (loss) on sale of asset	(1,500)
Tax impact of sale of asset (40%) = (1,500) × 0.4 =	(600) = a tax refund

Net cash flow from the sale of asset = $1,000 + 600 = $1,600

[b]The change in depreciation expense is computed by comparing the depreciation of the new asset with the depreciation that would have existed if the old asset was not replaced. The old asset has been depreciated on a straight line basis, with 5 years of $500 depreciation remaining. The new asset will be depreciated using the rates for the 3-year MACRS class (see Appendix 13A at the end of this chapter). The change in annual depreciation would be:

Year	New Asset Depreciation		Old Asset Depreciation		Change in Depreciation
2011	$12,000 × 0.33 = $ 3,960	–	$500	=	$3,460
2012	12,000 × 0.45 = 5,400	–	500	=	4,900
2013	12,000 × 0.15 = 1,800	–	500	=	1,300
2014	12,000 × 0.07 = 840	–	500	=	340
2015	= 0	–	500	=	(500)
Accumulated depreciation	= $12,000				

[c]The book value of the new asset in 2015 will be zero, because the entire $12,000 has been written off. The net salvage value of the new asset in 2015 is computed as follows:

Selling price (market value)	$ 2,000
Subtract book value	(0)
Gain (loss) on sale of asset	2,000
Tax impact of sale of asset (40%)	(800) = 2,000 × 0.4

Net salvage value of the new asset in 2015 = $2,000 – $800 = $1,200

Analysis of the Cash Flows

The initial investment outlay of $11,400 includes the cash flows associated with the cost of the new asset and the change in net working capital, which also is included in the initial investment computation for the expansion decision shown in Table 13-2. With a replacement decision, however, the cash flows associated with the disposal of the old asset must be considered when computing the initial investment outlay of the new asset, because the asset being replaced is removed from operations. In our example, the old asset has a book value equal to $2,500, but it can be sold for only $1,000. HEP will, therefore, incur a capital loss equal to –$1,500 = $1,000 – $2,500 if it replaces the lathe with the new machine. This loss will result in a tax savings equal to $600 = Loss × T = $1,500 × 0.4, which accounts for the fact that HEP did not adequately depreciate the old asset to reflect its true market value. Consequently, the disposal of the old asset will generate a positive cash flow equal to $1,600—the $1,000 selling price plus the $600 tax savings—that effectively reduces the amount of cash required to purchase the new machine and thereby the initial investment outlay.[5]

Next, we compute the incremental operating cash flow each year. Section II of Table 13-4 shows these computations. The procedure is the same as before: determine how operating cash flows will *change* if HEP purchases the new machine to replace the lathe. Recall that the new machine is expected to increase operating profits by $3,500 because less cash will be spent on its operation. Had the replacement also resulted in a change in sales or the annual savings been expected to change over time, these facts would have to be incorporated into the analysis.

We must calculate the change in depreciation expense to determine how such a change will affect the amount of taxes paid by the firm. If HEP purchases the new machine, the $500 depreciation expense associated with the lathe (old asset) will no longer be relevant for tax purposes; instead, the depreciation expense for the new machine will be used. For example, according to the percentages given in Appendix 13A (at the end of this chapter) for an asset in the 3-year MACRS class, the depreciation expense for the new machine will be $3,960 in 2011. The existing $500 depreciation from the old lathe will be replaced with the new machine's depreciation expense of $3,960, so depreciation will increase by $3,460 = $3,960 – $500. The computations for the remaining years are completed in a similar manner. Notice that the change in depreciation in 2015 is negative. The new machine will be fully depreciated at the end of 2014, so there is nothing left to write off in 2015—the $500 depreciation from the old machine is replaced with the new machine's depreciation of $0, which is a change of –$500.

The terminal cash flow includes $1,000 for the return of the original net working capital investment and the net salvage value of the new machine, which equals $1,200. It is expected that the new machine can be sold in 2015 for $2,000, but $800 in taxes will have to be paid on the sale because the new machine will be fully depreciated by the time of the sale.[6] Thus, the terminal cash flow equals $2,200 = $1,000 + $1,200.

---

[5]If you think about it, computing the initial investment outlay for replacement decisions is similar to determining the amount needed to purchase a new automobile to replace your old one. If the purchase price of the new car is $20,000 and the dealer is willing to give you $5,000 for your old car as a trade-in, then the amount you need is only $15,000. If you need to pay someone to take your old car out of the garage because you plan to keep the new car there at night, however, the total amount needed to purchase the new car is actually more than $20,000.

[6]In this analysis, the salvage value of the old machine is $0. If the old machine was expected to have a positive salvage value at the end of 5 years, replacing it now would eliminate this cash flow. In such a case, the after-tax salvage value of the old machine would represent an opportunity cost to the firm, and it would be included as a Year 5 cash outflow in the terminal cash flow section of the worksheet.

The following time line summarizes the cash flows we computed for HEP's replacement project.

Cash Flow Time Line for HEP's Replacement Project

Year Period	2010	2011	2012	2013	2014	2015
	0	1	2	3	4	5
	r = 15%					
Net Cash Flows	(11,400)	3,484	4,060	2,620	2,236	4,100

Now that we have identified the relevant cash flows associated with both an expansion project and a replacement project, we are ready to analyze these cash flows to determine whether the firm should purchase the projects. We discuss the analysis of the cash flows next.

Self-Test Questions

Explain and differentiate between the estimation of cash flows for expansion projects and for replacement projects.

A firm is evaluating a new machine to replace an existing, older machine. The old (existing) machine is being depreciated at $20,000 per year, whereas the new machine's depreciation will be $18,000. The firm's marginal tax rate is 30 percent. Everything else equal, if the new machine is purchased, what effect will the change in depreciation have on the firm's incremental operating cash flows?   (Answer: $600 reduction in operating CF)

CAPITAL BUDGETING EVALUATION TECHNIQUES

After we estimate the cash flows that are expected to be generated by a project, we must determine whether purchasing the project is desirable. That is, we need to evaluate how the project's purchase will affect the value of the firm. In this section, we introduce the basic techniques commonly used by financial managers to make capital budgeting decisions.

The three most popular methods used by businesses to evaluate capital budgeting projects are (1) net present value (NPV), (2) internal rate of return (IRR), and (3) payback period (PB).[7] We will explain how each evaluation criterion is calculated, and then we will determine how well each performs in terms of identifying those projects that will maximize the firm's stock price.

We use the tabular and time line cash flow data shown in Figure 13-1 for Projects S and L to illustrate each capital budgeting method. Throughout this section, we assume that both projects are equally risky. The expected cash flows, $\widehat{CF}_t$, shown in Figure 13-1

---

[7]For information about which methods firms use to make capital budgeting decisions, see John R. Graham and Campbell R. Harvey, "The Theory and Practice of Corporate Finance: Evidence from the Field," *Journal of Financial Economics* 60, 187–243, 2001. Another capital budgeting technique that was once widely used is the *accounting rate of return (ARR)*, which examines a project's contribution to the firm's net income. According to the Graham and Harvey study, only 20 percent of firms continue to calculate ARR when evaluating capital budgeting projects.

Because this method is not widely used and because it relies on income rather than cash flows, we do not discuss ARR here. For those who are interested, the ARR is computed by dividing the average net income expected to be generated by the project over its life by the investment's average value. In other words, the ARR is computed as follows:

$$ARR = \frac{\text{Average annual income}}{\text{Average book value of investment}}$$

A project would be considered acceptable if its ARR exceeded a certain return—perhaps the firm's required rate of return. For a discussion of ARR, see Chapter 12 in Eugene F. Brigham and Phillip R. Daves, *Intermediate Financial Management,* 9th ed. (Cincinnati, OH: South-Western/Cengage Learning, 2007).

FIGURE 13-1   Net Cash Flows for Projects S and L

Year (t)	Expected After-Tax Net Cash Flows, $\widehat{CF}_t$	
	Project S	Project L
0	$(3,000)	$(3,000)
1	1,500	400
2	1,200	900
3	800	1,300
4	300	1,500

Project S

	0	1	2	3	4
Net Cash Flow	(3,000)	1,500	1,200	800	300

Project L

	0	1	2	3	4
Net Cash Flow	(3,000)	400	900	1,300	1,500

represent the "bottom line" cash flows, which we assume occur at the end of the designated year. Incidentally, "S" stands for *short* and "L" stands for *long:* Project S is a short-term project in the sense that its cash flows tend to come in sooner than those for Project L. We use these two projects in our illustration to simplify our presentations.

Net Present Value (NPV)

Following the steps outlined earlier in the chapter, we can determine the acceptability of a capital budgeting project by computing its value and comparing the result to the purchase price. Remember from our previous discussions that the value of an asset can be determined by computing the present value of the cash flows it is expected to generate during its life. If we subtract the purchase price of the asset from (or add a negative cash flow) the present value of its expected future cash flows, the result is the net dollar value, or net benefit that accrues to the firm if the asset is purchased. This net benefit is called the asset's **net present value (NPV)**. The NPV shows by how much a firm's value, and thus stockholders' wealth, will increase if a capital budgeting project is purchased. *If the net benefit computed on a present value basis—that is, NPV—is positive, then the asset (project) is considered an acceptable investment.* In other words, to determine whether a project is acceptable using the NPV technique, we apply the following decision rule:

NPV DECISION RULE: A project is acceptable if NPV > $0.

We use the following equation to compute NPV:

$$NPV = \widehat{CF}_0 + \frac{\widehat{CF}_1}{(1+r)^1} + \frac{\widehat{CF}_2}{(1+r)^2} + \cdots + \frac{\widehat{CF}_n}{(1+r)^n}$$

net present value (NPV) A method of evaluating capital investment proposals by finding the present value of future net cash flows, discounted at the rate of return required by the firm.

13-2

Here $\widehat{CF}_t$ is the expected net cash flow at Period t, and r is the rate of return required by the firm to invest in this project.[8] Cash outflows (expenditures on the project, such as the cost of buying equipment or building factories) are treated as negative cash flows.

---

[8]The rate of return required by the firm generally is termed the firm's *cost of capital* because it is the average rate the firm must pay for the funds used to purchase capital projects. The concept of cost of capital is discussed in Chapter 12.

At a 10 percent required rate of return, Project S's net present value, NPV_S, is $161.33:

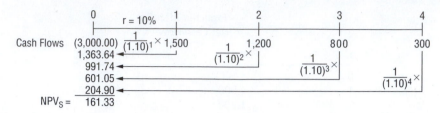

As the lower section of the cash flow time line shows, to find the NPV using Equation 13-2, we compute the present value of each cash flow, including $\widehat{CF}_0$, and sum the results. It is not difficult to calculate the NPV using Equation 13-2 and a regular calculator as we did here. Nevertheless, the most efficient way to find the NPV is by using a financial calculator. Different calculators are set up somewhat differently, but they all have a section of memory called the "cash flow register" that is used for computing the present value of uneven cash flows such as those in Project S (as opposed to equal annuity cash flows). As we saw in Chapter 9, a solution process for Equation 13-2 is literally programmed into financial calculators. Simply input the cash flows (being sure to observe the signs) in the order they occur, along with the value of $I/Y = r$. For Project S, enter $CF_0 = -3,000$, $CF_1 = 1,500$, $CF_2 = 1,200$, $CF_3 = 800$, $CF_4 = 300$, and $I/Y = r = 10\%$. At this point, you have entered in your calculator the cash flows and the interest rate shown on the cash flow time line for Project S. There is one unknown—NPV. Now you just ask the calculator to solve the equation for you; the answer, 161.33, will appear on the screen.[9] Using this same process for Project L, we find $NPV_L = \$108.67$.[10] On this basis, both projects should be accepted if they are *independent*, but Project S should be the one chosen if they are *mutually exclusive* because $NPV_S = \$161.33 > NPV_L = \$108.67$.

The rationale for the NPV method is straightforward. An NPV of $0 signifies that the project's cash flows are just sufficient to repay the invested capital and to provide the required rate of return (r) on that capital. If a project has a positive NPV, then it generates a return that is greater than is needed to pay for funds provided by investors, and this excess return accrues solely to the firm's stockholders. Therefore, if a firm takes on a project with a positive NPV, the position of the stockholders is improved because the firm's value increases.[11] In our example, shareholders' wealth would increase by $161.33 if the firm takes on Project S but by only $108.67 if it takes on Project L. Viewed in this manner, it is easy to see why Project S is preferred to Project L, and it also is easy to see the logic of the NPV approach. If the two projects are independent, both should be accepted because shareholders' wealth would

[9]Refer to the manual that came with your calculator to determine how the CF function is used.

[10]Appendix 13B at the end of this chapter shows how to compute the NPV for Project S using a spreadsheet. It also shows how to use a spreadsheet to compute the project's internal rate of return (IRR), which is discussed later in the chapter.

[11]The profitability index (PI) is a discounted technique similar to NPV. It is computed by dividing the sum of discounted cash flows by the initial investment:

$$\text{Profitability index} = \frac{\text{DCF}}{\text{Initial investment}}$$

Thus $PI_S = \$3,161.33/\$3,000 = 1.05$. A project is acceptable only if its $NPV = DCF - (\text{Initial investment})$ is greater than zero. It is logical, therefore, that the project's PI must be greater than 1.0. We do not discuss PI here because very few firms (about 12 percent) actually use this technique. For an indication of the capital budgeting techniques used by firms, see John R. Graham and Campbell R. Harvey, "The Theory and Practice of Corporate Finance: Evidence from the Field," *Journal of Financial Economics* 60, 187–243, 2001.

increase by $270 = \$161.33 + \$108.67$. *In general, a project is considered acceptable if its NPV is positive; it is not acceptable if its NPV is negative.*[12]

Internal Rate of Return (IRR)

In Chapter 10, we presented procedures for finding the yield to maturity (YTM), or rate of return, on a bond. Recall that if you invest in a bond and hold it to maturity, the average return you can expect to earn on the money you invest is the YTM. Exactly the same concept is employed in capital budgeting to determine the **internal rate of return (IRR),** which is the rate of return the firm expects to earn if a project is purchased and held for its economic (useful) life. The IRR is defined as the discount rate that equates the present value of a project's expected cash flows to the initial amount invested. *As long as the project's IRR, which is its expected return, is greater than the rate of return required by the firm for such an investment, the project is acceptable.* In other words, to determine whether a project is acceptable using the IRR technique, we apply the following decision rule:

internal rate of return (IRR) The discount rate that forces the present value of a project's expected cash flows to equal its cost. The IRR is similar to the yield to maturity on a bond.

> **IRR DECISION RULE:** A project is acceptable if IRR > r, where r is the firm's required rate of return.

We can use the following equation to solve for a project's IRR:

13-3

$$NPV = \widehat{CF}_0 + \frac{\widehat{CF}_1}{(1+IRR)^1} + \frac{\widehat{CF}_2}{(1+IRR)^2} + \cdots + \frac{\widehat{CF}_n}{(1+IRR)^n} = 0$$

or

$$\widehat{CF}_0 = \frac{\widehat{CF}_1}{(1+IRR)^1} + \frac{\widehat{CF}_2}{(1+IRR)^2} + \cdots + \frac{\widehat{CF}_n}{(1+IRR)^n}$$

For Project S, the cash flow time line for the IRR computation is as follows:

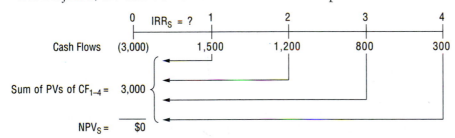

Using Equation 13-3, here is the setup for computing IRR_S:

$$(3,000) + \frac{1,500}{(1+IRR)^1} + \frac{1,200}{(1+IRR)^2} + \frac{800}{(1+IRR)^3} + \frac{300}{(1+IRR)^4} = 0$$

Although it is fairly easy to find the NPV without a financial calculator, the same is *not* true of the IRR. Without a financial calculator, you must solve Equation 13-3 by trial and error—that is, you must try different discount rates until you find the one that forces NPV equal to $0. This discount rate is the IRR.

---

[12]This description of the process is somewhat oversimplified. Both analysts and investors anticipate that firms will identify and accept positive NPV projects, and current stock prices reflect these expectations. Thus, stock prices react to announcements of new capital projects only to the extent that such projects were not already expected. In this sense, we can think of a firm's value as consisting of two parts: (1) the value of its existing assets and (2) the value of its "growth opportunities," or projects with positive NPVs.

Fortunately, it is easy to find IRRs with a financial calculator. To solve for IRR using a financial calculator, follow the steps used to find the NPV. First, enter the cash flows as shown on the preceding cash flow time line into the calculator's cash flow register. For Project S, enter $CF_0 = -3{,}000$, $CF_1 = 1{,}500$, $CF_2 = 1{,}200$, $CF_3 = 800$, and $CF_4 = 300$. In effect, you have entered the cash flows into Equation 13-3. You now have one unknown, IRR, or the discount rate that forces NPV to equal \$0. The calculator has been programmed to solve for the IRR, and you activate this program by pressing the key labeled "IRR." Following are the IRRs for Projects S and L found using a financial calculator:

$$IRR_S = 13.1\%$$
$$IRR_L = 11.4\%$$

required rate of return (hurdle rate)
The discount rate (cost of funds) that the IRR must exceed for a project to be considered acceptable.

A project is acceptable if its IRR is greater than the firm's **required rate of return,** or **hurdle rate.** For example, if the hurdle rate required by the firm is 10 percent, then both Projects S and L are acceptable. If they are mutually exclusive, Project S is more acceptable than Project L because $IRR_S > IRR_L$. On the other hand, if the firm's required rate of return is 15 percent, neither project is acceptable.

Notice from Equation 13-3 that *you do not need to know the firm's required rate of return (r) to solve for IRR.* However, you need the required rate of return to make a decision as to whether a project is acceptable once its IRR has been computed. Also, note that (1) the IRR is the rate of return that will be earned by anyone who purchases the project and (2) the IRR is dependent on the project's cash flow characteristics—that is, the amounts and the timing of the cash flows—not the firm's required rate of return.[13] As a result, *the IRR of a particular project is the same for all firms, regardless of their particular required rates of return.* A project might be acceptable to one firm (Project S would be acceptable to a firm that has a required rate of return equal to 10 percent), but not acceptable to another firm (Project S is not acceptable to a firm that has a required rate of return equal to 15 percent).

Why is a project acceptable if its IRR is greater than its required rate of return? Because the IRR on a project is the rate of return that the project is expected to generate, and if this return exceeds the cost of the funds used to finance the project, a surplus remains after paying for the funds. This surplus accrues to the firm's stockholders. Therefore, *taking on a project whose IRR exceeds its required rate of return, or cost of funds, increases shareholders' wealth.* On the other hand, if the IRR is less than the cost of funds, then taking on the project imposes a cost on current stockholders that decreases wealth.

Consider what would happen if you borrow funds at a 10 percent interest rate to invest in the stock market. The 10 percent interest is your *cost of funds,* which is what you *require* your investments to earn to break even. You lose money if you earn less than 10 percent, and you gain money if you earn more than 10 percent. This breakeven characteristic makes the IRR useful in evaluating capital projects.

Payback Period—Traditional (Nondiscounted) (PB) and Discounted (DPB)

traditional payback period (PB)
The length of time before the original cost of an investment is recovered from the expected cash flows.

Many managers like to know how long it will take a project to repay its initial investment (cost) from the cash flows it is expected to generate in the future. Thus, many firms compute a project's **traditional payback period (PB),** which is defined as the expected number of years required to recover the original investment (the cost

---

[13]In reality, the investment earns the internal rate of return only if the cash flows that are generated each year can be reinvested in the same project. In other words, the cash flows must be reinvested at the internal rate of return.

FIGURE 13-2   Traditional Payback Period (PB) for Projects S and L

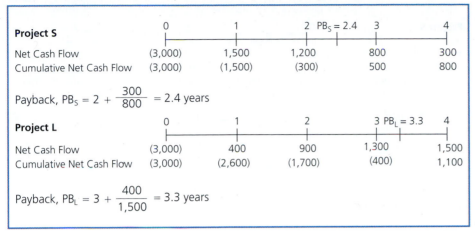

of the asset). Payback is the simplest and, as far as we know, the oldest *formal* method used to evaluate capital budgeting projects. To compute a project's payback period, simply add up the expected cash flows for each year until the cumulative value equals the amount that is initially invested. The total amount of time, including the fraction of a year if appropriate, that it takes to recapture the original amount invested is the payback period. Figure 13-2 shows the payback calculation process for Projects S and L.

The exact payback period can be found using the following formula:

$$\begin{array}{l} \text{Payback} \\ \text{period} \end{array} = \left(\begin{array}{c} \text{Number of years } \textit{before} \\ \text{the year of full recovery} \\ \text{of initial investment} \end{array} \right) + \left(\dfrac{ \begin{array}{c} \text{Amount of the initial investment that is} \\ \textit{unrecovered} \text{ at the start of the recovery year} \end{array} }{ \begin{array}{c} \text{Total cash flow generated} \\ \text{during the recovery year} \end{array} } \right)$$

13-4

As Figure 13-2 shows, the payback period for Project S is between 2 and 3 years. Using Equation 13-4, the exact payback period for Project S is computed as follows:

$$PB_s = 2 + \frac{300}{800} = 2.4 \text{ years}$$

Applying the same procedure to Project L, we find $PB_L = 3.3$ years.

Using payback to make capital budgeting decisions is based on the concept that it is better to recover the cost of (investment in) a project sooner rather than later. Therefore, Project S is considered better than Project L because it has a lower payback. *As a general rule, a project is considered acceptable if its payback is less than the maximum cost recovery time established by the firm.* In other words, to determine whether a project is acceptable using the traditional payback period method, we apply the following decision rule.

TRADITIONAL PAYBACK PERIOD (PB) DECISION RULE: A project is acceptable if PB < n*, where n* is the recovery period that the firm has determined is appropriate.

For example, if the firm requires projects to have a payback of 3 years or less, Project S would be acceptable but Project L would not.

The payback method is simple, which explains why payback traditionally has been one of the most popular capital budgeting techniques. But, because payback ignores the time value of money, relying solely on this method could lead to incorrect decisions—at

FIGURE 13-3   Discounted Payback Period (DPB) for Projects S and L

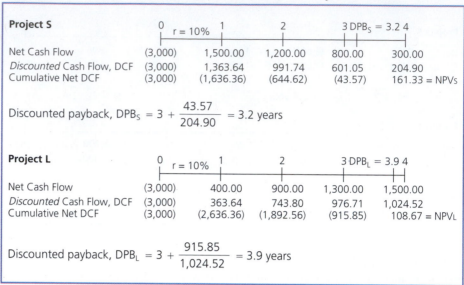

Project S

	0	1	2	3 DPB$_S$ = 3.2 4
	r = 10%			
Net Cash Flow	(3,000)	1,500.00	1,200.00	800.00	300.00
Discounted Cash Flow, DCF	(3,000)	1,363.64	991.74	601.05	204.90
Cumulative Net DCF	(3,000)	(1,636.36)	(644.62)	(43.57)	161.33 = NPV$_S$

Discounted payback, DPB$_S$ = $3 + \dfrac{43.57}{204.90}$ = 3.2 years

Project L

	0	1	2	3 DPB$_L$ = 3.9 4
	r = 10%			
Net Cash Flow	(3,000)	400.00	900.00	1,300.00	1,500.00
Discounted Cash Flow, DCF	(3,000)	363.64	743.80	976.71	1,024.52
Cumulative Net DCF	(3,000)	(2,636.36)	(1,892.56)	(915.85)	108.67 = NPV$_L$

Discounted payback, DPB$_L$ = $3 + \dfrac{915.85}{1,024.52}$ = 3.9 years

least if our goal is to maximize value. If a project has a payback of 3 years, we know how quickly the initial investment will be covered by the expected cash flows, but this information does not provide any indication of whether the return on the project is sufficient to cover the cost of the invested funds. In addition, when payback is used, the cash flows beyond the payback period are ignored. For example, even if Project L had a fifth year of cash flows equal to $50,000, its payback would remain 3.3 years, which is less desirable than the payback of 2.4 years for Project S. With the additional $50,000 cash flow, however, Project L most likely would be preferred.

To correct for the fact that the traditional payback method does not consider the time value of money, we can compute the **discounted payback period (DPB),** which is the length of time it takes for a project's *discounted* cash flows to repay the cost of the investment. Using the general payback concept, we can easily compute how long it takes to recapture the initial outlay of $3,000 using the present values of the project's cash flows. Figure 13-3 shows the discounted payback computations for Projects S and L. The sum of the *present values* of the cash flows for Project S for the first 3 years is $2,956.43 = $1,363.64 + $991.74 + $601.05, so all of the $3,000 cost is not recovered until 3.2 years = 3 years + [($3,000 − $43.57)/$204.90] years. Therefore, on a *present value basis*, it takes 3.2 years for Project S to recover, or pay back, its original cost. The discounted payback for Project L is 3.9 years, so Project S is more acceptable.

Unlike the traditional payback computation, the discounted payback computation considers the time value of money. If you look at the cash flow time line that shows the NPV computation for Project S, you can see the reason it has a positive NPV is because the initial investment of $3,000 is recovered on a present value basis prior to the end of the project's life. Thus, using the discounted payback method, a project should be accepted when its discounted payback is less than its expected life.

DISCOUNTED PAYBACK (DPB) DECISION RULE: A project is acceptable if DPB < Project's life.

As Figure 13-3 shows, when a project's discounted payback is less than its life, the present value of the future cash flows the project is expected to generate exceeds the initial cost of the asset—that is, NPV > 0.

discounted payback period (DPB)
The length of time it takes for a project's *discounted* cash flows to repay the initial cost of the investment.

Self-Test Questions

What are the principal methods for evaluating capital budgeting proposals?

Describe each method and give the rationale for its use. How do the methods differ?

Whole Wheat Bakery is considering purchasing a new machine that costs $75,000. The machine is expected to generate after-tax cash flows equal to $30,000, $38,000, and $28,000 during its 3-year life. Whole Wheat requires such investments to earn a return equal to at least 12 percent. What is the machine's net present value (NPV), internal rate of return (IRR), traditional payback period (PB), and discounted payback period (DPB)? Should the bakery purchase the machine?   (Answers: NPV = $2,009; IRR = 13.6%; PB = 2.25 years; DPB = 2.9 years; purchase the machine because NPV > 0, IRR > r = 12%, and DPB < machine's life)

COMPARISON OF THE NPV AND IRR METHODS

We found the NPV for Project S is $161.33, which means that the firm's value will increase by $161.33 if the project is purchased. The IRR for Project S is 13.1 percent, which means that the firm will earn a 13.1 percent rate of return on its investment if it purchases Project S. We generally measure wealth in dollars, so the NPV method should be used to accomplish the goal of maximizing shareholders' wealth. In reality, using the IRR method could lead to investment decisions that increase, but do not maximize, wealth. We choose to discuss the IRR method and compare it to the NPV method because many corporate executives are familiar with the meaning of IRR, it is entrenched in the corporate world, and it does have some virtues. For these reasons, it is important to understand the IRR method and be prepared to explain why a project with *a lower IRR might sometimes be preferable to one with a higher IRR.*

NPV Profiles

A graph that shows a project's NPV at various discount rates (required rates of return) is termed the project's **net present value (NPV) profile.** Figure 13-4 shows the NPV profiles for Projects S and L. To construct the profiles, we calculate the projects' NPVs at various discount rates—say, 0, 5, 10, and 15 percent—and then plot these values. The points plotted on our graph for each project are shown at the bottom of Figure 13-4.[14]

Because the IRR is defined as the discount rate at which a project's NPV equals $0, the point where its *NPV profile crosses the X axis indicates a project's internal rate of return.* Note that firms with different required rates of return can use the NPV profile to determine whether a project is acceptable. To determine a project's NPV using the NPV profile, simply locate the appropriate required rate of return on the graph and then identify the NPV that corresponds to that rate.

net present value (NPV) profile
A curve showing the relationship between a project's NPV and various discount rates (required rates of return).

---

[14]Note that the NPV profiles are curved—they are *not* straight lines. Also, the NPVs approach the cost of the project as the discount rate increases without limit. The reason is that, at an infinitely high discount rate, the PV of the future cash flows would be $0, so NPV at $r = \infty$ is CF_0, which in our example is –$3,000.

FIGURE 13-4   NPV Profiles for Projects S and L

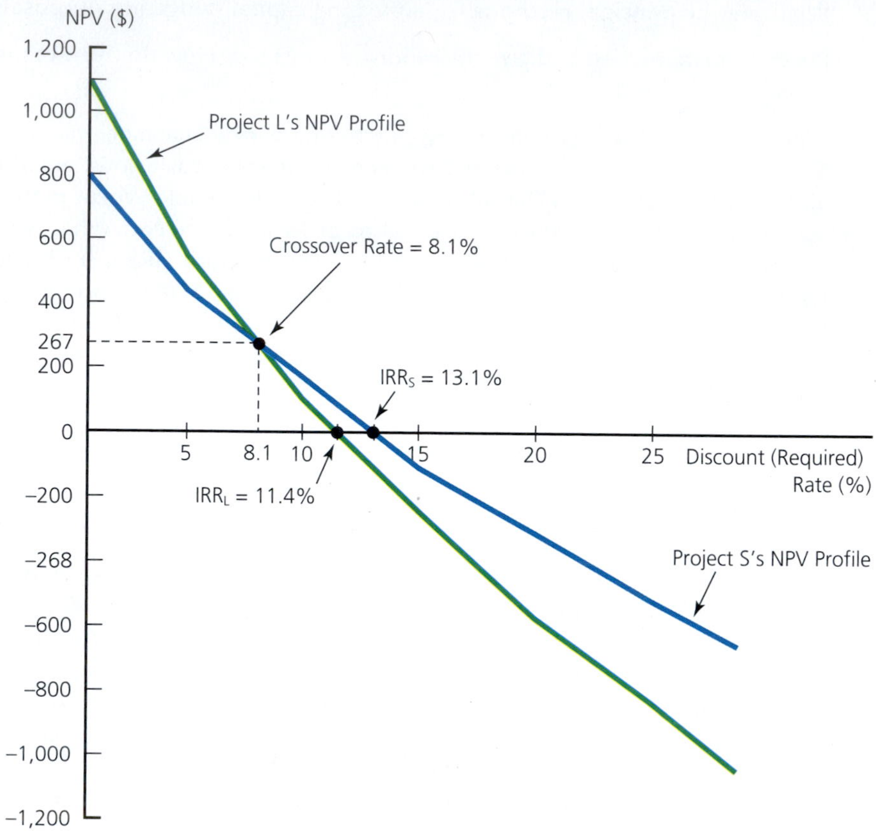

Discount Rate	NPV_S	NPV_L
0%	$800.00	$1,100.00
5	454.89	554.32
10	161.33	108.67
15	(90.74)	(259.24)
20	(309.03)	(565.97)

NPVs and the Required Rate of Return

crossover rate
The discount rate at which the NPV profiles of two projects cross and, therefore, at which the projects' NPVs are equal.

Figure 13-4 shows that the NPV profiles for Projects S and L decline as the discount rate (required rate of return) increases. Notice, however, that Project L has a higher NPV at low discount rates, whereas Project S has a higher NPV at high discount rates. According to the graph, $NPV_S = NPV_L = \$267$ when the discount rate equals 8.1 percent. We call this point the **crossover rate** because below this rate $NPV_S <$ NPV_L, and above this rate, $NPV_S > NPV_L$; but, $NPV_S = NPV_L$, and thus cross over, at 8.1 percent.[15]

---

[15]The crossover rate is easy to calculate. Simply go back to Figure 13-1, where we first show the two projects' cash flows. Now calculate the difference in the cash flows for Projects S and L in each year. The differences are computed as $\widehat{CF}_S - \widehat{CF}_L$. Thus, the cash flow differences for Projects S and L are $CF_0 = \$0$, $CF_1 = +\$1,100$, $CF_2 = +\$300$, $CF_3 = -\$500$, and $CF_4 = -\$1,200$, respectively. To compute the crossover rate using a financial calculator, enter these numbers in the order given here into the cash flow register, and then ask the calculator to compute the IRR. You should find IRR = 8.11%.

Figure 13-4 also indicates that Project L's NPV is "more sensitive" to changes in the discount rate than is Project S's NPV. That is, Project L's NPV profile has the steeper slope, indicating that a given change in r has a larger effect on NPV_L than on NPV_S. Project L is more sensitive to changes in r because the cash flows from Project L are received later than those from Project S. As a general rule, the impact of an increase in the discount rate is much greater on distant cash flows than on near-term cash flows.[16] Consequently, if most of its cash flows come in the early years, a project's NPV will not be lowered very much if the required rate of return increases. Conversely, a project whose cash flows come later will be severely penalized by high required rates of return. Accordingly, Project L, which has its largest cash flows in the later years, is hurt badly when the required rate of return is high, whereas Project S, which has relatively rapid cash flows, is affected less by high discount rates.

Independent Projects

Note that the IRR formula, Equation 13-3, is simply the NPV formula, Equation 13-2, solved for the particular discount rate that forces the NPV to equal zero. Thus, the same basic equation is used for both methods. Mathematically, the NPV and IRR methods will *always* lead to the same accept/reject decisions for independent projects: *If a project's NPV is positive, its IRR will exceed r; if NPV is negative, r will exceed the IRR.* To see why this is so, look back at Figure 13-4, focus on Project L's profile, and note that:

- The IRR criterion for acceptance is that the required rate of return is less than (or to the left of) the IRR (11.4 percent).
- Whenever the required rate of return is less than the IRR (11.4 percent), NPV > 0.

Thus, at any required rate of return less than 11.4 percent, Project L will be acceptable by both the NPV and the IRR criteria. Both methods reject the project if the required rate of return is greater than 11.4 percent. Project S—and all other independent projects under consideration—could be analyzed similarly, and *in every case, if a project is acceptable using the IRR method, then the NPV method also will show it is acceptable*.

Mutually Exclusive Projects

If Projects S and L are *mutually exclusive* rather than independent, then only one project can be purchased. If you use IRR to make the decision as to which project is better, you would choose Project S because $IRR_S = 13.1\% > IRR_L = 11.4\%$. If you use NPV to make the decision, you might reach a different conclusion depending on the firm's required rate of return. Note from Figure 13-4 that if the required rate of

---

[16]To illustrate, consider the present value of $100 to be received in 1 year versus $100 to be received in 10 years. The present values of each $100 discounted at 10 percent and at 15 percent are as follows:

Future Value	Year Received	PV @ 10%	PV @ 15%	Percent Difference
$100	1	$90.91	$86.96	−4.3%
$100	10	38.55	24.72	−35.9

As you can see, the farther into the future the cash flows are, the greater their sensitivity to discount rate changes.

return is less than the crossover rate of 8.1 percent, $NPV_L > NPV_S$, but $NPV_S > NPV_L$ if the required rate of return is greater than 8.1 percent. As a result of using the NPV technique, Project L would be preferred if the firm's required rate of return is less than 8.1 percent, but Project S would be preferred if the firm's required rate of return is greater than 8.1 percent.

As long as the firm's required rate of return is greater than 8.1 percent, using either NPV or IRR will result in the same decision—that is, Project S should be purchased—because $NPV_S > NPV_L$ and $IRR_S > IRR_L$. On the other hand, if the firm's required rate of return is less than 8.1 percent, a person who uses NPV will reach a different conclusion as to which project should be purchased than will a person who uses IRR. The person who uses NPV will choose Project L because $NPV_L > NPV_S$, whereas the person who uses IRR will choose Project S because $IRR_S > IRR_L$. Thus, in the case where the required rate of return is less than 8.1 percent, *a conflict exists*. Which capital budgeting technique should be used to choose the better project? Logic suggests that the NPV method is better because it selects the project that adds more to shareholder wealth.

Two basic conditions can cause NPV profiles to cross and thus lead to conflicts between NPV and IRR: (1) when *project size (or scale) differences* exist, meaning that the cost of one project is much larger than that of the other or (2) when *timing differences* exist, meaning that the timing of cash flows from the two projects differs such that most of the cash flows from one project come in the early years and most of the cash flows from the other project come in the later years, as occurs with Projects S and L.[17]

When either size or timing differences occur, the firm will have different amounts of funds to invest in the various years, depending on which of the two mutually exclusive projects it chooses. For example, if one project costs more than the other, then the firm will have more money at t = 0 to invest elsewhere if it selects the smaller project. Similarly, for projects of equal size, the one with the larger early cash inflows provides more funds for reinvestment in the early years. Given this situation, the rate of return at which differential cash flows can be invested is an important consideration.

The critical issue in resolving conflicts between mutually exclusive projects is this: How useful is it to generate cash flows earlier rather than later? The value of early cash flows depends on the rate at which we can reinvest these cash flows. *The NPV method implicitly assumes that the rate at which cash flows can be reinvested is the required rate of return, r, whereas the IRR method implies that the firm has the opportunity to reinvest at the project's IRR.* These assumptions are inherent in the mathematics of the discounting process. The cash flows can actually be withdrawn as dividends by the stockholders and spent on pizza, but the NPV method still assumes that cash flows could be reinvested at the required rate of return, whereas the IRR method assumes reinvestment at the project's IRR.

Which is the better assumption—that cash flows can be reinvested at the firm's required rate of return or that they can be reinvested at the project's IRR? To reinvest at the IRR associated with a capital project, the firm must be able to reinvest the project's cash flows in another project with an identical IRR. Such projects generally do not continue to exist, or it is not feasible to reinvest in

---

[17]Of course, it is possible for mutually exclusive projects to differ with respect to both scale and timing. Also, if mutually exclusive projects have different lives (as opposed to different cash flow patterns over a common life), this introduces further complications, and for meaningful comparisons, some mutually exclusive projects must be evaluated over a common life. Techniques used to compare projects with unequal lives are described in Chapter 12 in Eugene E. Brigham and Phillip R. Daves, *Intermediate Financial Management*, 9th ed. (Cincinnati, OH: South-Western/Cengage Learning, 2007).

such projects, because competition in the investment markets drives their prices up and their IRRs down. On the other hand, at the very least, a firm could repurchase the bonds and stock it has issued to raise capital budgeting funds and thus repay some of its investors, which would be the same as investing at its required rate of return. Thus, we conclude the *more realistic* **reinvestment rate assumption** *is that the firm's opportuinity cost is its required rate of return, which is implicit in the NPV method*. This, in turn, leads us to prefer the NPV method, at least for firms willing and able to obtain new funds at a cost reasonably close to their current cost of funds.

We should repeat that when projects are independent, the NPV and IRR methods both provide exactly the same accept/reject decision. However, when evaluating mutually exclusive projects, especially those that differ in scale or timing, the NPV method should be used to determine which project should be purchased.

> **reinvestment rate assumption**
> The assumption that cash flows from a project can be reinvested (1) at the cost of capital, if using the NPV method, or (2) at the internal rate of return, if using the IRR method.

 Self-Test Questions

Describe how NPV profiles are constructed.

What is the crossover rate, and how does it affect the choice between mutually exclusive projects?

Why do the NPV and IRR methods always lead to the same accept/reject decisions for independent projects?

What two basic conditions can lead to conflicts between the NPV and IRR methods?

If a conflict exists, should the capital budgeting decision be made on the basis of the NPV or the IRR ranking? Why?

CASH FLOW PATTERNS AND MULTIPLE IRRS

A project has a *conventional* cash flow pattern if it has cash outflows (costs) in one or more consecutive periods at the beginning of its life followed by a series of cash inflows during its life. If, however, a project has a large cash outflow at the beginning of its life and then another cash outflow either sometime during or at the end of its life, then it has an *unconventional* cash flow pattern. Projects with unconventional cash flow patterns present unique difficulties when the IRR method is used, including the possibility of **multiple IRRs.**[18] Following are examples of conventional and unconventional cash flow patterns:

> **multiple IRRs**
> The situation where a project has two or more IRRs.

Conventional Cash Flow Patterns: (1) − + + + + +   (2) − − − + + +

Unconventional Cash Flow Patterns: (1) − + + − + + +   (2) − − + + + − −

There exists an IRR solution for each time the *direction* of the cash flows associated with a project is interrupted—that is, inflows change to outflows. For example, each of the conventional cash flow patterns shown here has only one change (is interrupted) in the signs (direction) of the cash flows from negative (outflow) to positive (inflow), thus there is only one IRR solution. On the other hand,

---

[18]Multiple IRRs result from the manner in which Equation 13-3 must be solved to arrive at a project's IRR. The mathematical rationale and the solution to multiple IRRs will not be discussed here. Instead, we want you to be aware that multiple IRRs can exist because this possibility complicates capital budgeting evaluation using the IRR method.

FIGURE 13-5   NPV Profile for Project M

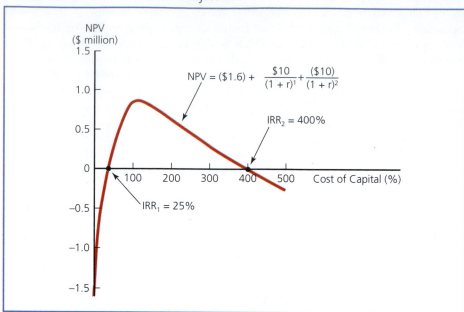

each of the unconventional cash flow patterns shown here has two "interruptions," and thus two IRR solutions.

Figure 13-5 illustrates the multiple IRR problem with a strip-mining project that costs $1.6 million. The mine will produce a cash inflow of $10 million at the end of Year 1, but $10 million must be spent at the end of Year 2 to restore the land to its original condition. Two IRRs exist for this project—25 and 400 percent. The NPV profile for the mine shows that the project would have a positive NPV, and thus be acceptable, if the firm's required rate of return is between 25 and 400 percent.

Self-Test Questions

How would you describe a conventional cash flow pattern? What is an unconventional cash flow pattern?

What is the multiple IRR problem, and what condition is necessary for its occurrence?

MODIFIED INTERNAL RATE OF RETURN

Despite a strong academic preference for NPV, surveys indicate that many business executives prefer IRR over NPV. It seems that many managers find it intuitively more appealing to analyze investments in terms of percentage rates of return than dollars of NPV. But remember from our earlier discussion that the IRR method assumes the cash flows from the project are reinvested at a rate of return equal to the IRR, which we generally view as unrealistic. Given this fact, can we devise a rate of return measure that is better than the regular IRR? The answer is yes—we can modify the IRR and make it a better indicator of relative profitability, hence better for use in capital budgeting. This "modified" return is called the **modified IRR, or MIRR,** and it is defined as follows:

13-5

$$\text{PV of cash outflows} = \frac{\text{FV of cash inflows}}{(1+\text{MIRR})^n} = \frac{\text{TV}}{(1+\text{MIRR})^n}$$

$$\sum_{t=0}^{n} \frac{\text{COF}_t}{(1+r)^t} = \frac{\sum_{t=0}^{n} \text{CIF}_t(1+r)^{n-t}}{(1+\text{MIRR})^n}$$

modified IRR (MIRR)
The discount rate at which the present value of a project's cost is equal to the present value of its terminal value, where the terminal value is found as the sum of the future values of the cash inflows compounded at the firm's required rate of return (cost of capital).

Here, COF refers to cash outflows (all negative numbers) and CIF refers to cash inflows (all positive numbers) associated with a project. The left term is simply the present value (PV) of the investment outlays (cash *outflows*) when discounted at the firm's required rate of return, r, and the numerator of the right term is the future value of the cash *inflows,* assuming that these inflows are reinvested at the firm's required rate of return. The future value of the cash inflows is also called the *terminal value,* or TV. The discount rate that forces the PV of the TV to equal the PV of the costs is defined as the MIRR.[19]

We can illustrate the calculation of MIRR with Project S:

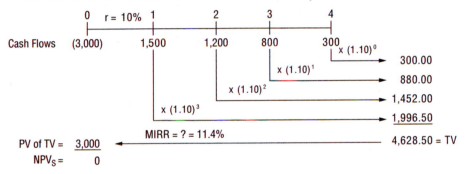

Using the cash flows as set out on the cash flow time line, first find the terminal value by compounding each cash inflow at the 10 percent required rate of return. Then, enter into your calculator PV = −3,000, FV = 4,628.50, and N = 4, and compute I/Y = 11.4% = MIRR$_S$. Similarly, we find MIRR$_L$ = 11.0%.

The modified IRR has a significant advantage over the traditional IRR measure. MIRR assumes that cash flows are reinvested at the required rate of return, whereas the traditional IRR measure assumes that cash flows are reinvested at the project's own IRR. Because reinvestment at the required rate of return (cost of funds) generally is more correct, the MIRR is a better indicator of a project's true profitability. MIRR also solves the multiple IRR problem. To illustrate, with r = 10%, the strip-mine project described in the chapter has MIRR = 5.6% versus the 10 percent required rate of return, so it should be rejected. This is consistent with the decision based on the NPV method because at r = 10%, NPV = −$0.77 million.

Is MIRR as good as NPV for choosing between mutually exclusive projects? If two projects are of equal size and have the same life, then NPV and MIRR will always lead

[19]There are several alternative definitions for the MIRR. The differences relate primarily to whether negative cash flows that occur after positive cash flows begin should be compounded and treated as part of the TV or discounted and treated as a cost. Our definition (which treats all negative cash flows as investments and thus discounts them) generally is the most appropriate procedure. For a complete discussion, see William R. McDaniel, Daniel E. McCarty, and Kenneth A. Jessell, "Discounted Cash Flow with Explicit Reinvestment Rates: Tutorial and Extension," *The Financial Review* (August 1988), 369–385.

to the same project selection decision. Thus, for any projects like our Projects S and L, if $NPV_S > NPV_L$, then $MIRR_S > MIRR_L$, and the kinds of conflicts we encountered between NPV and the traditional IRR will not occur. Also, if the projects are of equal size, but have different lives, the MIRR will always lead to the same decision as the NPV if the MIRRs for both projects are calculated using as the terminal year the life of the longer project. (Just fill in zeros for the shorter project's missing cash flows.) If the projects differ in size, however, then conflicts can still occur. For example, if we were choosing between a large project and a small mutually exclusive one, then we might find $NPV_{Large} > NPV_{Small}$ and $MIRR_{Large} < MIRR_{Small}$.

Our conclusion is that the MIRR is superior to the regular IRR as an indicator of a project's "true" rate of return, or "expected long-term rate of return," but the NPV method is still better for choosing among competing projects that differ in size because it provides a better indicator of the extent to which each project will increase the value of the firm; thus, NPV is still the recommended approach.

Self-Test Question

What is the primary advantage to using MIRR rather than IRR to evaluate an investment?

CONCLUSIONS ON THE CAPITAL BUDGETING DECISION METHODS

Earlier in this chapter, we compared the NPV and IRR methods to highlight their relative strengths and weaknesses for evaluating capital projects, and in the process we probably created the impression that "sophisticated" firms should use only one method in the decision process—NPV. However, because virtually all capital budgeting decisions are analyzed by computer, it is easy to calculate and list all the decision measures we discussed: traditional payback, discounted payback, NPV, IRR, and MIRR. In making the accept/reject decision, most large, sophisticated firms calculate and consider multiple measures because each provides decision makers with a somewhat different piece of relevant information. In fact, a recent survey revealed that approximately 75 percent of the respondent firms "always or almost always" use the NPV methods, about the same percent use the IRR method, and nearly 57 percent use the payback period approach to evaluate capital budgeting projects. These results show that firms do indeed use more than one technique to evaluate capital budgeting projects.[20]

Traditional payback and discounted payback provide information about both the risk and the *liquidity* of a project. A long payback means (1) that the investment dollars will be locked up for many years, hence the project is relatively illiquid, and (2) that the project's cash flows must be forecast far out into the future, hence the project is probably quite risky.[21] A good analogy for this is the bond valuation process. An investor should never compare the yields to maturity on two bonds without considering their terms to maturity because a bond's riskiness is influenced by its maturity.

NPV is important because it gives a direct measure of the dollar benefit (on a present value basis) to the firm's shareholders, so we regard NPV as the best single measure of *profitability*. IRR also measures profitability, but here it is expressed as a percentage rate of return, which many decision makers, especially nonfinancial managers, seem

---

[20]John R. Graham and Campbell R. Harvey, "The Theory and Practice of Corporate Finance: Evidence from the Field," *Journal of Financial Economics* 60, 187–243, 2001.

[21]We generally define *liquidity* as the ability to convert an asset into cash quickly while maintaining the original investment. Thus, in most cases, short-term assets are considered more liquid than long-term assets. We discuss liquidity in greater detail later in the book.

to prefer. Further, IRR contains information concerning a project's "safety margin," which is not inherent in NPV. To illustrate, consider the following two projects: Project T costs $10,000 at t = 0 and is expected to return $16,500 at the end of 1 year, while Project B costs $100,000 and has an expected payoff of $115,500 after 1 year. At a 10 percent required rate of return, both projects have an NPV of $5,000, so by the NPV rule we should be indifferent between the two. However, Project T actually provides a much larger margin for error. Even if its realized cash inflow were almost 40 percent below the $16,500 forecast, the firm would still recover its $10,000 investment. On the other hand, if Project B's inflows fell by only 13.5 percent from the forecasted $115,500, the firm would not recover its investment. Further, if no inflows were generated at all, the firm would lose only $10,000 with Project T but $100,000 if it took on Project B.

The NPV contains no information about either the safety margin inherent in a project's cash flow forecasts or the amount of capital at risk, but the IRR does provide "safety margin" information: Project T's IRR is a whopping 65 percent, while Project B's IRR is only 15.5 percent. As a result, the realized return could fall substantially for Project T, and it would still make money. Note, however, that the IRR method has a reinvestment assumption that probably is unrealistic, and it is possible for projects to have multiple IRRs. Both of these problems can be corrected using the MIRR calculation.

In summary, the different methods provide different types of information. Because it is easy to calculate them, all should be considered in the decision process. For any specific decision, more weight might be given to one method than another, but it would be foolish to ignore the information provided by any of the methods.

Finally, we note that all capital budgeting methods that consider the time value of money—that is, NPV, IRR, MIRR, and discounted payback—provide the same accept/reject decisions, but there could be ranking conflicts that might lead to different decisions about which project to purchase when they are mutually exclusive depending on which capital budgeting technique is used.

Self-Test Questions

Describe the advantages and disadvantages of the capital budgeting methods discussed in this chapter.

Should capital budgeting decisions be made solely on the basis of a project's NPV?

INCORPORATING RISK IN CAPITAL BUDGETING ANALYSIS

To this point we have assumed that the capital budgeting projects being evaluated have the same risk as the projects that the firm currently possesses, because such projects can be evaluated using the firm's average required rate of return (its WACC). In the real world, three types of project risk need to be considered to determine whether the required rate of return used to evaluate a project should be different than the firm's WACC:

1. The project's own **stand-alone risk,** or the risk it exhibits when evaluated alone rather than as part of a combination, or portfolio, of assets
2. The **corporate,** or **within-firm, risk,** which is the effect a project has on the total (overall) riskiness of the company
3. The **beta,** or **market, risk,** which is the project's risk assessed from the standpoint of a stockholder who holds a well-diversified portfolio

stand-alone risk
The risk that an asset would have if it were a firm's only asset. It is measured by the variability of the asset's expected returns.

corporate (within-firm) risk
The effect a project has on the total risk of the firm. It captures the risk relationships among the assets that the firm owns.

beta (market) risk
That part of a project's risk that cannot be eliminated by diversification. It is measured by the project's beta coefficient.

Evaluating the risk associated with a capital budgeting project is similar to evaluating the risk of a financial asset such as a stock. As we discovered in Chapter 11, an asset might have high stand-alone risk, often measured by its standard deviation, σ, yet taking it on might not dramatically alter the overall risk of a combination of assets because of portfolio, or diversification, effects.

In this section, we briefly examine how firms consider risk when evaluating capital budgeting projects. A more comprehensive discussion can be found in more advanced financial management texts.

Stand-Alone Risk

When we compute a project's NPV, we use cash flows that are forecasted by management. Unless management has perfect knowledge, the estimation of the cash flows included in capital budgeting analysis—for example, unit sales—will be expected values taken from probability distributions that define the outcomes that management considers viable. Of course, probability distributions could be relatively "tight," reflecting small standard deviations and low risk, or "flat," denoting a great deal of uncertainty, or high risk. Thus, the nature of the individual cash flow distributions determines a project's stand-alone risk.

scenario analysis
A risk analysis technique in which "bad" and "good" sets of financial circumstances are compared with a most likely, or base case, situation.

One method used by firms to assess a project's stand-alone risk is **scenario analysis,** a risk analysis technique that helps decision makers get an idea of the range of possible outcomes when a project is purchased. In a scenario analysis, the financial analyst asks operating managers to pick a "bad" set of circumstances (low unit sales, low sales price, high costs, and so on) and a "good" set. The NPVs under the bad and good conditions are then calculated and compared to the expected, or base case, NPV.

To see how this analysis works, let's return to the example introduced at the beginning of the chapter—the appliance control computer project being evaluated by Household Energy Products (HEP). We assume that HEP's managers are fairly confident their estimates of the project's cash flow variables are accurate, except for price and unit sales. They believe that the range for sales is 10,000 units to 20,000 units and the range for the sales price is $1,500 to $2,500. In this situation, 10,000 units at a price of $1,500 defines the lower bound, or the **worst-case scenario;** 20,000 units at a price of $2,500 defines the upper bound, or the **best-case scenario.** Recall that the **base case** values are 15,000 units selling for $2,000 each. Table 13-5 shows the NPVs for each scenario associated with the HEP project.[22]

worst-case scenario
An analysis in which all of the input variables are set at their worst reasonably forecasted values.

best-case scenario
An analysis in which all of the input variables are set at their best reasonably forecasted values.

base case
An analysis in which all of the input variables are set at their most likely values.

We can use the results of the scenario analysis to determine the expected NPV, the standard deviation of NPV, and the coefficient of variation. Table 13-5 shows the results of these computations, assuming there is a 20 percent probability of the worst-case scenario occurring, a 60 percent probability of the base case occurring, and a 20 percent probability of the best case occurring. The expected NPV is $4.475 million, and the coefficient of variation is 1.7.[23] The project's coefficient of variation can be compared with HEP's "average" coefficient of variation (CV) to get an idea of the relative riskiness of the appliance control computer project. If HEP's "average" CV is about 1.0, on the basis of this stand-alone risk measure, the appliance control project would be considered riskier than the firm's "average" project.

---

[22]We could have included worst- and best-case values for fixed and variable costs, income tax rates, salvage values, and so on. For illustrative purposes, we limited the changes to only two variables. Also, note that we treat sales price and quantity as independent variables here; that is, a low sales price could occur when unit sales were low, and a high sales price could be coupled with high unit sales, or vice versa. It is relatively easy to vary these assumptions if the facts of the situation suggest a different set of conditions.

[23]The expected NPV is *not* the same as the base case NPV, $3,790 (in thousands). The two uncertain variables—sales volume and sales price—are multiplied together to obtain dollar sales, which causes the NPV distribution to become skewed to the right. A big number times another big number produces a very big number, which in turn causes the average, or expected, value to be increased.

TABLE 13-5   Scenario Analysis ($ thousand, except sales price)

Scenario	Sales Volume (Units)	Sales Price	NPV	Probability of Outcome Pr_i	NPV $\times$ Pr_i
Best case	20,000	$2,500	$17,494	0.20	$ 3,499
Most likely case	15,000	2,000	3,790	0.60	2,274
Worst case	10,000	1,500	(6,487)	0.20	(1,297)
				1.00	Expected NPV = $ 4,475
					σ_{NPV} = $ 7,630
					CV_{NPV} = 1.7

$$\text{Expected NPV} = \sum_{i=1}^{n} Pr_i(NPV_i) = 0.2(\$17{,}494) + 0.6(\$3{,}790) + 0.2(-\$6{,}487) = \$4{,}475$$

$$\sigma_{NPV} = \sqrt{\sum_{i=1}^{n} Pr_i(NPV_i - \text{Expected NPV})^2}$$

$$= \sqrt{0.2(\$17{,}494 - \$4{,}475)^2 + 0.6(\$3{,}790 - \$4{,}475)^2 + 0.2(-\$6{,}487 - \$4{,}475)^2} = \$7{,}630$$

$$CV_{NPV} = \frac{\sigma_{NPV}}{\text{Expected NPV}} = \frac{\$7{,}630}{\$4{,}475} = 1.7$$

Corporate (Within-Firm Risk)

To measure corporate, or within-firm, risk, we must determine how the capital budgeting project is related to the firm's existing assets. Recall from our discussion in Chapter 11 that two assets can be combined to reduce risk if their payoffs move in opposite directions—that is, when the payoff from one asset falls, the payoff from the other asset generally rises. In reality, however, it is not easy to find assets with payoffs that move in opposite directions. As we also discovered in Chapter 11, however, as long as assets are *not* perfectly positively related ($\rho = +1.0$), we can still achieve some diversification, or risk reduction. Many firms use this principle to reduce the risk associated with their operations. That is, they know that adding new projects or new operations that are not highly related to existing assets can help reduce corporate risk. For example, if Microsoft acquires a food processing firm or a utility, it would be diversifying, and thus its overall (within-firm) risk would be expected to decline.

Beta (or Market) Risk

In Chapter 11, we developed the concept of beta, β, as a risk measure for individual stocks. In that discussion, we noted that systematic risk is the relevant risk of a stock, because unsystematic, or firm-specific, risk can be reduced significantly or eliminated through diversification. We can apply this same concept to capital budgeting projects, because the firm can be considered a composite of all the projects it has undertaken. The relevant risk of a project, then, can be viewed as the effect that it has on the firm's systematic risk. This line of reasoning leads to the conclusion that if the beta coefficient for a project, β_{proj}, can be determined, then the **project required rate of return, r_{proj},** can be found by using the following form of the CAPM equation:

$$r_{proj} = r_{RF} + (r_M - r_{RF})\beta_{proj}$$

project required rate of return, r_{proj}
The risk-adjusted required rate of return for an individual project.

To apply the CAPM to HEP's appliance control project, let's assume that the company is financed only with equity. As a consequence, the average required rate of return it needs to earn on capital budgeting projects is based solely on the average return demanded by stockholders (that is, there is no debt that might require a different return). HEP's existing beta = β_{HEP} = 1.5; r_{RF} = 5%; and r_M = 11%. Thus, HEP's cost of equity is 14% = r_S = 5% + (11% − 5%)1.5, which suggests that investors should be willing to give HEP money to invest in *average-risk projects* if the company expects to earn 14 percent or more on this money.[24]

Suppose, however, that the appliance control project has a beta greater than HEP's average beta of 1.5—say, β_{proj} = 2.0. Because the firm itself can be regarded as a "portfolio of assets," just like the beta of any portfolio, HEP's beta is a weighted average of the betas of its individual assets. If the firm accepts the project, then 80 percent of HEP's total funds will be invested in its basic operations and 20 percent in operations associated with the appliance control project. Accepting the project will increase HEP's beta to 1.6 = 0.8(1.5) + 0.2(2.0). This beta increase will cause its stock price to decline unless HEP earns at least 14.6 percent return on future investments because $r_{HEP\text{-}new}$ = 5% + (6%)1.6 = 14.6 percent. The firm can earn this higher *average* rate only if the new project generates a return *substantially* higher than that provided by HEP's existing assets. Of course, the opposite would be true if the project's beta was lower than 1.5 (HEP's current average).

With a beta of 2.0, the new appliance control project should be evaluated at a 17 percent required rate of return:

$$r_{proj} = 5\% + (6\%)2.0 = 17.0\%$$

If we compute the IRR for the appliance control device, we would find that it is 26.3 percent. Thus, this project is acceptable, even if the appropriate required return is 17 percent.

The major problem with evaluating beta risk is that it is difficult to measure betas for capital budgeting projects. One way that a firm can try to measure the beta risk of a project is to find *single-product* companies in the same line of business as the project being evaluated, and then use the average of the betas of those companies to determine the required rate of return for the proposed project. This technique is termed the **pure play method,** and the single-product companies that are used for comparisons are called *pure play firms*. Generally, this method can be used only for major projects such as whole divisions. Even then, however, it is often difficult to implement because pure play proxy firms are scarce.

pure play method
An approach used for estimating the beta of a project in which a firm identifies companies whose only business is the product in question, determines the beta for each company, and then averages the betas to find an approximation of its own project's beta.

Self-Test Questions

What are the three types of project risk?

What is meant by the term *average risk project*? How could you find the required rate of return for a project with average risk, low risk, and high risk?

Complete the following sentence: "An increase in a company's beta coefficient would cause its stock price to decline unless...."

---

[24]To simplify matters, we assume here that the firm uses only equity capital. If it uses debt, the cost of capital must be a weighted average of the costs of debt and equity. This point is discussed at length in Chapter 12.

How Project Risk Is Considered in Capital Budgeting Decisions

Financial managers would argue that it is difficult to quantify risk in capital budgeting analysis because it is difficult to develop a specific *measure* of project risk. Nevertheless, they would agree that it is possible to evaluate whether one project is riskier than another in a general sense. As a consequence, as we discussed in Chapter 12, most firms incorporate project risk in capital budgeting decisions by using the **risk-adjusted discount rate** approach. With this approach, the required rate of return used to evaluate a project is adjusted if its risk differs substantially from the firm's average risk. That is, average-risk projects would require an "average" rate of return (the firm's WACC); above-average-risk projects would require a higher-than-average rate; and below-average-risk projects would require a lower-than-average rate.

risk-adjusted discount rate
The discount rate (required rate of return) that applies to a particular risky stream of income. It is equal to the risk-free rate of interest plus a risk premium appropriate to the level of risk attached to a particular project's income stream.

Self-Test Question

How are risk-adjusted discount rates used to incorporate project risk into the capital budgeting decision process?

Multinational Capital Budgeting

Although the same basic principles of capital budgeting analysis apply to both domestic and foreign operations, some key differences need to be mentioned.

1. Cash flow estimation generally is much more complex for overseas investments. Most multinational firms set up a separate subsidiary in each foreign country in which they operate, and the relevant cash flows for these subsidiaries are the dividends and royalties **repatriated,** or returned, to the parent company. A foreign government might restrict the amount of cash that can be repatriated to the parent company, perhaps to force multinational firms to reinvest earnings in the host country or to prevent large currency outflows. The parent corporation cannot use cash flows blocked in the foreign country to pay current dividends to its shareholders, nor does it have the flexibility to reinvest cash flows elsewhere in the world. Therefore, from the perspective of the parent organization, *the cash flows relevant for the analysis of a foreign investment are the cash flows that the subsidiary legally can send back to the parent.*

repatriation of earnings
The process of sending cash flows from a foreign subsidiary back to the parent company.

2. Cash flows must be converted into the currency of the parent company, and thus are subject to future exchange rate changes. For example, General Motors' German subsidiary might make a profit of 150 million euro in 2010, but the value of these profits to GM will depend on the dollar/euro exchange rate when cash flows are repatriated.

3. Dividends and royalties normally are taxed by both the foreign and home-country governments.

4. In addition to the complexities of the cash flow analysis, *the rate of return required for a foreign project might be different than that for an equivalent domestic project because foreign projects might be more or less risky.* A higher risk could arise from two primary sources: exchange rate risk and political risk. A lower risk might result from international diversification.

    a. **Exchange rate risk** reflects the inherent uncertainty about the home currency value of cash flows sent back to the parent. In other words,

exchange rate risk
The uncertainty associated with the price at which the currency from one country can be converted into the currency of another country.

foreign projects have an added risk element that relates to what the basic cash flows will be worth in the parent company's home currency, because actual exchange rates might differ substantially from expectations.

political risk
The risk of expropriation of a foreign subsidiary's assets by the host country, or of unanticipated restrictions on cash flows to the parent company.

expropriation
The assets of a foreign subsidiary are seized, generally by the host government, without compensation to the company.

b. **Political risk** refers to any action (or the chance of such action) by a host government that reduces the value of a company's investment. At one extreme, it includes the **expropriation** (seizure) without compensation of the subsidiary's assets. Less drastic actions might reduce the value of the parent firm's investment in the foreign subsidiary through the imposition of higher taxes, tighter repatriation or currency controls, and restrictions on prices charged. The risk of expropriation of U.S. assets abroad is small in traditionally friendly and stable countries such as the United Kingdom or Switzerland. In Latin America and Africa, on the other hand, the risk might be substantial. Generally, political risk premiums are not added to the required rate of return to adjust for this risk. If a company's management is seriously concerned that a given country might expropriate foreign assets, it simply will not make significant investments in that country. Expropriation is viewed as a catastrophic or ruinous event, and managers have been known to be extraordinarily risk averse when faced with ruinous loss possibilities. Companies can take three major steps to reduce the potential loss from expropriation:

1. Finance the subsidiary with local capital
2. Structure operations such that the subsidiary has value only as a part of the integrated corporate system
3. Obtain insurance against economic losses from expropriation from a source such as the Overseas Private Investment Corporation (OPIC)

If the third step is taken, insurance premiums would have to be added to the project's cost.

Ethical Dilemma

This Is a Good Investment—Be Sure the Numbers Show That It Is!

Oliver Greene is the assistant to the financial manager at Cybercomp, Inc., a company that develops software to drive network communications for personal computers. Oliver joined Cybercomp 3 years ago, following his graduation from college. His primary responsibility has been to evaluate capital budgeting projects and make investment recommendations to the board of directors. Oliver enjoys his job very much; he often finds himself challenged with interesting tasks, and he is paid extremely well.

Last week, Oliver started evaluating the capital projects that have been proposed for investment this year. One proposal calls for Cybercomp to purchase NetWare Products, a company that manufactures circuit boards called network cards, which are required to achieve communication connectivity between personal computers. Cybercomp packages network cards with the software that it sells, but it currently purchases those circuit boards from another manufacturer. The proposal, which was submitted by Nadine Wilson, Cybercomp's CEO, suggests that the company might reduce costs and increase profit margins by producing the network cards in-house.

continues

Oliver barely had time to scan the proposal when he was summoned to Mrs. Wilson's office. The meeting was short and to the point. Mrs. Wilson instructed Oliver to "make the numbers for NetWare Products look good because we want to buy that company." She also gave Oliver an evaluation of NetWare completed 2 years ago by an independent appraiser that suggests NetWare might not be worth the amount that Cybercomp is willing to pay. Mrs. Wilson instructed Oliver to find a way to rebut the findings of the report.

Oliver was troubled by the meeting. His "gut feeling" was that something was wrong, but he hadn't yet had time to carefully examine the proposal. In fact, his evaluation was very cursory, and he was far from making a final decision about the acceptability of the proposed capital budgeting project. Oliver felt he needed much more information before he could make a final recommendation.

Oliver has spent the entire day examining the appraisal report provided by Mrs. Wilson and trying to gather additional information about the proposed investment. The report contains some background information concerning NetWare's operations, but crucial financial data are missing.

Further investigation into NetWare Products has produced little information. Oliver has discovered that the company's stock is closely held by a small group of investors. These investors own numerous businesses and contribute generously to the local university, which happens to be Mrs. Wilson's alma mater. In addition, Oliver's secretary has informed him that the gossip around the "water cooler" at Cybercomp suggests that Mrs. Wilson and the owners of NetWare are old college buddies, and she might even have a stake in NetWare.

This morning, Mrs. Wilson called Oliver and repeated her feelings concerning the purchase of NetWare. This time she said: "We really want to purchase NetWare. Some people might not believe so, but it's a very good deal. It's your job to make the numbers work—that's why we pay you the big bucks!" As a result of the conversation, Oliver has the impression that his job might be in jeopardy if he doesn't make the "right" decision. This added pressure has made Oliver very tense.

What should he do? What would you do if you were Oliver? Would your answer change if you knew Mrs. Wilson had recently sold much of her Cybercomp stock?

To summarize the key concepts, let's answer the questions that were posed at the beginning of the chapter:

Chapter Principles
–The Answers

- **What are the relevant cash flows associated with a capital budgeting project? How are these cash flows identified and used in capital budgeting analysis?** The cash flows that should be analyzed—that is, the relevant cash flows—in capital budgeting analysis are those that are affected by the investment decision. Any cash flow that changes if the firm purchases an asset is considered a relevant cash flow; any cash flow that is not affected by the purchase is irrelevant when evaluating the acceptability of the asset being evaluated. The three categories of relevant cash flows associated with a capital budgeting project are:

    1. *Initial investment outlay,* which includes cash flows that are associated with the purchase of the asset; these cash flows occur only at the time the asset is purchased.

    2. *Incremental operating cash flows* are those cash flows that change because the asset is purchased and continue throughout its life; these changes are generally seen in the day-to-day cash flows.

    3. *Terminal cash flow,* which includes cash flows that are associated with the disposal of the asset; these cash flows occur only at the end of the asset's useful life (to the firm).

- **How do firms make decisions about whether to invest in costly, long-lived real assets, such as buildings and equipment?** To make investment decisions, firms use decision-making methods that are based on the fundamental valuation concepts we discussed in earlier chapters. To make decisions about the acceptability of capital budgeting projects, which generally relate to such real assets as buildings and equipment, firms use techniques to evaluate the assets' values. Although the methods used in capital budgeting analysis have such names as net present value (NPV) and internal rate of return (IRR), they are based on the same concepts we discussed in Chapters 10 and 11. In other words, the decision is based on the present value of the cash flows an asset is expected to generate during its life. An asset's *NPV* is the present value of its expected future cash flows minus the initial investment that must be made to purchase the asset. If NPV > 0, the firm's value will increase if the asset is purchased. An asset's *IRR* is the rate of return that the asset is expected to provide if it is purchased. If IRR > r, which is the firm's required rate of return, the firm's value will increase if the asset is purchased. Most other capital budgeting methods used by firms are based on the same principles as NPV and IRR—that is, time value of money concepts.

- **How does a firm make a choice between two (or more) acceptable investments when only one can be purchased?** When a firm evaluates projects that are independent, all acceptable projects—that is, projects with NPVs > 0—can be purchased. However, when a firm evaluates projects that are mutually exclusive, only one of the acceptable projects can be purchased. If a firm evaluates two mutually exclusive projects, it is possible that the NPV and IRR methods yield conflicting results as to which project should be purchased. In some instances, we find that $NPV_1 > NPV_2$, which suggests that Project 1 is better than Project 2; at the same time, we might find that $IRR_1 < IRR_2$, which suggests that Project 2 is better than Project 1. How should this conflict be resolved? To make a decision that is consistent with the goal of maximizing the value of the firm, the NPV method should be used. As a result, in this case, Project 1 should be purchased.

- **How are different capital budgeting techniques related? Which methods do firms actually use?** In this chapter, we discussed five capital budgeting methods—net present value (NPV), internal rate of return (IRR), modified internal rate of return (MIRR), traditional payback period (PB), and discounted payback period (DPB). Except for PB, these methods are based on time value of money concepts. Thus, NPV, IRR, MIRR, and DPB will always yield the same accept–reject decision—that is, if a project is considered acceptable when evaluated using NPV, then it must also be considered acceptable when evaluated using IRR, MIRR, and DPB. As a result, when NPV > 0, IRR > r (the firm's required rate of return), MIRR > r, and DPB < the asset's life. Because the traditional payback period (PB) is not based on time value of money concepts, it is not related to the other capital budgeting methods.

  In practice, firms do not use a single method to evaluate capital budgeting projects; rather some combination of the techniques discussed in this chapter are used. Most firms rely heavily on NPV and IRR to make investment decisions, because decisions made using these methods are consistent with the goal of maximizing shareholders' wealth.

- **How is risk incorporated in capital budgeting analysis?** If a firm evaluates a project with a risk that differs significantly from its "average" investments, some adjustment must be made to account for the difference. Generally, projects that are much riskier than average are evaluated with higher required rates of return, whereas projects that have much less risk than average are evaluated with lower required rates of return. Failure to account for risk could lead to incorrect capital budgeting decisions.

- **How do capital budgeting analyses/decisions differ for multinational firms?** Such factors as exchange rate risk, political risk, and the ability to repatriate earnings make capital budgeting decisions more complicated when multinational firms evaluate foreign investments. The relevant cash flows for analysis of a foreign investment are those cash flows that can be returned to the parent company. Often, because the risk is greater, the required rate of return used to evaluate a foreign investment is higher than the required rate of return used to evaluate similar domestic investments.

The concepts presented in this chapter should help you to better understand how to make decisions when investing your money. If you understand the basic concepts we discussed, you should be able to determine whether an investment is acceptable or unacceptable. Some ways in which you can use the concepts presented in this chapter include:

CHAPTER PRINCIPLES
–Personal Finance

- **How can the NPV and IRR rules be applied to my investment decisions?** Determine the NPV of such investments as rental property and annuity payments. If you know or can estimate the future cash flows that you expect to receive from a particular investment, you should be able to compute its NPV using the rate of return you would like to earn on your invested funds. You should apply the same decision rule that businesses use to make your investment decisions—that is, purchase investments that have NPVs > 0. Similarly, you can compute the IRRs of your investments and compare these returns to the rate of return that you want to earn.

  When examining investments, make sure you evaluate the after-tax expected returns. Remember that you cannot spend or reinvest the dollars that must be paid to the government in taxes.

- **Can I apply the concepts that relate to estimating relevant cash flows to help me make better investment decisions?** When evaluating the purchase of an automobile or a house, you should be able to better estimate the relevant cash flows, especially the initial investment outlay and the incremental operating cash flows. For instance, when considering whether to purchase a new car to replace an older one, you should consider (1) whether you plan to trade in or sell your existing car and (2) the impact your purchase will have on your insurance premiums, gas expenses, and so forth during the time you own the car. If you are replacing an existing car, the purchase price of the new car (initial investment outlay) will be lower if you trade in or sell your existing car. For example, if the trade-in value of your current car is $5,000, and the purchase price of the new car you are considering is $25,000, then you need only $20,000 to purchase the new car. Depending on the type of car you buy and the age and coverage on your old car, your insurance premiums might increase, which will increase the incremental operating cash flows associated with the new car. On the other hand, the new car might be more fuel efficient, which will decrease its incremental operating cash flows compared to the existing car.

  You should apply the same reasoning to the purchase of a new house. If the purchase price is $250,000, is that all you need to move in? Generally the answer is no, because you need "up-front" funds (cash) for utility deposits, for needed appliances and other furnishings, and for other incidental expenses that must be covered at the time you purchase the house.

- **How can I determine the appropriate risk-adjusted return to use when evaluating my investments?** As we discussed in earlier chapters and continue to discuss throughout the book, you should always consider risk when evaluating investments. An easy way to incorporate risk in your analysis is to use a risk-adjusted required rate of return as suggested in this chapter. You can classify an investment's risk as "normal," "above normal," or "below normal" and make an appropriate adjustment to your required rate of return—that is, use a higher required rate of return to evaluate investments with above-normal risk, and vice versa.

QUESTIONS

13-1 Cash flows rather than accounting profits are listed in Table 13-1. What is the basis for this emphasis on cash flows as opposed to net income?

13-2 Look at Table 13-4 and answer these questions:

a. Why is the net salvage value shown in Section III reduced for taxes?

b. How is the change in depreciation computed?

c. What would happen if the new machine resulted in a reduction in net working capital?

d. Why are the cost savings shown as positive amounts?

13-3 Explain why sunk costs should not be included in a capital budgeting analysis but opportunity costs and externalities should be included.

13-4 Explain how net working capital is recovered at the end of a project's life and why it is included in a capital budgeting analysis.

13-5 Generosity Golf Equipment is considering whether to build a new manufacturing plant in Jacksonville, Florida, in an effort to increase sales of its golf products in the southeast. If it builds the plant, Generosity would not have to buy land because it owns sufficient land in a good location in Jacksonville. The land on which the plant will be built was bought for $100,000 5 years ago; its current value is $800,000. Before it decided that Florida would be a good location for a new plant, Generosity hired a company to provide the demographics of the Jacksonville area. The cost of the study was $200,000. It is estimated that $750,000 of the total sales generated by the new plant will be the result of existing customers shifting their business from other plants because Jacksonville is closer to their locations. How should the costs mentioned here be considered when Generosity performs its capital budgeting analysis?

13-6 Explain the decision rules—that is, under what conditions a project is acceptable—for each of the following capital budgeting methods:

a. Net present value (NPV)

b. Internal rate of return (IRR)

c. Modified internal rate of return (MIRR)

d. Traditional payback (PB)

e. Discounted payback (DPB)

13-7 After evaluating a capital budgeting project, Susan discovered that the project's NPV > 0. What does this information tell us about the project's IRR and discounted payback (DPB)? Can anything be concluded about the project's traditional payback period (PB)?

13-8 Explain why, if two mutually exclusive projects are being compared, the project that generates most of its cash flows in the beginning of its life might have the higher ranking under the NPV criterion if the required rate of return is high, whereas the project that generates most of its cash flows toward the end of its life might be deemed better if the required rate of return is low. Would changes in a firm's required rate of return ever cause a change in the IRR ranking of two such projects? Explain.

13-9 "If a firm has no mutually exclusive projects, only independent ones, and it also has both a constant required rate of return and projects with conventional cash flow patterns, then the NPV and IRR methods will always lead to identical capital budgeting decisions." Discuss this statement. What does it imply about using the IRR method in lieu of the NPV method? If the projects are mutually exclusive, would your answer be the same?

13-10 In what sense is a reinvestment rate assumption embodied in the NPV and IRR methods? What is the assumed reinvestment rate of each method?

13-11 Are there conditions under which a firm might be better off if it were to choose a machine with a rapid payback rather than one with a larger NPV? Explain.

13-12 Following is information for three *mutually exclusive* capital budgeting projects that the CFO of Universal Fire Systems (UFS) is currently evaluating:

Project	IRR	NPV	Discounted Payback
K	21.0%	$5,500	3.5 years
L	14.0	4,750	3.1
M	10.0	6,000	4.3

a. Which project(s) should be purchased (accepted)?

b. From the information given, what can be concluded about Universal's required rate of return, r?

13-13 "Two companies examined the same capital budgeting project, which has an internal rate of return equal to 19 percent. One firm accepted the project, but the other firm rejected it. One of the firms must have made an incorrect decision." Discuss the validity of this statement.

13-14 Following is a table Alice used to construct an NPV profile for Project K.

Rate of Return (r)	NPV
5%	$13,609
10	5,723
15	94
20	(4,038)
25	(7,147)

According to this information, which of the following statements is *incorrect*? Be prepared to discuss your answers.

a. Project K should be purchased if a firm has a required rate of return equal to 12 percent.

b. To determine whether Project K is acceptable, its internal rate of return (IRR) should be computed.

c. Project K has an internal rate of return that is between 15 and 20 percent.

d. Project K should be rejected if a firm has a required rate of return equal to 20 percent.

e. If one firm determines that Project K should be purchased, another firm might determine that it should not be purchased.

13-15 Distinguish between beta (or market) risk, within-firm (or corporate) risk, and stand-alone risk for a project being considered for inclusion in the capital budget. Which type of risk do you believe should be given the greatest weight in capital budgeting decisions? Explain.

13-16 Suppose Reading Engine Company, which has a high beta as well as a great deal of corporate risk, merged with Simplicity Patterns Inc. Simplicity's sales rise during recessions, when people are more likely to make their own clothes, and, consequently, its beta is negative but its corporate risk is relatively high. What would the merger do to the required rates of return in the consolidated company's locomotive engine division and in its patterns division?

13-17 Suppose a firm estimates its required rate of return for the coming year to be 10 percent. What are reasonable required rates of return for evaluating average-risk projects, high-risk projects, and low-risk projects?

SELF-TEST PROBLEMS

Solutions appear in Appendix B at the end of the book.

Key Terms **ST-1** Define each of the following terms:

    a. Capital budget; capital budgeting

    b. Cash flow; accounting income; relevant cash flow

    c. Incremental cash flow; sunk cost; opportunity cost; externalities; inflation bias

    d. Initial investment outlay; incremental operating cash flow; terminal cash flow

    e. Change in net working capital

    f. Expansion analysis; replacement analysis

    g. Independent projects; mutually exclusive projects

    h. Net present value (NPV) method

    i. Internal rate of return (IRR); modified internal rate of return (MIRR)

    j. Traditional payback period (PB); discounted payback period (DPB)

    k. NPV profile; crossover rate

    l. Unconventional cash flow patterns; multiple IRRs

    m. Reinvestment rate assumption; hurdle rate; required rate of return, r

    n. Stand-alone risk; within-firm risk; market risk

    o. Risk-adjusted discount rate; project required rate of return

    p. Project beta versus corporate beta; pure play method

    q. Exchange rate risk; political risk; expropriation

Expansion Project Analysis **ST-2** You have been asked by the president of Ellis Construction Company, headquartered in Toledo, to evaluate the proposed acquisition of a new earthmover. The mover's basic price is $50,000, and it will cost another $10,000 to modify it for special use by Ellis Construction. Assume that the earthmover falls into the MACRS 3-year class. (See Table 13A-2 at the end of this chapter for MACRS recovery allowance percentages.) It will be sold after 3 years for $20,000, and it will require an increase in net working capital (spare parts inventory) of $2,000. The earthmover purchase will have no effect on revenues, but it is expected to save Ellis $20,000 per year in before-tax operating costs, mainly labor. Ellis's marginal tax rate is 40 percent.

   a. What is the company's net initial investment outlay if it acquires the earthmover?

   b. What are the incremental operating cash flows in Years 1, 2, and 3?

   c. What is the project's terminal cash flow?

   d. If the firm's required rate of return is 10 percent, should the earthmover be purchased?

ST-3 The Dauten Toy Corporation currently uses an injection molding machine that was purchased 2 years ago. This machine is being depreciated on a straight line basis toward a $500 salvage value, and it has 6 years of remaining life. Its current book value is $2,600, and it can be sold for $3,000 at this time. Thus, the annual depreciation expense is ($2,600 – $500)/6 = $350 per year.   **Replacement Analysis**

     Dauten is offered a replacement machine that has a cost of $8,000, an estimated useful life of 6 years, and an estimated salvage value of $800. This machine falls into the MACRS 5-year class. (See Table 13A-2 at the end of this chapter for MACRS recovery allowance percentages.) The replacement machine would permit an output expansion, so sales would rise by $1,000 per year. In addition, the new machine's much greater efficiency would cause operating expenses to decline by $1,500 per year. The new machine would require that net working capital be increased by $1,500.

     Dauten's marginal tax rate is 40 percent, and its required rate of return is 15 percent. Should the old machine be replaced?

ST-4 You are a financial analyst for Damon Electronics Company. The director of capital budgeting has asked you to analyze two proposed capital investments, Projects X and Y. Each project has a cost of $10,000, and the required rate of return for each project is 12 percent. The projects' expected net cash flows are as follows: **Project Analysis**

Expected Net Cash Flows

Year	Project X	Project Y
0	$(10,000)	$(10,000)
1	6,500	3,500
2	3,000	3,500
3	3,000	3,500
4	1,000	3,500

   a. Calculate each project's traditional payback period (PB), net present value (NPV), internal rate of return (IRR), modified internal rate of return (MIRR), and discounted payback period (DPB).

   b. Which project or projects should be accepted if they are independent?

   c. Which project should be accepted if they are mutually exclusive?

   d. How might a change in the required rate of return produce a conflict between the NPV and IRR rankings of these two projects? Would this conflict exist if r were 5 percent? (*Hint:* Plot the NPV profiles.)

   e. Why does the conflict exist?

Risk Analysis   ST-5 The staff of Heymann Manufacturing has estimated the following net cash flows and probabilities for a new manufacturing process:

Net Cash Flows

Year	Pr = 0.2	Pr = 0.6	Pr = 0.2
0	$(100,000)	$(100,000)	$(100,000)
1	20,000	30,000	40,000
2	20,000	30,000	40,000
3	20,000	30,000	40,000
4	20,000	30,000	40,000
5	20,000	30,000	40,000
5*	0	20,000	30,000

Line 0 gives the cost of the process, Lines 1 through 5 give operating cash flows, and Line 5* contains the estimated salvage values. Heymann's required rate of return for an average-risk project is 10 percent.

a. Assume that the project has average risk. Find the project's expected NPV. (*Hint:* Use expected values for the net cash flow in each year.)

b. Find the best-case and worst-case NPVs. What is the probability of occurrence of the worst case if the cash flows are perfectly positively correlated over time? If they are independent over time?

c. Assume that all the cash flows are perfectly positively correlated; that is, there are only three possible cash flow streams over time: (1) the worst case, (2) the most likely, or base, case, and (3) the best case, with probabilities of 0.2, 0.6, and 0.2, respectively. These cases are represented by each of the columns in the table. Find the expected NPV, its standard deviation, and its coefficient of variation.

d. The coefficient of variation of Heymann's average project is in the range 0.8 to 1.0. If the coefficient of variation of a project being evaluated is greater than 1.0, two percentage points are added to the firm's required rate of return. Similarly, if the coefficient of variation is less than 0.8, one percentage point is deducted from the required rate of return. What is the project's required rate of return? Should Heymann accept or reject the project?

PROBLEMS

Disposal of an Asset   13-1 A company has collected the following information about a new machine that it is evaluating for possible investment:

Purchase price	$340,000
Salvage value at the end of 3 years	$ 15,000
Shipping and installation	$ 50,000
Book value at the end of 3 years	$ 5,000
Marginal tax rate	40%

a. What is the machine's *depreciable basis*—that is, the amount that can be depreciated during its life?

b. In 3 years, what will be the net cash flow generated by the disposal of the machine?

13-2   The Gehr Company is considering the purchase of a new machine tool to replace an obsolete one. The machine being used for the operation has both a book value and a market value of $0; it is in good working order, however, and will last physically for at least another 10 years. The proposed replacement machine will perform the operation so much more efficiently that Gehr's engineers estimate it will produce after-tax cash flows (cost savings) of $9,000 per year. The new machine will cost $40,000 delivered and installed, and its economic life is estimated to be 10 years. Its expected salvage value is $0. The firm's required rate of return is 10 percent, and its marginal tax rate is 40 percent. Should Gehr buy the new machine?   *Replacement Analysis*

13-3   Galveston Shipyards is considering the replacement of an 8-year-old riveting machine with a new one that will increase earnings before depreciation from $27,000 to $54,000 per year. The new machine will cost $82,500, and it will have an estimated life of 8 years and no salvage value. The new machine will be depreciated over its 5-year MACRS recovery period. (See Table 13A-2 at the end of this chapter for MACRS recovery allowance percentages.) The firm's marginal tax rate is 40 percent, and the firm's required rate of return is 12 percent. The old machine has been fully depreciated and has no salvage value. Should the old riveting machine be replaced by the new one?   *Replacement Analysis*

13-4   A firm is evaluating the acceptability of an investment that costs $90,000 and is expected to generate annual cash flows equal to $20,000 for the next 6 years. If the firm's required rate of return is 10 percent, what is the net present value (NPV) of the project? Should the project be purchased?   *NPV Computation*

13-5   What is the internal rate of return (IRR) of a project that costs $45,000 if it is expected to generate $15,047 per year for 5 years?   *IRR Computation*

13-6   Exit Corporation is evaluating a capital budgeting project that costs $320,000 and will generate $67,910 for the next 7 years. If Exit's required rate of return is 12 percent, should the project be purchased?   *NPV or IRR Computation*

13-7   If the firm's required rate of return is 14 percent, what is the net present value of the following project?   *NPV Computation*

Year	Cash Flow
0	$(75,000)
1	50,000
2	40,000

13-8   Compute the internal rates of return (IRRs) for the following capital budgeting projects: *IRR Computation*

Year	Project G	Project P	Project V
0	$(23,000)	$(48,000)	$(36,000)
1	7,900	0	(10,000)
2	7,900	0	0
3	7,900	0	0
4	7,900	81,000	75,000

Based on IRRs, under what conditions should each project be purchased?

IRR Computation   **13-9** Plasma Blood Services (PBS) is deciding whether to purchase a new blood cleaning machine that is expected to generate the following cash flows.

Year	Cash Flow
0	$(140,000)
1	60,000
2	60,000
3	60,000

What is the machine's IRR?

Payback Period   **13-10** Following is a table that shows the expected cash flows of a machine that QQQ Inc. is currently evaluating for possible purchase. Both the expected annual cash flows ($\widehat{CF}$) and the present values (PV) of the cash flows are shown in the table.

Year	Expected $\widehat{CF}$	PV of $\widehat{CF}$ Using the Firm's Required Rate of Return, r
0	$(10,000)	$(10,000)
1	6,000	5,455
2	3,000	2,479
3	1,000	751
4	5,000	3,415

Compute both the traditional payback period and the discounted payback period.

MIRR Computation   **13-11** If the firm's required rate of return is 12 percent, what is the modified internal rate of return (MIRR) for the following project?

Year	Cash Flow
0	$(105,000)
1	70,000
2	50,000

MIRR Computation   **13-12** Compute the internal rate of return (IRR) and the modified internal rate of return (MIRR) for each of the following capital budgeting projects. Assume that the firm's required rate of return is 14 percent.

Year	Project G	Project J	Project K
0	$(180,000)	$(240,000)	$(200,000)
1	80,100	0	(100,000)
2	80,100	0	205,000
3	80,100	375,000	205,000

Which project(s) should be purchased if they are independent? Which project should be purchased it they are mutually exclusive?

Capital Budgeting Decisions   **13-13** Project P costs $15,000 and is expected to produce benefits (cash flows) of $4,500 per year for 5 years. Project Q costs $37,500 and is expected to produce cash flows of $11,100 per year for 5 years.

   a. Calculate the NPV, IRR, MIRR, discounted payback, and traditional payback period for each project, assuming a required rate of return of 14 percent.

b. If the projects are independent, which project(s) should be selected? If they are mutually exclusive projects, which project should be selected?

13-14 Your company is considering two mutually exclusive projects—C and R— whose costs and cash flows are shown in the following table:

NPV and IRR Analysis

Expected Net Cash Flows

Year	Project C	Project R
0	$(14,000)	$(22,840)
1	8,000	8,000
2	6,000	8,000
3	2,000	8,000
4	3,000	8,000

The projects are equally risky, and their required rate of return is 12 percent. You must make a recommendation concerning which project should be purchased. To determine which is more appropriate, compute the NPV and IRR of each project.

13-15 The after-tax cash flows for two mutually exclusive projects have been esti- mated, and the following information has been provided:

NPV and IRR Analysis

Expected Net Cash Flows

Year	Machine D	Machine Q
0	$(2,500)	$(2,500)
1	2,000	0
2	900	1,800
3	100	1,000
4	100	900

The company's required rate of return is 14 percent, and it can get unlimited funds at that cost. What is the IRR of the *better* project? (*Hint:* Note that the better project might not be the one with the higher IRR.)

13-16 Diamond Hill Jewelers is considering the following independent projects:

NPV and IRR Analysis

Expected Net Cash Flows

Year	Project Y	Project Z
0	$(25,000)	$(25,000)
1	10,000	0
2	9,000	0
3	7,000	0
4	6,000	36,000

Which project(s) should be accepted if the required rate of return for the projects is 10 percent? Compute the NPVs and the IRRs for both projects.

13-17 Project K has a cost of $52,125, and its expected net cash inflows are $12,000 per year for 8 years.

Payback, NPV, and IRR

a. What is the project's payback period (to the closest year)?

b. If the required rate of return for the project is 12 percent, what is the project's NPV?

c. What is the project's IRR?

d. What is the project's discounted payback period, assuming a 12 percent required rate of return?

Risk Adjustment   **13-18** The risk-free rate of return is currently 5 percent and the *market risk premium* is 4 percent. The beta of the project under analysis is 1.4, with expected net cash flows estimated to be $1,500 per year for 5 years. The required investment outlay on the project is $4,500.

a. What is the required risk-adjusted return on the project?

b. Should the project be purchased?

Beta Risk   **13-19** Companioni Computer Corporation (CCC), a producer of office equipment, currently has assets of $15 million and a beta of 1.4. The risk-free rate is 8 percent and the *market risk premium* is 5 percent. CCC would like to expand into the risky home computer market. If the expansion is undertaken, CCC would create a new division with $3.75 million in assets. The new division would have a beta of 2.4.

a. What is CCC's current required rate of return?

b. If the expansion is undertaken, what would be the firm's new beta? What is the new overall required rate of return, and what rate of return must the home computer division produce to leave the new overall required rate of return unchanged?

Risk-Adjusted Discount Rate   **13-20** The capital budgeting manager of Conscientious Construction Company (CCC) submitted the following report to the CFO:

Project	IRR	Risk
A	9.0%	Low
B	10.0	Average
C	12.0	High

CCC generally takes risk into consideration by adjusting its average required rate of return (r), which equals 8 percent, when evaluating projects with risks that are either lower or higher than average. A 5 percent adjustment is made for high-risk projects, and a 2 percent adjustment is made for low-risk projects. If these projects are *independent*, which one(s) should CCC purchase?

Risk-Adjusted Discount Rate   **13-21** A college intern working at Anderson Paints evaluated potential investments using the firm's average required rate of return (r), and he produced the following report for the capital budgeting manager:

Project	NPV	RR	Risk
LOM	$1,500	12.5%	High
QUE	0	11.0	Low
YUP	800	10.0	Average
DOG	(150)	9.5	Low

The capital budgeting manager usually considers the risks associated with capital budgeting projects before making her final decision. If a project has a risk that is different from average, she adjusts the average required rate of return by adding or subtracting two percentage points. If the four projects listed are *independent*, which one(s) should the capital budgeting manager recommend be purchased?

13-22 Olsen Engineering is considering including two pieces of equipment—a truck and an overhead pulley system—in this year's capital budget. The projects are independent. The cash outlay for the truck is $22,430, and for the pulley system it is $17,100. Each piece of equipment has an estimated life of 5 years. The annual after-tax cash flow expected to be provided by the truck is $7,500, and for the pulley it is $5,100. The firm's required rate of return is 14 percent. Calculate the NPV, IRR, MIRR, traditional payback (PB) period, and discounted payback (DPB) period for each project. Indicate which project(s) should be accepted.

Independent Projects

13-23 Horrigan Industries must choose between a gas-powered and an electric-powered forklift truck for moving materials in its factory. Because both forklifts perform the same function, the firm will choose only one. The electric-powered truck will cost more, but it will be less expensive to operate; it will cost $22,000, whereas the gas-powered truck will cost $17,500. The required rate of return that applies to both investments is 12 percent. The life for both types of truck is estimated to be 6 years, during which time the net cash flows for the electric-powered truck will be $6,290 per year and those for the gas-powered truck will be $5,000 per year. Calculate the NPV and IRR for each type of truck, and decide which to recommend.

Mutually Exclusive Projects

13-24 You have been asked by the president of your company to evaluate the proposed acquisition of a spectrometer for the firm's R&D department. The equipment's base price is $140,000, and it would cost another $30,000 to modify it for special use by your firm. The spectrometer, which falls into the MACRS 3-year class, would be sold after 3 years for $60,000. (See Table 13A-2 at the end of this chapter for MACRS recovery allowance percentages.) Use of the equipment would require an increase in net working capital (spare parts inventory) of $8,000. The spectrometer would have no effect on revenues, but it is expected to save the firm $50,000 per year in before-tax operating costs, mainly labor. The firm's marginal tax rate is 40 percent.

Expansion Project Analysis

  a. What is the initial investment outlay associated with this project?

  b. What are the incremental operating cash flows in Years 1, 2, and 3?

  c. What is the terminal cash flow in Year 3?

  d. If the firm's required rate of return is 12 percent, should the spectrometer be purchased?

13-25 The Ewert Company is evaluating the proposed acquisition of a new milling machine. The machine's base price is $108,000, and it would cost another $12,500 to modify it for special use by the firm. The machine falls into the MACRS 3-year class, and it would be sold after 3 years for $65,000. (See Table 13A-2 at the end of this chapter for MACRS recovery allowance percentages.) The machine would require an increase in net working capital (inventory) of $5,500. The milling machine would have no effect on revenues, but it is expected to save the firm $44,000 per year in before-tax operating costs, mainly labor. Ewert's marginal tax rate is 34 percent.

Expansion Project Analysis

  a. What is the initial investment outlay of the machine for capital budgeting purposes?

  b. What are the incremental operating cash flows in Years 1, 2, and 3?

c. What is the terminal cash flow in Year 3?

d. If the firm's required rate of return is 12 percent, should the machine be purchased?

Replacement Analysis   **13-26** Atlantic Control Company (ACC) purchased a machine 2 years ago at a cost of $70,000. At that time, the machine's expected economic life was 6 years and its salvage value at the end of its life was estimated to be $10,000. It is being depreciated using the straight line method so that its book value at the end of its 6-year life is $10,000. In 4 years, however, the old machine will have a market value of $0.

A new machine can be purchased for $80,000, including shipping and installation costs. The new machine has an economic life estimated to be 4 years. MACRS depreciation will be used, and the machine will be depreciated over its 3-year class life rather than its 4-year economic life. (See Table 13A-2 at the end of this chapter for MACRS recovery allowance percentages.) During its 4-year life, the new machine will reduce cash operating expenses by $20,000 per year. Sales are not expected to change. But the new machine will require net working capital to be increased by $4,000. At the end of its useful life, the machine is estimated to have a market value of $2,500.

The old machine can be sold today for $20,000. The firm's marginal tax rate is 40 percent, and the appropriate required rate of return is 10 percent.

a. If the new machine is purchased, what is the amount of the initial investment outlay at Year 0?

b. What incremental operating cash flows will occur at the end of Years 1 through 4 as a result of replacing the old machine?

c. What is the terminal cash flow at the end of Year 4 if the new machine is purchased?

d. What is the NPV of this project? Should ACC replace the old machine?

Replacement Analysis   **13-27** The Boyd Bottling Company is contemplating the replacement of one of its bottling machines with a newer and more efficient one. The old machine has a book value of $600,000 and a remaining useful life of 5 years. The firm does not expect to realize any return from scrapping the old machine in 5 years, but it can be sold today to another firm in the industry for $265,000. The old machine is being depreciated toward a $0 salvage value, or by $120,000 per year, using the straight line method.

The new machine has a purchase price of $1,175,000, an estimated useful life and MACRS class life of 5 years, and an estimated market value of $145,000 at the end of 5 years. (See Table 13A-2 at the end of this chapter for MACRS recovery allowance percentages.) The machine is expected to economize on electric power usage, labor, and repair costs, which will save Boyd $230,000 each year. In addition, the new machine is expected to reduce the number of defective bottles, which will save an additional $25,000 annually.

The company's marginal tax rate is 40 percent and it has a 12 percent required rate of return.

a. What initial investment outlay is required for the new machine?

b. Calculate the annual depreciation allowances for both machines and compute the change in the annual depreciation expense if the replacement is made.

   c. What are the incremental operating cash flows in Years 1 through 5?

   d. What is the terminal cash flow in Year 5?

   e. Should the firm purchase the new machine? Support your answer.

   f. In general, how would each of the following factors affect the investment decision, and how should each be treated?

     (1) The expected life of the existing machine decreases.

     (2) The required rate of return is not constant but is increasing as Boyd adds more projects into its capital budget for the year.

13-28 Goodtread Rubber Company has two divisions: the tire division, which manufactures tires for new autos, and the recap division, which manufactures recapping materials that are sold to independent tire recapping shops throughout the United States. Because auto manufacturing fluctuates with the general economy, the tire division's earnings contribution to Goodtread's stock price is highly correlated with returns on most other stocks. If the tire division were operated as a separate company, its beta coefficient would be 1.5. The sales and profits of the recap division, on the other hand, tend to be countercyclical because recap sales boom when people cannot afford to buy new tires. The recap division's beta is estimated to be 0.5. Approximately 75 percent of Goodtread's corporate assets are invested in the tire division and 25 percent are invested in the recap division.

   Currently, the rate of interest on Treasury securities is 6 percent, and the expected rate of return on an average share of stock is 10 percent. Goodtread uses only common equity capital, so it has no debt outstanding.

   a. What is the required rate of return on Goodtread's stock?

   b. What discount rate should be used to evaluate capital budgeting projects for each division? Explain your answer fully, and, in the process, illustrate your answer with a project that costs $160,000, has a 10-year life, and provides expected after-tax net cash flows of $30,000 per year.

CAPM Risk Adjustment

13-29 Your firm, Agrico Products, is considering the purchase of a tractor that will have a net cost of $72,000, will increase pretax operating cash flows before taking account of depreciation effects by $24,000 per year, and will be depreciated on a straight line basis to $0 over 5 years at the rate of $14,400 per year, beginning the first year. (Annual cash flows will be $24,000 before taxes plus the tax savings that result from $14,400 of depreciation.) The board of directors is having a heated debate about whether the tractor actually will last 5 years. Specifically, Joan Lamm insists that she knows some tractors have lasted only 4 years. Alan Grunewald agrees with Lamm, but he argues that most tractors do provide 5 years of service. Judy Maese says she has known some to last for as long as 8 years.

   Given this discussion, the board asks you to prepare a scenario analysis to ascertain the importance of the uncertainty about the tractor's life span. Assume a 40 percent marginal tax rate, a $0 salvage value, and a required rate of return of 10 percent. (*Hint:* Here straight line depreciation is based on the MACRS class life of the tractor and is not affected by the actual life. Also, ignore the half-year convention for this problem.)

Scenario Analysis

NPV Profile   **13-30** Derek's Donuts is considering two mutually exclusive investments. The projects' expected net cash flows are as follows:

Expected Net Cash Flows

Year	Project A	Project B
0	$(300)	$(405)
1	(387)	134
2	(193)	134
3	(100)	134
4	500	134
5	500	134
6	850	134
7	100	0

a. Construct NPV profiles for Projects A and B.

b. What is each project's IRR?

c. If you were told that each project's required rate of return was 12 percent, which project should be selected? If the required rate of return was 15 percent, what would be the proper choice?

d. Looking at the NPV profiles constructed in part (a), what is the *approximate* crossover rate, and what is its significance?

Timing Differences   **13-31** The Southwestern Oil Exploration Company is considering two mutually exclusive plans for extracting oil on property for which it has mineral rights. Both plans call for the expenditure of $12 million to drill development wells. Under Plan A, all the oil will be extracted in 1 year, producing a cash flow at the end of Year 1 (t = 1) of $14.4 million. Under Plan B, cash flows will be $2.1 million per year for 20 years.

a. Construct NPV profiles for Plans A and B, identify each project's IRR, and indicate the approximate crossover rate of return. (To compute the exact crossover rate, see footnote 15 in this chapter.)

b. Suppose a company has a required rate of return of 12 percent, and it can get unlimited funds at that cost. Is it logical to assume that it would take on all available independent projects (of average risk) with returns greater than 12 percent? Further, if all available projects with returns greater than 12 percent are purchased, would this mean that cash flows from past investments would have an opportunity cost of only 12 percent because all the firm could do with these cash flows would be to replace money that has a cost of 12 percent? Finally, does this imply that the required rate of return is the correct rate to assume for the reinvestment of a project's cash flows?

c. Compute the MIRR for each project. Which project should Southwestern purchase? Why?

Scale Differences   **13-32** The Chaplinsky Publishing Company is considering two mutually exclusive expansion plans. Plan A calls for the expenditure of $40 million on a large-scale, integrated plant that will provide an expected cash flow stream of $6.4 million per year for 20 years. Plan B calls for the expenditure of $12 million to build a somewhat less efficient, more labor-intensive plant that has an expected cash flow stream of $2.72 million per year for 20 years. Chaplinsky's required rate of return is 10 percent.

a. Calculate each project's NPV, IRR, and MIRR.

b. Construct the NPV profiles for both Plans A and B. Using the NPV profiles, approximate the crossover rate.

c. Give a logical explanation, based on reinvestment rates and opportunity costs, as to why the NPV method is better than the IRR method when the firm's required rate of return is constant at some value such as 10 percent.

Integrative Problems

13-33 Argile Textiles is evaluating a new product, a silk/wool blended fabric. Assume that you were recently hired as assistant to the director of capital budgeting, and you must evaluate the proposed project.

  Capital Budgeting and Cash Flow Estimation

  The fabric would be produced in an unused building located adjacent to Argile's Southern Pines, North Carolina, plant; Argile owns the building, which is fully depreciated. The required equipment would cost $200,000, plus an additional $40,000 for shipping and installation. With the new project, inventories would rise by $25,000, and accounts payable would increase by $5,000. All of these costs would be incurred at t = 0. By a special ruling, the machinery could be depreciated under the MACRS system as 3-year property.

  The project is expected to operate for 4 years, then be terminated. The cash inflows are assumed to begin 1 year after the project is undertaken, or at t = 1, and to continue to t = 4. At the end of the project's life (t = 4), the equipment is expected to have a salvage value of $25,000.

  Unit sales are expected to total 100,000 5-yard rolls per year, and the expected sales price is $2 per roll. Cash operating costs for the project (total operating costs excluding depreciation) are expected to amount to 60 percent of dollar sales. Argile's marginal tax rate is 40 percent, and its required rate of return is 10 percent. Tentatively, the silk/wool blend fabric project is assumed to be of equal risk to Argile's other assets.

  You have been asked to evaluate this project and to make an accept–reject recommendation. To guide you in your analysis, your boss has asked you to answer the following questions:

a. What is capital budgeting? Are there any similarities between a firm's capital budgeting decisions and an individual's investment decisions?

b. What is the difference between independent and mutually exclusive projects? Between projects with conventional cash flows and projects with unconventional cash flows? Between replacement analysis and expansion analysis?

c. Draw a cash flow time line that shows when the net cash inflows and outflows will occur with Argile's proposed project, and explain how the time line can be used to help structure the analysis.

d. Argile has a standard form that is used in the capital budgeting process; it is shown in Table IP13-1. Part of the table has been completed, but you must compute the missing values. Complete the table in the following steps:

  (1) Complete the unit sales, sales price, total revenues, and operating costs (excluding depreciation) lines.

  (2) Complete the depreciation line.

TABLE IP13-1   Argile's Silk/Wool Blend Project ($ thousand)

End of Year:	0	1	2	3	4
Unit sales (thousands)			100		
Price/unit		$ 2.00	$ 2.00		
Total revenues				$200.0	
Costs excluding depreciation			($120.0)		
Depreciation				(36.0)	(16.8)
Total operating costs		(199.2)	(228.0)		
Earnings before taxes (EBT)				44.0	
Taxes (40%)		(0.3)			(25.3)
Net income				$ 26.4	
Depreciation		79.2		36.0	
Incremental operating cash flow		$ 79.7			$ 54.7
Equipment cost					
Installation					
Increase in inventory					
Increase in accounts payable					
Salvage value					
Tax on salvage value					
Return of net working capital					
Cash flow time line (net cash flow)	$(260.0)	$ 79.7			$ 89.7
Cumulative cash flow for payback	(260.0)	(180.3)			63.0
NPV =					
IRR =					
Payback =					

(3) Complete the table down to net income and then down to net oper-ating cash flows.

(4) Fill in the blanks under Year 0 and Year 4 for the initial investment outlay and the terminal cash flows, respectively. Next, complete the "cash flow time line" (net cash flow). Discuss the role of working capital. What would have happened if the machinery were sold for less than its book value?

e. (1) Argile uses debt in its capital structure, so some of the money used to finance the project will consist of debt. Given this fact, should you revise the projected cash flows to show projected interest charges? Explain.

(2) Suppose you learned that Argile had spent $50,000 to renovate the building last year, expensing these costs. Should this cost be re-flected in the analysis? Explain.

(3) Suppose you learned that Argile could lease its building to another party and earn $25,000 per year. Should that fact be reflected in the analysis? If so, how?

(4) Assume that the silk/wool blend fabric project would take away profitable sales from Argile's cotton/wool blend fabric business. Should that fact be reflected in your analysis? If so, how?

For the remainder of the questions, disregard all of the assumptions made in part (e) and assume there was no alternative use for the building over the next 4 years.

f. **(1)** What is the regular payback period and the discounted payback period for the project?

   (2) What is the rationale for the payback? According to the payback criterion, should Argile accept the project if the firm's maximum acceptable payback is 2 years?

   (3) Explain the main difference between the regular payback and the discounted payback.

   (4) What are the main disadvantages of the regular payback method? Is the payback method of any real usefulness in capital budgeting decisions?

g. **(1)** Define the term *net present value*. What is the proposed project's NPV?

   (2) What is the rationale behind the NPV method? Based on the results of your NPV analysis, should Argile accept the project?

   (3) Would the NPV change if the required rate of return changed? Explain.

h. **(1)** Define the term *internal rate of return*. What is the proposed project's IRR?

   (2) How is the IRR on a project related to the YTM on a bond?

   (3) What is the logic behind the IRR method? Based on the results of your IRR analysis, should Argile accept the project?

   (4) Would the project's IRRs change if the required rate of return changed? Explain.

i. **(1)** Define the term *modified internal rate of return (MIRR)*. What is each project's MIRR?

   (2) What is the rationale behind the MIRR method? According to MIRR, which project or projects should be accepted if they are independent? Mutually exclusive?

   (3) Would the MIRRs change if the required rate of return changed?

j. Draw the NPV profile for the proposed project. What information does the NPV profile provide?

k. If this project had been a replacement rather than an expansion, how would the analysis have changed? In answering this question, think about the changes that would occur in the cash flow table, but do not perform any calculations.

l. Assume that inflation is expected to average 5 percent over the next 4 years, that this expectation is reflected in the required rate of return, and that inflation will increase variable costs and revenues by the same percentage. Does it appear that the analysis has properly dealt with inflation? If not, what should be done and how would the required adjustment affect the decision?

13-34 Problem 13-33 contained the details of a new-project capital budgeting evaluation being conducted by Argile textiles. Although inflation was considered in the initial analysis, the riskiness of the project was not taken into **Risk Analysis**

account. Argile's required rate of return is 10 percent. You have been asked to answer the following questions:

a. Assume that you are confident about the estimates of all variables that affect the project's cash flows except unit sales. If product acceptance is poor, sales would be only 75,000 units per year, whereas a strong consumer response would produce sales of 125,000 units per year. In either case, cash costs would amount to 60 percent of revenues. You believe that there is a 25 percent chance of poor acceptance, a 25 percent chance of excellent acceptance, and a 50 percent chance of average acceptance (the base case).

   (1) What is the worst-case NPV? The best-case NPV?

   (2) Use the worst-case, most likely (base) case, and best-case NPVs and probabilities of occurrence to find the project's expected NPV, standard deviation (σ_{NPV}), and coefficient of variation (CV_{NPV}).

b. (1) Assume that Argile's average project has a coefficient of variation (CV_{NPV}) in the range of 1.25 to 1.75. Would the silk/wool blend fabric project be classified as high risk, average risk, or low risk? What type of risk is being measured here?

   (2) Based on common sense, how highly correlated do you think the project would be to the firm's other assets? (Give a correlation coefficient, or range of coefficients, based on your judgment.)

   (3) How would this correlation coefficient and the previously calculated σ combine to affect the project's contribution to corporate (within-firm) risk? Explain.

c. (1) Argile typically adds or subtracts three percentage points to the overall required rate of return to adjust for risk. Given this fact, should Argile accept the project?

   (2) What subjective risk factors should be considered before the final decision is made?

d. Assume that the risk-free rate is 10 percent, the market risk premium is 6 percent, and the new project's beta is 1.2. What is the project's required rate of return on equity based on the CAPM?

COMPUTER-RELATED PROBLEMS

Work the problems in this section only if you are using the computer problem spreadsheet.

NPV and IRR Analysis   **13-35** Use the model in File C13 to solve this problem. West Coast Chemical Company (WCCC) is considering two mutually exclusive investments. The projects' expected net cash flows are as follows:

Expected Net Cash Flows

Year	Project A	Project B
0	$(45,000)	$(50,000)
1	20,000	15,000
2	11,000	15,000
3	20,000	15,000
4	30,000	15,000
5	45,000	15,000

a. Construct NPV profiles for Projects A and B.

b. Calculate each project's IRR.

c. If the required rate of return for each project is 13 percent, which project should West Coast select? If the required rate of return is 9 percent, what would be the proper choice? If the required rate of return is 15 percent, what would be the proper choice?

d. At what rate do the NPV profiles of the two projects cross?

e. Project A has a large cash flow in Year 5 associated with ending the project. WCCC's management is confident of Project A's cash flows in Years 0 to 4 but is uncertain about what its Year 5 cash flow will be. (There is no uncertainty about Project B's cash flows.) Under a worst-case scenario, Project A's Year 5 cash flow will be $40,000, whereas under a best-case scenario, the cash flow will be $50,000. Redo parts (a), (b), and (d) for each scenario, assuming a 13 percent required rate of return. If the required rate of return for each project is 13 percent, which project should be selected under each scenario?

13-36 Use the computerized model in File C13 to work this problem. Golden State Bakers, Inc. (GSB) has an opportunity to invest in a new dough machine. GSB needs more productive capacity, so the new machine will not replace an existing machine. The new machine is priced at $260,000 and will require modifications costing $15,000. It has an expected useful life of 10 years, will be depreciated using the MACRS method over its 5-year class life, and has an expected salvage value of $12,500 at the end of Year 10. (See Table 13A-2 for MACRS recovery allowance percentages.) The machine will require a $22,500 investment in net working capital. It is expected to generate additional sales revenues equal to $125,000 per year, but its use also will increase annual cash operating expenses by $55,000. GSB's required rate of return is 10 percent, and its marginal tax rate is 40 percent. The machine's book value at the end of Year 10 will be $0, so GSB will have to pay taxes on the $12,500 salvage value.

Expansion Analysis

a. What is the NPV of this expansion project? Should GSB purchase the new machine?

b. Should GSB purchase the new machine if it is expected to be used for only 5 years and then sold for $31,250? (Note that the model is set up to handle a 5-year life; you need enter only the new life and salvage value.)

c. Would the machine be profitable if revenues increased by only $105,000 per year? Assume a 10-year project life and a salvage value of $12,500.

d. Suppose that revenues rose by $125,000 but expenses rose by $65,000. Would the machine be acceptable under these conditions? Assume a 10-year project life and a salvage value of $12,500.

Depreciation

APPENDIX 13A

Suppose a firm buys a milling machine for $100,000 and uses it for 5 years, after which it is scrapped. The cost of the goods produced by the machine each year must include a charge for using the machine and reducing its value. This charge is called *depreciation*. In this appendix we review some of the depreciation concepts covered in your accounting courses.

Companies often calculate depreciation one way when figuring taxes and another way when reporting income to investors: many use the *straight line* method for stockholder reporting (or "book" purposes), but they use the fastest rate permitted by law for tax purposes.

According to the straight line method used for stockholder reporting, you normally would take the cost of the asset, subtract its estimated salvage value, and divide the net amount by the asset's useful economic life. For an asset with a 5-year life that costs $100,000 and has a $12,500 salvage value, the annual straight line depreciation charge is ($100,000 − $12,500)/5 = $17,500. Note, however, as we discuss later in this appendix, that salvage value is not considered for tax depreciation purposes.

For tax purposes, Congress changes the permissible tax depreciation methods from time to time. Prior to 1954, the straight line method was required for tax purposes, but in 1954 accelerated methods (double declining balance and sum-of-years' digits) were permitted. Then, in 1981, the old accelerated methods were replaced by a simpler procedure known as the Accelerated Cost Recovery System (ACRS). The ACRS system was changed again in 1986 as a part of the Tax Reform Act, and it is now known as the Modified Accelerated Cost Recovery System (MACRS).

Tax Depreciation Life

For tax purposes, the *entire* cost of an asset is expensed over its depreciable life. Historically, an asset's depreciable life was determined by its estimated useful economic life; it was intended that an asset would be fully depreciated at approximately the same time that it reached the end of its useful economic life. However, MACRS totally abandoned that practice and set simple guidelines that created several classes of assets, each with a more-or-less arbitrarily prescribed life called a recovery period or class life. The MACRS class life bears only a rough relationship to the expected useful economic life.

A major effect of the MACRS system has been to shorten the depreciable lives of assets, thus giving businesses larger tax deductions and thereby increasing their cash flows available for reinvestment. Table 13A-1 describes the types of property that fit into the different class life groups, and Table 13A-2 sets

TABLE 13A-1   Major Classes and Asset Lives for MACRS

Class	Type of Property
3-year	Certain special manufacturing tools
5-year	Automobiles, light-duty trucks, computers, office machinery, and certain special manufacturing equipment
7-year	Most industrial equipment, office furniture, and fixtures
10-year	Certain longer-lived equipment and many water vessels
15-year	Certain land improvement, such as shrubbery, fences, and roads; service station buildings
20-year	Farm buildings
25-year	Property used in water treatment; municipal sewers
27½-year	Residential rental real property such as apartment buildings
39-year	All nonresidential real property, including commercial and industrial buildings

TABLE 13A-2   Recovery Allowance Percentages for Personal Property

Ownership Year	Class of Investment			
	3-Year	5-Year	7-Year	10-Year
1	33%	20%	14%	10%
2	45	32	25	18
3	15	19	17	14
4	7	12	13	12
5		11	9	9
6		6	9	7
7			9	7
8			4	7
9				7
10				6
11				3
	100%	100%	100%	100%

Notes: These recovery allowance percentages were taken from the Internal Revenue Service Web site: http://www.irs.ustreas.gov. The percentages are based on the 200 percent declining balance method prescribed by MACRS, with a switch to straight line depreciation at some point in the asset's life. For example, consider the 5-year recovery allowance percentages. The straight line percentage would be 20 percent per year, so the 200 percent declining balance multiplier is 2.0(20%) = 40% = 0.4. Because the half-year convention applies (see discussion), the MACRS percentage for Year 1 is 20 percent. For Year 2, 80 percent of the depreciable basis remains to be depreciated, so the recovery allowance percentage is 0.40(80%) = 32%. The same procedure is followed for subsequent years. Although the tax tables carry the allowance percentages to two decimal places, we have rounded to the nearest whole number for ease of illustration.

forth the MACRS recovery allowances (depreciation rates) for selected classes of investment property.

Consider Table 13A-1 first. The first column gives the MACRS class life, while the second column describes the types of assets that fall into each category. Property classified with lives equal to or greater than 27.5 years (real estate) must be depreciated by the straight line method, but assets classified in the other categories can be depreciated either by the accelerated method using rates shown in Table 13A-2 or by an alternate straight line method.

As we saw earlier in the chapter, higher depreciation expenses result in lower taxes, hence higher cash flows. Therefore, because a firm has the choice of using the alternate straight line rates or the accelerated rates shown in Table 13A-2, most elect to use the accelerated rates. Using MACRS, the yearly recovery allowance, or depreciation expense, is determined by multiplying each asset's *depreciable basis* by the applicable recovery percentage shown in Table 13A-2. Calculations are discussed in the following sections.

Half-Year Convention

Under MACRS, it is assumed that property is placed in service in the middle of the first year. Thus, for 3-year class life property, the recovery period begins in the middle of the year the asset is placed in service and ends 3 years later. The effect of the *half-year convention* is to extend the recovery period out 1 more year, so 3-year class life property is depreciated over 4 *calendar* years, 5-year property is depreciated over 6 calendar years, and so on. This convention is incorporated into Table 13A-2's recovery allowance percentages.[25]

Depreciable Basis

The *depreciable basis* is a critical element of MACRS because each year's allowance (depreciation expense) depends jointly on the asset's depreciable basis and its MACRS class life. The depreciable basis under MACRS is equal to the purchase price of the asset plus any shipping and installation costs. The basis is not adjusted for salvage value.

Sale of a Depreciable Asset

If a depreciable asset is sold, the sale price (salvage value) minus the then-existing undepreciated book value is added to operating income and taxed at the firm's marginal tax rate. For example, suppose a firm buys a 5-year class life asset for $100,000 and sells it at the end of the fourth year for $25,000. The asset's book value is equal to $100,000(0.11 + 0.06) = $17,000. Therefore, $25,000 − $17,000 = $8,000 is added to the firm's operating income and is taxed. If this difference were negative, the firm would effectively receive a tax refund, which would be recognized as a cash inflow.

Depreciation Illustration

Assume that Argile Textiles buys a $150,000 machine that falls into the MACRS 5-year class life asset and places it into service on March 15, 2011. Argile must pay an additional $30,000 for delivery and installation. Salvage value is not considered, so the machine's depreciable basis is $180,000. (Delivery and installation charges are included in the depreciable basis rather than expensed in the year incurred.) Each year's recovery allowance (tax depreciation expense) is determined by multiplying the depreciable basis by the applicable recovery allowance percentage. Thus, the depreciation expense for 2011 is 0.20($180,000) = $36,000, and for 2012 it is 0.32($180,000) = $57,600. Similarly, the depreciation expense is $34,200 for 2013, $21,600 for 2014, $19,800 for 2015, and $10,800 for 2016. The total depreciation expense over the 6-year recovery period is $180,000, which is equal to the depreciable basis of the machine.

As noted previously, most firms use straight line depreciation for stockholder reporting purposes but MACRS for tax purposes. For these firms, for capital budgeting, MACRS should be used because in capital budgeting we are concerned with cash flows, not reported income.

PROBLEM

Depreciation Effects **13A-1** Christina Manning, great-granddaughter of the founder of Manning Tile Products and current president of the company, believes in simple, conservative accounting. In keeping with her philosophy, she has decreed that

---

[25]The half-year convention also applies if the straight line alternative is used, with half of 1 year's depreciation taken in the first year, a full year's depreciation taken in each of the remaining years of the asset's class life, and the remaining half-year's depreciation taken in the year following the end of the class life. You should recognize that virtually all companies have computerized depreciation systems. Each asset's depreciation pattern is programmed into the system at the time of its acquisition, and the computer aggregates the depreciation allowances for all assets when the accountants close the books and prepare the financial statements and tax returns.

the company shall use straight line depreciation, based on the MACRS class lives, for all newly acquired assets. Your boss, the financial vice president and the only nonfamily officer, has asked you to develop an exhibit that shows how much this policy costs the company in terms of market value. Ms. Manning is interested in increasing the value of the firm's stock because she fears a family stockholder revolt that might remove her from office. For your exhibit, assume that the company spends $100 million each year on new capital projects, that the projects have on average a 10-year class life, that the company has a 9 percent required rate of return, and that its marginal tax rate is 34 percent. (*Hint:* Show how much the total NPV of the projects in an average year would increase if Manning used the standard MACRS recovery allowances.)

Using a Spreadsheet to Compute NPV and IRR

APPENDIX 13B

Using a spreadsheet to compute the net present value (NPV) of a capital budgeting project is straightforward if you understand what the spreadsheet function actually computes. To compute the NPV for Project S (described in the chapter) using Excel 2007, you could set up the spreadsheet as follows:

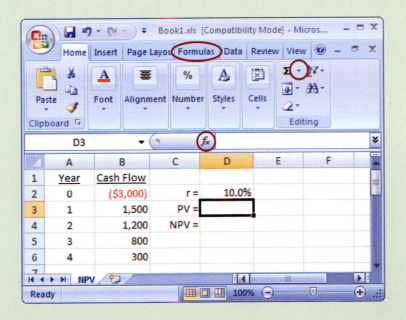

After setting up the spreadsheet as shown, place the cursor in cell **D3** and click one of the labels or symbols on the "Home" menu that is circled in the spreadsheet shown here—that is, the "Formulas" tab located at the top of the menu bar, the insert function icon, labeled f_x, located at the bottom of the menu, or the down arrow to the right of summation sign (Σ) that is located on the right side of the menu. When you find the Insert "Function" menu, click the "Financial function" category listed in the drop-down menu that is labeled "Or select a category:";

scroll down the "Select a function:" menu, select the "NPV function," and then click "OK." The following dialog box should appear:

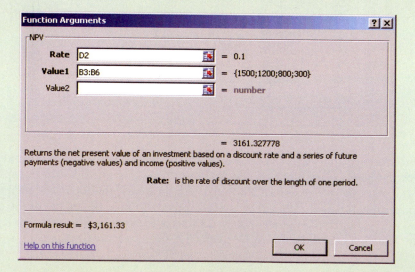

The description of this function indicates that the result of the computation is the present value of all the *future* cash flows—both inflows and outflows—associated with the investment. What this means is that the Excel function called "NPV" does not compute the net present value as described in this book; rather it computes the present value of all *future* cash flows. As a result, when you enter the cash flows or the locations for the cash flows, the spreadsheet will assume the first cash flow is $\widehat{CF}_1$, the second cash flow is $\widehat{CF}_2$, and so on. The NPV function actually computes the discounted cash flows (DCF), from which you need to subtract (or add a negative value to) the initial cost to determine the net present value described in the chapter.

Click the red arrow on the right side of the row labeled "Rate", place the cursor in the cell that contains the value for r (the required rate of return), and then press return. Then click the arrow on the right side of the row labeled "Value1", use the cursor to highlight the *future cash flows only*—that is, the cash flows from Year 1 through Year 4—located in cells B3 through B6, and then press return. Now the dialog box will look as follows:

You can see the result of the computation in the middle of the dialog box; it is 3161.327778. If you click the "OK" button, this result will appear in cell **D3** of your spreadsheet.

Now place the cursor in cell **D4** and enter the following relationship:

$$= \mathbf{D3} + \mathbf{B2}$$

This computation will add the initial investment, which is stated as a negative amount, to the result that is shown in cell **D3.** Your spreadsheet should now look as follows:

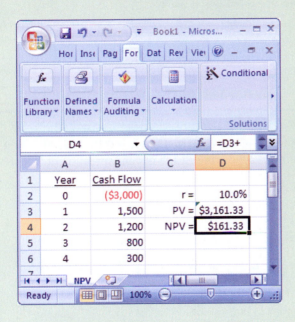

The result of the computation that is shown in cell **D4** is the same as the net present value we computed in the chapter.

To compute the internal rate of return (IRR) for the project using a spreadsheet, set up the problem as before, but type the label "IRR =" in cell **C5.** Place the cursor in cell **D5,** click f_x (Insert function), and then select the "IRR" function from the financial function category. The following dialog box should appear:

Function Arguments   ? X

IRR

    Values [   ] 🗐 = reference

    Guess [   ] 🗐 = number

                  =

Returns the internal rate of return for a series of cash flows.

            Values is an array or a reference to cells that contain numbers for which you want to calculate the internal rate of return.

Formula result =

Help on this function   OK   Cancel

Click the red arrow on the right side of the row labeled "Values," use the cursor to highlight *all* of the cash flows (including CF_0) located in column B—that is, cells B2 through B6—and then press return. Now the IRR dialog box will look as follows:

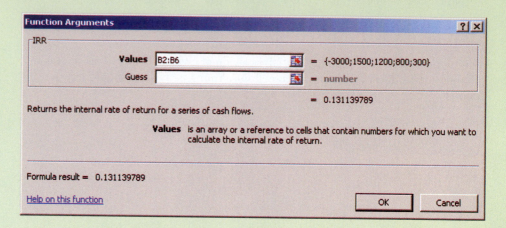

You can see the result of the computation; it is 0.131139789. If you click the "OK" button, this result will appear in cell **D5** of your spreadsheet, which will now look as follows:

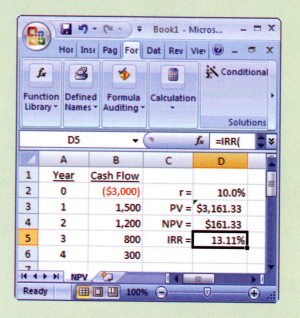

This is the same answer we computed in the chapter.

Now, use the same spreadsheet to compute the NPV and IRR for Project L; all you need to do is change the cash flows in column B. The results given for PV, NPV, and IRR will change as you change the values in cells **B2** through **B6.** The answers should be the same as we computed in the chapter.

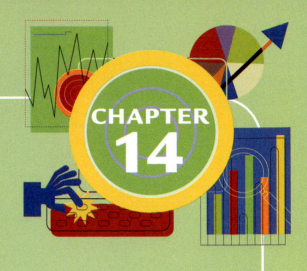

Capital Structure and Dividend Policy Decisions

A Managerial Perspective

A press release issued by United Parcel Service, Inc. (UPS) on January 9, 2008, stated that the board had approved plans for the company to change its capital structure in an effort to "enhance UPS's value to shareowners." The proposed change required the company to increase the amount of debt used to finance its assets such that the ratio of "funds-from-operations-to-total-debt" was in the range from 50 to 60 percent. The executives believed that the stability of the company's operations allowed it to use substantially more debt than it had in its capital structure at the time. In the 2007 annual report, the newly appointed CEO, D. Scott Davis, wrote: "After studying our options for some time, we determined we could significantly increase the debt component of the balance sheet and enhance shareowner value by reducing the company's cost of capital."

It might seem counterintuitive that a firm can decrease its cost of capital, and thus increase its value, by increasing the proportion of debt used to finance its assets. We generally associate more risk with more debt, and, as we discovered in Chapter 12, the cost of capital should increase when the riskiness of the firm increases. But remember that much of the risk that is associated with debt results from the fact that a fixed interest must be paid to debtholders. Also remember that firms benefit from debt financing when they are assured that the fixed interest payments can be covered,

because any amounts earned with the borrowed money that exceed the interest payments "belong" to the firm. As a result, as long as UPS's operations remain stable such that its operating cash flows are fairly predictable, the company can benefit by using a high proportion of debt in its capital structure. In 2008, UPS had a debt ratio (percent of debt) equal to almost 70 percent. To increase this debt ratio, the company planned to repurchase up to $10 billion of its common stock in 2008 and 2009.

Clearly, UPS believes that changing its capital structure to include a greater proportion of debt will benefit stockholders in the future by increasing the company's value. So, how did investors react to the January 9 press release? On January 10, the per-share price of UPS stock increased by $3, or 4.5 percent; and during the first 3 months of 2008, the stock price increased 11.5 percent to $74.50. Thus, at the beginning of 2008, it seemed that investors agreed with UPS executives that the change in capital structure would add to the value of the company. If investors "change" their minds about UPS's plan to increase the company's debt, however, a future price adjustment will take place.

In another announcement in May 2007, UPS stated that it intended to increase the quarterly dividend by $0.04 to $0.42 per share. This was not a surprise to stockholders because the company had

583

increased its dividend every year during the previous 4 years, and the annual dividend had either remained the same or been increased for nearly 40 years. As a result, on the day the dividend was declared, the price of the stock showed little movement because the announcement did not provide investors with new information.

As you read this chapter, keep in mind the reason UPS decided to increase the proportion of debt in its capital structure in 2008 and 2009. Also, consider the reaction of investors both to the announcement of the planned capital structure change and the 2007 dividend payment—that is, consider the effect that a particular capital structure or a dividend payment policy can have on the value of a firm.

Source: Press releases and the 2007 annual report of UPS. The press releases are located on the UPS Web site at http://www. pressroom. ups.com/pressreleases/archives/archive/0,1363, 4969,00.html and the annual reports are located at http://investor.shareholder. com/ups/.

CHAPTER PRINCIPLES –The Questions

After reading this chapter, you should be able to answer the following questions:

- What is a firm's capital structure?
- What is a firm's optimal capital structure? Can a firm have too little debt?
- How does a firm's capital structure affect its risk?
- Why do the capital structures of firms in different industries vary?
- What is an optimal dividend policy?
- What dividend payment policies are followed in practice?
- What factors affect dividend policy decisions?
- How does a stock split (dividend) work? Why would a firm initiate a stock split (pay a dividend in stock)?
- How do the capital structures and dividend payment policies of companies in the United States compare with those observed in foreign companies?

In Chapter 12, when we calculated the weighted average cost of capital (WACC) for use in making corporate investment decisions, we took the capital structure weights—that is, the mix of securities that the firm uses to finance its assets—as a given. However, if the weights are changed, the calculated cost of capital, and thus the set of acceptable investments, will change as well. Furthermore, changing the capital structure will affect the riskiness inherent in the firm's common stock, which will affect the return demanded by stockholders, r_s, and the stock's price, P_0. Therefore, the choice of a capital structure is an important decision. In addition, decisions concerning the amount of earnings that are paid to stockholders as dividends affect the amount of internal equity financing (retained earnings) that a firm has available to support its investments, which in turn affects capital structure decisions. In this chapter, we discuss concepts related to capital structure and dividend policy decisions.

THE TARGET CAPITAL STRUCTURE

capital structure
The combination of debt and equity used to finance a firm.

Firms can choose whatever mix of debt and equity they desire to finance their assets, subject to the willingness of investors to provide such funds. As we shall see, many different mixes of debt and equity, or **capital structures,** exist. In some firms, such as Ford Motor Company in 2008, debt accounts for more than 90 percent of the financing, whereas other firms, like Microsoft, have little or no long-term debt. In the next few sections, we will discuss factors that affect a firm's capital structure, and we will conclude that a firm should attempt to determine what its optimal, or best, mix of financing should be. It will become apparent that determining the exact optimal capital structure is not a science, so after analyzing a number of factors, a firm establishes a **target capital structure** that it believes is optimal, and which it uses as guidance for raising funds in the future. This target might change over time as conditions vary, but at any given moment the firm's management has a specific capital structure in mind, and individual financing decisions should be consistent with this target. If the actual proportion of debt is below the target level, new funds probably will be raised by issuing debt (or repurchasing stock), whereas if the proportion of debt is above the target, stock probably will be sold to bring the firm back in line with the target ratio.

> **target capital structure**
> The mix of debt, preferred stock, and common equity with which the firm plans to finance its investments.

Capital structure policy involves a tradeoff between risk and return. Using more debt raises the riskiness of the firm's earnings stream, but a higher proportion of debt generally leads to a higher expected rate of return. From the concepts we discussed in Chapter 11, we know that the higher risk associated with greater debt tends to lower the firm's stock price. At the same time, however, the higher expected rate of return makes the stock more attractive to investors, which, in turn, ultimately increases the stock's price. Therefore, *the optimal capital structure is the one that strikes a balance between risk and return to achieve the ultimate goal of maximizing the price of the stock.*

Four primary factors influence capital structure decisions.

1. *Business risk.* Business risk represents the riskiness that would be inherent in the firm's operations if it used no debt. The greater the firm's business risk, the lower the amount of debt that is optimal.

2. *Tax position.* A major reason for using debt is that interest is tax deductible, which lowers the effective cost of debt. However, if much of a firm's income is already sheltered from taxes by accelerated depreciation or tax loss carryovers from previous years, its tax rate will be low and debt will not be as advantageous as it would be to a firm with a higher effective tax rate.

3. *Financial flexibility.* The more able a firm is to raise capital on reasonable terms under adverse conditions, the more financial flexibility it has. Corporate treasurers know that a steady supply of capital is necessary for stable operations, which in turn are vital for long-run success. They also know that when money is tight in the economy, or when a firm is experiencing operating difficulties, a strong balance sheet is needed to obtain funds from suppliers of capital. Thus, it might be advantageous to issue equity to strengthen the firm's capital base and financial stability.

4. *Managerial attitude (conservatism or aggressiveness).* Some managers are more aggressive than others, hence some firms are more inclined to use debt in an effort to boost profits. This factor does not affect the optimal, or value-maximizing, capital structure, but it does influence the target capital structure a firm actually establishes.

These four points largely determine the target capital structure, but, as we shall see, operating conditions can cause the actual capital structure to vary from the target at any given time. For example, the proportion of debt that UPS had in its capital structure at the beginning of 2008 clearly was lower than desired (targeted), but the company planned to take corrective actions to adjust its financial position. (See "A Managerial Perspective" at the beginning of this chapter.)

Self-Test Questions

What are the four factors that affect a firm's target capital structure?

In what sense does capital structure policy involve a tradeoff between risk and return?

BUSINESS AND FINANCIAL RISK

When we examined risk in Chapter 11, we distinguished between *market risk,* which is measured by the firm's beta coefficient, and *total risk,* which includes both market (beta) risk and a type of risk that can be eliminated through diversification (*firm-specific risk).* In Chapter 13 we considered how capital budgeting decisions affect the riskiness of the firm. There again we distinguished between *beta risk* (the effect of a project on the firm's beta) and *corporate risk* (the effect of the project on the firm's total risk).

Now we introduce two new dimensions of risk:

business risk
The risk associated with projections of a firm's future returns on assets (ROA) or returns on equity (ROE) if the firm uses no debt.

financial risk
The portion of stockholders' risk, over and above basic business risk, resulting from the manner in which the firm is financed.

1. **Business risk** is defined as the uncertainty inherent in projections of future returns, either on assets (ROA) or on equity (ROE), if the firm uses no debt, or debt-like financing (i.e., preferred stock)—that is, it is the risk associated with the firm's operations, ignoring how the assets are financed (financing effects).

2. **Financial risk** is defined as the additional risk, over and above basic business risk, placed on common stockholders that results from using financing alternatives with fixed periodic payments, such as debt and preferred stock— that is, it is the risk associated with using debt, preferred stock, or both of these types of funds to finance assets.

Conceptually, the firm has a certain amount of risk inherent in its production and sales operations; this is its business risk. When it uses debt, it partitions this risk and concentrates most of it on one class of investors—the common stockholders—this is its financial risk.[1] Both business risk and financial risk affect the capital structure of a firm.

Business Risk

Business risk is the single most important determinant of capital structure because it is based on the uncertainty that a company's future operations exhibit. Some companies have fairly stable, and somewhat predictable operations—that is, production and sales patterns—whereas the operations of other companies are very unpredictable. It makes sense that firms with more stable operations generally can more easily take on, or "handle," the fixed interest payments that are associated with debt and therefore use more debt in their capital structures than firms with less stable operations (e.g., UPS). In other words, everything else the same, firms with more stable operations have lower business risk than firms with less stable operations, and firms with less business risk can take on more debt (fixed financial payments) than firms with greater business risk.[2]

---

[1]Using preferred stock also adds to financial risk. To simplify matters somewhat, in this chapter we assume that the firm is financed with debt and common equity only.

[2]We have avoided any discussion of market versus company-specific risk in this section. We note now that (1) any action that increases business risk will generally increase a firm's beta coefficient, but (2) a part of business risk as we define it will generally be company-specific and hence subject to elimination through diversification by the firm's stockholders.

Business risk depends on a number of factors, the more important of which include the following:

1. *Sales variability (volume and price).* The more stable (certain) the unit sales (volume) and prices of a firm's products, other things held constant, the lower its business risk.

2. *Input price variability.* A firm whose input prices—labor, product costs, and so forth—are highly uncertain is exposed to a high degree of business risk.

3. *Ability to adjust output prices for changes in input prices.* Some firms have little difficulty in raising the prices of their products when input costs rise; the greater the ability to adjust selling prices, the lower the degree of business risk. This factor is especially important during periods of high inflation.

4. *The extent to which costs are fixed: operating leverage.* If a high percentage of a firm's operating costs are fixed and hence do not decline when demand falls off, this increases the company's business risk. This factor is called *operating leverage.* We discussed operating leverage at length in Chapter 8; at that time, we concluded that *a firm with greater operating leverage has greater business risk than a firm with lower operating leverage, because its earnings will exhibit greater variability when sales vary.*

Each of these factors is determined partly by the firm's industry characteristics, but each also is controllable to some extent by management. For example, most firms can, through their marketing policies, take actions to stabilize both unit sales and sales prices. However, this stabilization might require either large expenditures on advertising or price concessions to induce customers to commit to purchasing fixed quantities at fixed prices in the future. Similarly, some firms can reduce the volatility of future input costs by negotiating long-term labor and materials supply contracts. Of course, they might have to agree to pay prices somewhat above the current price to obtain these contracts.

Financial Risk

We define *financial risk* as the additional risk, over and above basic business risk, placed on common stockholders that results from using financing alternatives with fixed periodic payments, such as debt and preferred stock. Thus, *financial risk* results from using **financial leverage,** which exists when a firm uses fixed-income securities, such as debt and preferred stock, to raise capital. When financial leverage is created, a firm intensifies the business risk borne by the common stockholders.[3] To illustrate, suppose 10 people decide to form a corporation to produce operating systems for personal computers. There is a certain amount of business risk in the operation. If the firm is capitalized only with common equity, and if each person buys 10 percent of the stock, then each investor will bear an equal share of the business risk. However, suppose the firm is capitalized with 50 percent debt and 50 percent equity, with five of the investors putting up their capital as debt and the other five putting up their money as equity. In this case, the cash flows received by the debtholders are based on a contractual agreement, so the investors who put up the equity will have to bear essentially all of the business risk, and their position will be twice as risky as it would have been had the firm been financed only with stock. Thus, *the use of debt intensifies the firm's business risk borne by the common stockholders.*

financial leverage
The extent to which fixed-income securities (debt and preferred stock) are used in a firm's capital structure.

---

[3]We discussed financial leverage at length in Chapter 8.

In the next section, we explain how financial leverage affects a firm's expected earnings per share, the riskiness of those earnings, and, consequently, the price of the firm's stock. The objective of our analysis is to determine the capital structure at which *value is maximized;* this point is then used as the target capital structure.[4]

Self-Test Questions

What is the difference between business risk and financial risk?

Identify and briefly explain some of the more important factors that affect business risk.

Why does business risk vary from one industry to another?

What creates financial risk?

DETERMINING THE OPTIMAL CAPITAL STRUCTURE

We can illustrate the effects of financial leverage using the data shown in Table 14-1 for a fictional company, which we will call OptiCap. As shown in the top section of the table, the company has no debt. Should it continue the policy of using no debt, or should it start using financial leverage? If it does decide to replace equity with debt, how far should it go? As in all such decisions, the correct answer is that it should *choose a capital structure—that is, a combination of debt and equity—that will maximize the price of the firm's stock.*

To answer the questions posed here, we examine the effects of changing OptiCap's capital structure while keeping all other factors, such as the total assets and the level of operations, constant. To keep all other factors constant, we assume that OptiCap changes its capital structure by *substituting* debt for equity—that is, as new debt is issued, the proceeds are used to repurchase an equal amount of outstanding stock.

EPS Analysis of the Effects of Financial Leverage

If a firm changes the percentage of debt used to finance existing assets, we would expect the earnings per share (EPS) and, consequently, the stock price to change as well. Remember that debt requires fixed payments, regardless of the firm's level of sales. To understand the relationship between financial leverage and earnings per share (EPS), we first examine how earnings per share are affected when our illustrative firm changes its capital structure to include greater relative amounts of debt.

---

[4]In this chapter we examine capital structures on a book value (or balance sheet) basis. An alternative approach is to calculate the market values of debt, preferred stock, and common equity, and then to reconstruct the balance sheet on a market value basis. Although the market value approach is more consistent with financial theory, bond rating agencies and most financial executives focus their attention on book values. Moreover, the conversion from book to market values is a complicated process, and because market value capital structures change with stock market fluctuations, they are thought by many to be too unstable to serve as operationally useful targets. Finally, exactly the same insights are gained from the book value and market value analyses. For all these reasons, a market value analysis of capital structure is better suited for advanced finance courses.

TABLE 14-1   Financial Information for OptiCap, 2009 ($ thousand, except per-share values)

I. Balance Sheet—12/31/09

Current assets	$100.0	Debt	$ 0.0
Net fixed assets	100.0	Common equity (10,000 shares)	200.0
Total assets	$200.0	Total liabilities and equity	$ 200.0

II. Income Statement for 2009

Sales	$ 200.0
Variable operating costs (60%)	(120.0)
Fixed operating costs	(41.0)
Earnings before interest and taxes (EBIT)	39.0
Interest	(0.0)
Earnings before taxes (EBT)	39.0
Taxes (40%)	(15.6)
Net income	$ 23.4
Common dividends	$ 23.4
Addition to retained earnings	$ 0.0

III. Per-Share Information

Earnings per share (EPS) = ($23,400/10,000 shares)	$ 2.34
Dividends per share (DPS) = ($23,400/10,000 shares)	$ 2.34
Market price per share (P$_0$)	$ 20.00

First, to simplify our example, we assume that OptiCap's level of operations—that is, production and sales—will not change if its capital structure changes.[5] Table 14-1 shows that OptiCap's net operating income (NOI), or earnings before interest and taxes (EBIT), was $39,000 in 2009. We expect that its EBIT will remain at this level when economic conditions are "normal" but will rise to $65,000 when the economy is booming and fall to $5,000 when the economy is in a recession. The probabilities associated with each of these economic states are 0.5, 0.3, and 0.2, respectively. We give the different economic states so that we can see what happens to OptiCap's financial risk when its capital structure is changed.

OptiCap asked its investment banker to help determine what the cost of debt, r$_d$, will be at various levels of debt. The results are shown in Table 14-2. Naturally, we would expect that as a firm increases the percentage of debt it uses, the lenders will perceive the debt to be riskier because the chance of financial distress is higher. As a result, lenders will charge higher interest rates to the firm as its percentage of debt increases, which is the pattern shown in the table.

---

[5]In the real world, capital structure *does* at times affect EBIT. First, if debt levels are excessive, the firm probably will not be able to finance at all if its earnings are low at a time when interest rates are high. This could lead to stop-start construction and a decrease in research and development programs, as well as to the necessity of passing up good investment opportunities. Second, a weak financial condition (i.e., too much debt) could cause a firm to lose sales. For example, prior to the time that its huge debt forced Eastern Airlines into bankruptcy, many people refused to buy Eastern tickets because they were afraid the company would go bankrupt and leave them holding unusable tickets. Third, financially strong companies can bargain hard with unions as well as with their suppliers, whereas weaker ones might have to give in simply because they do not have the financial resources to carry on the fight. Finally, a company with so much debt that bankruptcy is a serious threat will have difficulty attracting and retaining managers and employees, or it will have to pay premium salaries. For all these reasons, it is not totally correct to say that a firm's financial policy has no effect on its operating income.

TABLE 14-2   Cost of Debt, r_d, and Number of Common Shares Outstanding for OptiCap at Different Capital Structures ($ thousand)

Total Assets	Debt/Assets Ratio	Amount Borrowed[a]	Common Stock	Shares Outstanding[b]	Cost of Debt, r_d
$200	0%	$ 0	$200	10,000	—
200	10	20	180	9,000	8.0%
200	20	40	160	8,000	8.5
200	30	60	140	7,000	9.0
200	40	80	120	6,000	10.0
200	50	100	100	5,000	12.0
200	60	120	80	4,000	15.0

[a]We assume that the firm must borrow in increments of $20,000. We also assume that OptiCap cannot borrow more than $120,000, or 60 percent of assets, because of restrictions in its corporate charter.

[b]We assume that OptiCap uses the amount of funds raised by borrowing (issuing debt) to repurchase existing common stock at the current market value, which is $20 per share; thus, we assume that no commissions or other transaction costs are associated with repurchasing the stock. For example, if OptiCap's capital structure contains 40 percent debt, then $80,000 of the $200,000 total assets is financed with debt. We assume that if OptiCap borrows the $80,000, it will repurchase 4,000 shares = $80,000/$20 of its existing common stock, so 6,000 shares = 10,000 shares – 4,000 shares remain.

We assume that OptiCap does not retain any earnings for reinvestment in the firm—that is, all earnings are paid to shareholders, which currently consist of stockholders only. In addition, we assume that the size of the firm remains at its current level. As long as the firm pays all earnings to shareholders as dividends and no additional funds are raised, growth will equal 0 percent (g = 0), and future production and sales operations will continue as outlined previously. Thus, any changes in EPS that we observe when the proportion of debt is changed will be a direct result of changing the firm's capital structure, not its level of operations.

Table 14-3 compares OptiCap's expected EPS at two levels of financial leverage: (1) 0 percent debt, which is the existing capital structure, and (2) 50 percent debt. If OptiCap does not change its capital structure, all $200,000 of its assets will be financed with stock, so the interest expense will be $0 because no debt exists. Section II of Table 14-3 shows that EPS is expected to be $2.40 with this capital structure—EPS will be as high as $3.90 and as low as $0.30, but, on average, it will be $2.40. We also calculate the standard deviation of EPS and the coefficient of variation as indicators of the firm's risk with this capital structure: σ_{EPS} = $1.25, and CV_{EPS} = 0.52.[6]

Section III of Table 14-3 shows the effect on EPS of shifting OptiCap's capital structure so that the mix of financing is 50 percent debt and 50 percent equity—that is, when the $200,000 assets is financed with $100,000 debt and $100,000 equity. To accomplish this shift, OptiCap would issue $100,000 of debt and repurchase $100,000 of its existing equity. If we assume that stock can be repurchased at its current market price and transaction costs are negligible, then, using the information given in Table 14-1, we find that OptiCap can repurchase 5,000

---

[6]See Chapter 11 for a review of procedures for calculating standard deviations and coefficients of variation. Recall that the advantage of the coefficient of variation is that it permits better comparisons when the expected values of EPS vary, as they do here for the two capital structures.

TABLE 14-3   OptiCap: EPS at Different Capital Structures ($ thousand, except per-share values)

I. Economic States

Type of economy	Recession	Normal	Boom
Probability of occurrence	0.20	0.50	0.30

II. Debt/Assets = 0% (Current Capital Structure)

	Recession	Normal	Boom
EBIT	5.0	39.0	65.0
Interest	(0.0)	(0.0)	(0.0)
Earnings before taxes (EBT)	5.0	39.0	65.0
Taxes (40%)	(2.0)	(15.6)	(26.0)
Net income	$ 3.0	$ 23.4	$ 39.0
Earnings per share (EPS)—10,000 shares	$ 0.30	$ 2.34	$ 3.90
Expected EPS		$ 2.40	
Standard deviation of EPS (σ_{EPS})		$ 1.25	
Coefficient of variation (CV_{EPS})		0.52	

III. Debt/Assets = 50%

	Recession	Normal	Boom
EBIT	5.0	39.0	65.0
Interest = 0.12 × $100	(12.0)	(12.0)	(12.0)
Earnings before taxes (EBT)	(7.0)	27.0	53.0
Taxes (40%)	2.8	(10.8)	(21.2)
Net income	$(4.2)	$ 16.2	$ 31.8
Earnings per share (EPS)—5,000 shares	$(0.84)	$ 3.24	$ 6.36
Expected EPS		$ 3.36	
Standard deviation of EPS (σ_{EPS})		$ 2.50	
Coefficient of variation (CV_{EPS})		0.74	

shares = $100,000/$20 per share.[7] Thus, the number of shares outstanding will decrease from 10,000 to 5,000. At the same time, because the firm now has debt, it will have to pay interest, which, according to the schedule given in Table 14-2, will equal $12,000 = $100,000 × 0.12 per year. The $12,000 interest expense is a fixed cost—it is the same regardless of the level of sales. With a debt/assets ratio of 50 percent, the expected EPS is $3.36, which is $0.96 higher than if the firm uses no debt. Section III of Table 14-3 show that the EPS range is also greater; EPS can be as low as −$0.84 when the economy is poor or as high as $6.36 when the economy is booming. Thus, EPS has greater variability when the capital structure is 50 percent debt and 50 percent equity, which suggests that this capital structure is riskier than the capital structure of 100 percent equity financing. The standard deviation of EPS and the coefficient of variation computed for the capital structure with 50 percent debt are σ_{EPS} = $2.50 and CV_{EPS} = 0.74. As you can see, these computations support our suspicion that this capital structure is riskier than the capital structure shown in Section II of Table 14-3.

---

[7]We assume in this example that the firm could change its capital structure by repurchasing common stock at the current market value, which is $20 per share. However, if the firm attempts to purchase a large block of its stock, demand pressures might cause the market price to increase, in which case OptiCap would not be able to purchase 5,000 shares with the $100,000 that was raised with its debt issue. Also, we assume the flotation costs associated with the debt issue are negligible, so that OptiCap is able to use all $100,000 to repurchase stock. Clearly, the existence of flotation costs would mean OptiCap would have some amount less than $100,000 to repurchase stock. Neither of these assumptions affects the overall concept we are trying to provide with this illustration—only the numbers change.

FIGURE 14-1   OptiCap: Relationships among Expected EPS, Risk, and Financial Leverage

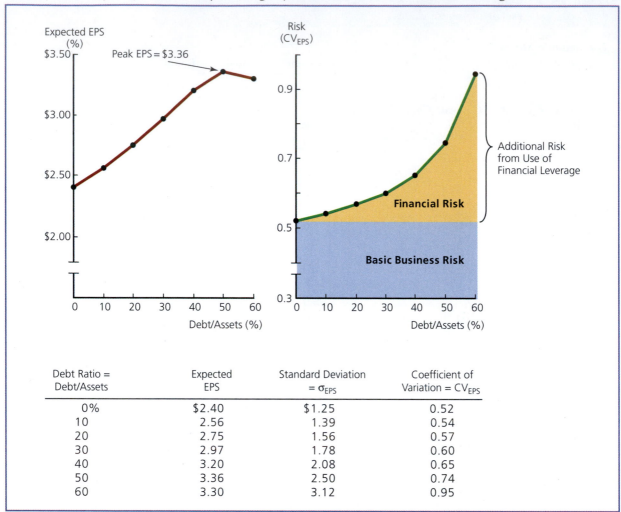

Debt Ratio = Debt/Assets	Expected EPS	Standard Deviation = σ_{EPS}	Coefficient of Variation = CV_{EPS}
0%	$2.40	$1.25	0.52
10	2.56	1.39	0.54
20	2.75	1.56	0.57
30	2.97	1.78	0.60
40	3.20	2.08	0.65
50	3.36	2.50	0.74
60	3.30	3.12	0.95

Figure 14-1 shows the relationships among expected EPS, risk, and financial leverage for OptiCap for the all-equity capital structure and the various capital structures given in Table 14-2. The tabular data in the lower section were calculated in the manner set forth in Table 14-3, and the graph plots these data. Here we see that expected EPS rises until the firm is financed with 50 percent debt. Interest charges rise, but this effect is more than offset by the declining number of shares outstanding as debt is substituted for equity. EPS peaks at a debt/assets ratio of 50 percent. Beyond this amount, interest rates rise so rapidly that EPS declines despite the smaller number of shares outstanding. The right panel of Figure 14-1 shows that risk, as measured by the coefficient of variation of EPS, rises continuously and at an increasing rate as debt is substituted for equity.

We see, then, that using leverage has both good and bad effects. Higher leverage increases expected earnings per share (in this example, until the firm is financed with 50 percent debt), but it also increases the firm's risk. Clearly, for OptiCap, the debt/assets ratio should not exceed 50 percent. But where in the range of 0 to 50 percent is the best debt/assets ratio for OptiCap? This issue is discussed in the following sections.

EBIT/EPS Examination of Financial Leverage

In the previous section, we assumed that OptiCap's EBIT had to be one of three possible values: $5,000, $39,000, or $65,000. Another way of evaluating alternative financing methods is to plot the EPS of each capital structure at many different levels of EBIT. Figure 14-2 shows such a graph for the two capital structures we considered for OptiCap in Table 14-3—that is, (1) 100 percent stock and (2) 50 percent stock and 50 percent debt. Notice that at low levels of EBIT, and hence low levels of sales, EPS is higher if OptiCap's capital structure includes only stock; at high levels of EBIT, however, EPS is higher with the capital structure that includes debt. Notice also that the "debt" line has a steeper slope, showing that EPS will increase more rapidly with increases in EBIT, and hence sales, if the firm uses debt. This relationship exists because the firm has a greater degree of financial leverage with the capital structure that includes 50 percent debt. In this

FIGURE 14-2   OptiCap's Earnings Per Share (EPS) for 100 Percent Stock Financing and for 50 Percent Debt Financing

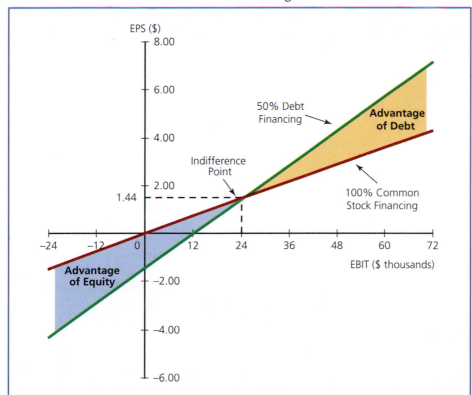

We can develop an equation to determine the EBIT level at which EPS is the same under different degrees of financial leverage:

$$EPS_1 = \frac{(EBIT - I_1)(1 - T)}{Shares_1} = \frac{(EBIT - I_2)(1 - T)}{Shares_2} = EPS_2$$

$$EBIT = \frac{(Shares_2)(I_1) - (Shares_1)(I_2)}{Shares_2 - Shares_1}$$

Here, EPS_1 and EPS_2 are the earnings per share at two debt levels; EBIT is the earnings before interest and taxes indifference point at which $EPS_1 = EPS_2$; I_1 and I_2 are the interest charges at the two debt levels; $Shares_1$ and $Shares_2$ are the shares outstanding at the two debt levels; and, T is the firm's marginal tax rate. In our example,

$$EBIT = \frac{(5,000)(0) - (10,000)($12,000)}{5,000 - 10,000} = \frac{-$120,000,000}{-5,000} = $24,000$$

case, the benefits of additional sales need not be shared with debtholders because debt payments are fixed; instead, any profits that remain after debtholders are paid "belong" to stockholders.

EPS indifference point
The level of sales at which EPS will be the same whether the firm uses debt or common stock financing.

The point on the graph where the two lines intersect is called the **EPS indifference point,** which is the level of sales where EPS is the same no matter which capital structure OptiCap uses. In Figure 14-2, the two lines cross where EBIT equals $24,000, which corresponds to sales equal to $162,500. If sales are below $162,500, EPS would be higher if the firm uses only common stock; above this level, the debt financing alternative would produce higher earnings per share. If we were certain that sales would never again fall below $162,500, bonds would be the preferred method of financing any increases in assets. We cannot know this for certain, however.

The Effect of Capital Structure on Stock Prices and the Cost of Capital

As we saw in Figure 14-1, OptiCap's expected EPS is maximized at a debt/assets ratio of 50 percent. Does this mean that OptiCap's optimal capital structure calls for 50 percent debt? The answer is a resounding No. *The optimal capital structure is the one that maximizes the price of the firm's stock, and this always calls for a debt/assets ratio that is lower than the one that maximizes expected EPS.* As we shall discover shortly, the primary reason this relationship exists is because P_0 reflects changes in risk that accompany changes in capital structures and affect cash flows long into the future, whereas EPS generally measures only the expectations for the near term. That is, current EPS generally does not capture future risk, whereas P_0 should be indicative of all future expectations. Our analysis to this point has, therefore, indicated that OptiCap's optimal capital structure should contain something less than 50 percent debt. The validity of this statement is demonstrated in Table 14-4, which develops OptiCap's estimated stock price and weighted average cost of capital at different debt/assets ratios. The debt cost and EPS data in Columns 2 and 3 were taken from Table 14-2 and Figure 14-1. The beta coefficients shown in Column 4 were estimated. Recall from Chapter 11 that a stock's beta measures its relative volatility compared with the volatility of an average stock. It has been demonstrated both theoretically and empirically that a firm's beta increases with its degree of financial leverage. The exact nature of this relationship for a given firm is difficult to estimate, but the values given in Column 4 show the approximate nature of the relationship for OptiCap.

If we assume that the risk-free rate of return, r_{RF}, is 4 percent and that the required return on an average stock, r_M, is 9 percent, we can use the CAPM equation to develop estimates of the required rates of return on equity, r_s, for OptiCap as shown in column 5. Here we see that r_s is 12 percent if no financial leverage is used, but r_s rises to 17 percent if the company finances with 60 percent debt, the maximum permitted by its corporate charter.

Figure 14-3 graphs OptiCap's required rate of return on equity, r_s, at different debt levels. The figure also shows the composition of OptiCap's required return: the risk-free rate of 4 percent and the premiums for both business risk and financial risk, which were discussed earlier in this chapter. As you can see from the graph, the business risk premium does not depend on the debt level. Instead, it remains constant at 8 percent, which is the difference between the 12 percent WACC when the firm is financed with 100 percent equity and the risk-free rate of 4 percent ($8\% = 12\% - 4\%$), at all debt levels. However, the financial risk premium

TABLE 14-4   Stock Price and Cost of Capital Estimates for OptiCap at Different Capital Structures

Debt/ Assets (1)	After-Tax Cost of Debt, r_{dT}[a] (2)	Expected EPS (and DPS[b]) (3)	Estimated Beta (β_s) (4)	Cost of Equity[c] $r_s = 4\% + 5\%(\beta_s)$ (5)	Estimated Stock Price[d] (6)	WACC[e] (7)
0%	—	$2.40	1.60	12.00%	$20.00	12.00%
10	4.8%	2.56	1.70	12.50	20.48	11.73
20	5.1%	2.75	1.80	13.00	21.12	11.42
30	5.4%	2.97	1.95	13.75	21.57	11.25
40	**6.0%**	**3.20**	**2.10**	**14.50**	**22.07**	**11.10**
50	7.2%	3.36	2.30	15.50	21.68	11.35
60	9.0%	3.30	2.60	17.00	19.14	12.20

[a]The after-tax cost of debt, r_{dT}, is the before-tax cost of debt, r_d, given in Table 14-2 adjusted for the taxes: $r_{dT} = r_d(1 - T)$. For example, at a capital structure of 40 percent debt, $r_{dT} = 10.0\%(1 - 0.4) = 6.0\%$.

[b]OptiCap pays out all earnings as dividends, so DPS = EPS.

[c]We assume that $r_{RF} = 4\%$ and $r_M = 9\%$, so $RP_M = 9\% - 4\% = 5\%$, and, at debt/assets equal to 40 percent, $r_s = 4\% + (5\% \times 2.10) = 14.5\%$. Other values of r_s are calculated similarly.

[d]Because all earnings are paid out as dividends, no retained earnings are available to be reinvested in the firm, and growth in EPS and DPS will be 0 ($g = 0$). Therefore, we use the zero growth model developed in Chapter 10 to compute the estimated stock price. To illustrate, at debt/assets equal to 40 percent, we have

$$\hat{P}_0 = \frac{DPS}{r_s} = \frac{\$3.20}{0.1450} = \$22.07$$

Other prices were computed similarly.

[e]The WACC, or weighted average cost of capital, is computed using the equation developed in Chapter 12. At a capital structure that has 40 percent debt, the computation is

$$WACC = w_d[r_d(1 - T)] + w_s r_s$$

$$= \left(\frac{Debt}{Assets}\right)r_{dT} + \left(1 - \frac{Debt}{Assets}\right)r_s = (0.40)6.00\% + (1 - 0.40)14.50\% = 11.10\%$$

The WACCs for the other capital structures were computed similarly.

varies depending on the debt level—the higher the debt level, the greater the premium for financial risk.

The zero growth stock valuation model developed in Chapter 10 is used in Table 14-4, along with the Column 3 values of dividends per share (DPS = EPS) and the Column 5 values of r_s, to develop the estimated stock prices shown in Column 6. Because OptiCap pays all earnings as dividends, its growth rate is 0 percent ($g = 0$), and thus we estimate the stock price by computing the present value of a constant dividend that will be paid forever (a perpetuity). Here we see that the expected stock price first rises with financial leverage, hits a peak of $22.07 at a debt/assets ratio of 40 percent, and then begins to decline. *Thus, OptiCap's optimal capital structure calls for 40 percent debt.*

Finally, Column 7 shows OptiCap's weighted average cost of capital (WACC), calculated as described in Chapter 12, at the different capital structures. If the company uses no debt, its capital is all equity, so WACC = r_s = 12%. As the firm begins to use lower cost debt, its weighted average cost of capital declines. As the debt/assets ratio increases, however, the costs of both debt and equity rise, and the increasing costs of the two components begin to offset the fact that larger amounts of the lower cost component are being used. At 40 percent debt, WACC hits a minimum at 11.1 percent, then it begins rising as the debt/assets ratio is increased.

FIGURE 14-3   OptiCap's Cost of Equity, r_s, at Different Capital Structures

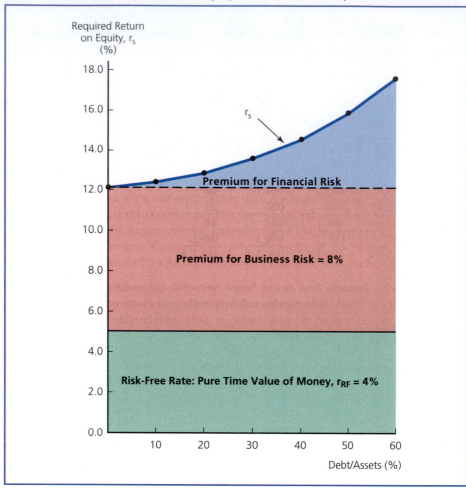

The EPS, cost of capital, and stock price data shown in Table 14-4 are plotted in Figure 14-4. As the graph shows, *the optimal capital structure calls for 40 percent debt and 60 percent equity. Management should set its target capital structure at these ratios, and if the existing ratios are off target, it should move toward the target when new security offerings are made.*

Self-Test Questions

Explain the following statement: "Using leverage has both good and bad effects."

What does the EPS indifference point show? What occurs at sales below this point? What occurs at sales above this point?

Is the optimal capital structure the one that maximizes expected EPS? Explain.

Explain the following statement: "At the optimal capital structure, a firm has minimized its cost of capital." Do stockholders want the firm to minimize its cost of capital?

FIGURE 14-4   Relationship between OptiCap's Capital Structure and Its Cost
of Capital and Stock Price

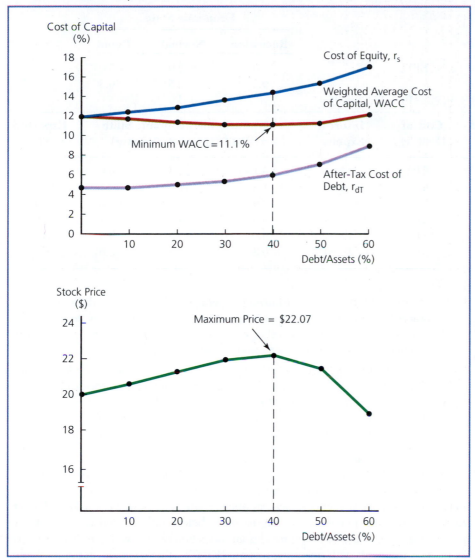

LIQUIDITY AND CAPITAL STRUCTURE

Some practical difficulties are associated with the type of analysis described in the previous section, including the following:

1. It is difficult to determine exactly how either P/E ratios or equity capitalization rates (r_s values) are affected by different degrees of financial leverage.

2. The managers might be more or less conservative than the average stockholder, so management might set a somewhat different target capital structure than the one that would maximize the stock price. The managers of a publicly owned firm never would admit this because, unless they owned voting control, they would be removed from office very quickly. However, in view of the uncertainties about what constitutes the value-maximizing capital structure, management could always say that the target capital structure employed is, in

TABLE 14-5 OptiCap's Times-Interest-Earned (TIE) Ratio at Different Capital Structures ($ thousand)

				Economic State			
				Recession	Normal	Boom	
Earnings before interest and taxes (EBIT)				$5.0	$39.0	$65.0	
Probability of occurrence				0.2	0.5	0.3	
Expected EBIT = 0.3($5.0) + 0.5($39.0) + 0.2($65.0) =					$34.0		

Debt/Assets Ratio	Amount of Debt	Cost of Debt, r_d	Interest Expense	TIE Ratio for Economic State = EBIT/(Interest Expense)			Expected TIE
10%	$ 20.0	8.0%	$ 1.60	3.1×	24.4×	40.6×	25.0×
20	40.0	8.5	3.40	1.5	11.5	19.1	11.8
30	60.0	9.0	5.40	0.9	7.2	12.0	7.4
40	80.0	10.0	8.00	0.6	4.9	8.1	5.0
50	100.0	12.0	12.00	0.4	3.3	5.4	3.3
60	120.0	15.0	18.00	0.3	2.2	3.6	2.2

its judgment, the value-maximizing structure, and it would be difficult to prove otherwise. Still, if management is far off target, especially on the low side, then chances are high that some other firm or management group will take over the company, increase its leverage, and thereby raise its value.

3. Managers of large firms, especially those that provide vital services such as electricity or communications, have a responsibility to provide continuous service. Therefore, they must refrain from using leverage to the point where the firms' long-run survivals are endangered. Long-run viability might conflict with short-run stock price maximization and capital cost minimization.[8]

For all these reasons, managers are concerned about the effects of financial leverage on the risk of bankruptcy, and an analysis of this factor is therefore an important input in all capital structure decisions. Accordingly, managers give considerable weight to financial strength indicators such as the **times-interest-earned (TIE) ratio,** which is computed by dividing earnings before interest and taxes (EBIT) by interest expense. The TIE ratio provides an indication of how well the firm can cover its interest payments with operating income (EBIT)—the lower this ratio, the higher the probability that a firm will default on its debt and be forced into bankruptcy.

Table 14-5 shows OptiCap's EBIT and sales under the three economic states described earlier and the expected TIE ratios at the different debt/assets ratios shown in Table 14-2. If the debt/assets ratio was only 10 percent, the expected TIE would be very high at 25 times, but the interest coverage ratio declines rapidly when the debt/ assets ratio is increased. Note, however, that these coverages are expected values at different debt/assets ratios; the actual TIE for any debt/assets ratio will be higher if EBIT exceeds the expected $34,000 level, but lower if EBIT falls below $34,000.

times-interest-earned (TIE) ratio
A ratio that measures the firm's ability to meet its annual interest obligations. It is calculated by dividing earnings before interest and taxes by interest charges.

---

[8]Recognizing this fact, most public service commissions that regulate utilities require these companies to obtain the commission's approval before issuing long-term securities, and Congress has empowered the SEC to supervise the capital structures of public utility holding companies. However, in addition to concern over the firm's safety, which suggests low debt ratios, both managers and regulators recognize a need to keep all costs as low as possible, including the cost of capital. Because a firm's capital structure affects its cost of capital, regulatory commissions and utility managers try to select capital structures that will minimize the cost of capital, subject to the constraint that the firm's financial flexibility not be endangered.

In general, with less debt, there is much lower probability of a TIE of less than 1.0, the level at which the firm is not earning enough to meet its required interest payments and thus is seriously exposed to the threat of bankruptcy.[9]

Self-Test Questions

Why do managers give considerable weight to the TIE ratio when they make capital structure decisions?

Why not just use the capital structure that maximizes the stock price?

CAPITAL STRUCTURE THEORY

Over the years, researchers have proposed numerous theories to explain what firms' capital structures should be and why firms have different capital structures. The general theories of capital structure have been developed along two main lines: (1) tax benefit/bankruptcy cost tradeoff theory and (2) signaling theory. These two theories are briefly discussed in this section.

Tradeoff Theory

Modern capital structure theory began in 1958, when Professors Franco Modigliani and Merton Miller (hereafter, together referred to as MM) published what is considered by many to be the most influential finance article ever written.[10] MM proved— under an extremely restrictive set of assumptions, including that there exist no personal income taxes, no brokerage costs, and no bankruptcy—that due to the tax deductibility of interest on corporate debt, a firm's value rises continuously as more debt is used, and hence its value will be maximized by financing almost entirely with debt.

Because several of the assumptions outlined by MM obviously were, and are, unrealistic, MM's position was only the beginning of capital structure research. Subsequent researchers, and MM themselves, extended the basic theory by relaxing the assumptions. Other researchers attempted to test the various theoretical models with actual data to see exactly how stock prices and capital costs are affected by capital structure. A summary of the theoretical and empirical research to date is expressed graphically in Figure 14-5. Here are the key points shown in the figure:

1. The fact that interest is a tax deductible expense makes corporate debt less expensive than common or preferred stock. In effect, the government pays, or subsidizes, part of the cost of debt capital; thus, using debt causes more of the firm's operating income (EBIT) to flow through to investors. So the more debt a company uses, the higher its value. Under the assumptions of the original MM paper, their analysis led to the conclusion that the firm's stock price will be maximized if it uses virtually 100 percent debt, and the line

---

[9]Note that cash flows can be sufficient to cover required interest payments even though the TIE is less than 1.0. Thus, at least for a while, a firm might be able to avoid bankruptcy even though its *operating income* is less than its interest charges. However, most debt contracts stipulate that firms must maintain the TIE ratio above some minimum level, say, 2.0 or 2.5, or else they cannot borrow any additional funds, which can severely constrain operations. Such potential constraints, as much as the threat of actual bankruptcy, limit the use of debt.

[10]Franco Modigliani and Merton H. Miller, "The Cost of Capital, Corporation Finance, and the Theory of Investment," *American Economic Review*, June 1958, 261–297, and "Corporate Income Taxes and the Cost of Capital," *American Economic Review*, June 1963, 433–443. Modigliani and Miller both won Nobel prizes for their work.

FIGURE 14-5   Effect of Leverage on the Value of OptiCap's Stock

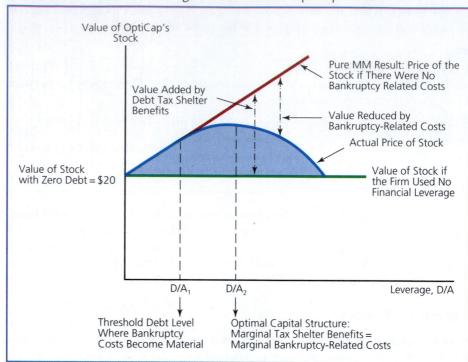

labeled "Pure MM Result" in Figure 14-5 expresses this relationship between stock prices and debt.

2. The MM assumptions do not hold in the real world. First, a firm pays higher interest rates as it uses greater amounts of debt. Second, expected tax rates fall at high debt levels, and this also reduces the expected value of the debt tax shelter. And, third, the probability of bankruptcy, which brings with it lawyers' fees and other costs, increases as the debt/assets ratio increases.

3. There is some threshold level of debt, labeled D/A_1 in Figure 14-5, below which the effects noted in Point 2 are immaterial. Beyond D/A_1, however, the bankruptcy-related costs, especially higher interest rates on new debt, become increasingly important, and they reduce the tax benefits of debt at an increasing rate. In the range from D/A_1 to D/A_2, bankruptcy-related costs reduce but do not completely offset the tax benefits of debt, so the firm's stock price rises (but at a decreasing rate) as the debt/assets ratio increases. However, beyond D/A_2, bankruptcy-related costs exceed the tax benefits, so beyond this point, increasing the debt/assets ratio lowers the value of the stock. Therefore, *D/A_2 is the optimal capital structure.*

4. Both theory and empirical evidence support the preceding discussion. However, researchers have not been able to identify points D/A_1 and D/A_2 precisely, so the graphs shown in Figures 14-4 and 14-5 must be taken as approximations, not as precisely defined functions.

Another perplexing aspect of capital structure theory as expressed in Figure 14-5 is the fact that many large, successful firms, such as Microsoft, use far less debt than the theory suggests. This point led to the development of signaling theory, which is discussed next.

Signaling Theory

MM assumed that investors have the same information about a firm's prospects as its managers—this is called **symmetric information** because both those who are inside the firm (managers and employees) and those who are outside the firm (investors) have identical information. However, we know that in fact managers generally have better information about their firms than do outside investors. This is called **asymmetric information,** and it has an important effect on decisions to use either debt or equity to finance capital projects. To see why, consider two situations, one in which the company's managers know that its prospects are extremely favorable (Firm F) and one in which the managers know that the future looks very unfavorable (Firm U).

Suppose, for example, that Firm F's research and development labs have just discovered a cure for the common cold, but the product is not patentable. Firm F's managers want to keep the new product a secret for as long as possible to delay competitors' entry into the market. New plants and distribution facilities must be built to exploit the new product, so capital must be raised. How should Firm F's management raise the needed capital? If the firm sells stock, then when profits from the new product start flowing in, the price of the stock will rise sharply and the purchasers of the new stock will have made a bonanza. The current stockholders (including the managers) also will do well, but not as well as they would have if the company had not sold stock before the price increased, because then they would not have had to share the benefits of the new product with the new stockholders. *Therefore, one would expect a firm with very favorable prospects to try to avoid selling stock and, rather, to raise any required new capital by other means, including using debt beyond the normal target capital structure.*[11]

Now, let's consider Firm U. Suppose its managers have information that new orders are off sharply because a competitor has installed new technology that has improved its products' quality. Firm U must upgrade its own facilities at a high cost, just to maintain its existing sales level. As a result, its return on investment will fall (but not by as much as if it took no action, which would lead to a 100 percent loss through bankruptcy). How should Firm U raise the needed capital? Here the situation is just the reverse of that facing Firm F, which did not want to sell stock so as to avoid having to share the benefits of future developments with new stockholders. *A firm with unfavorable prospects would want to sell stock, which would mean bringing in new investors to share the losses!*[12]

The conclusions from this example are that firms with extremely bright prospects prefer not to finance through new stock offerings, whereas firms with poor prospects do like to finance with outside equity. How would you, as an investor, react to these conclusions? You ought to say, "If I see that a company plans to issue new stock, this should worry me because I know that management would not want to issue stock if future prospects looked good, but it would want to issue stock if things looked bad. Therefore, I should lower my estimate of the firm's value, other things held constant, if I read an announcement of a new stock offering." Of course, the negative reaction would be stronger if the stock sale was by a large, established company such as General Electric or IBM, which surely would have many financing options, than if it were by a small company such as USR Industries. For USR, a stock

symmetric information
The situation in which investors and managers have identical information about the firm's prospects.

asymmetric information
The situation in which managers have different (better) information about their firm's prospects than do outside investors.

---

[11]It would be illegal for Firm F's managers to purchase more shares on the basis of their inside knowledge of the new product. They could be sent to jail if they did.

[12]Of course, Firm U would have to make certain disclosures when it offered new shares to the public, but it might be able to meet the legal requirements without fully disclosing management's worst fears.

sale might mean truly extraordinary investment opportunities that were so large that they just could not be financed without a stock sale.

If you gave the preceding answer, your views are consistent with those of many sophisticated portfolio managers of institutions such as Morgan Guaranty Trust. *Simply stated, then, the announcement of a stock offering by a mature firm that seems to have multiple financing alternatives is taken as a* **signal** *that the firm's prospects as seen by its management are not bright.* This, in turn, suggests that when a mature firm announces a new stock offering, the price of its stock should decline. Empirical studies have shown that this situation does indeed exist.

What are the implications of all this for capital structure decisions? The answer is that firms should, in normal times, maintain a **reserve borrowing capacity** that can be used in the event that some especially good investment opportunities come along. *This means that firms should generally use less debt than would be suggested by the tax benefit/bankruptcy cost tradeoff expressed in Figure 14-5.*

signal
An action taken by a firm's management that provides clues to investors about how management views the firm's prospects.

reserve borrowing capacity
The ability to borrow money at a reasonable cost when good investment opportunities arise. Firms often use less debt than the optimal capital structure to ensure that they can obtain debt capital later if necessary.

If you find our discussion of capital structure theory somewhat inexact, you are not alone. In truth, no one knows how to identify precisely the optimal capital structure for a firm or how to measure precisely the effect of the firm's capital structure on either its value or its cost of capital. In real life, capital structure decisions must be made more on the basis of judgment than numerical analysis. Nevertheless, an understanding of the theoretical issues as presented here is essential to making sound judgments on capital structure issues.

Self-Test Questions

What does it mean when one hears, "The MM capital structure theory involves a tradeoff between the tax benefits of debt and costs associated with actual or potential bankruptcy"?

Explain how asymmetric information and signals affect capital structure decisions.

What is meant by reserve borrowing capacity, and why is it important for firms?

VARIATIONS IN CAPITAL STRUCTURES AMONG FIRMS

As might be expected, wide variations in the use of financial leverage occur both across industries and among the individual firms in each industry. Table 14-6 illustrates differences for selected industries; the ranking is in descending order of common equity ratios, as shown in Column 1.

Drug and biotechnology companies do not use much debt (their common equity ratios are high). The uncertainties inherent in industries that are cyclical, oriented toward research, or subject to huge product liability suits normally render the heavy use of debt unwise. On the other hand, utilities traditionally have used large amounts of debt, particularly long-term debt. Their fixed assets make good security for mortgage bonds, and their relatively stable sales (operations) make it safe for them to carry more debt than would be true for firms with more business risk.

Particular attention should be given to the times-interest-earned (TIE) ratio because it gives a measure of how safe the debt is and how vulnerable the company is to

TABLE 14-6 Capital Structure Percentages, 2007: Five Industries Ranked by Common Equity Ratios[a]

Industry	Common Equity (1)	Preferred Stock (2)	Total Debt (3)	Long-Term Debt (4)	Short-Term Debt (5)	Times-Interest-Earned Ratio (6)	Return on Equity[b] (7)
Pharmaceuticals	79.8%	0.2%	20.0%	12.0%	8.0%	7.1×	−12.4%
Biotechnology	66.8	1.0	32.2	15.3	16.9	8.2	−10.3
Textiles	54.0	1.1	44.9	23.2	21.7	5.4	9.3
Restaurants	50.8	0.6	48.6	28.9	19.7	12.8	6.0
Utilities	27.2	0.6	72.2	55.0	17.2	2.9	9.4
Composite[c]	47.0	0.8	52.2	29.3	22.9	5.2	5.1

[a]These ratios are based on accounting, or book values. Stated on a market value basis, the equity percentages would be higher because most stocks sell at prices that are much higher than their book values.

[b]A negative ROE results because uncertain economic conditions in 2007 resulted in operating losses for many firms in the industry.

[c]These composite ratios include all industries, not just those listed above, except financial and professional service industries.

Source: *Standard & Poor's Research Insight*, 2008.

financial distress. Generally, the least leveraged industries, such as the drug and biotechnology industries, have the highest coverage ratios, whereas the utility industry, which finances heavily with debt, has a low average coverage ratio. Table 14-6 shows that companies that manufacture drugs and biotechnology research have high average TIEs, whereas utilities have a very low TIE.

Wide variations in capital structures also exist among firms within given industries. For example, although the average pharmaceutical firm had a capital structure consisting of approximately 20 percent debt in 2007, Genentech had approximately 25 percent debt in its capital structure and GlaxoSmithKline had greater than 70 percent debt in its capital structure. As you can see, factors unique to individual firms, including managerial attitudes, play an important role in setting target capital structures.

Self-Test Question

Why do wide variations in the use of financial leverage occur both across industries and among the individual firms in each industry?

DIVIDEND POLICY

Dividends are the cash payments, or distributions, made to stockholders from the firm's earnings, whether those earnings were generated in the current period or in previous periods. Consequently, a firm's *dividend policy* involves the decision to pay out earnings or to retain them for reinvestment in the firm. As a result, dividend policy decisions directly affect two aspects of the firm: (1) capital structure—all else equal, retaining earnings rather than paying out dividends increases common equity relative to debt and (2) cost of capital—financing with retained earnings, or internal equity, is less expensive than issuing new common equity.

In this section, we examine how dividend policy can impact the value of the firm.

dividends
Distributions made to stockholders from the firm's earnings, whether those earnings were generated in the current period or in previous periods.

Dividend Policy and Stock Value

How do dividend policy decisions affect a firm's stock price? Researchers have studied this question extensively for many years, but have yet to reach any definitive conclusions. On the one hand, some suggest that dividend policy is *irrelevant*. These researchers argue that a firm's value should be determined by the basic earning power and business risk of the firm, in which case value depends only on the income (cash) produced, not on how the income is split between dividends and retained earnings (and hence growth). Proponents of this line of reasoning, which is called the **dividend irrelevance theory,** would contend that investors care *only* about the *total returns* received, not whether they receive those returns in the form of dividends or capital gains. Thus, *if the dividend irrelevance theory is correct, there exists no* **optimal dividend policy** *because dividend policy does not affect the value of the firm.*[13]

On the other hand, it is quite possible that investors prefer one dividend policy over another; if so, a firm's dividend policy is *relevant*. For example, it has been argued that investors prefer to receive dividends "today" because current dividend payments are more certain than the future capital gains that *might* result from investing retained earnings in growth opportunities. Consequently, r_s should decrease as the dividend payout is increased.[14]

Another factor that might cause investors to prefer a particular dividend policy is the tax effect of dividend receipts. Investors must pay taxes when dividends and capital gains are received. Thus, depending on his or her tax situation, an investor might prefer either a payout of current earnings as dividends, which would be taxed in the current period, or capital gains associated with growth in stock value, which would be taxed when the stock is sold, perhaps many years in the future. Investors who prefer to delay the effects of taxes would be willing to pay more for low-payout companies than for otherwise similar high-payout companies, and vice versa.

Those who believe that the firm's dividend policy is relevant are proponents of the **dividend relevance theory,** which asserts that dividend policy can affect the value of a firm through investors' preferences.

dividend irrelevance theory
The theory that a firm's dividend policy has no effect on either its value or its cost of capital.

optimal dividend policy
The dividend policy that strikes a balance between current dividends and future growth and maximizes the firm's stock price.

dividend relevance theory
The value of a firm is affected by its dividend policy, with the optimal dividend policy being the one that maximizes the firm's value.

Self-Test Questions

Differentiate between the dividend irrelevance theory and the dividend relevance theory.

How might taxes affect investors' preferences concerning the receipt of dividends and capital gains?

INVESTORS AND DIVIDEND POLICY

Although researchers cannot tell corporate decision makers precisely how dividend policy affects stock prices and capital costs, their findings have generated some thoughts concerning investors' reactions to dividend policy changes and why

---

[13]The principal proponents of the *dividend irrelevance theory* are Miller and Modigliani (MM), who outlined their theory in "Dividend Policy, Growth, and the Valuation of Shares," *Journal of Business,* October 1961, 411–433. The assumptions that MM made to develop their dividend irrelevance theory are similar to those that they introduced in their capital structure theory, which was mentioned earlier in the chapter. Such assumptions are made so as to enable them to develop a manageable theory.

[14]Myron J. Gordon, "Optimal Investment and Financing Policy," *Journal of Finance,* May 1963, 264–272, and John Lintner, "Dividends, Earnings, Leverage, Stock Prices, and the Supply of Capital to Corporations," *Review of Economics and Statistics,* August 1962, 243–269.

firms have particular dividend policies. Three of these views are discussed in this section.

Information Content (Signaling)

As we discussed in Chapter 10, the value of a stock is based on the present value of the cash flows, or the dividends, that investors expect to receive during the life of the firm. Thus, if investors expect a company's dividend to increase by 5 percent per year, and if the dividend actually increases by 5 percent, the stock price generally will not change significantly on the day that the dividend increase is announced. In Wall Street parlance, such a dividend increase would be "discounted," or *anticipated*, by the market. If investors expect a 5 percent increase, but the company actually increases the dividend by 25 percent, this unexpected event ("good news") generally would be accompanied by an increase in the price of the stock. Conversely, a less-than-expected dividend increase, or a reduction ("bad news"), generally would result in a price decline.

It is a well-known fact that corporations are extremely reluctant to cut dividends and, therefore, *managers do not raise dividends unless they anticipate higher, or at least stable, earnings in the future to sustain the higher dividends.* For this reason, a larger-than-expected dividend increase is taken by investors as a "signal" that the firm's management forecasts improved future earnings, whereas a dividend reduction signals a forecast of poor earnings. It can be argued, therefore, that investors' reactions to changes in dividend payments do not show that investors prefer dividends to retained earnings; rather, the stock price changes simply indicate that important information is contained in dividend announcements. In effect, dividend announcements provide investors with information previously known only to management. This theory is referred to as the **information content,** or **signaling, hypothesis.**

Clientele Effect

It is very possible that a firm might set a particular dividend payout policy, which then attracts a *clientele* consisting of those investors who like that policy. For example, some stockholders, such as retired individuals, prefer current income to future capital gains, so they invest in firms that pay out higher percentages of their earnings. Other stockholders have no need for current investment income, so they favor firms with low payout ratios. In essence, a **clientele effect** might exist if stockholders are attracted to companies because they have particular dividend policies. That is, those investors who desire current investment income can purchase shares in high-dividend-payout firms, whereas those who do not need current cash income can invest in low-payout firms. Thus, we would expect the stock price of a firm to change if it changes its dividend policy because investors will adjust their portfolios to include firms with the desired dividend policy.

Free Cash Flow Hypothesis

If the financial manager intends to *maximize the value of the firm,* then investors should prefer that a firm *pay dividends only after all acceptable capital budgeting opportunities have been purchased.* We know that acceptable capital budgeting projects increase the value of the firm. We also know that, because flotation costs are incurred when a firm issues new stock, it costs a firm more to raise funds by issuing new common equity than by using retained earnings. To maximize its value, where possible, a firm should use retained earnings rather than issue new common stock to finance its capital budgeting projects. As a result, to maximize its value,

information content (signaling) hypothesis The theory that investors regard dividend changes as signals of management's earnings forecasts.

clientele effect The tendency of a firm to attract the type of investor who likes its dividend policy.

free cash flow hypothesis
All else equal, firms that pay dividends from cash flows that cannot be re-invested in positive net present value projects, which are termed *free cash flows,* have higher values than firms that retain free cash flows.

a firm should pay dividends only when *free cash flows* in excess of capital budgeting needs exist. According to the **free cash flow hypothesis,** therefore, the firm should only pay dividends out of earnings that cannot be reinvested in capital budgeting projects that earn rates that are greater than the investors' required rate of return, r_s.

The free cash flow hypothesis might help to explain why investors react differently to identical dividend changes made by similar firms. For example, a firm's stock price will not change dramatically if it reduces its dividend for the purposes of investing in capital budgeting projects with positive net present values. On the other hand, a company that reduces its dividend simply to increase free cash flows will experience a significant decline in the market value of its stock because the dividend reduction is not in the best interests of the stockholders. Therefore, the free cash flow hypothesis suggests that the dividend policy employed by a firm can provide information about its behavior with respect to wealth maximization.

 Self-Test Question
Define the *information content hypothesis, the clientele effect,* and *the free cash flow hypothesis,* and explain how each affects dividend policy.

DIVIDEND POLICY IN PRACTICE

Although no one has been able to develop a formula that can be used to determine precisely how a given dividend policy will affect a firm's stock price, management still must establish a dividend policy. This section discusses several alternative policies as well as experiences we observe in practice.

Type of Dividend Payments

The dollar amounts of dividends paid by firms follow a variety of patterns. In general, firms pay dividends using one of the four payout policies discussed in this section.

Residual Dividend Policy

residual dividend policy
A policy in which the dividend paid is set equal to the actual earnings minus the amount of re-tained earnings necessary to finance the firm's op-timal capital budget.

The **residual dividend policy** states that dividends should be paid only if more earnings are available than are needed to support the firm's optimal capital budget—that is, dividends should be paid only out of "leftover," or "residual," earnings. The basis of the residual policy is the fact that *investors prefer to have the firm retain and reinvest earnings rather than pay them out in dividends if the rate of return that the firm can earn on reinvested earnings exceeds the rate that investors, on average, can themselves earn on other investments of comparable risk.* According to the residual dividend policy, a firm that has to issue new common stock to finance capital budgeting needs does not have residual earnings, and these dividends will be $0. Also, because both the earnings level and the capital budgeting needs of a firm vary from year to year, strict adherence to the residual dividend policy would result in dividend variability. Following the residual dividend policy would be optimal only if investors were not bothered by fluctuating dividends.

Stable, Predictable Dividends

In the past, many firms set a specific annual dollar dividend per share and then maintained it, increasing the annual dividend only if it seemed clear that future

FIGURE 14-6   United Parcel Service (UPS): Earnings Per Share (EPS) and Dividends Per Share (DPS), 1991–2008

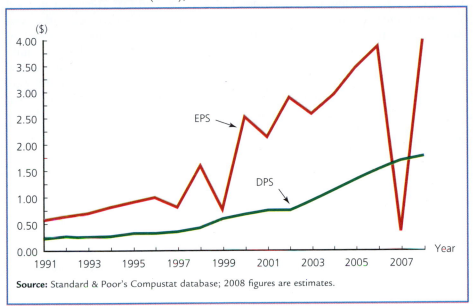

Source: Standard & Poor's Compustat database; 2008 figures are estimates.

earnings would be sufficient to maintain the new dividend. A corollary of that policy was the following rule: *never reduce the annual dividend.*

Figure 14-6 illustrates a fairly typical dividend policy, that of United Parcel Service (UPS). As you can see, UPS's earnings per share (EPS) fluctuated fairly substantially from 1996 through 2008, but its dividends steadily increased during this same period. UPS follows the **stable, predictable dividend policy;** its annual dividend has either stayed the same or increased each year since 1970.

There are two good reasons for paying stable, predictable dividends rather than following the residual dividend policy. First, given the existence of the information content (signaling) idea, a fluctuating payment policy would lead to greater uncertainty—and hence to a higher r_s and a lower stock price—than would exist under a stable policy. Second, many stockholders use dividends for current consumption, and they would be put to trouble and expense if they had to sell part of their shares to obtain cash if the company cut the dividend.

As a rule, *stable predictable dividends imply more certainty than variable dividends, and thus a lower r_s and a higher firm value.* Thus, most firms follow this dividend policy because they want investors to perceive stability in dividend payments.

Constant Payout Ratio

It would be possible for a firm to pay out a constant *percentage* of its earnings, but because earnings surely will fluctuate, this policy would mean that the dollar amount of dividends would vary. For example, if UPS had followed the policy of paying a constant percentage of EPS, say, 40 percent, the dividends per share paid since 1991 would have fluctuated exactly the same as the EPS graph shown in Figure 14-6, which means that the company would have had to cut its dividend in several years. Therefore, with the **constant payout ratio** dividend policy, if earnings fluctuate, investors have much greater uncertainty concerning the expected dividends each year, and chances are that r_s would also be greater, hence the firm's stock price would be lower.

stable, predictable dividends
Payment of a specific dollar dividend each year, or periodically increasing the dividend at a constant rate; the annual dollar dividend is relatively predictable for investors.

constant payout ratio
Payment of a constant *percentage* of earnings as dividends each year.

Low Regular Dividend Plus Extras

A policy of paying a low regular dividend plus a year-end extra payment in good years represents a compromise between a stable, predictable dividend and a constant payout ratio. Such a policy gives the firm flexibility, yet investors can count on receiving at least a minimum dividend. If a firm's earnings and cash flows are quite volatile, this policy might be a good choice. The directors can set a relatively low regular dividend—low enough so that it can be maintained even in low-profit years or in years when a considerable amount of retained earnings is needed—and then supplement it with an **extra dividend** in years when excess funds are available.

extra dividend
A supplemental dividend paid in years when the firm does well and excess funds are available for distribution.

Payment Procedures

Dividends normally are paid semiannually or quarterly, and an announcement, or declaration, of the dividend is made prior to its payment. For example, on May 8, 2008, the board of directors of United Parcel Service (UPS) declared a $0.45 quarterly common stock dividend. Earlier in the year the board had indicated that it anticipated the annual dividend to be $1.80. As a result, UPS's stockholders were not surprised when the $0.45 quarterly dividend was announced, but they would have been *shocked* if the dividend had been decreased because UPS had not decreased its dividend payment in nearly 40 years (in most years, the dividend increased).

When UPS *declared* the quarterly dividend that was to be paid on June 3, 2008, it issued the following statement:[15]

> **UPS BOARD DECLARES DIVIDEND**
>
> WILMINGTON, Del., May 8, 2008—The UPS (NYSE:UPS) Board of Directors today declared a regular quarterly dividend of $0.45 per-share on all outstanding Class A and Class B shares.
>
> The dividend is payable June 3, 2008, to shareholders of record on May 19, 2008. UPS has either increased or maintained its dividend every year for more than three decades.

The three dates mentioned in this announcement are important to current stockholders. These dates, as well as the ex-dividend date, are defined as follows:

declaration date
The date on which a firm's board of directors issues a statement declaring a dividend.

1. *Declaration date*. On the **declaration date** (May 8, 2008, in UPS's case), the board of directors meets and declares the regular dividend. For accounting purposes, the dividend becomes an actual liability on the declaration date. On UPS's balance sheet, the amount equal to $0.45 × (Number of shares outstanding) would appear as a current liability, and retained earnings would be reduced by a like amount.

holder-of-record date (date of record)
The date on which the company opens the ownership books to determine who will receive the dividend. The stockholders of record on this date receive the dividend.

2. *Holder-of-record date*. At the close of business on the **holder-of-record date, or date of record,** the company closes its stock transfer books and produces a list of shareholders as of that date; these are the stockholders who will receive the next dividend payment. Thus, if UPS was notified of the sale and transfer of shares of stock before 5 p.m. on Monday, May 19, 2008, then the new owner would receive the dividend. However, if notification was received after May 19, the previous owner of the stock would receive the dividend check because his or her name would appear on the company's ownership records.

3. *Ex-dividend date*. The securities industry has established a convention of declaring that the right to the dividend remains with the stock until two

---

[15]UPS posted the announcement as shown here on its Web site at http://investor.shareholder.com/ups/.

business days prior to the holder-of-record date. This policy is meant to ensure the company is notified of an ownership transfer in time to record the new owner and thus pay the dividend to him or her. The date when the right to receive the next dividend payment no longer goes with the stock—new purchasers will not receive the next dividend—is called the **ex-dividend date.** In the case of UPS, the ex-dividend date was Thursday, May 15, 2008, so any investor who purchased the stock on or after that date would not receive the next dividend payment associated with the stock. All else being equal, we would expect the price of UPS's stock to drop on the ex-dividend date by approximately the amount of the next dividend. Thus, assuming no other price fluctuations, the price at which UPS's stock opened on Thursday, May 15, 2008, should have been about $0.45 less than its price at the close of business on Wednesday, May 14.

4. *Payment date.* On June 3, 2008—the **payment date**—UPS will pay dividends to the holders of record. Recently, many firms have started paying dividends electronically.

ex-dividend date
The date on which the right to the next dividend no longer accompanies a stock. It is two working days prior to the holder-of-record date.

payment date
The date on which a firm actually mails dividend checks.

Dividend Reinvestment Plans (DRIPs)

Today, most large companies offer **dividend reinvestment plans (DRIPs),** whereby stockholders can automatically reinvest dividends they receive to purchase more stock of the paying corporation. As you will see, some DRIPs (referred to as "drips") directly affect the capital structures of firms that offer them.

dividend reinvestment plan (DRIP)
A plan that enables a stockholder to automatically reinvest dividends received back into the stock of the paying firm.

Two types of DRIPs exist:

1. *DRIP plans that involve "old" stock that already is outstanding.* Under the "old stock" type of plan, a bank, acting as trustee, takes the total funds available for reinvestment, purchases the corporation's stock on the open market, and allocates the shares purchased to the participating stockholders' accounts on a pro rata basis. This type of DRIP does not affect the capital structure of the firm because already outstanding stock is purchased from existing stockholders. The transaction costs of buying shares (brokerage costs) are low because of volume purchases, so these plans benefit small stockholders who do not need cash dividends for current consumption.

2. *DRIP plans that involve newly issued stock.* The "new stock" type of DRIP provides for dividends to be invested in newly issued stock, so these plans actually raise new capital for the firm. Many companies have used such plans to raise substantial amounts of *new* equity capital. Such DRIPs directly affect the capital structure of the firm: common equity is "issued," and the firm receives funds to invest in capital projects. No fees are charged to stockholders, and many companies offer stocks at discounts below the actual market prices. The companies absorb these costs, which represent a tradeoff against the flotation costs that would have been incurred had they sold stock through investment bankers rather than through the dividend reinvestment plans.[16]

Under either plan, the stockholder must pay income taxes on the amount of the cash dividend even though it is reinvested in stock.

---

[16]One interesting aspect of DRIPs is that they have forced corporations to reexamine their basic dividend policies. A high participation rate in a DRIP suggests that stockholders might be better off if the firm simply reduced cash dividends, as it would save stockholders some personal income taxes.

Self-Test Questions

Explain the logic of the residual dividend policy.

Describe the stable, predictable dividend policy and give two reasons why a firm might follow such a policy.

Describe the low-regular-dividend-plus-extras policy and explain why a firm might follow such a policy.

Describe the constant payout ratio dividend policy. Why is this policy probably not as popular as a stable, predictable dividend policy?

Why is the ex-dividend date important to investors?

Differentiate between the two types of dividend reinvestment plans.

FACTORS INFLUENCING DIVIDEND POLICY

In addition to management's belief concerning which dividend theory is most appropriate for a firm, a number of other factors must be considered when a particular dividend policy is chosen. The factors that firms take into account can be grouped into four broad categories:

Constraints on Dividend Payments

The amount of dividends that a firm can pay might be limited by three constraints:

1. Debt contract restrictions, which often stipulate that no dividends can be paid unless certain financial measures, such as the TIE ratio, exceed stated minimums.

2. The fact that dividend payments cannot exceed the balance sheet item "retained earnings." This restriction, which is known as the *impairment of capital rule*, is designed to protect creditors by prohibiting the company from distributing assets to stockholders before debtholders are paid.

3. Cash availability because cash dividends can be paid only with cash.[17]

Investment Opportunities

Firms that have large numbers of acceptable capital budgeting projects generally have low dividend payout ratios, and vice versa. If a firm can accelerate or postpone projects (that is, if it has flexibility), then it can adhere more closely to a target dividend policy.

Alternative Sources of Capital

When a firm needs to finance a given level of investment and its flotation costs are high, the cost of issuing new stock, r_e, will greatly exceed the cost of retained

---

[17]Another factor that some managers might consider is the restriction imposed by the IRS on improperly accumulated retained earnings. If the IRS can demonstrate that a firm's dividend payout ratio is being held down deliberately to help its stockholders avoid personal taxes, the firm is subject to heavy tax penalties. This factor is generally relevant only to privately owned firms.

earnings, r_s, making it better to set a low payout ratio and to finance through earnings retention rather than through the sale of new common stock. Also, if the firm can adjust its debt/assets ratio without raising its capital costs sharply, it can maintain a stable dollar dividend—even if earnings fluctuate—by using a variable debt/assets ratio.

Still another factor considered by management when making financing decisions is ownership dilution. If management is concerned about maintaining control, it might be reluctant to sell new stock, so the company might retain more earnings than it otherwise would.

Effects of Dividend Policy on r_s

The effects of dividend policy on r_s depend on four major factors:

1. Stockholders' desire for current versus future income
2. The perceived riskiness of dividends versus capital gains
3. The tax effects of capital gains versus dividends (rates and timing)
4. The information content of dividends (signaling)

Because we discussed each of these factors earlier, we need merely note here that the importance of each factor in terms of its effect on r_s varies from firm to firm, depending on the makeup of the individual organization's current and possible future stockholders.

It should be apparent from our discussions that dividend policy decisions truly are exercises in informed judgment, not decisions that can be quantified precisely. Even so, to make rational dividend decisions, financial managers must consider all of the points discussed in the preceding sections.

Self-Test Questions

Identify the four factors that affect dividend policy.

What constraints affect dividend policy?

How do investment opportunities affect dividend policy?

How does the availability and cost of outside capital affect dividend policy?

STOCK DIVIDENDS AND STOCK SPLITS

In this section, we discuss stock splits and stock dividends and their effects on capital structure and dividend policy decisions. Both actions are used to adjust the market price of a firm's stock, because, although little empirical evidence exists to support the contention, there is a widespread belief in financial circles that an *optimal, or psychological, price range* exists for stocks.

Stock Splits

If it is believed that the best price range for a firm's stock is from $30 to $80, then management probably would declare a 2-for-1 **stock split** when the price of the stock rises to greater than $80 per share. With a 2-for-1 split, each share of stock that

stock split
An action taken by a firm to increase the number of shares outstanding, such as doubling the number of shares outstanding by giving each stockholder two new shares for each one formerly held.

currently exists is replaced with two *new* shares. In this way, the number of shares outstanding is doubled, and all per-share values—including EPS, DPS, and market value—are halved. All else equal, after a stock split each stockholder would have more shares, but each share would be worth less than the per-share, pre-split value. If the post-split price were $40, stockholders would be *exactly as well off* as they were before the split because they would have twice as many shares at half the price as before the split. If the price of the stock stabilized above $40, however, stockholders would be better off.

Stock splits can be of any size. For example, the stock could be split 2-for-1, 3-for-1, or in any other way.[18]

Stock Dividends

stock dividend
A dividend paid in the form of additional shares of stock rather than in cash.

Stock dividends are similar to stock splits in that they "divide the pie into smaller slices" without affecting the fundamental position of the current stockholders. On a 5 percent stock dividend, the holder of 100 shares would receive an additional five shares (5 percent); on a 20 percent stock dividend, the same holder would receive 20 new shares; and so on. Again, the total number of shares is increased, so EPS, DPS, and the market price per share all decline, but the *total* value of all of the shares does not change.

If a firm wants to reduce the price of its stock, should it use a stock split or a stock dividend? Stock splits generally are used after a sharp price run-up to produce a large price reduction. Stock dividends typically are used on a regular annual basis to keep the stock price more or less constrained. For example, if a firm's earnings and dividends were growing at a rate of 10 percent per year, its stock price would tend to go up at approximately the same rate, and it would soon be outside the desired trading range. A 10 percent annual stock dividend would help maintain the stock price within the optimal trading range.

Effects of Stock Splits and Stock Dividends

Neither stock splits nor stock dividends affect the firm's capital structure—that is, the proportions of debt financing and equity financing do not change as a result of these actions. Further, stock splits and stock dividends have virtually identical economic effects—none.

Several empirical studies have examined the effects of stock splits and stock dividends on stock prices.[19] They suggest that investors see stock splits and stock dividends for what they are—*simply additional pieces of paper*. If stock dividends and splits are accompanied by higher earnings and higher cash dividends, then investors will bid up the price of the stock. If stock dividends are not accompanied by increases in earnings and cash dividends, however, the dilution of EPS and DPS

---

[18]Reverse splits, which reduce the shares outstanding, can be used as well. For example, a company whose stock sells for $5 per share might employ a 1-for-5 reverse split, exchanging one new share for five old ones and raising the value of the shares to about $25, which is within the optimal range. On June 16, 2003, for example, Priceline.com initiated a 1-for-6 reverse split to avoid being delisted from Nasdaq.

[19]See C. A. Barker, "Evaluation of Stock Dividends," *Harvard Business Review,* July–August 1958, 99–114. Barker's study has been replicated several times in recent years, and his results are still valid—they have withstood the test of time. Another excellent study, using an entirely different methodology, reached similar conclusions; see Eugene F. Fama, Lawrence Fisher, Michael C. Jensen, and Richard Roll, "The Adjustment of Stock Prices to New Information," *International Economic Review,* February 1969, 1–21.

causes the per-share price of the stock to drop by the same percentage as the stock dividend. Thus, the fundamental determinants of price are the underlying earnings and cash dividends per share, and stock splits and stock dividends merely cut the pie into thinner slices.

Self-Test Question

What is the rationale for a stock split? How do stock splits and stock dividends affect stock prices?

CAPITAL STRUCTURES AND DIVIDEND POLICIES AROUND THE WORLD

As you might expect, when we examine the capital structures of companies around the world we find wide variations. Table 14-7 illustrates differences for selected countries; the ranking is in descending order of common equity ratios, as shown in the column labeled Equity. As you can see, companies in Italy and Japan use a much greater proportion of debt than companies in the United States or Canada, and companies in the United Kingdom use the lowest proportion of debt of all the countries listed. Of course, different countries employ somewhat different accounting conventions, which make comparisons difficult. Even after adjusting for accounting differences, researchers still find that Italian and Japanese firms use considerably more financial leverage than their U.S. and Canadian counterparts. Note that the gap among the countries has narrowed somewhat during the past few decades. In the early 1970s, companies in Canada and the United States had debt/assets ratios of approximately 40 percent, whereas companies in Japan and Italy had debt/assets ratios of more than 75 percent (Japanese companies averaged nearly 85 percent leverage).

The dividend policies of companies around the world also vary considerably. A recent study found that the dividend payout ratios of companies range from

TABLE 14-7   Capital Structure Percentages for Selected Countries Ranked by Common Equity Ratios, 1995

Country	Equity	Total Debt	Long-Term Debt	Short-Term Debt
United Kingdom	68.3%	31.7%	N/A	N/A
United States	48.4	51.6	26.8%	24.8%
Canada	47.5	52.5	30.2	22.3
Germany	39.7	60.3	15.6	44.7
Spain	39.7	60.3	22.1	38.2
France	38.8	61.2	23.5	37.7
Japan	33.7	66.3	23.3	43.0
Italy	23.5	76.5	24.2	52.3

Note: The percentages were computed from financial data that were stated in domestic currency. For example, the amount of total assets for French companies was stated in francs, which was the currency used by France at the time.

Source: *OECD Financial Statistics, Part 3: Non-financial Enterprises Financial Statements,* 1996.

10.5 percent in the Philippines to nearly 70 percent in Taiwan.[20] Even the countries listed in Table 14-7 exhibit some great differences. For example, as a percentage of earnings, the dividends paid out in Canada, France, Italy, and the United States range from 20 to 25 percent; in Spain and the United Kingdom, the range is from 30 to 40 percent; in Germany, the rate is approximately 43 percent; and it is more than 50 percent for Japanese companies.

Why do international differences in financial leverage and dividend policies exist? It seems logical to attribute the differences to dissimilar tax structures. Although the interest on corporate debt is deductible in each country and individuals must pay taxes on interest received, both dividends and capital gains are taxed differently around the world. In some countries, capital gains, dividends, or both either are not taxed or are partially taxed. We would expect, therefore, that firms would tend to finance with capital that provided investors with the highest after-tax dollar returns. In fact, for the most part, this is exactly the opposite of the actual capital structures we observe. Thus, differential tax laws cannot explain the observed capital structure differences. Also, it has been found that differences in taxes do not explain the differences in dividend payout ratios observed among the countries.

If tax rates cannot explain the different capital structures or dividend policies, what else might be an appropriate explanation? Another possibility relates to risk, especially bankruptcy costs. Bankruptcy (even the threat of potential bankruptcy) imposes a costly burden on firms with large amounts of debt. Note, however, that the threat of bankruptcy is dependent on the probability of bankruptcy. In the United States, *equity* monitoring costs are comparatively low because corporations produce quarterly reports, pay quarterly dividends, and must comply with relatively stringent audit requirements. These conditions are less prevalent in the other countries. On the other hand, *debt* monitoring costs probably are lower in countries such as Germany and Japan than in the United States, because most of the corporate debt consists of bank loans as opposed to publicly issued bonds. More importantly, the banks in many European and developed Asian countries are closely linked to the corporations that borrow from them, often holding major equity positions in, and having substantial influence over the management of the debtor firms. Given these close relationships, the banks are much more directly involved with the debtor firms' affairs. As a result, they are also more accommodating than U.S. bondholders in the event of financial distress. This fact suggests that any given amount of debt gives rise to a lower threat of bankruptcy for such a firm than for a U.S. firm with the same amount of business risk. An analysis of both bankruptcy costs and equity monitoring costs therefore leads to the conclusion that U.S. firms should have more equity and less debt than firms in countries such as Japan and Germany—which is what we typically observe.

When we examine the differences in dividend policies among countries, we find that, all else equal, companies pay out greater amounts of earnings as dividends in countries with policies that help protect the rights of minority stockholders.[21] In such countries, firms with many growth opportunities tend to pay lower dividends, which is to be expected, because the funds are needed to finance the growth and shareholders are willing to forgo current income in hopes of greater future benefits. On the other hand, in countries where shareholders' rights are not well protected, investors prefer dividends because of the higher uncertainty regarding whether management will use earnings for self-gratification or for the benefit of the firm; investors in these countries accept any dividends they can get.

---

[20]Rafael La Porta, Florencio Lopez-de-Silanes, Andrei Shleifer, and Robert W. Vishny, "Agency Problems and Dividend Policies Around the World," *Journal of Finance*, February 2000, 1–33.

[21]*Ibid.*

We cannot state that one financial system is better than another in the sense of making the firms in one country more efficient than those in another. As U.S. firms become more involved in worldwide operations, they must become increasingly aware of worldwide conditions. In turn, they must be prepared to adapt to conditions in the various countries in which they do business.

Self-Test Questions

Why do international differences in financial leverage exist?

Why do dividend payout ratios of companies differ among different countries?

Ethical Dilemma

A Bond Is a Bond Is a Bond...Is a Stock...Is a Bondock?

To fund some of its expansion plans, Ohio Rubber & Tire (ORT) recently issued 30-year bonds with low coupon rates. Investors were willing to purchase the bonds despite the low coupon rates because ORT's debt has consistently been rated AAA during the past decade, which means that bond rating agencies consider the company's default risk to be extremely low.

Now ORT is considering raising additional funds by issuing new debt. The company plans to use the new funds to finance additional expansion. Unlike its previous expansion efforts, however, ORT now plans to grow the firm by purchasing young firms that just "went public" and are not in the tire and rubber industry.

Wally, who works closely with ORT's investment banker, has been assigned the task of determining how to best raise the desired funds. After speaking with the investment banker, some friends who work at other companies, and peers in ORT's international subsidiaries, Wally is seriously considering recommending to management that ORT issue a new security that has the characteristics of both debt and equity. The security, which was just recently introduced in the U.S. financial markets, is classified as debt because fixed interest payments that are tax deductible are paid every year. Unlike conventional bonds, however, these hybrid bonds, which are called "bondocks," have maturities of 50 to 60 years. In addition, the firm is not considered to be in default if it misses interest payments when the firm's credit rating drops below B+. Most experts consider bondocks to be quite complex financial instruments.

Through his research, Wally discovered that bondocks have been used for quite some time outside of the United States. Compared to conventional debt, companies that have used bondocks have increased their earnings per share (EPS) significantly. A major reason EPS increases is because the cost of a bondock generally is much lower than equity, but the instrument is comparable to equity financing with respect to maturity and default risk. For example, Wally discovered that ORT could issue bondocks with an after-tax cost equal to 5 percent, which is only slightly higher than the after-tax cost of issuing conventional debt and is approximately one-third the cost of issuing new equity. Although bondocks are considered risky, the actual degree of risk is unknown. The friends and coworkers with whom Wally consulted seem to think that there is a slight chance that investors—both stockholders and bondholders—would earn returns significantly lower than would be earned with conventional debt when the company performs extremely poorly. The opposite should occur when the company performs very well.

The major drawback to issuing bondocks is that they will significantly increase the financial leverage of ORT, and thus the value of the recently issued bonds will decrease substantially. On the other hand, Wally thinks that issuing bondocks can be a win-win proposition for ORT and its common stockholders. If the company's expansion

continues

plans are successful, stockholders will be nicely rewarded. If, the company's expansion plans are unsuccessful, however, the market values of both its debt and its equity would decrease to the point that it would be attractive for the firm to repurchase these financing instruments in the capital markets. If this is true, then issuing bondocks would benefit stockholders at the expense of bondholders. ORT's executives are major stockholders because their bonuses and incentives are paid in the company's stock. What should Wally do? What would you do if you were Wally?

CHAPTER PRINCIPLES
–The Answers

To summarize the key concepts, let's answer the questions that were posed at the beginning of the chapter

- **What is a firm's capital structure?** *Capital structure* refers to the combination of the long-term funds the firm uses to finance its assets. Thus, a firm's capital structure consists of the proportions of debt, preferred stock, and common equity the firm uses.

- **What is a firm's optimal capital structure? Can a firm have too little debt?** A firm's optimal capital structure is the combination of debt, preferred stock, and common equity that maximizes the value of its stock. A firm's value will be maximized when its weighted average cost of capital (WACC) is minimized.

  The tax deductibility of interest payments makes debt an attractive form of financing. The more debt a firm uses, however, the greater its chances of bankruptcy. As a result, firms find it desirable to finance with some debt. Firms that have little or no debt generally are not operating at their optimal capital structures, because they are not taking advantage of the tax deductibility of the interest payments on debt.

- **How does a firm's capital structure affect its risk?** Both debt and preferred stock require fixed financial payments. Because these payments do not vary with sales and operating profits, there is a risk that they cannot be paid when the firm performs poorly. As a result, everything else equal, we generally consider firms with higher proportions of fixed financial payments to have riskier financial positions than firms with less debt and preferred stock. And, in general, higher risk results in a higher WACC.

- **Why do the capital structures of firms in different industries vary?** Firms with more stable sales are able to take on greater proportions of debt than firms with more unpredictable sales. In general, then, we observe that firms with fairly predictable earnings have much higher proportions of debt than firms with uncertain earnings.

- **What is an optimal dividend policy?** Because the firm's goal is to maximize shareholders' wealth, the optimal dividend policy is the one that maximizes the value of the firm. When a firm pays dividends, it decreases the amount of earnings that can be used to invest in acceptable capital budgeting projects—that is, the amount that can be used to finance growth. As a result, firms that have many acceptable capital budgeting projects generally pay little or no dividends because earnings are retained to reinvest in the firm. On the other hand, firms with few acceptable capital budgeting projects generally pay out most of their earnings as dividends because not as much internal financing is needed.

- **What dividend payment policies are followed in practice?** The four policies that are observed in practice include (1) residual dividend, (2) stable, predictable dividend, (3) constant payout ratio, and (4) low regular dividend plus extras. According to the residual dividend policy, a firm should pay dividends only when earnings are greater than what is needed to finance the optimal capital budget. The stable, predictable dividend policy requires a firm to maintain a fairly stable dollar dividend from year to year, regardless of the earnings. If a firm follows the constant payout ratio dividend policy, it pays the same percentage of earnings as dividends each year. The low-regular-plus-extras dividend policy states that the firm should pay a low regular dividend each year, and this regular dividend should be supplemented with an extra (bonus) dividend in years when above-normal earnings are generated.

- **What factors affect dividend policy decisions?** Some factors that influence a firm's dividend policy decisions include constraints on payments, investment opportunities, ownership dilution, and the effect on the firm's cost of capital. (1) Factors that limit the amount of dividends that can be paid each year include any restrictions contained in the firm's debt contracts, the amount of cash that is available to pay dividends, and the firm's retained earnings. (2) Generally, the more good investment opportunities a firm has, the lower the proportion of its earnings that is paid as dividends, because the firm uses earnings to finance acceptable capital budgeting projects. (3) A firm that is concerned about diluting its ownership generally is inclined to retain earnings rather than to issue new common stock to finance investments. (4) Firms that face high flotation (issuing) costs generally prefer to use retained earnings rather than to issue new stock to fund capital budgeting needs.

- **How does a stock split (dividend) work? Why would a firm initiate a stock split (pay a dividend in stock)?** Both a stock split and a stock dividend increase the number of shares of outstanding stock. If a firm initiates a 2-for-1 stock split, then it will replace every one share of existing stock with two shares of new stock. If a firm declares a 10 percent stock dividend, then it "pays" a dividend in the form of stock (not cash) that consists of 10 percent of the firm's outstanding shares of stock. Neither action requires stockholders to invest any additional funds. Although both actions reduce the per-share value of the firm's stock, neither action by itself changes the *total* market value of the firm's stock.

- **How do the capital structures and dividend payment policies of companies in the United States compare with those observed in foreign companies?** An average U.S. firm has a debt/assets ratio equal to between 45 and 50 percent of its total capital, whereas the average debt ratio of firms in many other countries is above 60 percent. Differences in capital structures around the world can be explained primarily by the relationships firms have with their lenders. In many countries, banks own significant portions of both the stock and the debt of a firm. In such instances (1) it is easier to change the features of the debt and (2) the bank is more inclined to lend additional funds to a struggling firm in which it has ownership in an attempt to improve its finances than in the United States where a large number of investors owns the company's bonds.

   Both tax laws and the protection of stockholders' rights differ among countries throughout the world. The proportions of earnings that are paid as dividends generally are higher in countries where dividends are taxed at low rates and where stockholders' rights are not well protected.

The concepts presented in this chapter should help you to better understand how to determine the rate of return that you should demand when investing your money and why stock prices change when management changes the company's dividend policy or splits its stock. If you apply the concepts presented in this chapter, you should be able to make more informed investment decisions.

CHAPTER PRINCIPLES
–Personal Finance

- **How do I determine my capital structure?** Your capital structure can be defined as the mixture of the various loans (debt) that you have outstanding. Your capital structure determines your overall WACC, which affects your wealth. For example, if you use an expensive type of debt—perhaps credit cards—as a primary source of funds, then your WACC will be high compared to someone who uses less expensive debt. Similar to firms, there are steps you can take to lower your WACC. You can shift your capital structure, or mixture of loans, so that a greater proportion of cheaper debt is used. You can also shift your capital structure to alter your credit risk, which is the single most important variable that financial institutions use to determine the interest rate you are charged for borrowing funds. If you have too many credit cards, discontinue some of them; if you are habitually late (delinquent) with your bill payments, start paying on time; save a portion of your income each week; and don't become too leveraged (borrow too much). If you improve your credit, you will be able to borrow at better rates.

- **Do I have an optimal capital structure?** Many alternative loans with many different interest rates are available to individuals. When you need a loan, you should "shop around" and choose the alternative with the lowest interest rate. Also, because interest rates change continuously, you should monitor your loan portfolio to determine whether it is worthwhile to refinance existing loans at lower interest rates when market rates decline. Considering the variety of borrowing alternatives that exist, do you think it is wise to use your credit card as a source of borrowing for an extended period of time?   (Hint: The answer is no!)

- **Why should I have a basic understanding of a firm's dividend policy?** Based on the discussion in the chapter, you should understand that firms follow different dividend policies for different reasons. When determining whether to invest in the stock of a company, you should examine its dividend policy. Remember that the total return you earn when investing in a stock includes a yield that is based on dividend payments and a yield that is based on the firm's growth. Often firms that pay high dividends do not have good growth opportunities; thus, they generate high dividend yields, but fairly low capital gain (growth) yields. Therefore, you should be aware of the dividend policy of a firm before you purchase its stock.

- **How do stock splits and stock dividends affect my investments?** When you see the price of a stock drop dramatically from one day to the next, it could be the result of a stock split or a stock dividend. Keep in mind that neither action by itself changes the total market value of the outstanding stock. As a result, when a stock you own splits, your wealth position does not change; the per-share value of the stock declines, but the number of shares increases such that there is no economic effect (change in wealth).

- **Should I use DRIPs?** You should have a basic understanding of dividend reinvestment plans (DRIPs). Two characteristics that you should remember are (1) most large firms offer DRIPs, which permit you to have any dividends paid to you automatically reinvested in the firm's stock and (2) even though the dividend is "reinvested" in stock, you must pay taxes on the amount of the dividend you technically receive from the firm.

- **Why should I be concerned with the ex-dividend dates of stocks that I own?** As an investor, you should determine the ex-dividend date associated with a firm's stock. On the ex-dividend date, the value of the stock drops by an amount that approximately equals the next dividend payment. The reason for the price decrease is because the ex-dividend date signifies the date when the stock begins to sell "without the next dividend payment"—that is, stockholders who purchase the stock on or after the ex-dividend date will not receive the next dividend payment because there is not enough time to record their names on the company's ownership books before the names of those who will receive the next dividend payment are determined.

QUESTIONS

14-1 Explain why the following statement is true: "Other things equal, firms with relatively stable sales are able to carry relatively high debt/assets ratios."

14-2 If a firm went from 0 percent debt to successively higher levels of debt, why would you expect its stock price to first rise, then hit a peak, and then begin to decline?

14-3 Why is the debt level that maximizes a firm's expected EPS generally higher than the one that maximizes its stock price?

14-4 Why is EBIT generally considered to be independent of financial leverage? Why might EBIT actually be influenced by financial leverage at high levels of debt?

14-5 Explain how a firm might shift its capital structure so as to change its weighted average cost of capital (WACC). What would be the impact on the value of the firm?

14-6 Absolute Corporation currently has $50 million in liabilities and common equity in combination. The firm has no preferred stock. After careful evaluation, the CFO constructed the following table to show the CEO the effect of changing the firm's capital structure:

Amount of Debt in the Capital Structure	Earnings per Share (EPS)	Market Price Per Share (P_0)
$10,000,000	$5.00	$125.50
20,000,000	5.50	130.75
30,000,000	5.70	130.00
40,000,000	5.60	128.05

According to this information, what is Absolute's optimal capital structure? Explain your answer.

14-7 When the Bell System was broken up, the old AT&T was split into a new AT&T plus seven regional telephone companies. The reason the government required the company to break up was to increase the degree of competition in the telephone industry. At the time, AT&T had a monopoly on local service, long distance, and the manufacture of all equipment used by telephone companies, and the breakup was expected to open most of these markets to competition. In the court order that outlined the terms of the breakup, the capital structures of the surviving companies were specified, and much attention was paid to the increased competition that telephone companies could expect in the future. Do you think the optimal capital structure after the breakup should be the same as the pre-breakup optimal capital structure? Explain your position.

14-8 Your firm's R&D department has been working on a new process that, if it works, can produce oil from coal at a cost of $25 per barrel; the current market price for oil is $120 per barrel. The company needs $10 million of external funds at this time to complete the research. The results of this work will be known in about 1 year, and it has a 50-50 chance of success. If the research is successful, your company will need to raise a substantial amount of new money to put the idea into production. Your economists forecast that although the economy will be depressed next year, interest rates will be high because of international monetary problems. You must recommend how the currently needed $10 million should be raised—as debt or as equity. How would the potential implications of your project influence your decision?

14-9 As an investor, would you rather invest in a firm that has a policy of maintaining (1) a constant dividend payout ratio, (2) a stable, predictable dividend per share with a target dividend growth rate, or (3) a constant regular quarterly dividend plus a year-end extra payment when earnings are sufficiently high or corporate investment needs are sufficiently low? Explain your answer, stating how these policies would affect your required rate of return, r_s. Also, discuss how your answer might change if you were a student, a 50-year-old professional with peak earnings, or a retiree.

14-10 How would each of the following changes tend to affect the average dividend payout ratios for corporations, other things held constant? Explain your answers.

   a. An increase in the personal income tax rate that is applied to dividends

   b. A rise in general interest rates

   c. A decline in corporate investment opportunities

   d. Permission for corporations to deduct dividends for tax purposes as they now can do with interest charges

   e. A change in the tax code so that both realized and unrealized capital gains that investors earn in any year are taxed at the same rate as dividends

14-11 "The cost of retained earnings is less than the cost of new outside equity capital. Consequently, it is totally irrational for a firm to sell a new issue of stock and to pay dividends during the same year." Do you agree with this statement? Explain.

14-12 Would it ever be rational for a firm to borrow money to pay dividends? Explain.

14-13 One position expressed in the financial literature is that firms set their dividends as a residual after using income to support new investments.

   a. Explain what a residual dividend policy implies.

   b. Could the residual dividend policy be consistent with (1) a stable, predictable dividend policy, (2) a constant payout ratio policy, and/or (3) a low-regular-dividend-plus-extras policy? Answer in terms of both the short-run, year-to-year consistency, and long-run consistency.

14-14 What is the difference between a stock dividend and a stock split? As a stockholder, would you prefer to see your company declare a 100 percent stock dividend or a 2-for-1 split? Assume that either action is feasible.

14-15 If investors have the same information (symmetric information) as the managers/executives of a firm, then which of the dividend policies mentioned in the chapter should the firm follow to maximize value? Explain your answer.

14-16 Assume that *asymmetric* information exists in the financial markets. If a firm's earnings fluctuate every year, everything else equal, which of the dividend policies discussed in the chapter should be followed to provide investors with a perception of the least amount of risk? Explain your answer.

SELF-TEST PROBLEMS

Solutions appear in Appendix B.

Key Terms **ST-1** Define each of the following terms:

   a. Target capital structure; optimal capital structure

   b. Business risk; financial risk; total risk

   c. Financial leverage

   d. EPS indifference point

   e. Symmetric information; asymmetric information

   f. Tradeoff theory; signaling theory

   g. Reserve borrowing capacity

   h. Optimal dividend policy

   i. Dividend irrelevance theory; dividend relevance theory

   j. Information content (signaling) hypothesis; clientele effect; free cash flow hypothesis

   k. Residual dividend policy; stable, predictable dividend policy; constant payout ratio policy; low-regular-dividend-plus-extra policy

   l. Declaration date; holder-of-record date; ex-dividend date; payment date

   m. Dividend reinvestment plan (DRIP)

   n. Stock split; stock dividend

ST-2 Gentry Motors Inc., a producer of turbine generators, is in this situation: EBIT = $4 million; tax rate = T = 35%; debt outstanding = $2 million; r_d = 10%; r_s = 15%; shares of stock outstanding = 600,000; and book value per share = $10. Because Gentry's product market is stable and the company expects no growth, all earnings are paid out as dividends. The debt consists of perpetual bonds.   **Financial Leverage**

   a. What are Gentry's earnings per share (EPS) and its price per share (P_0)?

   b. What is Gentry's weighted average cost of capital (WACC)?

   c. Gentry can increase its debt by $8 million, to a total of $10 million, using the new debt to buy back and retire some of its shares of common stock at the current price. Its interest rate on debt will be 12 percent (it will have to call and refund the old debt), and its cost of equity will rise from 15 to 17 percent. EBIT will remain constant. Should Gentry change its capital structure?

   d. If Gentry did not have to refund the $2 million of old debt, how would this affect things? Assume that the new and the still outstanding debt are equally risky, with r_d = 12%, but that the coupon rate on the old debt is 10 percent.

   e. What is Gentry's TIE coverage ratio under the original situation and under the conditions in part (c) of this question?

ST-3 Components Manufacturing Corporation (CMC) has an all-common-equity capital structure. It has 200,000 shares of $2 par value common stock outstanding. When CMC's founder, who was also its research director and most successful inventor, retired unexpectedly to the South Pacific in late 2009, CMC was left suddenly and permanently with materially lower growth expectations and relatively few attractive new investment opportunities. Unfortunately, it had no way to replace the founder's contributions to the firm. Previously, CMC found it necessary to plow back most of its earnings to finance growth, which averaged 12 percent per year. Future growth at a 5 percent rate is considered realistic, but that level would call for an increase in the dividend payout. Furthermore, it now appears that new investment projects with at least the 14 percent rate of return required by CMC's stockholders (r_s = 14%) would amount to only $800,000 for 2010, compared   **Alternative Dividend Policies**

with a projected $2,000,000 of net income. If the firm continues its existing 20 percent dividend payout, retained earnings would be $1.6 million in 2010, but, as noted, investments that yield the 14 percent cost of capital would amount to only $800,000.

The one encouraging point is that CMC's high earnings from existing assets are expected to continue, and net income of $2 million is still expected for 2010. Given the dramatically changed circumstances, CMC's management is reviewing the firm's dividend policy.

a. Assuming that the acceptable 2010 investment projects would be financed entirely by earnings retained during the year, calculate DPS in 2010, assuming that CMC uses the residual payment policy.

b. What payout ratio does your answer to part (a) imply for 2010?

c. If CMC maintains a 60 percent payout ratio for the foreseeable future, what is your estimate of the present market price of its common stock? How does this price compare with the market price that should have prevailed under the assumptions existing just before the news about the founder's retirement? If the two values of P_0 are different, comment on why.

d. What would happen to the price of CMC's stock if it continued the old 20 percent payout policy? Assume that if this payout rate is maintained, the average rate of return on the retained earnings will fall to 7.5 percent and the new growth rate will be 6 percent.

PROBLEMS

Financial Leverage Effects

14-1   The firms HL and LL are identical except for their debt-to-total-assets ratios and interest rates on debt. Each has $20 million in assets, earned $4 million before interest and taxes in 2010, and has a 40 percent marginal tax rate. Firm HL, however, has a debt-to-total-assets ratio (D/TA) of 50 percent and pays 12 percent interest on its debt, whereas LL has a 30 percent debt-to-total-assets ratio and pays only 10 percent interest on debt.

a. Calculate the rate of return on equity (net income/equity) for each firm.

b. Observing that HL has a higher return on equity, LL's treasurer decides to raise the debt-to-total-assets ratio from 30 to 60 percent, which will increase LL's interest rate on all debt to 15 percent. Calculate the new rate of return on equity (ROE) for LL. ROE = (Net income)/(Common equity).

Dividend Payout

14-2   Open Door Manufacturer earned $100,000 this year. The company follows the residual dividend policy when paying dividends. Open Door has determined that it needs a total of $120,000 for investment in capital budgeting projects this year. If the company's debt-to-asset ratio is 50 percent, what will its dividend payout ratio be this year?

Dividend Payout

14-3   Last year the Bulls Business Bureau (BBB) retained $400,000 of the $1 million net income it generated. This year BBB generated net income equal to $1.2 million. If BBB follows the constant dividend payout ratio dividend policy, how much should be paid in dividends this year?

Dividend Payout

14-4   In 2010, Breaking News Company earned $15 million, and it paid $6 million in dividends. The company follows a constant payout ratio dividend policy. If the company would like to pay $8 million in dividends next year, how much must Breaking News earn?

14-5 HQ Company is considering a 1-for-3 reverse stock split. HQ's stock is currently selling for $3 per share.

   a. What will the price of the stock be after the stock split?

   b. HQ plans to pay a dividend equal to $0.60 per-share after the split. The company would like to pay an equivalent dividend per share even if the split does not take place. What would the per-share dividend have to be if the HQ doesn't split the stock?

Stock Split

14-6 After a 5-for-1 stock split, the Swenson Company paid a dividend of $0.75 per new share, which represents a 9 percent increase over last year's pre-split dividend. What was last year's dividend per share?

Stock Split

14-7 Northern California Heating and Cooling, Inc., has a 6-month backlog of orders for its patented solar heating system. To meet this demand, management plans to expand the firm's production capacity by 40 percent with a $10 million investment in plant and machinery. The firm wants to maintain a 40 percent debt/assets ratio in its capital structure; it also wants to maintain its past dividend policy of distributing 45 percent of last year's net income. In 2009, net income was $5 million. How much external equity must Northern California seek at the beginning of 2010 to expand its capacity as desired?

External Equity Financing

14-8 The Garlington Corporation expects next year's net income to be $15 million. The firm's debt/assets ratio currently is 40 percent. Garlington has $12 million of profitable investment opportunities, and it wishes to maintain its existing debt/assets ratio. According to the residual dividend policy, how large should Garlington's dividend payout ratio be next year?

Dividend Payout

14-9 The Scanlon Company's optimal capital structure calls for 50 percent debt. The interest rate on its debt is a constant 10 percent; its cost of common equity from retained earnings is 14 percent; the cost of equity from new stock is 16 percent; and its marginal tax rate is 40 percent. Scanlon has the following investment opportunities:

Dividend Payout

   Project A: Cost = $5 million; IRR = 20%

   Project B: Cost = $5 million; IRR = 12%

   Project C: Cost = $5 million; IRR = 9%

   Scanlon expects to have net income of $7,287,500. If Scanlon bases its dividends on the residual policy, what will its payout ratio be?

14-10 The Damon Company wishes to calculate next year's return on equity (ROE) under different leverage ratios. Damon's total assets are $14 million, and its marginal tax rate is 40 percent. The company can estimate next year's earnings before interest and taxes for three possible states of the world: $4.2 million with a 0.2 probability, $2.8 million with a 0.5 probability, and $700,000 with a 0.3 probability. Calculate Damon's expected ROE, standard deviation, and coefficient of variation for each of the debt-to-total-assets ratios in the following list and evaluate the results. ROE = (Net income)/(Common equity).

Financial Leverage Effects

Leverage (Debt/Assets)	Interest Rate
0%	—
10	9%
50	11
60	14

Risk Analysis   **14-11** **a.** Given the following information, calculate the expected value for Firm C's EPS. $E(EPS_A) = \$5.10$, and $\sigma_A = \$3.61$; $E(EPS_B) = \$4.20$, and $\sigma_B = \$2.96$; and $\sigma_C = \$4.11$.

	Probability				
	0.1	0.2	0.4	0.2	0.1
Firm A: EPS_A	($1.50)	$1.80	$5.10	$8.40	$11.70
Firm B: EPS_B	(1.20)	1.50	4.20	6.90	9.60
Firm C: EPS_C	(2.40)	1.35	5.10	8.85	12.60

b. Discuss the relative riskiness of the three firms' (A, B, and C) earnings.

Financing Alternatives   **14-12** Wired Communications Corporation (WCC) supplies headphones to airlines for use with movie and stereo programs. The headphones sell for $288 per set, and this year's sales are expected to be 45,000 units. Variable production costs for the expected sales under present production methods are estimated at $10,200,000, and fixed production (operating) costs at present are $1,560,000. WCC has $4,800,000 of debt outstanding at an interest rate of 8 percent. There are 240,000 shares of common stock outstanding, and there is no preferred stock. WCC pays out 70 percent of earnings as dividends and is in the 40 percent marginal tax bracket.

The company is considering investing $7,200,000 in new equipment. Sales would not increase, but variable costs per unit would decline by 20 percent. Also, fixed operating costs would increase from $1,560,000 to $1,800,000. WCC could raise the required capital by borrowing $7,200,000 at 10 percent or by selling 240,000 additional shares of stock at $30 per share.

a. What would be WCC's EPS (1) under the old production process, (2) under the new process if it uses debt, and (3) under the new process if it uses common stock?

b. At what unit sales level would WCC have the same EPS, assuming it undertakes the investment and finances it with debt or with stock? (*Hint:* V = variable cost per unit = $8,160,000/45,000$, and EPS = $[(P \times Q - V \times Q - F - I)(1 - T)]/\text{Shares}$. Set $EPS_{Stock} = EPS_{Debt}$ and solve for Q.)

c. At what unit sales level would EPS = 0 under the three production/financing setups—that is, under the old plan, the new plan with debt financing, and the new plan with stock financing? (*Hint:* Note that $V_{Old} = \$10,200,000/45,000$, and use the hints for part (b), setting the EPS equation equal to $0.)

d. On the basis of the analysis in parts (a) through (c), which plan is the riskiest, which has the highest expected EPS, and which would you recommend? Assume here that there is a fairly high probability of sales falling as low as 25,000 units, and determine EPS_{Debt} and EPS_{Stock} at that sales level to help assess the riskiness of the two financing plans.

Financing Alternatives   **14-13** Early next year, the Strasburg Company plans to raise a net amount of $270 million to finance new equipment and working capital. Two alternatives are being considered: common stock can be sold to net $60 per share, or bonds yielding 12 percent can be issued. The balance sheet and income statement of the Strasburg Company prior to financing are as follows:

The Strasburg Company
Balance Sheet as of December 31 ($ millions)

Current assets	$ 900.00	Accounts payable	$ 172.50
Net fixed assets	450.00	Notes payable to bank	255.00
		Other current liabilities	225.00
		Total current liabilities	$ 652.50
		Long-term debt (10%)	300.00
		Common stock, $3 par	60.00
		Retained earnings	337.50
Total assets	$1,350.00	Total liabilities and equity	$1,350.00

The Strasburg Company
Income Statement for Year Ended December 31 ($ millions)

Sales	$ 2,475.00
Operating costs	(2,227.50)
Earnings before interest and taxes (EBIT) (10%)	$ 247.50
Interest on short-term debt	(15.00)
Interest on long-term debt	(30.00)
Earnings before taxes (EBT)	$ 202.50
Taxes (40%)	(81.00)
Net income $	$ 121.50

The probability distribution for annual sales is as follows:

Probability	Annual Sales ($ millions)
0.30	$2,250
0.40	2,700
0.30	3,150

Assuming that EBIT is equal to 10 percent of sales, calculate earnings per share under both the debt financing and the stock financing alternatives at each possible level of sales. Then calculate expected earnings per share and σ_{EPS} under both debt and stock financing. Also, calculate the debt-to-total-assets ratio and the times-interest-earned (TIE) ratio at the expected sales level under each alternative. The old debt will remain outstanding. Which financing method do you recommend?

14-14 In 2009, the Sirmans Company paid dividends totaling $3,600,000 on net income of $10.8 million. The year 2009 was a normal one for the company, and for the past 10 years, earnings have grown at a constant rate of 10 percent. In 2010, earnings are expected to jump to $14.4 million, and the firm expects to have profitable investment opportunities of $8.4 million. It is predicted that Sirmans will not be able to maintain the 2010 level of earnings growth—the high 2010 earnings level is attributable to an exceptionally profitable new product line introduced that year—and the company will return to its previous 10 percent growth rate. Sirmans's target debt/assets ratio is 40 percent.

Alternative Dividend Policies

a. Calculate Sirmans's total dividends for 2010 if it follows each of the following policies:

   (1) Its 2010 dividend payment is set to force dividends to grow at the long-run growth rate in earnings.

   (2) It continues the 2009 dividend payout ratio.

   (3) It uses a pure residual dividend policy (40 percent of the $8.4 million investment is financed with debt).

   (4) It employs a regular-dividend-plus-extras policy. The regular dividend based on the long-run growth rate and the extra dividend is set according to the residual policy.

b. Which of the preceding policies would you recommend? Restrict your choices to the ones listed, but justify your answer.

c. Assume that investors expect Sirmans to pay total dividends of $9,000,000 in 2010 and to have the dividend grow at 10 percent after 2010. The total market value of the stock is $180 million. What is the company's cost of equity?

Dividend Policy and Capital Structure

14-15 Ybor City Tobacco Company has for many years enjoyed a moderate, but stable, growth in sales and earnings. In recent times, however, cigar consumption and consequently Ybor's sales have been falling, primarily because of the public's greater awareness of the health dangers associated with smoking. Anticipating further declines in tobacco sales in the future, Ybor's management hopes eventually to move almost entirely out of the tobacco business and into a newly developed, diversified product line in growth-oriented industries. The company is especially interested in the prospects for pollution-control devices because its research department has already done much work on the problems of filtering smoke. Right now, the company estimates that an investment of $15 million will be necessary to purchase new facilities and to begin production of these products, but the investment could earn a return of about 18 percent within a short time. The only other available investment opportunity costs $6 million and is expected to return about 10.4 percent.

The company is expected to pay a $3.00 dividend on its 3 million outstanding shares, the same as its dividend last year. The directors could be persuaded to change the dividend if there are good reasons for doing so. Total earnings after taxes for the year are expected to be $14.25 million; the common stock is currently selling for $56.25 per share; the firm's target debt/assets ratio is 45 percent; and its marginal tax rate is 40 percent. The costs of various forms of financing are as follows:

New bonds, $r_d = 11\%$ (the before-tax rate)

New common stock sold at $56.25 per share will net $51.25

Required rate of return on retained earnings, $r_s = 14\%$

a. Calculate Ybor's expected payout ratio, the break point at which the marginal cost of capital (MCC) rises, and its MCC above and below the point of exhaustion of retained earnings at the current payout. (*Hint:* r_s is given, and $\hat{D}_1/P_0$ can be found; then, knowing r_s and $\hat{D}_1/P_0$, you can determine g.)

b. How large should Ybor's capital budget be for the year?

c. What is an appropriate dividend policy for Ybor? How should it finance the capital budget?

d. How might risk factors influence Ybor's cost of capital, capital structure, and dividend policy?

e. What assumptions, if any, do your answers to the preceding parts make about investors' preferences for dividends versus capital gains (in other words, what are investors' preferences regarding the $\hat{D}_1/P_0$ and g components of r_s)?

Integrative Problems

14-16 Assume that you have just been hired by Adams, Garitty, and Evans (AGE), a consulting firm that specializes in analyses of firms' capital structures and dividend policies. Your boss has asked you to examine the capital structure of Campus Deli and Sub Shop (CDSS), which is located adjacent to a college campus. According to the owner, sales were $1,350,000 last year; variable costs were 60 percent of sales; and fixed costs were $40,000. Therefore, EBIT totaled $500,000. Because the neighboring university's enrollment is capped, EBIT is expected to be constant over time. As it does not require any expansion capital, CDSS pays out all of its earnings as dividends. The management group owns approximately 50 percent of the stock, which is traded in the over-the-counter market.

Optimal Capital Structure

CDSS currently has no debt—it is an all-equity firm—and its 100,000 shares outstanding sell at a price of $20 per share. The firm's marginal tax rate is 40 percent. On the basis of statements made in your finance text, you believe that CDSS's shareholders would be better off if the firm used some debt financing. When you made this suggestion to your new boss, she encouraged you to pursue the idea but to provide support for it.

From a local investment banker, you obtained the following estimates of the costs of debt and equity at different debt levels (in thousands of dollars):

Amount Borrowed	r_d	r_s
$ 0	—	15.0%
250	10.0%	15.5
500	11.0	16.5
750	13.0	18.0
1,000	16.0	20.0

If the firm were recapitalized, debt would be issued, and the borrowed funds would be used to repurchase stock. Stockholders, in turn, would use funds provided by the repurchase to buy equities in other fast-food companies similar to CDSS. To complete your report, answer the following questions:

a. **(1)** What is business risk? What factors influence a firm's business risk?

   (2) What is operating leverage, and how does it affect a firm's business risk?

b. **(1)** What is meant by the terms *financial leverage* and *financial risk*?

   (2) How does financial risk differ from business risk?

c. To develop an example that can be presented to CDSS's management as an illustration, consider two hypothetical firms: Firm U has $0 debt financing, and Firm L has $10,000 of 12 percent debt. Both firms have

$20,000 in total assets and a 40 percent marginal tax rate, and they face the following EBIT probability distribution for next year:

Probability	EBIT
0.25	$2,000
0.50	3,000
0.25	4,000

(1) Complete the following partial income statements and the set of ratios for Firm L ($ thousands):

	Firm U			Firm L		
Assets	$ 20,000	$ 20,000	$20,000	$20,000	$ 20,000	$ 20,000
Equity	$ 20,000	$ 20,000	$20,000	$10,000	$ 10,000	$ 10,000
Probability	0.25	0.50	0.25	0.25	0.50	0.25
Sales	$ 6,000	$ 9,000	$12,000	$ 6,000	$ 9,000	$ 12,000
Operating costs	(4,000)	(6,000)	(8,000)	(4,000)	(6,000)	(8,000)
Earnings before interest and taxes	$ 2,000	$ 3,000	$ 4,000	$ 2,000	$ 3,000	$ 4,000
Interest (12%)	(0)	(0)	(0)	(1,200)	_____	1,200)
Earnings before taxes	$ 2,000	$ 3,000	$ 4,000	$ 800	$	$ 2,800
Taxes (40%)	(800)	(1,200)	(1,600)	(320)	_____	(1,120)
Net income	$ 1,200	$ 1,800	$ 2,400	$ 480	$	$ 1,680
$\text{ROE} = \dfrac{\text{Net income}}{\text{Common equity}}$	6.0%	9.0%	12.0%	4.8%	%	16.8%
$\text{TIE} = \dfrac{\text{EBIT}}{\text{Interest}}$	∞	∞	∞	1.7×	×	3.3×
Expected ROE		9.0%			10.8%	
Expected TIE		∞			2.5×	
σ_{ROE}		2.1%			4.2%	
σ_{TIE}		0×			0.6×	

(2) What does this example illustrate concerning the impact of financial leverage on expected rate of return and risk?

d. With the preceding points in mind, consider the optimal capital structure for CDSS.

(1) Define the term *optimal capital structure*.

(2) Describe briefly, without using numbers, the sequence of events that would occur if CDSS decided to change its capital structure to include more debt.

(3) Assume that shares could be repurchased at the current market price of $20 per share. Calculate CDSS's expected EPS and times-interest-earned ratio at debt levels of $0, $250,000, $500,000, $750,000, and $1,000,000. How many shares would remain after recapitalization under each scenario?

(4) What would be the new stock price if CDSS recapitalizes with $250,000 of debt? $500,000? $750,000? $1,000,000? Recall that the payout ratio is 100 percent, so g = 0.

(5) Considering only the levels of debt discussed, what is CDSS's optimal capital structure?

(6) Is EPS maximized at the debt level that maximizes share price? Why?

(7) What is the WACC at the optimal capital structure?

e. Suppose you discovered that CDSS had more business risk than you originally estimated. Describe how this change would affect the analysis. What if the firm had less business risk than originally estimated?

f. What are some factors that should be considered when establishing a firm's target capital structure?

g. How does the existence of asymmetric information and signaling affect the firm's capital structure?

h. CDSS is considering either a stock split or stock dividend to lower its stock price. Explain how each action is applied, and the effect each action would have on CDSS's capital structure.

14-17 Now your boss wants you to evaluate the dividend policy of Information Systems, Inc. (ISI), which develops software for the health care industry. ISI was founded 5 years ago by Donald Brown and Margaret Clark, who are still its only stockholders. ISI has now reached the stage where outside equity capital is necessary if the firm is to achieve its growth targets, yet still maintain its target capital structure of 60 percent equity and 40 percent debt. To achieve this goal, Brown and Clark have decided to take the company public. Until now, the two owners have paid themselves reasonable salaries but routinely reinvested all after-tax earnings in the firm, so dividend policy has not been an issue. Before talking with potential outside investors, however, they must decide on a dividend policy.

Dividend Policy

Your boss has asked you to make a presentation to Brown and Clark in which you review the theory of dividend policy and discuss the following questions:

a. (1) What is meant by the term *dividend policy*?

(2) The terms *irrelevance* and *relevance* have been used to describe theories regarding the way that dividend policy affects a firm's value. Explain what these terms mean and briefly discuss the relevance of dividend policy.

(3) Explain the relationships between dividend policy and (i) stock price and (ii) the cost of equity under each dividend policy theory.

(4) What results have empirical studies of the dividend theories produced? How do these findings affect what we can tell managers about dividend policy?

b. Discuss (1) the information content, or signaling, hypothesis, (2) the clientele effect, (3) the free cash flow hypothesis, and (4) their effects on dividend policy.

c. (1) Assume that ISI has an $800,000 capital budget planned for the coming year. You have determined that its present capital structure (60 percent equity and 40 percent debt) is optimal, and its net income is forecasted at $600,000. Use the residual dividend policy approach to determine ISI's total dollar dividend and payout ratio. In the process, explain what the residual dividend policy is and use a graph to illustrate your answer. Also, explain what would happen if net income were forecasted at $400,000, or at $800,000.

(2) In general terms, how would a change in investment opportunities affect the payout ratio under the residual payment policy?

(3) What are the advantages and disadvantages of the residual policy? (*Hint:* Don't neglect signaling and clientele effects.)

d. What are some other commonly used dividend payment policies? What are their advantages and disadvantages? Which policy is most widely used in practice?

e. What is a dividend reinvestment plan (DRIP), and how does one work?

COMPUTER-RELATED PROBLEMS

Work the problem in this section only if you are using the computer problem spreadsheet.

Effects of Financial Leverage

14-18 Use the model in File C14 to work this problem.

a. Rework Problem 14-12, assuming that the old long-term debt will not remain outstanding, but rather must be refinanced at the new long-term interest rate of 12 percent. What effect does this change have on the decision to refinance?

b. What would be the effect on the refinancing decision if the rate on long-term debt fell to 5 percent or rose to 20 percent, assuming that all long-term debt must be refinanced?

c. Which financing method would you recommend if the stock price (1) rose to $105 or (2) fell to $30? (Assume that all debt will have an interest rate of 12 percent.)

d. With $P_0 = \$60$ and $r_d = 12\%$, change the sales probability distribution to the following:

Alternative 1		Alternative 2	
Sales	**Probability**	**Sales**	**Probability**
$2,250	0.0	$ 0	0.3
2,700	1.0	2,700	0.4
3,150	0.0	7,500	0.3

What are the implications of these changes?

Dividend Policy and Capital Structure

14-19 Refer back to Problem 14-15. Assume that Ybor's management is considering a change in the firm's capital structure to include more debt. Management would therefore like to analyze the effects of an increase in the debt/assets ratio to 60 percent. The treasurer believes that such a move would cause lenders to increase the required rate of return on new bonds to 12 percent and that r_s would rise to 14.5 percent.

a. How would this change affect the optimal capital budget?

b. If r_s rose to 16 percent, would the low-return project be acceptable?

c. Would the project selection be affected if the dividend was reduced to $1.88 from $3.00, still assuming $r_s = 16$ percent?

Working Capital Management

A MANAGERIAL PERSPECTIVE

In December 1993, Trans World Airlines (TWA) was labeled the best domestic airline for long flights and the second best for short flights by U.S. business travelers. TWA received this accolade just one month after emerging from bankruptcy. The future seemed rosy: employees had agreed to salary concessions in exchange for an equity position in the company, the airline had restructured its liabilities and lowered its cost structure, and the employees, with their new ownership position, appeared to possess a newfound motivation and concern for company success.

Unfortunately, the nation's seventh largest airline at the time soon discovered that its "new lease on life" was not a long-term contract. Because its liquidity position was tenuous, it wasn't long before TWA filed for bankruptcy a second time. To improve its liquidity, TWA reduced operating costs by laying off employees, eliminating unprofitable flights, and replacing outdated airplanes with more fuel-efficient airplanes.

TWA emerged from its second bankruptcy and regained its status as the best domestic airline for long flights, but its financial position was still tenuous. Unforeseen circumstances, including a tragic crash and labor difficulties, resulted in large losses in the late 1990s. As a result, TWA again took actions to improve its liquidity position. The benefits of its cost-cutting, revenue-increasing actions were short-lived.

TWA filed for bankruptcy a third time at the beginning of 2001, and in April 2001 TWA ceased to exist when it was acquired by American Airlines (AA). But the acquisition did not solve TWA's liquidity problems; it just passed them on to AA.

In 2005, all airlines were still trying to recover from the terrorist attacks on September 11, 2001. AA reported net losses that ranged from just under $1 billion to nearly $3 billion from 2001 through 2005. As a result of the significant decrease in air travel since the 2001 attacks, AA took measures to improve its liquidity. By improving its liquidity, the cost-cutting measures, which saved AA about $2 billion per year in 2002 and 2003, helped AA, the world's largest airline, to keep its "head above water"—although just barely.

Maintaining a healthy liquidity position is important if AA wants to overcome current financial challenges and continue operating in the future. Even though oil prices increased to record levels in 2006, AA's improved liquidity helped the company weather the financial storm. In 2006, AMR Corporation, AA's parent company, reported a profit ($231 million) for the first time since TWA was acquired. Analysts were confident that additional profits would follow in subsequent periods, primarily because AA's liquidity position was fairly strong. In 2007, despite continued fuel price increases, AA reported a profit ($504 million) for the second consecutive year. Unfortunately, AA recorded an operating loss in the first quarter of 2008. The loss resulted primarily from astronomically high fuel costs (prices were 65 percent higher than 1 year earlier) and the fact that AA had to ground planes for mandatory FAA inspections, which caused the cancelation of thousands of flights. Even so, AA's liquidity position remained strong, which suggested that the company would be able to survive such liquidity-draining events. In the midst of poor economic conditions and a looming struggle over wages with its unions, AA needs a strong liquidity position to weather the "financial storms" it is expected to face in the next few years.

Firms strive to maintain a balance between current assets and current liabilities, and between sales and each category of current assets, in an effort to provide sufficient liquidity to survive—that is, to live to maximize value in the future. As long as a good balance is maintained, current liabilities can be paid on time, suppliers will continue to provide needed inventories, and companies will be able to meet sales demands. If the financial situation gets out of balance, liquidity problems surface and often multiply into more serious problems, and perhaps even bankruptcy. As you read this chapter, consider how important liquidity—and thus proper management of working capital—is to the survival of a firm. Also, consider the fact that many start-up firms never make it past the first few months of business, primarily because they lack formal working capital policies.

Sources: Various articles from *The Wall Street Journal* at http://www.wsj.com, the investors' relations section of American Airlines Web site located at http://www.aa.com/content/amrcorp/investorRelations/main.jhtml, and Standard & Poor's Stock Reports (2008).

---

working capital management
The management of short-term assets (investments) and short-term liabilities (financing sources).

This chapter describes *short-term financial management*, also termed **working capital management**, which involves decisions that relate to the current (short-term) assets and current (short-term) liabilities of a firm. As you read this chapter, you will realize that a firm's value cannot be maximized in the long run unless it survives in the short run. In fact, the primary reason that firms fail is because they are unable to meet their working capital needs. Consequently, *sound working capital management is a requisite for firm survival*.

CHAPTER PRINCIPLES –The Questions

After reading this chapter, you should be able to answer the following questions:

- What is working capital and why is working capital management critical to the survival of a firm?
- What general strategies should a firm follow when managing its working capital accounts?
- How should the firm finance its working capital needs?
- What types of short-term credit do firms use?
- How is the cost of short-term credit determined? Why is it necessary to compute the cost of credit?
- Which assets are generally considered good security for collateralized short-term loans? What are some of the arrangements that exist with secured short-term loans?

WORKING CAPITAL TERMINOLOGY

working capital
A firm's investment in short-term assets—cash, marketable securities, inventory, and accounts receivable.

It is useful to begin the discussion of working capital policy by reviewing some basic definitions and concepts:

net working capital
Current assets minus current liabilities; the amount of current assets financed by long-term liabilities.

1. The term **working capital**, sometimes called gross working capital, generally refers to current assets.

2. **Net working capital** is defined as current assets minus current liabilities, with the *current ratio* being calculated by dividing current assets by current

liabilities. Both metrics are intended to measure a firm's liquidity. Neither a high current ratio nor a positive net working capital actually ensures that a firm will have the cash required to meet its needs. If inventories cannot be sold, or if receivables cannot be collected in a timely manner, then the apparent safety reflected by these measures could be illusory. The best way to get a comprehensive picture of a firm's liquidity position is to examine its *cash budget*, which forecasts cash inflows and outflows. The cash budget focuses on the firm's ability to generate sufficient cash inflows to meet its required cash outflows. Cash budgeting was discussed in Chapter 8.

3. **Working capital policy** refers to the firm's basic policies regarding (a) its target levels for each category of current assets and (b) the way in which current assets will be financed.

4. Only those current liabilities that are specifically used to finance current assets are included in working capital decisions. Current liabilities that resulted from past long-term debt financing decisions are not working capital decision variables in the current period. Examples include (a) the current maturities of long-term debt; (b) the financing associated with a construction program that will be funded with the proceeds of a long-term security issue after the project is completed; and (c) the use of short-term debt to finance fixed assets. Although such accounts are not part of the working capital decision process, they cannot be ignored because they are *due in the current period*. As a result, they must be taken into account when managers assess the firm's ability to meet its current obligations using expected cash inflows.

working capital policy Decisions regarding the target levels for each current asset account and the way in which current assets will be financed.

Self-Test Question

Why is it important to properly manage short-term assets and liabilities?

THE REQUIREMENT FOR EXTERNAL WORKING CAPITAL FINANCING

In this section and throughout the chapter, we will use the financial statements of Argile Textiles, the North Carolina textile manufacturer that was introduced in Chapter 7, to illustrate working capital analyses and decisions. First, we will examine balance sheets constructed for Argile at three different dates, which are given in Table 15-1. According to the definitions given earlier, Argile's December 31, 2010, working capital was $235 million, its net working capital was $170 million, and its current ratio was 3.6. Argile's operations are very seasonal, typically peaking in September and October. Thus, at the end of September, Argile's inventories are significantly higher than they are at the end of the calendar year. As a result of this sales surge, Argile's accounts receivable balance is much higher at the end of September than it is at the end of December.

Consider what is expected to happen to Argile's current assets and current liabilities from December 31, 2010, to September 30, 2011. Current assets are expected to increase from $235 million to $345 million, or by $110 million; this growth must be supported with new financing. The higher volume of purchases, plus labor expenditures associated with increased production, will cause the firm's accounts payable and accruals to increase spontaneously from a total of $45 million ($15 million payables and $30 million accruals) to $95 million

TABLE 15-1   Argile Textiles: Historical and Projected Financials ($ million)

	12/31/10 Historical	9/30/11 Projected	12/31/11 Projected
I. Balance Sheets			
Cash	$ 10.0	$ 15.0	$ 11.0
Accounts receivable	90.0	125.0	99.0
Inventories	135.0	205.0	148.5
Total current assets (CA)	$235.0	$345.0	$258.5
Net plant and equipment	190.0	205.0	209.0
Total assets	$425.0	$550.0	$467.5
Accounts payable	$ 15.0	$ 45.0	$ 16.5
Accruals	30.0	50.0	33.0
Notes payable	20.0	64.5	23.6
Total current liabilities (CL)	$ 65.0	$159.5	$ 73.1
Long-term bonds	152.0	152.5	156.8
Total liabilities	$217.0	$312.0	$229.9
Common Stock	66.0	78.0	81.5
Retained earnings	142.0	160.0	156.1
Total owners' equity	$208.0	$238.0	$237.6
Total liabilities and equity	$425.0	$550.0	$467.5
Net working capital = CA − CL	$170.0	$185.5	$185.4
Current ratio = CA/CL	3.6×	2.2×	3.5×

	2010		2011
II. Partial Income Statements			
Sales	$ 750.0		$ 825.0
Cost of goods sold	(600.0)		(660.0)
Fixed costs	(85.0)		(93.5)
Earnings before interest and taxes	$ 65.0		$ 71.5

($45 million payables and $50 million accruals), or by only $50 million. This increase leaves a projected $60 million ($110 million − $50 million) current asset financing requirement—the amount not covered by the increase in payables and accruals. Argile expects to finance this requirement primarily through a $44.5 million increase in notes payable (from $20 million to $64.5 million). Note that from December 2010 to September 2011, Argile's net working capital is expected to increase from $170 million to $185.5 million, but its current ratio is expected to decline from 3.6 to 2.2. This shift occurs because most, but not all, of the additional funds invested in current assets ($110 million) are expected to come from increases in current liabilities ($94.5 million). Thus, *when the current ratio is greater than 1.0 and current liabilities increase (decrease) by the same (or nearly the same) dollar amount as current assets, the current ratio decreases (increases).*

The fluctuations in Argile's working capital position shown in Table 15-1 result from seasonal variations. Similar fluctuations in working capital requirements, and hence in financing needs, also occur during business cycles. For example, working capital needs typically decline during recessions and increase during booms. For some companies, such as those involved in agricultural products, seasonal fluctuations are much greater than business cycle fluctuations. For other firms, such as appliance or automobile manufacturers, cyclical fluctuations are larger. In the following sections, we will look in more detail at the requirements for working capital financing and examine some alternative working capital policies.

Self-Test Question

Under normal circumstances, when does a firm's working capital position change? Explain why.

THE CASH CONVERSION CYCLE

To summarize the working capital management process that Argile Textiles and most other companies face, consider the following activities:

1. Argile orders and then receives materials needed to produce the products that it sells. The company purchases from its suppliers on credit, so an account payable is created for the credit purchase. The purchase has no immediate cash flow effect because payment is not made until some later date.

2. Labor is used to convert the materials (cotton and wool) into finished goods (cloth products, thread, and so forth). Wages are not fully paid at the time when the work is done, so accrued wages build up, perhaps for a period of 1 or 2 weeks.

3. The finished products are sold, but on credit. Thus sales create receivables, not immediate cash inflows.

4. At some point during the cycle, Argile pays its suppliers and employees. If these payments are made before Argile has collected cash from its receivables, a net cash outflow will occur, and the firm must finance this outflow.

5. The cycle is completed when Argile's receivables are collected (perhaps in 30 days). At that time, the company is in a position to pay off the credit that was used to finance the manufacture of its products, and it can then repeat the cycle.

The activities outlined here give an indication of the relationships among the various working capital accounts. To illustrate these relationships, we can formalize the process Argile faces by examining its *cash conversion cycle*, which focuses on the length of time between when the company makes cash payments, or invests in the manufacture of inventory, and when it receives cash inflows, or realizes a cash return from its investment in production.[1] The following terms are used in the model:

1. The **inventory conversion period** (age of inventory) is the average length of time required to convert raw materials into finished goods, and then to sell those goods; it is the amount of time that the product remains in inventory in

inventory conversion period
The length of time required to convert raw materials into finished goods and then to sell those goods.

---

[1]See Verlyn Richards and Eugene Laughlin , "A Cash Conversion Cycle Approach to Liquidity Analysis," *Financial Management*, Spring 1980, 32–38.

various stages of completion. The inventory conversion period is calculated as follows:

15-1

$$\text{Inventory conversion period} = \frac{\text{Inventory}}{\text{Cost of goods sold per day}} = \frac{\text{Inventory}}{\left(\dfrac{\text{Annual cost of goods sold}}{360 \text{ days}}\right)}$$

Because Argile's cost of goods sold was $600 million in 2010, its inventory conversion period was:[2]

$$\text{Argile's inventory conversion period} = \frac{\$135.0 \text{ million}}{\left(\dfrac{\$\ 600 \text{ million}}{360 \text{ days}}\right)} = \frac{\$135.0}{\$1.667} = 81.0 \text{ days}$$

Thus, in its 2010 operations, it took Argile 81 days to manufacture and sell its products.

receivables collection period
The length of time required to collect cash following a credit sale.

2. The **receivables collection period** (age of receivables) is the average length of time required to convert the firm's receivables into cash—that is, to collect cash following a credit sale. The receivables collection period is also called the days sales outstanding (DSO), and it is calculated as follows:

15-2

$$\text{Receivables collection period (DSO)} = \frac{\text{Receivables}}{\text{Average daily credit sales}} = \frac{\text{Receivables}}{\left(\dfrac{\text{Annual credit sales}}{360}\right)}$$

In 2010, Argile generated $750 million in sales, so its DSO was:

$$\text{Argile's receivables collection period (DSO)} = \frac{\$90.0 \text{ million}}{\left(\dfrac{\$750.0 \text{ million}}{360}\right)} = \frac{\$90.0}{\$2.083} = 43.2 \text{ days}$$

Thus, on average, the cash payment associated with a credit sale was not collected until approximately 43 days after the sale.

payables deferral period
The length of time from when the firm purchases raw materials and when it pays for the purchase.

3. The **payables deferral period** (age of payables) is the average length of time between the purchase of raw materials and labor and the payment of cash for them. Also called days payables outstanding (DPO), it is computed as follows:

15-3

$$\text{Payables deferral period (DPO)} = \frac{\text{Accounts payable}}{\text{Average daily credit purchases}} = \frac{\text{Accounts payable}}{\left(\dfrac{\text{Cost of goods sold}}{360}\right)}$$

---

[2]In the computations that follow, as well as other ratio computations in this book, we assume that there are 360 days in the year. This assumption is made to simplify computations only—360 is divisible by more integer values than 365. This assumption changes neither the meaning nor the application of the computations.

FIGURE 15-1   The Cash Conversion Cycle for Argile Textiles

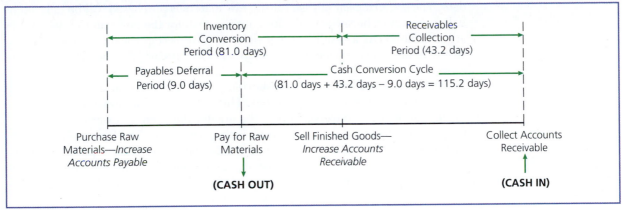

Argile's payables deferral period was:

$$\text{Argile's payables deferral period (DPO)} = \frac{\$15 \text{ million}}{\left(\dfrac{\$600 \text{ million}}{360}\right)} = \frac{\$15.0}{\$1.667} = 9.0 \text{ days}$$

Therefore, on average, Argile paid its suppliers 9 days after materials were purchased.[3]

4. The **cash conversion cycle** computation nets out the three periods just defined, resulting in a value that equals the length of time from when the firm pays for (invests in) productive resources (materials and labor) and when it receives cash (a return) from the sale of products. Thus, the cash conversion cycle equals the average length of time that a dollar remains tied up in current assets.

We can now use these definitions to analyze Argile's cash conversion cycle. First, the concept is diagrammed in Figure 15-1. Each component is given a number, and the cash conversion cycle can be expressed by the following equation:

cash conversion cycle
The length of time from the payment for the purchase of raw materials needed to manufacture a product until the collection of accounts receivable associated with the sale of that product.

$$\begin{array}{c} \text{Cash} \\ \text{conversion} \\ \text{cycle} \end{array} = \left[\left(\begin{array}{c} \text{Inventory} \\ \text{conversion} \\ \text{period} \end{array}\right) + \left(\begin{array}{c} \text{Receivables} \\ \text{collection} \\ \text{period} \end{array}\right) \right] - \left(\begin{array}{c} \text{Payable} \\ \text{deferral} \\ \text{period} \end{array}\right)$$

15-4

$$= \quad 81.0 \text{ days} \quad + \quad 43.2 \text{ days} \quad - \quad 9.0 \text{ days}$$
$$= 115.2 \text{ days}$$

In this case, the cash conversion cycle is approximately 115 days. The *receipt* of cash from manufacturing and selling the products will be delayed by approximately 124 days because (1) the product will be "tied up" in inventory for 81 days

---

[3]The computation for the payables deferral period shown here is the traditional method used to determine the value used in the calculation of the cash conversion cycle. If we recognize that the intention of the computation is to determine the length of time between the purchase of raw materials *and* the labor used to produce inventory and the payment for these inputs, then the payables deferral period might more appropriately be written to include consideration of accrued wages.

and (2) cash from the sale will not be received until about 43 days after the selling date. The *disbursement* of cash for the raw materials purchased will be delayed by 9 days, however, because Argile does not pay cash for the raw materials when they are purchased. As a result, the net delay in cash receipts associated with an investment (cash disbursement) in inventory is 115 days, which is nearly one-third of a year.

The firm's goal should be to shorten its cash conversion cycle as much as possible without hurting its operations. This effort would improve profits because the longer the cash conversion cycle, the greater the need for external financing—for example, bank loans—and such financing has a cost. The firm can shorten its cash conversion cycle by (1) reducing the inventory conversion period by processing and selling goods more quickly, (2) reducing the receivables collection period by speeding up collections, and (3) lengthening the payables deferral period by slowing down payments made to suppliers. To the extent that these actions can be taken *without harming the return* associated with the management of these accounts, they should be carried out. More specific actions that can be taken to reduce the length of the cash conversion cycle are discussed later in the chapter. As you read the chapter, you should keep the cash conversion cycle concept in mind.

Self-Test Questions

What steps are involved in estimating the cash conversion cycle?

Define the following terms: *inventory conversion period, receivables collection period, payables deferral period.*

How can the cash conversion cycle be used to improve current asset management?

WORKING CAPITAL INVESTMENT AND FINANCING POLICIES

Working capital policy involves two basic questions:

- What is the appropriate level for investment in current assets, both in total and for specific accounts?
- How should current assets be financed?

Alternative Current Asset Investment Policies

Figure 15-2 depicts three alternative policies for the total amount of current assets carried. Essentially, these policies differ in that different amounts of current assets are carried to support a particular level of sales. The line with the steepest slope represents a **relaxed current asset investment** (or "fat cat") **policy,** in which relatively large amounts of cash, marketable securities, and inventories are carried and sales are stimulated by the use of a credit policy that provides liberal financing to customers and a corresponding high level of receivables. With the **restricted current asset investment** (or "lean-and-mean") **policy,** the amounts of current assets are minimized. The **moderate current asset investment policy** lies between these two extremes.

---

relaxed current asset investment policy
A policy in which relatively large amounts of cash and marketable securities and inventories are carried, and sales are stimulated by a liberal credit policy that results in a high level of receivables.

restricted current asset investment policy
A policy in which holdings of cash and marketable securities, inventories, and receivables are minimized.

moderate current asset investment policy
A policy that lies between the relaxed and restrictive current asset investment policies.

FIGURE 15-2   Alternative Current Asset Investment Policies ($ million)

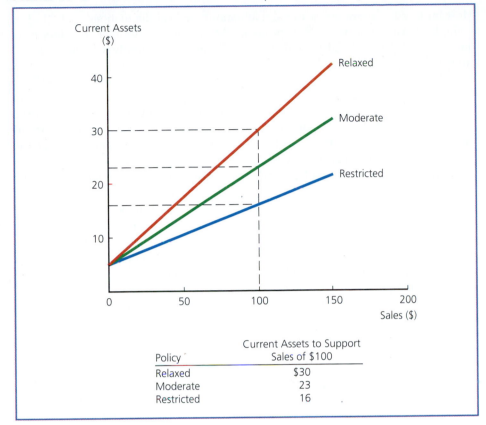

Policy	Current Assets to Support Sales of $100
Relaxed	$30
Moderate	23
Restricted	16

The more certain a firm is about its sales, costs, order lead times, payment periods, and so forth, the lower the level of current assets that is required to support operations. If there is a great deal of uncertainty about operations, however, the firm will require some minimum amount of cash and inventories based on expected payments, expected sales, expected order lead times, and so on, plus additional amounts, or *safety stocks*, that enable it to deal with departures from the expected values. Similarly, accounts receivable levels are determined by credit terms: the tougher the credit terms, the lower the accounts receivable for any given level of sales. With a restricted current asset investment policy, the firm would hold minimal levels of safety stocks for cash and inventories, and it would have a tight credit policy even though such a policy would mean running the risk of losing sales. A restricted, lean-and-mean current asset investment policy generally provides the highest expected return on investment, but it entails the greatest risk. The reverse is true under a relaxed policy. The moderate policy falls in between the two extremes in terms of both expected risk and return.

In terms of the cash conversion cycle, a restricted investment policy would tend to reduce the inventory conversion and accounts receivable collection periods, resulting in a relatively short cash conversion cycle. Conversely, a relaxed policy would create higher levels of inventories and accounts receivables, longer inventory conversion and accounts receivable collection periods, and a relatively long cash conversion cycle. A moderate policy would produce a cash conversion cycle somewhere between the two extremes.

Alternative Current Asset Financing Policies

Most businesses experience seasonal fluctuations, cyclical fluctuations, or both. For example, construction firms have peaks in the spring and summer, retailers peak during the Christmas holidays, and the manufacturers that supply both construction companies and retailers follow similar patterns. Similarly, virtually all businesses must build up current assets when the economy is strong, but they then sell off inventories and have net reductions of accounts receivable when the economy slacks off. Even so, current assets rarely drop to $0, and this realization has led to the development of the idea that some current assets should be considered **permanent current assets** because their levels remain stable (at some minimum level) no matter the seasonal or economic conditions.

Temporary current assets, on the other hand, are those amounts of current assets that vary with respect to the seasonal or economic conditions of a firm. During off-season periods, temporary assets will be $0; during peak-season periods, they will be very high. Table 15-1 shows that the level of current assets for Argile Textiles is expected to be $345 million in September 2011 and only $258.7 in December 2011. Because the height of Argile's selling season occurs in the fall, most of the difference between the levels of current assets at these two dates results from changes in temporary current assets.

The manner in which the permanent and temporary current assets are financed is called the firm's *current asset financing policy.* In general, the approach that a firm uses to finance its current assets is referred to as *maturity matching, conservative,* or *aggressive.*

Maturity Matching (Self-Liquidating) Approach

The **maturity matching,** or **"self-liquidating," approach** calls for matching asset and liability maturities. This strategy minimizes the risk that the firm will be unable to pay off its maturing obligations *if* the liquidations of the assets can be controlled to occur on or before the date the obligations reach maturity. At the limit, a firm could attempt to match exactly the maturity structure of its assets and liabilities. Inventory expected to be sold in 30 days could be financed with a 30-day bank loan; a machine expected to last for 5 years could be financed by a 5-year loan; and so forth. Of course, two factors make it impossible to match maturities exactly: (1) there is uncertainty about sales and the lives of the firm's assets, thus when cash inflows will be received, and (2) some common equity, which has no maturity, must be used to finance the firm.

Conservative Approach

With the **conservative approach,** permanent, or long-term, capital is used to finance all permanent asset requirements and to meet much (perhaps all) of the seasonal demands, and hence to finance temporary current assets. At the extreme, a firm could finance all of its seasonal needs with long-term financing alternatives, thereby eliminating the need to use short-term financing. This would be a difficult, if not impossible, task to accomplish. Most firms that follow this approach use some amounts of short-term credit to meet financing needs during peak-season periods. Even so, they will have "extra" permanent funds during off-peak periods, which allows them to "store liquidity" in the form of short-term investments, called marketable securities, during the off-season. As its name implies, this approach is a safe, conservative, current asset financing policy, and it generally is not as profitable as the other two approaches discussed here.

Sidebar definitions:

permanent current assets
Current assets' balances that do not change due to seasonal or economic conditions; balances that exist even at the trough of a firm's business cycle.

temporary current assets
Current assets that fluctuate with seasonal or economic variations in a firm's business.

maturity matching (self-liquidating) approach
A financing policy that matches asset and liability maturities—considered a moderate current asset financing policy.

conservative approach
A policy in which all of the fixed assets, all of the permanent current assets, and some of the temporary current assets of a firm are financed with long-term capital.

Aggressive Approach

A firm that follows the **aggressive approach** finances *all* of its fixed assets and some of its permanent current assets with long-term capital; the remainder of the permanent current assets and all of the temporary current assets are financed with such short-term financing as bank loans. Several different *degrees* of aggressiveness are possible. For example, one firm might finance nearly all of its permanent current assets with short-term credit, while another firm might finance relatively little of its current permanent assets with the same type of credit. The aggressive approach is riskier than either of the other two approaches because the short-term credit used to finance the permanent current assets must be renewed each time it comes due. As a consequence, the firm faces the threat of rising interest rates as well as loan renewal problems. Because short-term debt often is less expensive than long-term debt, however, some firms are willing to sacrifice safety for the chance of higher profits.

aggressive approach
A policy in which all of the fixed assets of a firm are financed with long-term capital, but some of the firm's permanent current assets are financed with short-term, nonspontaneous sources of funds.

Self-Test Questions

What two key issues does working capital policy involve?

What are three alternative current asset investment policies? Is one best?

What are three alternative current asset financing policies? Is one best?

What distinguishes *permanent current assets* from *temporary current assets?*

ADVANTAGES AND DISADVANTAGES OF SHORT-TERM FINANCING

The three different financing policies just described are distinguished by the relative amounts of short-term debt used under each policy. The aggressive policy calls for the greatest use of short-term debt, the conservative policy requires the least, and maturity matching falls in between. This section considers some of the pros and cons of short-term financing.

Speed

A short-term loan can be obtained much faster than long-term credit. Lenders will insist on a more thorough financial examination before extending long-term credit, and the loan agreement will have to be spelled out in considerable detail, because much can happen during the life of a long-term loan.

Flexibility

If the needs for funds are seasonal or cyclical, a firm might not want to commit itself to long-term debt for three reasons:

1. The cost of issuing long-term debt is considerably greater than the cost of using short-term credit.
2. Some long-term loans charge expensive penalties for paying off the debt prior to maturity.
3. Long-term loan agreements contain provisions, or covenants, that restrict the firm's future actions, whereas short-term credit agreements usually are much less onerous in this regard.

In general, then, short-term financing alternatives are more flexible than long-term financing alternatives.

Cost of Long-Term versus Short-Term Debt

As discussed in Chapter 5, the yield curve normally is upward sloping, indicating that interest rates generally are lower on short-term debt than on long-term debt. Thus, interest costs normally will be lower if the firm borrows on a short-term rather than on a long-term basis.

Risk of Long-Term versus Short-Term Debt

A major disadvantage of short-term debt is that it subjects the firm to more risk than does long-term debt. This greater risk occurs for two reasons:

1. If a firm borrows on a long-term basis, its interest costs will be relatively stable—perhaps even fixed—over time. If it uses short-term credit, its interest expense will fluctuate, at times reaching very high levels.

2. If a firm borrows heavily on a short-term basis, it could find itself unable to repay this debt, and it might be in such a weak financial position that the lender will not extend the loan. Such an event could force the firm into bankruptcy.

Self-Test Questions

What are some advantages of short-term debt over long-term debt as a source of capital?

What are some disadvantages of short-term debt?

SOURCES OF SHORT-TERM FINANCING

short-term credit
Any liability originally scheduled for repayment within 1 year.

Statements about the flexibility, cost, and riskiness of short-term debt versus long-term debt depend, to a large extent, on the type of short-term credit used. **Short-term credit** is defined as any liability originally scheduled for payment within 1 year. Numerous sources of short-term funds exist. In this section, we briefly describe five major types: accruals, accounts payable (trade credit), bank loans, commercial paper, and secured short-term loans.

Accruals

accruals
Continually recurring short-term liabilities; liabilities such as wages and taxes that increase spontaneously with operations.

A firm generally pays employees on a weekly, biweekly, or monthly basis, so its balance sheet typically shows some accrued wages. Similarly, the firm's own estimated income taxes, the Social Security and income taxes withheld from employee payrolls, and the sales taxes collected generally are paid on a weekly, monthly, or quarterly basis, so the balance sheet typically also shows some accrued taxes. These **accruals** increase (decrease) automatically, or spontaneously, as a firm's operations expand (contract). This type of debt generally is considered "free" in the sense that no explicit interest is paid on funds raised through accruals. Ordinarily, a firm cannot control its accruals: the timing of wage payments is set by economic forces and industry custom, whereas tax payment dates are established by law.

Accounts Payable (Trade Credit)

Most firms purchase from their suppliers on credit, recording the debt as an *account payable*.[4] Representing approximately 40 percent of the current liabilities for the average nonfinancial corporation, this type of financing—called **trade credit**—is the largest single category of short-term debt. Trade credit is a *spontaneous* source of financing in the sense that it arises from ordinary business transactions. The amount of trade credit used by a firm depends on the terms of the credit purchase and the size of the firm's operations. For example, lengthening the credit period, as well as expanding sales and purchases, generates additional trade credit.

trade credit
The credit created when one firm buys on credit from another firm.

Short-Term Bank Loans

Commercial banks, whose loans generally appear on a firm's balance sheet as notes payable, are second in importance to trade credit as a source of short-term financing.[5] The banks' influence actually is greater than it appears from the dollar amounts they lend because banks provide *nonspontaneous* funds. That is, as a firm's financing needs increase, it specifically requests additional funds from its bank. If the request is denied, the firm might be forced to abandon attractive growth opportunities. Bank loans include the key features described next.

Maturity

Bank loans to businesses frequently are written as 90-day notes, so the loan must be repaid or renewed at the end of 90 days. Of course, if a borrower's financial position has deteriorated at that point, the bank might refuse to renew the loan.

Promissory Note

When a bank loan is approved, the agreement is executed by signing a **promissory note** that specifies (1) the amount borrowed, (2) the interest rate, (3) the repayment schedule, (4) whether collateral, or security, is required, and (5) any other terms and conditions to which the bank and the borrower have agreed.

promissory note
A document specifying the terms and conditions of a loan, including the amount, interest rate, and repayment schedule.

Compensating Balances

Banks often require a firm to maintain an average checking account balance, called a **compensating balance (CB),** as a requirement of getting a loan. The funds that are used to maintain a compensating balance, which generally equals 10 to 20 percent of the loan amount, cannot be used by the firm to pay its bills or to invest. A compensating balance does not earn interest. As a result, a compensating balance essentially represents a charge by the bank for *servicing* the loan (bookkeeping, maintaining a line of credit, and so on).

compensating balance (CB)
A minimum checking account balance that a firm must maintain with a bank to borrow funds—generally 10 to 20 percent of the amount of loans outstanding.

---

[4]In a credit sale, the seller records the transaction as a receivable, and the buyer records it as a payable. We examine accounts receivables as an investment later in the chapter. Note that if a firm's accounts payable exceeds its accounts receivable, it is said to be *receiving net trade credit*. If its accounts receivable exceeds its accounts payable, it is *extending net trade credit*. Smaller firms frequently receive net credit; larger firms generally extend it.

[5]Although commercial banks remain the primary source of short-term loans, other sources are available. For example, in 2008, GE Capital Corporation (GECC) had several billion dollars in commercial loans outstanding. Firms such as GECC, which was initially established to finance consumers' purchases of GE's durable goods, often find business loans to be more profitable than consumer loans.

Line of Credit

line of credit
An arrangement in which a bank agrees to lend up to a specified maximum amount of funds during a designated period.

revolving credit agreement
A line of credit in which the funds are guaranteed, or committed, by the bank or other lending institution.

commitment fee
A fee charged on the *unused* balance of a revolving credit agreement to compensate the bank for guaranteeing that the funds will be available when needed by the borrower.

commercial paper
Unsecured, short-term promissory notes issued by large, financially sound firms to raise funds.

A **line of credit** is an agreement between a bank and a borrower indicating the maximum credit that the bank will allow the borrower to have outstanding at any point in time. For example, a bank loan officer might indicate to a financial manager that the bank regards the firm as being "good" for a maximum of $200,000 during the forthcoming year. That is, the firm can have at most a $200,000 balance of loans outstanding from this source at any time during the year. When a line of credit arrangement is *guaranteed,* it is called a **revolving credit agreement.** With a revolving credit agreement, the bank has a *legal obligation* to provide funds requested by the borrower. The bank generally charges a **commitment fee** for guaranteeing the availability of the funds. This fee is usually charged on the unused balance of the credit line because, to guarantee that the funds will be available when requested, the funds must be accessed quickly, and, as a consequence, the bank must invest these funds in liquid instruments that provide relatively low returns. Neither the legal obligation nor the fee exists under a "regular," or general, credit line because this type of credit provides the funds only if they are available at the bank.

Commercial Paper

Commercial paper is a type of unsecured promissory note *issued* by large, financially strong firms. It is sold primarily to other firms, insurance companies, pension funds, money market mutual funds, and banks. The use of commercial paper is restricted to a comparatively small number of firms that are *exceptionally* good credit risks. Maturities of commercial paper vary from 1 to 9 months, with an average of about 5 months.[6] Using commercial paper permits a corporation to tap a wider range of credit sources, including financial institutions across the country, which can reduce interest costs. One potential problem with commercial paper is that a debtor who is in temporary financial difficulty might receive little help from "lenders" because commercial paper dealings generally are less personal than are bank relationships.

Secured Loans

secured loans
Loans backed by collateral. For short-term loans, the collateral often consists of inventory, receivables, or both.

pledging receivables
Using accounts receivable as collateral for a loan.

factoring
The outright sale of accounts receivable.

Most loans can be secured, or collateralized, if it is deemed necessary or desirable. Given a choice, it is usually better to borrow on an unsecured basis because the bookkeeping costs of **secured loans** often are high. Nevertheless, weak firms might find that they can borrow only if they put up some type of security or if using security allows them to borrow at a lower rate.

Most secured, short-term business loans involve the use of short-term assets, such as accounts receivable and inventories, as collateral. When receivables are used as collateral, the firm is said to be **pledging** its **receivables.** Sometimes, receivables are actually *sold* to financial institutions. With this arrangement, the firm is said to be **factoring** its receivables, and the buyer is called a *factor.* In both cases, the dollar amount the firm receives is less than the full value of the receivables—that is, either the amount borrowed (pledged) on the receivables or the amount for which the receivables are sold (factored) is less than the face, or total, value of the receivables. When receivables are pledged, the difference between the loan value and

---

[6]The maximum maturity without SEC registration is 270 days. Also, commercial paper can be sold only to "sophisticated" investors; otherwise, SEC registration would be required even for maturities of 270 days or less.

the face value of the receivables represents a cushion to protect the lender against "bad" receivables (bad debts); when receivables are factored, the difference represents the potential gross profit to the factor (purchaser). A principal difference between the two arrangements is that when receivables are pledged, the lender has both a claim against the receivables and **recourse** to the borrower. Thus, if one of the borrowing firm's credit customers, which represents an account receivable, does not pay, the borrowing firm rather than the lending institution takes the loss. With most factoring arrangements, the factor that buys the receivables must take the loss. Therefore, it is not uncommon for the factor to provide credit department personnel for the borrower to carry out the credit investigation of its customers.

recourse
A situation in which the lender can seek payment from the borrowing firm when the accounts receivable used to secure a loan is uncollectable.

A substantial amount of credit is secured by business inventories. If a firm is a relatively good credit risk, the mere existence of the inventory might be a sufficient basis for receiving an unsecured loan. If the firm is a relatively poor risk, the lending institution might insist on security in the form of a *lien* against the inventory. The three major types of inventory liens include the following:

1. A *blanket lien* gives the lending institution a lien against all of the borrower's inventories without limiting the borrower's ability to sell the inventories. This type of lien generally is used when the inventory put up as collateral is relatively low priced, fast moving, and difficult to identify individually.

2. A *trust receipt* is an arrangement in which the goods are held in trust for the lender, perhaps stored in a public warehouse or held on the premises of the borrower. Such an arrangement generally is used for goods that are relatively high priced, slow moving, and easy to identify individually using serial numbers or some other distinguishing characteristic. When the goods that are affected by this lien are sold, proceeds from the sale must be given to the lender. Automobile dealer financing is one of the best examples of trust receipt financing.

3. *Warehouse receipt* financing refers to an arrangement in which inventory used as collateral is physically separated from the borrower's other inventory and then stored in a secured site located either on the premises of the borrower (*field warehousing*) or in an independent warehouse (*terminal warehousing*). To provide inventory supervision, the lending institution employs a third party in the arrangement—a warehousing company—that acts as its agent in the oversight and the sale of the inventory.

Self-Test Questions

What types of short-term sources of funds are classified as accruals?

What is trade credit?

How does a revolving line of credit differ from a regular line of credit?

What is commercial paper? What types of companies can use commercial paper to meet their short-term financing needs?

What is a secured loan? What two types of current assets are pledged as security for short-term loans?

Differentiate between pledging accounts receivable and factoring accounts receivable.

Describe three arrangements in which inventory is used as collateral for a short-term loan.

COMPUTING THE COST OF SHORT-TERM CREDIT

In this section, we describe how the cost of short-term credit is determined. To start, we compute the percentage cost of using the funds for a given period, r_{PER}:

15-5

$$\text{Percentage cost per period} = r_{PER} = \frac{\text{Dollar cost of borrowing}}{\text{Amount of usable funds}}$$

In this equation, the numerator represents the dollar amount that must be paid for using the borrowed funds. This cost includes the interest paid on the loan, application fees, charges for commitment fees, and so forth. The denominator represents the amount of the loan that actually can be used (spent) by the borrower. This amount is not necessarily the same as the principal amount of the loan, because discounts, compensating balances, or other costs might reduce the amount of the loan proceeds that the firm can use. We will soon discover that *when loan restrictions prevent the borrower from using the entire amount of the loan, the effective annual rate paid for the loan is higher than the stated interest rate.*

Using Equation 15-5 and the concepts described in Chapter 9, the effective annual rate (EAR) and the annual percentage rate (APR) for short-term financing can be computed as follows:

15-6

$$\text{Effective annual rate (EAR)} = r_{EAR} = (1 + r_{PER})^m - 1.0$$

15-7

$$\text{Annual percentage rate (APR)} = r_{PER} \times m = r_{SIMPLE}$$

where m is the number of borrowing periods per year (that is, if the loan is for 1 month, m = 12). Recall from our discussion in Chapter 9 that the EAR incorporates interest compounding in the computation, but the APR does not. Both computations adjust the percentage cost per period so that it is stated on an annual basis. We annualize the cost to make it easier to compare short-term credit instruments that have different maturities—that is, to compare borrowing costs on the same annual basis.

To illustrate the application of these equations, consider the credit terms of 2/10, net 30, which allows the firm to take a 2 percent discount from the purchase price of raw materials if payment is made on or before Day 10 of the billing cycle; otherwise, the entire bill is due by Day 30. If it does not take the discount, then for each $1 of purchases, the firm effectively pays 2¢ to borrow 98¢ for a 20-day period, so the cost of using the funds for the additional 20 days is:

$$\text{Percentage cost per period} = r_{PER} = \frac{2¢}{98¢} = 0.020408 \approx 2.041\%$$

Because there are m = eighteen 20-day periods in a 360-day year, the APR, or simple interest rate, associated with the trade credit is:

$$\text{APR} = r_{SIMPLE} = 2.0408\% \times 18 = 36.73\%$$

The effective annual cost (rate), EAR, of using trade credit with these terms as a source of short-term financing is:

$$r_{EAR} = (1 + 0.020408)^{18} - 1.0 = 1.43856 - 1.0 = 0.43856 = 43.86\%$$

According to this computation, if the firm chooses to pay its bill on Day 30, then it will "forgo" the 2 percent cash discount, which is equivalent to borrowing funds at a rate of nearly 44 percent per year.[7]

Next, let's consider what happens when a firm finances with a **discount interest loan** from the bank. With this type of loan, the interest due is deducted "up front" so that the borrower receives less than the principal amount, or face value, of the loan. Assume that Argile Textiles received a $10,000 discount interest loan with an 8 percent quoted (simple) interest rate to be used for a period of 9 months. The interest payment on this loan is $10,000 \times 0.08 \times (9/12) = \$600$. Note that interest is paid only for the portion of the year during which the loan is outstanding—9 months in this case. Because the interest is paid in advance, Argile has only $9,400 = \$10,000 - \$600$ available for use. Thus, the 9-month interest rate paid for the loan is:

> **discount interest loan**
> A loan in which the interest, which is calculated on the amount borrowed (principal), is paid at the beginning of the loan period—that is, interest is paid in advance.

$$r_{PER} = \frac{\text{9-month}}{\text{interest rate}} = \frac{\$10{,}000 \times 0.08 \times \left(\frac{9}{12}\right)}{\$10{,}000 - \left[\$10{,}000 \times 0.08 \times \left(\frac{9}{12}\right)\right]}$$

$$= \frac{\$600}{\$9{,}400} = 0.06383 = 6.38\%$$

The APR for the loan is:

$$APR = r_{SIMPLE} = 6.383\% \times \left(\frac{12}{9}\right) = 8.51\%$$

The EAR is:

$$r_{EAR} = (1.06383)^{(12/9)} - 1.0 = 0.08600 = 8.60\%$$

What do you think the cost of the loan described here would be if Argile's bank charged a $50 fee to cover the costs of processing the loan? To answer this question, first look at Equation 15-5 and determine whether the payment affects the numerator (that is, the dollar cost of borrowing), the denominator (that is, the amount of usable funds), or both. The general rule is that the numerator is affected by any expense associated with the loan, and the denominator is affected if funds must be put aside (for example, to satisfy a compensating balance requirement) or if costs are paid out of the proceeds at the beginning of the loan period. Thus, if Argile uses the proceeds from the loan to pay the $50 fee, both the numerator and the denominator are affected, and the 9-month interest rate would be:

$$r_{PER} = \frac{\text{9-month}}{\text{interest rate}} = \frac{\$600 + \$50}{\$9{,}400 - \$50} = \frac{\$650}{\$9{,}350} = 0.06952 = 6.95\%$$

---

[7]We assume that the firm pays its supplier on the last day possible. That is, if it takes the discount, payment is made on Day 10; if it doesn't take the discount, payment is made on Day 30. This pattern constitutes rational business behavior. If the firm does not take the discount, but pays on Day 20 (or any other time before the final due date), then the cost associated with using this source of financing is higher than computed here. The funds cost more because the firm pays the same dollar cost, but uses the funds for a shorter period.

Check to see that the APR and the EAR are now 9.27 percent and 9.37 percent, respectively.

From the examples presented here, you should recognize that the percentage cost of short-term financing is higher when the dollar expenses (such as those associated with interest, clerical efforts, loan processing, and so forth) are higher or when the net proceeds from the loan are less than the principal amount. In most cases, then, the effective interest rate (cost) of short-term financing is greater than its stated (quoted) interest rate. The effective interest rate of a loan is equal to the quoted (simple) rate only when the entire principal amount borrowed can be used by the borrower for an entire year and the only dollar cost is interest charged on the outstanding balance of the loan.

Self-Test Questions

What is the difference between APR and EAR?

All else equal, what causes the APR and EAR to increase?

MANAGING CASH AND MARKETABLE SECURITIES

In Chapter 10, we discovered that value, which the firm's management should want to maximize, is based on cash flows. Consequently, managing cash flows is an extremely important task for a financial manager. Part of this task involves determining how much cash a firm should have on hand at any time to ensure that normal business operations can continue uninterrupted. This section describes factors that affect the amount of cash held by firms and some of the cash management techniques currently used by businesses.

Cash Management

For the purposes of the discussion here, the term *cash* refers to the funds a firm holds that can be used for immediate disbursement—it includes the amount a firm holds in its checking account as well as the amount of actual currency it has. Cash is a "non-earning, or idle, asset" that is needed to pay bills. When possible, cash should be "put to work" by investing in assets that have positive expected returns. Thus, the goal of the cash manager is to minimize the amount of cash held by the firm for use in conducting its normal business activities, while simultaneously ensuring that the firm has sufficient cash to support its operations.

Firms hold cash for the following reasons:

transactions balance
A cash balance necessary for day-to-day operations; the balance associated with routine payments and collections.

1. The primary reason that firms maintain cash balances is because payments must be made in cash and receipts are deposited in a cash account. Cash balances associated with routine payments and collections are known as **transactions balances.**

2. A bank often requires a firm to maintain a *compensating balance* on deposit to help offset the costs of providing services such as check clearing, cash management advice, and so forth.

precautionary balance
A cash balance held in reserve for unforeseen fluctuations in cash flows.

3. Because cash inflows and outflows are somewhat unpredictable, firms generally hold some cash in reserve to ensure against random, unforeseen fluctuations in cash flows. These "safety stocks" are called **precautionary balances.** The less predictable the firm's cash flows, the larger such balances

should be. However, if the firm has quick and easy access to borrowed funds, perhaps through an established line of credit, its need for precautionary balances is reduced.

4. At times, cash balances are held to enable the firm to take advantage of bargain purchases that might arise. These funds are called **speculative balances.** As with precautionary balances, firms that have easy access to borrowed funds are likely to rely on their ability to borrow quickly rather than use cash balances for speculative purposes.

Although the cash accounts of most firms can be envisioned as consisting of transactions, compensating, precautionary, and speculative balances, we cannot calculate the amount needed for each purpose, sum them, and produce a total desired cash balance because the same money often serves more than one purpose. For instance, precautionary and speculative balances can also be used to satisfy compensating balance requirements. Firms do, however, consider all four factors when establishing their target cash positions.

In addition to the four motives given here, a firm maintains cash balances to preserve its credit rating by keeping its liquidity position in line with those of other firms in the same industry. A strong credit rating enables the firm to purchase goods from suppliers on favorable terms and to maintain an ample line of credit with its bank.

Cash Management Techniques

Most cash management activities are performed jointly by the firm and its primary bank, but the financial manager ultimately is responsible for the effectiveness of the cash management program. Effective cash management encompasses proper management of both the cash inflows and the cash outflows of a firm, which entails consideration of the factors discussed in this section.

Cash Forecasts

The most critical ingredient of proper cash management is the cash forecast, often referred to as the cash budget. A firm needs to predict the timing of its cash inflows and cash outflows to plan for its investment and borrowing activities. If a cash shortfall is projected to occur during a particular period, arrangements can be made to borrow the needed funds before a crisis erupts. At the same time, if a cash surplus is projected, the firm can plan to temporarily invest the funds rather than letting them sit idle. The cash budget is discussed in greater detail in Chapter 8.

Cash Flow Synchronization

Companies try to arrange matters so that their cash inflows and cash outflows are matched as well as possible—that is, customers are billed so that their "billing cycles" will coordinate with when the firm pays its own bills. Having **synchronized cash flows** enables the firm to reduce its cash balances, decrease its bank loans, lower its interest expenses, and boost its profits. The more predictable the timing of the cash flows, the greater the synchronization that can be attained. Notably, utilities and credit card companies generally have high degrees of cash flow synchronization.

Float

Float is defined as the difference between the balance shown in a firm's (or individual's) checkbook and the balance on the bank's records. For example, suppose

speculative balance
A cash balance held to enable the firm to take advantage of any bargain purchases that might arise.

synchronized cash flows
A situation in which cash inflows coincide with cash outflows, thereby permitting a firm to hold low transactions balances.

float
The difference between the balance shown in a firm's (or individual's) checkbook and the balance on the bank's records.

a firm writes checks in the amount of $5,000 each day, and it normally takes 4 days from the time the check is mailed until it is cleared and deducted from the firm's bank account. This particular delay causes the firm's own checkbook to show a balance $20,000 = ($5,000 × 4 days) less than the balance on the bank's records; this difference is called **disbursement float.** Now suppose the firm receives checks in the amount of $6,500 daily, but it loses 2 days while the checks are being processed, deposited, and cleared. This delay results in $13,000 = ($6,500 × 2 days) of **collections float.** Together, the firm's **net float**—the difference between the $20,000 positive disbursement float and the $13,000 negative collections float—will be $7,000. Thus, the net balance that the bank shows in the firm's checking account is $7,000 greater than the balance that the firm shows in its own checkbook.

Delays that cause float arise because it takes time for checks to be (1) delivered to the payee (receiver) via mail or electronically *(transit delay)*, (2) processed by the receiving firm *(processing delay)*, and (3) cleared through the banking system *(clearing, or availability, delay)*. Basically, the size of a firm's net float is a function of its ability to speed up collections on checks *received* and to slow down collections on checks *written*. Efficient firms go to great lengths to speed up the processing of incoming checks (receipts), thereby putting the funds to work more quickly, and they try to delay their own payments for as long as possible.

Acceleration of Receipts

A firm cannot use customers' payments until they are received *and* converted into a spendable form, such as cash or an increase in a checking account balance. Not surprisingly, it would benefit the firm to accelerate the collection of customers' payments and the conversion of those payments into cash.

Although the firm cannot directly control some of the delays that cause float, it can use the following techniques to manage collections:

1. A **lockbox arrangement** requires customers to send their payments to a post office box located in the area near where they live rather than directly to the firm (when payments are mailed). The firm arranges for a local bank to collect the checks from the post office box, perhaps several times each day, and to immediately deposit them into the company's checking account. Float is reduced in two ways. First, the transit delay is less than if the payment has to travel farther. Second, checks are cleared more rapidly because the banks on which the checks are written are located in the same Federal Reserve district.

2. If a firm receives regular, repetitious payments from its customers, then it might want to establish a **preauthorized debit system** (sometimes called *preauthorized payments*). With this arrangement, the collecting firm and its customer (paying firm) enter into an agreement whereby the paying firm's bank periodically transfers funds from the paying firm's account to the collecting firm's account, even if that account is located at another bank. The transfer of funds is accelerated because transit and check-clearing delays are eliminated and the processing delay generally is reduced significantly.

3. **Concentration banking** is a cash management arrangement used to mobilize funds from decentralized collection locations, whether they are lockboxes or decentralized company locations, into one or more central cash pools. The cash manager then uses these pools for short-term investing or reallocation of funds among the firm's banks. By pooling its cash, the firm can take maximum advantage of economies of scale in cash management and investment. For example, commissions are often less per dollar on large

---

disbursement float
The value of the checks that have been written and disbursed, but have not yet fully cleared through the banking system and thus have not been deducted from the account on which they were written.

collections float
The value of checks that have been received and deposited, but have not yet been credited to the account in which they were deposited.

net float
The difference between disbursement float and collections float; the difference between the balance shown in the firm's (or individual's) checkbook and the balance shown on the bank's books.

lockbox arrangement
A technique used to reduce float by having payments sent to post office boxes located near the customers.

preauthorized debit system
A system that allows a customer's bank to periodically transfer funds from its account to a selling firm's bank account for the payment of bills.

concentration banking
A cash management technique in which funds from many bank accounts are moved to a more central cash pool so as to more effectively manage cash.

investments, and investments of larger dollar amounts sometimes earn higher returns than do smaller investments.

Disbursement Control

Accelerating collections represents one side of cash management, and controlling cash outflows, or disbursements, represents the other side. Three methods are commonly used to control disbursements:

1. Centralizing the processing of accounts payable permits the financial manager to evaluate the payments coming due for the entire firm and to schedule the availability of funds so as to meet these needs on a company-wide basis. It also permits more efficient monitoring of accounts payable and the effects of float. A disadvantage associated with centralized disbursement systems is that regional offices might not be able to make prompt payments for services rendered, which can create ill will and raise the company's operating costs. As payment systems become more electronically advanced, the centralization of disbursements can be coordinated more effectively, and such situations should occur much less often.

2. A **zero-balance account (ZBA)** is a special disbursement account that has a balance equal to $0 when no disbursement activity occurs. Typically, a firm establishes several ZBAs in its concentration bank and funds them from a master account. As checks are presented to a ZBA for payment, funds are automatically transferred from the master account.

3. Whereas ZBAs are typically established at concentration banks, **controlled disbursement accounts (CDAs)** can be set up at any bank. These accounts are not funded until the day's checks are presented against the account. The firm relies on the bank that maintains the CDA to provide information in the morning (generally before 11 a.m. New York time) concerning the total amount of the checks that will be presented for payment that day. This notification permits the financial manager to (a) transfer funds to the controlled disbursement account to cover the checks presented for payment or (b) invest excess cash at midday, when money market trading is at its peak.

Float, both collection and disbursement, has been reduced significantly with the introduction of electronic payment systems. As these systems become more sophisticated and widespread, float will continue to decrease, perhaps to the point where it is virtually nonexistent.

Marketable Securities

Realistically, the management of cash and marketable securities cannot be separated. Management of one implies management of the other because the amount of marketable securities held by a firm depends on its short-term cash needs.

Marketable securities, or *near-cash* assets, are extremely liquid, short-term investments that permit the firm to earn positive returns on cash that is not needed to pay bills immediately, but will be needed sometime in the near term, perhaps in a few days, weeks, or months. Although such investments typically provide much lower yields than do operating assets, nearly every large firm has them. Firms cite two basic reasons for owning marketable securities:

1. Marketable securities serve as a *substitute for cash balances.* Firms often hold portfolios of marketable securities, liquidating part of the portfolio to increase

zero-balance account (ZBA)
A special checking account used for disbursements that has a balance equal to $0 when no disbursement activity occurs.

controlled disbursement account (CDA)
A checking account in which funds are not deposited until checks are presented for payment, usually on a daily basis.

marketable securities
Securities that can be sold on short notice without loss of the principal or original investment.

the cash account when cash is needed, because the *marketable securities offer a place to temporarily put cash balances to work earning a positive return.* In such situations, the marketable securities could be used as a substitute for transactions balances, precautionary balances, speculative balances, or all three.

2. Marketable securities are used as a *temporary investment* (a) to finance seasonal or cyclical operations and (b) to amass funds to meet financial requirements in the near future. For example, if the firm has a conservative financing policy (as discussed earlier), then its long-term capital will exceed its permanent assets, and marketable securities will be held when inventories and receivables are low.

Because marketable securities are temporary investments, financial assets that are considered appropriate investments include those sold in the money (short-term) markets. Examples of such securities (as described in Chapter 2) include Treasury bills, commercial paper, negotiable certificates of deposit, and Eurodollar time deposits. Depending on how long these instruments will be held, the financial manager decides on a suitable set of securities, and a suitable maturity pattern, to hold as *near-cash reserves* in the form of marketable securities. Long-term securities are not appropriate investments for marketable securities as described in this section. Instead, safety—especially maintenance of principal—should be the paramount concern when putting together a marketable securities portfolio.

Self-Test Questions

Why is cash management important?

What are the motives for holding cash?

What is float? How do firms use float to increase cash management efficiency?

What are some methods that firms can use to accelerate receipts?

What are some techniques employed for controlling disbursements?

Why do firms hold marketable securities?

CREDIT MANAGEMENT

Firms prefer to sell for cash only because payment is certain and immediate. Why, then, do firms sell for credit? The primary reason is because their competitors offer credit. Consider what you would do if you had the opportunity to purchase the same product for the same price from two different firms, but one firm required cash payment at the time of the purchase whereas the other firm allowed you to pay for the product 1 month after the purchase without any additional cost. From which firm would you purchase the product? Like you, firms prefer to delay their payments, especially if no additional costs are associated with the delay.

Effective credit management is extremely important because too much credit is very costly in terms of the investment in, and maintenance of, accounts receivables. Conversely, too little credit might result in the loss of profitable sales. Carrying accounts receivables has both direct and indirect costs, but it also provides an important benefit: granting credit should increase profits. Thus, to maximize shareholders' wealth, a financial manager needs to understand how to effectively manage the firm's credit activities.

This section describes the factors considered important when determining the appropriate credit policy for a firm, procedures for monitoring the credit policy to ensure that it is being administered properly, and ways to evaluate whether credit policy changes will benefit the firm.

Credit Policy

The major controllable variables that affect demand for a company's products are sales prices, product quality, advertising, and the firm's **credit policy.** The firm's credit policy, in turn, includes the following factors:

1. **Credit standards** refer to the financial strength and creditworthiness that a customer must exhibit to qualify for credit. The firm's credit standards are applied to determine which customers qualify for the regular credit terms and how much credit each customer should receive. Major factors considered when setting credit standards relate to the likelihood that a given customer will pay slowly or perhaps even end up as a bad debt loss. Determining the credit quality—that is, creditworthiness—of a customer is probably the most difficult part of credit management. Nevertheless, credit evaluation is a well-established practice, and a good credit manager can make a reasonably accurate judgment of the probability of default by examining a customer's (firm's) current financial position and evaluating factors that might affect this position in the future.

2. **Terms of credit** are the conditions of the credit sale. The most important aspect of the terms of credit deals with the payment arrangements. Firms need to determine when the **credit period** will begin, how long the customer will have to pay for credit purchases before the account is considered delinquent, and whether a cash discount for early payment should be offered. An examination of the credit terms offered by firms in the United States shows great variety across industries: credit terms range from cash before delivery (CBD) and cash on delivery (COD) to **cash discounts** offered for early payment. Because of the competitive nature of trade credit, most financial managers follow the norm of the industry in which they operate when setting credit terms.

3. The **collection policy** refers to the procedures followed by the firm to collect its credit accounts. The firm needs to determine when, and how, notification of the credit sale will be conveyed to the buyer. The more quickly a customer receives an invoice, the sooner the bill *can* be paid. In today's world, many firms have begun to use electronic methods to "send" invoices to customers.

Receivables Monitoring

Once a firm sets its credit policy, it must operate within that policy's limits. To ensure that the policy is applied appropriately, the firm must examine its receivables periodically to determine whether customers' payment patterns have changed to the extent that credit operations are outside the credit policy limits. **Receivables monitoring** refers to the process of evaluating the credit policy to determine whether a shift in customers' payment patterns has occurred.

credit policy
A set of decisions that includes a firm's credit standards, credit terms, methods used to collect credit accounts, and credit monitoring procedures.

credit standards
Standards that indicate the minimum financial strength a customer must have to be granted credit.

terms of credit
The payment conditions offered to credit customers. The terms include the length of the credit period and any cash discounts offered.

credit period
The length of time for which credit is granted; after that time, the credit account is considered delinquent.

cash discount
A reduction in the invoice price of goods offered by the seller to encourage early payment.

collection policy
The procedures followed by a firm to collect its accounts receivable.

receivables monitoring
The process of evaluating the credit policy to determine whether a shift in customers' payment patterns has occurred.

TABLE 15-2   Argile Textiles: Receivables Aging Schedule for 2010

Age of Account (days)	Net Amount Outstanding ($ million)	Fraction of Total Receivables	Average Days
0–30	$37.8	42%	22
31–60	45.0	50	55
61–90	5.4	6	75
Over 90	1.8	2	98
	$90.0	100%	

$$\text{DSO} = 0.42(22 \text{ days}) + 0.50(55 \text{ days}) + 0.06(75 \text{ days}) + 0.02(98 \text{ days})$$
$$= 43.2 \text{ days}$$

Traditionally, firms have monitored accounts receivable by using methods that measure the length of time credit remains outstanding. Two such methods are the *days sales outstanding (DSO)* and the *aging schedule.*

days sales outstanding (DSO)
The average length of time required to collect accounts receivable; also called the average collection period.

1. The **days sales outstanding (DSO),** also called the *average collection period*, represents the average time it takes to collect credit accounts. Equation 15-2 shows the computation for DSO (average collection period). Recall that we found that the DSO for Argile was 43.2 days in 2010. If Argile's credit terms are 2/10, net 30, then we know that some customers are delinquent when paying their accounts. In fact, if many customers are paying within 10 days to take advantage of the cash discount, the others would, on average, have to be taking much longer than 43.2 days. One way to check for this possibility is to use an aging schedule.

aging schedule
A report showing how long accounts receivable have been outstanding. The report categorizes receivables into specified periods, which provides information about the proportion of receivables that are current and the proportion that are past due for given lengths of time.

2. An **aging schedule** is a breakdown of a firm's receivables by age of account. Table 15-2 shows the December 31, 2010, aging schedule for Argile Textiles. The standard format for an aging schedule generally includes age categories broken down by month. Even more precision, and hence better monitoring information, can be attained by using narrower age categories (for example, 1 or 2 weeks).

According to Argile's aging schedule, only 42 percent of the firm's credit sales are "current" because they have been outstanding for 30 days or less; 58 percent of the credit sales collections are delinquent. Some of the payments are delinquent by only a few days, whereas others are delinquent by three to four times the 30-day credit period.

Management should constantly monitor the DSO and the aging schedule to detect trends; this information can be used to see how the firm's collection experience compares with its credit terms as well as how effectively the credit department is operating in comparison with other firms in the industry. If the DSO starts to lengthen or if the aging schedule begins to show an increasing percentage of past-due accounts, then the firm might need to tighten its credit policy.

You must use care when interpreting changes in the DSO or the aging schedule. If a firm experiences sharp seasonal variations, or if it is growing rapidly, then both measures could be distorted. Recall that Argile's peak selling season occurs at the end of summer. Table 15-1 shows that forecasted receivables are expected to be high ($125 million) in September 2011, but much lower ($99 million) at the end of December 2011. Because sales are expected to amount to $825 million in 2011,

Argile's DSO will be 54.5 days = $125/($825/360) on September 30, but only 43.2 days = $99/($825/360) on December 31. This decline in DSO would not indicate that Argile had tightened its credit policy, but merely that its sales had declined due to seasonal factors. Similar problems arise with the aging schedule when sales fluctuate widely.

A change in either the DSO or the aging schedule should be taken as a signal to investigate further, but not necessarily as a sign that the firm's credit policy has weakened. If a firm generally experiences widely fluctuating sales patterns, some type of modified aging schedule should be used to account for these fluctuations.[8] Even with this caveat, the DSO measure and the aging schedule still represent useful tools for evaluating credit customers' payment behaviors.

Analyzing Proposed Changes in Credit Policy

The key question when deciding on a proposed credit policy change is this: How will the change affect the firm's value? If the added benefits expected from a credit policy change do not exceed the added costs on a present value basis, then the firm should *not* make the policy change.

To illustrate how to evaluate whether a proposed change in a firm's credit policy is appropriate, let's examine what would happen if Argile Textiles made changes to reduce its average collection period. The company's financial manager has proposed that this task be accomplished in 2011 by taking two steps: (1) billing customers sooner and exerting more pressure on delinquent customers to pay their bills on time and (2) examining the accounts of existing credit customers and suspending the credit of those who are considered "habitually delinquent." Clearly, these actions will increase the costs associated with Argile's credit policy. At the same time, even though Argile has an extremely loyal customer base, it is expected that some sales will be lost to competitors as the result of some customers having their credit eliminated. Because the credit policy changes will have little, if any, effect on the "good" credit customers, the financial manager does not expect there to be a change in the payments of those customers who currently take advantage of the cash discount. If the proposed credit policy changes are approved, the average collection period (DSO) for receivables is expected to be reduced from 43.2 days to 34.9 days, which is more in line with the credit terms offered by Argile (2/10, net 30) and closer to the industry average of 32 days. Also, if the average collection period is reduced, the amount "carried" in accounts receivable will be reduced, which means that fewer funds will be "tied up" in receivables.

Table 15-3 provides information relating to Argile's existing credit policy and the financial manager's proposed changes. According to the table, if the company changes its credit policy, its sales will drop by $2 million per year, or $5,556 per day. Notice that only the amount paid by customers who do not currently take the cash discount will be affected by this decrease. This group of customers includes the "habitually delinquent" payers, which is the category of customers that the credit policy change is intended to affect. As a result, on a daily basis, the amount paid by the nondiscount customers will decrease by $5,556, from $1.9022 million to $1.8967 million, if the proposed credit policy is adopted; the amount paid by the discount customers, however, will remain at $0.3817 million.

To determine whether Argile should adopt the financial manager's proposal, we need to evaluate how the proposed changes will affect the value of the firm.

---

[8]See Eugene F. Brigham and Phillip R. Daves, *Intermediate Financial Management*, 9th ed. (Cincinnati, OH: South-Western Cengage Learning, 2007), Chapter 22, for a more complete discussion of the problems with the DSO and aging schedule and how to correct for them.

TABLE 15-3 Argile Textiles: Existing and Proposed Credit Policies, 2011

	Existing Policy	Proposed Policy
I. General Credit Policy Information		
Credit terms	2/10 net 30	2/10 net 30
Days sales outstanding (DSO) for all customers[a]	43.2 days	34.9 days
DSO for customers who take the cash discount (17%)	10.0 days	10.0 days
DSO for customers who forgo the cash discount (83%)	50.0 days	40.0 days
II. Annual Credit Sales and Costs ($ millions)		
Net credit sales[b]	$ 825.0	$ 823.0
Amount paid by discount customers[c]	$ 137.4	$ 137.4
Amount paid by nondiscount customers[c]	$ 684.8	$ 682.8
Variable operating costs (80 percent of *net* sales)[d]	$ 660.0	$ 658.4
Bad debts	$ 0.0	$ 0.0
Credit evaluation and collection costs[d]	$ 8.0	$ 9.0
III. Daily Credit Sales and Costs ($ thousands)		
Net sales	$2,291.7	$2,286.1
Amount paid by discount customers	$ 381.7	$ 381.7
Amount paid by nondiscount customers	$1,902.2	$1,896.7
Variable operating costs (80 percent of net sales)	$1,833.3	$1,828.9
Bad debts	$ 0.0	$ 0.0
Credit evaluation and collection costs	$ 22.2	$ 25.0

[a]With the existing policy, 17 percent of the customers take the cash discount and pay on Day 10 and the remaining customers (83 percent) pay, on average, on Day 50; thus, the DSO for all customers is 43.2 days = 0.17(10 days) + 0.83(50 days).

[b]In Chapter 8, we determined that Argile's 2011 net *forecasted* sales is $825 million, which represents what the firm expects to collect from credit sales, net of cash discounts. The gross sales, which includes cash discounts, can be computed as follows:

$$\text{Net sales} = 0.83(\text{Gross sales}) + 0.17(1 - 0.02)(\text{Gross sales}) = \$825 \text{ million}$$
$$= (\text{Gross sales})[0.83 + 0.17(0.98)] = \$825 \text{ million}$$
$$\text{Gross sales} = \frac{\$825 \text{ million}}{0.9966} = \$827.8 \text{ million}$$

[c]Currently, 17 percent of Argile's customers pay on Day 10, taking advantage of the 2 percent cash discount. As a result, the amount expected to be paid by this group of customers is $137.4 million = $0.17 \times (1.0 - 0.02) \times$ $825 million. Customers who take the discount will not be affected by the credit policy changes that are intended to affect delinquent customers; thus, the amount paid by customers who take the discount will be the same under either policy—$137.4 million. Consequently, the $2 million decrease in sales associated with the proposed credit policy will reduce the amount paid by customers who do not take the discount from $684.8 million (= 0.83 × $825 million) to $682.8 million (= $684.8 million – $2 million).

[d]The variable operating costs are paid at the time of the credit sale. Fixed operating costs are not included in the analysis because the amount does not change if the credit policy is changed. Expenses related to credit sales (evaluation and collection costs) are also paid at the time of the credit sale. These assumptions are made to simplify the analysis.

[e]Daily figures are required to evaluate whether the proposal should be adopted. See Table 15-4 for the actual analysis. For consistency, we use a 360-day year to compute the daily figures.

TABLE 15-4 Argile Textiles: NPV Analysis of Credit Policies ($ thousand)

I. Existing Credit Policy

Cash Flow Time Line

0	r = (10% ÷ 360) = 0.02778%	10		50 Days
(1,833.3)		381.7	...	1,902.2
(22.2)				
(1,855.5)				

$$\text{NPV}_{\text{Existing}} = (1,855.5) + \frac{381.7}{\left(1 + \frac{0.10}{360}\right)^{10}} + \frac{1,902.2}{\left(1 + \frac{0.10}{360}\right)^{50}}$$

$$= (1,855.5) + \quad 380.6 \quad + \quad 1,876.0 \quad = 401.1$$

II. Proposed Credit Policy

Cash Flow Time Line

0	r = (10% ÷ 360) = 0.02778%	10		40 Days
(1,828.9)		381.7	...	1,896.7
(25.0)				
(1,853.9)				

$$\text{NPV}_{\text{Proposal}} = (1,853.9) + \frac{381.7}{\left(1 + \frac{0.10}{360}\right)^{10}} + \frac{1,896.7}{\left(1 + \frac{0.10}{360}\right)^{40}}$$

$$= (1,853.9) + \quad 380.6 \quad + \quad 1,875.7 \quad = 402.4$$

III. Effect on Firm's Value If Proposal Is Adopted

ΔNPV on a daily basis = $402.4 − $401.1 = $1.3

$$\Delta\text{Value} = \frac{\$1.3}{\left(\frac{0.10}{360}\right)} = \$4,680.0$$

Thus, we must compare the net present values (NPV) of the two credit policies. To complete the analysis, we make two simplifying assumptions:

1. Sales occur evenly throughout the year.

2. Each production/selling cycle is constant such that cash inflows and cash outflows occur at the same point in time relative to the credit sale, no matter what time of the year is examined.

These assumptions allow us to evaluate the cash inflows and cash outflows associated with credit sales for 1 day to determine whether the proposed credit policy change should be made.

Table 15-3 gives specific assumptions concerning the timing of the cash flows, and Table 15-4 shows the results of the NPV analysis (r = 10%). According to these results, the NPV for the existing credit policy is $401,100 per day, whereas the NPV for the proposed credit policy is $402,400 per day. If the company changes its credit policy, the change in the daily NPV (ΔNPV in Section III of Table 15-4) is $1,300. Given the assumptions we have stated previously as well as the assumptions given in Table 15-3, we would expect that this change will have a permanent, or continuing, effect on the firm. Thus, the $1,300 change represents a daily perpetuity, which, according to Section III of Table 15-4, will increase the value of the firm by $4.68 million. Clearly, then, the proposed changes should be made.

The analysis in Table 15-4 provides Argile's managers with a vehicle for considering the effects of credit policy changes on the firm's value. They must apply a great deal of judgment to the final decision, however, because both customers' and competitors' responses to credit policy changes are difficult to gauge. Nevertheless, this type of analysis is essential.

Self-Test Questions

What are the four credit policy variables? Describe how each variable affects sales and profitability.

Define days sales outstanding (DSO). What can you learn from it? How is it affected by sales fluctuations?

What is an aging schedule? What can you learn from it? How is it affected by sales fluctuations?

Describe the procedure used to evaluate a change in credit policy.

INVENTORY MANAGEMENT

If it could, a firm would prefer to have no inventory. After all, while products are in inventory, they do not generate returns and must be financed. Nevertheless, most firms find it necessary to maintain inventory in some form for two reasons: demand cannot be predicted with certainty, and it takes time to get a product ready for sale. Although excessive inventories can be costly to the firm, so are insufficient inventories; customers might purchase from competitors if products are not available when demanded, and future business could be lost.

Although inventory models are covered in depth in production management courses, it is important to understand the basics of inventory management. Thus, in this section we briefly describe the concepts of inventory management.

raw materials
The inventories purchased from suppliers, which ultimately will be transformed into finished goods.

work-in-process
Inventory in various stages of completion. Some work-in-process is at the very beginning of the production process, whereas other work-in-process is at the end of the process.

finished goods
Inventories that have completed the production process and are ready for sale.

Types of Inventory

An inventory item can be classified according to its stage of completion:

1. **Raw materials** include new inventory purchased from suppliers; a firm purchases these materials so it can transform them into finished products for sale. As long as the firm has an inventory of raw materials, delays in ordering and delivery from suppliers will not affect the production process.

2. **Work-in-process** refers to inventory items that are at various stages of completion. If a firm has work-in-process at every stage of the production process, then it will not have to completely shut down production if a problem arises at one of the earlier stages.

3. **Finished goods** inventory represents products that are ready for sale. Firms carry finished goods to ensure that orders can be filled when they are received. If there are no finished goods, the firm must wait for the completion of the production process before inventory can be sold, so demand might not be satisfied when inventory arrives. When a customer arrives and no inventory is

available to satisfy that customer's demand, a **stockout** exists. In such a situation, the firm might lose the customer to its competitors, perhaps permanently.

Optimal Inventory Level

The goal of inventory management is to provide the inventories required to sustain operations at the lowest possible cost. The first step in determining the optimal inventory level is to identify the costs involved in purchasing and maintaining inventory. Next, we must determine at what point those costs are minimized.

Inventory Costs

We generally classify inventory costs into three categories: those associated with carrying inventory, those associated with ordering and receiving inventory, and those associated with running short of inventory (stockouts). First, let's look at the two costs that are most directly observable: carrying costs and ordering costs.

1. **Carrying costs** include any expenses associated with having inventory, such as rent paid for storage space, insurance on the inventory, and so forth. Carrying costs generally increase in direct proportion to the average amount of inventory carried: total carrying costs increase with greater amounts of inventory.

2. **Ordering costs** include those expenses associated with placing and receiving an order for new inventory, such as the costs of generating memos, fax transmissions, and so forth. For the most part, the costs associated with each order are fixed regardless of the order size.[9]

If we assume that the firm knows how much inventory it needs and sales are distributed evenly during each period, then we can combine the total carrying costs (TCC) and the total ordering costs (TOC) to find total inventory costs (TIC) as follows:

15-8

$$\begin{aligned} \text{Total inventory} \atop \text{costs (TIC)} &= \quad\text{Total carrying costs} \quad + \text{ Total ordering costs} \\[2mm] &= \begin{pmatrix} \text{Carrying} \\ \text{cost per unit} \end{pmatrix} \times \begin{pmatrix} \text{Average units} \\ \text{in inventory} \end{pmatrix} + \begin{pmatrix} \text{Cost per} \\ \text{order} \end{pmatrix} \times \begin{pmatrix} \text{Number} \\ \text{of orders} \end{pmatrix} \\[2mm] &= \quad (C \times PP) \quad \times \quad \left(\frac{Q}{2}\right) \quad + \quad O \quad \times \quad \left(\frac{T}{Q}\right) \end{aligned}$$

The variables in the equation are defined as follows:

C = Carrying costs as a percentage of the purchase price of each inventory item

PP = Purchase price, or cost, per unit

Q = Number of units purchased with each order

T = Total demand, or number of units sold, per period

O = Fixed costs per order

According to Equation 15-8, the average investment in inventory depends on how often orders are placed and the size of each order. If we order every day,

stockout
A situation in which a firm runs out of inventory *and* customers arrive to purchase the product.

carrying costs
The costs associated with having inventory, which include storage costs, insurance, the cost of tying up funds, depreciation costs, and so on. These costs generally increase in proportion to the average amount of inventory held.

ordering costs
The costs of placing an order. The cost of each order generally is fixed, regardless of the average size of the inventory.

[9]In reality, both carrying and ordering costs can have variable and fixed cost elements, at least over certain ranges of average inventory. For example, security and utilities charges probably are fixed in the short run over a wide range of inventory levels. Similarly, labor costs in receiving inventory could be tied to the quantity received, and hence could be variable. To simplify matters, we treat all carrying costs as variable and all ordering costs as fixed.

FIGURE 15-3   Determination of the Optimal Inventory Order Quantity

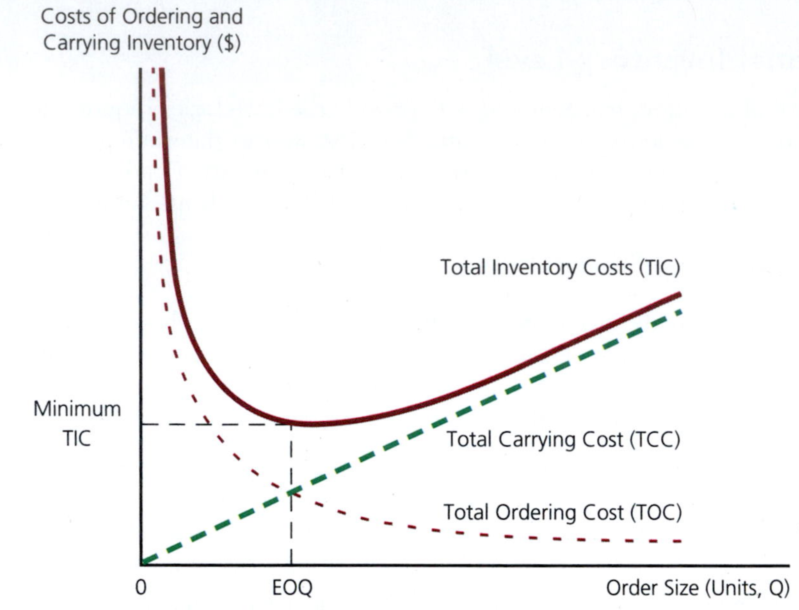

Costs of Ordering and
Carrying Inventory ($)

Total Inventory Costs (TIC)

Minimum
TIC

Total Carrying Cost (TCC)

Total Ordering Cost (TOC)

0   EOQ   Order Size (Units, Q)

average inventory will be much smaller than if we order once per year, and inventory carrying costs will be low, but the number of orders will be large and inventory ordering costs will be high. We can reduce ordering costs by ordering greater amounts less often, but then average inventory, and hence the total carrying cost, will be high. This tradeoff between carrying costs and ordering costs is shown graphically in Figure 15-3. Note from the figure that there is a point where the total inventory cost is *minimized;* this point is called the **economic (optimum) ordering quantity (EOQ).**

economic (optimum) ordering quantity (EOQ)
The optimal quantity that should be ordered; the quantity that will minimize the total inventory costs.

The Economic Ordering Quantity (EOQ) Model

The EOQ is determined by using calculus to find the point where the slope of the TIC curve in Figure 15-3 is perfectly horizontal—that is, where the slope equals 0. The result is the following equation:

15-9

$$\text{Economic ordering quantity} = \text{EOQ} = \sqrt{\frac{2 \times O \times T}{C \times PP}}$$

EOQ model
A formula for determining the order quantity that will minimize total inventory costs.

The primary assumptions of the **EOQ model** given by Equation 15-9 are that (1) sales are evenly distributed throughout the period examined and can be forecasted perfectly, (2) orders are received when expected, and (3) the purchase price (PP) of each item in inventory is the same regardless of the quantity ordered.[10]

---

[10]The EOQ model can also be written as:

$$\text{EOQ} = \sqrt{\frac{2 \times O \times T}{C^*}}$$

where C* is the carrying cost per unit expressed in dollars.

To illustrate the EOQ model, consider the following data supplied by Cotton Tops, Inc., a distributor of custom-designed T-shirts that supplies concessionaires at Daisy World:

T = 78,000 shirts per year

C = 25 percent of inventory value

PP = $3.84 per shirt (The shirts sell for $9, but this information is irrelevant for computing EOQ under our assumptions.)

O = $260 per order

Substituting these data into Equation 15-9, we find an EOQ of 6,500 units:

$$EOQ = \sqrt{\frac{2 \times \$260 \times 78{,}000}{0.25 \times \$3.84}} = \sqrt{42{,}250{,}000} = 6{,}500 \text{ units}$$

If Cotton Tops orders 6,500 shirts each time it needs inventory, it will place $78{,}000/6{,}500 = 12$ orders per year and carry an average inventory of $6{,}500/2 = 3{,}250$ shirts. Thus, at the EOQ amount, Cotton Tops' total inventory costs would equal $6,240:

$$\begin{aligned}\text{Total inventory costs (TIC)} &= (C \times PP)\left(\frac{Q}{2}\right) + O\left(\frac{T}{Q}\right) \\[4pt] &= (0.25 \times \$3.84)\left(\frac{6{,}500}{2}\right) + \$260\left(\frac{78{,}000}{6{,}500}\right) \\[4pt] &= \$3{,}120 + \$3{,}120 = \$6{,}240\end{aligned}$$

Note the following two points:

1. Because we assume that the purchase price of each inventory item does not depend on the amount ordered, TIC does *not* include the annual cost of purchasing the inventory itself, which is $299{,}520 = 78{,}000(\$3.84)$.

2. As we see in Figure 15-3 as well as in the computation here, at the EOQ, total carrying cost equals total ordering cost. This property is not unique to our Cotton Tops illustration; it always holds with the assumptions outlined earlier.

Table 15-5 contains the total inventory costs that Cotton Tops would incur at various order quantities, including the EOQ level. As the amount ordered increases, the total carrying costs increase but the total ordering costs decrease, and vice versa. Also, if less than the EOQ amount is ordered, then the higher ordering costs more than offset the lower carrying costs. Conversely, if more than the EOQ amount is ordered, the higher carrying costs more than offset the lower ordering costs.

EOQ Model Extensions

It should be obvious that some of the assumptions necessary for the basic EOQ to hold are unrealistic. To make the model more useful, we can apply some simple extensions.

First, if a delay occurs between the time when inventory is ordered and when it is received, the firm must reorder before it runs out of inventory. For example, if it normally takes 2 weeks to receive orders, then Cotton Tops should reorder when it has 2 weeks of inventory remaining. The firm sells $78{,}000/52 = 1{,}500$ shirts per week, so its **reorder point** would occur when inventory drops to 3,000 shirts.

reorder point
The level of inventory at which an order should be placed.

TABLE 15-5 Cotton Tops, Inc.: Total Inventory Costs for Various Order Quantities

	Quantity	Number of Orders	Total Ordering Costs	Total Carrying Costs	Total Inventory Costs
	3,000	26	$ 6,760	$ 1,440	$ 8,200
	5,200	15	3,900	2,496	6,396
	6,000	13	3,380	2,880	6,260
EOQ	**6,500**	**12**	**3,120**	**3,120**	**6,240**
	7,800	10	2,600	3,744	6,344
	9,750	8	2,080	4,680	6,760
	13,000	6	1,560	6,240	7,800
	78,000	1	260	37,440	37,700

T = Annual sales = 78,000 shirts
C = Carrying cost = 25 percent
PP = Purchase price = $3.84/shirt
O = Ordering cost = $260/order

Even if Cotton Tops orders additional inventory at the appropriate reorder point, unexpected demand might cause it to run out of inventory before the new inventory is delivered. To avoid this problem, the firm could carry **safety stocks,** or additional inventory that helps guard against stockouts. The amount of safety stocks held by a firm generally *increases* with three factors:

1. Greater uncertainty of demand forecasts
2. Higher costs (in terms of lost sales and lost goodwill) of stockouts
3. Greater chance that delays will occur in receiving shipments

The amount of safety stock *decreases* as the cost of carrying this additional inventory increases.

Another factor that a firm might need to consider when determining appropriate inventory levels is whether its suppliers offer discounts for purchasing large quantities. For example, if Cotton Tops' supplier offered a 1 percent discount for purchases equal to 13,000 units or more, the total reduction in the annual cost of purchasing inventory would be $[0.01(\$3.84)] \times 78,000 = \$2,995.20$. Looking at Table 15-5, we see that the costs of carrying existing inventory and ordering new inventory at 13,000 units equal $7,800, which is $1,560 = $7,800 − $6,240 greater than the costs at the EOQ level of 6,500 units. The net benefit of taking advantage of the **quantity discount** is $1,435.20 = $2,995.20 − $1,560.00. Therefore, in this case, each time Cotton Tops orders inventory, it will be more beneficial to order 13,000 units rather than the 6,500 units prescribed by the basic EOQ model.

In cases in which it is unrealistic to assume that the demand for the inventory will remain uniform throughout the year, the EOQ should not be applied on an annual basis. Rather, it would be more appropriate to divide the year into the periods within which sales are relatively constant—for example, the summer, the spring and fall, and the winter. The EOQ model can then be applied separately to each period.

Although we did not explicitly incorporate the extensions mentioned here into the basic EOQ, this discussion should give you an idea of how the EOQ amount should be adjusted to determine the optimal inventory level if any of these conditions exist.

Inventory Control Systems

The EOQ model can be used to help establish the proper inventory level, but inventory management also involves the establishment of an *inventory control system.* Inventory control systems run the gamut from very simple to extremely complex, depending on the size of the firm and the nature of its inventories. One simple control procedure is the **red-line method.** With this method, inventory items are stocked in a bin, a red line is drawn around the inside of the bin at the level of the reorder point, and the inventory clerk places an order when the red line becomes visible. This procedure works well for parts such as bolts in a manufacturing process or for many items in retail businesses.

Most firms employ some type of **computerized inventory control systems.** Large companies, such as Wal-Mart, often have fully integrated computerized inventory control systems in which the computer adjusts inventory levels as sales are made, orders inventory when the reorder point is reached, and records the receipt of an order. The computer records also can be used to determine whether the usage rates of inventory items have changed, and adjustments to reorder amounts can be made accordingly. Increased use of electronic technologies has allowed firms to better coordinate orders with suppliers, thereby enabling them to follow the **just-in-time system,** which was refined by Japanese firms many years ago. With this system, materials are delivered to the company at about the same time they are needed—perhaps only a few hours before they are used.

Another important development related to inventories is **outsourcing,** which is the practice of purchasing components rather than making them in-house. For example, if GM arranged to buy radiators rather than making them itself, it would be outsourcing. Outsourcing is often combined with just-in-time systems to reduce inventory levels.

Inventory control systems require coordination of the inventory policy with the manufacturing/procurement policies. Companies try to minimize *total production and distribution costs,* and inventory costs are just one part of these total costs. Nevertheless, they are an important cost, and financial managers should be aware of the determinants of inventory costs and ways to minimize them.

red-line method
An inventory control procedure where a red line is drawn around the inside of an inventory-stocked bin to indicate the reorder point level.

computerized inventory control system
A system of inventory control in which a computer is used to determine reorder points and to adjust inventory balances.

just-in-time system
A system of inventory control in which a manufacturer coordinates production with suppliers so that raw materials or components arrive just as they are needed in the production process.

outsourcing
The practice of purchasing product components rather than making them in-house.

Self-Test Questions

What are the types of inventory?

What are the three categories of inventory costs?

What is the purpose of the EOQ model?

What are safety stocks, and why are they needed?

Describe some inventory control systems used in today's businesses.

MULTINATIONAL WORKING CAPITAL MANAGEMENT

For the most part, the methods used to manage short-term assets and liabilities in multinational corporations are the same as those used in purely domestic corporations. Multinational corporations face a far more complex task, however, because they operate in many different business cultures, political environments, economic conditions, and so forth. This section describes some of the differences between multinational and domestic working capital management.

Cash Management

Like a purely domestic company, a multinational corporation (MNC) has the following goals: (1) speed up collections and slow down disbursements where possible, (2) shift cash as rapidly as possible to those areas where it is needed, and (3) put temporary cash balances to work earning positive returns. Multinational companies use the same general procedures for achieving these goals as do their domestic counterparts, but because of the longer distances and more serious mail delays encountered by MNCs, lockbox systems and electronic funds transfers are even more important to them.

One potential problem faced by a multinational company is the chance that a foreign government will restrict transfers of funds out of the country. Such restrictions are intended to encourage domestic investment. Even if funds can be transferred without limitation, deteriorating exchange rates might discourage a multinational from moving these funds to its operations in other countries.

Once it has been determined what funds can be transferred out of the various nations in which a multinational corporation operates, it is important to get those funds to locations where they will earn the highest returns. Whereas domestic corporations tend to think in terms of domestic securities, MNCs are more likely to be aware of investment opportunities all around the world. Most multinational corporations use one or more global concentration banks, located in money centers such as London, New York, Tokyo, Zurich, or Singapore. They also work with international bankers to take advantage of the best rates available globally.

Credit Management

Credit policy generally is more important for a multinational corporation than for a purely domestic firm for two reasons. First, much U.S. trade takes place with poorer, less-developed nations; in such situations, granting credit is typically a necessary condition for doing business. Second, and in large part as a result of the first point, developed nations whose economic health depends on exports often help their manufacturing firms compete internationally by granting credit to foreign customers. In Japan, for example, government agencies help firms identify potential export markets and potential customers to arrange credit for purchases from Japanese firms. The U.S. government has implemented some programs that help domestic firms to export products, but it does not provide the degree of financial assistance that many multinationals based in other countries receive from their local governments.

When granting credit, the multinational firm faces a riskier situation than the purely domestic firm because, in addition to the normal risks of default, it must deal with two potential problems:

1. Political and legal environments might make it more difficult to collect on defaulted accounts.
2. The multinational corporation must worry about exchange rate changes between the time a sale is made and the time a receivable is collected.

Hedging can reduce the latter type of risk, albeit at a cost.

By pointing out the risks in granting credit internationally, we do not mean to suggest that such credit is bad. Quite the contrary—the potential gains from international operations far outweigh the risks, at least for companies that have the necessary expertise.

Inventory Management

Inventory management in a multinational setting is more complex than that in a purely domestic market because of the logistical problems associated with handling inventories. For example, if a firm concentrates its inventories in a few strategic centers located worldwide, it might minimize the total amount of, and hence the investment in, inventories needed to operate globally. Of course, the firm might also incur delays in getting goods from the central storage locations to user locations all around the world. It is clear that both working stocks and safety stocks must be maintained at each user location, as well as at the strategic storage centers.

Exchange rates can also significantly influence the MNC's inventory policy. For example, if a country's currency is expected to rise in value against the U.S. dollar, a U.S. company operating in that country would want to increase its stocks of local products before the rise in the currency, and vice versa.

Another factor that must be considered is the possibility of import or export quotas or tariffs. Quotas restrict the quantities of products that firms can bring into a country. Tariffs, like taxes, increase the prices of products that are allowed to be imported. Both quotas and tariffs are designed to restrict the ability of foreign corporations to compete with domestic companies. At the extreme, foreign products are excluded altogether.

Another danger in certain countries is the threat of expropriation, or government takeover of the firm's local operations. If the threat of expropriation is large, inventory holdings will be minimized, and goods will be brought in only as needed.

Taxes also must be considered when deciding on a multinational inventory management policy, for two reasons. First, countries often impose property taxes on assets, including inventories. Second, any such tax will be based on holdings as of a specific date. Such rules make it advantageous for a multinational firm to schedule production so that inventories are low on the assessment date. If assessment dates vary among countries in a region, the company could find it beneficial to hold safety stocks in different countries at different times during the year.

In general, then, multinational firms use techniques similar to those described in this chapter to manage working capital. Their job is more complex, however, because business, legal, and economic environments can differ significantly from one country to another.

Self-Test Questions

What are some factors that make cash management especially complicated in a multinational corporation?

Why is granting credit especially risky in an international context?

What are some factors that make inventory management in multinational firms more complex than in purely domestic firms?

Ethical Dilemma

Money-Back Guarantee, No Questions Asked

TradeSmart, Inc., operates 1,200 discount electronics stores throughout the United States. TradeSmart has been quite successful in a highly competitive industry, primarily because it has been able to offer brand-name products at prices lower than can be found at other discount outlets. Because of its size, the firm can purchase bulk inventory directly from manufacturers, and the economies of scale it derives from such purchases can be passed on to consumers in the form of lower prices.

In addition to low prices, TradeSmart offers an extremely liberal product return policy. Customers are permitted to return products for virtually any reason, with little regard to the time period covered by manufacturers' warranties. In fact, just a few days ago, a customer returned a digital pager that was more than 2 years old. TradeSmart gave the customer a full refund even though the pager appeared to have been run over by a car, which, if true, certainly would have voided the manufacturer's warranty. In another instance, a customer was given a refund when he returned the camcorder he had purchased 3 days earlier to record his daughter's wedding festivities. The customer could not describe the camcorder's malfunction—he said "It just didn't work right." The customer refused an offer to replace the camcorder; instead, he insisted on a full refund, which he was given. The manager of the customer relations department suspected that the customer had "purchased" the camcorder intending all along to return it after his daughter's wedding.

TradeSmart's return policy does not dissuade customers from returning goods for *any* reason. According to Ed Davidson, vice president of customer relations, TradeSmart is willing to stand behind every product it sells, regardless of the problem, because the company believes that such a policy is needed to attract and keep loyal customers in such a competitive industry. The company's motto—"Customer Satisfaction Is Our Business"—is displayed prominently throughout TradeSmart stores.

With such a liberal return policy, how does TradeSmart keep its prices so low? Actually, the firm ships the returned products back to the manufacturers as defective products, so the return costs are passed on to the manufacturers. According to manufacturers, only one out of every six products returned by TradeSmart is really defective. When manufacturers complain about returns of used products or products that have no mechanical problems, TradeSmart reminds them that the company does not have a service department, so its personnel are not knowledgeable concerning the technical circuitry of the products. Instead, the products are returned to the manufacturers with the customers' complaints attached. TradeSmart's inventory manager would contend that the company does not intentionally deceive or take advantage of the manufacturers' return policies and warranties.

Do you agree with TradeSmart's return policy? Is it ethical? What action would you take if you were one of TradeSmart's suppliers?

CHAPTER PRINCIPLES –The Answers

To summarize the key concepts, let's answer the questions that were posed at the beginning of the chapter:

- **What is working capital and why is working capital management critical to the survival of a firm?** Working capital refers to the short-term, or current, assets of a firm. Poor working capital management generally results in financial distress, and perhaps bankruptcy. Liquidation of working capital accounts produces the cash that is needed to pay current bills. If a firm cannot pay its current bills, it cannot survive the long term.

- **What general strategies should a firm follow when managing its working capital accounts?** Everything else equal, a firm wants to put its funds to work earning positive returns so as to maximize value. Consequently, the general working capital policy that a firm should follow is to collect funds that it is owed as quickly as possible and to delay payments that it owes for as long as possible. Of course, any actions taken should not be detrimental to the value of the firm.

In general, a firm prefers to hold $0 balances of (1) cash, because cash is considered an idle asset that does not earn interest, (2) inventory, because inventory requires funds to be tied up until items are sold, and (3) accounts receivables, because receivables represent sales for which cash payments have not been received. As a result, firms try to minimize the balances in these accounts that are required to maintain optimal operations. That is, firms try to hold just enough cash to ensure that day-to-day obligations can be paid (transactions balances), to take advantage of bargain purchases that might arise (speculative balances), and to meet minimum cash balances required by the bank (compensating balances). Firms carry sufficient inventories to ensure that demand is met when it arrives, because a sale cannot be made unless inventory exists. Firms sell on credit primarily because competitors sell on credit, but also because some customers are not able to buy products unless they are extended credit.

- **How should the firm finance its working capital needs?** Often a firm has to pay for the materials and labor that are needed to manufacture and sell its products before customers pay for their purchases. During the period from when the firm invests in the product—that is, pays for materials and labor—until it receives cash payment from the sale of the product, external financing is needed to support operations. These financing needs can be satisfied using either short-term or long-term debt instruments.

   Short-term financing generally is riskier, but cheaper than long-term financing. Thus, a firm must determine what level of financing risk it can handle. Firms that are able to handle good amounts of financial risk are likely to finance current assets with more short-term debt (aggressive approach) than firms that are not able to handle much financial risk (conservative approach). Most firms follow a maturity matching, or "self-liquidating," approach, a moderate approach that specifies firms should finance spontaneous, self-liquidating assets with temporary debt and finance more permanent assets with more permanent debt.

- **What types of short-term credit do firms use?** Firms generally purchase raw materials from suppliers who permit such purchases to be made on credit. This type of credit, which is called trade credit, is spontaneous and self-liquidating in the sense that the amount of credit that is outstanding at any point during the year automatically (spontaneously) increases or decreases with the production needs of the firm that purchases the raw materials, and payment generally is made from the proceeds that are received when the firm sells the finished products that are made from the raw materials.

   Banks also offer a variety of short-term loans. Two notable financing arrangements include a note that has a maturity that is less than 1 year and a line of credit. If a firm borrows a specific amount from a bank, it must sign a promissory note. A line of credit gives the firm the ability to borrow at any time as long as the total amount that is outstanding does not exceed some maximum specified by the bank. Both types of loans are nonspontaneous in the sense that the firm must formally request funds from the banks. Such loans might require the firm to maintain a compensating balance at the bank. The bank uses the compensating balance to earn returns that effectively help to recover fees that would otherwise be charged for the various services it offers.

- **How is the cost of short-term credit determined? Why is it necessary to compute the cost of credit?** The percentage cost of credit per period, r_{PER}, is equal to the total dollar cost of borrowing divided by the amount of funds that the borrower can actually use. The percentage cost per period is annualized by computing the APR, which is a noncompounded rate, or the EAR, which recognizes the effects of compounding. The percentage cost of credit is higher (lower) when the dollar cost of borrowing is higher (lower), the amount available for use is lower (higher), or both. When the entire principal amount of a loan cannot be used by the borrower, the cost of the loan is higher than the quoted, or simple, interest rate.

- **Which assets are generally considered good security for collateralized short-term loans? What are some of the arrangements that exist with secured short-term loans?** Both accounts receivable and inventory are considered good collateral for short-term loans because they are liquid operating assets. Accounts receivable represent sales that have been made but have not been collected. Thus, the accounts receivable balance is an indication of the cash that the firm expects to collect (be paid) in the near future. Firms can use receivables to raise funds before the accounts are actually collected by (1) pledging the accounts as collateral for a loan or (2) factoring the receivables, in which case the receivables are sold to a factor.

  Inventory represents products that the firm expects to sell in the near term. The attractiveness of inventory as collateral depends on its characteristics—nonperishable inventory that is easy to sell is considered better inventory than hard-to-sell inventory that is perishable.

CHAPTER PRINCIPLES
–Personal Finance

The concepts presented in this chapter should help you to understand actions that you can take to better manage your liquidity position, and thus to better handle decisions about your current obligations.

- **Can the cash conversion cycle help me make better personal financial decisions?** Although you are not a business, you do have a "personal" cash conversion cycle. When you purchase items using your credit card, your cash conversion cycle *might* be similar to the following:

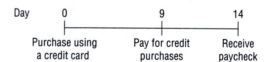

In this example, the payment for your credit card purchases is due before you get your next paycheck. When this is the case, to pay your credit card bill you must have alternative sources of funds (e.g., savings). Given this situation, you should want to reduce your cash conversion cycle as much as possible. To do so, you can delay the credit purchase, delay payment for the credit purchase, or take both actions. If you choose to delay the credit payment, however, you must ensure that payment is made when it is due—you want to neither harm your credit position nor pay exorbitant interest.

- **How liquid should I be?** Like businesses, you should evaluate your liquidity position. If your income is variable and uncertain, you probably should be more liquid than if your income is stable. Because you do not want to jeopardize your ability to pay current bills, you should ensure that you have sufficient liquidity—that is, cash in a checking account, savings, and short-term investments—to be able to meet your current obligations. You shouldn't be too liquid, however, because short-term investments generally earn lower returns than long-term investments, which are riskier and less liquid. As a result, you should balance your liquidity position so that you have an appropriate combination of short-term and long-term investments.

- **Which financing policy should I follow when looking for loans?** It generally is best to match the maturity of the loan used to finance an asset with the life of the asset. For example, although you could finance a house purchase with a series of 1-year loans that are turned over every year for 30 years, such a strategy is very risky. Interest rates change from year to year, and at some point you might not be able to turn over the 1-year loan because personal or economic factors harm your financial position. As a result, when financing a house, it is better to use a 30-year mortgage rather than a 1-year mortgage that is renewed every year for 30 years.

- **How much cash should I hold?** Most of us use cash primarily to pay for such daily purchases as gas, lunch, groceries, and so forth (transactions balances). Often we also hold some safety (precautionary) cash in case unexpected purchases arise, and in some cases we hold cash that can be used to take advantage of bargains (speculative balances). Regardless of the reasons you hold cash, you should be aware of the fact that cash is an idle asset that is not working for you to earn a positive return. Thus, you should learn how to effectively manage your cash position.

- **What philosophy should I take when paying my bills?** Like businesses, you should collect amounts owed to you as soon as possible and pay your bills as late as possible (but on time). Keep in mind that you do not have to pay your bills at the time the billing statement arrives. As long as you pay your bills by the due date, you will not harm your credit and you can keep *your money* working for you earning positive returns.

- **How do inventory management concepts apply to my personal financial decisions?** To apply the inventory management principles discussed in the chapter to your personal situation, consider the food and other necessary items that you purchase during the year. You might go to the grocery store every day, whereas your friends might go once each week or every other week. But how often you should go to the grocery store depends on (1) how much storage space you have in your home or apartment (carrying cost), (2) how convenient it is to go to the grocery store (ordering cost, which includes the cost of gas), and (3) how you react when you are hungry and cannot find the food you want in your house or apartment (stockout cost). By considering these factors, you can decide which food inventory management policy is best for you and your family.

- **How do bank charges such as compensating balances, application fees, and so forth affect me?** At some point in your life, you will borrow money, perhaps to buy a car, to finance a house, or to invest. After reading this chapter, you should realize that the cost of borrowing is significantly affected by application fees, processing costs, and other charges that are included in the loan. In cases where the stated interest rate is low, look for "hidden" costs that increase the effective rate that you are paying on the loan. You should always evaluate the cost of a loan by computing its EAR.

    Banks often require customers to maintain "compensating balances" to avoid fees and other charges. For example, many banks charge a service fee if you don't carry a minimum amount in your checking account. The amount of the compensating balance that is needed to avoid such fees is determined by the bank based on the costs of the services provided to you—for example, with a checking account, you receive check-cashing services and the bank clears the checks you write and the checks you deposit.

QUESTIONS

15-1   Describe the relationships among accounts payable, inventories, accounts receivable, and the cash account by tracing the effects on these accounts of a product manufactured and sold by a company. Start with the purchase of raw materials and conclude with the collection for the sale of the product.

15-2   Describe the cash conversion cycle. How can a financial manager use knowledge of the cash conversion cycle to better manage the firm's working capital?

15-3   What are the advantages of matching the maturities of assets and liabilities? What are the disadvantages?

15-4   What are the two principal reasons for holding cash? Can a firm estimate its target cash balance by summing the cash held to satisfy each of these reasons?

15-5   Why is it important for a financial manager to understand the concept of float to effectively manage the firm's cash?

15-6   Why would a lockbox plan make more sense for a firm that makes sales all over the United States than for a firm with the same volume of business but for which the sales are concentrated where the firm's corporate headquarters are located?

15-7   In general, does a firm want to speed up or slow down collections of payments made by its customers? Why? How does the same firm want to manage its disbursements? Why?

15-8   When selecting securities for portfolio investments, corporate treasurers must make a tradeoff between risk and returns. Is it true that most treasurers are willing to assume a fairly high exposure to risk to gain higher expected returns with marketable securities?

15-9   What are the elements of a firm's credit policy? To what extent can firms set their own credit policies as opposed to having to accept policies that are dictated by "the competition"?

15-10 What are aging schedules, and how can the credit manager use them to more effectively manage accounts receivable?

15-11 Describe the three classifications of inventory and indicate the purpose of holding each type.

15-12 "Every firm should use the EOQ model to determine the optimal level of inventory to maintain." Discuss the accuracy of this statement with respect to the form of the EOQ model presented in this chapter.

SELF-TEST PROBLEMS

Solutions appear in Appendix B.

Key Terms   **ST-1**   Define each of the following terms:

    a. Working capital; net working capital; working capital policy

    b. Cash conversion cycle; inventory conversion period; receivables collection period (DSO); payables deferral period

    c. Relaxed current asset investment policy; restricted current asset investment policy; moderate current asset investment policy

d. Permanent current assets; temporary current assets

e. Moderate (maturity matching) current asset financing policy; aggressive current asset financing policy; conservative current asset financing policy

f. Accruals; trade credit

g. Promissory note; line of credit; revolving credit agreement

h. Compensating balance (CB); commitment fee

i. Commercial paper; secured loan

j. Pledging receivables; factoring; recourse

k. Discount interest loan

l. Transactions balance; compensating balance; precautionary balance; speculative balance

m. Float; disbursement float, collections float, and net float

n. Lockbox arrangement; preauthorized debit; concentration banking

o. Zero-balance account; controlled disbursement account

p. Marketable securities

q. Credit policy; credit standards; terms of credit; cash discount

r. Receivables monitoring; collection policy; aging schedule

s. Inventory carrying costs; ordering costs; total inventory costs

t. Raw materials; work-in-process; finished goods

u. Economic ordering quantity (EOQ); EOQ model; reorder point; safety stocks

v. Just-in-time system; outsourcing

ST-2 The Calgary Company is attempting to establish a current assets policy. Fixed assets are $600,000, and the firm plans to maintain a 50 percent debt/assets ratio. The interest rate is 10 percent on all debt. The three alternative current asset policies under consideration are to carry current assets that total 40, 50, or 60 percent of projected sales. The company expects to earn 15 percent before interest and taxes on sales of $3 million. Calgary's marginal tax rate is 40 percent. What is the expected return on equity (ROE) under each alternative? (*Hint:* ROE is computed by dividing net income by the dollar amount of equity.)   **Working Capital Policy**

ST-3 Gallinger Corporation projects an increase in sales from $1.5 million to $2 million, but it needs an additional $300,000 of current assets to support this expansion. The money can be obtained from the bank with a discount interest loan with a simple interest of 13 percent; no compensating balance is required. Alternatively, Gallinger can finance the expansion by no longer taking discounts, thereby increasing its accounts payable. The company makes purchases under terms of 2/10, net 30, but it can delay payment for an additional 35 days—paying on Day 65 and thus becoming 35 days past due—without a penalty because of its suppliers' current excess capacity problems.   **Trade Credit versus Bank Credit**

a. Based strictly on effective annual interest rate comparisons, how should Gallinger finance its expansion?

b. What additional qualitative factors should Gallinger consider before making a decision?

ST-4 The Boca Grande Company expects to have sales of $10 million this year under its current operating policies. Its variable costs as a percentage of sales   **Change in Credit Policy**

are 80 percent, and its cost of short-term funds is 16 percent. Currently, Boca Grande's credit policy is net 25 (no discount for early payment), but its customers pay on average in 30 days. Boca Grande spends $50,000 per year to collect its credit accounts. It collects all receivables (that is, it has no bad debts), and its marginal tax rate is 40 percent. All costs associated with the manufacture of the product and with the credit department's operations are paid when the product is sold.

The credit manager is considering two alternative proposals for changing Boca Grande's credit policy. Should a change in credit policy be made?

Proposal 1. Lengthen the credit period by going from net 25 to net 30. Collection expenditures will remain constant. Under this proposal, sales are expected to increase by $1 million annually, and the DSO is expected to increase from 30 to 45 days on all sales.

Proposal 2. Shorten the credit period by going from net 25 to net 20. Collection expenses will remain constant, but sales are expected to decrease by $1 million per year and the DSO is expected to decline from 30 to 22 days.

EOQ and Total Inventory Costs   **ST-5**   The Homemade Bread Company buys and then sells (as bread) 2.6 million bushels of wheat annually. The wheat must be purchased in multiples of 2,000 bushels. Ordering costs are $5,000 per order. Annual carrying costs are 2 percent of the purchase price of $5 per bushel. The delivery time is 6 weeks.

  a. What is the EOQ?

  b. At what inventory level should the firm place an order for more wheat?

  c. What are Homemade Bread's total inventory costs?

PROBLEMS

Inventory Conversion Period   **15-1**   The Cristo Candy Corporation carries an average balance of inventory equal to $400,000. The company's cost of goods sold averages $4.5 million. What are Cristo's (a) inventory turnover and (b) inventory conversion period?

Inventory Conversion   **15-2**   Wally's Motors generally has inventory that equals $48 million. If the inventory turnover for the company is 8, what are its (a) inventory conversion period and (b) cost of goods sold?

Receivables Collection Period (DSO)   **15-3**   Small Fry Pools generally carries an amount of receivables equal to $80,000, and its annual credit sales equal $2.4 million. What are Small Fry's (a) receivables turnover and (b) receivables collection period (DSO)?

Receivables Collection Period (DSO)   **15-4**   Unique Uniforms generally has accounts receivables that equal $480,000. If the accounts receivables turnover for the company is 12, what are its (a) receivables collection period (DSO) and (b) annual credit sales?

Payables Deferral Period (DPO)   **15-5**   At any point in time, Grandiron Fertilizer generally owes its suppliers $180,000. The company's cost of goods sold averages $2.52 million. What are Grandiron's (a) payables turnover and (b) payables deferral period (DPO)?

Payables Deferral Period (DPO)   **15-6**   The accounts payables of Momma's Baby, Inc., generally equal $1.6 million. If the turnover of accounts payables is 20, what are its (a) payables deferral period (DPO) and (b) annual credit purchases?

15-7   Clearwater Glass Company examined its cash management policy and found that it takes an average of 5 days for checks that the company writes to reach its bank, and thus be deducted from its checking account balance—that is, disbursement delay, or float, is 5 days. On the other hand, it is an average of 4 days from the time Clearwater Glass receives payments from its customers until the funds are available for use at the bank—that is, collection delay, or float, is 4 days. On an average day, Clearwater Glass writes checks that total $70,000, and it receives checks from customers that total $80,000.   **Computation of Float**

    a.   Compute the disbursement float, collection float, and net float in dollars.

    b.   If Clearwater Glass has an opportunity cost equal to 10 percent, how much would it be willing to spend each year to reduce collection delay (float) by 2 days? (*Hint:* Assume any funds that are freed up will be invested at 10 percent annually.)

15-8   The McCollough Company has a variable operating cost ratio of 70 percent, its cost of capital is 10 percent, and current sales are $10,000. All of its sales are on credit, and it currently sells on terms of net 30. Its accounts receivable balance is $1,500. McCollough is considering a new credit policy with terms of net 45. Under the new policy, sales will increase to $12,000, and accounts receivable will rise to $2,500. Compute the days sales outstanding (DSO) under the existing policy and the proposed policy.   **Credit Policy Change**

15-9   Calculate the APR and the r_{EAR} of non-free trade credit under each of the following terms. Assume payment is made either on the last due date or on the discount date.   **Cost of Trade Credit**

    a.   1/15, net 20

    b.   2/10, net 60

    c.   3/10, net 45

    d.   2/10, net 45

    e.   2/15, net 40

15-10   **a.**   If a firm buys under terms of 3/15, net 45, but actually pays on the twentieth day and still takes the discount, what is the APR of its non-free trade credit?   **Cost of Credit**

    b.   Does the firm receive more or less credit than it would if it paid within 15 days?

15-11   Boles Corporation needs to raise $500,000 for 1 year to supply capital to a new store. Boles buys from its suppliers on terms of 3/10, net 90, and it currently pays on Day 10 and takes discounts; but it could forgo discounts, pay on Day 90, and get the needed $500,000 in the form of costly trade credit. Alternatively, Boles could borrow from its bank on a 12 percent discount interest rate basis. What is the EAR of the lower cost source?   **Cost of Credit**

15-12   Gifts Galore Inc. borrowed $1.5 million from National City Bank (NCB). The loan was made at a simple annual interest rate of 9 percent a year for 3 months. A 20 percent compensating balance requirement raised the effective interest rate because the company does not maintain a checking balance at NCB.   **Cost of Bank Credit**

    a.   The APR on the loan was 11.25 percent. What was the EAR?

    b.   What would the EAR of the loan be if the note required discount interest?

Cash Conversion Cycle

15-13 The Saliford Corporation has an inventory conversion period of 60 days, a receivables collection period of 36 days, and a payables deferral period of 24 days.

    a. What is the length of the firm's cash conversion cycle?

    b. If Saliford's annual sales are $3,960,000 and all sales are on credit, what is the average balance in accounts receivable?

    c. How many times per year does Saliford turn over its inventory?

    d. What would happen to Saliford's cash conversion cycle if, on average, inventories could be turned over eight times a year?

Receivables Balance and DSO

15-14 Morrissey Industries sells on terms of 3/10, net 30. Total sales for the year are $900,000. Forty percent of the customers pay on Day 10 and take discounts; the other 60 percent pay, on average, 40 days after their purchases.

    a. What is the days sales outstanding?

    b. What is the average amount of receivables?

    c. What would happen to average receivables if Morrissey tightened its collection policy with the result that all nondiscount customers paid on Day 30?

Tightening Credit Terms

15-15 Helen Bowers, the new credit manager of the Muscarella Corporation, was alarmed to find that Muscarella sells on credit terms of net 50 days whereas industry-wide credit terms have recently been lowered to net 30 days. On annual credit sales of $3 million, Muscarella currently averages 60 days' sales in accounts receivable. Bowers estimates that tightening the credit terms to 30 days would reduce annual sales to $2.6 million, but accounts receivable would drop to 35 days of sales, and the savings on investment in them should more than overcome any loss in profit.

    Muscarella's variable cost ratio is 70 percent, and its marginal tax rate is 40 percent. If the interest rate on funds invested in receivables is 11 percent, should the change in credit terms be made? All operating costs are paid when inventory is sold.

EOQ

15-16 Green Thumb Garden Centers sells 240,000 bags of lawn fertilizer annually. The optimal safety stock (which is on hand initially) is 1,200 bags. Each bag costs Green Thumb $4, inventory carrying costs are 20 percent, and the cost of placing an order with its supplier is $25.

    a. What is the economic ordering quantity (EOQ)?

    b. What is the total inventory cost at the EOQ level?

    c. What is the maximum inventory of fertilizer?

    d. What will Green Thumb's average inventory be?

    e. How often must the company order?

Disbursement Float

15-17 The Garvin Company is setting up a new checking account with Barngrover National Bank. Garvin plans to issue checks in the amount of $1.6 million each day and to deduct them from its own records at the close of business on the day they are written. On average, the bank will receive and clear (that is, deduct from the firm's bank balance) the checks at 5 p.m. the fourth day after they are written. For example, a check written on Monday will be cleared on Friday afternoon. The firm's agreement with the bank requires it to maintain a $1.2 million average compensating balance, which is $400,000 greater than the cash balance the firm would otherwise have on deposit. Garvin will make a $1.2 million cash deposit at the time it opens the account.

a. Assuming that the firm makes cash deposits at 2 p.m. each day (and the bank includes them in that day's transactions), how much must it deposit daily to maintain a sufficient balance once it reaches a steady state? (To find the answer, set up a table that shows the daily balance recorded on the company's books and the daily balance at the bank until a steady state is reached.) Indicate the required deposit, if any, on Day 1, Day 2, Day 3, Day 4, and each day thereafter, assuming that the company will write checks for $1.6 million on Day 1 and each day thereafter.

b. How many days of float does Garvin carry?

c. What ending daily balance should the firm try to maintain (1) on the bank's records and (2) on its own records?

d. Explain how net float can help increase the value of the firm's common stock.

15-18 The Flamingo Corporation is trying to determine the effect of its inventory turnover ratio and days sales outstanding (DSO) on its cash flow cycle. Flamingo's 2009 sales (all on credit) were $180,000, and it earned a net profit of 5 percent, or $9,000. The cost of goods sold equals 85 percent of sales. Inventory was turned over eight times during the year, and the DSO, or average collection period, was 36 days. The firm had fixed assets totaling $40,000. Flamingo's payables deferral period is 30 days.

Cash Conversion Cycle and Asset Turnover

a. Calculate Flamingo's cash conversion cycle.

b. Assuming Flamingo holds negligible amounts of cash and marketable securities, calculate its total assets turnover and return on assets (ROA).

c. Suppose Flamingo's managers believe that the inventory turnover can be raised to 10×. What would Flamingo's cash conversion cycle, total assets turnover, and ROA have been if the inventory turnover had been 10× for 2009?

15-19 Durst Corporation began operations 5 years ago as a small firm serving customers in the Denver area. Its reputation and market area grew quickly, however, and today Durst has customers throughout the United States. Despite its broad customer base, Durst has maintained its headquarters in Denver and keeps its central billing system there. Durst's management is considering an alternative collection procedure to reduce its mail time and processing float. On average, it takes 5 days from the time customers mail payments until Durst is able to receive, process, and deposit them. Durst would like to set up a lockbox collection system, which it estimates would reduce the time lag from customer mailing to deposit by 3 days—bringing it down to 2 days. Durst receives an average of $1,400,000 in payments per day.

Lockbox System

a. How many days of collection float now exist (Durst's collection float) and what would it be under the lockbox system? What reduction in cash balances could Durst achieve by initiating the lockbox system?

b. If Durst has an opportunity cost of 10 percent, how much is the lockbox system worth on an annual basis?

c. What is the maximum monthly charge Durst should pay for the lockbox system?

Relaxing Collection Efforts

15-20 The Pettit Corporation has annual credit sales of $2 million. Current expenses for the collection department are $30,000, bad debt losses are 2 percent, and the days sales outstanding is 30 days. Pettit is considering easing its collection efforts so that collection expenses will be reduced to $22,000 per year. The change is expected to increase bad debt losses to 3 percent and to increase the days sales outstanding to 45 days. In addition, sales are expected to increase to $2.2 million per year.

Should Pettit relax collection efforts if the opportunity cost of funds is 12 percent, the variable cost ratio is 75 percent, and its marginal tax rate is 40 percent? All costs associated with production and credit sales are paid on the day of the sale.

Easing Credit Terms

15-21 Bey Technologies is considering changing its credit terms from 2/15, net 30 to 3/10, net 30 to speed collections. At present, 40 percent of Bey's paying customers take the 2 percent discount. Under the new terms, discount customers are expected to rise to 50 percent. Regardless of the credit terms, half of the customers *who do not take the discount* are expected to pay on time, whereas the remainder will pay 10 days late. The change does not involve a relaxation of credit standards; therefore, bad debt losses are not expected to rise above their present 2 percent level. However, the more generous cash discount terms are expected to increase sales from $2 million to $2.6 million per year. Bey's variable cost ratio is 75 percent, the interest rate on funds invested in accounts receivable is 9 percent, and the firm's marginal tax rate is 40 percent. All costs associated with production and credit sales are paid on the day of the sale.

a. What is the days sales outstanding before and after the change?

b. Calculate the costs of the discounts taken before and after the change.

c. Calculate the bad debt losses before and after the change.

d. Should Bey change its credit terms?

Inventory Cost

15-22 Computer Supplies Inc. must order memory sticks from its supplier in lots of one dozen boxes. Given the information provided here, complete the following table and determine the economic ordering quantity of memory sticks for Computer Supplies Inc.

Annual demand	26,000 dozen
Cost per order placed	$ 30.00
Carrying cost	20%
Price per dozen	$ 7.80

Order Size (dozens)	250	500	1,000	2,000	13,000	26,000
Number of orders	___	___	___	___	___	___
Average inventory	___	___	___	___	___	___
Carrying cost	___	___	___	___	___	___
Order cost	___	___	___	___	___	___
Total cost	___	___	___	___	___	___

EOQ and Inventory Costs

15-23 The following inventory data have been established for the Thompson Company:

(1) Orders must be placed in multiples of 100 units.

(2) Annual sales are 338,000 units.

    (3) The purchase price per unit is $6.

    (4) Carrying cost is 20 percent of the purchase price of goods.

    (5) Fixed order cost is $48.

    (6) Three days are required for delivery.

  a. What is the EOQ?

  b. How many orders should Thompson place each year?

  c. At what inventory level should an order be made?

  d. Calculate the total cost of ordering and carrying inventories if the order quantity is (1) 4,000 units, (2) 4,800 units, or (3) 6,000 units. (4) What are the total costs if the order quantity is the EOQ?

15-24 Look back in the chapter to Table 15-1, which showed the balance sheets for Argile Textiles on three different dates. Argile's sales fluctuate during the year due to the seasonal nature of its business; however, we can calculate its sales on an average day as total sales divided by 360, recognizing that daily sales will be much higher than this value during its peak selling season and much lower during its slack time. Argile's projected sales for 2011 are $825 million, so daily sales are expected to average $2.29 million. The projected cost of goods sold for 2011 is $660 million, so daily credit costs associated with production are expected to average $1.83 million. Assume all sales and all purchases are made on credit.

Cash Conversion Cycle

  a. Calculate Argile's inventory conversion period as of September 30, 2011, and December 31, 2011.

  b. Calculate Argile's receivables collection period as of September 30, 2011, and December 31, 2011.

  c. Calculate the payables deferral period as of September 30, 2011, and December 31, 2011.

  d. Using the values calculated in parts (a) through (c), calculate the length of Argile's cash conversion cycle on the two balance sheet dates.

  e. In part (d), you should have found that the cash conversion cycle was longer on September 30 than on December 31. Why did these results occur?

  f. Can you think of any reason why the cash conversion cycle of a firm with seasonal sales might be different during the slack selling season than during the peak selling season?

15-25 Verbrugge Corporation is a leading U.S. producer of automobile batteries. Verbrugge turns out 1,500 batteries a day at a cost of $6 per battery for materials and labor. It takes the firm 22 days to convert raw materials into a battery. Verbrugge allows its customers 40 days in which to pay for the batteries, and the firm generally pays its suppliers in 30 days.

Working Capital Investment and Cash Conversion Cycle

  a. What is the length of Verbrugge's cash conversion cycle?

  b. If Verbrugge always produces and sells 1,500 batteries a day, what amount of working capital must it finance?

  c. By what amount could Verbrugge reduce its working capital financing needs if it was able to stretch its payables deferral period to 35 days?

15-26 Susan Visscher, owner of Visscher's Hardware, is negotiating with First Merchant's Bank for a $50,000 1-year loan. First Merchant's has offered

Cost of Bank Credit

Visscher the following alternatives. Calculate the effective interest rate (EAR) for each alternative. Which alternative has the lowest EAR?

a. A 12 percent annual rate on a simple interest loan with no compensating balance required and interest due at the end of the year.

b. A 9 percent annual rate on a simple interest loan with a 20 percent compensating balance required and interest again due at the end of the year.

c. An 8.75 percent annual rate on a discounted loan with a 15 percent compensating balance.

Effective Cost of Credit   **15-27** The Meyer Company must arrange financing for its working capital requirements for the coming year. Meyer can (a) borrow from its bank on a simple interest basis (interest payable at the end of the loan) for 1 year at a 12 percent simple rate; (b) borrow on a 3-month, renewable loan at an 11.5 percent simple rate; or (c) obtain the needed funds by no longer taking discounts and thus increasing its accounts payable. Meyer buys on terms of 1/15, net 51. What is the EAR of the least expensive type of credit, assuming 360 days per year?

Cost of Bank Credit   **15-28** The UFSU Corporation intends to borrow $450,000 to support its short-term financing requirements during the next year. The company is evaluating its financing options at the bank where it maintains its checking account. UFSU's checking account balance, which averages $50,000, can be used to help satisfy any compensating balance requirements the bank might impose. The financing alternatives offered by the bank include the following:

Alternative 1. A discount interest loan with a simple interest of $9\frac{1}{4}$ percent and no compensating balance requirement.

Alternative 2. A 10 percent simple interest loan that has a 15 percent compensating balance requirement.

Alternative 3. A $1 million revolving line of credit with simple interest of $9\frac{1}{4}$ percent paid on the amount borrowed and a $\frac{1}{4}$ percent commitment fee on the unused balance. No compensating balance is required.

a. Compute the effective cost (rate) of each financing alternative assuming UFSU *borrows* $450,000. Which alternative should UFSU use?

b. For each alternative, how much would UFSU have to borrow to have $450,000 available for use (to pay the firm's bills)?

Integrative Problems

Cash Management   **15-29** Ray Smith, a retired librarian, recently opened an outdoor recreation shop called Smitty's Sports Paradise (SSP). Ray decided that, at age 62, he wasn't quite ready to stay at home living the life of leisure. It had always been his dream to open an outdoor recreation shop, so his friends convinced him to go ahead. Because Ray's educational background was in literature and not in business, he hired you, a finance expert, to help him with the store's cash management. Ray is eager to learn, so he has asked you to develop a set of questions to help him understand cash management. Answer the following questions:

a. What is the goal of cash management?

b. For what reasons do firms hold cash?

c. What is meant by the terms *precautionary balance* and *speculative balance*?

d. What are some specific advantages for a firm in holding adequate cash balances?

e. How can a firm synchronize its cash flows, and what good would this effort do?

f. You have been going through the store's checkbook and bank balances. In the process, you discovered that SSP, on average, writes checks in the amount of $10,000 each day and that it takes approximately 5 days for these checks to clear. Also, the firm receives checks in the amount of $10,000 daily, but loses 4 days while they are being deposited and cleared. What is the firm's disbursement float, collections float, and net float?

g. How can a firm speed up collections and slow down disbursements?

h. Why would a firm hold marketable securities?

i. What factors should a firm consider in building its marketable securities portfolio? What are some securities that should be held and some that should not be held?

15-30 Ray now asks you to examine his company's credit policy to determine whether changes are needed. One of his employees, who recently graduated with a finance degree, has recommended that the credit terms be changed from 2/10, net 30, to 3/20, net 45, and that both the credit standards and the collection policy be relaxed. According to the employee, such a change would cause sales to increase from $3.6 million to $4.0 million.

    Currently, 62.5 percent of SSP's customers pay on Day 10 of the billing cycle and take the discount, 32 percent pay on Day 30, and 5.5 percent pay (on average) on Day 60. If the firm adopts the new credit policy, Ray thinks that 72.5 percent of customers would take the discount, 10 percent would pay on Day 45, and 17.5 percent would pay late, on Day 90. Bad debt losses for both policies are expected to be trivial.

    SSP's variable operating costs are currently 75 percent of sales, its cost of funds is 10 percent, and its marginal tax rate is 40 percent. None of these factors would change as a result of a credit policy change. All cash payments associated with the production and sale of products (including credit costs) are made on the day the products are sold.

    To help him decide whether to adopt the new policy, Ray has asked you to answer the following questions:

a. What variables make up a firm's credit policy? In what direction would each be changed if the credit policy were tightened? How would each variable tend to affect sales, the level of receivables, and bad debt losses?

b. How are the days sales outstanding and the average collection period related? What would the DSO be if SSP maintains its current credit policy? If it adopts the proposed policy?

c. What is the dollar amount of discounts granted under the current and the proposed credit policies?

d. Should SSP make the change?

e. Suppose the company makes the proposed change, but its competitors react by changing their own credit terms, with the net result being that

Credit Policy

SSP's gross sales remain at the $3.6 million level. How would this situation affect the company's value?

f. **(1)** What does the term *monitoring accounts receivable* mean?

(2) Why would a firm want to monitor its receivables?

(3) How might the DSO and the aging schedule be used in this process?

EOQ Model   **15-31** Now Ray asks you to look at the company's inventory position. He thinks that inventories might be too high as a result of the manager's tendency to order in large quantities. Ray has decided to examine the situation for one key product—fly rods that cost $320 each to purchase and prepare for sale. Annual sales of the product are 2,500 units (rods), and the annual carrying cost is 10 percent of inventory value. The company has been buying 500 rods per order and placing another order when the stock on hand falls to 100 rods. Each time SSP orders, it incurs a cost equal to $64. Sales are uniform throughout the year.

a. Ray believes that the EOQ model should be used to help determine the optimal inventory situation for this product. What is the EOQ formula, and what are the key assumptions underlying this model?

b. What is the formula for calculating total inventory costs?

c. What is the EOQ for the fly rods? What will the total inventory costs be for this product if SSP orders the EOQ amount?

d. What is SSP's added cost if it orders 500 fly rods rather than the EOQ amount? What if it orders 750 rods each time?

e. Suppose it takes 3 days for SSP to receive its orders and package the rods before they are ready for sale. Assuming certainty in production time and usage, at what inventory level should SSP order more fly rods? (Assume a 360-day year, that SSP is open every day, and that SSP orders the EOQ amount.)

f. Of course, there is uncertainty in SSP's usage rate as well as in order delays, so the company must carry a safety stock to avoid running out of the fly rods and having to lose sales. If SSP carries a safety stock of 50 rods, what effect would this policy have on total inventory costs?

g. For most of SSP's products, inventory usage is not uniform throughout the year, but rather follows some seasonal pattern. Could the EOQ model be used in this situation? If so, how?

h. How would the following factors affect the use of the EOQ model?

(1) Use of "just-in-time" procedures

(2) The use of air freight for deliveries

(3) Computerized inventory control systems

Short-Term Financing   **15-32** Ray has asked you to review the company's short-term financing policies and prepare a report to help him with SSP's future working capital financing decisions. To assist you in getting started, he has prepared some questions that, when answered, will give Ray a better idea of the company's short-term financing policies.

a. What is short-term credit, and what are the major sources of this credit?

b. Is there a cost to accruals, and do firms have much control over them? What is trade credit?

c. Like most small companies, SSP has two primary sources of short-term debt: trade credit and bank loans. One supplier, which supplies SSP with $50,000 of materials each year, offers purchases on terms of 2/10, net 50.

(1) What are SSP's net daily purchases from this supplier?

(2) What is the average level of SSP's accounts payable to this supplier if SSP takes the discount? What is the average level if it does not take the discount?

(3) What is the approximate cost of financing if SSP does not take the discount? What is its effective annual cost?

d. In discussing a possible loan with the firm's banker, Ray has found that the bank is willing to lend SSP a maximum of $800,000 for 1 year at a 9 percent simple, or quoted, rate. Unfortunately, he forgot to ask what the specific terms would be.

(1) Assume that the firm will borrow $800,000. What would be the effective interest rate if the loan required interest to be paid at the end of the year (not a discount interest loan)? If the loan had been an 8 percent interest loan for 6 months rather than for 1 year, would that change affect the effective annual rate?

(2) What would be the effective rate if the loan were a discount interest loan? Assume the loan is a 1-year loan.

(3) Assume that the bank requires interest to be paid at the end of the year and it requires the firm to maintain a 20 percent compensating balance. What is the effective annual rate on the loan? Assume that SSP does not have any funds in a checking account at the bank.

e. SSP is considering using secured short-term financing. What is a secured loan? What two types of current assets can be used to secure loans?

f. What are the differences between pledging receivables and factoring receivables? Is one type generally considered better?

g. What are the differences among the three forms of inventory financing? Is one type generally considered best?

COMPUTER-RELATED PROBLEM

Work the problem in this section only if you are using the computer problem spreadsheet.

15-33 Use the model in File C15 to solve this problem.

Tightening Credit Terms

a. Refer to Problem 15-15. When Bowers analyzed her proposed credit policy changes, she found that they would reduce Muscarella's value and, therefore, should not be enacted. Bowers has reevaluated her sales estimates because all other firms in the industry have recently tightened their credit policies. She now estimates that sales would decline to only $2.8 million if she tightens the credit policy to 30 days. Would the credit policy change be profitable under these circumstances?

b. On the other hand, Bowers believes that she could tighten the credit policy to net 45 days and pick up some sales from her competitors. She estimates that sales would increase to $3.3 million and that the days sales outstanding (DSO) would fall to 50 days under this policy. Should Bowers enact this change?

c. Bowers also believes that if she leaves the credit policy as it is, sales will increase to $3.4 million and the DSO will remain at 60 days. Should Bowers leave the credit policy alone or tighten it as described in either part (a) or part (b)? Which credit policy produces the highest value for Muscarella Corporation?

Investor Decision Making

Investment Concepts

A MANAGERIAL PERSPECTIVE

"**M**aximize return and minimize risk." Should this be the battle cry of all investors? Perhaps. But not all individuals invest for the same reasons, and not all investors manage their portfolios in the same way. Many investors are relentless when it comes to achieving their investment goals. They brag that they can consistently outperform the market; indeed, they can back up their claims. How do they do it?

Many investors do not make decisions about specific securities to include in their portfolios when pursuing their goals, but rather employ the services of professional investment advisers. Also, because there are a great number of investment professionals competing for investors' funds, investors have been known to create competitive environments among the various advisers who handle their money by continuously monitoring their positions and then, at least indirectly, letting each professional know how well he or she has performed relative to the others. The advisers/managers who lag behind the others are then asked to explain why their performances are not "up to par." If investment returns do not improve within a particular period—say, 6 months or 1 year—the funds are moved to other firms. If you were the adviser who was in jeopardy of losing an investment account, you would "bend over backward" to find a way to keep it, especially if the account was worth millions of dollars. In addition, you wouldn't want it known that you lost the account due to lackluster performances because "reputation" is everything in this milieu.

Investors can be savvy about their investment positions even if they don't make specific decisions about which securities to include in their portfolios, as long as they understand the fundamentals of investing. In most cases, experts would suggest that investment positions should be fairly consistent. That is, although investing is a dynamic process, making a number of substantial changes to a portfolio's composition to chase exorbitant returns could prove disastrous. This possibility does not mean that you must be overly conservative. It *does* mean that you should not exceed your risk tolerance level: take only those risks that are in line with your risk attitudes. Follow the advice that has proved successful for others who use investment advisers: (1) ask friends for advice about their experiences with investment professionals, (2) examine past performances, and (3) interview prospective candidates. Look for consistency in performance, a disciplined and focused work ethic, and a high degree of enthusiasm for the profession.

This chapter introduces some basic investment concepts. As you read it, think about why the approach to managing investments described here might help you achieve your investment goals.

**CHAPTER
PRINCIPLES**

–The Questions

After reading this chapter, you should be able to answer the following questions:

- What process should individuals follow when investing their money?
- What types of orders can investors place to buy or sell securities?
- How is the return on an investment determined?
- What is the difference between the arithmetic average return and the geometric average return? Which is a better measure of the true return on an investment?
- How are market returns measured?
- What are margin trading and short selling? When should each be used?

From an economic standpoint, we can define an investor as a person who forgoes current consumption to increase future wealth and thus to increase future consumption. If you ask investors why they invest, you will get many different responses: retirement, savings, house purchase, supplemental income, and so forth are some of the reasons people give. If you really think about it, however, there are two general types of "investors," and thus two major reasons why people purchase financial assets:

1. Most people view investments as instruments that produce growth over a long period of time. Individuals who take on "normal" risks by purchasing investments that they anticipate will exhibit relatively stable growth on average (in the long run), and thus generate normal, as opposed to abnormal, returns, are usually referred to as **investors.**

2. Some people are willing to take on relatively large risks expecting to earn quick abnormal risk-adjusted returns on "investments" that they believe to be incorrectly valued in the financial markets. Persons who fit this description generally are called **speculators** because they gamble, or *speculate,* on whether financial assets are mispriced and market prices will adjust accordingly. Speculating is riskier than investing.

investors
Individuals who purchase investments with current savings in anticipation of relatively stable growth on average or in the long term.

speculators
Individuals who take relatively large risks hoping to earn quick abnormal returns; they gamble on whether the prices of financial assets believed to be mispriced will be adjusted accordingly in the market.

In this chapter and in Chapter 17, we describe some investment concepts and evaluation techniques. Our discussions focus on investing, not speculating, and on individuals rather than institutions, such as pension funds and insurance companies. These chapters provide only a general overview of investing. You can learn more about investing by taking a course that is devoted solely to investment topics.

THE INVESTMENT PROCESS

Investing should be viewed as a continuous process that includes the steps outlined in this section and shown in Figure 16-1.

Investment Objectives

As we discovered in Chapter 2, many different financial instruments exist, each of which serves a somewhat different purpose. Before any investor decides which investments to purchase, he or she should identify the reason(s) for investing. Some of the more common reasons given for investing include the following:

1. The major reason why people invest relates to *retirement planning.* Even though most of us do not begin retirement planning early enough, when we do, we generally make choices about how to best invest to supplement Social Security or pension and retirement plans set up by employers or other organizations. The point in your career at which you start planning for your own retirement will significantly influence the strategy that you follow. If you

FIGURE 16-1 The Investment Process

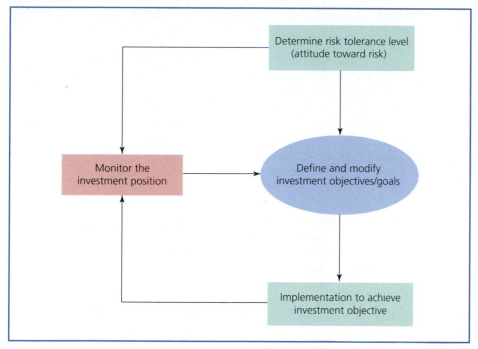

begin planning early in your career, you can invest in instruments that promise long-term growth; if you don't begin planning until later, you might have to invest in instruments that offer greater short-term stability.

2. People use investments to *supplement their current income*, especially if they are already retired. Appropriate investments include those that offer steady dividend or interest payments, which are called **income securities.** Preferred stock and interest-bearing bonds generally are considered good income-producing investments.

3. People invest to *shelter current income from taxes* using tax write-offs or other provisions of the Tax Code. Often, investors will attempt to legally defer or avoid paying taxes on income if it is not needed in the current period. For example, the Tax Code provides that contributions to qualified employee pension plans and individual retirement accounts (IRAs) can be made from pretax income dollars such that taxes do not have to be paid until withdrawals are made at retirement. In addition, some investments, such as rental property, might allow you to take advantage of tax write-offs, such as depreciation, which reduce the amount of taxes paid on income generated from the investments.

4. People save current income to *achieve future goals* such as purchasing a house, sending their children to college, traveling around the world, and so forth. If the need for, or the dedication toward, the future goal is great, an investor probably will select financial instruments that are safe enough to ensure that the financial needs are met.

income securities
Investments, such as preferred stock and corporate bonds, that offer steady dividend or interest payments.

Investors' Attitudes Toward Risk

When we first discussed risk in Chapter 11, we indicated that, for the most part, investors are *risk averse;* thus, they demand greater returns for taking on greater levels of risk. We also stated that the degree of risk aversity exhibited by investors varies among individuals at any point in time and changes for individuals across time. For example, if you ask the students in your class what investments they would choose if they had $10,000 to invest, you would receive a wide range of answers. Some would be willing to take on great risks in an effort to increase their investment quickly, whereas others would be more conservative because they want to preserve their investment and achieve steady, long-term growth. If you posed the same question at a reunion of your class 40 years later, you would receive very different answers, however. Even those individuals who were willing to take great risks 40 years earlier would be more conservative, most likely preferring to hold relatively safe income-producing instruments to help supplement their retirement income rather than riskier, high-growth-oriented investments.

To determine what instruments are appropriate to achieve your investment objectives, you must examine your ability and willingness to take risk when investing. Clearly, everyone strives to maximize the returns associated with their investments. Remember, however, that higher returns are accompanied by higher risks. For most people, a good rule of thumb to follow when determining risk tolerance is this: *if you lose sleep over your investments or are more concerned about the performance of your portfolio than your job performance, then your investment position probably is too risky.* Generally speaking, your ability and willingness to tolerate risk, which is called your **risk tolerance level,** depend on existing economic conditions, your current socioeconomic position (wealth, income, and other factors), and your expectations about your socioeconomic position in the future.[1] For instance, when the economy is performing well and you have funds that are not needed for current expenses or existing investment goals, you probably are willing to invest in riskier securities than when the economy is performing poorly and the funds are needed for specific reasons.

risk tolerance level
An investor's ability and willingness to tolerate, or accept, risk.

Implementation to Achieve Investment Objectives

Once realistic goals have been formulated based on investment objectives and risk attitudes, it is necessary to implement the decisions that have been made. Implementation involves the selection and purchase of specific investment instruments to achieve the desired goals. This process can be costly because transaction costs, or commissions, must be paid to acquire investments. The **transaction costs** of some investment instruments, including savings accounts, certificates of deposit, and so forth, are small and indirect because only time, effort, and gas or telephone calls are involved; other transaction costs are more direct and larger because, in addition to time, effort, and telephone calls, broker commissions are incurred. Of course, unless the investment strategy is implemented, these investment goals cannot be accomplished.

transaction costs
The costs associated with trading securities, which include the costs of time, effort, and telephone calls, as well as any broker commissions incurred.

Depending on your risk tolerance level and your propensity to control your investment decisions, you might prefer to either select your own investments or rely on the advice of an investment professional when implementing your investment strategy. If you choose to *actively manage* your investment portfolio, you must be able to commit the time and effort necessary to properly examine and select investment instruments that are appropriate to meeting your investing goals. If you cannot make such a commitment or are not confident that you have the ability to make cogent investment decisions, you probably should follow a more *passive*

[1]If you would like to know your risk tolerance level, you can take an online risk tolerance quiz, such as the one located on the MSN Money Web site at http://moneycentral.msn.com/investor/calcs/n_riskq/main.asp.

TABLE 16-1	Recommended Asset Allocations Based on Risk Tolerance/Position in Life			
Risk Tolerance	**Description**	**Stocks**	**Bonds**	**Cash**[a]
High risk	Young Investors	70–80%	15–25%	0– 5%
Moderate risk	Investors Near Retirement	60	30–40	0–10
Low risk	Retired Investors	40–50	40–50	5–20
	Investors older than 70	20–30	60	10–20

[a]*Cash* refers to checking accounts, savings accounts, and money market (short-term) investments.

Source: William Reichenstein, "Basic Truths About Asset Allocation: A Consensus View Among Experts," *American Association of Individual Investors,* October 1996.

management style by purchasing investments that are managed by professionals, such as mutual funds, or by hiring a professional investment adviser.

Whether you are active or passive in the management of your investments, you should always be aware of the composition of your **investment portfolio,** or the combination of investment assets that you hold, because the allocation of your investment funds to various types of assets in your portfolio is an important decision. When determining the appropriate **asset allocation,** or proportion of funds invested in various types of assets, you should always keep your investment goal in mind. If your investment goal is to generate income, then your portfolio should include more income-producing investments than assets with returns that are primarily based on capital gains, or growth.

In most cases, investors allocate their funds to three basic categories of financial assets:

1. Short-term debt instruments, or money market securities (cash and near-cash items)

2. Long-term debt, or bonds

3. Stocks

You might think that asset allocation would be an easy task because there are only three general categories among which your funds need to be allocated. In reality, the asset allocation decision is extremely important because it affects the return that you will earn on your investment portfolio. In addition, asset allocation is a dynamic process. As conditions in the financial markets change, so should your asset allocations in investment portfolios. For instance, when the markets become more unstable and unpredictable than normal, many professional investment managers shift their allocations into the asset categories that are considered safer, such as money market instruments and debt. Similarly, as noted earlier, as individuals move through life, they have a tendency to become more conservative and, therefore, to shift funds into less risky asset categories.

Table 16-1 shows the asset allocations recommended by investment experts. Notice that the allocation recommendations shift from riskier investments (that is, stocks) to less risky investments (that is, bonds and cash) as the individual investor gets closer to retirement.

Monitoring the Investment Position

After the investment strategy has been implemented, the investment position must be monitored to ensure that the goals are being met. Because economic and legal

investment portfolio
A combination of investment instruments.

asset allocation
The proportion of funds invested in various categories of assets, such as money market instruments, long-term debt, stocks, and real estate.

conditions change continuously and new investment instruments are created periodically, investors should reevaluate their investment positions periodically to determine whether they are in the best positions to achieve their objectives. In
addition, as individuals' attitudes toward risk or their socioeconomic positions
change, their investment strategies should change as well. For these reasons, it is
vitally important for investors to regularly reexamine their goals and strategies and
their investment positions to determine whether modifications are needed.

Self-Test Questions

What steps are involved in the investment process?

Explain why risk attitudes differ among investors at a particular point in time
and why the risk attitude of an individual investor changes over time.

Why is it important to monitor, or periodically evaluate, your investment
position?

INVESTMENT ALTERNATIVES

Recall from our description of financial assets in Chapter 2 that many different
instruments are available to help individuals meet their investment goals. For example, individuals who prefer low risk and want to invest for short periods can
purchase money market instruments, such as Treasury bills, certificates of deposit,
and so forth. Those who have longer term goals can purchase capital market instruments that are expected to exhibit stable, long-term growth, such as the stocks or
bonds of large, well-established firms. Investors who prefer greater risk can gamble
with their money in the derivatives markets by purchasing options or futures.

Although there are so many different types of investment instruments that it
might seem an investment exists to meet any investment goal imaginable, new
investments continue to evolve as investors' needs (demands) change. For example,
money market mutual funds were created in the mid-1970s when investors withdrew from the capital markets because interest rates were relatively high and the
stability of the long-term financial markets was uncertain. Clearly, new financial
instruments will continue to evolve in the future as investors' demographics change
and as their financial needs and strategies are adjusted accordingly.

Self-Test Question

Do you believe that new investment alternatives (instruments) will be created
in the future? For what reasons?

SECURITIES TRANSACTIONS

broker
A middleman, or agent,
who helps investors trade
financial instruments
such as stocks, bonds,
and derivatives.

Most of the investment transactions that are not related to savings instruments from
financial institutions require the help of a middleman, or agent, called a **broker.**
The role of the broker is to help his or her clients trade financial instruments,
especially stocks, bonds, and derivatives. For example, *stockbrokers*, or account
executives as they are called by many brokerage firms, help both individual and
institutional investors buy and sell financial assets, and they earn commissions in the

process. To trade securities, and thus to be a broker, an individual must be licensed by the exchanges on which the traded securities are listed. In addition, a broker must abide by any licensing or registration requirements of the state in which he or she trades and by ethical standards established by the Securities and Exchange Commission.

Because brokerage firms play an important role in the financial markets and the implementation of individuals' investment goals, this section describes some of the services such organizations traditionally provide. In addition, it indicates how securities trades are accomplished.

Brokerage Firms versus Financial Intermediaries

In the strictest sense of the term, a brokerage firm is not considered a "financial intermediary." Recall from the definition and descriptions provided in Chapter 4 that financial intermediaries literally *manufacture* a variety of financial products, such as mortgages, automobile loans, NOW accounts, or pension funds, thereby allowing savers to *indirectly* provide funds to borrowers (users of funds). By comparison, the traditional role of a brokerage firm is not to create savings instruments, or financial securities; rather, it is to help investors trade such securities, which are created by corporations and governments. In this way, brokers allow savers to *directly* provide their funds to users of those funds; this process is not part of the intermediation process discussed in Chapter 4. For instance, if you call a broker and purchase Microsoft common stock, you have invested in a security created by Microsoft, not by a bank, thrift institution, or other financial intermediary. In contrast, if you purchase a mutual fund that includes Microsoft stock, then you participate in the intermediary process because you do not actually own Microsoft stock; instead, your investment is in the security (shares) created by the mutual fund company that actually owns the Microsoft stock.

Although their traditional role has been to help investors buy and sell stocks, bonds, and other securities, many brokerage firms have ventured into areas that have been customarily associated with financial intermediaries. For example, many brokerage firms offer their own money market funds with limited checking privileges, credit cards, and other services that have traditionally been viewed as products of banks, mutual funds, or other financial intermediaries. In the future, brokerage firms will undoubtedly offer even more financial products that are considered "nontraditional" in an effort to better compete in the financial marketplace.

Types of Brokerage Firms

In general, we classify brokerage firms into one of two categories: *full-service brokerage firms* or *discount brokerage firms*. As the name implies, a **full-service brokerage firm** offers a variety of services to its clients, including the results from various research projects, monthly publications that contain investment recommendations, and advisory services. In contrast, a **discount brokerage firm** offers its clients only the basic services associated with trading securities; in some cases, the services provided include only trade executions and related reporting requirements.

Because discount brokers offer fewer amenities than full-service brokers and their operations are less costly, they charge substantially lower commissions to execute trades. In fact, sometimes the commissions charged by a "bare-bones" discount broker are only 15-20 percent of the commissions charged by a full-service broker. The commissions charged by full-service brokers average nearly $90 for 100

full-service brokerage firm
A brokerage firm that offers a variety of services to its clients, including research information, monthly publications that contain investment recommendations, advisory services, and so forth.

discount brokerage firm
A brokerage firm that offers clients only the basic services associated with trading securities; in some cases, the services provided include only trade executions and related reporting requirements.

shares of stock with a purchase price of $50 per share. Conversely, the commissions charged by discount brokers for the same transaction might range from $10 to $55, with an average of about $30. "Deep-discount" brokers often offer execution of similar trades for commissions of less than $10.

Although most security trades are still completed either by telephone or in person, large brokerage firms also offer electronic trading. One advantage to trading electronically is that you can place an order any time, even when the markets are closed. Although orders placed when the markets are closed generally are not executed until the beginning of the next trading day, the ability to place orders at any time provides convenience to investors. Another advantage to electronic trading is that commissions generally are lower than those charged by a traditional stock-broker (even a discount broker) because, in effect, electronic orders can be placed directly with the representative of the brokerage firm that completes the trade. It is estimated that most of the commissions generated by discount brokers and more than 15 percent of full-service brokerage commissions are produced by online trading activities. Although most commissions are still derived from traditional trading mechanisms, it is evident that a "virtual Wall Street" is evolving.

Trading Securities

Whether you use a full-service broker, work with a discount broker, or trade electronically, executing a trade involves the same general process: instructions must be given concerning the security to be traded. Generally speaking, besides identifying the security to be traded, trade instructions include an indication of the number of units, or shares, to be traded, the time at which the trade should take place, and any limitations associated with the trade.

Trading Quantities

round lots
Multiples of 100 shares of a security.

When securities are traded on exchanges, they are traded in **round lots,** or multiples of 100 shares. This restriction does not mean that an investor must buy or sell 100 shares, or multiples of 100 shares, each time he or she trades. Investors can trade in **odd lots,** the term given to trades with shares that are not in multiples of 100. Because only round lots are traded on the exchanges, odd-lot trades are handled by special dealers called *odd-lot dealers*. Odd-lot dealers effectively "bundle together" odd lots to create round lots that can be traded on the exchanges. As you might imagine, odd-lot trading involves additional processing that often increases the relative cost compared to round-lot trades.

odd lots
Numbers of shares that are not in multiples of 100.

Types of Orders

market order
An order to execute a transaction at the best price available when the transaction reaches the market.

Transactions to buy and sell stocks are executed according to orders submitted by investors. Many different types of orders are available to the investing public. The most common type is a **market order,** which is an order to execute a transaction at the best price available when the transaction reaches the market. Thus, if an investor submits a market order to buy IBM stock, he or she has instructed the broker to buy IBM stock at the lowest possible price as soon as the transaction reaches the trading floor.

An order might also include conditions and limitations concerning how and when a buy or sell transaction can be executed. For example, *stop orders* and *limit orders* are used to specify the price at which a market order is executed or to restrict the price of the transaction.

A **stop order** specifies the price at which a market order is initiated. If IBM stock is currently selling at $129 per share and an investor submits an order to *BUY IBM 130 STOP*, the market order to buy IBM stock will not be initiated until the per-share price reaches $130. A stop order instructs the broker when to begin executing a transaction, but it does not guarantee or limit the price of the transaction. For example, the stop order to buy IBM stock simply instructs the broker to begin executing a market buy order when the price of the stock reaches $130. By the time the order actually is executed, the price of IBM might be much higher or much lower than $130.

To restrict the price of a transaction, an investor can use a **limit order,** which is an order to buy or sell a stock at no worse than a specified price. For example, an investor who wants to buy IBM stock, but does not want to pay more than $132 per share, can submit an order to *BUY IBM 132 LIMIT.* This order instructs the broker to buy the stock as long as the per-share price is no higher than $132. If the price of IBM is $132.25 when the order reaches the market, it will not be executed.

Sometimes, a stop order and a limit order are combined into a single order. If the previous orders for IBM are combined, for example, the investor would submit an order to *BUY IBM 130 STOP 132 LIMIT.* In this case, a buy market order would be initiated when the price of IBM stock reaches $130, but the stock will not be purchased if its price exceeds $132 when the order reaches the market.

Orders that have price restrictions can also have time limitations. For example, a stop order can be placed so that it will be canceled if the price conditions are not met by the end of the trading day; this type of order is called a **day order (DO).** Alternatively, the order might be **good 'til canceled (GTC),** which means that the order remains active until the price limitations are met or until the investor cancels it. In reality, the broker reconfirms a GTC order periodically (perhaps every 6 months) to ensure that the investor wants the order to remain outstanding. An investor can also place a **fill or kill order,** which instructs the broker that the order should be canceled if it cannot be executed immediately. Sometimes a time limit, such as 15 minutes, is placed on a fill or kill order.

Evidence of Ownership

When you buy stock from a broker, you will be asked whether you want the stock certificate, which is evidence of ownership, to be delivered to you or to be kept by the brokerage firm. If you choose to have the certificate delivered to you, then you will have physical possession of shares that are registered in your name. If you sell the stock in the future, you will have to transfer ownership just as you would if you were selling a car (that is, you need notarized signatures and so forth). On the other hand, if you allow the brokerage firm to hold your stock for you, generally it will be kept in **street name,** which means that the stock will be registered to the brokerage firm. The brokerage firm's records will indicate that you are the "real" owner of the stock, and evidence of your ownership will be sent to you via periodic statements from the broker. Dividends, annual reports, and other information that the company distributes to its shareholders will be sent to the brokerage firm, which will then distribute the payment or materials to its clients who own the stock. Thus, even though the stock is held in street name, you will receive the same distributions as all other owners, regardless of how their shares are held.

Generally, it is better to allow the brokerage firm to hold your stock in street name for two reasons. First, it is easier to transfer the shares when they are sold than if they are registered in your name (that is, you have the stock certificate). Second, by retaining custody of the stock, in effect, the brokerage firm offers safekeeping for your stock certificates and other investments' documents.

stop order
An order that specifies the price at which a market order is initiated.

limit order
An order to buy or sell a stock at no worse than a specified price.

day order (DO)
An instruction to cancel an order if the price conditions are not met by the end of the trading day.

good 'til canceled (GTC)
An instruction to keep an order active until the price limitations are met or until the investor cancels it.

fill or kill order
An instruction to cancel the order if it is not executed immediately.

street name
A situation in which stock is registered to the brokerage firm, rather than to the individual investor.

Security Insurance

Nearly every brokerage firm, including discount brokers, purchases insurance through the Securities Investor Protection Corporation (SIPC), which insures the cash and securities of investors held by the brokerage company from theft or loss (loss of the security, not loss in value). Each investor is covered to a maximum of $500,000 ($100,000 for cash holdings). Some firms also purchase additional coverage from private organizations.

Self-Test Questions

How does a traditional brokerage firm differ from the financial intermediaries described in Chapter 4?

What are the two major types of brokerage firms? What is the primary difference between them?

What is a round-lot trade? What is an odd-lot trade?

What types of instructions can investors specify when placing security orders?

Why would investors allow the stocks they purchase to be kept in street name by the brokerage firm?

What is SIPC insurance?

INVESTMENT INFORMATION

Whether you choose to actively manage your investments or hire an investment adviser/manager, you should be informed about your choices. *Ignorance can be extremely costly when it comes to making investment decisions.* It is important that you understand what you are investing in before committing large sums of money. As a general rule, you should investigate both the advantages and disadvantages of any investment you are contemplating. In Chapter 2, we described some of the more common investment instruments. In this section, we examine some of the sources and the uses of investment information related to those investments.

Sources of Investment Information

Many sources and forms of investment information exist. Newspapers, magazines, company reports, investment research organizations, and the Internet all provide volumes of data and information about various investments. For example, as discussed in Chapter 7, a publicly traded company is required to prepare and publish annual reports that contain financial statements and other information about the firm and the nature of its operations during the year. Such sources as *Value Line Investment Survey, Moody's Investment Services,* and *Standard & Poor's,* among others, provide similar financial data as well as the results from analyses conducted by their research staffs. General business and economic news and quotations for stocks, bonds, and other securities can be found in local and national newspapers. The newspapers published in larger cities, such as the *New York Times,* have large sections devoted entirely to financial reporting. *The Wall Street Journal, Barron's,* and *Investor's Business Daily* are "newspapers" that report only financial news and related business information for investors. More general business news and information can be found in magazines such as *BusinessWeek, Forbes, Fortune,* and *Money,* to name a few.

In addition to newspapers and business magazines, the Internet provides a mechanism for investors to find and contact numerous other sources. Most large companies have Web sites that provide information about their operations, products, and personnel, as well as current and recent historical financial statements.[2] Also, many brokerage firms and investment services have Web sites that provide specific information about companies and more general information about the economy and various financial markets. The U.S. government and its various agencies are good sources of data relating to economic and general financial conditions. For example, the SEC and the Federal Reserve both have extensive amounts of data that can be downloaded and evaluated by anyone with a personal computer (PC).

As investors have become more proficient at moving information electronically, the PC has evolved as an important part of investment decision making. Numerous databases and programs to analyze those databases are available on the Internet. Some of the services require a subscription, but others are free. In any event, the PC has dramatically expanded the ability of individual investors to evaluate investment strategies and the alternatives available to meet investment goals. A consequence of the proliferation of PCs and greater accessibility to software packages and financial databases is that individual investors are able to perform much more sophisticated investment analyses today than was possible 20 or 30 years ago. As a result, they can make more informed investment decisions. As the electronic processing of information improves in the future, these analyses are certain to become even more sophisticated.

Price Information—Quotations

In the next section, we describe how to compute the return associated with an investment. First, however, we have to determine the price of the investment—that is, we have to be able to read the investment's price quotation. For the most part, it is easy to look in any financial newspaper or on the Internet and determine the current price of a stock or bond. Nevertheless, some items presented in the quotations deserve explanation. This section focuses on stock and bond quotes, noting what the numbers actually mean.

The Wall Street Journal traditionally has been considered to be the premier source of daily quotations for stocks and bonds.[3] Because stock quotes are readily available on various sites on the Internet, *The Wall Street Journal* does not publish as many stock and bond quotations as it did previously; rather, quotations are provided for an abbreviated list of stocks and bonds. For example, stock quotes are provided for the "Biggest 1,500 Stocks" rather than for all of the stocks listed on the New York Stock Exchange and Nasdaq. Much of the financial numbers that are currently published in *The Wall Street Journal* are in the form of summary data that provide information about general movements in the various financial markets. As a result, in this section we describe the quotations that appear in *The Wall Street Journal* as well as quotations that can be found on the Internet.

---

[2]Companies normally post their annual reports on their Web sites in sections labeled Investor Relations (or some similar wording).

[3]*The Wall Street Journal* is published every day on which the stock markets are open during the year. An edition of the *Journal* is also published on Saturday. Thus *The Wall Street Journal* is published Monday through Saturday, except on holidays.

FIGURE 16-2 Stock Price Quotations from *The Wall Street Journal*, Published May 30, 2008

STOCK	SYM	CLOSE	NET CHG
TAM SA	**TAM**	**21.48**	**1.13**
Target	**TGT**	53.75	1.43
❗ TataMtrs ADS	**TTM**	13.85	−0.68
♣ TaubmanCtr	**TCO**	53.88	0.46
TeckCominco B	**TCK**	47.92	−2.30
▲ **TecoEngy**	**TE**	**20.59**	**1.10**
Teekay	**TK**	49.69	−0.05
TelNoLeste	**TNE**	26.34	0.71
TlcmArg ADS	**TEO**	18.58	0.29
TeleNZ ADS	**NZT**	15.47	0.04

Common footnotes and emphases to stock quotations:

<u>Underlined quotations</u>—trading volume is much larger than average during the past 65 days. The trading volume for TECO Energy was larger than normal on Thursday, May 29, 2008.

Bolded quotations—the one-day price change was equal to or greater than 5 percent. The closing price of TECO's stock on Thursday, May 29, 2008, which was $20.59, was 5.6 percent higher than the closing price on Wednesday, May 28, 2008.

▲ The closing price for the day represents a new 52-week high. TECO's closing price of $20.59 was higher than any price during the past 52 weeks.

❗ The closing price for the day represents a new 52-week low.

h The stock issue fails to meet the requirements to continue to be listed on the exchange.

v Trading in the stock has been halted on the primary market.

vj The company is in bankruptcy or is being reorganized under the bankruptcy laws.

♣ Indicates that the company's annual reports are available through The Wall Street Journal's Annual Report Service, which is located at http://wsj.ar.wilink.com

Source: *The Wall Street Journal*, May 30, 2008.

Stock Quotes

Figure 16-2 shows a portion of the quotations published on Friday, May 30, 2008, for stocks that are included in the "Biggest 1,500 Stocks" section of *The Wall Street Journal*. Because these quotes appeared in *The Wall Street Journal* on May 30, they represent trading activity that occurred on Thursday, May 29, 2008.

As you can see from the quotes in Figure 16-2, stock prices are denominated in decimal form such that they are reported in dollars and cents.[4] To explain the information contained in the stock quotations, let's look at the quote for TECO Energy, which is highlighted. TECO, which is based in Tampa, Florida, produces electricity, gas, and coal.

The quotes given in Figure 16-2 are fairly easy to "read" because the labels above the columns indicate what the data represent. Following is the interpretation of the information in each column:

STOCK   The name of the stock, which is abbreviated where necessary. For instance, TECO Energy is abbreviated "TecoEngy."

---

[4]The minimum price movement, called the tick size, allowed by the NYSE was changed from 1/8 to 1/16 on June 24, 1997. At about the same time, the NYSE approved future implementation of the decimal form of quote. The decimal form was implemented for all stocks on January 29, 2001. From its inception more than 200 years ago, the minimum variation in price had been 1/8. Consequently, both of these changes were historical occasions for the NYSE.

SYM   The company's **stock symbol,** which represents the trading initials of the company. TECO's stock symbol is TE. The stock symbol is the reference used by brokers when trades are made and when price quotes are retrieved. The "running" market quotations that you see at the top or the bottom of your television screen on financial channels, in brokers' offices, or on the Internet are reported using company stock symbols because it is less cumbersome to include initials than the full names of the stocks.[5]

CLOSE   At the end, or "close," of the trading day on Thursday, May 29, 2008, TECO's stock traded for $20.59.

NET CHG   The closing price on Thursday, May 29 was $1.10 higher than the price at the end of the previous day (Wednesday, May 28, 2008), when TECO's stock closed at $19.49—that is, the net change in price from the close of trading on the previous day to the close of trading on the day of the quote was an increase equal to $1.10.

stock symbol
The trading initials of a company; the reference used by brokers when trades are made and price quotes are retrieved.

Some of the quotes given in Figure 16-2 include symbols, such as ↑ and ♣, which are used to disclose special information about the stock. The definitions for the symbols are given in the explanatory notes that are published along with the stock quotes. A few of the footnotes are described at the bottom of Figure 16-2.

In addition to the symbols and letters included in the quotes, note that some of the quotations are either boldfaced or underlined. Boldfaced quotes indicate that the company's stock price changed by at least 5 percent compared with the previous closing price. Underlined quotes highlight stocks that show significant trading volume compared with their averages during the past 65 trading days. The quote for TECO is both bold and underlined, which means that the price of the stock increased by 5 percent or more from the previous day's close and the trading volume was high compared to the stock's average volume. The actual increase in TECO's stock price on Thursday, May 29, 2008, was 5.6 percent [= ($20.59 − $19.49)/ $19.49].[6]

Although serious investors read such publications as *The Wall Street Journal,* many investors choose to get their stock quotations from the Internet because these quotes represent the results of the most recent trades (perhaps with a 15 to 20 minute delay). Following is an example of a quote that you might see for TECO on the Web site of an electronic brokerage firm, such as Charles Schwab or TD Ameritrade:

	Last	Change	Bid	Ask	High	Low	Vol
TE	20.60	−0.03	20.59	20.61	20.88	20.51	3,359,562

This quote was retrieved at 2 p.m., Friday, May 30, 2008. The meaning of the number in each column is:

Last   The price at which the last trade was performed equaled $20.60.

Change   The price of the last trade was $0.03 lower than the previous trade.

Bid   Dealers are willing to buy the stock for $20.59, thus they offer a "bid" of this amount to investors who might be considering selling their TECO stock.

---

[5]Stock symbols are also called *ticker symbols* because the first device used to continuously report stock prices to brokers' offices made a "ticking" sound when the quotes were printed.

[6]Although our explanations of stock quotes were applied to stocks listed on the NYSE, they are also valid for stocks listed on the American Stock Exchange, the Nasdaq, most regional stock exchanges, and the OTC.

FIGURE 16-3   Corporate Bond Quotations from *The Wall Street Journal*, Published May 30, 2008

| Issuer | Symbol | Coupon (%) | Maturity | BOND PRICE as % of face value | | | STOCK PERFORMANCE | |
				Current	One-day change	Last week	Close ($)	% chg
Countrywide Financial	**CFC**	6.250	May15,'16	86.500	8.00	80.000	5.39	8.23
Trump Entertainment Resorts	**TRMP**	8.500	June1,'15	67.000	7.63	59.740	3.56	23.18
Standard Pacific	**SPF**	7.750	March15,'13	85.875	3.88	75.000	3.14	−4.56
Momentive Performance Mtrls	**APOLO**	10.125	Dec.1,'14	88.750	2.25	93.375	...	...
Albertsons	**SVU**	7.450	Aug.1,'29	98.500	2.07	96.125	...	...
K Hovnanian Enterprises	**HOV**	6.375	Dec.15,'14	70.250	2.00	n.a.	8.10	1.63
Penske Automotive	**PAGXZ**	7.750	Dec.15,'16	94.375	1.88	n.a.	...	...
Bowater Canada Finance	**ABH**	7.950	Nov.15,'11	69.500	1.50	68.000	...	...

Ask   Dealers are willing to sell stock that they own for $20.61, thus they are "asking" investors who might want to buy TECO to pay this amount.

High   The highest price that TECO traded to this point of the day was $20.88.

Low   The lowest price that TECO traded to this point of the day was $20.51.

Vol   To this point of the day, 3,359,562 shares of TECO have been traded. This number will increase as the day progresses and more trades are completed.

Bond Quotes

Figure 16-3 shows some quotes for corporate bonds that were reported in *The Wall Street Journal* on May 30, 2008. The interpretation of the bond quotations is somewhat different than for the stock quotations.

Following is the interpretation of the information given in the first four columns for Countrywide Financial, which is highlighted in the figure:

Issuer   The name of the issuer, which is Countrywide Financial, the largest home loan organization in the United States in 2008.

Symbol   The ticker symbol for the company, which is CFC for Countrywide Financial Corporation.

Coupon (%)   The coupon rate of interest, which indicates the interest that bondholders will be paid each year. Because the coupon rate is "6.250%," investors in this Countrywide bond will receive $62.50 for each $1,000 face value bond they hold (= 0.0625 × $1,000). Countrywide bonds pay interest semiannually, so bondholders will receive $31.25 every 6 months.

Maturity   The date the bond matures, which is the date the face value of the bond must be paid to bondholders. The Countrywide bonds mature on May 15, 2016.

The next three columns in Figure 16-3 fall under the general heading of "BOND PRICE as % of face value," which gives information about the market price of the bond.

Current   The closing price of the bond stated as a percent of its face value. The price at which the Countrywide bond traded at the end of the day on Thursday, May 29, 2008, was 86.500 percent of its face value. Thus, a bond that had a face value of $1,000 sold for $865 = $1,000(0.8650).

One-day change   Indicates the change in the bond's price from the closing of trade on the previous day. Thus, the closing price of Countrywide's bond on Wednesday, May 27, 2008, was 78.5 percent of face value, which is eight percentage points lower than the closing price of 86.5 percent on Thursday, May 30. In dollar amounts, the Wednesday closing price for a $1,000 face value bond was $785, which is $80 ($= 0.08 \times \$1,000$) lower than Thursday's closing price of $865.

Last week   The price of the bond stated as a percent of face value 1 week earlier. At the close of trading on Thursday, May 22, 2008, Countrywide's $1,000 face value bond sold for $800 $= 0.800 \times \$1,000$.

The final two columns in Figure 16-3, which fall under the general heading of "STOCK PERFORMANCE," give information about the performance of the company's common stock.

Close ($)   The price of the company's stock at the close of trading on Thursday, May 29, 2008. Countrywide's common stock closed at $5.39.

% chg   The percent change in the stock price from the previous day's closing. On Wednesday, May 28, 2008, Countrywide's stock closed at $4.98. Thus, on Thursday, May 29, 2008, the change in the stock price was 8.23 percent—that is, $0.0823 = (\$5.39 - \$4.98)/\$4.98$.

Like stock quotes, many investors choose to get their bond quotations from the Internet because the quotes represent the results of the most recent trades (perhaps with a 15- to 20-minute delay) and the prices for more bonds are available electronically. Following is an example of a quote that you might see for Countrywide Financial's bond on such Web sites as Yahoo!Finance or Financial Industry Regulatory Authority (FINRA):

Type	Issue	Price	Coupon	Maturity	YTM	Current Yield	Rating	Callable
Corp	Countrywide Financial	86.50	6.250	15-May-2016	8.57	7.23	A	No

This quote was retrieved at 4:30 p.m., Thursday, May 29, 2008. The meaning of the number in each column is:

Type   The type of bond, which could be coporate, U.S. government, municipal, and so forth.

Issue   The name of the issue, which is generally the company's name.

Price   The price of the bond stated as a percent of its face value. Because this quote was retrieved at the close of trading on Thursday, May 29, 2008, this quote is the same as the one shown in Figure 16-3.

Coupon   The coupon rate of interest.

Maturity   The date the bond matures, which is the date that the face value must be paid to bondholders.

YTM   Yield to maturity, which represents the return that investors would earn if they buy the bond at the current price and hold it until maturity. We discussed YTM in Chapter 10. In the case of the Countrywide bond, to determine the YTM with your financial calculator, do the following: (1) enter $N = 16 = 8 \times 2$, $PV = -865$,

PMT = 31.25 = 62.50/2, and FV = 1,000; (2) compute I/Y = 4.31, which is the YTM stated on a 6-month basis; and (3) annualize the result, which gives an annual YTM = 8.62 = 4.31 × 2. Our result differs slightly from the quoted YTM because there are not exactly 8 years (16 compounding periods) remaining until maturity.[7]

Current Yield   Current yield, which equals the annual interest payment divided by the current price of the bond. For the Countrywide bond, current yield = $62.50/$865 = 0.07225 = 7.23%.

Rating   The bond rating, which gives an indication of the creditworthiness of the issuing company. Countrywide's bond has an A rating, which means that the company is judged to be a fairly good credit risk; AAA is the top rating. (See Chapter 2 for a discussion of bond ratings.)

Callable   Indicates whether the bond is callable by the issuer at some date prior to maturity. The Countrywide bond is not callable. (See Chapter 2 for a discussion of call provisions.)

Self-Test Questions

Name some sources of financial and investment information. Does each source provide daily investment information?

How might an investor use information that is reported about common stock prices when evaluating the relative attractiveness of stocks?

How are bond prices reported?

COMPUTING INVESTMENT RETURNS

An important part of monitoring investments includes determining the return that has been earned. In this section, we discuss techniques used to calculate the *historical* return earned by holding an individual investment and an investment portfolio over a period of time.

Computing the Return on an Individual Security

As we discovered in Chapter 11, the return on an investment is generated by (1) the *income* produced by the investment and (2) any *change in the value,* or the price, of the investment. Thus, the dollar return earned from an investment is simply the income received plus any change in value, which can be stated as follows:

16-1

$$\text{Dollar return} = (\text{Dollar income}) + (\text{Capital gains})$$
$$= (\text{Dollar income}) + \left(\begin{array}{c}\text{Ending value} \\ \text{of investment}\end{array} - \begin{array}{c}\text{Beginning value} \\ \text{of investment}\end{array}\right)$$
$$= \quad \text{INC} \quad + (\quad P_1 \quad - \quad P_0 \quad)$$

---

[7]Because the last interest payment for this bond was May 15 and the date for the current price quote is May 29, an investor who buys the bond on May 29 will have to pay the current bondholder the equivalent of 2 weeks' interest in addition to the market price of $865. Thus, the total cost to the new investor (excluding commissions and other costs) will be $867.40 = $865 + (2/52)$62.50. Using this amount as the present value of the bond, we find that the YTM is 8.57 percent.

In this equation, INC represents the dollar income received from the investment, whether it is interest from a bond or dividends from a stock; P_1 is the investment's value at the end of the period for which the return is computed; and P_0 is the value of the investment at the beginning of the period for which the return is computed.

The *rate of return* on an investment for a particular period can then be computed as follows:

16-2

$$\text{Yield (\% return)} = \ddot{r} = \frac{\text{Dollar return}}{\text{Beginning value of investment}} = \frac{\text{Dollar income} + \text{Capital gains}}{\text{Beginning value of investment}}$$

$$= \frac{\text{INC} + (P_1 - P_0)}{P_0} = \text{Holding period return (HPR)}$$

The computation given in this equation is often referred to as the **holding period return (HPR)** because we use it to calculate the return earned over the period of time that the investment was held, which might be 6 months, 5 years, or some other period. The holding period return is the *actual*, or *realized, rate of return* described in Chapter 11; thus, we use the same designation here, $\ddot{r}$. As you can see from the equation, the numerator includes both the income received from the investment and the change in value, or the *capital gain (loss)*, associated with the investment.

To illustrate how to compute the HPR, let's examine the performance of Ingersoll-Rand, which is the world's leading manufacturer of air compressors and related equipment, from January 2, 2008, through May 30, 2008. During this period, Ingersoll-Rand paid its stockholders a dividend equal to $0.18 on March 3. On Friday, May 30, 2008 (the last trading day in May), the company's stock price was $44.04. Any investors who purchased Ingersoll-Rand stock at the beginning of trading on January 2, 2008, when the price was $46.47 earned a 6-month HPR equal to:

$$\text{5-month HPR}_{\text{Ingersoll}} = \frac{\$0.18 + (\$44.04 - \$46.47)}{\$46.47}$$

$$= \frac{\$0.18}{\$46.47} + \frac{(-\$2.43)}{\$46.47}$$

$$= 0.00387 + (-0.05229)$$

$$= -0.0484 = -4.84\%$$

holding period return (HPR)
The return earned over the period of time that an investment is held, which might be 6 months, 1 year, or 5 years.

This computation shows that investors who purchased Ingersoll-Rand stock at the beginning of 2008 and held it through May 2008 earned a 5-month return equal to −4.84 percent. In our calculation, we broke the return into two components: the part of the return associated with the dividends paid by the firm, which is called the **dividend yield**, and the change in the market value of the stock, which is called the **capital gain (loss)**. Note that dividend payments contributed 0.387 percent to the return, but the value of Ingersoll-Rand's stock *decreased* by $2.43, which generated a 5.229 percent capital loss. Thus, the total return associated with holding the stock for the first 5 months of 2008 was −4.84 percent.

In most cases, we prefer to state returns on an annual basis so that the returns on alternative investments can be more easily compared. Therefore, we need to adjust Equation 16-2 to account for the possibility that an investor's holding period does

dividend yield
The part of the total return associated with the dividends paid by the firm. It is computed by dividing the amount of dividends paid by the current stock price.

capital gain (loss)
A change in the market value of a security.

not equal exactly 1 year. To "annualize" the return, Equation 16-2 can be rewritten as follows:

16-3

$$\text{Annualized rate of return} = \frac{\text{INC} + (P_1 - P_0)}{P_0} \times \left(\frac{360}{T}\right)$$

In Equation 16-3, all of the variables are as previously defined, and T represents the number of days that the investment is held such that $360/T$ "annualizes" the HPR (that is, adjusts the return so that it is stated on an annual basis). We use 360 days in our computation for simplicity only—that is, the number 360 is divisible by more values than 365.[8] The return we compute using Equation 16-3 is the annual percentage rate (APR) described in Chapter 9—it does not include compounding effects.

Returning to the Ingersoll-Rand example, we found that the return for the first 5 months of 2008 was −4.84 percent. Thus, the equivalent annual return is $-4.84\% \times 360/150 = -11.62\%$.[9] The same result is found by applying Equation 16-3:

$$\text{Annualized return} = \frac{\$0.18 + (\$44.04 - \$46.47)}{\$46.47} \times \left(\frac{360}{150}\right)$$
$$= -0.0484 \times 2.4 = -0.1162 = 11.62\%$$

Generally, when we examine the returns associated with an investment that has been held for many years, we want to know the *average annual return*. For instance, you may have heard someone state that an investment he or she has owned for a long time—say, 5 or 10 years—has earned an average return, or grown by an average, of 15 percent per year. How do we calculate the average annual return (return per period)? First, we must compute the annual HPR for each year during which the investment was held. For example, if an investment was held for 5 years, we would compute five annual returns. Next, we find the average. There are two techniques for computing the average return on an investment that has been held for more than 1 year (period): the *simple arithmetic average* and the *geometric average*.[10]

Simple Arithmetic Return

simple arithmetic average return
A technique for computing the average return on an investment that sums each return and then divides by the number of returns; it does not consider compounding.

The **simple arithmetic average return** is computed by summing each return and then dividing by the number of returns included in the sum. Thus, the calculation for the simple arithmetic average return is:

16-4

$$\text{Simple arithmetic average return} = \bar{r}_A = \frac{\ddot{r}_1 + \ddot{r}_2 + \cdots + \ddot{r}_n}{n}$$

---

[8]Equation 16-3 can be applied to holding periods longer than 1 year—the last term will still "annualize" the return. To illustrate, suppose an investment earned a 20 percent return over a 2-year period. The annualized return for this investment would be $10\% = 20\% \times (360/720)$.

[9]In this case, $T = 150$ was computed as follows: January, 30 days, because the stock was purchased on January 2; February, 29 days, because 2008 was a leap year; March, 31 days; April, 30 days; and, May 30 days because we computed the return on the last trading day of the month, which was Friday, May 30, 2008.

[10]Both the simple arithmetic average and the geometric average can be applied to holding periods other than 1 year—for example, 1 month, 6 months, and so forth. Because it is more common to compare average returns on an annual basis, our calculations are based on annual returns only.

TABLE 16-2   Market Prices and Returns for TreeTop Landscape Services, 2004–2009

Year	End-of-Year Price	One-Year Holding Period Return[a]
2004	$200.00	—
2005	300.00	50.0%
2006	330.00	10.0
2007	343.20	4.0
2008	350.06	2.0
2009	200.00	−42.9

[a]TreeTop Landscape paid no dividends during this period, so the annual holding period returns are based on price changes only.

In this equation, $\bar{r}$ is the simple arithmetic average return, $\ddot{r}_t$ is the holding period return for Year t, and n is the number of years the investment was held.

To illustrate the application of Equation 16-4, let's consider the data given in Table 16-2, which shows the end-of-year market prices from 2004 through 2009 and the annual holding period returns for the common stock of TreeTop Landscape Services for this period. The firm's simple arithmetic average return is:

$$\bar{r}_{A_{TreeTop}} = \frac{50.0\% + 10.0\% + 4.0\% + 2.0\% + (-42.9\%)}{5} = \frac{23.1\%}{5} = 4.6\%$$

This result suggests that the average return per year was 4.6 percent during the 5-year period from January 2005 to December 2009. Note, however, that the computation for the simple arithmetic average return does not include consideration of compounded rates.

Geometric Average Return

The **geometric average return** does consider compounded rates because it assumes that a dollar invested today will grow to $1(1 + \ddot{r}_1)$ at the end of 1 year; this amount will be reinvested to grow to $1(1 + \ddot{r}_1)](1 + \ddot{r}_2)$ at the end of the second year, and, so on. Thus, the multiple by which an investment of $1 (or any other amount) grows over many years is $[(1 + \ddot{r}_1)(1 + \ddot{r}_2)\ldots(1 + \ddot{r}_n)]$. For example, as we discovered in Chapter 9, if $1 is invested today at a 15 percent rate for 5 years, it will grow by 2.0114 times, which equals $(1.15) \times (1.15) \times (1.15) \times (1.15) \times (1.15) = (1.15)^5$. To find the annual average, then, we have to reverse the compounding process by taking the nth root of the growth multiple and subtracting 1.0. Therefore, we can state the geometric average return as follows:

geometric average return
A technique for computing the average return on an investment that involves taking the nth root of the growth multiple $(1 + \ddot{r}_1) \times (1 + \ddot{r}_2) \times \cdots \times (1 + \ddot{r}_n)$ and subtracting 1.0. It does consider compounding.

$$\text{Geometric average return} = \bar{r}_G = [(1 + \ddot{r}_1) \times (1 + \ddot{r}_2) \times \cdots \times (1 + \ddot{r}_n)]^{\frac{1}{n}} - 1.0$$

16-5

In this equation, $\bar{r}_G$ is the geometric average return and all of the other variables are the same as defined in Equation 16-4. When an equation is raised to the 1/n power, it means take the nth root of the result, which can be accomplished by using the $\boxed{y^x}$ key on your calculator.[11]

---

[11]See Chapter 9 for further discussion about using the $\boxed{y^x}$ key on your calculator.

If we apply Equation 16-5, the geometric average return for TreeTop Landscape Services is computed as follows:

$$\ddot{r}_{G_{TreeTop}} = [(1 + 0.500)(1 + 0.100)(1 + 0.040)(1 + 0.02)(1 - 0.429)]^{\frac{1}{5}} - 1.0$$

$$= [(1.500)(1.100)(1.040)(1.020)(0.571)]^{\frac{1}{5}} - 1.0$$

$$= (1.00)^{0.2} - 1.0 = 0.0 = 0.0\%$$

This result indicates that TreeTop Landscape showed no growth from January 2005 to December 2009.

As you can tell from our results, the computations for the simple arithmetic average return and the geometric average return give different answers—4.6 percent versus 0.0 percent, respectively. Which one is correct? In this case, we can find the answer very simply by computing the 5-year holding period return. Remember that the $200 price that existed when the stock market closed at the end of 2004 (Friday, December 31) was also the price of the stock when the market reopened at the beginning of 2005 (Monday, January 3). Therefore, if an investor bought TreeTop Landscape stock on Monday, January 3, 2005, he or she would have paid $200 per share. Because an investor could have bought the stock for the same price on Thursday, December 31, 2009 (or, when the market opened on Monday, January 4, 2010), the actual growth over the 5-year holding period was 0 percent (and $0). The per-share price fluctuated during each of the 5 years, but any investor who purchased TreeTop Landscape stock at the beginning of 2005 and then sold it 5 years later was returned the amount originally invested; thus, the investor earned nothing from the investment. Consequently, we can conclude that the geometric average shows the correct return that was earned during the 5-year period.

Because the simple arithmetic average return does not consider compounding, its value will always be equal to or greater than the geometric average return. From your knowledge of time value of money concepts (which were presented in Chapter 9), you should understand that this relationship exists because, all else equal, it takes a greater rate of return to reach a particular future value if funds are not compounded. The simple arithmetic average return and the geometric average return will be equal only if annual returns are constant (the same every year).

Although you should not use the simple arithmetic average return to compute the average annual return for an investment over a multiple-year period, such as 5 years, you can use it to compute the average return for a group of investments at one point in time. For example, to determine the average return on stocks from a particular industry, you would use the simple arithmetic average because you are not concerned with growth over time; instead, you are examining the returns of several investments at a specific point in time.

Computing the Return on a Portfolio

In Chapter 11, we stated that the *expected return* on a portfolio is the weighted average of the expected returns on the individual stocks included in the portfolio. The same principle applies when computing the *historical return* of a portfolio. That is, we simply determine the weighted average of the actual returns that were earned on each individual stock, with the weights being the fraction of the total portfolio invested in each stock at the *beginning of the investment (holding) period.* We compute the historical return of a portfolio using the following equation:

16-6

$$\ddot{r}_p = \left(\frac{\text{Value of Security 1}}{\text{Total value of portfolio}}\right)\ddot{r}_1 + \left(\frac{\text{Value of Security 2}}{\text{Total value of portfolio}}\right)\ddot{r}_2 + \cdots + \left(\frac{\text{Value of Security n}}{\text{Total value of portfolio}}\right)\ddot{r}_n$$

$$= w_1\ddot{r}_1 + w_2\ddot{r}_2 + \cdots + w_n\ddot{r}_n$$

Here the w values are the weights based on market values at the beginning of the investment period, and the portfolio includes n stocks.

To illustrate the use of Equation 16-6, let's examine Sue Hogan's portfolio of stocks for the last 2 years. The brokerage firm has provided Sue with the following information:

| | **Market Value** | | |
Stock	12/31/07	12/31/08	12/31/09
Microtech	$1,500	$1,800	$1,980
Unicity	2,500	2,750	3,300
Hywall	1,000	950	1,425
Portfolio value	$5,000	$5,500	$6,705

To help Sue evaluate her investments, we can first compute the annual holding period returns for each stock using Equation 16-2. These computations yield the following results:

| | **Return** | |
Stock	2008	2009
Microtech	20.0%	10.0%
Unicity	10.0	20.0
Hywall	−5.0	50.0

If we apply Equation 16-6, Sue's portfolio return for 2008 is calculated as follows:

$$\ddot{r}_{p,\,2008} = \left(\frac{\$1,500}{\$5,000}\right)(20.0\%) + \left(\frac{\$2,500}{\$5,000}\right)(10.0\%) + \left(\frac{\$1,000}{\$5,000}\right)(-5.0\%)$$

$$= 0.3(20.0\%) + 0.5(10.0\%) + 0.2(-5.0\%)$$

$$= 6.0\% + 5.0\% + (-1.0\%)$$

$$= 10.0\%$$

Although Hywall lost 5 percent in 2008, because the amount invested in Hywall represented only 20 percent of Sue's entire portfolio, her total portfolio return was reduced by only 1 percent by holding this stock.

To compute the 2009 portfolio return, we again apply Equation 16-6. This time, the weights for each stock are based on their values at the beginning of 2009 (end of

2008) rather than the original values. Because Hywall's value decreased during 2008, its weight, or influence on the portfolio's return, will also decrease. The computation of the 2009 portfolio return is:

$$\ddot{r}_{p,\,2009} = \left(\frac{\$1,800}{\$5,500}\right)(10.0\%) + \left(\frac{\$2,750}{\$5,500}\right)(20.0\%) + \left(\frac{\$950}{\$5,500}\right)(50.0\%)$$

$$= 0.3273(10.0\%) + 0.5000(20.0\%) + 0.1727(50.0\%)$$

$$= 3.3\% + 10.0\% + 8.6\%$$

$$= 21.9\%$$

Note that the weight of Hywall dropped from 20 percent at the beginning of 2008 to 17.3 percent at the beginning of 2009. Consequently, even though the price of Hywall's stock increased by 50 percent during 2009, its contribution to the portfolio return was less than that of Unicity, which earned 20 percent and contributed to one-half (50 percent) of the portfolio's funds.

We could have computed the annual returns for the portfolio by determining the change in the total value of the portfolio each year. In other words, we could have computed the portfolio returns by applying Equation 16-2 as follows:

$$\ddot{r}_{p,\,2008} = \left(\frac{\$5,500 - \$5,000}{\$5,000}\right) = 0.100 = 10.0\%$$

$$\ddot{r}_{p,\,2009} = \left(\frac{\$6,705 - \$5,500}{\$5,500}\right) = 0.219 = 21.9\%$$

The returns are the same as we found using Equation 16-6. When we aggregate the returns, however, it is not necessary to compute the weights associated with each stock because this information is included in the aggregated value. Therefore, if we simply want to compute an overall return for a portfolio, we can use Equation 16-2. If we want to determine the returns associated with the individual stocks and their contribution to the portfolio's return, then we should use Equation 16-6.

Self-Test Questions

What does it mean when an investor says that his or her holding period return was 15 percent?

What is a capital gain (loss)?

Differentiate between the simple arithmetic average return and the geometric average return. Under what circumstances should each be used?

What is the difference between computing the return on a portfolio using Equation 16-2 versus computing the return using Equation 16-6?

Suppose that Stock A earned the following returns during the past 4 years: 4%, 8%, −5%, 15%. What are the arithmetic average return and the geometric average return that investors earned on this stock?   (Answers: $\bar{r}_A = 5.5\%$, $\bar{r}_G = 5.2\%$)

Indexes—Measuring Market Returns

In the previous section, we examined methods used to measure returns on individual assets such as stocks and bonds and portfolios of investments. In this section, we discuss market indexes, which are used to measure the returns for combinations of securities, or "baskets" of investments, such as stock markets and bond markets.

Market indexes measure performance in the financial markets just as economic indexes measure performance in the economy. One of the most often quoted market indexes is the Dow Jones Industrial Average (DJIA), which measures the aggregate return, or performance, for the 30 largest industrial firms in the United States. Started by Charles Dow in 1896, the DJIA is the oldest known stock market index. This index, which originally included only 12 large firms, was created to gauge the overall performance of the stock market. Table 16-3 shows the composition of the Dow when it was started and the companies included in the DJIA in 2008. Only one company that was in the original DJIA is still in the index today: General Electric. Even though the DJIA includes only 30 stocks, or less than 1 percent of the total number of stocks listed on the NYSE, many people believe that it provides a very good picture of the stock market's performance, because the companies in the Dow are extremely large industrial firms that account for greater than 20 percent of the total market value of NYSE firms.

Many other market indexes either have been created to measure different "baskets" of investments or use different methods of computation. For example, another well-known family of indexes includes those published by Standard & Poor's—S&P 500, S&P 400, S&P Industrials, and so forth. The S&P indexes are more general, with broader coverage, than the DJIA because they include more companies. Indexes with even broader coverage also exist. For example, the major stock markets have composite indexes that include all of the stocks listed on the exchanges; there is the NYSE composite index, the AMEX composite index, and the Nasdaq composite index. In addition, the Russell 3000 (includes 3,000 securities) and the Wilshire 5000 (acutally includes many more than 5,000 securities) are indexes that were created to measure the performance of more general groups of stocks, not just those listed on particular exchanges.

Despite the proliferation of indexes, you will probably hear the DJIA quoted more often than any other index. It is published in nearly every newspaper, and local and national newscasts quote the Dow every night to provide listeners with an indication of the daily performance of the stock markets. The Dow is considered the stock market's bellwether barometer.

Table 16-4 lists a few of the market indexes that are published each day in *The Wall Street Journal* as well as on the Internet and gives the return on stocks in 2008 as specified by each index measure.[12] Although all of the indexes indicate that a declining market existed, the computed returns differ substantially. There are two major reasons for these differences. First, as we indicated earlier, not every index measures the same group of stocks, so it makes sense that the index results would vary to some extent. For example, compared with the firms that are included in the DJIA, the firms included in the Nasdaq index are very small in size (assets). Second, even if the indexes contained the same "basket" of securities, some differences in the results would still occur because not all indexes are computed in the same

---

[12]The 2008 returns that are reported in Table 16-4 are based on the market performance through May 2008, which is prorated through the remainder of the year. The actual performance of the stock market for the remainder of 2008 could have turned out quite different.

TABLE 16-3 Composition of the Dow Jones Industrial Average (DJIA), 1896 and May 2008

Company	What Happened to the Company?
I. Original DJIA, 1896	
American Cotton Oil	Became CPC International; now named Bestfoods
American Sugar	Became Amstar Holdings, which became Long Wharf Maritime Center
American Tobacco	A 1911 antitrust action resulted in a breakup—American Brands and RJR Tobacco evolved from it
Chicago Gas	Acquired in 1897 by Peoples Gas, which is now a subsidiary of TECO Energy, Inc.
Distilling & Cattle Feeding	Became Quantum Chemical, which became a subsidiary of Millennium Chemicals, Inc.
General Electric	Still part of the DJIA
Laclede Gas	Operates under the same name; removed from the DJIA in 1899
National Lead	Named NL Industries today
North American	A utility monopoly that was broken up in the 1940s
Tennessee Coal & Iron	Acquired by U.S. Steel in 1907; U.S. Steel is now USX
U.S. Leather (preferred)	Liquidated in 1952
U.S. Rubber	Became Uniroyal, which is now a subsidiary of Michelin

Company	Date First Included	Comments
II. Current DJIA, May 2008		
3M Company	1976	In 2002, Minnesota Mining & Manufacturing changed its name to 3M
Aluminum Co. of America	1959	
American Express Co.	1982	
American International Group (AIG)	2004	
AT&T Inc.	1912	Replaced in 1928; included again in 1939; renamed from American Telephone & Telegraph in 1994; replaced in 2004; included again in 2005 after merging with SBC Communications
Bank of America	2008	
Boeing Co.	1987	
Caterpillar, Inc.	1991	
Chevron Corp.	2008	
Citigroup	1997	Renamed in 1998 when Travelers Group and Citicorp merged
Coca-Cola Co.	1932	Replaced in 1935; included again in 1987
DuPont Co.	1924	Replaced in 1925; included again in 1935
Exxon/Mobil Corp.	1928	Changed name from Standard Oil of New Jersey in 1972; companies merged in 1999
General Electric	1896	Replaced in 1898; included again in 1899; replaced in 1901; included again in 1907
General Motors Corp.	1915	Replaced in 1916; included again in 1925
Hewlett-Packard Co.	1997	
Home Depot	1998	
IBM	1932	Replaced in 1939; included again in 1979
Intel	1998	
Johnson & Johnson	1997	
J. P. Morgan Chase & Co.	1991	J. P. Morgan and Chase Manhattan merged in 2000
McDonald's Corp	1985	
Merck & Co.	1979	
Microsoft	1998	
Pfizer Incorporated	2004	
Procter & Gamble Co.	1932	
United Technologies Corp.	1933	Replaced in 1934; included again in 1939; changed name from United Aircraft in 1975
Verizon Communications	2004	
Wal-Mart Stores Inc.	1997	
Walt Disney Co.	1991	

Notes: (1) In the comments, the term *replaced* indicates that the stock was taken out of the DJIA.

(2) The number of stocks included in the DJIA increased from 12 to 20 in 1916.

(3) The number of stocks included in the DJIA increased from 20 to 30 in 1928.

Sources: Dow Jones Company Web site, http://averages.dowjones.com, and *The Dow Jones Averages, 1885–1995*, Phyllis S. Pierce, ed. Irwin Professional Publishing, 1996.

TABLE 16-4   Selected Market Indexes, 2008

Index Name	Composition	Method of Computation	2008 Return
Dow Jones Industrial Average	30 largest industrial firms in the United States	Price-weighted	−11.33%
NYSE composite	More than 3,000 common stocks traded on the NYSE (excludes some types of securities)	Value-weighted	−8.36
S&P 500	500 large companies traded on the NYSE and Nasdaq from different industrial sectors	Value-weighted	−11.11
Nasdaq composite	All common stocks of domestic companies traded on Nasdaq	Value-weighted	−11.73
Russell 3000	3,000 largest companies in the United States based on market capitalization—represents about 98 percent of all investable stocks	Value-weighted	−9.16
Dow Jones Wilshire 5000	Greater than 5,000 common stocks (originally 5,000) traded on the NYSE, AMEX, and OTC—the broadest market measure	Value-weighted	−9.05

Note: The 2008 return is an annualized rate based on the change in the value of the index from January 2, 2008, (the first trading day of 2008) through May 30, 2008.

manner. A detailed discussion of the computational differences among the various indexes is beyond the scope of this book, but this section does provide an indication of how indexes differ by considering a simple example.

Table 16-5 shows information for the prices associated with three fictional companies. We use this information to construct two types of indexes: a price-weighted index and a value-weighted index.

To construct a simple *price-weighted index,* we add the price of one share of each stock, and then divide by the number of stocks in the index. With the values given in Table 16-5, the value of this type of index was 80 at the end of 2008 and 77 at the end of 2009. According to this measure, the three stocks generated a 3.75 percent loss during 2009. If you look at the column in the table labeled "1-Year Return," you can see that only one stock actually had a loss; the other two stocks earned rather substantial positive returns. Because Wotterup is a high-priced stock, however, its price change influenced the index more than the other two stocks, which have much smaller values (Wotterup's price was more than 80 percent of the combined prices in 2008). This issue has prompted major criticism of price-weighted indexes.

One way to mitigate the influence of high-priced securities on the value of a price-weighted index is to compute a value-weighted index. A *value-weighted index* is based on the total market value of the stock of each firm rather than the price of a single share. For example, according to the information in Table 16-5, the total

TABLE 16-5 Constructing Market Indexes

| Stock | Shares Outstanding | 2008 | | 2009 | | 1-Year Return |
		Price	Market Capital	Price	Market Capital	
Amber, Inc.	5,000	$ 10	$ 50,000	$ 15	$ 75,000	50.0%
B&B Design	500	30	15,000	36	18,000	20.0
Wotterup, Inc.	200	200	40,000	180	36,000	−10.0
Totals		$240	$105,000	$231	$129,000	

I. Calculating a simple price-weighted index, I_W:

$I_{W,2008} = \$240/3 = 80$

$I_{W,2009} = \$231/3 = 77$

2009 return based on $I_W = (77 - 80)/80 = -0.0375 = -3.75\%$

II. Calculating a simple value-weighted index, I_V:

$I_{V,2008} = \$105,000/3 = 35,000$

$I_{V,2009} = \$129,000/3 = 43,000$

2009 return based on $I_V = (43,000 - 35,000)/35,000 = 0.2286 = 22.86\%$

Notes: Values are from the end of the year.

The value-weighted index is often computed by dividing the combined market value of the stocks from 1 year by the market value of the previous year; the result is then multiplied by 100. In our illustration, the computation would be:

$$I_V = (129,000/105,000) \times 100 = 122.86$$

As you can see, this result is 22.86 percent greater than a base-year value of 100.

market capitalization
The total market value of a firm's stock, which can be computed by multiplying the number of shares outstanding by the market price per share.

market value, or **market capitalization,** of Amber, Inc., was $50,000 in 2008; the value of Wotterup in the same year was $40,000. Even though Amber's per-share stock price was $190 less than, or 5 percent of, Wotterup's stock price, Amber's total market capitalization was $10,000, or 25 percent, greater than Wotterup's total market capitalization.

The value-weighted index shown in Table 16-5 is in a very simple form. Nevertheless, it demonstrates that the method used to construct an index can make a considerable difference in the results that are computed for market performance. The value-weighted index suggests that the combined performance of the three companies was very good in 2009—the return for the year was almost 23 percent. This result is significantly different from that given by the price-weighted index, primarily because the loss experienced by Wotterup did not influence the index as much as the positive returns associated with the other two stocks; in 2008, the market value of Wotterup was less than 40 percent of the combined market capitalization of the three stocks.

We have described these two methods of constructing market indexes to make you aware that the indexes reported in the newspapers or on the nightly newscasts do not always measure the same event. If you hold an equal number of shares of every stock in your portfolio, then you might want to compare the returns on your portfolio with a price-weighted index such as the DJIA; otherwise, it might be better to use a value-weighted index such as the S&P 500 for the comparison. In reality, market indexes are very highly correlated, regardless of how they are constructed or the specific group of securities that is used. Figure 16-4 shows the movements of five indexes since 1975. As you can see, for the most part, the indexes have moved in tandem. If we showed a single graph of the annual market returns measured by each

FIGURE 16-4   Market Indexes, 1975–2008

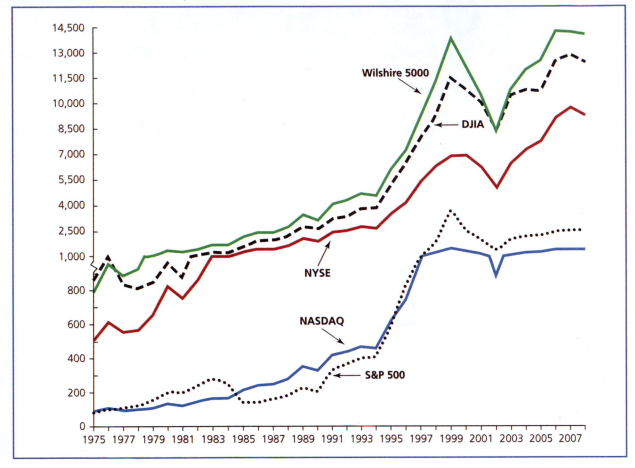

index (that is, changes in the values given in Figure 16-4), it would be difficult to identify the returns of the individual indexes because their lines would overlap for most of the years.

Indexes have several important uses. First, because indexes are used as gauges for determining how well the stock market is performing, they also provide investors with an indication of the health of the general economy. When the market is rising, we call it a **bull market,** which suggests that the economy is performing well. When the market is falling, we call it a **bear market,** which suggests that the economy is performing poorly.

bull market
A rising stock market.

bear market
A falling stock market.

In addition to gauging the economy, market indexes are used as benchmarks by individual investors and mutual fund managers to determine how well their portfolios have performed. Have you ever heard someone say that he or she outperformed the market? To make such a statement, the investor must have compared his or her portfolio's return with the return on the market by using one of the market indexes.

Indexes are also used to estimate the betas for securities. Recall from the discussion in Chapter 11 that the beta coefficient represents the relationship between a stock's returns and the market's returns; that is, it measures the systematic risk associated with the stock. Finally, indexes are used as investment instruments and as the basis for other investments, such as options.

Self-Test Questions

What does a market index measure?

What are some examples of market indexes that are published in *The Wall Street Journal*?

Are the market returns computed by using different indexes always the same? Why or why not?

What are some uses for market indexes? How might you as an individual investor use indexes?

ALTERNATIVE INVESTMENT STRATEGIES

buy-and-hold strategy
When investors purchase securities with the intention of holding them for a number of years.

Investors construct investment portfolios by holding different positions in different financial assets. To achieve their investment goals, most individual investors follow a **buy-and-hold strategy,** which means that they purchase securities with the intention of holding them until either their goals are met or modifications are needed in their portfolios to ensure that future goals can be met. A buy-and-hold strategy is usually considered a long-term, rather than a short-term, investment position. When investors buy securities, regardless of the intended holding period, they are said to be *going long* and, clearly, they hope that prices increase. On the other hand, when investors sell securities that they already own, they are said to be *going short,* which generally occurs when they believe prices will drop in the future.

When investors expect prices to increase, they can go long and magnify their return by borrowing funds (leveraging) from brokerage firms, which is called *margin trading*. This strategy enables investors to invest amounts greater than they have saved. On the other side of the coin, when investors expect prices to decline, they can make money by *short selling,* which involves selling securities that they do not own and replacing them at some future date. If prices fall, the securities can be repurchased at lower prices and investors can keep the difference between short selling prices and the repurchase prices.

In this section, we describe margin trading and short selling to give you an idea of alternative investment arrangements that can be made with a broker. We must caution you, however, that such arrangements should not be used unless they are fully understood. In other words, *caveat investor*—let the investor beware!

margin trading
When an investor borrows from his or her broker some portion of the funds used to purchase an investment.

Margin Trading

margin requirement
The minimum percentage of the total purchase price that an investor must "put up" to buy stock (or other investments) on margin.

Margin trading permits an investor to borrow from his or her broker some portion of the funds used to purchase securities. The amount that can be borrowed is based on the **margin requirement,** which represents the minimum amount of personal funds (initial equity) that an investor must "put up" to purchase securities. For example, if the margin requirement is 60 percent, the investor must provide at least 60 percent of a security's purchase price; in this case, the maximum amount that the broker will lend the investor is 40 percent. The minimum margin requirement, which is set by the Federal Reserve, is currently 50 percent.[13]

---

[13]In 1946, the margin requirement was 100 percent, meaning that an investor could not borrow to make stock purchases. The lowest margin requirement was 40 percent in the late 1930s. With a 40 percent margin, an investor could borrow 60 percent of the amount of stock purchased. The margin requirement has been 50 percent since 1974.

When an investor borrows funds from a brokerage firm to purchase securities, he or she signs a **hypothecation agreement,** which assigns the securities as collateral for the margin loan. In essence, the hypothecation agreement allows the broker to liquidate the stocks to repay the loan if the investor defaults. Like other borrowers, investors who borrow funds to purchase securities are charged interest on their margin loans. The interest rate, which is called the **broker loan rate,** is based on the rate that a brokerage firm is charged by its lenders. Because an investor pays a specified (fixed) rate to borrow funds from his or her broker, margin trading magnifies the gains when the value of the investment increases at a rate *greater than* the broker loan rate; conversely, margin trading magnifies losses associated with a decline in value.

> **hypothecation agreement**
> A contract that assigns securities as collateral for a margin loan.
>
> **broker loan rate**
> The rate charged by brokers to borrow funds for margin trading.

To see how margin trading works, consider the case of Karen Lambert. Karen has $6,000 of her own funds to invest in MVP Corporation, which is currently selling for $50 per share. Using only her funds, Karen can purchase 120 shares ($6,000/$50) of MVP stock. MVP does not pay dividends. Thus, if the value of MVP's stock increases to $60 in 1 year, Karen will gain $10 per share and the total gain on her investment will be $1,200, or 20 percent (0.20 = $1,200/$6,000). If the value of MVP's stock drops to $40, Karen will lose $10, and the value of her investment will decrease by 20 percent to $4,800.

The brokerage firm that handles Karen's trades allows margin trading with a margin requirement equal to 60 percent plus a 10 percent broker loan rate.[14] If Karen *margins* her position, she can purchase more than the 120 shares of MVP stock than she could buy using only her own funds. To determine the amount of MVP stock that Karen can purchase on margin, let's first consider how the actual margin, or percent investor's equity, is computed:

$$\frac{\text{Actual}}{\text{margin}} = \frac{\text{Percentage of}}{\text{investor's equity}} = \frac{\text{Investor's equity}}{\text{Market value of investment}}$$

 16-7

When the stock is purchased, the *actual margin* cannot be lower than the margin requirement. Thus, the maximum amount of MVP that Karen can purchase is:

$$\frac{\text{Actual}}{\text{margin}} = 0.60 = \frac{\$6,000}{\text{Market value of investment}}$$

$$\frac{\text{Market value}}{\text{of investment}} = \frac{\$6,000}{0.60} = \$10,000$$

Therefore, Karen can purchase $10,000, or 200 shares, of MVP if she fully margins her position. To do so, she must borrow $4,000 from the broker to add to her $6,000. If the value of MVP's stock increases to $60, the total value of the 200 shares will equal $12,000. Karen cannot keep the entire $12,000 if she liquidates her position, however, because she must give the broker $4,400 to repay the $4,000 that she borrowed, plus the $400 (= 0.10 × $4,000) interest charged on the loan. In this case, Karen can keep $7,600 = $12,000 − $4,400, which is $1,600 more than the $6,000 she had to invest. The return on *her* funds is

---

[14] A brokerage firm can establish its margin requirement at greater than the amount set by the Federal Reserve, but it cannot offer a lower margin requirement.

26.7 percent, which is greater than the 20 percent that she would earn without margin trading.

$$\text{1-year HPR} = \frac{(\$12,000 - \$4,400) - \$6,000}{\$6,000} = \frac{\$1,600}{\$6,000} = 0.267 = 26.7\%$$

Conversely, if the value of MVP's stock drops to $40, the value of Karen's 200 shares will be $8,000. Karen must still pay the broker $4,400 to repay the loan with interest, so she is left with $3,600 (= $8,000 − $4,400) of her original $6,000, which represents a 40.0 percent loss on her investment (−$2,400/ $6,000).

As this example shows, both gains and losses are magnified by margin trading. From our discussion of leverage (operating and financial) in Chapter 8, you should have expected that such a magnification would occur.

Note that the amount Karen owes the broker does not change when the market value of the stock changes. Thus, when the stock price increases, Karen has greater equity, or ownership, in the investment position. When the stock price decreases, she has less equity. At any point, an investor's equity position is represented by the actual margin associated with the existing market price of the stock. To compute an investor's equity position, Equation 16-7 can be expanded such that:

16-8

$$\begin{aligned}
\frac{\text{Actual}}{\text{margin}} &= \frac{\text{Percentage of}}{\text{investor's equity}} = \frac{\text{Investor's equity}}{\text{Market value of investment}} \\[2mm]
&= \frac{\left[\left(\begin{array}{c}\text{Number of}\\\text{shares}\end{array}\right) \times \left(\begin{array}{c}\text{Price per}\\\text{share}\end{array}\right)\right] - (\text{Amount borrowed})}{\left(\begin{array}{c}\text{Number of}\\\text{shares}\end{array}\right) \times \left(\begin{array}{c}\text{Price per}\\\text{share}\end{array}\right)}
\end{aligned}$$

Thus, when the value of MVP's stock is $60, Karen has an equity position equal to 66.7 percent. That is, the actual margin is:

$$\frac{\text{Actual margin}}{(\text{Price} = \$60)} = \frac{(200 \times \$60) - \$4,000}{(200 \times \$60)} = \frac{\$8,000}{\$12,000} = 0.667 = 66.7\%$$

When the value of MVP's stock is $40, her actual margin is 50 percent because Karen owes the broker half of the $8,000 value of the MVP stock.

If the price of a stock drops too much, a margined investor might be tempted to abandon his or her position in the stock and not repay the broker's loan. To guard against this possibility, the broker requires the investor to provide additional funds when the *actual margin* decreases to a certain percentage or lower. That is, the broker *calls* for more funds by issuing a **margin call.** The price at which a margin call is issued depends on the **maintenance margin,** which represents the lowest actual margin, or percentage equity, that the brokerage firm permits its margined investors to have at any time after the investment is made. To determine the price at which a margin call will be issued, we can set the *actual*

margin call
A call from the broker to add more funds to a margined account.

maintenance margin
The lowest actual margin that the broker will permit margined investors to have at any time.

margin in Equation 16-8 equal to the *maintenance margin* and rearrange the equation as follows:[15]

$$\text{Margin call price (per share)} = \frac{\text{Amount borrowed}}{\left(\text{Number of shares}\right)\left(1 - \text{Maintenance margin}\right)} \qquad 16\text{-}9$$

If the maintenance margin is 45 percent, Karen Lambert will receive a margin call when the price of MVP stock falls to $36.36 per share:

$$\text{Margin call price (per share)} = \frac{\$4{,}000}{200 \times (1 - 0.45)} = \$36.36$$

If the price of MVP stock drops below $36.36, the total value of the 200 shares purchased by Karen will be less than $7,272 (= 200 × $36.36), and her actual margin position will be less than the 45 percent maintenance margin. If Karen does receive a margin call, she must provide additional funds to increase the actual equity that she has in the margin position; if she fails to provide the funds, some or all of her stock will be liquidated to satisfy the margin call. Remember, in margin trading the stock is put up as collateral for the investment position, so the broker can sell it if necessary.

Of course, Karen would prefer for the price of MVP stock to increase so that her return will be magnified by margin trading. If she thought that MVP's stock was going to decrease in value, she might decide to *short sell*, which is the investment arrangement described next.

Short Selling

If an investor believes that the price of a stock (or other security) will decrease in the future, he or she could make a profit by **short selling** the stock.[16] To *short sell*, an investor borrows the stock of another investor and then sells it, promising to replace, or repay, the borrowed stock at a later date. If the price of the borrowed stock falls, the investor can buy it back and replace it at the lower

short selling
A situation in which an investor borrows the stock of another investor and then sells it, but promises to replace the stock at a later date.

---

[15]Equation 16-9 is derived as follows:

$$\text{Maintenance margin} = \frac{\left[\left(\text{Number of shares}\right) \times \left(\text{Price per share}\right)\right] - \text{Amount borrowed}}{\left(\text{Number of shares}\right) \times \left(\text{Price per share}\right)} = 1 - \frac{\text{Amount borrowed}}{\left(\text{Number of shares}\right) \times \left(\text{Price per share}\right)}$$

$$\left[1 - \left(\text{Maintenance margin}\right)\right] = \frac{\text{Amount borrowed}}{\left(\text{Number of shares}\right) \times \left(\text{Price per share}\right)}$$

$$\left[1 - \left(\text{Maintenance margin}\right)\right] \times \left(\text{Number of shares}\right) \times \left(\text{Price per share}\right) = \text{Amount borrowed}$$

$$\text{Price per share} = \frac{\text{Amount borrowed}}{\left(\text{Number of shares}\right) \times \left[1 - \left(\text{Maintenance margin}\right)\right]} = \text{Margin call price}$$

[16]Securities other than stock can be *shorted*. Because it generally is easier to discuss short selling with respect to stock trading, we discuss only stocks here.

price, thereby making a profit. In essence, then, the objective of short selling is to "sell high and buy low."[17]

To illustrate, if Karen expects MVP's stock to decrease in value, she could borrow 100 shares from her broker and sell them for the current price of $50 each. If the price per share decreases to $40, Karen would buy back the shares at $40 each and return them to her broker. Her profit, not considering commissions and other costs, would be $10 per share, or $1,000 total. If the price of MVP increases to $60, however, Karen would lose $10 per share, or $1,000 because she would have to repurchase the stock for $10 per share more than it was shorted.

The initial proceeds generated from the short sale cannot be used freely by the investor; instead, the proceeds are kept by the broker as collateral for the stock that was borrowed. In addition, the investor must "deposit" funds with the brokerage firm to ensure that the stock can be repurchased if its price increases. The amount of the deposit generally is a function of the margin requirement, subject to some minimum amount—say, $2,000. For example, if Karen wants to short sell 100 shares of MVP stock when the price is $50, the proceeds from the sale would be $5,000. Not only would the broker keep this money in a deposit account, but Karen probably would have to deposit $3,000 (= $5,000 × 0.60) of her own funds with the broker to ensure that the short position can be covered if the stock's price should actually increase. If the price of the stock rises by too much, the investor will receive a "margin call" from the brokerage firm that will require him or her to provide additional funds to cover possible future price increases.[18]

Any amount left in the brokerage account will be given to the investor when the short position is covered, which occurs when the stock is returned to its original owner.

Actually, when an investor short sells a stock, the owner of the stock generally does not know that his or her stock has been sold because street name stock is used. Because the owner of the stock technically does not have the shares any longer, the short seller must pay any dividends distributed by the company during the period in which the stock is shorted. Given this fact, investors whose stocks are shorted should not be concerned that they technically do not own the shares during the shorting period.

The unpredictability of stock price movements make this investment strategy very risky. Short selling is an investment strategy used by sophisticated investors.[19] If you ever consider short selling a security, be sure that you understand what you are doing and realize that you can lose large amounts of money. How much can you lose on a short sale? To answer this question, we pose another question: How high can the value of a stock rise?

---

[17]Prior to 2007, short selling had "price restricitions" that prohibited an investor from short selling unless the previous transaction associated with the stock resulted in either a price increase (called an uptick) or no price change after a price increase from one trade earlier (called a zero-plus tick). The SEC eliminated this limitation (Rule 10a–1) in 2007.

[18]The accounts in which funds or securities are held as collateral for, or to ensure the safety of, various investment positions are usually referred to as margin accounts. Even if the investor is not specifically margin trading, such a position involves some type of borrowing or leverage activity. For instance, short selling involves borrowing securities.

[19]Prior to 1997, there were times when investors would short sell stock that they also owned, which is referred to as shorting against the box. This term originated in earlier times, when an investor held securities in a safety-deposit box at the bank or a strong box at home or work; this investment strategy involved short selling the same stock that was held in "the box." In the past, investors "shorted against the box" to delay tax payments associated with liquidating an investment until some future period. But revisions made to the Tax Code in 1997 have eliminated the tax benefits associated with such an investment strategy.

Self-Test Questions

What is a buy-and-hold investment strategy?

What do we mean when we say an investor is "going long"? What does "going short" mean?

What is margin trading? How can margin trading help magnify returns?

How do investors short sell? What are some restrictions applied to short selling?

Andy currently has $5,400 that he wants to invest in Best Sell Company's stock, which currently is selling for $30 per share. The brokerage firm through which Andy invests has a 60 percent margin requirement and a 50 percent maintenance margin. If he margins the maximum amount, how many shares of Best Sell can Andy buy? At what price will Andy receive a margin call?   (Answers: 300 shares; $24)

Ethical Dilemma

Drip, Drip, Drip . . . Should We Call a Plumber?

Freeman Plumbing Supplies has decided to re-examine its existing dividend policy, which was established 30 years ago when the firm first started paying dividends. Freeman's operations have changed significantly during the past 30 years, so the CEO wants to determine whether its dividend policy is still appropriate.

The CEO suggested that it might be a good idea for the firm to begin a dividend reinvestment plan (DRIP), because he believes that the company is a good investment and that most of the firm's stockholders would prefer to have their dividends reinvested in the company's stock rather than paid to them in cash. As a result, Ed Davidson, Freeman's CFO, was assigned the task of evaluating the feasibility of starting a DRIP program.

It is Mr. Davidson's opinion that Freeman should pay dividends to maintain its market value, and thus also maintain stockholders' wealth. Since the tax rate on dividends was lowered a few years ago, most companies in Freeman's industry have either increased their dividends or started paying dividends for the first time. So, Ed is convinced that Freeman must continue to pay dividends; in fact, he thinks that the amount of dividends should be increased.

When Ed was assigned the task of evaluating the possibility of starting a DRIP program, he was excited. He knew that the program would be administered in his department, which would give him and his colleagues a chance to showcase the quality of work they perform. As his evaluation progressed, however, Mr. Davidson started to get concerned that the CEO had a personal ulterior motive in mind when he suggested the DRIP program. Ed's concerns increased when he found out that Freeman's executives receive huge bonuses each year that are normally paid in the form of the company's stock. His research indicates that a DRIP program would permit executives to receive their bonuses in the form of dividends that are reinvested in the company's stock, which would have the same effect as the existing bonus-payment system. However, because they actually receive a dividend payment, the executives would be taxed differently if their bonuses "pass through" a DRIP program. If executives are paid their bonuses using the existing plan, any stock they receive is taxed at the same rate as their ordinary, or "regular," income, whereas qualified dividends are taxed at lower rates. In other words, stock that is

continues

purchased through a DRIP plan qualifies as a dividend payment that would be taxed at a more favorable rate than ordinary income.

With the additional information that he has collected, Ed is concerned that the CEO wants to initiate a DRIP program only because it will be beneficial to Freeman's executives. Although Ed is still in the beginning stages of his evaluation, he doesn't think the company should initiate programs just because they benefit executives. At this point, Ed is trying to decide whether he should abandon his evaluation and tell the CEO to "go jump in the lake" or continue with an evaluation that might give the CEO the justification he needs to start a program that will benefit top management. What should he do? What would you do if you were Ed?

CHAPTER PRINCIPLES
–The Answers

To summarize the key concepts, let's answer the questions that were posed at the beginning of the chapter:

- **What process should individuals follow when investing their money?** When investing, one of the first decisions that an investor must make is to determine his or her investment objective. Is the purpose of the investment to save for retirement or to build funds that will help buy a house in 5 or 10 years, or is there another goal? Next, the investor must determine the amount of risk he or she is willling to take to achieve the investment objective. Although taking greater amounts of risk could permit the investor to reach the investment objective more quickly, such a position might also result in a substantial loss in the value of the investment position. Once the investment objective and acceptable risk are determined, the investment plan has to be implemented—that is, the appropriate investment position must be created. Finally, the investment position must be monitored continuously so that it can be changed when necessary.

- **What types of orders can investors place to buy or sell securities?** There are numerous instructions, or orders, that investors can "place" when executing investment transactions. The most common type of order is the market order, which instructs the broker to execute the order at the best price available when the transaction reaches the market. Investors can use stop orders, limit orders, or combinations of the two orders to restrict the prices at which transactions take place. A stop order specifies the price at which a market order should be initiated, whereas a limit order specifies the "worst" price at which the order can take place. Investors can also place a time limit on their orders—a day order is good for the remainder of the trading day, a good 'til canceled order remains in effect until it is canceled by the investor, and a fill or kill order instructs the broker to cancel the order if it cannot be executed immediately.

- **How is the return on an investment determined?** Two components determine the return on an investment: (1) the dollar income—interest or dividend—that is paid during the investment holding period and (2) the change in the value of the investment. Thus, to determine the yield, or rate of return, that an investment earns, we must compute the income yield and the capital gains yield that the investment generates during a particular period. Generally, so that we can easily compare different investments, we state their rates of return on an annual basis.

- **What is the difference between the arithmetic average return and the geometric average return? Which is a better measure of the true return on an investment?** To compute an investment's arithmetic average return, we simply add all of the annual returns and then divide by the number of returns. To compute the geometric average return, we follow these steps: (1) add 1.0 to each annual return; (2) multiply each of the results obtained in Step 1—that is, $(1 + \ddot{r}_1) \times (1 + \ddot{r}_2) \times \cdots \times (1 + \ddot{r}_n)$, where $\ddot{r}_1$ is the return from the first year; (3) take the nth root of the result obtained in Step 2; and (4) subtract 1.0 from the result obtained in Step 3. Equation 16-4 gives the equation that is used to compute the arithmetic average return, and Equation 16-5 gives the equation that is used to compute the geometric average return. The arithmetic average return provides a simple, noncompounded average, whereas the geometric average return provides an average that considers the effects of compounding over time. Thus, because most investors permit the returns on their investments to compound, we conclude that they should compute the geometric average returns on their investments to determine the true returns of the investments.

- **How are market returns measured?** Generally, market returns are measured by computing market indexes, such as the Dow Jones Industrial Average, the Standard & Poor's 500, or some other market index. These indexes represent certain segments of the market. Although some indexes represent broader segments than other indexes, each index is used to determine how well either the market or a particular part of the market is performing. Many investors use market indexes as benchmarks to determine how well their portfolios of investments are performing relative to some standard. Market indexes are also used as barometers to indicate how markets might perform in the future.

- **What are margin trading and short selling? When should each be used?** When investors trade on margin, they borrow from their brokers some of the money that they invest. The investors must pay interest on the money that is borrowed. Even so, because margin trading involves leverage, this type of position produces a magnification effect on returns—both gains and losses are greater than they would be without margin trading. Leverage is discussed in Chapter 8. When investors short sell stock, they borrow and sell the stocks of other investors with the promise that the stocks will be returned to the original owners at some later date. The investors "short" the stocks in the hopes that the prices will decline, and thus they will be able to buy back and replace the stocks at lower prices at some later date.

The concepts presented in this chapter should help you to better understand personal investing. If you apply the concepts presented in this chapter, you should be able to make more informed investment decisions whether you hire a professional to manage your investments or you make your own investment decisions.

CHAPTER PRINCIPLES

–Personal Finance

- **Why should I set investment goals and then monitor my investment position?** You should follow the "investment process" that is given at the beginning of the chapter to make sure that you formulate realistic investment goals that consider your risk attitudes. Because the financial markets are very dynamic, you must continuously (not every day) monitor your investment position to ensure that your objectives are being met. If the condition of your portfolio has changed so significantly that your investment goals are not being met, you must take corrective action that might require you to replace some existing investments with new securities that are more appropriate for meeting your objectives.

- **Aren't all brokers alike?** Shop for brokerage and information services. There are many types of brokers and many different types of investment services available. Investment services range from "bare bones" to full service with all the frills. Because there are so many different types of brokers—both live (human) and online—you should determine what services you need/want to ensure that you select a brokerage firm that provides and charges you for only what you use/need.

- **Why should I understand how rates of return on investments are computed?** You must understand how rates of return are determined so that you (1) know what the return that is reported on your broker statements represents and (2) can compute returns yourself. Many of the decisions that investors make with regard to what types of securities are appropriate to meet certain investment goals are based on the returns that those investments are expected to generate. If you do not understand how returns are determined and what the numbers mean, your interpretation of numbers reported by investment organizations might lead to decisions that are not appropriate for your investment objectives.

- **How can I use market indexes when making investment decisions?** Market indexes are often used as benchmarks to "grade" the performance of investment portfolios. If you understand what the benchmarks measure, you will be able to reach more informed conclusions about the performances of your investments.

- **Should I take advantage of alternative investment strategies?** At the end of the chapter, we mentioned a couple of alternative investment positions/strategies— that is, margin trading and short selling. Many other alternatives exist, which means that investors do not always have to put themselves in "plain vanilla" types of investment positions. But, a warning should be attached to all investments, regardless of what they are called: NEVER invest in something you do not understand. Risky, complex investments might promise to generate extremely high gains, but they also can lose significant amounts of your investment—this is the definition of risk. Don't take on risk that you cannot handle just because there is a possibility that you will earn a high return. Many investors lose considerable amounts because they don't follow this advice. Consider those investors that invested in subprime mortgages in 2006 and 2007; most, if not all, of their money was lost, and a majority of these investors did not know why.

QUESTIONS

16-1 Outline the "investment process" and indicate the types of decisions that are necessary at each step of the process.

16-2 Why is it important for every investor to monitor his or her investment position on a continuous basis? What would happen if the monitoring function is ignored?

16-3 In its traditional role, why is a stock brokerage firm not considered a financial intermediary? Differentiate between the role of a brokerage firm and that of an intermediary.

16-4 Identify some of the instructions that investors can give brokers when trading securities. Under what circumstances would a limit order be appropriate? Why would an investor ever use a good 'til canceled (GTC) order?

16-5 What types of information can investors get from stock and bond quotations?

16-6 Explain the difference between a dividend yield and a capital gain (loss). Which is preferable from an investor's standpoint?

16-7 What is the difference between the simple arithmetic average return and the geometric average return? Under what circumstances is it appropriate to use each method?

16-8   What are the major uses of market indexes?

16-9   When they are used to measure returns, do all market indexes yield the same results? Why might different indexes give different results? Give some examples.

16-10 What is the difference between a price-weighted index and a value-weighted index? Which is a better computational method?

16-11 Explain how margin trading magnifies an investor's returns.

16-12 How, and why, does an investor short sell a security?

16-13 What are the possible gains and losses that can occur when an investor short sells a security?

16-14 How do you think transaction costs affect decisions about implementing investment goals?

16-15 What advice would you give your friends about taking risk when investing their hard-earned money?

SELF-TEST PROBLEMS

Solutions appear in Appendix B.

ST-1   Define each of the following terms: **Key Terms**

    a. Investors; speculators

    b. Risk tolerance level

    c. Transaction costs

    d. Asset allocation

    e. Full-service brokerage firm; discount brokerage firm

    f. Market order; stop order; limit order; day order; fill or kill order

    g. Street name stock

    h. Stock symbol

    i. Holding period return (HPR); dividend yield; capital gain

    j. Market index; bull market; bear market

    k. Margin requirement; maintenance margin; margin call

    l. Hypothecation agreement; broker loan rate

    m. Margin trading; short selling

ST-2   Lance Underwood is considering his options for investing the $19,800 in-   **Margin Trading**
heritance he just received, so he contacted a broker who was recommended by a friend. The broker told Lance that he could either invest the $19,800 or borrow from the brokerage firm and invest more. The margin requirement at the brokerage firm is 55 percent, the maintenance margin is 40 percent, and the broker loan rate is 12 percent. Lance has decided to invest in Megasoft because his close friends have told him how well the stock has performed in the past 15 years. Currently, Megasoft has a market price equal to $120; the company does not pay dividends.

    a. Assuming that Lance does not margin, how many shares of Megasoft stock could he purchase? What holding period return would he earn if the price of Megasoft increases to $150 in 1 year? What would the return be if the price drops to $105?

b. Assuming that Lance margins by borrowing the maximum amount allowed by the broker, how many shares of Megasoft stock could he buy? What holding period return would he earn if the price of Megasoft increases to $150 in 1 year? What would the return be if the price drops to $105?

c. If Lance margins, how far can the price of Megasoft stock drop before he could expect a margin call? Assume that Lance margins the maximum amount.

Portfolio Return   **ST-3**   Lucy Ramissaw invested $10,000 in four stocks 4 years ago. She just received a statement from Bestvest Brokerage, Inc. (the firm with which she trades), that summarized her investment portfolio as follows:

	Date				
Investment Name	**12/31/05**	**12/31/06**	**12/31/07**	**12/31/08**	**12/31/09**
Mateo Computers	$ 2,000	$ 2,400	$ 2,760	$ 2,484	$ 3,726
Northern Water	4,000	4,100	4,900	5,635	6,762
AMN Motors	1,000	900	1,080	1,350	1,404
Farley Agricorp	3,000	2,850	3,420	3,762	3,762
Portfolio value	$10,000	$10,250	$12,160	$13,231	$15,654

a. Compute the 4-year holding period return and the annual returns for each stock. That is, compute the overall return for the entire 4-year period, and then compute the return for each year.

b. Based on the market values given in the table, compute the weights (proportion) of each stock in the portfolio for each year.

c. Compute the 4-year holding period return and the annual returns for the portfolio based on (1) the market values given for the total portfolio and (2) the annual returns for each individual stock computed in part (a) and the weights computed in part (b).

PROBLEMS

The problems in this section do not take into consideration the effects of taxes or commissions on investment returns. For simplicity, we assume that there are no taxes and no commissions.

Short Selling   **16-1**   Assume that IBM stock is selling for $110 per share and that you short sell 200 shares of the stock.

a. What would be your dollar return if the price of IBM stock drops to $95 per share?

b. What would be your dollar return if the price of IBM stock increases to $120 per share?

c. Is there a limit to your gains? Is there a limit to your losses? Explain.

Margin Trading   **16-2**   Robin wants to purchase 1,000 shares of Anatop, Inc., which is selling for $5 per share. Anatop does not pay dividends because all earnings are reinvested in the firm to maintain its successful R&D department. The brokerage firm will allow Robin to borrow funds with an initial margin requirement of

70 percent and a maintenance margin of 35 percent. The broker loan rate is 14 percent. Assume that Robin borrows the maximum allowed by the brokerage firm to purchase the Anatop stock.

  a. How much of her own money must Robin provide to purchase 1,000 shares of Anatop?

  b. To what price can Anatop drop before Robin will receive a margin call from her broker?

  c. If the price of Anatop's stock is $7.50 in 1 year, what rate of return would Robin earn from her investment position?

  d. If the price of Anatop's stock is $4 in 1 year, what rate of return would Robin earn from her investment position?

16-3 Mary Anderson bought 250 shares of Dishport stock when it was selling for $50 per share, and she sold the stock for $55 per share 6 months later. During the time she held the stock, Mary received two $1 dividend payments from the firm.

  a. What was Mary's 6-month holding period return?

  b. On an annual basis, what return did Mary earn?

Holding Period Return

16-4 Ralph Saunderson's portfolio includes both stocks and a corporate bond. The total amount of funds that Ralph has invested is $50,000, with $40,000 of this amount invested in the stocks. The names of the stocks and their most recent 1-year returns are given in the following table:

Portfolio Return

Stock	Return
Abbott, Inc.	20.1%
Randicorp	12.5
Salvidore Co.	−2.4

Of the $40,000 invested in the stocks, 50 percent is invested in Randicorp and the rest is divided equally between Abbott, Inc., and Salvidore Company. The most recent 1-year return on the bond was 6 percent.

  a. How much does Ralph have invested in each of the stocks?

  b. If Ralph's portfolio included only the stocks, what would be his most recent 1-year return?

  c. What is the most recent 1-year return earned by Ralph on the entire portfolio?

16-5 Nancy Cotton bought 400 shares of NeTalk for $15 per share. One year later, Nancy sold the stock for $21 per share, just after she received a $0.90 cash dividend from the company.

  a. What is the total *dollar* return earned by Nancy for the year?

  b. What is the *rate* of return earned by Nancy?

  c. Separate the rate of return computed in part (b) into the dividend yield and the capital gain. In other words, compute the dividend yield and the capital gain that Nancy earned by holding NeTalk for 1 year.

Rates of Return

16-6 Janis Rafferty purchased 100 shares of Gold Depot common stock at the beginning of January for $25.00 per share. Janis received a $1.25 dividend payment from the company at the end of December. At that time, the stock was selling for $27.50 per share.

  a. Compute the *dollar* return earned by Janis during the year.

  b. Compute the *rate* of return earned by Janis.

Rates of Return

c. What was the dividend yield and the capital gain generated by Gold Depot during the year?

d. Compute the rate of return that Janis would have earned if she had purchased 500 shares instead of 100 shares of Gold Depot stock at the beginning of the year.

Arithmetic and Geometric Returns

16-7 According to the NYSE Composite Index, the stock market returns from 2005 through 2009 were as follows:

Year	NYSE Return
2005	3.0%
2006	−13.5
2007	−0.5
2008	−8.0
2009	8.0

a. Compute the simple arithmetic average return for the NYSE for the 5-year period.

b. Compute the geometric average return for the NYSE for the 5-year period.

c. Based on your answer in part (b), compute the dollar value that an investor would have at the end of 2009 if he or she invested $2,000 in the NYSE index at the beginning of 2005.

d. Using the annual returns given in the table, compute the value of a $2,000 initial investment at the end of each year.

Rates of Return

16-8 George Rice is reviewing the performance of the portfolio that he has held for the past 5 years. He has decided to compare his portfolio returns with the market returns measured by the S&P 500 Index. The market *values* of his portfolio and the S&P 500 Index from 2004 through 2009 are given in the following table:

End of Year	Portfolio Value	S&P 500 Index
2004	$17,000.00	1212
2005	20,400.00	1250
2006	22,440.00	1420
2007	23,562.00	1410
2008	27,096.30	1360
2009	37,934.82	1440

a. Compute the annual return for both the portfolio and the market.

b. Compute the simple arithmetic average return for both the portfolio and the market.

c. Compute the geometric average return for both the portfolio and the market.

d. Explain why the simple arithmetic average return is greater than the geometric average return for both the portfolio and the market.

e. Evaluate the performance of George's portfolio compared with the market.

16-9 Abby Deere took the advice of a close friend and short sold 100 shares of Techware common stock when its market price was $105.   **Short Selling**

    a. How much will Abby gain or lose (in dollars) if the price of Techware is $120 when she repurchases the stock to close her short sale position?

    b. How much will Abby gain or lose (in dollars) if the price of Techware is $95 when she repurchases the stock to close her short sale position?

    c. What is the most that Abby can gain from her short sale position? Explain why.

    d. What is the most that Abby can lose from her short sale position? Explain why.

16-10 Harold Rawlings has computed the returns he earned last year from each of the stocks he holds in his portfolio. The individual returns and the amounts he had invested in each stock at the beginning of the year are shown in the following table: **Portolio Return**

Stock	Return	Amount Invested
AT&T	22.5%	$5,200
GM	12.3	5,520
Danka	−44.7	1,200
Suiza Foods	100.0	3,080

    a. Compute the return that Harold earned on his portfolio during the year.

    b. Harold has decided to keep Danka in his portfolio, even though it has experienced financial difficulties and performed very poorly last year, because he expects a significant turnaround that will generate a 25 percent return next year. Suppose that Harold is correct. Assuming that the returns from the other stocks remain the same as last year, compute the return on the portfolio for next year. (*Hint:* The portfolio weights for the stocks change based on the returns earned last year, so the values of the stocks at the end of the year should be used to compute the new weights.)

16-11 Assume that the stock of Warner-Lambert Company, a pharmaceutical manufacturer, is currently selling for $75 per share. You have $7,500 of your own funds to invest. The brokerage firm that you use for your stock trades will allow you to borrow funds to buy the stock with an initial margin equal to 62.5 percent, a maintenance margin of 40 percent, and a broker loan rate equal to 12 percent. In 1 year, you expect the per-share price of Warner-Lambert's stock to be 20 percent higher than it is today. At that time, the company will pay shareholders a cash dividend equal to $2.00 per share.   **Margin Trading**

    a. If your expectations for the coming year are correct, what return would you earn if you invested your $7,500 and did not borrow any funds from the brokerage firm?

    b. If you borrowed the maximum amount allowable from the brokerage firm, how much can you invest in Warner-Lambert?

    c. If your expectations for the coming year are correct, what return would you earn if you invested your $7,500 and borrowed the maximum funds allowable from the brokerage firm?

    d. Compute the return that you would earn if the stock's price drops to $70 per share at the end of the year and you borrowed to invest the maximum amount possible to purchase the stock at the beginning of the year.

Holding Period Return

16-12 Three years ago, Sparky Lewis purchased 200 shares of Andrinap, Inc., for $80.00 per share. The company does not pay dividends. Now the market value of the stock is $128.08.

    a. Compute the total *dollar* return earned by Sparky since he bought Andrinap.

    b. Compute Sparky's *3-year* holding period return.

    c. Compute the *average annual return* earned by Sparky. (*Hint:* You know the beginning value and ending value of the stock, so you can use the time value of money concepts discussed in Chapter 9 to solve this problem.)

Margin Trading, Short Selling, and Returns

16-13 Angie Cowler bought 300 shares of INV stock 4 years ago when it was selling for $10 per share. At that time, she really believed that the stock was "a diamond in the rough," so she borrowed to purchase the maximum amount possible. The initial margin requirement was 55 percent, and the broker loan rate was 10 percent. Today, the stock is selling for $30 per share, and the margin requirements are the same as when Angie first purchased INV. INV reinvests all of its earnings in capital budgeting projects, so it has not paid dividends since its stock began trading publicly.

    Even though INV's stock is now selling for $30, its price has dropped from a historically high price of $38 just a few months ago. Angie doesn't want to sell the stock because she believes that the stock price will return to its upward trend within the next few months. For that reason, Angie is considering taking the advice of one of her friends, who has suggested that she short sell 100 shares of INV to protect a portion of her gains if the stock price drops further in future months. Her friend has explained that if she decides to sell her stock after more declines, the short sale position will help offset some of the losses she will earn on her long position in the stock.

    a. Assume that the price of INV is $20 per share in 1 year and that Angie *does not* short sell the stock. What return would she earn on the stock for the year? Remember that Angie is in a margined position.

    b. Assume that the price of INV is $20 per share in 1 year and that Angie short sells 100 shares of the stock at the beginning of the year. What return would she earn on the stock for the year?

    c. Compute Angie's 5-year holding period return given the situation presented in part (a).

    d. Compute Angie's 5-year holding period return given the situation presented in part (b).

    e. Rework parts (a) through (d) assuming that the price of INV is $40 in 1 year.

Constructing Market Indexes

16-14 The following table gives information about the five stocks that have traded on the Small Investors Stock Exchange (SISE) since it started 2 years ago:

		Price per Share		
Stock	Number of Shares	Beginning of Year 1	End of Year 1	End of Year 2
Startab	500	$ 75.00	$ 82.50	$100.00
Oakorn	100	450.00	454.50	460.00
Teeduff	1,000	30.00	40.00	38.50
Amxy	5,000	7.50	6.75	13.50
Zaxive	300	150.00	165.00	148.50

None of the stocks pays a dividend.

a. Using all of the stocks, construct a simple price-weighted market index and compute the market returns for each year.

b. Using all of the stocks, construct a value-weighted market index and compute the market returns for each year.

c. Explain why the returns computed in parts (a) and (b) are not identical.

Integrative Problem

16-15 You have just been hired by Jamestown Financial Services (JFS) as an investment adviser. Your boss, Susan Canton, must write a report for an important client, so she has decided to give you "on-the-job training" by asking you to answer the following questions and complete the appropriate computations:

Rates of Return, Margin Trading, and Short Selling

a. What questions would you ask JFS's client to determine her investment objectives and how to best achieve them?

b. How would you determine the appropriate asset allocation for the client? Under what conditions should the asset allocation be changed?

c. What is a stockbroker, and what role does a broker play in securities transactions?

d. Should JFS recommend that the client use a full-service broker or a discount broker when she trades securities in her portfolio?

e. What types of orders can be placed with a broker? When should restrictions—either time limits or price limits—be used when placing trading orders?

f. Where can JFS's client get investment and other financial information so that she can stay current with her investment position?

g. One year ago the client inherited a portfolio of stocks. The following table gives information about the inherited stocks:

Stock	Number of Shares Inherited	Value of Shares When Inherited	Current Value of Shares[a]
Borman	3,000	$ 45,500	$ 43,225
Capnow	185	18,500	24,050
Exytor	500	30,000	33,000
Orteck	120	6,000	9,000
		$100,000	$109,275

[a]Includes any dividends paid during the year.

What return did the client earn on each stock and on the portfolio?

h. JFS's client wants to compare the returns on her stocks with the market return. JFS generally uses the S&P 500 Index for such comparisons. When the client received her inheritance, the value of the S&P 500 was 1017.01; today, its value is 1080.53. What was the market's return for the year?

i. The client's stockbroker has told her that his firm allows margin trading and short selling. Because the client does not know what these investment positions are, explain the concepts of margin trading and short selling so that she can better understand what risks she would be taking by pursuing either position.

j. JFS's client is quite interested in purchasing MacroTech, because she has observed the extraordinary growth experienced by the stock during the past decade. In particular, she wants to know what returns she could earn if she borrowed from her brokerage firm to buy MacroTech. The brokerage firm has an initial margin requirement equal to 60 percent, a maintenance margin of 35 percent, and a broker loan rate of 10 percent. Assume that the client borrows the maximum amount possible from the broker. Also, assume that MacroTech does not pay a dividend.

(1) If she margins, how much can the client invest in MacroTech if she has $18,600 of her own money to invest? How many shares of MacroTech can she buy if the stock price is $100?

(2) If the price of MacroTech stock increases from $100 to $125 over a 1-year period, what rate of return would the client earn?

(3) If the price of MacroTech stock decreases from $100 to $90 over a 1-year period, what rate of return would the client earn?

(4) What is a margin call? At what price would the client receive a margin call for the MacroTech stock?

(5) If the price of MacroTech drops to $61 and a margin call is issued such that the client must provide enough funds to increase her actual margin to 50 percent, how much money must she give to the broker?

k. JFS's client is thinking about short selling 200 shares of TNT Fireworks, which is currently selling for $35 per share. TNT does not pay dividends.

(1) If the brokerage firm requires the client to provide a deposit, or "good faith funds," based on the initial margin requirement, how much money must she give to the broker to short sell TNT?

(2) What will be her dollar return on the short sale position if the price of TNT drops to $28 per share?

(3) What will be her dollar return on the short sale position if the price of TNT increases to $40 per share?

l. If you had to give this client one piece of advice about investing, what would it be?

COMPUTER-RELATED PROBLEM

Work the problem in this section only if you are using the computer problem spreadsheet.

Rates of Return   **16-16** Use the model in File C16 to work this problem.

a. Refer back to Problem 16-8. Assume that George Rice has another investment portfolio that he set up to help pay for his daughter's college education. The market values of his daughter's portfolio from 2004 through 2009 are as follows:

End of Year	Portfolio Value
2004	$5,500
2005	5,000
2006	5,510
2007	6,010
2008	6,705
2009	6,945

Compute both the simple average return and the geometric average return. How does this portfolio compare to the portfolio that is given in Problem 16-8?

b. Assume that the values for both portfolios and the S&P 500 Index are as follows during the next 5 years:

End of Year	George's Portfolio	Daughter's Portfolio	S&P 500 Index
2010	$44,850	$7,350	1450
2011	50,250	7,105	1550
2012	40,250	7,800	1675
2013	45,120	8,210	2080
2014	50,150	9,000	1955

Compute both the simple average return and the geometric average return for the portfolios during the 5-year period. Compare the portfolios' performances.

c. Compare the risk/return relationships of the portfolios.

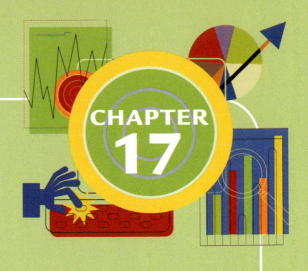

CHAPTER 17

Security Valuation and Selection

Throughout history, the investment adage "buy low, sell high" has been repeated again and again. Following this advice is not as difficult as it might seem because, historically, the stock market has trended upward over the long term. Thus, if you invest in a basket of securities today and you hold your position for a long period (say, 10 to 20 years), chances are that you will be able to sell the securities for much higher prices. In fact, if you earn the historical market average return, your original investment will double every 6 to 8 years.

In today's world, the many technological advances that have been made in processing and delivering information have increased the interests of average individuals in managing their own investment portfolios. Of course, every person who manages his or her own investments wants to find stocks that will become "winners" after they are purchased, which will result in investment bonanzas. Some investors go to extreme measures in their attempts to identify such stocks. Recognizing this fact, perhaps the old adage should be revised to "Beat the market—buy lower, sell higher."

Investors who try to "beat the market" on a risk-adjusted basis use various approaches in their attempts to identify stocks that either are mispriced or promise very high growth rates. These two groups of stocks are referred to as *value stocks* and *growth stocks*. Some professional investors believe that value stocks produce greater return potentials than growth stocks; other professionals believe just the opposite. Which side is correct?

Most evidence suggests that value stocks, which are defined as stocks that are undervalued and have high dividend yields and fairly low price/earnings ratios, generally outperform growth stocks, which are defined as stocks that have potential for high earnings growth and have low dividend yields and fairly high price/earnings ratios. For example, for the period from January 2003 through January 2008, value stocks generated a compounded annual return equal to 11.5 percent and growth stocks generated a 9.6 percent return. And, during the past 30 years, value stocks outperformed growth stocks by an average of 1.5 to 3.0 percent.

Why haven't growth stocks performed as well as value stocks? The answer is not clear-cut. Although the strategy of investing in growth stocks is founded on a well-grounded principle—invest in stocks of companies with growth rates that exceed the norm—most growth stocks sell for prices that exceed 20 to 30 times their earnings, which is quite a premium for future growth that is not guaranteed today. Of course, future growth could turn out to be greater than originally forecasted, in which case the investor would realize substantial gains. The opposite could also occur, in which case the returns would be substantially less than expected. Lower-than-expected growth *in any future period* lowers the forecasts of all subsequent cash flows, even if the growth predictions of later years come true.

Value stocks, by comparison, tend to be stocks of firms that do not offer the same glamour as growth stocks because, few, if any, analysts or professional investors follow them. These types of companies likely produce above-average returns because most of the information that comes out of them is considered "good news" and surprises the market; in response, their stock prices often increase significantly. In addition, there appears to be more value stocks than growth stocks, which suggests that the prices of value stocks are less likely to be inflated relative to the prices of growth stocks.

Proponents of growth stocks and proponents of value stocks will remain on opposite sides of the fence for years to come. It has been shown that substantial returns can be made in either camp if investors can time their strategies correctly. Many experts believe that value stocks perform significantly better that growth stocks when the market is lackluster or in a downturn, because earnings are low. On the other hand, growth stocks perform much better when the stock market is booming, especially toward the end of business peaks, because companies are growing earnings at rates that are above normal. Regardless as to who is correct, most professional advisers tell investors to look for both good growth prospects and bargains. Thus, it seems that every investor wants the same question answered: How can I pick the "winners"? Unfortunately, there is no clear answer to this question. In fact, you might discover that it really cannot be answered. Even so, in this chapter, we attempt to give you an idea of some approaches used by investors to value and select securities—that is, to pick the "winners."

Note: The returns that are reported here were determined by examining historical data for the Russell 1000 Growth Index, the Russell 1000 Value Index, the S&P/Barra Growth Index, and the S&P/Barra Value Index.

Chapter Principles
–The Questions

After reading this chapter, you should be able to answer the following questions:

- What is fundamental analysis? What is technical analysis? How do these two stock analyses differ?
- What general factors should investors examine when evaluating the attactiveness of investments?
- What are some techniques that can be used to value the common stock of a corporation?
- What general rules do professionals advise individuals to follow when investing their money?

In Chapter 10, we described the concept of valuation and its general application to both financial assets, such as stocks and bonds, and real assets, such as buildings and equipment. As we learned then, the value of any asset can be described simply as the present value of the cash flows expected to be generated by the asset during its life. Unfortunately, as we discovered in Chapters 10 and 13, predicting future cash flows is not always an easy task. Estimating cash flows is much easier in situations where a legal contract obligates an individual or a firm to make specific payments at specific times than in cases where there is an implied contract that cash distributions eventually will be made at some point in the future. For instance, we know that a traditional corporate bond obligates the firm to make interest payments that are defined in a legal document called an *indenture;* the future cash flows associated with a bond are, therefore, generally easy to estimate. Conversely, issuing common stock does not legally obligate the firm to make any future cash distributions; rather, investors view common stock as an *implied contract* in which the firm "promises" that value will be maximized and cash distributions will be made when the firm exhausts its positive growth opportunities. Thus, even though the concept of valuation is fairly intuitive, trying to determine the value of investments such as common stock is not so straightforward in the real world; in fact, it can be a formidable task.

This chapter describes some of the approaches that are used to value and select securities such as common stock. It provides only an overview of available valuation and selection methods; it is beyond the scope of this chapter to provide detailed discussions of such techniques. You can get more detailed descriptions by taking a course that is specifically dedicated to the subject of investments.

FUNDAMENTAL ANALYSIS VERSUS TECHNICAL ANALYSIS

Traditionally, the techniques used to value common stock have been classified into one of two categories: *fundamental analysis* or *technical analysis.* We begin our discussion by examining both of these approaches, and then we introduce some popular valuation techniques used by both types of analysts.

Fundamental analysis is the practice of evaluating the information contained in financial statements, industry reports, and economic factors to determine the *intrinsic value* of a firm. The term **intrinsic value** refers to the "true," or economic, value of the firm. If the market value and the intrinsic value are not the same, then the stock is said to be *mispriced.* **Fundamentalists**—analysts who utilize fundamental analysis—attempt to forecast future stock price movements by examining factors that are believed to be related to the market values of stocks. The factors that are examined can be grouped into one of three categories:

1. Company conditions, such as earnings, financial strength, products, management, labor relations, and so forth

2. Industry conditions, such as maturity, stability, competitive conditions, and so forth

3. Economic and market conditions, such as interest rates, inflation, unemployment and so forth

Thus, fundamental analysis entails integrating evaluations of the company, its industry, and the economy as a whole.

In a general sense, technical analysis includes any method that does not incorporate the fundamental investment concepts and evaluation of those factors believed to be the basis for establishing the market values of securities. More specifically, **technical analysis** is based on analyses of supply/demand relationships for securities to determine trends in price movements of stocks or financial markets. Technical analysts, who are called **technicians,** search for trends by examining charts or by using computer programs that evaluate information about historical movements in trading volume and prices for stocks and for financial markets as a whole. In the past, technicians were dubbed *chartists* because they were known to pore over charts, or plots, that contained historical trading volume and prices in an attempt to find patterns that could be expected to be repeated in the future. In fact, if technical analysts have a rallying cry, it would be "history repeats itself."

The approach that technicians take reflects their belief that movements in the financial markets are caused by investors' attitudes toward various economic and financial factors and other psychological circumstances; in many instances, these attitudes result in actions that, although not always rational, are fairly predictable. According to technicians, investors' actions are predictable because humans are creatures of habit. That is, when faced with situations resembling ones that occurred in the past, today's investors will take similar actions as past investors did. For example, reactions to emotions such as greed and fear generally can be anticipated: in bull markets, investors pour more and more money into the stock market as a

fundamental analysis
The practice of evaluating the information contained in financial statements, industry reports, and economic factors to determine the intrinsic value of a firm.

intrinsic value
The "true," or economic, value of the firm.

fundamentalists
Analysts who utilize fundamental analysis in an attempt to forecast future stock price movements.

technical analysis
Examination of supply and demand for securities over time to determine trends in price movements of stocks or financial markets.

technicians
Analysts who examine stocks and financial markets using technical analysis.

result of their greed; in bear markets, fear causes these same investors to pull their money out of the markets. In essence, investors have a tendency to "jump on the bandwagon" when the markets are performing well, but they quickly "abandon ship" when the markets turn around.

The sections that follow describe some techniques used by both fundamentalists and technicians to make decisions about the values of stocks and financial markets. Most of the chapter is devoted to discussion of those methods (analyses) that are generally considered part of fundamental analysis, principally because such approaches are consistent with the general concepts of valuation that we espouse in this book. Later in the chapter, we provide a brief overview of those methods used in technical analysis. Although this chapter focuses on stocks, most of the techniques described here can also be used for evaluation of debt instruments and other financial assets.

Self-Test Questions

Differentiate between the approaches that a fundamental analyst and a technical analyst would take to value a particular security or financial market.

Is the market value of a stock always equal to its intrinsic value? What do you think will happen if the two values are not equal?

ECONOMIC ANALYSIS

Clearly, the condition of the economy affects the performances of businesses and thus their securities in the financial markets. When the economy is growing, financial markets generally increase because individuals are willing to invest their savings in stocks and bonds; this investment, in turn, provides firms with the funds needed for expansionary projects. Of course, the opposite occurs when the economy is stagnant or declining. For this reason, it is important to assess the future of the economy when forecasting movements in the financial markets and the performances of firms. In this section, we provide a brief overview of areas that should be examined when analyzing economic conditions.

Forecasting Business Cycles

business cycle
The movement in aggregate economic activity as measured by the gross domestic product.

expansion
Increasing economic activity.

contraction
Declining economic activity.

gross domestic product (GDP)
A measure of all goods and services produced in the economy during a specific time period.

When we forecast economic conditions, what we really want to determine is when to expect changes in the *business cycle.* The **business cycle** is defined as the direction in which aggregate economic activity is moving. Increasing economic activity is called an **expansion,** and declining economic activity is called a **contraction.** Economic activity generally is measured using the **gross domestic product (GDP),** which includes all of the goods and services produced in the economy during a specific time period. The GDP is stated both in nominal terms, which means that the value *is not* adjusted for inflation, and in real terms, which means that the value *is* inflation-adjusted. The real GDP allows economists to determine the actual growth in the economy.

Movements in the financial markets are closely related to business cycles. Consequently, if we can get good estimates of changes in the business cycle, we should be able to forecast movements in financial markets such as the stock market and the bond market. Unfortunately, past business cycles have been irregular, which makes it difficult to use historical economic information to predict future cycles. To make matters worse, the financial markets are not perfectly related to business cycles.

FIGURE 17-1   Recessions and Stock Market Movements, 1975–2008

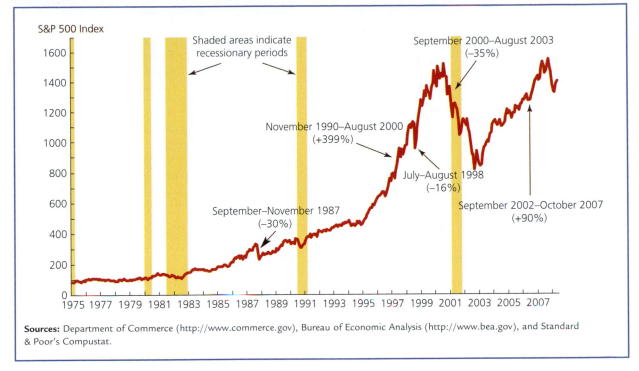

Sources: Department of Commerce (http://www.commerce.gov), Bureau of Economic Analysis (http://www.bea.gov), and Standard & Poor's Compustat.

Figure 17-1 shows the movements in the stock market since 1975; those periods when the economy was in a recession are shaded. Economists define a **recession** as two consecutive quarters of economic contraction, or decline in the GDP. According to the National Bureau of Economic Research, five recessions have occurred since 1975. Notice in Figure 17-1 that the value of the stock market decreased during each of the recessions, but that the three most notable declines in the market within the last 25 years actually occurred during economic expansions: stocks declined 30 percent from September 1987 through November 1987, 16 percent from July 1998 through August 1998, and 18 percent from September 2000 through February 2001 (35 percent from September 2000 through August 2003, a period that included a recession). As you can also see from the graph, the stock market performed very well during the 1990s; its value increased nearly 316 percent from the beginning of 1990 until the end of 1999. From the middle of the 1990–1991 recession, when the market began a general rebound, until August 2000, this value increased almost 400 percent. Unfortunately, the market declined from September 2000 through August 2003 before beginning its current general upward trend. At the time we write this book in May 2008, the economy is stagnant and the stock market is fairly flat, which might be an indication of a near-term recessionary period.

Table 17-1 gives more information about the recessions that have occurred since 1975. As you can see, there is no pattern associated with these recessions. Their lengths and effects as well as the times between recessions (expansionary periods) vary considerably. As of May 2008, (when we write this book), even though the economy had been fairly unstable, experts were predicting that stable growth would return in about 6 months. But if no pattern governs when and how long expansions or recessions occur, how can analysts make such predictions? The answer can be found by examining economic indicators published by the government and by determining the general tenor of professional analysts' commentary.

recession
Two consecutive quarters of economic contraction in the GDP.

TABLE 17-1   Recessionary Periods Since 1975

Recession Period				Time Since Previous Recession (months)	Average Annual Change in Real GDP (%)
Beginning Date		Ending Date	Recession Duration		
November 1973		March 1975	16 months	36 months	−2.97%
January 1980		July 1980	6	58	−1.92
July 1981		November 1982	16	12	−1.12
July 1990		March 1991	8	92	−2.67
March 2001		November 2001	8	120	−0.29

Source: National Bureau of Economic Research located at http://www.nber.org.

Economic Indicators

The Bureau of Economic Analysis (BEA), which is part of the U.S. Department of Commerce, collects a number of economic measures, such as the GDP, price indexes, personal and business income figures, and so on. These measures, as well as various analyses performed by the BEA, are published in the *Survey of Current Business*, which is available at nearly every university library and in most public libraries.[1] Perhaps the most often cited barometers of business activity are the *composite indexes,* which were previously reported by the BEA and now are published by The Conference Board in their monthly economic reports. These aggregate measures include various economic variables grouped into one of three categories—leading, lagging, or coincident—depending on the timing of their movements relative to business cycles. Rather than rely on a single indicator in each category, composite indexes are constructed that repesent a combination of numerous individual indicators. These composites provide better gauges of general economic patterns because spurious movements are averaged out.

leading economic indicators
Economic measures that tend to move prior to, or precede, movements in the business cycle.

As their name implies, movements in **leading economic indicators** tend to precede, or lead, movements in the economy. Similarly, movements in **lagging economic indicators** generally follow, or lag behind, economic movements. The **coincident indicators** tend to mirror, or move at the same time as, business cycles. The economic indicators that make up each of the three composite indexes reported by The Conference Board are shown in Table 17-2.

lagging economic indicators
Economic measures that tend to move after, or follow, movements in the business cycle.

The composite index of leading indicators includes 10 measures, such as manufacturers' new orders, new building permits for residential housing, and the money supply. Perhaps the most familiar leading indicator included in this composite index is stock prices. Stock prices have long been considered a leading economic indicator because, as was pointed out in Chapter 10, the prices of stocks are based on *forecasted* future cash flows. As you can imagine, the composite index of leading indicators receives a great deal of attention, especially from the news media, because it is viewed as a prophecy of the future of the economy. Unfortunately, it is difficult to predict the timing of economic movements relative to changes in the composite index of leading indicators, because the lead time has not been consistent over time.

coincident indicators
Economic measures that tend to mirror, or move at the same time as, business cycles.

---

[1]The Bureau of Economic Analysis also has a Web site located at http://www.bea.doc.gov.

TABLE 17-2   Business Cycle Indicators—Leading, Coincident, and Lagging Composite Indexes

Index and Measures Included	Rationale/Explanation
I. Index of Leading Indicators	
Average workweek production	Workweek hours increase (decrease) as firms try to produce more (less) to meet forecasted higher (lower) future demand.
Average first-time claims for unemployment insurance	Claims for unemployment decrease (increase) when recoveries (contractions) are expected.
New orders of manufacturers—consumer goods and materials	As the economy expands (contracts), new orders increase (decrease).
Manufacturers' new orders of nondefense capital goods	As the economy expands (contracts), companies expand (contract) plant and equipment.
Vendor delivery performance	Deliveries slow (speed up) during expansion (contraction) periods because products are not as (more) readily available.
New private building permits	Expectations of good (bad) times entice individuals to build new (stay in their existing) homes.
Money supply, M2	An increase (decrease) in the money supply causes interest rates to decrease (increase), affecting the economy.
Interest-rate spread: 10-year Treasury bonds yield less federal funds rate	Interest rates are based on expectations—when longer term and shorter term rates converge (diverge), investors have greater (less) confidence in the financial markets and are willing to take greater (less) risks.
Stock prices—S&P 500 index	The prices of stocks depend on cash flows expected in the future.
Index of consumer expectations	Constructed by the Survey Research Center at the University of Michigan—if consumers expect an improved (worse) economy, they will spend more (less).
II. Index of Coincident Indicators	
Number of employees on nonagricultural payrolls	Employees are hired (let go) as business improves (deteriorates).
Personal income—salaries	Salaries generally increase (decrease) as the economy expands (contracts).
Industrial production	Most significant movements in the manufacture of products occur at the same time as economic movements; orders precede actual production.
Manufacturing and trade sales	Increased (decreased) sales to distributors, retailers, and so on, occur during economic expansions (contractions).
III. Index of Lagging Indicators	
Average length of unemployment	As the economy rebounds from an economic contraction, laid-off employees are rehired, and vice versa; those unemployed for longer periods are called first.
Ratio of inventories divided by sales—manufacturers and trade	Sales begin to increase (decrease) and inventories decrease (increase) as the economy recovers from a contraction (expansion).
Change in labor costs per unit	Lower (higher) unemployment causes labor costs to increase (decrease) as the economy of output for manufacturers rebounds from a contraction (expansion).
Prime rate at banks	Banks usually don't change the prime rate until the general demand for funds (loans) changes.
Loans to commerce and industry	Borrowing increases (decreases) to support financing required for *sustained* increases (decreases) in operations.
Percentage of personal income consumers have outstanding in installment loans/credit	Individuals borrow more (less) based on their personal incomes during expansions (contractions), but only after they recognize the economic situation/conditions.
Change in the consumer price index for services	Prices change only after business conditions change.

Source: Bureau of Economic Analysis, located at http://www.bea.doc.gov.

FIGURE 17-2   Business Cycle Indicators—Composites, 1975–2008

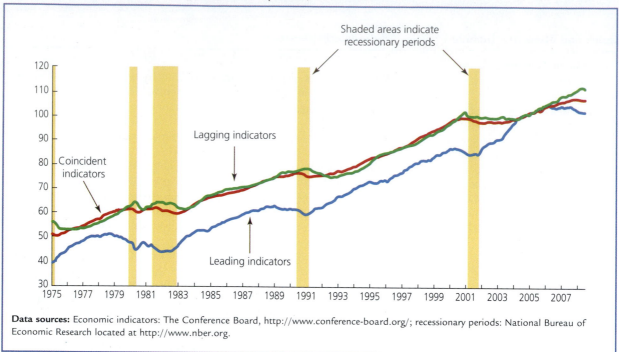

Data sources: Economic indicators: The Conference Board, http://www.conference-board.org/; recessionary periods: National Bureau of Economic Research located at http://www.nber.org.

Figure 17-2 shows a graph of the three composite indexes published by The Conference Board. For the most part, the indexes have performed as expected: the index of leading indicators has declined prior to the start of recessionary periods, the index of coincident indicators has declined at the start of recessions, and the index of lagging indicators has declined after the beginning of recessions and sometimes not until after the end of recessions. As you can see, for the most part, the composite indexes seem to provide indications of general business cycles. Nevertheless, the timings and magnitudes of the cycles remain difficult to forecast because the lead and lag times vary from one recession to another.

Professional Forecasters' Opinions

In addition to the economic information published by the government, most large brokerage firms and financial service organizations have divisions that analyze economic data and provide the results to their clients with estimates of future business activity. Although the detailed results of the analyses are usually available only to clients, these companies often release their general economic forecasts to the public. By examining a number of experts' forecasts, you can form your own opinion about expected economic movements based on the consensus of professionals' analyses.

Business Cycles and Monetary and Fiscal Policy

monetary policy
The means by which the Federal Reserve influences economic conditions by managing the U.S. money supply.

The monetary policy carried out by the Federal Reserve and the fiscal policy of the government can significantly affect business cycles. Recall from the discussion in Chapter 4 that **monetary policy** refers to the means by which the Federal Reserve influences economic conditions by managing the U.S. money supply. The Fed changes the money supply through reserves at financial institutions in an effort to promote stable economic conditions with moderate growth. For example, when the economy is in a recession, the Fed generally attempts to increase business activity by easing credit via lower interest rates, which is accomplished by increasing reserves (money supply). Although the actions taken by the Fed have not always been the same in similar economic situations, investors should evaluate existing economic conditions and form opinions about future actions that the Fed might take, because, clearly, the financial markets will be affected by those actions. For example, in the 20 months prior to May 2008, the Fed decreased interest rates by 3.25 percent in an attempt to stimulate a stagnant economy. At the same time, the Fed took actions to combat inflationary pressures, especially in the oil market, where the cost of oil had reached record highs (greater than $130 per barrel in May 2008).

Fiscal policy encompasses government spending, which is primarily supported by its ability to tax individuals and businesses. Conceptually, fiscal policy should have the same goal as monetary policy: to promote economic stability with moderate growth. Since the 1960s, the fiscal policy in the United States has been dominated by **deficit spending,** which occurs when the government spends more funds than it collects in taxes—that is, its expenses exceed its revenues. Many economists believe that deficit spending results in higher than normal prices or interest rates because the government must either print more money or borrow greater amounts to finance the additional spending. Clearly, evaluating the government's spending behavior is important when determining economic expectations.

Such an assessment is especially critical when examining a multinational corporation. For instance, in the late 1990s, exposure of the corrupt practices of governments in southeast Asia resulted in substantial declines in stock markets throughout the world. Even in the United States, the market declined considerably because investors feared that Asian companies would dump products at "cut-rate" prices, thereby making international markets less accessible to U.S. firms.

From our discussion here, it should be apparent that economic conditions affect financial markets, making it important to perform an economic analysis—even if it is only cursory—when making investment decisions. The next step in this analysis is to determine how industries are influenced by economic conditions and to ascertain their general financial and competitive positions.

fiscal policy
Government spending, which is primarily supported by the government's ability to tax individuals and businesses.

deficit spending
When the government spends more funds than it collects in taxes.

Self-Test Questions

What is a business cycle? Identify two types of business cycles.

Describe the three types (categories) of economic indicators.

How do monetary and fiscal policies affect the economy?

Why is it important to perform an economic analysis before making investment decisions?

INDUSTRY ANALYSIS

The business economy consists of many different segments called industries, which include companies with similar characteristics. Although industries are usually defined by product classifications, we also differentiate firms based on their general sectors—industrial, service, technology, financial, and so forth. As you can imagine, all industries do not perform the same in different business cycles. That is, some industries perform better than others during expansionary periods, and vice versa. For this reason, we need to examine industry conditions to determine the attractiveness of firms classified in a particular industry relative to firms in other industries. A basic industry analysis should include evaluations to determine (1) the relationship between the general performance of the industry and economic conditions and (2) the potential for future growth with respect to the industry's current position in its life cycle.

Industry Performance and Economic Conditions

cyclical industries
Industries that tend to perform best during expansions and worst during contractions.

defensive (countercyclical) industries
Industries that tend to be the best performers when the economy is in a contraction or recession, and the worst performers in expanding economies.

In Chapter 11, we mentioned that every firm is affected by economic, or market, conditions. We also noted that changes in business cycles do not affect every firm in the same way. Clearly, because industries simply represent combinations of firms with similar characteristics, we would expect different industries to react differently to shifts in the economy. For example, industries that include durable goods manufacturers, such as home builders and automobile manufacturers, generally are more sensitive to interest rate changes than are industries that include staple goods firms, such as food retailers and consumer services. **Cyclical industries** tend to perform best during expansions and worst during contractions. In contrast, **defensive,** or **countercyclical, industries** tend to be the best performers when the economy is in a contraction or recession, but generally perform poorly compared to other industries in expanding economies. Can you think of examples of both cyclical and countercyclical industries? Automobile manufacturing and construction usually are considered cyclical industries, whereas automobile parts manufacturers and home improvement suppliers are more countercyclical in nature.

To determine the sensitivity of an industry to the economy, we can use computer models that are based on sophisticated statistical methods or we can simply observe the direction in which an industry's stock prices move when major economic factors, such as interest rates and consumer prices, change. It is an easy task to use a spreadsheet to plot the relationship between industry sales and a particular economic variable or to run a relatively simple regression analysis. As an example, Figure 17-3 gives the results of fitting a trendline showing the relationship between housing starts and mortgage rates. Notice that the line has a negative slope, which indicates that housing starts increase as interest rates fall, and vice versa. This graph suggests that individuals are more (less) inclined to purchase houses when interest rates are low (high) than when rates are high (low). Of course, other factors, such as salary levels and prices, also affect housing starts. Nevertheless, Figure 17-3 gives you an idea of one method that we can use to determine the relationship between economic conditions and industry activity.

Industry Life Cycle

industry life cycle
The various phases of an industry with respect to its growth in sales and its competitive conditions.

When we examine the history of business and industry, we discover that industries go through life cycles that are comparable to the human life cycle. The cycle begins when the industry is born and firms are weak and susceptible to competition; it then progresses through periods of strengthening and growth; and finally it ends with the death of the industry. More specifically, the **industry life cycle** follows the various stages of growth with respect to the industry's products and the competitive conditions within the industry. We can identify three distinct stages in the life of an industry, as depicted in Figure 17-4:

1. The *introductory stage* begins with the birth of the industry. In this stage, growth is rapid, few barriers exist to keep new competition from entering

FIGURE 17-3   Trendline—Relationship between Housing Starts and Mortgage Rates 1975–2007

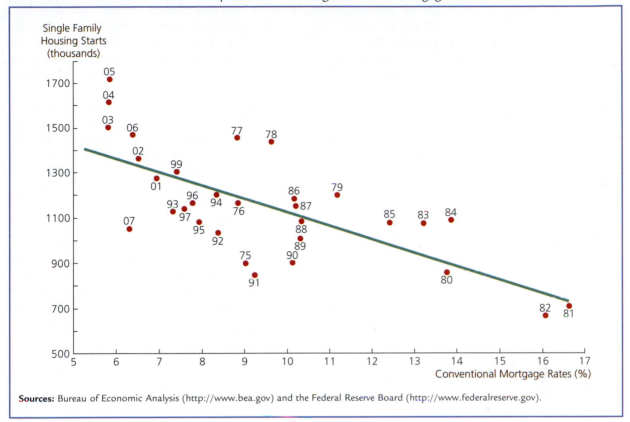

Sources: Bureau of Economic Analysis (http://www.bea.gov) and the Federal Reserve Board (http://www.federalreserve.gov).

FIGURE 17-4   The Industry Life Cycle

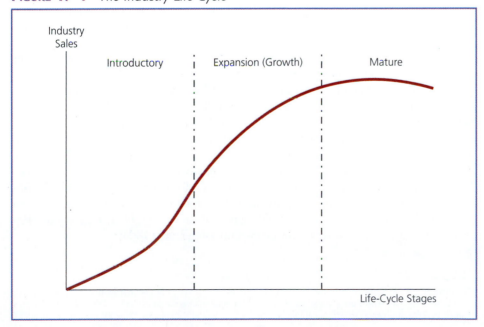

the industry, and survivorship is relatively low. Most firms have "bare-bones" operations because they are trying to carve out competitive niches. For this reason, all earnings are typically reinvested in the firm to support growth. Notice from Figure 17-4 that industry sales are growing at an increasing rate in this stage of the life cycle, which suggests that numerous growth opportunities (that is, investments with positive net present values) are available.

2. At the *expansion stage,* the industry includes those firms that have survived the introductory stage. Operations become more sophisticated as firms move into larger facilities to meet their expanded needs. Growth begins to slow, however, because the product is no longer a novelty. Sales continue to increase, albeit at a diminishing rate (see Figure 17-4). Competitive barriers increase because firms begin to carve out their competitive niches and customers become more brand loyal. Because fewer investment growth opportunities are available, it is in this stage (probably near the end) that firms generally begin to pay dividends.

3. In the *mature stage,* the industry is characterized by firms that are well entrenched, because, in essence, they have "paid their dues." It is difficult for newcomers to enter the market because competitive niches that are difficult to penetrate have been established—competitive barriers are high. Growth in the industry begins to flatten, so much of the earnings are paid out as dividends.

Industries do not progress through these life-cycle stages at the same pace. Some industries, such as biotechnology, move through the stages relatively quickly compared with industries such as automobile manufacturing or utilities. Also, industries that continuously produce large amounts of innovative technology might never reach the mature stage of the industry life cycle.

It is important for an investor to understand the point in the life cycle at which an industry is operating. The survivorship rate in the industry, its chances for growth, and expectations about its future depend on the life-cycle stage in which the industry is positioned. Furthermore, investors should evaluate the characteristics of the investment opportunities in each of the three stages. The introductory stage is characterized by small, growth-oriented firms, many of which will not survive and move to the expansion stage. Therefore, investing in this stage is considered extremely risky, but potentially extremely rewarding because those that do survive generally grow extremely rapidly.

Consider, for example, the gain you would have earned if you had purchased Microsoft stock when it was first sold to the public in March 1986 for $21 per share. Since it first went public, Microsoft's stock has been split nine times, such that one original share of stock is now the equivalent of 288 shares of existing stock. The market value of one share of the *existing* stock was $28.30 at the end of May 2008; thus, the equivalent value of one *original* share of stock was $8,150 \approx $28.30 \times 288.[2] The total 22-year holding period return for the stock was approximately 38,700 percent. Conversely, if you had purchased the stock of another start-up software company that existed in 1986, your holding period gain would likely have been −100 percent because many of those companies no longer exist today.

---

[2]Since the time it was first sold to the public in March 1986, Microsoft's stock has been split nine times. There were seven 2-for-1 splits and two 3-for-2 splits. One share of the original stock is the equivalent of 288 ($= 2^7 \times 1.5^2$) shares of stock in 2008.

As you can imagine, investing in industries in the expansion and mature stages is less risky than investing in industries in the introductory stage. In fact, industries in the mature stage are often characterized by large, stable firms with income-producing stocks (that is, stable dividends).

Self-Test Questions

Describe the characteristics of a cyclical industry and a defensive industry.

What stages does an industry go through during its life cycle?

Explain why the introductory stage of the industry life cycle is considered the riskiest stage for investors.

EVALUATING THE FIRM'S FINANCIAL POSITION

Remember that the ultimate goal of investment analysis is to value the firm's security. As we already know, valuation requires an estimation of the future cash flows expected to be generated by the investment. Therefore, the next step in investment analysis is to examine the current financial condition of the firm issuing the security and to forecast its future prospects.

To evaluate the financial condition of a firm, we generally use financial statement analysis like that described in Chapter 7. It is important for investors to examine the financial reports prepared by the firm to judge its performance in the current period and in past periods in an effort to determine its future direction. From an investor's standpoint, the purpose of financial statement analysis is to determine the attractiveness of an investment by identifying the strengths and weaknesses of the firm and projecting how its operations will change in the future.

Because we discussed financial statement analysis in detail in Chapter 7, in this section we simply summarize the general concepts of such analyses. Recall that, in general, financial statement analysis involves a comparison of a firm's operating performance and financial position with that of other firms in the same line of business. Investors can use this financial statement analysis to form expectations about the firm's future, especially with regard to its cash flow distributions.

Even though financial statement analysis is based on examinations of accounting statements, which often do not represent economic earnings, such assessments are useful in investment analysis for the following reasons:

1. We can compare a firm's business conditions with the conditions faced by other, similar firms to determine whether its current operations are average, below average, or above average.

2. Based on business conditions both in the current period and in recent past periods, we can forecast the direction that the firm is likely to take in the future. In some instances, firms that are performing below average in the current period are considered attractive investments because their futures are forecasted to be much brighter, and vice versa.

3. By developing forecasts about the company's future financial condition, we can predict earnings and dividends that can then be used in security valuation models.

4. We can use our examinations of current and forecasted business conditions to form expectations regarding the risk of the firm's future operations. Recall that risk is an important ingredient in the determination of the rate of return

that investors require to invest in the firm's securities. This required rate of return is used as the discount rate when calculating the present value of the future cash flows associated with the investment—that is, finding its value.

From our discussion here, it should be apparent that the primary use of financial statement analysis as an analytical tool is to help investors form expectations about the future cash flows and the risks associated with an investment. Before we leave our current discussion, however, we would be remiss if we didn't repeat the comment made in Chapter 7 concerning financial statement analysis: *the most important and most difficult input to successful financial statement analysis is the judgment used when interpreting the results to reach an overall conclusion about the firm's financial position.*

In addition to looking at financial statements, fundamental analysts examine qualitative factors, such as labor conditions, management tenure, brand loyalty, and so forth, when forming opinions about a firm's financial position. Examining the nature of existing qualitative factors such as these is important in predicting the future strength of the firm's financial position. Unfortunately, incorporating qualitative factors into the analysis of companies requires the analyst to apply a great deal of judgment.

Self-Test Question

What are some of the reasons financial statement analysis should be included in investment analysis?

STOCK VALUATION TECHNIQUES

As we indicated earlier, individual investors and professional analysts use a number of valuation methods to evaluate common stocks. In this section, we describe three basic techniques used to value stock. These approaches are used by investors in their efforts to find mispriced stocks and fast-growing stocks, as well as to make strategic decisions about the general compositions of their portfolios.

Dividend Discount Models

dividend discount model (DDM)
A model that utilizes the discounted cash flow principle to value common stock. Value is represented by the present value of the dividends expected to be received from investing in the stock.

In Chapter 10, we discovered that the cash flows derived from investing in a common stock are called dividends. In addition, we determined that the market value of a stock can be found by computing the present value of all dividends expected to be paid by the firm in the future. Clearly, based on our discussions throughout the book, finding the present value of, or discounting, future cash flows is the most appropriate approach to valuation.

Most existing sophisticated stock valuation models were derived in someway from the **dividend discount model (DDM),** which applies the discounted cash flow principle to the dividends expected to be received from investing in a stock. In Chapter 10, we presented the general dividend discount model, which we restate here:

17-1

$$\text{Value of stock} = V_s = \hat{P}_0 = \text{PV of expected future dividends}$$

$$= \frac{\hat{D}_1}{(1 + r_s)^1} + \frac{\hat{D}_2}{(1 + r_s)^2} + \cdots + \frac{\hat{D}_\infty}{(1 + r_s)^\infty}$$

In this equation, $\hat{D}_t$ represents the dividend payment expected in Period t, and r_s is the rate of return that investors require for similar risk stocks. Recall that if we assume the firm grows at a constant rate, the DDM is rewritten in the following simplified form:

$$\hat{P}_0 = \frac{\hat{D}_1}{r_s - g}$$

17-2

where g represents the constant growth rate in dividends. Although this is a simple equation, applying it to obtain a good estimate of a stock's value is anything but simple for two reasons. First, correct application of the equation requires that the firm's growth be fairly constant today and remain so long into the future. In reality, there probably is not one company in the world that strictly meets this criterion. Second, we must be able to estimate three variables: (1) next period's dividend payment, (2) the constant growth rate, and (3) the appropriate required rate of return. Thus, although this valuation process seems quite simple, its application is generally a formidable task.

Even with its problems and the inherent difficulties associated with forecasting the inputs necessary for its application, the DDM model can be used to obtain a "ballpark" value for common stock. For instance, if we can predict with some confidence the dividends expected to be paid by a firm for, say, the next 10 years $(\hat{D}_1, \ldots, \hat{D}_{10})$, and we can use the Capital Asset Pricing Model (CAPM) described in Chapter 11 to determine the appropriate rate of return (r_s), then we can apply the nonconstant growth version of the DDM to estimate what the current stock price $(\hat{P}_0)$ should be.

In Chapter 10 we discovered that we could value a stock that currently has nonconstant growth, but is expected to attain constant growth at some point in the future, by proceeding as follows:

1. Compute the present value of the dividends that experience nonconstant growth, and then sum the results.
2. Find the price of the stock at the end of the nonconstant growth period, at which point it has become a constant growth stock; discount this price back to the present.
3. Add the results of these two computations to find the intrinsic value of the stock, $\hat{P}_0$.

Summarizing these three steps, the nonconstant growth DDM is written as follows:

$$\hat{P}_0 = \frac{\hat{D}_1}{(1+r_s)^1} + \frac{\hat{D}_2}{(1+r_s)^2} + \cdots + \frac{\hat{D}_N + \hat{P}_N}{(1+r_s)^N}$$

$$= \frac{\hat{D}_1}{(1+r_s)^1} + \frac{\hat{D}_2}{(1+r_s)^2} + \cdots + \frac{\hat{D}_N}{(1+r_s)^N} + \frac{\hat{P}_N}{(1+r_s)^N}$$

17-3

Here:

$$\hat{D}_1 \dots \hat{D}_N = \text{Expected dividends that are affected by nonconstant growth}$$

$$\hat{P}_N = \frac{\hat{D}_N(1 + g_{norm})}{r_s - g_{norm}} = \text{Future stock price at the point where constant}$$

growth, g_{norm}, begins (or, when nonconstant growth ends)

$$r_s = \text{Cost of equity, or the required rate of return of the stockholders}$$

To illustrate the use of the DDM technique for stock valuation, let's consider Altria Group (formerly Philip Morris). The company paid a dividend of $3.05 per share in 2007. Based on analysts' forecast, we estimate that Altria's earnings in 2009 will be $2.09. Altria's beta coefficient was 0.85 in 2008, which we assume will not change in the foreseeable future. To evaluate Altria, let's assume that all dividend payments are made at the end of the year. Examining the past 10 years of growth in earnings and dividends, we find that the growth in both earnings and dividends has averaged approximately 7 percent per year. This growth rate most certainly will change somewhat in the future, because Altria completed the spin-off of Kraft Foods in 2007 and it is currently restructuring its operations. As a result, experts estimate that the growth rate will remain about the same for the next few years. Therefore, let's make a simple assumption that the firm's earnings will continue to grow at 7 percent for the next 3 years, grow at 6 percent the following 2 years, and then decline by 1 percent each year until it settles at 3 percent, the rate at which it will continue to grow from that time on. An examination of the firm's dividend policy shows that Altria has consistently paid approximately 50 percent of earnings as dividends during the past few years. Thus, we assume this practice will continue. In addition, let's assume that economic conditions will be such that the expected market returns will be about 9 percent in the future and the yield on Treasury bonds will be 4 percent; both of these rates are in line with market conditions that exist in a fairly normal market. We now have sufficient information to apply the DDM method to value Altria stock. Table 17-3 shows the steps we took to value the stock and the results of the valuation.

Using the DDM, we estimate the value of Altria to be $22.90 in 2008. The actual market price of Altria stock in May 2008 was about $22.50 per share. Does this price mean that the stock is incorrectly valued (slightly undervalued) in the market? Perhaps. Of course, not everyone will predict the same growth rates as we did; thus, because different analysts might reach completely different conclusions, different forecasts are likely.

If we find that analysts arrive at substantially different predictions, which one is most reliable? It is difficult—if not impossible—to answer this question. We do know that valuation methods such as the DDM are most effective when forecasts of future dividends are accurate and when the assumptions associated with the CAPM and the DDM are not violated. For example, to apply the constant growth model to find the price of Altria stock in 2015, we had to assume that dividends would grow at a constant rate of 3 percent from 2016 until infinity. Clearly, this assumption is not reasonable. Even so, the DDM approach provides analysts with estimates of the values of common stocks. Professional analysts, however, employ much more complex computations than we used in our example; more detailed information is used to better predict the future performance of a firm.

P/E ratio
A ratio computed by dividing the current market price per share, P_0, by the earnings per share, EPS_0.

Valuation Using P/E Ratios

Many analysts consider the P/E ratio, or earnings multiplier, to be a good indicator of the value of a stock in relative terms. The **P/E ratio** mentioned here is the same

> **TABLE 17-3**   Using the DDM Technique to Value Altria Group (formerly Philip Morris)

Step 1. Compute the required rate of return associated with Altria Group (MO) using the CAPM.

$$r_{Altria} = r_{RF} + (r_M - r_{RF})\beta_{PM}$$
$$= 4.0\% + (9.0\% - 4.0\%)0.85 = 8.25\%$$

Step 2. Forecast the dividends based on the assumed future growth rates for the periods when nonconstant growth is expected. At the same time, we can find the present values of the dividends using the required return.

Year	Assumed Growth	Forecasted Earnings[a]	Forecasted Dividend (50% of EPS)	PV of the Dividend at 8.25%
2009	0.07	2.09	$\hat{D}_1 = 1.045$	0.965
2010	0.07	2.23	$\hat{D}_2 = 1.115$	0.952
2011	0.07	2.39	$\hat{D}_3 = 1.195$	0.942
2012	0.06	2.53	$\hat{D}_4 = 1.265$	0.921
2013	0.06	2.68	$\hat{D}_5 = 1.340$	0.901
2014	0.05	2.82	$\hat{D}_6 = 1.410$	0.876
2015	0.04	2.93	$\hat{D}_7 = 1.465$	0.841

PV of dividends (2009–2015) = $6.398

Step 3. Compute the price of the stock after nonconstant growth ends in the year 2015.

$$\hat{P}_{2015} = \frac{\hat{D}_{2016}}{r_s - g_{norm}} = \frac{\$1.465(1.03)}{0.0825 - 0.03} = \frac{1.509}{0.0525} = \$28.742$$

Step 4. Compute the current price of the stock, which is the present value of the dividends computed in Step 2 plus the present value of the future price computed in Step 3.

$$\hat{P}_0 = \$6.398 + \frac{\$28.742}{(1.0825)^7} = \$6.398 + 16.501 = \$22.90$$

[a]The 2009 earnings estimate is based on forecasts for Altria that were published on the Internet at sites such as Zacks Investment Research, Charles Schwab, and *The Wall Street Journal*.

as that described in Chapter 7; it is computed by dividing the current market price per share, P_0, by the earnings per share, EPS_0. The higher (lower) the P/E ratio, the more (less) investors are willing to pay for each dollar earned by the firm.

In a sense, the P/E ratio is similar to the payback method we used in capital budgeting. For example, if a firm's P/E ratio is 12, then, assuming that the firm distributes all of its earnings as dividends, it would take 12 years for an investor to recover his or her initial investment. If we view P/E ratios as measures of payback, all else equal, lower earnings multipliers are better. In fact, it has been suggested that firms with low P/E ratios relative to other firms in the same industries can earn above-average, risk-adjusted returns, and vice versa. The rationale is that if a company's P/E ratio is too low relative to that of similar firms, its earnings have not been fully captured in the existing stock value; thus, the price will be bid up in the future.

Similarly, if the firm's P/E ratio is too high relative to that of similar firms, the market has overvalued its current earnings and its stock price should decrease.

How can we use P/E ratios to value common stocks? Generally speaking, we examine whether the stock's P/E ratio is considered to be higher or lower than "normal" to decide whether the price is too high or too low. If we can determine what value is appropriate for the P/E ratio, we can then multiply that value by the firm's EPS to estimate the appropriate stock price. Determining the appropriate P/E requires judgment, so analysts do not always agree about what the preferred P/E ratio for a firm should be.

Depending on the company analysis, such as evaluation of the firm's financial statements, the P/E ratio might need to be adjusted to reflect expectations about the firm's performance in the future. It might be adjusted downward if the firm's future is considered less promising than the recent past, because investors might not be willing to pay the same multiple for the earnings that are expected to be generated in the future. Although the adjustment process is somewhat arbitrary, we know that P/E ratios are higher (lower) for firms with higher (lower) expected earnings growth and lower (higher) expected required rates of return. For example, investors will place a higher value on the current earnings if the firm is expected to grow at a higher than normal rate.

To illustrate the use of P/E ratios to determine the price of a stock, let's again examine Altria. According to *The Wall Street Journal* online (http://www.wsj.com), Altria had a P/E ratio equal to 15 at the end of May 2008, which was approximately the same as the industry average. If we examine the firm's P/E ratios for the past 5 years, we find that the values have ranged from 5 to 14, with an average of approximately 12. Because the most recent trend has been for the P/E ratio to hover around 12, we can assume that this value is the appropriate future P/E ratio for Altria. We therefore multiply the EPS expected for 2008 by 12 to estimate the price of the stock. According to Zacks Investment Research, Charles Schwab online research, and *The Wall Street Journal* online company research, analysts estimate that the EPS should be about $1.95 in 2008. Thus, using the P/E ratio method to value Altria stock, we estimate the stock price to be $23.40 = $1.95 × 12, which is slightly higher than the actual stock price ($22.50) at the end of May 2008.

Evaluating Stocks Using the Economic Value Added Approach

economic value added (EVA)
An analytical method that seeks to evaluate the earnings generated by a firm to determine whether they are sufficient to compensate the suppliers of funds—both the bondholders and the stockholders.

Economic value added (EVA) is a fairly new approach that is used to measure financial performance and thus evaluate the attractiveness of a firm's stock. The basic approach, which was developed by Stern Stewart Management Services, is to use basic financial principles to analyze a company's performance to value the firm. Companies that have used EVA include Coca-Cola, Eli Lily, AT&T, Sprint, and Quaker Oats, to name a few. Some companies, such as Coca-Cola, have used EVA since the early 1980s. So what is EVA and how is it applied to make investment decisions?

EVA is based on the concept that the earnings from actions taken by a company must be sufficient to compensate the suppliers of funds—both the bondholders and the stockholders. If this idea sounds familiar, it should; it is closely related to the concept that projects must earn at least the firm's weighted average cost of capital (WACC) to be acceptable, which we discussed in Chapters 12 and 13. What is different with the EVA approach, however, is that we adjust the operating earnings figure reported on the income statement to account for the costs associated with both the debt and the equity issued by the firm.

The general concept underlying the EVA is a determination of how much a firm's economic value is increased by the decisions it makes. Thus, we can write the basic EVA equation as follows:

17-4

$$\text{EVA} = (\text{IRR} - \text{WACC}) \times (\text{Invested capital})$$
$$= \text{EBIT}(1 - T) - [\text{WACC} \times (\text{Invested capital})]$$

In this equation, IRR represents the firm's internal rate of return, WACC is the firm's weighted average cost of capital, T is the marginal tax rate, and Invested capital is the amount of funds provided by investors. Equation 17-4 can be used to evaluate the value of the firm as a whole or individual projects. If the EVA is positive, the actions of the firm should increase its value; conversely, if the EVA is negative, the actions of the firm should decrease its value. Recall from Chapter 13 that capital budgeting projects with IRR > WACC are acceptable because they increase the firm's value. The same holds for EVA: when IRR > WACC, EVA > 0.

To illustrate the use of the EVA approach, let's again examine Altria Group. First, we gather the following information from the financial statements published by the company at the end of March 2008:

Operating income, EBIT	$ 1.21 billion
Total capital = long-term debt + equity	$13.76 billion
Shares outstanding	2.81 billion
Marginal tax rate	37%
Debt/assets ratio	82%

In addition, using information about the interest paid during the year and the amount of debt outstanding, we estimate that Altria had a before-tax cost of debt, r_d, equal to 6.8 percent. Assuming that the cost of equity we computed earlier using the CAPM is correct, the WACC is computed as follows:

$$\text{WACC} = [6.8\%(1 - 0.37)](0.82) + 8.25\%(0.18) = 5.00\%\,.$$

If we apply Equation 17-4, we find the EVA as follows:

$$\text{EVA} = [\$1.21 \text{ billion} \times (1 - 0.37)] - (0.0500 \times \$13.76 \text{ billion})$$
$$= \$0.762 \text{ billion} - \$0.688 \text{ billion}$$
$$= \$0.074 \text{ billion} = \$74 \text{ million}$$

According to this computation, the EVA approach suggests that investors demanded $688 million in compensation for providing funds to the firm. Because the firm generated $762 million in net operating profits after taxes to cover the compensation associated with financing, we can conclude that Altria was able to use its funds to earn higher returns than those demanded by investors in 2007. Thus, the firm should be attractive to investors. Altria stock should be especially attractive to common stockholders because they have the right to any amounts earned in excess of the required rate of return.

We can use the EVA concept to determine the maximum dividend that can be paid to stockholders before we would expect the firm's value to be threatened. The computation is simple—just divide the computed EVA by the number of out-standing shares. In the case of Altria Group, the maximum per share dividend suggested by EVA is $0.03 = $0.074 billion ÷ 2.81 billion shares. Philip Morris paid a dividend equal to $3.05 in 2007 and was expected to pay a dividend equal to approximately $1.80 in 2008. Thus, the actual dividend is substantially greater than the EVA dividend. This finding might suggest that the firm is overvalued. Like the other analytical techniques discussed in this section, however, the EVA approach requires additional computations and predictions to achieve greater precision in the final result. For instance, Stern Stewart indicates that it has identified more than 160 possible adjustments to accounting values contained in financial statements that can be used to better estimate the true economic value of the firm's performance.

The EVA approach has gained attention as a valuation technique because it is based on the fundamental principle of wealth maximization, which should be the goal of every firm. It is also attractive because it allows us to outline the value creation process in simple terms: (1) changing the capital structure can change value because the WACC is affected and (2) increasing the efficiency of the firm through reductions in operating expenses or increases in revenues will increase operating income and thus increase value. Prospective EVA users should be aware that to obtain a precise estimate of the economic performance of a firm, it might be necessary to make many adjustments to the accounting numbers contained in the firm's financial statements. Knowing how to apply such adjustments often takes considerable expertise.

Self-Test Questions

Describe the general procedure for using the dividend discount model (DDM) to value stock.

How are P/E ratios used to estimate the value of common stock?

What is EVA? How can you use the EVA approach to determine the attractiveness of a firm?

In general, what are some of the difficulties associated with the application of the valuation techniques described in this section?

Suppose that the last dividend paid by a company was $2.20, dividends are expected to grow at a constant rate equal to 5 percent forever, and stockholders require 16 percent to invest in similar types of investments. What is the value of the company's stock? (Answer: $21)

TECHNICAL ANALYSIS

The valuation techniques described in the previous section rely on basic valuation principles that focus on *which* factors determine values and *why* values change. As a result, these techniques are considered to be part of fundamental analysis. Technical analysis, on the other hand, focuses on predicting *when* values will change. Technical analysts believe that it is possible to identify shifts in the supply/demand relationships associated with investments that result in persistent trends for either individual stocks or the market as a whole. More importantly, they believe that investors behave in a predictable manner when faced with current situations similar to ones that occurred in the past—that is, "history repeats itself."

Technical analysts probably would not disagree with fundamental analysts who believe that they can find the intrinsic values of firms. They would argue, however, that by the time fundamentalists complete their evaluations of the economy, the respective industries, and the companies, it is probably too late to take advantage of any mispricings that are discovered. Therefore, technical analysts believe that methods other than those used by fundamental analysts are needed to determine which investments should be bought and sold. In this section, we describe some of the approaches employed by technical analysts to evaluate stocks and the stock market. This section is intended to give you a general overview of technical analysis, so only a few of the numerous methods used by technical analysts are included here.

Charting—Using Charts and Graphs

As noted earlier, technical analysis is based primarily on the belief that trends exist in the stock market. One of the ways in which technical analysts attempt to identify trends is by examining charts and graphs of historical prices, trading volume, and so on.

To illustrate the use of charts, let's examine a **bar chart,** which is simply a graph that indicates the daily, weekly, or monthly high, low, and closing price movements for a firm's stock during a specified period. Figure 17-5 shows a bar chart for a hypothetical company named Jacrad Corporation. In the graph, the trading line that is plotted for each day includes three pieces of information: (1) the high price, which corresponds to the top of the line; (2) the low price, which corresponds to the bottom of the line; and (3) the closing price, which is represented by the tick mark that protrudes horizontally from the line. As you can see from the graph, the height of the line indicates the range within which the stock's price traded during the day. For example, on the sixth day of trading, Jacrad's highest trading price was $33, its lowest trading price was $32, and the closing price was $32.50; thus, the price range was very narrow. On the other hand, on Day 32, the high price was $49, the low price was $40, and the closing price was $43. This wider trading range suggests greater volatility occurred on Day 32 than on Day 6.

Figure 17-5 includes a **trendline,** which indicates the direction of the stock price movement. The line in Figure 17-5 was drawn so that it touches the lowest

bar chart
A graph that indicates the high, low, and closing price movements for a stock during a specified period.

trendline
A line that indicates the direction of the stock price movement. It is drawn so that it touches either the high prices or the low prices for some of the trading days.

FIGURE 17-5   Bar Chart for Jacrad Corporation

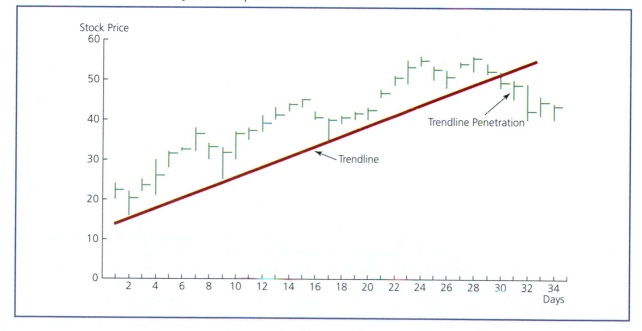

prices for the trading days. According to this trendline, the stock shows a pattern of increased prices for the first 29 trading days included on the chart. On Day 30, however, the trading line crosses the trendline; on Days 31 through 33, the trading lines actually fall below the trendline. The point at which the trading line crosses the trendline is called the **trendline penetration.** If the penetration is either significant or persistent, the suggestion is that there is pressure for the previous trend to reverse its direction. Therefore, according to the bar chart given in Figure 17-5, an investor should think about selling Jacrad Corporation on Day 31 or 32, even though the price is higher than $40 per share, which is more than twice its price 1 month earlier.

trendline penetration
The point at which the trading line crosses the trendline.

Here, we have given only one example of the numerous types of charts that technical analysts might use. This illustration should, however, give you an idea of the basic approach that is involved in charting. Note that most of the graphs examined by technical analysts are much more complex and much more difficult to interpret than the example given in Figure 17-5. The most critical—and most difficult—part of charting is interpreting the graphs in an attempt to find trading patterns and to determine the timing reversals in any patterns that are found.

Measures and Indicators Used by Technical Analysts

Technical analysts work with more than just charts and graphs to formulate their investment predictions. They also use measures and indicators that they believe gauge both the trading activity and the tenor of the market. In this section, we describe some of the more common measures used by technical analysts.

The Dow Theory

Dow theory
A technique used to predict reversals in market patterns by examining the movements of the Dow Jones Industrial Average and the Dow Jones Transportation Average.

As far as we know, structured technical analysis was introduced in the late 1890s by Charles Dow, who developed the **Dow theory.** According to this theory, three types of market movements are possible:

1. A primary, or broad, trend that lasts from several months to many years

2. A secondary, or intermediate, trend that lasts from a few weeks to 3 or 4 months

3. A short-term movement, which is represented by daily price movements

The primary objective of the Dow theory is to identify the reversal of primary trends by examining the movements of the Dow Jones Industrial Average, which includes stocks of the 30 largest industrial firms, and the Dow Jones Transportation Average, which includes stocks of 20 transportation firms. Proponents of the Dow theory believe that these two indexes reflect the most important factors that drive market movements, including market psychology, or the general attitude of investors. In essence, the theory states that as long as the industrial index and the transportation index move in the same direction, the market will continue its current trend. For example, in a bull market, if the two indexes consistently increase, then this pattern suggests that the market is strong and should continue its increase. When the indexes move in opposite directions, the suggestion is that the market is weakening and a reversal of the current trend might be imminent. The underlying principle of the Dow theory is the notion that industrial products must be transported to the end users; thus, when transportation increases (decreases) coincide with production increases (decreases), this is a sign that the economy is expected to move in the same direction.

Moving Averages

Technical analysts often examine the patterns of average stock prices for a fixed time frame, or window, over a particular period of time. Such measures are called **moving averages.** For example, suppose we want to compute a 3-day moving average using the following series of prices:

moving averages
Stock price averages for a fixed time frame (say, 100 days) computed for a particular period of time.

Day	Price	3-Day Moving Average
1	$44.00	—
2	44.24	—
3	44.90	$44.38
4	45.02	44.72
5	45.14	45.02

The first 3-day average that we can compute includes the prices for Days 1 through 3. The result of the computation is $44.38 = ($44.00 + $44.24 + 44.90)/3. The second 3-day average that we can compute includes the prices for Days 2 through 4; the computation is the same as the first 3-day average, except that we omit the price for Day 1 and include the price for Day 4. As you can see, the window of prices used to compute the averages is always 3 days. Because this window "moves" through time, however, only the prices from the most recent 3 days are used.

The windows for the moving averages used by technical analysts generally range from 30 days to 1 year. For example, they might compute a 100-day moving average. The results of the moving average computations for a particular time period—say, 6 months—are then graphed. Such graphs are interpreted much like bar charts: when the moving average crosses over, or penetrates, a previously established series, a reversal in the trend might be expected.

Technical Indicators

Technical indicators are measures that technical analysts use to help forecast future movements in stock prices. Technicians believe that these indicators behave much like the leading economic indicators discussed earlier in the chapter. Although many variations of technical indicators are possible, two basic types of indicators exist: those that measure the *breadth* of the market and those that measure the *sentiment* of the market.

technical indicators
Measures used by technical analysts to forecast future movements in stock prices.

Market breadth indicators are used to measure the trading volume and the range of trading that takes place in the market. For example, one of the most often quoted measures is the **advance/decline line,** which is constructed by graphing the difference between the number of advancing stocks and the number of declining stocks over some time period. The advance/decline line is used to track whether the market is experiencing upward or downward pressure. As long as the advance/decline line moves in the same direction as the market, technicians generally conclude that the market will continue in that same general direction. If the advance/decline line moves opposite the market trend, the trend might be weakening and a reversal might occur soon. Other breadth indicators, such as the overbought/oversold index, the traders index, and various other volume indexes, are used by technical analysts as well. In essence, such analysts believe that changes in trading volume—and thus measures based on trading volume—provide indications of future price changes in the market.

market breadth indicators
Technical indicators that are used to measure the trading volume and the range of trading that takes place in the market.

advance/decline line
A graph that depicts the difference between the number of advancing stocks and the number of declining stocks over some time period.

sentiment indicators
Technical indicators that are used to monitor the "mood," or psychology, of the market.

Sentiment indicators are used to monitor the "mood," or psychology, of the market. One group of sentiment measures is based on observations of the recommendations made to, and the behavior of, the average individual investor. Many technical analysts believe that the average investor makes decisions to buy or sell in the stock market at the wrong time. Therefore, when odd-lot buying (an indication of the behavior of small investors) increases or recommendations made by investment newsletters subscribed to by individual investors are bullish, technical analysts would suggest that the market is expected to decline in the near term.[3] Another group of sentiment measures is based on observations of the trading behavior of investment experts and sophisticated investors. For example, technical analysts believe that the amount of short selling positions held by professional investors is a good indicator of which direction they expect the market to move. That is, when the professionals increase their short positions, it is a sign that the market might decline in the future, and vice versa.

Even though this section has described only briefly a few of the many approaches used by technical analysts, you should have a general idea of the basic factors that technicians believe provide important signals about movements in stock prices. For the most part, fundamental analysts would argue that technical analysis can reveal only what we already know—the movements of historical prices—rather than what we want to know—the movement of future prices.

Self-Test Questions

Why are technical analysts often referred to as chartists?

What is a trendline?

How do you compute moving averages?

Which types of indicators are used by technical analysts?

STOCK SELECTION CRITERIA

Through the years, many different criteria, or screening techniques, for selecting stocks have been developed by numerous investment professionals. Some of the approaches emphasize growth potential, whereas others focus on value and stability. Most of the factors that are evaluated are considered part of fundamental analyses, but some of the measures clearly would be classified as technical indicators. Even with their differences, the stock selection approaches used by well-known investment professionals do have some commonalities.

The discussion in this section focuses on an article contained in the November 1998 issue of the *AAII Journal*, which is published by the American Association of Individual Investors.[4] The article summarized and compared the stock selection criteria applied by 10 well-known investment professionals. Some of the techniques, such as those developed by Benjamin Graham and T. Rowe Price, were proposed

---

[3]In Chapter 16, we defined an odd-lot trade as a trade where the number of shares involved is not a multiple of 100. For instance, if an investor buys 60 shares of a particular stock, he or she is involved in an odd-lot trade. Only individuals trade odd-lot shares. Thus, when odd-lot trading increases, we know that trading by individuals has increased.

[4]Maria Crawford Scott, "The Common Traits of Successful Investment Strategies," *AAII Journal*, November 1998, 11–15.

decades ago, but still evoke interest today. This section briefly describes the general approaches and indicates the commonalities of the approaches included in the *AAII Journal* article. Before we begin, however, we should make it clear that, to date, no one has discovered the "perfect" stock selection technique.

Many investors use the screening, or selection, techniques referred to in this section in hopes that they can find stocks that will "beat the market" on a risk-adjusted basis. Such stocks can be classified into two categories: *growth stocks* and *value stocks* (see "A Managerial Perspective" at the beginning of the chapter). Technically, **growth stocks** are defined as stocks of firms that have many positive net present value opportunities—that is, the firms' values should increase (grow) as these projects are undertaken. More generally, we define growth stocks as the stocks of firms that exhibit sales and earnings growth rates that significantly exceed the industry averages. **Value stocks,** by comparison, are defined as stocks of firms that are mispriced, especially those that are undervalued.

Table 17-4 lists the 10 investment professionals discussed in the *AAII Journal* article and summarizes their general investment philosophies and the stock selection criteria they believe should be applied to achieve particular investment goals. The table provides only a very general indication of the investment philosophy of each professional. Consequently, you should note that each of the individuals listed in Table 17-4 outlines very clear-cut investment goals and recommends that every investor should be disciplined in pursuit of his or her investment goals.

If we examine the quantitative and qualitative criteria presented in the table, we find some interesting similarities among the different approaches. First, note that each stock selection criteria requires some type of evaluation of the firm's earnings and that the P/E ratio appears to be the most commonly used valuation measure. It should not come as a surprise that professional investors prefer firms that exhibit stable growth in earnings. Nor should it surprise you to learn that the criteria favor firms with financial strength: the best firms seem to be those that have low amounts of debt relative to the industry norm and the ability to meet current obligations. One element that is not consistent among the criteria is the amount of institutional ownership—ownership by pension funds, insurance companies, and so forth—that should be present. Those professionals who favor institutional ownership believe that it adds liquidity to a firm's stock, whereas those who prefer a lower institutional presence believe that it is easier to find stocks that are selling at bargain prices if institutional ownership is relatively low.

In examining the qualitative factors included in Table 17-4, we find a general consensus that an investor should have some knowledge and understanding of a company's product line and general operations before investing in it. In fact, most of the professionals listed in the table would argue that you should not invest in companies you cannot understand, because there is a good chance you will not be able to understand the reasons for stock price movements, even after they occur. The professionals also seem to favor firms that have carved out competitive niches due to patents, brand loyalty, or other competitive barriers. If a company faces little competition, its future growth generally is more certain than that of a company that operates in a very competitive industry.

Perhaps the most interesting piece of information contained in Table 17-4 appears in the last column, which is labeled "Investment Horizon." This column summarizes the general feelings of the professionals with respect to the length of time for which an investment should be held. Clearly, none of these professionals recommends that investors speculate or try to time market movements; instead, the common theme is to hold an investment until it no longer satisfies the investor's

growth stocks
Stocks of firms that have many positive net present value opportunities. In general, these firms exhibit sales and earnings growth rates that significantly exceed the industry averages.

value stocks
Stocks of firms that are mispriced, especially those that are undervalued.

TABLE 17-4   Stock Selection Criteria of Investment Professionals (listed alphabetically)

Name	Investment Philosophy	Types of Stock Included
Warren Buffett	Use the intrinsic value to select companies expected to generate long-run earnings	Any stock, but the selection criteria require the stocks to be from older companies
David Dreman	Examine investors' attitudes; trade on overreactions	Large and medium firms
Phillip Fisher	Look for firms that show growth higher than the market	Any stock
Benjamin Graham	Find firms with prices below their intrinsic values	Quality dividend-paying firms or unpopular large firms with good subsidiaries
Peter Lynch	Select firms that have good growth prospects at reasonable prices	Any stock
William O'Neil (CANSLIM)	Seek firms that exhibit favorable conditions for future price increases	Any stock, but smaller firms are preferred
James O'Shaughnessy	Whichever strategy is used, be disciplined; use an approach that has exhibited success	Depends on the strategy used
T. Rowe Price	Select firms positioned early in their life cycle with good long-term growth prospects	Any stock, but smaller firms offer greater growth opportunities
Ralph Wanger	Find firms that have good value based on financial strength and growth prospects	Established firms that are relatively small
Geraldine Weiss	Select quality firms that pay dividends and are undervalued	Dividend-paying firms; high quality; great number of outstanding shares

goals. Thus, the consensus of the professionals is to "buy and hold" until either personal goals or market conditions change.

We can summarize the common factors contained in the advice of the investment professionals as follows:

1. Be disciplined with your investment approach—give a particular strategy a chance to work; don't flip-flop between approaches because you don't see immediate results.

Quantitative Characteristics	Qualitative Characteristics	Investment Horizon
Strong earnings with consistent upward trend; high retained earnings; high returns for 5 of the last 10 years	Firms should be easy to understand; have a competitive edge due to patents, brands, etc.	Hold until the firm's features are no longer attractive
Low P/E ratios with high dividend yields; high earnings growth compared with market; high ROE and current ratio; low debt	Understand the firm's business and which factors most affect earnings	Hold for a long term; sell if P/E ratios are near the market's P/E
Low P/E ratios relative to growth; good capital position; above-average profits and strong, stable growth in sales	Look for good R&D firms; depth in personnel; good relations with investors; strong market prospects	Hold until growth falls or firm's general features change
Low P/E and price-to-book ratios; stable growth in earnings; current ratio greater than 2.0; long-term debt less than 110 percent of current assets	Prefers to rely on quantitative measures, but seeks firms that are well managed historically	Hold for a long term; sell if price is well above intrinsic value
Low P/E ratios relative to industry and firm's historical growth, low debt/equity ratios, and low institutional ownership; stable earnings	Firms should be established and known by investor; boring; demand for product exists in all economies	Hold for a long term; sell when investment doesn't fit into goals
High, increasing earnings and growth in earnings; low debt; prices achieving new highs; low institutional ownership	Seek leading firms in innovative, growth-oriented industries	Monitor continuously; sell worst performers each quarter
For value-based strategies, choose market leaders with above-average sales, dividend yields, etc.; for growth-based strategies, firms should have capitalizations greater than $150 million, stable earnings, and high price strength	–	Hold stocks until they no longer meet investment goals
P/E low compared with historical norm; stable EPS growth; retains earnings to increase capital base; above-average profit margins	High degree of management ownership; in growth industry; good labor relations	Hold for a long term; sell when firm is no longer a growth firm
P/E ratio low relative to growth potential; cheap price relative to assets; good working capital; low debt; low institutional ownership	Good management; competitive edge; provide needs for future social and economic trends	Hold for a long term; sell when investment no longer fits goals
Stable earnings and dividends; low P/Es; dividend yields within 10 percent of all-time high; high current ratio; low debt/equity ratio; high institutional ownership	Have a knowledge of the firm's product, R&D, and marketing efforts	Hold until the dividend yield is within 10 percent of historical low

2. Know the company in which you invest—make sure that you have a basic understanding of the company and its operations before you invest.

3. Choose firms that are in strong financial positions and have good potential for future growth.

4. Stay with the investment until it no longer satisfies your investment goals—but don't use short-term performance evaluations to determine whether your investment goals are being met.

Self-Test Questions

According to the investment selection criteria presented in Table 17-4, which measure is used most often by professionals to value stocks?

What is the most common qualitative factor included in the stock selection criteria?

How long do the professionals listed in Table 17-4 recommend that investors hold stocks chosen by using their selection criteria?

INVESTMENT SELECTION IN EFFICIENT MARKETS

In Chapter 3, we described the concept of information efficiency in the financial markets. Recall that if the markets are efficient with respect to information, then investors should not be able to use investment selection criteria to *consistently* earn **abnormal returns,** which are defined as returns that exceed the returns earned by investments with similar risks. Investors who believe that the markets are efficient might also believe that it is a waste of time to use the valuation and stock selection approaches discussed in the previous sections in an attempt to find mispriced securities. For that reason, in this section, we discuss the concept of information efficiency in the financial markets and the use of stock valuation and selection techniques suggested by both technical analysts and fundamental analysts.

abnormal returns
Returns that exceed the returns earned by investments with similar risks.

Market Efficiency and Stock Analysis

The three general forms of market efficiency include weak-form efficiency, semistrong-form efficiency, and strong-form efficiency.

Weak-form Efficiency

weak-form efficiency
Asserts that current market prices reflect all historical information, including any information that might be provided by examining past price movements and trading volume data.

If **weak-form efficiency** exists, then existing market prices reflect all historical information, including any information that might be provided by examining past price movements and trading volume data. Most empirical tests of this form of market efficiency indicate that the markets are weak-form efficient. This result suggests that the charting techniques and other approaches used by technical analysts cannot be used to earn abnormal returns. In fact, some tests show that investors could do just as well if they selected stocks randomly and followed a simple buy-and-hold strategy. Most fundamental analysts would agree that the markets are weak-form efficient because they believe that the approaches used by technical analysts are analogous to sorcery or witchcraft.

Semistrong-form Efficiency

semistrong-form efficiency
Asserts that existing market prices reflect all publicly available information, including information contained in historical data and information contained in current financial statements.

Semistrong-form efficiency asserts that existing market prices reflect all publicly available information, including information contained in historical data and information contained in current financial statements. If the markets are semistrong-form efficient, then using fundamental analysis techniques, such as examining financial statements, industry life cycles, and so on, to earn abnormal returns will prove futile. To date, tests of this form of market efficiency have been somewhat inconclusive: many empirical tests seem to prove that semistrong-form efficiency exists, but other tests indicate that such efficiency does not exist. Many fundamental analysts would argue that it is their evaluations and the information they provide that help make the markets efficient. Some of the empirical evidence suggests that this argument might be flawed, however, because pockets of information inefficiency are present in the markets. For instance, some researchers believe that stocks with low P/E ratios produce abnormal returns; others believe that small firms perform better than large firms on a relative basis. Still others suggest that those who find such anomalies in the market are examining the wrong events or are using the wrong types of statistical tests.

Strong-form Efficiency

Strong-form efficiency asserts that existing market prices reflect all information, whether it is public or private. Thus, if the markets achieve this form of efficiency, then even corporate insiders would be unable to earn abnormal returns on a consistent basis. In a strong-form efficient market, investors could not earn abnormal returns even if they had inside information. For the most part, empirical tests of the strong form of market efficiency have produced results that suggest insiders can consistently earn abnormal returns; thus, the evidence fails to prove that strong-form efficiency exists.

strong-form efficiency
Asserts that existing market prices reflect all information, whether it is public or private.

Investment Analysis and Strategy in Efficient Markets

What does the evidence about the efficiency of the financial markets suggest about selecting investments? If you believe that the markets are efficient, should you randomly select securities and follow a buy-and-hold strategy? In an efficient market, are the approaches discussed in this chapter useless? In general, the answer to the latter two questions is a resounding no. The approaches included in this chapter are useful for more reasons than simply trying to earn abnormal returns. Of course, investors would love to earn abnormal returns if they could. Unfortunately, the evidence suggests that it is difficult, if not impossible, to accomplish this objective on a consistent basis. Even if we accept that abnormal returns can be earned only with diligent evaluation of both fundamental and technical information, most of us would be inclined to follow buy-and-hold investment strategies because we are unable or unwilling to put the time and effort into seeking out mispriced securities, knowing that we could be wrong.

If we accept that abnormal returns cannot be earned on a consistent basis, we still need to evaluate the investments we select to ensure that our investment goals are being met. If you invest without conducting appropriate investment analysis, you might find that the resulting investment portfolio is either too risky or not risky enough. The valuation and selection approaches described in this chapter can be used to evaluate particular investments to determine whether you should include them in your portfolio. Thus, unless your goal is to earn about the same return as the market by investing in a portfolio with a large number of different securities, then it generally would not be wise to randomly select stocks. In summary, *you should always do your "investment" homework so that you know what risks you are taking and whether your investment goals are being met.*

?   **Self-Test Questions**
What are the three forms of market efficiency?

If the markets are considered to be informationally efficient, is there a need to evaluate investments using the approaches described in this chapter?

Ethical Dilemma

Mary Mary Quite Contrary, What Makes Your Sales Forecasts Grow?

Saskatchewan Mining and Steel (SMS) Corporation is evaluating whether it should produce a new synthetic steel, which will require billions of dollars to develop. According to Bill Bates, the CEO of SMS, the synthetic steel should boost sales such that the company's total net income is increased substantially. Mary, who has worked in the capital budgeting area for 6 years, was asked to estimate the relevant cash flows that the synthetic steel is expected to generate.

During the past few weeks, Mary has had quite a few conversations with the company's engineers, its production manager, and its vice president of marketing. With the information she compiled through her conversations with these persons and additional information she received from independent sources, Mary put together a rather detailed forecast of the synthetic steel's relevant cash flows. The final report, which includes only the forecasted cash flows and explanations for the forecasts, was submitted to the chief investment officer yesterday. The report does not include analyses of the overall attractiveness of the investment because such analyses are conducted by the investment officer.

Today, the investment officer called Mary to tell her that he thought that the forecasts she submitted were incorrect. Mary explained that her forecasts were based on a large amount of information that she had collected and corroborated in combination with analysts' predictions concerning the potential success of the synthetic steel. As she told the investment officer, her forecasts were based on optimistic growth rates in sales for the synthetic steel during the next

15 years. The investment officer said that he thought the growth of such a revolutionary product could be higher than Mary estimated, so he asked her to reconsider her cash flow estimates. Although she had reviewed the numbers dozens of times and she is convinced that her forecasts are reliable, Mary agreed to "go over" the forecasts one more time. Being a "team player" is important to Mary because she wants to move up the "corporate ladder" as quickly as possible, and she believes that her rise to the executive suite will be enhanced if she cooperates with her superiors, including the investment officer.

Because she set up her forecast on a spreadsheet, Mary knew that it would be easy to change the growth rate of sales to get new cash flow forecasts for the synthetic steel. But Mary didn't think that growth rates higher than the ones she used in her original forecasts could be achieved, even if the synthetic steel proved to be a huge success. She did, however, use the higher growth rates that the investment officer had suggested to generate a new set of forecasted cash flows for the synthetic steel. Even though she is convinced that the new growth rates are likely not attainable, Mary sent her new forecasts to the investment officer a little while ago. She figured: "What's the difference? I don't make the final decision anyway."

Do you believe that Mary should have changed her forecasts? What would you have done if you were in Mary's position? What impact might such information have on investors who own, or are considering purchasing, SMS's common stock?

CHAPTER PRINCIPLES
–The Answers

To summarize the key concepts, let's answer the questions that were posed at the beginning of the chapter:

- **What is fundamental analysis? What is technical analysis? How do these two stock analyses differ?** Those who conduct fundamental analysis—the fundamentalists—evaluate the economy, the industry in which a firm operates, and the firm itself in an attempt to determine the firm's intrinsic, or "true" economic value. When evaluating the firm, fundamentalists examine such factors as financial statements, labor relations, management effectiveness, and so forth. Technical analysts—the technicians—examine past trends and patterns that might exist in the financial markets in an attempt to determine the direction the markets and various investments will move in the future. Technicians believe that "history repeats itself" because humans are "creatures of habit." As a result, technicians believe that investors will exhibit behavior in the current period that is similar to behavior observed in the past when they recognize conditions that are familiar.

- **What general factors should investors examine when evaluating the attractiveness of investments?** Suppose that you are considering investing your hard-earned money in the common stock of a particular company. Most professional investors would advise that you should be aware of the condition of the economy, the company's industry, and the company. As a result, you should perform three "types" of analyses when determining the attractiveness of the company: (1) economic analysis, where you form expectations about the future condition of the economy and its effect on the company; (2) industry analysis, where you form expectations about the future of the industry in which the company operates, as well as where the company will be positioned in the industry in the future; and (3) company analysis, where you form expectations about the future financial position of the company to determine its attractiveness as an investment.

- **What are some techniques that can be used to value the common stock of a corporation?** Three stock valuation techniques are described in the chapter: (1) the dividend discount model (DDM), which requires you to compute the present value of the dividends that the stock is expected to pay during its life; (2) the P/E ratio technique, which suggests that the appropriate value of a stock can be determined by multiplying expected earnings per share by a "normal" P/E ratio for the firm or its industry; and (3) the economic value added (EVA) approach, which is based on the concept that, to maintain its value, the firm's earnings must be sufficient to compensate those who provide its funds—that is, the firm must earn a high enough return to sufficiently reward stockholders and bondholders for using their funds.

- **What general rules do professionals advise individuals to follow when investing their money?** Successful investment professionals would recommend that individual investors (1) be disciplined by giving a particular investment strategy a chance to work, (2) have a basic understanding of the company in which he or she invests, (3) select firms with strong financial positions that have good potential for growth in the future, and (4) get out of an investment when it no longer satisfies specific investment goals, but don't make this decision based on the short-term performance of the company.

The concepts presented in this chapter should help you understand actions that you can take to make better decisions about your personal investments. The material in the chapter was presented in a manner that permits you to relate its application to personal financial decision making. Some of the concepts that you should use when making personal investment decisions are:

CHAPTER PRINCIPLES
–Personal Finance

- **Understand what you are doing!** When you invest your hard-earned money, you want to make good decisions. To do so, you should understand what you are doing. Although you don't have to be an expert to invest, you should have a decent understanding of the financial markets and the investments that you might be interested in purchasing. There are numerous resources available to you, both hard copy and electronic, that provide information about personal investing.

- **Do your homework!** To make informed decisions about investing, you should examine the attractiveness of the investments you are considering. Because a company does not operate in isolation, when evaluating common stock, not only should you determine how financially sound it is, but you must also determine how industry and economic activities affect the firm's operations.

- **Keep current!** After you invest your money, you must still keep current with the activities that take place in the company, its industry, and the economy. Investing is a dynamic process. As a result, to ensure that your investment objectives are being met, you must continue to monitor events and factors that affect your investment position and make changes when necessary.

- **Be aware of the advice of professionals!** Professionals recommend that you follow a disciplined investment strategy. In other words, don't flip-flop with your decisions just because you don't see the intended results immediately. Most professionals would advise that investing should be driven by long-term objectives, not by short-term greed.

QUESTIONS

17-1 Differentiate between the fundamental analysis and technical analysis approaches used for stock valuation and selection.

17-2 For each of the following cases, identify whether the economic variable leads, lags, or is coincidental with economic movements. Discuss your reasoning.

Economic Variable	Leading	Lagging	Coincident
a. New building permits	_____	_____	_____
b. Stock market	_____	_____	_____
c. Money supply	_____	_____	_____
d. Prime interest rate	_____	_____	_____
e. Consumer prices	_____	_____	_____
f. Industrial production	_____	_____	_____
g. Personal wages/salaries	_____	_____	_____

17-3 Explain how the Federal Reserve manages the monetary policy of the United States. If the economy was in a recession characterized by high interest rates, what actions might the Fed take to exert downward pressure on those interest rates?

17-4 Some economists contend that the deficit spending practices followed by the U.S. government artificially inflate prices and interest rates. Explain their rationale. Can you think of any arguments that can be used to defend deficit spending as a means to support economic activity?

17-5 Indicate whether the industries in the following list should be classified as cyclical, defensive, or neither. As you make your classifications, consider the reasons why you would make such designations.

	Cyclical	Defensive	Neither
a. Automobile manufacturing	_____	_____	_____
b. Debt collection services	_____	_____	_____
c. Jewelry	_____	_____	_____
d. Food processing/groceries	_____	_____	_____
e. Personal computer software	_____	_____	_____
f. Appliance manufacturing	_____	_____	_____

17-6 Given the circumstances in the following list, determine which stage of the industry life cycle individual investors would prefer. Include your rationale.

	Life-Cycle Stage		
	Introductory	Expansion	Mature
a. The purpose of the investments is to supplement retirement income.	_____	_____	_____
b. Susan recently graduated from college and is just beginning her career.	_____	_____	_____
c. Steve wants to use some of his lottery winnings to speculate in stocks.	_____	_____	_____
d. An investor wants a stock that pays dividends and also promises high future growth.	_____	_____	_____
e. Skyler, who now is 12 years old, just received a small inheritance from her aunt.	_____	_____	_____

17-7 Describe the dividend discount model (DDM), P/E ratio, and economic value added (EVA) approaches used to value common stock. Under what conditions does each approach provide a good estimate of a stock's value?

17-8 Discuss the basic concepts upon which technical analysis is founded. What information do technicians hope to glean from their charts and graphs and the technical indicators?

17-9 Discuss the common themes that are found in the investment philosophies and selection criteria of the professional investors named in Table 17-4. Do these commonalties suggest anything about investment strategies and behaviors that should be followed by average investors?

17-10 Assume that the financial markets are strong-form efficient. Would there be any reason for investors to conduct investment analyses? Why?

SELF-TEST PROBLEMS

Solutions appear in Appendix B.

ST-1 Define each of the following terms: **Key Terms**

a. Fundamental analysis; fundamentalists

b. Technical analysis; technicians

c. Intrinsic value

d. Economic analysis; industry analysis; company analysis

e. Business cycle; expansion; contraction; recession

    f. Economic indicators; leading economic indicators; lagging economic indicators; coincident economic indicators

    g. Monetary policy; fiscal policy; deficit spending

    h. Cyclical industry; defensive industry

    i. Industry life cycle

    j. Growth stocks; value stocks

    k. Dividend discount model (DDM); P/E ratio; economic value added (EVA)

    l. Bar chart; trendline; trendline penetration

    m. Dow theory; moving averages

    n. Market breadth indicators; advance/decline line; sentiment indicators

    o. Abnormal returns; weak-form efficiency; semistrong-form efficiency; strong-form efficiency

Valuation Using EVA and P/E Ratio

ST-2 American Transmitter (AT) is a telecommunications firm that currently does not pay a dividend. The following information about AT has been gathered from various sources:

Before-tax cost of debt	8.0%
Cost of equity	15.0%
EBIT	$ 600,000
Total capital	$2,000,000
Debt/assets ratio	65.0%
EPS	$ 2.64
Shares outstanding	100,000
Marginal tax rate	40.0%

    a. Compute AT's weighted average cost of capital.

    b. Compute the economic value added (EVA) for AT in the current operating period. Is AT a good investment?

    c. Given the answer from part (b), compute the EVA dividend that AT could pay without harming the value of the firm.

    d. Estimate the market price per share assuming that AT normally has a P/E ratio equal to 15×.

Moving Averages

ST-3 The following table contains the closing prices for the common stock of Banquet Caterers for the last 10 days of trading:

Day	Price
1	$76.00
2	76.50
3	76.75
4	77.10
5	77.20
6	77.85
7	78.20
8	77.95
9	77.90
10	78.10

    a. Compute a 5-day moving average for the entire period. (*Hint:* You should have six moving average values when you are finished.)

b. Based on your series of moving averages, comment on whether you believe the stock price is trending upward or downward.

ST-4 Anchor Shipping has paid a dividend for more than 50 years, and this practice is expected to continue for a long time to come. Analysts have evaluated the financial position of Anchor and discovered that past dividends have grown by a constant rate of 6 percent each year. The most recent dividend payment, which was made yesterday, was $3.40 per share. The company has not been able to compute the rate of return required by its shareholders. The following information about market conditions has been gathered:

Stock Valuation Using DDM

Risk-free rate	8.0%
Market return	18.0%
β for Anchor Shipping	1.6

a. According to the capital asset pricing model, what is the rate of return required by Anchor's stockholders?

b. Using the constant growth version of the dividend discount model (DDM), what should be the current value of Anchor's common stock?

PROBLEMS

17-1 The current price of ADM's stock, P_0, is $20, and the company is expected to pay a $2.20 dividend next year. If the appropriate required rate of return for ADM's stock is 15 percent, what should be the price of the stock in 1 year, $\hat{P}_1$? Assume that the company has achieved constant growth.

Stock Valuation Using DDM

17-2 Steel Safety Corporation is in the introductory stage of the industry life cycle, so its sales and earnings have grown rapidly in recent years. To date, the company has chosen to retain all of its earnings rather than pay dividends. Analysts have projected that Steel Safety will continue to retain all of its earnings for another 10 years. Eleven years from today, the company is expected to pay its first dividend, which is predicted to be $25 per share. Analysts have also determined that the appropriate required rate of return on Steel Safety's stock is 16 percent.

Nonconstant Growth Stock Valuation

a. Compute the value of the stock today assuming that once the dividend payments start, the dollar amount will remain constant at $25 per share per year. (*Hint:* The first dividend is not paid until 11 years from today.)

b. Assuming the dividend will grow at a constant rate of 5 percent per year once the payments begin, what is the value of the stock today?

17-3 J. D. Agribusiness has $500,000 invested capital, 60 percent of which is in the form of debt. With this capital structure, the company has a weighted average cost of capital equal to 12 percent. According to J. D.'s latest income statement, the firm's operating income is $100,000 and its marginal tax rate is 40 percent. Under the EVA approach, is J. D. Agribusiness a good company in which to invest?

EVA Analysis

17-4 The stock of East/West Maps is currently selling for $122.40, which equates to a P/E ratio of 30×.

Valuation Using P/E Ratios

a. Using the P/E ratio, compute the current EPS of East/West.

b. Assume that earnings next year increase by 20 percent, but the P/E ratio drops to 25×, which is more in line with the industry average. What will be the price of East/West's stock next year?

c. If an investor purchases the stock today for $122.40 and sells it in 1 year at the price computed in part (b), what rate of return would be earned?

EVA Analysis   17-5 RJS Foods reported that its net income was $65,000 last year. The firm's interest expense was reported to be $40,000, and its marginal tax rate was 35 percent. According to the company's balance sheet, invested capital equals $800,000.

a. Compute the operating income (EBIT) that RJS Foods generated last year.

b. If the WACC for RJS Foods is 12 percent, what was its EVA last year?

Constant Growth Stock   17-6 Zycard, Inc., has determined that stockholders require a 15 percent rate of
Valuation return to invest in its common stock. The last dividend paid by the company was $2.50 per share.

a. What will be the value of Zycard's stock if investors expect future dividends to grow at a constant annual rate of (1) 0 percent, (2) 5 percent, and (3) 10 percent?

b. Describe what steps you might take to estimate the appropriate future growth rate for Zycard.

Nonconstant Growth   17-7 Consumer Friendly Collections (CFT) has grown at a rate of 30 percent in
Stock Valuation each of the last 5 years. This same growth rate is expected to continue for the next 3 years. After 3 years, growth will decline to 15 percent, where it will remain for 5 years; growth will then decline to 5 percent, the rate at which the firm will grow for the remainder of its life. CFT's beta coefficient is 1.5, the expected market return is 14 percent, and the risk-free rate of return is 6 percent. Currently, the economy is experiencing normal growth, and economists' projections indicate that this type of economy will continue at least for the next 5 years.

a. Using the Capital Asset Pricing Model, compute the required rate of return for CFT stock.

b. If it just paid a dividend equal to $2.40 per share, what should be the market value of CFT's stock today?

c. If you suspected the economy was going to enter into a long-term recessionary period 1 year from now, would you make any adjustments to the expected growth rates given here? Explain why or why not.

Computing Moving   17-8 The S&P 500 end-of-month closing prices from June 2006 through May 2008
Averages follow:

Date	S&P 500	Date	S&P 500
Jun-06	1270.20	Jun-07	1503.35
Jul-06	1276.66	Jul-07	1455.27
Aug-06	1303.82	Aug-07	1473.99
Sep-06	1335.85	Sep-07	1526.75
Oct-06	1377.94	Oct-07	1549.38
Nov-06	1400.63	Nov-07	1481.14
Dec-06	1418.30	Dec-07	1468.36
Jan-07	1438.24	Jan-08	1378.55
Feb-07	1406.82	Feb-08	1330.63
Mar-07	1420.86	Mar-08	1322.70
Apr-07	1482.37	Apr-08	1385.59
May-07	1530.62	May-08	1400.38

   a. Compute the 6-month moving averages associated with this series of data.

   b. Plot the results of your computations in part (a). Describe any patterns, or trends, that are apparent.

   c. According to your interpretations of the graph, in which direction do you think the market should move during the last half of 2008? (*Note:* At the time you work this problem, you should be able to compare your prediction to what actually happened in the market.)

17-9 Georgetown Motorcars (GM) common stock currently is selling for $71.44, which is 19 times its earnings per share (EPS). The most recent dividend paid by GM was $2.00 per share.   **P/E Ratios and Valuation**

   a. What is GM's current EPS?

   b. What is GM's current dividend payout ratio? (*Hint:* The payout ratio refers to the percentage of earnings that is paid as dividends.)

   c. Assume that GM does not expect to grow in the future and investors require a 12 percent return to invest in the company's stock. Compute both the dividend yield and the growth provided by GM's stock. (*Hint:* The dividend yield is the dividend divided by the current market price of the stock.)

   d. The industry P/E ratio normally varies from around 11× to 14×. Using these industry averages, estimate the price at which GM should sell.

   e. Discuss some factors that might justify GM's P/E ratio being greater than the industry average.

17-10 Consider the following operating information gathered from three firms that are identical except for their capital structures: **EVA Analysis**

	Firm A	Firm B	Firm C
Total invested capital	$100,000	$100,000	$100,000
Debt/assets ratio	0.80	0.50	0.20
Shares outstanding	6,100	8,300	10,000
Cost of debt	14%	12%	10%
Cost of equity	26%	22%	20%
Operating income, EBIT	$ 25,000	$ 25,000	$ 25,000
Net income	$ 8,970	$ 12,350	$ 14,950
Marginal tax rate	0.35	0.35	0.35

   a. Compute the weighted average cost of capital (WACC) for each firm.

   b. Compute the economic value added (EVA) for each firm.

   c. Based on the results of your computations in part (b), which firm would be considered the best investment? Why?

   d. Assume the industry P/E ratio generally is 15×. Using the industry norm, estimate the price for each stock.

   e. What factors might cause you to adjust the P/E ratio value used in part (d) so that it is more appropriate?

17-11 Backhaus Beer Brewers (BBB) just announced that the current fiscal year's income statement reports its net income to be $1.2 million. BBB's marginal tax rate is 40 percent, and its interest expense for the year was $1.5 million. The company has $8 million of invested capital, of which 60 percent is debt.   **EVA Analysis**

In addition, BBB tries to maintain a weighted average cost of capital (WACC) near 12 percent.

a. Compute the operating income (EBIT) that BBB earned in the current year.

b. What is BBB's economic value added (EVA) for the current year?

c. BBB has 500,000 shares of common stock outstanding. According to the EVA value you computed in part (b), how much can BBB pay in dividends per share before the value of the firm would start to decrease? If BBB doesn't pay any dividends, what would you expect to happen to the value of the firm?

Valuation Using DDM and P/E Ratios

17-12 The investment public has shown great interest in the stock of Rollover Beds Corporation, because the company has been growing at an average annual rate equal to 25 percent. Jason Jackson decided to evaluate the company to determine whether he should include the stock in his investment portfolio. Jason's analysis has led him to conclude that the current rate of growth will not end within the next 30 years. He also has determined that the appropriate required rate of return for Rollover Beds' stock is 20 percent. Following is some other information that Jason examined:

EBIT	$300,000
Net income	$120,000
Total dividends paid	$ 72,000
Shares outstanding	100,000
Industry P/E ratio	25×

a. Compute the most recent dividend per share, D_0. What is the dividend expected to be next year, $\hat{D}_1$?

b. Using the information provided in the problem and the result of your computation in part (a), apply the constant growth DDM to determine the current price of Rollover Beds.

c. Does your answer in part (b) make sense? Explain why you arrived at the answer you did. Given the information available, is there a more appropriate approach to estimating the price of the stock?

d. Apply the P/E ratio approach to value Rollover Beds' stock. Compare the result of this computation to the result from part (b). Which would you consider a better estimate for the price?

Integrative Problem

Stock Valuation and Selection

17-13 Michelle Delatorre, the professional tennis player first introduced in the Integrative Problem in Chapter 4, has returned to your office at Balik and Kiefer to ask some questions about stock valuation and selection. Ms. Delatorre intends to retain your services as her investment adviser and manager, but she wants to "dabble" in the stock market with a small amount of the winnings she earned in tournaments last year. She has posed some questions relating to stock valuation and selection that she would like help answering.

a. What is the difference between evaluating stocks using fundamental analysis and technical analysis?

b. What is a business cycle? What does it mean when we say that the economy is in an expansion? What does it mean when we say that the economy is in a contraction?

c. What approaches can we use to forecast business cycles? Is it difficult to predict business cycles? Why?

d. How are business cycles affected by the monetary policy carried out by the Federal Reserve and by the fiscal policy followed by the government?

e. Why is it necessary to evaluate the industry within which a company operates before making an investment decision? What factors should an investor examine when conducting an industry analysis?

f. How can knowledge of the industry life cycle concept aid an individual with his or her investment decisions?

g. What is the primary reason an investor needs to examine the financial position of a firm?

h. Describe the three valuation techniques discussed in this chapter and indicate when it is appropriate to use each one.

i. Ms. Delatorre has been following a company (Omega Optical) that was recommended by one of her fellow tennis players. The more she investigates the company, the greater her interest becomes. Right now, she does not know how to estimate the value of Omega Optical's stock. Ms. Delatorre has collected quite a bit of information about the company through her own analysis. The results of her investigations have yielded the following information:

EBIT	$110,000
Net income	$ 60,060
Marginal tax rate	35%
Invested capital	$550,000
Before-tax cost of debt, r_d	8.0%
Cost of equity, r_s	18%
Debt/assets ratio	40%
Shares outstanding	40,000
Current dividend per share, D_0	0

In addition to this information, Ms. Delatorre has given you some analysts' forecasts that she has gathered from various investment information subscriptions she receives. The consensus of the experts is that Omega will initiate its first dividend payment 5 years from today, when it pays each investor $4 per share. In the following year, the dividend payment will increase by 25 percent, then the growth in dividends will decrease by 2 percent per year until it stabilizes at the constant, or normal, growth of 5 percent. In other words, dividend growth in Year 6 will be 25 percent, it will decrease to 23 percent in Year 7, it will decrease to 21 percent in Year 8, and so on, until Year 16, when dividend growth settles at 5 percent for the remaining life of the firm.

(1) Using the dividend discount model, compute the value of Omega's common stock.

(2) Ms. Delatorre's cache of information indicates that the average P/E ratio for firms with operations similar to Omega's is 25.

Using the P/E valuation approach, what would be the estimate for the price of the stock?

(3) Compute Omega's EVA. According to this computation, is Omega a good investment? Why?

j. Explain why the results you found in part (i) are not the same for each computation. What do you believe the value for the stock should be?

k. Describe some measures used by technical analysts that might be helpful to Ms. Delatorre's effort to value Omega's stock.

l. If you had to summarize the advice of the experts contained in Table 17-4 and give Ms. Delatorre three pieces of general advice about investing, what would you tell her?

m. Describe the concept of informational efficiency in the financial markets. If the markets are efficient, of what use is investment analysis? What investment advice would you give Ms. Delatorre about investing in an efficient market?

COMPUTER-RELATED PROBLEM

Work the problem in this section only if you are using the computer problem spreadsheet.

EVA Analysis   **17-14** Use the model in File C17 to solve this problem. Refer back to Problem 17-10. Rework parts (a) through (d) using the computerized model, but make the following changes. Consider each change to be independent of the others; that is, in each case, assume all values except those to be changed remain the same as originally stated in Problem 17-10.

a. All else equal, except the debt/assets ratio is 70 percent for Firm A, 40 percent for Firm B, and 30 percent for Firm C.

b. All else equal, except the EBIT for each firm is $15,000.

c. All else equal, except the marginal tax rate for each firm is 40 percent.

Using Spreadsheets to Solve Financial Problems

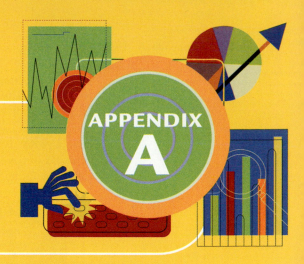

APPENDIX A

Like calculators, spreadsheets were developed to make mathematical computations easier to solve. In this appendix, we provide a brief tutorial on how to use spreadsheets to solve the problems discussed in the book. In the explanations that follow, we use Excel 2007 to illustrate the spreadsheet applications.

SETTING UP MATHEMATICAL RELATIONSHIPS

It is easy to set up relationships to solve mathematical problems that require you to use such arithmetic operators as addition, subtraction, multiplication, division, and so forth. Following are the common arithmetic operators used by Excel:

Operator	Description	Function
+	Plus sign	Addition
−	Minus sign	Subtraction
*	Asterisk	Multiplication
/	Forward slash	Division
^	Caret	Exponentiation

To solve a problem, put the cursor in the cell that you want to contain the final answer, type an equal sign (=), enter the relationship that you want to solve, and then press "Enter" to generate the result. For example, suppose that you want to compute how much $100 invested today will grow to in 3 years if it earns 6 percent interest compounded annually. This problem can be easily solved by entering into one of the cells of a spreadsheet the relationship shown in Equation 9-1 in Chapter 9. Following is the solution:

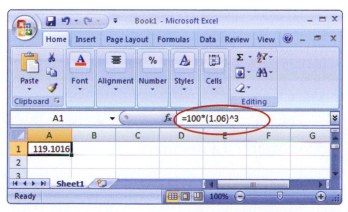

The equation that was input into cell **A1,** which is shown in the circled area, is $FV = 100*(1.06)^3$, which solves for $100(1.06)^3 = 119.1016$.

Although it is easy to a solve problem by defining the relationship and entering numbers in a cell, it is better to create a table that contains the values needed to solve a particular relationship and then set up a general solution that refers to the locations of the specific cells that contain the needed values. For example, for the current computation, the spreadsheet might be set up as follows:

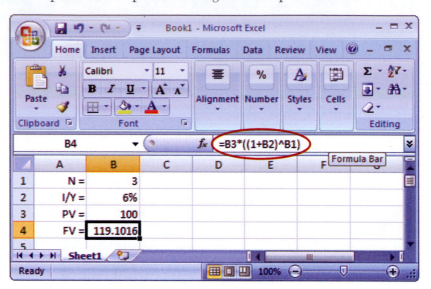

As you can see by the equation that is shown in the circled area, cell **B4** contains the relationship that computes the future value of the $100 investment. But the equation that is contained in cell **B4** refers to the cells where the values that are needed to solve the problem are located. By setting up the solution in this manner, you can change any of the input values and the answer using the new value(s) will be shown immediately in cell **B4.** Try setting up your spreadsheet as shown here. You should get the answer shown previously. Now change the interest rate to 10 percent. When you input 0.10 and press "Enter," you will see the result in cell **B4** change to 133.1, or $133.10. Note that when you input a percent into the spreadsheet, you must either enter the number in decimal form—for example, 0.10—or as a number followed by a % sign—for example, 10%. If you enter the number without a % sign, the spreadsheet interprets the number literally and solves the problem accordingly. For example, if you enter 6 rather than 0.06 or 6% in the original computation, the result shown in cell **B4** will be:

$$FV = 100(1 + 6)^3 = 100(7)^3 = 34,300$$

which is an incorrect answer for the situation we set up.

Although it is fairly easy to set up relationships for most of the problems presented in Chapter 9, it is even easier to use the preprogrammed functions contained in the spreadsheet. In the remainder of this appendix we show you how to use the time value of money functions that are programmed into spreadsheets to solve the problems introduced in Chapter 9.

Solving Time Value of Money (TVM) Problems Using Preprogrammed Functions

The functions that are programmed into spreadsheets are the same as those programmed into financial calculators. In this section, we show how to use an Excel spreadsheet to solve some of the examples given in Chapter 9. Remember that in Chapter 9 we showed only the spreadsheet setup and the final solution to each problem. Here we show the specific steps that should be followed when using the TVM functions. Note that we label the values entered into the cells of the spreadsheet (Column A) the same as the TVM keys on a Texas Instruments BAII Plus financial calculator, which is the same calculator that was used to solve the problems presented in Chapter 9.

Using Excel 2007, you can access the TVM functions from either the "Home" menu or the "Formulas" menu. To access the functions from the "Formulas" menu, click the "Insert Function" icon that appears on the far left of the horizontal menu bar. To access the functions from the "Home" menu, either click the f_x icon on the formula bar or click the *down arrow* that is to the right of the Σ sign in the "Editing" box on the far right of the horizontal menu bar that appears on the "Home" menu. The following screenshot shows the location of the f_x icon (circled in green) and Σ sign (circled in red) on the "Home" menu:

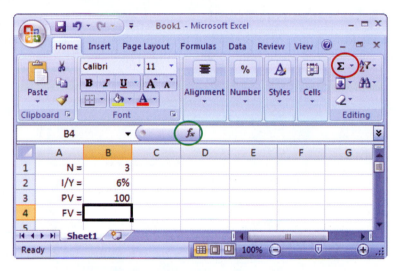

A small menu will appear after you click the *down arrow* next to the Σ sign; click the "More Functions..." options at the bottom of this menu. Whether you enter through the "Home" menu or the "Formulas" menu, the following functions menu will appear when you enter the "Insert Functions" option:

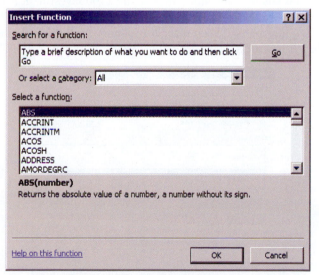

The "Search for a function:" option at the top of the menu allows you to search for all of the functions that fit the type of computation that you want to perform. You can also select a particular category of computations by using the drop-down menu labeled "Or select a category:". Because we are going to use the financial functions, click the "Or select a category:" drop-down menu, and then click the category labeled "Financial," which will give you access to the financial functions that are needed to solve time value of money problems. These financial functions will appear in the large menu labeled "Select a function:", which is located in the middle of the "Insert Function" menu.

Solving for Future Value (FV): Lump-Sum Amount and Annuity

The same spreadsheet function—FV—is used to solve for the future value of a lump-sum amount and the future value of an annuity.

FV of a Lump-Sum Amount

If you want to find the FV in 3 years of $100 invested today at 6 percent compounded annually, you might want to set up your spreadsheet as follows:

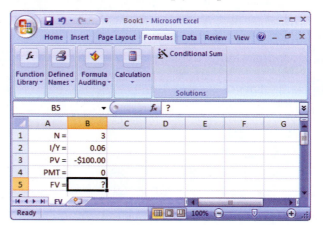

Note that in this case, we entered the interest rate as a decimal. Also, the amount invested, $100, is entered as a negative number, just as it is when solving this problem using a financial calculator—that is, the $100 investment is a cash outflow.

To solve for the future value, place the cursor in cell **B5,** click the "Insert Function" (f_x) option on the "Formulas" menu, and scroll down the list of functions that are included in the "Select a function:" menu until you reach FV.

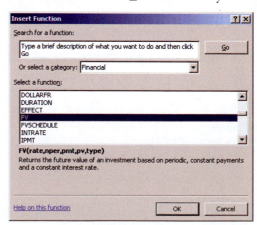

When you click "OK," or double-click "FV," the following dialog box will appear:

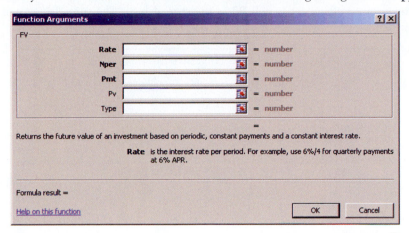

"Rate" represents the interest rate per period, "Nper" is the number of periods interest is earned, "Pmt" is the periodic, or annuity, payment (we will use this later), "Pv" is the present value of the amount, and "Type" refers to the type of annuity payment (0 = ordinary annuity; 1 = annuity due). You can view the definition of each variable by placing the cursor in the row in which the variable is located. For example, the definition for "Rate" is shown in the dialog box above.

To solve our problem, you should refer to the appropriate cells in the spreadsheet that contain the values requested. As a result, you should insert **B2** in the first row of the dialog box (Rate), **B1** in the second row (Nper), **B4** in the third row (Pmt), and **B3** in the fourth row (Pv), and you should leave the last row blank so that the dialog box looks like the following:

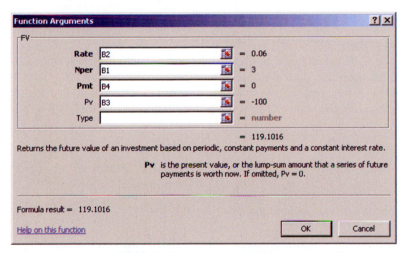

Note that you can also insert the appropriate location for each row in the dialog box by clicking the small box that contains a red arrow on the right side of the row, placing the cursor in the cell that contains the value, and then pressing "Enter." Also note that the content of each cell to which you refer is given to the right of the row in which the cell is referenced. For example, to the far right of the row that contains the cell reference for "Rate" the number 0.06 appears, which indicates that the numerical value for the rate of return that is used in the computation of the future value is 6 percent. When enough information is entered in the dialog box, you will see the result of the computation at the bottom left of the box (as shown above).

Once the locations of all the appropriate values are in the dialog box, click "OK," and the answer will appear in cell **B5** in the spreadsheet. The spreadsheet will now appear as follows:

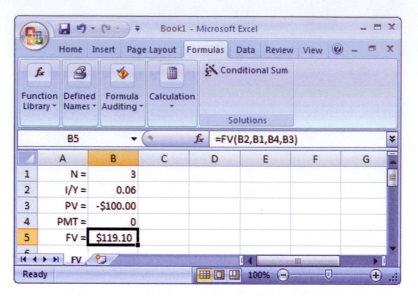

The future value amount we computed here, $119.10, is the same result as we found in the previous section. If you press the F2 key, you will see the contents of cell **B5,** which should be = FV(B2,B1,B4,B3).

FV OF AN ANNUITY

To solve for the future value of an annuity, we use the same financial function that we discussed in the previous section—that is, FV. For example, in Chapter 9, we solved for a 3-year $100 annuity with an opportunity cost equal to 5 percent. Using the same spreadsheet setup shown earlier, change the values so that N = 3, I/Y = 0.05, PV = 0, and PMT = −100. You will see that the value for FV changes so that it is equal to $315.25, which is the same result we found in Chapter 9—that is, FVA = $315.25.

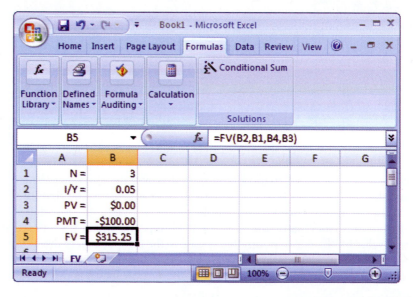

The result given here is the future value of an ordinary annuity. To find the future value of an annuity due, place the cursor in cell **B5** and click the "Insert Function" option on the "Formulas" menu. When the dialog box appears, place a 1 in the last row, which is labeled "Type," so that the inputs are as follows:

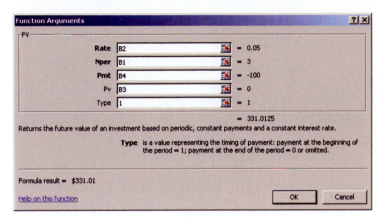

You will notice that the result shown in the menu changes to $331.01, and when you click "OK," the result appears in cell **B5**. As you can see on the menu, when you enter 1 in the last row, you change the timing of the cash flows from the end of the period to the beginning of the period for the purposes of the computation. You can also create another cell in your main spreadsheet—perhaps cell **B6**—labeled Type, enter a 0 when computing the value of an ordinary annuity or a 1 when computing the value of an annuity due, and reference this cell location in the "Function Arguments" dialog box shown here. The result of the computation is the same as we found in Chapter 9.

Solving for Present Value (PV): Lump-Sum Amount and Annuity

To find the PV using a spreadsheet, follow the same steps as described to solve for FV, except use the PV financial function. The menus are the same as in the previous section, except the value for the future value (labeled "Fv" in the menu) is a required input rather than the present value (labeled "Pv") that was required previously. For example, if you want to determine the present value of $315.25 to be received in 3 years if your opportunity cost is 5 percent, the spreadsheet setup and the PV function window would be:

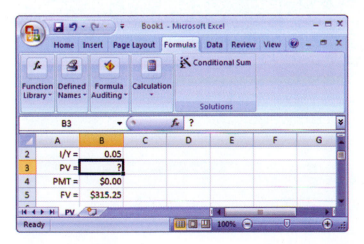

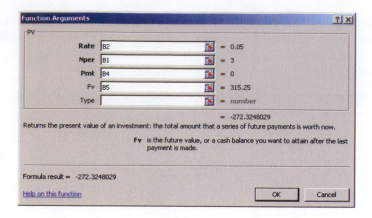

The result is the same as was reported in Chapter 9, $272.32.

Solving for r: Lump-Sum Amount and Annuity

Suppose you want to determine the rate of return that would be earned if you purchase an investment for $78.35 that will pay $100 after 5 years. To solve this problem using a spreadsheet, use the "Rate" function. The spreadsheet might be set up as follows:

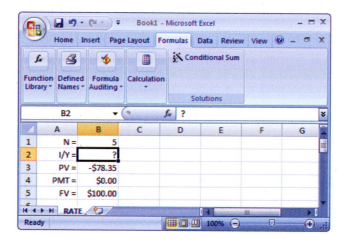

Once the appropriate cell locations are entered, the "Rate" function dialog box should appear as follows:

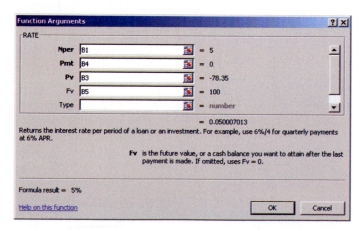

As you can see, the result of the computation is 5 percent, which will appear in cell **B2** when you press "OK." You would use the same function to find the interest rate, r, for an annuity.

Solving for n: Lump-Sum Amount and Annuity

Suppose you want to determine how many years it will take $68.30 invested today to grow to $100 if the interest rate is 10 percent. To solve this problem using a spreadsheet, use the "Nper" function. The spreadsheet might be set up as follows:

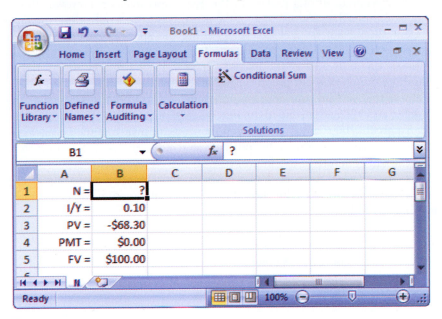

Once the appropriate cell locations are entered, the "Nper" function dialog box will appear as follows:

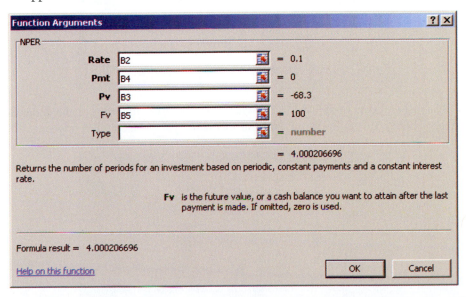

As you can see, the result of the computation is 4 years, which will appear in cell **B1** when you press "OK." You would use the same function to solve for n, the number of periods, for an annuity.

Solving for Present Value and Future Value: Uneven Cash Flows

To solve for the PV of an uneven cash flow stream, use the NPV function. Take care, however, to ensure that you understand what this spreadsheet function actually computes. The computation of NPV as we presented in Chapter 13 in this book represents the net present value of a series of cash flows that include the initial amount that is invested in Period 0 and the *future* cash flows that the investment is expected to generate during its life. In the Excel spreadsheet, however, the NPV function computes the present value of the *future* cash flows only; thus, the current investment should not be included when using the spreadsheet's NPV function. Here we use the NPV function to compute the present value of a series of uneven cash flows. Appendix 13B at the end of Chapter 13 shows how to use the NPV function to compute the net present value of a capital asset.

Suppose that you are considering purchasing an investment that promises to pay $500, $800, and $300 at the end of the next 3 years, respectively. If your opportunity cost is 8 percent, how much should you pay for the investment? To answer this question, you need to determine the present value of the series of cash flows that the investment will generate in the future.

To compute the present value of a series of uneven cash flows using a spreadsheet, we must use the NPV function. For the current situation, we can set up the spreadsheet as follows:

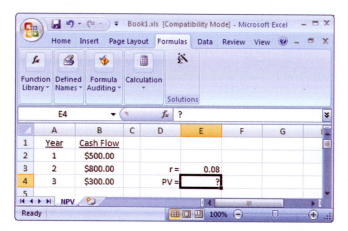

Place the cursor in cell **E4** as shown, select the NPV function in the financial category of the Insert Function, and the following dialog box should appear:

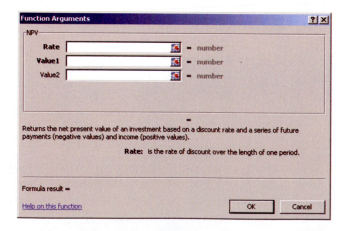

The description of this function indicates that the result of the computation is the present value of all the *future* cash flows—both inflows and outflows—associated with the investment. Enter the appropriate cell locations for the values needed to compute the present value of the cash flows given in the spreadsheet. In the dialog box, Value1 refers to the series of cash flows. You can click the arrow on the right side of the row labeled Value1 and use the cursor to highlight cells **B2** through **B4.** Now the dialog box shows the cell locations of the needed values and it will appear as follows:

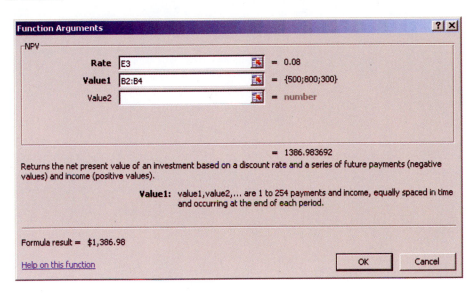

The result of the computation, which is shown at the bottom of the dialog box, is $1,386.98. When you click the "OK" button, this result will appear in cell **E4** of the spreadsheet. Thus, the present value of the series of cash flows is $1,386.98, which is the same result we found in Chapter 9 using a financial calculator.

To compute the future value of the series of uneven cash flows, first compute its present value, and then compound this value to the future period at the appropriate opportunity cost. For our example, the future value would be:

$$FV = \$1,386.98(1.08)^3 = \$1,747.20$$

This relationship can be entered into the spreadsheet so that it is automatically computed.

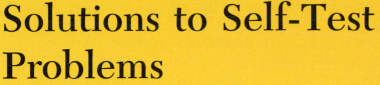

Solutions to Self-Test Problems

Note: We do not show an answer for ST-1 problems because they are verbal rather than quantitative in nature. For the ST-1 problems, you can refer to the marginal glossary definitions or relevant chapter sections to check your responses.

CHAPTER 2

ST-2 a. $100,000,000/10 = $10,000,000 per year. Because the $10 million will be used to retire (repay) the bonds immediately, no interest will be earned on it.

b. The debt service requirements will decline. As the amount of bonds outstanding declines, so will the interest payments each year (amounts are in millions of dollars):

Payment Period (1)	Amount of Outstanding Bonds (2)	Sinking Fund Payment (3)	Interest Payment 0.12 × (2) = (4)	Total Debt Service (3) + (4) = (5)
1	$100	$10	$12.0	$22.0
2	90	10	10.8	20.8
3	80	10	9.6	19.6
.	.	.	.	.
.	.	.	.	.
.	.	.	.	.
10	10	10	1.2	11.2

Note from the table that the total cash debt service requirement decreases by $1.2 million each year because there is $10 million less debt at the beginning of each year, which means $1.2 million less interest has to be paid each year.

c. Annual debt service costs will be $100,000,000(0.12) + $6,582,009 = $18,582,009.

d. If interest rates rose, causing the bond's price to fall, the company would use open market purchases. This would reduce its debt service requirements.

CHAPTER 3

ST-2 **a.** Net proceeds = $150,000,000 − 0.07($150,000,000) − $225,000

$$= \$139{,}275{,}000$$

b. Number of shares = $150,000,000/$25 = 6,000,000

c. Needs = $150,000,000 = Amount issued − 0.07(Amount issued) − $225,000

$$= (\text{Amount issued}) \times (1.0 - 0.07) - \$225{,}000$$

$150,000,000 + $225,000 = 0.93(Amount issued)

Amount issued = $150,225,000/0.93 = $161,532,258.10

Number of shares = $161,532,258.10/$25

$$= 6{,}461{,}290.3 \approx 6{,}461{,}291$$

To see that this is the correct number of shares to issue, compute the net proceeds the firm would receive if 6,461,291 shares are issued at $25 per share:

Net proceeds = (6,461,291 × $25) − 0.07(6,461,291 × $25) − $225,000

$$= \$161{,}532{,}275 - \$11{,}532{,}259.25 = \$150{,}000{,}015.80$$

The additional $15.80 results because the firm has to issue a full share rather than 0.3 shares.

CHAPTER 4

ST-2 **a.** If the Fed wants to increase the money supply, it should *buy* Treasury securities because it pays for the securities by increasing reserves at financial institutions. The amount of securities the Fed should buy is solved as follows:

$$\frac{\text{Maximum change in}}{\text{the money supply}} = \frac{\Delta \text{ Excess reserves}}{\text{Reserve requirement}} = \$110 \text{ billion}$$

$$= \frac{\Delta \text{ Excess reserves}}{0.10}$$

Δ Excess reserves = $110 billion × 0.10 = $11.0 billion

$$= \Delta \text{ Reserves}(1 - \text{Reserve requirement})$$

$$\Delta \text{ Reserves } = \frac{\Delta \text{ Excess reserves}}{\left(1 - \dfrac{\text{Reserve}}{\text{requirement}}\right)} = \frac{\$11.0 \text{ billion}}{(1 - 0.10)} = \$12.2 \text{ billion}$$

Thus, the Fed must purchase $12.2 billion in Treasury securities. This action would create immediate excess reserves equal to $11.0 billion, which would then create ($11.0 billion)/(0.10) = $110 million in additional money.

b. Solve this problem the same as above, except substitute $50 billion for the $110 million. The answer should be $5.6 billion, which represents the amount of securities the Fed needs to *buy* to reduce the money supply by $50 billion.

CHAPTER 5

ST-2 **a.** Dollar return = (100 shares)($78 − $80) + (100 shares)($5) = $300

      b. Yield = $300/(100 × $80) = $300/$8,000 = 0.0375 = 3.75%

ST-3 **a.** Average = (2% + 3% + 5% + 6%)/4 = 16%/4 = 4.0%

      b. $r_{\text{T-bond}} = r^* + IP = 3.0\% + 4.0\% = 7.0\%$

      c. If the 5-year T-bond rate is 11 percent, the inflation rate is expected to average approximately 8% − 3% = 5% during the next 5 years. Thus, the implied Year 5 inflation rate is 9 percent:

$$IP_5 = 5\% = (2\% + 3\% + 5\% + 6\% + Infl_5)/5$$
$$25\% = 16\% + Infl_5$$
$$Infl_5 = 9\%$$

CHAPTER 6

ST-2

	2010	2011	2012
Thompson's taxes as a corporation:			
Income before salary and taxes	$60,000.0	$ 90,000.0	$110,000.0
Less: Salary	(40,000.0)	(40,000.0)	(40,000.0)
Taxable income, corporate	20,000.0	50,000.0	70,000.0
Total corporate tax	($ 3,000.0)[a]	($ 7,500.0)	($ 12,500.0)
Salary	$40,000.0	$ 40,000.0	$ 40,000.0
Less: Exemptions and deductions	(22,500.0)	(22,500.0)	(22,500.0)
Taxable personal income	17,500.0	17,500.0	17,500.0
Total personal tax	($ 1,822.5)[b]	($ 1,822.5)	($ 1,822.5)
Combined corporate and personal tax	$ 4,822.5	$ 9,322.5	$ 14,322.5
Thompson's taxes as a proprietorship:			
Total income	$60,000.0	$ 90,000.0	$110,000.0
Less: Exemptions and deductions	(22,500.0)	(22,500.0)	(22,500.0)
Taxable personal income	37,500.0	67,500.0	87,500.0
Tax liability of proprietorship	$ 4,822.5	$ 9,562.5[c]	$ 14,562.5
Advantage to being a corporation	$ 0.0	$ 240.0	$ 240.0

[a]Corporate tax in 2010 = (0.15)($20,000) = $3,000.

[b]Personal tax (if Thompson incorporates) in 2010 = $1,605.0 + ($17,500.0 − $16,050.0) × 0.15 = $1,822.5.

[c]Proprietorship tax in 2010 = $8,962.50 + 0.25 × ($67,500 − $65,100) = $9,562.5.
The corporate form of organization allows Thompson to pay the lowest taxes in 2011 and 2012; therefore, on the basis of taxes over the 3-year period, Thompson should incorporate his business. However, note that to get money out of the corporation so he can spend it, Thompson must have the corporation pay dividends, which will be taxed as personal income to him. Therefore, sometime in the future, Thompson will have to pay additional taxes when corporate distributions are made.

CHAPTER 7

ST-2 Billingsworth paid $2 in dividends and retained $2 per share. Because total retained earnings rose by $12 million, there must be 6 million shares outstanding. With a book value of $40 per share, total common equity must be $40(6 million) = $240 million. Because Billingsworth has $120 million of debt, its debt ratio must be 33.3 percent:

$$\frac{\text{Debt}}{\text{Assets}} = \frac{\text{Debt}}{\text{Debt} + \text{Equity}} = \frac{\$120 \text{ million}}{\$120 \text{ million} + \$240 \text{ million}} = \frac{\$120}{\$360}$$

$$= 0.333 = 33.3\%$$

ST-3

(1) Operating cash flow = Net income + Depreciation
$$= \$120,000 + \$25,000 = \$145,000$$

(2) Free cash flow = Operating cash flow − Investments
$$= \$145,000 - \$150,000 = -\$5,000$$

(3) EVA = NOI(1 − Tax rate) − [(Invested capital) × (After-tax cost of capital as a percent)]

$$= \$120,000(1 - 0.40) - [\$500,000(0.12)]$$
$$= \$72,000 - \$60,000 = \$12,000$$

ST-4 a. In answering questions such as this, always begin by writing down the relevant definitional equations, then start filling in numbers. Note that the extra zeros indicating millions have been deleted in the following calculations. The results are not rounded until the final answer.

(1)
$$\text{DSO} = \frac{\text{Accounts receivable}}{(\text{Sales}/360)}$$

$$40 = \frac{\text{Accounts receivable}}{(\$1,000/360)}$$

$$\text{A/R} = 40(\$2.778) = \$111.1 \text{ million}$$

$$\text{Quick ratio} = \frac{\text{Current assets} - \text{Inventories}}{\text{Current liabilities}}$$

$$= \frac{\text{Cash securities} + \text{A/R}}{\text{Current liabilities}} = 2.0$$

$$2.0 = \frac{\$100 + \$111.1}{\text{Current liabilities}}$$

(2) Current liabilities = ($100 + 111.1)/2 = $105.55

(3)
$$\text{Current ratio} = \frac{\text{Current assets}}{\text{Current liabilities}} = \frac{\text{CA}}{\$105.55} = 3.0$$

Current assets = 3.0($105.55) = $316.65

(4) Total assets = Current assets + Fixed assets = $316.7 + $283.5
$$= \$600.2 \text{ million}$$

(5) ROA = Profit margin × Total assets turnover

$$= \frac{\text{Net income}}{\text{Sales}} \times \frac{\text{Sales}}{\text{Total assets}} = \frac{\$50}{\$1,000} \times \frac{\$1,000}{\$600.2}$$

$$= 0.05 \times 1.667 = 0.0833 = 8.33\%$$

(6)

$$\text{ROE} = \text{Net income/Equity}$$
$$12\% = 0.12 = \$50/\text{Equity}$$
$$\text{Equity} = \$50/0.12 = \$416.67$$

(7)

Total assets = Total claims = \$600.1 million

Current liabilities + Long-term debt + Equity = \$600.1 million

\$105.6 + Long-term debt + \$416.7 = \$600.1 million

Long-term debt = \$600.2 − \$105.6 − \$416.7 = \$77.9 million

b. Kaiser's average sales per day were \$1,000/360 = \$2.778 million. Its DSO was 40, so A/R = 40(\$2.778) = \$111.1 million. Its new DSO of 30 would result in A/R = 30(\$2.778) = \$83.3 million. The reduction in receivables would be \$111.1 − \$83.3 = \$27.8 million, which would equal the amount of cash generated.

(1)

New equity = Old equity − Stock bought back

= \$416.7 − \$27.8 = \$388.9 million

Thus,

$$\text{New ROE} = \frac{\text{Net income}}{\text{New equity}} = \frac{\$50}{\$388.9}$$

$$= 12.86\% \text{ (versus old ROE of 12.0\%)}$$

(2) New ROA $= \dfrac{\text{Net income}}{\text{Total assets} - \text{Reduction in A/R}}$

$$= \frac{\$50}{\$600.2 - \$27.8} = 8.74\% \text{ (versus old ROS of 8.33\%)}$$

(3) The old debt is the same as the new debt:

Debt = Total claims − Equity

= \$600.2 − \$416.7 = \$183.5 million

Old total assets = \$600.2 million

New total assets = Old total assets − Reduction in A/R

= \$600.2 − \$27.8

= \$572.4 million

Therefore,

$$\frac{\text{Debt}}{\text{Old total assets}} = \frac{\$183.4}{\$600.2} = 0.306 = 30.6\%$$

while

$$\frac{\text{New debt}}{\text{New total assets}} = \frac{\$183.4}{\$572.4} = 0.32 = 32.0\%$$

CHAPTER 8

ST-2 **a.** **(1)** Determine the variable cost per unit at present, using the following definitions and equations:

Q = units of output (sales) = 5,000
P = average sales price per unit of output = \$100
F = fixed operating costs = \$200,000
V = variable costs per unit

$$\text{EBIT} = P(Q) - F - V(Q)$$
$$\$50,000 = \$100(5,000) - \$200,000 - V(5,000)$$
$$5,000V = \$250,000$$
$$V = \$50$$

(2) Determine the new EBIT level if the change is made:

$$\text{New EBIT} = P_2(Q_2) - F_2 - V_2(Q_2)$$
$$= \$95(7,000) - \$250,000 - \$40(7,000)$$
$$= \$135,000$$

(3) Determine the incremental EBIT:

$$\Delta\text{EBIT} = \$135,000 - \$50,000 = \$85,000$$

(4) Estimate the approximate rate of return on the new investment:

$$\Delta\text{ROA} = \frac{\Delta\text{EBIT}}{\text{Investment}} = \frac{\$85,000}{\$400,000} = 0.2125 = 21.25\%$$

Because the ROA exceeds Olinde's average cost of capital, this analysis suggests that Olinde should go ahead and make the investment.

b.
$$\text{DOL} = \frac{Q(P - V)}{Q(P - V) - F}$$

$$\text{DOL}_{\text{Old}} = \frac{5,000(\$100 - \$50)}{5,000(\$100 - \$50) - \$200,000} = 5.00\times$$

$$\text{DOL}_{\text{New}} = \frac{7,000(\$95 - \$40)}{7,000(\$95 - \$40) - \$250,000} = 2.85\times$$

This indicates that operating income will be less sensitive to changes in sales if the production process is changed; thus, the change would reduce risks. However, the change would increase the breakeven point. Still, with a lower sales price, it might be easier to achieve the higher new breakeven volume.

$$\textit{Old: } Q_{\text{OpBE}} = \frac{F}{P - V} = \frac{\$200,000}{\$100 - \$50} = 4,000 \text{ units}$$

$$\textit{New: } Q_{\text{OpBE}} = \frac{F_2}{P_2 - V_2} = \frac{\$250,000}{\$95 - \$40} = 4,545 \text{ units}$$

c.   The incremental ROA is:

$$\Delta \text{ROA} = \frac{\Delta \text{Profit}}{\Delta \text{Sales}} \times \frac{\Delta \text{Sales}}{\Delta \text{Assets}}$$

Using debt financing, the incremental profit associated with the investment is equal to the incremental profit found in part (a) minus the interest expense incurred as a result of the investment:

$$
\begin{aligned}
\Delta \text{Profit} &= \text{New profit} - \text{Old profit} - \text{Interest} \\
&= \$135{,}000 - \$50{,}000 - 0.08(\$400{,}000) \\
&= \$53{,}000
\end{aligned}
$$

The incremental sales is calculated as:

$$
\begin{aligned}
\Delta \text{Sales} &= P_2 Q_2 - P_1 Q_1 \\
&= \$95(7{,}000) - \$100(5{,}000) \\
&= \$665{,}000 - \$500{,}000 \\
&= \$165{,}000
\end{aligned}
$$

$$
\begin{aligned}
\text{ROA} &= \frac{\$53{,}000}{\$165{,}000} \times \frac{\$165{,}000}{\$400{,}000} \\
&= 0.1325 = 13.25\%
\end{aligned}
$$

The return on the new equity investment still exceeds the average cost of funds, so Olinde should make the investment.

d.

$$
\begin{aligned}
\text{DFL} &= \frac{\text{EBIT}}{\text{EBIT} - \text{I}} \\[2mm]
&= \frac{\$135{,}000}{\$135{,}000 - \$32{,}000} = 1.31\times
\end{aligned}
$$

CHAPTER 9

ST-2   a.   (1)

$$\text{FV}_n = \text{PV}(1 + r)^n$$

$$\$7{,}020 = \$5{,}500(1 + r)^5$$

$$(1 + r)^5 = \frac{\$7{,}020}{\$5{,}500} = 1.2764$$

To solve for the rate, use your calculator or solve algebraically. Using your calculator, enter $N = 5$, $FV = 7{,}020$, $PV = -5{,}500$, and then solve for $I/Y = r = 5.001$. To solve algebraically, recognize that, according to the above computations, $(1 + r)^5 = 1.276364$ (carried to six places).

Therefore,

$$(1+r)^5 = 1.276364$$

$$r = (1.276364)^{1/5} = 0.05001 = 5.001\%$$

(2)

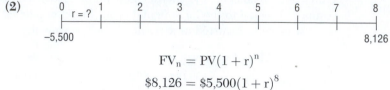

$$FV_n = PV(1+r)^n$$

$$\$8,126 = \$5,500(1+r)^8$$

$$(1+r)^8 = \frac{\$8,126}{\$5,500} = 1.4775$$

$$r = (1.4775)^{1/8} - 1.0$$

$$= 1.05000 - 1.0$$

$$= 0.050 = 5.0\%$$

Using your calculator, enter N = 8, FV = $8,126, PV = −5,500, and then solve for I/Y = r = 5.00. Because both investments yield the same return, you should be indifferent between them.

b. If you believe there is greater uncertainty about whether the 8-year investment will pay the amount expected ($8,126) than about whether the 5-year investment will pay the amount expected ($7,020), then you should prefer the shorter term investment. We discuss the effects of risk on value in Chapter 11.

ST-3   a.

$1,000 is being compounded for 3 years, so your balance on January 1, 2014, is $1,259.71:

$$FV_n = PV(1+r)_n = \$1,000(1+0.08)^3 = \$1,259.71$$

Using a financial calculator, input N = 3, I/Y = 8, PV = −1,000, PMT = 0, and FV = ? = $1,259.71.

b.

$$FV = PV\left(1 + \frac{r}{m}\right)^{n \times m}$$

$$= \$1,000\left(1 + \frac{0.08}{4}\right)^{4 \times 3} = \$1,000(1.26824) = \$1,268.24$$

Using a financial calculator, input N = 12, I/Y = 2, PV = −1,000, PMT = 0, and FV = ?; FV = $1,268.24.

c.

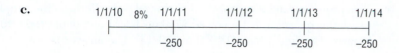

Using a financial calculator, input N = 4, I/Y = 8, PV = 0, PMT = −250, and FV = ? = $1,126.53.

d.

N = 4; I/Y = 8%; PV = 0; FV = $1,259.71; PMT = ? = $279.56

Therefore, you would have to make four payments of $279.56 each to have a balance of $1,259.71 on January 1, 2014.

ST-4   **a.** Set up a time line like the one in the preceding problem:

```
1/1/10   8%   1/1/11      1/1/12      1/1/13      1/1/14
├─────────────┼───────────┼───────────┼───────────┤
         PV = ?                               1,000
```

Note that your deposit will grow for 3 years at 8 percent. The fact that it is now January 1, 2010, is irrelevant. The deposit on January 1, 2011, is the PV, and the FV is $1,000. Here is the solution:

N = 3; I/Y = 8%; PMT = 0; FV = $1,000; PV = ? = $793.83

$$PV = \$1,000 \left[\frac{1}{(1.08)^3} \right] = \$1,000(0.79383) = \$793.83$$

b.

```
1/1/10   8%   1/1/11      1/1/12      1/1/13      1/1/14
├─────────────┼───────────┼───────────┼───────────┤
         PMT         PMT         PMT         PMT
                                        FV = 1,000
```

Here we are dealing with a 4-year annuity whose first payment occurs 1 year from today, on 1/1/11, and whose future value must equal $1,000. You should modify the time line to help visualize the situation. Here is the solution:

N = 4; I/Y = 8%; PV = 0; FV = $1,000; PMT = ? = $221.92

$$FVA_4 = PMT \left[\frac{(1.08)^4 - 1}{0.08} \right] = \$1,000$$

$$PMT = \frac{\$1,000}{4.50611} = \$221.92$$

c. This problem can be approached in several ways. Perhaps the simplest is to ask this question: If I received $750 on 1/1/11 and deposited it to earn 8 percent, would I have $1,000 on 1/1/14? The answer is no:

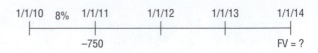

$$FV_3 = \$750(1.08)^3 = \$944.78$$

This indicates that you should let your father make the payments rather than accept the lump sum of $750.

You could also compare the $750 with the PV of the payments:

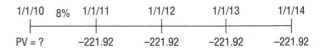

$$N = 4; I/Y = 8\%; PMT = -\$221.92; FV = 0; PV = ? = \$735.03$$

$$PVA_4 = \$221.92 \left[\frac{1 - \frac{1}{(1.08)^4}}{0.08} \right] = \$221.92(3.31212) = \$735.03$$

This is less than the $750 lump sum offer, so your initial reaction might be to accept the lump sum of $750. However, this would be a mistake. The problem is that when you found the $735.03 PV of the annuity, you were finding the value of the annuity *today*, on January 1, 2010. You were comparing $735.03 today with the lump sum of $750 1 year from now. This is, of course, invalid. What you should have done was take the $735.03, recognize that this is the PV of an annuity as of January 1, 2010, multiply $735.03 by 1.08 to get $793.83, and compare $793.83 with the lump sum of $750. You would then take your father's offer to make the payments rather than take the lump sum on January 1, 2011. If you solved the PV for an annuity due, you would find the same answer.

d.

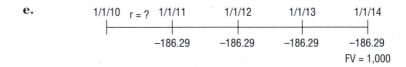

$$N = 3; PV = -\$750; PMT = 0; FV = \$1,000; I/Y = ? = 10.0642\%$$

e.

1/1/10   r = ?   1/1/11   1/1/12   1/1/13   1/1/14

            −186.29   −186.29   −186.29   −186.29

                                                           FV = 1,000

$$N = 4; \ PV = 0; \ PMT = -186.29; \ FV = 1,000; \ I/Y = ? = 20.00\%$$

You might be able to find a borrower willing to offer you a 20 percent interest rate, but there would be some risk involved—he or she might not actually pay you your $1,000 on January 1, 2014.

f.

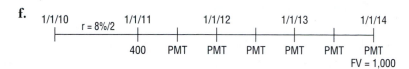

Find the future value of the original $400 deposit: $FV_6 = 400(1.04)^6 = \$400(1.26532) = \$506.13$. This means that on January 1, 2014, you need an additional sum of $493.87:

$$\$1,000.00 - \$506.13 = \$493.87$$

This will be accumulated by making six equal payments that earn 8 percent compounded semiannually, or 4 percent each 6 months: $N = 6; \ I/Y = 4\%; \ PV = 0; \ FV = \$493.87; \ PMT = ?; \ PMT = 74.46.$

g.

$$\text{Effective annual rate} = \left(1 + \frac{r_{\text{SIMPLE}}}{m}\right)^m - 1.0$$

$$= \left(1 + \frac{0.08}{2}\right)^2 - 1.0$$

$$= 1.0816 - 1 = 0.0816 = 8.16\%$$

ST-5 Bank A's effective annual rate is 8.24 percent:

$$\text{Effective annual rate} = \left(1 + \frac{0.08}{4}\right)^4 - 1.0$$

$$= (1.02)^4 - 1 = 1.0824 - 1$$

$$= 0.0824 = 8.24\%$$

Now Bank B must have the same effective annual rate:

$$\left(1 + \frac{r}{12}\right)^{12} - 1.0 = 0.0824$$

$$\left(1 + \frac{r}{12}\right)^{12} = 1.0824$$

$$1 + \frac{r}{12} = (1.0824)^{1/12}$$

$$1 + \frac{r}{12} = 1.00662$$

$$\frac{r}{12} = 0.0062$$

$$r = 0.07944 = 7.944\%$$

Thus, the two banks have different quoted rates—Bank A's quoted rate is 8 percent, while Bank B's quoted rate is 7.94 percent; however, both banks have the same effective annual rate of 8.24 percent. The difference in their quoted rates is due to the difference in compounding frequency.

CHAPTER 10

ST-2 **a.** Pennington's bonds were sold at par; therefore, the original YTM equaled the coupon rate of 12%.

b. Five years have passed; with 25 years remaining until maturity, $25 \times 2 = 50$ interest payments remain:

$$V_d = \sum_{t=1}^{50} \frac{\left(\$120/2\right)}{\left(1 + \frac{0.10}{2}\right)^t} + \frac{\$1,000}{\left(1 + \frac{0.10}{2}\right)^{50}} = \$60 \left[\frac{1 - \frac{1}{(1.05)^{50}}}{0.05}\right] \$1,000 \left[\frac{1}{(1.05)^{50}}\right]$$

$$= \$60(18.25593) + \$1,000(0.08720) = \$1,095.36 + \$87.20 = \$1,182.56$$

Alternatively, with a financial calculator, input the following: N = 50, I/Y = 5, PMT = 60, FV = 1000, and PV = ? PV = $1,182.56.

c.
$$\text{Current yield} = \text{Annual coupon payment/Price}$$
$$= \$120/\$1,182.56$$
$$= 0.1015 = 10.15\%$$

$$\text{Capital gains yield} = \text{Total yield} - \text{Current yield}$$
$$= 10\% - 10.15\% = -0.15\%$$

d.
$$\$916.42 = \sum_{t=1}^{19} \frac{\$60}{\left(1 + \frac{r_d}{2}\right)^t} + \frac{\$1,000}{\left(1 + \frac{r_d}{2}\right)^{19}}$$

Using a financial calculator, input the following: N = 13, PV = −916.42, PMT = 60, FV = 1,000, and $r_d/2$ = I/Y = ? Calculator solution = $r_d/2$ = 7.0%; therefore, r_d = 14.0%.

e.
$$\text{Current yield} = \$120/\$916.42 = 13.09\%$$
$$\text{Capital gains yield} = 14.00\% - 13.09\% = 0.91\%$$

ST-3 The first step is to solve for g, the unknown variable, in the constant growth equation. Because $\hat{D}_1$ is unknown but D_0 is known, substitute $D_0(1 + g)$ as follows:

$$\hat{P}_0 = P_0 = \frac{\hat{D}_1}{r_s - g} = \frac{D_0(1 + g)}{r_s - g}$$

$$\$36 = \frac{\$2.40(1 + g)}{0.12 - g}$$

Solving for g, we find the growth rate to be 5 percent:

$$\$4.32 - \$36g = \$2.40 + \$2.40g$$
$$\$38.4g = \$1.92$$
$$g = 0.05 = 5\%$$

The next step is to use the growth rate to project the stock price 5 years hence:

$$\hat{P}_5 = \frac{D_0(1+g)^6}{r_s - g}$$

$$= \frac{\$2.40(1.05)^6}{0.12 - 0.05} = \frac{\$3.2162}{0.07} = \$45.95$$

Therefore, Ewald Company's expected stock price five years from now, $\hat{P}_5$, is $45.95.

ST-4   a.   (1) Calculate the PV of the dividends paid during the supernormal growth period:

$$\hat{D}_1 = \$1.1500(1.15) = \$1.3225$$

$$\hat{D}_2 = \$1.3225(1.15) = \$1.5209$$

$$\hat{D}_3 = \$1.5209(1.13) = \$1.7186$$

PV of $\hat{D} = \$1.3225(0.89286) + \$1.5209(0.79719) + \$1.7186(0.71178)$

$$= \$1.1809 + \$1.2124 + \$1.2233$$

$$= \$3.6167 \approx \$3.62$$

(2) Find the PV of Snyder's stock price at the end of Year 3:

$$\hat{P}_3 = \frac{\hat{D}_4}{r_s - g} = \frac{\hat{D}_3(1+g)}{r_s - g}$$

$$= \frac{\$1.7186(1.06)}{0.12 - 0.06}$$

$$= \$30.36$$

PV of $\hat{P}_3 = \$30.36(0.71178) = \$21.61$

(3) Sum the two components to find the value of the stock today:

$$\hat{P}_0 = \$3.62 + \$21.61 = \$25.23$$

Alternatively, the cash flows can be placed on a time line as follows:

Enter the cash flows into the cash flow register, $I/Y = 12$, and press the NPV key to obtain $P_0 = \$25.23$.

b. $\hat{P}_1 = \$1.5209(0.89286) + \$1.7186(0.79719) + \$30.36(0.79719)$

$$= \$1.3580 + \$1.3701 + \$24.2027$$

$$= \$26.9308 = \$26.93$$

(Calculator solution: $26.93)

$$\hat{P}_2 = \$1.7186(0.89286) + \$30.36(0.89286)$$
$$= \$1.5345 + \$27.1072$$
$$= \$28.6418 = \$28.64$$
(Calculator solution: \$28.64)

c.

Year	Dividend Yield	+	Capital Gains Yield	=	Total Return
1	$\dfrac{\$1.3225}{\$25.23} \approx 5.242\%$	+	$\dfrac{\$26.93 - 25.23}{\$25.23} \approx 6.738\%$	=	12%
2	$\dfrac{\$1.5209}{\$26.93} \approx 5.648\%$	+	$\dfrac{\$28.64 - 26.93}{\$26.93} \approx 6.350\%$	=	12%
3	$\dfrac{\$1.7186}{\$28.64} \approx 6.000\%$	+	$\dfrac{\$30.36 - 28.64}{\$28.64} \approx 6.000\%$	=	12%

ST-5 **a.** This is not necessarily true. Because G plows back two-thirds of its earnings, its growth rate should exceed that of D, but D pays higher dividends (\$6 versus \$2). We cannot say which stock should have the higher price.

b. Again, we just do not know which price would be higher.

c. This is false. The changes in r_d and r_s would have a greater effect on G—its price would decline more.

d. The total expected return for D is $\hat{r}_D = \hat{D}_1/P_0 + g = 15\% + 0\% = 15\%$. The total expected return for G will have $\hat{D}_1/P_0$ less than 15 percent and g greater than 0 percent, but $\hat{r}_G$ should be neither greater nor less than D's total expected return, 15 percent, because the two stocks are stated to be equally risky.

e. We have eliminated a, b, c, and d, so e should be correct. On the basis of the available information, D and G should sell at about the same price, \$40; thus, $\hat{r}_s = 15\%$ for both D and G. G's current dividend yield is \$2/\$40 = 5%. Therefore, g = 15% − 5% = 10%.

CHAPTER 11

ST-2
$$\beta_P = w_A\beta_A + w_B\beta_B$$
$$0.95 = 0.3(2.0) + 0.7(\beta_B)$$
$$\beta_B = (0.95 - 0.6)/0.7$$
$$= 0.5$$

ST-3
$$r_s = r_{RF} + (r_M - r_{RF})\beta s$$
$$= 4\% + (12\% - 4\%)2.5$$
$$= 4\% + 20\%$$
$$= 24\%$$

ST-4   **a.**

			Returns 50/50	
Year	Stock A	Stock B	Portfolio	
2005	−10.00%	−3.00%	−6.50%	$= 0.5(-10.00\%) + 0.5(-3.00\%)$
2006	18.50	21.29	19.90	$= 0.5(18.50\%) + 0.5(21.29\%)$
2007	38.67	44.25	41.46	$= 0.5(38.67\%) + 0.5(44.25\%)$
2008	14.33	3.67	9.00	$= 0.5(14.33\%) + 0.5(\ 3.67\%)$
2009	33.00	28.30	30.65	$= 0.5(33.00\%) + 0.5(28.30\%)$
$\bar{r}$	18.90%	18.90%	18.90%	$= 0.5(18.90\%) + 0.5(18.90\%)$

$$\bar{r}_A = \frac{-10.0\% + 18.50\% + 38.67\% + 14.33\% + 33.00\%}{5} = 18.90\%$$

b. The standard deviation of returns is estimated as follows:

$$\text{Estimated } \sigma = s = \sqrt{\frac{\sum\limits_{t=1}^{n} (\ddot{r}_t - \bar{r})^2}{n - 1}}$$

or Stock A, the estimated σ is 19.0 percent:

$$\sigma_A = \sqrt{\frac{(-10.00 - 18.9)^2 + (18.50 - 18.9)^2 + (38.67 - 18.9)^2 + (14.33 - 18.9)^2 + (33.00 - 18.9)^2}{4}}$$

$$= \sqrt{\frac{1{,}445.92}{4}} = \sqrt{361.48} = 19.01\%$$

The standard deviation of returns for Stock B and the portfolio are similarly determined, and they are as follows:

	Stock A	Stock B	Portfolio AB
Standard deviation	19.0%	19.0%	18.6%

c. Because the risk from diversification is small—the standard deviation falls only from 19.0 to 18.6 percent—the most likely value of the correlation coefficient is 0.9. If the correlation coefficient were −0.9, the risk reduction would be much larger. In fact, the correlation coefficient between Stock A and Stock B is 0.92.

ST-5   **a.**

$$\hat{r}_R = 0.5(-2\%) + 0.1(10\%) + 0.4(15) = 6.0\%$$
$$\hat{r}_S = 0.5(20\%) + 0.1(12\%) + 0.4(2\%) = 12.0\%$$

b.

$$\hat{r}_P = w_R \hat{r}_R + w_S \hat{r}_S$$
$$\hat{r}_P = 0.5(6.0\%) + 0.5(12.0\%) = 9.0\%$$

Alternative computation: Compute the portfolio return for each possible stock outcome.

		Returns	
Probability	Stock R	Stock S	50/50 Portfolio
0.5	–2%	20%	9.0% = 0.5 (–2%) + 0.5 (20%)
0.1	10	12	11.0 = 0.5 (10%) + 0.5 (12%)
0.4	15	2	8.5 = 0.5 (15%) + 0.5 (2%)

Then compute the expected return based on the probability of the outcome.

$$\hat{r}_P = 0.5(9.0\%) + 0.1(11.0\%) + (0.4)(8.5\%) = 9.0\%$$

c.

$$\text{Standard deviation} = \sigma = \sqrt{\sigma_A} = \sqrt{\sum_{i=1}^{n} (r_i - \hat{r})^2 Pr_i}$$

$$\sigma_R = \sqrt{0.5(-2\% - 6\%)^2 + 0.1(10\% - 6\%)^2 + 0.4(15\% - 6\%)^2}$$

$$= \sqrt{32 + 1.6 + 32.4} = \sqrt{66} = 8.12\%$$

$$\sigma_S = \sqrt{0.5(20\% - 12\%)^2 + 0.1(12\% - 12\%)^2 + 0.4(2\% - 12\%)^2}$$

$$= \sqrt{32 + 0 + 40} = \sqrt{72} = 8.49\%$$

$$\sigma_P = \sqrt{0.5(9\% - 9\%)^2 + 0.1(11\% - 9\%)^2 + 0.4(8.5\% - 9\%)^2}$$

$$= \sqrt{0 + 0.4 + 0.1} = \sqrt{0.5} = 0.71\%$$

Stock S is riskier because its standard deviation is higher than that of Stock R. Clearly, however, the portfolio, or combination of the two stocks, has the lowest risk.

d.

$$\text{Coefficient of variation} = CV = \frac{\text{Risk}}{\text{Return}} = \frac{\sigma}{\hat{r}}$$

$$CV_R = 8.12\%/6\%\ = 1.35$$
$$CV_S = 8.49\%/12\% = 0.71$$

According to the coefficient of variations computed here, Stock R is riskier than Stock S. Although Stock S has a higher amount of total risk, it also has a much higher expected return than Stock R. The coefficient of variation for the portfolio is $0.08 = 0.71\%/9\%$, which is much lower than for either stock.

e. In this case, because the standard deviation for the two-stock portfolio is close to 0 percent, we would expect that initially there would be little change in the riskiness of the portfolio as additional stocks are added. But as the number of stocks in the portfolio increases substantially, we would expect that the risk associated with the portfolio should approach the standard deviation of the market, or average, portfolio, which is near 15 percent. See Figure 11-8.

Chapter 12

ST-2   a. A break point will occur each time a low-cost type of capital is used up. We establish the break points as follows, after first noting that LEI has

$24,000 of retained earnings:

$$\text{Retained earnings} = (\text{Total earnings})(1.0 - \text{Payout})$$
$$= \$34,285.72(0.7)$$
$$= \$24,000$$

$$\text{Break point} = \frac{\text{Maximum amount of low-cost capital of a given type}}{\text{Proportion of this type of capital in the capital structure}}$$

Type of Capital	Break Point Calculation	Break Point	Break Number
Retained earnings	$\text{BP}_{RE} = \dfrac{\$24,000}{0.60}$	$= \$40,000$	2
10% flotation common equity	$\text{BP}_{10\%E} = \dfrac{\$24,000 + \$12,000}{0.60}$	$= \$60,000$	4
5% flotation preferred stock	$\text{BP}_{5\%PS} = \dfrac{\$7,500}{0.15}$	$= \$50,000$	3
12% debt	$\text{BP}_{12\%D} = \dfrac{\$5,000}{0.25}$	$= \$20,000$	1
14% debt	$\text{BP}_{14\%D} = \dfrac{\$10,000}{0.25}$	$= \$40,000$	2

Summary of break points:

(1) There are three common equity costs and hence two changes and, therefore, two equity-induced breaks in the MCC. There are two preferred costs and hence one preferred break. There are three debt costs and hence two debt breaks.

(2) The numbers in the fourth column of the table designate the sequential order of the breaks, determined after all the break points were calculated. Note that the second debt break and the break for retained earnings both occur at $40,000.

(3) The first break point occurs at $20,000, when the 12 percent debt is used up. The second break point, $40,000, results from using up both retained earnings and the 14 percent debt. The MCC curve also rises at $50,000 and $60,000, as preferred stock with a 5 percent flotation cost and common stock with a 10 percent flotation cost, respectively, are used up.

b. Component costs within indicated total capital intervals are as follows:

Retained earnings (used in interval $0 to $40,000):

$$r_s = \frac{\hat{D}_1}{P_0} + g = \frac{\hat{D}_0(1+g)}{P_0} + g$$
$$= \frac{\$3.60(1.09)}{\$60} + 0.09$$
$$= 0.0654 + 0.09 = 0.1554 \qquad\qquad = 15.54\%$$

Common with F = 10% ($40,001 to $60,000):

$$r_e = \frac{\hat{D}_1}{P_0(1.0 - F)} + g$$

$$= \frac{\$3.924}{\$60(0.9)} + 0.09$$

$$= 0.0727 + 0.09 = 0.1627 \qquad\qquad = 16.27\%$$

Common with F = 20% (over $60,000):

$$r_e = \frac{\$3.924}{\$60(0.8)} + 0.09$$

$$= 0.08175 + 0.09 = 0.17175 \qquad\qquad = 17.18\%$$

Preferred with F = 5% ($0 to $50,000):

$$r_{ps} = \frac{\hat{D}_p}{P_0(1.0 - F)}$$

$$= \frac{\$11}{\$100(0.95)}$$

$$= 0.1158 \qquad\qquad = 11.58\%$$

Preferred with F = 10% (over $50,000):

$$r_{ps} = \frac{\$11}{\$100(0.9)}$$

$$= 0.1222 \qquad\qquad = 12.22\%$$

Debt at r_d = 12% ($0 to $20,000): $r_{dT} = r_d(1 - T) = 12\%(0.6) = 7.20\%$

Debt at r_d = 14% ($20,001 to $40,000): $r_{dT} = 14\%(0.6) = 8.40\%$

Debt at r_d = 16% (over $40,000): $r_{dT} = 16\%(0.6) = 9.60\%$

c. WACC calculations within indicated total capital intervals:

(1) $0 to $20,000 (debt = 7.2%, preferred = 11.58%, and retained earnings [RE] = 15.54%):

$$WACC_1 = w_d r_{dT} + w_{ps} r_{ps} + w_s r_s$$

$$= 0.25(7.2\%) + 0.15(11.58\%) + 0.60(15.54\%) = 12.86\%$$

(2) $20,001 to $40,000 (debt = 8.4%, preferred = 11.58%, and RE = 15.54%):

$$WACC_2 = 0.25(8.4\%) + 0.15(11.58\%) + 0.60(15.54\%) = 13.16\%$$

(3) $40,001 to $50,000 (debt = 9.6%, preferred = 11.58%, and equity = 16.27%):

$$WACC_3 = 0.25(9.6\%) + 0.15(11.58\%) + 0.60(16.27\%) = 13.90\%$$

(4) $50,001 to $60,000 (debt = 9.6%, preferred = 12.22%, and equity = 16.27%):

$$\text{WACC}_4 = 0.25(9.6\%) + 0.15(12.22\%) = 0.60(16.27\%) = 14.00\%$$

(5) Over $60,000 (debt = 9.6%, preferred = 12.22%, and equity = 17.18%):

$$\text{WACC}_5 = 0.25(9.6\%) + 0.15(12.22\%) + 0.60(17.18\%) = 14.54\%$$

d. Expected return calculation for Project E using a financial calculator:

$$N = 6, \, PV = -20,000, \, PMT = 5,427.84; \, I/Y = ? = 16.00\%$$

e. See the graph of the MCC and IOS schedules for LEI.

LEI: MCC and IOS Schedules

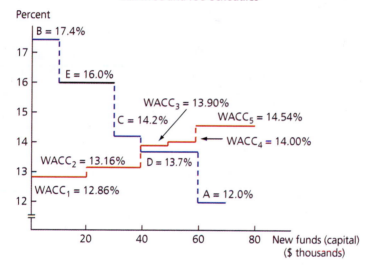

f. LEI should accept Projects B, E, and C. It should reject Projects A and D because their IRRs do not exceed the marginal costs of funds needed to finance them. The firm's capital budget would total $40,000.

CHAPTER 13

ST-2   a. *Estimated investment outlay*

Price	($50,000)
Modification	(10,000)
Change in net working capital	(2,000)
Total investment outlay	($62,000)

b. *Incremental operating cash flows*

	Year 1	Year 2	Year 3
1. After-tax cost savings[a]	$12,000	$12,000	$12,000
2. Depreciation[b]	19,800	27,000	9,000
3. Depreciation tax savings[c]	7,920	10,800	3,600
Net cash flow (1 + 3)	$19,920	$22,800	$15,600

[a]$20,000 (1 − T).

[b]Depreciable basis = $60,000; the MACRS percentage allowances are 0.33, 0.45, and 0.15 in Years 1, 2, and 3, respectively; hence, depreciation in Year 1 = 0.33($60,000) = $19,800, and so on. There will remain $4,200, or 7 percent, undepreciated after Year 3; it would normally be taken in Year 4.

[c]Depreciation tax savings = T(Depreciation) = 0.4($19,800) = $7,920 in Year 1, and so on.

c. *Terminal cash flow*

Salvage value	$ 20,000
Tax on salvage value[a]	(6,320)
Net working capital recovery	2,000
Terminal cash flow	$ 15,680

[a]Sales price	$ 20,000
Less book value	(4,200)
Taxable income	$ 15,800
Tax at 40%	$ 6,320

Book value = Depreciable basis − Accumulated depreciation
= $60,000 − ($19,800 + $27,000 + $9,000) = $4,200

d. *Project NPV*

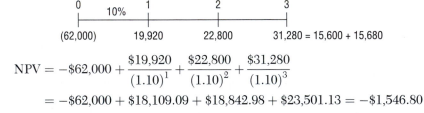

$$NPV = -\$62,000 + \frac{\$19,920}{(1.10)^1} + \frac{\$22,800}{(1.10)^2} + \frac{\$31,280}{(1.10)^3}$$

$$= -\$62,000 + \$18,109.09 + \$18,842.98 + \$23,501.13 = -\$1,546.80$$

Alternatively, using a financial calculator, input the cash flows into the cash flow register, enter I = 10, and then press the NPV key to obtain NPV = −$1,546.81. Because the earthmover has a negative NPV, it should not be purchased.

ST-3 *First determine the initial investment outlay:*

Purchase price	($8,000)
Sale of old machine	3,000
Tax on sale of old machine	(160)[a]
Change in net working capital	(1,500)
Total investment	($6,660)

[a]The market value is $3,000−$2,600 = $400 above the book value. Thus, there is a $400 recapture of depreciation, and Dauten would have to pay 0.40($400) = $160 in taxes.

Now, examine the operating cash inflows:

Sales increase	$1,000
Cost decrease	1,500
Increase in pretax operating revenues	$2,500

After-tax operating revenue increase:
$$\$1,500 = \$2,500(1 - T) = \$2,500(0.60)$$

Depreciation:

Year	1	2	3	4	5	6
New[a]	$1,600	$2,560	$1,520	$960	$880	$480
Old	350	350	350	350	350	350
Change	$1,250	$2,210	$1,170	$610	$530	$130
Depreciation tax savings[b]	$ 500	$ 884	$ 468	$244	$212	$ 52

[a]Depreciable basis = $8,000. Depreciation expense in each year equals depreciable basis times the MACRS percentage allowances of 0.20, 0.32, 0.19, 0.12, 0.11, and 0.06 in Years 1–6, respectively.

[b]Depreciation tax savings = T(Depreciation) = 0.4(Depreciation).

Now recognize that at the end of Year 6 Dauten would recover its net working capital investment of $1,500, and it would also receive $800 from the sale of the replacement machine. However, because the machine would be fully depreciated, the firm must pay 0.40($800) = $320 in taxes on the sale. Also, by undertaking the replacement now, the firm forgoes the right to sell the old machine for $500 in Year 6; thus, this $500 in Year 6 must be considered an opportunity cost in that year. No tax would be due because the $500 salvage value would equal the old machine's Year 6 book value.

Finally, place all the cash flows on a time line:

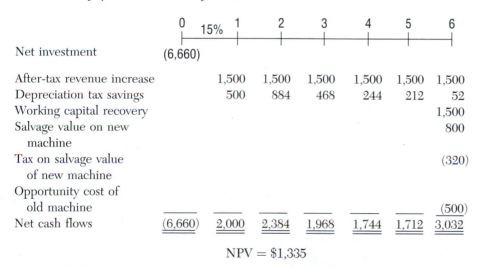

	0 15%	1	2	3	4	5	6
Net investment	(6,660)						
After-tax revenue increase		1,500	1,500	1,500	1,500	1,500	1,500
Depreciation tax savings		500	884	468	244	212	52
Working capital recovery							1,500
Salvage value on new machine							800
Tax on salvage value of new machine							(320)
Opportunity cost of old machine							(500)
Net cash flows	(6,660)	2,000	2,384	1,968	1,744	1,712	3,032

NPV = $1,335

The net present value of this incremental cash flow stream, when discounted at 15 percent, is $1,335. Thus, the replacement should be made.

ST-4   **a.** *Payback*

To determine the payback, construct the cumulative cash flows for each project:

	Project X		Project Y	
Year	Cash Flows	Cumulative CF	Cash Flows	Cumulative CF
0	($10,000)	($10,000)	($10,000)	($10,000)
1	6,500	(3,500)	3,500	(6,500)
2	3,000	(500)	3,500	(3,000)
3	3,000	2,500	3,500	500
4	1,000	3,500	3,500	4,000

$$\text{Payback}_X = 2 + \frac{\$500}{\$3,000} = 2.17 \text{ years}$$

$$\text{Payback}_Y = 2 + \frac{\$3,000}{\$3,500} = 2.86 \text{ years}$$

Net present value (NPV)

$$NPV_X = -\$10,000 + \frac{\$6,500}{(1.12)^1} + \frac{\$3,000}{(1.12)^2} + \frac{\$3,000}{(1.12)^3} + \frac{\$1,000}{(1.12)^4}$$

$$= -\$10,000 + \$5,803.57 + \$2,391.58 + \$2,135.34 + \$635.52 = \$966.02$$

$$NPV_Y = -\$10,000 + \frac{\$3,500}{(1.12)^1} + \frac{\$3,500}{(1.12)^2} + \frac{\$3,500}{(1.12)^3} + \frac{\$3,500}{(1.12)^4}$$

$$= -\$10,000 + \$3,125.00 + \$2,790.18 + \$2,491.23 + \$2,224.31 = \$630.72$$

Alternatively, using a financial calculator, input the cash flows into the cash flow register, enter I = 12, and then press the NPV key to obtain $NPV_X = \$966.01$ and $NPV_Y = \$630.72$.

Internal rate of return (IRR)

To solve for each project's IRR, find the discount rates that equate each NPV to $0:

$$IRR_X = 18.0\%$$
$$IRR_Y = 15.0\%$$

Modified internal rate of return (MIRR)

$$\text{PV of cash outflows} = \frac{\text{TV}}{(1 + \text{MIRR})^n}$$

$$\text{Cost} = \frac{\sum_{t=1}^{n} \text{CIF}_t(1 + r)^{n-t}}{(1 + \text{MIRR})^n}$$

$$\$10,000 = \frac{\$6,500(1.12)^3 + \$3,000(1.12)^2 + \$3,000(1.12)^1 + \$1,000(1.12)^0}{(1 + \text{MIRR}_X)^4}$$

$$\$10,000 = \frac{\$17,255.23}{(1 + \text{MIRR}_X)^4}$$

$$(1 + \text{MIRR}_X)^4 = \frac{\$17,255.23}{\$10,000} = 1.725523$$

$$\text{MIRR}_X = (1.725523)^{1/4} - 1.0$$

$$= 0.1461 = 14.61\%$$

$$\$10,000 = \frac{\$3,500(1.12)^3 + \$3,500(1.12)^2 + \$3,500(1.12)^1 + \$3,500(1.12)^0}{(1 + MIRR_Y)^4}$$

$$\$10,000 = \frac{\$16,727.65}{(1 + MIRR_Y)^4}$$

$$(1 + MIRR_Y)^4 = \frac{\$16,727.65}{\$10,000} = 1.672765$$

$$MIRR_Y = (1.672765)^{1/4} - 1.0$$

$$= 0.1373 = 13.73\%$$

Discounted Payback Period (DPB)

To determine the discounted payback, construct the cumulative discounted cash flows for each project:

	Project X		Project Y	
Year	PV CF @ 12%	Cumulative CF	PV CF @ 12%	Cumulative CF
0	($10,000.00)	($10,000.00)	($10,000.00)	($10,000.00)
1	5,803.57	(4,196.43)	3,125.00	(6,875.00)
2	2,391.58	(1,804.85)	2,790.18	(4,084.82)
3	2,135.34	330.49	2,491.23	(1,593.59)
4	635.52	966.01	2,224.31	630.72

$$DPB_X = 2 + \frac{\$1,804.85}{\$2,135.34} = 2.85 \text{ years}$$

$$DPB_Y = 3 + \frac{\$1,593.59}{\$2,224.31} = 3.72 \text{ years}$$

b. The following table summarizes the project rankings by each method:

	Project that Ranks Higher
Traditional Payback	X
NPV	X
IRR	X
MIRR	X
PB_{Disc}	X

Note that all methods rank Project X over Project Y. In addition, both projects are acceptable under the NPV, IRR, MIRR, and DPB criteria. Thus, both projects should be accepted if they are independent.

c. In this case, we would choose the project with the higher NPV at r = 12%, or Project X.

d. To determine the effects of changing the cost of capital, plot the NPV profiles of each project. The crossover rate occurs at about 6 percent (6.2%).

If the firm's required rate of return is less than 6 percent, a conflict exists because $NPV_Y > NPV_X$, but $IRR_Y < IRR_X$. Therefore, if r were 5 percent, a conflict would exist.

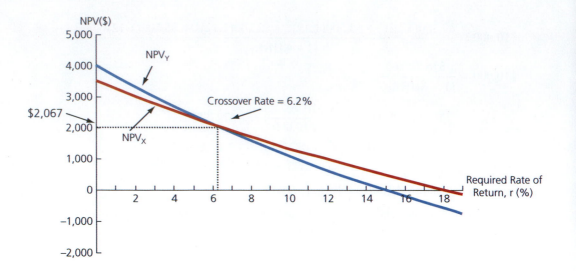

Required Rate of Return	NPV$_X$	NPV$_Y$
0%	$3,500	$4,000
4	2,545	2,705
8	1,707	1,592
12	966	631
16	307	(206)
18	5	(585)

e. The basic cause of the conflict is differing reinvestment rate assumptions between NPV and IRR. NPV assumes that cash flows can be reinvested at the cost of capital, whereas IRR assumes reinvestment at the (generally) higher IRR. The high reinvestment rate assumption under IRR makes early cash flows especially valuable, and hence short-term projects look better under IRR.

ST-5 a. First, find the expected cash flows:

Year	Expected Cash Flows	
0	0.2(−$100,000) + 0.6(−$100,000) + 0.2(−$100,000)	= ($100,000)
1	0.2($20,000) + 0.6($30,000) + 0.2($40,000)	= $ 30,000
2		= $ 30,000
3		$ 30,000
4		$ 30,000
5		$ 30,000 ⎤
		⎢ $48,000
5*	0.2($0) + 0.6($20,000) + 0.2($30,000)	= $ 18,000 ⎦

0		1		2		3		4		5
	10%									
(100,000)		30,000		30,000		30,000		30,000		48,000

Next, determine the NPV based on the expected cash flows:

$$NPV = -\$100,000 + \frac{\$30,000}{(1.10)^1} + \frac{\$30,000}{(1.10)^2} + \frac{\$30,000}{(1.10)^3} + \frac{\$30,000}{(1.10)^4} + \frac{\$48,000}{(1.10)^5}$$

$$= -\$100,000 + \$27,272.73 + \$24,793.39 + \$22,539.44 + \$20,490.40$$
$$+ \$29,804.22 = \$24,900.18$$

Using a financial calculator, input the cash flows in the cash flow register, enter I = 10, and then press the NPV key to obtain NPV = $24,900.19.

b. For the worst case, the cash flow values from the cash flow column farthest on the left are used to calculate NPV:

Next, determine the NPV based on the expected cash flows:

$$NPV = -\$100,000 + \frac{\$20,000}{(1.10)^1} + \frac{\$20,000}{(1.10)^2} + \frac{\$20,000}{(1.10)^3} + \frac{\$20,000}{(1.10)^4} + \frac{\$20,000}{(1.10)^5}$$

$$= -\$100,000 + 18,181.82 + 16,528.93 + 15,026.30 + 13,660.27$$
$$+ 12,418.43 = -\$24,184.25$$

Using a financial calculator, input the cash flows in the cash flow register, enter I = 10, and then press the NPV key to obtain NPV = −$24,184.26.

Similarly, for the best case, use the values from the column farthest on the right. Here the NPV is $70,259.

If the cash flows are perfectly dependent, then the low cash flow in the first year will mean a low cash flow in every year. Thus, the probability of the worst case occurring is the probability of getting the $20,000 net cash flow in Year 1, or 20 percent. If the cash flows are independent, the cash flow in each year can be low, high, or average, and the probability of getting all low cash flows will be as follows:

$$0.2(0.2)(0.2)(0.2)(0.2) = 0.2^5 = 0.00032 = 0.032\%$$

c. The base case NPV is found using the most likely cash flows and is equal to $26,142. This value differs from the expected NPV of $24,900 because the Year 5 cash flows are not symmetric. Under these conditions, the NPV distribution is as follows:

Pr	NPV
0.2	($24,184)
0.6	26,142
0.2	70,259

Thus, the expected NPV is 0.2(−$24,184) + 0.6($26,142) + 0.2($70,259) = $24,900. As is generally the case, the expected NPV is the same as the NPV of the expected cash flows found in part (a). The standard deviation is $29,904:

$$\sigma^2_{NPV} = 0.2(-\$24,184 - \$24,900)^2 + 0.6(\$26,142 - \$24,900)^2$$
$$+ 0.2(\$70,259 - \$24,900)^2$$
$$= 894,261,126$$
$$\sigma_{NPV} = \sqrt{894,261,126} = \$29,904$$

The coefficient of variation, CV, is $29,904/$24,900 = 1.20.

d. Because the project's coefficient of variation is 1.20, the project is riskier than average, and hence the project's risk-adjusted required rate of return is 10% + 2% = 12%. The project now should be evaluated by finding the NPV of the expected cash flows, as in part (a), but using a 12 percent discount rate. The risk-adjusted NPV is $18,357, and therefore the project should be accepted.

CHAPTER 14

ST-2   **a.**

EBIT	$ 4,000,000
Interest ($2,000,000 × 0.10)	(200,000)
Earnings before taxes (EBT)	$ 3,800,000
Taxes (35%)	(1,330,000)
Net income	$ 2,470,000

$$EPS = \$2,470,000/600,000 = \$4.12$$
$$P_0 = \$4.12/0.15 = \$27.47$$

b.

$$Equity = 600,000 \times (\$10) = \$6,000,000$$
$$Debt = \$2,000,000$$
$$Total\ capital = \$8,000,000$$

$$WACC = w_d[r_d(1 - T)] + w_s r_s$$
$$= (2/8)[(10\%)(1 - 0.35)] + (6/8)(15\%)$$
$$= 1.63\% + 11.25\%$$
$$= 12.88\%$$

c.

EBIT	$ 4,000,000
Interest ($10,000,000 × 0.12)	(1,200,000)
Earnings before taxes (EBT)	$ 2,800,000
Taxes (35%)	(980,000)
Net income	$ 1,820,000

Shares bought and retired:

$$\Delta Shares = \Delta Debt/P_0 = \$8,000,000/\$27.47 = 291,227$$

New outstanding shares:

$$Shares_1 = Shares_0 - \Delta Shares = 600,000 - 291,227 = 308,773$$

New EPS:

$$EPS = \$1,820,000/308,773 = \$5.89$$

New price per share:

$$P_0 = \$5.89/0.17 = \$34.65 \text{ versus } \$27.47$$

Therefore, Gentry should change its capital structure.

d. In this case, the company's net income would be higher by $(0.12 - 0.10)(\$2,000,000)(1 - 0.35) = \$26,000$ because its interest charges would be lower. The new price would be

$$P_0 = \frac{(\$1,820,000 + \$26,000)/308,733}{0.17} = \$35.17$$

In the first case, in which debt had to be refunded, the bondholders were compensated for the increased risk of the higher debt position. In the second case, the old bondholders were not compensated; their 10 percent coupon perpetual bonds would now be worth

$$\$100/0.12 = \$833.33,$$

or $\$1,666,667$ in total, down from the old $\$2$ million, or a loss of $\$333,333$. The stockholders would have a gain of

$$(\$35.17 - \$34.65)(308,773) = \$160,562.$$

This gain would, of course, be at the expense of the old bondholders. (There is no reason to think that bondholders' losses would exactly offset stockholders' gains.)

e.

$$TIE = \frac{EBIT}{I}$$

$$\text{Original TIE} = \frac{\$4,000,000}{\$200,000} = 20\times$$

$$\text{New TIE} = \frac{\$4,000,000}{\$1,200,000} = 3.33\times$$

ST-3   a.

Projected net income	$\$2,000,000$
Less projected capital investments	$(\ 800,000)$
Available residual	$\$1,200,000$
Shares outstanding	$200,000$

$$DPS = \$1,200,000/200,000 \text{ shares} = \$6 = \hat{D}_1$$

b. $EPS = \$2,000,000/200,000 \text{ shares} = \$10$

Payout ratio $= DPS/EPS = \$6/\$10 = 60\%$, or

Total dividends/NI $= \$1,200,000/\$2,000,000 = 60\%$

c. $\text{Currently, } P_0 = \dfrac{\hat{D}_1}{r_s - g} = \dfrac{\$6}{0.14 - 0.05} = \dfrac{\$6}{0.09} = \$66.67$

Under the former circumstances, $\hat{D}_1$ would be based on a 20 percent payout on \$10 EPS, or \$2. With $r_s = 14\%$ and $g = 12\%$, we solve for P_0:

$$P_0 = \frac{\hat{D}_1}{r_s - g} = \frac{\$2}{0.14 - 0.12} = \frac{\$2}{0.02} = \$100$$

Although CMC has suffered a severe setback, its existing assets will continue to provide a good income stream. More of these earnings should now be passed on to the shareholders, as the slowed internal growth has reduced the need for funds. However, the net result is a 33 percent decrease in the value of the shares.

d. If the payout ratio were continued at 20 percent, even after internal investment opportunities had declined, the price of the stock would drop to \$2/(0.14 − 0.06) = \$25 rather than to \$66.67. Thus, an increase in the dividend payout is consistent with maximizing shareholder wealth.

Because of the downward-sloping IOS curve, the greater the firm's level of investment, the lower the average ROE. Thus, the more money CMC retains and invests, the lower its average ROE will be. We can determine the average ROE under different conditions as follows:

Old situation (with founder active and 20 percent payout):

$$g = (1.0 - \text{Payout ratio})(\text{Average ROE})$$
$$12\% = (1.0 - 0.2)(\text{Average ROE})$$
$$\text{Average ROE} = 12\%/0.8 = 15\% > r_s = 14\%$$

Note that the *average* ROE is 15 percent, whereas the *marginal* ROE is presumably equal to 14 percent.

New situation (with founder retired and a 60 percent payout):

$$g = 6\% = (1.0 - 0.6)(\text{ROE})$$
$$\text{ROE} = 6\%/0.4 = 15\% > r_s = 14\%$$

This suggests that the new payout is appropriate and that the firm is taking on investments down to the point at which marginal returns are equal to the cost of capital.

CHAPTER 15

ST-2   The Calgary Company: Alternative Balance Sheets

	Restricted (40%)	Moderate (50%)	Relaxed (60%)
Current assets	\$1,200,000	\$1,500,000	\$1,800,000
Fixed assets	600,000	600,000	600,000
Total assets	\$1,800,000	\$2,100,000	\$2,400,000
Debt	\$ 900,000	\$1,050,000	\$1,200,000
Equity	900,000	1,050,000	1,200,000
Total liabilities and equity	\$1,800,000	\$2,100,000	\$2,400,000

The Calgary Company: Alternative Income Statements

	Restricted	Moderate	Relaxed
Sales	$ 3,000,000	$ 3,000,000	$ 3,000,000
EBIT (15% of sales)	450,000	450,000	450,000
Interest (10%)	(90,000)	(105,000)	(120,000)
Earnings before taxes (EBT)	$ 360,000	$ 345,000	$ 330,000
Taxes (40%)	(144,000)	(138,000)	(132,000)
Net income	$ 216,000	$ 207,000	$ 198,000
ROE	24.0%	19.7%	16.5%

ST-3 **a.**
$$\frac{\text{Cost of}}{\text{bank loan}} = \frac{\text{Principal} \times 0.13}{\text{Principal}(1 - 0.13)} = \frac{0.13}{0.87} = 0.1494 = 14.94\%$$

Terms of trade credit: 2/10, net 30. But the firm plans delaying payments 35 additional days, which is the equivalent of 2/10, net 65.

$$55\text{-day rate on the trade credit} = \frac{2}{98} = 0.020408163$$

$$\text{Effective rate} = (1.0204082)^{360/55} - 1.0 = 0.14138 = 14.14\%$$

Comparing interest costs, the Gallinger Corporation might be tempted to expand its payables rather than obtain financing from a bank. (For reason, see solution to part [b].)

b. Although the interest rate comparison favors trade credit, Gallinger Corporation should take into account how its trade creditors would look upon a 35-day delay in making payments. Gallinger would become a "slow pay" account, and in times when suppliers were operating at full capacity, Gallinger would be given poor service and also probably would be forced to pay on time.

ST-4 Analysis of change:

	Current	Proposal 1	Proposal 2
Annual amounts			
Sales	$10,000,000	$11,000,000	$9,000,000
Operating expenses (80%)	($ 8,000,000)	($ 8,800,000)	($7,200,000)
Collection expense*	($ 50,000)	($ 50,000)	($ 50,000)
Bad debt losses*	($ 0)	($ 0)	($ 0)
Days sales outstanding (DSO)	30 days	45 days	22 days
Required return, r	16%	16%	16%
Daily amounts			
Sales = (Annual sales)/360	$ 27,778	$ 30,556	$ 25,000
Operating costs (80%)	($ 22,222)	($ 24,444)	($ 20,000)
Required return = 12%/360	0.0444%	0.0444%	0.0444%

*Because bad debt losses and collection expenses do not change, they are not considered in the analysis.

Current policy:

$$
\begin{array}{ll}
0 & 30 \\
\vdash\!\!\!\text{—} \;\; r = 0.0444\% \;\; \text{———} & \dashv \\
(22,222) & 27,778
\end{array}
$$

$$
\text{NPV}_{\text{Current}} = -\$22{,}222 + \frac{\$27{,}778}{\left(1 + \dfrac{0.16}{360}\right)^{30}} = \$5{,}188
$$

Proposal 1:

$$
\begin{array}{ll}
0 & 45 \\
\vdash\!\!\!\text{—} \;\; r = 0.0444\% \;\; \text{———————} & \dashv \\
(24,444) & 30,556
\end{array}
$$

$$
\text{NPV}_{\text{Proposal 1}} = -\$24{,}444 + \frac{\$30{,}556}{\left(1 + \dfrac{0.16}{360}\right)^{45}} = \$5{,}507
$$

Proposal 2:

$$
\begin{array}{ll}
0 & 22 \\
\vdash\!\!\!\text{—} \;\; r = 0.0444\% \;\; \text{——} & \dashv \\
(20,000) & 25,000
\end{array}
$$

$$
\text{NPV}_{\text{Proposal 2}} = -\$20{,}000 + \frac{\$25{,}000}{\left(1 + \dfrac{0.16}{360}\right)^{22}} = \$4{,}757
$$

The NPV is greatest with Proposal 1, so the firm should change its terms of credit from net 25 to net 30.

ST-5 a.

$$
\text{EOQ} = \sqrt{\frac{2 \times O \times T}{C \times PP}}
$$

$$
= \sqrt{\frac{2(\$5{,}000)(2{,}600{,}000)}{(0.02)(\$5.00)}}
$$

$$
= 509{,}902 \text{ bushels}
$$

Because the firm must order in multiples of 2,000 bushels, it should order in quantities of 510,000 bushels.

b.

$$
\text{Average weekly sales} = 2{,}600{,}000/52
$$
$$
= 50{,}000 \text{ bushels}
$$
$$
\text{Reorder point} = 6 \text{ weeks' sales}
$$
$$
= 6(50{,}000)
$$
$$
= 300{,}000 \text{ bushels}
$$

c. Total inventory costs:

$$\text{TIC} = (\text{C})\text{PP}\left(\frac{Q}{2}\right) + \text{O}\left(\frac{T}{Q}\right)$$

$$= (0.02)(\$5)\left(\frac{510{,}000}{2}\right) + \$5{,}000\left(\frac{2{,}600{,}000}{510{,}000}\right)$$

$$= \$25{,}500 + \$25{,}490.20 = \$50{,}990.20$$

CHAPTER 16

ST-2 **a.** Number of shares $= \dfrac{\$19{,}800}{\$120} = 165$ shares

If $P_1 = \$150$,

$$\text{HPR} = \frac{(\$150 - \$120)165}{\$120(165)} = \frac{\$4{,}950}{\$19{,}800} = \frac{\$30}{\$120} = 0.250 = 25.0\%$$

If $P_1 = \$105$,

$$\text{HPR} = \frac{(\$105 - \$120)165}{\$120(165)} = \frac{-\$2{,}475}{\$19{,}800} = \frac{-\$15}{\$120} = -0.125 = -12.5\%$$

b. If Lance borrowed the maximum amount allowed, he could purchase $36,000 worth of Microsoft stock.

$$\frac{\text{Maximum that}}{\text{can be invested}} = \frac{\$19{,}800}{\text{Margin requirement}}$$

$$= \frac{\$19{,}800}{0.55} = \$36{,}000$$

Thus, Lance can purchase $36,000/$120 = 300 shares of Microsoft.

Because Lance borrows $36,000(1 − 0.55) = $16,200, he will have to pay interest equal to $16,200 × 0.12 = $1,944 at the end of the year. Therefore, the return he will earn if Microsoft's price is $150 or $105 at the end of the year is:

If $P_1 = \$150$,

$$\text{HPR} = \frac{(\$150 - \$120)300 - \$1{,}944}{\$19{,}800} = \frac{\$7{,}056}{\$19{,}800} = 0.356 = 35.6\%$$

If $P_1 = \$105$,

$$\text{HPR} = \frac{(\$105 - \$120)300 - \$1{,}944}{\$19{,}800} = \frac{-\$6{,}444}{\$19{,}800} = -0.325 = -32.5\%$$

c.
$$\frac{\text{Margin}}{\text{call price}} = \frac{\text{Amount borrowed}}{(\text{Number of shares})\left(1 - \dfrac{\text{Maintenance}}{\text{margin}}\right)}$$

$$= \frac{\$16,200}{300(1 - 0.40)} = \$90.00$$

ST-3   **a.** The annual return is computed as follows:

$$\text{Annual return} = \frac{P_1 - P_0}{P_0}$$

Thus, the 2006 return for Mateo Computers is:

$$\text{Mateo Computers' 2006 return} = \frac{\$2,400 - \$2,000}{\$2,000} = \frac{\$400}{\$2,000} = 0.20 = 20.0\%$$

Using the same approach, the annual returns for the stocks are:

	2006	2007	2008	2009
Mateo Computers	20.0%	15.0%	−10.0%	50.0%
Northern Water	2.5	19.5	15.0	20.0
AMN Motors	−10.0	20.0	25.0	4.0
Farley Argicorp	−5.0	20.0	10.0	0.0
Portfolio	2.5	18.6	8.8	18.3

The 4-year HPR for Mateo Computers is

$$\frac{\text{Mateo Computers'}}{\text{4-year return}} = \frac{P_{1/31/09} - P_{1/31/05}}{P_{1/31/05}} = \frac{\$3,726 - \$2,000}{\$2,000} = 0.863 = 86.3\%$$

The 4-year HPRs for the other companies and the portfolio are:

Northern Water $= \$\ 6,762/\$\ 4,000 - 1 = 69.1\%$

AMN Motors $\ \ = \$\ 1,404/\$\ 1,000 - 1 = 40.4\%$

Farley Argicorp $= \$\ 3,762/\$\ 3,000 - 1 = 25.4\%$

Portfolio $\qquad = \$15,654/\$10,000 - 1 = 56.5\%$

b. The weights for the stocks each year are computed by dividing the beginning-of-the-year market value of the stock by the market value of the portfolio.

2006 Weights (2005 end-of-year values)

Mateo Computers $= \$\ 2,000/\$10,000 =\ \ 20.0\%$

Northern Water $\ \ = \$\ 4,000/\$10,000 =\ \ 40.0\%$

AMN Motors $\quad = \$\ 1,000/\$10,000 =\ \ 10.0\%$

Farley Argicorp $\ = \$\ 3,000/\$10,000 =\ \ 30.0\%$

Portfolio $\qquad = \$10,000/\$10,000 = 100.0\%$

2007 Weights (2006 end-of-year values)

Mateo Computers = $ 2,400/$10,250 =   23.4%

Northern Water   = $ 4,100/$10,250 =   40.0%

AMN Motors   = $ 900/$10,250 =   8.8%

Farley Argicorp = $ 2,850/$10,250 =   27.8%

Portfolio   = $10,250/$10,250 = 100.0%

2008 Weights (2007 end-of-year values)

Mateo Computers = $ 2,760/$12,160 = 22.7%

Northern Water   = $ 4,900/$12,160 = 40.3%

AMN Motors   = $ 1,080/$12,160 =   8.9%

Farley Argicorp = $ 3,420/$12,160 = 28.1%

Portfolio   = $12,160/$12,160 = 100.0%

2009 Weights (2008 end-of-year values)

Mateo Computers = $ 2,484/$13,231 = 18.8%

Northern Water   = $ 5,635/$13,231 = 42.6%

AMN Motors   = $ 1,350/$13,231 = 10.2%

Farley Argicorp = $ 3,762/$13,231 = 28.4%

Portfolio   = $13,231/$13,231 = 100.0%

c. The 4-year HPR and the annual returns for the portfolio based on the market values given in the table are shown with the earlier computations. Using the weights for each stock each year to compute the annual returns, we have:

$$2006 \text{ portfolio return} = 20.0\%(0.20) + 2.5\%(0.40) + (-10.0\%)(0.10)$$
$$+ (-5.0\%)(0.30) = 2.5\%$$
$$2007 \text{ portfolio return} = 15.0\%(0.234) + 19.5\%(0.400) + 20.0\%(0.088)$$
$$+ 20.0\%(0.278) = 18.6\%$$
$$2008 \text{ portfolio return} = (-10.0\%)(0.227) + 15.0\%(0.403) + 25.0\%(0.089)$$
$$+ 10.0\%(0.281) = 8.8\%$$
$$2009 \text{ portfolio return} = 50.0\%(0.188) + 20.0\%(0.426) + 4.0\%(0.102)$$
$$+ 0.0\%(0.284) = 18.3\%$$

These results are the same as reported earlier. Using this same method, the 4-year HPR is:

$$4\text{-year HPR} = 86.3\%(0.20) + 69.1\%(0.40) + 40.4\%(0.10) + 25.4\%(0.30)$$
$$= 56.6\%(\text{rounding difference})$$

CHAPTER 17

ST-2 **a.** If $r_d = 8.0\%$, $r_s = 15.0\%$, $T = 40.0\%$, and Debt/Assets $= 65.0\%$,

$$\text{WACC} = [8.0\%(1 - 0.40)](0.65) + 15.0\%(0.35) = 8.37\%.$$

b.

$$
\begin{aligned}
\text{EVA} &= \text{EBIT}(1 - T) - (\text{WACC} \times \text{Invested capital}) \\
&= \$600,000(1 - 0.40) - (0.0837 \times \$2,000,000) \\
&= \$360,000 - \$167,400 \\
&= \$192,600; \text{ thus, AT is a good investment.}
\end{aligned}
$$

c.

$$
\begin{aligned}
\text{EVA dividend} &= \text{EVA}/(\text{Shares outstanding}) \\
&= \$192,600/100,000 \\
&= \$1.93
\end{aligned}
$$

d. First, we must compute the net income for American Transmitter:

EBIT	$600,000
Interest[a]	(104,000)
Earnings before taxes	496,000
Taxes (40%)	(198,400)
Net income	$297,600

[a]Remember $r_d = 8.0\%$. But, to compute interest, we need to know the amount of debt, which equals $2,000,000 \times 0.65 = \$1,300,000$. Therefore, the annual interest expense is $1,300,000 \times 0.08 = \$104,000$.

$$\text{EPS} = (\text{Net income})/(\text{Shares outstanding})$$

$$= \$297,600/100,000 = \$2.98$$

$$\hat{P}_0 = \text{EPS} \times \text{P/E}$$

$$= \$2.98 \times 15 = \$44.70$$

ST-3 **a.** The average price for the first series, Day 1 through Day 5, is computed as follows:

$$\frac{\text{Average price for}}{\text{Day 1 through Day 5}} = \frac{\$76.00 + \$76.50 + \$76.75 + 77.10 + 77.20}{5}$$

$$= \$76.71$$

The average price for each 5-day period is computed as a simple average such as above. The results are given in the following table:

Series	5-day Period	Average
1	Day 1–Day 5	$76.71
2	Day 2–Day 6	77.08
3	Day 3–Day 7	77.42
4	Day 4–Day 8	77.66
5	Day 5–Day 9	77.82
6	Day 6–Day 10	78.00

b. If you plot the series of 5-day moving averages, you will find that the line is upward sloping, which suggests the stock price is trending upward.

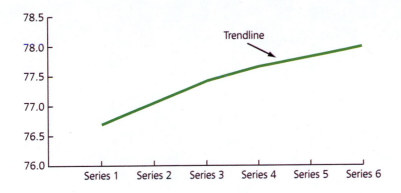

ST-4   **a.** $r_{Anchor} = 8\% + (18\% - 8\%)\,1.6 = 24.0\%$

b.
$$P_0 = \frac{\$3.40(1.06)}{0.24 - 0.06} = \$20.02$$

Answers to End-of-Chapter Problems

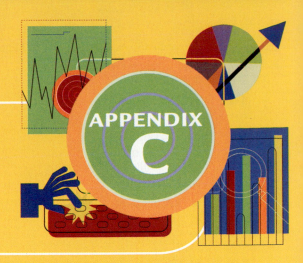

We present here final answers to selected end-of-chapter problems. Please note that your answer might differ slightly from ours due to rounding differences. Also, although we hope not, some of the problems might have more than one correct solution, depending upon what assumptions are made in working the problem. Finally, many of the problems involve some verbal discussion as well as numerical calculations; this verbal material is not presented here.

2-1	**a.** $40	
2-2	**a.** $4	
	b. $12.50	
2-3	**a.** 7,931 bonds	
	b. Annual debt service = $0	
2-4	**a.** +$300	
	b. −$200	
	c. At $P_0 = \$18$, −$300; at $P_0 = \$13$, +$200	
2-5	**b.** $1,000	
	c. −$1,000	
2-6	**b.** 20,000 shares	
	d. $EPS_{Meyer} = \$2.52$; $EPS_{Haugen} = \$2.50$	
2-7	**c.** Plan 1 EPS = $0.58; Plan 2 EPS = $0.62	
	d. Plan 2	
2-8	**a.** $35.00	
	b. $34.18	
2-9	**b.** $522,500	
	c. At $0.10/yen, cost = $550,000; at $0.085/yen, cost = $467,500	
3-1	**a.** $1,050,000	
	c. −$3,450,000	

3-2	**b.** $36,270,000	
	c. $41,935,484	
3-3	600,000 shares	
3-4	5,000,000 shares	
3-5	Number of bonds = 77,784	
	Proceeds = $75,000,480	
3-6	**a.** 6 million shares	
	b. $138 million	
3-7	**a.** $10,325,000	
	b. $10,085,000	
3-8	**a.** $4,200,000	
	b. $2,300,000	
3-9	**a.** $35,280,000	
	b. 10,000,000 shares	
4-1	**a.** 7.0%	
	b. 12.0%	
	c. $1.43 trillion	
4-2	$1,035 billion	
4-3	**a.** $2,280 billion	
	c. $120 billion	
	d. $0	
4-4	**a.** −$2,280 billion	
	b. −$1,080 billion	
4-5	$12 billion	

4-6 $55.8 billion

4-7 **a.** $20 billion
     b. $12 billion

4-8 **a.** $451 billion
     b. $1.051 trillion
     c. $3.0 billion
     d. $57.1 billion

4-9 **a.** $225 billion
     b. 25.0%
     c. −$150 billion

5-1 57.1%

5-2 −10%

5-3 **a.** r_1 in Year 2 = 10%

5-4 r_{RF1} in Year 2 = 15%; Year 2 inflation = 11%

5-5 6.0%

5-6 $Infl_2$ = 3.4%

5-7 DRP = 1.5%

5-8 r_{2014} = 5.4%

5-9 r_1 in Year 3 = 7.0%

5-10 **a.** r_1 = 9.2%; r_5 = 7.2%

5-11 **a.** $Infl_5$ = 4.6%
     b. MRP_5 = 0.8%
     c. r_5 = 8.4%
     d. r_{10} = 8.1%

5-12 **a.** 0.3%
     c. r^* = 1.5%

5-13 **a.** 11.1%
     c. 3.7%

5-15 **a.** 4.8%
     b. 6.8%
     c. 5-yr bond = 7.3%

6-1 **a.** Tax = $61,250
     b. Tax = $15,600
     c. Tax = $4,680

6-2 **a.** Tax = $107,855; Net income = $222,145
     b. Average tax rate = 33.76%

6-3 **a.** Tax = $125
     b. Tax = $150
     c. Tax = $1,050

6-4 **a.** Tax = $30
     b. Tax = $30
     c. Tax = $70

6-6 Tax_{2009} = $0; Initial tax_{2011} = $4,500;
Initial tax_{2012} = $15,450;
Final tax_{2012} = $0

6-7 **a.** 2010 advantage as a corporation = $0
        2011 advantage = $640
        2012 advantage = −$1,160

6-8 **a.** Personal tax = $14,793.75
     c. IBM after-tax yield = 8.25%;
        Choose the Florida bonds
     d. 18.18%

6-9 **a.** Personal tax = $4,531.25
     b. Loan interest is not tax deductible

6-10 **a.** Taxes = $9,750.00
     b. Taxes = $4,387.50

7-1 $262,500; 1.19×

7-2 Sales = $2,511,628; DSO = 37 days

7-3 TIE = 3.5

7-4 ROE = 24.5%; ROA = 9.8%

7-5 $230,000

7-6 **a.** $2.8 million
     b. $950,000

7-7 −$20,000

7-8 Net profit margin = 2%; Debt/Assets = 40%

7-9 **a.** +5.54%
     b. **2)** +3.21%

7-10 Total sources = $102;
Net increase in cash & marketable
securities = $19

7-11 **a.** NOI after taxes = $900,000; CF = $2,400,000
     b. CF = $3,000,000

7-12 **a.** Current ratio = 3.8×; DSO = 41.1 days;
        FA turnover = 4.0×; Debt ratio = 48.1%

7-13 **a.** Current ratio = 1.98×; DSO = 75 days;
        Total assets turnover = 1.7×; Debt ratio
        = 61.9%

7-14 A/P = $90,000; Inv = $67,500;
FA = $160,500

7-15 **b.** Net profit margin = 3.4%;
        TA turnover = 1.77×; ROA = 6.0%

7-16 **a.** Quick ratio = 0.85×; DSO = 38 days;
        ROE = 13.1%; Debt ratio = 54.8%

8-1 **a.** $80,000
     b. Q_{OpBE} = 6,000

8-2 Q_{OpBE} = 200

8-3	$30,000	9-10	**a.** $2,703.61
8-4	DFL = 1.8×	9-11	PVP at 7% = $1,428.57; PVP at 14% = $714.29
8-5	**a.** **(1)** −$75,000		
	(2) $175,000	9-12	**a.** Stream A: $973.57
	b. Q_{OpBE} = 140,000	9-13	**a.** $881.17
	c. **(1)** −8.3		**b.** $895.42
	(2) 15.0		**c.** $903.06
	(3) 5.0		**d.** $908.35
8-6	**a.** $480,000	9-14	**b.** $279.20
	b. $18,750		**c.** $276.84
8-7	**a.** 40,000		**d.** $275.22
	b. ($0.30)	9-15	**a.** $5,272.32
	c. DOL = 3.0×; DFL = 1.7×		**b.** $5,374.07
8-8	AFN = $360	9-16	**a.** $2,944.03
8-9	**a.** Notes payable = $31.44 million		**b.** $2,975.49
	b. Current ratio = 2.0×; ROE = 14.2%	9-17	**a.** $101,616.34
	c. **(2)** Current ratio = 4.25×;		**b.** $78,729.48 and $0
	ROE = 10.84%	9-18	$1,205.55
8-10	**a.** Total assets = $33,534;	9-19	n ≈ 15 years
	AFN = $2,128	9-20	5 years; $1,885.09
	b. Notes payable = $4,228;	9-21	PVA(DUE) = $46.8 million; take the annuity
	AFN = $70; Interest = $213		
8-11	**a.** DOL = 2.5×; DFL = 3.0×	9-22	**a.** PVA = $51.1 million; take the lump-sum payment
8-12	**a.** First pass AFN = $667		**b.** 5.4%
	b. Increase in notes payable = $51;	9-23	**b.** 7%
	Increase in CS = $368		**c.** 9%
8-13	**a.** **(1)** −$60,000		**d.** 15%
	b. Q_{OpBE} = 14,000	9-24	**a.** 1st City = 7%; 2nd City = 6.66%
	c. **(1)** −1.33	9-25	APR = 8.0%; EAR = 8.24%
8-14	**a.** **(2)** $125,000	9-26	12%
	b. Q_{OpBE} = 7,000	9-27	9%
8-15	**a.** Feb = $2,000	9-28	**a.** $7,350
	b. Feb = −$58,000		**b.** PMT(Bank of South Alaska) = $1,425.46
8-16	**a.** Oct = −$22,800		**c.** 3.07%
9-1	$561.80	9-29	$984.88
9-2	$747.26	9-30	**b.** PMT = $6,594.94
9-3	**(1)** $499.99		**c.** $13,189.87
	(2) $867.13	9-31	**a.** Z = 9%; B = 8%
9-4	at 7%, n ≈ 10 years		**b.** Z = $558.39; $135.98; 32.2%;
9-5	$1,000 today is worth more		B = $548.33; $48.33; 9.7%
9-6	14.87%	9-32	**a.** $260.73
9-7	**a.** $6,374.97		**b.** $263.34
9-8	**a.** $7,012.47	9-33	r_{SIMPLE} = 15.19%
9-9	**a.** $2,457.83	9-34	**a.** 26.51 months
	b. $865.90		**c.** 9.81 months

9-35 **a.** $854.74
     c. 14.3 years

9-36 **b.** $493.19
     d. Credit union loan: $11,127.78

9-37 **a.** $61,204
     b. $11,020
     c. $6,841

9-38 **a.** $176,792
     b. $150,259

9-39 $1,901

9-40 $4,971

10-1 $823.32

10-2 $841.15

10-3 **a.** $1,251.22

10-4 **a.** $813.07

10-5 $85

10-6 $150

10-7 $100

10-8 $65

10-9 $15.30

10-10 $23.75

10-11 $1.96

10-12 **a.** V_L at 5 percent = $1,518.99;
      V_L at 7 percent = $1,273.24;
      V_L at 11 percent = $928.09

10-13 **b.** $30

10-14 $25.03

10-15 P_0 = $19.89

10-16 $35.28

10-17 12%

10-18 12%

10-19 7.6%

10-20 8.0%

10-21 **a.** YTM at $829 = 15%

10-22 0.5%

10-23 **a.** 13.3%
      b. 10%
      c. 8%
      d. 5.3%

10-24 IBM bond = 9.33%

10-25 10.2%

10-26 Total return = 46%

10-27 Total return = 15%

10-28 12%

10-29 Total return = 5% = dividend yield

10-30 **a.** 7%
      b. 5%
      c. 12%

10-31 **a.** 10.54%
      c. Capital gains = 17.2%;
         total return = 26.2%

10-32 Capital gains = −0.7%;
      total return = 7%

10-33 **a.** $1,250
      b. $833.33
      d. At 8%, V_d = $1,196.36

10-34 **a.** $1,000
      b. V_{GM} = $888.42
      c. IBM capital gains = −6.8%
      d. IBM current yield = 5.0%
      e. IBM total return = −1.8%
      g. V_{IBM} = $965.35

10-35 **a.** **(1)** $9.50
         (2) $13.33
      b. **(1)** Undefined

10-36 **a.** $22.50
      b. $27.79
      d. $42.59

10-37 **a.** Dividend 2012 = $2.66
      b. P_0 = $39.43
      c. Dividend yield 2010 = 5.10%;
         2014 = 7.00%

10-38 **a.** P_0 = $54.11

11-1 17%

11-2 10%

11-3 2.0

11-4 15.5%

11-5 14%

11-6 CV_E = 0.667

11-7 r_{RF} = 2.5%

11-8 17%

11-9 **a.** $\hat{r}_M$ = 13.5%; $\hat{r}_S$ = 11.6%
      b. σ_M = 3.85%; σ_S = 6.22%
      c. CV_M = 0.29; CV_S = 0.54

11-10 19%

11-11 **a.** $\hat{r}_Y$ = 14%
       b. σ_X = 12.20%

11-12 r_K = 19%

11-13 $\beta_{New} = 1.4$

11-14 $\beta_{Stock} = 1.2$

11-15 $\beta_{New} = 1.16$

11-16   **a.** $\beta_B = 2$
   b. $r_B = 12.5\%$

11-17   **a.** $r_X = 15.5\%$
   b. **(1)** $r_X = 16.5\%$
   c. **(1)** $r_X = 18.1\%$

11-18 4.5%

11-19 $\beta_P = 0.7625$; $r_p = 12.1\%$

11-20   **a.** $\hat{r}_C = 8\%$
   b. $\sigma_A = 9\%$
   c. $CV_A = 0.50$; $CV_B = 0.97$;
         $CV_C = 0.41$

11-21   **a.** 0.5 million
   d. **(2)** 15%

11-22   **a.** 13.5%
   b. 1.8
   c. $r_F = 8\% + 5.5\%\beta_F$
   d. 17.9%

11-23   **a.** $\ddot{r}_A = 11.3\%$
   c. $s_A = 20.8\%$
   d. $CV_A = 1.84$

12-1 6.12%

12-2 7.92%

12-3 7.64%

12-4 11.94%

12-5 12.37%

12-6 13.0%

12-7 $r_e = 14.0\%$

12-8   **a.** $F = 10\%$
   b. $r_e = 15.8\%$

12-9   **a.** 13.6%
   b. 14.2%

12-10 7.2%

12-11 $r_e = 16.5\%$

12-12 $80,000

12-13 $BP_{RE} = 500,000$;
         $BP_{7.8\%\,debt} = 1,500,000$

12-14 9.8%

12-15 $WACC = 15\%$; purchase Projects E and F

12-16 7.0%

12-17 $WACC = 12.72\%$

12-18 $10 million

12-19 $42,000

12-20 $62,000

12-21   **a.** 14.40%
   b. 10.62%

12-22   **a.** 16.3%
   b. 15.4%
   c. 16%

12-23   **a.** 8%
   b. $2.81
   c. 15.8%

12-24   **a.** $18 million
   b. $BP = 40 million
   c. $BP_1 = 21.8$ million; $BP_2 = 43.6$ million

12-25   **a.** $g = 3\%$
   b. $EPS = 5.562

12-26   **a.** $35,000,000
   c. $r_s = 12\%$; $r_e = 12.4\%$
   d. $27,000,000
   e. $WACC_1 = 9\%$; $WACC_2 = 9.2\%$

12-27   **a.** $r_{dT} = 5.4\%$; $r_s = 15.1\%$
   b. $WACC = 11.22\%$
   d. $WACC = 11.70\%$

12-28   **a.** Three breaks; $BP_{D1} = 1,111,111$;
         $BP_{RE} = 1,818,182$; $BP_{D2} = 2,000,000$
   b. $WACC_1 = 10.96\%$; $WACC_2 = 11.50\%$;
         $WACC_3 = 12.14\%$; $WACC_4 = 12.68\%$
   c. $r_1 = 16\%$; $r_3 = 14\%$

13-1   **a.** $390,000
   b. $11,000

13-2 $NPV = 15,301$; Buy the new machine

13-3 $NPV = 22,329$; Replace the old machine

13-4 $NPV = -2,894.79$

13-5 20%

13-6 $NPV = -10,075.29$

13-7 -361.65

13-8 $IRR_G = 14.04\%$; $IRR_P = 13.98\%$;
         $IRR_V = 13.75\%$

13-9 13.7%

13-10 $PB_{Disc} = 3.39$ years

13-11 $MIRR = 10.6\%$

13-12 $IRR_G = 15.96\%$; $MIRR_G = 15.25\%$
         $IRR_J = 16.04\%$; $MIRR_J = 16.04\%$
         $IRR_K = 15.53\%$; $MIRR_K = 15.10\%$

13-13 **a.** $NPV_P = \$448.86$; $NPV_Q = \$607.20$;
$IRR_P = 15.24\%$; $IRR_Q = 14.67\%$;
$DPB_P = 4.81$ years; $DPB_Q = 4.89$ years

13-14 $NPV_C = \$1,256$; $IRR_C = 17.3\%$;
$NPV_R = \$1,459$

13-15 $IRR_Q = 15.6\%$

13-16 $NPV_Y = \$886$; accept Project Y

13-17 **b.** $NPV = \$7,486.68$
d. $DPB = 6.51$ yrs

13-18 **a.** 10.6%
b. $NPV = \$1,100$; Accept

13-19 **a.** 15%
b. 1.48; 15.4%; 17%

13-20 Accept A and B

13-21 Accept QUE and DOG

13-22 $NPV_P = \$409$; $IRR_P = 15\%$; Accept;
$NPV_T = \$3,318$; $IRR_T = 20\%$; Accept

13-23 $NPV_E = \$3,861$; $IRR_E = 18\%$;
$NPV_G = \$3,057$; $IRR_G = 18\%$;
Purchase electric-powered forklift; it has a higher NPV

13-24 **a.** ($178,000)
b. $52,440; $60,600; $40,200
c. $48,760
d. $NPV = -\$19,549$; Do not purchase

13-25 **a.** ($126,000)
b. $42,560; $47,477; $35,186
c. $51,268
d. $NPV = \$11,385$; Purchase

13-26 **a.** ($52,000)
b. $18,560; $22,400; $12,800; $10,240
c. $1,500
d. $NPV = \$1,021$; Replace the old machine

13-27 **a.** ($776,000)
c. $199,000; $255,400; $194,300;
$161,400; $156,700
d. $115,200
e. $NPV = \$436.77$;
Purchase the new machine

13-28 **a.** 11%

13-29 $NPV_5 = \$4,422$; $NPV_4 = (\$4,161)$;
$NPV_8 = \$26,658$

13-30 **b.** $IRR_A = 17.8\%$; $IRR_B = 24.0\%$

13-31 **a.** $IRR_A = 20\%$; $IRR_B = 16.7\%$;
Crossover rate $\approx 16\%$

13-32 **a.** $NPV_A = \$14,486,808$;
$NPV_B = \$11,156,893$;
$IRR_A = 15.03\%$; $IRR_B = 22.26\%$

13A-1 $PV = \$1,273,389$

14-1 **a.** $ROE_{LL} = 14.6\%$; $ROE_{HL} = 16.8\%$
b. $ROE_{LL} = 16.5\%$

14-2 Payout = 40%

14-3 $720,000

14-4 $20,000,000

14-5 **a.** $0.20

14-6 $D_0 = \$3.44$

14-7 $3,250,000

14-8 Payout = 52%

14-9 Payout = 31.39%

14-10 No leverage: $ROE = 10.5\%$; $\sigma = 5.4\%$;
$CV = 0.51$; 60% leverage: $ROE = 13.7\%$;
$\sigma = 13.5\%$; $CV = 0.99$

14-11 **a.** $5.10

14-12 **a.** $EPS_{Old} = \$2.04$;
New: $EPS_D = \$4.74$; $EPS_S = \$3.27$
b. 33,975 units
c. $Q_{New,Debt} = 27,225$ units

14-13 Debt used: $E(EPS) = \$5.78$;
$\sigma_{EPS} = \$1.05$; $E(TIE) = 3.49\times$
Stock used: $E(EPS) = \$5.51$;
$\sigma_{EPS} = \$0.85$; $E(TIE) = 6.00\times$

14-14 **a.** **(1)** $3,960,000
(2) $4,800,000
(3) $9,360,000
(4) Regular = $3,960,000;
Extra = $5,400,000
c. 15%

14-15 **a.** Payout = 63.16%;
$BP_{with\ dividend} = \$9.55$ million;
$WACC_1 = 10.67\%$; $WACC_2 = 10.96\%$
b. $15 million

15-1 **a.** $11.25\times$
b. 32 days

15-2 **a.** 45.0 days
b. $384,000,000

15-3 **a.** $30.0\times$
b. 12 days

15-4 **a.** 30 days
b. $5,760,000

15-5   a. $14.0\times$
      b. 25.7 days

15-6   a. 18 days
      b. $32,000,000

15-7   a. Net float = $30,000
      b. $16,000

15-8 $DSO_{Existing} = 54$ days,
      $DSO_{Proposal} = 75$ days

15-9   b. APR = 14.69%; $r_{EAR} = 15.66\%$
      d. APR = 20.99%; $r_{EAR} = 23.10\%$

15-10 a. 44.54%

15-11 N/P = 13.64%

15-12 a. 11.73%
      b. 12.09%

15-13 a. 72 days
      b. $396,000
      d. Decrease to 57

15-14 a. DSO = 28 days
      b. $70,000

15-15 $NPV_{Existing} = \$2,349$,
      $NPV_{Proposal} = \$2,089$

15-16 a. EOQ = 3,873
      c. 5,073 bags
      d. 3,137 bags
      e. Every 6 days

15-17 a. $1,600,000
      c. Bank = $1,200,000;
           Books = −$5,200,000

15-18 a. 51 days
      b. Turnover = $2.33\times$; ROA = 11.67%;
      c. CCC = 42 days; Turnover = 2.46;
           ROA = 12.3%

15-19 b. $420,000
      c. $35,000

15-20 $NPV_{Existing} = \$1,141$; $NPV_{Proposal} = \$1,196$

15-21 a. $DSO_{Old} = 27$ days; $DSO_{New} = 22.5$ days
      b. $D_{Old} = \$15,680$; $D_{New} = \$38,220$
      c. $BD_{Old} = \$40,000$; $BD_{New} = \$52,000$
      d. $NPV_{Old} = \$1,197$; $NPV_{New} = \$1,514$

15-22 EOQ = 1,000

15-23 a. EOQ = 5,200
      b. 65
      c. Every 5.5 days
      d. $TIC_{Q=6,000} = \$6,304$

15-24 a. (1) 112 days
         (2) 79 days

d. (1) 142 days
     (2) 113 days

15-25 a. 32 days
      b. $288,000
      c. $45,000

15-26 a. 12%
      b. 11.25%
      c. 11.48%

15-27 b. 12.01%
      d. 10.57%

15-28 a. Alternative 3 EAR = 9.56%
      b. Alternative 2 = $470,588

16-1   b. −$2,000

16-2   a. $3,500
      b. $2.31
      d. −34.6%

16-3   a. 14.0%

16-4   a. Invest in Randicorp = $20,000
      b. 10.675%
      c. 9.74%

16-5   a. $2,760
      b. 46%
      c. Capital gains = 40%;
           Dividend yield = 6%

16-6   a. $375
      b. 15%
      d. 15%

16-7   a. $r_A = -2.2\%$
      b. $r_G = -2.5\%$
      d. $FV_{2009} = \$1,761.64$

16-8   a. $r_{p,2008} = 15.0\%$;
         $r_{S\&P,2008} = -3.55\%$
      b. $\bar{r}_{A,P} = 18.00\%$;
         $\bar{r}_{A,S\&P} = 3.67\%$
      c. $\bar{r}_{G,P} = 17.41\%$;
         $\bar{r}_{G,S\&P} = 3.51\%$

16-9   a. −$1,500
      b. +$1,000

16-10 a. 29.28%
      b. 43.94%

16-11 a. 22.7%
      b. $12,000
      c. 29.1%
      d. −13.6%

16-12 a. $9,616.00
      b. 60.1%
      c. 17%

16-13   **a.** −41.0%
         b. −27.9%
         c. 140.9%
         d. 201.5%

16-14   **a.** $r_{W,2} = 1.57\%$
         b. $r_{V,1} = 7.67\%$

17-1 $P_1 = \$20.80$

17-2   **a.** $P_0 = \$35.42$
         b. $P_0 = \$54.09$

17-3   EVA = $0

17-4   **a.** $EPS_0 = \$4.08$
         b. $P_0 = \$122.40$
         c. r = 0%

17-5   **a.** EBIT = $140,000
         b. EVA = −$5,000

17-6   **a.** (2) $P_0 = \$26.25$

17-7   **b.** $46.42

17-9   **a.** $3.76
         c. Divided yield = 2.8%
         d. At P/E = 14, $P_0 = \$52.64$

17-10 **a.** $WACC_A = 12.48\%$; $WACC_B = 14.90\%$;
            $WACC_C = 17.30\%$
         b. $EVA_A = \$3,770$; $EVA_B = \$1,350$;
            $EVA_C = -\$1,050$
         d. $P_B = \$22.32$

17-11 **a.** $3.5 million
         b. EVA = $1.14 million

17-12 **a.** $D_0 = \$0.72$; $\hat{D}_I = \$0.90$
         b. $P_0 = -\$18$, which does not make sense

Selected Equations

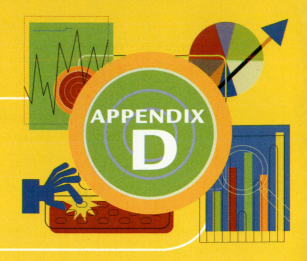

CHAPTER 2

$$\text{Conversion price} = \frac{\text{Face value}}{\text{Conversion price}}$$

CHAPTER 3

Proceeds from issue = (Market value of issue) × (1 − Percent flotation costs)

Investment banker profit = Flotation costs − Expenses

CHAPTER 4

$$\frac{\text{Maximum change}}{\text{in money supply}} = \frac{\text{Excess reserves}}{\text{Reserve requirement}}$$

CHAPTER 5

Dollar return = (Dollar income) + (Capital gains)

$\qquad\qquad$ = (Dollar income) + (Ending value − Beginning value)

$$\text{Yield} = \frac{\text{Dollar return}}{\text{Beginning value}} = \frac{\text{Dollar income} + \text{Capital gains}}{\text{Beginning value}}$$

$$= \frac{\text{Dollar income} + (\text{Ending value} - \text{Beginning value})}{\text{Beginning value}}$$

Rate of return = r = Risk-free rate + Risk premium

Rate of return = r = r_{RF} + RP = r_{RF} + [DRP + LP + MRP]

$\qquad\qquad\qquad$ = [r* + IP] + [DRP + LP + MRP]

$$\frac{\text{Yield on a}}{\text{2-year bond}} = \frac{\left(\begin{array}{c}\text{Interest rate} \\ \text{in Year 1}\end{array}\right) + \left(\begin{array}{c}\text{Interest rate} \\ \text{in Year 2}\end{array}\right)}{2} = \frac{R_1 + R_2}{2}$$

CHAPTER 6

$$\frac{\text{Equivalent pretax yield}}{\text{on a taxable investment}} = \frac{\text{Yield on a tax-free investment}}{1 - \text{Marginal tax rate}}$$

$$\frac{\text{Yield on}}{\text{tax-free investment}} = \left(\begin{matrix}\text{Pretax yield on}\\\text{taxable income}\end{matrix}\right) \times (1 - \text{Marginal tax rate})$$

$$\text{Average tax rate} = \frac{\text{Tax liability}}{\text{Taxable income}}$$

CHAPTER 7

$$\text{Net cash flow} = \text{Net income} + \text{Depreciation and amortization}$$

$$\text{Net working capital} = \text{NWC} = \text{Current assets} - \text{Current liabilities}$$

$$\frac{\text{Net operating}}{\text{working capital}} = \text{NOWC} = \left(\begin{matrix}\text{Current assets}\\\text{required for operations}\end{matrix}\right) - \left(\begin{matrix}\text{Non-interest-bearing}\\\text{current liabilities}\end{matrix}\right)$$

$$\frac{\text{Operating}}{\text{cash flow}} = [\text{NOI}(1 - \text{Tax rate})] + \left(\begin{matrix}\text{Depreciation and}\\\text{amortization expense}\end{matrix}\right)$$

$$= \left(\begin{matrix}\text{Net operating}\\\text{profits after taxes}\end{matrix}\right) + \left(\begin{matrix}\text{Depreciation and}\\\text{amortization expense}\end{matrix}\right)$$

$$\text{Free Cash Flow (FCF)} = \text{Operating cash flow} - \text{Investments}$$
$$= \text{Operating cash flow} - (\Delta \text{ in fixed assets} + \Delta \text{NOWC})$$

$$\text{EVA} = \text{NOI}(1 - \text{Tax rate}) - [(\text{Invested capital}) \times (\text{After-tax cost of capital as a percent})]$$

$$\text{Current ratio} = \frac{\text{Current assets}}{\text{Current liabilities}}$$

$$\text{Quick (acid-test) ratio} = \frac{\text{Current assets} - \text{Inventory}}{\text{Current liabilities}}$$

$$\text{Inventory turnover ratio} = \frac{\text{Cost of goods sold}}{\text{Inventory}} = \frac{\text{Variable operating costs}}{\text{Inventory}}$$

$$\text{Days sales outstanding (DSO)} = \frac{\text{Accounts receivable}}{\text{Average daily sales}} = \frac{\text{Accounts receivable}}{\left[\dfrac{\text{Annual sales}}{360}\right]}$$

$$\text{Fixed assets turnover ratio} = \frac{\text{Sales}}{\text{Net fixed assets}}$$

$$\text{Total assets turnover ratio} = \frac{\text{Sales}}{\text{Total assets}}$$

$$\text{Debt ratio} = \text{Debt-to-total-assets ratio} = \frac{\text{Total liabilities}}{\text{Total assets}}$$

$$\text{D/E} = \frac{\text{D/A}}{1 - \text{D/A}}, \quad \text{and} \quad \text{D/A} = \frac{\text{D/E}}{1 - \text{D/E}}$$

$$\text{Times interest earned ratio (TIE)} = \frac{\text{Earnings before interest and taxes}}{\text{Interest charges}}$$

$$\text{Fixed charge coverage ratio} = \frac{\text{EBIT} + \text{Lease payments}}{\begin{array}{c}\text{Interest} \\ \text{charges}\end{array} + \begin{array}{c}\text{Lease} \\ \text{payments}\end{array} + \left[\dfrac{\text{Sinking fund payments}}{(1 - \text{Tax rate})}\right]}$$

$$\text{Net profit margin} = \frac{\text{Net profit}}{\text{Sales}}$$

$$\text{Return on total assets (ROA)} = \frac{\text{Net income}}{\text{Total assets}}$$

$$\text{Return on equity (ROE)} = \frac{\text{Net income available to common stockholders}}{\text{Common equity}}$$

$$\text{Earnings per share (EPS)} = \frac{\text{Net income available to common stockholders}}{\text{Number of common shares outstanding}}$$

$$\text{Price/Earnings (PE) ratio} = \frac{\text{Market price per share}}{\text{Earnings per share}}$$

$$\text{Book value per share} = \frac{\text{Common equity}}{\text{Number of common shares outstanding}}$$

DuPont model:

$$\text{ROA} = \text{Net profit margin} \times \text{Total assets turnover}$$

$$= \frac{\text{Net income}}{\text{Sales}} \times \frac{\text{Sales}}{\text{Total assets}}$$

$$\text{ROE} = \text{ROA} \times \text{Equity multiplier}$$

$$= \frac{\text{Net income}}{\text{Total assets}} \times \frac{\text{Total assets}}{\text{Common equity}} = \frac{\text{Net income}}{\text{Sales}} \times \frac{\text{Sales}}{\text{Total assets}} \times \frac{\text{Total assets}}{\text{Common equity}}$$

CHAPTER 8

$$\text{Full capacity sales} = \frac{\text{Sales level}}{\left(\begin{array}{c}\text{Percent of capacity used} \\ \text{to generate current sales level}\end{array}\right)}$$

Total operating costs = Total fixed operating costs + Total variable operating costs

$$\text{TOC} = \qquad \text{F} \qquad + \qquad \text{VC}$$

$$= \qquad \text{F} \qquad + \qquad (\text{V} \times \text{Q})$$

At the operating breakeven point:

$$\frac{\text{Sales}}{\text{revenues}} = \frac{\text{Total operating}}{\text{costs}} = \frac{\text{Total}}{\text{variable costs}} + \frac{\text{Total}}{\text{fixed costs}}$$

$$(\text{P} \times \text{Q}) = \qquad \text{TOC} \qquad = \qquad (\text{V} \times \text{Q}) \quad + \quad \text{F}$$

$$Q_{\text{OpBE}} = \frac{\text{F}}{\text{Contribution margin}} = \frac{\text{F}}{\text{P} - \text{V}}$$

$$S_{\text{OpBE}} = \frac{\text{F}}{\text{Gross profit margin}} = \frac{\text{F}}{1 - \left(\frac{\text{V}}{\text{P}}\right)}$$

$$\text{DOL} = \frac{\text{Gross profit}}{\text{NOI}} = \frac{(\text{Q} \times \text{P}) - (\text{Q} \times \text{V})}{(\text{Q} \times \text{P}) - (\text{Q} \times \text{V}) - \text{F}} = \frac{\text{S} - \text{VC}}{\text{S} - \text{VC} - \text{F}}$$

$$\text{DFL} = \frac{\text{EBIT}}{\text{EBIT} - \left[\text{I} + \dfrac{\text{D}_{\text{ps}}}{(1 - \text{T})}\right]}$$

$$\text{DFL} = \frac{\text{EBIT}}{\text{EBIT} - \text{I}}; \text{ if preferred stock} = 0$$

$$\text{DTL} = \quad \text{DOL} \quad \times \text{DFL}$$

$$= \frac{\text{Gross profit}}{\text{EBIT}} \times \frac{\text{EBIT}}{\text{EBIT} - \text{I}} \qquad \left.\begin{array}{l} \\ \\ \\ \\ \\ \end{array}\right\} \text{ if preferred stock} = 0$$

$$= \frac{\text{Gross profit}}{\text{EBIT} - \text{I}} = \frac{\text{S} - \text{VC}}{\text{EBIT} - \text{I}} = \frac{\text{Q}(\text{P} - \text{V})}{[\text{Q}(\text{P} - \text{V}) - \text{F}] - \text{I}}$$

CHAPTER 9

$$\text{FV}_n = \text{PV}(1 + r)^n$$

$$\text{PV} = \text{FV}_n \left[\frac{1}{(1 + r)^n}\right]$$

$$\text{FVA}_n = \text{PMT}\left[\sum_{t=0}^{n-1}(1 + r)^n\right] = \text{PMT}\left[\frac{(1 + r)^n - 1}{r}\right]$$

$$\text{FVA(DUE)}_n = \text{PMT}\left[\sum_{t=1}^{n}(1 + r)^t\right] = \text{PMT}\left[\left\{\frac{(1 + r)^n - 1}{r}\right\} \times (1 + r)\right]$$

$$PVA_n = PMT \sum_{t=1}^{n} \left[\frac{1}{(1+r)^t} \right] = PMT \left[\frac{1 - \frac{1}{(1+r)^n}}{r} \right]$$

$$PVA(DUE)_n = PMT \sum_{t=0}^{n-1} \left[\frac{1}{(1+r)^t} \right] = PMT \left\{ \left[\frac{1 - \frac{1}{(1+r)^n}}{r} \right] \times (1+r) \right\}$$

$$PVP = \frac{\text{Payment}}{\text{Interest rate}} = \frac{PMT}{r}$$

$$PV = \frac{CF_1}{(1+r)^1} + \frac{CF_2}{(1+r)^2} + \cdots + \frac{CF_n}{(1+r)^n} = \sum_{t=1}^{n} \frac{CF_t}{(1+r)^t}$$

$$\begin{matrix} \text{Periodic} \\ \text{rate} \end{matrix} = r_{PER} = \frac{\text{Stated annual interest rate}}{\text{Number of interest payments per year}} = \frac{r_{SIMPLE}}{m}$$

$$\text{Effective annual rate (EAR)} = r_{EAR} = \left(1 + \frac{r_{SIMPLE}}{m} \right)^m - 1.0 = (1 + r_{PER})^m - 1.0$$

$$APR = r_{SIMPLE} = r_{PER} \times m$$

CHAPTER 10

$$\begin{matrix} \text{Asset} \\ \text{value} \end{matrix} = V = \frac{\widehat{CF}_1}{(1+r)^1} + \frac{\widehat{CF}_2}{(1+r)^2} + \cdots + \frac{\widehat{CF}_{n-1}}{(1+r)^{n-1}} + \frac{\widehat{CF}_n}{(1+r)^n}$$

$$\begin{matrix} \text{Bond} \\ \text{Value} \end{matrix} = V_d = \left[\frac{INT}{(1+r_d)^1} + \frac{INT}{(1+r_d)^2} + \cdots + \frac{INT}{(1+r_d)^N} \right] + \frac{M}{(1+r_d)^N} = \left[\sum_{t=1}^{N} \frac{INT}{(1+r_d)^t} \right] + \frac{M}{(1+r_d)^N}$$

$$= INT \left[\frac{1 - \frac{1}{(1+r_d)^N}}{r_d} \right] + M \left[\frac{1}{(1+r_d)^N} \right]$$

$$V_d = \left(\frac{INT}{2} \right) \left[\frac{1 - \frac{1}{\left(1 + \frac{r_d}{2} \right)^{2 \times N}}}{\left(\frac{r_d}{2} \right)} \right] + \frac{M}{\left(1 + \frac{r_d}{2} \right)^{2 \times N}} ; \text{ if interest is paid semiannually}$$

$$V_d = \frac{INT}{(1+r_d)^1} + \frac{INT}{(1+r_d)^2} + \cdots + \frac{INT + M}{(1+r_d)^N} = \frac{INT}{(1+YTM)^1} + \frac{INT}{(1+YTM)^2} + \cdots + \frac{INT + M}{(1+YTM)^N}$$

$$\begin{matrix} \text{Approximate} \\ \text{yield to maturity} \end{matrix} = \frac{\left(\begin{matrix} \text{Annual} \\ \text{interest} \end{matrix} \right) + \left(\begin{matrix} \text{Accrued} \\ \text{capital gains} \end{matrix} \right)}{\text{Average value of the bond}} = \frac{INT + \left(\frac{M - V_d}{N} \right)}{\left[\frac{2(V_d) + M}{3} \right]}$$

$$V_d = \frac{INT}{(1 + r_d)^1} + \frac{INT}{(1 + r_d)^2} + \cdots + \frac{INT + Call\ price}{(1 + r_d)^{N_c}}$$

$$= \frac{INT}{(1 + YTC)^1} + \frac{INT}{(1 + YTC)^2} + \cdots + \frac{INT + Call\ price}{(1 + YTC)^{N_c}}$$

$$Bond\ yield = Current\ (interest)\ yield\ +\ Capital\ gains\ yield$$

$$= \frac{INT}{V_{d,Begin}} + \frac{V_{d,End} - V_{d,Begin}}{V_{d,Begin}}$$

$$\begin{array}{c} \text{Expected rate} \\ \text{of return} \end{array} = \hat{r}_s = \frac{\hat{D}_1}{P_0} + \frac{\hat{P}_1 - P_0}{P_0} = \frac{\hat{D}_1}{P_0} + g = \begin{array}{c} \text{Expected} \\ \text{dividend yield} \end{array} + \begin{array}{c} \text{Expected growth rate} \\ \text{(capital gains yield)} \end{array}$$

$$\begin{array}{c} \text{Stock} \\ \text{Value} \end{array} = V_s = \hat{P}_0 = \frac{\hat{D}_1}{(1 + r_s)^1} + \frac{\hat{D}_2}{(1 + r_s)^2} + \cdots + \frac{\hat{D}_{\infty-1}}{(1 + r_s)^{\infty-1}} + \frac{\hat{D}_{\infty}}{(1 + r_s)^{\infty}}$$

$$= \sum_{t=1}^{\infty} \frac{\hat{D}_t}{(1 + r_s)^t}$$

$$\hat{P}_0 = \frac{D}{(1 + r_s)^1} + \frac{D}{(1 + r_s)^2} + \cdots + \frac{D}{(1 + r_s)^{\infty-1}} + \frac{D}{(1 + r_s)^{\infty}} = \frac{D}{r_s}$$

$$= \text{Value of a zero growth stock}$$

$$\hat{r}_s = \frac{D}{P_0} ; \text{zero growth stock}$$

$$\hat{P}_0 = \frac{D_0(1 + g_1)}{(1 + r_s)^1} + \frac{D_0(1 + g_2)}{(1 + r_s)^2} + \cdots + \frac{D_0(1 + g_N)}{(1 + r_s)^N} + \frac{\hat{P}_N}{(1 + r_s)^N}$$

$$= \text{Value of a nonconstant growth stock}$$

$$\text{where } \hat{P}_N = \frac{\hat{D}_N(1 + g_{norm})}{r_s - g_{norm}} = \frac{\hat{D}_{N+1}}{r_s - g_{norm}}$$

$$\hat{P}_0 = \frac{D_0(1 + g)^1}{(1 + r_s)^1} + \frac{D_0(1 + g)^2}{(1 + r_s)^2} + \cdots + \frac{D_0(1 + g)^{\infty-1}}{(1 + r_s)^{\infty-1}} + \frac{D_0(1 + g)^{\infty}}{(1 + r_s)^{\infty}} = \frac{D_0(1 + g)}{r_s - g}$$

$$= \frac{\hat{D}_1}{r_s - g} = \text{Value of a constant growth stock}$$

CHAPTER 11

$$\text{Expected rate of return} = \hat{r} = Pr_1 r_1 + Pr_2 r_2 + \cdots + Pr_n r_n = \sum_{i=1}^{n} Pr_i r_i$$

$$\text{Variance} = \sigma^2 = (r_1 - \hat{r})^2 Pr_1 + (r_2 - \hat{r})^2 Pr_2 + \cdots + (r_n - \hat{r})^2 Pr_n = \sum_{i=1}^{n} (r_i - \hat{r})^2 Pr_i$$

$$\text{Standard deviation} = \sigma = \sqrt{(r_1 - \hat{r})^2 Pr_1 + (r_2 - \hat{r})^2 Pr_2 + \cdots + (r_n - \hat{r})^2 Pr_n}$$

$$= \sqrt{\sum_{i=1}^{n} (r_i - \hat{r})^2 Pr_i}$$

$$\text{Estimated } \sigma = s = \sqrt{\frac{\sum_{t=1}^{n} (\ddot{r}_t - \bar{r})^2}{n - 1}}$$

$$\bar{r} = \frac{\ddot{r}_1 + \ddot{r}_2 + \cdots + \ddot{r}_n}{n} = \frac{\sum_{t=1}^{n} \ddot{r}}{n}$$

$$\text{Coefficient of variation} = CV = \frac{\text{Risk}}{\text{Return}} = \frac{\sigma}{\hat{r}}$$

$$\text{Portfolio return} = \hat{r}_p = w_1 \hat{r}_1 + w_2 \hat{r}_2 + \cdots + w_N \hat{r}_N = \sum_{j=1}^{N} w_j \hat{r}_j$$

$$\text{Portfolio beta} = \beta_p = w_1 \beta_1 + w_2 \beta_2 + \cdots + w_N \beta_N = \sum_{j=1}^{N} w_j \beta_j$$

$$r_j = r_{RF} + (RP_M)\beta_j = \text{Capital Asset Pricing Model (CAPM)}$$

$$= r_{RF} + (r_M - r_{RF})\beta_j$$

CHAPTER 12

$$\begin{array}{l} \text{After-tax component} \\ \text{cost of debt} \end{array} = r_{dT} = \begin{pmatrix} \text{Bondholders' required} \\ \text{rate of return} \end{pmatrix} - \begin{pmatrix} \text{Tax} \\ \text{savings} \end{pmatrix}$$

$$= \qquad r_d \qquad - \quad r_d \times T$$

$$= r_d(1 - T)$$

$$\text{Bond value} = V_d = \frac{INT}{(1 + r_d)^1} + \frac{INT}{(1 + r_d)^2} + \cdots + \frac{INT + M}{(1 + r_d)^N}$$

$$\begin{array}{l} \text{Component cost} \\ \text{of preferred stock} \end{array} = r_{ps} = \frac{D_{ps}}{NP_0} = \frac{D_{ps}}{P_0 - \text{Flotation costs}} = \frac{D_{ps}}{P_0(1 - F)}$$

$$\text{Required rate of return} = \text{Expected rate of return}$$

$$r_s \qquad = \qquad \hat{r}_s$$

$$r_{RF} + RP \qquad = \qquad \frac{\hat{D}_1}{P_0} + g$$

$$r_s = r_{RF} + \quad RP$$

$$= r_{RF} + (r_M - r_{RF})\beta_s$$

$$\hat{r}_s = \frac{\hat{D}_1}{P_0} + g = r_s$$

$$r_s = \text{Bond yield} + \text{Risk premium}$$

$$\hat{r}_e = \frac{\hat{D}_1}{NP_0} + g = \frac{\hat{D}_1}{P_0(1-F)} + g$$

$$\text{WACC} = \left[\begin{pmatrix}\text{Proportion} \\ \text{of} \\ \text{debt}\end{pmatrix} \times \begin{pmatrix}\text{After-tax} \\ \text{cost of} \\ \text{debt}\end{pmatrix}\right] + \left[\begin{pmatrix}\text{Proportion} \\ \text{of preferred} \\ \text{stock}\end{pmatrix} \times \begin{pmatrix}\text{Cost of} \\ \text{preferred} \\ \text{stock}\end{pmatrix}\right] + \left[\begin{pmatrix}\text{Proportion} \\ \text{of common} \\ \text{equity}\end{pmatrix} \times \begin{pmatrix}\text{Cost of} \\ \text{common} \\ \text{equity}\end{pmatrix}\right]$$

$$= [\quad w_d \quad \times \quad r_{dT} \quad] + [\quad w_{ps} \quad \times \quad r_{ps} \quad] + [\quad w_s \quad \times \quad (r_s \text{ or } r_e)]$$

$$\text{Break point} = \frac{\text{Maximum amount of lower cost of capital of a given type}}{\text{Proportion of this type of capital in the capital structure}}$$

CHAPTER 13

$$\text{Incremental operating CF}_t = \Delta\text{Cash revenues}_t - \Delta\text{Cash expenses}_t - \Delta\text{Taxes}_t$$
$$= \Delta NOI_t \times (1-T) + \Delta Depr_t$$
$$= (\Delta S_t - \Delta OC_t - \Delta Depr_t) \times (1-T) + \Delta Depr_t$$
$$= (\Delta S_t - \Delta OC_t) \times (1-T) + T(\Delta Depr_t)$$

$$\text{NPV} = CF_0 + \frac{\widehat{CF}_1}{(1+r)^1} + \frac{\widehat{CF}_2}{(1+r)^2} + \cdots + \frac{\widehat{CF}_n}{(1+r)^n}$$

$$\text{Profitability index} = \frac{\text{DCF}}{\text{Initial investment}}$$

$$\text{NPV} = CF_0 + \frac{\widehat{CF}_1}{(1+IRR)^1} + \frac{\widehat{CF}_2}{(1+IRR)^2} + \cdots + \frac{\widehat{CF}_n}{(1+IRR)^n} = 0$$

or

$$CF_0 = \frac{\widehat{CF}_1}{(1+IRR)^1} + \frac{\widehat{CF}_2}{(1+IRR)^2} + \cdots + \frac{\widehat{CF}_n}{(1+IRR)^n}$$

$$\text{Payback period} = \begin{pmatrix}\text{Number of years } before \\ \text{the year of full recovery} \\ \text{of initial investment}\end{pmatrix} + \begin{pmatrix}\text{Amount of the initial investment that is} \\ \dfrac{unrecovered \text{ at the start of the recovery year}}{\text{Total cash flow generated}} \\ \text{during the recovery year}\end{pmatrix}$$

$$\text{PV of cash outflows} = \frac{\text{FV of cash inflows}}{(1+MIRR)^n} = \frac{\text{TV}}{(1+MIRR)^n}$$

$$\sum_{t=0}^{n} \frac{COF_t}{(1+r)^t} = \frac{\displaystyle\sum_{t=0}^{n} CIF_t(1+r)^{n-t}}{(1+MIRR)^n}$$

$$E(NPV) = \sum_{i=1}^{n} Pr_i(NPV_i)$$

$$\sigma = \sqrt{\sum_{i=1}^{n} Pr_i[NPV_i - E(NPV)]^2}$$

$$CV_{NPV} = \frac{\sigma_{NPV}}{E(NPV)}$$

$$r_{Project} = r_{RF} + (r_M - r_{RF})\beta_{Project}$$

CHAPTER 14

$$EPS = \frac{(S - F - VC - I)(1 - T)}{\text{Shares outstanding}} = \frac{(EBIT - I)(1 - T)}{\text{Shares outstanding}}$$

$$TIE = \frac{EBIT}{I}$$

$$\begin{array}{l}\text{Dollars transferred} \\ \text{from retained earnings}\end{array} = \begin{pmatrix}\text{Number of shares} \\ \text{outstanding}\end{pmatrix} \times \begin{pmatrix}\text{Stock dividend} \\ \text{as a percent}\end{pmatrix} \times \begin{pmatrix}\text{Market price} \\ \text{of the stock}\end{pmatrix}$$

CHAPTER 15

$$\begin{array}{l}\text{Account} \\ \text{balance}\end{array} = \begin{pmatrix}\text{Amount of} \\ \text{daily activity}\end{pmatrix} \times \begin{pmatrix}\text{Average life} \\ \text{of the account}\end{pmatrix}$$

$$\begin{array}{l}\text{Inventory} \\ \text{conversion period}\end{array} = \frac{\text{Inventory}}{\text{Cost of goods sold per day}} = \frac{\text{Inventory}}{\left(\dfrac{\text{Annual cost of goods sold}}{360 \text{ days}}\right)}$$

$$\begin{array}{l}\text{Receivables} \\ \text{collection period (DSO)}\end{array} = \frac{\text{Receivables}}{\text{Average daily credit sales}} = \frac{\text{Receivables}}{\left(\dfrac{\text{Annual credit sales}}{360}\right)}$$

$$\begin{array}{l}\text{Payables} \\ \text{deferral period (DPO)}\end{array} = \frac{\text{Accounts payable}}{\text{Average daily credit purchases}} = \frac{\text{Accounts payable}}{\left(\dfrac{\text{Cost of goods sold}}{360}\right)}$$

$$\begin{array}{l}\text{Cash} \\ \text{conversion} \\ \text{cycle}\end{array} = \left[\begin{pmatrix}\text{Inventory} \\ \text{conversion} \\ \text{period}\end{pmatrix} + \begin{pmatrix}\text{Receivables} \\ \text{collection} \\ \text{period}\end{pmatrix}\right] - \begin{pmatrix}\text{Payables} \\ \text{deferral} \\ \text{period}\end{pmatrix}$$

$$\text{Percentage cost per period} = r_{PER} = \frac{\text{Dollar cost of borrowing}}{\text{Amount of usable funds}}$$

$$\text{Effective annual rate (EAR)} = r_{EAR} = (1 + r_{PER})^m - 1.0$$

$$\text{Annual percentage rate (APR)} = r_{PER} \times m = r_{SIMPLE}$$

$$\begin{aligned}
\text{Total inventory costs (TIC)} &= \quad\text{Total carrying costs} \quad + \quad\text{Total ordering costs} \\
&= \begin{pmatrix}\text{Carrying cost}\\ \text{per unit}\end{pmatrix} \times \begin{pmatrix}\text{Average units}\\ \text{in inventory}\end{pmatrix} + \begin{pmatrix}\text{Cost per}\\ \text{order}\end{pmatrix} \times \begin{pmatrix}\text{Number of}\\ \text{orders}\end{pmatrix} \\
&= \quad(C \times PP) \quad \times \quad \left(\dfrac{Q}{2}\right) \quad + \quad O \quad \times \quad \left(\dfrac{T}{Q}\right)
\end{aligned}$$

$$\text{Economic ordering quantity} = EOQ = \sqrt{\dfrac{2 \times O \times T}{C \times PP}}$$

CHAPTER 16

$$\begin{aligned}
\text{Dollar return} &= (\text{Dollar income}) + (\text{Capital gains}) \\
&= (\text{Dollar income}) + (\text{Ending value of investment} - \text{Beginning value of investment}) \\
&= INC + (P_1 - P_0)
\end{aligned}$$

$$\text{Yield (\% return)} = \ddot{r} = \dfrac{\text{Dollar return}}{\text{Beginning value of investment}} = \dfrac{\text{Dollar income} + \text{Capital gains}}{\text{Beginning value of investment}}$$

$$= \dfrac{INC + (P_1 - P_0)}{P_0} = \text{Holding period return (HPR)}$$

$$\text{Annualized rates of return} = \dfrac{INC + (P_1 - P_0)}{P_0} \times \left(\dfrac{360}{T}\right)$$

$$\text{Simple arithmetic average return} = \bar{r}_A = \dfrac{\ddot{r}_1 + \ddot{r}_2 + \cdots + \ddot{r}_n}{n}$$

$$\text{Geometric average return} = \bar{r}_G = [(1 + \ddot{r}_1) \times (1 + \ddot{r}_2) \times \cdots \times (1 + \ddot{r}_n)]^{\frac{1}{n}} - 1.0$$

$$\begin{aligned}
\ddot{r}_p &= \begin{pmatrix}\dfrac{\text{Value of Security 1}}{\text{Total value of portfolio}}\end{pmatrix}\ddot{r}_1 + \begin{pmatrix}\dfrac{\text{Value of Security 2}}{\text{Total value of portfolio}}\end{pmatrix}\ddot{r}_2 + \cdots + \begin{pmatrix}\dfrac{\text{Value of Security n}}{\text{Total value of portfolio}}\end{pmatrix}\ddot{r}_n \\
&= \quad w_1\ddot{r}_1 \quad + \quad w_2\ddot{r}_2 \quad + \cdots + \quad w_n\ddot{r}_n
\end{aligned}$$

$$\text{Price-weighted index} = I_{w,t} = \dfrac{\sum\limits_{j=1}^{n} P_{j,t}}{n}$$

$$\text{Value-weighted index} = I_{v,t} = \dfrac{\sum\limits_{ji=1}^{n} (P_{j,t} \times \text{Shares})}{n}$$

$$\text{Actual margin} = \text{Percentage of investor's equity} = \dfrac{\text{Investor's equity}}{\text{Market value of investment}}$$

$$\frac{\text{Actual}}{\text{margin}} = \frac{\text{Percentage of}}{\text{investor's equity}} = \frac{\text{Investor's equity}}{\text{Market value of investment}}$$

$$= \frac{\left[\left(\begin{array}{c}\text{Number of}\\\text{shares}\end{array}\right) \times \left(\begin{array}{c}\text{Price per}\\\text{share}\end{array}\right)\right] - (\text{Amount borrowed})}{\left(\begin{array}{c}\text{Number of}\\\text{shares}\end{array}\right) \times \left(\begin{array}{c}\text{Price per}\\\text{share}\end{array}\right)}$$

$$\begin{array}{c}\text{Margin call price}\\(\text{per share})\end{array} = \frac{\text{Amount borrowed}}{\left(\begin{array}{c}\text{Number of}\\\text{shares}\end{array}\right)\left(1 - \begin{array}{c}\text{Maintenance}\\\text{margin}\end{array}\right)}$$

CHAPTER 17

$$\text{Value of stock} = V_s = \hat{P}_0 = \text{PV of expected future dividends} = \frac{\hat{D}_1}{(1+r_s)^1} + \frac{\hat{D}_2}{(1+r_s)^2} + \cdots + \frac{\hat{D}_\infty}{(1+r_s)^\infty}$$

$$\hat{P}_0 = \frac{\hat{D}_1}{(1+r_s)^1} + \frac{\hat{D}_2}{(1+r_s)^2} + \cdots + \frac{\hat{D}_N + \hat{P}_N}{(1+r_s)^N} = \frac{\hat{D}_1}{(1+r_s)^1} + \frac{\hat{D}_2}{(1+r_s)^2} + \cdots + \frac{\hat{D}_N}{(1+r_s)^N} + \frac{\hat{P}_N}{(1+r_s)^N}$$

$$\hat{P}_N = \frac{\hat{D}_N(1+g_{\text{norm}})}{r_s - g_{\text{norm}}}$$

$$\text{EVA} = (\text{IRR} - \text{WACC}) \times (\text{Invested capital})$$
$$= \text{EBIT}(1-T) - [\text{WACC} \times (\text{Invested capital})]$$

Index

Note: Page numbers referencing figures are italicized and followed by an "*f*". Page numbers referencing tables are italicized and followed by a "*t*".

F

I